THE CAMBRIDGE HISTORY OF JAPAN

General editors
JOHN WHITNEY HALL, MARIUS B. JANSEN, MADOKA KANAI,
AND DENIS TWITCHETT

Volume 2
Heian Japan

THE CAMBRIDGE HISTORY OF JAPAN

Volume 2
Heian Japan

Edited by
DONALD H. SHIVELY
and
WILLIAM H. McCULLOUGH

CAMBRIDGE
UNIVERSITY PRESS

PUBLISHED BY THE PRESS SYNDICATE OF THE UNIVERSITY OF CAMBRIDGE
The Pitt Building, Trumpington Street, Cambridge, United Kingdom

CAMBRIDGE UNIVERSITY PRESS
The Edinburgh Building, Cambridge CB2 2RU, UK   http://www.cup.cam.ac.uk
40 West 20th Street, New York, NY 10011-4211, USA http://www.cup.org
10 Stamford Road, Oakleigh, Melbourne 3166, Australia

© Cambridge University Press 1999

This book is in copyright. Subject to statutory exception
and to the provisions of relevant collective licensing agreements,
no reproduction of any part may take place without
the written permission of Cambridge University Press

First published 1999

Printed in the United States of America

Typeface Plantin 11/13 pt.   *System* Quark   [HVG]

*A catalog record for this book is available from
the British Library.*

Library of Congress Cataloging-in-Publication Data
(Revised for volume 2)
The Cambridge history of Japan.
Includes bibliographical references and index.
Contents: v. 1. Ancient Japan / edited by Delmer M.
Brown – v. 2. Heian Japan / edited by Donald H. Shively and
William H. McCullough – v. 3. Medieval Japan / edited by Kozo Yamamura –
v. 4. Early modern Japan / edited by John Whitney Hall – [etc.]
1. Japan – History.   I. Hall, John Whitney, 1916–1997
DS835.C36   1998   952   88-2877

ISBN 0-521-22353-9 (v. 2) hardback
     0-521-22352-0 (v. 1) hardback
     0-521-22354-7 (v. 3) hardback
     0-521-22355-5 (v. 4) hardback
     0-521-22356-3 (v. 5) hardback
     0-521-22357-1 (v. 6) hardback
     0-521-65728-8 hardback set

GENERAL EDITORS' PREFACE

Since the beginning of this century the Cambridge histories have set a pattern in the English-reading world for multivolume series containing chapters written by specialists under the guidance of volume editors. Plans for a Cambridge history of Japan were begun in the 1970s and completed in 1978. The task was not to be easy. The details of Japanese history are not matters of common knowledge among Western historians. The cultural mode of Japan differs greatly from that of the West, and above all there are the daunting problems of terminology and language. In compensation, however, foreign scholars have been assisted by the remarkable achievements of the Japanese scholars during the last century in recasting their history in modern conceptual and methodological terms.

History has played a major role in Japanese culture and thought, and the Japanese record is long and full. Japan's rulers from ancient times have found legitimacy in tradition, both mythic and historic, and Japan's thinkers have probed for a national morality and system of values in their country's past. The importance of history was also emphasized in the continental cultural influences that entered Japan from early times. Its expression changed as the Japanese consciousness turned to questions of dynastic origin, as it came to reflect Buddhist views of time and reality, and as it sought justification for rule by the samurai estate. By the eighteenth century the successive need to explain the divinity of the government, justify the ruler's place through his virtue and compassion, and interpret the flux of political change had resulted in the fashioning of a highly subjective fusion of Shinto, Buddhist, and Confucian norms.

In the nineteenth century the Japanese became familiar with Western forms of historical expression and felt the need to fit their national history into patterns of a larger world history. As the modern Japanese state took its place among other nations, Japanese history faced the task of reconciling a parochial past with a more catholic present. Historians familiarized themselves with European accounts of the course of civilization and described Japan's nineteenth-century turn from military to civilian bureaucratic rule under monarchical guidance as part of a larger, worldwide pattern. Buckle, Guizot, Spencer, and then Marx successively provided interpretative schema.

The twentieth-century ideology of the imperial nation-state, however, operated to inhibit full play of universalism in historical interpretation. The growth and ideology of the imperial realm required caution on the part of historians, particularly with reference to Japanese origins.

Japan's defeat in World War II brought release from these inhibitions and for a time replaced them with compulsive denunciation of the pretensions of the imperial state. Soon the expansion of higher education brought changes in the size and variety of the Japanese scholarly world. Historical inquiry was now free to range widely. A new opening to the West brought lively interest in historical expressions in the West, and a historical profession that had become cautiously and expertly positivist began to rethink its material in terms of larger patterns.

At just this juncture the serious study of Japanese history began in the West. Before World War II the only distinguished general survey of Japanese history in English was G. B. Sansom's *Japan: A Short Cultural History*, first published in 1931 and still in print. English and American students of Japan, many trained in wartime language programs, were soon able to travel to Japan for study and participation with Japanese scholars in cooperative projects. International conferences and symposia produced volumes of essays that served as benchmarks of intellectual focus and technical advance. Within Japan itself an outpouring of historical scholarship, popular publishing, and historical romance heightened the historical consciousness of a nation aware of the dramatic changes to which it was witness.

In 1978 plans were adopted to produce this series on Japanese history as a way of taking stock of what has been learned. The present generation of Western historians can draw upon the solid foundations of the modern Japanese historical profession. The decision to limit the enterprise to six volumes meant that topics such as the history of art and literature, aspects of economics and technology and science, and the riches of local history would have to be left out. They too have been the beneficiaries of vigorous study and publication in Japan and in the Western world.

Multivolume series have appeared many times in Japanese since the beginning of the century, but until the 1960s the number of professionally trained historians of Japan in the Western world was too small to sustain such an enterprise. Although that number has grown, the general editors have thought it best to draw on Japanese specialists for contributions in areas where they retain a clear authority. In such cases the act of translation itself involves a form of editorial cooperation that requires the skills of a trained historian whose name deserves acknowledgment.

The primary objective of the present series is to put before the English-reading audience as complete a record of Japanese history as possible. But the Japanese case attracts our attention for other reasons as well. To some it has seemed that the more we have come to know about Japan, the more we are drawn to the apparent similarities with Western history. The long continuous course of Japan's historical record has tempted historians to look for resemblances between its patterns of political and social organization and those of the West. The rapid emergence of Japan's modern nation-state has occupied the attention of comparative historians, both Japanese and Western. On the other hand, specialists are inclined to point out the dangers of being misled by seeming parallels.

The striking advances in our knowledge of Japan's past will continue and accelerate. Western historians of this great and complex subject will continue to grapple with it, and they must as Japan's world role becomes more prominent. The need for greater and deeper understanding of Japan will continue to be evident. Japanese history belongs to the world, not only as a right and necessity but also as a subject of compelling interest.

JOHN WHITNEY HALL
MARIUS B. JANSEN
MADOKA KANAI
DENIS TWITCHETT

This is the final volume of *The Cambridge History of Japan*, of which the first to be published appeared in 1988. Professor John W. Hall, A. Whitney Griswold Professor Emeritus of Yale University, died in October 1997 and, sadly, was unable to see the completion of this project. As one of the general editors and as editor of Volume 4, *Early Modern Japan*, he played a central role in shaping and executing every facet of this undertaking, and his loss is mourned by all historians of Japan.

MARIUS B. JANSEN
MADOKA KANAI
DENIS TWITCHETT

CONTENTS

General editors' preface	page v
List of maps, figures, and tables	xiii
Preface to Volume 2	xv
Chronology	xviii

	Introduction by DONALD H. SHIVELY and WILLIAM H. MCCULLOUGH, *Department of East Asian Languages, University of California, Berkeley*	1
1	The Heian court, 794–1070 by WILLIAM H. MCCULLOUGH, *Department of East Asian Languages, University of California, Berkeley*	20
	Kammu to Nimmyō, 781–850	20
	Evolution of the statutory government	37
	The establishment of Fujiwara ascendancy, 850–969	45
	The Fujiwara regency, 970–1070	64
	Regency government	74
	Foreign relations, 794–1070	80
2	The capital and its society by WILLIAM H. MCCULLOUGH, *Department of East Asian Languages, University of California, Berkeley*	97
	Site of the new capital	97
	Plan of the city	102
	Greater Imperial Palace	108
	Emperor's Residential Compound	113
	Other public buildings and spaces	116
	Residential districts and population	119
	Imperial clan and court nobility	123

The noble family, marriage, and the position of women	134
Life in the mansion of a great noble	142
Officialdom and its functions	159
The city's economy	161
City administration	170
Changes in the city plan	172
New imperial and Fujiwara buildings	173
Ceremony and ritual	180

3 Land and society 183
by DANA MORRIS, *Department of History, University of California, Berkeley*

Agrarian technology	184
Peasant community	194
Tax structure	199
Landholding	215
Shōen	224

4 Provincial administration and land tenure in early Heian 236
by CORNELIUS J. KILEY, *Department of History, Villanova University*

Regional administration	254
The establishment of custodial governorship	265
Land and taxes	272
The surrender of central control to provincial authorities	283
Discretionary taxation and elite wealth	298
Local elites as a political force	326

5 Chinese learning and intellectual life 341
by MARIAN URY, *Comparative Literature Program, University of California, Davis*

Introduction and assimilation of Chinese learning	341
Ideal of the sage-king	355
Six National Histories	359
Compilation of statutes	364
State Academy	367
Scholars and their accomplishments	375

6	Aristocratic culture by HELEN CRAIG MCCULLOUGH, *Department of East Asian Languages, University of California, Berkeley*	390
	Domestic architecture and furnishings	390
	Textiles and costumes	394
	Diet	398
	Aristocratic occupations and pastimes	400
	Secular painting	409
	Calligraphy and paper	415
	Buddhist art	418
	Music	424
	Literature: Poetry	431
	Literature: Narrative prose	441
7	Aristocratic Buddhism by STANLEY WEINSTEIN, *Department of East Asian Languages and Literatures, Yale University*	449
	The prelude to Heian Buddhism	449
	The assertion of government control over the Buddhist church	454
	Saichō	462
	Kūkai	473
	The Tendai school after Saichō	478
	The Shingon school after Kūkai	497
	The growth of Pure Land Buddhism	507
8	Religious practices by ALLAN G. GRAPARD, *Department of Religious Studies, University of California, Santa Barbara*	517
	The association of Shinto shrines with Buddhist temples	520
	Ritualized and ritualizing activities	532
	Dealing with the forces of nature	547
	The association of *kami* with buddhas	564
	Late Heian developments	572
9	*Insei* by G. CAMERON HURST, III, *Department of Asian and Middle Eastern Studies, University of Pennsylvania*	576
	Abdication, regency, and the Japanese throne, 645–1068	576

Go-Sanjō and the prelude to *insei*, 1068–1073	583
Shirakawa and the normalization of *insei*, 1073–1129	595
The hegemony of Toba, 1129–1156	608
Go-Shirakawa and the Taira, 1156–1185	618
Foreign relations, 1070–1185	632
The *insei* in retrospect	637

10 The rise of the warriors   644
   by TAKEUCHI RIZŌ, *Faculty of Literature, Waseda University*

Origins of the warriors	644
Revolts of Masakado and Sumitomo	653
Revolt of Tadatsune	664
Earlier Nine Years' War	670
Later Three Years' War	675
Conditions in the capital	679
Hōgen Disturbance	688
Heiji Disturbance	691
Taira rise to power	695
Gempei War	700

Works cited	711
Glossary-index	741

MAPS, FIGURES, AND TABLES

MAPS

	Japan in the Heian period	*page* XXIV
10.1	Battle sites in the northeast	672
10.2	The Gempei War	701

FIGURES

1.1	Genealogy of Heian emperors	22
1.2	Genealogy of the four Fujiwara houses	27
1.3	Genealogy of the Northern House of the Fujiwara	46
2.1	The Heian capital (Heian-kyō)	104
2.2	Greater Imperial Palace (Daidairi)	110
2.3	Major Heian governmental organs	112
2.4	The Emperor's Residential Compound (Dairi)	114
2.5	Plan of Ononomiya	145
2.6	Plan of Hōjōji	178
3.1	Eighth- and ninth-century house sites at the Hiraide site	196
3.2	Houses in Wakatsuki-no-shō	196
3.3	Houses in Kohigashi-no-shō	197
3.4	Tax structure in the late seventh and eighth centuries	210
3.5	Tax structure in the ninth century	211
3.6	Tax structure in the tenth century	211
9.1	Genealogy of emperors during the *Insei* period	584
9.2	Genealogy of the Murakami Genji (Minamoto)	587
9.3	Family relations of Go-Sanjō	594
9.4	Family relations of Shirakawa	597

9.5	Structure of the *in-no-chō*	605
9.6	Family relations of Toba	609
9.7	Genealogy of the Kammu Heishi (Taira)	615
10.1	Genealogy of the Seiwa Genji	651
10.2	The Kiyohara and Ōshū Fujiwara	676

TABLES

1.1	Heian emperors	52
3.1	Distribution of iron tools in farm households	190
3.2	Land tax rates in the late tenth century	213
4.1	Provincial officials mandated by the *ritsuryō*	256
4.2	*Gun* officials mandated by the *ritsuryō*	258
4.3	Stipend grants from stored rice in Izumo	315
8.1	The Twenty-two Shrine-temples sponsored by the imperial government	527
9.1	Reigning and retired emperors in the *Insei* period	610

PREFACE TO VOLUME 2

Heian (794–1185) is regarded as Japan's classical age. The imperial court was at its height as a political power and patron of aristocratic culture in its most brilliant time. The Heian period has received special attention from Japanese historians through the centuries, as might be expected, and became an important subject of modern scholarship following the restoration of the imperial government in 1868. Japanese historians have been thorough and tireless in their investigations of the era. All of the primary materials known to have survived from Heian times have been published in modern editions. Japanese scholars have shared their erudition in a daunting wealth of detailed monographs and articles as well as interpretive studies. The chapters of this volume, in their content and notes, give evidence of our debt to them. None contributed more to research on Heian history than the late Professor Takeuchi Rizō, who wrote a chapter for this volume.

In this volume, Japanese is romanized according to the Modified Hepburn system, and Chinese according to Wade-Giles. Japanese and Chinese personal names follow their native form, with family or clan name preceding given name, except in citations of Japanese authors writing in English. Characters for Japanese and Chinese names and terms appear in the Glossary-Index. References cited in the footnotes are listed in alphabetical order by author in the list of Works Cited.

In footnotes Japanese dates are abbreviated as, for example, Jōwa 9 (842) 3/6, meaning the ninth year of the Jōwa era (dated to 842 in the Western calendar), the sixth day of the third lunar month. Years of the Heian lunar calendar and the Julian calendar do not correspond exactly. When the date of an event occurring late in the lunar-calendar year is known to fall at the beginning of the next year in the Julian calendar, conversion is made to the next year, following the practice of the *Kodansha Encyclopedia of Japan*, 9 vols. (Tokyo: Kōdansha, 1983). When a person's age is given, it is expressed according to the Western method of counting full years, rather than the Japanese practice of counting the calendar years in which the individual lived.

The Japanese sovereign is usually referred to as "emperor," the conventional translation of *tennō*, his official title. The generally recognized "names" of Japanese emperors are actually titles or toponymic cognomens, sometimes bestowed posthumously, as in the case of Kammu and Kōnin, and sometimes acquired during the person's lifetime or reign. For ease of identification, such names are employed in the present volume to refer to their holders both before and after their accession to the throne, and also after their retirement.

In the translation of official titles, we generally follow the translations descending from Sir George Sansom's pioneering study, "Early Japanese Law and Administration," *Transactions of the Asiatic Society of Japan*, 2nd series, 9 (1932), as modified and expanded by Helen C. McCullough and William H. McCullough, translators, *A Tale of Flowering Fortunes*, 2 vols. (Stanford, Calif.: Stanford University Press, 1980), with further modification as deemed necessary. In another terminological matter, we sometimes refer to the system of law and government known to Japanese historians as the *ritsuryō sei* by a romanized form, the "*ritsuryō* system," and sometimes by a translated form, the "statutory system." For confirmation of dates and readings of Heian names and offices, we consulted *Kokushi daijiten*, 15 vols. (Tokyo: Yoshikawa kōbunkan, 1979–97).

I should like to express my particular appreciation of the contributors for their chapters and their remarkable patience during the long delay in publication. I am grateful to Dr. Patricia Sippel for her translation of Chapter 10, and to Dr. Regine Johnson for her care in adapting and expanding the chapter. Among those who assisted in the preparation of the volume I should like to thank Professor Robert Borgen for his collegial assistance to Marian Ury in attending to the final revisions of her chapter when she fell ill. In 1985, when other responsibilities left me inadequate time to devote to editing, William H. McCullough, whom I had recently joined on the Berkeley faculty, generously consented to join me as coeditor. Author of the first two chapters of this volume, he made important contributions to several other chapters before he was unexpectedly stricken by a debilitating illness that eventually took his life in April 1997. I am deeply indebted to William McCullough.

The costs of publishing this book have been supported in part by an award from the Hiromi Arisawa Memorial Fund (named in honor of the renowned economist and the first chairman of the Board of the University of Tokyo Press) and financed by the generosity of Japanese citizens and Japanese corporations to recognize excellence in scholarship on Japan. On behalf of the contributors to this volume, I would also like to express our gratitude to the United States–Japan Friendship Commission for a grant that funded a workshop for the authors when we were planning the volume and that supported the translation of Takeuchi's chapter.

I join the editors of the other five volumes in thanking the Japan Foundation for funds that facilitated the production of this series.

Donald H. Shively

CHRONOLOGY

794 Emperor Kammu (r. 781–806) transfers the capital to Heian-kyō. Ōtomo no Otomaro, appointed the first *seii taishōgun* ("Barbarian-subduing Generalissimo"), is commander of a campaign against the Emishi in Mutsu.

796 Resettlement of 9,000 people from the eastern and northern provinces to Iji Fort in Mutsu.

797 Sakanoue no Tamuramaro appointed *seii taishōgun*, commander of forces to subjugate the Emishi.

Shoku Nihongi, second of the national histories, covering 697–791, completed.

798 Provincial administrators ordered to register Buddhist monks and lay practitioners.

Appointment of an embassy to Silla.

799 Provincial governors and bishops ordered to purge the *kokubunji* (provincial branch temples) of corrupt monks.

801 Tamuramaro subjugates the Emishi, constructs Isawa Fort, and moves the Pacification and Defense Headquarters (*chinjufu*) there. Four thousand vagrants settled at the fort.

804 Embassy to the T'ang court accompanied by monks Saichō and Kūkai.

805 Abolition of the Office of Palace Construction.

More than one hundred princes and princesses reduced from imperial to noble status and given clan names.

806 Monopolization of the use of uncultivated land by princely and noble families and by Buddhist temples prohibited.

807 Purge of officials of the Southern House of the Fujiwara.

809 Emperor Saga (r. 809–23) succeeds his brother Heizei.

810 Establishment of the *kurōdodokoro* (Chamberlains' Office).

Attempt by Heizei to regain the throne fails and the Ceremonials House of the Fujiwara is discredited.

Kamo Shrine Vestal first appointed.

811 Victorious campaign against the Emishi ends thirty years of conflict.

Hereditary district magistrates (*gunryō*), previously abolished by Kammu, are reinstated.

812 Buddhist monks and nuns cautioned by imperial decree against depravity.

813 Sillan attack on the island of Ochika in Hizen.

814	Princes and princesses given the clan name of Minamoto no ason.
	Ryōunshū, an imperial anthology of poems in Chinese, completed.
815	An order issued directing the planting of tea in Kinai and other provinces.
816	*Kebiishi* (Imperial Police) office established.
	Saga approves Kūkai's plan to build a Shingon monastery on Mount Kōya, the beginning of Kongōbuji.
818	The court uniform for ordinary and ceremonial occasions changed to the T'ang style.
	Bunka shūreishū, an imperial anthology of poems in Chinese completed.
823	Saga puts Kūkai in charge of Tōji in Kyoto as a Shingon temple.
825	Circulating inspectors (*junsatsushi*) appointed to examine the performances of provincial and district administrators.
827	Māhāyana ordination hall is completed at Enryakuji, the central Tendai monastery founded by Saichō on Mount Hiei.
	Keikokushū, an imperial anthology of poems and prose in Chinese, completed.
832	Kūkai establishes a Shingon chapel within the imperial palace.
838	The monk Ennin travels with the embassy to T'ang; he returns in 847 with esoteric scriptures and ritual implements and introduces Tendai and Mikkyō practices at the court.
842	Jōwa Incident, a plot resulting in the deposition of Crown Prince Tsunesada. He is replaced by a nephew of Fujiwara no Yoshifusa, head of the Northern House of the Fujiwara.
848	Ennin begins to establish Amida worship on Mount Hiei.
857	Yoshifusa appointed Chancellor (*daijō daijin*) and becomes de jure regent for his nephew, Emperor Montoku.
858	Yoshifusa's grandson, Seiwa, becomes emperor, the first of many child emperors.
866	The scandal of the burning of Ōtemmon discredits the Ōtomo and Ki clans. Yoshifusa the first person not of the imperial family to receive the title of regent (*sesshō*). Thereafter the Northern House monopolizes the office.
873	Fujiwara no Mototsune appointed regent and continues for four reigns.
875	Reizeiin, a detached palace, destroyed by fire with loss of books and documents.
878	Emishi revolt in Dewa.
887	Mototsune appointed regent with the title *kampaku*.
	He embarrasses Emperor Uda in the Akō Controversy.
889	First Kamo Shrine Special Festival.
891	Upon Mototsune's death, Uda appoints the scholar-official Sugawara no Michizane Head of the Chamberlains' Office to check the power of the Fujiwara.
	Compilation of *Nihonkoku genzai shomokuroku*, a bibliography of texts, mostly Chinese, existing in Japan.
894	The plan to send an embassy to T'ang is canceled.

	Sillan "bandits" attack Tsushima.
	Catapult experts deployed to Noto and their number increased in Kyushu.
899	Uda instructs Fujiwara no Tokihira and Michizane to share the supervision of government as Ministers of the Left and Right, respectively.
901	Tokihira succeeds in plotting the demotion and exile of Michizane to Kyushu, where he dies in 903.
	Nihon sandai jitsuroku, the last of the Six National Histories (*Rikkokushi*), covering 858–87, completed.
903	Private purchase of Chinese goods by princes and nobles is forbidden.
905	*Kokin(waka)shū*, the first imperial anthology of poems in Japanese, compiled.
920	Last Po-hai embassy at court. Cessation of official relations with the continent.
923	Michizane posthumously pardoned and returned to office to placate his vengeful ghost.
926	Po-hai destroyed by the Khitan. Two centuries of diplomatic relations end.
927	*Engi shiki*, a compilation of 3,300 statutes, completed, enacted 967.
931	Quarrel between Taira no Masakado and his uncle Taira no Yoshikane in Shimōsa.
935	Beginning of the Jōhei–Tengyō Disturbance: Masakado said to have killed his uncle, Taira no Kunika, a Hitachi official.
	Ki no Tsurayuki composes a travel journal, *Tosa nikki*.
	Minamoto no Shitagō completes *Wamyō ruiju shō*, a large dictionary-encyclopedia, about this date.
936	Reunification of Korea under Koryŏ.
938	Kūya preaches in the streets of Kyoto.
939	Fujiwara no Sumitomo, an official turned pirate, causes havoc in the Inland Sea.
	Emishi revolt in Dewa.
	(or 940) Masakado, joined by Prince Okiyo, seizes several eastern province headquarters and styles himself the "New Emperor" (*shinnō*).
940	Masakado is killed by his cousin, Kunika's son, Taira no Sadamori and Fujiwara no Hidesato.
941	The pirate Sumitomo is hunted down and killed.
	Fujiwara no Tadahira resigns the office of *sesshō* and is appointed *kampaku*; hereafter the title *kampaku* is used for regent of an adult emperor.
949	First major violent demonstration in the capital by warrior monks (*sōhei*), these from Tōdaiji.
953	A Chinese merchant from Wu-yüeh takes the monk Nichien to China.
967	Fujiwara no Saneyori appointed *kampaku*, beginning the full regency period (to 1068), during which heads of the Northern House are regents almost continuously.
969	Anna Incident results in the exile of Minamoto no Takaakira.

CHRONOLOGY

985	Genshin writes *Ōjō yōshū* (*Anthology on Rebirth in Pure Land*).
986	Emperor Kazan abdicates, succeeded by Ichijō. Fujiwara no Kaneie's high-handed rule as regent to 990.
	Printed edition of the Tripitaka is brought from China.
988	Petition of district magistrates and farmers of Owari Province requesting the removal of the governor for gross misconduct.
995	Michinaga receives *nairan* ("private inspection") regental powers; his control of the court until his death in 1028 is the height of Fujiwara power.
997	Pirates from Koryŏ and Amami Islands attack Tsushima, Iki, and Kyushu.
1000	Two daughters of Michinaga become empresses of Ichijō concurrently: Teishi as *kōgō*, Shōshi as *chūgū*.
1002	Sei Shōnagon completes *Makura no sōshi* (*Pillow Book*) by this year.
1005	Arrival of Sung traders in Kyushu.
1019	Michinaga falls ill and takes holy orders, but continues to dominate the court.
	Toi (Jurchen) pirates in fifty or more ships ravage Tsushima, Iki, and the northern coast of Kyushu.
1020	*Genji monogatari* (*The Tale of Genji*) completed by Murasaki Shikibu about this date.
1022	Completion of the Golden Hall at Michinaga's Hōjōji.
1028	Taira no Tadatsune of Kazusa and Shimōsa plunders tax receipts and revolts. Taira no Naokata appointed commander of a punitive force but fails to capture him.
1030	Cedar-bark shingles and earthen walls forbidden to those of Sixth Rank or lower.
1031	Tadatsune surrenders to Minamoto no Yorinobu without a fight, raising the prestige of the Seiwa Genji.
1035	Onjōji warrior monks attack Enryakuji.
1039	Enryakuji monks protest at the regent's residence and set it on fire.
1050	Governor of Yamato and his son exiled for failure to curb the violence of the Kōfukuji monks.
1051	Beginning of the Earlier Nine Years' War, Minamoto no Yoriyoshi's attempt, on imperial orders, to discipline Abe no Yoritoki in Mutsu.
1052	Regent Yorimichi converts his Uji villa into a Buddhist temple, the Byōdōin, and constructs the Hōōdō (Phoenix Hall) in 1053.
1057	Yoritoki is killed, but the Abe continue a dogged resistance.
1062	Kiyohara no Takenori of Dewa, with a large force, joins Yoriyoshi and his son Yoshiie and ensures the defeat of Abe no Sadatō, ending the Earlier Nine Years' War.
1063	Yoriyoshi, in gratitude for his victory, secretly builds a shrine dedicated to Hachiman at Yui-no-gō, Sagami. (His descendant, Yoritomo, moves the shrine to Kamakura in 1191 as the Tsurugaoka Hachimangū.)
1066	A Sung merchant presents rare medicines and a parrot to the court.

1068	Emperor Go-Sanjō exercises direct rule (to 1073), the first emperor in 170 years whose mother is not a Fujiwara.
1069	Go-Sanjō establishes the Office for Investigation of Estate Documents (*Kiroku shōen kenkeijo*) and confiscates *shōen* (estates) established since 1045 as well as earlier *shōen* with questionable deeds.
1073	Forty-two Japanese merchants visit Koryŏ, presenting gifts to the king and beginning an active, quasi-legal trade.
1074	Sung court lifts the prohibition on exporting Sung coins, which become widely used in Japan.
1075	Monks of Enryakuji and Onjōji fight over Onjōji's petition to establish an ordination platform.
1078	Chinese merchants arrive in Kyushu with a message from the Sung court.
1081	Enryakuji monks and laymen burn Onjōji temples.
	Emperor Shirakawa visits the Iwashimizu and Kamo shrines, guarded by Minamoto no Yoshiie and Yoshitsuna against attack by Onjōji monks.
1083	Yoshiie intervenes in a quarrel among the Kiyohara and the Later Three Years' War begins.
1087	Shirakawa, after fourteen years of strong rule, abdicates and opens the Senior Retired Emperor's Office (*in-no-chō*), through which he dominates the court until his death in 1129.
	Yoshiie finally defeats Kiyohara no Iehira, ending the Later Three Years' War. Mutsu and Dewa are united under Kiyohara no Kiyohira, who assumes Fujiwara, his father's clan name, at Hiraizumi (the Ōshū Fujiwara).
1091	The court is alarmed by the threat of a clash between forces of Yoshiie and his brother Yoshitsuna near the capital.
	Provincial troops forbidden to come up to the capital.
	Landholders forbidden to commend land to Yoshiie.
1095	Shirakawa establishes a guard unit (*in-no-hokumen*) for the Senior Retired Emperor's Office.
1105	Fujiwara no Kiyohira begins building a temple in Hiraizumi later known as Chūsonji.
1108	Taira no Masamori, favored by Shirakawa, successfully leads a punitive mission against Yoshiie's son Yoshichika. The martial reputation of the Ise Heishi begins to rival the Minamoto's.
1113	A force of 2,000 Enryakuji warrior monks comes to Shirakawa's residence, where they are confronted by Imperial Police led by Masamori and Minamoto no Tameyoshi.
1115	Shirabyōshi female dancers are said to have made their first appearance.
1126	The Chūsonji in Hiraizumi is dedicated.
1129	Upon Shirakawa's death, his grandson Toba follows him as the senior retired emperor and proves to be equally strong-willed. Toba relies on the Ise Heishi for military support.
1135	Masamori's son, Tadamori, captures pirates in the Inland Sea and parades them in the capital.
1155	Because of the lawless conduct of Minamoto no Tametomo, his father, Tameyoshi, is dismissed from office.

	Enthronement of Go-Shirakawa.
1156	Toba, the senior retired emperor, dies.
	Hōgen Disturbance results from rivalries within both the imperial and Fujiwara families that bring mounted warriors into Kyoto for battle. The faction supporting Go-Shirakawa, including Taira no Kiyomori and Minamoto no Yoshitomo, is victorious. Ex-emperor Sutoku is exiled to Sanuki.
1158	Go-Shirakawa abdicates and plays a strong role at court as senior retired emperor through the reigns of five emperors, all children but one, until his death in 1192.
1160	In the Heiji Disturbance, Yoshitomo's coup fails and Kiyomori, who is again victorious, decimates the Minamoto leaders.
	Kiyomori is appointed to the Third Rank, the first warrior to become a senior noble (*kugyō*).
1167	Kiyomori appointed Chancellor, the first warrior to rise to the First Rank. His kinsmen monopolize court offices.
1168	Kiyomori falls ill, resigns, and takes holy orders, but continues to dominate the government.
1172	A Chinese merchant arrives as an emissary from the Sung and gifts are exchanged.
1175	Hōnen preaches Pure Land teaching in Kyoto, leading to the formation of the first sect of popular Buddhism, the Jōdo Sect.
1177	Shishigatani plot of Go-Shirakawa's supporters to overthrow Kiyomori is exposed and crushed.
1179	Kiyomori, with a show of military strength against Go-Shirakawa, seizes full control of the government.
1180	Kiyomori's two-year-old grandson, Antoku, is enthroned.
	Prince Mochihito, a son of Go-Shirakawa, issues a call for warriors everywhere to rise against the Taira.
	Minamoto no Yoritomo raises an army and the Taira army flees from a confrontation at Fujigawa.
	A Taira force torches the Nara temples.
1181	Kiyomori dies.
1183	Minamoto no Yoshinaka (Kiso Yoshinaka) defeats a Taira army at Kurikara in Etchū and marches on Kyoto.
	The Taira with Antoku flee to Kyushu.
	Go-Shirakawa has Go-Toba, his grandson, enthroned, even though Antoku is emperor.
1184	Minamoto no Yoshitsune, half brother of Yoritomo, defeats Yoshinaka.
	Yoshitsune surprises and destroys the Taira force at Ichinotani.
1185	Yoshitsune defeats the Taira at Yashima and in the final sea battle at Dannoura, where Antoku drowns.
1189	Yoritomo destroys the Ōshū Fujiwara and extends his military control to all of Japan.

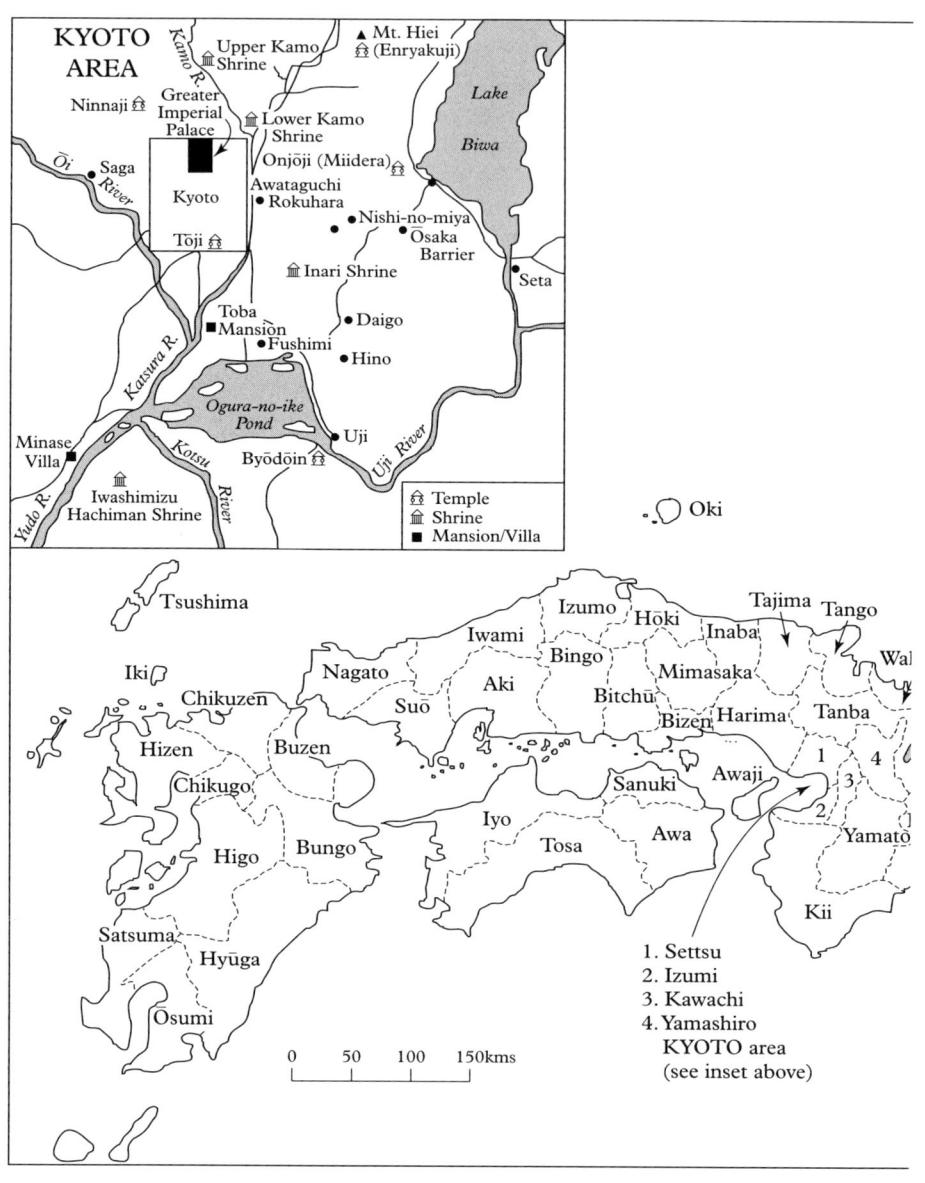

Japan in the Heian period. Adapted from Helen McCullough, *Classical Japanese Prose*, 1990.

INTRODUCTION

The Heian period opened in 794 with the building of a new capital, Heian-kyō, later known as Kyoto. The grand plan of the new city, on a larger scale than earlier capitals, expressed the ambitious vision of Emperor Kammu. No other Japanese emperor had ever taken into his own hands so decisively the absolute powers of the emperor as conceived in Chinese theory. He and some of his immediate successors not only asserted the authority of the throne; they took positive measures designed to improve the effectiveness of the central government in administering the country. Theirs was a dedicated attempt to revitalize the system of administration modeled on the governmental machinery of T'ang China and operate it effectively. Throughout the four centuries of the Heian era the imperial court continued as the only political center, but the effectiveness of its administration declined gradually. The title of emperor continued in the imperial line without dynastic change, as it does to this day, but many of the reigning emperors were reduced to figureheads, manipulated by noble families at court, notably the Fujiwara, and later by senior retired emperors. The Heian period closed in 1185 when the struggle for hegemony among the warrior families resulted in the victory of Minamoto no Yoritomo and most political initiatives devolved into his hands at his headquarters at Kamakura. The imperial court continued at Kyoto, playing a largely ceremonial and legitimizing role, while political power was exercised by military overlords until the Meiji Restoration of 1868.

During Heian times, however, there was no challenge to the central position of the imperial court; rather, there was a gradual decline in its ability to derive adequate income from the provinces to sustain itself in the style it had designed. Similarly, although the principle of monarchical rule was unquestioned, actual political power was usually exercised, after the first century and a half, by a Fujiwara or by a senior imperial relative acting in the name of the emperor. In fact, historians, both medieval and modern, of loyalist sympathies regard as the golden age of Japanese history those decades of direct rule by enlightened, "virtuous" emperors – Kammu (781–806) and Saga (809–23), and again Uda and Daigo (887–930). For loyalists, these were the years when Japanese rulers most closely approached the ideal reigns of the sage-kings of ancient China. Probably the direct rule that these emperors exercised was praised, without close inquiry into how wise their policies may have been.

The system of government at the beginning of the Heian period was a remarkable copy, somewhat modified, of the Chinese institutions of the Sui (581–618) and T'ang (618–907) dynasties. The emperor was expected to rule with absolute authority. He was served by high ministers and a council of state, overseeing an elaborate centralized bureaucracy arranged in ministries (eight in the Japanese version) and numerous bureaus and offices. Japan, with a population estimated at 6 or 7 million, was divided into sixty-eight provinces (*kuni*), including two island provinces, as of 823, each with a provincial headquarters overseen by a governor. Provinces were subdivided into districts (*gun* or *kōri*), eight or nine on the average, each with an administrative office. In China the bureaucratic structure was staffed by officials selected for appointment on the basis of qualifications as determined by examinations. The examination system was not properly instituted in Japan. Some students at the state Academy (*Daigaku-ryō*) did take examinations, but appointment to office was determined largely by the court rank of the candidate's family and by family and marital connections rather than by qualifications or ability. The Chinese prohibition against appointment in one's native district was not observed in Japan.

Rice land was nationalized, in principle, and it was allotted to families of cultivators according to the ages and sex of family members. Allotments were subject to revision and adjustment every six years. Uniform taxes were levied on the basis of rice-field holdings, payable in grain, and there were handicraft-produce taxes frequently payable in textiles, a corvée, and a military service tax. In order to operate the land system, it was essential to survey the rice fields and prepare current registers of land allotted and a census at six-year intervals. The procurement of a literate and efficient staff, dedicated to the government's interests, to operate this complex land and tax system may well have been beyond the country's human resources. Provincial administration required the building and maintenance of a network of highways and a post system. It is not known when and how extensively the facilities were completed in areas distant from the capital, especially in the eastern provinces.

The T'ang system of government is referred to by Japanese historians as the *ritsuryō* (statutory) system: *ritsu* is the penal code, specifying punishments for various offenses, and *ryō* is the administrative code that provides detailed regulations and instructions for the operation of government and society. The Taihō code, completed in 701, and its revision, the Yōrō code, in 718 (but not put into effect until 757), generally followed the T'ang code. The *ryō* of Yōrō had over nine hundred articles. It was later amplified by supplementary rules. *Kyaku* were new orders or modifications of existing law, while *shiki* were issued to provide additional detail for provisions of the *ritsuryō* and *kyaku*. These supplements, designed to make the *ritsuryō* system operate more effectively by expanding on existing provisions or sometimes overruling them, were compiled diligently in early Heian into the tenth century.

When Chinese institutions were introduced from the beginning of the seventh century, they were seriously compromised by native traditions of aristocratic privilege. The elite class had long been organized in *uji* (clans or lineage groups), bound together by descent from a common ancestor, the clan deity (*ujigami*). Among the large clans in Yamato in central Japan, one rose above the others and assumed a kingly role. Claiming descent from the Sun Goddess, its chief, in his sacerdotal function, interceded with the deities on behalf of all of the clans. He also mediated relations among clans. In the sixth century, by conquest and negotiation, this Sun line extended its authority over much of Japan in league with its supporting clan chiefs, who performed specialized services as warriors, ritualists, administrators, and fiscal agents, functioning increasingly like ministers of a king.

The relative status level of the leading *uji* chiefs was recognized by hereditary court titles (*kabane*) conferred by the king of the Sun line to honor superior lineages. Competitiveness among the chiefs for status was the source of considerable turbulence within the Yamato group. It is significant that one of the first Chinese institutions to be adopted in 604 was the system of twelve cap-ranks, designating the colors of caps in official court dress. The scheme of court ranks was elaborated several times during the seventh century, increasing the number of gradations to nineteen, then to twenty-six, and in 685 to an eight-rank system with forty-eight steps, demonstrating the care with which gradations in hierarchy among the clan chiefs and their followers were adjusted to proclaim their relationship to the Yamato king.

This king came to be called *tennō* (literally, "heaven [descended] luminance"), conventionally translated "emperor." Like the Chinese Son of Heaven, he claimed absolute authority to all of the land. Private titles to rice fields were abolished in principle, as were agricultural and craft support groups that had served and supported the clans. To gain the acquiescence of the affiliated clans, he appointed their members to new Chinese-style official positions and assigned lands and households for their support. Rice land was granted according to court rank, office held, and meritorious service. Powerholders of regional clans whose cooperation was needed were also given grants and official positions. Court rank gave honored status and assurance of eligibility for hereditary appointments. The awarding of lower grades of rank restricted the number of lineages that could compete for high office. In effect, a new court aristocracy was formed selectively from the *uji* at great expense to the public domain. In the eighth century this was a large group, for more than 120 clans can be recognized, but by mid-Heian only about 10 of the clans were playing a significant role.

The first chapter of this volume, by William McCullough, describes the politics of the Heian court, beginning with the strong rule of Emperor Kammu and continuing until the reassertion of direct imperial rule by Go-Sanjō in 1068. During the first half-century the highest officials were drawn mostly from the imperial clan. Thereafter, in the competition for appointment to high office, the Northern Branch of the Fujiwara clan increasingly succeeded in excluding from high office other clans and also the other branches of the Fujiwara. This predominance came in good part from their success in providing emperors with Fujiwara daughters who produced heirs to the throne. The practice of a Fujiwara head, as grandfather of a young emperor, serving as his grandson's regent began in 866 and became the regular pattern. (Hitherto only imperial princes had served as regent.) Emperors were often persuaded to abdicate before reaching manhood. Early abdication had been common since the middle of the seventh century. It was often a welcome escape from the ceremonial demands of the position, palace intrigue, and the constant requests for favors from imperial relatives and families which had supplied women for the harem. It became a regular practice for Fujiwara relatives to serve as regent for adult as well as child emperors, and after 967 an unbroken succession of Fujiwara held the office of regent. This was possible because the Fujiwara played the game of marriage politics with consummate skill, aided by the good fortune of usually having available a supply of eligible imperial consorts.

The few strong emperors who ruled directly in early Heian proved to be the exception in Japanese history. The actual power of political initiative was delegated to (or usurped by) Fujiwara relatives. The emperor's role again became largely ceremonial and sacerdotal as he receded to a position above politics. The preference for indirect rule that had been evident since the clan period prevailed again. The domination of the court by the Fujiwara leader reached its height with Michinaga, especially in the years from 1016 to 1028.

During this time when the aristocracy was ascendant, the number favored with privilege was not large, perhaps only two or three hundred principal male members of the nobility at any one time. Those who actually wielded power may have numbered only a dozen or two and were almost all Fujiwara, except for a few Minamoto (of courtier, nonwarrior families). The five or six highest offices were reserved for lineages that traditionally might reach the first three court ranks, senior nobles known as *kugyō*, a group that also included men of the Fourth Rank who served on the Council of State. Lower on the scale, but also among the privileged nobles, were those of the Fourth Rank (ministers, for example) and Fifth Rank (governors of large provinces, among others).

Although the wealth of the aristocracy came from a variety of sources, well into the eleventh century its mainstay was income attached to rank and office. In the eleventh century, however, the lower ranks of the nobility seem often to have received little or nothing in the way of official income, depending for their livelihood on service in the households of the great aristocrats, who had concentrated most of the government's resources in their own hands. There was, in addition, some income obtained from landed proprietorships called *shōen* (estates). It was this small, ancient, completely urbanized society of aristocratic civil officials, living mostly on appointive incomes, that produced either directly or through patronage most of what we think of as Heian aristocratic culture, which is discussed in Chapter 6 by Helen McCullough.

The monopoly of power held by the Fujiwara continued until 1068, when Go-Sanjō came to the throne, the first emperor in 170 years whose mother was not a Fujiwara. During his short reign he reasserted monarchical powers. For the next century until the end of the Heian period, the Fujiwara, while continuously holding the post of regent and other high offices, had little actual power, being kept in check by three strong emperors (Shirakawa, Toba, and Go-Shirakawa). Each of these three, after a relatively short reign, abdicated, took up residence in a "cloister" (*in*), and established the Administrative Office of the Senior Retired Emperor (*in-no-chō*). This office, in its peculiar mixture of private and public functions, resembled the Administrative office (*mandokoro*) that had been created much earlier by the Fujiwara and other noble families to manage their family affairs, even to the formation of a guard unit and client relationships with warrior families. This organization enabled the retired emperors to develop more effectively landholding and other resources for the support of the imperial family and to hold the upper hand over the Fujiwara and dominate the court as few emperors had. As father or grandfather of the reigning emperor, the senior retired emperor played a regental role, dominating not only the emperor but also any younger retired emperors. He displaced the Fujiwara regent as the acknowledged authority in national affairs. This practice of political domination by the senior retired emperor, known as *insei*, "cloister government," is the subject of Chapter 9 by G. Cameron Hurst. The shift of power to the ex-emperors can be viewed as another phase in the ebb and flow of political strength between the imperial line and noble families with which it intermarried, a pattern that was already familiar in the Yamato clan period and in the Nara court.

Perhaps the greatest attribute of the Chinese state was its capital, an enormous walled city laid out in a symmetrical grid pattern dominated by the huge buildings of the imperial palace compound. The city plan was a most impressive symbolic representation of imperial grandeur. Kammu's new capital, Heian-kyō, following this model, was designed to make a powerful statement. True, it was overly ambitious and too costly, for it was never possible to fill out the complete grid. But while earlier capitals were all short-lived, Kyoto remained the imperial capital for more than a thousand years, from 794 to 1869. Until the seventeenth century it was the only real city in Japan. Chapter 2, by William McCullough, is devoted to a description of the capital, its plan and architecture, its economy and commerce, its population and the social world of noble households.

For the major policy and administrative problems engaged by the early Heian emperors, we turn again to the first chapter. In addition to building a new capital, Kammu may also have had in mind the T'ang example of mounting military campaigns to subjugate and absorb "barbarian" border areas. Since early Nara there had been numerous expeditions to subdue the ethnic people in the northeast. Kammu intensified the effort and by 804 finally met with success. However, the great expense of the expeditions together with the building of the new capital exhausted the treasury.

Among measures of fiscal retrenchment taken by Kammu was to restrict the large number of imperial princes and princesses receiving government support under provisions of the statutory system. In 805, more than one hundred were reduced to noble status, a measure taken by several succeeding emperors. Some sons of high-ranking consorts were granted the clan name Minamoto, and a few imperial grandchildren were given such clan names as Taira, Ariwara, and others. Some of these imperial descendants found careers as court nobles and others joined the provincial gentry.

Kammu and his immediate successors attempted to make their administrations more effective by introducing several new offices. To check misappropriation of tax rice and other assets from the provincial account by an outgoing governor, a board of agents known as *kageyushi* was appointed in Kammu's reign to audit a governor's accounts and the transfer of property to the incoming governor. Both parties were held accountable for discrepancies.

In 810, Emperor Saga established the *kurōdodokoro* (Chamberlains' Office), staffed by trusted men, to ensure confidentiality in the handling of important documents. Later it transmitted imperial edicts and supervised the imperial archives. In time it also came to handle the emperor's household affairs.

Also in Saga's time, in response to lawlessness in the capital and the surrounding region, a new police organization known as *kebiishi* ("Offenses Investigation Agents") gradually evolved. The functions of the Imperial Police included not only security matters and the arrest of miscreants but also the investigation, trial, sentencing, and imprisonment of criminals, thus replacing some of the duties of several existing offices. Later, branches were placed in some provinces and its *kebiishi* agents investigated land ownership, tax evasion, and other matters.

These new offices were established, one may conjecture, because the functions they served were not being performed satisfactorily by the existing *ritsuryō* offices. Or, in some instances, the emperor and his circle may have aimed to bring the functions in question under more immediate control. Many of the offices provided for by the statutory code were languishing, either because they were not considered essential or because the government had insufficient revenues to keep them in operation. By the end of the ninth century half of the central government's *ritsuryō* offices had been abandoned and the number of officials was much reduced.

The primary mission of the provincial government office and its subunits, the district offices, was to collect local products in the form of taxes and forward them to the capital. These products, including rice and other foodstuffs, were all of the goods and services needed to support officials of the central government and supply the specific needs of the capital and its elites: textiles, handicrafts, and local products such as salt, iron, paper mulberry, and many other goods. Rice was collected not only by direct taxation, but also as rental on rice land lent out by the provincial government. Rice was also collected on seed rice lent to cultivators for planting in the spring. At the beginning, corvée and military service were also part of tax obligations. In Chapter 3, "Land and Society," Dana Morris discusses how this all-important tax structure of the beginning of Heian underwent continual changes during the following centuries.

The provincial capitals were designed as small versions of the grid plan of the Heian-kyō. Detailed regulations for the staffing and operation of the provincial government, described by Cornelius Kiley in Chapter 4, "Provincial Administration and Land Tenure in Early Heian," indicate the importance central officials attached to the province's mission. A directive of 822 specifies a large and specialized staff for the provincial office to perform various administrative functions and compile the required annual reports, tax-grain inventory, list of tribute, number of taxable households, acreage under cultivation, percentage of crop damage, and so forth.

Responsibility for the administration of a province was entrusted to a governor selected from the middle ranks of the Kyoto nobility and appointed usually for four years. He was accompanied to his post by a number of staff members, but most of the officeholders in the provincial headquarters were members of the local elites in positions that, by and large, were permanent and hereditary. It was usually difficult for the governor to prevail against the interests of the locally based officials. Increasingly the governors were absentee, the position a sinecure, and the executive function left to a deputy.

The subprovincial district offices were staffed entirely by local gentry. As a consequence, the administration of land and the collection of taxes were carried out by locals who, backed by governmental authority, benefited greatly from their positions in income and landholding. Although the mission of a provincial office was to marshal local resources for the benefit of the central government, it developed into a bargaining place for the division of resources between capital and country. Some governors sought the post, even purchased it, with the expectation of enriching themselves. As a consequence of these competing interests, the share that went to Kyoto declined steadily.

In the attempt to ensure its income, the government set a revenue quota for each province, charging the governor with the responsibility of meeting the contracted amount. In effect this policy recognized the provincial government as a semiautonomous unit with tax obligations to the central government. It was permitted to make certain changes in the tax system, adding new taxes or occasional levies, to meet its quota. This was a significant departure from the principle of the statutory code of a national, uniform tax system. Morris argues that the modifications in the tax system, while abandoning provisions of the code, were changes that better met the capital's needs and, at the same time, were more efficient and better fitted the rural economy. The changes succeeded at length in stabilizing the government's income. However, the quotas were set using the tax base as it stood about the year 900. As a consequence, Morris points out, the central government did not benefit from the increase in agricultural output brought about by expansion of acreage and by higher yields produced by improvements in agricultural methods. Among the improvements were the introduction of an animal-drawn plow with moldboard, the use of draft animals, better fertilizer, and other innovations discussed by Morris.

The system of allotting rice fields on the basis of census registration operated reasonably well in the Nara period, but reallocations came to a halt about 840. Scholars have suggested a variety of causes for the suspension of reallocation. Morris demonstrates that the primary reason was the shortage of land available for distribution. Population had increased by more than a million during Nara, creating a demand for allocations that the government could not meet.

Since early in the Nara period the government had encouraged the opening of new rice fields, and much land continued to be reclaimed. Because of the high cost of developing irrigated rice land, the government was obliged in 743, as an incentive, to grant developers permanent possession of reclaimed land, the source of many of the first *shōen* (estates). In the Heian period, however, *shōen* were created, in effect, when the central government ordered the transfer of tax payments on segments of land from the provincial government to a religious institution or a noble family in the capital. Subsequently there was an increase in the number of *shōen* established by commendation. Local magnates or land managers were often in conflict with provincial officials over land rights, management authority, and tax immunities. They tried to prevent the interference of provincial authorities by commending rights (*shiki*) to the land under their control to a Kyoto aristocrat or a major religious institution as "proprietor" (*ryōke*) while retaining hereditary rights of management and control of the cultivators. In return for a fee or a share of the *shōen*'s income, the *ryōke* sought to protect the rights claimed by the local manager. If the *ryōke* could not command enough influence at court to accomplish this task, he might make a further commendation to a member of the imperial family or one of the most powerful Fujiwara or to a great temple (*honke*). By late Heian, nearly half of the agricultural land had become *shōen* in this way. This privatization of land, or rights to land, was carried out, for the most part, within the provisions of the statutory code and was usually well supported by documentation.

The greater part of the agricultural land may have remained in the public domain under the administration of the provincial headquarters – designated as *kokugaryō* (provincial domains) – but *shōen* probably provided most of the economic support of court nobles, religious institutions, and even the imperial family. Emperor Go-Sanjō in 1069 ordered a major nationwide registration of *shōen* to examine their legality and rule on their tax exemption claims. Such inquiries, which had begun as early as the ninth century, continued periodically until the end of Heian. Sorting out claims of land parcels to *shōen* or *kokugaryō* status was a continuous process. Also in frequent dispute was the question of which parcels of *shōen* land were liable for which provincial levies. Issues such as these were usually present in the centuries-long struggle of the central government to control local officials and landholders. But, lacking effective means of coercion, the authorities gradually lost ground. Thus, landholding and tax systems changed slowly but significantly in the course of the Heian period. Through these changes, as Kiley states, the provincial governments "proved to be among the most durable of the *ritsuryō* institutions, probably because from the beginning they served to integrate the interests of local elites, capital officials, and court nobility."

Japan was a preliterate society until the adoption of Chinese as a system of writing. This probably occurred several centuries before the writing of the first complete books that have come down to us, two histories: the *Kojiki*, traditionally dated 712; and the first of the official histories modeled on Chinese dynastic histories, the *Nihon shoki* of 720. The latter work reveals a high degree of assimilation of Chinese civilization: the writing of a historical chronicle in literary Chinese, the citing of earlier sources, a Confucian worldview and ethics, and, of course, the re-creation of the complex T'ang organization of government already spelled out in the codes of 702 and 718.

By this time the study of Chinese civilization had certainly had a long history. The first study of Chinese texts is conventionally associated with the arrival of Wani, a Korean scholar from the kingdom of Paekche who is thought to have arrived about 400 to tutor the crown prince. Early in the sixth century, Paekche began sending, in rotation, scholars of the classics as well as specialists in music, medicine, divination, and the calendar. The introduction of Buddhist statues and sutras in 552 (or 538) is also attributed to the king of Paekche. Knowledge of Chinese-style governmental institutions as adapted in Korea came from several Korean states and informed the measures taken by the prince regent Shōtoku Taishi in 604 to introduce cap ranks and other Chinese institutions.

Regular relations with China began in 607 and 608 when official embassies were sent to the Sui court, followed by many embassies to the T'ang, beginning in 630 and continuing until 834. These missions enabled the court to send students to China, some for many years of specialized study. Upon their return they made an invaluable contribution to the political and cultural transformation of Japan on the Chinese model.

The invasion of the Korean peninsula by T'ang armies and the overthrow of Paekche in 663 and Koguryŏ in 668 precipitated the flight to Japan of many Koreans. Among the refugees were officials and scholars who had knowledge of such fields as administration, law, court ceremonial, military tactics, Chinese literature, and other subjects. That well over a hundred of the immigrants were appointed to court rank and absorbed into the nobility is evidence of the value placed on their knowledge and talents.

The court followed the Chinese example of opening an Academy (*Daigaku-ryō*) in the capital to train officials. The written language of the Academy was Chinese, as was the written language of government, the law codes, the surviving records and inscriptions, and the national histories. The ability to compose Chinese poems became an essential skill at court banquets, as it was at receptions for visiting Chinese and Korean officials. Banquet poems in Chinese were represented in the earliest known anthology, the *Kaifūsō* of 751. It was followed in the early decades of the Heian period by three anthologies of poems in Chinese compiled by imperial order. The only written works in the Japanese language surviving from the Nara period are written with Chinese characters used phonetically, that is, for their sound, ignoring their meaning. However, there were exceptions when Chinese constructions were used, pronounced in the Japanese approximation of their meaning. This cumbersome mixture of Chinese and Japanese is found in the *Kojiki* and the great anthology of Japanese poetry, the *Man'yōshū* (after 759), and in records of imperial proclamations (*semmyō*) and Shinto prayers (*norito*).

The Japanese elite appears to have been eager to adopt all aspects of Chinese civilization, not merely governmental institutions, law, and the written language, but also Chinese thought and ethics, Buddhism and its sculpture, painting, and architecture, continental forms of music and dance, and many branches of Chinese knowledge, arts, and crafts.

These remarkable advances in acquiring and assimilating Chinese culture in the two centuries leading up to the Heian period are described by Edwin Cranston in his chapter in Volume 1 of *The Cambridge History of Japan*. In the present volume, Marian Ury's Chapter 5 continues the account of the absorption of Chinese learning and intellectual life. Sons of aristocrats were tutored using Chinese primers that were compilations of quotations drawn from the classics and other edifying texts. While memorizing the characters, children also learned moral maxims to live by. The more talented or better-connected boys went on to private schools or the Academy to prepare for careers as officials. The curriculum included Chinese classics, histories, and belles lettres.

Many noblemen recorded their activities in diaries, written in Chinese or hybrid Chinese, which have come down to us. Parts of the personal diaries of emperors Uda and Murakami of the eighth and ninth centuries have survived. Anthologies of prose written in Chinese began to appear. Ury traces the careers of professional scholars of Chinese patronized by emperors and Fujiwara leaders. Among the scholars were a number of men of experience and insight who, when commissioned to submit reports detailing the ills of society and government and their recommendations for reform, came forward with trenchant proposals, most of which were not adopted. Some of the early Heian rulers, however, tried to legislate an orderly and harmonious society by compiling detailed regulations supplementing the *ritsuryō* statutes, culminating in the voluminous *Engi shiki*, completed in 927. Scholars continued to record the histories of past reigns, completing the last of the Six National Histories (*Rikkokushi*) in 901 to serve as mirrors in which to read the successes and failures of past administrations.

During the ascendancy of the Chinese cultural style at the beginning of Heian, poetry composed in Japanese may have lost temporarily its role on public occasions. But an important change came about 900 with the development of the *hiragana* syllabary. This was the practice of using a limited number of the cursive, simplified forms of characters for their sound to write Japanese phonetically. The graceful and fluid *kana* were an efficient and elegant way to write Japanese, a major improvement over the cumbersome method of writing characters in their formal, angular style. Men as well as women used *hiragana* to write poetry and informal prose.

There was a resurgence of attention to Japanese poetry, especially the *waka* (thirty-one-syllable) form. The first and most celebrated of the imperial anthologies of poems in Japanese, the *Kokinshū*, was compiled in 905. One of the compilers, Ki no Tsurayuki, added a preface in Japanese in which he seemed to imply that Japanese poetry could stand its ground with Chinese poetry. From about the same date came the earliest surviving work of narrative prose, *Taketori monogatari*. In 935, Tsurayuki wrote a travel journal (*Tosa nikki*), in which the Japanese prose serves as a setting for his poems; in it he adopted the persona of a woman, a nod to the convention that Japanese prose was woman's language. In these prose works, as in the *Kokinshū*, there is a confident assertion of the Japanese style at the same time that Chinese stylistic influences are evident. The blend of Japanese and Chinese elements is characteristic of the best of the arts of aristocratic culture. The importance of *hiragana* was that both women and men could now write fluently in their native language. It was especially liberating for the women, ladies of the court, to find voices in which they could express their feelings about their experiences – relationships between women and between men and women.

The aesthetics of court society received its most sensitive expression in *The Tale of Genji* (early eleventh century) of Murasaki Shikibu. This acclaimed masterpiece of Japanese literature, together with the *Pillow Book* (completed about 1001), a miscellany by Sei Shōnagon, and contemporary historical accounts (*Eiga monogatari* and *Ōkagami*) of the Fujiwara at their height, provide us with extraordinarily rich descriptions of aristocratic culture of the early eleventh century. Helen McCullough's Chapter 6 draws on this range of literary sources to detail the artistic accomplishments and entertainments of this privileged society in its most brilliant period. This was the culture of a small circle of the highest-ranking nobles and their associates. And yet we are better informed about their lives and careers, their etiquette and ceremonies, their ideals of beauty and aesthetic sensibilities, their romantic affairs and yearnings, than we are about any other group in Japanese history, at least until the seventeenth century.

Of the many elements of Chinese and continental civilization introduced into Japan, one that was embraced with special enthusiasm and had profound and lasting importance in Japanese culture is Buddhism. Following the arrival of Buddhist texts and statues from Paekche in the middle of the sixth century, the Nakatomi clan, with its Shintō ritualists, opposed the reception of Buddhism by the court. In 587 the dying emperor Yōmei was converted to Buddhism. In the succession struggle that followed, Soga no Umako and the future Prince Shōtoku defeated the Nakatomi. To commemorate divine assistance in their victory, Shōtoku founded the Shintennōji Temple (in present day Osaka).

Buddhist sutras and images were considered to have magical powers akin to but greater than those of the native religion. They were regarded as beneficial in preventing and curing disease and safeguarding against famine and natural disasters. Buddhism's gorgeous vestments and mysterious rites had a strong appeal, as did the grandeur of its temple buildings with their statues and wall paintings. Buddhism was an important vehicle for the transmission of many aspects of continental culture. In addition to the literate, intellectual tradition and the large corpus of texts, it also carried with it beneficial practical knowledge: medicine, architecture, bridge building, and road construction. The imperial clan and great families were extravagant in supporting Buddhism, founding temples and endowing them with large landholdings. At the same time, the government tried to maintain control of temples by appointing the high clerics, restricting the number of ordinations, and disciplining wayward monks and nuns.

The government recognized the value of Buddhism as a means of spreading the spiritual authority of the state, following the practice in China and Korea. In 741, Emperor Shōmu ordered the establishment of a temple (*kokubunji*) and nunnery in each province as branches of the central Tōdaiji in Nara. They were staffed by clerics from the capital who served as religious agents of the central government and performed rituals for the protection of the state. Buddhism became, in effect, a state religion. It was brought under the administration of the central government in somewhat the same way that Shinto shrines were in the Taihō code that established the *Jingikan* (Department of Shrines) as a government office. The emperor presided over both temples and shrines while continuing to perform his historical role as chief priest in the worship of his ancestors and the national deities.

The government's attempt to check the uncontrolled increase of temples and monks in early Nara was undercut by the lavish support of temples by Emperor Shōmu (r. 724–49) and his daughter, who succeeded him as Kōken (r. 749–58) and reigned again later as Shōtoku from 764 to 770. The large temples in Nara appeared to surround and overwhelm the imperial palace. The scandal of the priest Dōkyō's influence over Shōtoku, which threatened even the imperial succession, brought a sharp reaction that profoundly affected the course of Heian Buddhism. The danger of Buddhist interference in government was a factor in Emperor Kammu's decision to move the capital first to Nagaoka, and it certainly determined his policy to forbid the Nara sects from establishing temples in Heian-kyō.

Stanley Weinstein, in Chapter 7, "Aristocratic Buddhism," traces the imperial patronage of the newly introduced esoteric sects, Tendai and Shingon, which were permitted to establish temples in and near the new capital. These sects were adapted to Japanese needs. Their rituals soon came to have an integral role in the spiritual as well as ceremonial life of the imperial family and court aristocrats. Tendai monks introduced from China recent developments in Pure Land teachings that assured believers that the repeated recitation of Amida's name would lead to rebirth in the Western Paradise. Buddhism emerged from the monasteries to give direction to the spiritual lives of the aristocrats, especially in their later years, with the promise of immediate salvation. Nobles patronized the copying of illuminated sutras, and the great Fujiwara constructed private chapels and commissioned large gilded statues of Amida Buddha. On his deathbed the believer waited holding strings in his hands, stretched to a statue or painting of Amida descending to welcome him (*raigō*), to ensure that his soul would be conducted to paradise. At the same time, itinerant monks preaching the faith attracted an ecstatic following among the common people. In the twelfth and thirteenth centuries, Pure Land teachings emerged from Tendai to become independent sects: the Jōdo and Jōdo Shin.

In Heian times, Buddhism diverged from its sources on the continent, and became a naturalized Japanese religion. It has continued to this day to be the prominent religion in Japan, in contrast to its history in China and Korea, where its following gradually declined.

Allan Grapard's Chapter 8, on religious practices, introduces recent findings by Japanese and Western scholars that have broadened our conception of Heian religion. One theme the chapter traces is the relationship that evolved between Buddhism and Shinto, as the native religious practices came to be called. Beginning in mid-Nara and increasingly in early Heian, Buddhist temples were built on the grounds of important Shinto shrines. Buddhist monks administered the temples and performed Buddhist rites in front of the native deities (*kami*). There was no incongruity seen in monks worshipping both buddhas and *kami*. Not only were temples associated with shrines in this way, but buddhas and bodhisattvas came to be associated with individual ancestral *kami* of the imperial and clan lineages. In many instances *kami* came to be regarded as local manifestations of the more universal buddhas and bodhisattvas. A number of shrines to which temples were added were distant from the capital and were dedicated to the worship of deities associated with lineages other than the imperial clan. Not only were *kami* co-opted in this way and linked to Buddhist deities, but measures were taken to establish a uniformity in the rites that were performed. The primary rituals were those for the protection of the state and for the health and protection of the emperor as the embodiment of the state. This was, like the network of provincial branch temples, yet another strategy for extending throughout the country the religious representation of the emperor and the central government, and for presenting rites that had a recognizable, consistent pattern.

Grapard opens his chapter with a quotation from the tenth-century testament of Fujiwara no Morosuke, who, as Minister of the Right, held one of the highest offices of state. His words of guidance for his heirs include advice on how they should conduct themselves in their daily activities. He provides a remarkable illustration of the variety of religious, cosmological, and ethical beliefs that guided the Heian noble's actions. Morosuke's daily observances included reciting the names of buddhas and worshipping various *kami*. He was mindful each day of cosmological and geomantic constraints, according to Chinese calendrical lore, on his movements and activities. The testament proceeds to advocate at length some of the Confucian principles of behavior – rectitude, moderation, self-control, frugality, and a single-minded concern for his family's physical and material welfare. Heian prose literature and nobles' diaries provide numerous instances of a noble's appeal to rites to ensure protection from disease, recovery from illness, safe childbirth, success in projects, and progress in his career. A noble gentleman was expected to cultivate knowledge of and skill in the correct performance of rites and ceremonies which were akin to religious practices.

The professional warrior class (*bushi*), its evolution and rise to dominance at the end of Heian, is the subject of Chapter 10 by Takeuchi Rizō. When the government ended military conscription as a national requirement in 792, it ceased to maintain a standing army. To keep order in the countryside, it recruited *kondei* ("stalwart youths"), mounted fighters drawn from the families of the regional gentry. A prescribed number of *kondei*, ranging from twenty to two hundred, was specified for each province. Perhaps because they were so few, they do not appear frequently in the literature. Little is known about their employment, and they are rarely mentioned by mid-Heian. In the capital, for the defense of the Greater Imperial Palace, there were six guard units provided by law. Led by aristocrats, they became largely ceremonial and decorative. For the security of the palace and to check crime in the capital and its environs, the Imperial Police (*kebiishi*) were formed early in the ninth century. A number of government units, like the new Chamberlains' Office, and later the Senior Retired Emperor's Office (*in-no-chō*), found it expedient to recruit private guard units for security.

Lawlessness was prevalent in the countryside, for the central government had in effect ceded to the landed classes responsibility for the preservation of the public peace. By the late ninth century, provincial governors, first in the eastern provinces, requested permission to recruit warriors to protect themselves from attack and also to employ as needed to enforce their orders. Landowners and *shōen* managers engaged armed men to help them defend their claims. Predominant among the professional fighters were relatives of district magistrates and other prominent provincial families. Only those in this class had the resources to maintain the horses, saddles, armor, and weapons that distinguished them as professional warriors. Descended from regional *uji*, these mounted archers, skilled in hunting, had been the effective forces in the campaigns to the northeast. Members of this class held appointments as provincial or district officials, or involved themselves as self-appointed land managers or tax collection agents, ever ready and equipped to defend their land claims and perhaps to trespass on others' holdings. Military preparedness was a necessary adjunct to land management.

When a local strongman defied a provincial governor by refusing to forward tax revenues or by intruding on government land, the imperial court, lacking a military force of its own, deputized the governor or, if more strength was needed, the leader of a court-related warrior family – a Taira or Minamoto – with a military or police title and commissioned him to mount a force against the offender. The revolt of Taira no Masakado in the 930s was the first major disturbance of this kind. The Taira or Minamoto chief who was victorious as commander of a punitive expedition attracted followers to his warrior band from among the provincial elite. These noble families of imperial descent sought their fortunes by landholding and police actions in the provinces while maintaining ties with the capital. They were used as intimidators by Fujiwara regents and senior retired emperors. When rival factions at court brought mounted warriors of the Minamoto and Taira chiefs into the capital to stage a coup in 1156, the gates to political power were opened for the *bushi*. The issue still to be resolved was which of the network of warrior bands would dominate. That was determined in the Gempei (i.e., Minamoto – Taira) War of 1180–85, when armies organized by Minamoto no Yoritomo defeated the Taira forces.

At the outset of the war, Yoritomo attracted supporters by proposing a bold plan. On his own authority he confirmed rights to land and office of warriors in the eastern region who would pledge allegiance to him. By usurping in this way the authority of the imperial government over land, he guaranteed enduring tenures that the provincial warrior-gentry class had long sought. As he rose to military supremacy, he gradually put in place an administrative organization that supplemented the existing system of provincial government. From the independent headquarters he maintained in Kamakura in the east, Yoritomo exercised, with imperial sanction, broad military and police powers and, through his involvement in land rights, civil authority as well.

This revolutionary transfer of power brought the Heian period to an end. The court nobility, together with the imperial line, had monopolized political power and enjoyed all of its material benefits for more than five centuries since the beginning of the Nara period. With the end of Heian, the substance of the civil aristocracy's privilege was gone, although as a class it continued to survive in reduced circumstances. From this time political initiatives were taken only by *bushi* rulers. As one warrior regime followed another in the Kamakura (1185–1333), Muromachi (1333–1568), Azuchi-Momoyama (1568–1600), and Edo (1600–1868) periods, the imperial family and nobility were sustained on meager allowances by *bushi* overlords who continued to relish appointment to court rank and empty *ritsuryō* titles. Some of the vestiges of court traditions were preserved, along with the lineages of the Fujiwara and other noble families, to be resurrected following the Meiji Restoration of 1868.

CHAPTER 1

THE HEIAN COURT, 794–1070

KAMMU TO NIMMYŌ, 781–850

The man known to history as Emperor Kammu (737–806, r. 781–806) was an obscure official in his mid-thirties when the exigencies of Nara politics catapulted his almost equally obscure father, Kōnin (702–82, r. 770–81), onto the imperial throne in 770 and elevated Kammu himself to the position of crown prince three years later.[1] In 781 his father abdicated, and the former director of the state Academy, who may have been passed over originally in the selection of Kōnin's heir apparent because of the humble immigrant origins of his mother's patriline (a Korean-descended lineage, the Yamato), now found himself installed as Emperor of Japan – a learned peer of his illiterate contemporary Charlemagne and of the famous Abassid caliph Harun Al-Rashid at the new capital of Baghdad. Governmental reform and retrenchment, coupled with vigorous action against Buddhist and secular opponents, had laid a sound basis for imperial power during Kōnin's reign, and Kammu quickly demonstrated that he was capable of exercising and enhancing that power.

After efficiently suppressing a plot against the throne in 782 by high-ranking adherents of the imperial lineage displaced by Kōnin's accession (the line of Emperor Temmu), the new emperor and his advisers apparently decided the time had come to leave the capital, which was the handiwork of the old imperial line and the stronghold of both that line's adherents and the Buddhist forces that seem to have very nearly succeeded in usurping imperial authority in the time of Kōnin's immediate predecessor, Empress Shōtoku (718–70;

---

1 Among the surveys of Heian history consulted in the writing of this chapter, one of the most useful is Inoue Mitsusada, Nagahara Keiji, Kodama Kōta, and Ōkubo Toshiaki, eds., *Nihon rekishi taikei*, vol. 1: *Genshi. Kodai* (Tokyo: Yamakawa shuppansha, 1984). See also George Sansom, *A Short Cultural History of Japan*, rev. ed. (New York: Appleton-Century, 1943); Sansom, *A History of Japan to 1334* (Stanford, Calif.: Stanford University Press, 1958); James Murdoch, *A History of Japan*, vol. 1 (London: Routledge & Kegan Paul, 1949; first published 1910), and John Whitney Hall, *Japan from Prehistory to Modern Times* (New York: Delacorte Press, 1970).

r. 749–58, 764–70). In the early summer of 784, Kammu directed that a site for a new capital be surveyed at Nagaoka, an area near the Katsura River about twenty miles northwest of Nara (Heizei-kyō or Heijō-kyō) and approximately a half mile northwest of the point where the Meishin Highway now first crosses the Tōkaidō Shinkansen south of Kyoto. At the end of the same year, he moved into his new palace there, his haste to be gone from Nara inspired perhaps by fear of interference in, or resistance to, the move by forces in the old capital facing economic loss or ruin because of the court's abandonment of the city.

Nagaoka was in an area associated politically and economically with Kammu's family line ever since the time of his great-grandfather Emperor Tenji (626–72, r. 661–72), but it was doubtless particularly attractive to him as the home of his matriline. (His mother, as already noted, was a Yamato, and her mother was a Korean-descended Haji, or Hanishi, based in the same general area.) The new imperial seat was more conveniently located for land and water communication than the capital at Nara had been, but its cramped and flood-prone site near a large marsh may have made it unsuitable for long-term occupancy. In any case, a series of inauspicious political events that accompanied the city's founding probably further condemned it in the eyes of a court that set great store by omens and spirits.[2]

Fujiwara no Tanetsugu (737–85), although not the senior minister at court in 784, was Kammu's chief adviser and, apparently, the leading advocate of the transfer of the capital to Nagaoka. (His maternal family, the Hata, was, like Kammu's, also of Korean lineage and also based in the Nagaoka area.) He probably owed his influential position at court to his being a nephew of Fujiwara no Momokawa (732–79), who had almost certainly been instrumental both in the selection of Kōnin as successor to Empress Shōtoku in 770, and also in the appointment of Kammu as Kōnin's heir in 773. Moreover, Tanetsugu's cousin Otomuro (760–90) was Kammu's consort and the mother of his eldest son, the future Emperor Heizei (774–824, r. 806–9). (See Figure 1.1: Genealogy of Heian emperors.)

On a night in the autumn of 785, while Emperor Kammu was temporarily absent from the city, Tanetsugu was killed at Nagaoka. Because of his position it seems likely that the murder was a political

---

2 On the removal of the imperial seat to Nagaoka, see Ronald P. Toby, "Why Leave Nara? Kammu and the Transfer of the Capital," *Monumenta Nipponica* 40 (1985): 331–47. On floods at Nagaoka, see Hirakawa Minami, "Zōto to seii," in Hashimoto Yoshihiko, *Komonjo no kataru Nihon shi*, vol. 2: *Heian* (Tokyo: Chikuma shobō, 1991), pp. 27–32.

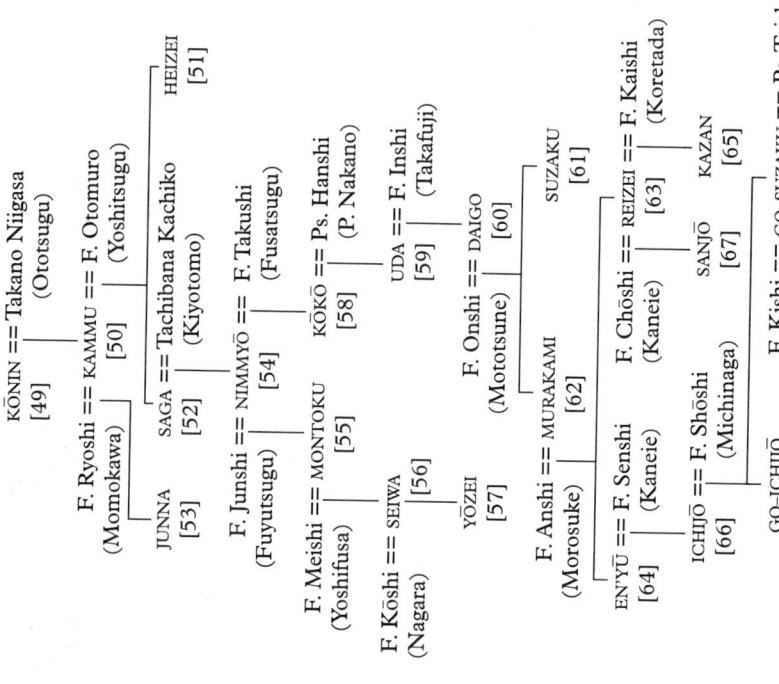

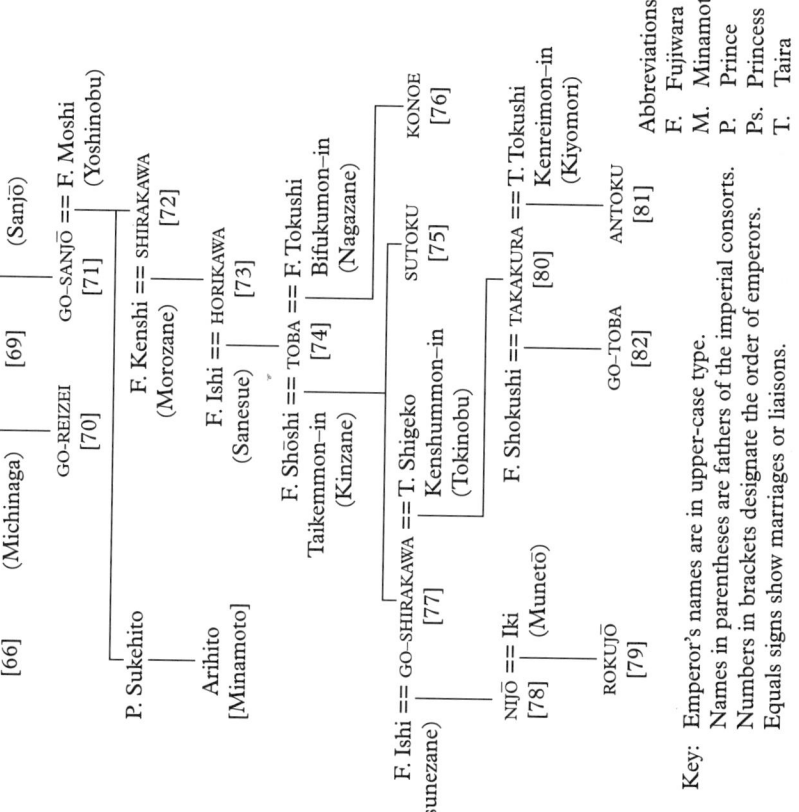

Figure 1.1. Genealogy of Heian emperors.

act, as the spare account in the chronicles suggests. It could have been instigated by entrenched interests at Nara opposed to the move to Nagaoka, by elements excluded from power after the ascendancy of the Momokawa line of the Fujiwara clan at court (i.e., by members of the Ōtomo and Saeki clans), and by friction between Tanetsugu and the heir apparent, Kammu's younger full brother, Prince Sawara (d. 785), who appears to have clashed with Tanetsugu earlier, and who may have felt that his own position was endangered by Tanetsugu's familial connection with Heizei. Tanetsugu may in fact have been looking for an opportunity to depose Sawara and establish Heizei in his place as crown prince, a step that might well have had Kammu's backing. In any case, Sawara was soon implicated in the assassination, deposed, and condemned to exile – which he avoided, the chronicle alleges, by starving himself to death. That outcome served what may be presumed to have been Kammu's interests – so well, indeed, that one might suspect the emperor himself of having manipulated the affair from the outset. However, no evidence supports such a view, and Kammu does not appear otherwise to have pursued his ends with so ruthless a disregard of his nobles' lives.

Tanetsugu's assassination, Sawara's suicide, and the execution of the assassins were soon followed by famine, devastating floods, epidemic disease, and a series of deaths and illnesses in Kammu's family, which diviners had no difficulty in interpreting as the revenge of Sawara's angry spirit. It may have been the inauspiciousness of all those circumstances, together with a lively fear of what the prince's spirit might do in the future, that helped Kammu decide in the early spring of 793 to accept the advice of his longtime confidant Wake no Kiyomaro (733–99), who, reportedly dismayed by the unfinished state of Nagaoka after ten years of effort and untold expenditures, had urged the emperor to seek a new location for the capital in the Kadono area northeast of Nagaoka. The choice of a site in what is now the city of Kyoto was soon made, and the fifty-seven-year-old Kammu moved into his new palace at Heian-kyō in the tenth month of 794.

The move to Heian marked the end of a temporally long peregrination that had taken Japanese rulers and their courts from one site to another ever since the inception of the statutory (*ritsuryō*) system of government in the seventh century. Like the earlier transfers, the moves to Nagaoka and Heian doubtless served to strengthen the position of the political leaders at the imperial court, increasing the dependence of the nobility on the government because of the great personal cost of the moves; and we can perhaps assume that such was one of Kammu's chief objectives.[3] The move to Heian was both a continuation of, and a conclusion to, a century and a half of homogeneous historical development – in that sense, an apt symbol for the reign of the sovereign who presided over the construction of the new capital and occupied the throne for the first dozen years of its life. Kammu was the last of a line of puissant, capital-building monarchs who were able to mobilize the entire country's wealth and military power for national or dynastic purposes. After him, the limelight of central political history shifted steadily and rapidly away from the person of the sovereign toward erstwhile holders of nominally subordinate court posts, roles men whose growing power at length confined their suzerains to largely ritualistic and ceremonial functions. By the time death ended the reign of Kammu's grandson Nimmyō (810–50, r. 833–50), the Northern House of the Fujiwara clan was well on its way to complete domination of both the emperor and the organs of his statutory government.

Kammu may have been the most powerful ruler the imperial line ever produced. He was a mature man and an experienced official when he came to the throne in 781, trained in the Confucian pedagogic tradition to what appears to have been a sober passion for government. The official chronicler notes that he had no use for "literary floweriness," and he appears to have been equally uninterested in the kind of extravagant Buddhistic devotion that had nearly bankrupted the state under Shōmu and Kōken/Shōtoku. It is characteristic of him that his reign is remembered chiefly not because of grand temples, magnificent art, or superlative literature, but for its accomplishments in city building, war, and governmental reform.

Kammu was able to impose his will on the imperial court not only because of his personal qualities, but also because of circumstances, partly fortuitous and partly of his own making, that left him relatively free of influence from the old-line high nobility. Political history until the middle of the eighth century had been characterized by the interaction between, on the one hand, an emperor who was thought of as possessing absolute authority, and, on the other, a powerful body of noble clans, based in the Council of State (*Daijōkan* or *Dajōkan*), who wielded the government's executive authority. But after the downfall of Fujiwara no Nakamaro (706–64) of

---

[3] Sasayama Haruo, ed. *(Kodai o kangaeru) Heian no miyako* (Tokyo: Yoshikawa kōbunkan, 1991), pp. 1–5.

the Southern House (Nanke) in 764 and the reconstitution of the government under Dōkyō (d. 772), men of lesser, "bureaucratic" clans (Kibi, Ishikawa, Isonokami, etc.) entered the central councils of government, and the ability of the Council of State to control and gainsay the emperor was markedly reduced.

Heir to that development, Kammu carried it to its furthest extent. Both he and his father owed their positions to the backing of Fujiwara leaders – notably Nagate (714–71) of the Northern House (Hokke) and Momokawa of the Ceremonials House (Shikike) – who, in concert with other nobles, seem to have sought a change of imperial line as a means of checking the decay associated with Empress Kōken/Shōtoku (in the Temmu line of emperors), a process that was threatening both their political and their economic well-being. (See Figure 1.2: Genealogy of the Four Fujiwara Houses.) But by the early years of Kammu's reign, Momokawa and most of the other influential Fujiwara were dead, and Kammu subsequently saw to it that a new generation of clan leaders was not given the opportunity to establish its hegemony at court. He was aided by the enormous costs to the nobility of the successive moves of the capital, and by great military campaigns in the northeastern part of the country. His success in maintaining ascendancy may also have been related to his lack of blood-kinship ties with the Fujiwara or any of the other leading clans; and it must have been aided, too, by his skillful creation of a small, privileged group of supporters tied to him by kinship, by marital alliances, and by the large land grants he had begun making to his favorites as early as 793. (He was particularly generous in his treatment of relatives of his mother and grandmother.)

That Kammu enjoyed substantial freedom from clan control may be inferred from the fact that leading governmental offices were either left vacant or entrusted to imperial family members during much of his reign. The post of Minister of the Left, the highest regularly filled office in the court government, remained vacant throughout all but the first year of Kammu's rule; after the death in 796 of Tsugutada (the Southern House Fujiwara who may have been the chief promoter of the move to Heian), the post of Minister of the Right was similarly vacant until 798 and was then occupied until the end of the reign by Kammu's cousin Prince Miwa (737?–806); the post of Palace Minister was vacant at Kammu's accession and never thereafter filled; and the post of Major Counselor, the fourth highest in the government, was held from 796 on by another of Kammu's cousins, who shared it with Ki no Kosami

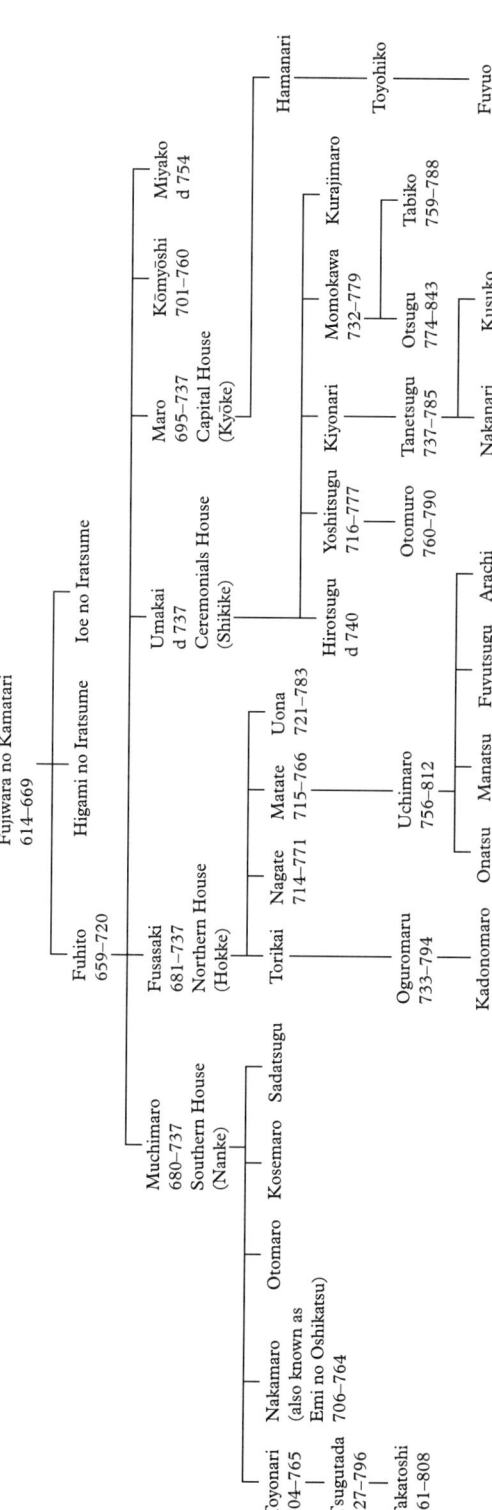

Figure 1.2. Genealogy of the four Fujiwara houses. Adapted from *Kodansha Encyclopedia of Japan*.

(733–97) until 797. There was not a single Fujiwara officeholder above the level of Middle Counselor during the final decade of the reign (796–806). Although influential lower officials restricted the emperor's role to something considerably less than that of an absolute despot, it seems, nevertheless, to have been true that the final decision in major matters was his, both in name and in fact.

Under Kammu's domination, the imperial court addressed itself to the political, social, and economic problems of the day with a vigor and dedication that did credit to the emperor's Confucian training. Among those problems, none was more pressing than the security of the country's northeastern frontier.

At the time of Kammu's accession to the throne in 781, the Japanese government had reached a crisis in its relations with a nonsubject people who lived in the general area of Honshu now known as Fukushima and Niigata prefectures, and also farther north. Little is known with certainty about those people: even their name is a matter of dispute. The logographic orthography commonly used in reference to them until around the beginning of the ninth century is generally thought to have been read as both "Emishi" (see Glossary-Index) and "Ebisu" (also "Ezo" after the mid-Heian period), but other readings ("Kai" and "Ainu") are still advocated in scholarly circles. After 800 the orthography itself was replaced by others, especially "Fushū" (literally, "war captives"), a term that presumably reflected the Japanese view of the Emishi after their subjugation early in the ninth century.[4] Nor do we know anything more of Emishi physical characteristics than that the mighty T'ang emperor Kao-tsung (r. 649–83) was surprised by the "oddity" of the bodies and faces of two introduced to him by a Japanese embassy in 659 (but "odd" in what way?), that both women and men did up their hair in the shape of a "small mallet," and that men's beards might be four or more feet long. The Emishi may, in fact, have been quite hirsute, as the frequent occurrence of the epithet "hairy people" suggests. On the other hand, that usage, it is suspected by some, may have been simply an acknowledgment of an ancient Chinese notion that the realm of the "hairy people" was in the northeast, which in Japan's case was the direction of the Emishi homeland. Alternatively, "hairy" may have had reference to their fur clothing.

Culturally, some Emishi were clearly hunters and gatherers; but

---

[4] For a survey of the problems surrounding the name of the Emishi, see Araki Yoichirō, "Emishi no kōshō, hyōki o meguru shomondai," *Kokushi kenkyū* (Hirosaki Daigaku) 87 (1989).

others were agriculturalists at least as early as the eighth century and possibly from Yayoi times (roughly 300 B.C.E.–300 C.E.).[5] For the Japanese, however, their most notable cultural characteristic may have been their fierce, brutish nature. This attitude seems to underlie an imperial order, quoted in the *Nihon shoki* (the first official history of 720), which dispatched the legendary Yamatotakeru no Mikoto against the Emishi during the reign of Keikō (traditionally, r. 71–130). In its description of Emishi character and custom the order is an almost verbatim reproduction of Chinese descriptions of barbarian people. But though it is doubtless anachronistic or wholly apocryphal, its contents may be taken as an expression of a view commonly accepted at court in the latter half of the seventh century – one perhaps discernible even today in histories accounting for the distinctive "brutality" (*zangyaku*) of Japan's eastern warriors by reference to their experiences in battles against these foes:[6]

> I hear that the eastern outlanders are by nature fierce and wild, and that their chief interest is violent assault. Their villages lack chiefs, their settlements lack heads. Coveting territory, they all rob each other. Further, there are evil deities in the mountains and perverse devils on the plains. They obstruct passage at intersections and block the roads, causing great affliction on people.
> The fiercest of those eastern outlanders are the Emishi. Men and women live mixed together, nor is there distinction between father and son. In winter they lodge in holes; in summer they dwell in nests. They wear furs and drink blood; eldest and younger brothers are distrustful of each other. Climbing mountains they are like flying birds; running through grass they are like furry beasts in flight. They forget benefits received but always requite wrongs suffered and for that purpose conceal an arrow in their topknots and wear a sword under their robes. Sometimes they band together and invade the border regions; sometimes they spy out opportune times in agriculture and sericulture and rob the people. If attacked, they hide in the grass; if pursued, they go into the mountains. Consequently, they have never since ancient times been subject to the transforming royal influence.[7]

The Emishi lived for the most part in tribal groups, but Japanese cultural and political influences, which had penetrated the Fuku-

---

[5] Takahashi Takashi, *Emishi: kodai tōhokujin no rekishi*, Chūkō shinsho 804 (Tokyo: Chūō kōronsha, 1986), pp. 7–8.
[6] See, for example, Inoue et al., eds., *Nihon rekishi taikei*, p. 857.
[7] *Nihon shoki*, ed. Sakamoto Tarō, Ienaga Saburō, Inoue Mitsusada, and Ōno Susumu, vol. 67 of *Nihon koten bungaku taikei* (Tokyo: Iwanami shoten, 1967), p. 302; passage cited in Takahashi, *Emishi*, p. 9; translated by W. G. Aston, *Nihongi: Chronicles of Japan from the Earliest Times to A.D. 697*, reprint of 1896 ed. (London: George Allen & Unwin, 1956), part 1, p. 203 (translation revised).

shima area as early as the fourth century,[8] impelled some of them to become agriculturalists, with leaders who might hold appointments as local officials of the statutory regime. As the Japanese pushed their administration and settlers farther northward and eastward after the Taika Reforms of the mid-seventh century, relations with the Emishi deteriorated, and there were sporadic eruptions of violence – isolated attacks of one upon the other, killings, and warfare. But it was not until 780, the year before Kammu's accession to the throne, that matters came to a head. In that year, just as Japanese forces were preparing to attack the Emishi stronghold of Isawa (about fifteen miles due north of modern Hiraizumi in Iwate Prefecture), they were confronted by the revolt of a powerful Emishi ally named Koreharu no Azamaro, who held a Japanese provincial title. Their leaders were slain, and in the ensuing turmoil the chief military seat of the region, Taga Fort, was taken by Emishi and put to the torch. The Japanese then found themselves confronted by a sudden dangerous threat to their presence in the northeastern territories.[9]

Azamaro's revolt in 780 was the beginning of more than thirty years of large-scale warfare between the Emishi and the Japanese. Major Japanese military campaigns against the Emishi in 780–81, 788–89, and 794 met with either defeat or inconclusive success. Not until 801–2 were Japanese forces under the command of the red-visaged, yellow-bearded warrior "giant" Sakanoue no Tamuramaro (758–811) able to defeat the main Emishi leader, Aterui, and permanently occupy and garrison his base at Isawa.[10] A relatively limited action under Fun'ya no Watamaro (765–823) against two Emishi areas, in what is now the eastern part of Iwate Prefecture and along the Aomori–Iwate border, brought the Emishi Wars to a tentative conclusion in 811, and in the following year most of the Japanese armies in the northeast were demobilized.

Although the back of armed Emishi resistance to Japanese encroachment was broken during the three decades of fighting from

---

8 A century or two earlier than commonly believed until recently. See "Kōkogaku: kono ichinen," *Yomiuri shimbun*, 22 December 1990.
9 On the vexing question of the reading of Azamaro's surname, which has commonly been read "Iji," see Inoue, *Nihon rekishi taikei*, p. 692, n. 2.
10 At about five feet ten inches, Tamuramaro was six inches taller than the inferred average height of Japanese men during the Ancient-Tomb (*kofun*) period – i. e., from the end of the third or the beginning of the fourth to the mid-sixth century, – and he may well have looked like a giant to his contemporaries. His ancestors are said to have come from China. A short, perhaps nearly contemporaneous, biography of him has been preserved: *Tamuramaro denki*, in *(Shinkō) Gunsho ruijū*, Hanawa Hokiichi, comp. (Tokyo: Meicho fukyūkai, 1977), kan 64, vol. 3, p. 699. On the heights of early Japanese, see Joseishi Sōgō Kenkyūkai, *Nihon josei shi*, vol. 1: *Genshi. Kodai* (Tokyo: Tōkyō daigaku shuppankai, 1982), p. 15.

780 to 811, the conflict was by no means finally resolved. Revolts by Emishi against Japanese authority in Dewa Province in 878–79 and 939, the threat of further revolt, and outbreaks of fighting among the Emishi themselves kept the area in an almost continuous state of alarm and tension during the following century and a half. Then, as central government control weakened and the assimilation of the Emishi proceeded, with Emishi leaders coming to play a growing role in local government, the conflict was internalized in Japanese society, erupting again in open warfare during the Earlier Nine Years' War of 1051–62 and the Later Three Years' War of 1083–87, when Emishi-descended leaders sought to assert their independence of the central government (see Chapter 10). The area subsequently developed into the private satrapy of a local Fujiwara line that had intermarried with an Emishi family, remaining independent of central control until the time of Minamoto no Yoritomo's conquest in 1189, more than four centuries after Azamaro's revolt in 780. By that time the unassimilated Emishi were confined generally to the northernmost tip of Honshu and to Hokkaido.

Japanese penetration of the northeastern part of Honshu was marked by the establishment of forts (*jō*) and palisades (*saku*) throughout the area as the line of colonization and conquest moved east and north. The aim was not merely to provide strongholds for defense against the Emishi but also to create administrative centers through which the central government could exercise control over the Japanese colonists who were sent en masse to the region from the Kanto and central Honshu. In 796, for example, 9,000 people from Sagami, Musashi, and seven other provinces are said to have been moved to the Iji Fort region (in what is now Miyagi Prefecture) and established as "palisade households" (*sakuko*) to cultivate the land there.

As both military and administrative centers, the forts and palisades at least sometimes rivaled the administrative seats of provinces (*kokufu*) in their size and complexity, as archaeological excavation has shown. The site of the famous Taga Fort, for instance, was a square nearly 3,000 feet on each side surrounded by an earthen wall over two miles long. Several administrative buildings on an elevation at the center of the site were enclosed within their own earthen wall, which measured 330 feet east to west and 390 feet north to south. Elsewhere within the site were other groups of buildings, including storehouses and what are thought to have been quarters for artisans and soldiers. Five distinct periods in the history of the site can be identified, from the founding of the fort in the first half of the eighth century through the Heian period.

Although the Emishi Wars consolidated and extended Japanese control over the northern part of Honshu, their enormous cost must have also contributed significantly to the weakening of the statutory regime. Even allowing for exaggeration by the chroniclers, the armies mustered for the campaigns were huge in relation to the contemporary population and economy, numbering in one instance, it is said, as many as 100,000 men. The creation and supply of such forces placed what ultimately proved to be an intolerable burden on the resources of the government, both in direct expenses and presumably also in the removal of men from productive employment, and in 805 Kammu decided to terminate the campaigns specifically because of their cost. Fujiwara no Otsugu (774–843), whose recommendation it was that brought the large-scale campaigns to an end, asserted that the wars against the Emishi and construction work in the new capital at Kyoto were the two chief causes of distress among the peasantry.

The wars and their aftermath were also apparently a stimulus to the growth of private warrior forces in the eastern provinces of Honshu, whose men had borne the chief burden of the fighting, and they further affected the social fabric of Japan as a result of the forced resettlement of captured and subjugated Emishi in almost every area of the main islands. Although it is not possible to estimate the number of Emishi involved in the resettlement, it is clear that a major shift of population was involved, undertaken almost certainly to remove rebellious and unassimilated Emishi elements from their still restless homelands. Some of the transported Emishi became slaves attached to noble households or government offices, but most apparently were forced to live in their own special communities, supported at least in part by governmental subsidies and experiencing the problems familiar to minority peoples everywhere submerged in a hostile dominant culture. Some communities quickly died out, others were involved in armed clashes with Japanese neighbors and rebellions against the government, and still others seem to have moved fairly expeditiously toward full assimilation to Japanese society. The warlike skills of the resettled Emishi were put to good use in Kyushu, where they were employed in coastal defense, and it is possible that Emishi also became ancestors of warrior families elsewhere in Japan.

The Emishi wars and the construction of the capital were made economically possible by the close attention that Kammu gave to the government's revenue base in the countryside, which is discussed later in the chapter.

After the death of Kammu in the spring of 806, the leading noble clans, and especially the Fujiwara, began almost immediately to move again into the highest offices of government, but the balance of power at court until about the middle of the century seems to have consistently favored the emperors, who thus continued to maintain at least the semblance of rule in their own right. Although Kammu's three immediate successors on the throne, his sons Heizei, Saga (786–842, r. 809–23), and Junna (786–840, r. 823–33), each had a Fujiwara mother, they were able during their reigns to steer relatively independent courses, thanks at least in part apparently to rivalries within the Fujiwara clan itself. It was only after the death of the retired emperor Saga in 842 that the exercise of court power began to shift back and forth between emperors and Fujiwara leaders, initiating the process that ended with the firm establishment of Fujiwara ascendancy in the first half of the tenth century.

Insofar as imperial rule was maintained during the three or so decades following Kammu's death, the chief credit is usually given to Saga, who appears to have inherited his father's erudition and also his skill in government. The reign of Saga's predecessor, his sickly and possibly neurotic full brother Heizei, does not seem to have been promising from that point of view.

Even before Heizei's accession in 806, he is said to have established a scandalous liaison with his consort's mother, Fujiwara no Kusuko (d. 810), a daughter of the Tanetsugu who was assassinated at Nagaoka in 785, and after he became emperor he seems to have been much guided by her and her brother Nakanari (774?–810). The official chronicle says, in fact, that Heizei was completely under Kusuko's sway, although that may be no more than another case of the misogynistic scapegoating common in Chinese and Chinese-derived historiography. The unfavorable view often taken of Heizei may be mistaken. His reign was actually notable for its attention to government and finances, so attentive, in fact, that the emperor may have provoked the hostility of his nobility. Saga's illustrious reputation, by contrast, seems based more on his literary and cultural accomplishments than on his actual effectiveness as a ruler.

Nakanari and Kusuko may have been behind the most dramatic event of Heizei's brief reign, the forced suicides in 807 of the emperor's younger half brother, Prince Iyo, and the prince's Southern-

House mother following their imprisonment on the probably false charge of plotting rebellion against the government. The incident became the occasion for a purge of the leading members of the Southern House of the Fujiwara clan from the influential positions in government they had held since the days of Emperor Kammu, the pretext for the purge being that the Southern-House men were closely related to Prince Iyo through his mother. Since the purge removed from the court important rivals of Nakanari and Kusuko who belonged to the Ceremonials House of the clan, it is plausible to suppose, as the official chronicle seems to suggest, that the brother and sister were responsible for the charges against Prince Iyo and the implication of his maternal relatives. However, the incident may have also been inspired at least in part by personal animosities of the violent-tempered Heizei. The emperor is said to have long been resentful of the marked favor his father, Kammu, had shown Prince Iyo and his mother during the last half of his reign. Heizei is also known to have borne a particular grudge against one of the purged Southern-House officials, Takatoshi (761–808), who, while Heizei was still crown prince, had treated him with less than the respect the future emperor felt was his due.

If Nakanari and Kusuko were involved in the downfall of Iyo and his kin, their maneuvering gained them very little in the end. Just two years later Emperor Heizei was forced by ill health to abdicate in favor of Saga, leaving Nakanari and Kusuko isolated in a government whose chief minister was Fujiwara no Uchimaro (756–812), the head of the clan's Northern House. Heizei withdrew to the old capital at Nara, but in the following year, 810, he began issuing governmental orders again in his own name, decreeing finally in the late fall of the year that the capital was to be moved back to Nara. The step was seen as a move on the part of the ex-emperor to reclaim the throne, and Saga moved swiftly against the pair held responsible for his actions. Kusuko was relieved of her court rank and ordered expelled from Heizei's palace, and her brother Nakanari was arrested and demoted to a provincial office. Heizei attempted to make his way with Kusuko to the eastern provinces to raise an army in his defense there, but his route was blocked by government forces, and he returned to Nara and took Buddhist holy orders. Nakanari was executed, his sister Kusuko committed suicide, and the crown prince, a son of Heizei, was replaced by Junna, a half brother of Saga and Heizei. Removed from the influence of Nakanari and Kusuko, the chastened ex-emperor thereafter led a pious, docile life until his death fourteen years later.

Following the deaths of Kusuko and Nakanari and the hasty ordination of Heizei in 810, the imperial court enjoyed a thirty-year period of relative peace and stability, undisturbed by great enterprises, which had taxed the regime to its limits under Kammu, or by the kind of political and dynastic rivalries that had sent Prince Iyo to his death under Heizei. The Fujiwara, as always, posed a threat to the authority and independence of the emperors, but Saga and Junna managed to avoid marital ties with that powerful clan, thus limiting its direct, personal influence on the throne. They also succeeded in maintaining a balance of competing families and clans in the higher ranks and offices of the government. For example, of the thirteen men who occupied the highest government offices in 841, the year before Saga's death, only four were Fujiwara, two from the Ceremonials line (one of whom was the ranking court officer, the Minister of the Left) and two from the Northern. Equally important to note is that among that select group of thirteen were four members of the imperial clan or descendants thereof (Minamoto), and four men from lower-ranking families who were known chiefly for their sinitic learning or administrative abilities. The presence of learned men and practical administrators in the highest offices of government not only is a clear reflection of Saga's well-known interest in, and emphasis on, Chinese learning and Chinese conceptions of government, but is also evidence of a desire to maintain a group of leaders in the government amenable to imperial direction.

During Saga's time the personal material fortunes of the emperor, of his family, and of the privileged group of nobles closest to him began to acquire a generous and independent foundation. This was the result of large-scale grants to them of agricultural lands developed or reclaimed by provincial governments and worked with the labor of local farmers. In the case of emperors and retired emperors, the lands so granted, known for historical reasons as "later close" (*goin*), grew into a substantial patrimony that became a chief support for the reassertion of imperial rule (chiefly in the person of the retired emperor) toward the end of the eleventh century.

Although the political energies of the court during the time of Saga and Junna were expended for the most part on efforts to adapt the institutions of the statutory regime to changing social and economic circumstances, their success was limited. Even that limited success was placed in jeopardy just one week after Saga's death in 842, when the crown prince was deposed and replaced by a nephew of Fujiwara no Yoshifusa (804–72), the head of the Northern House. The events surrounding the crown prince's removal from office, which are sometimes referred to collectively as the Jōwa Incident (*Jōwa no hen*) after the name of the calendar era in which they occurred, marked the beginning of the end of imperial rule in Japan. The emperor remained an important and sometimes controlling force at court into the tenth century, but the main focus of political interest after 842 is the rise to power of the Northern House of the Fujiwara.

At the time of Saga's death, there appear to have been two rival groups at court, one centered around the emperor, Saga's gifted son Nimmyō, and the other around the crown prince, Tsunesada (825–84), Junna's son by a daughter of Saga. The core of Nimmyō's party was the emperor himself; his mother, Saga's consort Tachibana no Kachiko (786–850); his son, the fifteen-year-old future Emperor Montoku (827–58; r. 850–58); and Montoku's uncle Fujiwara no Yoshifusa. Most important among Tsunesada's supporters were the officials in his household office, especially Tomo no Kowamine and Tachibana no Kachiko's cousin Hayanari (d. 842), and his father-in-law, Yoshifusa's uncle Arachi (787–843). It is noteworthy that the rival groups were not defined by family or clan lines: it was Tachibana (Kachiko) against Tachibana (Hayanari), Northern House (Yoshifusa) against Northern House (Arachi), and imperial grandmother (Kachiko) and uncle (Nimmyō) against grandchild and nephew (Tsunesada).

The situation was ripe for conflict. Nimmyō, who doubtless wished to see his own son succeed him on the throne, was no longer restrained by the wishes of his father, and Tsunesada, whose position had been greatly weakened by the loss of his own father (Junna) two years earlier, now found himself in an even more precarious position as a result of the death of his last protector, his grandfather Saga. Furthermore, and perhaps even more to the point, Nimmyō's son Montoku was the nephew of Fujiwara no Yoshifusa, who not only could expect to prosper greatly upon Montoku's accession to the throne but who may have also feared that the leadership of the Northern House would permanently pass to the line of his uncle Arachi if Tsunesada became emperor. The crown prince was married to Arachi's daughter, and his accession would almost certainly have given Arachi control of the court.

It seems more likely on the whole that the ambitions and fears of the Nimmyō party lay behind the events of 842, but according to the chronicles, it was Tsunesada and his supporters who actually precipitated the upheaval by plotting a coup aimed at deposing Nimmyō and placing Tsunesada on the throne. The plot was reported to Nimmyō's mother, Kachiko, on the very next day after Saga's death, and she immediately informed Yoshifusa, indicating perhaps that he was already by that time the leading figure at court despite his junior position (he was a Middle Counselor, outranked by three other men not associated with the plot). The government moved quickly against the plotters, arresting and exiling the alleged ringleaders, Tomo no Kowamine and Tachibana no Hayanari, dismissing from office or demoting some sixty officials connected with Tsunesada, including Arachi, and deposing Tsunesada himself. A few days later Nimmyō's son was appointed crown prince, and the Northern House of the Fujiwara under Yoshifusa stood on the threshold of the period of its greatest power.

EVOLUTION OF THE STATUTORY GOVERNMENT

The statutory regime from its outset underwent numerous modifications in the details of its operations and structure as governmental leaders sought to correct past failings and respond to new needs, opportunities, and pressures, but it was particularly in the ninth century, when the regime began to falter badly because of changing social, economic, and political conditions, that major alterations of the governmental structure itself took place. The chief problems seem to have been declining, or at least less adequate, revenues and a concomitant narrowing scope of political action. The main solutions attempted were retrenchment and a simplification of the governmental machinery, the operations of which were less and less concerned with nationwide projects and policies and increasingly concentrated on the capital area and the court itself.

It is difficult to pinpoint with certainty the reasons for the central government's financial difficulties. Although overspending on the construction of new capitals and on wars against the Emishi during the reign of Kammu undoubtedly contributed to the problem, that may not have been the basic cause. The decay of the state system of allocated rice land, accompanied in some cases by the abandonment of capitatim rice tillages (*kubunden*), and the growth of various kinds of private landed proprietorships or estates (*shōen*, "rural garths") enjoying a degree of tax immunity (legal or otherwise) must have also contributed to the government's straitened circumstances. But perhaps most important was the emergence in the provinces of a powerful and wealthy class that the central authorities were unable fully to control or to exploit. That class, whose members frequently held appointments in the district and provincial administrations, appears to have absorbed an ever-growing share of the country's wealth.

Whatever the reasons, the central government during the first century of the Heian period appears clearly to have been faced with a worsening financial situation, to which it responded in two chief ways. On the one hand, it sought to adjust the tax structure to the changed conditions of the countryside, hoping thereby no doubt to preserve such sources of income as were still available to it; and, at the same time, it attempted to improve its control over provincial governments, where the largest losses in income were occurring. There was thus during the reigns of Kammu, Heizei, Saga, and Junna – that is, from the beginning of the period to 833 – an almost constant tinkering with the tax laws and unremitting attention to provincial government, especially to the means of ensuring provincial compliance with central law. But despite all efforts, revenues appear to have continued to decline in quality and quantity (they were mostly rendered in kind), and the central government's control over the provinces steadily weakened.

At the same time that the government was seeking to avoid further erosion of its fiscal base, it was also taking various measures to reduce expenditures. The decisions to terminate the campaigns against the Emishi and to halt construction work at the capital in 805 were evidently motivated by economic concerns, as noted earlier, and similar considerations probably lay behind efforts to reduce the size of the central government that continued from the time of Kōnin to the beginning of the tenth century. During the time of Kōnin and Kammu, government retrenchment policy was concentrated on eliminating special posts and offices that had proliferated outside the framework established by law, but in the reigns of Kammu's sons (Heizei, Saga, and Junna) an attack on unneeded offices and posts within the statutory structure itself began. By the end of the ninth century, approximately half of the central offices originally provided for by statute had been abolished. The resulting savings were offset to some extent, it is true, by a simultaneous increase in the number of supernumerary officials, but since supernumerary positions appear to have been restricted to the more senior titles, there was likely overall a substantial reduction in the size of Heian officialdom. The result presumably was not only economic but also social. Displaced officials and disappointed aspirants to such status were forced to look elsewhere for a living, and some, at least, must have sought their fortunes outside Kyoto, where they would have found and no doubt frequently joined the provincial gentry.

Even the imperial clan itself was not immune to the budget cutter's blade. By the beginning of the Heian period the clan had greatly increased in size, including by legal definition descendants of emperors down to the fifth, and in some instances the sixth, generation. The generous economic treatment of imperial princes and princesses provided for by statute placed a heavy burden on the government's shrinking revenues, and even as early as Kammu's reign steps to reduce the size of the clan began to be taken. In 798 membership was redefined to exclude imperial descendants in the fifth generation and after (thus restoring the original statutory definition of the clan), and in 805, the same year in which the Emishi campaigns and construction at Heian were halted, more than one hundred princes and princesses were reduced to noble status and given clan names, thus removing them from the imperial family. Individual princes had been similarly removed from the family in the Nara period, and Kammu himself had earlier taken the unprecedented step of reducing sons of emperors (one of Kōnin and two of his own) to noble status, but the action in 805 was the first instance of wholesale exclusion. Emperor Saga continued his father's policy, in 814 going so far as to reduce all of his numerous children except those by higher-ranking consorts to noble status with the bestowed clan name of Minamoto, an example that was followed by succeeding emperors down to Yōzei (869–949, r. 876–84). Second- or later-generation descendants of emperors who were reduced to noble status in Saga's time and after seem regularly to have received clan names other than Minamoto, such as Taira and Ariwara, which conferred less prestige on their holders than Minamoto. The last grant of noble status to imperial clan members occurred in the reign of Murakami (926–67, r. 946–67). Thereafter the absence of remunerative bureaucratic openings for demoted princes and the smaller number of imperial children that seems to have resulted from Fujiwara control of the emperor and his harem probably made the practice mostly unnecessary. When an excess of imperial children did occur after the tenth century, Buddhist holy orders provided a convenient, dignified refuge.

Although the growth of the imperial clan may have been checked by the measures adopted by Kammu and his successors, it was not necessarily stopped. In the latter half of the ninth century, at any rate, the clan still numbered more than five hundred members who had a claim on state revenues, a burden so heavy that the government felt obliged to reduce the level of its support, leaving some peripheral members of the clan in what appears to have been dire straits. It was those poorer imperial relatives, presumably, who joined their Minamoto and Taira kindred in the exodus to the provinces that was enlarging and strengthening the gentry class there.

At the same time that the government was seeking to retrench and preserve its fiscal base, it was also attempting to reshape the central governmental structure in order to meet the changing conditions of the day. The concern of the emperors and their courts seems to have been increasingly restricted to the control and support of the internal workings of the court itself. There was consequently an overall tendency in government toward simplification of operations, with focus on the person of the emperor, and a shift toward dependence of emperors and governmental offices alike on revenues from specific pieces of land that were taking on some of the characteristics of private proprietorships. The process is sometimes thought of as the partial conversion of a semibureaucratic regime supported by general tax revenues to a more personal type of rule by emperors and their close associates dependent on private or individualized sources of income.

At the very beginning of the Heian period, the major business of government seems still to have been conducted as prescribed in the statutory code, the emperor and his ministers gathering each morning to attend to business in governmental councils (*chōsei*) at the Court of Government (Chōdōin), a large complex of buildings just inside the Gate of the Vermilion Sparrow (Suzakumon), the main entrance gate of the Greater Imperial Palace on its south-central side (on the imperial palace and its structures, see Chapter 2). By the beginning of Saga's reign, however, the business of such councils may have already so dwindled in quantity and scope that they were becoming anachronistic in any case. When the emperor established a new office at the time of the Kusuko Incident in 810 that gave him more direct control over the bureaucracy, the councils rapidly withered away, remaining then simply as biannual court rituals.

The new governmental organ created by Saga in or about 810 was probably designed to help the emperor cope with Heizei's attempt to regain the throne. Called the Chamberlains' Office (*kurōdodokoro*, "Repositors' Office"), it was placed in charge of the emperor's personal storehouse, which was within the compound of his residential palace and included the imperial archives. Initially, the chief duties of the office apparently were to handle legal disputes, to ensure the confidentiality and integrity of imperial documents, and possibly also to secure the personal safety of the emperor. But its duties and officers rapidly expanded in number and importance during the reigns of Kōkō (r. 884–87) and Uda (r. 887–97), when it became a veritable pivot of court government that Uda was able to employ in his attempt to check Fujiwara power, at least until the clan leaders gained control of that office, too. Staffed by men who were personally close to the emperor (they had often served in his household office when he was crown prince), the office took over many of the functions of the Council of State relating to communication with the emperor and the issuance of imperial orders, decrees, and rescripts, sidestepping thereby the cumbersome mechanisms of the Council and giving the emperor better access to the operating offices of the government. At the same time, the office also took charge of the administration of many of the emperor's personal or household affairs, supervising functions at the residential palace and the daily activity of the imperial audience chamber, providing for the emperor's personal needs, and otherwise generally functioning in the capacity of a steward's office.

The appearance and evolution of the Chamberlains' Office into one of the chief instruments by which the emperor exercised control over the court and the government reflected the atrophy of governmental activity in the ninth century and a shift of political power away from the public, semibureaucratic institutions of the statutory regime toward a more personal kind of rule that depended chiefly on the emperor and a narrow circle of his intimates. The joining of state and household functions in the office, clearly signaled by the location of the office itself at the emperor's residence, further blurred the distinction between the imperial position and the imperial person, thus perhaps rendering the court more easily controllable by those with personal ties to the emperor. Although the office was an important expression of imperial determination to rule as well as reign, in the end it may have contributed significantly to the success of the Northern Fujiwara House in establishing its supremacy at court.

After the near disappearance of the daily governmental councils (*chōsei*) and the establishment of the Chamberlains' Office, the emperor seldom met with the ministers of the Council of State to transact court business, but the Council itself continued to fulfill most of its original functions as the highest organ of government, advising the emperor, recommending policies, issuing directives to subordinate offices in at least nominal compliance with imperial orders, and in general directing and supervising the operations of the regime. Major policies and issues now were discussed mostly not with the emperor (or his regent), but in meetings of the ministers themselves. These evolved through various arrangements and places of meeting, but from the last half of the ninth century increasingly took the form of what were usually called "Guard-Post Judgments" (*jinnosadame*). Following the general shift of government toward the emperor's residential palace, Guard-Post Judgments were held at one of the posts (Left or Right) of the Imperial Guards located in the residential compound. The choice of meeting site may have reflected a concern for security, the palace itself by that time having become a prime target for robbers and arsonists. The meetings were usually convened by the emperor or regent two or three times a month through the Chamberlains' Office to consider specific problems. The decisions of the meetings, made by the senior minister present after discussion with the others, were reported back through the Chamberlains' Office as recommendations to the emperor or regent, who then caused such orders as were necessary to be issued. The business of the meetings covered the range of court concerns: imperial accessions, foreign relations, military uprisings, appointments to court rank and office, Buddhist and Shinto rites, tax matters, provincial government, and so on. Despite the eventual domination of court government by the Fujiwara regents, Guard-Post Judgments remained a vital instrument of court decision-making into the latter half of the eleventh century.

A similar shrinkage or rationalization of structure also occurred in the military, police, and judicial organs of government during the first century or so of the Heian period. The military conscript system provided for under the statutory code had already been recognized as ineffective by the end of the Nara period, and it was probably nearly moribund when in 792 Kammu formally abolished the system outside Kyushu, the northern part of Honshu, and the island of Sado. The dismantlement of the conscript system came in the midst of the campaigns against the Emishi, suggesting that these campaigns may have relied less on regular peasant conscripts than on the specially mobilized forces of vagrants and elite fighting men mentioned in the official chronicles. In the provinces where the conscript system was abolished, Kammu established small bands of armed men (called "stalwart youths," *kondei*), selected from among the families of district officials to serve on a rotating basis as guards at provincial administrative seats and other governmental installations in the area. They were few in number, however, and in themselves could not have constituted a significant military force. When military action was undertaken, the government relied instead on the private forces that were developing in the provinces and that eventually usurped the authority of the imperial court (on that subject, see Chapter 10).

In the aftermath of the Emishi campaigns and the Kusuko Incident, the safety of the capital itself seems to have become more precarious than ever: unrest, violence, and rumors of rebellion kept the city in a more or less constant state of alarm. It may have been for this and other reasons that, probably during Saga's reign, a new imperial police force, whose members were called *kebiishi* ("Offenses Investigation Agents"), was established at the emperor's residential palace. The new force appears initially to have been restricted mostly to police work and the maintenance of public order within the city of Kyoto and its immediate environs. After the force became an independent entity in 834, its powers gradually expanded to include almost all police and judicial authority throughout Kyoto and surrounding areas and also the administration of prisons in the city. The office became involved additionally in the resolution of disputes concerning agricultural lands, in the collection of unpaid land rents, in the establishment of *shōen* (estate) boundaries, and in other similar police, inspection, and judicial functions relating to land and land revenues. Eventually it seems to have even taken on some street repair and maintenance duties in the capital.

The success of the *kebiishi* in controlling crime is difficult to judge, especially since the depredations of the agents themselves may have occasionally equalled or surpassed those of the criminals they were supposed to control, but the bureaucratic success of the office, as measured in terms of expanding powers and growing numbers of officers, was undoubted. It was soon imitated in the provinces, where *kebiishi* agents are found as early as the 850s; in one province at least (Musashi), such officers are known to have been established even as far down the administrative scale as the district (*gun*).

Kebiishi agents were a powerful and ubiquitous force in Heian life through the eleventh century, providing such security as the capital city had and playing an important role in the functioning of the land system that supported it. Their success was the result of a rationalization of the statutory structure that brought together under a single authority police, judicial, and prison functions that had formerly been divided among several offices: the Board of Censors, the Capital Offices, the Punishments Ministry, and the Imperial Guards. But the success achieved by that rationalization was also another instance of the concentration of governmental authority in and around the person of the emperor and the narrowing of governmental concern to the immediate interests of the court, developments antithetical to basic principles of the statutory regime.

At the same time that the organizational structure of the central government was changing in important ways, the financial support of the structure also underwent alterations in order to accommodate governmental needs to a persistent insufficiency of income. From the point of view of the central government, the most striking development in that respect was the beginning of a shift away from reliance on general revenues for the support of central offices and their staffs toward the establishment of designated pieces of land as sources of revenue for particular offices. In 879 the government set aside about 12,000 acres of rice tillage in provinces near the capital for direct operation by the government or for rental, a portion of the income in either case becoming revenue for the central government itself. Within twenty years, over half of those lands had been permanently allocated to particular central offices for their exclusive use and exploitation. It is noteworthy that it was generally the less important, lower-ranking offices that received such grants of land, but even so the creation of offices with independent sources of support led inevitably to a weakening of the regime's control over its own subordinate organs. The offices endowed with land became in essential respects institutional equivalents of the *shōen* proprietors, whose growth otherwise was already affecting the structure of the statutory fiscal system.

Parallel to the growth of *shōen* and the appearance of land-endowed offices was the emergence during this same period of large personal land- and other economically valuable holdings of the emperor himself, as noted earlier. The accumulation of personal land-holdings by emperors seems to have begun at least as early as the reign of Saga, and the process continued in Junna's reign, accelerating after the death of the Northern House leader Fujiwara no Fuyutsugu (775–826), who may have acted as a restraint on the imperial appetite for private wealth. The holdings grew rapidly thereafter, and in Nimmyō's reign considerable acreages of waste and vacant land were also granted to other members of the imperial clan for their use. As personal imperial wealth grew, the Chamberlains' Office and the household offices established for retired emperors acquired important functions in the management and administration of the imperial property.

THE ESTABLISHMENT OF FUJIWARA ASCENDANCY, 850–969

The accession of Emperor Montoku in 850 was a critical turning point in the fortunes of the Northern House of the Fujiwara, placing on the throne the thirteen-year-old maternal nephew of the house's leader, Yoshifusa, at forty-six the most powerful figure at court. By the time of his death in 872, Yoshifusa had become the first regent to the emperor in Japanese history to be appointed from outside the imperial clan, establishing a claim to the post for the Fujiwara Northern-House line that was never thereafter successfully challenged by any other clan or family. He was also by that time well along in the process of excluding other clans from the ranks of the government's senior ministers (*kugyō*). In 850 four of the nineteen senior ministers were Fujiwara; at Yoshifusa's death in 872, seven of eighteen were; a century later, in 972, eleven of nineteen were; and at the time of Michinaga's death in 1028, the ratio stood at twenty-two of twenty-five, while the remaining three, all Minamoto, were closely related by marriage to Michinaga. The genealogies of the emperors (Figure 1.1) and the Northern House of the Fujiwara (Figure 1.3) reveal the domination of the Fujiwara.

But the ascendancy of the Fujiwara was in another sense nothing new. From the very beginning of the statutory regime in the seventh century the clan had been much more than just another ministerial lineage at court. It had usually been the leading noble clan in the central government, its men often occupying the highest or most powerful positions there and its women sometimes exercising great influence in the imperial harem. The clan's founder, Kamatari (614–69), had played a dominant role in the events surrounding the Taika Reforms of 645; Kamatari's son Fuhito (658 or 659–720) had been a key figure in the institution and codification of the statutory system; Fuhito's daughter Kōmyōshi (701–60) had been empress of Shōmu and one of the most influential figures in

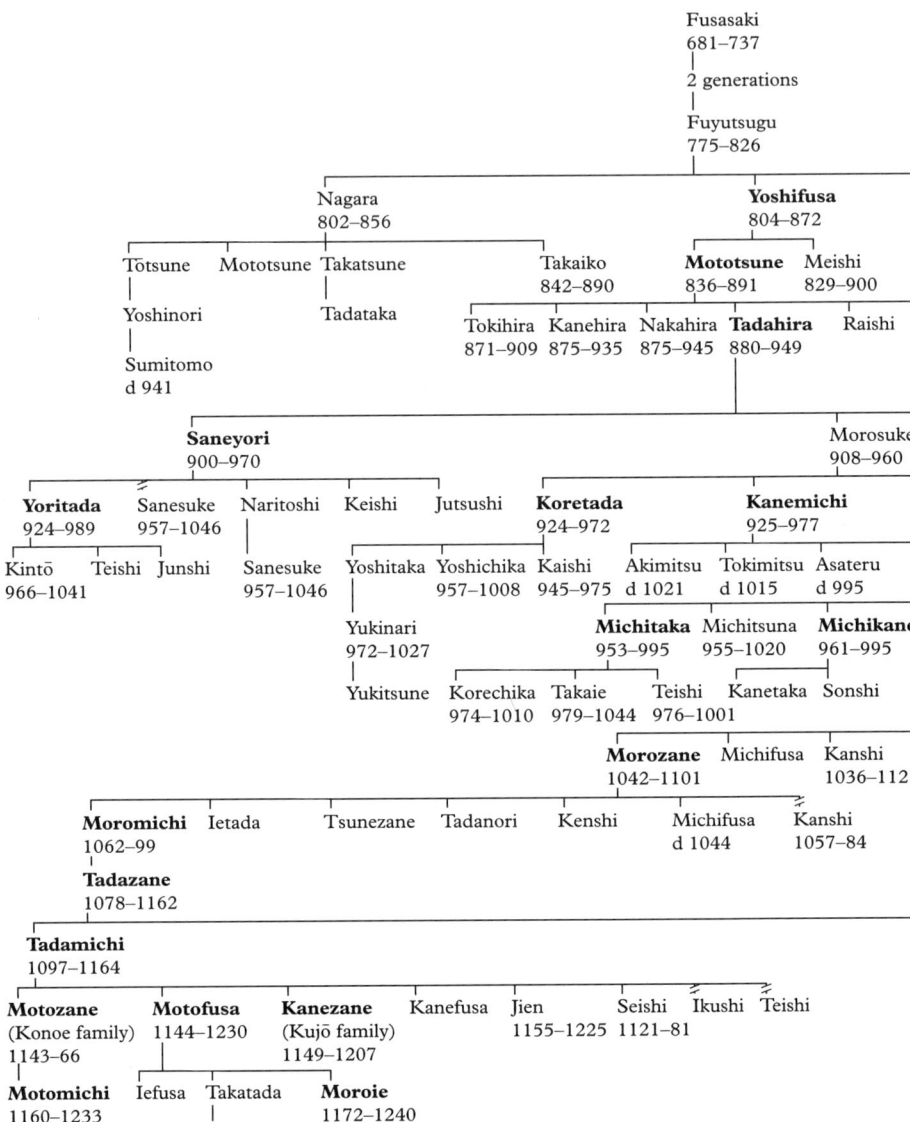

Figure 1.3. Genealogy of the Northern House of the Fujiwara. Adapted from *Kodansha Encyclopedia of Japan*.

the mid-Nara period; Fuhito's grandson Momokawa had been instrumental in the selection of Kōnin as emperor and Kammu as crown prince; Fuhito's great-granddaughter Otomuro (760–90) had been empress of Kammu and mother of Heizei and Saga; and

THE FUJIWARA ASCENDANCY

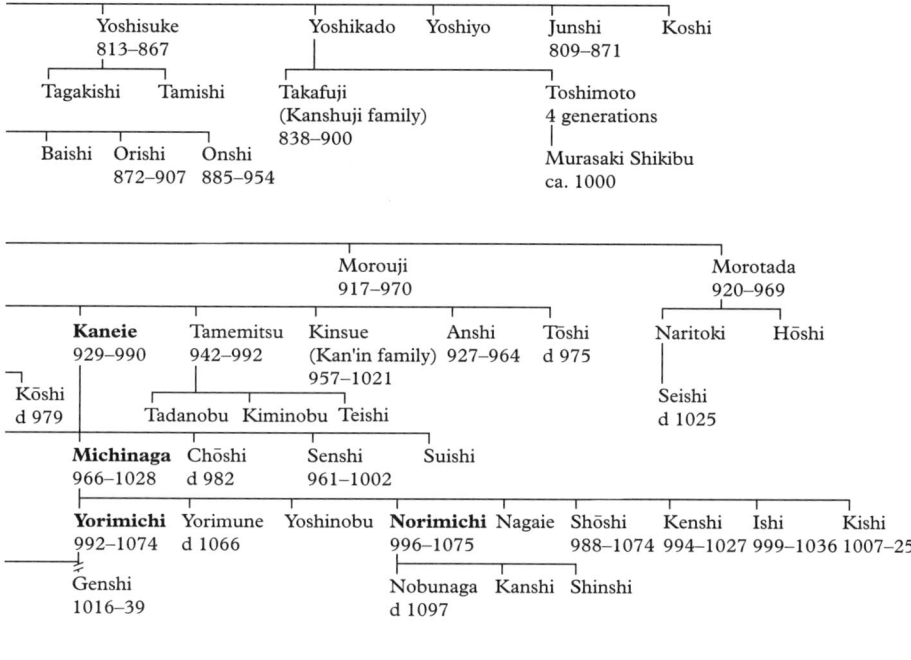

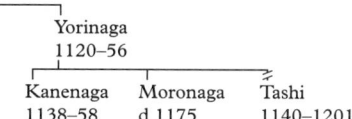

Regents in boldface
⇒ Adoption

for most of the period from the time of Heizei's accession in 806 up to 850 the chief court minister in title or in fact had been a Fujiwara.

The special position of the clan at court was also marked in economic and social terms. Kamatari and Fuhito received altogether 16,000 households of heritable sustenance grants (*jikifu*) from the court both as rewards for their services to the throne and also, it has been suggested, in order to strengthen their position against wealthy clans resisting implementation of the Taika reforms. That largesse gave the two men an enormous personal fortune over and above the huge stipends and emoluments they received from their official ranks and posts. Although the sustenance grants were all returned to the court in 820, during the time of Yoshifusa's father, Fuyutsugu, the decline of other court clans in the meantime and the prominence of Fujiwara men in the higher ministerial ranks suggest that the clan's relative economic standing may have remained largely unchanged. The special social status occupied by the Fujiwara was given formal recognition in 729 when Kōmyōshi became the first woman not of imperial descent to receive the title of empress (*kōgō*), and again in 792 when Kammu issued a directive permitting men of the clan to marry daughters of emperors (that is, female descendants in what was calculated as the second generation of descent), while limiting other noblemen to granddaughters (third generation) or after.

Yoshifusa's position in 850 was based, however, not only on a long history of Fujiwara leadership, preeminence, and preference at court, but also more specifically on the favorable situation in which the Northern House of the clan found itself in the post-Kammu years. Members of the house were the chief governmental ministers during the reigns of Heizei, Saga, and Junna, and during the latter two reigns Yoshifusa's father, the astute Fuyutsugu, laid the groundwork of a nearly impregnable position for his son. Fuyutsugu had been close to Saga ever since the emperor's days as crown prince, and after Saga's accession he rose rapidly, becoming with Kose no Notari (794–817) the first head of the Chamberlains' Office in 810 and then, as Major Counselor, the chief minister in the government on the death of his senior clansman Sonohito (756–819). He buttressed his own position and prepared the way for lasting Northern-House domination of the court by establishing close marital links with the imperial clan, giving a daughter, Junshi (809–71), to Saga's son, the future emperor Nimmyō, and taking one of Saga's daughters as a wife for his own son Yoshifusa. Fuyutsugu's premature death in 826 left the young and still relatively low-ranking Yoshifusa in a somewhat precarious position, but after the Jōwa Incident in 842 the future clearly belonged to him and his house, and he did not hesitate to claim it.

Yoshifusa demonstrated his power at court and his willingness to use it in his own and his family's interests during the very first year of Montoku's reign. The emperor had taken Yoshifusa's daughter Meishi (829–900) as a consort while he was still crown prince, and in the month of Nimmyō's death and Montoku's accession, Meishi had borne to her husband a son, the future emperor Seiwa (850–81, r. 858–76). Montoku already had a son by a woman of the Ki clan, the six-year-old Prince Koretaka (844–97), but eight months after the birth of Seiwa, Yoshifusa appears to have forced his nephew Montoku to pass over Koretaka's claims and declare Meishi's infant son crown prince, thus assuring Yoshifusa even greater power in the next reign as maternal grandfather of the emperor.

During most of Montoku's reign the chief ministerial post (Minister of the Left) was held by a powerless son of Saga named Minamoto no Tokiwa (812–54), but after Tokiwa's death Yoshifusa became in title as well as in fact the leading minister at court. In 857 he was named Chancellor (*daijō daijin* or *dajō daijin*), a momentous appointment that is regarded by some as the beginning of the Fujiwara regency under which Japan was ruled during most of the next two centuries or more.

According to the provisions of the statutory code, the office of Chancellor was the highest post in the government, but it was supposed to remain vacant unless a man could be found whose outstanding character and moral probity qualified him to serve as a model of conduct for the emperor and for the officialdom of the regime. Although the functions of a Chancellor were formally limited to the role of exemplar, the prestige of the post was unmatched by any other office at the government's disposal, and it had been filled in the past either by influential imperial princes, or, exceptionally, by imperial favorites with extraordinary power at court (that is, Fujiwara no Nakamaro [706–64] and the Buddhist monk Dōkyō [d. 772]). The significance of Yoshifusa's appointment as Chancellor was emphasized by the fact that the office had remained vacant ever since the time of Dōkyō, ninety years earlier.

With his appointment as Chancellor, Yoshifusa became probably in everything but name regent to the emperor, and on the accession of his grandson Seiwa in the following year (858), his control of the court was virtually complete. Not until eight years later, however, was he formally invested with the title of regent (*sesshō*). In that year, 866, the Gate of Obedience to Heaven (Ōtemmon), the main gate to the imperial palace's Court of Government, burned under mysterious circumstances. One of the two Major Counselors at the time, Tomo no Yoshio (809–68), charged that his adversary and rival, the

Minister of the Left Minamoto no Makoto (810–69), an affinal relative of Yoshifusa, was responsible for the burning of the gate, and he persuaded Yoshifusa's brother, the Minister of the Right Yoshimi (or Yoshisuke, 813–67), to issue an order for Makoto's arrest. At the time, Yoshifusa was living in seclusion at Shirakawa just outside the capital, but he intervened immediately on Makoto's behalf and halted the proceedings against him. Shortly thereafter a witness with a grudge against Yoshio opportunely turned up to swear that the fire was actually the work of Yoshio and his confederates, who included a man from the Ki clan. After investigation, Yoshio, his son, and a number of other Tomo and Ki men were found guilty and sent into exile, bringing to a decisive end the long struggle of those ancient clans to maintain the important positions they had once occupied at court. (Yoshio was a member of the Ōtomo clan, but since the time of Emperor Junna clan members had used a shortened form of the name – Tomo, or "Ban" in the Sino-Japanese reading of the character – in order to avoid Junna's personal name, Ōtomo.)

The events and motives involved in the burning of the Gate of Obedience to Heaven are by no means clear, and even insofar as we have a record of them, their authenticity cannot be assumed, since they are contained in a chronicle compiled under the editorship of Yoshifusa's grandson. The results of the series of events that flowed from the fire are, however, quite clear. Two of the oldest clans at court were removed from the path of Fujiwara ambition, and in the midst of it all, following Yoshio's arrest and interrogation but before his exile, Yoshifusa was formally appointed regent by the sixteen-year-old emperor, who may have been anxious to make amends for his too ready acceptance of Yoshio's charge against Makoto.

Individual clans (the Kazuragi, Wani, Heguri, Ōtomo, Mononobe, and Soga) had come to exercise preponderant power at court in the sixth century as the emperor's strength seems steadily to have waned in relation to the constituent clans of the Yamato state. In that sense, Fujiwara domination of the court had ample historical precedent. But the institution of the statutory regime in the seventh century, while by no means giving despotic authority to the imperial line, brought some restitution of the line's authority, an authority that was markedly expanded in the late eighth and the ninth century under emperors Kammu and Saga on the basis of governmental reform and retrenchment, and it was the newly expanded power that Yoshifusa exercised as regent to the emperor.

By the time of his death in 872, Yoshifusa had achieved heights of power and prestige unprecedented for a court noble, his position differing but little in form or substance from that of the emperor himself. His chief failing, his inability to produce a son, had been remedied by the adoption of Mototsune (836–91), a son of his brother Nagara (or Nagayoshi, 802–56), who succeeded Yoshifusa as the principal power at court, with appointment to the title of regent coming at the beginning of 873. Emperor Seiwa, now in his early twenties, sought to rule in his own right for a while, but bothered by bad health and a series of ominous portents, he abdicated in 876 in favor of the seven-year-old Yōzei, his son by Nagara's daughter. Mototsune, who was also the emperor's maternal uncle, was reappointed regent.

Yōzei's accession at the age of seven and Seiwa's at the age of eight marked a significant turning point in the history of the imperial clan. They were the first child-emperors to come to the throne in Japan, clearly indicating that by their time the imperial position was distinct from the power to rule. In the Nara period and earlier, when an emperor died before a male heir, or the preferred male heir, had come of age, it seems to have been the custom for the mother or a sister to take the throne until the heir had reached a suitable age. Now, however, with regency power at court in the hands of Northern-House leaders, such precautions were apparently no longer thought necessary; they were indeed, from the point of view of the Fujiwara, undesirable, since mature emperors were generally more difficult to control. We find, consequently, that of the thirteen emperors who reigned from the time of Seiwa to Go-Ichijō (1008–36, r. 1016–36), nine were seventeen or younger at the time of their accessions, and seven, or more than half, were no older than twelve. It may also be observed that among that group of thirteen, with the exception of Kōkō (830–87, r. 884–87), whose special circumstances are noted later in the chapter, it was the emperors who came to the throne at the age of twenty or more who were most independent of, or clashed most seriously with, the Fujiwara: Uda (867–931, r. 887–97), Murakami, and Sanjō (976–1017, r. 1011–16).

Despite his youth, Emperor Yōzei seems to have been more than Mototsune could easily handle. Although the official chronicle of his reign is discreet to the point of obscurity, it appears that the young emperor was wild in the pursuit of unorthodox interests, perhaps not quite a Japanese Caligula but possibly sharing the attitude re-

TABLE 1.1
Heian emperors

Numerical order	Emperor	Birth and death dates	Reign dates
50	Kammu	737–806	781–806
51	Heizei	774–824	806–809
52	Saga	786–842	809–823
54	Nimmyō	810–850	833–850
55	Montoku	827–858	850–858
56	Seiwa	850–881	858–876
57	Yōzei	869–949	876–884
58	Kōkō	830–887	884–887
59	Uda	867–931	887–897
60	Daigo	885–930	897–930
61	Suzaku	923–952	930–946
62	Murakami	926–967	946–967
63	Reizei	950–1011	967–969
64	En'yū	959–991	969–984
65	Kazan	968–1008	984–986
66	Ichijō	980–1011	986–1011
67	Sanjō	976–1017	1011–1016
68	Go-Ichijō	1008–1036	1016–1036
69	Go Suzaku	1009–1045	1036–1045
70	Go-Reizei	1025–1068	1045–1068
71	Go-Sanjō	1034–1073	1068–1073
72	Shirakawa	1053–1129	1073–1087
73	Horikawa	1079–1107	1087–1107
74	Toba	1103–1156	1107–1123
75	Sutoku	1119–1164	1123–1142
76	Konoe	1139–1155	1142–1155
77	Go-Shirakawa	1127–1192	1155–1158
78	Nijō	1143–1165	1158–1165
79	Rokujō	1164–1176	1165–1168
80	Takakura	1161–1181	1168–1180
81	Antoku	1178–1185	1180–1185
82	Go-Toba	1180–1239	1183–1198

Source: Kodansha Encyclopedia of Japan (1983), vol. 2, p. 202.

vealed in that vicious despot's warning: "Remember that I can do anything to anybody."[11] Although not so bloodthirsty as his Roman predecessor, Yōzei was very likely the murderer of one of his own courtiers. It was in protest of such behavior, no doubt, that Mototsune sought to resign his regency powers on several occasions and in 883 refused for a number of months to appear at the palace, bringing government to a standstill. The murder appears to have been the final straw, however, and shortly thereafter Mototsune expelled from

---

11 John Boardman, Jasper Griffin, and Oswyn Murray, eds., *The Oxford History of the Classical World* (Oxford and New York: Oxford University Press, 1986), pp. 9–10.

court the emperor's more flamboyant companions, forced the emperor himself to abdicate, and installed in his place on the throne a fifty-four-year-old son of Nimmyō, Emperor Kōkō.

If it is assumed that Mototsune was pursuing chiefly his own interests and those of his family, his choice of Kōkō was at first sight extraordinary and in some respects inexplicable. A more natural choice from that point of view, one might have thought, would have been one of the two younger brothers of Yōzei who were related through their mothers to Mototsune, one a ten-year-old nephew (a son of Kōshi) and the other a six-year-old grandchild. But perhaps in order to avoid another regency and to help bring the court back to a certain normalcy after the bizarre events of Yōzei's reign, Mototsune selected a prince with a reputation for intelligence and probity and who was related to him only rather distantly (they were cousins through their mothers). The choice therefore may have been at least partially an act of statesmanship, as subsequent historians have sometimes treated it, but it was perhaps at the same time also firmly rooted, after all, in a clear calculation of family self-interest. Before the new emperor's accession to the throne, his seventh son (later Emperor Uda) had been adopted by Mototsune's childless adoptive sister, Shukushi. The decisive influence that sisters seem often to have exercised on their brothers in Heian society provides grounds for thinking that her Machiavellian hand may have been involved in the choice of the aged emperor, whose early demise, she might have correctly foreseen, would lead under Mototsune's influence to the elevation of her adopted son to the imperial title and to exceptional honors for herself. (She became, in fact, the first woman to hold the Junior First Rank, a rank so high that it had been rarely awarded to anyone.) Kōkō's selection may also be interpreted to mean, on the one hand, that the power of the Northern House was so firmly entrenched by this time that it did not need to depend on a close blood relationship with the emperor, and, on the other, that Kōkō was not personally inclined toward the assertion of his authority. The latter is illustrated by his decision (if the decision was indeed his) to reduce all his sons to noble status, including the son adopted by Shukushi – rendering them at least formally ineligible as heirs to the throne and thus avoiding possible conflict with the Fujiwara – and also by his investment of Mototsune with what amounted to regency powers.

Kōkō's reign was brief, and an heir to the throne had still not been chosen when he lay on his deathbed in 887. According to a nearly contemporaneous document, the emperor had frequently sought to make Uda his crown prince, but Mototsune did not act, and it was thanks largely to the efforts of Shukushi that her adopted son was finally restored to his princely title and raised to the throne on the same day that he was named imperial heir. The selection of Uda, as we shall see, eventually led to some difficulties for the Northern House in its domination of the court, but as long as Mototsune lived, the absence of a close blood connection with the emperor seems to have made no more difference than in the days of Kōkō. One of Uda's first acts was, in fact, to invest Mototsune with regency powers, the edict of investment employing for the first time the title *kampaku* ("internuncio"), the name by which a regent came to be called when the emperor was an adult, contrasting with *sesshō* ("vice-regent"), the title of a regent to a minor emperor.

That there was, nevertheless, at least some friction between Uda and Mototsune is suggested by a curious and seemingly trivial controversy about nomenclature that erupted following Motosune's appointment as *kampaku*. In offering the post to Mototsune a second time after he had formally declined the first edict of appointment as required by custom, Uda – or, rather, Tachibana no Hiromi (837 or 838–90), the erudite of Chinese letters who drafted Uda's edict – equated *kampaku* with the Chinese title *a-heng* (Japanese *akō*), which in early China had designated the chief governmental minister. Although the same word had been used of Mototsune without incident in an imperial rescript three years earlier, this time Mototsune's steward, a Fujiwara named Sukeyo (d. 897 or 898), also learned in Chinese, persuaded the Northern-House leader that *akō* actually referred to a purely nominal post without substantive duties and that the equation of the two titles implied the dismissal of Mototsune from government. Mototsune thereupon refused to take further part in court affairs, bringing major governmental business to a halt, just as he had done during Yōzei's reign. The controversy raged on for six or seven months, with one group of literati supporting Hiromi and another supporting Sukeyo, but finally the chastened Uda was forced to apologize and delete the offending word from his edict.

Although the Akō Controversy was perhaps fueled chiefly by the ambitions of rival learned families, Mototsune may have also welcomed it as an opportunity to rid Uda's court of the influential literati with whom he had surrounded himself. It may have also had some other important political results. In the first place, although on the one hand it clearly demonstrated to Uda his inability to oppose

Mototsune's wishes, at the same time it seems to have left a legacy of imperial bitterness that encouraged a brief challenge to the Northern House's control of the court during the generation of Mototsune's sons. Furthermore, the controversy ended in disgrace for Hiromi, who as the father of Uda's consort and the grandfather of her two sons posed at least a potential threat to the Fujiwara position. It may have been to allay Mototsune's fears in that respect that just four months after Uda's forced apology, Mototsune's daughter Onshi (872–907) was allowed to become a consort of the emperor. Finally, among the learned men defending Hiromi was Sugawara no Michizane (845–903), who after Mototsune's death figured prominently in the efforts of Uda to free himself and the imperial clan from Fujiwara control. Michizane's defense of Hiromi took the form of a written statement of opinion addressed to Mototsune and dated after the incident had already been resolved. He argued that persecution of Hiromi for what he contended was an unintended affront would have a chilling effect on the learned world, and also that it was not in the interests of the Fujiwara to attack a man who was grandfather to two of the emperor's children.[12]

The death of Mototsune in 891 ushered in about a decade of imperial ascendancy at court. Immediately after Mototsune's death, an aged, ineffective brother of Yoshifusa became the senior Fujiwara minister; and Mototsune's eldest son, Tokihira (871–909), was still too young and too junior in status to control the senior ministers, whose ranks were dominated by Minamoto men. Effective leadership in the Council of State was in the hands of a Minamoto Major Counselor who was a son of Emperor Montoku, which left Uda with a freedom of rule that had not been enjoyed by an emperor since the days of Saga and Junna. In his determination to control his own court and to maintain his independence of Fujiwara power, Uda strengthened the Chamberlains' Office, expanding its staff and codifying its procedures, greatly enlarged the *kebiishi* office, and also created landholdings for the personal use of retired emperors. To assist him, he employed men from the middling ranks of the nobility unconnected, or only distantly connected, with the Fujiwara leaders, men like the literati-official Sugawara no Michizane, who was appointed head of the Chamberlains' Office in the month following Mototsune's death, and the celebrated provincial administrator Fu-

---

12 For Michizane's role in the Akō Controversy, see especially Robert Borgen, *Sugawara no Michizane and the Early Heian Court*, Harvard East Asian Monographs, 120 (Cambridge, Mass.: Council on East Asian Studies, Harvard University, 1986), pp. 173–81.

jiwara no Yasunori (825–95), whose series of provincial appointments testify to his remoteness from the center of Fujiwara power. (He belonged to the Southern House of the clan.)

Michizane, in particular, became a key instrument in Uda's quest for control of the Council of State, perhaps having earned the emperor's confidence and gratitude by his letter to Mototsune in the Akō Controversy (although, in fact, it is not known whether either Mototsune or Uda ever saw the letter). With Uda's backing, Michizane found himself suddenly elevated from the status of an unemployed ex-provincial official at the time of Mototsune's death to the ranks of the senior ministers just two years later. By 896, when one of his daughters entered Uda's harem, Michizane had risen to the post of Middle Counselor, and before his imperial patron abdicated in the following year he had been appointed Provisional Major Counselor, just a step behind his junior by twenty-six years, Fujiwara no Tokihira. When Uda abdicated in favor of his twelve-year-old son Daigo (885–930, r. 897–930), whom he had earlier named crown prince in consultation with Michizane and who had no direct family relationship with Tokihira, Michizane and Tokihira were directed to share the supervision of the government with powers similar to those of *kampaku* (that is, *nairan*, or "private inspection," powers). In 899, on the same day that Tokihira became Minister of the Left, Michizane was appointed Minister of the Right, the second highest regularly filled office in the government and a totally unprecedented honor for a member of the Sugawara clan. In an age when clan and family membership had come generally to determine the offices for which a man was eligible, Michizane was understandably alarmed by his newfound prominence, which even he considered beyond his station in life.

Michizane's rise to eminence not only implied a weakening of the Fujiwara position at court but also represented the emergence in high court councils of a man with practical experience in provincial administration, source of the most critical governmental problems of the day. Much against his will, he had served a term as governor of Sanuki (on Shikoku) from 886 to 891, acquiring there, and also in his association with Fujiwara no Yasunori and other experienced provincial governors, a practical knowledge of the problems confronting provincial administrators that made him unique among the court's chief ministers. Those problems centered on the question of how to collect revenues from and administer a province under social and economic conditions strikingly different from the ones envisioned in the statutory code. Although the virtual abandonment of the land distribution system, the emergence of a provincial gentry possessed of large landholdings, a conspicuous increase in the vagrant population, and the corruption of population registers had made much of the statutory provincial administrative structure inoperable or useless, the court under Fujiwara leadership had continued to insist for the most part on the literal observance of statutory law and procedures. Caught between those demands and the actualities of local conditions, provincial administrators seem regularly to have resorted, even at the risk of punishment, to subterfuge and illegal or extralegal measures in order to fulfill their governmental responsibilities. Needless to say, private gain was no doubt also sometimes the object of such measures. If a single instance relating to the dispatch of provincial tax inspectors can be accepted as indicative of the general lines of Michizane's thought on the subject, he argued at court that the provincial administrators were entirely justified in the freedoms they were taking with the law. He said in essence that the provinces were ungovernable under the existing provisions of the statutory code and that it was necessary to adjust provincial administrative aims and procedures to existing local circumstances. That pragmatic view seems to have found little favor in court councils during Michizane's own day, but not many years later, shortly before Tokihira's death in 909, it became the policy of the court, contributing vitally to the survival of that institution as a functioning organ of government.

Despite Uda's abdication, which may have been a political tactic designed to strengthen his own position and that of his heir, the direction of court affairs apparently remained largely in his hands. But by that time (897) Tokihira was approaching thirty and beginning to demonstrate the gift for leadership and decisive action that had made his father and grandfather before him such dominant figures. It had probably been clear to him for some time that if Fujiwara control of the court was to be firmly reestablished and maintained, Michizane, as an instrument of imperial power and possibly also as a contender for power in his own right, would have to be removed from his influential position. But it was not until 901 that Tokihira found, or perhaps created, an opportunity to move against the upstart Minister of the Right. His action may have been precipitated by a proposal that, according to a twelfth-century source, Uda and Emperor Daigo had made to Michizane the previous year suggesting that the dual leadership shared by him and Tokihira be ended and that supervision of governmental matters be entrusted exclusively to Michizane. Although Michizane prudently refused to consider the proposal, Tokihira, if he learned of it, could not have been pleased by so marked a sign of imperial favor. At any rate, early in 901 he persuaded the sixteen-year-old emperor that Michizane was conspiring with a deluded Uda to force Daigo to abdicate, presumably in favor of Uda's son and Michizane's son-in-law Prince Tokiyo (886–927), and an imperial decree was hastily issued demoting Michizane and exiling him to Kyushu. There is some evidence to suggest that the chief architect of the conspiracy, assuming that a conspiracy did in fact exist, may have been Uda himself. If so, the ex-emperor's defeat and humiliation were complete, for when he raced to the imperial palace on learning too late what had happened to Michizane, he was refused access to, or communication with, the emperor, despite the all-day vigil he mounted in the palace courtyard.

In the years following Michizane's death in exile, calamities at court and in Tokihira's family – including especially a spectacular lightning storm that struck the imperial palace in 930, killing or injuring several high-ranking courtiers – were attributed to Michizane's angry spirit. In an effort to placate the spirit, Daigo rescinded the rescript ordering Michizane's exile and restored him to his original office and rank. It was probably for the same reason that perhaps as early as the 940s Michizane had begun to be worshiped at Kitano in Kyoto, an area earlier associated with a god of thunder and lightning. By the 980s he had acquired the name Heavenly Deity Temman ("Heaven Filling") and was being called the "ancestor of the Way of Letters," becoming thus the divinity of a cult that has survived vigorously to the present day.[13]

After the ouster of Michizane and the isolation of Uda from governmental affairs, Tokihira enjoyed a period of unchallenged power at court as the sole possessor of "private inspection" authority until his death in 909, although he never received appointment as regent. It is worthwhile noting that Tokihira's line of the Northern House seems to have been so powerful by this time that he was able to continue the family's ascendancy at court despite the presence on the Council of State of a member of a collateral line of the house who was both senior in age to him and also the maternal uncle of Daigo. Northern-House lineage, a blood relationship with the emperor, se-

---

[13] On Michizane and his cult, see Borgen, *Sugawara no Michizane and the Early Heian Court*, pp. 307–36.

niority, and ministerial rank were not necessarily sufficient to give a man control of the court.

Tokihira was succeeded in family and governmental affairs not by his eldest son, who was only about seventeen at the time of Tokihira's death, but by his younger brother Tadahira (880–949), who dominated the court during the remainder of Daigo's reign but seems to have been a somewhat less powerful or autocratic figure than his brother had been, never wholly succeeding in usurping the emperor's authority. He had to contend not only with the emperor himself, who was in his mid-twenties by that time, but also with the ex-emperor Uda, who had become a Buddhist monk in 899 and had remained in seclusion at Ninnaji Temple following Michizane's exile. Uda now reasserted himself and through Tadahira, who was married to the ex-emperor's daughter (or possibly his half sister – there is a question about the exact relationship), exercised a powerful influence at court and in the government. Tadahira did succeed, however, in imposing his nephew, Daigo's son by Mototsune's daughter Onshi, on the emperor as his crown prince, and when that prince became emperor at the age of seven in 930, Tadahira was appointed regent (*sesshō*). When the emperor, Suzaku (923–52, r. 930–46), was eighteen in 941, Tadahira's regency title was changed to *kampaku*, beginning the practice observed thereafter of distinguishing a regent for a minor emperor (*sesshō*) from that of an adult emperor (*kampaku*). From 944 until Tadahira's death in 949, the three highest offices in the government (regent and Chancellor, Minister of the Left and Minister of the Right) were held by Tadahira, his brother Nakahira (875–945), or his sons Saneyori (900–70) and Morosuke (908–60). The Fujiwara in the line of Mototsune were firmly in the saddle of power, seemingly impregnable to almost any challenge from within the court.

During most of Tokihira's time at the head of the central government, the court, ignoring Michizane's prescient advice, continued a basic policy of attempted institutional revival or restoration first adumbrated in Uda's reign. It sought in a flurry of Council of State orders to check the growth of a wealthy landed gentry class in the provinces, and to restore and maintain the system of taxes and publicly allotted rice tillage provided for by the statutory code. Toward the end of Tokihira's life, however, he and his court seem finally to have recognized the futility of that policy and to have sought instead to adapt governmental practice to provincial reality. In pursuit of that aim, three basic changes in past policy were instituted:

1. A de facto abandonment of the statutory land allotment system and a substitution of land taxes for capitatim taxes.
2. A new approach to private landed proprietorships that accepted their existence and growth but also attempted to limit the expansion of tax-exempt land within the proprietorships in return for increased exemptions on legally exempt land.
3. The recognition of provincial governments as quasi-autonomous entities with contractual tax obligations to the central government, a notable weakening of a cardinal principle of the statutory system, which had established a centrally defined uniform tax system and a thoroughgoing centralized control over the provinces based on the appointment of central officials to the chief administrative posts.

Pushed forward also under Tadahira, the court's new, more pragmatic approach to land, taxes, and provincial administration enabled the regime to survive the outbreak of large-scale revolt and piracy in the eastern and western parts of the country in the late 930s and early 940s, and to evolve and endure for another two centuries or more as the nation's central instrument of government. The change in governmental policy seems in large part to have been simply a confirmation of earlier tentative steps in the same direction and a recognition of practices that had already been adopted by the provincial governors themselves acting on their own authority. If the change was not therefore particularly sudden or radical, it represented nevertheless a major political turning point. The new policies brought the last period of the old statutory regime to an end, recognizing, and in part creating, a new organization of the country in which the political system was increasingly characterized by personalized rule at court, descent-determined office, and provincial autonomy. The land allotment system was gone and the main tax burden had shifted from individuals to land; large private landed proprietorships had become an ever more prominent feature of the economy; and the society was marked by a growing military class in the provinces. Modern historians often use the term "Royal-Court State" (ōchō kokka) to distinguish the new system from the early statutory regime.

A quarrel among the Kammu Taira descended from the Emperor Kammu, who had become great landowners in the eastern provinces, escalated from small armed conflicts in 935 to a full-blown rebellion when Taira no Masakado in 939 seized the provincial headquarters of Hitachi. He grandiosely set forth to control all of the eight provinces of the Kanto region and began to appoint new provincial officials. Even more shocking, he declared himself the "New Emperor" (*shinnō*) and claimed imperial powers for himself throughout the east. The court, greatly alarmed, appointed a military commander to lead an expedition force against Masakado, but before it reached the east, Masakado was attacked and killed by Taira no Sadamori, his cousin, and Fujiwara no Hidesato.

Just at the height of the Masakado crisis late in 939, the court was beset by a resurgence of piracy in the Inland Sea (Seto Naikai) to the west. Fujiwara no Sumitomo, once an official in Iyo Province, carried out audacious raids on ports and ships in the Inland Sea, disrupting the transportation of tax revenues and products from the western regions to the capital. It was not until 941 that an expeditionary force organized by the court, with the assistance of defectors from the pirate bands, was able to corner and defeat Sumitomo.

The Masakado revolt and the Sumitomo piracy are referred to by modern Japanese historians as the "Discord of the Jōhei [931–38] and Tengyō [938–47] Eras." Masakado's rebellion was the more significant as a harbinger of future developments. It was the first attempt by a local leader to challenge the authority of the central government by trying to establish an autonomous government. The suppression of the revolt did not establish the central government's authority in the eastern provinces but, rather, confirmed the strength of the local provincial leaders who defeated Masakado. In the conflicts among the eastern warriors can be seen an early stage in the development of the *bushidan,* the private "warrior bands," based on family alliances and mutual regional interests, that shaped warrior society in the eleventh and twelfth centuries. (For a fuller account of the Jōhei–Tengyō disturbances, see Chapter 10.)

In 944 when Emperor Suzaku was twenty-one years old and still had not produced an heir, his mother, Onshi, persuaded him to appoint his younger brother crown prince, and two years later he abdicated.

The new emperor, Murakami (926–67, r. 946–67), was twenty at the time of his accession and inclined to take a stronger hand in government than his brother had, trying, mostly unsuccessfully, to improve the government's financial situation and to restore security in the provinces and the capital. The period centering on his reign is notable as the graveyard of several important activities of the statutory regime. The last official chronicle of the state was commissioned then but never completed; the last attempt at compiling governmental laws and procedures was undertaken but also abandoned before completion; and the last coins of the regime were minted. By Murakami's time, much of the statutory system survived only as an empty shell.

Following Tadahira's death in 949, the office of regent fell vacant, but the court continued to be dominated by the Northern House, as represented then by Tadahira's sons Saneyori, Morosuke, and Morotada (920–69), all of whom placed daughters in Murakami's crowded harem. Morosuke's daughter Anshi (927–64) was the most successful of the Northern-House imperial consorts, bearing three sons – Prince Tamehira (952–1010) and the two future emperors Reizei (950–1011, r. 967–69) and En'yū (959–91, r. 969–84)–and also, according to a twelfth-century source, exercising an unusually powerful influence over the emperor himself. Reizei was named crown prince just two months after his birth, passing over a luckless elder half brother, Motokata (888–953), whose mother was a daughter of the Southern-House Fujiwara. Reizei, however, was a sickly and perhaps mentally disturbed child, and after the birth of Anshi's second and favorite son, Tamehira, in 952, she and Murakami came to feel, with most of the court, that Tamehira should replace Reizei as crown prince. But nothing had been done by the time of Anshi's death in 964, and after 966, when Tamehira made the mistake of marrying a non-Fujiwara (a daughter of his mother's learned brother-in-law and confidant, Daigo's son Minamoto no Takaakira [914–83]), the Fujiwara were opposed to Tamehira's selection as crown prince at any time. When Reizei came to the throne in 967, the new crown prince therefore was not Tamehira but his younger brother En'yū.

Morosuke had been the ablest and most influential of Tadahira's sons, but his early death in 960, when his eldest son Koretada (or Koremasa, 924–72) was still relatively junior in rank and office, left the senior Council of State positions in the hands of his older brother Saneyori (Minister of the Left), Tokihira's son the Minister of the Right Akitada (898–965), and Minamoto no Takaakira (Major Counselor). Thus, when Reizei came to the throne following Murakami's death in 967 and it became necessary to name a regent for the ailing emperor, the choice fell on Saneyori, an aged and somewhat weak figure who was not closely related to Reizei. So much of the actual power at court during Saneyori's time seems to have been in the hands of others, especially those of his younger brother Morotada, that even Saneyori referred to himself in his diary as a "nominal" regent. It is nevertheless from 967, the year of his appointment to that post, that historians often date the beginning of the "Regency Period" (*sekkan jidai*), since the office of regent, which had been established only sporadically until that time, was thereafter almost continuously in existence, occupied invariably by a Northern-House leader holding the title of *sesshō* or *kampaku*, or exercising "private inspection" (*nairan*) authority. The Regency Period is usually thought of as lasting to the accession of Emperor Go-Sanjō in 1068.

Although it seems unlikely that Minamoto no Takaakira posed any real threat to the interests of the Northern House, his abilities, his sway at court, his marital connection with a possible imperial heir (Tamehira), and his high pedigree and office (he became Minister of the Left at the beginning of 968) could scarcely have endeared him to Saneyori and the other Northern-House men. His eventual downfall in the Anna Incident of 969 (so named after the current era name), however, may have occurred at least in part because of his position. This made him a convenient target of an ambitious military leader in the capital at that time who seems to have been seeking closer ties with the Northern House as well as a means of reducing or eliminating the influence of his military rivals of Kyoto.

The military leader in question, Minamoto no Mitsunaka (912–97), was the son of a warrior who had fought against Masakado and Sumitomo. He had latterly been employed by the court in police and military functions in the capital area together with Fujiwara no Chiharu, a son of the Hidesato who had helped defeat Masakado. In the early spring of 969, Mitsunaka and another man reported to the government that Minamoto no Tsuranu and others were plotting treason. In the absence of sources, it is impossible to say with any certainty what the plot was about, if it existed at all, but since Tsuranu was closely related to Takaakira, who was both his cousin and his brother-in-law, it is possible that an attempt (fictional or otherwise) to place Tamehira on the throne was involved. In any case, Takaakira and a number of others, including Mitsunaka's chief rival for military leadership in the capital, Chiharu, were implicated in the plot and sent into exile. Chiharu went to the island of Oki, and Takaakira, following in the footsteps of Sugawara no Michizane, another Fujiwara victim, to Kyushu, where he remained for three years before being allowed to return to a quiet life of study at the capital. The immediate result of the Anna Incident was thus the removal of the last real or potential rivals of the Northern House and Mitsunaka, but the long-term importance of the affair is probably that it marked the first significant appearance of warrior figures in the politics of the capital. It was also the beginning of an alliance between the Northern House and Mitsunaka's warrior family, the Seiwa Genji line of the Minamoto, from which eventually came the founder of the Kamakura Bakufu.

A few months after Takaakira's exile, the sickly emperor Reizei abdicated the throne to his younger brother En'yū, and on the same day Reizei's infant son by Fujiwara no Koretada's daughter Kaishi (945–75), the future emperor Kazan (968–1008, r. 984–86), was named crown prince. Reizei's decision to abdicate was encouraged by Koretada, who was anxious to see his grandson appointed crown prince before a competitor for the position could be produced by another of the emperor's consorts, Chōshi (d. 982), a daughter of Koretada's younger brother Kaneie (929–90).

THE FUJIWARA REGENCY, 970–1070

In the year following En'yū's accession in 969, the aged regent Saneyori died, and the regency passed to Morosuke's eldest son, Koretada, who was the maternal uncle of the emperor and the maternal grandfather of the crown prince. But three years later Koretada himself was dead, and another shift in the regency was required, the choice lying between Koretada's brothers, Kanemichi (925–77) and Kaneie. (For a genealogy of the Fujiwara Northern House and its regents, see Figure 1.3.)

Although Kanemichi was four years Kaneie's senior, he had not been well thought of by Murakami, Reizei, or Saneyori, and his career had languished behind that of his vigorous and able younger brother, who had been head of the Chamberlains' Office under Reizei and had progressed rapidly up the Council of State ladder to the post of Major Counselor by the year of Koretada's death. The choice of Kaneie as Koretada's successor may therefore have been regarded as a foregone conclusion by the courtiers, but the wily Kanemichi, a late source asserts, had obtained from his influential sister Anshi before her death in 964 a statement written in her own hand declaring that the regental succession was to follow the order of seniority among her brothers. Kanemichi is supposed to have shown the document to Anshi's son, Emperor En'yū, while Koretada lay dying at the end of 972, and the emperor, it is implied, felt constrained to honor his mother's wishes. When Koretada resigned his offices a few days before his death, Kanemichi, who held the comparatively lowly post of Provisional Middle Counselor, was ordered to take charge of the government. At the beginning of 973, a few weeks after Koretada's death, he was promoted over the heads of six other nobles, including his brother Kaneie, to the office of Palace Minister and named regent (*kampaku;* the regental appointment may not have come until the next year).

Following his precipitous rise to the regency, Kanemichi ruled the court in cooperation with his cousin, Saneyori's son Yoritada (924–89), and prepared the way for an eventual blood link with the imperial line by marrying a daughter to the young emperor. But his plans for the future and the enjoyment of his triumph over Kaneie were cut short by his premature death at the age of fifty-two in 977. Just before his death, however, Kanemichi exacted a final revenge on Kaneie, arranging matters so as to humiliate him and, as he no doubt hoped, to permanently debar him from the regency. In debarring Kaneie, Kanemichi violated that same testament of Anshi by which he is said to have won the post for himself. Angered, a late source says, by the unfeeling haste with which Kaneie presented himself at the imperial palace to claim the regency when he mistakenly concluded that his brother was already dead, Kanemichi roused himself from his deathbed, rushed to the imperial palace, and obtained the appointment of Yoritada as regent and the demotion of Kaneie from Major Captain of the Right (a distinguished post that he held concurrently with his office of Major Counselor) to the inferior title of Minister of Popular Affairs. Whatever the precise circumstances, it seems likely that by Yoritada's appointment and Kaneie's demotion Kanemichi was paying off old scores accumulated during the years of humiliation he had suffered before becoming regent.

Yoritada, who may have been an innocent pawn in the angry rivalry between Kanemichi and Kaneie, had no blood ties with the emperor and little stomach for confronting Kaneie in a struggle for power at court. He soon moved to make amends to his powerful kinsman, appointing him Minister of the Right in 978, the year following Kanemichi's death, and the two seem to have got along together amicably enough thereafter. But it was undoubtedly a frustrating time for the ambitious Kaneie, whose marital links with the imperial line placed him in an excellent position eventually to claim the regency and leadership at court. His daughter Chōshi, a consort of the ex-emperor Reizei, had already borne three potential heirs to the throne. Another daughter, Senshi (or Akiko; later titled Higashisanjō-in; 962–1002), produced Emperor En'yū's first son in 980.

A break in the impasse, as Kaneie must have thought of it, occurred in 984, when Emperor En'yū, acting under pressure from Kaneie, abdicated the throne to Reizei's son Kazan, and Senshi's son by En'yū, the future Emperor Ichijō (980–1011, r. 986–1011), was appointed crown prince. Kaneie was then but a single abdication or death away from the status of maternal grandfather to an emperor.

The mother of the new emperor had been Koretada's daughter Kaishi (she had died in 975). In the absence of strong leadership from Yoritada, who now retreated almost entirely from active involvement in government, it was, according to a thirteenth-century source, Koretada's son Yoshichika (957–1008) who, as a maternal uncle of Kazan, wielded the principal power at court, though never himself holding high ministerial office or the post of regent. A young and active man, Yoshichika is reputed to have plunged with enthusiasm into the business of government, aided by an equally young and vigorous distant kinsman, Fujiwara no Koreshige (953–89), whose exceptional authority during Kazan's reign earned him the sobriquet of Fifth-Rank Regent. During the reign of Kazan the court attacked some of the major governmental problems of the day, attempting to increase the supply of currency, stabilize prices, and regulate the growth of *shōen,* and it is possible that those measures were the handiwork of Yoshichika and Koreshige. But however much influence they may have actually wielded at court (and there is reason to doubt that it was as extensive as late sources would suggest) their power was of brief duration. After less than two years on the throne, Kazan abdicated; two days later, on the same day that Yoshichika and Koreshige joined the newly tonsured ex-emperor in holy orders, Kaneie was appointed regent, the first maternal grandfather of a reigning emperor to hold that post since Yoshifusa's time.

The circumstances surrounding Kazan's abdication are not recorded in contemporary sources, but a twelfth-century work attributed it to the machinations of Kaneie. He is said to have employed his son Michikane (961–95) to play upon Kazan's grief following the death of a well-loved consort and persuade him to abdicate the throne for Buddhist monkhood. Whatever the truth of that famous story may be, the identification of Kaneie as the chief instigator of the abdication seems plausible, given his ambition, his ruthlessness, and the rewards he reaped from the change of emperors. With the new reign, he became maternal grandfather of the emperor; a few weeks after Ichijō's accession, another of Kaneie's grandsons was appointed crown prince (the future Emperor Sanjō, Reizei's son by Kaneie's daughter Chōshi); and still another of Kaneie's daughters immediately became a consort of the new crown prince (who was also her nephew). The accession of Ichijō clearly marked the beginning of the high tide of Fujiwara fortunes.

Following his elevation to the post of regent, Kaneie operated with a high hand at court, treating the emperor himself as the cipher he was, rapidly promoting his three sons over the heads of other nobles to high posts in the Council of State, and further blurring the distinction between public weal and private fortune. When he fell fatally ill and resigned his offices in 990, after four years of extravagant and often arrogant rule, his powers did not pass in bureaucratic fashion to the senior officials in the Council of State but devolved in royal style on the family heir, his eldest son, Michitaka (953–95).

Michitaka continued the marital and family politics of Kaneie, favoring his relatives, especially his second son, Korechika (974–1010), in official appointments and promoting his daughter Teishi (976–1001) from the position of imperial consort to empress. When the hard-drinking regent fell ill in 995 and was no longer able to attend to court business, he obtained private inspection powers for Korechika but failed in his attempt to have his son named regent, possibly because of the opposition of his sister Senshi, the emperor's influential mother. Michitaka was succeeded as regent, therefore, by his disgruntled younger brother Michikane, who, a late source says, had earlier expected to follow Kaneie in the post because of the service he had rendered in persuading Kazan to abdicate. Michikane, however, was already gravely ill at the time of his appointment, and he enjoyed the office for only nine days before his own death raised the question of regental succession again. (Counting from the date on which he formally accepted appointment as regent in audience with the emperor, Michikane's tenure lasted only seven calendar days; he is thus sometimes called the "Seven-Day Regent.")

The contenders for the regency following Michikane's death were his nephew Korechika and his younger brother Michinaga (966–1028). Korechika was eight years Michinaga's junior but senior to him in office. Thanks to an epidemic that had decimated the ranks of the senior court officers, he was also, as Palace Minister, the highest-ranking member of the Council of State. His claims to the regency, later sources say, were supported by his sister Teishi, Ichijō's empress, while those of Michinaga were forcefully pressed by the emperor's mother, Michinaga's sister Senshi. Whatever doubt there may have actually been about the choice was resolved three days after Michikane's death when Michinaga was granted private inspection powers, beginning a thirty-year rule that marked the apex of Fujiwara power and influence. Although Michinaga is usually regarded as the Fujiwara regent par excellence, he actually held that post for only a little more than a year in 1016 and 1017 and otherwise exercised his control of the government mainly through the private inspection authority he held and through his ministerial posts, or, following his resignation from office and entrance into holy orders, through his son.[14]

By the time of Michinaga's investiture with private inspection powers in 995, rivalry between him and Korechika over offices and family succession seems to have led to such deep and open hostility between the two kinsmen that both could not remain comfortably together at court. It was not long before Michinaga found, or was given, a means of consigning his nephew to the same fate that had overtaken Sugawara no Michizane and Minamoto no Takaakira: demotion and exile to Kyushu.

Korechika's fall began with an armed attack instigated by him against the ex-emperor Kazan, the result apparently of Korechika's mistaken belief that Kazan, despite his holy orders, was a rival for the affections of a lady in whom Korechika was interested. The ex-emperor was not injured and is said to have had no interest in pressing charges against his assailants, especially since the attack occurred as he was returning from a tryst with the sister of Korechika's lady. Even so, the court, led by Michinaga, launched an investigation. Evidence of wrongdoing by Korechika – including the harboring of warriors in the capital, the use of black magic against Senshi, and the performance of Buddhist esoteric rites forbidden to all but the imperial house – was soon uncovered, and Korechika, his brother Takaie (979–1044), and others were condemned and exiled for treason. The banishment of Korechika and Takaie left their sister Teishi, Ichijō's consort, isolated at court, and she soon took Buddhist holy orders. The brothers were pardoned in a general amnesty in 997 and allowed to return to the capital, but Korechika never succeeded in regaining his position at court.

14 Michinaga's diary, *Midō kampaku ki*, survives in large part and has been translated by Francine Hérail, *Notes journalières de Fujiwara no Michinaga, ministre à la cour de Heian (995–1018): Traduction du Midō kanpakuki*, Hautes études orientales II, 23, Institut des hautes études japonaises (Geneva: Librairie Droz, 1987).

With Korechika safely out of the way, Michinaga turned his attention to marital politics. In 999 Teishi, nun though she had become, bore Emperor Ichijō's first son, but just a few days before the birth Michinaga had placed his eldest daughter Shōshi (or Akiko; later titled Jōtōmon-in; 988–1074) in the emperor's harem. In the following year he shocked even his admirers by arranging for the unprecedented appointment of Teishi (or Sadako) and Shōshi as concurrent empresses of the same emperor, Teishi holding the usual title of "Lustrous Heir-bearer" (*kōgō*) and Shōshi that of "Inner Palatine" (*chūgū*), a toponymically derived equivalent coined for the occasion. By the time of Ichijō's abdication in 1011, Shōshi had borne him two sons, the eldest of whom, the future Emperor Go-Ichijō, then became crown prince under the new emperor, Sanjō, Reizei's son by Michinaga's sister Chōshi. Although Teishi's son was Ichijō's eldest and also a favorite of Shōshi, who had raised him after his mother's death in 1001, he had little or no chance of ever being chosen heir apparent, since he lacked powerful maternal relatives at court.

The new emperor, Sanjō, at thirty-five was four years older than his predecessor and less closely connected with Michinaga because his mother, Michinaga's sister, had been dead for nearly thirty years. It was perhaps for that reason and also because Sanjō stood between the Northern-House leader and the status of imperial maternal grandfather – just as his half brother, the unfortunate Kazan, had in Kaneie's day – that relations between him and Michinaga seem to have been strained. Before his accession, Sanjō had taken as consort a daughter of Michinaga's cousin Fujiwara no Naritoki (941–95), who had borne him four sons, including his eldest, Prince Atsuakira (994–1051). In the years just before Sanjō's accession, however, Michinaga had given the emperor as a consort one of his daughters, Kenshi (994–1027), and soon after the accession Kenshi, despite her youth and lack of children, was appointed empress (*chūgū*), clearly at the behest of Michinaga. Two months later, Naritoki's daughter Seishi (972–1015) was also appointed empress (*kōgō*), but under humiliating circumstances arranged by Michinaga, who made certain that virtually no one attended the ceremony of appointment.

That kind of pressure on Sanjō seems to have been nearly constant. Michinaga and his intermediaries took every opportunity to impress on the emperor the wisdom of abdication, especially after his eyesight failed. Sanjō was resentful of the pressure, but at last agreed in 1016 to do as Michinaga wished in exchange for the designation of Atsuakira, his son by Naritoki's daughter Seishi, as the next crown prince. Michinaga's maternal grandson Go-Ichijō then came to the throne at the age of eight, fourteen years younger than his heir apparent. Atsuakira's only hope of ascending the throne probably lay in the survival of his father until the death or abdication of Go-Ichijō, but Sanjō died in the year following his abdication (1017), and just three months later Atsuakira, probably succumbing to pressure from Michinaga, renounced his title in return for appointment to the status of a retired emperor (he was known then as Koichijō-in) and marriage to still another of Michinaga's numerous daughters. The new crown prince was Go-Ichijō's brother, Go-Suzaku (1009–45, r. 1036–45), who, like him, was a son of Shōshi and a grandson of Michinaga.

Michinaga was now at the peak of his power. He had been appointed regent (*sesshō*) on the day of Go-Ichijō's accession, and he ruled over a Council of State composed almost entirely of relatives by blood or marriage. His ties with the imperial line were as complex as they were close, involving at times relations that were just short of incestuous. Two of his daughters, the highly influential Shōshi and Sanjō's willfully extravagant consort, Kenshi, were ex-empresses; the emperor (Go-Ichijō) and the crown prince (Go-Suzaku) were his grandsons; in 1018 his nineteen-year-old daughter, Ishi (999–1036), became the empress (*chūgū*) of her ten-year-old nephew Go-Ichijō, who thus became son-in-law as well as grandson to Michinaga. Three years later the same complicated set of relationships resulted when another daughter, Kishi (1007–25), became a consort of the crown prince. At the same time, Michinaga's eldest son, Yorimichi (992–1074), was being promoted in office and rank with unprecedented speed, becoming a senior noble (*kugyō*) at the age of fifteen (his peers were mostly in their thirties, forties, fifties, and sixties) and receiving appointment as Provisional Middle Counselor at eighteen.[15] It was during this period that the great regent composed his most famous poem, a crow of pride on the occasion of the appointment of his daughter Ishi as Go-Ichijō's empress: "No waning in the glory of the full moon – this world is indeed my world!" His own diary also shows him a happy and triumphant man a few days later when he received at his Tsuchimikado mansion simultaneous visits from his grandsons, the emperor and the crown prince, and his daughters, the three empresses.[16]

15 Tsuchida Naoshige, *Ōchō no kizoku*, vol. 5 of *Nihon no rekishi* (Tokyo: Chūō kōronsha, 1981), pp. 113–14, 279–301.
16 *Shōyūki*, part 10, vols. 1–11 of *Dai Nihon kokiroku* (Tokyo: Tokyo Daigaku Shiryō Hensanjo, 1959–86), vol. 5, p. 55, Kannin 2 (1018)/10/16.

Michinaga carried all before him at Kyoto, crushing his enemies, disposing of people and official posts mostly as he saw fit, and on occasion employing state resources for his own private purposes: for example, in the rebuilding of his mansion following a fire in 1016 and in the construction of his great temple, the Hōjōji, after he had become a Buddhist monk in 1019. He and his principal wife, Minamoto no Rinshi (964–1053), whose family wealth and connections may have paved the way for Michinaga's initial successes, were granted almost every imaginable court honor, stopping barely short, it sometimes seemed, of the imperial position itself. So complete was the family's domination of the court and the capital, so luxurious its life, and so rich the civilization its patronage spawned, that subsequent generations of the Fujiwara nobility tended to look back on Michinaga's time as the golden age of court society and to draw from it the standards and precedents by which court and noble life were regulated. It was in that important sense the classical age of Japan.

Michinaga resigned the regency to his eldest son, Yorimichi, in 1017 and took Buddhist holy orders because of a grave illness in 1019, but his domination of the court continued nearly unchanged until his death early in 1028, as his sobriquet "the Sacred Hall Regent" suggests. Much of his success may be attributed to the fertility of his wives, who produced seven sons and eight daughters for him, and also to the remarkable ability of his daughters to bear male offspring to their imperial husbands. His heir, Yorimichi, was not so fortunate. Yorimichi's adopted daughter was married to Go-Suzaku but managed to produce only girls, and the single daughter that he himself fathered during his long life proved barren when she was placed in the harem of Go-Suzaku's successor Go-Reizei (1025–68, r. 1045–68). Yorimichi's brother Norimichi (996–1075) also attempted to preserve the family's maternal link with the imperial house by giving a daughter to Go-Reizei, but she had no better luck than Yorimichi's daughter. Consequently, although Yorimichi's position remained secure during the reigns of Go-Ichijō, Go-Suzaku, and Go-Reizei, who were all sons of his sisters, when Go-Suzaku abdicated the throne to Go-Reizei in 1045, the former emperor, in the absence of a Fujiwara grandchild, was able to install as crown prince his son by an imperial princess. The next accession, that of Go-Sanjō (1034–73, r. 1068–73), brought to the throne therefore the first emperor born of a non-Fujiwara mother since the accession of Uda in 887. Because neither Yorimichi nor Norimichi, who succeeded his brother as regent in 1068, seems to have been an able enough politician to maintain the position of the Northern House without the support of blood ties to the emperor, control of the court slipped from regental hands as the imperial line, chiefly under the leadership of retired emperors, reasserted its authority for the final century of court rule and brought to an end the period of the Fujiwara regency. (On rule by retired emperors, see Chapter 9.)

Despite Yorimichi's failure in marital politics, he was not, apparently, the inconsequential figure that historians have sometimes painted him. It was during his time and probably under his leadership that an important reform of the land and tax system took place. This reform recognized further contraction of the government's fiscal base, but also seems to have succeeded in containing the growing strength of the provincial gentry and in securing the revenues with which the court supported itself during the final century of its autonomous rule.

The reform was initiated in the 1040s, probably in response to strong pressure from cultivators and landholders in the provinces closer to Kyoto. At least some of them had been in open conflict with the provincial governors since the last part of the tenth century and, by about the beginning of the eleventh century, were abandoning at an alarming rate tillage in the public realm for other occupations or for newly opened lands that had been commended to Kyoto patrons as privately established (i.e., taxable, not officially sanctioned) *shōen*. The chief causes of complaint, as registered in one famous appeal addressed to the central government in 988, were high taxes and illegal exactions. Provincial governors since the beginning of the tenth century had had the legal authority to set tax rates at their own discretion. Impelled by the need to meet the demands of the central government and of their patrons at the capital, and no doubt also by a desire to fill their own pockets, they seem frequently to have resorted to higher and higher taxes, or to exploitive measures that had the same effect as higher taxes. The court government, probably generally ignorant of the conditions in the provinces that bred the conflict, initially responded vigorously to complaints brought against especially greedy governors, disciplining them by dismissal from office. Under Michinaga, however, there seems to have been a realization that the court's revenues depended on just such rapacious officials, and a more lenient attitude appeared, encouraging some governors to suppress complaints against them by force. But continuing pressure from the cultivators and landholders, sometimes accompanied by violent assaults on the governors or arson at their Kyoto residences, convinced the court eventually that relief had to be given. The result, it is thought, was the reform of the 1040s, which can be seen as an attempt to appease the cultivators and landholders in the provinces while preserving a more assured, if reduced, income for the government and its officials. The chief known features of the reform were the initiation of fixed taxation rates not subject to change by provincial administrators and recognition by the central government of all but the most recent *shōen* that had been formally established with tax immunities by the authority of provincial administrators. The reform seems also to have required the return to the public realm of the privately established, taxable *shōen* that had been set up in great numbers in the name of the regent and other powerful patrons at the capital after the beginning of the tenth century.

The official recognition of all but the most recent *shōen* represented an important retreat from the court's long-standing effort to restrict *shōen* to those officially established before 902. That retreat, together with the fixed taxation rates, must have been especially well received in the provinces. In return for those concessions, the government obtained a certain measure of peace, probably better cooperation in the collection of taxes, and an increase in the taxes leviable on *shōen* lands returned to the public realm.

Whether the reform actually changed the total amount or distribution of revenue flowing into Kyoto is unknown. Insofar as the exploitive habits of the provincial governors were checked (and success in that respect was by no means complete), the regent's house, in particular, may have suffered a loss of income, but if the efficiency of tax collection was in fact increased by the more willing cooperation of the provincial gentry, who were the primary tax agents, and if the privately established *shōen* were actually incorporated into the public realm, revenues may have held steady or perhaps even increased. On the other hand, further court efforts in 1055 and 1069 to halt the growth of provincially authorized, tax-immune *shōen* suggest that despite the government's policies, its tax base continued to erode.

The reforms of the 1040s also included the beginning of the transformation of the statutory administrative-area system that led eventually in most areas outside the east to the elimination of subprovincial districts (*gun*) as functioning administrative units and the direct subordination of lesser units with various designations (known generally as *betsumyō*, "special nominals") to the provincial governor's office. It was during the same period that the several specific names of statutory taxes also disappeared from use.

Following the suppression of Taira no Masakado's revolt in 940, his conqueror, Taira no Sadamori, and his descendants were the leading warriors of the eastern provinces. The next serious incident in the east began with the seizure of tax revenues in Kazusa and Shimosa by the warrior Taira no Tadatsune (d. 1031) in 1027, which escalated into a revolt not unlike that of Masakado's. The court sent a punitive force led by Taira no Naokata, but when, after several years of campaigning, Naokata had failed to capture the rebel, he was relieved of his command and replaced by Minamoto no Yorinobu (968–1048), a son of Mitsunaka of the Anna Affair, who immediately effected Tadatsune's surrender. From this feat the reputation of the Seiwa Genji rose as a major force in the east.

Later in the eleventh century, more extensive campaigns were fought in the far northeast against the Emishi (or Ezo) who had halted the payment of taxes. Two long campaigns were mounted, known as the Earlier Nine Years' War (1051–62) and the Later Three Years' War (1083–87), before a stable order was reestablished in the region. The first campaign was ordered by the court, which appointed Minamoto no Yorinobu's son Yoriyoshi (988–1075) as commander, but the second war was an enterprise of the latter's son, Yoshiie (1039–1106), which the court refused to authorize or support. (A detailed account of this military history can be found in Chapter 10.)

REGENCY GOVERNMENT

The Fujiwara regency was in many aspects simply a prolonged and institutionalized phase in the cyclically shifting balance of power between the imperial line and the noble clans that had for shorter periods and in less formal ways been characteristic of Japanese government since at least the seventh century. It was distinguished from earlier phases of noble domination of the court by its long history, by its inheritance in a single family line, by the greater absoluteness of its domination, and by its coinciding with a period when changing economic and social conditions had much reduced the scope of the central government's authority and made personal relationships and private purposes salient features of governmental operations. Its essential legitimacy, however, continued to be derived from the person of the emperor and from the by then hallowed, if much truncated and changed, framework of the statutory regime. Its authority and power were, moreover, never absolute: not even the most powerful regent was able to govern autocratically in complete disregard of the emperor and the Council of State. The view of perhaps most modern historians is, in fact, that the terms "regency government" and "regency period" are misnomers in the sense that the regency was not the significant distinguishing characteristic of the period but simply an adjustment in, or relatively limited transformation of, the central government mechanism centering on the Council of State. It was, in that view, the change in the government's policies toward provincial administration and taxes at the beginning of the tenth century that marked a genuinely new phase in Heian history.

The period of the regency was a conservative time when the chief object of the court was to preserve such authority and resources as it had, rather than to strike out on radically new paths or to seek expanded wealth and power. Within those limits, however, the government played an active and often effective role in directing the affairs of the nation. It is undeniably true, as has often been observed, that much of the central government's attention was focused on the internal affairs of the court itself, especially on ceremonial and ritual, which were conceived to be essential, and indeed perhaps the most essential, elements of governmental operations. That was inevitable perhaps in a society of hereditary nobility where status defined all roles and where the chief means of coping with any major crisis, whether political, economic, social, or personal, was recourse to divine intervention, which all agreed was superior in efficacy to anything that man might otherwise do. But the court, its ceremonies, and its rituals were by no means the whole of regency government, as has sometimes been alleged. The regent and the Council of State ministers were actively engaged in the formulation and implementation of practical, mundane policy for a broad range of problems with nationwide import. It was they in their Guard-Post Judgments and other councils who directed Japan's diplomatic, cultural, and commercial relations with foreign states and supervised defenses against foreign piratical invaders; who oversaw efforts to cope with domestic revolt and warfare in the provinces; who instituted a series of attempts to regulate and halt the growth of *shōen;* who continuously adjusted the statutory institutions to the evolving social and economic conditions of the day in order to preserve a flow of income from the lands remaining under public control; and who dealt with countless other major governmental, judicial, and police matters. The quest for the regency and control of the court was not an empty game played simply for honors and personal advantage. Although the statutory regime was by this time but a pale shadow of its former self, the regency still represented the greatest concentration of governmental power and wealth in Japan.

The establishment of the first Fujiwara regency seems to have been the result of a search for a means of giving institutional recognition to the overwhelmingly dominant position occupied by Yoshifusa at court. It did not represent, in other words, the seizure of new power through an existing office but, rather, the confirmation of existing power through the creation of a new office. The uniquely sovereign powers Yoshifusa exercised were first formally recognized by his appointment to the post of Chancellor in 857. But the vague, exemplary duties given to that post by the code may have come to seem inadequate after Yoshifusa's grandson, Emperor Seiwa, came to the throne in 858, and especially after the emperor reached adulthood. It was therefore probably to give more substantive content to the Chancellor's position that an imperial rescript was issued in 866 specifically directing Yoshifusa to take charge of the government as regent, the title itself (*sesshō*), however, being only implied in the rescript. That was an ad hoc arrangement without legal basis in the statutory code or in any of the amendments thereto, and it is important to note that even after the regency was firmly established, its ad hoc nature persisted. The holder of the title had to be reappointed to his post by each succeeding emperor, instead of continuing from reign to reign, as with regular governmental appointees.

The problem of defining the Fujiwara leader's position at court seems to have continued in the time of Mototsune, and was perhaps in some way a chief cause of the otherwise rather mysterious Akō Controversy in 887 (see earlier in this chapter) and the similar impasse that developed when Mototsune was appointed Chancellor in 880. Mototsune evidently wanted to create a position that stood apart from and superior to the regular statutory organs of government but was not rendered ineffective by isolation from them. His solution was basically the same as Yoshifusa's: a combination of the ad hoc office of regent with a statutory ministerial post. The chief difference was that after Mototsune's appointment as regent in 876 while holding the title of Minister of the Right, the chancellorship was clearly differentiated from the regental position. Eventually it was even possible for the regency and the chancellorship to be held by different men, as when Yoritada retained his title of Chancellor after Kaneie succeeded him in the regency in 986. That the regency continued for some time, nevertheless, to be viewed chiefly as the definition of the duties of a regular statutory minister is suggested by the fact that until the time of Kanemichi a regent who held, for instance, the title of Minister of the Right was considered inferior for protocol and other purposes in the Council of State to a nonregental Minister of the Left (the senior title). The same view is reflected also in the fact that before Kaneie's day the chieftainship of the Fujiwara clan was always held by the clansman with the highest statutory office and rank, regardless of who was regent. But the position of regent had become fully independent of Council of State offices by the time of Kaneie, who resigned his office of Minister of the Right after he was appointed regent and during most of his tenure held no other Council title.

It was in Tadahira's time that a clear distinction was made between the titles of *sesshō*, a regent to a minor emperor, and *kampaku*, regent to an adult emperor. Initially, the distinction was a significant one, since the *sesshō* was able to act *as* the emperor in approving official documents, in the conduct of ceremonies, and in all other official capacities, whereas the *kampaku* only acted *for* the emperor in his dealings with the Council of State and was not otherwise empowered to represent him. The *sesshō* in effect became the emperor, as a twelfth-century courtier said, while the *kampaku* remained a minister to the emperor. The practical significance of the distinction seems to have been lost, however, as the post of regent came to be regularly filled and the alternation between the titles of *sesshō* and *kampaku* became simply a mechanical function of the emperor's age. The terminological distinction itself, nevertheless, was always faithfully maintained.

A third regental title, *nairan* ("private inspection"), first employed in the time of Tokihira and Sugawara no Michizane, gave its holders powers mostly identical with those of a *kampaku*. It appears to have been of lower official status, though, and to have differed significantly in that a *nairan* regent regularly took an active part in the business and meetings of the Council of State, unlike regents holding the titles of *sesshō* and *kampaku*, who were generally removed from direct involvement in the Council's affairs. There was probably always a danger, recognized perhaps as early as Mototsune's day, that as a result of its isolation from the operating organs of the government, the regency might, like the imperial throne, become largely a figurehead or honorary position devoid of actual power. It was perhaps because of such considerations that an active politician and leader like Michinaga preferred the *nairan* title during most of his regental career. He took advantage of the freedom it gave him to exercise direct administrative leadership over the Council of State, appearing at court almost daily and presiding over most important Council meetings. There was consequently little of importance that went on in the government of which he was not directly aware, which no doubt helps explain the extraordinary power he enjoyed as regent.

Government finances under the Fujiwara regency continued to depend on tax revenues derived through the provincial administrations from public lands, but the period saw substantial growth in the areas of rice tillage under private control, and *shōen* came consequently to play an important role in the economy of the capital. Most of the new privately controlled tillage seems to have been land recently opened to cultivation by provincial gentry, who, to prevent incorporation of their lands into the tax units of public land called "nominals" (*myō*), commended them as privately established *shōen* to influential nobles and religious institutions in the capital area. Such *shōen* were not officially recognized by the provincial governments and were therefore still subject to the taxes levied on newly opened tillage, but by their exclusion from the "nominal" system, they escaped the heavy taxes based on the public land in the units of that system. The most influential potential patron of *shōen* was, of course, the regent, who became therefore the beneficiary of what was undoubtedly the largest share of such commendations. Chiefly by that process, apparently, the regent's house accumulated such a large number of *shōen* in Michinaga's time that one of his contemporaries complained hyperbolically that there was not a needle's breadth of land in the country that did not belong to him. Nevertheless, despite the size of the regent's *shōen* holdings in the time of Michinaga and Yorimichi, most of the commendations appear to have been largely fictitious arrangements, and only a few *shōen* actually yielded significant income to the regental purse. Until past the middle of the eleventh century, the family probably still obtained the major part of its income from the official posts and ranks of its leaders. The middle and lower ranks of the nobility, on the other hand, who had been the first to suffer when the decline in governmental revenues in the ninth and tenth centuries forced a curtailment of expenditures, relied heavily on *shōen* income during this time to replace or supplement their governmental stipends. A similar fate awaited the regent's house itself in the following century, when control of the central government passed into other hands.

The regent's income was supplemented by gifts of labor and

goods that he frequently received from provincial officials. The tax system adopted at the beginning of the tenth century and the quasi-autonomy of provincial administration seem to have made provincial posts so highly lucrative that the provincial administrator became a common metaphor in the contemporary literature for ostentatious new wealth. Since the regent usually exercised a controlling influence in the selection and appointment of such officials, it may be assumed that their munificent gifts were made in recognition of past favors and in hopes of future appointment. Michinaga, for example, received a nearly continuous stream of horses and oxen from provincial officials, and, as mentioned earlier, much of the financial responsibility for the reconstruction of his Tsuchimikado mansion and for the construction of his Hōjōji Temple was assigned to provincial governors. The governor of Iyo, Minamoto no Mitsunaka's son Yorimitsu (948–1021), supplied all the furnishings for the reconstructed Tsuchimikado mansion, which were so fabulously extravagant that they left even the wealthiest nobles agog, and there was competition in the nobility to obtain copies of the catalogue of gifts that accompanied the furnishings. A wall of onlookers, straining to get a glimpse of the gifts, is said to have lined the streets when they were transported from Yorimitsu's house to Tsuchimikado. Such income, however, was only as reliable as the provincial officials' control of their provinces and the regent's control over appointments, and both types of control suffered drastic change in the last half of the eleventh century.

Probably as a direct consequence of the growth of their *shōen* holdings, the Fujiwara regents found it necessary to expand greatly the household administrative office that they were allowed to staff and maintain under the provisions of the statutory code. As provided for under the code, such offices were staffed by at most half a dozen titled officials holding various court ranks, some as high as the ranks held by the heads of regular government bureaus or governors of provinces. By Yorimichi's day, however, the staff of the regent's household office had grown to include at least twenty court-ranked officials, who held a wide variety of specialized titles and managed what was clearly a large private empire of mansions, palaces, and land. Under Michinaga, most such officials were at the same time provincial administrators, who must have been especially useful in filling the coffers of the house and in enforcing its orders at the *shōen* level. But from Yorimichi's time on, the number of provincial administrators on the household staff decreased and the posts tended to become hereditary. This reflected perhaps both the expanding role of *shōen* in the economy of the regent's house and the consequent increased need for experienced administrators, as well as the loss of regental control over the appointment of provincial officials during the reign of Go-Sanjō and afterward.

Perhaps because of the size and far-ranging activities of the regent's household office, which may have occasionally impinged on governmental prerogatives, and because of the central position occupied by the regent in Kyoto political life, one eleventh-century diarist asserted that in his day the regent's house had become the imperial court. There was probably a good deal of truth in that observation, since political power flowed from the regent and much governmental business was transacted at his house. But it is also true that the court, with its regularly established offices, its fixed procedures and its documents, remained both the formal and, for the most part, the actual center of government.

FOREIGN RELATIONS, 794–1070

Japan's relations with the other countries of East Asia during the Heian period were driven by the familiar twin engines of fear of external power, on the one hand, and desire for material and cultural gain on the other, and they were typically structured by trilateral interrelationships among Japan, China, and the Korean peninsula. The proximate source of the fear tended to be Korea, in the affairs of which Japan had at times been deeply involved since early historical times. The source of desire, although more evenly distributed, was mostly concentrated on the riches of China, either directly or as filtered through the states of Northeast Asia. During the period of present concern, the desire never developed into territorial ambition, and therefore Japan's neighbors did not become the victims of aggression by forces of the Japanese government. Nevertheless, the poorly informed Kyoto authorities were sometimes alarmed by rumors of impending foreign assaults on Japan, and raids on Iki, Tsushima, and Kyushu by Korean and other pirates occasionally brought those fears to a white heat.

Japan's earliest substantial foreign relations were with the Korean peninsula. When those relations first dimly appear in historical sources for the fourth century, the peninsula was occupied by the three principal kingdoms of Koguryŏ in the north, Paekche in the southwest, and Silla in the southeast. In the latter half of the fourth century, the early Japanese kingdom of Yamato appears to have held or occupied in some fashion a territorial base (called Mimana in Japanese sources) at the south-central tip of the peninsula between Paekche and Silla (the area called Kaya). What the nature of the Japanese interest in Korea was at that time is unknown (ethnic and cultural affinities may have been the main elements), but it led first to military alliances with both Paekche and Silla against the expansionist pressure of Koguryŏ, and then, when Silla leagued itself with Koguryŏ, to support of Paekche against the other two. The Japanese launched repeated attacks on Silla, apparently both from their Korean base and also directly from Tsushima. But at the beginning of the fifth century their activities in Korea were checked by a major defeat at the hands of Koguryŏ armies, and they were expelled from the peninsula in the mid-sixth century.

Beginning in the late sixth century, Koguryŏ came under attack by Chinese armies (first those of the Sui dynasty [581–618], then of T'ang [618–907]), giving Paekche an opportunity to launch an assault on its longtime enemy Silla, now unsupported by the otherwise occupied Koguryŏ forces. In response, Silla allied itself with China, which in 660 sent a naval force against Paekche. The Paekche king sought and received military support from Japan, but in 663 the Japanese forces were crushed by the Chinese in a naval engagement off the southwest Korean coast at the mouth of the Kum River (the Battle of Hakusuki, or Hakusan, Estuary, as it is known to Japanese historians), and Japanese military intervention in the peninsula was soon at an end, not to be renewed for some nine centuries.

With the destruction of Paekche and Koguryŏ by Chinese and Sillan attacks in the 660s, Silla was finally able to unite the peninsula south of P'yongyang under its rule, the former territory of Koguryŏ to the north being then occupied by the Tungusic state of Po-hai, as it is generally known (Parhae in modern Korean). It was that resulting distribution of power in the peninsula, together with the long history of Japanese-Sillan hostility, that provided some of the chief determinants of Japanese foreign relations until as late as the last half of the tenth century.[17]

Japan's relations with China began very early but did not rival

---

17 There is disagreement among historians, especially between Korean and Japanese historians, about the nature and extent of early Japanese involvement in Korean affairs. The present account owes more to the commonly accepted Japanese interpretation, as summarized, for example, in Inoue, *Nihon rekishi taikei*, pp. 16–18 and 273–93, which also presents the chief alternative views.

those with Korea in practical importance until the reunification of China under the Sui and T'ang dynasties made Chinese cultural and military influence throughout East Asia so overwhelming that even a seagirt nation like Japan was compelled to place China at the forefront of its attention. As Sui and T'ang armies became involved in the complicated affairs of the Korean peninsula, threatening Japanese allies and interests there, and as Japan became ever more deeply involved in the assimilation of sinitic culture and institutions, official relations with the Chinese court became indispensable. In 600, when a Japanese army was confronting Sillan forces in territory at the southern tip of the Korean peninsula claimed by the Japanese court, a Chinese chronicle records the arrival of an embassy from Japan at the Sui court, which was allied with Silla against their common enemy Koguryŏ. From that time on for more than two centuries the Japanese government, spurred by military and cultural concerns, maintained official relations with the Chinese court, becoming in form a tributary state in the Chinese system of international relations.

But by the end of the eighth century much had changed, internally as well as externally. The compilation of the Taihō and Yōrō codes at the beginning of the century had put a capstone on the sinitically inspired structure of the statutory regime and rendered less pressing the need for study and observation of the operations of the Chinese government. Several generations of officials had provided a base of experience and learning, and it was no longer as necessary for student-officials to undertake the long journey to the Chinese capital at Ch'ang-an in search of the knowledge, books, and techniques required by the court's governmental machinery. National amour propre and pragmatic diplomatic aims had been served by Chinese recognition of Japan's high status in the Chinese tributary system.[18] If Japan could still benefit greatly from intercourse with China, that was less in the realm of government, where official relations might be most useful, than in economic, cultural, and intellectual matters, which were perhaps more amenable to private routes of exchange.

Externally, whatever justification there may have been for Japanese fears of the T'ang armies in Korea after the Japanese defeat in 663, such concerns were presumably much ameliorated in the following decade when the Chinese forces in Korea withdrew north of

---

[18] Charlotte von Verschuer, *Les Relations officielles du Japon avec la Chine aux viiiᵉ et ixᵉ siècles*, Hautes études orientales, 21 (Geneva: Librairie Droz, 1985).

the Taedong River (at P'yongyang), leaving a unified peninsula under the rule of Silla. True, the outbreak of the An Lu-shan rebellion in China in 755 worried the Nara court sufficiently to cause it to look to its defenses in Kyushu, and Japanese suspicions about Sillan intentions reached such a feverish pitch at the same time that the government even laid plans for a punitive military expedition against the peninsula. Fortunately, however, nothing came of them, and, in fact, internal troubles in both Silla and China were making it less and less likely that either state would ever again be able to menace even its nearest neighbors, much less a nation like Japan, whose main islands were protected from the continent by over a hundred miles of intervening sea.

Japanese geography placed the country in the enviable position of being able to regulate its relations with the adjacent continent largely according to its own internally generated needs and desires. Although the court sometimes convinced itself that invasion by continental forces was imminent, Japanese defenses before the thirteenth century were never tested by anything more formidable than marauding pirates, and, even more important, the country never faced an enemy invasion. The court thus was generally able to determine the pace and depth of its official relations with the outside world unrestricted by the fierce pressures that characterized relations between states on the continent. For the same reason it could also continue a certain semblance of equality with the Chinese court, which had been expressed by Empress Suiko in 607 when she began her message to Yang-ti, the mighty emperor of the Sui dynasty, with the famous salutation, "The Child of Heaven of the land where the sun rises sends a message to the Child of Heaven of the land where the sun sets."

The relative freedom of action that the Japanese government enjoyed in that respect, lessened the need for, and attraction of, official relations with China. Possibly other more humdrum factors, such as the great cost of equipping and dispatching an embassy of several hundred people to the continent and the perils of sea travel for a people who apparently did not yet fully understand the prevailing winds of the East China Sea, combined in the eighth century to reduce the frequency of embassies to the T'ang court from one every fifteen or sixteen years in the early part of the century (itself a quadrupling of the interval in the immediate post-Taika years) to the leisurely rate of one in every twenty-five or more years toward the end of the century. And the trend continued after the establishment of the capital of

Heian. Emperor Kammu sent his first and only embassy to the T'ang court in 804, twenty-seven years after the dispatch of the previous embassy in 777; and another thirty-four years passed before the next and final Japanese embassy to China for many centuries departed in 838.[19] Nearly sixty years later, in 894, Sugawara no Michizane was chosen to head another embassy to China, perhaps in response to a request relayed from Chinese officials (or so it was made to seem), but before the embassy could be dispatched Emperor Uda and the Council of State accepted Michizane's recommendation that official relations with China be terminated. Japanese intercourse with China thereafter was abandoned entirely to private hands, except for a few exchanges of messages with the king of the southern Chinese coastal state of Wu-yüeh around the middle of the tenth century and another exchange with the Sung court in the 1070s.

By the beginning of the Heian period, the chief remaining reason for maintaining state relations with the T'ang court seems to have been trade. The earlier quest for knowledge of Chinese culture and institutions and the desire to keep abreast of the developments in the East Asian international world, and to participate as a leading member in the Chinese diplomatic order, had been largely fulfilled. With the growing disorder in China after the middle of the eighth century, the attraction of, and need for, relations waned. The material wealth of the continent was as eagerly sought as ever, but private trade was available to supply that need at no cost to the court and without the personal and diplomatic risks of official missions. Under those circumstances, it was not in intent a particularly momentous decision when the court canceled Michizane's mission of 894. There is no indication that that decision represented the adoption of a new policy of permanent diplomatic withdrawal. Official relations with China had been petering out for more than a century, and under different subsequent historical conditions in both Japan and China they might, in the natural course of things, have eventually been resumed. But such was not the case. The cancellation of the embassy of 894 turned out to be, in fact if not in intent, the end of the exchange of official envoys between the two nations that had begun in 630 and numbered by the end more than thirty missions to China from Japan (including the "sending-off" missions that accompanied Chinese embassies back to the T'ang court). The century of turmoil in China

---

19 On the mission of 838, see Edwin O. Reischauer's two volumes: *Ennin's Travels in T'ang China* and *Ennin's Diary: The Record of a Pilgrimage to China in Search of the Law* (New York: Ronald Press, 1955).

that followed the collapse of the T'ang empire at the beginning of the tenth century and the shift of an impoverished statutory regime's attention to internal affairs left little room for the practice of traditional diplomacy. In his proposal of 894, Michizane cited as justification for jettisoning a foreign policy that had endured by his time for nearly three centuries the chaotic disorder accompanying the decline of the T'ang dynasty. He also mentioned the hazards of travel to China:

> A Request That the Members of the Council of State Decide on the Dispatch of a Mission to the T'ang
> Last year in the third month, the merchant Wang No brought a letter from the monk Chūkan, who is in China. It described in detail how the Great T'ang is in a state of decline, and reported that the emperor is not at court [because of the rebellion] and foreign missions have ceased to come. Although Chūkan is merely a wandering monk, he has shown great loyalty to our court....
> Investigating records from the past, we have observed that some of the men sent to China have lost their lives at sea and others have been killed by pirates. Still, those who arrived safely in China have never yet had to suffer there from hunger and cold. According to Chūkan's letter, however, that which has never yet happened now seems likely to occur. We humbly request that his letter be distributed to all members of the Council of State and the professors at the university so that they may carefully read it and consider the merits of this proposal. This is a matter of national importance and not merely of personal concern....
> The fourteenth day of the ninth month, in the sixth year of the Kampyō era [894].[20]

Although it may be suspected that Michizane did no more than state a generally accepted view of the current diplomatic situation, and although he submitted his request simply to provide a basis for the formal adoption of a policy that had already been decided on, the implied reasoning was fundamentally sound and especially convincing, very likely, to a somewhat impecunious court that may have been less than eager to undertake the huge expenses of outfitting and dispatching an embassy.

By 894 the T'ang dynasty was tottering toward its final collapse in 907, dragging with it the remnants of the relatively stable and orderly empire of which it had been the founder and center. The hard-pressed Chinese court at the time was in no shape to receive foreign embassies, and its once great empire was no longer the military threat it had been in the seventh and eighth centuries, when it and

---

20 Robert Borgen, *Sugawara no Michizane and the Early Heian Court*, pp. 242–43, slightly modified.

its Sillan allies seemed at times on the verge of attacking Japan. War, revolt, banditry, and piracy were endemic in the continental countries of East Asia, preparing the way for the vast upheavals of the tenth century, when all the old regimes were swept away by new and sometimes very different powers. It was a dangerous, confusing world, and a country that could elect to stay clear of it was doubtless well advised to do so.

The perils of the voyage to China mentioned by Michizane were, as he himself recognized, nothing new. Only one of the earlier Japanese embassies to the T'ang court seems to have made the crossing and return completely unscathed, and some suffered catastrophic losses of life and property. But the dangers of the trip may well have been even more intimidating in Michizane's day than they had been in the seventh century, when most embassies seem to have followed the longer but safer northern route across the Korea Strait, along the west coast of Korea, and then over to the vicinity of Teng-chou at the base of the north coast of the Shantung peninsula. The seventh century was also a period of relative stability in East Asia, when strong governments in China and Korea were presumably able to exercise some control over the piracy that Michizane cited two centuries later as one of the hazards of sea travel.

In the 660s, however, the west coast of the Korean peninsula fell under the control of Japan's longtime adversary, the increasingly hostile state of Silla. Thereafter, embassies apparently found it prudent usually to follow a southerly route, making for ports on the coast of central China either indirectly via the islands south of Kyushu or, later, directly across the East China Sea. The latter direct route could be quicker if all went well but was also more dangerous, involving two hundred miles or more of navigation across a body of water notorious for its great storms. The route became even more hazardous after the middle of the eighth century as disorder grew in China and Silla, relaxing whatever restraints had been imposed on piratical activity, and travel within China itself was dangerous and hard. By the last half of the ninth century, pirates were making even the passage along the Seto Naikai from Naniwa (in present-day Osaka) to Hakata unsafe for official travelers.[21]

21 On Japan's official relations with China in the eighth and ninth centuries, see the work by Charlotte von Verschuer cited in note 18. Chapter 5 (pp. 161–86) examines in some detail the circumstances of the Japanese decision to cancel Michizane's embassy and constructs a narrative that reconciles apparent inconsistencies in the sources and speculates about additional reasons for the cancellation. On the same subject and to much the same purpose, see Robert Borgen's study of Michizane, pp. 240–53.

The cessation of official relations with China did not bring a halt to intercourse between the two countries. Private Chinese traders had been a familiar sight in the Dazaifu's port on the Bay of Hakata since the first half of the ninth century, and they continued to come now as before carrying the material and intellectual products of the continent and also providing incidentally transport for Japanese Buddhist monks traveling to China for study. During the first half of the turbulent tenth century, it is true, the Japanese government, apparently for reasons of economy and in response to fears of piratical incursions and foreign attack, adopted a semi-isolationist policy severely restricting the frequency with which Chinese traders were allowed to visit Japan; by the second half of the century unauthorized travel overseas by Japanese had also been banned. But by the end of the century enforcement of trade and travel restrictions, which had been sporadic in any case, was being further undermined by a weakening of the central government's control of the provinces and by the emergence of alternative ports free to some extent from the supervision and exactions of government officials. Although the trade seems to have been picayune compared, for instance, to that conducted by contemporary Arab traders of the Umayyad and Abassid empires, it meant that Japan remained open to the stimulation and influence of its surrounding world.

Under the statutory system of private foreign trade that the government sought to enforce in the tenth century, Chinese merchants were restricted entirely to the Dazaifu port in Kyushu, which they were allowed to visit only once in three years. The conditions under which trade was conducted at the port worked further to the disadvantage of merchants, forcing them to sell their choicest goods on interest-free credit to the government at prices determined by it. Thus they were exposed to the often realized threat of confiscation and placed at the mercy and whim of corrupt officials. The appearance of unofficial ports within *shōen* partially immune from government taxes and law offered Chinese merchants a more attractive and profitable alternative to the Dazaifu trade. By the eleventh century they had begun to take full advantage of that opportunity, providing through the *shōen*-port proprietors in and around the court a supply of imported goods for Kyoto noble society that was quite possibly steadier and more abundant than anything the purposely restrictive official system of trade had ever permitted. The principal private ports engaged in the China trade during the eleventh century were at Hakata, Hakozaki, and Kashii, all just across an intervening river from the Dazaifu trading and diplomatic office (the Kōrokan) on the Bay of Hakata, but there were similar ports elsewhere in Kyushu and also opposite the capital on the Japan Sea coast of Honshu.

The China trade seems to have brought to Japan mainly aromatics, medicines, fancy silk fabrics and other luxury items, and manuscript and printed texts in book format (the latter imported as early as 986, when a Japanese monk returned from China with a printed edition of the Buddhist Tripitaka), but it also may have included some items like those exchanged during the eighth and ninth centuries between the Japanese and Chinese courts in their official relations or purchased by individual members of the embassies in China: court costumes, arms and armor, musical instruments, and such utilitarian objects as an iron measuring rule. In return, the Japanese are known to have sent to China by the same official and semiofficial routes pearls, yellow amber, and agate; and Japanese regulations specified silver, silk thread, "prisms," camellia oil, liana juice (a sweetener), and gilt lacquerware as part of an embassy's "tribute" to the Chinese court.[22]

In the first half of the tenth century, following the collapse of the T'ang empire, Japan's chief commercial and cultural ties with China appear to have been concentrated in the successor state of Wu-yüeh (907–70), one of the "Ten Kingdoms" occupying an economically rich area in southern China – the Chekiang area, which included the premier overseas trading ports of Ming-chou (the modern Ningpo, south of Shanghai) and Kuei-chou. It also included the famous Buddhist complex on Mount T'ien-t'ai, which, together with the Wu-t'ai mountains in the north, was a principal pilgrimage objective of Japanese Buddhist monks during the Heian period. Perhaps encouraged by the founder of the state, Ch'ien Liu (852–932), himself a former salt merchant, aggressive traders from the area early on established commercial relations with the Khitan, Po-hai, Silla, and Koryŏ. Soon they were also in Japan, where their vessels are recorded as having arrived on nine occasions between 935 and 959. More than once the Wu-yüeh king sought to establish official relations with the Japanese court, dispatching personal letters and gifts to the emperor and his ministers; but the gifts for the emperor were returned and the king's overtures rebuffed.

The kings of Wu-yüeh were devout Buddhists, and the fifth in the line, Ch'ien Shu (r. 948–78), seeking to reassemble the texts of the

---

22 Von Verschuer, *Les Relations officielles*, pp. 134 ff.

T'ien-t'ai school lost during the proscription of Buddhism instituted in 845 by the T'ang emperor Wu-tsung (r. 840–46), sent a request for replacement texts to the Enryakuji Temple, headquarters of the Tendai (T'ien-t'ai) school in Japan. In 953 the temple responded by dispatching the monk Nichien with an unspecified number of texts for the king. Nichien returned to Japan four years later, bringing with him Buddhist and other texts and also one of the 84,000 small stupas made by Ch'ien Shu in an act of devotion imitating the great Indian king Asoka, who was celebrated for his piety.

China during the early Heian period posed little or no real military threat, but in contrast, the court was apprehensive about its immediate continental neighbor Silla, which lay on the other side of the Korea Strait just thirty-five or so miles distant from the island of Tsushima. In the last half of the eighth century and throughout the ninth century the government repeatedly ordered the strengthening of coastal defenses in anticipation of Sillan attacks. Fears were fueled in one instance in 870 by a Japanese fowler who escaped a Sillan jail (he had been caught in Sillan waters) and brought back stories of large-scale Sillan military preparations for an attack on Tsushima. Ancient animosities, exacerbated by Japan's pretensions to suzerainty over Silla, by the latter's preference for its strong tributary ties to China, and by the increasingly bold attacks of Sillan corsairs on the Japanese coast in the ninth century were at the root of the prickly and sometimes hostile relations between the two countries.

Official relations between Japan and Silla had been close, closer than between Japan and China, in the early part of the eighth century. But the last Sillan envoy to reach the Japanese court arrived in 779, and thereafter the relationship became fairly remote and strictly unilateral, continued only by the inclusion of envoys to Silla in the Japanese embassies to China of 804 and 838. (The last full-scale Japanese embassy to Silla was dispatched in 799.) Intercourse between the two countries during the ninth century was maintained chiefly by Sillan traders, by large numbers of refugees from the revolts and banditry that were bringing the kingdom to its end in 935, and by the ever-present Sillan pirates. The historic hostility between the two states seems to have been replicated even among the Sillan refugees in Japan, who were first settled in the eastern provinces of Honshū, where harsh conditions and treatment led to uprisings and revolts (a revolt of 820 is reported to have involved 700 Koreans),[23]

---

23 Inoue, *Nihon rekishi taikei*, p. 741.

and then in 824 resettled in the even more remote former Emishi territories of Mutsu.

The number of Sillan traders visiting Japan grew from the 820s on, their principal partners in trade being the Kyoto nobility and local magnates in the Kyushu area. Alarmed especially by the prospect of alliances between Sillans with their advanced weapons technology and Kyushu and Tsushima magnates, suspicious as always of Sillan territorial ambitions, and shaken by Sillan piratical raids and rumors of a Sillan invasion of Tsushima, the court sought to limit the trade and retreat within its semi-isolationist walls.

The coolness in Sillan–Japanese relations stood in contrast to the warm relations between Japan and Po-hai. Bordering China on the west and Silla south of P'yongyang, Po-hai was a large state that at its greatest extent occupied the area of present-day northeastern China (in Chi-lin and Hei-lung-chiang), North Korea, and the Russian Maritime Province. Po-hai claimed to be the legitimate heir to the old state of Koguryŏ, from which a powerful Tungusic leader in the present area of Chi-lin Province had declared his independence in 698 and in 713 had been enfeoffed king of the Po-hai Commandery by the T'ang court. As the state expanded in the reign of the second Po-hai king, it came into conflict with its tributary lord T'ang China and also with the T'u-chüeh, or "Turks," to the north and Silla to the south. Pressed on all sides by hostile forces, the Po-hai government dispatched an embassy to Japan in 727, apparently intending to ally itself with what it considered a tributary equal in the East Asian international system. But the Japanese court seems to have misunderstood Po-hai intentions, mistakenly concluding that the Koguryŏ successor was submitting tribute in recognition of the imperial court's suzerainty. That misunderstanding led to various diplomatic contretemps, but by the last half of the eighth century Japan was accepted as the tributary lord in the relationship. In any case, by that time Po-hai's relations with the T'ang court had improved, the emphasis of the relationship with Japan shifting to trade.

The official relations between the two states that had begun in 727 continued at a brisk pace until the destruction of Po-hai by the Khitan in 926. During that time, more than thirty official envoys arrived in Heian from Po-hai, reciprocated by some fifteen Japanese missions to Po-hai.[24] The Po-hai embassies, sailing directly across the Sea of Japan from ports south of present-day Vladivostok, succeeded

---

24 Ueda Takeshi, *Bokkaikoku no nazo*, Kōdansha gendai shinsho, 1104 (Tokyo: Kōdansha, 1992), pp. 64–66.

in making land mostly in the provinces closest to the capital (somewhere between Izumo and Noto), but a number landed far north in Dewa, and one came ashore as far south as Tsushima. Although the Japanese government stopped dispatching its own officials to Po-hai after 811, Po-hai envoys continued to arrive in Japan until 920, when the last of the state's diplomatic missions landed in Wakasa.

The later embassies were, as the Japanese themselves recognized, primarily trading missions. Japanese enthusiasm for them seems to have waned, however, as the men from Po-hai reaped the profits of the trade while the Japanese court bore the heavy expenses of transporting, feeding, housing, and receiving in suitable style the hundred or so persons who made up an average embassy. At any rate, beginning in 824 the court tried with limited success to impose a rule restricting Po-hai embassies to one in every twelve years, but by 871 it had found it expedient to permit Po-hai trading in the capital of Heian itself. To judge by scanty evidence, the embassies brought for trade chiefly furs (tiger, leopard, bear), honey, ginseng, and other domestic goods and products; but they also may have regularly supplied items from China, like the copy of the Chinese Hsüan-ming calendar that was brought by an embassy in 859 and remained the official calendar of Japan, with growing inaccuracy, from 862 to 1684. (It was replaced in China at the end of the ninth century.) The Po-hai embassies took home with them a variety of luxury products and goods acquired in Japan: silk fabrics, silk wadding, silk thread, gold, mercury, lacquer, camellia oil, crystal prayer beads, and other goods.

Po-hai played what was clearly a vital intermediary role in Japan's relations with China, including the importation of Chinese culture, although most details of that role are missing. Po-hai itself, both as a successor state to Koguryŏ and in its own right, was under heavy sinitic influence. The Po-hai governmental structure and its chief capital, the walled Upper Capital at Lung-ch'üan-fu (in present Hei-lung-chiang Province), were both modeled on T'ang prototypes, and its officials were versed in Chinese and Chinese poetry. Goods from even more exotic sources arrived in Japan through Po-hai. A record is preserved, for instance, of a *sake* cup made of tortoiseshell that had originated in the vaguely defined "South Seas." (The shell was that of the hawksbill tortoise, a widely distributed denizen of tropical and subtropical seas.) Musk is also known to have reached Japan by the same route.[25] Japanese dancing girls, goshawks, falcons, and

---

25 Tajima Isao, "Bokkai to no kôshô," in Hashimoto Yoshihiko, *Komonjo no kataru Nihon shi*, vol 2: *Heian*, p. 255.

at least one fine chalcedony chest figure in the tributary gifts proferred by Po-hai to the T'ang court, and these or similar goods may have also been items in the Po-hai-Japanese trade.[26] Communication with Japanese living or studying in China and the transmission of goods to them was sometimes accomplished through the use of Po-hai intermediaries, and Japanese in China were able to use Po-hai visitors there to communicate with, or send goods to, Japan. On at least one occasion a Japanese monk traveled to China aboard a Po-hai ship. Japanese are also mentioned as having been resident in Po-hai for study purposes.

During the Heian period, embassies from foreign countries were mostly similar in their personnel and received much the same kind of treatment in Japan. Their chief formal purpose was usually purely diplomatic and ceremonial: to convey expressions of goodwill and to observe, or avoid, as circumstances dictated, the linguistic niceties of an established suzerain–subject relationship. That purpose was fulfilled in the conveyance of a message or messages between the foreign and Japanese courts, always couched in the ornate language of Chinese diplomatic intercourse. We may assume that more substantive communication sometimes took place at the banquets and receptions regularly held for embassies in Heian. Despite linguistic barriers, discussions between members of the embassies and more senior Japanese officials must have taken place on such occasions, aided by interpreters (both foreign and native are known to have existed) and especially by written Chinese being a language common to all embassies and familiar to Japanese courtiers. All that remains to whatever informal discussions that did take place, however, is a few poems exchanged between embassy members and lower-ranking Japanese court officials, poetry that succeeds in avoiding mention of, or allusion to, any diplomatic or governmental matter.[27]

The embassies might consist of one hundred or more members, including, in addition to the envoy who headed it and his assistant, miscellaneous officials and clerks, interpreters, traders, a goodly number of seamen, and, in the absence of the mariner's compass, astronomers to navigate the embassy's ships to Japanese shores. The many traders could account for more than half the embassy mem-

---

26 Edward H. Schafer, *The Golden Peaches of Samarkand: A Study of T'ang Exotics* (Berkeley and Los Angeles: University of California Press, 1963), pp. 56, 94, 228.
27 For examples of the poems, see *Bunka shūrei shū* in Kojima Noriyuki, ed., *Kaifūsō. Bunka shūrei shū. Honchō monzui*, vol. 69 of *Nihon koten bungaku taikei* (Tokyo: Iwanami shoten, 1964), pp. 228–29, 225.

bers, at least in the missions from Po-hai. They landed at various ports in Japan, the Chinese mostly in northern Kyushu or at the western tip of Honshu – but sometimes on the Sea of Japan coast of Honshu at about the latitude of Heian or a little north of there – the Po-hai ships almost entirely along the Sea of Japan coast of Honshu. When their arrival was reported to the court at Heian, minor officials were appointed to look after and supervise them during their stay in Japan. In dealing with the Po-hai embassies, one of those officials was dispatched to the port of arrival to obtain copies of the embassy's official messages in order to send the copies to the court in Heian so that their language might be checked for acceptability. (An earlier verbal miscue of 772 was the origin of that cautious practice.)

After permission to enter the capital was granted by the court, the embassy began its journey to Heian. A few miles outside the city they were met by an official deputed for their care and supervision, who performed for them a ceremony of welcome and expressed the court's concern for their welfare. Under his guidance, the embassy then entered Heian and was lodged in the two Kōrokan buildings on Suzaku Avenue. From the time of the embassy's appointment until its arrival at the Kōrokan, as much as half a year or more might have elapsed.

During the days immediately after the embassy's arrival at the Kōrokan, the court sent frequent messengers to inquire after its members and to transmit provisions of food and clothing, which had also been supplied at the time of the welcoming ceremonies on the outskirts of the city. But soon the embassy was escorted to the imperial palace, where an audience with the emperor was held (usually in the Chōdōin), and the envoy presented the chest containing the message from his own sovereign. In the case of the Po-hai embassies, in the ninth century it became customary for the king's message to be accompanied, or to be replaced, by a message from a responsible office in the Po-hai government, which might be turned over to Japanese officials at the Kōrokan before the palace audience. Gifts from the foreign ruler were also presented on the occasion of the audience, and the envoy might later make his own private gifts of "local products" to the court. Two formal banquets for an embassy were provided: one by the emperor himself, at which it was customary to award court rank to the envoy and other embassy members; the other by the Council of State. There often may have been private banqueting as well. Subsequently, the envoy was entrusted with gifts for the foreign sovereign and a message of reply, the conveyance of the latter to the envoy marking the final ceremony of the visit.[28]

The fall of Po-hai in 926 was followed just nine years later by the final collapse of Silla, and in 936 by the reunification of the Korean peninsula under the new state of Koryŏ (918–1392). The Koryŏ king immediately sought to establish official relations with Japan, but his overtures were twice rejected by the wary Japanese court, and intercourse was left as before in the hands of Korean refugees, pirates, and merchants, who were joined occasionally by Japanese traders in defiance of the court's ban on unauthorized overseas travel by its subjects.

After decades of disunity, China was finally reunified under the Sung dynasty during the years between 960 and 979 and entered a period of rapid agricultural and handicraft-industrial development that stimulated vigorous trade with all the nations of East Asia. This trade was actively fostered by the Sung court, where the imperial coffers depended heavily on customs duties collected from overseas traders and on the monopoly the court reserved for itself in the sale of aromatics and other luxury items. Based chiefly around the port of Ming-chou, the Sung merchants early made their way to Japan, crossing the East China Sea to Hakata in Kyushu. There the Kyushu authorities at the Dazaifu determined the status of the merchant, the object of his visit, and what cargo he carried, reporting the information to the court in Kyoto, which determined the allowed length of the merchant's stay in Japan and whether or not he would be permitted to trade. If trade was permitted, the Kyoto government exercised its right of first purchase either directly through a specially dispatched official, the Foreign Goods Commissioner (*karamono no tsukai*), or indirectly and increasingly through the Dazaifu office. It was the growing authority of the Dazaifu in the trade that encouraged the Sung merchants to seek out private ports in Kyushu.

After the cessation of its official relations with the continent, which can be dated to the year 920, when a Po-hai embassy is last known to have reached Kyoto, the Japanese court's chief foreign problem apart from trade was piratical brigandage. Large-scale attacks by Koryŏ and Amami Island pirates on Tsushima, Iki, Kyushu, and other nearby islands between 997 and 999 resulted in heavy losses of life and property.

28 For official messages presented by the Po-hei mission of 841–42, see *Shoku Nihon kōki* in *Nihon kōki. Shoku Nihon kōki. Montoku jitsuroku (Shintei zōho) Kokushi taikei*, ed. Kuroita Katsumi, vol. 3 (Tokyo: Yoshikawa kōbunkan, 1934), *kan* 11, pp. 129–30, Jōwa 9 (842)/3/6. See also Tajima, "Bokkai to no kōshō," pp. 243–58.

Twenty years later, the ferocious attacks of a people previously unknown to the Japanese spread even greater havoc. The Japanese called the mysterious new marauders "Toi," a Korean term, it is said, meaning "barbarian" borrowed from Koryŏ prisoners who had been impressed into Toi service. It was only subsequently that the Japanese authorities learned from the Koryŏ government that their attackers were actually a Tungusic Jurchen people from the maritime region northeast of the Korean peninsula. The attacks came in the spring of 1019, when fifty large ships loaded with several thousand Toi pirates ravaged Tsushima, Iki, and the northern coastal areas of Kyushu for seventeen days, killing more then 350 people, including the governor of Iki, taking nearly 1,300 prisoners, and looting and burning countless buildings. Dazaifu forces at the Bay of Hakata and local warriors in Hizen put up a stiff resistance and finally succeeded in expelling the invaders. Koryŏ, which had also earlier suffered from Toi depredations, deployed armed ships at several places along the Korean coast and inflicted heavy damage on the piratical fleet as it sailed homeward. The Koryŏ forces captured eight of the Toi ships and sent back home 270 or so Japanese prisoners on board (mostly women), a friendly gesture that the Japanese authorities at the Dazaifu acknowledged with a gift of gold.

Trade between Koryŏ and Japan grew during the tenth and eleventh centuries despite the refusal of the Japanese court to enter into formal relations with the Korean government, the trade forming part of a significant, if unquantifiable, volume of trilateral commerce among China, Koryŏ, and Japan. It was presumably at least in part the importance of the trade and the more favorable Japanese attitudes toward the Koryŏ government following the Toi attacks that finally forced the court at Kyoto to emerge somewhat from its isolationist shell in the last half of the eleventh century. At that time the Sung court in China, its treasury strained by the southward pressure of the Khitan state of Liao (916–1125), repeatedly sent envoys to Japan seeking the opening of state relations and trade (the latter, as usual, under the fiction of tribute rendered to the Sung emperors, with "gifts" sent in exchange). Although the Japanese were still unwilling to enter into a formal relationship, they now at least responded to the Chinese imperial messages and sent gifts in return.

Insofar as the content of the China–Korea–Japan trade is known (and that is not very far at all), the Japanese exported such natural products as gold and gold dust, mercury, pearls, sulfur, pine, cryptomeria, and hinoki cypress, and also various handicraft items, including different types of fancy lacquerware, hinoki cypress folding fans, folding screens, and swords. They imported from China brocades, damasks and other rich silks, ceramics, writing implements, books, paintings, and copper coins; from Koryŏ came chiefly ginseng and saffron; from Southeast Asia, dyes, medicines, aloeswood, and other aromatics. The items of trade, in other words, seem to have been chiefly low in bulk and high in cost, as would be expected.

The general nature of Japanese foreign commerce remained much the same in the twelfth century, except that domestic and external problems in Koryŏ lessened the level of trade with that state, creating an almost entirely bilateral trading relationship between Japan and Sung China, which by that time had lost its northern territories to the Chin and was centered on the valley of the Yangtze River. The importance of the trade to Japanese leaders at Kyoto grew markedly when the imperial court came increasingly under the domination of Taira no Kiyomori (1118–81) and his family in the last half of the century. Much of the Taira military strength was in the Inland Sea and Kyushu areas, where local warrior leaders were often heavily involved either directly or indirectly in overseas trade, and it clearly served Taira interests to protect and develop that trade. Kiyomori himself was notably active in that regard, undertaking a large-scale redevelopment of Ōwada-no-tomari, the port for his estate at Fukuhara on the Inland Sea coast near modern Kobe, where he succeeded in developing a brisk commerce with Sung merchants and, according to literary sources, reaping rich rewards for his efforts. In 1171, Kiyomori and the retired emperor Go-Shirakawa received one of the Sung merchants in an audience at Fukuhara, much to the dismay of some conservative courtiers at Kyoto, and in the following year he and the retired emperor were also recipients of messages and gifts from the Sung emperor. (For a more detailed discussion of foreign relations at the end of the Heian period, see Chapter 9.)

CHAPTER 2

THE CAPITAL AND ITS SOCIETY

SITE OF THE NEW CAPITAL

When Emperor Kammu dispatched Fujiwara no Oguromaro (733–94) and Ki no Kosami (733–97) to determine the auspices of a site for a new capital in the spring of 793, he took the first official step in creating one of the longer continuous urban traditions in world history, stretching nearly twelve hundred years down to the present day.[1] The site was at Uta, the mausolea area for Kammu's imperial lineage (that of Tenji) in the upper end of what is now called the Kyoto basin, 115 square miles of land and water. The area had attracted human habitation ever since Jōmon man had settled down on the edges of its marshes and swamps to harvest aquatic life there while continuing to hunt and gather in the thickly forested hills and steep valleys surrounding the basin on the east, north, and west. As the watery areas retreated and dried up, the basin became ideal rice-growing country, relatively flat, blessed with rich alluvial soil, and well watered by streams flowing out of the mountains to the north, which caught moist winds from the Sea of Japan only 35 miles away. Rice agriculture appeared in the basin in Yayoi times, followed by Tomb culture with its more complex social and political institutions, its greater wealth, and its expanding intellectual horizons. The area appears to have been incorporated into the Yamato state in the fourth or fifth century, and with the establishment of the statutory regime in the seventh century it became the heart of what was called Yamashiro Province. The rice lands there were eventually brought under the public land system with its checkerboard pattern of fields, which can still be traced in the agricultural areas of the basin today.

By the time the basin emerged on the historical scene in the sixth

[1] The chief source for the physical description and history of Heian presented here is Kyoto-shi, comp., *Kyōto no rekishi*, vol. 1 (Tokyo: Gakugei shorin, 1970). A much older but still mostly reliable English-language study is R. A. B. Ponsonby-Fane, *Kyoto: The Old Capital of Japan, 794–1869* (Kyoto: The Ponsonby Memorial Society, 1956; first published in article form 1925–28).

and seventh centuries, its most prominent inhabitants were the Hata, members of a rich and powerful clan that claimed Chinese descent but seems to have come most immediately from Korea. No doubt making use of the technology of the continent, the Hata appear to have brought under control the streams and rivers in the western and southeastern parts of the basin and developed the area into prime agricultural land. They were especially connected with silk making and weaving, but they were also *sake* brewers and probably accomplished hydraulic and construction engineers. An early Heian source associates them with the building of a large weir (*ōi*) on the Katsura River, whence perhaps the present name of the river west of central Kyoto (Ōi). Hata men built the palace wall and the wall around the Council of State compound at Nagaoka.

The neighbors of the Hata in the southern part of the basin were members of another powerful clan, the Haji, who had been known as clayworkers in earlier times and had long enjoyed close ties with the imperial line. The presence of the Hata and Haji in the basin may have been one of its chief attractions for Kammu and his advisers. Kammu himself was the maternal grandson of a Haji woman and seems to have lived with her in his youth; and two of his closest associates, Fujiwara no Tanetsugu and Oguromaro, were intimately connected with the Hata, Tanetsugu's maternal grandmother and Oguromaro's wife having been women of that clan. Tanetsugu had been a leading advocate of the move to Nagaoka, which was on the southern edge of the basin in Haji territory. Oguromaro, who had been appointed with Tanetsugu in 784 to determine the auspices of the Nagaoka site, seems to have played a similar, if somewhat less central, role in the move to Heian, where the imperial residential palace, a tenth-century source says, was eventually located on the site of a Hata leader's house.

When Oguromaro and Kosami reported the results of their survey to Kammu at Nagaoka, they informed him that the site at Uta was a natural fortress formed by surrounding mountains and streams, and that it matched the geomantically auspicious features of "corresponding-to-the-four-gods" topography: a great river on the east, a great highway on the west, a mountain in the north, and marshy lowlands to the south. Apart from its geomantic virtues, Uta was indeed in many ways well situated for a capital city. The steep, thickly timbered hills and mountains on the east, west, and north formed a skyline generally between 1,500 and 2,500 feet above the basin floor and in combination with the lake and marsh region known as Oguranoike to the south (now reclaimed and dry) and the river systems that converged on that area (chiefly the Kamo from the northeast, the Katsura from the northwest, and the Uji from the east) provided defensible positions against hostile attack. At the same time, there is reason to think that there were already well-established roads leading out of the basin in all directions, making communication with the rest of the country reasonably convenient, and the Yodo River in the south gave easy water access to the Inland Sea (Seto Naikai). The site was, moreover, mostly level, easing problems of layout and construction, and it was well irrigated by numerous streams and easily tapped underground water, which served not only mundane needs but also made possible the creation of elaborate gardens.

The site's chief disadvantages were its climate and inadequate drainage. Modern residents of Kyoto, it is said, endure the miseries of summer and winter in return for the glories of the spring and fall, and one can easily imagine that both miseries and glories were greatly intensified by the more natural environment of the eighth century. Although the average temperature in Kyoto now through the year is an equitable fifty-seven degrees Fahrenheit, hot, breathless summers, with high temperatures in the upper eighties and often climbing into the high nineties, and relatively cold winters that bring the thermometer down into the low twenties or below, combine with high humidity (averaging over 70 percent throughout the year) to make the Kyoto basin famous for its muggy, unbearable heat and its piercing cold. It was probably more the pains of the climate than its pleasures that moved the eleventh-century poet Izumi Shikibu to write:

> If only the world
> Into spring and fall
> We could forever make
> And summer and winter
> Were never more.[2]

Heavy precipitation (over 60 inches a year in modern times) and heavy runoff from the surrounding hills place severe demands on the drainage system in the Kyoto basin. The general slope of the land in a southwesterly direction and underlying strata of gravelly sand gave most of the eastern half of the Heian site fairly good drainage. But the western half, which was low-lying and generally underlain by

---

2 *Izumi Shikibu shū*, in *Zoku kokka taikan*, ed. Matsushita Daizaburō (Tokyo: Kadokawa shoten, 1963), no. 40575.

clay or clayey sand, must have often been so wet and marshy as to be scarcely fit for human habitation under the engineering and architectural conditions of the day. A story from a twelfth-century source tells about a rich and clever man who succeeded in building a house on a fill of rushes and earth at a watery site in the western part of the capital. Few ordinary people, though, could have managed so ambitious an engineering feat, and one wonders even so how long the foundations of the clever man's house lasted.

Following the advice of Wake no Kiyomaro (733–99), Kammu himself two or three months before the dispatch of Oguromaro and Kosami had twice used the pretext of a hunting expedition to visit and inspect the Uta area. His decision, just a few days after the submission of their report, to transfer the capital to the new site suggests he was simply waiting for geomantic confirmation of a choice already made. Oguromaro, who was immediately appointed to supervise the construction of the new imperial palace, was faced by a multitude of difficult and complex tasks. One of the first and greatest must have been the diversion and control of the numerous streams that flowed through the site, a project in which his Hata in-laws, with their wealth, experience, and engineering skills, may have proved indispensable.

The Kyoto basin at one time had been an inlet of the Inland Sea and it was still in the late eighth century a very watery place: streams and rivers ran across it at the site of the new capital in a generally southwesterly direction, and ponds and marshes dotted the landscape throughout. One of the more prominent bodies of water would have been the famous pond that was later incorporated in the great imperial preserve south of the palace called the Park of the Divine Spring (Shinsen'en), a remnant of which precariously survives in modern Kyoto. A small river called the Kamo ran along the eastern edge of the site, its course shifting within a broad bed that directly adjoined what was to become the eastern limit of the city.[3] Perhaps to simplify bridge building and to reclaim usable land, the riverbed was narrowed and straightened with the aid of dikes. That task and the work of eliminating or realigning other smaller streams at the site presumably began early and may have continued for many

---

3 Ishida Shirō, "Kyōto bonchi hokubu no senjōchi: Heian-kyō sentoji no Kyōto no chisei," *Kodai bunka* 34, 12 (December 1982): 1–14, has demonstrated that the Kamo and Takano rivers have occupied what are substantially their present courses ever since Jōmon times, thus laying to rest a previously widely held belief that the rivers originally flowed directly across the site of the new capital.

decades. At any rate, parts of the Kamo were still being diked and moved eastward as late as the eleventh century, resulting in an elevated streambed and frequent flooding of the city when the dikes were breached or flood water clogged the bridges spanning the river.

Although his palace was still in the early stages of construction, Emperor Kammu, anxious perhaps to be gone from the gloomy and threatening atmosphere of his already half-dismantled palace at Nagaoka, moved to the new imperial seat in the late autumn of 794. Two or three weeks later he issued an edict conferring on the capital city its official name and renaming (or, rather, selecting different Chinese characters for the name of) the province in which the site was located:

Enclosed collar-and-sash by mountains and streams, the province here makes a natural citadel. Because of that configuration, we devise a new designation for it: let this Postmontane [Yamashiro] Province be renamed the Province of the Mountain Citadel [Yamashiro]. Moreover, the joyfully flocking people and the singers of praise raise their different voices in identical words, naming this the Capital of Peace and Tranquillity [Heian-kyō].[4]

Despite the supposedly popular origin of the new capital's name, it seems never to have enjoyed much vogue except among latter-day historians, most people in the following centuries preferring to call it simply "the Capital" (*miyako;* more literally, "imperial seat"). *Kyōto,* a sinitic synonym of *miyako,* had been applied as a common noun to earlier Japanese capitals and was similarly used of Heian during the first centuries of its existence. But the term also began to function sporadically as a proper noun in the late tenth and eleventh centuries and had become a fairly common name for the city in everyday types of writing by the thirteenth century. There were several other Chinese-derived names used of the city, mostly in fancy or learned writing. Among the most common were "Rakuyō" and "Raku," the latter an abbreviation of the first.

"Rakuyō" is the Sino-Japanese reading of the characters for Loyang, the name of the Eastern Capital of the T'ang dynasty as paired with the Western Capital at Ch'ang-an. Since Heian was modeled on neither Ch'ang-an nor Lo-yang, as often erroneously supposed, but on the earlier Japanese capital at Fujiwara – which seems to have taken its inspiration from the capital of the southern Chinese dynasties at Chien-k'ang (Nanking) – the application of "Rakuyō" to Heian is unexpected. But Japan had also known a period of dual

4 Quoted in translation from *Nihon kiryaku* in *Kyōto no rekishi,* vol. 1 (1970), p. 238.

capitals at Heizei and Naniwa, and although that period had passed with the establishment of the capital at Nagaoka, the tradition was revived in terminology about the time of the sinophile emperor Saga, when the literati started referring to the western half of the city (Ukyō) as Chōan (i.e., Ch'ang-an) and the eastern half as Rakuyō (Lo-yang).[5] As the western half withered and failed and the eastern half became the heart of the capital, Rakuyō began to function as a name for the whole. (The abbreviation "Raku" much later became especially familiar in Western art history circles because of the brilliant sixteenth-century paintings of scenes in and around Kyoto called "*Rakuchū rakugai zu*.")

PLAN OF THE CITY

Knowledge of early Heian and its palace rests chiefly on a collection of government regulations and procedures dating from the early tenth century (*Engi shiki*), on twelfth- or thirteenth-century plans and maps thought to reflect the city mainly as it existed in the ninth and tenth centuries, and on some other literary and documentary evidence. Since every surface vestige of Heian disappeared long ago, and since the site is now overlaid by the densely populated city of Kyoto, severely limiting archaeological investigation, physically verifiable knowledge of the city is far more restricted than in the case of the earlier capital, Heizei-kyō (Nara). This capital for the most part quickly reverted to agricultural land after the removal of the imperial seat to Nagaoka and remained therefore not only relatively undisturbed for the modern archaeologist but also more easily accessible. Consequently, although it is possible to describe Heian toward the date of its founding with considerable confidence in the general reliability of the detail, one must bear in mind in reading the following account that the city plan as a whole and some particular features, such as the walls that are said to have lined the streets and avenues, may have been only partially realized in practice.

The site of the new capital, after an extension of its northern boundary in the last half of the ninth century, was a rectangle measuring approximately 3.3 miles north and south and 2.8 miles across, or 9.24 square miles, which gave it roughly the same area as that of the

---

5 Kishi Toshio, *Tojō no seitai*, vol. 9 of *Nihon no kodai* (Tokyo: Chūō kōronsha, 1987), pp. 54–58, and 23–37.

old capital at Nara or of small modern university towns like Berkeley (10.4 sq. miles) and Cambridge, Massachusetts (6.2 sq. miles), but just one-third the size of Ch'ang-an, at the time perhaps the largest metropolis in the world. A rectangular space of about 1,300 by 1,500 yards (six-tenths of a sq. mile) at the north-central edge of the site was reserved for the Greater Imperial Palace (Daidairi), the location and general contours of the area being identical to those of the imperial palaces at Ch'ang-an and at previous statutory capitals in Japan. The modern city of Kyoto includes the entire area of what was Heian, but it is, of course, much larger. The geographical center of Heian was located at about what is now the intersection of Shijō and Sembondōri Streets in Kyoto, its northeast corner corresponding almost exactly to the southern parts of the site presently occupied by the Imperial Palace (Gosho) and the Kyoto Imperial Gardens, its southern border lying on a line extending along the southern edge of Tōji Temple, and its northwest corner falling a short distance northwest of the Myōshinji. The southeast corner of the Heian Greater Imperial Palace was at almost the exact center of the present Nijō Castle.

Outside the Greater Imperial Palace, the layout of the city was modeled fairly closely on the grid system used in the allocation of agricultural land. Thirty-three north-south and thirty-nine east-west streets (*kōji*) and avenues (*ōji*) traversed the site at regular intervals, intersecting at right angles and dividing the site checkerboard-fashion into blocks (*machi*) of equal size. Low earthen walls about 6 feet wide at their bases lined both sides of each street or avenue. Except in two instances where streams shared the roadway (Horikawa and Nishihorikawa), the streets were of uniform width, measuring nearly 35 feet across, or about the width of a modern street accommodating two lanes of automobile traffic and parallel parking on both sides. Most of the twenty-four avenues (thirteen running east and west, eleven north and south) were a little more than twice the width of the streets, but several in more prominent positions (at the city limits and leading to or past palace gates) were between 90 and 110 feet wide. The avenue paralleling the south face of the palace (Nijō) measured a little over 160 feet across; and the great axial avenue (Suzaku) that ran north to south at the exact center of the city and led to the main palace gate was a mall-like thoroughfare 270 feet wide. One street lay between every pair of parallel avenues in the sections of the city due west, east, and south of the imperial palace; elsewhere the street interval between avenues was three.

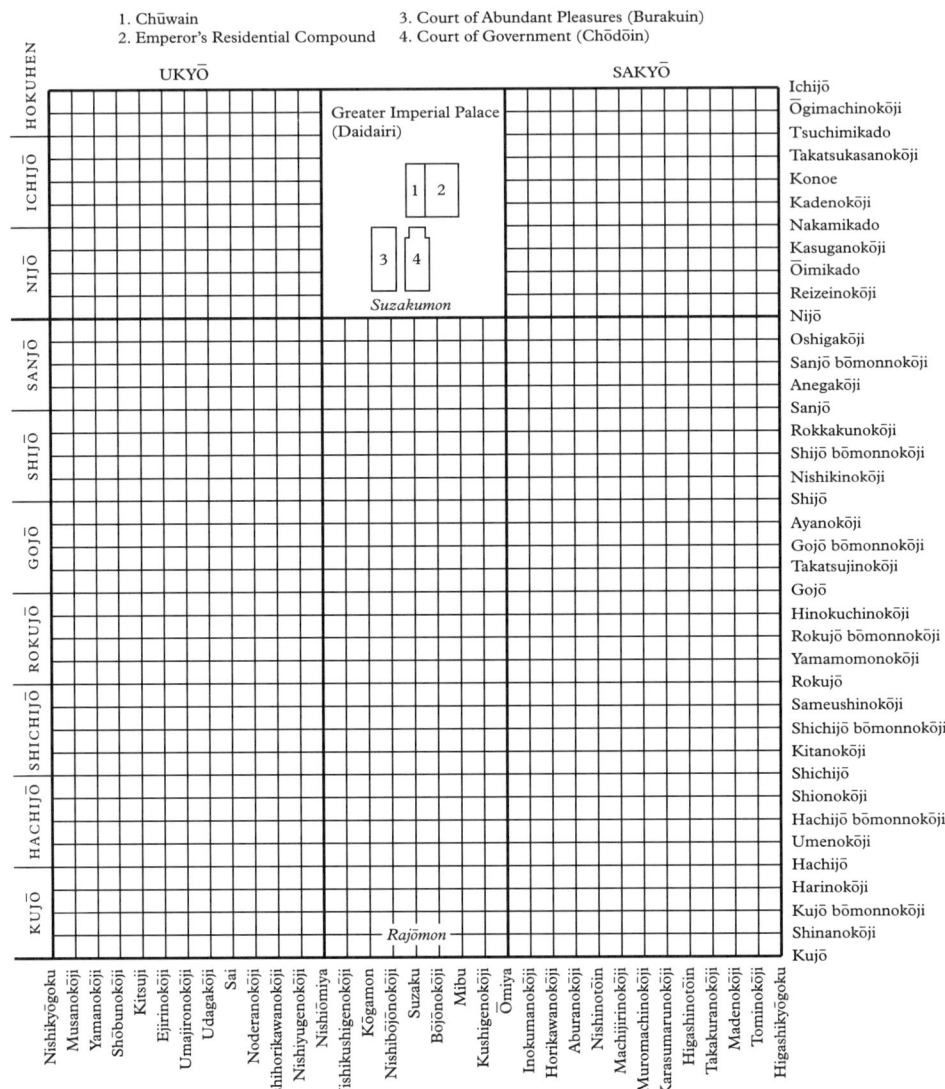

Figure 2.1. The Heian capital (Heian-kyō). Names in capital letters are districts; names in italics are gates. Adapted from McCullough and McCullough, *A Tale of Flowering Fortunes*, p. 834.

It must be added, however, that Heian streets and avenues were not entirely devoted to traffic. All were lined on both sides by ditches and narrow paths or strips of vacant land (called "dog runs," *inubashiri*) that occupied from 15 to 35 percent of the total width. In the case of a street, for example, the area next to the walls on either side was occupied by a "dog run" 3 feet wide and beyond that by a ditch of the same width, leaving a usable roadway of about 23 feet between the ditches. The median roadway on Suzaku Avenue was similarly constricted to a width of about 230 feet. The avenues on the four sides of the Greater Imperial Palace were even further restricted where they passed the palace, which was separated from them by a vacant space 26 feet wide and an 8-foot fosse.

The capital outside the Greater Imperial Palace was divided physically and administratively into western and eastern halves, the line of demarcation being Suzaku Avenue and, north of its terminus at Nijō Avenue, the Greater Imperial Palace. (Suzaku Avenue corresponded mostly with the modern Sembondōri Street in Kyoto, except that it ended at the imperial palace 200 to 300 yards due north of what is now Nijō Station.) The avenue was on a line that ran due south from Funaoka, a low (368-foot) hill less than a mile outside the northern city limit that seems to have served as a chief reference point in the orientation and planning of the city. Since the geographical perspective of the city was, in keeping with Chinese practice, southward-facing from the palace, its eastern half was frequently called the Left Capital (Sakyō) and the western half the Right Capital (Ukyō). The two halves, Left and Right, were further divided by avenues into nine parallel east-west belts of equal area called "zones" (jō) and a single narrower belt at the city's northern edge called the North Edge (Kitanobe). Numbered in order from north to south, the nine zones straddled the city from border to border except where interrupted by the Greater Imperial Palace, each being about 560 yards wide on its north-south axis (the North Edge, however, was just half that).

Each zone south of the palace was divided by north-south avenues into eight equal "quarters" (bō), each about 17 acres in area. The four in each half of the city were numbered separately in order beginning with the quarter next to Suzaku Avenue. Zones One and Two, which were interrupted by the palace, contained only six quarters each, three on either side of the palace. Each quarter was usually divided by intersecting north-south and east-west streets or avenues into sixteen blocks (machi) numbered boustrophedonically (as in the route of a plow ox) from north to south away from Suzaku Avenue, and each block was further divided into thirty-two rectangular house lots (henushi). There were eight house lots north to south in a block and four east to west. Each lot measured in theory about 49 by 98 feet, but some were apparently reduced in size to accommodate the one to three 10- or 15-feet-wide alleyways that penetrated the blocks north to south and gave access to interior lots. Lots were identified within each block by a grid system of four numbered columns (*kō*) and eight numbered "gates" (*mon*), the columns running east to west in the Right Capital and west to east in the Left Capital, and the gates, which corresponded to individual house lots, running north to south. It was thus possible to identify precisely any piece of property in the capital after the fashion of the following description, which comes from a deed of sale dated in 912: "A single area of four house lots in all (located in Gates 4, 5, 6, and 7 North, Column 1 West, Block 15, Quarter 1, [Zone Seven, Left Capital])."

Thanks to the precision and clarity of the system, we can determine that the four lots here described were in a row facing Kushige Street just west of the present site of Nishihonganji and that they measured altogether approximately 98 by 196 feet.

The broad, straight streets and avenues of the new capital must have lent an agreeable air of openness and spaciousness to its vistas, affording unobstructed views of the surrounding mountains and creating small and large squares at road intersections throughout the city. The largest such square was directly in front of the Vermilion Sparrow Gate (Suzakumon) at the palace, where the intersection of Suzaku and Nijō Avenues created an open space 160 feet north to south and 270 feet across (just about an acre in area). Another, measuring 270 by 110 feet, was at the intersection of Suzaku and Kujō on the southern edge of the city just inside Rampart Gate (Rajōmon, also Rashōmon),[6] formally the main entranceway to Heian.

The openness of the city was enhanced by the low profile of its prevailing architecture, which was with but few exceptions uniformly single-storied, and especially by the absence of encompassing city walls. In the tradition of Heizei and earlier statutory capitals in Japan, but unlike the heavily fortified major cities of medieval Europe and China, Heian itself was almost certainly unwalled, except for a small garden-like structure about 6 feet high on the city's southern border that served as a setting for Rampart Gate. That extremely modest "rampart," only about a third as high as the great walls that surrounded Ch'ang-an, was paralleled by two ditches or

---

6 The original pronunciation of the gate's name seems to have been "Raseimon." A common pronunciation since the fifteenth or sixteenth century has been "Rashōmon," as in the cinema title.

moats a little less than 10 feet wide, one inside the wall and the other outside. The remainder of the city's boundaries is thought to have been delineated by nothing more formidable than extensions of those moats and perhaps some kind of simple earthwork. Permanent, fixed bridges apparently spanned the moats at various points, leaving the city open to the countryside.

The builders of Heian may have also deviated from their Chinese model in the disposition of walls within the city. The walls on either side of streets and avenues formed enclosures for each block (*machi*), but inconclusive evidence suggests that, unlike at Ch'ang-an, the quarter (*bō*) may have been walled and gated only where it abutted Suzaku Avenue south of the imperial palace and at the city's eastern and western limits (Higashikyōgoku and Nishikyōgoku). Suzaku Avenue, which exactly bisected the Heian site north to south and led directly from Rampart Gate to the main entrance of the palace at Vermilion Sparrow Gate, was the chief ceremonial thoroughfare in the city. If quarter walls were erected only along the sides of that avenue, their chief function may have been to enhance the dignity of the main approach to the palace. A foreign envoy entering Rampart Gate was undoubtedly meant to be impressed by the resemblance of the city to its Chinese prototypes, especially Ch'ang-an, the acknowledged queen of East Asian capitals. The great, two-storied Rampart Gate, 110 feet wide, 25 feet deep, and perhaps 70 feet high; the Chinese-style bridge spanning the moat outside the gate; the vastness of willow-lined Suzaku Avenue, flanked near at hand by two imposing temples (Saiji and Tōji) and in the middle distance by the paired lodgings for foreign embassies (the Kōrokan), and bounded on either side by continuous rows of quarter walls pierced at regular intervals by gates; and, finally, far in the distance at the northern end of the avenue, the soaring, two-storied Vermilion Sparrow Gate – all would have been reassuringly familiar to an official visitor from the continent, confirming Japan's vaunted reputation as a country of sinitically learned "superior men" (*chün-tzu*) who could be counted on to understand Confucian rites and principles.[7] He might not have ever fully realized that the city's southern "rampart," the quarter walls, and the tiled roofs of the buildings along the southern edge of the palace precincts were mostly ambitious facade.

7 Charlotte von Verschuer, *Les Relations officielles du Japon avec la Chine aux viiie et ixe siècles* (Geneva: Librairie Droz, 1985).

GREATER IMPERIAL PALACE

Not much is known about the actual process of construction at the new capital, the sources for the years in question being particularly meager, but there can be little doubt that the scene of greatest activity was at the Greater Imperial Palace itself, which was both the residence of the emperor and his household and the seat of the government's central administrative organs. Work there was directed at first by specially appointed commissioners, and then from 796 by a semipermanent Office of Palace Construction staffed by some 150 officials and technicians, who employed and oversaw a larger labor force levied for one year of recompensed service from the provinces. In the early stages of construction before public labor levies were organized, noble families were also obliged to contribute laborers for work on palace and city projects, and prisoners were used as well. The chief responsibilities of the Office of Palace Construction were, apart from the construction of palace buildings and government offices, the expropriation of land for the city's site, the construction of streets and the layout of house lots in the city, the diking and channelization of streams and rivers, and the organization of labor for those various tasks. The office remained in existence until early 805, when economic exhaustion led to its abolition. Even then, it appears, not all of the projected palace buildings had been completed. The size of its task and the burden the office placed on the economy are suggested by an early-tenth-century estimate that during Kammu's reign three-fifths of the central government's expenditures were devoted to the construction of the Heian palace and princely residences.

The spacious site of the palace was surrounded at its periphery by an outer fosse 8 feet wide, a median strip of vacant land 26 feet across, and an inner earthen wall a little over 6 feet high. Fourteen gates provided access to the grounds, the largest and most impressive by far being the tile-roofed Vermilion Sparrow Gate, whose fanciful name was borrowed from a corresponding structure at the Ch'ang-an palace. The "vermilion sparrow," a mythical creature associated in Chinese thought with the south, was said to appear to holy men and rulers of exceptional merit and power as a harbinger of good, and it served therefore as an auspiciously apt symbol for the main southern entrance of an emperor's palace.[8] It was the Yōmei

---

8 Edward H. Schafer, *The Vermilion Bird: T'ang Images of the South* (Berkeley and Los Angeles: University of California Press, 1987), p. 267. Although the Chinese-derived names by which the main palace buildings and gates at Heian are commonly known were mostly

("Brilliance," "Sun") Gate, however, standing on the east side of the site at the entrance most convenient to the Emperor's Residential Compound (Dairi, "penetralia"), that the emperor and his courtiers most commonly used in their comings and goings. The senior nobles in particular tended to live in the quarter of the city that lay directly east of the palace, and by using the Yōmei Gate they were within a ten- to twenty-minute walk of the Emperor's Audience Hall, less than half the distance of the route through Vermilion Sparrow Gate.

As construction progressed, the palace grounds were filled with perhaps as many as two hundred or more buildings, gateways, towers, and connecting corridors situated within numerous walled enclosures in a setting of courtyard gardens, winding streams, ancient trees, and occasional broad, open spaces. Space within the grounds was differentiated functionally both in the general layout and in the details of particular areas. Reflecting the dual character of the palace as an imperial residence and administrative seat, the buildings were arranged in two principal groups: (1) government offices and facilities, which occupied most of the southern two-fifths of the site; and (2) the imperial residence and associated household offices, which were located in an area of equal size north of the first group. A third group of buildings, consisting mainly of governmental storehouses, was concentrated on the remaining land at the northern extremity of the site.

The first group of buildings provided space for both the workaday and ceremonial business of government, but it was the ceremonial space that, characteristically of the age, received the greatest emphasis in the palace plan. The two chief compounds of ceremonial buildings, the Court of Government (Chōdōin) and the Court of Abundant Pleasures (Burakuin), were the largest of all the walled enclosures in the palace; their buildings were the grandest and most ornate of all palace structures; and the more important of the two, the Court of Government, was centered exactly in the north-south median line of the palace grounds directly opposite Vermilion Sparrow Gate to the south.

The Court of Government (or Court of the Eight Ministries – Hasshōin – as it was also called) was on a generally rectangular site surrounded by its own wall, the main entrance through which was the celebrated Obedient-to-Heaven Gate (Ōtemmon) on the south-

adopted about twenty-five years after the founding of the city (during the reign of Emperor Saga), Vermilion Sparrow Gate was probably so called from the beginning.

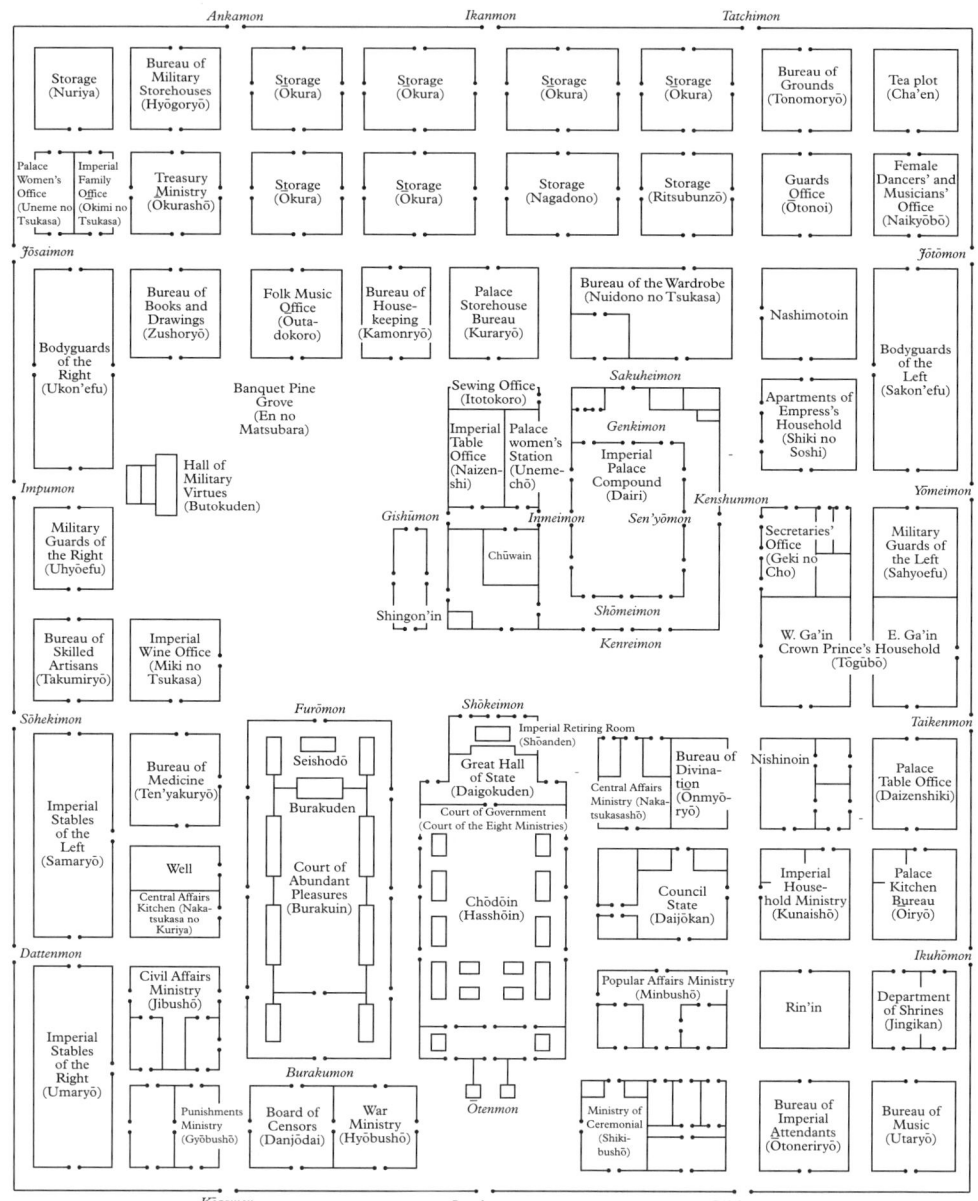

Figure 2.2. Greater Imperial Palace (Daidairi). Names in italics are gates. Adapted from McCullough and McCullough, *A Tale of Flowering Fortunes*, p. 835.

central side of the enclosure. Originally designed as the center of statutory government, the place where the emperor was to meet in daily audience with his chief ministers to conduct the business of the state, where foreign envoys were to be received, and where the great state ceremonies and rituals were to be conducted, the Court consisted of three subprecincts. The smallest, at its southern end, was occupied by two buildings used as waiting rooms by senior nobles. The middle and largest area contained a broad courtyard surrounded on its eastern, western, and southern sides by twelve symmetrically arranged buildings where members of the bureaucracy assembled when business was being conducted at the Court; and finally a somewhat smaller section at the northern end was the site of the imperial-throne building, the Great Hall of State (Daigokuden). The latter, a soaring Chinese-style edifice of vermilion pillars, green roof tiles, and dolphin roof finials, was the most magnificent building in the entire palace complex, measuring nearly 175 feet east to west and 65 feet north to south. (The present Heian Shrine in Kyoto is a five-eighths scale replica of a 1072 reconstruction of the hall. It was built in 1895 to commemorate the eleven-hundredth anniversary of the founding of the city.) The peculiar name of the hall (literally, "grand culmen"), borrowed from the T'ang imperial palace, was derived from one of the appendices to the *I-ching* (Book of Changes), where "grand culmen" was used to signify the source of the universe, or absolute existence. The name implied a view of the emperor as the source of all things, a veritable pivot of the world.

The Court of Abundant Pleasures also stood within its own walled enclosure about 90 feet west of the Court of Government, occupying an area slightly larger than the latter's. Built as the principal imperial banquet facility, the site of the chief festivals (*sechie*), and a center of court cultural life, the Court contained ten buildings disposed in a pattern similar to that of the Court of Government. The main structure was the Celestial Presidence Pavilion (Kenrinkaku), which corresponded in position and function to the Great Hall of State. (The Pavilion was later renamed the Hall of Abundant Pleasures, Burakuden; its site is one of the few in the palace that have been excavated by modern archaeologists.) From there the emperor presided over banquets and festivals, watched archery contests and wrestling matches, and participated in other events on the regular court calendar.

The remainder of the southern area of the Greater Imperial Palace was given over mostly to buildings housing governmental

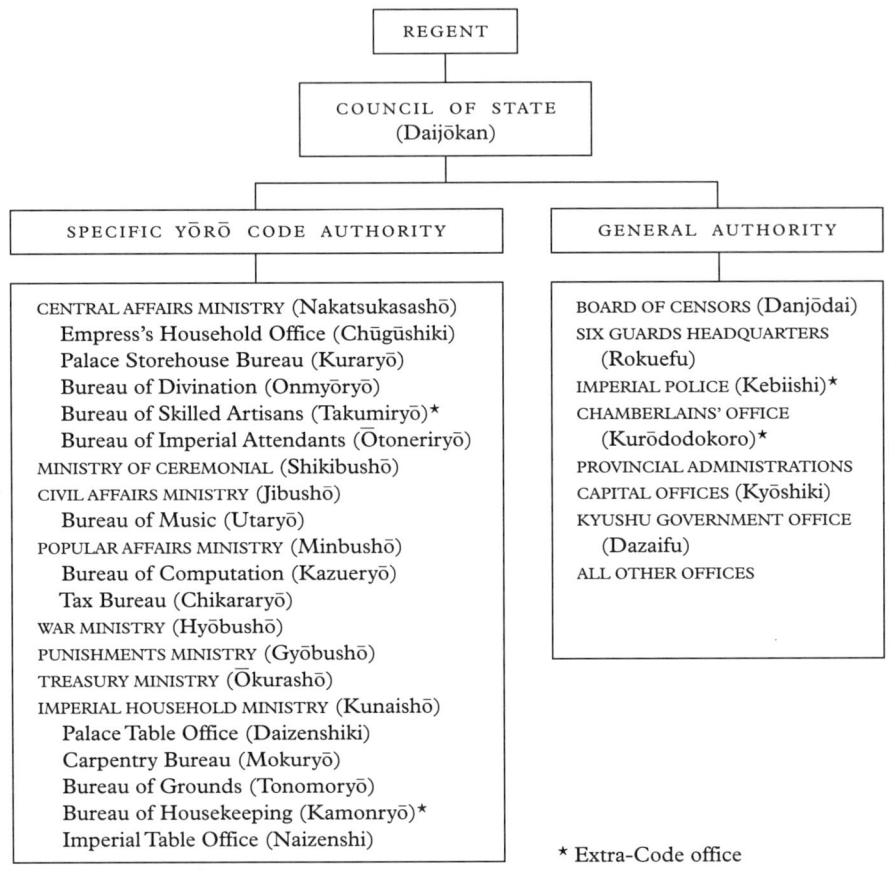

Figure 2.3. Major Heian governmental organs, ca. C.E. 1000. Adapted from McCullough and McCullough, *A Tale of Flowering Fortunes*, p. 801.

ministries, bureaus, and offices arranged left and right of the Court of Government according to the statutory table of organization. A walled compound lying directly east of the Court of Government was the administrative heart of the government, containing the three connected buildings of the Council of State. The positions of ceremonial prominence on either side of Vermilion Sparrow Gate were occupied by the Ministries of Ceremonial and War, while the bureaucratically superior Department of Shrines was relegated to the southeastern edge of the site.

EMPEROR'S RESIDENTIAL COMPOUND

The most radical departure of the Heian imperial palace from its predecessor at Nara was in the physical separation of the Emperor's Residential Compound from the Court of Government. At Nara the residential compound had stood on the palace's north-south median line directly north of the Court, and its outer encircling wall had included the Great Hall of State itself, thus linking in an obvious way the person of the emperor and the imperial position. At Heian, however, the residential compound, following the example of the Nagaoka palace, was not only completely distinct from the Court of Government but also removed to a directionally intermediate position in the eastern half of the grounds off the median north-south line.

It is tempting to see in that physical arrangement of the palace a symbolic expression of a newly conceived, or more clearly recognized, distinction between the emperor as a man and as an institution, a distinction that became important, no doubt, as regents imposed broadly on imperial authority after the middle of the ninth century. The removal of the residential compound from a position astride a cardinal axis of the palace site might even be interpreted as a diagrammatic subordination of the imperial person to the imperial position. But it may be closer to the truth to view the repositioning of the residential compound at Heian as having less to do with the symbolization of abstract political notions than with a practical desire to avoid the frequent moves and rebuildings of the imperial palace that had characterized Japanese history since early times.

The reasons for those moves are unknown, but most speculation centers around considerations of ritual purity or the short life-span of the lightly constructed wooden palace buildings. In the case of ritual purity, the motive would have been to remove the ritual pollution caused by the death of a previous emperor or to maintain purity through periodic rebuilding, after the manner of the similar custom still practiced at some Shinto shrines. Although the early "palaces" were presumably quite simple buildings that could have been rebuilt at manageable cost, the growing size and complexity of the palace from the sixth century on must have caused a vast increase in the financial burden of reconstruction. It would have been natural for a politically ambitious emperor like Kammu to seek a way of containing palace-building costs, just as he was also seeking retrenchment in expenditures elsewhere in his government.

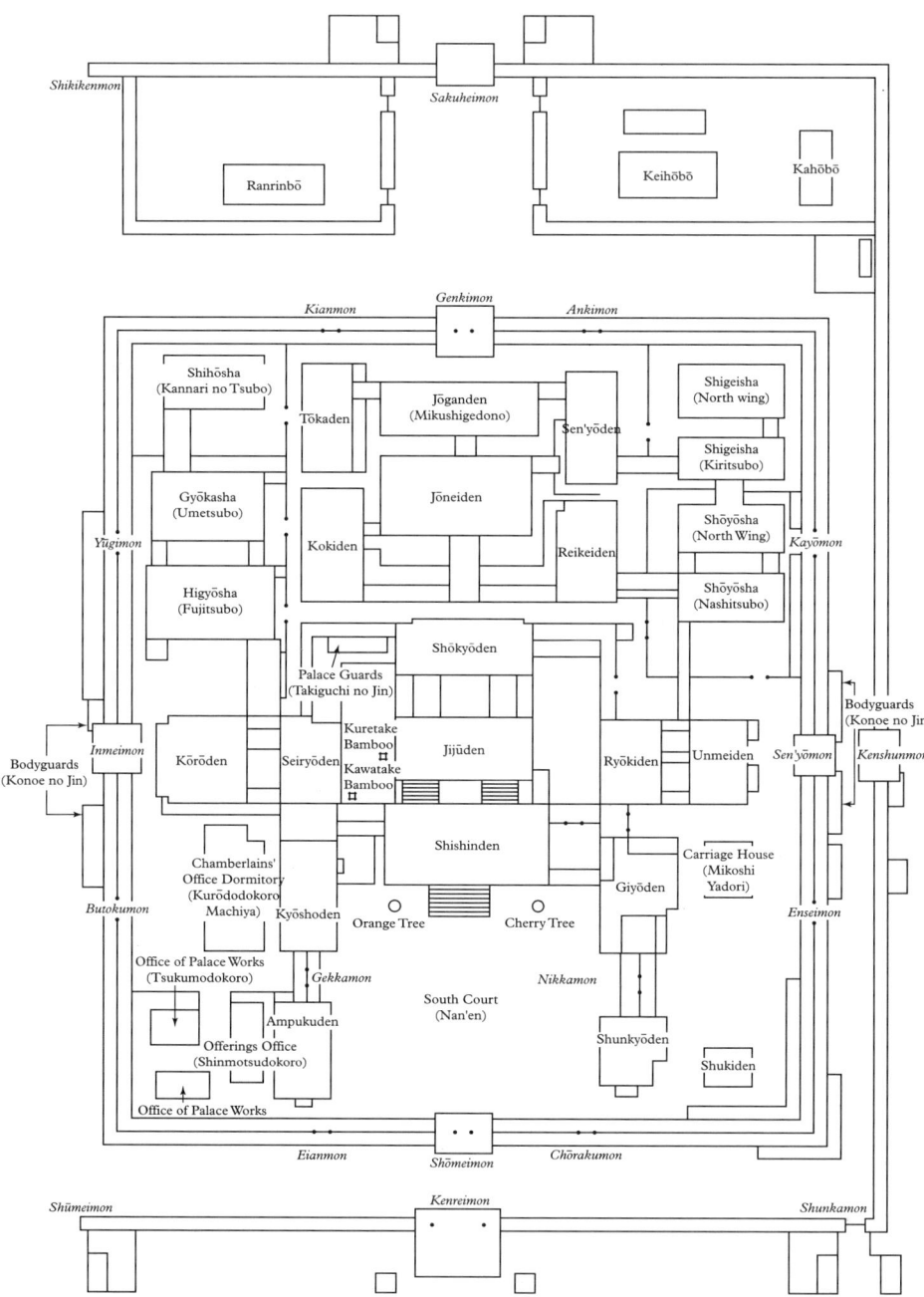

Figure 2.4. The Emperor's Residential Compound (Dairi). Names in italics are gates. Adapted from McCullough and McCullough, *A Tale of Flowering Fortunes*, p. 840.

West of the median north-south axis of the Heian palace, in a position corresponding exactly to the residential compound on the east, was a large open space called the Banquet Pine Grove (En no Matsubara). The arrangement was strongly reminiscent of those Shinto shrines where a vacant space is reserved as a site for the next periodic rebuilding of the shrine's sanctuary. At such shrines, when a new sanctuary is built the old sanctuary is disassembled and its site left vacant until the next rebuilding, the location of the sanctuary thus shifting back and forth regularly between the two sites. Given that model, which originated in pre-Heian times, it is possible to conclude that the designers of the Heian palace may have shifted the position of the residential palace compound in order to create a balanced pair of sites, one in the known position of the compound on the east and the other at Banquet Pine Grove on the west, where rebuildings of the compound could be alternated after the fashion of the Shinto shrines. If that inference is correct, the positioning of the residential compound and the Banquet Pine Grove can be seen as an attempt to integrate into the structure of the palace the conflicting native tradition of a shifting imperial seat and the sinitic concept of a fixed capital, an issue that was by no means fully resolved at the beginning of the period.

The expanded scale of the statutory government and its capital made frequent transfers of the capital intolerably costly, and the planners of Heian may have seen in the Banquet Pine Grove site a convenient means of bringing them to a permanent end while still providing for whatever was achieved, or thought to be achieved, through new construction. If so, the failure in practice to use the alternative site for a new residential compound is puzzling. It might be attributed to the straitened finances of the regime at the time of Kammu's death and possibly also to changing attitudes toward native custom during the reigns of his sons, when Chinese cultural influence was exceptionally strong, but the absence of contemporary comment on the problem is difficult to explain.

The residential compound was enclosed within a double set of walls and gates, the outer set also encompassing household offices, storage areas, and the Court of Central Harmony (Chūwain), a small, walled area of Shinto ritual buildings that included the geographical center of the Greater Imperial Palace. The residential compound proper, measuring about 710 feet north and south and 560 feet east and west, contained more than thirty named buildings. Those in the northern two-fifths of the site housed the various imperial consorts and female officials; the remainder in the southern portion were devoted to the imperial residence itself, a ceremonial building, and various household offices and storage structures.

The core of the residential compound consisted of two buildings: the Purple Sanctum Hall (Shishinden), said to have been on the site of the residence of a seventh-century Hata leader named Kawakatsu; and the Benevolent Longevity Hall (Jijūden).

The name of the Purple Sanctum Hall was borrowed from a similar structure at the T'ang imperial palace, "purple sanctum" signifying the presence chamber or building of an emperor. The largest structure in the compound, measuring about 100 by 85 feet, the hall served as the site for lesser rites and ceremonies involving the emperor, occupying a position in the south-central portion of the compound physically and functionally analogous to that of the Great Hall of State within the Greater Imperial Palace. Facing south across a courtyard toward the main entrance gate to the compound, the large, simple building contrasted sharply, however, with the grandiloquently sinitic lines of the Court of Government building, its unpainted surfaces, cypress-bark roof, and high plank floors echoing the architecture of Shinto shrines. The imperial-throne chair occupied the central chamber of the hall, facing south in front of the Panels of the Sages, a series of removable partitions decorated with representations of meritorious Chinese ministers that may not have been installed, however, until the reign of Emperor Saga. Complementing the Great Hall of State, where the great ceremonies of state were held, the Purple Sanctum Hall and its southern courtyard were used to accommodate such events as Buddhist services, coming-of-age ceremonies for the emperor and crown prince, and the ordinary ceremonies and rituals of the court's annual calendar.

The Benevolent Longevity Hall, its name alluding to a Chinese classic that associated the Confucian virtue of benevolence or humanity with longevity, was a cypress-bark-shingled building located directly north of the Purple Sanctum Hall at the exact center of the compound. With perhaps 15 percent less space than the Purple Sanctum Hall, it was the usual residence of the emperor, its somewhat cramped central chamber being further divided into two rooms separated by a corridor. On the north, it communicated through another building with the quarters of the imperial harem.

OTHER PUBLIC BUILDINGS AND SPACES

Outside the palace, the city was occupied chiefly by individual residences, but there were also a number of public buildings, facilities, and spaces that in their sum accounted for perhaps as much as 5 to 10 percent of the total area. The public facilities included the city's two prisons, disposed slightly asymmetrically east and west of the palace; the building of the government's Academy of Chinese learning (*Daigaku-ryō*, "Bureau of the Greater Learning") and an official granary directly south of the palace; the Carpentry Bureau near the southeastern corner of the palace; the lodgings and work space for the labor levies allocated to the various government offices, concentrated east and west of the palace; the offices of the city's administrative organs on either side of Suzaku Avenue just south of the palace; and probably some charitable institutions for the sick, destitute, and the orphaned that are known to have existed from at least the 820s on. But the most prominent public spaces were the paired foreign embassy lodgings, the markets, and the Buddhist temples that flanked Suzaku Avenue in the southern half of the city, and the spacious Park of the Divine Spring (Shinsen'en) directly south of the palace on the eastern side of Suzaku.

Two temples, the only Buddhist institutions permitted in Heian, were at the southern edge of the city on four blocks (over 14 acres) of land each, about 300 yards east and west of Rampart Gate. Commonly known because of that arrangement as the West and East Temples (Saiji and Tōji), the two establishments were built at government expense and under government supervision to obtain divine protection for the state and its capital and to serve other official needs, such as the performance of mourning rites for emperors. Athough construction of the multitude of buildings required for the temples may have begun as early as 796, progress was slow, hindered partly by the large scale and luxuriousness of some of the structures, but chiefly no doubt by the competing demands of construction at the palace and by the financial strains of the Emishi Wars. Both temples appear to have been in operation by about 816, but construction continued long after that, the pagoda of the East Temple not being completed perhaps until the 870s or 880s and that of the West Temple not until 906. The heights of the pagodas are unknown, but once completed they must have been among the most conspicuous features on the Heian skyline. The East Temple survives on its original site in modern Kyoto, but all of its buildings are much later reconstructions, its famous 180-foot pagoda, for many the symbol of historical Kyoto, dating from 1644. The West Temple disappeared in the thirteenth century, but the site has been extensively excavated, and the general features of the temple are known.

About a half-mile north of the temples lay two official markets, similarly called the East and West Markets, about 600 yards east and west of Suzaku Avenue. The markets were, interestingly, among the earliest features of the Heian landscape, having been transferred there from Nagaoka three or four months before the arrival of Emperor Kammu in 794. Walled and gated, it appears, and distinguished architecturally by a tower or loft structure, each market was four blocks in area, the same size as the temple sites, and contained, in addition to the stalls, warehouses, and residences of the merchants, the offices of the market administrators.

At the same distance north of the temples but facing each other directly across Suzaku Avenue in Shichijō ("Zone Seven") were the two Kōrokan Lodgings, the government's residences for visiting foreign embassies. The name of the lodgings, which was borrowed from the title of a Chinese ministry in charge of foreign relations, is said to have meant "transmission of the voice," implying direction and assistance of (presumably) foreign peoples. Falling administratively under the Bureau of Buddhism and Aliens, the residences occupied walled sites that were probably equal in size to those of the temples and markets. Since the lodgings were used only for the very occasional embassy from Po-hai, they usually stood empty, and special supervision by the city's administrative offices was required in order to prevent vandalism and occupation by squatters. The East and West Markets lay due east and west of the lodgings, separated from them by little more than 300 yards. Given the highly commercial nature of the Po-hai embassies, it may be assumed that the propinquity of lodgings and markets was not coincidental. A medieval statement that the Kōorokan originally occupied the sites of the East and West Temples and were moved to their Shichijō locations to make way for the temples appears to be mistaken, but if such a move did in fact take place, it may have been as much to bring the foreign embassies closer to the markets as to accommodate the temples.

Finally, east of the northern terminus of Suzaku Avenue directly south of the palace lay the Park of the Divine Spring, a 30-odd-acre stretch of water and woods that probably preserved something of the original natural landscape of the Kyoto basin. On the shores of the spring-fed pond stood the park's chief architectural feature, the Celestial Presidence Pavilion (Kenrinkaku), a central building with two connected wing structures on either side where the emperor and his courtiers gathered for banqueting, archery exhibitions, flower and autumn-leaf viewing, music, dance, and poetry composition, or simply to escape the heat of a summer day. Hunting and fishing also occasionally took place in the park, the latter perhaps from an angling hall that stood near the main pavilion, and visitors could enjoy the view of a waterfall from another nearby structure. There was an island in the pond, probably connected to the shore by a bridge. The water deity later known as the Good Dragon Queen (Zennyoryūō) may have already been enshrined there, perhaps providing the impetus that during the course of the ninth century transformed the park from an imperial pleasure ground into a sacred place where holy men prayed for rain or for the cessation of rain, or sought to soothe the angry spirits that caused epidemic disease.

RESIDENTIAL DISTRICTS AND POPULATION

An allocation of house lots was made to prospective residents of the city in the fall of 793, and since most of the court must have accompanied Emperor Kammu when he transferred his seat to Heian a year later, it may be assumed that the construction of private dwellings on the lots proceeded rapidly. Little is known about individual land occupancy and use in the early days of the city, but if the practices associated with the agricultural land system were applied, house lots may initially have been allotted to families for limited periods of time. If so, the system soon broke down, for by the beginning of the tenth century lots were being treated as private property that could be inherited and sold. Although it is not clear that commoners (those who did not hold court rank) were provided for at all in the original city plan, or, if they were, how and where they acquired dwelling sites, the administrative nomenclature itself – house lot (*henushi*) – seems to suggest that each family was entitled to one lot. If commoners did in fact receive house lots, they were almost certainly those located farthest from the imperial palace and off the major avenues.

In accordance with a Nara-period precedent, individuals who held court rank may have been entitled to varying amounts of land, depending on their ranks. According to the earlier usage, the very highest ranks (First to Third), which in 793 were held by only five men, were supposed to receive a maximum of thirty-two house lots, the area of an entire city block (3.5 acres). The next highest ranks (Fourth and Fifth), numbering perhaps seventy-five or so men in 793, were entitled to a maximum of half that amount, and those with lower ranks (Sixth or below) to half that again, that is, to a maximum of eight lots.[9] If the Nara-period precedents were in fact followed, it is clear that not everyone received his maximum share of lots, since the five thousand to seven thousand lower-ranking officials estimated to have been in the capital would alone have been entitled to over forty thousand lots, and there were only about thirty-two thousand lots available in the entire city plan. We may suspect that most of the senior ranks received approximately the maximum areas to which they were entitled, as a certain amount of later evidence suggests, whereas the lowest ranks rarely, if ever, did so. However, even if the lower ranks received just one house lot each, their residences accounted for about a sixth of all the lots in the city plan. Their prominence in the capital would, in fact, have been even greater than that fraction suggests because, as we shall see, only about half of the city area seems actually to have been fully developed and inhabited.

Such in outline were the physical circumstances of Heian during its first decades of existence. The city clearly was devoted to but one purpose: the provision of living and work space for people associated with the workings of the central government, from the emperor down to the lowliest laborer. It was to be a capital city and nothing more, and its plan revealed that exclusive goal with exquisite clarity. The largest single area, amounting to nearly 7 percent of the total space, was occupied by the Greater Imperial Palace, which sat at the end of Suzaku Avenue, the great thoroughfare that led directly from the city's main entranceway at Rampart Gate. The palace was the symbolic center of the city, and the symbolic center of the palace was the ceremonial center of government, the Court of Government and its Great Hall of State, which lay on a line extending due north from Suzaku Avenue just beyond the main entrance to the palace precincts. One could scarcely imagine a more graphic representation of the city's function.

At the same time, there was little else except government buildings and private residences in the rest of the city. Religion, as represented in the East and West Temples at the city's southern edge, was confined to less than 1 percent of the area; commerce existed in limited form on similarly narrow sites at the East and West Markets, and industry outside the government's own workshops was not represented at all in the city plan.

Despite the narrowness of its conception and flaws in its planning,

---

9 Yoshioka Saneyuki, "Kizoku shakai no seijuku," in Hashimoto Yoshihiko, ed., *Komonjo no kataru Nihon shi,* vol. 2: *Heian* (Tokyo: Chikuma shobō, 1991), pp. 93–138.

Heian may rightly be called the first successful city in Japan, not only because it survived and prospered, but also because it is there that we can see clearly for the first time in Japanese history the distinctive characteristics of what may have been the most important product of the statutory system of government: urban life and civilization. The capital at Heizei was undoubtedly urban in essential ways, but the brevity of its life and the paucity of sources leave only scant knowledge about actual conditions in the city. Thanks to the work of archaeologists, the physical layout of Heizei and its palace is generally well known; the Shōsōin and the older temples of the Nara area reveal in their structures and treasures much about the physical, artistic, and intellectual environment of the imperial court and the Buddhist clergy; and written sources tell about government and its problems. But there is little that can be learned with certainty about the society of Heizei itself, about what it meant in concrete terms to be an inhabitant of the city. With Heian, however, and especially from the tenth century on, an increasingly abundant and varied supply of written sources begins to reveal at least the outlines of life at the capital, a picture skewed certainly toward the imperial court and the nobility but full enough nevertheless for us to recognize in it an ever more urban society.

The distinctively urban character of the society appears in several ways, but the most fundamental were, on the one hand, the diversity of the population, and, on the other, the population's removal, for the most part, from primary modes of production.

How large that population was at the city's founding or at any other time during its first few centuries of existence can be estimated only in the crudest fashion, but one can at least say that the frequently cited figure of 200,000 is almost certainly too high for the early decades of the city's life. (Inflation of early-city population figures seems to be a common failing of historians, who often mistakenly extrapolate from the size of households determined either on the analogy of much later social history or by guesswork.)[10] There is reliable evidence to show that in 829 there were only a little over 580 blocks (*machi*) in the city, or, in other words, not much more than half of the approximately 1,100 blocks originally planned in the area outside the imperial palace. Since a fairly large number of blocks was reserved, as we have seen, for public institutions and spaces, residential space in the city probably amounted to only about 500

---

10 Several urban historians have made the point, including Gideon Sjoberg, *The Preindustrial City, Past and Present* (Glencoe, Ill.: Free Press, 1960), pp. 80–85.

blocks, which, at thirty-two lots (*henushi*) per block, would have contained sixteen thousand lots. If we assume for the moment that one household occupied one house lot, as the city's planners may have envisaged, and if we accept somewhat uncertain evidence for 665 households in the year 871 indicating that the average size of a Heian household was 6.2 persons, we can calculate that the maximum population of the city outside the imperial palace during the ninth century was around 100,000. It may be true that many house lots were occupied by more than one household, but since there were other households that occupied several lots each, and since it also seems probable that there were unoccupied lots even in the developed areas of the city, the assumption that there was an average of one household per lot is perhaps as reasonable as any other. It is also true that the average household size may have been larger than the figures for 871 indicate. There is evidence to suggest that the average household size in the western section of Heizei during the Nara period was 9.4, but even if we use that figure in our calculations, the population of Heian would still be no more than 150,000.

In sum, the maximum population of Heian proper outside the imperial palace in the ninth century seems most likely to have been somewhere in the neighborhood of 100,000 to 150,000. If we accept a more conservative estimate based chiefly on the number of government officials and employees in the city, the figure may have actually been as low as 70,000. Such numbers are unimpressive by the standards of present-day megalopolises, but if they are even approximately correct in indicating the size of the city's population, they made Heian one of the larger cities in the world of its time and gave it an urban role that was even more central to the country than huge cities like Paris and Tokyo are to their modern-day societies. Just as a Wyoming city of 50,000 is, because of its physical and demographic context, a more important urban place in almost every sense than a bedroom town of similar size on the outskirts of London, so also undoubtedly was a ninth-century capital of 100,000 people, located in a country otherwise sparsely inhabited and almost wholly rural in population, a more significant center of urban civilization than a metropolis of millions is in a modern industrial state.

It has been estimated on the basis of fairly good evidence that at the beginning of the tenth century there were between 5,000 and 10,000 people who held titles in the organs of government at Heian or were employed at the imperial palace. If that figure is correct, most of the population in the city during its early days must have been either directly in the service of the court and its governmental apparatus or resident as family members or servants in the households of those who were so employed, numbering altogether perhaps as many as 50,000 to 60,000 people. Although that population was uniform in the sense that it was employed by, or was indirectly dependent on, the court and the government, the uniformity encompassed a diversity of occupations and social distinctions. These clearly distinguished the society from that of the countryside, where in any particular location one occupation (usually agriculture) tended to monopolize the economy, and specialization of labor and social differentiation were limited.

IMPERIAL CLAN AND COURT NOBILITY

The most conspicuous and best-known part of that large official or courtly population was, of course, the political and social elite: the imperial clan and the court nobility.

It is possible that the statutory regime is more accurately characterized as a rein on imperial power than as an expression of it. The emperor was far from being a despot under the regime's code, which in rule and practice gave great power to the nobility, who controlled entry to their own and the lower ranks of officialdom and were the conduit for most official documents issued under the imperial seal. If the regime was not quite the creature of the nobles, it seems to have served them nearly as well as it did their sovereign. But the emperor stood unquestionably at the apex of the social and political structure. Although his position and authority were defined chiefly by implication in the statutory code, all governmental action was taken ultimately in his name, and the more important actions required his direct, personal approval, or that of his regent. The emperor presided over the chief court rituals and ceremonies, which were widely considered the most significant contribution a ruler could make to his own and the general welfare, lying as they did at the very foundation of a healthy state. And the emperor was the universally acknowledged arbiter of social status, a recognized incarnation of divinity, greater or lesser proximity to whom usually defined the standing of his subjects. His authority and prestige were nearly as absolute as his power and influence were inconsequential later under the Fujiwara regents, which may be a principal reason that the line survived.

Succession to the throne was not regulated by law, but custom provided unmistakably clear guidance. Although there had been a number of reigning empresses in the eighth century and before bearing the imperial title of *tennō*, the throne throughout the Heian period was occupied exclusively by males, all of whom were sons of emperors and succeeded one another in the masculine line: from father to son in a bare majority of cases, but also frequently from brother to brother and exceptionally from uncle to nephew or nephew to uncle, cousin to cousin, or to a great-uncle (a great-grandfather's son). The chief qualification was that of imperial son, and the preferred succession was from father to son or brother to brother, but any line was possible in case of need or for the sake of political convenience. (Kammu's father, Kōnin, was, it will be remembered, an exception in the Nara period to the rule of succession by imperial sons: he was the paternal grandson of an emperor but not the son; similar exceptions had occurred earlier.) Imperial succession was unusually flexible. For example, a brother might succeed to the throne even when a son was available, and yet he did not necessarily do so. Such flexibility made almost any imperial son a potential heir to the throne and thus sometimes led to, or was used as a device for the creation of, conflict, but it worked on the whole with surprising smoothness during the Heian period, which was spared the war and bloody intrigue among imperial sons that might have been expected from such circumstances. One or two attempts on the throne may have been made during the period (the details are not altogether clear), but succession to the position was never sullied by bloodshed or physical violence.

The imperial clan shared materially, socially, and sometimes politically in the emperor's exalted position. Until 798, the clan included by law male and female descendants of emperors in the male line down to the fifth generation, but in that year, probably for reasons of economy, the original provision of the statutory code excluding the fifth generation and beyond was restored. The clan remained very large, including all patrilineal descendants of an emperor down to the generation of his great-grandchildren's children, so that a relative as remote from a reigning emperor as the child of the great-grandchild of the father of the emperor's great-grandfather (his fourth cousin?) was a member. Those numerous imperial relatives were distinguished by their titles into two groups according to the degree of lineal proximity to the emperor: (1) the "near-princes" (*shinnō*) or "near-princesses" (*naishinnō*), and (2) the "princes" (*ō*) or "princesses" (*nyoō*). The near-princes and -princesses were imperial children and siblings, and originally all relatives of that degree of relationship received one of the titles. But, again for reasons of economy, during the course of the Heian period it came to be the practice that only those children of an emperor who had been specifically granted the titles by imperial decree were allowed to use them and enjoy their emoluments and perquisites. All other members of the clan bore the lesser title of prince or princess, titles that might also be used by descendants in the fifth generation but without the right to court support. Male descendants in the sixth generation and beyond sometimes used the title of prince, but the text of the statutory code is not clear on the legality of that practice.

By law, the clan had originally tended toward endogamy, as had apparently many of the nonimperial clans, but the emperor himself early took the lead in ignoring legal restrictions, and in the Heian period emperors and their male descendants married freely outside the clan. Female imperial descendants, on the other hand, seem to have been bound by endogamy rules until well into the period. The first known instance of the marriage of a princess to a man outside the clan did not occur until the generation of Emperor Nimmyō's granddaughter, and the first known marriage of a near-princess to an outsider occurred in the reign of Emperor Daigo (897–930). Thereafter, however, such marriages were common.

The size of the imperial clan at any particular time in the early part of the Heian period is unknown, but in the latter half of the ninth century, when efforts had already been made to reduce its number, there were over five hundred people with princely titles that qualified them for government support, and toward the beginning of the tenth century there were upward of seven hundred. The level of support was generous, sometimes amounting, through appointment to high court rank and remunerative offices, to an annual income of as much as twelve hundred times that of an ordinary agriculturalist. That support, which often included as well valuable perquisites other than those derived from rank and office, became a very heavy burden on the court, and steps were taken, as we have seen, to reduce the level of support and further check the clan's growth. A critical turning point came in the reign of Emperor Saga (809–23), when for the first time large numbers of imperial sons and daughters were removed from the clan and reduced to the level of the court nobility. That step had the effect not only of immediately paring the size of the clan by seventeen near-princes and fifteen near-princesses, but also of eliminating the possibly two hundred or more princes (ō) and princesses (*nyoō*) who might have sprung from the lines of the imperial sons during the next three generations. Saga's policy, continued by succeeding emperors down to Murakami (r. 946–67), the smaller size of the imperial harem under the Fujiwara regents, and the immaturity of many emperors after the tenth century so greatly reduced the size of the clan that only a single prince is known to have been alive in 1143. It is symptomatic of the clan's changed circumstances that although the imperial genealogy lists a total of eighty-two descendants with princely titles in the first two generations under Emperor Kammu, it shows only sixteen for the same span of generations under Go-Sanjō (r. 1068–73).

An imperial consort, like all Heian wives, remained a member of her natal clan and was not formally assimilated to that of her husband. But her status even when she was not of imperial origin was in most ways equivalent to that of imperial clan members both during the lifetime of her husband and, if she survived him, after his death as well. The statutory code provided for ten imperial consorts hierarchically arranged under four titles of descending prestige conferred by decree of the emperor. The highest-ranking title, that of empress (*kōgō*), was held by only one consort at a time, a woman of the imperial clan chosen from among the two women holding the next lower title in the hierarchy, who were also members of the imperial clan. The rule restricting the two upper titles to women of the imperial clan had already been breached in the eighth century, however, and the empress was in fact normally a Fujiwara woman throughout the Heian period. As indicated by the literal meaning of the empress's title, "Lustrous Heir-bearer," it was originally conferred on a consort who had already borne the emperor a son, but in the reign of Reizei (967–69) an exception was made for the cherished only daughter of Emperor Suzaku, and thereafter it was common for childless women to receive the title. It remained the case, however, that no woman was ever directly appointed empress, always first holding one of the lower consort titles. Until the time of Ichijō (r. 986–1011) it was also the case that not every emperor had an empress.

The lesser consort titles of the code, which were held by women from the clans of the court nobility, disappeared and were replaced by other, office-derived designations (notably *nyōgo*, "female attendant") during the ninth and tenth centuries. As a result of Fujiwara political need a second empress's position and title (*chūgū*, "Inner Palatine") became available at the beginning of the eleventh century.

But despite such changes in substance and nomenclature, the code's system of a hierarchically arranged group of imperial consorts drawn from a restricted group of clans remained basically intact, usually making at least half a dozen princely and noble consorts simultaneously available to a mature emperor.

Those women lived with their ladies-in-waiting, their servants, and the numerous female court officials and servants in the twelve connected buildings of the "rear palace" (*kōkyū*) north of the emperor's residential palace, where, especially from the tenth century on, they presided over one of the chief centers of noble social life. The total female population of the rear palace in the Heian period has been estimated at one thousand, but that seems high for the available space. Those living and employed there may have numbered that many, but it seems unlikely that all would have been present at one time, since the rather small buildings would otherwise have been virtually wall-to-wall with people.

Although the rear palace was by no means freely accessible to any noble, neither was it a sultan's seraglio jealously guarded and disciplined by a corps of eunuchs. The consorts were not prisoners of the palace, and even while there they were not isolated from society. They frequently returned for visits or childbirth to the homes of their parents or other close relatives, and while at court they were freely visited in their quarters by a variety of male and female relatives. There were probably few higher-ranking nobles who did not have some kind of access to the rear palace. Since each consort usually sought to make the physical trappings of her quarters as attractive as possible and to surround herself with particularly accomplished and beautiful ladies-in-waiting, the result was at least sometimes a highly stylish salon where men and women were able to meet and entertain themselves with considerable freedom. The parentage of many nobles and the literature of the period suggest that the freedom frequently enough included sexual trysts, and it is clear that the consorts themselves were not always blameless in that respect.

Principal consorts during the Heian period came from a handful of noble clans in the capital that ranked in social status below the imperial clan but included in their number the great Fujiwara lineage and its Northern House, whose power and wealth for much of the time rivaled or eclipsed that of the emperor. The term "Northern House" (Hokke), which does not appear in sources until about the twelfth century, refers to the Fujiwara line descending from Fuhito's son Fusasaki (681–737), the line of the Fujiwara regents. There were three other lines descending from Fusasaki's brothers: (1) the Southern House (Nanke) from Muchimaro (680–737); (2) the Ceremonials House (Shikike) from Umakai (694–737); and (3) the Capital House (Kyōke) from Maro (695–737). Of the three, only the Southern and Ceremonial houses figured prominently in Heian history, and even they quickly faded from view as the Northern House established its ascendancy at court. (For Fujiwara genealogy, see Figures 1.2 and 1.3.)

The "clan" in the early part of the period and during the Fujiwara regency was a loosely knit, patrilineal kin group of nobles whose members shared an ancestral or guardian deity, bore a common patronymic (except for the imperial clan, which had no name) and hereditary title of status, acknowledged a common clan chieftain (*uji no chōja*), and were usually buried together in a clan cemetery. It was a survival of what very scanty and problematical evidence suggests to have been in pre-Taika days a more substantive and powerful kin and fictive-kin organization with hereditary political and economic functions that seems to have been created in the consolidation of central rule in Japan as an instrument of imperial power. "Clan" is used here conventionally to refer to what was called in Japanese the *uji*, a term of possibly Korean origin. Since it is clear that the pre-Taika *uji* was not characterized by some of the major features of the clan, as that term is traditionally used (it was not, for instance, exogamous and may not have been unilineal), some have been reluctant to call it a clan at all. But the concept of P. Kirschoff's "conical clan" seems to fit the early Japanese *uji* fairly well, and the use of the term may be less misleading than sometimes supposed.[11] It should be noted, however, that the early *uji* differed significantly from the conical clan in that succession to the chieftainship was not primogenitary but shifted continuously among collateral lines.[12]

The inauguration of the statutory code deprived the *uji* clan of most of its direct political role, but it remained the broadest kin group to which a noble belonged and continued to play an important role in the lives of individual clan members. Membership in a clan was itself a definition of nobility in the broadest sense of the

---

11 Paul Wheatley and Thomas See, *From Court to Capital: A Tentative Analysis of the Japanese Urban Tradition* (Chicago: University of Chicago Press, 1978), pp. 94–95, appear to have been the first to call attention to the conical clan in connection with the *uji*, but scholars in Japan have since reached the same conclusion.
12 Pointed out by Yoshida Takashi, "Uji to ie," Sasaki Junnosuke and Ishii Susumu, eds., *Shimpen Nihon shi kenkyū nyūmon* (Tokyo: Tōkyō Daigaku shuppankai, 1982), pp. 31–58.

term; it determined the court positions to which a member might reasonably aspire; in part it made possible the achievement of those positions; and it was a controlling influence in the religious life of members. The clan chieftain – whose position was not hereditary in a direct line but passed by imperial decree usually to the clan member holding the highest court rank and office – was responsible for the worship of the clan deity or deities; for the administration of clan shrines and temples, including fairly extensive police and judicial functions; for the execution of imperial orders addressed to the clan (orders requiring, for example, the presentation of clan women for service at court); for the discipline of members by expulsion from the clan; and, to some ill-defined extent, for the physical and educational welfare of clan members. (In the case of the Fujiwara, the Kangakuin, the "Learning Promotion Court," a clan dormitory and school for members enrolled in the government's Academy of Chinese learning, was under the chieftain's jurisdiction.) He also enjoyed certain privileges symbolic of distinction, such as burial in the manner usually reserved for holders of the Third Rank or above. But from at least the tenth century his most important prerogative was the nomination each year of a Sixth-Rank clan member for promotion to the Fifth Rank. That prerogative in effect gave him the power to create a primary member of the nobility, for it was the elite stratum of holders of the Fifth Rank and above who supported their clans with their incomes, controlled the government, and led society.

It is important to note that the clan seems neither in its earlier history nor in the Heian period to have been an organization found throughout Japanese society. It is thought to have been restricted from the outset mainly to nobles at, or closely tied to, the court of the emperor, and in the Heian period the clans, insofar as they are known, were all centered on the capital. By the middle of that period only a few survived: chiefly the Fujiwara, the Taira, the Tachibana, the Sugawara, the Ōtomo (Tomo), the Takashina, the Ōnakatomi, the Imbe, the Urabe, the Wake, and the Ochi. There was also the recently founded Minamoto clan – a single clan despite the diverse imperial origins of its various lineages; its clan chieftainship was held in the Saga line up through the mid-Heian period, then by the Murakami line, and finally by what is usually identified as the Seiwa line, that is, the line of the Ashikaga and Tokugawa shoguns. The imperial, or "princely" (ō), clan, consisting of the princes and princesses (near and otherwise), also survived, of course, but it was distinguished from the noble clans by the special conditions attaching to membership in it (descendants in the fifth generation and beyond outside the direct line of imperial succession were excluded); by its lack of a patronymic; and by its peculiar relationship to the focus of kinship in the clan, the emperor, who seems himself not to have been a member. There were, in addition, many other presumably patronymic lineages found among the lower reaches of officialdom and in private employment and occupations (over eighty such names can be found, for example, in the diary of Fujiwara no Michinaga), but although little can be said with certainty about them, it is nearly certain that they were not clans of the sort just described.

All members of the clans were "noble" in the sense that they bore imperially conferred hereditary titles of honor called *kabane* that seem in practice to have been the essential qualification for appointment to one of the five highest court ranks. Although those ranks were not hereditary in law and often not in fact, the statutory regulations governing appointment to rank ensured that once a member of a clan had been appointed to the Fifth Rank or above, his lineage would continue to receive appointment at that level. The hereditary nature of rank was the result of a system of preferential treatment for men whose fathers or grandfathers held, or had held, noble rank (Fifth or above). Such men on reaching the age of twenty-one calendar years were entitled by the fact of their birth to appointment to relatively high rank (Fifth down to Eighth), the precise rank depending on the rank of the father or grandfather. That privilege gave even those appointed to the Sixth Rank or below (the overwhelming majority) practical assurance of promotion to noble rank, their rise being accelerated by other kinds of preferential treatment, and their eventual appointment to the critical Fifth Rank facilitated by the direct control over such appointments that seems to have been exercised by the Council of State, where sympathetic kinsmen were frequently to be found. Sons of men who never rose above the Sixth Rank, on the other hand, started at the bottom court rank at the age of twenty-five calendar years (four years older than noble sons at the time of their initial appointment to rank) and moved slowly up the ladder through an elaborate review and evaluation process that effectively barred all but the most exceptional or fortunate from the upper ranks. It might take a man starting at the bottom rank as long as thirty or more years to reach the rank at which the son of a Fifth-Rank noble began his career (the Junior Eighth Rank Lower).

As a result of such privileges, the number and identity of noble clans (those whose male members regularly achieved the Fifth Rank or above) varied little from the beginning of the statutory system up to the early Heian period. The highest and mightiest nobles, who held the Third Rank or above and were distinguished under the code as "the august" (*ki*), came from only about 20 clans, while holders of the lower noble ranks (the Fourth and Fifth), who were known under the code as "the august equivalent" (*tsūki*), represented another 150 to 200 clans. Few new clans were admitted to the noble ranks, and few of the established clans lost status before the ninth century, when the atrophy and decline of the statutory system and the growing monopolization of offices by the Fujiwara began to reduce the number of clans to the dozen or so already mentioned. Even then, however, the system of preferential appointment to rank continued to operate in defining the nobility, although Fujiwara power and the inflation of ranks soon led to much higher initial ranks for noble sons at much earlier ages.

But the formal definition of the nobility in terms of court rank was no longer entirely valid by the tenth and eleventh centuries, for by then shrinking governmental revenues and a tendency toward inflation of ranks had erased much of the sharp difference that had separated the Fifth from lower ranks. More appointments were being made to the noble ranks, and the lower ranks, deprived very often of any economic meaning at all, were falling into disuse. Reflecting the personalization of government and the shift of the center of governmental activity to the Emperor's Residential Compound, the chief distinguishing feature of the nobility then was a combination of rank (Fifth or above) with the privilege of attendance in the imperial audience chamber, a privilege that was enjoyed ex officio by holders of the top three court ranks and by Consultants (*sangi*) of the Fourth Rank (a group known collectively as the *kugyō*, "lords and ministers") and that was granted by imperial decree to selected holders of the Fourth and Fifth Ranks and to certain other officers who required access to the audience chamber in the performance of their duties.[13]

The nobility at the beginning of the Heian period was still generally what it had become under the impact of the Taika Reforms and the

---

13 In the years around 1000 there appears to have been a fixed number of senior nobles (*kugyō*): sixteen. The number radically increased thereafter. Senior nobles holding appointment at the level of Consultant (*sangi*) or above were called "currently active" (*gennin*), and it was they who took part in the deliberations of the Council of State (*daijōkan*). Yoshioka, "Kizoku shakai no seijuku," p. 112. See also William H. and Helen Craig McCullough, *A Tale of Flowering Fortunes: Annals of Japanese Aristocratic Life in the Heian Period*, 2 vols. (Stanford, Calif.: Stanford University Press, 1980), pp. 790–91.

institution of the statutory state: a partially bureaucratized social and economic elite concentrated in the capital and almost totally divorced from the direct use and exploitation of rural land. It was the core of the urban population whose culture defined the civilization of the period, controlling the governmental apparatus, reaping the major economic rewards of that apparatus, dominating society, setting standards of behavior that were recognized by most as the society's ideals, writing the literature, practicing and patronizing the arts, and creating the religious and intellectual life of the day. It fluctuated in size through the period but seems usually to have consisted of somewhere between 100 and 125 men, who together with their families may have accounted for 1 or 2 percent of the capital's population. Women also held ranks among the nobility, but since they normally acquired those ranks only as consanguinal or affinal relatives of an emperor or regental noble and did not usually hold substantive office within the statutory structure, they are perhaps better excluded from a tally of the nobility's primary members.

Although the statutory government was in law a largely meritocratic bureaucracy, insofar as the regime survived in the mid-Heian period and after, its offices tended to become hereditary in particular sublineages of clans called "houses." That was especially true initially of those lower offices requiring what might be regarded as specialized or technical skills. The subjects of Chinese history and poetry at the Academy of Chinese learning, for example, were taught by a Professor of Literature (*monjō hakase*), an office hereditary in the Sugawara or Ōe houses; key posts in the Secretaries' Office (*gekikyoku*) of the Council of State requiring a knowledge of Confucian texts went to Nakahara and Kiyohara men; and *yin-yang* professors expert in calendrical and astronomical matters were drawn from the Abe and Kamo. Such hereditary "house status" (*kakaku*) determined not only the houses of clans from which appointments to particular titles could be made, but also usually the careers to which a man might aspire. A Sugawara noble did not, if he was prudent, aim to be a Minister of State (*daijin*). A "house status" designated, in fact, an entire career, both a hereditary office and the particular route of promotion thereto. The system eventually extended also to the major governmental posts, evoking a nomenclatural system that by the late Heian period in the twelfth century and after included in descending order of rank and prestige: (1) the "five regental houses" (*gosekke*) of the Northern House of the Fujiwara clan; (2) the "limpid flower" (*seika*) houses whose members were the hereditary holders of Minister of State posts; and (3) the "feather grove" (*urin*) and "name" (*mei*) houses whose members similarly held the Middle and Major Counselor posts.[14]

The senior nobles, those "august" ones who held the highest three ranks and occupied the chief positions of the court government, numbered a scant five at the beginning of the period, but economics and family ambition had quadrupled that figure by the eleventh century. At the same time, the several old-line clans that had still been represented among the senior nobles in the early part of the period were gradually excluded from their number as the Northern House of the Fujiwara established its ascendancy. By the last half of the ninth century the group was made up almost entirely of Fujiwara clan members and men of the imperial Minamoto families, who were often marital kin of the Fujiwara.

The ordinary nobles of the "august equivalent" Fourth and Fifth Ranks (or, in the mid-Heian period, those of them who held audience chamber privileges) were not usually directly involved in the highest councils of government. However, they commonly held key administrative or ceremonial positions that gave them access to, and influence with, the emperor or his chief ministers, and they were full participants in court life, "dwellers above the clouds" (*unjō-bito*) at the very apex of society. From the ninth century on, however, the shrinkage of the statutory regime and its revenues made them increasingly dependent on the favor, protection, and patronage of the senior nobles, whom they sometimes served in personal capacities.

The differences in status among the nobility and the lower officialdom (those whose highest ranks were the Sixth or below) were numerous and profound, and there was a similar, if slightly less sharp, difference within the nobility itself among the senior and ordinary nobles. The differences occurred in the treatment accorded each group in criminal law, in mortuary matters, in imperial audience privileges, in marital access to the imperial clan, in ceremonial behavior, in the size of residences, in costumes, and in almost every other branch of life. The nature of the differences, which, of course, always favored the superior strata, is most easily seen in the income allotted to the various ranks under the statutory code. According to the provisions of the code, the lowest-ranking noble (one of the Fifth Rank) received approximately ten times the income of the highest-ranking lower official (one of the Sixth Rank), and there was an

14 Yoshioka, "Kizoku shakai no seijuku," p. 126.

equally great difference in income between the lowest rank of the senior nobles (the Third Rank) and the highest of the ordinary nobles (the Fourth Rank). Those incomes changed markedly during the period as the government's economic situation deteriorated, but it is probably safe to assume that the disparity in wealth between the two levels of the nobility remained at least as pronounced as in the code's provisions, and that the gap between the nobles and whatever remained of the lower officialdom by that time was similarly maintained or widened.

THE NOBLE FAMILY, MARRIAGE, AND THE POSITION OF WOMEN

Despite the continuing importance of the clan in the early and mid-Heian periods, the chief focus in the day-to-day life of the nobility was the clan sublineage and the coresidential family or household, the partial divorce of which from each other distinguished both from the medieval and later "house" (*ie*). Sublineages within a clan seem to have been referred to most commonly as "gates" (*kado*) or "houses" (*ie*), the latter a term excessively familiar to students of Japanese social history. The word *ie* was used in Heian vernacular texts up to the eleventh century mainly in the meaning of "house" or "home" (the physical place, including the various buildings and grounds), but sometimes also in reference to the dwellers in a house, or, in other words, to a family or household. The *ie* as family had genealogical but not to any very important degree proprietary continuity. One spoke, for example, of a noble or base house, but not of a rich or poor one; of house lineage but not of house patrimony. Misapplication of the later *ie* concept to Heian noble society has led to some confusion on the subject.

An examination of the Heian noble family may begin, therefore, with the observation that the family residence was unconnected with income or income-producing property. A noble had neither a country seat that was the administrative center of a surrounding landed estate nor, of course, any kind of urban commercial, trading, or manufacturing enterprise. His income came almost entirely from governmental revenues or the revenues from scattered pieces of agricultural land, most of which he never saw, and with the operation and oversight of which he usually had little or nothing to do. Status and income were totally divorced from family residence, adhering instead to individuals, and residential arrangements were therefore free to follow other principles. A man acquired rank and office largely through the patriline, but since that rank and office, with the attendant income, followed him wherever he chose to live, his residence could be, and perhaps even ordinarily was, unrelated to lineage. Residence was determined partly by social convention and partly by circumstance.

A chief determinant of Heian noble residence was the nature of the marriage institutions of the time. Before taking up the direct bearing of marriage on residence, however, three preliminary points may be made.

One is the very early age at which initial marriages frequently occurred, often at about the age of puberty (girls might be only eleven or twelve, boys a year or two older). In such marriages, the ages of the bride and groom were usually fairly close to each other, but the bride was often two or three years older than her husband, and in some cases as much as seven to ten years older. In second and subsequent marriages, men often married women much junior to themselves (sometimes mere children), and the marriage was apt to be the first for the bride. Women were apparently less likely to marry a second time (their high mortality rate in childbirth and the general absence of violence between men accounts undoubtedly for part of the difference – there must have been many fewer widows than widowers), but when they did, the husband seems typically to have been older and the marriage seldom, if ever, his first.

A second feature of the period's marriage institutions was the practice of polygyny. Men were permitted to have more than one wife, although by no means all of them did, even among the wealthiest and most puissant. Women, on the other hand, were not permitted to engage in polyandrous marriage. They could, through divorce or by the death of a spouse, have more than one husband, but not two or more at the same time. When a man had more than one wife, the woman first married seems to have had a strong presumptive claim to be a principal wife in the sense that (1) her husband's usual or expected residence was with her, (2) her male children rose higher in the official hierarchy than the sons of other wives, and (3) the title used of her by others was that associated with a wife distinguished by the first two characteristics. The title of a principal wife, "northern quarter" (*kita no kata*), was defined and confirmed, however, neither by law nor by sacred writing, and the status of such wives may have been as vague in practice as it seems in modern formulation. Although the ranked titles of the imperial harem might lead one to expect a similar hierarchy of wives in noble polygynous marriages, there are quasi-historical cases of polygynous marriages in which the principal-wife title was used of concurrent wives of a single husband, suggesting equal or nearly equal status for the wives.

A final point about Heian marriages is that they were accomplished solely through domestic rites, and, as far as is known, neither the government nor any religious authority played a role in sanctioning or confirming them. Furthermore, there appears to have been no written marriage contract or other similar instrument executed by the families or the principals – the existence of a union rested entirely on familial and social recognition. There was consequently no legal or moral bastardy, and there is also no evidence that children of informal unions who were recognized by their fathers suffered greater social or career disadvantages than was the common lot of children by secondary wives. Perhaps, in fact, paternal recognition of children was the necessary condition for social regularization of a sexual relationship, in other words, for marriage.

From a social point of view, the most critical aspect of a marriage – apart from its basic function of uniting a man and woman for the production and rearing of children – is apt to be the location of the married couple's residence. Anthropologists and sociologists often identify four chief types of marital residence found among the diverse societies of the world: (1) at or near the husband's parental home (virilocal, or patrilocal, residence); (2) at or near the wife's parental home (uxorilocal or matrilocal); (3) at a house separate from either spouse's parental home (neolocal); and (4) at the respective parental homes of the wife and husband, the husband visiting his wife at her house but continuing to live at his own (duolocal). Other types of residence are, of course, possible, and there may be shifting from one type of residence to another in the course of a single marriage (especially likely in the case of duolocal residence, it seems), but societies appear usually to exhibit a preference either in practice or in the ideal for one of the above four chief types. It should be noted, however, that few if any societies follow exclusively one type of residence pattern. Each of the four residential types and their various combinations is undoubtedly found at least occasionally, for example, in present-day American society, where neolocal marriage is, nevertheless, usually the goal and practice. Individual circumstances and needs seem commonly able to overrule social norms in such matters.

During most of the Heian period, and especially during its middle century and a half (950–1100), the prevailing modes of marital residence in noble society at the capital were uxorilocal, neolocal, and duolocal. It appears that the society's ideal marriage, the marriage that took place when all things were normal and as they should be, was uxorilocal, or uxorilocal followed by neolocal residence, and it is likely that such marriages were also numerically predominant. They were, in any case, very common among the nobility.[15]

When a marriage was the first for both bride and groom and the bride's parents were present and leading nonreligious lives, the typical residence rule seems to have been uxorilocal. Such marriages began with a period of duolocal residence that lasted for varying periods of time, from a few days up to a year or more (the birth of the first child may have usually marked the upper limit of the duolocal phase), but eventually the husband took up residence at the house of his wife's parents. As the youthful couple matured and began to assume greater responsibility for their own lives, the wife's parents often moved into another house, usually nearby, or provided a separate house for the couple, and sometimes the husband supplied a new house for himself and his wife.

The uxorilocal and uxorilocal–neolocal unions were the marriages that might be regarded as the most orthodox. The extreme youth of the bride and groom, together with the general absence of opportunities for social intercourse between high-ranking boys and girls, meant inevitably that such marriages were arranged by the families of the couples. The wishes of the principals in the matter were but little if at all consulted (the couple often, perhaps even regularly, met for the first time during their wedding rites, which involved lying together but not necessarily the consummation of the marriage). The primary considerations were, rather, the usual ones of noble societies: rank, political or social advantage, wealth, and so on. The bride's family was especially interested in obtaining a husband whose family connections promised high rank and office for him at court and thus eventually a large income and broad influence. The groom's family looked for a wife whose family could provide adequate support and care for their son and assist him in his career at court. Both families also sought to strengthen their political and social standing through marital ties with leading court figures. The natural result of such considerations was fairly strict class endogamy and, as the Fujiwara came to control most of the choice

---

15 William H. McCullough, "Marriage Institutions in the Heian Period," *Harvard Journal of Asiatic Studies* 27 (1967): 103–67.

court offices, even a tendency toward clan endogamy, especially at the upper levels of the nobility. (Incest rules were narrowly drawn, the only clearly disapproved marriages being those with a direct ascendant or descendant and with a full or half sibling.)

If a family had more than one daughter, the second and subsequent daughters might be married uxorilocally, either in the same residence with the first daughter or in the house to which the parents later removed, or, especially perhaps when the groom was an adult, they might be provided by the parents with neolocal residences. As one would assume, when the groom was still a child, the initial marital residence seems never to have been neolocal.

It was not uncommon for an adult groom or his parents also to provide the initial residence for a neolocal marriage. That was least often the case, probably, when special circumstances (a fire, for example, at the wife's parents' house) made the arrangement necessary or convenient even under what might otherwise be considered normal circumstances (i.e., when the wife's parents were alive and of the noble group from which the husband might be expected to take a principal wife). Groom-supplied neolocal residences may have been the rule, on the other hand, for imperial princes, and also when the bride was severely disadvantaged: an orphan, or of a station or situation so inferior to that of the groom that her parents could not provide living quarters and support commensurate with their son-in-law's superior status. If uxorilocal marriages were the most orthodox and the least sentimental in origin, the latter type of neolocal marriage, in which the husband supplied the residence for an orphaned girl or a woman of inferior rank or circumstances, was the most romantic, and it is perhaps inevitable that much of the fiction of the period centered on such unions. They originated almost exclusively, the fiction and inference tell us, in the man's affection for the woman, since there was otherwise nothing to attract him to a marriage that yielded neither important economic nor social benefit to him. The woman, on the other hand, had much to gain from such a marriage: economic support, a rise in social status, and perhaps even some promise of long-term security. It was in her interest clearly to encourage and maintain her husband's love.

If a man took a secondary wife, the marriage was almost always duolocal, since wives did not usually share houses and the husband normally resided with his principal wife. There is no historical support for the well-known fictional case in *The Tale of Genji* where the living quarters of three wives are found disposed on three sides of the husband's mansion, nor is there any undisputed historical case of permanent duolocal marriage with a principal wife. A woman in a duolocal marriage was typically inferior in status to her husband, and it was no doubt as often the promise of an improved economic and social situation as of love that induced her to accept the position of a secondary wife. For the husband, on the other hand, the chief motive for the marriage was again likely to be affection, although family politics or the desire for children also sometimes played a role.

The absence from literary and historical sources of a single, unequivocal case of virilocal residence among the Heian nobility, except in imperial marriages, is striking and noteworthy.[16] We may assume that virilocal marriage did occur exceptionally – just as, for example, duolocal marriage occurs exceptionally in modern Western societies – but the circumstances giving rise to it must have been very special indeed. The near absence of virilocal residence meant that as a rule a noble wife never lived with her husband's parents. Since children remained with the mother in case of divorce and often with a maternal relative in the event of the mother's death, it meant also that grandchildren seldom lived with their paternal grandparents. A further consequence was that most men left their parental homes at an early age, often while still children.

The matrimonial residence patterns of the Heian nobility produced, in combination with other characteristics of the marriage institutions and of the society, distinctive common patterns of personal relationships. The most important pattern emerged from the uxorilocal marriages, where the chief potential family members were the primary couple (the maternal grandparents), their married daughters and the husbands and children thereof, and their unmarried children. Since the unmarried sons of the grandparents could be expected soon to marry out of the household, and since the second and subsequent daughters were often established in marriages elsewhere (a separate uxorilocal or neolocal residence), the long-term core of the house tended to be composed of maternal grandparents, a daughter of the grandparents, and the daughter's husband and children, and it was between them that the strongest family ties seem to have been found. The relationship between the maternal grandparents and grandchildren was often particularly close, perhaps because the grandparents played an especially large role in rais-

---

16 The existence of such virilocal residences has been alleged by, among others, Sumi Tōyō, *Zenkindai Nihon kazoku no kōzō* (Tokyo: Kōbundō, 1983), but the cases cited in support of that view all seem to be neolocal.

ing the children when the parents themselves were still very young, as was often the case. Father and daughter were also often particularly close, the result, perhaps, of living together longer than any other family members. The mother frequently died early in childbirth, leaving the father as the sole parent (except when he remarried and moved to his new wife's residence or to a neolocal establishment). And while a son married out at an early age, a daughter married uxorilocally and might continue living with her father until she was well into her adult years. The relations between sisters and brothers also seem usually to have been close, as were those between the husband and his wife's parents (the husband was, however, never adopted by his in-laws, as happened in later Japanese history and sometimes even today). On the other hand, the ties with paternal grandparents, uncles, and aunts, who almost always lived elsewhere, were usually fairly remote. Even those between father and son and brother and brother seem to have been somewhat distant, the result in each case very likely of separate residence or of only a short period of coresidence.

The particular pattern of personal relationships characteristic of uxorilocal marriages varied somewhat with neolocal and duolocal marriages, but the closeness of familial ties through, among, and to females and the relative remoteness of the corresponding male connections remained basically unchanged. Those characteristics of noble society had a pervasive influence on the period's history and civilization (as seen most dramatically in the example of the Fujiwara regency), exercised partly through the control of infant and child emperors by their maternal relatives, and perhaps also in the flourishing of female letters, which depended in part on a recognition of feminine worth that must have been supported and encouraged by the women-centered relationships of the society.

A summary of Heian noble marriage residence rules draws particular attention to the social and economic position of the wife. The general tenor of the marriage institutions and the nature of the resulting personal relationships within the family suggest a fairly elevated status for a principal wife vis-à-vis her husband, and that impression is strengthened and confirmed by several additional considerations.

To begin with, the psychological position of a principal wife in an orthodox, uxorilocal marriage must have been fairly strong. Instead of moving to a strange house among the unfamiliar and possibly cold or hostile relatives and servants of her husband's family, she remained in her natal home. There she still very likely played in the early years of her marriage as much or more the role of daughter as of wife, and was surrounded by brothers, sisters, and faithful servants. Marriage meant for her no radical shift of physical or social scene, and thus she escaped the severe psychological trauma that was a common fate of Japanese brides in the virilocal marriages of later periods. It was the husband who became the guest or intruder, although even for him the transition was eased to some extent by the period of duolocal residence that preceded his move to his bride's house.

The wife's position was also buttressed by a degree of economic autonomy. Under prevailing inheritance custom, a daughter shared in the estate of her parents, often or regularly receiving the family residence and also a share of the other property, a share that sometimes, at least, included almost the whole of the estate. That was a logical, pragmatic arrangement, since it could be expected that a son would be largely supported by his court income and that he would live uxorilocally or in a neolocal residence supplied by his wife's family. A woman's control over the property she inherited was absolute in the sense that she could sell or transfer it at will (it was not a lifetime holding that reverted elsewhere on the woman's death, as in later periods). Because there are instances of marital residences that passed down from mother to daughter through as many as four generations, it may be that real and other property was often inherited in the maternal line. That point, however, is uncertain. Although female ownership and bequeathal of property is clearly established in surviving documents, no case of an actual inheritance of a residence and property by a noble daughter from her mother has been found. It is possible that the seemingly matrilineal succession to houses was at least in some cases actually accomplished through and at the discretion of the husband, into whose hands at some point the uxorilocal residence seems often to have passed, a development that negotiations leading to the marriage may conceivably have provided for.

The Heian noble wife also enjoyed certain other customary rights that tended to give additional substance to the degree of her social and economic autonomy. She retained her own clan name at marriage and was eventually buried with members of her natal clan (she did not become, in other words, a member of her husband's clan). She had and used the right of divorce, and she kept her children in case of divorce or the death of her husband. Furthermore, she had a limited measure of sexual freedom in the sense that although premarital sex and adultery were not socially condoned in women, they seem not to have been uncommon, and even if the relationship was discovered, the woman was not ordinarily subjected to physical or other punishment. If she was discovered in adultery, her husband might divorce her, but that was not certain, and perhaps not even customary.

Finally, the general nature of the surrounding society in which the Heian noblewoman found herself provided relatively favorable conditions for the growth and exercise of her talents. The society was intensely urban, thoroughly civil, generally pacific and nonviolent, and inclined heavily toward aesthetic, literary, and learned pursuits. The conditions of society may not have been "feminine" in any essential sense, but they were far more promising for women than those of, for example, a feudal society geared for war, where the high value placed on muscle and meanness led inevitably, no doubt, to harsher conditions for women.

It is clear that the Heian noblewoman enjoyed a relatively high and strong position in her society, in sharp contrast with the women of feudal Japan. It is important, however, to stress that her position remained distinctly and absolutely inferior to that of noblemen. She did not occupy what were clearly the preeminent positions in the society: there were no reigning Japanese empresses during the Heian period, no female government ministers, no female heads of Buddhist sects, no female chieftains of noble clans. The relative position of men and women is well illustrated by the names commonly used of women, names frequently drawn from their roles as daughters, wives, or mothers (as, for instance, "the Mother of Michitsuna," the name of a famous writer who was the mother of a totally undistinguished son); those, indeed, were the chief functions in life for most women. Moreover, it must be admitted that the noblewoman's concept of herself was usually as an inferior being: unintelligent, emotional, incompetent, and dependent.

LIFE IN THE MANSION OF A GREAT NOBLE

The houses in which the Heian nobility married and lived were highly perishable wooden structures that fire and war completely obliterated centuries ago, leaving not a single physical trace of their existence for the historian. But thanks to abundant literary and pictorial evidence and to scanty architectural survivals in religious institutions outside Kyoto, the chief features of the houses are well known. Modern scholars have even been able to produce with some exactitude floor and ground plans of several of the chief noble residences in the mid-Heian period, and scale models are found in more than one Japanese museum. The plans and models are based, of course, on a fair amount of guesswork and inference, but their degree of reliability appears to be generally high. It is unlikely that a resurrected Heian courtier would have much difficulty in identifying them as the species of house in which he had once lived.

The architectural style of the Heian noble mansion deriving ultimately, it is said, from China, has been known since the nineteenth century as "dwelling hall construction" (*shindenzukuri*), taking its name from the building, the "dwelling hall" (*shinden*), where the main inhabitant or inhabitants slept and lived. A fully developed establishment consisted of several buildings, whose construction was much the same as that of the common Japanese domestic architecture of more recent times: rectangular, single-story, post-and-beam structures with probably unpainted surfaces, gable or hip roofs, and plank floors elevated several feet above the ground on posts. The roofs were plank or, in the better establishments, shingled with cypress bark; tile seems not to have been used except on roof ridges. Interior space in the major buildings was for the most part undivided by permanent partitions or walls, but the configurations of post alignment, supplemented as occasion required by curtains, blinds, and sliding or freestanding screens, created a large central chamber (called the *moya*) surrounded on four sides by oblong "eave chambers" (*hisashi*), beyond which, but still beneath the eaves, were open verandas running the entire length and breadth of the building. The eave chambers were divided from the verandas by board-backed latticework partitions that were usually opened or entirely removed during the day, leaving the occupants protected from the elements only by standing paper screens, curtains, or bamboo blinds. Living took place mostly on the plank floors, which were bare except for cushions and movable mats, and furniture was minimal: armrests (used by people seated on the floor), screens, oil-lamp stands, an occasional cabinet or table, a curtained dais for sleeping, charcoal braziers (the only artificial source of heat), and apparently little else.[17]

Many ordinary nobles may have had to content themselves with

---

17 The recognized authority on *shindenzukuri* is Ōta Seiroku, *Shindenzukuri no kenkyū* (Tokyo: Yoshikawa kōbunkan, 1987).

unelaborated dwelling halls on cramped sites in the back streets of the city, and some may have been unable to manage even that. But we know little of such houses, since it is only the grander mansions of the senior nobles that the literary and historical sources describe in any detail. Those establishments were distinguished by sites of generous dimensions (usually up to about 3.5 acres) facing on major avenues near the grounds of the imperial palace in the northeastern part of the city, and by a multiplicity of linked and independent structures that, together with their accompanying gardens and courtyards, accommodated the ceremonial and ritual, as well as the domestic, needs of government and clan leaders, and also produced residences that must have been as singularly pleasing to the eye as they were uncomfortable to the other senses.

Although there was considerable variation in detail among the great noble mansions, a basic identity of plan and function allows a description of one to serve as a guide to the others. For the present purpose, which is to observe the noble family in its physical context, the well-studied Ononomiya residence of Fujiwara no Sanesuke (957–1046) is particularly suitable: Sanesuke was powerful and wealthy enough to allow his family and residence to attain a maximum development, but he did not marry a daughter to an emperor, and the family structure and the functions of the residence were not complicated by the exceptional arrangements attendant on imperial marriages. His case, it may be reasonably assumed, was fairly typical of the senior nobility, except that he was wealthier than most, lived to be nearly ninety, and was not remarkably successful in the fathering of children.[18]

Ononomiya, at the peak of its development during Sanesuke's time, consisted of a main site roughly 400 feet square in the northeastern section of the city and additional adjacent pieces of property of unknown dimensions across the streets that bounded the site on four sides. It was a five- or ten-minute walk west from there to the nearest gate of the imperial palace and only two or three minutes longer in the opposite direction to Michinaga's famous Tsuchimikado mansion on the northeast.

The main site, which had come to Sanesuke from his grandfather

---

18 On Ononomiya and Sanesuke's family, see Yoshida Sanae, "Fujiwara no Sanesuke to Ononomiya-tei: shindenzukuri ni kan-suru ichikōsatsu," *Nihon rekishi* 350 (July 1977): 50–69, and "Fujiwara no Sanesuke no kazoku," *Nihon rekishi* 330 (November 1975): 69–85. Both studies are based mainly on Sanesuke's diary, *Shōyūki*, in part 10, vols. 1–11 of *Dai Nihon kokiroku* (Tokyo: Tokyo Daigaku Shiryō Hensanjo, 1959–86).

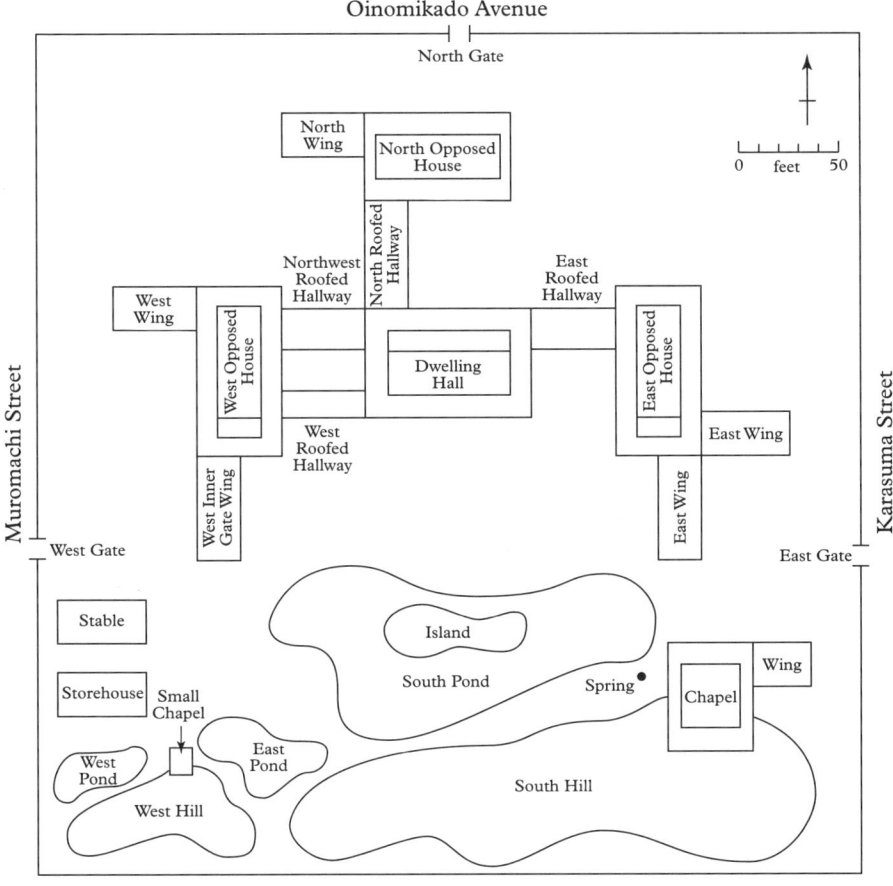

Figure 2.5. Plan of Ononomiya. Adapted from Yoshida Sanae, "Fujiwara no Sanesuke to Ononomiya-tei," p. 51.

and adoptive father, Saneyori, was developed over a period of about twenty-five years following a fire in 997 that destroyed most of the original structures. Sanesuke seems to have lived in the residences of his first two wives while they were alive, but within a few years of the death of the second wife in 998 he took up permanent residence at Ononomiya, never again formally marrying and moving to the residence of a principal wife.

The chief residential quarters, situated in the northern two-thirds of the square site, consisted eventually of a central "dwelling hall" and three adjacent "opposed houses" (*tai no ya*) on the east, west, and north, each connected with the dwelling hall across a space of about 40 or 45 feet by one, or, as in the western house, by two roofed hallways (*watadono*). Steps descended to the main courtyard from the southern of the two hallways leading to the western house, suggesting that the hallway there was open on the sides. The rectangular design of the opposed houses was the same as that of the dwelling hall, but each also included one (in the case of the northern house) or two (the eastern and western houses) rectangular wings ("corridors," *rō*) extending from corners of the structures at right angles. Since the houses are assumed to have faced the dwelling hall, as their name suggests, the wings are believed to have been on the sides of the houses away from the central structure.

The dwelling hall itself faced south toward a courtyard formed by the southern wings (*rō*) of the eastern and western houses. One or more apricot trees (*ume*, commonly misidentified as plum trees) grew in the courtyard, and south of there, occupying about a third of the entire site, were the man-made ponds and hills of an extensive garden. The largest of the ponds, broad enough to contain an island on which a banquet for a sizable group of people could be held, was directly south of the courtyard; the two smaller ponds seem to have been west and south of there, near the corner of the property. Two hills stood at the southern edge of the site, rising behind the ponds and providing for observers in the residential quarters displays of foliage and blossoms across the intervening water. The ponds were probably fed both by an irrigation stream brought in beneath the roofed hallway connecting the eastern opposed house to the dwelling hall and by a spring southeast of the largest pond.

The garden contained two Buddhist chapels, the larger one at the foot of the hill next to the spring southeast of the main pond, and the smaller apparently between the two ponds in the southwest corner. A stable and a building used for storage stood on the southwestern edge of the site, just inside a wall that encircled the entire property. There were three gates in the encircling wall, one each on the east, west, and north. The west gate, a relatively large, roofed passageway of the kind described as quadripedal (*yotsuashi*), was the main formal entrance to the site. Inside the west gate, at the southern end of the western house and its southern corridor wing, was another gate (the "inner gate," *chūmon*) leading into the courtyard south of the dwelling hall.

Such were the known major structures and features of the main Ononomiya site as they existed in about the year 1030. It was a large and handsome establishment, laid out and executed with a sophistication of taste and sensibility uncommon, surely, in the world of medieval domestic architecture. A source from the following century claimed that the mansion was kept in such beautiful repair that there was never a day when seven or eight carpenters were not busy there: the two places where one was always certain to hear the sound of adzes, the narrator in the source asserts, were the Tōdaiji Temple at Nara and the Ononomiya mansion. But it must be kept in mind that the spaciousness of the site did not necessarily result in commensurately spacious living quarters for the inhabitants. The overall dimensions of the largest structure measured perhaps 80 by 50 feet; the opposed houses on the east and west were probably about 80 by 40 feet; and the northern opposed house approximately 70 by 40 feet. (All of those measurements are rough estimates.) The total floor space in the main buildings thus amounted to something over 13,000 square feet, and the hallways and corridors wings may have added another 5,000 to 6,000, a grand total of nearly 19,000 square feet of usable space.

Lower-ranking nobles lived in much less spacious surroundings than those of Sanesuke, of course. A will from the end of the eleventh century, for example, seems to show that the main residence of an otherwise unknown but obviously wealthy man named Ōe no Kiminaka was crowded onto eight house lots of one of his three large properties in Heian (each listed at one *chō,* or about 3.5 acres). The property on which the main residence stood also included in its other sections a library, which would have been especially appropriate for a member of the learned Ōe family, and a chapel.[19]

The physical traces of another more humble, probably noble, establishment were revealed at the time of the reconstruction of a Kyoto high school in 1979. Located in the northeastern corner of Heian, the site showed in excavation the outline of a rectangular main hall about 21 by 16 meters, with two smaller buildings on either side and another at the rear. The plan seems to represent the *shindenzukuri* design at an incipient stage.[20]

The Ononomiya compound, in addition to its chief half-dozen or so inhabitants, also housed, temporarily or permanently, ladies-in-waiting, servants, and miscellaneous workers and hangers-on, so

19 Yoshioka, "Kizoku shakai no seijuku," pp. 134–36.
20 Yoshioka, "Kizoku shakai no seijuku," p. 137.

that the total twenty-four-hour population of the site may have been counted in three figures. There was, furthermore, a daily stream of visitors: kinsmen, court officials, and religious, who came at all hours of the day and night, often accompanied by their own companions and servants. Between the resident population and the visitors, the chambers, corridors, and wings of Ononomiya must have been constantly alive with what to modern sensibilities might seem veritable hordes of people.

The relatively high density of site population and the openness of interior space would have combined to produce a public style of living. Sleeping or waking, the individual was rarely if ever very far removed from companions, and the occasions when one was completely alone were probably exceptional indeed. Darkness, sleep, and curtains seem often to have been all that protected even a couple's sexual relations from kin and attendants in the same room. To be alone, or nearly so, at night in a dark building was enough to make even the bravest man feel the sharp talons of goblins snatching at him, or to frighten a timid girl quite literally to death.

Large numbers of people living together in a relatively limited space with little provision or opportunity for privacy may have created two partially contradictory tendencies in the personal relationships of family members. On the one hand, the frequency and intimacy of association may have helped strengthen certain ties, especially those with personal attendants, who sometimes were also family kin or related through fosterage. (The child of a wet nurse might become a personal attendant of its mother's nursling.) Sanesuke's diary is too impersonal a document to provide examples of such relationships, but contemporary fiction contains frequent instances suggesting that the degree of intimacy (if not its precise nature) approached what a modern observer might expect to find between congenial siblings. On the other hand, the multifariousness of relationships within a very large household, the strength of particular ties with household members outside the family nucleus, and the absence of a special nourishing privacy for relationships among nuclear family members would have presumably diffused and somewhat weakened affective relationships between nuclear members themselves. It may be noteworthy that in a society where genealogy and kinship played such decisive roles there was not a single word or customary phase in the spoken language that designated the nuclear (or elementary) family (parents and their unmarried children).

Nuclear family relationships may have been further weakened by the practice of wet-nursing, which appears to have been nearly universal among at least the more exalted noble households; few if any ladies of distinction ever suckled their own children even for the briefest period. The practice differed radically, however, from a form of it found at one time in Europe, where a newborn infant of the wealthier classes might be sent away to a poor, usually peasant, household for one or two years of nursing by a woman whose poverty, ignorance, and inattention seems frequently enough to have led to the infant's death. The Heian custom was to select one or more wet nurses for an infant from among women of relatively good birth (often from Fifth-Rank families) and, if she was not already in service at the house, to bring the nurse (or nurses) there, where she might then remain more or less indefinitely, even after her charge had been weaned. The natural mother was not physically separated from her child, but her relationship with it would have usually been weakened, one must suppose, insofar as she delegated nursing and care to another woman. There was no doubt a good deal of individual variation in the degree of maternal responsibility delegated to a nurse, ranging from simply a year or two of breast-feeding on up to what may have amounted at times to a nearly complete surrender of maternal duties, but the overall tendency would have been toward some loosening, at least, of the link between a child and its natural mother.

Nuclear family ties were similarly affected by the presence in the household of other close relatives, regularly a daughter's husband (the son-in-law) and her children (the grandchildren), but also occasionally, according to individual circumstances, a brother or sister of one of the parents. In such cases, however, the effect on nuclear relationships may have been slight, since the nonnuclear kin are known sometimes to have lived in subhouseholds in detached or semidetached buildings. For example, when Sanesuke's daughter Chifuru married in 1029, she and her husband lived together in the eastern opposed house at Ononomiya, which had its own household offices and kitchen in the corridor wings and was probably also equipped to function otherwise as at least a semiindependent establishment. When Sanesuke's sister moved to Ononomiya in 1005, she was not housed at the main site but in the Western Residence, which lay across the street bounding the site on the west. That residence also presumably functioned more or less independently of the residential quarters of Sanesuke's immediate family.

The ties of the nuclear family could be further loosened by the practice of polygyny. Sanesuke, like many or most Heian noblemen, seems to have been formally married to only one wife at a time, but some, like Michinaga, had two wives, and it was common for men to have continuing relations with women other than their principal and secondary wives, either within or outside their own households. All such relations, but especially with a secondary wife in a separate household, would have reduced the frequency of association between a man and his principal wife and between him and their children, leading ordinarily to some weakening of nuclear family relationships.

Early mortality had the same general effect, limiting the lifespan of a nuclear family and reducing the measure of common history and association that lies at the base of personal relationships. In Heian noble society, where social violence was relatively rare and warfare almost unknown, the chief danger to parental life apart from disease was probably childbirth, and it was therefore the link with the wife and the mother that was most likely to be severed by early death. Although statistics are lacking, the frequency with which death in, or shortly following, childbirth appears in the literature and sources of the period suggests that at the very least a large proportion of all marriages ended in that fashion. This, taken together with the undoubtedly high mortality rate from disease, may mean that it was the exception for a husband and wife in their first marriage to live beyond their twenties together. For instance, Sanesuke's first marriage ended with the death of his wife in 986 shortly after the birth of their first child, in the twelfth or thirteenth year of the marriage, when Sanesuke was twenty-nine. Had the wife borne a child earlier, there is an excellent chance that the marriage would have lasted no longer than Sanesuke's second marriage, which was brought to an end in its fifth year by the death of his wife. Sanesuke also had two children by a woman who may have been in the service of his sister; she, too, died shortly after the birth of her second infant, which had died immediately after birth.

Such personal histories may have been more nearly the rule than the exception, and a child probably had to count itself fortunate if it reached adolescence with even one parent alive. Since the death of young women in childbirth was so common as to be almost normal, and since childhood mortality was especially high, the Heian noble child also often found itself with neither a natural mother nor any full siblings. Many children, and perhaps a majority, lived for longer or shorter periods of their lives in foster or adoptive families, or became stepchildren in the household of a remarried surviving parent.

It is entirely possible that the nuclear family as a rule was even less stable among the Heian nobility than it is in present-day societies, where the frequency of divorce may be at least partly a function of improved physical health and increased longevity. If stepchildren and adopted children are excluded, it may also be true that the Heian nuclear family was little larger than its counterpart today in Japan or the West: few Heian couples seem to have had more than two or three children who lived past infancy.

Finally, ties within the family were probably also affected by the tendency of the Heian noble to change residences often. The divorce of residence from income and status, the relative simplicity and ephemerality of the noble house, and the prevailing pattern of marital residence led to a high degree of residential mobility within the narrow confines of the capital city. A great nobleman like Michinaga or Sanesuke was likely to live in a succession of houses as one marriage followed another, new houses were acquired by purchase or transfer, and fire destroyed the old. Michinaga, for instance, owned or controlled seven houses in the capital, three acquired through his marital connections and four otherwise, and he had villas at Katsura (near the present Katsura Detached Palace) and Uji (on the site of the Byōdōin), in most of which he is known to have lived at one time or another. Fire, storm, and family vicissitude probably also made it rare even for a woman to reach old age in the house in which she was born and married. Such absences were occasioned by the interdictions of *yin-yang* lore,[21] by the requirements of official duty at court, by ceremonial or ritual functions at other noble households, by childbirth and its attendant ritual pollution, and sometimes simply by inclination. Although it is true that the range of physical movement was restricted, usually involving no more than a few hundred yards of travel and often simply a shift from one structure to another on the same property, the frequency of moves and absences from home and of new construction presumably contributed to at least some diffusion of personal relationships outside the household and a corresponding loosening within. That process would not, however, have affected the two sexes equally. Since the woman was far less likely to move or to absent herself from home than the man, the overall effect must have been to reinforce the uxorilocal nature of many households by centering the closest, most intense personal ties on women.

---

21 See Bernard Frank, *Kata-imi et kata-tagae: Étude sur les interdits de direction à l'époque Heian*, Bulletin de la Maison Franco-Japonaise, Nouvelle Série, Tome 5, 2–4 (Tokyo and Paris, 1958).

The foregoing suggests there were circumstances in Heian noble society tending toward a diffusion of affective ties away from the nuclear family and a weakening of relationships within it. There is also at least one small piece of objective evidence that may confirm the existence of that tendency with respect to children. The death of a Heian noble adult was marked by a considerable amount of ceremony and ritual leading to and following the cremation or interment of the body. However, when children under eight calendar years of age died, parents were advised by experts in such matters that the proper course was simply to abandon the body in the open, which seems to have been a frequent practice among commoners even in the case of adults. References in contemporary sources to the abandonment of children's corpses are frequent enough to indicate that the practice was commonly observed. The high rate of childhood mortality undoubtedly argued in favor of a simple, inexpensive method of disposing of the corpses, and in an age accustomed to the sights and smells of death and mostly unacquainted with the origins of disease, abandonment in the open may have seemed the simplest and most practical means available. But the custom seems to imply, nevertheless, a certain callousness toward, or distance from, children, a view of them as somehow less important or less human than the adults who were sent off with elaborate obsequies and mourning.

It seems legitimate to conclude that, generally speaking, the affective ties of the Heian noble with members of his immediate family were neither so strong nor so enduring as those among members of a reasonably successful modern family in Japan or the West, and that those ties were therefore more easily severed or shared than they usually are nowadays. The implications were not usually quite the same as they would be for modern family members when, for example, a Heian spouse ended a marriage by taking holy orders or by divorce, or when a husband took a secondary wife, or when a son left his family to live at his bride's house, or when a child was given up for adoption. The break may often have been more easily accomplished at that time than now, the sharing more willingly undertaken.

One should not infer from this, of course, that nuclear family relations were unimportant in the practical or emotional life of the Heian noble. Although a noble husband and wife seem normally to have been less closely bound by association and affection to each other and to their children than we like to think the modern married couple should be, there was usually no other set of relationships that was of comparable strength. For most people of that age and class the deepest and most durable emotional ties were still undoubtedly within the confines of the immediate family. In individual cases, moreover, the bond between husband and wife or between parent and child was as strong as any such relationship commonly is in the modern family. Or so, at least, the contemporary literature tells us and some of the historical sources suggest. We may perhaps infer from Sanesuke's diary, for instance, that he was strongly attached to his first wife, whom he married when he was sixteen and lived with for twelve or thirteen years. Although the diary, as usual, says nothing about the author's personal feelings at the time of his wife's death in 986, it does reveal that he continued to hold annual mourning services on the date of her death for many years thereafter, evidence perhaps of an uncommon degree of devotion (or fear of the spirit of the deceased?). Sanesuke was even more deeply attached to a daughter he had by a woman who had been in the service of his second wife. He was in his mid-fifties when the daughter, Chifuru, was born, childless except for adopted children and a clerical son in whom he had never evinced much interest, and he seems to have poured all of his thwarted parental affection into his daughter's care and upbringing. He kept her with him constantly, took her on outings, catered seemingly to her every whim, reconstructed and refurbished the eastern opposed house at Ononomiya for her marriage, and willed both Onomomiya and most of the rest of his estate to her. There is no indication in any of this that he ever considered using Chifuru to further his own political ambitions at court. Her mother's relatively low birth may have made hopes for an imperial marriage impractical in any case, and for a man in Sanesuke's high position (he was Minister of the Right during most of her life), there was no other marital alliance that could have been of much interest to him. Unhappily, he outlived that daughter, too: she died at about the age of twenty-seven, when he was eighty-one, leaving behind a two-year-old daughter who eventually inherited Onomomiya.

The literary and quasi-historical sources for the period frequently describe domestic scenes that would entirely agree with what can be seen in, and inferred from, Sanesuke's diary: a husband and wife in free and affectionate converse about their everyday lives; a fond father holding his infant daughter and being amused when his clothes are wet by her; a father playing horse with his little son; a mother moved to tears by the beauty of her children; sisters assisting each other in the conduct of love affairs; or the searing grief caused by a death in the family, including that of an infant or small child. The affective ties between parent and daughter seem to have been especially strong, and Sanesuke's devotion to Chifuru may also in that respect be regarded as typical of noble family relationships.

The ways in which space was employed at Ononomiya were also inevitably related to human relations there. Each area of the establishment tended to be associated with particular functions, although the functional definitions of space were neither so detailed nor so strictly applied as one might find in the great houses of the wealthy in recent times, where many or most rooms may be reserved individually for some one particular activity or purpose: dining, breakfasting, gaming, dancing, sleeping, reading, and so on. At Ononomiya, the main functional divisions had to do with whether space was chiefly employed for everyday private living or for the more public and ceremonial or ritual aspects of life. At the same time, in limited areas of the establishment, space was also defined by fairly specific functional criteria. The division of space into public and private parts mostly concerned the principal family members; the more specific functional divisions mainly involved the household staff.

The greatest part of the main site at Ononomiya was reserved for the use of Sanesuke and the members of his family. The space allotted for that purpose consisted of the dwelling hall, all of the opposed houses, the corridor wing extending south from the western opposed house, and one or both of the hallways connecting that house with the dwelling hall.

The central chamber and the northern and eastern eave chambers of the dwelling hall, together with the opposed houses on the east and north, were used by family members for everyday living, but beyond that minimal definition the space was not, for the most part, further differentiated by function: the inhabitants slept, ate, and pursued most of the activities of their waking hours in the same undifferentiated areas. Latrine arrangements of the period are not well understood, but since there were servants responsible for the removal and cleaning of pots of human waste, perhaps those needs, too, were often or usually met in the regular living quarters. The central chamber of Sanesuke's dwelling hall included a walled room that was probably used for storage or possibly as sleeping quarters, but commonly in noble residences, the chief inhabitant or inhabitants slept on a slightly raised movable platform enclosed simply by curtains and blinds suspended on a lightly constructed frame, and the attendant ladies-in-waiting slept nearby on the floor. In the normal course of affairs, the only visitors to the living quarters seem to have been close relatives, one's official subordinates, and household retainers, attendants, and servants. However, in the case of a highly placed man like Sanesuke, whose household was large and to whom almost everyone else in the government was subordinate, that group was very numerous.

Although Sanesuke was at one with his modestly reticent age in not mentioning the details of his sexual life, it appears that none of his mistresses or secondary wives ever shared the dwelling hall with him as a permanent resident after he took up residence at Ononomiya. The mother of his daughter Chifuru may have lived in the northern opposed house, which is thought to have been a common location for the quarters of noble wives, who were therefore generally removed from the scene of social intercourse centering on their husbands in the dwelling hall. Such women, moreover, had far less occasion than their husbands did to venture forth from their houses. The chief centers of social intercourse among Heian nobles were the imperial court and the mansions of the leading court figures, and since noble wives did not normally participate in the life of the court or visit other residences, they remained perforce for the most part in their own living quarters among their children, ladies-in-waiting, and servants. An occasional pilgrimage to a Buddhist temple or a Shinto shrine, an outing to witness a festival procession through the streets of the capital, transfer to another residence for childbirth, a visit to a parent or sister, and in rare cases a trip to the imperial court at the time of a daughter's marriage to an emperor – such limited occasions constituted the bulk of the usual noblewoman's experience of the outer world. The eleventh-century tale that describes a noble girl alone in the streets of Kyoto and unable to find her way to her own nearby house may not be a wholly fanciful representation of contemporary female knowledge of the world outside the home gates.

As a small child, Sanesuke's daughter Chifuru seems to have occupied the eastern eave chamber of the dwelling hall (she lived, in other words, in the same building with her father), but when she grew up, she moved to the eastern opposed house and after her marriage continued living there and in one of the house's corridor wings with her husband and daughter. How living space was shared in the house and wing is unknown, but the general lack of functional differentiation remained no doubt very much the same as in the dwelling hall. A common development would have been the removal of Chifuru's family to the dwelling hall upon the death, retirement, or entry into holy orders of Sanesuke, but that was forestalled by Chifuru's early demise and Sanesuke's long life. Chifuru's husband returned to his father's house for a while after her death but came back to live again in the eastern house with his and Chifuru's small daughter, who had probably remained there during his absence. He had been only thirteen or so when he married Chifuru in about 1029, five years younger than his wife, and he had lived at Ononomiya with her for nearly ten years. How much longer he remained at the mansion is unknown, but circumstantial evidence suggests that his residence may have been more or less indefinite.

The northwest corner of the northern opposed house is known to have been the residence of one of Sanesuke's five adopted sons, and others of those five may have also lived there until they married. As already noted, the northern house is thought to have commonly been occupied by a man's principal wife and by her small children, but circumstances frequently altered that arrangement. Sanesuke himself, for instance, lived for a while in the northern house at Ononomiya while his dwelling hall was under construction.

The remainder of the family space at the main site (i.e., the southern and western eave chambers of the dwelling hall, and the western opposed house and its southern wing and hallway) appears to have been used chiefly for formal occasions, such as the reception of an imperial envoy or one of the many *rites de passage* that marked the life of a great noble family. The chief ceremonial entrance to the estate was the western gate, the side nearest the imperial palace, and it may have been because of that geographical circumstance that the western side of noble houses generally was often the place where receptions were held and ceremonies conducted, most such houses having been, like Ononomiya, located east of the palace. On very great occasions, such as the visit of an emperor, the marriage of a daughter, or the celebration of a major Buddhist ritual, the central chamber of the dwelling hall might also be used. At Ononomiya, the rites and ceremonies held in the public space were not only for members of the immediate family but for more distant kin as well.

It was in the corridor wings (*rō*) of the opposed houses that the function of space seems to have been given its narrowest definition. There were located the offices and work areas of the household staff: the attendants' office (*saburaidokoro*), the escorts' office (*zuijindokoro*), the administrative office (*mandokoro*), the repairs office (*shuridokoro*), the servants' office (*zōshikidokoro*), the pages' office (*kodoneridokoro*), the kitchens (*daibandokoro*), and the pantry (*zen-*

sho). The eastern opposed house had its own separate kitchen and attendants' offices, and probably some of the other offices as well. If Sanesuke had had a principal wife living in the northern opposed house, she, too, might have had some of her own separate offices.

Sanesuke tells us little about the roofed hallways (*watadono*) connecting his dwelling hall to the opposed houses, but if their use was similar to that of hallways in other noble mansions, they functioned not only as passageways between the buildings but also, suitably outfitted with screens and curtains, as the living quarters of the mansion's ladies-in-waiting.

The ponds and gardens occupying the southern part of the property seem to have been designed largely for the pleasures of contemplation and strolling. Sanesuke, like others of his noble contemporaries, also personally participated in the layout, construction, and upkeep of his garden, and he frequently took his ease there, especially, on hot days, near the spring at the southeastern corner of the largest pond. The garden also occasionally became an extension of the formal space at Ononomiya, serving as the site for a banquet or some other type of entertainment. Sanesuke, to judge by his diary, seems to have been little interested in the more vigorous kinds of amusements, but at other mansions of the aristocracy the courtyard immediately south of the dwelling hall was sometimes the site of cockfighting or kickball (*kemari*). At Michinaga's establishment, for instance, part of the garden was given over to a horseracing course.

The Buddhist chapels in the garden were devoted, of course, to religious purposes, but not exclusively so. The larger chapel near the spring had quarters for the chapel monks in a corridor wing and had its own kitchen and bathing facilities, functioning thus independently of the main buildings. Perhaps because of the nearby spring and the pleasant surroundings, Sanesuke spent considerable time at the chapel, using it as an extension of his regular living space and sometimes taking his meals there. It is possible that the building also served as a library. That would explain the absence of any mention of a library in Sanesuke's diary, although he was a learned man, and men of far lesser means than he managed to maintain a separate library building in their gardens.

A twelfth-century source gives particular attention to the larger Buddhist chapel in a description of Ononomiya narrated by a fictional contemporary of Sanesuke's:

The mansion [Sanesuke] has erected is a splendid sight. Wings, a main hall, and galleries are common enough, but he also has a Buddha Hall to the southeast, three bays long on each of its four sides, with monks' quarters in all the corridors. The monks' bathhouse is furnished with two huge three-legged cauldrons, plastered with earth, under which fires are lighted every day. In the Buddha Hall itself, there are innumerable golden images, and the receptacles in front of them always contain thirty *koku* [about sixty bushels] of rice. People walk to the Buddha Hall from the front lake, following a path through a great park laid out to resemble a wild meadow, which is filled with trees and plants chosen for their seasonal flowers and autumn color – or else they can row across the lake. Those are the only ways of approaching it. Every one of the monks is either a distinguished scholar, a special sutra chanter, or an expert in the mystic Shingon rites. Sanesuke gives them summer and winter vestments and sustenance allowances, and tells them to pray for the extinction of his sins, the growth of his virtues, and the safety of Her Ladyship his daughter.[22]

Although relatively little is known about the subsidiary Ononomiya properties across the streets bounding the main site on four sides, they seem to have had two distinct uses. The properties on the west and north – referred to sometimes by Sanesuke as the Western Hall (*nishidono*) and the Northern Residence (*hokutaku*) – seem to have been reserved for use by members of the family as occasion required. Sanesuke himself and Chifuru and her husband made some use of the Western Hall, but it seems to have been occupied chiefly by, first, Sanesuke's sister, then by a nephew (an elder brother's son), after whose marriage it may have been used by one or more of Sanesuke's five adopted sons, all of whom were sons or grandsons of his two elder brothers. All that is known about the Northern Residence is that Sanesuke ceded it to his adopted son Sukehira. The properties on the east and south contained, on the other hand, dwellings of household staff members and perhaps also the storehouses, kitchens, and workshops that seem commonly to have been grouped together in great mansions in a separate area of their own called the "storehouse row" (*mikuramachi*). The storehouses there and elsewhere in a noble establishment contained both the everyday necessities – food, cloth, clothing, paper, dyestuffs, household furniture, dishes, utensils, and so forth – and also various luxury items and treasures: aromatics, precious metals, religious statuary and paintings, Buddhist scriptures, medicines, ritual ware and objects, heirlooms, musical instruments, and the like. Workshops known to have been associated with noble mansions included those of seamsters, hatters, pictorial artists, lacquerworkers, carpenters, joiners, metalworkers, and metal

---

22 Helen Craig McCullough, trans., *Ōkagami, The Great Mirror: Fujiwara Michinaga and His Times* (Princeton, N.J.: Princeton University Press, 1980), p. 110.

casters, but not all of those were necessarily staffed with full-time artisans. Metal casters, for example, seem to have been called in only as the need arose.

OFFICIALDOM AND ITS FUNCTIONS

Although the great nobles in Sanesuke's elevated sphere of society – the Ministers of State (*daijin*), the Counselors (*nagon*), and the Consultants (*sangi*) – were the chief makers of governmental decisions and often prided themselves on their detailed knowledge of court procedures, ceremonies, and rituals, it was the nobles whose careers culminated at the Fourth or Fifth Rank who provided most of the workaday administrative direction of the governmental offices and much of the special knowledge and skills that fueled their operations. They were the working (as well, usually, as the titular) heads of the eight ministries that directed the activities of all central organs of the government under the Council of State. They were, as well, the chief officers in a host of other key administrative or technical offices and bureaus, including those responsible for the administration of the capital; the reception of foreign embassies; the computing, budgeting, and disbursement of government revenues; the construction and repair of public buildings; the supervision of the Academy of Chinese learning; divination, purification, and other matters relating to *yin-yang* arts; the management of Buddhist and Shinto affairs and of imperial mortuary matters; the maintenance of the imperial library; the teaching and performance of court music and dance; the direction of the hundreds of Imperial Attendants who saw to the domestic and personal needs of the court; house- and groundskeeping at the palace; medical treatment and the preparation of medicines; the supply of furniture and other crafted items to the court; and the provision of food and drink for official banquets. Their number also included the secretariat or principal staff for the Council of State and in the Chamberlains' Office; they held other pivotal posts, professional and administrative, in the various ministries, offices, and bureaus; and they sometimes attended in person on the emperor. It is perhaps not too much to say that most of the day-to-day practical work of the court and its government fell in the first instance on their shoulders.

During the first several decades of the Heian period, the roughly 95 percent of the capital's population that belonged to neither the princely nor the noble ranks was, nevertheless, largely official, and perhaps overwhelmingly so. Those were the people who occupied at the peaks of their careers one of the court ranks below the Sixth or worked in menial government jobs without court rank. The higher ranks of that large group included the heads of suboffices in charge of such matters as the imperial clan register, the East and West Markets, the two government prisons, the palace weavers, and various domestic or housekeeping tasks concerned with the emperor, the crown prince, or the palace (i.e., meals for the emperor or crown prince, drinking water, *sake* making, women servants in the imperial residential compound, the crown prince's stable and equestrian equipage, etc.). The middling and lower ranks held secretarial and subordinate administrative positions in the ministries or the higher offices and bureaus, and they shared with the higher ranks the many professional, technical, or skilled-labor posts that supported government operations and palace life. They were teachers of the various subjects at the Academy of Chinese learning (Chinese letters, Confucian classics, Chinese pronunciation, calligraphy, law, and mathematics), physicians, *yin-yang* practitioners, acupuncturists, astrologers, calendrical specialists, herbalists, healers by incantation, masseurs, veterinarians, musicians and dancers, painters, dyers, weavers of fancy silks, investigators and judges of crime, disbursing officers, storekeepers, and so forth. Below them and under the control and supervision of diverse superiors was the army of servants, guards, armed men, attendants, and laborers who supplied much of the skilled manual work in the palace and its organs, kept the watches and walked the patrols, and performed all the menial tasks. Most of the laborers, guards, and armed men seem to have been levied from the general population, but the servants and attendants were regularly recruited from among the children of officials.

By the mid-Heian period, however, a large part of the official class had disappeared; its income and duties had either vanished in the contraction of the statutory regime or been absorbed by superior offices. The Seventh and lower ranks seem rarely, if ever, to have been used anymore, and many offices either ceased to exist or remained as little more than paper organizations. Government workshops closed or curtailed operations, and the great number of menials, laborers, and guards that had once populated the palace seem to have been sharply reduced, leaving many palace buildings outside the residential compound uncared for and unprotected. The absence of guards at most of the palace gates (especially at night) gave free run of the grounds to arsonists and robbers, and even the personal safety of the courtiers was no longer assured.

The shrinkage of the official class probably resulted in the departure from the capital of large numbers of people, especially those who had been brought in on labor levies, most of whom presumably returned to their rural homes and were not replaced, but also some of whom were descendants of court-rank officials who failed to obtain substitute employment in the city and found themselves forced to seek their fortunes elsewhere. Key segments of the class remained, however, and contributed importantly to the diversification of the general, non-noble and nonofficial population, which toward the date of the city's founding had been small and also, in contrast with the highly diversified noble and official population, fairly uniform in composition. The largest part of the early general population may have consisted of the swarms of servants and laborers employed by the great princely houses, the nobility, and the more elevated members of the official class. A few other elements can also be identified or surmised to have existed, including a scattering of artisans and skilled laborers, who for the most part do not appear in the sources but must have been available to some extent for private construction and other similar needs in the city (some or most may have been moonlighters from the palace); a small group of merchants, to whom we shall return; and a priestly class, which was very small within the city proper, confined mostly to the Buddhist monks at the East and West Temples, but considerably larger if the many Shinto shrines and the growing number of Buddhist temples in the immediate neighborhood of Heian are taken into account.

THE CITY'S ECONOMY

The relative uniformity of the general population in early Heian was a product of the city's peculiar economy which, in its nearly complete dependence on the court and the government, was more like that of a large military base than of a fully evolved city. As a purely political center of administration, Heian was almost exclusively a city of consumers, drawing into itself the produce, manufactures, and labor of the countryside; sending back little in return except orders, officials, and superfluous members of its own society; and producing solely (or virtually so) for its own uses.

The city's basic source of income was governmental tax revenues in kind and labor levies, which supplied in themselves through the individual incomes of princely personages, nobles, and officials most of the goods and services required by the population. A description of the early city economy becomes therefore primarily an account of the distribution of income.

Under the statutory system, all holders of rank and office received varying amounts of goods and services according to their particular ranks and offices. The system was complex in detail and underwent numerous modifications, but in outline there were three primary categories of payment. For the noble ranks and offices and for certain specialists (physicians, *yin-yang* experts, teachers at the Academy of Chinese learning, etc.), the tax revenues from specified amounts of land or from specified numbers of households were assigned to the holders of the ranks and offices. Those revenues consisted of handicraft items (especially cloth) as well as rice and other food products. A second type of payment, again for the noble and princely ranks only, consisted of specified numbers of household officials, servants, and guards, provided in part through the government's labor levies. Finally, all levels of officials received outright stipends paid from the government's treasuries in cloth, iron implements, salt, rice, other foods, and at times limited amounts of cash. (There were twelve small mintings of primarily copper coins in Japan, the last in 958; by the twelfth century, the chief currency was Chinese copper cash.)

The income received by great nobles and the leading princely personages was very large, supplemented sometimes by special grants of land from the emperor, by privately acquired landholdings, and, in the tenth century and after, also by commended *shōen,* the revenues from all of which would similarly have been in goods and services. The ordinary noble was also amply rewarded, receiving enough, it is thought, to support comfortably many or most of the families in his clan. The large incomes of the nobility and the princely houses were used in substantial part to employ the great numbers of servants, laborers, nurses, guards, estate managers, and so on, that high social position both required and made possible. The pay received by such dependents would, of course, have also usually been in goods.

Most of the early population of Heian therefore received many or most of the necessities of life directly in their incomes and not through commerce. Residents at that time also held capitatum tillages (*kubunden*) from which they derived income in kind. The income of many at the lower levels of the economy may have been further supplemented by small vegetable gardens and by fishing and hunting on the outskirts of the capital. Some residents of the city also cultivated rice and barley fields immediately adjacent to the city or on vacant city land.

Although the early economy of Heian functioned primarily on income in kind or in labor, not all needs could be met for all people through their incomes alone, and a certain amount of commerce was thus provided for at the East and West Markets. The only places in the capital where trading was permitted, the markets were closely supervised and regulated by a special organ of the city administration, the Market Office, which fixed prices, weights, and measurements, determined the types of goods to be sold in the markets, and controlled merchant access, only those merchants registered by the Market Office and living in the market area being permitted to trade there. The markets were periodic, but since they alternated with each other at half-monthly intervals, one or the other was always open for business.

Both markets, East and West, were subdivided into shop areas (*ichikura*), each of which was devoted to a single kind of merchandise.[23] There was one and only one shop area for each kind of good offered in the market, and every area was required to display a sign indicating what was sold there. The number of shop areas and the types of goods sold at the time of the founding of the city are unknown, but a century later sixty-seven different kinds were provided for in official regulations. Some were common to the two markets and some were restricted to one or the other, so that, with duplications excluded, the total number of shop areas in both markets was eighty-four: fifty-one in the East and thirty-three in the West. Most goods sold were fairly practical items: food (rice, barley, salt, bean paste, a kind of vermicelli, fruits and nuts, seaweed, pungent bulbs, sweet gluten, etc.); many types of cloth, clothing, and dyestuffs; tools and implements of various sorts (combs, needles, writing brushes, charcoal ink, iron and gold implements, lacquerware, wooden implements, pottery); transport animals (horses and oxen); oils; and equestrian gear. But there were also shops specializing in less humdrum goods, such as jewels (pearls and jade), weapons and armor (swords, bows, arrows, etc.), medicines and medicinal ingredients

---

23 Abe Takashi, "Heiankyō no keizai kōzō," in Itō Tasaburō, ed., *Kokumin seikatsu shi kenkyū*, vol. 2: *Seikatsu to shakai keizai* (Tokyo: Yoshikawa kōbunkan, 1959), p. 74, shows that *ichikura* did not refer to "shop" or "stall," as often thought, but to an area of stalls or shops dealing in the same kind of goods.

(herbs, cinnabar, etc.), and aromatics. The goods sold in the markets came mainly, no doubt, from surplus governmental and private incomes in the city, but also apparently to a certain extent from individual producers and merchant suppliers who began to appear in the market area and on the outskirts of Heian, and perhaps also from foreign trade. Some cash circulated in the markets during the ninth and tenth centuries while the government was still minting coins, but even then the chief means of trade was undoubtedly barter.

In the quest for recognition as a civilized society by the seemingly advanced countries of the adjacent continent, Japanese leaders followed the example of Korea and China in minting the government's own coinage, despite the apparent absence of a vigorous domestic commerce in need of money currency. The leaders also probably hoped thereby not only to encourage and facilitate such commerce as existed, but perhaps as well to reap the profits that currency manipulation made possible. The first minting was the well-known Wadō kaihō coin of 708, which was produced just seven years after the adoption of the Taihō code of 701. Eleven new coins followed in the next two and a half centuries (until 958), eight of them during the Heian years. Minting at various places but mainly in copper-producing regions like Suō and Nagato, they were mostly made of brass, but some were silver, and there was one gold coin, the Kaiki shōhō coin of 760.

The coins were legally valued at more than the worth of their metallic content. At the time of new mintings they were also customarily exchanged at the rate of one new coin for ten old coins, the result being that the authorities experienced considerable difficulty in getting them accepted, resorting frequently to fiats and rewards directed toward that purpose. Their cause was not helped, one assumes, as the coins were steadily debased in the ninth century, becoming smaller and lighter, with more lead and less tin, and eventually what were in effect lead coins. Gresham's law no doubt led to the hoarding of more valuable coins, and despite draconian measures against it, private minting was also practiced, further confusing an already chaotic currency situation. The government seems to have tried to regain control of the currency by its frequent minting of new coins, and also by reducing the disparity between the legal value of the coinage and its actual metallic worth. But despite all efforts, the coins fell rapidly out of use after the last minting in 958, replaced in the late Heian period by imports of Chinese coins, especially the copper coins of Northern Sung.

The government used coins in its own transactions and in payment of its obligations, and the coins also circulated publicly, mainly in the Heian region, but also to some extent in the outer provinces, where they were sometimes hoarded as treasure or treated as magical objects. The currency of trade in the Heian markets was a mixed affair, the trade relying at times on straight barter, at other times on values expressed in units of rice or fabrics, and at other times partly on cash, either Japanese or Chinese.

The relatively uniform nature of the economy and of the general population in the early part of the period was an obvious consequence of the origins of Heian, a city thrust on a rural landscape practically overnight to serve a single, wholly political purpose. But even as the Heian palace was being built, the statutory regime it was intended to serve was changing, and the pace and depth of the change only intensified in the following century, soon leading to correspondingly major alterations in the capital's economy and population. The main economic changes were a contraction of government revenues and the growth in importance among the nobility of private or quasi-private sources of income, chiefly directly owned land; gifts of goods and labor made by wealthy provincial governors to leading nobles; and dues from people and land under tax protection by noble houses, the protected people sometimes very likely including merchants and artisans. The most notable population changes were the radical reduction in the size of the official class already mentioned and a diversification of the general population, in part a consequence of the diminished fortunes of the government.

As the government experienced increasing difficulty in collecting revenues and levying labor in the quantity and kind called for by statutory law, it tended to concentrate its remaining resources in the imperial family and the senior nobility, leaving the ordinary nobility in what were often perilous financial straits and completely depriving the greater part of officialdom of any income at all. To survive in the capital, it became necessary for the ordinary nobles and officials to attach themselves in some fashion to the senior nobles, the chief source of disposable income in the city outside the government itself. At the same time, as the wealth of the senior nobility – and especially that of the Fujiwara regents and their kin – grew, and as their economic affairs were made more complex by the acquisition of *shōen* and possibly other types of private income-producing rights and property, their mansions increasingly demanded larger and more professional household administrative staffs. We find, consequently, that by the eleventh century some considerable part of the ordinary nobility and the upper officialdom had been converted into at least partial dependents of senior nobles, and especially of the regents. Some became formal members of senior-noble households, where they served with appropriate administrative titles on a regular basis, tending to the wide range of economic, political, religious, ceremonial, ritual, domestic, and personal business that occupied a great noble house. Others served noble patrons in such particular professions as the *yin-yang* arts, calligraphy, Chinese learning, the healing arts, or the like, while many ordinary nobles simply attended on the comings and goings of senior nobles, participated in their ceremonies, rituals, and religious observances, and played the courtier at their festivities, for all of which rewards were regularly received (commonly, silk fabrics or wadding, sets of costly female robes, and horses – clothing and horses also being the items that seem to have most attracted Heian robbers). If it was the privilege of a leading noble to monopolize the more lucrative ranks and posts and to be the recipient of gifts from those seeking his favor, it was also his obligation to be generous in his treatment of the men and women who served and attended on him.

Since most of the officials and ordinary nobles patronized by, or in the service of, senior nobles continued to hold government titles and ranks entailing some official duties, they are perhaps better thought of as intermediate in social and economic status, neither strictly government officeholders nor entirely private persons. The same may be said of another important element of the population that was making a similar transition from public to private status in the mid-Heian period: the artisan or skilled-labor class. We know by inference – and from the Heian *sake* brewers whose vats were sealed in 806 because of a drought-induced inflation of rice prices – that even in the early years of the city's history a certain amount of private industry and skilled labor existed to meet everyday needs of the population that were not supplied in their incomes or through their own labor, but it was at the palace and in its workshops that industry, and especially the more skilled forms of industry, appears to have been concentrated. There were found the makers of most of the material culture of the Heian court: the furnishings and draperies for palace chambers, utensils of all types and materials (lacquer, silver, bamboo, pottery, wood, etc.), weapons, tools and implements, palanquins and carriages, balls and clay dolls, cloth and clothing, roof tiles, paintings, paper and writing materials, and so on in an almost endless list. And when nobles had need of specially crafted objects, it was (fiction from the ninth and tenth centuries tells us) to the palace artisans that they sometimes turned, supplying them with the necessary materials and rewarding them for their work.

By the beginning of the tenth century, the number of palace artisans had been drastically reduced, perhaps by as much as half or more. The chief causes of the reduction were probably declining governmental revenues (including a diminished supply of the materials used in the workshops) and the avoidance of, or flight from, palace duty by artisans who were finding more favorable working conditions at or under the protection of great noble and princely houses. By the eleventh century the wealthier households of princely personages and senior nobles (especially the regents) regularly included a number of artisans and workshops. The artisans, it is thought, came mostly from government shops or traced their lineages to government artisans, and some at least may still have been formally liable for duty at the palace. The weavers of fancy silks, for instance, remained in the service of the palace perhaps longer than any other artisans, preserving a monopoly of their trade until the middle of the eleventh century, but already in 1013 one of their number was working concurrently in the household of a near-prince. Few if any such workers achieved autonomous status during the period, however, since an artisan still had to be attached to the palace, to a noble or princely house, or to a temple or shrine in order to receive the support and protection that made his work possible or profitable. His first duty, therefore, was to meet the requirements of his patron or patrons, but beyond that his work could be, and perhaps often was, for the market.

The emergence of the artisan from the palace was very likely among both the causes and effects of the more open market and the expanded scope of commercial operations that had developed by the eleventh century. The market by then had long ceased to be the minutely regulated, carefully controlled institution the government had sought to impose on the city at its founding. The simple dynamics of urban life, with its constantly shifting social and economic patterns, almost immediately generated powerful forces for change in the rigid concept of commerce embodied in the East and West Markets. The trend was toward decreased interference in, and control of, the market by the government and significant overall expansion of commerce, leading eventually in the twelfth century to the emergence of the characteristic form of medieval market organization, the guild.

The official market system was already in trouble by 835, when the government was forced to take steps to shore up the faltering West Market. Its location in the sparsely populated western half of the city seems to have affected its fortunes from the outset, and evidence of near anarchic conditions in the markets suggests that even at that early date the government's control of them may have been tenuous at best. Thirty years later, the Market Office reported to the Council of State that merchants were placing themselves under the protection of princely personages and nobles, forming "gangs" (*shūrui,* possibly a forerunner of the guild) and running roughshod over the officials. Attempts were still being made at the beginning of the tenth century to control trade and to restrict it to the official markets, but by then, or certainly not long afterward, such attempts had become largely futile, and private need or convenience was probably the chief determinant of the content, the location, and the agents of trade in the city.

No doubt the government's inability to maintain the official market system was generally the result of its own growing weakness and the opposing strength of more or less natural market forces; but one specific factor also must have contributed greatly to the process. That was the government's loss of control over the bulk of the goods moving in commerce in the capital. Under the statutory system, as we have seen, most of the identifiable wealth entering Heian during its early years came in the form of governmental revenues. It was the surplus from those revenues and the surplus production of the government's own workshops that are thought to have constituted, in one way or another, the major part of the goods traded in the official markets. The shrinkage of revenues and the curtailment of operations in government workshops in the ninth and tenth centuries must have entailed, therefore, an at least proportionate contraction in the quantity of official goods in the market. At about the same time, there seems to have been a marked increase of goods in private trade, coming chiefly from the growing private incomes of the nobility (including goods imported from the continent); from the riches brought or sent to the capital by provincial administrators; from the provincial gentry to whom much of the government's former revenues had been transferred; and from the emerging class of semiautonomous artisans. In short, merchants were no longer so heavily dependent on the government for the goods of their business, and control of their activities was neither so advantageous to the court nor so readily accomplished.

The collapse of the official market system seems to have been accompanied by an expansion of commerce in the city, marked in the tenth century by a tripling of the physical area of the markets themselves and in the following century by the growth of commerce and industry in areas outside the markets. The latter development had already led by the middle of the eleventh century to the appearance of several new street names that probably derived from local concentrations of merchants and artisans in the southeastern part of the city, names like Salt Street, Oil Street, Needle Street, Brocade Street, and Damask Street. The official markets were converted to private ownership and disappeared in all but name during the course of the twelfth century, the chief commercial and industrial quarters shifting to a north-south street near the center of the eastern half of the city called Machi (the modern Shimmachi), and especially to areas near the intersections of that street with Sanjō, Shijō, and Shichijō Avenues.

The deregulation and degovernmentalization of Heian introduced many new elements into the population or gave added prominence to previously existing groups. Most conspicuous perhaps was the greatly increased presence of Buddhist monks in and around the city, subverting the highly secular atmosphere imposed in the days of the Confucian-trained emperor Kammu. The founding of chapels on the estates of great nobles like Sanesuke, the erection of large temples by Fujiwara leaders on the eastern and northern edges of the capital, the appearance of other temples nearby, and the growth of the Tendai establishment on Mount Hiei must have resulted in a vast increase in the population of Buddhist monks in the city or within a day's walk of it, their numbers almost certainly reaching into the thousands. They were by then a vital economic and cultural force in the capital, omnipresent in the life of the court and in the personal affairs of the nobility. They supported a wide variety of artisans in the construction, decoration, furnishing, and operation of their temples, creating an informed demand for art and books, playing the role of cultural mediators between China and Japan, and serving generally as intellectual and cultural catalysts. The great bulk of them were probably of fairly humble origins, but noble sons were found frequently in the higher Buddhist ranks and offices, and most of the monks who figured directly in the lives of the court and the nobility seem to have been of that class. The noble presence in Buddhist temples and the catering of Buddhism to noble interests and needs were so pronounced that historians sometimes speak of the "nobilization of Buddhism" in this period.

Other new or expanded elements that can be identified in the eleventh-century population of Heian include a small but important group of warriors up from the provinces to serve chiefly in the *kebiishi* office or under regimental command; gangs of robbers, among whom were found Buddhist monks, declassé or renegade nobles, and probably also others whose livelihoods had vanished in the contraction of the statutory government; a flourishing society of beggars; male and (especially) female peddlers who roamed the city streets selling a variety of goods; transport workers, who had grown in numbers and importance as the flow of goods from the provinces passed from government to private hands; entertainers, wonder-workers, gamblers, and, at least on the outskirts of the city, prostitutes; rich former provincial administrators whose houses were sometimes assaulted by infuriated (or possibly calculating) citizenry of their former provinces; and, of course, as always the huge numbers of servants and manual laborers with which the nobility surrounded itself. In its diversity and complexity, it was a truly urban population, the most urban that Japan had ever known.

CITY ADMINISTRATION

The population in the early days of Heian was governed by two Capital Offices (*Kyōshiki*), the Left and Right, which were responsible respectively the Left and Right halves (the eastern and western halves) of the city. Classified with the provincial administrations as regional organs, each office communicated directly with the Council of State and the central ministries under a chief official of the Fourth Rank, who directed an administrative staff of 7 and an armed force of 240 men. Like their provincial counterparts, the offices were responsible for the entire range of government in their jurisdictions, including the compilation and maintenance of household registers; the collection of taxes; police and judicial matters; the repair and maintenance of canals, ditches, bridges, and quarter walls; the cleaning of streets; the dispatch of the abandoned sick and orphaned to governmental institutions (it seems to have been the practice to eject ailing menials from the houses where they were employed, perhaps to avoid the ritual pollution of death); the removal and disposal of corpses (an onerous duty in times of epidemic disease, when as many as 5,000 bodies might be collected from the streets and riverbeds of Heian); and the distribution of aid to the indigent.

The authority of the Capital Offices was exercised at the local level through an officer in each zone (*jō*) called the quarter, or zone, magistrate (*bōrei, jōrei*), who was supposed to be an influential local resident of good character. Beneath him was a chief (*bōchō*) in each quarter of the zone and also a ward chief (*hochō*) for every five households. Although the quarter magistrate was a key official intimately involved in the daily lives of Heian residents, the government experienced continuing difficulty in finding suitable men for the post. This must have been partly because of the scanty emoluments attached to it, but perhaps it was mainly because of the frustrations and dangers the job might involve for a low-ranking magistrate, who had to cope with high officials and members of the imperial family living under his jurisdiction. It would have required a brave, even foolhardy, magistrate, for example, to admonish a mighty court minister or a prince of the blood for failure to clean up the streets in the vicinity of his house, an obligation imposed by law on all residents of the city. Yet the magistrate was liable to punishment if he were remiss in the enforcement of the law.

The problem of recruiting effective quarter magistrates seems to have been one of the chief causes of the atrophy that affected the Capital Offices during the course of the tenth century and led eventually to their replacement by other organs of government, chiefly the *kebiishi* office. The emergence of the latter as the chief administrative organ for the capital probably also reflected the increasing insecurity of the city from the tenth century on, when arson, robbery, and murder were epidemic and the exercise of police power became perhaps the first concern in city government. But even that office was unable to control the growing criminality of Heian, especially since its own agents were sometimes themselves involved in the crime they were supposed to suppress. By the eleventh century the city was, if not lawless, at least a freewheeling place compared to the carefully governed and regulated capital envisioned under statutory law.

Almost every aspect of life in Heian was minutely legislated at the founding of the city, from the symmetrical layout of the city itself down to the number of trees (seven) to be planted in the blocks surrounding the Park of the Divine Spring, the architecture of private houses, the cleaning of streets, the colors and materials of costumes, behavior in social intercourse, the tethering of horses and oxen, and so on in nearly infinite detail. In its orderliness, its discipline, and its nearly uniform dependence on a single industry, the city reminds one again of a military post or company town. And as with a military post or company town, the withdrawal of its single industry (the court and its government) during the early years of Heian's existence would have surely resulted, as at Nara and Nagaoka, in the almost immediate disappearance of the city. But the court remained, and by the eleventh century the capital had acquired in some measure a life of its own, forcing great changes in the plans and conceptions of its founders. The city of Kyoto had begun to emerge through the debris of the collapsing ideal of Heian.

CHANGES IN THE CITY PLAN

The greatest physical departure from the original city plan was an eastward and northward shift of the population that left the western and southern parts of the site only thinly populated, tending toward a geography in which the principal division was no longer east and west, but north and south (or, in the parlance of later centuries, Upper and Lower). The shift was in considerable part chimerical, representing not an actual movement of people but a simple disjunction between the original plan and its realization in practice. As noted earlier, it appears that only about half of the total area planned for the city was actually laid out and developed, and it is clear that most of the land thus left unoccupied or under cultivation was concentrated in the damp, low-lying western and southern parts of the planned site. But those sections were by no means totally devoid of urban development, and their loss of population to the eastern and northern parts of the city seems to have been real, as the opening lines of a short essay written in 982 by the religiously inclined Yoshishige no Yasutane (d. 1002) indicate:

> For the past twenty years and more I have observed the situation throughout the eastern and western sections of the capital. In the western part of the capital the houses have become fewer and fewer till now it's almost a deserted wasteland. People move out of the area but no one moves in; houses fall in ruin but no new ones are ever built. Those who don't have any other place to move to, or who aren't ashamed to be poor and lowly, live there, or people who enjoy a life of obscurity or are hiding out, who

ought to return to their native mountains or countryside hut but don't. But anyone who hopes to pile up a fortune or whose heart is set on rushing around on business wouldn't be able to stand living there even for a day.[24]

Spurred also probably by a cluster of communication routes along the eastern edge of the city and by the attraction of the imperial palace and the mansions of the great nobles in the north, the demographic shift noted by Yasutane (doubtless with exaggeration) carried the population beyond the capital's official borders into the alluvial plain of the upper Kamo River to the north and across to the foot of the Higashiyama Hills on the other side of the river where it flowed past the eastern city limit. The western edge of the urban area meanwhile retreated eastward, by the end of the latter half of the twelfth century coming to rest, it is thought, somewhere between Suzaku Avenue and the avenue (Ōmiya) that bordered the eastern side of the Greater Imperial Palace. The geographical center of the city was shifting toward the eastern reaches of Sanjō and Nijō Avenues, and the symmetry of the city's original plan was gone. With it went the earlier zone, quarter, block, and house-lot land divisions, the zone and quarter ceasing to function as administrative areas, and the house lot made meaningless by repeated divisions and sales. By the end of the eleventh century, property was being identified both by the old land divisions and by a new system of street coordinates (Nishinotōin and Shijō, for example), and it was not long before the older system disappeared altogether from documents.

NEW IMPERIAL AND FUJIWARA BUILDINGS

The eastward and northward shift of the population left the Greater Imperial Palace stranded on the western edge of the capital, its changed position relative to the city an almost too neat symbol of the changed status of the regent-ridden emperors. Yet despite frequent fires, the major structures of the palace itself seem to have remained much the same until past the middle of the eleventh century. The original Court of Government and its Great Hall of State were destroyed by fire in 876 but were almost immediately rebuilt. Although they burned once again in 1058 and fourteen years elapsed before reconstruction was completed, they remained a usual part of the palace landscape until their final destruction in the great Kyoto fire

---

24 From "Chiteiki" (Record of the Pond Pavilion), trans. Burton Watson, in *Japanese Literature in Chinese*, vol. 1 (New York: Columbia University Press, 1975), pp. 57–58.

of 1177. The original Court of Abundant Pleasures survived unscathed for more than two and a half centuries, but it, too, finally succumbed to fire in 1063 and was never rebuilt, adding greatly to what was probably by that time the growing vacant space within the palace walls. Even though the two great ceremonial courts of the palace survived until well into the eleventh century or beyond, their functions had long been almost entirely usurped by the Emperor's Residential Compound (or the substitutes therefor). Only the imperial accession ceremony seems still to have been regularly conducted at the Great Hall of State.

Although not quite so fortunate as the Court of Abundant Pleasures, the Emperor's Residential Compound also led a charmed life for a century and a half after the founding of Heian, escaping the numerous conflagrations that were a nearly inescapable part of life in a city where all structures were wooden; curtains, bamboo blinds, and paper or cloth screens were the chief partitions; and open flame or coals were the only means of illumination, heating, and cooking. But at last, in 960, fate caught up with it, too, and the entire compound, along with the many art treasures, heirlooms, and documents and books stored there, went up in smoke. The buildings were soon rebuilt, but the disaster was repeated so frequently thereafter (fourteen times, or an average of a little less than once a decade, between 960 and 1082) that politically or larcenously inspired arson is generally assumed. The residential compound continued to be used by most emperors until past the middle of the twelfth century, but by the end of that century it and the Greater Imperial Palace seem to have been largely abandoned. A fire in 1227 put a finish to what remained of the buildings in the compound, and the old palace site turned eventually into vegetable gardens famed especially for their turnips.

Although the Emperor's Residential Compound seems to have been rebuilt according to its original plan following the fire of 960, the use of the buildings within the compound differed in one important respect. At the founding of the capital, the emperor's personal residence within the compound, it will be remembered, was the Benevolent Longevity Hall (Jijūden). But for unknown reasons emperors by the middle of the ninth century were living not only there but also frequently in other buildings within, and even on occasion outside, the compound, and not until after the fire of 960 did a single building again come to be identified as the usual imperial residence. The building so favored was called the Limpid Cool Hall (Seiryōden), a name derived from that of an imperial summer palace in Han dynasty China. Facing east (rather than south) and located off the north-south median line of the compound directly across an enclosed courtyard from the Benevolent Longevity Hall to the west, the Limpid Cool Hall was, according to Chinese notions, appropriate neither in name nor position for the residence of a reigning emperor. It was even more cramped than its predecessor. The dimensions of the largest chamber in the building, the chamber where the emperor apparently spent most of his time, seem to have been about 50 by 25 feet; the imperial bedchamber was about a third of that; and the audience chamber at the southern end of the building where the emperor received the nobility was a hall only 10 to 15 feet wide and perhaps 60 feet long. Servants, female officials, ladies-in-waiting, consorts, and courtiers crowded the building day and night, and the emperor, like his subjects in the noble mansions, was probably never alone or more than a few feet from other people even in his most intimate moments.

An emperor who found himself without living quarters as a result of the frequent fires at the residential compound after 960 usually took up temporary residence outside the Greater Imperial Palace at a mansion, or part of a mansion, vacated and placed at his disposal by a Fujiwara maternal or marital relative, where he remained until the reconstruction of the compound was completed. The period of residence in such "town palaces" (*sato dairi*), as they were usually called, varied anywhere from several months to several years, but until the end of the eleventh century the emperor always eventually returned to the residential compound of the Greater Imperial Palace. By the beginning of the twelfth century, however, emperors were beginning to live permanently in "town palaces" especially constructed for the purpose, returning to the Greater Imperial Palace only for ceremonial occasions, and after the final destruction of the Emperor's Residential Compound in 1227, such palaces became the regular imperial residence. It is from a "town palace" of the fourteenth century just west of the site of Fujiwara no Michinaga's residence in the northeastern corner of the old capital that the present Kyoto imperial palace (Gosho) descends.

The architectural landscape outside the imperial palace also changed in conspicuous ways. Rampart Gate, the towering entranceway to the capital at the southern end of Suzaku Avenue, had been rebuilt after its destruction by wind in 816, less than twenty-five years after the city's founding, but it collapsed again during a great storm in 980 and seems never again to have been restored. The "rampart" along the city's southern border was probably already gone by that time, as were very likely many of the city's interior walls. The Kōrokan Lodgings must have been in an advanced state of decay by the end of the tenth century, their function lost with the cessation of relations with Po-hai in the 920s, but some evidence suggests that the buildings themselves may have survived into the twelfth century. Gone, too, most likely by about the beginning of the eleventh century or before, were the governmental charity institutions, the public granary, and the imperial pleasure buildings in the Park of the Divine Spring. The park had been much favored by the early Heian emperors, but imperial visits declined sharply as the space began to be employed for public religious rites in the latter half of the ninth century. The frequent use of the large pond there to provide drought relief for the rural population south of the capital may have further reduced the natural attractions of the place for its courtly patrons. Left a wasteland by the great fire of 1177, the park seems at times thereafter to have become a peculiarly noisome site for the dumping of garbage, human waste, and corpses. The northern half of the park was incorporated into the site of the Nijō Castle at the beginning of the seventeenth century; its surviving remnant in modern Kyoto is less than 5 percent of its original size.

The decay and disappearance of the symbols and monuments of the old statutory capital were accompanied by the emergence of the architectural landmarks of the city of the regents, most notably the luxurious mansions and the great temples of the Fujiwara leaders.

The mansions were located exclusively in the northeastern quarter of the capital, northeast of the intersection of Shijō and Ōmiya Avenues, an area that because of them became perhaps the most vital center of political and social life in the capital. The site of constant ceremony, ritual, and entertainment, of the birth and upbringing of imperial children, of imperial visits, of great economic strength, and of much of the substance (as opposed to the formal aspects) of political power, the mansions exercised a centripetal influence on the life of the city. They did not by any means replace the imperial palace, but heavily diluted its once unrivaled role in shaping the capital's civilization. Physically, the Fujiwara dwellings were all generally of the same mold and on the same scale as Sanesuke's Ononomiya establishment. The best known, of course, were those of the most powerful regents: Kaneie's Higashi sanjō residence, Michinaga's Tsuchimikado mansion, and Yorimichi's great Kayanoin, which was twice as extensive as the others, a place (in Sanesuke's words) of "incomparable magnificence," polished with peach pits until it shone like a mirror, and so grand that it seemed to another contemporary observer as if it belonged to a different world. Grand and brilliant as such mansions may have been, however, their grounds were only a fraction of the size of the Greater Imperial Palace, and only Yorimichi's Kayanoin rivaled even the much smaller dimensions of the Emperor's Residential Compound. The regental world was on a smaller scale than that of the statutory emperors.

The Fujiwara regents founded two Buddhist temples dedicated chiefly to Amidist faith at the eastern edge of the city on the narrow strip of land between Higashikyōgoku Avenue, the eastern city limit, and the Kamo River. One, called the Hokoin (or Hōkōin), was founded in the dwelling hall of a mansion owned by Kaneie just north of Nijō Avenue, shortly before his death in 990; the other, the Hōjōji, was established by Michinaga directly east of his Tsuchimikado mansion and a short distance north of the Hokoin in 1019. Illness and apprehension of approaching death were the direct motives for the founding of both temples, but whereas Kaneie died almost immediately after the founding of the Hokoin, leaving its further development in the hands of descendants, Michinaga made a good recovery from his illness and was able to devote most of the last decade of his life to the construction, decoration, and outfitting of the Hōjōji, which became in consequence the larger and more famous of the two temples.

Lavishing wealth and attention on the temple, the great ex-regent turned the 14 or so acres of the site (the same size as the sites of the East and West Temples) into the scenic and architectural wonder of his age, creating elaborate gardens and constructing over a dozen major halls and chapels there. A probably contemporary source provides an impressionistic description of the construction in its early stages:

A great tile-capped wall was thrown around a four-block area. Michinaga urged the work on with floods of orders, chafing at the slowness of dawn and bemoaning the gathering shadows of night. He turned ideas over in his mind all night long. How should the artificial hill be built up? The lake laid out? The garden designed? He must go on to construct a whole series of impressive halls. Nor could the images be run-of-the-mill affairs; there would be great numbers of golden buddhas sixteen feet tall, arranged in a row with a passageway running from north to south in front of them. Paths and walks would be needed, and corridors and galleries. . . . Daily levies of laborers, amounting to from 500 or 600 to 1,000 men, came from the sustenance households and private estates of Michinaga's male connections

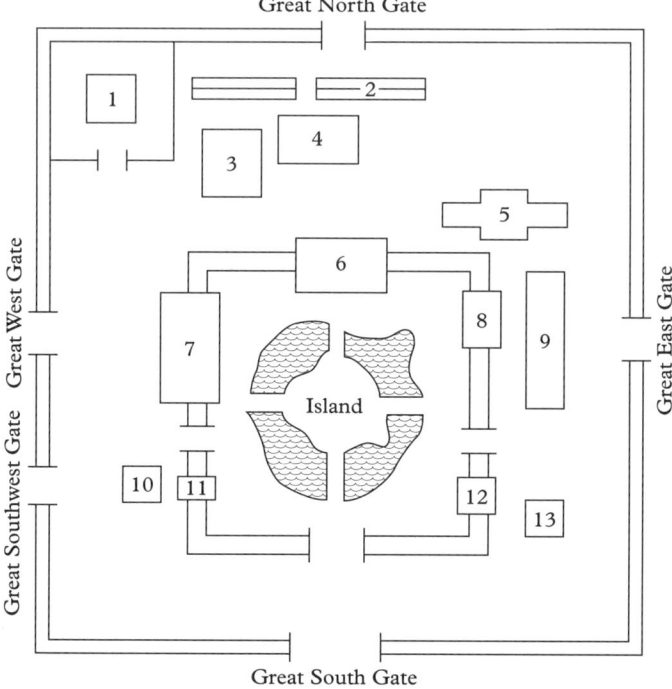

Figure 2.6. Plan of Hōjōji. From McCullough and McCullough, *A Tale of Flowering Fortunes*, p. 782.

and the Imperial personages, and everyone was immensely heartened by the availability of so many hands. Provincial governors competed to provide the most labor, timber, cypress bark, and tiles for the hall, even at the cost of falling behind with their rental taxes and tribute commodities; and artisans flocked from near and far, making themselves useful in capacities and places suited to their callings. In one place, master joiners worked on sacred images, assisted by a huge crew of 100 image-carvers. What assignment could be more splendid for an artisan! Near the top of the building 200 or 300 carpenters were at work, shouting *"Esa! Masa!"* in unison, as they raised massive beams attached to thick cables. In the interior, where gorgeous thrones for the images were being built, forty or fifty men were polishing the plank floors with scouring rushes, *muku* leaves, and peach pits. Countless cypress-bark roofers, plasterers, and tile makers worked away, and venerable monks and other aged men were cutting and laying three-foot rocks. Some 400 or 500 men had descended to excavate the lake, and another 500 or 600 had climbed up onto the artificial hill and were adding to its height, layer by layer. On the avenues, shouting laborers pulled immense tree trunks roped to work carts; on the Kamo River, raftsmen sang cheerful, lusty songs as they poled their loads of lumber upstream....Crews tugged at fragile rafts, which somehow managed to keep afloat under the weight of mighty rocks as big as cliffs.[25]

The same source also describes the dedication of the temple's main building, the Golden Hall, which was attended by Michinaga's grandson, Emperor Go-Ichijō:

Very much at ease, the Emperor gazed at the scene inside the temple compound. The garden sand glittered like crystal; and [artificial] lotus blossoms of varying hues floated in ranks on the fresh, clear surface of the lake. Each blossom held a buddha, its image mirrored in the water, which also reflected, as in a buddha domain, all the buildings on the east, west, south, and north, even the sutra treasury and the bell tower. Jeweled nets hung from every branch on the trees bordering the lake; fragile blossoms quivered in the still air. Green-pearl leaves shone with the hue of beryl; elegant glass branches appeared on the bottom of the lake; delicate clusters of flowers hung as though about to fall. There were leaves of many kinds and colors – green pearl, like pine trees at the height of summer; gold, like late autumn foliage; amber, like mid-autumn foliage; white glass, like a winter garden mantled in snow. Ripples washed the lake's golden jeweled shores when a breeze stirred the trees. A bridge made of the seven treasures spanned the golden jeweled lake, jeweled boats glided in the shade under the trees, and [artificial] peacocks and parrots played on the island.[26]

(On the dedication ceremony see also the section "Music" in Chapter 6.)

In a bit of ironical symbolism that even Michinaga may have appreciated, some of the old foundation stones of Rampart Gate were used in the construction of Hōjōji.

A final new element in the city landscape, and one that would grow in significance in the twelfth century, was the small group of palaces used by retired emperors. In the Nara period, the abdicated emperors had continued to live at the Greater Imperial Palace, but when Emperor Saga gave up the throne in 823, he took up residence at Reizeiin, a spacious four-block establishment at the southeastern corner of the Greater Imperial Palace. Subsequent abdicated em-

---

25 William H. and Helen Craig McCullough, *A Tale of Flowering Fortunes*, pp. 499–501.
26 *Flowering Fortunes*, pp. 553–54.

perors and their empresses followed his example, using either the Reizeiin or one of several other palaces scattered through the city, including the largest of them all, the six-block Suzakuin directly south of the Greater Imperial Palace. Landed property was attached to some or all such palaces, and that wealth and the household organization established for each abdicated emperor are generally thought to have provided part of the impetus that led to the brief revival of imperial-family power in the twelfth century.

CEREMONY AND RITUAL

Heian, as a political administrative seat for an imperial line and its hereditary nobility, was perhaps inevitably an intensely ceremonious and ritualistic city. Whether in the early Heian of Kammu and his immediate successors on the throne or in the Heian of Michinaga's time, ceremony and ritual were primary concerns of government and private citizens alike. During the period of the Fujiwara regency, in particular, it might even be argued that ceremony and ritual were conceived to be at the very center of life and government, more time and wealth being expended on them than on perhaps any other single category of public or social activity at court and among the nobility.

An order of ritual and ceremony at the imperial court had been established at least as early as the ninth century, and precedential rules providing detailed instructions for the conduct of individual participants were evolving by the tenth century, when knowledge of the rules became the *sine qua non* of a successful career at court. A key figure was Fujiwara no Mototsune, the imperial regent whose observances became the basis, through his sons Saneyori (Ononomiya) and Morosuke (Kujōdono), of two ritual-ceremonial schools (*ryū*), the Ononomiya and the Kujō. An initial dominance of the Ononomiya (founded by Saneyori's son Sanesuke) came to an end with the revival of the Kujō under Michinaga, from whom descended a ritual-ceremonial line known as the Midō school, which was a mixture of Ononomiya and Kujō elements with Michinaga's own particular contributions. A number of learned treatises were written on the subject by eminent authorities like Minamoto no Takaakira for the reference of courtiers, and when a man was called learned and able, it often had to do with his knowledge of ritual and ceremony. The existence of such schools and the extraordinary intellectual attention to their subject matter by senior government ministers may baffle or appall the casual modern observer, but they were the rational product of minds that conceived of ritual and ceremony as the chief means by which nature could be controlled, society regulated, and personal success achieved in a mysterious, imperfectly understood world.

In the life of Heian, no ritual or ceremony was more representative of the capital and its society than the regular Kamo Festival, which took place every year in the fourth month. The festival was both ritual and ceremony, functioning on the one hand to guard the city and its people, and on the other to affirm and display the bonds that held the community together. It was also, as almost all rituals and ceremonies were in part, an entertainment, providing one of the great spectacles of the city's year. In short, it was the Heian equivalent of the famous Gion Festival that later came to symbolize Kyoto under warrior rule as a city of artisans, merchants, temples, and shrines.

The explicit purpose of the Kamo Festival was to pay homage to the Kamo deities and to secure their protection of the court and the capital. Originally worshiped as deities of the ancient Kamo clan, the gods were enshrined in two locations in the northern part of the Kyoto basin: at the Lower Shrine near the confluence of the Kamo and Takano rivers and at the Upper Shrine a couple of miles farther north on the east bank of the Kamo.

There were two central figures in the festival: the Kamo Vestal and the Imperial Messenger. The Vestal was a near-princess chosen by divination at the beginning of each reign, or whenever the post fell vacant. Her role is not altogether clear, although it is obvious that it was modeled on that of the Ise Vestal, who was considered the Chief Priestess of the Ise Shrines and lived there. The Kamo Vestal, who was first appointed in the reign of Emperor Saga, lived at a special palace called Murasakinoin on the northwest outskirts of the capital. Her role seems to have been simply to maintain ritual purity and to represent the emperor at the festival. The Imperial Messenger was a Fifth-Rank courtier holding the office of Middle or Lesser Captain of the Imperial Guards, and thus usually a man destined for high office. He read an imperial rescript at the shrines and presented the emperor's offerings, which was the chief object of the festival. The Vestal and the Messenger were accompanied by ten dancers and twelve musicians, who were also courtiers from the Imperial Guards. Their duty was to perform an ensemble of music, dance, and song called "Eastern Music" (*Azumaasobi*) at the shrines.

The great festival procession began from the Vestal's palace and proceeded along Ichijō Avenue on the northern edge of the city toward the shrines. It was made up of a huge throng of military and civil officials, court ladies, and attendants, some walking and others mounted on elaborately caparisoned horses or riding in ox-drawn carriages, and all brilliantly costumed in formal robes, with headgear, mounts, and carriages decorated with flowers and leaves. The chief figures in the procession were the Vestal carried in a large palanquin by twenty bearers and surrounded by numerous male and female attendants; the Imperial Messenger dressed in black silk robes, wearing a sword and riding horseback; the Messenger's retinue carrying the official vermilion umbrella and an umbrella covered with artificial flowers; the mounted musicians and dancers; an officer from the Storehouse Bureau in charge of white chests containing the offerings for the shrines, and bearing himself the imperial rescript to the shrine enclosed in a brocade bag; an officer from the Stables Bureau in charge of fourteen horses that were to be paraded before the shrines; the vice-governor of Yamashiro Province, the province in which the shrines were located, riding at the head of troops; and *kebiishi* police to clear the way for the procession and to provide ceremonial guard at the shrines.

Along the route of the procession, crowds of townsmen and countrymen filled the streets and overflowed onto housetops and trees. Gorgeously attired ladies, courtiers, and exalted personages sat in their lacquered carriages or luxurious viewing stands, while their lackeys jostled against the commoners in an excited, unruly mass through which *kebiishi* agents, marching in the vanguard, cleared a passage. Houses along the way were all decorated with garlands of real and artificial flowers, with leaves of the *katsura* tree, and, especially, with the *aoi* or "heartvine" leaves (*Asarum caulescens* Maxim) that gave the festival its popular name.[27]

The ritual at the shrines themselves was simple. At both sites the Vestal paid her respects while the Imperial Messenger intoned the imperial rescript praising the gods and requesting their continued favor. The offerings (silk, hemp, etc.) and the dances and songs were presented, and the horses were paraded and raced. The Vestal spent the night at the Upper Shrine, and on the following day there was a less elaborate procession of return to the capital, culminating in a lavish banquet at the imperial palace, with rewards for all participants.

27 "Heartvine" is the ingeniously apt neologistic translation by Edward Seidensticker.

CHAPTER 3

LAND AND SOCIETY

Social and economic change in premodern times is seldom rapid. But even by premodern standards, change in rural Heian Japan must at first glance seem glacial. Population did increase moderately and with it the area of land under cultivation. Millet gave way to barley as the second grain most grown, but rice retained its place as the primary and most prestigious grain. Irrigation networks, both simple and intricate, grew to feed the expansion in arable land, but with no discernible advance in irrigation technology – indeed, the great state-sponsored water projects of previous centuries found no echo in the Heian period. Provincial handicraft industry grew but little, and there may even have been a decline in the production of silk. House construction remained little changed through most of the country, although in the home provinces there may have been some shift from excavated floors ("pit dwellings") to raised foundations. All in all, there is little to show for the passage of four centuries.

Or so it must seem to the modern observer. Yet to an eighth-century peasant, agricultural life in twelfth-century Japan would have seemed significantly altered. Iron tools were much more abundant, and included tools and uses unfamiliar to him. Households would have seemed smaller and less independent than in his own age, and the force of local elite families on economic life much stronger. Most of all, he would have found a dramatically changed tax structure, with taxes now managed by an extensive class of local, regional, and provincial notables and officials whose powers, initiatives, and frequently only quasi-official status would have struck him as bewildering and, no doubt, intimidating.

Change is not always progress: of the changes in technology, social structure, taxation, and landholding to be discussed, perhaps only the diffusion of the plow can be seen as an unequivocal advance. But most of these changes worked toward a restructuring of rural Japanese society and economy that was at least as significant in premodern terms as straightforward technological advances and quantitative growth. The greater complexity of rice farming in the Heian period drew households together in greater interdependence, and so began the slow growth that was to culminate in the highly political and cooperative Tokugawa village many centuries later. Changes in farming also brought more power to wealthy families, just as developments in taxation rendered the central and provincial governments more dependent on these local notables to keep the ruling class in the capital properly supplied with the goods and services on which it relied. The greater power and influence that thus devolved on local notables did not of itself create the provincial warrior class of *bushi* that dominated medieval Japan. But *bushi* growth could hardly have proceeded in quite the same manner without this restructuring of rural Heian society.

If a single factor can be assessed as most responsible for this restructuring, the leading candidate must be the brisk growth in population experienced in the first third of the Heian period – a growth that, significantly, was most marked in the eastern and outer provinces where *bushi* development became strongest. By putting pressure on agricultural resources, growth in population stimulated a search for means of increasing crop yields, stabilizing cultivation, and, at the very least, lessening the extreme losses in harvests during bad years. Growth in population and in agricultural production also increased the potential tax income that could be collected by local officials – an increased income most available in provinces distant from the capital, and hence out of sight of a ruling class dependent on local officials and notables for even a straightforward continuation of existing levels of tax income.

AGRARIAN TECHNOLOGY

In Chapter 26 of *Konjaku monogatari-shū* there is a tale, most likely from the early Heian period, that begins as follows:

> At a time now past, there was a lowly person who lived in Hata District in Tosa Province. This person held rice fields both on the shore where he lived and on the shore opposite. To cultivate the fields on the opposite shore, he planted seed rice in the fields near his home, then carried the seedlings by boat to be transplanted on the opposite shore. With the seedlings, he brought by boat hired farm laborers, food provisions for these and for his family, a single-stem plow (*maguwa*), a full plow (*karasuki*), a scythe, hoe, ax, and other cutting tools.[1]

---

1 *Konjaku monogatari-shū*, vols. 22–6 of *Nihon koten bungaku taikei* (Tokyo: Iwanami shoten, 1962), vol. 25, *kan* 26, story 10, p. 443.

In this tale we can see the adoption of a rice regime that joined seedbeds and summer transplanting, preparation of the soil by animal-drawn cultivating tools, and, by implication, draining of fields midseason to allow the crop to mature in dry soil.[2] Rice cultivation was introduced to Japan about the second century B.C.E.; the use of seedbeds and the transplanting of seedlings to flooded fields in early summer can be found as early as the second century C.E.;[3] both the simple and full plows were brought to Japan from the continent in the fourth or fifth century.[4] The use of seedbeds and the plow produced greater rice yields; equally important, each allowed rice to be grown in a greater variety of soils. But both also required a considerable cost, in labor as well as in capital expense. Transplanting seedlings was extra work and had to be done quickly while water was diverted into each field – hence requiring the extra expense of hired help. Purchasing and maintaining a plow and draft animal was a greater expense still. These costs hampered the full adoption of an improved rice regime available to the Japanese in the fifth century until as late as the tenth century.

Evidence of planting first in seedbeds, then transplanting to flooded fields in early summer – a practice known as *taue* – has been noted in the famous Toro site in Shizuoka Prefecture as early as the second century. Some scholars further feel that *taue* must have been well known even before this period.[5] Yet the simpler practice of direct seeding was still familiar in the seventh and eighth centuries. A poem, "Where ricefields have been planted along the Sumiyoshi coast / Alas, that I do not see you from planting even to harvest!" in the eighth-century anthology the *Man'yōshū*, for example, seems clearly to imply that the rice had matured in the same field in which it had been first planted.[6]

Under conditions of primitive rice agriculture, the higher yields resulting from the practice of *taue* did not offset the greater amount of labor required to transplant seedlings. In fact, it is probable that *taue* was first adopted not for its higher yields, but to conserve water during the spring growing season and to concentrate seedlings into

---

2 Iinuma Jirō, *Nihon nōgyō gijutsu ron* (Tokyo: Miraisha, 1971), p. 88, describes this regime.
3 This has been shown at the Hiraide site; see Hiraide iseki chōsakai, ed., *Hiraide* (Tokyo: Asahi shimbunsha, 1955).
4 Kinoshita Tadashi, "Nōgu," in Wajima Seiichi, ed., *Nihon no kōkogaku*, vol. 3 (Tokyo: Kawade shobō, 1966), p. 246.
5 Kondō Yoshirō and Okamoto Akio, "Nihon no suitō nōkō gijutsu," in Ishimoda Shō, ed., *Kodai no kōza*, vol. 3 (Tokyo: Gakuseisha, 1962), p. 344. Also see Kinoshita, "Nōgu," p. 240.
6 *Man'yōshū*, vols. 4–7 of *Nihon koten bungaku taikei*, vol. 6, p. 131 (poem 2,244).

a smaller area that could be better protected from the elements.[7] With improved control of irrigation – a notable area of agrarian advance in the fourth to sixth centuries – practice of *taue* also resulted in superior yields, however, for seedlings grown in seedbeds were hardier and more evenly distributed than those sown by direct broadcast.

Furthermore, fields to which seedlings were transplanted could be richly prepared by either plow or manual cultivation. This is indicated in the *Konjaku* tale just quoted by the mention of two such cultivating tools, the single-stem plow (*maguwa*) – basically a heavy hoe drawn by a horse or ox – and the more substantial plow known as *suki* or *karasuki*. Conceivably the single-stem plow found some use after its introduction to Japan in the fourth century, but its employment was confined, of course, to those few who owned draft animals.[8] The more effective full plow, however, remained rare for the first three to four centuries after its introduction. In an era of iron scarcity, it was far more effective to use the iron that would have been needed to make one heavy plowshare to make instead several hoe or spade blades. It is also likely that the advantages of plow use in rice farming were not well understood at first.

We should not be surprised by this, for the plow in Asia (as elsewhere) was essentially a tool of dry-field farming. Originally used in north India and north China for cultivation of millet and barley, the plow was only later transferred to wet rice culture.[9] This association of the plow with dry field farming retarded its diffusion in Japan, where for several reasons the greatest importance was always attached to the cultivation of rice. One reason was that the introduction of rice to Japan in fact preceded that of other grains by at least two centuries. Beyond this, however, rice was actively promoted by the developing aristocratic government from the early centuries C.E. Aristocrats preferred rice because of its high and relatively secure productivity, its effect on settling – indeed, tying down – a population into narrow regions easier to control, and because of their own preference for rice as the staple of their diet. As a result, the best fields were reserved for rice culture; fields growing other crops, though perhaps as extensive as those growing rice,[10]

---

7 Kondō and Okamoto, "Nihon no suitō," p. 343.
8 Okamoto Akio, "Nōgyō seisan," in Kondō Yoshirō and Fujisawa Chōji, eds., *Nihon no kōkogaku*, vol. 5 (Tokyo: Kawade shobō, 1966), p. 34.
9 Iinuma, *Nihon nōgyō*, pp. 73 and 92.
10 Dana Morris, "Peasant Economy in Early Japan, 650–950," Ph.D. diss., University of California, Berkeley, 1980, pp. 137–38.

were largely confined to marginal lands and to land not conveniently located for irrigation.[11]

With the continued moderate growth in population, arable land planted to rice continued to expand in the eighth and ninth centuries. Nonetheless, there is reason to believe that expansion of land planted to dry-field crops such as millet, barley, and soybeans may have more than just kept pace with expansion in rice fields. Growth of paddy was limited by the still primitive state of irrigation technology; this was particularly the case in the more heavily cultivated home provinces (Kinai).[12] In addition, the widespread failure of land projects sponsored by the aristocracy in the eighth century led to the withdrawal of aristocrats from land reclamation efforts in the Heian period. Whereas the ruling class was most anxious to create new rice fields, the local land developers who took their place were more likely to respond to peasant demand, and hence create dry fields in at least equal number to paddy. Also significant was the imposition of a higher land tax in the tenth century. Because it was applied to rice fields of all kinds, including those developed privately, the higher land tax increased the advantage of developing tax-free dry fields.

From this impression of the increased importance of dry-field cultivation in Heian Japan, we may deduce the means by which the utility of the plow in rice farming came to be recognized. As dry-field cultivation received more attention, perhaps even constituting a larger percentage of all fields, it made increasing sense to invest in a plow and animal, since the advantages of plow use in dry-field farming probably were well known. The rising role of local notables in land development was crucial, for such entrepreneurs were best able to afford plows and draft animals.

Once brought into use on dry fields, it was a logical extension to apply the plow to rice fields, particularly considering the magnitude of the plow investment. Leading an animal through carefully prepared rice fields may have seemed risky at first, but the extra time spent repairing damage to embankments was more than offset by the time saved with the plow. When it became apparent that deeper tillage benefited the soil and increased yields as well, the advantages of the plow in rice cultivation should have been soon evident.

---

11 Toyoda Takeshi, ed., *Sangyō shi*, vol. 10 of *Taikei Nihon shi sōsho* (Tokyo: Yamakawa shuppansha, 1964), pp. 163–69.
12 Kinda Akihira, "Heian-ki no Yamato bonchi ni okeru jōri jiwari naibu no tochi riyō," *Shirin* 61,3 (May 1978): 75–112. Also see Furushima Toshio, *Nihon nōgyō gijutsu shi*, vol. 1 (Tokyo: Jichōsha, 1947), pp. 142–46.

The kind of plow best suited to rice culture, however, was not that best for dry-field crops. Dry-field farming required a light plow to minimize dehydration of the soil – most especially on the Asian continent, where the Japanese plow originated. (Because of its wet summers and volcanic soil, Japan was better suited for use of a heavier plow even for dry-field farming.) By contrast, a heavier plow, which cultivated deeper, could be used to advantage when growing rice because the flooding of fields during the first half of the growing season prevented soil dehydration. It was also possible to use a plow with a moldboard, an attachment set at an angle to the top of the plowshare to turn over the earth as it is loosened. The action of the moldboard helped aerate the upper layer of the soil, further renewing fertility. But this action also allowed the soil to dry out, rendering it undesirable in dry-field farming.

References to the plow are few in both Nara and Heian literature. Despite this, historians have been able to delineate a chronology of its diffusion on which there is general agreement. There is little sign of use of the plow in the Nara period, at least in rice culture, and literary evidence of its use is virtually nonexistent.[13] Two simple eighth-century plows survive in the Tōdaiji warehouse, Shōsōin, but their use appears to have been ceremonial.[14] Both the Shōsōin plows lack moldboards. As already noted, plows without moldboards were better suited to dry-field culture, suggesting that plows of the Shōsōin type were not intended for use in rice culture.

Heian sources, by contrast, reveal much greater use of the plow. The early tenth-century sources *Engi shiki* and *Wamyō ruiju shō* both speak of the plow as in common use, at least as farming was viewed from the capital.[15] Use of the plow in rice farming also is described in the tenth-century romance *Utsuho monogatari* and, as noted, in *Konjaku*.[16] The *Konjaku* story does not reveal whether the plow in use had a moldboard or how many animals were used to draw it. Both *Engi shiki* and *Wamyō ruiju shō*, however, describe the plow as being equipped with a moldboard. This is significant as evidence that the plow was used in Heian times not only in dry-field farming but also in rice farming.

13 Furushima, *Nihon nōgyō*, vol. 1, pp. 94–95.
14 Iinuma Jirō, "Nihon-shi ni okeru suki to kuwa" (Kyōto daigaku jimbun kagaku kenkyūjo), *Jimbun gakuhō* 32 (March 1971): 10.
15 *Engi shiki*, in (*Shintei zōho*) *Kokushi taikei*, 60 vols. in 66 (Tokyo: Yoshikawa kōbunkan, 1929–64), vol. 26, *kan* 39, pp. 878–81; *Wamyō ruiju shō*, 3 vols. (Tokyo: Kazama shobō, 1954), vol. 2, *kan* 15, 8b.
16 *Utsuho monogatari*, vols. 10–12 of *Nihon koten bungaku taikei*, vol. 10, pp. 339–40.

The plow described in *Engi shiki* was heavier than the Shōsōin plows, and consequently required two persons to operate. The moldboard, which tends to pull the plow off balance, no doubt was one reason for this. Nonetheless, the Japanese plow was pulled by a single animal, unlike the four to six needed to pull the very heavy plows of northern European agriculture. The relative lightness of the Asian plow was a legacy of its origins in dry-field farming in regions where dehydration of the soil was a major problem. The need to restrict the number of animals led over rice fields during plowing made it undesirable to develop a heavier plow even for rice farming, where deeper tilling would have been advantageous. Hence the plow of Japanese agriculture was more akin to the lighter plow of Mediterranean agriculture than the heavy plow of northern Europe.

Why did the plow, known for centuries before, not become widely used until the Heian period? Increased attention to dry-field farming was certainly a catalyst leading to its use in rice culture, but this might have occurred before the Heian period. Knowledge of the moldboard and its utility in rice cultivation might have been delayed, but we do not know this for sure: there is, for example, a reference to the moldboard as early as 772.[17] The limited number of oxen raised in Japan before the Heian period no doubt slowed diffusion of the plow. But the early ninth-century collection of tales *Nihon ryōiki* amply demonstrates that Japanese peasants were familiar with oxen in the Nara period, although in no case does it show oxen being used to draw plows.[18]

Almost certainly the main impediment to diffusion of the plow before the Heian period was the severely limited supply of iron. A plowshare required much more iron than a simple hoe or spade blade. Furthermore, the plow was a luxury tool that duplicated, albeit more elegantly, the cultivating job of the hoe.

The spread of iron tools among farm households can be seen in figures gathered by Harashima Reiji showing the distribution of iron tools in archaeological sites from the fifth to ninth centuries. It should be noted that most of these sites are in eastern Japan; iron use was greater in the central and western parts of the country. Most of the sites owe their preservation to destruction by natural disaster followed by failure to resettle. Harashima notes that many iron tools left in these sites must have been lost through corrosion. An even

---

17 Furushima, *Nihon nōgyō*, vol. 1, p. 94. The reference occurs in a poem in *Kakyō hyōshiki* (771), cited in Takeuchi Rizō, ed., *Nara ibun*, vol. 2 (Tokyo: Yagi shobō, 1943), pp. 930–37.
18 See Furushima, *Nihon nōgyō*, vol. 1, p. 59.

TABLE 3.1
Distribution of iron tools in farm households, fifth to ninth centuries

Period[a]	Houses in sample	Houses with iron tools	Percentage	Adjusted percentage (approximate)
Goryō (early 5th C.)	225	5	2.2	5
Izumi/Yakuradai (late 5th C.)	118	10	8.5	20
Onidaka (6th to early 7th C.)	223	35	15.7	40
Mama (late 7th to 8th C.)	135	25	18.5	40
Kokubun (9th C.)	206	78	37.9	100

[a]Periods refer to the pottery eras to which the sites belong; the time spans in parentheses are widely accepted approximations, but should not be taken as incontestable.
Source: Harashima Reiji, *Nihon kodai shakai no kiso kōzō* (Tokyo: Miraisha, 1966), pp. 30 and 314.

more important cause of loss, however, was salvage by the displaced population, since iron implements were just about the only possessions capable of surviving fire or other natural disaster unharmed. Hence Harashima's adjustment factor of 2.5 to estimate actual iron tool rates seems a reasonable minimal adjustment. Harashima uses this adjustment figure only on his ninth-century figures, but in Table 3.1 it has been extended to earlier periods as well; there seems no reason to believe the discrepancy between original tool use and what survives today would have varied from one period to another.

Although the extrapolation from iron tool incidence in archaeological sites to actual tool possession must of necessity be rather rough, it appears that by the ninth century virtually every farm household had at least one minor iron tool. (This is so particularly when we bear in mind how few iron tools must have been abandoned even after homes were destroyed.) It is clearly this increase in the supply of iron that enabled the diffusion of the plow in the Heian period. Specifically, it appears that the takeoff point for plow diffusion after the nearly plowless eighth century came only after lesser iron tools were within the grasp of most peasant households. From this we may speculate that the principal spur to plow diffusion in the

Heian period was not excess local elite wealth but a wide demand among peasants for a more advanced level of technology.

The second major agrarian development of the Heian period was the practice of keeping animals year-round in stables instead of pasturing them on wasteland. Two factors made this change in animal husbandry necessary: an increase in number of animals raised owing to the diffusion of the plow, and a decrease in wasteland available for pasture. Both factors reduced the capacity of available wasteland to sustain the number of horses and oxen raised. But of the two, it was the decrease in available wasteland that most strongly forced owners to keep and feed their animals year-round in stables.

The early Japanese state, like the aristocracy of medieval Europe, posed as guardian of the right of public use of wasteland. In 706, for example, the government issued a decree forbidding monopolization of public land for private use. Aristocrats were not to block peasant access to wasteland to collect grasses or firewood, nor were peasants themselves to block others from free use of uncultivated land other than land immediately adjacent to their homes and graveyards.[19] Public use of wasteland included hunting, food gathering, pasturing of animals, and collection of wood for building and firewood. Aristocrats, however, were also interested in taking over wasteland for most of these same uses. Consequently, Nara and Heian aristocrats, like their European counterparts, began to appropriate large tracts of waste for private use.

One means of doing this derived from the laws of 743 permitting permanent possession of rice fields that had been brought under cultivation privately. State-supported temples and some upper aristocratic houses were given large grants of wasteland that they were to develop into landed estates. Although efforts to create rice fields from waste often proved fruitless, the land granted these institutions was nonetheless withdrawn from public access.

From the late eighth century, the central government granted waste for nonagricultural uses as well. The major recipients of these grants were temples, shrines, and the imperial household. Significantly, all three were considered part of the "public interest" that had a natural claim to wasteland use. All three, however, often had interests that came into conflict with the "lesser" public of peasant farmers, for the products derived from wasteland grants were the

---

19 *Shoku Nihongi*, in *Kokushi taikei*, vol. 2, Jingo-keiun 3/3/14, pp. 362–63.

same as those peasants expected to get from communal wasteland, such as firewood, lumber, salt, fish, vegetable oils, clay, and chestnuts.[20] Private wasteland reserves were also used to pasture animals and even to raise falcons, although occupation of waste for private hunting reserves, a major cause of aristocratic encroachment on public wasteland in Europe, was not a factor in Buddhist Japan.

Appropriation of waste for private use, reclamation for rice cultivation by both estate owners and local notables, and a probable expansion in the proportion of farmland devoted to dry-field crops all worked to decrease wasteland that could be used by peasants for pasture of animals. This decrease seems to have been most pronounced in the ninth century. Most wasteland grants were in this period;[21] so, too, are the first signs of the changes in tax structure that made dry fields more attractive to local land developers. By the midtenth century, when plow use had increased greatly, the amount of wasteland where peasants or even local notables could freely pasture their animals had been much reduced.

Consequently it became necessary to keep and feed animals in enclosures throughout the year. The most logical source of animal feed was the stalks of rice and other grains after they had dried to hay. Because allowing animals to forage freely on rice fields after harvest would have destroyed many of the embankments, rice was harvested at the ground and the stalks after threshing were brought to the animals as feed. This required an extra step at harvest to separate stalks from the head. For this reason, rice in earlier times had been harvested at about 15 centimeters from the tip (where the kernels were concentrated), and the stalks left in the field. The practice came about partly because ground-level harvesting required the use of a scythe with an extended handle (known as *tokama*), which was more difficult to operate than the simple sickle (*kama*). Like the plow, the scythe had been known since the fifth and sixth centuries but was not widely used until the Heian period.[22] Another reason to favor the simpler harvest method was that rice stalks left in the ground rotted during winter and could be plowed under in the spring, enriching the soil. Only the need to keep animals year-round in stables, or to clear the ground after harvest to plant a winter crop, provided a sufficient inducement to harvest rice at ground level.

20 Okuno Nakahiko, "Hachi kyū seiki ni okeru shiteki tochi shoyūsei no rekishiteki seikaku," *Nihon rekishi*, 279 (August 1971): 53–69.
21 See Takeuchi Rizō, ed., *Tochi seido shi*, vol. 6 of *Taikei Nihon shi sōsho*, pp. 124–28.
22 Furushima, *Nihon nōgyō*, vol. 1, p. 57.

In the Nara period rice was still harvested near the tip with a sickle. An eighth-century register of ceremonies at Ise Shrine describes use of the long-handled scythe, but only to cut grass.[23] The varieties of mortars and pestles used to process rice harvested with stalks are not to be found until the ninth century. By contrast, Heian sources clearly show the harvesting of rice at ground level: both *Engi shiki* and *Makura no sōshi* indicate straw was a by-product of threshing, as would only be the case were rice harvested at the ground.[24] It is unlikely that rice was harvested at ground level to clear the ground for a second crop. Since planting both a summer and a winter crop required a great increase in fertilizer if the soil was not to be quickly depleted, it is probable that few fields were double-cropped until well into the medieval period. Adoption of the more cumbersome method of harvesting rice at the ground, therefore, may be taken as a sign of the need to harvest rice stalks to feed animals kept in enclosures.

Even with the increased use of the plow, it is likely that only a small number of Heian farm households owned draft animals. But those who raised animals in stables would have needed more hay than fields farmed by their own families could have provided. Hence we may assume that farmers who did not raise animals could sell or barter hay to those who did. The spread of animal husbandry thus indirectly created a new source of income for even the poorest farm households.

An equally important consequence of year-round stabling was the collection of manure previously lost on wasteland pasture. If the new harvest method robbed the soil of rice stalks that up to then had rotted and been plowed under, this was surely compensated by the beneficial effects of fertilizing rice fields with manure.

Use of the plow, harvesting of rice at ground level, an increase in animal husbandry, and the stabling of animals year-round worked together to transform Heian agrarian life. With the plow it was possible to work heavier soils than could be worked with hand tools, as well as to loosen and turn soil better and faster. With the plow's greater speed, it was also possible to turn the soil more frequently before planting, with a direct effect in increased yields. Greater use of animals, and most especially their stabling at home, provided manure that also significantly increased soil fertility. Stabling of animals altered peasant society in other ways as well. Pasturing animals on

23 *Kōtai jingū gishiki chō*, in *Gunsho ruijū*, vol. 1 (Tokyo: Keizai zasshisha, 1904), p. 3. Also see Furushima, *Nihon nōgyō*, vol. 1, p. 58.
24 See Furushima, *Nihon nōgyō*, vol. 1, pp. 57 and 96.

wasteland of necessity took some family members away from the farm for a substantial part of the year. Now both animals and their tenders were available year-round at home, thus integrating animal husbandry more thoroughly into Japanese peasant life.

Perhaps the most valuable single effect of increased use of both the plow and fertilizer was the securing of year-to-year cultivation of fields that before had been left fallow after one or more years of cultivation. As use of the plow spread, it became possible to revitalize fields through better aeration of the soil, more frequent working of soil before planting, and greater use of fertilizer. This was a considerable improvement in Japanese farming, for the high costs of constructing rice fields were best recovered by continuous year-to-year cultivation.

PEASANT COMMUNITY

The task of transplanting rice seedlings in early summer was arduous, but could not be time-consuming: as each field was flooded and the soil worked into a mush, the full complement of seedlings had to be planted while the soil was neither too hard nor too liquid, and before the next field, flooded at no little expense, required similar attention. The intensive work of harvest in autumn could be staggered by planting both early- and late-maturing rice, a technique well known in the Heian period.[25] But the work of transplanting rice seedlings required more hands than even a large peasant household could muster. In more recent times Japanese farmers commonly pooled labor for transplanting, the entire village turning out to plant first one field, then another, until all were planted. Such communal effort did not come just from a desire for cooperation: it came from a strong village organization. Such an organization is nowhere evident in Heian or pre-Heian Japan, and in fact does not develop until the fifteenth and sixteenth centuries.[26]

Instead, transplanting was accomplished with the help of hired labor. The Tosa farmer in the *Konjaku* story quoted earlier took hired laborers and food provisions to the "opposite shore" along with rice seedlings, a plow and other tools, and his own family. The very term for the labor organization used in transplanting, *yui*, was associated

---

25 Furushima, *Nihon nōgyō*, vol. 1, pp. 161–63; also Toyoda, *Sangyō shi*, pp. 189–91.
26 Nagahara Keiji (with Kozo Yamamura), "Village Communities and Daimyo Power," in John Whitney Hall and Toyoda Takeshi, eds., *Japan in the Muromachi Age* (Berkeley and Los Angeles: University of California Press, 1977), pp. 107–23.

with the term *yatou*, "to hire."²⁷ Government rice loans in the early summer (discussed in the next section) quite evidently were related to the need to pay laborers in rice to help with early summer transplanting.

Very likely farmers hired their neighbors to help in rice transplanting, and were in turn hired to help transplant their neighbor's crop. Such exchange did not develop into an overall communal labor organization, however, because the political "village" unit by and through which to organize such exchange did not yet exist. Households were often grouped into identifiable hamlets, with shared economic interests and even shared worship at the same shrine, but no village structure arose to integrate hamlets into separate, corporate territorial bodies, nor was any imposed from above by the government. The units of local administration created by central and provincial governments in the Nara and Heian periods bear no relation to any imagined "natural village" unit.²⁸

As a result, Heian peasant households were larger than those of more recent times, maintained a larger and steadier supply of labor within the household, and generally maintained a greater degree of independence one from the other. This relative independence is evident even in the physical layout of Heian hamlets. Instead of lying tightly clustered, as in most Tokugawa and modern communities, houses were distributed in small, loose clumps, or else stood entirely apart from each other.²⁹

The well-excavated site at Hiraide in Nagano prefecture reveals a community of sixteen houses dating from the eighth or the ninth century. As shown in Figure 3.1, the sixteen houses were spread over an arc of nearly 800 meters. Only in one area, near a shrine, are seven found loosely grouped together. Yet even this group was spread over an area about the size of a modern city block, and nearly five city blocks separate the two extreme houses of the hamlet.

A similar distribution of houses can be found in other archaeological sites from this period.³⁰ The scattered nature of peasant hamlets can be seen also in land surveys from the late Heian period. Two of the best-studied cases are shown in Figures 3.2 and 3.3. Although the twenty households of Wakatsuki-no-shō lie within a 300-meter radius of each other, they show only the loosest of clustering. The

---

27 Toyoda, ed., *Sangyō shi*, pp. 192–93.   28 Morris, "Peasant Economy," pp. 108–19.
29 Kinda Akihiro, "Nara Heian-ki no sonraku keitai ni tsuite," *Shirin* 54, 3 (May 1971): 80–108.
30 Kinda, "Nara Heian-ki," p. 114.

Figure 3.1. Eighth- and ninth-century house sites at the Hiraide site. Adapted from Hiraide iseki chōsakai, ed., *Hiraide*, pp. 258–59.

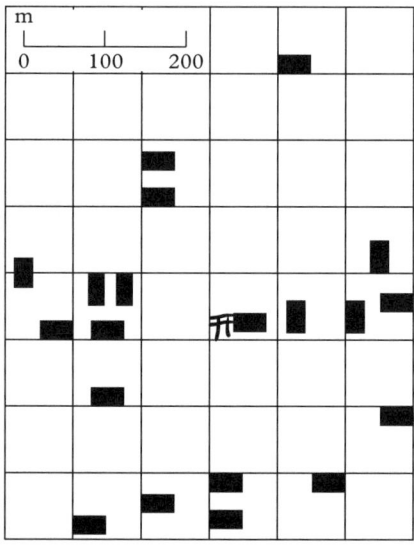

Figure 3.2. Houses in Wakatsuki-no-shō, Yamato Province (twelfth century). Adapted from Kinda Akihiro, "Nara Heian-ki no sonraku keitai ni tsuite," p. 88.

eighteen households of Kohigashi-no-shō are even more scattered: only in two areas can three houses be found within 150 meters of each other.

Without organized communal labor cooperation, peasant households had to be as economically self-sufficient as they were physi-

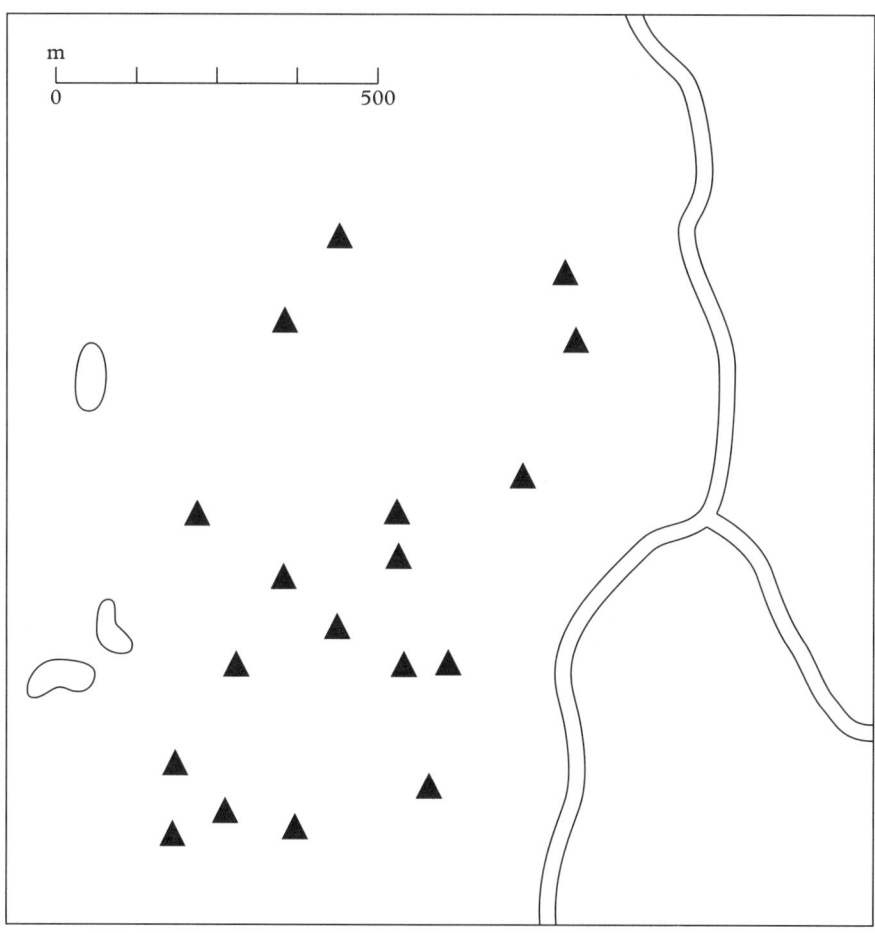

Figure 3.3. Houses in Kohigashi-no-shō, Yamato Province (1144). Adapted from Inagaki Yasuhiko, "Shoki myōden no kōzō," p. 10.

cally separate. This can be seen in the great size of Nara and Heian households. The stem family pattern of Tokugawa Japan produces an average household size of four to, at most, seven persons; under the modern nuclear family pattern the average is far less. By contrast, surviving population records from the early eighth century (the only source for such information) reveal an average household size of eight to ten persons.[31] While not as large as the average of nearly twenty persons that the appearance of these records has led some

---

[31] Morris, "Peasant Economy," pp. 67–73.

historians to surmise, this is still half again larger than the average size of early modern Japanese households, and larger still than any found in premodern Europe.

The principal cause of this enlarged household size was the practice of duolocal marriage. In this pattern, familiar among the Heian aristocracy, husband and wife continued to live in their households of birth even after marriage, but the husband visited the wife periodically at night. The children of the marriage were raised in the mother's household.

In some of the communities found in eighth-century population records the duolocal pattern of marriage is found for several years after marriage, after which the wife and children were brought into the husband's household. But in other communities husbands and wives lived apart for most or all of the marriage. Of the four regions found in this sample, the incident of duolocal marriage among newlyweds varied from 25 percent (Kyushu) to 95 percent (Shimōsa, in the east), and the average length of the duolocal phase from five or six years (Kyushu) to more than fifteen years (the home provinces).[32]

The effects of duolocal marriage on peasant family life must have been profound. Children were raised in a household where there were always other adults to care for them, freeing the mother for farmwork. The mother, in turn, was likely to have greater autonomy in her own natal household than in a household headed by her husband or by in-laws. Her husband, held in his household of birth when he might otherwise have founded an independent household of his own, was allowed correspondingly less autonomy. Overall, duolocal marriage served to strengthen and prolong control by the older generation over the fortunes of the young.

By delaying the departure of married children, practice of duolocal marriage served to retain adult labor in the household. At the same time, splitting of households by noninheriting sons was delayed until the branch households consisted of a more substantial body of individuals. It was this double effect that produced the enlarged average household size of Japanese peasant families. Instead of splitting apart as children reached adulthood and married, setting up branch households too small to manage a farm independently, households retained an ample supply of labor during exactly that stage in the family cycle when labor supply would otherwise have been at its lowest. The practice of duolocal marriage by some family

---

32 Morris, "Peasant Economy," pp. 76–80.

members thus led not only to an enlarged household labor supply overall, but to a steadier supply of labor throughout the family cycle.[33]

In an era when the diffuseness of the peasant community offered only limited support to the individual family, such labor considerations were essential if households were to survive as successful farming units. By the late Heian period, however, households with access to use of a plow and draft animal may have been able to function with correspondingly less human labor. Since a single plow and animal could be spread among several households – indeed, had to be if it were to be cost-effective – shared plow use must have promoted a more tightly organized sense of community than is evident at the beginning of the Heian period. Hence, greater cooperation during the transplanting season when plows were in use, led by the plow owner, may have spread to other periods of the agricultural calendar as well. We might therefore expect to find signs of more tightly organized peasant communities by the end of the Heian period.

There are, in fact, some signs of more tightly clustered hamlets in the late Heian period, but these cases are exceptional. Over most of Japan, compact physical communities did not appear until after the fourteenth century.[34] If plow use promoted greater cooperation of labor and hence a stronger sense of peasant community, we must wait for signs of this in the Kamakura period, when plow and animal use spread most rapidly through Japanese agriculture.[35] Until then, Japanese peasant households continued to maintain a striking level of physical and economic autonomy from each other.

TAX STRUCTURE

Japan's first national tax system, conceived in the late seventh century, reflected what might be called a manorial view of the economy. The state claimed ownership of all rice fields, and expected that they would be planted with seed provided by an ancient system of rice loans known as *suiko*. State revenue was to be collected in kind, as raw materials, handicraft items, and labor. By expressing their tax needs in terms of industrial products and labor, aristocrats in the capital were spared the necessity of obtaining from an uncertain market products essential to their way of life. The new tax levies were

---

33 Morris, "Peasant Economy," pp. 92–95.   34 Kinda, "Nara Heian-ki," pp. 86–103.
35 Furushima, *Nihon nōgyō*, vol. 1, pp. 197–200.

all related to rights traditional to the state from ancient times: the right to direct and promote rice culture, the right to demand tribute from regions not under direct imperial control, and the right to demand corvée labor or payment in lieu of labor from all adult male commoners.

Far from turning Japan into a kind of giant manor, however, the new tax system helped stimulate industrial and commercial development to the point that the manorial conception became no longer necessary to meet the aristocracy's needs. An increasing awareness of this in the Heian period led the central government to adopt a more functional view of the nation's economy and tax structure. Aristocrats in the capital started to view the extraction of tax revenue as a problem between the central and provincial governments rather than between the capital and the commoner population. They came to make their demands for increased revenue not directly of peasants, but of provincial governments. Provincial officials were given incentives to increase the amount of rice lent as *suiko* – the most flexible source of revenue – and new local officials were deputized to expand *suiko* and ensure steady production of other tax income. Tax quotas were set for each province, with provincial officials responsible for seeing that they were met. To a great extent the capital abandoned the actual means of tax collection to provincial and local government. This distanced the central government from the peasantry and greatly enlarged the autonomy of provincial officials in tax collection.

Traditionally, these changes in tax structure have been seen as just so many steps in the breakdown of centralized, bureaucratic government. Yet each change in taxation in the Nara and Heian periods – that is, the expansion of *suiko* loans, the provincial quota system, the manufacture or purchase of handicraft products at the provincial rather than the local level, and the conversion of *suiko* to a direct land tax – was a change that better suited the capital's revenue needs, better ensured that these needs would be met, and increased the efficiency of tax assessment and collection. Far from indicating a breakdown in the organs of government, these changes should be seen as elements of a rationalization of the national tax structure, better fitting it to the Heian rural economy.

Suiko

From ancient times Japanese governments at the local and national levels had made rice loans in the spring or summer that were repaid after the autumn harvest at a substantial rate of interest – 50 percent, in the eighth century. These loans came to be known as *suiko*. Their chief purpose seems to have been the promotion of rice culture. But they had long become equally important as a source of government revenue. Since neither objective – rice planting and state revenue – was considered optional, the loans involved some degree of coercion, although there was frequently also peasant demand for *suiko*. In times of famine, borrowers were often excused from paying interest, which allowed *suiko* to function occasionally as a welfare system as well.

By the early eighth century, income from *suiko* interest was at least equal to the revenue from the second source of income in rice, the land tax (*denso*). In the 730s the central government decided to increase *suiko* income still more, as the growing capital and the expanding provincial governments found existing tax revenues inadequate. This it did by directing provincial officials to increase sharply the amount of rice lent as *suiko,* allowing them to keep a portion of the new interest income as a supplement to their stipends.[36] In 745 rough quotas of *suiko* were set for each province, and a variety of stipend-*suiko* (called *kugetō*) was devised that made permanent the use of *suiko* income as a supplement to the stipends of provincial officials. The idea was that officials would make up from stipend income any deficiencies in the *suiko* quotas that had been set for meeting provincial expenses; anything that remained could then be divided among them as supplemental income.[37]

Unhappy with the job provincial officials were doing as tax collectors, the central government at the beginning of the Heian period tightened the stipend-*suiko* system to prevent officials from taking their supplemental stipends without first making up deficiencies in meeting *suiko* quotas. In 790 it was decreed that a minimum of 10 to 15 percent of stipend-*suiko* (varying by province) was to be applied to *suiko* deficiencies from previous years for as long as such shortfalls were outstanding.[38] A measure of 803 extended this approach to the use of stipend-*suiko* income to pay wage and travel expenses of provincial corvée laborers.[39] These measures served to make standard the amounts from stipend-*suiko* income that were to be used to make up *suiko* deficiencies. The remainder was thus allowed to be-

---

36 Sonoda Kōyū, "Suiko: Tempyō kara Engi made," in Ōsaka rekishi gakkai, ed., *Ritsuryō kokka no kiso kōzō* (Tokyo: Yoshikawa kōbunkan, 1960), pp. 412–17.
37 *Shoku Nihongi*, Tempyō 17/10/5, pp. 184–85.   38 *Shoku Nihongi*, Enryaku 9/11/3, p. 549.
39 *Enryaku kōtai shiki*, in *Kokushi taikei*, vol. 26, Enryaku 22/2/20, p. 15.

come what many officials apparently treated the *suiko* stipend as from the beginning: a simple, and very lucrative, stipend system.

With the institution of stipend-*suiko*, the central government began contracting provincial governments to collect tax revenue by quota rather than by assessment of the tax base. This could be justified because *suiko*, although it acted as a harvest tax, was in theory a loan rather than a tax. Hence, increased *suiko*, however coercive, could be justified by the legal fiction that peasants needed the extra loans. In the course of the ninth century, with this precedent, no further legal fictions were deemed necessary to extend provincial quotas to other taxes as well.

Of equal importance were changes in how *suiko* loans were made. In 795 the interest charge was reduced from 50 to 30 percent; at the same time, *suiko* debts were no longer forgiven when borrowers died before repayment.[40] This latter policy had, in the 730s, reduced the effective return on *suiko* to about 40 percent, largely because of canny borrowers who took out loans in the names of persons already dead.[41] It is entirely possible that by 795 the effective return had dropped to close to 30 percent, so that there may have been little change in actual *suiko* income under the new rules. The new approach had a major impact nonetheless, for it was no longer necessary that *suiko* loans be secured only by individual borrowers.

This meant that *suiko* could now be "levied" as a straight tax. In 807, for example, the circuit inspector for the northern Tōsandō provinces recommended that *suiko* be levied by household size.[42] The following year the central government proposed a more complex approach: each adult male taxpayer would be lent 10 to 100 *soku* (36 to 360 liters) of rice, half in spring and half in summer, on a sliding scale according to wealth – that is, the wealthier, though less needy, would be lent more because of their greater ability to repay.[43]

The growing recognition of *suiko* as a tax made it possible to assess *suiko* by unit of rice cultivation. Levy by land area presented several advantages over securing loans by individuals. As long as *suiko* was lent to individuals, it was tied to its traditional justification as a

---

40 *Ruijū sandai kyaku*, in *Kokushi taikei*, vol. 25, *kan* 14, Enryaku 14/int.7/1, p. 396; *Ruijū kokushi*, in *Kokushi taikei*, vol. 5, *kan* 83, Enryaku 15/int.7/21, p. 451. There was a brief return to 50 percent interest from 806, a year of crop failure, until 810, the first year of good harvest after 806: *Nihon kōki*, in *Kokushi taikei*, vol. 3, Daidō 1/1/29, p. 51; and *Ruijūsandai kyaku*, *kan* 14, Kōnin 1/9/23, p. 396.
41 See Funao Yoshimasa, "Suiko no jittai ni kansuru ichikōsatsu: Bitchū no kuni taizei o ōtaru shibōnin chō o chūshin to shite," *Shirin* 56,5 (September 1973): 74–102.
42 *Ruijū kokushi*, *kan* 83, Daidō 2/9/21, p. 455.
43 *Ruijū sandai kyaku*, *kan* 14, Daidō 3/9/26, pp. 395–96.

welfare measure and so might be resisted by unwilling borrowers. But once *suiko* was assessed by unit of rice cultivation, the welfare pretense was abandoned and *suiko* became a variety of harvest tax. Administration of *suiko* was also made simpler, for it was now assessed on the same basis as the land tax.

The first evidence of *suiko* assessment by land area is from Kawachi Province in 822.[44] By the end of the ninth century requests from provinces for permission to levy *suiko* at the rate of 5 *soku* (18 liters) of rice per *tan* of land (0.1 hectare) had become common.[45] In 901 the central government instructed all provinces to lend *suiko* at this rate as necessary to ensure that *suiko* quotas were met.[46] At 30 percent, *suiko* interest at the official rate of levy came to 1.5 *soku* per *tan*, which was identical to the land tax (*denso*) rate.

The central government welcomed the levy of *suiko* loans, as this better ensured that provincial *suiko* quotas would be met. After 900, provinces were held much more strictly responsible for seeing that these quotas were met. Quotas were now known as *shiki* quotas (*shikisū*), after the administrative guidebooks, most particularly *Engi shiki* (927), in which the quotas were set. From about 905 provinces were required to petition for permission to lend and collect interest on less than the quota amounts.[47] The amount of the reductions allowed in these quotas is known for seven provinces between 945 and 1093: reductions varied from 10 to 70 percent and were greatest in the home provinces, and least in the east.[48]

The next step after levy of *suiko* loans by land area was to delete the loan entirely and levy the interest as a direct tax.[49] In concept this was a giant departure from the use of *suiko* as a welfare measure and aid to agriculture. In practice, however, it was the logical outcome of the attitude, two centuries old, that acceptance of *suiko*

---

44 *Ruijū kokushi*, kan 83, Kōnin 13/12/28, pp. 456–57.
45 *Sandai jitsuroku*, in *Kokushi taikei*, vol. 4, Genkei 5/3/14, p. 495; *Ruijū sandai kyaku*, kan 14, Kampyō 6/2/23, p. 402, and kan 20, Shōtai 4/int.6/25, pp. 636–37.
46 *Sandai jitsuroku*, Genkei 5/3/14, p. 495.
47 *Ruijū sandai kyaku*, kan 14, Engi 5/12/25, p. 398, and kan 15, Engi 5/12/25, pp. 397–98; *Besshū fusenshō*, in *Kokushi taikei*, vol. 27, Engi 7/8/11, suppl. p. 4.
48 See Abe Takeshi, *Ritsuryō kokka kaitai katei no kenkyū* (Tokyo: Shinseisha, 1966), pp. 123–27.
49 Levy of *suiko* interest without loan of principal is reported by Owari Province in 988: Takeuchi Rizō, ed., *Heian ibun*, 13 vols. (Tokyo: Tōkyōdō, 1963:b274), vol. 2, no. 339 (Eien 2/11/8), pp. 473–85; by Yamashiro Province in 1001: *Chōya gunsai*, in *Kokushi taikei*, vol. 29,1, kan 26, Chōhō 3, pp. 533–34; by Tosa Province in 1004: *Chōya gunsai*, kan 26, Kankō 1/11/20, pp. 534–35; by Kōzuke Province in 1030 or 1031: *Heian ibun*, vol. 9, no. 4609 (Chōgen 3 or 4), pp. 3511–12; by Kōzuke Province again in 1076: *Chōya gunsai*, kan 26, Jōhō 3/12/15, p. 541; and by Sagami Province in 1093: *Chōya gunsai*, kan 26, Kanji 7/6, pp. 539–40.

loans was an obligatory benevolence, and that the state could legitimately count on collecting the same level of *suiko* interest income each year regardless of peasant demand or need for loans.

But however logical from the point of view of government needs, such a major departure from the traditional justification of *suiko* was not easily made. What led to the transformation of *suiko* into a direct land tax was not just central government demand for steady "interest" income, but, rather, this factor coupled with the depletion or loss of *suiko* principal. Time and again, mid-Heian provincial government documents explain that *suiko* principal was no longer lent because it was either "totally nonexistent" or in the hands of local tax managers.[50] Most commonly, provincial officials transferred *suiko* principal to local tax managers in return for promise of a guaranteed level of "interest" income. Whether local tax managers chose to lend rice to produce this interest or to keep it and extract "interest" as a direct land tax was up to them. In the latter case the *suiko* supplies became "totally nonexistent," but the provincial government received the same level of *suiko* income nonetheless.

It is not clear how early the transfer of *suiko* rice from provincial to local officials occurred, but eleventh-century sources speak of this transfer as already "long ago."[51] From the early ninth century we find references to two related practices by which local *suiko* lenders took control of *suiko* rice stores to become thereafter permanent managers of local tax collection.[52] The first, known as "partial repayment" (*hankyo*), is explained by Sugawara no Michizane: a portion of the *suiko* supply, theoretically half but possibly more, was kept by the local tax manager, but interest was delivered in full.[53] The practice of the second, "falsified repayment" (*kyonō*), was similar: lesser grains, or even straw, were substituted for *suiko* principal, but interest was delivered properly in rice. In both cases *suiko* principal was retained by local tax collectors with provincial cooperation, but undoubtedly the idea originated with local officials.

At first the central, and some provincial, governments looked askance at local control of *suiko* principal. But by the eleventh cen-

---

50 For example, *Heian ibun* vol 9, no. 4609 (Chōgen 3 or 4), pp. 3511–12.
51 *Heian ibun*, vol. 9, no. 4609 (Chōgen 3 or 4), pp. 3511–12.
52 The first reference to these practices (*hankyo* and *kyonō*) is *Nihon kōki*, Kōnin 6/12/29, pp. 136–37.
53 *Kanke bunsō*, kan 4, Kampyō 3/7/5; quoted in Murai Yasuhiko, *Kodai kokka kaitai katei no kenkyū* (Tokyo: Iwanami shoten, 1965), pp. 30–31.

tury high officials no longer seem concerned over the loss of *suiko* principal, even that which local officials themselves admitted was long gone. This is clear, for example, from a document of 1080 or 1081 from the eastern province of Kōzuke, which shows that local tax managers were committed to certain levels of *suiko* payment to the provincial government regardless of the presence or absence of *suiko* principal.[54] This source, in fact, also claims that the capital authorized transfer of provincial *suiko* rice to local officials as early as 966.

It appears it was local tax managers, then, who initiated the collection of *suiko* interest as a direct land tax without loan of principal. Already in the ninth century the "true" land tax (*denso*), was coupled with provincial *suiko* (generally known as *shōzei*) to form a single land tax known as *sozei*.[55] At 30 percent interest, as we saw, the return on *suiko* levied at 5 *soku* per *tan* was 1.5 *soku* per *tan*. This was identical to the rate at which the *denso* land tax was levied, so that the combined *sozei* tax came to 3 *soku* per *tan*. This amounted to 8 to 9 percent of a typical crop yield of 35 *soku* per *tan*.

It was clearly to the advantage of local tax managers to levy *suiko* "interest" without making actual loans, as this freed them to put *suiko* rice stores to their own private use. Less obvious, perhaps, is that this was to the provincial government's advantage as well, as it freed provinces to transfer tax collection authority to new officials if earlier tax managers failed to deliver the level of land tax income assessed of their districts. Were the lending of *suiko* principal still necessary to collect *suiko* interest, provincial governments would have been unable to transfer local tax collection authority without somehow inducing former officials to give up *suiko* stores to new officials. Without provincial support, local officials might have been unable to force peasants to pay *suiko* interest as a direct land tax without first making *suiko* loans. But with provincial and, ultimately, central government officials backing local tax managers, there was little the tenth-century peasant could do to resist the transformation of *suiko* into a direct land tax – the obligation to accept *suiko* loans and pay *suiko* interest regardless of peasant need had been a recognized state right for at least two and a half centuries.

---

54 *Heian ibun*, vol. 9, no. 4609 (Chōgen 3or 4), pp. 3511–12 12f.
55 See, for example, *Montoku jitsuroku*, in *Kokushi taikei*, vol. 3, Kajō 3/4/17, pp. 7–8, and 3/4/24, p. 9; *Ruijū sandai kyaku*, kan 8, Kampyō 5/5/17, p. 343; and *Heian ibun*, vol. 2, no. 339 (Eien 2/11/8), pp. 473–85.

The handicraft-produce taxes

The eighth-century tax structure included two taxes that were paid in handicraft or industrial products such as silk cloth, silk floss, linen or paper mulberry cloth, iron, salt, fish, seaweed, and many other local products. One part of Japan, however, departed sharply from this essentially manorial approach to taxation: in the central provinces, both taxes were commonly paid in cash.

The *chō* tax was assessed on adult taxable men, with a full share paid by men aged 21 to 60, a half share by men 61 to 65, and lesser amounts by men 17 to 20 according to a separate schedule. The *yō* tax, paid in a lesser variety of goods, was set generally at half the *chō* rate, and was due from men aged 21 to 65 only, assessed as for *chō*. Technically, *yō* was the commutation of a corvée labor requirement of ten days a year (five days for men 61 to 65), but, as in China, the corvée requirement seems to have been only theoretical. From the beginning, therefore, the two taxes were of one nature. Although the requirement could be satisfied by products in kind as well as by handcrafted items, for convenience we will refer to the *chō* and *yō* taxes as handicraft taxes, after their most important element.

The original plan was that handicraft items would be produced by the taxpayers from whom they were due. But already in the eighth century there is evidence that taxpayers pooled their resources to hire handicraft specialists to make the items required.[56] This soon became the key principle by which the handicraft-tax system was transformed in the ninth and tenth centuries.

From about 770 the central government began to complain of a serious decline in both the quality and quantity of handicraft tax products. In 785 several provincial officials were punished for sending payments that were both late and of poor quality.[57] In 797 the capital complained that hoes sent as handicraft payments were so thin and of such poor material that they were utterly unsuited to agricultural use; provincial and district officials were accused of keeping all the good hoes for themselves.[58]

Several steps were taken to prod provincial officials to more diligent delivery of the handicraft taxes. Officials were to pay more attention to registering migrants (*furōnin*) to be sure that persons farming land in *shōen* (estate) property did not evade tax payments. More

---

56 Abe, *Ritsuryō kokka*, p. 141.
57 *Shoku Nihongi*, Enryaku 4/5/24, p. 508, and 4/7/28, p. 511.
58 *Ruijū sandai kyaku, kan 7*, Enryaku 16/4/16, p. 330.

concretely, the government required that provincial officials after 795 make up from their *suiko* stipends any deficiencies in payments of silk (due from handicraft taxes) or rice (due from the land tax).[59]

Nonetheless, complaints continued that deliveries of the handicraft taxes were late, incomplete, and of poor quality. This led the central government to institute a major overhaul of the handicraft tax system in the 840s. At some time before 846, each province was instructed to make a final measurement of its number of taxable men, to be used thereafter as a fixed rate by which each province's handicraft tax liability was to be calculated. As with later *suiko* quotas, each province had to petition the capital for permission to reduce the number of taxable men used to calculate its handicraft dues.[60] In 846 provinces were also instructed to levy each year 10 percent of the accumulated deficiencies in previous years' payments of the two handicraft taxes, to be paid on top of what was required for the current year.[61]

At either the same time or somewhat later, the central government also set for each province minimum quotas of specific products that were to be included in its annual handicraft tax payments; these quotas can be found in *Engi shiki*.[62] By these measures the central government withdrew from concern with the assessment and collection of the two handicraft taxes, and left the provincial governments responsible only for meeting specified handicraft tax quotas. The new system was apparently a success: from this time the capital rarely complained of lateness or poor quality in handicraft tax products.[63]

By setting quotas for the handicraft taxes, the central government left provincial and local officials free to jettison assessment by population in favor of more efficient methods of collection. Tax liability could be commuted to payments in rice, which were used to purchase products required by the quotas at the marketplace, or pay for their manufacture at workshops run by provincial or local officials.

By the early tenth century the central government had set provincial quotas for products outside of the handicraft taxes proper. *Engi*

---

59 *Ruijū sandai kyaku*, kan 8, Enryaku 4/12/9, pp. 339–40, Enryaku 16/8/3, p. 340, and Enryaku 21/8/27, p. 331; *Enryaku kōtai shiki*, Enryaku 14/7/27, pp. 15–17.
60 Nishibeppu Motoka, "Kyū seiki chūyō ni okeru kokusei kichō no tenkan ni tsuite," *Nihonshi kenkyū* 169 (September 1976): 30–54.
61 *Ruijū sandai kyaku*, kan 8, Shōwa 13/8/17, p. 342.
62 The quotas of items provinces were to include in their annual *chō* and *yō* payments are found in *Engi shiki*, kan 24, pp. 597–622.
63 Nishibeppu, *Kyū seiki chōyō*," pp. 42–43.

shiki records quotas of paper, brushes, raw linen, leather, and tools that were to be purchased by provinces with income from *suiko*.[64] These quotas belong to a developing category of taxation, known as "miscellaneous offerings" (*kōeki zōmotsu*), that first attained real importance in the tenth century. Originally such exactions were "tribute" offerings by district officials (*gunji*), who were to purchase them with income from the *suiko* stores under their control (*guntō*). When district *suiko* was added to provincial *suiko* stores in 712, the responsibility for miscellaneous offerings was transferred to the provincial governments. By the tenth century there seem to have been at least three ways to meet quotas for miscellaneous offerings: provincial governments either sent directly to the capital the rice necessary to purchase the products required, or levied an additional land tax equivalent to price of miscellaneous offerings and used the proceeds to purchase these at the marketplace, or levied the items required directly as a tax in kind.[65]

In short, quotas for miscellaneous offerings were met in just the same way as quotas for the handicraft taxes proper: direct levies in kind, indirect levies as an added land tax, purchase at the marketplace, or, in at least some areas, manufacture in government workshops. Despite their different origins, therefore, beginning in the tenth century the original handicraft taxes and the newer (though with roots as old) miscellaneous offerings may be considered as one system. "Tribute" from local officials (*kōeki zōmotsu*), "tribute" from the commoner population (*chō*), and commutation payments for labor owed the state by commoners (*yō*) had all been transformed into a shopping list of quotas of goods that provinces were to deliver to the capital.

Corvée

The final component of the eighth-century tax structure to be considered is the provincial corvée labor requirement (*zōyō*). Corvée duty was not to exceed sixty days a year for taxable men 21 to 60 (or thirty days for men 61 to 65, fifteen for men 17 to 20). A taxpayer could hire others to serve in his place. Generally, it is thought,

---

64 "*Nenryō bekkō zōmotsu*" and "*nenryō zakki*": see *Engi shiki*, kan 26, pp. 586–87.
65 *Heian ibun*, vol. 2, no. 339: Eien 2/11/8, pp. 473–85, and *Seiji yōryaku*, in *Kokushi taikei*, vol. 28, kan 57, Tengyō 2/int.7/5, pp. 437–38. *Kōeki zōmotsu* quotas are given in *Engi shiki*, kan 26, pp. 591–94.

corvée labor was at first uncompensated, although the evidence either way is rather thin.[66] In the course of the eighth century, however, an increasing number of corvée laborers were paid at least subsistence wages.

In 795 the central government complained that provincial and local officials invariably used corvée labor up to the maximum sixty days allowed per adult male taxpayer. Since wealthy peasants could pay others to serve for them, only the poor were actually taken away from personal business by labor service. This encouraged officials to levy the maximum so as to collect the commuted payments of those who could afford not to serve. For this reason, the central government reduced the maximum corvée levy from sixty to thirty days a year.[67]

From 808 the central government began to require that provincial officials submit annual reports to all uses of corvée labor. This brought a temporary halt to the long tradition of local freedom in the levy of corvée.[68] In 822, for the first time since the Taihō code a century earlier, a national remission of corvée was declared. Ostensibly so that arrangements could be made to hire wage labor this year, each province was instructed to report for what uses corvée labor was absolutely essential. But, in fact, the central government used these reports to prepare a table of legitimate uses of corvée labor and the number of workers who could be employed for each use. A few categories of work – repair of government buildings, construction of irrigation canals and embankments, courier service for government business, and the like – were left to the discretion of provincial officials. To use more than the prescribed number of workers for any other purpose, however, provinces had to apply for permission from the capital.[69]

With its newly established control over corvée labor, the central government issued in the 840s and 850s a series of reductions in the maximum labor requirement. In 864 the requirement was reduced permanently to twenty days a year.[70] As a result of these strictures on the use of corvée, an increasing amount of government work was handled by more highly compensated hired labor, financed by income from *suiko* interest. By the tenth century the levy of corvée properly speaking had all but disappeared.

66 Abe, *Ritsuryō kokka*, pp. 210–12.
67 *Ruijū sandai kyaku*, kan 17, Enryaku 14/int.7/15, p. 517.
68 *Nihon kōki*, Daidō 3/8/6, p. 76.
69 *Ruijū sandai kyaku*, kan 6, Kōnin 13/int.9/20, pp. 278–80.
70 *Sandai jitsuroku*, Jōgan 6/1/7, pp. 121–3, Jōgan 6/1/9, p. 124, and Jōgan 6/1/29, p. 130.

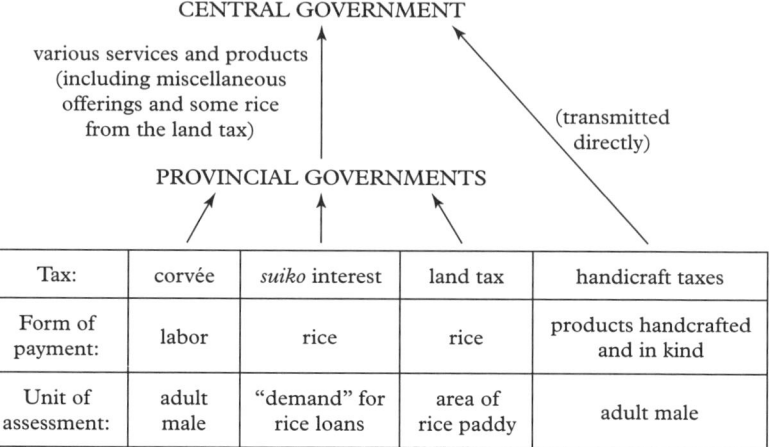

Figure 3.4. Tax structure in the late seventh and eighth centuries.

The new tax structure of the tenth century

The changes in Japanese tax structure from the seventh to tenth centuries that have just been discussed are summarized in Figures 3.4, 3.5, and 3.6. It will be noted that in the tenth century the former taxes on land (*denso*), on handicraft produce (*chō* and *yō*), and the quasi-tax *suiko* were all reorganized into a single, enlarged land tax (*nengu*, or *kammotsu*). To this unified land tax was added a new set of duties, levied primarily by provincial and local officials, that were known variously as "occasional exactions" (*rinji zōyaku*) or "public duties" (*kuji*, or *kuniyaku*).

The most detailed source for the rate and structure of the enlarged land tax of the tenth century is the famous Owari Province petition of 988, in which Owari district officials and other local notables requested that their governor, Fujiwara no Motonaga, be removed from office for gross misconduct.[71] Because of the nature of the petition, it is necessary to disentangle those taxes described which were the norm for all provinces from levies that were the particular excesses of Motonaga. Fortunately, the petitioners made clear comparisons to neighboring provinces and gave the total land tax rate for both Owari and neighboring provinces.

The land tax described in the first six articles of the Owari

---

71 *Heian ibun*, vol. 2, no. 339: Eien 2/11/8, pp. 473–85. Also see Abe Takeshi, *Owari no kuni gebumi no kenkyū* (Tokyo: Shinseisha, 1971).

TAX STRUCTURE

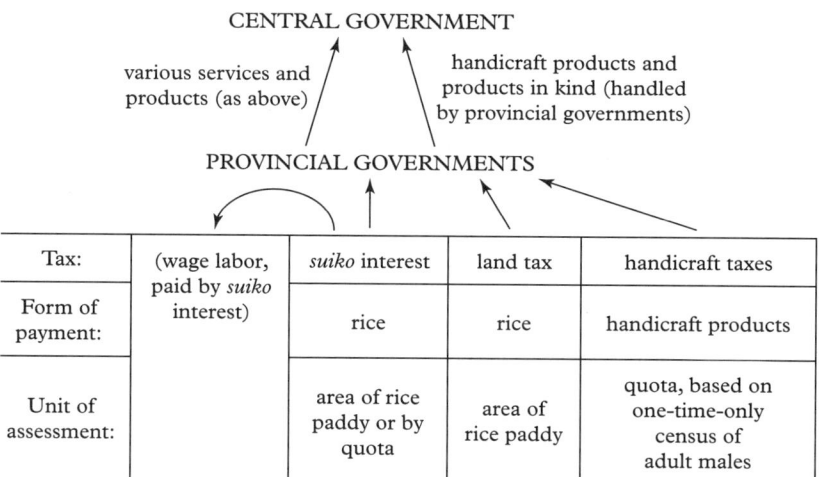

Figure 3.5. Tax structure in the ninth century.

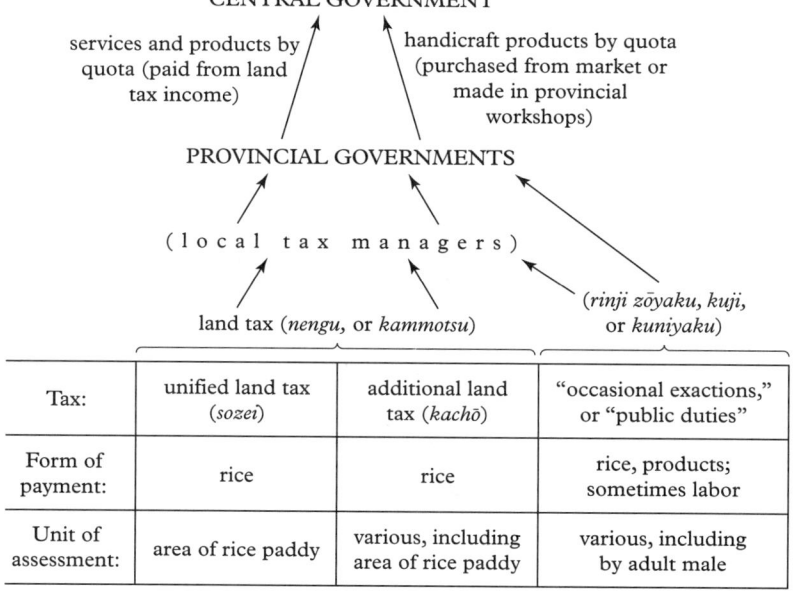

Figure 3.6. Tax structure in the tenth century.

province petition was composed of five parts. The first, the old land tax (*denso*), was imposed at 1.5 *soku* per *tan*. The second, the regular *suiko* levy, was based on the *suiko* quotas set for Owari by the capital. The original quota, as found in *Engi shiki*, would have produced a levy of 4 *soku* per *tan* of "loan," or 1.2 *soku* of interest.[72] This had been officially reduced, however, to a quota producing a levy of 0.6 *soku* per *tan* of "interest" for which no principal was loaned (Article One). There was also, however, an "additional *suiko* levy" of 2.8 *soku* per *tan* to be used for government expenses (Article Four). Other provinces also levied such additional *suiko* dues; the complaint of the Owari petitioners was that Motonaga pocketed the additional levy for himself. On top of these three legitimate taxes, Motonaga was accused of levying a "secret extra *suiko* levy" that came to 1.1 *soku* per *tan* (Article One).

The fifth and final element of the tenth-century land tax was an "additional levy" (*kachō*) used to purchase the handicraft products required by central government quotas. In Owari the *chō* handicraft tax was assessed by assigning 24 *tan* of rice fields to produce, at 4 *soku* per *tan*, the rice necessary to purchase each bolt of silk required. In fact, Motonaga manipulated this system so that only 11 *tan* of land was to pay for one bolt of silk, forcing local officials to extract over twice the proper levy (Article Six). In addition, Motonaga forced producers of handicraft items to accept only half the market price for silk and other cloth, and to deliver bonus cloth for his own use (Article Five). Motonaga also made local officials levy *kachō* twice, collecting rice a second time to be ground into brown rice (*shōmai*) that met other state quotas (Article Three). These brown rice quotas should have been met from the first additional *suiko* levy (2.8 *soku* per *tan*), but, again, Motonaga was accused of keeping this income for himself. Hence the total *kachō* levy of 7.2 *soku* per *tan* was nearly twice what it was supposed to be and was augmented by further illicit payments extracted by Motonaga. For other provinces it is said the *kachō* levy was between 3 and 4 *soku* per *tan* (Article Three).

The above land tax information from the Owari Province petition is summarized in Table 3.2. The total for Owari, 13.2 *soku* per *tan*, is given in Article Five of the petition itself.

It is a measure of the central government's degree of reliance on

---

72 The twelfth-century work *Shōchūreki*, in *Zoku gunsho ruijū* (Tokyo: Zoku gunsho ruijū kanseikai, 1923–30), vol. 32, part 1, p. 101, gives the land area planted to rice in the early tenth century in Owari Province as 119,400 *tan*. *Engi shiki* gives a *suiko* quota for Owari of 472,000 *soku* of rice, which would have come to 4 *soku* per *tan*.

TABLE 3.2
Land tax rates in the late tenth century

Land tax components	Tax rate per tan of rice field (in *soku*)	
	Owari Province	Other Provinces
land tax (*denso*)	1.5	1.5
regular *suiko* levy	0.6	0.6
additional *suiko* levy	2.8	2.8
"secret" extra *suiko* levy by Motonaga in Owari	1.1	—
additional levy (*kachō*), to pay miscellaneous offerings, handicraft taxes, and other quota items	7.2	4.0[a]
Total land tax	13.2	8.9[b]

[a] "3 to 4 *soku* per *tan*" (Article Three).
[b] "8 to 10 *soku* per *tan*" (Article Five).
Note: 1 *soku* = 3.6 liters; 1 *tan* = 0.1 hectare. A good annual yield in this period was 50 *soku* per *tan*; an average yield, 35 *soku* per *tan*.
Source: "Owari no kuni gunji hyakusei ra ge," in Takeuchi Rizō, ed., *Heian ibun* (Tokyo: Tōkyōdō, 1974), vol. 2, no. 339, Eien 2/11/8.

provincial officials, local officials, and quasi-official tax managers in the mid-Heian period that for the first time in at least two centuries they were permitted to levy new exactions of their own that were not in any way connected with central government revenue. Somewhat euphemistically known as "occasional exactions" (*rinji zōyaku*), these new taxes were generally levied on individuals rather than by land unit, and included, significantly, a reappearance of the institution of corvée labor, which in its earlier form (*zōyō*) had been all but regulated out of existence in the ninth century.

The earliest reference to occasional exactions is in 889, where they are described as "new"[73] – and, indeed, we do not hear of them again until 924. For after 924, references become more numerous: "occasional" or not, occasional exactions became a permanent part of the provincial tax structure from about the mid-tenth century on. In contrast to the unified, expanded land tax (*nengu*, or *kammotsu*), occasional exactions were levied entirely for the benefit of local and provincial officials. They came under central government control only indirectly, when *shōen* proprietors in

[73] *Heian ibun*, vol. 9, no. 4549: Kampyō 1/12/26, pp. 3464–70.

the capital requested that officials on their estates be excused from all locally imposed duties. In the tenth century occasional exactions were levied only on products such as silk and other cloths, lamp oil, *sake*, and cedar bark.[74] Again, unlike the land tax, they were generally assessed by population rather than land area, and were most likely due only from adult males.

After 1000, however, occasional exactions were expanded to include both a land tax in rice (*tammai*), separate from the regular land tax, and corvée labor. It also became increasingly common to assess occasional exactions by land unit rather than by population.[75] The most common term for occasional exactions in the eleventh century was "public duties" (*kuji*), a somewhat misleading term, inasmuch as these so-called public duties were permitted mainly in order to reward local and provincial officials for providing through land tax income the goods and services required by quota by the central government. One warning, however: "public duties" sometimes denoted all "occasional exactions," and sometimes all but the corvée element, which is called "labor services" (*buyaku*); at other times the term is used more broadly still to include that portion of the land tax used to meet quotas for handicraft and industrial products.

By whatever name, the privilege to levy occasional exactions was part of the price the central government allowed for the successful functioning of its provincial quota system. For the direct levy of land tax (*denso*), *suiko* loans, and handicraft taxes (*chō* and *yō*) in the eighth century, the central government by the tenth century had substituted the indirect levy of their equivalents on provincial governments. These indirect levies were translated by the provincial governments into a broad land tax payable by peasants in rice that, as shown in Table 3.2, brought together all the exactions of the earlier tax system. Through this system the central government at length succeeded in stabilizing its income in the course of the ninth and tenth centuries, but at a cost: quotas were all but frozen at levels that fit the tax base as it stood about the year 900. After 900, agricultural output continued to increase through expansion of arable land, especially in the eastern provinces, and even more through the greater security of cultivation and higher yields promoted by the diffusion of the plow and by the agrarian regime associated with it. But as a general rule, it may be argued that none of this growth in pro-

---

74 Abe, *Ritsuryō kokka*, pp. 215–31; Okuno Nakahiko, "Rinji zōyaku no seiritsu to tenkai," *Nihon rekishi*, 255 (August 1969): 32–49.
75 Okuno, "Rinji zōyaku," pp. 32–49.

duction was captured as increased tax revenue for the central government; nor should it be thought that estate proprietors (discussed in the next section) captured more than a small share. Instead, increases garnered from agrarian expansion were captured by local tax managers as land on which they did not pay public land tax (*kammotsu*), and by both provincial and local officials through the new "occasional exactions" (*rinji zōyaku; kuji*).

LANDHOLDING

In the eighth century, tenure of rice-producing farmland took three forms: household fields (*kubunden*), public fields (*kōden*), and reclaimed fields (*konden*). Household fields were allotted, or rearranged, each six years under the allotment system known as *handen*, which apportioned rice fields according to each household's size and composition. Household fields could not be sold or exchanged, or used as security in making loans, although their crop potential could be mortgaged.[76] Despite these restrictions, household fields were legally classified as "private fields," as they were held by households as long as they had labor to cultivate them. This is in accord with other evidence that private ownership of land in early Japan was recognized only so long as land was actively in use.[77] There seems every reason to believe, therefore, that the allotment system in early Japan, though inspired by Chinese example, had traditional roots that explain the extraordinary differences between the Japanese practice, which was basically a success, and its Chinese prototype, which quickly failed.[78]

Rice fields that remained after the first full national application of the allotment system in the 690s were classified as "public fields" (*kōden*). A sizable proportion of these were set aside to support rank-holders, officeholders, temples or shrines, or were awarded to individual aristocrats. It is known that in the early eighth century public fields set aside for these purposes came to 20,000 to 25,000 hectares, which was somewhat under 5 percent of the total area under rice cultivation, estimated as between 600,000 and 700,000 hectares.[79] A very small proportion of these (some 750 hectares, in the home provinces and in Kyushu) were at first farmed with corvée labor; after ex-

---

[76] Takeuchi, *Tochi seido shi*, p. 56.
[77] See, for example, the laws relating to land tenure codified in *Ryō no shūge*, in *Kokushi taikei*, vol. 24, "Den-ryō," pp. 370, 372–73.
[78] Morris, "Peasant Economy," pp. 31–33. [79] Takeuchi, *Tochi seido shi*, pp. 69–77.

penses, about half of the crop went to the holder of the fields. A much larger group, some 9,000 hectares, was assigned to district officials as supplemental "private fields" (on top of their assigned household fields). Like household and reclaimed fields, these could be either farmed by the holder's family or rented to others. The remainder of public fields, 50 to 60 percent of the total, was leased by provincial governments to peasant farmers at a rent set at 20 percent of the assessed yield of each field. These rents were collected by the provincial governments and forwarded along with other tax income to the beneficiaries of the public fields in the capital.

The great bulk of public fields, however, were not assigned to specific beneficiaries but were simply rented at large by provincial governments to local farmers in this same manner – at 20 percent of assessed yield. The rent from these fields was added to the general tax income forwarded from the provinces to the capital. No figures survive for the total area of public fields nationwide, but for one district to Tōtōmi Province in 740 the ratio of public to household fields was 1:5; for the entire island of Kyushu in 823, it was 1:6.[80]

All rice fields brought under cultivation after the first land distribution in the 690s were classified as reclaimed fields (*konden*). The original idea, expressed in the codes, was that reclaimed fields would be held privately for the remainder of the developer's life, but after his death would be added to the pool of rice fields available for distribution as household fields. But in 723 the term for which reclaimed fields could be held was first extended to include descendants through the original developer's great-grandchildren. Then in 743, before any fields could have passed so far, reclaimed fields were made the personal property of the holder and his heirs in perpetuity. From this time on they also could be freely bought and sold.

In view of the central government's tremendous concern with the allocation and taxation of rice fields, it is a surprising fact that fields growing other crops were regulated hardly at all until at least the eleventh century. Dry fields – those planted to crops other than rice – resembled reclaimed fields in that they could be freely disposed of by sale or inheritance. At the same time, they resembled household fields in that they generally could be claimed by a family only so long as they were actively cultivated. But dry fields were not directly taxed, nor did the government concern itself with their tenure. Not the least important purpose of government regulation of

---

80 *Nara ibun*, vol. 1, pp. 281–88; *Ruijū sandai kyaku*, kan 15, Kūnin 14/2/21, pp. 434–37.

rice culture was to ensure that adequate rice was produced to satisfy the aristocratic diet. Other grains grown in the Nara and Heian periods – in rough order of importance, these were millet, barley, wheat, and buckwheat – were probably of more importance to the peasant diet than rice, as were soybean and vegetable crops. But all of these products concerned the central government only marginally, as "miscellaneous exactions" that could be purchased with provincial rice income.

Two major changes in land tenure marked the early Heian period: the cessation of the distribution of household fields, and the reorganization of farmland to meet the changes in tax structure already discussed. The characteristic product of this reorganization was the unit of tax assessment and management known as *myō*.

Under the allotment system instituted in the seventh century, household fields were adjusted to fit changes in household size and composition shortly after each population registration (*koseki*), every six or seven years. This system worked for about a century. Then in 794 – the year of the move to the Heian capital – distribution of household fields was held up, and did not take place until 800. The distribution of 800 was the first to include the provinces of Satsuma and Ōsumi on the extreme southern frontier. It thus became both the first and last land distribution to be carried out through the entire country.[81]

After 800, distributions were carried out only sporadically. Distribution in 828 can be verified for only the home provinces and the province of Kōzuke in the east. After 828, household fields in the home provinces were not adjusted for fifty years, until 881, when fields were redistributed principally to enable the establishment of 4,000 hectares of new imperial fields mandated in 879.[82] Some distributions occurred in other provinces in this period, but none at all, it seems, in the 830s or 840s. The national histories report that land registers were made in 843 and 844, but that officials were unable to carry out a redistribution of household fields.[83]

The process by which the distribution system was terminated in the ninth century is revealed in two population registers that survive from the early tenth century.[84] These two registers tell a rather re-

---

81 Torao Toshiya, *Handen shujū-hō no kenkyū* (Tokyo: Yoshikawa kōbunkan, 1961), pp. 307–16.
82 Nishibeppu, "Kyū seiki chūyō," p. 43. 83 Torao, *Handen shujū-hō*, p. 326.
84 *Heian ibun*, vol. 1, no. 188: Engi 2, pp. 224–40, and no. 199: Engi 8, pp. 289–305. See Hirata Shūji, "Heian jidai no koseki ni tsuite," in Toyoda Takeshi kanreki kinenkai, ed., *Nihon kodai chūsei no chihō-teki tenkai* (Tokyo: Yoshikawa kōbunkan, 1973), pp. 59–96.

markable story that, surprisingly, tends to disprove traditional contentions that the land distribution system broke down in the ninth century because of the resistance of local officials and the misappropriation of public land by aristocrats and temples. The process was, in fact, rather more orderly than that.

The two registers, from Awa Province in 902 and Suō Province in 908, list an enormous preponderance of women – 88 and 73 percent of the population, respectively – and of aged persons, including a number aged over 100. The distribution of ages above 70, however, is not unlike the curve expected in a normal population starting at age 1. The distribution from 40 to 70 is nearly stable. Below age 40, in defiance of demographic logic, the population shrinks with descending age until, below age 10, no younger persons are recorded.[85]

This remarkable pattern, found in two registers from widely separate provinces, could not have come about through random fabrication. It would appear that local officials, following directives from above, ceased to record new births from about 830 to 870. During this period the registered population was regularly advanced in age, but without note of births or deaths. Then in the 870s births were again added, but at a declining rate until 894, after which no new persons were added. It is likely these births were added to take the place of persons in the register whose recorded age had become improbably advanced.

By making no changes in registered population after the 830s, other than regular advances in ages, household fields as then distributed were made permanent household possessions. Although redistributions were ostensibly resumed in the 870s and 880s, new persons were added to the registers only to replace names that had to be removed because of improbably high age. This guaranteed that there would be no net change in household field eligibility. To further ensure that households would not appear eligible for increased allotments, officials altered the registration of most men to women, who were eligible for only two-thirds the allotment due men. This was clearly done after men had first been registered by their correct gender: "children" (of whatever age) were listed in two descending sequences, as in earlier registers, but whereas in the eighth-century registers the first sequence was of sons and the second of daughters, in the tenth-century registers both are of daughters.

Manipulation of population registers after the 830s was made pos-

---

85 Hirata, "Heian jidai no koseki," pp. 71–77.

sible by the policy changes in the early 840s, already discussed, that fixed the number of taxable males in each province at then-current figures. This fixed the liability of each province for handicraft and labor taxes. As no further adjustments to the number of men liable to taxation were to be made, there was no longer any need to keep population registers other than to determine eligibility for household fields. From the way population registers were handled, it is clear eligibility for household fields was also to be held constant. The conclusion seems inescapable, therefore, that in the latter part of the ninth century the central government decided to allow household fields to remain as permanent possessions of the households then in possession of them – and not just in a piecemeal or haphazard way, but as a concerted policy implemented throughout the country.

Hence, the argument that men were disguised as women to avoid taxes is mistaken. So, too, is the contention that manipulation of population registers made it impossible to carry out field redistribution. On the contrary, by a curious but consistent bureaucratic compulsion, population registers were manipulated to make the distribution system work on paper in an age when physical redistribution of household fields was no longer desired.

It is clear, therefore, that household field "redistribution" had lost any real content after 830. Sporadic "distributions" continued to take place on paper for some decades thereafter, but ceased even as a paper institution after 902.[86]

The underlying cause of the cessation of the land distribution system was an expansion of population without any corresponding expansion in the pool of rice fields available for distribution as household fields. As noted at the beginning of this chapter, the total area planted to rice in Japan increased by about a third between 740 and 900, from about 650,000 hectares to 875,000 hectares. This suggests a growth of perhaps 2 million in population (from between, perhaps, 5 and 6 million to between 7 and 8 million). The codes in the early eighth century had intended that new rice fields would become available for distribution as household fields after the developer's death, ensuring a steady increase in the pool of household fields as population increased. But once this policy was abandoned, and reclaimed fields were allowed to remain permanently as private possessions, population increase could not but lead to a shortage in available household fields. By the ninth century the government thus

---

86 Takeuchi, *Tochi seido shi*, p. 109.

had little choice but to bring the distribution system to an end. The only alternative would have been to convert most public fields to household fields, a clearly unpalatable alternative, as the rent charged on public fields was roughly four times the land tax received from household fields.

Many other arguments have been offered to explain the cessation of the eighth-century land distribution (*handen*) system. As changing land and tax policy was clearly the central social issue of ninth-century Japan, it is important to consider some of these arguments individually:[87]

1. Malfeasance by provincial and local officials, and the fabrication of population register data, are most often cited as causes of the decline of the distribution system, but are difficult to verify. As has been seen, population registers were certainly manipulated, but in specific and orderly ways designed to implement central government policy. It is interesting to consider how much of what has traditionally been seen as brazen illegality by provincial officials in Heian Japan was in fact legitimate behavior by officials from the capital loyally implementing changing central policy.
2. Another popular theory is that the occupation of land by aristocrats, temples, and shrines led to a shortage of household fields. For all its importance, however, the percentage of the nation's land monopolized by aristocratic households and religious institutions was never great. And since these holdings consisted largely of nonagricultural waste and newly created fields, the household field system should not, technically, have been affected. Illegal conversion of household to reclaimed fields, while in theory possible with provincial government help, is nonetheless a supposition that has never been verified.
3. The argument that population expansion led to a shortage of household fields comes closer to the argument presented here, but it is rarely noted that the reason for this was that increases in population were served by increases in reclaimed fields that, after the new laws of the early eighth century, could no longer be converted into new household fields.
4. Perhaps the weakest argument commonly found is that massive migration removed peasants from population registers and so made land redistribution difficult. It first of all is presupposed that the government viewed migration as illegal, which it had not

---

[87] These traditional arguments are listed in Torao, *Handen shujū-hō*, pp. 424–6.

since the beginning of the eighth century. Migration led to the loss of eligibility for household fields, but it did not lead to loss of taxes, as migrants were registered for tax assessment where they settled. And since migrants did not receive allotments of household fields, any extensive migration would have made land distribution easier, not more difficult.
5. Finally, the argument that cultivators themselves resisted redistribution of household fields because they desired a more secure (that is, private) form of tenure is difficult to accept, for the form of tenure that replaced household fields provided no more secure rights to the tiller than had been enjoyed under the previous system.

With the cessation of distribution of household fields, it was no longer as important to distinguish household from reclaimed fields. Since both were (and always had been) liable to the same tax rate, late-tenth-century documents such as the 988 Owari Province petition discussed earlier group the two forms of tenure together as "land tax fields" (*sozeiden*). The same sources refer to public fields as "rental fields" (*jishiden*). The rent (*jishi*) paid on the latter, ranging from 6 to 10 *soku* per *tan*, had now been matched, however, by the enlargement of the land tax paid on other fields. Thus, from a tax standpoint there was little reason to maintain a distinction between rental (public) and other fields, and after the late tenth century no distinction was made. From the eleventh century, all rice fields came to be known simply as "public fields" (*kōden*), unless they were certified by central government document as tax-exempt "private fields" (*shiden*), in which case their tax income was delivered to a private "proprietor" within the central government. (These are the *shōen* "estates" discussed in the next section.) This later use of the term "public fields" should not be confused with the earlier use of the very same term, for the word was now applied to all fields liable to the provincial land tax, thus grouping together what had earlier been distinguished as household, public (in the old sense), and reclaimed fields.

From the late ninth century, distribution of rice land ceased to be dictated by the government. It would be a mistake, though, to assume that farmers could now claim full "private" tenure to the land they tilled. On the contrary, it was the government view that all rice land, no matter what its designation, was rented from the provincial government, unless rent was transferred to designated *shōen* proprietors, and that rent was paid in the form of the provincial land tax. This is why some historians, putting the cart before the horse, speak of land liable to provincial taxation as essentially identical in character to private *shōen* land. In fact, it was the system of tenure and taxation on public land that provided the model for *shōen* rental systems, not the reverse.

The unit of taxation, on public and estate land alike, was the *myō* – a term that does not yield to translation; a literal rendition would be "nominal." It used to be common to view *myō* as units of land tenure. To some extent they became so in later times, but not in the Heian period. *Myō* were simply the units on which taxes were assessed and collected. As tax liability was calculated by land area, provincial governments were concerned only with recording the area of taxable land within each *myō*, not the number of people tilling this land or the distribution of cultivation rights among them.

Two examples of the variation in the relationship of *myō* to land tenure can be seen in Figures 3.2 and 3.3. The twenty households of Wakatsuki-no-shō were grouped into fifteen *myō*. In ten cases *myō* were identical with solitary tenures; in the other five, *myō* included the holdings of two households, which in only one case were geographical neighbors. By contrast, the holdings of the eighteen households in Kohigashi-no-shō were originally grouped into a single *myō* (later reorganized into several *myō*).[88] Thus, *myō* were at times equivalent to units of land tenure, or else might as easily hold a number of separate tenures. Furthermore, farm families could, and frequently did, hold tenures in more than one *myō*.

The taxes owed by the farmers of land in a *myō* were collected by a local tax manager (known most simply as *fumyō*). Some of the tax revenue was used immediately to purchase special products as required; the balance was then forwarded with the products purchased to the provincial government. For *myō* owing dues to a shōen proprietor the procedure was essentially the same, the dues being forwarded by the tax manager to the proprietor instead of to the provincial government.[89] *Myō* tax managers came in time to be known as *myōshu* ("*myō*-holders"), a term that first appears in 1047.[90] It must be kept in mind that these *myōshu* were not the own-

---

88 Inagaki Yasuhiko, "Shoki myōden no kōzō: Yamato no kuni Ōta-no-inumaru-myō ni tsuite," in Inagaki Yasuhiko and Nagahara Keiji, eds., *Chūsei no shakai to keizai* (Tokyo: Tōkyō daigaku shuppansha, 1962), pp. 40–41.
89 See examples in *Heian ibun*, vol. 2, nos. 388–403, pp. 527–31, and vol. 9, nos. 4579–97, pp. 3495–3500, dated from Chōhō 1 to Chōhō 3 (999–1001).
90 *Heian ibun*, vol. 3, no. 646: Eijō 2/10/27, pp. 779–80.

ers or landlords of the land in a *myō*, but were tax managers who reported *myō* land area, collected the taxes assessed by the provincial government, and delivered these in the forms requested. In many cases a single tax manager collected taxes from several *myō*.[91] In others, such as that of Kohigashi-no-shō, several evidently shared responsibility for tax collection.[92] In these latter cases (Kohigashi included) it was common to use a fictitious name as *myōshu* – this seems to be the case, in fact, in the 1047 document in which the term "*myōshu*" is first found.[93]

Right to control cultivation of a given parcel of land was granted by either provincial governor *shōen* proprietor to persons known as *tato*, who may or may not have also held the tax management privilege (*fumyō*) for the same land. A *tato* could assign cultivation rights to others, for whom he would serve as landlord. But in many cases the amount of land controlled by a *tato* was no more than enough for him and his family to farm alone. The one to whom a *tato* assigned cultivation rights was known as *sakushu* or *sakujin* – "cultivator." If a *tato* retained cultivation rights for himself, the terms *tato* and *sakushu* might be, and frequently were, used interchangeably. Otherwise, *sakushu* were tenants of *tato*, although it must be borne in mind that *tato* did not actually "own" land itself, but only cultivation rights to land.

Tato and *sakushu* are terms that define legal relationships to land tenure, not social classes. A *tato* exercising control over the cultivation rights to one parcel of land might at the same time rent other land as *sakushu* to another *tato*. Only when a *tato* also held the right of tax collection as well did he stand indisputably in a higher, and more lucrative, position than other cultivators.

The right of *tato* to control cultivation of land was revocable at any time by the provincial government or *shōen* proprietor. Hence cultivators who obtained *tato* appointments were not automatically able to treat land that had been household fields as fully partible and alienable. On the contrary, even holders of fields that had been developed as reclaimed fields were often less able to assert the full possessory rights that had attached to reclaimed fields in the eighth and ninth centuries. This was because provincial governments after the year 900 no longer issued the certificates of ownership (*kugen*) that had earlier guaranteed these rights to the developers of new

---

91 One example is *Heian ibun*, vol. 1, no. 240: Jōhei 2/9/22, pp. 354–55.
92 Takeuchi, *Tochi seido shi*, p. 147. 93 Inagaki, "Shoki myōden," p. 70.

farmland.[94] This change in policy – part of the overall adjustments in central government land and tax policies in this period – inaugurated a period of at least a century and a half during which land "ownership" per se was not recorded in the all-important provincial land surveys (*kokuzu*). Holders of reclaimed fields who obtained appointment to deliver taxes from the *myō* containing their holdings were generally better able to protect their possessory rights. But others often stood in danger of being dispossessed of the land they cultivated.

In the eleventh century some cultivators were able to exert sufficient leverage to win a stronger recognition of their rights to the land they tilled. These cultivators were known as "permanent cultivators" (*eisakushu*) of the land to which they were granted this privilege. In theory, they were able to sell, exchange, or bequeath their land in perpetuity.[95] Although many more cultivators may have been able to hold similar privileges in practice, full "permanent cultivator" rights were not granted routinely by provincial governments or *shōen* proprietors, but, rather, were an exceptional concession. Full legal recognition of the right to secure, private land tenure was to develop only very gradually during the succeeding Kamakura and Muromachi periods.

SHŌEN

In 743 the central government decreed that rice fields brought under cultivation privately – that is, reclaimed fields (*konden*) – were to be held in perpetuity. The maximum acreage of reclaimed fields to be held by aristocrats of various ranks, and – at the bottom – by commoners, was specified. In 749 similar, but much higher, ceilings were set for the nation's temples. Starting in 749, the government actively assisted the major temples, most especially Tōdaiji, in finding land that could be developed into estates of reclaimed fields. These estates were the first to be called *shō*, or *shōen* (although there is some use of the term, not entirely relevant, in earlier periods).

These early *shōen* must be distinguished from those of the Heian period, when the term applied not just to land actually owned by the *shōen* proprietor, but primarily to the transfer of tax income from the provincial government to a designated aristocratic household or re-

---

94 Takeuchi, *Tochi seido shi*, p. 150.
95 The *eisakushu* privilege is first seen in a document of 1037: *Heian ibun*, vol. 2, no. 570: Chōryaku 1/12/8, p. 734.

ligious institution. In early usage, *shōen* may fairly be translated as "estate." But in the later, far more important use of the term as a unit of tax revenue, the term "estate" would be utterly misleading. For this reason, the term *shō* or *shōen* (used interchangeably) is used without translation.

It would be safe to say that the main reason there were a significant number of estates of reclaimed fields developed in the eighth century was that the central government actively sought their development. This was especially true for the largest of the early *shōen* proprietors, Tōdaiji. Between 749 and 756 Tōdaiji dispatched officials to several provinces where, with the help of provincial officials, they located suitable land for development. Tōdaiji was further granted several large tracts of wasteland that they might develop into reclaimed fields. By 770, when the main impetus to Tōdaiji land development was over, the great temple held ninety-two *shōen* in twenty-three provinces, most in the home provinces and the Hokuriku region to the northwest. Convenience of location was all-important; hence, no *shō* were developed on Tōdaiji's behalf in either the eastern (Kanto) provinces or in Kyushu. About half of the Tōdaiji *shō* had their origin in commendation by the central government.[96]

Land development by aristocrats, apart from the temples, was important too. Several bills of sale survive that show acquisition of reclaimed fields by aristocrats in the home provinces, and in such nearby provinces as Ōmi and Kii. Whether aristocrats ever financed land reclamation directly, as temples did, is far less clear. It seems likely that aristocrats, even more than temple proprietors, had to depend on hired local managers to acquire fields developed by others, and to find tenants for them, even when fields were located close to the capital.

Temples could manage their estates either by sending out their own representatives or by engaging local notables; the latter were most often also local officeholders in the government. Generally, temples preferred to use their own representatives; but even then it was necessary to win local cooperation. Reclaimed fields in early *shōen* were farmed by tenants. In the case of the well-documented Kuwahara-no-shō in Echizen Province, fields were rented at either 6 or 8 *soku* per *tan*, to which was added the land tax of 1.5 *soku*. When fields could be certified as "temple fields" (*jiden*), the land tax por-

---

96 Takeuchi, *Tochi seido shi*, pp. 128–9; see also Kishi Toshio, *Nihon kodai seiji shi kenkyū* (Tokyo: Hanawa shobō, 1966), pp. 317–99.

tion could be kept by the temple, but the government granted this exemption very sparingly. On most reclaimed fields owned by temples – and on all fields owned by aristocrats – the regular land tax (*denso*) was paid to the provincial government.

With the exception of some estates in the home provinces, these eighth-century estates did not thrive in the Heian period. Little is known of most temple estates in the ninth century. But by the tenth century it is apparent that most consisted of uncultivated waste, or had disappeared from the landscape entirely. In a 950 Tōdaiji register, three estates in Asuwa District in Echizen were still listed with 450 hectares of reclaimed fields. Yet a year later the Asuwa chief magistrate reported that the first two of these estates had long been uncultivated, while no one in recent years had so much as heard of the third.[97] Of forty-one Tōdaiji *shō* listed in the surviving fragment of a 998 register, only ten were in operation; the others were entirely waste.[98]

There were a number of reasons for the decline of temple reclamation estates. One was the withdrawal of central government support. From having assisted in their growth, the government in the late eighth century turned to limiting any expansion in estates of reclaimed fields. In the ninth century few grants were made to the old Nara temples. Estates belonging to temples of the now-favored Tendai and Shingon sects were given preferential tax treatment denied such old temples as Tōdaiji.[99] But even the favored temples did not receive substantial land grants in the ninth century, as they had in the eighth. Instead, these grants were made to the imperial house or to individual members of the imperial family: between 828 and 886, mostly in the 830s, the imperial house was granted nearly 7,000 hectares of land. About 20 percent had already been developed as farmland; the rest was to be developed into farmland whenever possible. Similarly, from 795 to 878 over 3,700 hectares were granted to some thirty-three imperial princes and princesses, also to be developed where possible into farmland.[100] In the eighth century most such land would have been given to Tōdaiji and other temples.

A second reason for the decline of early *shōen* was lack of cooperation by local officials and estate managers. Proprietors depended on

---

[97] *Heian ibun*, vol. 1, no. 257: Tenryaku 4/11/20, pp. 372–84, and no. 263: Tenryaku 5/10/23, p. 386.
[98] *Heian ibun*, vol. 2, no. 377: Chōtaku 4, pp. 511–13.
[99] Yasuda Motohisa, *Nihon shōen shi gaisetsu* (Tokyo: Yoshikawa kōunkan, 1957), pp. 52–53.
[100] Takeuchi, *Tochi seido shi*, pp. 124–28.

the loyalty of their estate managers, who might derive more profit from developing reclaimed fields for their own use. Managers sent out from the temple might be more trustworthy, but were less likely to obtain the local cooperation necessary to enlist tenants for estate land. Nor were all temple managers reliable: one such manager, sent by Tōdaiji to manage Takaba-no-shō in Tamba Province in 842, proceeded to embezzle the rents he was to have delivered to the temple, then disappeared into a neighboring province.[101] As a general rule, the estates that most often failed were those in which the proprietor played the most active role: those managed by monks or others sent from the home office, those in which fields were brought under cultivation by the proprietor, and those (found only in Echizen) where the proprietor attempted to form a geographically compact estate by trading outlying temple fields for fields at the center of the estate that had belonged to others. By contrast, estates formed by purchase of fields developed by others, and managed by local notables, had a greater chance of lasting into the tenth century and beyond. But even these survived only if they were fitted into the new tax structure.

The final, and perhaps crucial, reason for the decline of early *shōen* was the transformation of the tax structure in the late ninth century. As *suiko* came to be levied as a land tax, it was applied (like the land tax, *denso*) to reclaimed and household fields alike. This grew in the tenth century to a greater land tax that, since it was derived from *suiko*, was also applied equally to reclaimed fields and to those that had been household fields. The application of a large land tax made reclaimed fields far less profitable to the *shōen* proprietor unless the estate was also made tax-exempt. Hence, tax exemption, not land development, became the key to *shōen* formation in the tenth century.

Most new *shōen* in the tenth century were formed along a pattern that has come to be known as the "Kinai *shō*" pattern. To ensure that government-supported temples and shrines received their proper dues from provincial governments, segments of provincial public land (*kōden*) were designated to provide these dues directly, on either a permanent or a floating basis. Fields so designated were "excused" other taxes so that their tax yield could be forwarded directly to the temple or shrine. Such fields were known as the temple's (or shrine's) "exempt fields" (*menden*); when different fields each year were designated for this purpose, they were known as "floating ex-

---

101 See Abe Takeshi, *Nihon shōen shi* (Tokyo: Ohara shinseisha, 1972), p. 46.

empt fields" (*ukimen*). Aggregates of exempt fields were called *shōen* because local tax managers for these fields reported directly to the proprietor rather than forwarding revenue by way of the provincial government office. Because most such fields were in the Kinai (home provinces) region, historians have come to refer to these *shōen* as "Kinai *shō*." The term refers, however, not to the location of a *shō*, but to its origin in the designation of fields to yield taxes to support a given religious institution.

Kinai *shō* proprietors had no direct contact with the land designated as exempt fields, nor with the farmers who paid the taxes they received as *shōen* dues. Nor did they determine how much they could collect each year; this was arranged by the provincial government. Furthermore, the taxes forwarded to the *shōen* proprietor constituted only the land tax (*kammotsu*) component. The balance of "miscellaneous exactions" (*rinji zōyaku*) were still paid to the provincial government.

Both Kinai *shō* and those earlier land-development *shōen* that survived into the tenth century had to be certified by the central government. These certificates (called *kanshōfu*) specified the limits to the location (if fixed) and extent of fields that were exempt from land tax for each of the 1-hectare grid squares (*tsubo*) by which land was divided for survey and registration purposes. Provincial governments, for their part, recorded the number of such exempt fields per grid square in their provincial land registers (*kokuzu*). Each year local officials reported to the provincial government the area in each grid square under actual rice cultivation that year. Taxes for the area exempted were then forwarded to the proprietor; taxes from excess cultivated fields, if any, over the limit of exempt fields allowed by central government certificate were paid in full to the provincial government.[102]

There were three ways *shōen* proprietors could expand their influence over *shōen* land and cultivators to embrace more than just receipt of rents equivalent to the land tax that would otherwise have gone to the provincial government. The first was to levy an additional rent (*kajishi*) on all exempt fields, parallel to the added exactions provincial governments themselves levied. Frequently these additional rents could still be collected even when *shōen* privileges were withdrawn and the basic *shōen* dues proper reverted to the

---

[102] Sakamoto Shōzō, *Nihon ōchō kokka taisei ron* (Tokyo: Tōkyō daigaku shuppansha, 1972), pp. 19–28.

provincial government.¹⁰³ Proprietors might also gain limited exemptions from the second component of provincial taxation, the "occasional" or "miscellaneous" exactions, which they could then collect themselves. Since these exactions lay entirely outside the purview of the central government, such exemptions were not covered by *shōen* certificates and had to be negotiated directly with the provincial government. In the tenth century, when miscellaneous exactions were levied on individuals, proprietors argued that their *shōen* personnel should not have to pay these taxes to the provincial government. Later, as the exactions came to be assessed by land area, some argued that *shōen* land already exempt from land tax should be exempt from miscellaneous exactions as well. All such requests for exemption were granted solely at the pleasure of the provincial governor, and exemptions granted by one governor could be, and frequently were, overturned by his successor.

A final avenue for the expansion of proprietary influence over *shōen* land was to assume control of the granting of cultivation rights to *shō* fields. In *shōen* that originated in the development of reclaimed fields such control was implicit. But for *shōen* of the Kinai type, the right to control cultivation rights – the right to *tato* – was still assigned by provincial officials. Proprietors might gain the right to appoint their own *tato*, though, through a policy of consolidation of exemptions of both land tax and miscellaneous exactions, obtaining fixed rather than floating exempt fields, and then using the argument that the right to receive all major taxes due from a fixed parcel of land implied with it the right to assign cultivation rights to that land. For, as should by now be abundantly clear, this concept, which is so familiar in the West, was not at all a given assumption in Heian Japan.

It is also important to bear in mind that only a minority of *shōen* were developed toward the goals of expansion and consolidation of tax and cultivation rights. Frequently, the conflict with provincial governments that such expansion programs inevitably entailed resulted in more losses than gains. Most *shōen* of the Kinai pattern remained administered through local officials and *myōshu*, therefore, with little or no involvement by the proprietor in the actual management of local agricultural affairs. Like provincial governments, proprietors were generally concerned only with the assessment of taxable land, as organized into *myō*, not in the distribution of culti-

---

103 Sakamoto, *Nihon ōchō kokka*, p. 44.

vation rights with *myō*, or even with the identity of tillers. In fact, for simplicity of administration, it was common to assign *myō* uniform *shōen* dues, although *myō* themselves were of greatly uneven size, an approach that was known as "equalized *myō*" (*kintō-myō*). While certainly simpler, such proprietor distance left little possibility for full maximization of additional rents (*kajishi*), let alone expansion into new revenue areas. But for many *shōen* proprietors, just to maintain a steady income from fields that had been properly certified by central government decrees required a constant struggle with provincial governments.

In the eighth and ninth centuries the central government had expected *shōen* to expand through the development of new lands. After about 900, however, high officials came to feel that no further expansion in the area exempted from provincial taxation was desirable. In part this was because the new land tax of this period had expanded far beyond the simple 1.5 *soku* per *tan* that had been the limit of *shōen* tax exemption earlier.[104] But the main reason to oppose further expansion in exempt fields was that under the new provincial quota system the maximum revenue due the capital from each province had been fixed and was, in fact, subject to reduction upon provincial petition. Hence, any further expansion in the area of exempt fields directly reduced the ability to meet provincial tax quotas, and thus gave the province a perfect rationale to request reductions in these quotas. This concern was certainly on the minds of high officials when they inaugurated the first of what was to be a series of campaign to hold back *shōen* growth and revoke certificates of exemption that were not in order. There was, moreover, a direct line between this campaign in 902 and the inauguration after about 915 of the system just outlined for the registration and control of exempt fields through annual assessment and review by provincial and local officials.[105]

Accreditation of exempt fields was always by the central government, not by provincial officials. But under the new system of registration, provincial governments gained the power to recognize or deny recognition to any new land development claims by *shōen* proprietors or by other land developers, who most commonly were local officials or tax managers. Provincial governments thus made the crucial decisions in three areas that greatly affected the fate of *shōen:* the recognition of the certification of exempt fields, the recognition of

---

104 Sakamoto, *Nihon ōchō kokka*, p. 90.   105 Sakamoto, *Nihon ōchō kokka*, p. 122.

new reclaimed fields, and the exemption of *shōen* personnel or, later, *shōen* land from provincial miscellaneous exactions. In the first matter proprietors could appeal provincial decisions to the central government. The other two areas, however, were entirely under provincial jurisdiction, and a favorable decision by one governor might be, and frequently was, reversed by a subsequent governor.

The uneasy relationship between *shōen* proprietors and provincial governments entered a new stage in the 1040s. In response to a series of squabbles over *shōen* tax rights – most particularly the case of the Tōdaiji estate Kuroda-no-shō in Iga Province – the central government set a standard rate for the provincial land tax at 6 *soku* per *tan*. *Shōen* proprietors were permitted to collect as rent either all or part of this rate for those fields certified as exempt fields, but in either case the amount allowed was always to be spelled out as a standard rate. Any provincial land-tax exactions above 6 *soku* per *tan* (and by this time there were many) were to go unequivocally to the provincial government.[106]

This did much to clarify the terms of discourse between *shōen* holders and provincial governments – generally in favor of the latter. During this same period the levy of miscellaneous exactions shifted definitively from persons to land units, and the exactions themselves came to be known most commonly as "provincial levies" (*kuniyaku*), or simply "miscellaneous levies" (*zōyaku*). This simplified method for the assessment and collection of taxes favored *shōen* proprietors as well as provincial officials: before, *shōen* proprietors had to argue case by case the relevance of *shō* personnel to temple support before miscellaneous exactions were exempted. Now they could make the far simpler argument that any field already exempt from (some) land tax should by extension be exempt from provincial levies as well.

For many proprietary institutions the development of *shōen* made up for the decline, or loss altogether, of revenue from provincial government tax receipts. This was perhaps most explicit for the largest proprietor, Tōdaiji, whose efforts to establish Kinai-style *shō* in the tenth and eleventh centuries followed directly from the failure of provincial governments to forward income properly due them from "support households" (*fuko*), whose regular tax income was to be set aside for support of the great Nara temple.[107] Since all *shōen* proprietors were entitled to state tax support, *shōen* established to make up for previous tax sources now lost were a legal part of the tax

---

106 Sakamoto, *Nihon ōchō kokka*, pp. 226–29.   107 Inagaki, "Shoki myōden," p. 77.

structure, and hence were never challenged on grounds of principle by the central government.

What did lead to challenge by high officials in the capital was the competition for limited tax sources, a competition in which organized temple bureaucracies held a distinct advantage over the aristocrat-bureaucrats who staffed the civil government proper. With the institution of provincial tax quotas, and particularly after 900 when governors were allowed to request each year reductions in these quotas, aristocrats were forced to divide an ever shrinking pie of provincial revenue to pay their own stipends and emoluments, the daily expenses of government operation, the support of the imperial household, and the maintenance of the Heian capital. The major political households of the capital, none of them ones to watch their income dry up for want of proper contacts, were thus at pains to develop ties with career provincial governors and, where possible, to establish direct links to the source of tax income by setting up *shōen*, which they could do either in their own names or through temples and shrines with which they were associated. The first concerted effort to check *shōen* growth, in 902, had clearly reflected a land policy aimed at holding all *shōen* growth in abeyance. Later efforts at *shōen* regulation, however, were in fact much more commonly partisan efforts designed to check the growth of some temple *shōen*, the better to enable households currently enjoying political power, and their clients, to compete for increasingly limited tax resources.

The rise of *shōen* in its major function as a tax instrument (as distinct from its earlier role as a land-development estate) thus followed naturally from the evolution of a tax structure centered on shrinking provincial quotas. From the first important period of *shōen* development in the middle decades of the tenth century to the end of the eleventh century, the various elements of the central government, whether they were government offices, aristocratic households, or the imperial household itself, received a mixture of support, mostly indirect at first by way of the provincial governments, and the rest direct, forwarded by local officials and tax managers from fields designated as *shōen*.

It would be difficult to calibrate exactly the mixture of these indirect and direct revenue sources, but there seems little doubt that reliance on direct *shōen* and *shōen*-like revenue sources increased steadily in the tenth and eleventh centuries. This was true not only for the great temples, which became nearly wholly reliant on *shōen* for support, but also for the great aristocratic households and their clients, the holders of bureaucratic posts in the capital, most government offices and agencies, and, finally, even the imperial household.

Hence it even seems inevitable, although nonetheless remarkable, that there would come a point when the much-atrophied provincial quota system would be jettisoned altogether in favor of wholesale reliance on *shōen* and *shōen*-like support for virtually all the elements of the ruling hierarchy. This point came during the last part of the Heian period, the Insei period (see Chapter 9). Those portions of "public land" (*kōden*) that had not yet been made into *shōen* – a proportion that has been variously estimated at between 40 and 60 percent of the nation's tax base – were now assigned province by province to support government offices or household patronage clusters, including the imperial household, in just the same manner as *shōen*. As with *shōen* proper, the proprietors of a given province's public land (known as its *kokugaryō*) received its tax revenue as personal rents, could communicate directly with local tax officials regarding tax delivery, and could appoint officials of their own to supervise local tax collection and accounting.

The key figures in any transfer of tax rights from a provincial government to a *shōen* proprietor were the local officials and tax managers (*fumyō* and their equivalents) who controlled local tax and land management. Provincial governments were totally dependent on local tax managers to see that taxes were properly assessed, collected, and delivered. Because of that dependence, beginning from about the 1040s, local officials and *myōshu* were able to exercise a rather remarkable right: provided they found a qualified and receptive proprietor, they could "commend" the tax unit (usually a *myō*) for which they were responsible to a *shōen* proprietor, on their own authority transferring land from provincial administration to inclusion in a *shōen*.

Owners of privately developed rice land (reclaimed fields) had always been able to commend their land to a religious institution, which then administered the land as a *shōen*. In these cases the commendation was an outright gift by a private party for religious merit or, not uncommonly, by a priest who had developed the land for the express purpose of commending it to his employer. Commendation by tax managers in the late Heian period, however, was quite another matter. What was commended in the later instance was not land owned outright by the commender, but units of public taxation for which the commender served merely as tax collector, albeit in the expanded role of tax manager. The commender was, as it were, simply exchanging one master for another. Tax rates and application remained essentially the same, and, of course, the tax manager retained his lucrative position as the assessor and collector of these taxes, now deemed *shōen* dues. What made such an act possible in the late Heian period was the growing central government support of *shōen* growth and the provincial governments' near total reliance on local officials as the only people who could guarantee that taxes would be duly assessed and collected. While provincial officials certainly did not welcome the removal of territory from their tax rolls, there was frequently little they could do when the land was being transferred to *shōen* proprietors who outranked them socially and politically and enjoyed increasing support from the highest quarters to expand *shōen*.

A number of factors might lead a tax manager to commend the unit of tax base for which he was responsible to a qualified *shōen* proprietor. One was simply the matter of tax rates. *Shōen* dues duplicated provincial tax rates, but generally lagged behind in terms of the additional levies provincial officials were able to exact on top of the land tax proper (*kammotsu*), which after 1040 was set at a nationally uniform rate. This was simply because provincial officials were closer to the scene than *shōen* proprietors. Where *shōen* levies lagged behind provincial taxation, the margin for tax manager profit increased correspondingly. For the same reasons, most, though certainly not all, *shōen* proprietors were at a disadvantage in supervising dues collection because of their distance from the *shō* in question. This must have been of particular advantage to commenders in the distant Kanto and Kyushu provinces. The commender's position in office was also likely to be far more secure under a *shōen* proprietor who was entirely in his debt for gaining a new *shō*.

Hence, financial advantage was a considerable factor in motivating a commendation of provincial "public land" to a *shōen* proprietor. But even more considerable in a great many cases was the matter of patronage. By commending a tax source to a central temple, shrine, or aristocrat household, the commender forged an alliance with a powerful source of political support. Some profited substantially from the association; others were eventually dispossessed by their new masters, as indeed they might have been under provincial administration. And for every case of commendation, there must have been many other tax managers who used the leverage of potential commendation to win still greater concessions from provincial officials. Local tax managers most certainly did not have the power to keep tax revenues for themselves – any attempt to do so soon put them in rebellion against the imperial government, as rebels from Taira no Masakado on discovered (see Chapter 10). But through the power of commendation they could determine through which route the taxes they collected made their way to the ruling class and thereby jockey for the best possible financial and patronage position.

All of this adds up to a tremendous growth in the power and influence of local magnates. This growth, the central development of rural society in Heian Japan, was favored by several factors: a significant expansion in population and, consequently, in the utilization of land resources; the spread of use of the plow and of related agrarian improvements in the use of animals and fertilizer; and the realization by provincial and central government officials that the farming-out of tax contracts provided the most secure source of national tax assessment and collection. And in the outlying provinces of both east and west (but especially in the east, where population expansion was greatest) there was a further development: the growth of a warrior-class identity that lent unity and purpose to the aspirations of developing tax managers and local magnates. The power to commend the tax land they controlled to the political master of their choice was both the symbol and the measure of the growing power of this local tax manager class. More than this: it was the very substance of power.

CHAPTER 4

PROVINCIAL ADMINISTRATION AND LAND TENURE IN EARLY HEIAN

The Heian era, as correctly portrayed in current studies, was characterized by a progressive weakening of centralized control over regional areas. Most of the administrative offices that had been established in the late seventh and eighth centuries for the purpose of maximizing state power declined rapidly during the early Heian period, with the notable exception of the headquarters offices at the capitals (*kokufu*) of the sixty-five (or sixty-six) provinces into which the country was divided. While the central government declined, these provincial offices (*kokuga*) retained, and even increased, their power over local land and people as local elites took over their functions: the collection of taxes, the administration of land, and the "promotion of agriculture" (*kannō*). The changes resulted in large part from movement from below, and, at least in the first two centuries of Heian times (the ninth and tenth centuries), had little to do with warriors or *shōen* (estates). The following discussion concentrates largely on those two centuries in an attempt to explain these changes. A more detailed inquiry, however, requires a preliminary discussion of local problems during the Heian period as a whole, and the problems they raise for us.

Managed by officials dispatched for short terms from the capital, the provincial offices were intended to be a new meeting ground for capital and local elites, enabling the dynastic state to marshal local resources and the loyal services of local aristocrats,[1] but in practice the provincial governments turned out to be unique bargaining

---

[1] The following abbreviations are used for works cited in this chapter: *HIB* for Takeuchi Rizō, comp., *Heian ibun*, 15 vols. (Tokyo: Tōkyō-dō shoten, 1968–81); *IK* for Ienaga Saburō, Ishimoda Shō, Inoue Kiyoshi, Inoue Mitsusada, eds., *Iwanami kōza: Nihon rekishi*, 23 vols. (Tokyo: Iwanami shoten, 1962–64); *KT* for Kuroita Katsumi et al., eds., (*Shintei zōho*) *kokushi taikei*, 60 vols. in 66 (Tokyo: Yoshikawa kōbunkan, 1929–64); *NKBT* for *Nihon koten bungaku taikei*, 102 vols. (Tokyo: Iwanami shoten, 1957–69). The most authoritative work on Heian provincial administration is Yoshimura Shigeki, *Kokushi seido hōkai ni kansuru kenkyū* (Tokyo: Tōkyō Daigaku shuppankai, 1979 reprint). See also Morita Tei, "Heian chūki gunji ni tsuite no ichikōsatsu," in Hayashi Rokurō, ed., *Ronshū: Nihon rekishi*, vol. 3 (Tokyo: Yūseidō, 1976), pp. 208–17.

grounds for the division of resources between capital and countryside, and that function, combined with the functions of the governments as repositories and redistributors of wealth, ensured their survival well beyond the Heian period. Provincial governments did indeed marshal economic resources, but the share falling to the nobility in the capital steadily diminished. In the meantime, control over labor and land use fell largely into the hands of local elites, whose authority was, at the highest level, reinforced by provincial office titles unheard of in the eighth century. The structure of provincial authority changed drastically as local power grew.

The rise of a quasi-autonomous warrior elite in late Heian times and the proliferation of tax-immune landholdings called *shōen* weakened most provincial administrations and paralyzed one or two, but 60 to 70 percent of the landed wealth remained under provincial jurisdiction until the founding of the Kamakura bakufu in 1185.[2] Up to that time, when the Kamakura regime began to thrust itself between capital and province, the provincial governments remained unchallenged as centers of local administration, but were profoundly transformed. This transformation was primarily the result of social changes in rural society that tended to strengthen purely local power.[3] Changes in local administration have also been seen as reflecting change in the political order as a whole, from centralized empire to patrimonial state and ultimately to feudalism. Those changes, including most notably the rise of the warrior class as the dominant force, occurred at different rates in different places, but the course of events can, in the light of recent Japanese scholarship, be divided into three fairly distinct stages.

The first of the stages, which lasted through the ninth century and most of the tenth, was marked by government edicts for the benefit of a rural stratum of petty gentry, often called "the rich and powerful" (*fugō*), who, despite existing rules to the contrary, were able to insert themselves between the tax-collecting officials and the tax-rendering peasantry by assuming the latter's various burdens for the convenience of the former. By about 900 those de facto arrange-

---

2 Murai Yasuhiko, *Kodai kokka kaitai katei no kenkyū* (Tokyo: Iwanami shoten, 1965), pp. 237–65.
3 Major works propounding this view include, among others, Miyahara Takeo, *Nihon kodai no kokka to nōmin* (Tokyo: Hōsei daigaku shuppankyoku, 1973); Morita Tei, *Heian jidai seijishi kenkyū* (Tokyo: Yoshikawa kōbunkan, 1978); Murai, *Kodai kokka*; Sakamoto Shōzō, *Nihon ōchō kokka taisei ron* (Tokyo: Tōkyō daigaku shuppankai, 1972); Satō Shin'ichi, *Nihon no chūsei kokka* (Tokyo: Iwanami shoten, 1983); and Toda Yoshimi, *Nihon ryōshusei seiritsushi no kenkyū* (Tokyo: Iwanami shoten, 1967).

ments had been granted almost full legal recognition as "provincial precedents" by the government in Kyoto.⁴

"Riches and power" in early Heian provincial life were inextricably bound up with the official taxation system. Wealth, moreover, was not yet based primarily on the power of landownership. The nature of wealth at the very beginning of Heian times is well illustrated by the following passage from the *Nihon ryōiki*, an early-ninth-century collection of pious Buddhist stories. The story concerns an impoverished orphaned girl whose problems are solved by the miraculous intervention of Kannon:

> When her parents were alive, they enjoyed abundant wealth and goods and constructed numerous sheds and granaries . . . after the parents died, the slaves ran away and the horses and cattle died, so that the goods were lost and the house impoverished.⁵

The same story, retold in the twelfth-century *Konjaku monogatari-shū*, presents a revised version of the kind of prosperity that was lost:

> In that region lived a district magistrate. . . . The underlings who served him all left, and the fields he had held in domain were all seized by others so that there was no place left in her possession, and her distress grew worse day by day.⁶

Early Heian texts do sometimes include land among the constituents of riches and power, along with slaves, animals, and stored grain, but lands held as a "domain" (*ryō*) are never an element where provincial figures are concerned. Power over grain, livestock, or sources of labor like slaves or, more commonly, dependent clients, had not yet become incidental to power over land.

Provincial governments during this first phase came to be headed by a chief executive dispatched from the capital for a short term, usually four years. That official, holding the formal title of governor or vice-governor, was the "custodial governor." He alone among the higher executive staff of the provincial administration assumed responsibility for the rendering of the province's taxes and the conservation of its assets. He was called a *zuryō* (literally, "custodian") and could not be discharged from his office on the completion of his

---

4 Toda, *Ryōshusei*, pp. 25–45.
5 Kyōkai, comp., *Nihon ryōiki*, in Endō Yoshimoto and Kasuga Kazuo, eds., *Nihon ryōiki*, vol. 70 of *NKBT*, pp. 276–81; translated by Kyoko Motomichi Nakamura as *Miraculous Stories from the Japanese Buddhist Tradition: The Nihon ryōiki of the Monk Kyokai* (Cambridge, Mass.: Harvard University Press, 1972), pp. 173–74. Cited in Toda, *Ryōshusei*, pp. 32–33.
6 Minamoto no Takakuni et al., comps., *Konjaku monogatari-shū*, 16, 8, in Yamada Yoshio, Yamada Tadao, Yamada Hideo, and Yamada Toshio, eds., *Konjaku monogatari*, vols. 32–36 of *NKBT* at 34:438–41. Cited in Toda, *Ryōshusei*, p. 33.

term without a release from his successor certifying that an audit of his account showed no irregularities.[7] This concentration of responsibility in a single officeholder, rather than in the provincial officials as a group, relieved many other appointees of any significant obligation whatever, converting their posts to virtual sinecures. The *zuryō* system of specially designated custodial officials, a radical departure from the principles of collective responsibility established by the organic (or statutory) codes (*ritsuryō*), originated during the Nara period, and by Heian times a complex network of regulations had grown up around the transfer of custodial authority from one accountable governor to the next in order to circumscribe the resulting opportunities for misuse of public resources.

Fiscal and custodial responsibilities in the provinces were further complicated by the two-tiered system prescribed by the organic code. The upper tier was made up of the governors and their official staffs, all capital aristocrats appointed for a short term, usually four years. But each province was further subdivided into districts called *gun* (or *kōri*), and each *gun* had its own magistrates who were selected from registered lineages of local nobility to serve for life terms.[8] The most important government stores were dispersed among the various *gun,* whose magistrates exercised custody of the stores jointly with the provincial officers, and during the course of the ninth and tenth centuries custodial authority for governmental stores on the local level was further fragmented among other rich and powerful persons. The income generated by official grain lent out from such stores for interest was a major source of income for officials at both *gun* and provincial levels, making conflicts between them inevitable, conflicts that were further exacerbated by the demands of the petty gentry for a greater share in these resources.

Although weak, the provincial governments of the ninth and tenth centuries remained generally under central control. Governors were sometimes killed in disagreements with local residents, and the more distant from the capital a province was, the more dangerous it was likely to be. Nevertheless, governors from the capital continued to travel to their provinces and extract most, if not all, of the revenue needed to support the capital and its nobles. The rich and powerful

---

7 On *zuryō* governors generally, see Abe Takeshi, *Heian zenki seijishi no kenkyū* (Tokyo: Shinseisha, 1974), pp. 143–250, 301–41; Izumiya Yasuo, "Zuryō kokushi to nin'yō kokushi," in Hayashi Rokurō, ed., *Ronshū: Nihon rekishi*, vol. 3, pp. 173–84.
8 Sakamoto Tarō, *Nihon kodaishi no kisoteki kenkyō* (Tokyo: Tōkyō Daigaku shuppankai, 1964), vol. 2, pp. 142–51.

were too well integrated into the existing system of official taxation to revolt against it. Property, as an institution, was still weak. In the second stage proposed here, that is, the eleventh century, the rich and powerful members of provincial society consolidated their control over peasant labor but did not usually legitimate their control in terms of landholding. Generally known as *tato* (probably "field man"), they were primarily managers, rather than owners, of agricultural land, and the term *tato* designated the performer of a function, not the holder of a claim.[9]

But, beginning in the late eleventh century, there occurred a general sorting out of agricultural areas into two major categories: provincial domains (*kokugaryō*) and *shōen*. *Shōen*, the specially designated landed estates of high nobles or religious institutions, had existed even in Nara times, but now that land management had been largely taken over by local field managers (*tato*), disengagement from the authority of provincial officials could be much more complete. The provincial governors had, during the earlier phase, lost control of their original function of promoting agriculture (*kannō*) to the local land managers, a loss that in itself meant the end of the *ritsuryō* state. The provincial headquarters had nevertheless retained its power to maintain public order and collect revenue. The removal of a *shōen* from the province's fiscal authority meant that its lands and the obligations of its field managers "belonged" to the *shōen* lord and not to the province, making it, in the language of modern scholars, a mature *shōen*. *Shōen* and province enjoyed a de facto, though incomplete, administrative independence that inevitably led to conflict.

The position of the field manager is fairly well illustrated by a decree of the government of Izumi Province issued in 1012 instructing *gun* magistrates as follows:

The only basis for reclamation must be the promotion of agriculture; public and private profit similarly depend on the cultivation of fields. Now although this province is small in area, the people living here are numerous. Half concentrate on fishing and have no liking for farm work. Migrants may sometimes want [to farm], but since they have no claim to the land, they are unable to contract for its cultivation. The rich and powerful who have always had fields in their control leave them fallow for years, claiming the land is infertile. The failing prosperity of the province and the reduced benefits to the people are mostly due to this. Now in considering the situation, it appears that policies can be adjusted, there being times for laxity and

---

9 Yoshida Akira, "Tato no seiritsu ni tsuite," *Hisutoria*, 16 (September 1956): 35–46.

times for strictness. *But how can there be private holding of what is public field?* Consequently, in the case of public fields that have been abandoned since the fifth year of Kankō [1008], petitions of lesser people to cultivate them are to be allowed *even if the fields are claimed as old cultivations of "great nominees."* However, if an "original nominee" who has not abandoned the cultivation of his old fields wishes to bring more land under cultivation, the *gun* magistrate must, after an accurate survey of the grid-parcels containing the new and old parcels, deny the petitions of other nominees.[10]

The division here of the subject population into residents and "migrants" (*rōnin*) originates from a classification of the *ritsuryō* census system, but had by this time become a kind of legal artifice. *Rōnin* (literally "wave people") were not necessarily hapless wanderers, and could be both affluent and of long-standing residence. More significant is the phrase "great and small field managers" in the heading of the order and the corresponding terms "the rich and powerful," "great nominees," "lesser people," and "original nominee." For both the terms "field manager" and "nominee" one might, without much distortion, substitute the word "occupant." There was nonetheless an important difference of connotation, since the word "nominee," literally "name" (*na*), primarily signified a name on a list of licensed cultivators, guarantors of official revenue from land they had undertaken to cultivate. Being a "name" did not mean holding title to land, but, rather, having responsibility, viewed as a function, for paying taxes on it.[11]

"How can there be private holding of what is public field?" That rhetorical question, echoing the *ritsuryō* rule that each parcel of agricultural land had to be either "public" or "private" and that only private land could be privately possessed or enclosed, actually betrays some uncertainty about the position of the field manager and his authority to withdraw a parcel from cultivation, an arrogation of the *kannō* power of the provincial administration. By the terms of this order, it must be noted, the possessory rights of old cultivators are, albeit indirectly, given considerable recognition. Despite their legally precarious position, the field-manager cultivators whenever possible treated their holdings as if they were private and heritable, and, not surprisingly, relations between them and their administrative overlords were marked by persistent struggles over both tenure and revenue. By the middle of the eleventh century, a rule called "the law

---

10 Izumi provincial order of Kankō 9(1012)/1/22, in *HIB* 2:630, doc. 462.
11 Murai, *Kodai kokka*, pp. 292–97; Toda, *Ryōshusei*, pp. 247–56.

of apportionment" (*rippō*) was established in every province, setting some limits to the dues that could be extracted from holders of provincial public lands.¹²

During this period, radical changes occurred within the provincial administration. In the late eleventh century, for example, in the absence of the governor, vice-governor, or any other member of the officially appointed executive staff, the provincial headquarters began to issue orders that were everywhere accepted as valid, a sign that the power of the *zuryō* was passing its peak. The *ritsuryō* concept of responsible officeholding was totally abandoned as governors ceased to visit their provinces at all, and the interests of the capital were represented locally by gubernatorial delegates, or "deputy supervisors" (*mokudai*).

The provincial headquarters of this period always had a chief executive office, if not a chief executive. Called the "administrative office" (*mandokoro*), it was sometimes renamed the *rusudokoro*, or "custodial office," a term fictively implying the governor's imminent return. From that office the deputy supervisor could maintain control of the local officialdom.

Starting in the ninth century, the structure of the provincial headquarters changed dramatically. Except for the governor or acting governor, the vice-governor and other regular officials mandated by the codes lapsed into insignificance, and instead the officialdom was divided into a series of functionally differentiated suboffices, such as the land office (*tadokoro*) and the militia office (*kondeidokoro*). This functional compartmentalization of authority and privilege, although to some extent inevitable in any system, was fundamentally contradictory to the basic premise of the *ritsuryō* state, that government should be carried out by an upper stratum of omnicompetent, generalistic officials.

Such divisions had probably existed even during the eighth century, but, now completely staffed by local irregulars, these offices (*wkoro*) had eclipsed the regular staff. The custodial-office system brought the offices and their officials into unprecedented prominence. Called "resident officials" (*zaichō kanjin*), these functionaries represented the provincial, as distinguished from the national, elite. Some came from local lineages, others were descended from capital nobles who first arrived in the province in an official capacity and

---

12 On *rippō*, see Katsuyama Seiji, "Kōden kammotsu rippō no seiritsu to sono zentei," *Shirin* 70 (February 1987): 1–43; Murai, *Kodai kokka*, pp. 320–36; Sakamoto, *Nihon ōchō kokka taisei ron*, pp. 223–40.

then stayed on, but all tended to regard their posts as heritable. The offices of the *gun* magistrates, whose prerogatives had been in a steady decline, were in effect amalgamated into a broad provincial hierarchy through the officials-in-residence posts that many held concurrently.[13]

Resident officials belonged to a corporate hierarchy centering on the *kokuga*, and by the eleventh century had developed quasi-hereditary estatist interests in their posts. Their privileges, relatively safe from cancellation by the Kyoto government, served to reinforce the new type of landed property that appeared late in the eleventh century.[14]

By the time of the second stage, in the eleventh century, provincial governments were, without permission from the capital, beginning to license certain holdings as the specially chartered possessions of their "cultivators," endowed with specific tax preferences. Such holdings were generally termed *betsumyō* or *beppu myō*, literally, "names by special order," but actually meaning something like "specially named holding." A "named holding," or *myō*, could cover an extensive area, including residences as well as both cultivated and uncultivated fields, and by the late twelfth century the *myō* had become a major component of larger *shōen*.

"Names" had been units of tax responsibility for several decades. Originally, the names referred to were those of provincial gentry listed as responsible for tax payments from specific areas or groups. The earliest record of the word "name" (*na*) in that sense dates to 947.[15] By the middle of the eleventh century the *myō* had become a unit of specially administered land bearing the name of a fictitious person. Despite the presumption of the Izumi decree of 1012, such private holdings in public (i.e., provincial) domain were now in the making.

The establishment of specially chartered nameholdings was legally justified in a variety of ways, but usually the principal ground for granting a provincial special decree was that the founder had opened the area to cultivation. Reclamation projects on the scale of nameholdings required, however, the cooperation of the provincial authorities, as when from 1075 to 1079 one Hata no Tametatsu re-

---

13 Morita, "Heian chūki gunji ni tsuite no ichikōsatsu," pp. 208–17; Yoneda Yūsuke, "Gigunji kō," in Kodaigaku kyōkai, ed., *Engi Tenryaku jidai no kenkyū* (Tokyo: Yoshikawa kōbunkan, 1960), pp. 215–46.
14 The development of the estatist office is fully discussed in Satō, *Nihon no chūsei kokka*. See also Toda, *Ryōshusei*, pp. 116–65.
15 *HIB* 3:838–39, doc. 708. See, inter alia, Morita, *Heian jidai seijishi kenkyū*, pp. 300–316.

opened about 80 *chō* (1 *chō* = 11,900 sq. meters) of abandoned rice paddy in Harima Province using more than five thousand local peasant laborers to restore the irrigation facilities. The holder of minor *gun* and provincial titles, Tametatsu became the certified reclaimer, or "opening lord" (*kaihatsu ryōshu*) of the Hisatomi Settlement (*hō*). Although the term *hō*, translated here as "settlement," at first meant a subunit of the *ritsuryō* village, or *gō*, in late Heian times it always referred to a special proprietorship created for the benefit of opening-lord reclaimers or their sponsors in Kyoto. The private landholding rights of such people were validated by a customary rule, as yet only tacitly acknowledged by the capital government, permitting reclaimers of agricultural land to treat it as alienable property.[16]

Specially created settlements, of which the Hisatomi is the earliest known example, were internally complex, as were their equivalents, the specially organized *myō*. There were subtenures held by a lord's "followers," the cultivation and residential rights of which were normally heritable but subject to the obligation to pay taxes to the lord. That quasi-feudal structure was reinforced by the concept of rights and powers expressed by the term *shiki*, usually translated into English as "office," but which had always denoted official function rather than official title or status (*kan*). In 1098, when Tametatsu passed on his rights to his son, his bequest included as a constituent of his proprietorship "the documentation *shiki*" of Hisatomi Settlement.[17] The appearance of the *shiki* in the late eleventh century was an essential step in the development of the medieval domain, and of the medieval Japanese state.

Despite its literal meaning of "office" or, perhaps better, "commission," *shiki* in Tametatsu's case indicated rights to possession and income as much as it did official responsibilities. By its incorporation of economic benefice into the exercise of administrative power and management, the term reinforced the still weak concept of domanial property in land, making the enjoyment of lordly powers into a sort of official delegation of authority. Locally, it integrated the do-

---

16 On Hisatomi *ho* and Tametatsu, see Tametatsu's petitions of Enkyū 3(1071)/6/25, *HIB* 3:1077, doc. 1059; Jōhō 2(1075)/3/12, *HIB* 3:1122, doc. 1109; Jōhō 2(1075)/4/26, *HIB* 3:1126, doc. 1113; Jōryaku 3(1079)/11/3, *HIB* 3:1177, doc. 1171; his bequest of Jōtoku 2(1098)/2/10, *HIB* 4:1351, doc. 1389; the decree of Retired Emperor Toba's chancery of Hōen 2(1136)/2/11, *HIB* 5:1982–83, doc. 2339; and the discussion in Toda, *Ryōshusei*, pp. 201–25.

17 *HIB* 4:1351, doc. 1387; on the *shiki*, see Nagahara Keiji, "Shōensei ni okeru 'shiki' no seikaku," in Hōgetsu Keigo Sensei kanreki kinenkai, ed., *Nihon shakai keizai shi kenkyū, Kodai chūsei hen* (Tokyo: Yoshikawa kōbunkan, 1967), pp. 249–78; Nakada Kaoru, *Shōen no kenkyū* (Tokyo: Shōkō shoin, 1949), pp. 185–93; Satō Shin'ichi, *Nihon no chūsei kokka*, pp. 41–45.

manial holding into a larger official network dominated by the provincial officials in residence. The introduction of a concept of office into the area of landholding, however, also linked it firmly into the surviving framework of *ritsuryō* authority in a way that muted the autonomy of the landholder vis-à-vis the capital nobility. Officeholding still came before property per se.

Long before the *shiki* appeared, the steady growth of local power was severely weakening the provincial governors. Another related challenge to the authority of custodial governors and deputy supervisors, and to the provincial headquarters itself, was the proliferation of *shōen*. Although large estates of high nobles or powerful religious institutions had existed for centuries, now in the eleventh century they provided certain local lords with a chance to withdraw their holdings entirely from the fiscal authority of the province. Private holdings in "public" lands could be transferred to a temple or noble house at the capital, while the transferor retained hereditary rights of management and control over the cultivators. That process, called *kishin*, or commendation, had a long history, but the transfer of office rights gave it a new significance. When a local lord (*ryōshu*) conveyed his land title to a high noble, reserving a supervisory office right for himself, he brought his holding into the sphere of direct courtier authority, which impaired the bargaining power of the provincial government when tax and other immunities were asserted later. Custodial governors and deputy supervisors reaped immediate profits by their sponsorship of such arrangements, but created problems for their successors in office.

The rapid militarization of the eleventh-century rural elite was intricately related to the development of domanial landholding.[18] A critical step in both processes was the reinforcement of title to land secured by reclamation with the holding of *shiki* rights. A secondary development, the incorporation of *shiki* rights into the *shōen* structure and the act of commendation that often accompanied the incorporation,[19] facilitated *shōen*-holding among court nobles, which, in turn, stimulated the court in 1069 to issue the first of a series of decrees requiring nationwide registration and certification of tax-immune *shōen*. In the ensuing century and a half, similar edicts were periodically issued by the court of the retired emperor (*in*) as that

---

18 Taniguchi Kengo, "Mino no kuni Ōi no shō ni okeru shōkan ichizoku no ryōshusei: Ōnakatomi-shi no geshishiki sōron o megutte," *Hōsei shigaku* 28 (1976): 24–37; Yasuda Motohisa, "Bushidan no keisei," in *Kodai*, vol. 4 of Ienaga Saburō, *IK*, pp. 121–60.
19 Nagahara Keiji, "Shōensei ni okeru 'shiki' no seikaku," pp. 249–78.

newly invigorated organ steadily expanded its judicial authority over rights in land, an authority that up to that time had been almost entirely within the control of each provincial government.

One purpose of the new *shōen* registration system was the elimination of ambiguity concerning the legality of *shōen* through insistence on clear documentation of their establishment,[20] and that, together with the judicial decisions of the retired emperor's court, led to a gradual sorting out of lands into the two categories of *shōen* and provincial domain (*kokugaryō*). In the process the fiscal authority of the provincial governments was largely confined to the provincial domains, which those governments were obliged to maintain and, if possible, expand.

What has here been designated the second phase of development of Heian-period provincial administration (late tenth to early twelfth centuries) can be seen as the time when domanial property supplanted administrative authority as the dominant factor in the organization of local power. But despite the development of domanial tenures, the completely tax-immune *shōen* was still a thing of the future, and the distinction between provincial domain and *shōen* was far from clear in many cases. It was not until the twelfth century that the medieval type of local administration and land tenure became pervasive. That necessary preliminary to the foundation of the Kamakura bakufu constitutes the third phase of Heian provincial history as presented here.

During the third stage (the first half of the twelfth century), the system of land tenure sometimes called "the *shōen* system" reached maturity.[21] *Shōen* almost certainly never occupied the greater portion of Japanese landholdings, but historically they enjoy the advantage of better documentation, a record that throws considerable light on the tenurial system generally. Although many Kamakura warriors were resident officials (*zaichō kanjin*) and private lords on technically provincial domains, the nobility in the capital in the twelfth century was clearly almost entirely dependent on *shōen*, giving the latter a political importance far in excess of their relative area.[22] Nobles in Kyoto could, by prearrangement, enjoy a share in the income of the

20 See Murai Yasuhiko, "Shōensei no hatten to kōzō," in *Kodai*, vol. 4, *IK*, pp. 41–88.
21 Murai "Shōensei no hatten to kōzō," pp. 41–88; Murai, *Kodai kokka*, pp. 237–65; Nagahara "Shōensei ni okeru 'shiki' no seikaku," pp. 249–78.
22 Inagaki Yasuhiko, "Ritsuryōseiteki tochi seido no kaitai," in Takeuchi Rizō et al., eds., *Taikei Nihonshi sōsho*, vol. 5 (Tokyo: Yamakawa shuppansha, 1973), pp. 139–72; Takeuchi Rizō, *Ritsuryōsei to kizoku seiken*, vol. 2 (Tokyo: Ochanomizu shobō, 1958), pp. 436–75; Toda, *Ryōshusei*, pp. 241–77; Yoshimura, *Kokushi seido*, pp. 684–91.

custodial governors, but revenues from the provincial domains were no longer freely available for the stipends of the court nobility.

The long career of Emperor Shirakawa (1053–1129), who reigned from 1072 to 1087 and exercised the power of retired emperor from 1087 to 1129, straddles the second and third phases defined here, and in many ways his regime marked the final transition from bureaucratic to estatist forms of political organization. His *shōen*-limitation edicts of 1075, 1099, 1107, and 1127 were a major factor in the growing body of law concerning *shōen* and their immunities vis-à-vis the provincial authorities. Indeed, the announced restrictions and registration requirements operated as invitations to litigate, and *shōen* proprietors in the capital could sometimes be major beneficiaries of such contests, which were adjudicated under the guidance of the many legal experts on the retired emperor's staff.[23] The *zuryō* governorships came to be treated by the court as mere sources of income, and indeed provinces themselves, in the view of the courtiers, were becoming mere estates, analogous to *shōen*. One aging courtier, reviewing Shirakawa's career on his death in 1129, made a short list of the more regrettable abuses established during his time, including the simultaneous granting of gubernatorial posts to three or four children of the same father, the appointment of boys not much over ten years old, the steep rise in fees, *jōgō*, to be paid to the court for an appointment, and the refusal of such governors to pay religious institutions or noble houses the shares of provincial revenues they were entitled to. The use of governorships to provide sources of official income for court nobles had been fairly common during the eleventh century and earlier. Concurrent appointments to gubernatorial posts could be granted to capital officials as a kind of compensation. As a means of supplementing their incomes, high nobles and royalty were also given the power to nominate appointees to certain provinces, that is, power to sell the appointments. In addition, a governor could assure himself of a renewal of his appointment, or perhaps a reappointment to an even more rewarding province, by making a special contribution to the court, typically in the form of financial support for some official project. This meant the increasing

---

23 See Koizumi Yoshiaki, "Todaijiryō Akanabe-no-shō," in Gifu ken, ed., *Gifu kenshi, Tsushihen: chūsei* (Gifu: Taishū shobō, 1969), pp. 430–548, for a case where the *shōen* registration process resulted in greatly increased immunities and prerogatives for the proprietary temple. Works on the *shōen* registration efforts of retired emperors and the functioning of *kirokusho* include Ishii Susumu, "Insei jidai," in Rekishigaku kenkyūkai and Nihonshi kenkyūkai, eds., *Kōza: Nihon shi* (Tokyo: Tōkyō daigaku shuppankai, 1970), vol. 2, pp. 193–220; Takeuchi Rizō, "Insei no seiritsu," in *Kodai*, vol. 4 of *IK*, pp. 89–120.

politicization of the *zuryō* office, released by the retired sovereigns from the bureaucratic oversight to which it had been subjected by the government of the Fujiwara regency.[24]

At some time early in the twelfth century a new means of diverting the income of custodial governors to the upkeep of the capital officialdom appeared in the form of *chigyōkoku,* or "possessory provinces." Possessory provinces were first awarded to court Counselors (*nagon*) in lieu of income from "support household" (*fuko*) revenues that governors could easily avoid turning over to their designated recipients in the capital. Holders of possessory provinces, who were never themselves governors, could dispatch "deputy supervisors" to look after their interests. These agents sometimes provoked the hostility of the officials in residence. The large number of possessory provinces held by members of the Taira clan later in the twelfth century was an important factor in the uprisings of 1181–85 that ushered in the Kamakura period. In a sense, the *zuryō* system had within it the seeds of its own destruction; increasingly, the newly consolidated (and militarized) local elites could deal with the capital nobility directly, without the governor as intermediary.[25]

It is a major aim of the following discussion to show how, during the first two centuries of the Heian era, custodial governors acquired so much access to free-floating resources in the provinces. That they did so is beyond argument, and during the eleventh and twelfth centuries their posts were routinely regarded as assets to be tapped for the redistribution of wealth in the capital. As the appointment of minor children to these posts indicates, the nominal holder of the office was not necessarily the person responsible for actually collecting the revenue. The administrative functions of child governors were carried out by the household superintendents (*keishi*) of their noble fathers or grandfathers, and the accountability of the gubernatorial office was no longer directed primarily toward the offices of the *ritsuryō* state, but to the persons or institutions that had, in effect, been given a prior claim on the tax income collected.

In the provinces, claims on the land, including those of the provincial government, were to some degree sorted out by the chancery of the retired emperors. In 1114, for example, the newly opened Record-

---

24 Hashimoto Yoshihiko, *Heian kizoku shakai no kenkyū* (Tokyo: Yoshikawa kōbunkan, 1976), pp. 172–90; Takeuchi, *Ritsuryōsei to kizoku seiken*, vol. 2, pp. 587–640; Yoshimura, *Kokushi seido*, pp. 383–401, 548–649; Fujiwara no Munetada, *Chūyūki*, entry of Daiji 4(1129)/7/25, cited in Toda Yoshimi, *Chūyūki* (Tokyo: Soshiete, 1979), pp. 245–48.
25 On *fuko*, see Katsuyama Seiji, "Fukosei no saihen to kaitai: jū-jūni seiki no fukosei," *Nihonshi kenkyū* 194 (October 1978): 1–41.

ing Office, or *kirokusho,* of Retired Emperor Shirakawa decided a lawsuit between Tōji, a major Kyoto temple, and the governor of the province of Tamba concerning a property called Ōyama-no-shō. The previous governor had rejected the claims of the *shōen,* limiting Tōji to three *chō* of land that had been officially certified exempt from taxes in the ninth century. Tōji's complaint recounted a long history of fluctuating provincial policies toward its claims to tax-exempt property, and the nine-year-old governor replied through his representative that most of the estate consisted of "newly established" *shōen* lands of the sort prohibited by the retired emperor's edict.

But after further litigation, the Recording Office decided in favor of the temple in every respect, finding that the earlier documentation was clear despite the intermittent efforts of governors (and probably officials in residence) to restrict the tax immunities of the holding.[26] The Recording Office, purportedly established to control *shōen,* had in the careful exercise of its judicial impartiality actually reinforced, and probably increased, the tax immunities of the Ōyama *shōen.* The holdings brought before the tribunal were likely to either win complete fiscal immunity or lose all claim to any immunity whatever.

That development was part of a general trend leading to the emergence of the totally immune *shōen* from which agents of the provincial headquarters were legally barred. The mature *shōen,* as it has been called,[27] was usually created through acts of commendation. In the late eleventh century high-ranking courtiers had been the most common objects of commendation by local proprietors, but in the twelfth, the successors of those courtiers were often unable to maintain influence enough to fend off provincial authorities and were therefore themselves required to commend their lordships to higher powers, reserving *shiki* rights for themselves. Those highers usually turned out to be temples or shrines favored by the retired emperor's court.[28]

In *shōen* holdings that had reached the mature stage of development, an original local proprietorship had typically evolved into a three-tiered hierarchy of tenures. On the lowest level was the successor of the original local proprietor, who was often called the "sub-officer" (*geshi*) or "custodian" (*azukaridokoro*). Above him was the

---

26 See Miyagawa Mitsuru, *Ōyama sonshi, Hommon hen* (Tokyo: Hanawa shobō, 1964), pp. 77–103; and Takeuchi Rizō, *Bushi no tōjō,* vol. 6 of Inoue Mitsusada et al., eds., *Nihon no rekishi* (Tokyo: Chūō kōron sha, 1973), pp. 155, 263–67.
27 Yoshimura, *Kokushi seido,* pp. 684–91.
28 Ishii, "Insei jidai," pp. 193–220; Murai, "Shōensei no hatten to kōzō," pp. 41–88; Murai, *Kodai kokka,* pp. 373–402.

lord (*ryōshu* or *ryōke*) and often, at an even higher level, stood a chief tenant, almost always a religious institution, called the "principal" (*honjo*).

That core structure supported many variations of detail, the authority of higher tenants over lower differing widely from case to case in both degree and kind.[29] The principal institution (*honjo*) typically exercised judicial authority over lower tenancies. It frequently was entitled to dues of various kinds but in some instances enjoyed no substantial economic benefits, serving merely as a fiduciary for the lord's interests so as to preserve the holding's immunities.[30] When proprietors commended their land, they reserved to themselves suboffice, custodial, or lordship tenancies, promising faithfully to render dues to the commendee. The subofficer and custodian categories of tenure, almost always designated as *shiki* (office) in the source materials of the period, were generally treated as property interests in land, leading some scholars to regard the *shiki* as primarily a legal "right" to income from *shōen* lands. The power and privileges of *shōen* officers, however, were not entirely insulated from those of the high proprietors. Rather, relations between the two levels were fluid, and the proprietors could in some cases exercise overwhelming power.[31]

Shiki still retained, however, some of the characteristics of the local offices from which they had evolved. Most importantly, they required certification of appointment (*bunin*) by a higher authority, usually the recipient of the original commendation of his successors. In 1164, for example, a litigant defending his custodian's *shiki* against a rival for the same position with prior claim to the title, maintained that "when a private domain has been commended to another, whatever kinds of promises may have been made on the occasion, the prevailing practice is to replace a commender who turns against the lord." However "private" the holding of the original domain, and regardless of the prerogatives reserved by the commender, typically the right to treat his position as hereditary, the customary law of the twelfth century gave the *shōen* lord the power to cancel a *shiki* if the holder committed a breach of *fides*.

The commendation pact was not merely a matter of private property rights. The newly recognized authority of the major proprietary

---

29 Murai, "Shōensei no hatten to kōzō," pp. 41–88.
30 Nakada, *Shōen no kenkyū*, pp. 60–301.
31 Nakada, *Shōen no kenkyū*, pp. 98–100, 185–90, and references cited in note 17, above; *HIB* 8:2948–50, doc. 3836.

lords to award *shiki* marked a decisive step in the gradual assimilation of state power by particular groups. To be sure, the exercise of authority over land and people, even on a moderate scale, could not possibly be regarded as private in the modern sense. Throughout the eleventh century, for example, dues collected locally on *shōen* were fixed by precedent and provincial rules, as if the proprietor were somehow a surrogate tax collector. But the certification of immune *shōen* by the retired emperor's court and the *shiki*-commendation procedures of the late eleventh and early twelfth centuries marked the final step in the appropriation of official power by local and central elites.[32]

The lands of the mature twelfth-century *shōen* were made up chiefly of units called names (*myō*) or name-fields (*myōden*). Typically, each such unit was called by a personal name, so that the designation of entire areas by names like Sanefuji, Motoshige, and so on, became commonplace by the late twelfth century. *Myō* holders (*myōshu*), like their predecessors the field managers (*tato*), took charge of cultivation and the rendering of the dues owed on account of their holdings. These holdings were not ordinarily called domains (*ryō*), but the term *shiki* was, in the century following, often used in connection with *myōshu* rights.

Areas not preempted by *shōen*, that is, the provincial domains, were similarly organized. *Shiki* proprietorships in fact originated in the provincial domain as the holdings of the more powerful resident officials, particularly holdings reinforced by claims of reclamation, came to be identified with their office functions. In the final analysis, *shiki* entitlements, on or off *shōen* territories, were part of a single network of authority centering on the imperial court. In the case of the provinces, the retired emperor's court, the absentee custodial governor, the beneficial holder (in the case of possessory provinces), and the provincial officials in residence were interrelated in a way not unlike the linkages between principals, lords, and subofficers.

The powers of landed proprietorship on the local level were undoubtedly enhanced by the general delegation of tax collecting authority to local gentry, both on *shōen* and provincial domain. In both, there was a great variety of taxes and dues, but legal pleas for exemptions in the eleventh century gradually divided them all into two broad categories. First was the "official goods" (*kammotsu*) tax, con-

---

32 The document of 1164 quoted above is *HIB* 7, doc. 3318, pp. 2634–35; on the appropriation of state authority, see Takeuchi, *Bushi no tōjō*, pp. 269–70.

sisting of a specified quantity of rice and other commodities, and second were the "irregular," and partially discretionary, taxes (*zōkuji*), including labor, that the provincial headquarters or *shōen* lord demanded annually. The appearance of this new mode of taxation signaled the emergence of truly domanial property. By the late twelfth century, the ultimate responsibility for both types often fell on the landholding *myōshu*.

Not all lands were *myōshu* holdings, but these holdings, and their proprietors, were the ultimate surety that taxes or dues would be forthcoming from local communities, and the *myō* was the basic unit of taxation. The provincial domain, which usually contained most of the arable land, centered on a headquarters dominated by officials in residence who presided over a number of *myō* or other *shōen*-like entities, many bearing older official designations like *gun* or "village," but in fact managed by *shōen*-type proprietors.

On both provincial domains and *shōen*, a new form of levy appeared based merely on residence within a given proprietorship. Collected by the authorities of *gun*, *shōen*, *myō*, or village from cultivating households on the next lower level, the "resident-householder levy" (*zaikeyaku*), including both labor and commodities, could be required of resident households (*zaike*) on several occasions during the year. *Zaikeyaku* had a distinct resemblance to European feudal dues; on certain holdings, for example, cultivators were expected to provide the proprietor with the traditional eggplants and cucumbers needed on the Festival of Souls (*bon*). The resident-household levy has been seen as a natural outgrowth of a established domanial system. Nevertheless, it more likely developed from older practices. These dues became incidents of residence only after earlier obligations of personal subjection were assimilated into the system of domanial property that matured only in the late eleventh and early twelfth centuries. The underlying question, then, is: at what time *was* domanial lordship established? The discussion that follows is mainly concerned with the ninth and tenth centuries, when the domain itself was not a dominant feature. It cannot, however, completely sidestep this problem, as it aims to point out developments that ultimately led to the medieval Japanese domain. The distinction between burdens of tenure and personal obligation is far from apparent in many of the sources, particularly those of the eleventh century, and it is most likely that there was often little consciousness of it, but, as in the Izumi document of 1012 already cited, what might be called latent domains appeared early in the second phase defined here.³³

It must also be noted that the provincial headquarters, despite the restrictions on its fiscal powers imposed by *shōen*, remained the political focal point of the province, especially in police and constabulary affairs. By the middle of the eleventh century, each provincial headquarters had a resident constabulary, reinforced and countered by the forces accompanying the acting governor (*zuryō*) or his deputies (*mokudai*). This meant that the more eminent military chiefs had their own regional bases in addition to commissions to represent court authority in other provinces.³⁴ The gradual division of local territory and people between provincial domain and *shōen* was an important and final step in the development of estate patrimonialism in early medieval Japan. When this is viewed as a culmination of the changes that took place in the preceding centuries, the importance of provincial office and the *kokuga* becomes clear. The provincial governments themselves proved to be among the most durable of *ritsuryō* institutions, probably because from the beginning they served to integrate the interests of local elites, capital officials, and court nobility.

One crucial issue is how the relationship of provincial government to local elites changed over time. In the early Heian years, when provinces were still repositories of national wealth in the form of stored grain, the governments could stand apart from local chiefs as centers of commodity redistribution, public works, and agricultural development. Then during the ninth and tenth centuries (the first phase proposed here) those functions of the provincial governments were appropriated by locally based authorities, a development that did not, however, undermine the governments. Provincial authority was gradually reconstituted as the resident officials assumed more and more authority. From the late tenth to early twelfth centuries (the second phase), a domanial landholding system evolved and, by about the year 1100, the subject populace had also been reorganized, bringing whole communities of cultivators under the patrimonial control of domanial lords or proprietary officeholders. The stage was thus set for the third phase, the division of both territory and people between the provincial domains and *shōen*.

33 On the *myōshu, zaike,* and village of late Heian, see Toda, *Ryōshusei,* pp. 190–277, 379–402.
34 See Toda Yoshimi, "Kokuga gunsei no keisei katei," in Nihonshi kenkyūkai, eds., *Chūsei no kenryoku to minshū* (Osaka: Sōgensha, 1970), pp. 3–45.

The transition from the despotic *ritsuryō* polity of the eighth century to the Kamakura Bakufu at the end of the twelfth was not the result of uniform, gradual, and continuous change. The course of change was always sporadic, and not all changes took place everywhere in the country at the same time. The suggested three-stage periodization is consequently highly approximate, based chiefly on documentation from the home provinces (Kinai) and vicinity, the area that most Japanese scholars regard as more advanced in development than the "peripheral" provinces of the south and northeast. In those areas more distant from the capital, local authority, including that created by military power, grew up more rapidly than in the central regions, whereas nearer the capital, in the provinces of Kii and Yamashiro, the overwhelming presence of temple *shōen* holdings had a distorting effect on historical development. Within that erratic, regionally differing, discontinuous course of change, perhaps the single most important development was the takeover of provincial governments by the local officials in residence.

REGIONAL ADMINISTRATION

By the time Emperor Kammu began construction of the Heian capital, the territorial division of the country into provinces and districts had nearly reached the form that was to endure for many centuries. The last major change occurred in 823 when the province of Kaga, on the Sea of Japan north of the capital, was created from the two northernmost *gun* of Echizen Province, which were then further split into four. In the following year the provincial-level island of Tane (now called Tanegashima) was merged into the nearby province of Ōsumi in southern Kyushu.[35] No further alterations of provincial boundaries were made after that, and the total of sixty-six provinces and two islands persisted into the nineteenth century, albeit in an attenuated sense. The *gun* units into which provinces were subdivided were slightly less stable. The total slowly rose from 555 in the early eighth century to 592 in the early tenth.[36]

The *ritsuryō* system had established a rigid classification for both provinces and *gun,* based on magnitude of land area, population, and strategic importance. The sixty-eight Heian provinces (including the two islands, Tsushima and Iki) were designated as either great, upper, medium, or lower. This determined the number and ranks of officials

---

35 Yoshimura, *Kokushi seido*, pp. 157–58.   36 Yoshimura, *Kokushi seido*, pp. 219–35.

dispatched from the capital to take command of each provincial government. Great and upper provinces had a provincial administration (*kokushi*) containing all four levels of officials provided for in *ritsuryō* law: a chief, an assistant chief, and major and minor administrators. Thirty-five, or slightly more than half, of the provinces belonged to the upper category, which had one officer at each level of officialdom: a governor (*kami*), a vice-governor (*suke*), an executive officer (*jō*), and an inspector (*sakan*).[37] The prescribed rank of the governor was Lower Junior Fifth; that of the vice-governor, Upper Junior Sixth; that of the executive officer, Upper Junior Seventh; and that of the inspector, Lower Junior Eighth. Like all other classes of provinces, the upper province was also given three clerks (*shishō*) for whom formal rank was not required, although it might be held. Lower provinces, by contrast, had only a governor (Lower Junior Sixth Rank), an inspector (Upper Lesser Starting Rank), and the three clerks. This meant that in the nine smallest provincial units a mere clerk might function as acting governor if both his superiors were absent or incapacitated. The complete scheme of provincial administration is represented in Table 4.1.[38]

In addition to administrative officials, the organic law provided that a physician and a professor be appointed to each provincial capital, selected either from the lower officialdom of the capital or from the local population. (During the Nara period, at least, such officers were ordinarily dispatched from the capital.) Like the three clerks, they were part of the higher official staff of the provincial government, even though they did not fit into the formal four-tier hierarchy of *ritsuryō* office structure and were therefore "irregular appointees" (*zōnin*).[39]

Divided among eight large administrative regions called circuits (*dō*), the provinces included all the territory of the country outside the capital. A total population of somewhat less than 5 million persons was distributed over capital and provinces. Among the provinces, Hitachi and Mutsu in the far northeast had the largest populations, estimated respectively at about 217,000 and 186,000 in the eighth century.[40] They also had the largest recorded areas of culti-

---

37 Yoshimura, *Kokushi seido*, pp. 115–46.
38 Taken from Abe Takeshi, *Owari no kuni gebumi no kenkyū* (Tokyo: Shinseisha, 1971), p. 60.
39 Nyūya Tetsuichi, "Zaichi tone no keisei to rekishiteki ichi," in Ōsaka rekishi gakkai, ed., *Chūsei shakai no seiritsu to tenkai* (Tokyo: Yoshikawa kōbunkan, 1976), pp. 141–224; Yamada Hideo, "Sammi no kenkyū," in Sakamoto Tarō hakushi kanreki kinenkai, ed., *Nihon kodaishi ronshū*, vol. 2 (Tokyo: Yoshikawa kōbunkan, 1962), pp. 89–128.
40 Population figures for Hitachi and Mutsu are based on Sawada Goichi, *Fukkoku: Naracho jidai minsei keizai no sūteki kenkyū* (Tokyo: Kashiwa shobō, 1972), pp. 47–310.

TABLE 4.1
Provincial officials mandated by the ritsuryō

	Great Province *Daikoku*	Upper Province *Jōkoku*	Medium Province *Chūkoku*	Lower Province *Kakoku*
Governor *Kami*	One: Junior 5th Rank Upper Grade	One: Junior 5th Rank Lower Grade	One: Senior 6th Rank Lower Grade	One: Junior 6th Rank Lower Grade
Vice-governor *Suke*	One: Senior 6th Rank Lower Grade	One: Junior 6th Rank Upper Grade	None	None
Executive Officer *Jō*	Two: One Chief Executive Officer, *Daijō*, Senior 7th Rank Lower Grade; one Assistant Executive Officer, *Shōjō*, Junior 7th Rank Upper Grade	One: Junior 7th Rank Upper Grade	One: Senior 8th Rank Upper Grade	None
Inspector *Sakan*	Two: One Chief Inspector, *Daimoku* Junior 8th Rank Upper Grade; one Assistant Inspector, *Shōmoku*, Junior 8th Rank Lower Grade	One: Junior 8th Rank Lower Grade	One: Senior Initial Rank Lower Grade	One: Junior Initial Rank Upper Grade
Clerk *Shishō*	Three: No Specified Rank	Three: No Specified Rank	Three: No Specified Rank	Three: No Specified Rank

vated land: according to a dictionary compiled in about 935, there were approximately 40,000 *chō* in Hitachi and 51,000 in Mutsu. Although those figures are not trustworthy enough to warrant any conclusions about agricultural productivity,[41] they surely indicate a large concentration of manpower in an area quite remote from the capital and help to explain why the region quickly became the most difficult for Heian officialdom to govern.

Kyushu presented special difficulties, not only because of its distance from the capital and its ample potential for hostility toward the

---

41 Minamoto no Shitagō, comp., *Wamyō ruijūshō* (Tokyo: Kazama shobō, 1974 facsimile ed.) part 5, pp. 15b–16a, 18a–18b.

central government, but also because of its proximity to Silla, an often unfriendly state, and the potential for foreign trade afforded by its accessibility to the East Asian mainland. To cope with those problems, a Kyushu Government Headquarters (Dazaifu) was established in Chikuzen Province near the present Bay of Hakata. That large, militarized bureau, headed by a governor general (*sotsu*) whose prescribed rank was Junior Third, had a complex structure that in many ways replicated that of the central government on a reduced scale. Authorized to exercise broad political control over the nine provinces of Kyushu and the two island provinces of Iki and Tsushima, the Kyushu Headquarters could affect fiscal policy in the entire area.[42]

The *gun*, of which there were at least two in every province, could not, according to the organic code, contain more than one thousand "households." Census households were large, somewhat artificial groupings of related persons, on rare occasions numbering over one hundred persons. One thousand households thus represented a substantial population, but the code's restriction on *gun* population size probably did, nevertheless, set limits on concentration of power in the hands of the local aristocratic families from which *gun* magistrates were recruited. Those lifetime appointees, whose office usually presupposed a documented lineage (*fudai*) from earlier chieftains, were something of an anomaly within the *ritsuryō* bureaucracy, since in fact, if not in theory, meritocratic norms had little to do with their selection. Officially certified pedigrees did not always guarantee obedience. As the gentry stratum grew, holders of lineage were sometimes challenged by other prosperous peasants who lacked the proper genealogy.[43] The organic code established five classes of *gun* according to size (great, upper, middle, lower, and small), and for the three larger sorts, at least one officer on all four administrative levels: chief magistrate (*dairyō*), assistant magistrate (*shōryō*), administrative officer (*shusei*), and secretary (*shuchō*). The official complements of each type are shown in Table 4.2.[44]

The actual work of governing a province in accordance with *ritsuryō* standards required hundreds of irregular appointees and auxiliary personnel at the provincial capitals, the *gun* (district) headquarters, and throughout the provincial territories. In 822 the central

---

42 On the *Dazaifu*, see Sasaki Keisuke, "Dazaifu no kannai shihai henshitsu ni kansuru shiron: omo ni zaiseiteki sokumen kara," in Tsuchida Naoshige Sensei kanreki kinenkai, eds., *Nara Heian jidaishi ronshū* (Tokyo: Yoshikawa kōbunkan, 1984), vol. 2, pp. 245–90.
43 See note 1, above.   44 Taken from Abe, *Owari no kuni gebumi no kenkyū*, p. 60.

TABLE 4.2
Gun officials mandated by the ritsuryō

	Great *Gun* Daigun	Upper *Gun* Jōgun	Middle *Gun* Chūgun	Lower *Gun* Kagun	Small *Gun* Shōgun
Chief Magistrate *Dairyō*	1	1	1	1	One Magistrate *Ryō*
Assistant Magistrate *Shōryō*	1	1	1	1	
Administrative Officer *Shusei*	3	2	1	none	none
Secretary *Shuchō*	3	2	1	1	1

government in Heian-kyō issued a directive aimed at standardizing the number of corvée helpers, including craftsmen and a variety of quasi-official functionaries, who could be fed at public expense while working for the political authorities. The document reads in part:

> Impressed workers to whom food may be granted: General attendants for the four annual messengers (four for the court report messenger and two each for the other three).
> Scribes for the major-report and tax-grain-report offices (eighteen for great provinces, sixteen for upper provinces, fourteen for middle provinces, and twelve for lower provinces).
> Paper makers for provincial supplies (sixty for great provinces, fifty for upper provinces, forty for middle provinces, and thirty for lower provinces).
> Brush makers (two per province), ink makers (one per province) and paper craftsmen (six for great provinces, five for upper provinces, four for middle provinces, and three for lower provinces).
> Chief maker of annual arms supplies (1 per province) and workmen (120 for great provinces, 90 for upper provinces, 60 for middle provinces, and 30 for lower provinces).
> Provincial corvée directors (320 for great provinces, 260 for upper provinces, 200 for middle provinces, and 150 for lower provinces).
> Guardians of local branch storehouses receiving tax-grain and the like (twelve per branch).
> Gatherers of black kudzu (two per province; not applicable to provinces that do not contribute to the imperial table).
> Laborers for each member [of the provincial-officer staff] (four serving men).
> Two keyholders, the tax-grain chief, and the officers of official storehouses (three men for each branch granary).

Tax-grain collectors (two per village), two tribute-tax chiefs, and assistant chiefs (one per village).

Commutation-tax chiefs (one per village) and corvée workers (fifteen for a great *gun*, twelve for an upper *gun*, ten for a middle *gun*, and eight for a lower *gun*).

One kitchen chief, fifty corvée workers, two vessel makers, and two paper-making workers.

Three hay workers, workers providing equipment for two post-station riders (four for each *gun* and post station), and grooms for spare horses (one per *gun*).

Petitions from the various provinces concerning the aforesaid have not been uniform, and accordingly the standards have been determined as stated. Not included in this ruling are master weavers and apprentices making tribute-tax figured silk, shuttle makers (this does not apply to provinces that do not render tribute of figured silk), transport directors and bearers delivering miscellaneous tax items to the Council of State, workers accompanying incoming or outgoing provincial officers, or provincial and *gun* officers delivering tribute taxes, and workers bringing the associated documents, kitchen workers and station workers for post riders together with grooms, ferrymen and the like, and gatherers of sweet kudzu, honey, and boar fat, or those delivering such items to the Council of State.[45]

Although this particular directive is far from complete in its coverage of local government activities, its emphasis being only on those functions for which the legal corvée-overhead was still unclear, it tells a good deal about the scope and organization of provincial government in early Heian times. The first two items, dealing with the "four annual messengers" (*yodo no tsukai*),[46] are noteworthy for the light they shed on how the provincial government prepared and delivered its reports to the capital. The messengers in question were always, in early Heian times, regular officials of province or *gun*. The four reports they delivered to the capital at different times of the year were:

1. The court report (*chōshūchō*), which detailed the conduct of the provincial administration over the course of the previous year, including the state of public buildings, irrigation facilities, etc.
2. The major accounting report (*daikeichō*), also called the major report (*daichō*), which gave the population of taxable households and able-bodied workers, indicating thereby the theoreti-

---

45 Ordinance (*kyaku*) of Kōnin 13(822)/int. 9/20, *Ruijū sandai kyaku*, KT, vol. 25, pp. 279–81. See also Nyūya, "Zaichi tone no keisei to rekishiteki ichi," pp. 141–224.
46 On *yodo no tsukai*, see Hérail, Francine, *Yodo no Tsukai ou le Système des Quatre Envoyés* (Paris: Presses Universitaires de France, 1966). See also Sakamoto, *Nihon kodaishi no kisoteki kenkyū*, vol. 1, pp. 163–204; Satō Sōjun, *Heian zenki seijishi josetsu* (Tokyo: Tōkyō Daigaku shuppankai, 1977), pp. 57–71.

cal capacity of the province to render tribute (*chō*) and labor-commutation (*yō*) taxes.
3. The tax-grain fund report (*shōzeichō*) which gave a complete inventory of tax grain on hand and amounts collected or disbursed.
4. The tribute-tax report (*kōchōchō*) which itemized the tribute commodities actually delivered to the capital at the time of delivery.

The second and third reports are of special concern because they dealt almost exclusively with taxable people and stored grain, regarded by all officials of the time as major capital assets belonging to the country as a whole but subject to the custodial authority of province and *gun*. In this area fraught with potential conflict of interest, liaison with the capital demanded special exertions, and preparation of the major accounting and tax-grain reports, neither of which was mandated by the organic code, and the many supplementary documents that were also demanded, had come to require special secretariats or offices, called *tokoro* (literally, "places"), at the provincial headquarters.[47]

Those scribes and many of the other workers listed by the directives were clearly not ordinary corvée laborers, despite their designation as "impressed workers" (*yōtei*) in the heading of the document. They were among the hundreds of "irregular officials" (*zōshiki*) drawn from the upper stratum of the local populace to complete the myriad tasks that government regulations imposed on the officials of province and *gun*.[48] These petty gentry thus had from the very beginning substantial representation in the headquarters of both province and *gun*. *Ritsuryō* rules prohibiting the provincial-officer staff from bringing private assistants with them from the capital, generally disregarded by the early tenth century, originally made local collaborators all the more necessary. As responsibility for the tax revenues from each province came to be wholly concentrated in a single governor, fiscal, and often military, assistants were an absolute necessity

---

47 See Kikuchi Kyōko, "Tokoro no seiritsu to tenkai," in Hayashi Rokurō, ed., *Ronshū: Nihon rekishi*, vol. 3, pp. 100–54; Morita, *Heian jidai seijishi kenkyū*, pp. 51–78; Sakamoto, *Nihon kodaishi no kisoteki kenkyū*, vol. 2, pp. 163–204; Satō, *Heian zenki seijishi josetsu*, pp. 67–98.
48 Eleventh-century customary rules regarding *zōshiki* may be found in Miyoshi no Tameyasu, comp., *Chōya gunsai*, KT 29A:517–25; see also Hōjō Hideki, "Heian zenki chōzei kikō no ichikōsatsu," in Inoue Mitsusada hakushi kanreki kinenkai, ed., *Kodaishi ronsō* (Tokyō: Yoshikawa kōbunkan, 1978), vol. 3, pp. 121–64; Izumiya Yasuo, "Chōyōsei no henshitsu ni tsuite," in Kodaigaku kyōkai, ed., *Engi Tenryaku jidai no kenkyū*, pp. 175–308; Yoneda, "Gigunji kō," pp. 215–46.

in dealing with the local elites permanently ensconced in the provincial headquarters.⁴⁹

As indicated by the directive of 822, among the irregular officials were various kinds of tax gatherers, and such officials were, ultimately, the providers of the labor power needed to maintain such public facilities as irrigation works and post stations, as well as to provide housekeeping services for provincial officers. Custody of official granaries and of branch granaries (*in*) was, as noted earlier, of special importance because the grain in the granaries, let out for interest annually, was a major capital asset, providing the wherewithal for ordinary provincial expenses, including compensation for the provincial officers.⁵⁰ *Gun* magistrates, acting jointly, presumably, with the officers in the provincial capital, had been primarily responsible for the granaries, but very early it was decided to disperse the holdings within the *gun*, thus diffusing responsibility over a far greater number of minor functionaries.

Although the reasons given for the change were geographic convenience in the collection and disbursal of tax-rice, as well as the reduction of damage in case of fire, the measure was in fact intended to appease disgruntled local elites jealous of the *gun* magistrates' monopoly over a major source of financial power. By conferring public legitimacy on privately held grain, it systematized the petty gentry's power over peasant labor by making their residences official centers for the distribution of rice to a client population. This delegation of official power to "promote agriculture" (*kannō*) was an important step in the development of the gentry, whose residences and granaries would later become nuclei for rural domains like that of Hata no Tametatsu discussed earlier.⁵¹

The numerous irregular officials listed in connection with branch granaries, village tax collection, and the like were officials of the *gun*, rather than of the provincial headquarters, and such persons sometimes appear in documents of the period as provisional *gun* magistrates.⁵² Although irregular officials could be regarded as menials by

---

49 Abe, *Heian zenki seijishi no kenkyū*, pp. 311–18; *Chōya gunsai*, KT 29A:517–25, "Kokumu jōjō no koto," esp. articles. 5, 6, 34, 39, and 40.
50 Nakano Hideo, *Ritsuryōsei shakai kaitai katei no kenkyū* (Tokyo: Hanawa shobō, 1979), pp. 258–59; Sonoda Kōyū, "Suiko: Tempyō kara Engi made," in Ōsaka rekishi gakkai, ed., *Ritsuryō kokka no kiso kōzō* (Tokyo: Yoshikawa kōbunkan, 1960), pp. 397–466.
51 Abe, *Heian zenki seijishi no kenkyū*, pp. 30–35; Murai, *Kodai kokka*, pp. 37–59; Toda, *Ryōshusei*, pp. 94–99.
52 Yoneda, "Gigunji kō," pp. 15–246.

the capital officialdom, as in the document just quoted, their authority within their districts was undoubtedly great: they had the power to allocate tax burdens, distribute grain revenues, and supervise the manufacture of fine fabrics and other high-quality tribute tax items required by the court from each province. Other profit-making opportunities for them included participation in the official barter called "exchange" (*kōeki*),[53] in which tax-grain was used to purchase silks and other goods for shipment to Kyoto.

Most irregular officials enjoyed immunity from personal taxation, adding to the material rewards they were able to gain for themselves as providers of goods and services. They also sometimes held a grade of court-appointed rank, obscuring somewhat the distinction in rank-hierarchy between them and the regular officers of province and *gun*. There were several reasons for discrepancies in rank-hierarchy between local residents and provincial and *gun* officers. Some local men earned rank status through official employment as guards or service workers in the capital, which they were allowed to retain on their return home. Their ranks set them above the lower *gun* officials, who were usually rankless, and at times they held ranks higher even than those of some regular provincial officials (although protocol required that local magistrates dismount in deference to regular provincial officers, regardless of whose rank was higher).[54]

The distribution of privilege among this numerous local elite, often masked by superficially demeaning functional designations, was thus far from congruent with the hierarchical order presumed by the organic code. To the wide variety of local people enjoying some degree of tax exemption must be added the unregistered, or separately registered, migrants (*rōnin*) whose services were specially reserved for specific purposes, irregular officials,[55] Buddhist monks and nuns, Shinto priests and priestesses, militiamen (*kondei*), and the twenty to fifty students admitted to each provincial academy.[56]

Provincial capitals and *gun* headquarters were built on a scale appropriate to the number and status of functionaries quartered there. A provincial capital differed from the national capital of Heian in that it was never, in the census system, taken to be the official residence of a subject household. In theory, all present were merely on temporary duty. All provincial capitals shared the symmetrical grid

---

53 Murai, *Kodai kokka*, pp. 80–116.   54 Yamada, "Sammi no kenkyū," pp. 89–128.
55 For rules on legal exemptions, see *Buyaku ryō*, especially *Toneri shishō no jō*, Koremune no Naomoto, comp., *Ryō no shūge*, KT 23:416–18.
56 Abe, *Heian zenki seijishi no kenkyū*, pp. 143–248.

pattern typical of *ritsuryō* planning. The scheme replicated the Heian capital on a miniature scale, with the provincial headquarters standing in the place of the imperial palace buildings.[57] The *gun* seats (called *gunke*, or sometimes *miyake*) were also surrounded by walls or moats. Besides the headquarters buildings and official residences, they included a stable of post horses and official granaries, which, as the document of 822 implies, required strict guarding.[58]

Although surviving official regulations provide scant information about how all the mandated official work at the provincial level was organized, it is reasonable to assume that it was thoroughly departmentalized. Some evidence appears in the directive of 822 where it mentions the offices (*tokoro*) of clerks assigned to prepare the major accounting report and the tax-grain report. Ancillary evidence of departmentalization is found in the case of the Tōdaiji Construction Office, the largest government bureau in the late Nara capital, which was functionally divided into *tokoro*.[59] It is thus possible that already at the beginning of the ninth century most irregular appointees of the provincial headquarters were attached to some such office. By the middle of the tenth century, though, such was definitely the case, and the offices had become permanent institutions, subordinate to the governors sent from the capital but also possessing a certain degree of autonomy. The irregular officials of the headquarters were, more clearly than before, representatives of the locally privileged class.

One source describes the reception prescribed for a newly arrived governor in the following way (the *-sho* in the document is the Sino-Japanese allomorph of *tokoro*):

On this day, the irregular appointees of the offices come forward and pay their respects (offices means the tax-grain office [*zeisho*], the major [accounting] report office [*daichōsho*], the court report office [*chōshūsho*], the militia office [*kondeisho*], the provincial management office [*kokushōsho*], and the like). In this ceremony, those of the administrative office (*mandokoro*) lead the scribes and others standing in ranks in the courtyard. One by one, each tells his office, rank, and full name, and after those statements, all bow down again. The chief official [i.e., the governor] then commands, saying, "You are appointed . . ."[60]

The concentration of local elites in the provincial headquarters as irregular officials, and their extralegal division of fiscal and military

57 Fujioka Kenjirō, *Kokufu* (Tokyo:Yoshikawa kōbunkan, 1974).
58 See Yamanaka Toshiji and Satō Kōi, *Kodai no yakusho* (Tokyo: Iwanami shoten, 1984), for a general description of *gun* headquarters, provincial temples, and barrier posts.
59 Kikuchi, "Tokoro no seiritsu to tenkai," pp. 100–54.   60 *Chōya gunsai, KT* 29A:520.

functions into *tokoro*, show a degree of corporate autonomy quite antithetical to the original *ritsuryō* order. The balance between province and *gun* established by the organic code was fatally upset, and the *gun* and its officers merged into the corporate structure of the provincial headquarters. As members of the local elite rose to eminence at the provincial level, there was a corresponding dilution of status and function of the *gun* offices. During the eighth century, *gun* magistrates had to be examined by the Ministry of Ceremonial in the capital before being appointed, reflecting the importance of the positions, but in 812 the government abandoned that procedure and allowed the headquarters of each province full authority to make the evaluations. In 822 the government further stipulated that candidates for *gun* magistracies first be appointed provisionally for three years of probationary service before becoming eligible for regular office. From that time onward, the orderly pattern of officeholding prescribed for the *gun* by the organic code was a dead letter. Provisional magistrates tended to outnumber regular appointees, perhaps because without formal tenure they were more firmly under the governors' control. The new system also permitted the total number of *gun* magistrates to exceed the quotas of the code. Although provisional *gun* magistrates still ranked above the provincial irregular officials during the ninth century, both groups were merging into a single dominant stratum of provincial gentry, overseers of *tato* for whom *gun* boundaries meant very little.

The most striking structural change, however, took place on the highest level of provincial government. The administration of provincial areas presented officers dispatched from the capital with unique opportunities for private enrichment, and the original *ritsuryō* framework of rules soon proved inadequate to curb official rapacity. Early in the Nara period the government had sought to strengthen its control of provincial governments by demanding, in addition to the already staggering volume of correspondence required from provincial headquarters, the yearly tax-grain and great accounting reports mentioned earlier. Those accounts were rigorously checked against accumulated prior reports at the capital, and their acceptance by the relevant bureaus certified the provincial officers' good conduct. In the case of the tax-grain report, the government specified its acceptance by issuing a certificate of receipt (*henshō*) indicating that the officers of both province and *gun* and the province itself had discharged all tax-grain obligations. Both levels of officer could be held responsible for deficiencies and their own public-allowance rice (*kugetō*), confiscated to make up shortages.[61]

The organic code also provided for the occasional dispatch of very high-ranking officials as circuit inspectors (*junsatsushi*) to make on-the-spot inspections of provincial administrations and report on the conduct of the officers. The reports were basically personnel evaluations and could result in promotion, demotion, or dismissal for the officers concerned.[62] There were thus two kinds of sanctions that could be used against unscrupulous officers. The government could threaten their career interests by poor personnel evaluations, and it could impose immediate financial penalties by forcing offenders to make restitution for shortages in official stores.

THE ESTABLISHMENT OF CUSTODIAL GOVERNORSHIP

In 731 a new system of policing provincial officers was put into operation. Possibly inspired by T'ang-dynasty procedures, the new requirement obliged outgoing provincial officials to submit to an accounting by their newly appointed successors. New arrivals were to incur responsibility for deficiencies they failed to detect, and officers whose terms were expiring were ineligible for further appointments until their replacements had issued discharge certificates (*geyujō*). This innovation had profound effects on the *ritsuryō* system of provincial office. It stressed the custodial aspects of office, forcing incoming governors to seek out and take charge of all government assets that were supposed to be on hand, particularly tax-grain. This meant that some officers, usually the governor, had to assume complete responsibility for all such capital assets, leading in time to deterioration of the corporate integrity of the provincial-government officer staff as the lower-level officers escaped all fiscal responsibility. The "discharge" (*geyu*) system also differed from earlier techniques of official oversight in its fundamentally adversarial, although still bureaucratic, nature. It often resulted in lengthy disputes between incoming and outgoing officers of approximately equal rank over whether or not a discharge certificate could legally be issued. By the early ninth century, regulations governing this transfer of custo-

---

61 Sonoda, "Suiko," pp. 397–466. The term *kuge* occurs in the *ryō; Zōryō, kuge no jō*, Kiyowara no Natsuno et al., comps., *Ryō no gige, KT* 22B:340.
62 Nagayama Yasutaka, *Ritsuryō futan taikei no kenkyū* (Tokyo: Hanawa shobō, 1976), pp. 219–45; Abe, *Heian zenki seijishi no kenkyū*, pp. 47–62.

dial responsibility had attained an amazing volume and complexity, and every provincial headquarters of importance needed a clerk specializing in transfer procedures.[63]

These problems were already acute as early as 761, when legal doctors (*myōbō hakase*), ordered to give an opinion on the criminal aspects of delays in transfer of office, and reasoning by analogy from provisions of *ritsu* and *ryō*, concluded that if a new gubernatorial appointee could not obtain a satisfactory accounting from his predecessor within 120 days, he should bring his complaint to the Council of State, or else forfeit his appointment and be held guilty of collusion in misappropriation of official property. That opinion was enacted into law by decree. A new appointee, under these rules, was now required to impeach his recalcitrant predecessor before the Council of State, explaining to that body why he had refused to issue the discharge. The Council of State in its new supervisory role was thus forced to duplicate the functions of the Tax Bureau (*Shuzeiryō*), the Accounting Bureau (*Shukeiryō*), and other offices in the capital assigned to oversee the reports of the governors. The need for some way to regularize the processing of the disputes arising from the discharge system became increasingly clear in the latter half of the eighth century, when several ad hoc attempts were made to deal with them.[64]

At the center of many such disputes was the system of public-allowance rice (*kugetō*), first established in 745.[65] "*Kuge* rice" was in fact a rice fund from which "seed rice" was lent to cultivators at an annual rate of 30 percent, the proceeds of the loan being assigned as stipends to provincial officials. Interest from such loans accounted for many of the expenses of the provincial administration, as well as some of the tax obligations owing to the central government. Called *suiko*, the loans became an ever more important financial source for both the imperial government and its local officials in the late Nara period, each household within the jurisdiction of a provincial headquarters being compelled to accept its share of the loans, regardless of need.

In 757 each type of provincial officer was allowed a specific number of shares in public-allowance rice as follows:[66]

---

63 For examples (the earliest from 959), see *Chōya gunsai*, *KT* 29A:529–33; See also Nagayama, *Ritsuryō futan taikei no kenkyū*, pp. 194–218.
64 Sugano no Mamichi and Fujiwara no Tsugutada, comps., *Shoku Nihongi*, Tempyō Hōji 2(758)/9/8, *KT* 2:255–56; Yoshioka Saneyuki, "Fuyogeyujō to kageyushi ni kansuru shiron," in Inoue Mitsusada hakushi kanreki kinenkai, ed., *Kodaishi ronsō*, vol. 3, pp. 87–120.
65 *Shoku Nihongi*, Tempyō 17(745)/11/27, *KT* 2:185. See Murai, *Kodai kokka*, pp. 11–36.
66 *Shoku Nihongi*, Tempyō Hōji 1(757)/11/11, *KT* 2:243; Sugano no Mamichi et al., comps., *Enryaku kōtai shiki*, *KT* 17:10–11; Sonoda, "Suiko," pp. 397–466.

Governor	6
Vice-governor	4
Executive officer	3
Inspector	2
Clerk	1
Provincial professor	1
Physician	1

Although the scheme of apportionment changed slightly in Heian times, the rights to public-allowance rice for provincial officers remained basically the same. They accrued both to those with substantive functions in the provincial government and also to provincial officers whose lack of real fiduciary responsibility under the *zuryō* system had deprived them of any administrative role. Thus arose a special class of nominal officers having a claim on revenue from provincial stores.

Public-allowance rice had developed out of an earlier accounting category called the provincial account (*kokucho*), established in 724 to pay certain local clerical expenses. The capital dedicated to this account was reapportioned several times during the Nara period, and part of the income was always reserved for *kuge* stipends. During Kammu's reign, in a reapportionment of 804, one-tenth the original amount was to be devoted as before to pay the local clerks and the remainder disbursed to the higher officials. The province itself, the edict illustrates, had become a major source of official emolument distinct from the central government. It is also clear that in the period from 724 to 803, when the following order was issued, the category "provincial account" had become a subcategory of *kuge* (public-allowance rice). The original account now meant a subsidiary portion, here one-tenth, of total *kuge*.

Determination of the portion of public-allowance rice to be reserved as provincial account.

Great provinces: 12,000 sheaves. (In a general calculation of public-allowance-rice interests, from 10,000 sheaves, 1,000 sheaves should be set aside for the provincial account. If the public-allowance rice is greater or lesser in amount, always follow the same ratio. Upper, middle, and lower provinces are also to follow this principle.)

Upper provinces: 9,000 sheaves.

Middle provinces: 5,000 sheaves.

Lower provinces: 3,000 sheaves. (The province of Shima and the three islands of Iki, Tsushima, and Tane are not within this rule.)

This matter has been examined. In the ordinance of the first year of Jingi [724], third month, twentieth day, it is stated: "A portion of the tax-grain fund (*shōzei*) should be set aside and let out for interest. This is to be designated provincial earnings and is to be allotted to the court-report messenger while he is away from the province, to unscheduled expenses, and the clerks who proofread and copy reports, and also to the provision of supplies for bearers delivering articles other than tribute and commutation-tax articles to the capital. The amounts used for lending are to be, for a great province, 40,000 sheaves, and for a lower province, 10,000 sheaves."[67]

Note that the amounts of rice in ear authorized for each category of province (12,000 sheaves, 9,000 sheaves, etc.) represent interest to be distributed, rather than principal, and that they are all exactly 30 percent of the principal amounts given by the quoted order of 724. By the standard specified in the document, an officer of a great province could expect to enjoy a share in an annual income of 10,800 sheaves, the size of the share depending on his status.

That income, however, was not free and clear. According to the regulations, any shortages in the main tax-grain fund (*shōzei*) would have to be made up out of the public-allowance fund before any distribution of it to local officers. Furthermore, provincial earnings were to have priority over distributions to officers. Most interest income from the main tax-grain fund, meanwhile, was reserved as income for officials in the capital. The use of government rice for the benefit of regional officers was originally regarded as a kind of interest-free loan to provincial officials out of the main tax-grain fund, and logic as well as fiscal policy required that local public-allowance beneficiaries receive last priority.[68]

Enforcing those priorities was, understandably, a major difficulty, prompting the elaborate oversight mechanisms already described. The discharge system was probably moderately effective in checking misappropriations of public wealth. An incoming governor had an incentive to see that the entire tax-grain fund was intact and that his predecessor had not wasted any "government rice" (*kantō*). Assignment of primary responsibility for loss was a complex task. If there was a shortage in a given granary, for example, under what circumstances should the loss be charged against the general public-allowance account, and when should the local officials in immediate custody of the granary be charged? Such problems, repeatedly adjudicated, generated a substantial body of law.[69]

To expedite the litigation, the Kammu regime installed a new

---

67 *Enryaku kōtai shiki*, KT 17:14–15; Murao Jirō, *Ritsuryō zaiseishi no kenkyū* (Tokyo: Yoshikawa kōbunkan, 1961), pp. 279–323; Abe, *Heian zenki seijishi no kenkyū*, pp. 49–51.
68 Murao, *Ritsuryō zaiseishi no kenkyū*, pp. 392–418.
69 Abe, *Heian zenki seijishi no kenkyū*, pp. 47–62.

board, the Board of Discharge Examiners (*Kageyushi*), probably at some time between 795 and 797. It was headed by Fujiwara no Uchimaro (756–812), then an official of Fourth Rank but destined later to attain the title of Minister of the Right and Junior Second Rank. In 803 he participated in the compilation of *Enryaku kōtai shiki* (Enryaku Regulations on the Transfer of Office), a compendium of rules concerned with the administration of the discharge system by the Board of Discharge Examiners. A copy was to be kept at every provincial headquarters.

The new board was organized as a regular office with four levels of officials: one chief, two assistant chiefs, three senior clerks, and three junior clerks. Under such influential figures as Uchimaro and later Sugano no Mamichi (738–811) the board was in a position to exercise unchallenged authority over provincial officers. That authority took the form of compulsory arbitration and adjudication, rather than administrative inspection of supervision.[70]

The establishment of the board appears to have been part of a wholesale revision of the provincial administrations. During the 790s the government forbade provincial officers the cultivation of any local land whatever, and although it quickly modified its stand on the issue, it took every conceivable measure to restrict the degree of private control the officers could exercise over the use of labor or the exchange of goods. That policy prompted edicts in 795 and 797 that transformed the system of public-allowance rice. The first ruled that deficiencies in tribute articles from a province would be a general charge against the public-allowance fund, and the second set a limit on the degree to which income from that fund could be impaired by prior deficiencies, guaranteeing all provincial officials not personally responsible for loss a minimum public-allowance income regardless of the total deficit.

Although probably first established as a temporary expedient, the Board of Discharge Examiners continued to function, not reaching its full development until sometime after Kammu's reign. It was disbanded in 806 but reinstituted in 825 and was a permanent office thereafter. During the nineteen-year hiatus in the Board's existence, Circuit Inspectors were again appointed to oversee provincial administrations and their handling by the Controller's Office (*benkan*) of the Council of State. A procedural change of 807 required a new gubernatorial appointee first to present a charge of deficiency in the

---

70 Abe, *Heian zenki seijishi no kenkyū*, pp. 52–55.

provincial accounts to the incumbent governor before appealing to the Controller's Office. That was intended to speed up the adjudication process by permitting the Office to disallow any new questions not raised by the new appointee at the time of the original charge. Only one such presentation of charges could be made, and the incumbent was required to reply to each charge. The process resulted in a refusal-of-discharge statement (*fuyogeyujō*) containing all changes and responses and signed by both parties. The discharge process was also imposed on certain officers in the capital, resulting in a work load too heavy for the Controllers' Office and its legal staff, and the Board of Discharge Examiners was reestablished in 825, continuing the procedures instituted during its temporary demise.[71]

As noted earlier, the adoption of the discharge system gradually accentuated the distinction within the provincial headquarters between officers with custodial responsibility (*zuryō kokushi*) and those without, that is, between the custodial and the merely commissioned provincial officials. The government of the late eighth and early ninth centuries did not, to be sure, anticipate this strict differentiation between commissioned and custodial officials, and the collective responsibility of all officials serving in the same headquarters or bureau was still stressed by the directives of the 790s empowering the Board of Discharge Examiners. In early Heian times, moreover, both the governor and the vice-governor of a province were considered responsible for official properties, and both needed a discharge certificate for the properties when vacating office.

Yet power was quickly centered in the hands of a single *zuryō* governor. In 879 the governor of Bungo Province complained to the Council of State that his commissioned assistants were obstructing his administration, stating in part:

The welfare of a province always depends on the chief official, and the conduct of affairs is not ordered by assistants. Furthermore, as for crimes by *gun* magistrates, the law has its provisions: there is reduction in rank, also confiscation of office land, and in the case of the severest penalty, there is deprivation of rank and office. But the commissioned appointees are not the officials for this [i.e., the enforcement of the law]. They take their personal concerns into public affairs and express their resentment. Sometimes trusting the word of lackeys, they wrongly judge *gun* officers, and sometimes opposing the will of their chief, they commit violent crimes against the clerks. Because of this, people capable of doing service are all afraid to

---

71 Order of Enryaku 14(795)/7/27, *Enryaku kōtai shiki*, KT 17:16–17; order of 797, Enryaku 16(797)/8/3, *Enryaku kōtai shiki*, KT 17:13–14; Yoshioka, "Fuyogeyujō to kageyushi ni kansuru shiron," pp. 87–120.

work, and only a few unreliable people take office. Even if the governor is an honest leader and leads with skill, if the *gun* magistrates are not aligned with him, his authority will be unavailing. How much worse, then, when the officials and the people are not at peace and the district is in turmoil. When one cannot change the old ruts, one cannot expect a new government. I respectfully petition that commissioned appointees not be permitted to pass judgment. If irregular appointees are at fault and must be judged, let the chief official pass judgment and afterwards enforce it.[72]

The petition was granted, marking an important step in the rise of the *zuryō* governor. The Council of State in its order granting the petition, after exempting Fifth and higher ranking officials from the governor's judicial monopoly, condemned the exercise of judicial authority by the commissioned officers as injurious to the prestige of officials sent out from the capital. The activities of the commissioned officers clearly were seen as a complicating factor in the often adversary relations between the "chief official" and the local peerage. Another important consequence of the Council of State order, and one that the original petitioner must have intended, was that governors could now feel at least somewhat justified in bringing their own personal staffs of assistants, including military assistants, with them to their posts, something that the organic code had prohibited. The Council took a decisive step in 897 by ruling that mere commissioned officers were entirely unaccountable to the Board of Discharge Examiners.[73]

The concentration of functional authority in the *zuryō* governor, and consequent abandonment of the provincial staff as a bureau of the central government, led in the early tenth century to a revised picture of the ideal good official. The emphasis shifted decisively from magisterial benevolence toward the people at large to effective negotiation of taxes with local elites, not excluding the use of force where needed. These elites, in turn, often conflicted, sometimes violently, with the *zuryō* governor over the distribution of official and unofficial benefices within the province.[74]

Provincial officers, whose appointments were mere conferrals of public-allowance rice (*kugetō*), had existed ever since the Nara period, when acting or concurrent provincial posts were first awarded as benefices to officials in the capital. To those "remote appointments" (*yōnin*) may be added, by way of contrast, the unstipended

---

72 Order of Gangyō 3(879)/9/4, *Ruijū sandai kyaku*, KT 25:318–19.
73 *Kyaku* of Gangyō 9(885)/4/9, *Ruijū sandai kyaku*, KT 25:246–47.
74 *Chōya gunsai*, KT 29A:517–25, "Kokumu jōjō no koto," esp. articles. 5, 6, 34, 39, and 40; Satō, *Heian zenki seijishi josetsu*, pp. 149–59; Toda, *Ryōshusei*, pp. 115–65.

assignments to distant provinces that served as a form of exile.[75] A famous instance is the posting of Sugawara no Michizane (845–903) to the Kyushu Government Headquarters in 901. Except for such exiles, supernumerary officials were forbidden by a decree of 766 to visit their provinces.[76] A ruling of 826, departing apologetically from the established taboo against appointing high royalty to subordinate positions in the bureaucracy, sanctioned the appointment of princes of the blood to stipendary governorships of the eastern provinces of Kazusa, Hitachi, and Kōzuke, which remained prince-of-the-blood provinces (*shinnō ninkoku* or *shinnō koku*) for the next century and a half. The somewhat loftier title of supreme governor (*taishu*) and the income from the governorship were awarded to a series of major imperial princes who, as before, were barred from leaving the capital area. The vice-governor of a prince-of-the-blood province, called a great vice-governor (*ōsuke*), was the custodial governor.[77] This new form of sharing provincial revenues, later to be extended to other nobles in the capital, was among the more important outgrowths of the *zuryō* institution.

LAND AND TAXES

Although the administration of stored tax-grain came first among the financial concerns of provincial officers in the ninth century, control over land use and revenues was undoubtedly a close second. The *ritsuryō* system recognized a bewildering variety of land tenures, but from the viewpoint of finance, there were three broad categories of rice lands: taxable fields (*yusoden*), tax-exempt fields (*fuyusoden*), and rental fields (*chishiden*). The tax from taxable fields, called *so*, was legally 1.5 sheaves of unthreshed rice ears per *tan*, which was only 3 percent of the yield from a top-grade field, but perhaps 5 to 6 percent in the case of average land.[78] When the registered "owner" rented a field out, the *so* tax was always collected from the actual cultivator. Tax-exempt land included fields allocated to official temples and high officials. Rental fields, from the standpoint of the provincial governments, were state land that had not yet been distributed as allotment fields (*kubunden*) to cultivators. Such land was let out

---

75 On *yōnin*, see Yoshimura, *Kokushi seido*, pp. 350–81.
76 Sakamoto Tarō, *Sugawara no Michizane* (Tokyo: Yoshikawa kōbunkan, 1962), pp. 109–15.
77 Ordinance (*kyaku*) of Tenchō 3(826)/9/6, *Ruijū sandai kyaku*, KT 25:198; on *shinnōkoku* generally, Yoshimura, *Kokushi seido*, pp. 373–76.
78 On the *so* tax and Heian measures, see the appendix to this chapter, "Note on Heian Measures."

(in Nara-period terminology, "sold") on a yearly basis for a price equivalent to one-fifth of the putative yield. That price or ground rent was called *chishi*. In the terminology of the *ritsuryō* commentators, taxable fields of all kinds, including peasant allotment fields, were "private." The allotment-field holdings of each household were to be readjusted every six years in accordance with changes in household population, yet they were considered in law as "owned," that is, managed, by the household members to whom they had been allotted.[79]

There was one category of fully alienable rice land called *konden* (reclaimed fields). In 743 the government ruled that rice paddy opened to irrigation at the reclaimer's expense *on land never before registered as cultivated* should, up to a maximum area depending on the status of the reclaimer, become his private chattel (*shizai*) free from the prospect of reallotment. By the early Heian period such land was treated as freely heritable and alienable as long as kept under cultivation. As with all other private and public lands, registration of reclaimed fields was required. The reclamation and transfer of fields had to be approved by both *gun* and province. The law concerning reclaimed fields facilitated the opening of large tracts of land under private auspices during the Nara and early Heian periods. Principal beneficiaries were rich and powerful local elites with private rice stores to invest in reclamation. Small-scale "cleared fields" called *chiden* (or *harita*) were an important development of the early Heian period, but the massive projects typical of Nara times were not to resume until the eleventh century, when they were invariably carried out on the initiative of local, rather than central, elites.[80]

Private *suiko* loans were perhaps the major bulwark of the rich and powerful stratum. The interest rate on such loans was commonly 50 percent, significantly higher than the 30 percent for a public loan from the tax-grain fund (*shōzei*).[81] Private loans were a potent means of control, as is suggested by the following excerpt from an early-ninth-century tale of a *gun* magistrate's greedy wife:

Or, when she lent rice, she used a light-weighing scale, but when she collected it, she used a heavy-weighing scale. She did not show any mercy in forcibly collecting interest, sometimes ten times and sometimes a hundred

---

[79] Torao Toshiya, *Handen shūju no hō no kenkyū* (Tokyo: Yoshikawa kōbunkan, 1961).
[80] *Kyaku* of Tempyō 15(743)/5/27, *Ryō no shūge, Denryō, kōhai no jō*, KT 23:372; *Shoku Nihongi*, KT 2:372; *Ruijū sandai kyaku*, KT 25:441.
[81] Miyahara, *Nihon kodai no kokka to nōmin*, pp. 137–48.

times as much as the original loan. She was strict in collecting debts, never being generous. Because of this, many people worried a great deal and abandoned their homes to escape from her, wandering to other provinces. There had never been anybody so greedy.[82]

Private *suiko* loans could be secured by the pawning of family members, and creditors could distrain the property and the labor of those in arrears. In 751, creditors' rights were severely restricted and seizures of debtors' lands were forbidden, but the efficacy of these legal restrictions seems to have been quite limited.[83] Under such circumstances, the power of the rice lender was easily extended to power over the land cultivated by the borrower.

Reclaimed fields and private *suiko* loans were among the major factors leading to the breakdown of the land allotment system established by the organic code.[84] Reclaimed fields did not, however, preempt existing allotment land, as the regulations for the reclamation of land applied only to land never before cultivated, not to abandoned or ruined paddy.[85] Loans, on the other hand, were a means of de facto exploitation of every kind of land. That was recognized by the central government, which occasionally forbade private loans. The issue became even more acute when public loans from stored tax-grain became a prime source of state revenue in late Nara times. The conflict of local and central interests was most certainly a factor in the incidents of arson (*shinka*, literally "divine fire") that destroyed numerous tax-grain granaries in the late Nara and early Heian periods.[86]

The collection of the *ritsuryō* tribute (*chō*) and labor-commutation (*yō*) taxes could work to the advantage of proprietors of private granaries. According to a petition of 823,[87] peasants needing food in the months immediately before harvest time obtained it from private granaries in return for cloth and other commodities that would later be needed for payments of those taxes. When the taxes were due and

---

82 Kyōkai, *Nihon ryōiki*, pp. 392–97; trans Nakamura, *Miraculous Stories*, pp. 206–8. Cited in Nakada, *Shōen no kenkyū*, pp. 276–83.
83 *Kyaku* of Tempyō shōhō 3(751)/9/4, *Ruijū sandai kyaku*, KT 25:403–4; Sakanoue Akikane et al., comps., *Hossō shiyōshō*, in Hanawa Hokinoichi et al., eds., *Shinkō gunsho ruijū*, vol. 4 (Tokyo: Naigai shoseki, 1983 reprint), pp. 164–211; Satō, *Nihon no chūsei kokka*, pp. 52–55; Murao, *Ritsuryō zaiseishi no kenkyū*, pp. 288–92. *Ryō* rules on *suiko* are found in Zōryō, provisions 18, 19, 20, and 21, *Ryō no gige*, KT 22B:336–37.
84 Nakada, *Shōen no kenkyū*, pp. 276–83.
85 Iyanaga Teizō, "Ritsuryōseiteki tochi shoyū," *Kodai*, vol. 3 of *IK*, pp. 33–78.
86 Murao, *Ritsuryō zaiseishi no kenkyū*, pp. 392–438, 49–257.
87 On these taxes, see Hōjō, "Heian zenki chōzei kikō no ichikōsatsu," pp. 121–64; Izumiya, "Chōyōsei no henshitsu ni tsuite," pp. 175–308. The petition of 823 is recorded in a *kyaku* of Kōnin 14(823)/2/2, *Ruijū sandai kyaku*, KT 25:434–37.

the harvest was in, the granary proprietors resold the tax commodities to the same peasants at much higher grain prices than they had paid for them. The official system of acquiring tax commodities and goods in exchange for grain afforded provincial officers comparable opportunities for profit. The officers purchased the requisite items from local producers at the low grain prices that prevailed before harvest but forwarded them to the central government in quantities equivalent to the higher postharvest values.

The close relationship between administration of rice lands and rice lending prompted the Kyushu Government Headquarters in 823 to propose a novel way of replenishing dwindling tax-grain stores in the nine provinces of Kyushu.[88] The petition conveying the proposal to the central government stated that the total area of allotment fields in Kyushu was about 65,700 *chō*, which under good conditions produced field tax revenues (*so*), and that there were about 10,900 *chō* of unallotted public fields (*kōden*), or extra fields (*jōden*), that were a potential source of ground rent. Those figures, showing an approximate six-to-one ratio of allotted to unallotted land, were typical of Japan as a whole. Extra fields, it appears, were so firmly established as an element of the provincial economy that their conversion to allotment fields was infeasible. From the total landed resources of about 76,600 *chō*, the petitioners recommended the expropriation of 12,100 *chō* of "good" fields not subject to flood or drought and their establishment as "publicly operated fields" (*kueiden*).

The amounts of allotment and extra fields to be expropriated were about equal; all were to yield *so* revenues, as dictated by the codes, of fifteen sheaves per *chō*, for a total of about 181,400 sheaves. The term "operated" is explained by this statement in the petition:

Impress five corvée laborers to operate each *chō*, giving them compensation and food, and just as is done among the people, allocate stored tax-grain for operating expenses. After the autumn harvest, restore [the grain] to the original granaries.

The clear inference here that grain stores were the source "among the people" of labor power to work private fields is one of several indications of on what terms the rich and powerful had their land cultivated, and what local officials and magistrates did when they were said to "cultivate" (*den*) their office lands directly. The same method

---

88 *Kyaku* of Kōnin 14(823)/2/2, *Ruijū sandai kyaku*, KT 25:434–37; Murai, *Kodai kokka*, pp. 61–79.

was clearly being employed at about the same period by the temple proprietor Gangōji on parts of its Echi *shōen* in Ōmi, where overseers from local *gun*-magistrate families supervised the operation.[89]

For the convenience of administering publicly operated fields in the manner just described, small branch granaries (*shōin*) were to be located throughout the areas involved. The petitioners in 823 also integrated the collection of the tribute and labor-commutation taxes into their plan, maintaining that the new system would ensure the delivery of such taxes equal to the amount due from 60,240 able-bodied male subjects. Mollifying the exploitative "private" practices then prevailing, the local administration under the proposed system would offer a more reasonable price for the tax articles during the growing season, namely, twenty sheaves for tribute tax items and fifteen sheaves for the labor-commutation tax items owed by each able-bodied male. The projected annual budget was:

Total anticipated harvest	5,054,120 sheaves
Expenses	
Cultivators' compensation	1,451,400
Cultivators' food	723,084
Repair of facilities	110,000
Price of tax commodities	1,507,790
Field tax [*so*]	181,425
Total expenses	3,973,699 sheaves
Surplus for storage as tax-grain	1,080,421 sheaves

The expected annual return of slightly over 21 percent, although less than the 30 percent authorized for "public *suiko*," was undoubtedly less risky and also covered expenses for repairs of buildings and irrigation facilities that were normally covered by a separate stored tax-grain account called "miscellaneous rice" (*zōtō*). The field tax was not normally merged into the stored tax-grain account, and it was therefore taken as a deduction from that account. It was destined for the "nonmoving" (*fudō*) stores of permanent reserves, which were not to be lent out.

The Kyushu Government Headquarters' publicly-operated-fields project required the labor of 60,257 corvée laborers, or about five per *chō*, each man to work for thirty days, which was the limit set by the

---

89 The term *den*, meaning land under direct supervisory control, including rights to the entire harvest, first occurs in a document relating to Echi no *shō*; Murai, *Kodai kokka*, pp. 255–58.

code for the local corvée service called "irregular corvée" (*zōyō*). To oversee the work, the proposal recommended:

> selecting capable men from the villages, make each one a director. Assessing his capacities, entrust him with one *chō* or more of land, and insofar as field work is concerned, leave it entirely to him. If damage from wind, insects, or hail occurs, excuse him in accordance with the facts.[90]

Requiring five workers per *chō* and one "director" (*shōchō*) for a "*chō* or more," the scheme reflected the scattered dispersal of the publicly operated fields, which made necessary the services of several thousand corvée overseers. The capacities of the villagers to be chosen as directors are nowhere explained, but almost certainly authority within the local community was a factor in determining the amount of land to be left in a director's care.

The proposal recommended continuing the system of publicly operated fields for thirty years, permitting a total accumulation of over 32 million sheaves of stored tax-grain, but the Council of State, while acknowledging the merits of the idea, permitted it to be put into effect for four years only, remarking, "what has been done since past times surely should not be changed abruptly." Among the likely reasons for the Council's reluctance is the probability that the approximately 20 percent rental (*chishi*) paid by local lessees to use the "extra" public fields had been going to the Kyushu Government Headquarters, and merging that land into the publicly operated fields would have the institutionally disruptive effect of diverting this income to the several Kyushu provincial capitals. Furthermore, the buying-in of tribute and labor-commutation tax commodities under the system of publicly operated fields probably annoyed private lenders who had profited by taking those goods as security for food loans.

Trading tax articles for grain was clearly a major source of income for the petty gentry, a source that the new scheme was deliberately designed to coopt. The radical reduction in the area of "extra" rental lands, moreover, must have also resulted in substantial losses for rent-paying tenants. A glance at the figures shows that the "good" fields selected as publicly operated fields had an average expected yield of about 421 sheaves per *chō*. Even if a 20 percent rental were charged, a renter could have still profitably operated the land with paid labor, that is, the same kind of direct cultivation the state was

---

[90] Yoshida Takashi, "Ritsuryō ni okeru zōyō no kitei to sono kaishaku," in Sakamoto Tarō hakushi kanreki kinenkai, eds., *Nihon kodaishi ronshū*, vol. 2, pp. 223–62.

now undertaking. In sum, the scheme of publicly operated fields would have undoubtedly improved the accumulation of stored tax-grain at the provincial level, but it would have also made the utilization of private granaries for control of peasant labor that much more difficult.

"Extra fields" (*jōden*) had been, in *ritsuryō* terms, publicly owned but privately operated by the lessees. In the new system proposed in 823, publicly operated land was in fact to be publicly exploited land, with all reasonably predictable revenues going to public stores. The exploitation of land, as distinguished from labor, was probably not at this time the major revenue source for either provincial or central governments, but it was gradually becoming so as the government's share of this labor power came under the control of the petty gentry. The rationale behind the old field-allotment system of the *ritsuryō* had been, as Miyoshi Kiyoyuki (847–918) stated in his famous sealed memorial of 914, to enable the peasant to produce tribute and labor-commutation taxes and tax-grain for storage.[91] Peasant land holdings were ultimately a form of compensation to the people for paying taxes. Publicly-operated-field projects of various kinds, including provincial fields, continued throughout the ninth and tenth centuries. The commitment to land allotment as the best way to acquire revenues was, by Kiyoyuki's time, all but abandoned.

A ruling of 801 decided that reallotment of fields would take place once every twelve years rather than, as earlier, once every six, the excuse being the difficulty of surveying the land.[92] Another attempt at nationwide reallotment was made in 806, but thereafter reallotment on that scale ceased, and each province followed a history of its own in allotment matters. The major cause of the failure of land reallotment was very probably resistance on the part of the many local irregular officials (*zōshiki*), themselves members of the petty gentry, on whose cooperation government surveyors had to depend.

More important, if the scattered small-scale operations contemplated under the publicly-operated-fields plan were, as stated in the petition, patterned on the kind of management found on "private" land, "among the people," it is likely that however often private allotment titles were reassigned, the actual distribution of labor over

---

91 Tokoro Isao, *Miyoshi Kiyoyuki* (Tokyo: Yoshikawa kōbunkan, 1970); Tokoro, "Ritsuryō jidai ni okeru ikenfūshin seido no jittai," in Kodaigaku kyōkai, ed., *Engi Tenryaku jidai no kenkyū*, pp. 162–97. For a text of Kiyoyuki's memorial with commentary, see Abe, *Heian zenki seijishi no kenkyū*, pp. 228–48.

92 *Kyaku* of Enryaku 20(801)/6/5, quoted in *kyaku* of Jōgan 1(859)/2/3, *Ruijū sandai kyaku*, KT 25:427; Torao, *Handen shūju no hō no kenkyū*, pp. 281–414.

the land would not have been much affected. Census registers were also taking on a fictional character that would have added considerably to the difficulties of reallotment. At the same time, publicly-operated-field experiments demonstrated that rice fields cultivated by peasants who were assured of food and seed supplies produced more than allotment fields. Large-scale publicly-operated-fields projects, however, were likely to irritate the petty gentry, who were beginning to challenge the *gun*-magistrate class.[93]

Varieties of publicly-operated-fields projects were carried out from time to time in Kyushu and elsewhere, but as the ninth century progressed those schemes became decidedly more accommodating to local elites. In 879, 4,000 *chō* of rice paddy in the home provinces were designated office fields (*kanden*), to be "publicly operated" and the anticipated proceeds to be applied to stipends of certain minor officials.[94] This marked deviation from the *ritsuryō* order of things, where the central treasury had been the designated source of all such stipends, was part of a general effort by the capital government to divest itself of fiscal burdens by shifting them to specifically designated sources of income. At first, shares in provincial *suiko* funds had been awarded to the officials, but when that source proved unreliable, stored provincial tax-grain was appropriated outright for the purpose, and, at last, the office fields were established.

Two years later, in 881, a new directive ordered a reduction in the mandated rice revenue from the office fields. This reduction in amounts collectible was entirely for the benefit of the local land managers. Retreating from the original plan of direct cultivation for the entire bloc, the new plan instead provided for leasing, for the legally stipulated rent of 20 percent of estimated yield, of half the area to the managers and direct cultivation, through their agency, of the rest. This concession to the petty gentry was one that, fifty-eight years earlier, had not occurred to the architects of the Kyushu scheme. The land managers, *tato*, were now, in a sense, sharing the proceeds of cultivation with the government. More important, the price for the management of publicly administered land was now the granting of possessory interests in part of the land to be managed. The text of the directive fully acknowledges that a concession has been made:

---

93 Hirata Kōji, "Heian jidai no koseki ni tsuite," in Toyoda Takeshi kyōju kanreki kinenkai, ed., *Nihon kodai chūseishi no chihōteki tenkai* (Tokyo: Yoshikawa kōbunkan, 1973), pp. 59–96.
94 *Kyaku* of Gangyō 5(891)/2/8, *Ruijū sandai kyaku*, KT 25:439–41. Murai, *Kodai kokka*, pp. 129–44; Nagayama, *Ritsuryō futan taikei no kenkyū*, pp. 258–74; Satō, *Heian zenki seijishi josetsu*, pp. 187–210.

Although we are strongly desirous of direct cultivation, we are concerned that it will be difficult for officials and people to bear, and yet if the whole is rented out, we fear that the profit for the court officers will be but slight.

The land-managing *tato* was to become an increasingly significant force over the next three centuries.[95]

Another, closely related change in the office-fields system in 881 was that the appointment of labor chiefs or directors was no longer restricted to native residents of an area but could include migrants (*rōnin*) as well. *Tato* could come from anywhere. Although being a migrant was not in itself illegal, their regular employment away from home contributed to the weakening of the original *ritsuryō* household registration system. Nor was this the first time that migrants had been employed as petty officials in a government project. In 873 orders for the establishment of publicly operated fields in Kyushu for the support of local defense directed the governor to select capable chiefs regardless of whether they were natives or migrants.[96]

Although partially obscuring the importance of the rural elite, the diffuse language of the sources ultimately confirms it. Gentry land managers were occasionally termed *rikiden no yakara*, "those who maintain the fields." Borrowed from T'ang China, this phrase indicated commendable peasant worthies. It was used regularly for persons who, having contributed their private wealth to public projects, had merited official recognition, usually accompanied by tax remissions, along with other exemplary subjects like filial sons and chaste widows. For *rikiden* farmers, the assumption of burdens was the key to privilege, and, indeed, this was the underlying rationale of all privileges enjoyed by the gentry. The use of grain wealth to make private *suiko* loans and thereby command peasant labor power, as may be seen here, was not always disapproved, and contributions of wealth to agricultural projects or famine relief, even under compulsion, could sometimes lead to rank status as well as tax exemptions. *Rikiden no yakara* were, for purposes of rural administration, the indispensable allies of the officials among the "people." The term rich and powerful (*fugō no yakara*), on the other hand, expressed disapproval of the same class of gentry when they displeased the provincial authorities above them. In the 881 ruling on office fields, the simple word "people" was inferentially applied to gentry managers when

---

95 Murai, *Kodai kokka*, pp. 217–39; Toda, *Ryōshusei*, pp. 18–87, 241–77.
96 Fujiwara no Tokihira et al., comps., *Sandai jitsuroku*, Jōgan 15(873)/12/17, *KT* 4:333–34; on the legal status of *rōnin*, see Morita Tei, *Nihon kodai ritsuryōhō shi no kenkyū* (Tokyo: Bunken shuppan, 1986), pp. 274–96; Murai, *Kodai kokka*, pp. 246–55.

the government stated that direct cultivation of all the new office-field holdings would be "hard for officials and people to bear."[97]

The employment of local gentry as estate directors, and the consequent need to assure them a share in the revenues, was not limited to publicly administered land. It was common to all landholdings of absentee proprietors, that is to say, *shōen* in the broadest sense of the term. In the tenth century the term for legally privatized rice fields so managed was *shōden* (estate fields). This new category demonstrated the increasing importance of land as a form of wealth that accompanied the growth of the gentry.[98] Some of the migrant land managers were drawn from former low-ranking "commissioned" (*nin'yō*) provincial officers who had (illegally) taken up permanent residence in their provinces on the expiration of their terms. Such resettlement of minor nobles from the capital in the countryside had been noticed and condemned as early as 797 in an order to the Kyushu Government Headquarters. That prohibition was repeated, apparently without notable effect, at least nine more times during the next hundred years.[99]

The authorities of the *ritsuryō* state generally discouraged private linkages between central and local elites. In 744, and again in 868, for example, provincial officers were forbidden to contract marriage alliances with *gun* magistrates or other persons under their jurisdiction, and capital officials were repeatedly prohibited from traveling privately to the provinces.[100] Despite these prohibitions, powerful migrants, many of them from the capital, were a generally acknowledged feature of the late-ninth-century countryside, and legally irregular transactions between local gentry and Kyoto aristocrats proliferated. A petition in 881 from the vice-governor of Hizen Province complained about the conduct of "former provincial officers, sons or grandsons of princes and ministers." The petitioner stated that such rich and powerful migrants lived together, seized "the cultivation

---

97 On *rikiden no yakara*, see Abe Takeshi, "Sekkanki ni okeru chōzei taikei to kokuga," in Kodaigaku kyōkai, ed., *Sekkan jidaishi no kenkyū* (Tokyo: Yoshikawa kōbunkan, 1965), pp. 29–55; Kameda Takashi, *Nihon kodai yōsuishi no kenkyū* (Tokyo: Yoshikawa kōbunkan, 1973), pp. 340–61; Satō, *Heian zenki seijishi josetsu*, pp. 130–34; Toda, *Ryōshusei*, pp. 14–32. On privilege and assumption of burdens, "liturgy," see Max Rheinstein, *Max Weber on Law in Economy and Society* (Cambridge, Mass.: Harvard University Press, 1954), p. 163.
98 See Takeuchi, *Ritsuryōsei to kizoku seiken*, vol. 2, pp. 371–91.
99 *Kyaku* of Enryaku 16(797)/4/29, quoted in *kyaku* of Saikō 2(855)/6/25, *Ruijū sandai kyaku*, KT 25:383–84; Yoshimura, *Kokushi seido*, pp. 338–39 and 654–56; Toda, *Ryōshusei*, pp. 139–44.
100 On intermarriage with local elites, see *kyaku* of Tempyō 16(744)/10/14, *Ruijū sandai kyaku*, KT 25:302, and *kyaku* of Jōgan 10(868)/6/28, *Ruijū sandai kyaku*, KT 25:303; Yoshimura, *Kokushi seido*, pp. 61, 219–28.

rice funds" of the people, did not accept official rice loans, made private rice loans, and at harvest time obstructed public business. He proposed the following remedy:

> In accordance with the provincial precedent of Chikugo, without distinction between former officers and migrants, let stored tax-grain be distributed to both in proportion to the extent of the fields they operate, and let them [also] be required like natives to cultivate publicly operated fields. If the powerful among them do not comply with this decision, let them be expelled from the district and refused residence there.[101]

The management of proprietary or publicly operated fields, the petitioner's argument implies, must be subject to the same burdens in the case of both natives and migrants, and the presence in the area of the latter should be conditional on acceptance of those burdens, specifically: (1) the cultivation of publicly operated fields, as a sort of compulsory public service due from all *rikiden*-type chiefs; and (2) acceptance of stored-tax-grain loans, here viewed as a kind of surtax on land, to be assessed in proportion to the area cultivated, a practice that was gradually undermining the old *ritsuryō* grain-banking system. As loans from stored tax-grain came to be regularly distributed in proportion to land under cultivation without regard to the need of the cultivator, the actual transfer of loan funds from the government was becoming a needless formality. In the late ninth century, the responsible cultivator merely paid the interest on the assigned tax-grain loan while actually receiving only about half the principal.[102]

Rikiden were basically small-scale operators, but their resistance to tax-grain loans was nevertheless having an effect. Custody of official grain stores was now shared by the local gentry, who were also given interest-free loans from provincial stores unlisted in the annual Tax Grain Report. A related threat to the official loan system came from the private grain stores of the noble households and great religious institutions, also administered with the collaboration of regional gentry. They could function as shelters for gentry holdings against the demands of local authorities.[103]

---

101 *Sandai jitsuroku*, Gangyō 5 (881)/3/14, *KT* 4:495–96, discussed in Toda, *Ryōshusei*, pp. 18–24.
102 Edict of Jōgan 4(862)/3/26, *Sandai jitsuroku, KT* 4:89–90, discussed in Murao, *Ritsuryō zaiseishi no kenkyū*, pp. 297–99, 435–38; Murai, *Kodai kokka*, pp. 232–46.
103 Abe, *Heian zenki seijishi no kenkyū*, pp. 325–27; Takada Minoru, "Chūsei shoki no kokka kenryoku to sonraku" *Shichō* 99 (June 1967): 6–25; Toda, *Ryōshusei*, pp. 144–65. The sheltering of local grain wealth is attested by *kyaku* of Jōgan 10(868)/6/28, *Ruijū sandai kyaku*, *KT* 25:603–4, *kyaku* of Kampyō 7(895)/9/27, *Ruijū sandai kyaku*, *KT* 25:604–5 and *kyaku* of Engi 2(902)/3/13, *Ruijū sandai kyaku*, *KT* 25:605.

THE SURRENDER OF CENTRAL CONTROL TO PROVINCIAL AUTHORITIES

The allegation in the Hizen petition of 881 that provincial precedent, or practice, in the nearby province of Chikugo justified the use of migrants and former officers as land managers, notwithstanding repeated prior edicts to the contrary, demonstrates the qualified withdrawal of the central authority from the field of local regulation in late-ninth-century Japan. As a valid legal norm taking precedence in individual cases over *ritsuryō* law and even recent imperial edicts, provincial precedent first gained broad recognition from the Council of State in connection with local finances. An early instance occurred in 873, when the Kyushu Government Headquarters was ordered after a nineteen-year lapse to redistribute allotment fields in the province of Chikuzen according to a new apportionment plan. When the Headquarters reported its compliance with the order, it also noted some surprising modifications it had made on its own authority. It had, to begin with, expropriated 950 *chō* of good land for publicly operated fields in order to achieve a more reliable source of tribute taxes than allotment fields provided. Even though that meant eliminating the ordered distribution of allotment shares to women, the Headquarters explained, the allotment fields in the province were still double those of other provinces. The Headquarters also established large blocks of rental fields for "miscellaneous expenses," and it provided for the appointment of migrants as field managers. By the end of the ninth century, similar provincial precedents had been recognized for the provinces of Shimōsa, Mino, and Harima.[104]

The surrender to provincial precedent of Council of State authority to distribute tax burdens was to continue steadily in the following centuries. At bottom a concession to the interests of the provincial gentry, it contributed substantially to the discretionary powers of the *zuryō* governors. Although land was important, especially to the *gun* magistrates, who were permitted extensive office lands, the main force of irregular officials in the provincial governments depended heavily on the income from loans of stored tax-grain and the labor power it represented. Despite the many difficulties reported in official petitions and edicts, tax-grain stores and *suiko*-loan revenues probably grew during the ninth century, even as actual custody of

---

104 Ishimoda Shō, "Kodai hō," in *Kodai*, vol. 4 of *IK*, pp. 255–87. The term occurs frequently throughout *Ruijū sandai kyaku*. For the allotment of 873 in Chikuzen, see Decree of Jōgan 15(873)/12/17, *Sandai jitsuroku*, *KT* 4:333–34.

the stores fell more and more into private hands and official reports became cluttered with legal fictions intended to reconcile official standards with intractable fact. By the end of the century, conflicting demands on these grain stores from central government and local elites had become acute. This partially explains the practice of reporting rice not really in official custody as let out in *suiko* loan when, in fact, "interest" payments were being made on receipt of a fraction of the reported amount. The Tax Grain Report was becoming more a means for evaluating the incumbent local official than a tool of actual financial supervision.[105]

The attempts of middle-status nobles and officials to augment their dwindling incomes by exploiting local rice stores and cultivating provincial fields in absentia (i.e., by establishing *shōen*) threatened the local officialdom and, in the final decade of the ninth century, prompted a flurry of prohibitory edicts intended to preserve the authority of the provincial officials and of the *ritsuryō* order generally.[106] One of the more troublesome problems confronting the reformist regime was that of imperial grant fields (*chokushiden*). Mostly wasteland or abandoned paddy reclaimed with the use of provincial tax-grain stores by authority of an imperial decree (*chokushi*), these lands were directed by the palace treasury and often (but not necessarily) dedicated to the support of high-ranking imperial family members. Widely distributed throughout the country, by the late ninth century they could be found in nearly every province, mostly in blocks of one hundred *chō* or more. The force of the decree gave such fields priority rights to irrigation water and immunity from the field tax (*so*). They were operated in the same general way as so-called publicly operated fields, but under the ultimate protection of the palace authorities. For that reason, the dominant Fujiwara leaders seem to have seen *chokushiden* as a threat to their own power as well as an unwelcome intrusion into the government's provincial base.[107]

In one of a famous series of edicts in 902 aimed at restricting intrusion into the provincial economies by great families and religious

---

[105] On the critical increase in declared provincial *suiko* funds, see Murao, *Ritsuryō zaiseishi no kenkyū*, pp. 232–46; on *gunji* benefices, Sakamoto, *Nihon kodaishi no kisoteki kenkyū*, vol. 2, pp. 142–51. On the evaluation of *zuryō*, Murai, *Kodai kokka*, pp. 70–86.

[106] Satō, *Heian zenki seijishi josetsu*, pp. 264–73.

[107] See Kōchi Shōsuke, "Chokushiden ni tsuite," in Tsuchida Naoshige sensei kanreki kinenkai, ed., *Nara Heian jidaishi ronshū* (Tokyo: Yoshikawa kōbunkan, 1984), vol. 2, pp. 291–327; Miyamoto Tasuku, "Ritsuryōseiteki tochi seido," in Takeuchi Rizō et al., eds., *Taikei Nihonshi sōsho* (Tokyo: Yamakawa shuppansha, 1973), vol. 6, pp. 49–138; Murai, "Shōensei no hatten to kōzō," pp. 41–88.

institutions in the capital area, the government ordered the abolition of imperial grant fields, the cessation of collusive sale or gift of lands and dwellings by farmers to members of the imperial family or upper-ranking courtiers for the implied purpose of establishing *shōen*, a halt to the occupation of vacant and abandoned land by the same imperial and noble figures for similar purposes, and a return of peasant lands held by temples and shrines to their original owners of record. The stated purpose of this order, to restrict the extent of privately reserved land and granary holdings, was nevertheless subject to one important qualification. The order exempted from its scope any *shōen* headquarters, or "estate house" (*shōke*), that would otherwise come under its provisions if its head – that is, the *shōen* manager – had obtained his position through "transmission" (*sōden*) from an ancestor. This concession conferred on the hereditary *shōke* head, as distinguished from the self-established one, a quasi-proprietary right. *Shōden* management was becoming a protected household occupation (*kagyō*), in other words, a kind of estate.

Collusion between the capital elites and prosperous peasants in the reclamation of rice lands and the establishment of *shōen* was not new, but government orders of the late ninth century show that the scale of such activity was steadily increasing. Wealthy peasants could more often than before choose to evade the provincial headquarters and become *shōen* managers for the nobility, thus removing their rice wealth and the labor power at their command from provincial control. A *shōen* manager's establishment was, as the order of 902 shows, a place where harvested rice was stored, and also a depot for private *suiko* loans and a source of payment for the labor costs of field work and reclamation.[108]

There was a growing tendency in the ninth century for provincial governments to use the owners of private storehouses as intermediaries in the operation of the *suiko*-loan system. Tax-grain was loaned to such owners, who reloaned it at 50 percent interest to farmers in the area, returning 30 percent in interest (the generally prevailing public *suiko*-loan rate) to the provincial authorities. From the tenth century on, the process was simplified: the tax-grain was paid in directly to the private storehouses, instead of going first to the provin-

---

108 *Kyaku* of Engi 2(902)/3/13, *Ruijū sandai kyaku*, KT 25:607–9. The other eight *kyaku* of this series, all promulgated on Engi 2/3/12 or 2/3/13, are recorded in either *Ruijū sandai kyaku* or Koremune no Tadasuke, comp., *Seiji yōryaku*, KT 28; Inagaki, "Ritsuryōseiteki tochi seido no kaitai," pp. 139–72; Satō, *Heian zenki seijishi josetsu*, pp. 295–305; Takeuchi, *Ritsuryōsei to kizoku seiken*, vol. 2, pp. 371–91; Toda, *Ryōshusei*, pp. 74–113.

cial granaries, and the operators of the storehouses simply paid 30 percent interest on the rice to the province. The practice was generally, if tacitly, condoned, and the discharge system did not substantially inhibit it. The result was a diminution of direct involvement by the provincial governments in the operation of the tax system that provided it with much of its revenue.

A legal requirement that each province keep on hand a designated amount of tax-grain, with specified quantities dedicated to the stipends of provincial officers (public-allowance rice) and miscellaneous use (such as upkeep of provincial temples), may not have been literally observed, but it did impose on the provincial governments high minimum quotas of *suiko*-loan interest to be collected. That burden could be spread over the inhabitants of a province in a number of ways. Early in the ninth century, the government had intended that the compulsory *suiko* loans be made on a per capita basis, but differences of wealth made that impractical. A natural response to the difficulty was to apportion the loans in accordance with the wealth of the borrowers, but that opened up too many opportunities for abuse by the minor provincial officers who actually toured the districts imposing the loans, and resulted in a level of *suiko* defaults that prompted over half of the recorded ninth-century sales of privately reclaimed fields.

By the end of that century, the area of land under cultivation in each province had, in the government's accounting, become highly fictionalized. There was provincial precedent in most areas for the imposition of *suiko* loans, but despite general agreement on that standard, responsibility for *suiko* payments continued also to be imposed on any others who were able to pay, and the apportionment of the burden still involved a degree of local discretion somewhat inconsistent with the *ritsuryō* model of a capital-centered economy.

A redistribution of the state's economic resources under the direction of central authority was undoubtedly a major ideal underlying the nine reformist Council of State orders of 902, of which the example cited above is typical. Fujiwara no Tokihira (871–909), then the prevailing voice on the Council, was attempting through the reforms to reinforce the function of the court treasury as the principal source of income for the nobles and officials in the Heian capital, and to restore the *ritsuryō* structure generally. For the last time in history the Council called for a nationwide distribution of allotment fields and insisted that undeveloped areas be kept open for both public and private use. It revived the old emphasis on labor-commutation and tribute taxes, commodities produced and delivered to the capital by provincial farmers' households. These orders attest to a somewhat belated recognition of the *ritsuryō* distributive system as essential to the solidarity of the courtier class.

Fields designated as allotment land continued to make up a large share of the arable in provincial accounts up to the year 1000. Such fields were still monitored closely by both provincial and national governments at the beginning of the ninth century, and periodic reallotment was merely one of several control devices employed. Cultivated fields were registered by owner or allottee and their location and ownership indicated on official maps. They were to be surveyed annually by provincial officers, who prepared the register of standing crops (*seibyōbo*), listing each household eligible to receive an allotment of land, which of their fields were leased out and which cultivated directly, and what lands had been rented from others. The register thus showed the actual cultivator of each plot who, regardless of ownership status, was the person responsible for the payment of the field tax (*so*) to be reported later in the field-tax report (*sochō*). Basically a device meant to assure centralized control over all rice cultivation, the register was also to report all cases of land and crop damage, a justification for partial tax remission for the affected households and reduction of tax receipts expected by the capital from the province. An early concession to the local gentry may be seen in an 845 Council of State ruling that the register, which was in any case being neglected, would no longer be required by the capital except as evidence of crop damage requiring tax remission. The government thereby declared an end to its policy of centralized monitoring of all leasing arrangements. Such arrangements were, however, crucial to the changes taking place in the countryside, as the government acknowledged in its edicts of 902.[109]

The government sought to prevent high-ranking nonprovincials from acquiring land in the provinces, where their local estate managers were said to have imposed harsh and cruel regimes on the peasantry. The acquisition of legally transferrable land by capital elites, moreover, was only a small part of an essentially local problem. The fields that were available for purchase, mostly reclaimed fields (*konden*), provided local magnates or *shōden* directors with a

---

109 Fujiwara no Tokihira et al., comps., *Engi shiki, Shuzeishiki, Seibyōbo no jō*, KT 26:690–97; *kyaku* of Jōwa 9(842)/6/9, *Ruijū sandai kyaku*, KT 25:327–28; *kyaku* of Jōwa 12(845)/9/10, KT 22:328, *Seiji yōryaku*, KT 28:330–31; comments to *Buyaku ryō, Suikan no jō* in *Ryō no shūge*, KT 23:392–403; Murai, *Kodai kokka*, pp. 327–36.

base from which to exert economic dominance over the legally registered cultivators of inalienable fields such as *kubunden*. The legal holders of *kubunden* were forbidden to transfer the land to others but could transfer cultivation rights on a year-by-year basis. Rice-loan indebtedness, a major reason for the sale of alienable land, could lead to the loss of control over *kubunden* to the holders of local rice storehouses, so that inalienability of land afforded little real protection. Official records of landholding took on an increasingly fictitious character as the ninth century wore on, and reallotment of rice fields became even more difficult as the authorities in the capital grew preoccupied with checking suspicious census data. With control of allotment field cultivation steadily passing from the capital to the provinces, the central government's reviews of allotment data submitted by *zuryō* governors became in effect negotiations between countryside and capital about the amounts of taxes due. By the end of the century the central government was accepting patently fictitious census data in which women and children vastly outnumbered taxable males, data that justified the occupation of extensive areas of allotment fields by households of record with very little accompanying liability for tribute-commodity or labor-commutation taxes.[110]

The original presumption of the architects of the *ritsuryō* system seems to have been that the crop yields from allotment fields would be almost entirely consumed as food by the allottees. The fields were therefore left ungraded as to fertility (unlike the public extra fields rented out by provincial governments) and taxed at a low uniform rate. The government's chief revenue source was thus not *so*, the field tax, but the tribute-commodities and labor taxes. That situation changed, however, as the government began to impose additional taxes on crop yields, first through the public *suiko*-loan system, and occasionally by the same direct cultivation methods it condemned in 902 when applied by nobles of the capital to provincial lands.

Another step in that direction was attempted in 862 when the Council ordered a general revision of the taxation system in the home provinces. The three major features of the plan were:

1. An increase in *so* from the long-established rate of 1.5 to 3 sheaves per *tan* for all allotment fields, and 2 sheaves per *tan* for most other fields subject to the tax (excluding reclaimed fields).
2. A reduction in provincial corvée obligations from thirty to ten

---

110 On the fictionalization of census and tax reports, see Hirata, "Heian jidai no koseki ni tsuite," pp. 59–96.

days, and a complete exemption of households in the capital from the obligation. Labor paid out of the increased *so* was to be used instead.
3. The abolition of compulsory provincial *suiko*-loan quotas, except for provinces short of the land and rice funds needed for the support of large Buddhist temples.[111]

Although the scheme was intended to remain in effect for an experimental three years, it lasted only two. The two prevailing objections were (1) that most allotment fields were of "lower lower" quality, making increases in the *so* difficult to collect and causing land to go uncultivated when increases of the tax were added to an existing rental payment; and (2) that outlays of tax-grain could not defray the increased labor costs without a depletion of official stores, shortages in which would be made even more acute by the lowered grain revenues from *suiko* loans. The interrelatedness of *so*, *suiko*-loan revenues from stored tax-grain, and provincial corvée presumed by the experiment came about because, unlike the tribute and labor-commutation taxes, they were the foundations of the revenue system of the provincial headquarters rather than of the central government. We may suspect, moreover, that the failure of the new system resulted less from the infertility of allotment fields than from the reluctance of local gentry authorities to accept the plan. A century later grain taxes against allotment fields had nearly quadrupled, and the burden was being sustained by the cultivators, albeit reluctantly. This could not have been due to a sudden surge in productivity. The more plausible explanation is that land had become easier to tax because of the abandonment of the allotment system, which left the distribution of cultivation rights to those fields entirely in local hands, as well as the absorption of large numbers of the local elites into the provincial-headquarters structure.

The Council of State in 902 thus faced two major problems: first, the maintenance of central control over allotment land and public fields; and second, the restriction of *shōen* formation. At the time, the two problems were fairly distinct. Allotment fields and other lands subject to *so* and *suiko* fees (*sozeiden*) and the public or "extra lands" leased out annually (*chishiden*) were not then in much danger of misappropriation, remaining firmly within the distributive control of the provincial governments. Newly reclaimed rice paddy, however, could be sold freely by the reclaimer or his successors. Reclamation

111 On these changes in the land tax, see Murai, *Kodai kokka*, pp. 312–27.

projects and land so reclaimed diverted local labor and resources away from provincial control and into the hands of nobles from the capital and their agents. For this reason, the Council wished to prevent the further development of *shōen*, which were a focus of private reclamation efforts.[112]

The type of *shōen* that was the object of the Council of State's restrictions in 902 was not the same as the very large temple *shōen* established in Nara times, which declined precipitously in the ninth century. The earlier *shōen* had been almost completely dependent on the support of the central government, and as extensions of central authority to the local scene, they were highly vulnerable, soon being abandoned by their mostly nonresident cultivators. The new *shōen* that evolved in the ninth century were more clearly private in origin, representing typically a cooperative relationship between, on the one hand, a high-ranking noble or member of the imperial family and, on the other, a local magnate or official. Although they did not always enjoy formalized tax exemptions, *shōen*-based gentry could expect special consideration from the fiscal authorities. The increasing prominence of the local gentry in the tenth century resulted in a new sort of *shōen* that, like Ōyama-no-shō, could support an adversary relationship with the provincial headquarters.[113]

The *ritsuryō* system had never totally banned nobles or temples from having special interests in local economies. Such interests, however, were usually well differentiated from the ordinary holdings of provincial farmers. Very high nobles and official temples, for example, were given "support households" (*fuko*) by the government. The recipient of such households was entitled to the tribute and labor-commutation taxes from them and to part of the field tax from their allotment fields.[114] Originally controlled entirely by the provincial officers on the recipient's behalf, some of the support household grants evolved into *shōen*, but others seem simply to have reverted to the provincial domain as the importance of commodity taxes in personal income declined.

The greatest number of new *shōen* probably originated from collusive agreements between upper-level peasants and middle-ranking nobles. In the countryside, peasant gentry sought to avoid forced

---

112 Nagayama, *Ritsuryō futan taikei no kenkyū*, pp. 304–9; Satō, *Heian zenki seijishi josetsu*, pp. 294–319.
113 Nakano, *Ritsuryōsei shakai kaitai katei no kenkyū*, pp. 278–79; Sakamoto, *Nihon ōchō kokka taisei ron*, pp. 66–95.
114 On *fuko*, see note 25, above.

suiko loans and other burdens. In the capital, a shortage of available posts and stipends forced downwardly mobile nobles to develop private estates of their own. Middle-ranking officials in the capital, who did not receive grants of support households, had to rely entirely on disbursements from the central treasury. The four thousand *chō* of rice fields appropriated in 879 to sustain their stipends, while helpful, could not totally offset the steady reduction in commodity tax revenues. Minor royals and nobles seeking new sources of income could, however, offer the protection from forced *suiko* loans that the upper peasantry needed. The consequence was a proliferation of regional *shōen* holdings, accompanied by the quasi-legal resettlement of capital gentility in the provinces. Already alarmed by these developments, the central government in 902 made renewed efforts to check estate growth.

Shōen holdings by individuals were not necessarily prohibited; if the "documentation was clear," as the order of 902 put it, the tenure was legal. A condemnation of the "private administration" of provincial land by capital nobles issued by the Council in 895 also recognized the legality of certain types of *shōen* holding, but prohibited new acquisitions.

Officials of the Fifth Rank and above already have high position, their responsibilities are not unimportant and each of them has a stipend independent of cultivation. Why then should they covet the profits of the fields? Accordingly, the various imperial, princely, and ministerial houses and persons of Fifth Rank and above are absolutely prohibited from cultivating any land other than their estate fields (*shōden*), imperial rank fields, rank fields, and office fields.[115]

The legality of estate fields was, as implied in the Council orders of 902, certified jointly by representatives of both the central and the provincial governments. The precise distinctions made in the Council's orders are far from clear, but the *shō* houses mentioned there seem to have been an essential element of both legal and prohibited *shōen*. The recognition later given to *shō* houses with a history of two or more generations shows the hereditary patron–client relationship that could develop between capital nobles and rural gentry. The *shō* house was an extension of the noble house. Its chief, under the patron's protection, could disrupt the provincial government's control of peasant agriculture, as the edict of 902 suggests, by lending rice to neighboring farmers and thus reducing them to dependent-debtor

---

115 *Kyaku* of Kampyō 8(896)/9/2, *Ruijū sandai kyaku*, KT 25:444–45.

status. This also led to control over the circulation of commodity-tax items, and the government quite naturally saw this as a major threat to its authority.[116]

Shō houses were substantial residences that usually included privately reclaimed fields as well as granaries. Whether old or new, the houses reflected the emergence of a new and numerous stratum of wealthier peasants, operators of private granaries and leaders of reclamation projects both for themselves and for patrons in the capital. More than the purchase of provincial lands by nobles, it was the emergence of that elite peasant stratum that made the taxes mandated by the codes harder to collect and goaded the Council of State into attempts at reform.

The Heian government's policies toward the rich and powerful were far from consistent. Some high officials, like Miyoshi Kiyoyuki, regarded them with undisguised hostility, but the Council of State often acted to protect their interests. In 896, for example, the Council modified the ordinance of 743 permitting permanent possession of reclaimed fields in order to make the titles of smallholders of such fields more secure against takeover by powerful nobles. The earlier ordinance, while recognizing the permanent ownership of reclaimed fields by their developers, also specified that if wasteland awarded by a provincial government for reclamation was not in fact brought under cultivation within three years, the award could be revoked and reassigned to another petitioner. In 824 a similar restriction had been placed on the reopening of permanently abandoned allotment fields (jōkōden). The rule of noncultivation for three years (sannen fukō) was abused by powerful figures in the capital in order to deprive smallholders of partially reclaimed fields. This was explained in a complaint by gun magistrates addressed to a Circuit Inspector that became the occasion for the ruling in 896:

> The peasants of the villages petition for abandoned or unreclaimed land and, following the ordinances, bring it into cultivation. Then later some temple, shrine, prince, or ministerial house, claiming that the land has not been cultivated for three years, notifies the provincial government and requests reassignment of that land. The provincial government, relying on the wording of the ordinances, grants the requests and reassigns the land. The nobles go into occupation with no interest in [further] development but only in the profits of the land [from renting out already developed parts]. Having respectfully surveyed the situation, the gun magistrates suggest that when a peasant opens three or four tan of a chō of land [that is, 30 or 40

---

116 Murai, Kodai kokka, pp. 232–38, 270–80.

percent] that he has received [for reclamation], but is unable to open it completely because of his poverty and weakness, it is a grievous thing to award the land to another merely because of the terms of the ordinances. The peasant is greatly to be pitied. We pray for a decision from the Inspector quickly granting relief.[117]

The Council, after reviewing the history of land reclamation law, decided that the basic principle of promoting agriculture (*kannō*) required the protection of local farmers. It accordingly ruled that as long as one-fifth of the land claimed was under cultivation, the three-year rule was not to be applied.

A survey in 859 of the Echi *shōen*, a holding of Gangōji Temple, revealed the same struggle between local and capital elites over "the profits of the land" so strongly implied in the Council of State orders of 902. Located in Ōmi Province, the Echi *shōen* grew into a fairly large domain by the eleventh century, but in 859 it probably did not exceed ten *chō* of arable field, divided like most *shōen* in the ninth century between fields let out for a fixed rent and directly cultivated fields (*eiden*). In addition to a local superintendent (*bettō*), there were on the domain two field managers (*tato*) who rented fields in the *shōen* for cultivation. Contemporary documents from the same area show that these managers were members of a local elite, and had the status of irregular officers in the local government, collecting taxes and witnessing land transfers in that capacity. They had reclaimed-field holdings of their own, but it is clear that their property was not very secure, and *suiko*-loan debts often required them to sell off their land. Such sales account almost entirely for the steady growth of the Echi *shōen*.

The field managers principally responsible for the cultivation of Gangōji's fields were not part of the temple's administrative framework. Their status depended on their position in the local community, not on delegation from the *shōen* proprietor, whose fields simply happened to be located in the area. Their interests conflicted with those of the temple, and they and the other renting cultivators on the *shōen* took every possible opportunity to increase their own holdings at the temple's expense and to minimize rent payments. The survey report of 859, written by Empō, the temple's representative, records his efforts, beginning eleven years earlier in 848, to help the superintendent vindicate the temple's proprietary claims.

One frequently disputed issue was the amount of rent due from

---

117 *Kyaku* of Kampyō 8(896)/4/2, *Ruijū sandai kyaku*, KT 25:486–87.

leased fields. Legally, the amount of rent depended on the assessment of the fertility of each field in terms of upper, middle, or lower grades, an assessment made by the provincial authorities. Even when a field was part of a *shōen*, the rent to be paid by field managers or other cultivators was fixed by the provincial government. That control, which lasted into the eleventh century, meant that in principle leased *shōen* fields were the equivalent of leased public fields, and both could be called rental fields (*chishiden*). Empō's efforts to increase rents was therefore a campaign to have official assessments raised, as he reported in the case of two particular parcels.

> The aforesaid two grid-parcels were originally classified as middle-quality fields. At present, an on-site survey shows that they are clearly upper-grade. We accordingly summoned the field manager . . . Echi-no-Hata-no-Kimi Yasuo for questioning, and the assessor said, "This is clearly upper-grade field. Why do you render only middle-grade rent? How can that not be the crime of violating goods of the Buddhist clergy?" He answered, "This was decided long ago and is not a recent matter. There is no deliberate act of offense, so how can there be a crime?" I, the representative, pressed him, saying, "Even if the officials negligently fail to recognize the grade, why do field managers not correct it? In accord with what is proper, the fields should be made upper-grade." He answered, "It will be done in accord with what is proper. How can there be any resistance?"[118]

Empō's disputes over land ownership illustrate the temple's lack of control over vacant lands in the vicinity of its fields. Echi *shōen* at the time consisted solely of buildings and arable fields either in or out of cultivation. The temple had no firm prior option on reclaiming new rice paddies on undeveloped land and no legal right to enclose it, regardless of proximity to its own fields. The *shōen* was merely a complex of estate fields (*shōden*) registered with the provincial government, which kept maps on which all fields were located in a grid of one *chō* survey squares called grid squares (*tsubo*).

Renters of the temple's fields, on the other hand, were free to reclaim paddy land on their own account and were thus enabled to hold property in reclaimed fields adjacent to those of the *shōen*. Ambiguities could arise, and Empō seems to have felt, probably correctly, that they were likely to be resolved by local officials in the cultivator's favor. Typical of the several ownership disputes summarized in his survey report is one in which the issue at stake was the illegal merger of temple fields into the adjacent reclaimed fields of a local

118 Survey report of Jōgan 1(859)/12/25, *HIB* 1:107–10, doc. 128; on Echi-no-shō (the Gangōji domain); Miyamoto, "Ritsuryōseiteki tochi seido," pp. 49–138, especially 131–36.

cultivator. The original temple fields were registered as permanently uncultivated and thus unproductive of revenue for the temple. The document reads as follows (note that the field manager in the rental dispute already mentioned appears again here to defend the cultivator against Empō's charges):

In the case of this grid square, the original notation is "permanently uncultivated." Now on viewing the land, we found that it had become the reclaimed field of . . . Echi-no-Hata-no-Kimi Otonaga. Whereupon I as representative disputed this, saying, "This grid square originally consisted of 1 *tan* 160 *bu* [1 *bu* = 3.3 sq. meters] of temple field and 60 *bu* of reclaimed land. But now temple fields are claimed to be permanently uncultivated, and reclaimed land, originally small in quantity, is presently cultivated in large quantity. I surmise from this that the original fields of the temple have wrongfully been designated reclaimed land." It was said in answer, "The original fields of the temple are described as being to the east, but the present reclaimed land is in the center of the grid square. Since the direction is not the same, how can you say it is temple field?" (The person making this answer was . . . Yasuo.) I, the representative, disputed this, saying, "There were originally in this grid square 1 *tan* 160 *bu* of temple field and 60 *bu* of reclaimed field. The meaning of 'east' is that, as between the two, the temple field is to the east and the reclaimed field to the west. It does not mean that the temple fields are on the eastern edge of the grid square. Furthermore, rice paddies are opened from the bottom land first. How can the temple fields be on a hillside and the reclaimed land in the valley? Here the owner of the reclaimed field is twisting reason."

The temple's *shōen* holdings here had originated partly from alienable residence- or garden-land donated or sold by individual owners. As in other such cases, there probably was an original core of temple fields already established by donation from the government or imperial family. But the addition of new fields to the core holdings was not perfected until the provincial authorities registered the acquisitions on its official maps, a process in which local elders played a crucial role. Their testimony, moreover, was usually decisive in cases where records were ambiguous. As Empō's report illustrates, the official maps did not indicate the precise location of any holding within a single square. Empō's investigations disclosed three cases where fraudulently redesignated temple fields belonging to Gangōji were sold to third parties. He reported success in recovering not only that property but also other temple *shōen* land that had been misrepresented as public fields owing rent to the government. Although the net gain was a mere 3.86 *chō*, the temple's managers, by a vigorous policy of purchase and exchange, consolidated the scattered holdings into a sold block, thus laying the foundation for the somewhat more extensive *shōen* revealed by a document of 1051.[119]

This later document shows another significant change. Empō's statement shows that the Gangōji holdings of 877 were being treated by the officials of Ōmi Province as *chishiden*, to be rented at one-fifth the putative yield, and for this purpose all such land was classified as upper, middle, lower, or lowest. All public – in other words, unallotted – land was classified in this way under the *ritsuryō* system, but in the tenth century such meticulous control over the land by the central government could no longer be maintained. In 1050, all fields actually under cultivation in Echi-no-shō yielded a uniform *chishi* rental of 3 *to* (1 *to* = 7.2 liters) of hulled rice per *tan*, minus *so*, still calculated in accord with the *ritsuryō* rate of 7.5 *shō* per *tan*.

Early *shōen* proprietors, as we see from this example, had very weak support in the local community. Their fields were for the most part let out for rent, a procedure that seems often to have required annual written lease agreements registered with provincial authorities, with rates determined by provincial assessment. There was some, probably not very extensive, directed cultivation on behalf of the absentee proprietors of the *shōen*. In another Echi *shōen*, this one a holding of Tōdaiji, only about two of the twelve *chō* under cultivation were operated under direction of the proprietor in the late ninth century.[120] Early *shōen*, unlike those of the eleventh and twelfth centuries, mostly lacked their own proprietor-appointed operators, and there was not a strong community of interest binding field-manager lessees to proprietors. By 1060, however, when Echi *shōen* had grown to more than sixty *chō* of rice paddy and was provided with a resident official staff, the *shōen* had become a domain in the true sense, and the temple proprietor was threatening to expel cultivators who resisted an increase in rental.[121]

Cultivation by field managers dominated agriculture in the tenth century, gradually displacing allotment-field holdings as the single major source of labor power from land. It was possession by field managers that made land, rather than people, the major object of taxation by both provincial headquarters and *shōen* proprietors. That development meant that the *ritsuryō* system of allotment of land and

---

119 Dues assessment of Eishō 5(1051)/1/28, *HIB* 3:822, doc. 687; Morita, *Heian jidai seijishi kenkyū*, p. 232.
120 Inagaki, "Ritsuryōseiteki tochi seido no kaitai," pp. 139–72, 154–56.
121 *Shōen* supervisor's petition of Kōhei 3(1060)/4/21, *HIB* 3:1005–8, doc. 931.

direct taxation of each household had failed. Tax revenues were no longer available except through the rich and powerful, who by the late tenth century were, as far as agriculture was concerned, the field managers.

The same trend toward reliance on field managers was also affecting the system of local granaries and stored tax-grain. By the late ninth century, not all of the tax-grain legally presumed to be in official granaries was actually there. A substantial portion of it consisted of merely paper obligations, debts to the province assumed by consignees called "named obligees" (*fumyō*). Commenting on that situation in 891, the famous scholar-official Sugawara no Michizane, in the course of opposing the dispatch of tax-grain auditors from the capital to the provinces, wrote:

> If, for example, a certain province has stored tax-grain to the amount of 1 million, in actuality an amount of 500,000 will be counted as lent back. On the day for the collection of *suiko* loans, with respect to lent-back grain, only the interest, not the principal, will be returned. The principal is allowed to remain in the custody of private people and will be lent back again in the following year. Precedents like this are long established and cannot suddenly be changed.[122]

Michizane argued that demands for strict accounting by the tax-grain auditors (*kenzeishi*) would do more harm than good. His fear of disrupting provincial administrations and violating precedent shows the development of a new relationship between provincial headquarters and capital. The governor's formal accounting, as a tacit confirmation of private proprietorship over allegedly government grain stores, had to be accepted as valid without authorization from above. Custody of official grain and the imposition of *suiko* loans had always been sources of controversy, and in the early ninth century destruction of official stores by arson had become a serious problem. The dispersal of tax-grain stores away from *gun* headquarters to branch granaries and the appointment of village irregular officials to dispense tax-grain loans were intended to diffuse local resentments. The lending-back system mentioned by Michizane, allowing local gentry to hold and lend out tax grain as if it were their own, was an inevitable concession to gentry growth, rationalized in terms of provin-

---

[122] Memorial of Kampyō 8(896)/7/5, Sugawara no Michizane, comp., *Kanke bunsō*, in Kawaguchi Hisao, ed., *Kanke bunsō, Kanke kōshū*, vol. 72 of *NKBT*, pp. 569–70; Murai, *Kodai kokka*, p. 235; Abe, *Heian zenki seijishi no kenkyū*, pp. 210–14; Robert Borgen, *Sugawara no Michizane and the Early Heian Court* (Cambridge, Mass.: Harvard University Press, 1986), pp. 134–36, 208–10, 357.

cial precedents.[123] The need of provincial governors to come to terms with local power structures, regardless of the prescriptions of the *ritsuryō* system, widened the cleavage between capital and provincial regimes. Arguing against the dispatch of tax-grain inspectors, who would have forced restitution of missing grain to official granaries, Michizane insisted that the proper conduct of provincial affairs sometimes demanded departure from the letter of the law. Provincial precedent, he implied, did not always need to be confirmed by the Council of State, and governors should be allowed to exercise considerable discretionary power in fiscal matters.

DISCRETIONARY TAXATION AND ELITE WEALTH

"Precedent" as used here referred not to the customary law of the local people as such, but to the established practices of provincial headquarters (*kokuga*). A Council order of 902, for example, acknowledged that because of the proliferation of personal tax exemptions among the provincials, it had been provincial precedent (*kokurei*) since the Jōgan era (859–77) for the governors to impose irregular levies (*zōyaku*) on them.[124] *Rinji zōyaku*, the extraordinary irregular levies that were to become one of the two principal categories of late Heian taxation, most probably originated in this way. As the code-mandated tax structure collapsed, the discretionary autonomy of the *kokuga* increased. It is important here not to be misled by the word "extraordinary" (*rinji*). Extraordinary levies were in fact routine, as implied by their justification by provincial precedent.

Loosening regulatory supervision over the governors led to a series of legal fictions meant to establish limits beyond which they were not to go. One such fiction, sanctioned by Council order on the same day Kiyoyuki presented his memorial, was the "rule of sevenths" (*shichibumpō*), establishing artificial standards for tax remission claims based on crop damage. Only one-seventh of damaged public land was to be deemed upper grade, and assessments of middle, lower and lowest were to be ascribed, regardless of actual fact, in equal amounts to the remaining six-sevenths. Similarly, a stipulated grain value was assigned, province by province, to tax com-

---

123 Murai, *Kodai kokka*, pp. 47–59, and Nakano, *Ritsuryōsei shakai kaitai katei no kenkyū*, pp. 252–71.
124 *Kyaku* of Engi 2(902)/4/11, *Ruijū sandai kyaku*, KT 25:635–36, cited in Toda, *Ryōshusei*, p. 30.

modities purchased by the *kokuga* in exchange for tax-rice. In a sense, the *kokuga* itself was becoming the principal object of taxation, and the central government was defining its minimum share.[125]

In his sealed memorial of 914, Miyoshi Kiyoyuki voiced the same opinion as his former rival Michizane, declaring, "The administration of a provincial governor cannot in every instance be bound by the formal law." Kiyoyuki's memorial stresses the importance of reinforcing the authority of the governor against unruly locals and complains bitterly of the latter's numerous techniques of escaping tribute and labor taxes, techniques that usually included the acquisition of such official or quasi-official titles as those of priests at official shrines and temples, constables, *kebiishi*, and palace guards, posts that were often mere sinecures and could be obtained or renewed by purchase.

In recommending that the numbers of tax-exempt persons be limited to about 10 percent of those then existing, Kiyoyuki's aims were not entirely fiscal. He was very much concerned that governors were not being accorded proper respect. One article in his twelve-point memorial begins:

Lately subordinate officers bearing a private grudge have brought false accusations against the chief official of their province; local people have also lodged complaints against their governor under the pretense of public duty. Sometimes the charge is misappropriation of public goods, sometimes illegal acts of administration.

Kiyoyuki, who clearly felt it outrageous to subject governors to such abuse, proceeds to relate how one Tachibana no Mamiki, falsely accused by an underling while he was governor of Awa, was subjected to investigation by an official sent out from the capital, a humiliation that thereafter rendered him a "cripple" without real authority in his province. "With the like of this, what gentleman of honor will seek office?" Kiyoyuki asked. Only in cases of treason or high crimes, he insisted, should a governor in office be embarrassed in this way. Besides, he added, "the time is now one of decline, and public duty is difficult to accomplish."

During Kiyoyuki's time, a provincial governor could be penalized in three different ways. First, he could be reprimanded bureaucratically by central government agencies, often for failure to meet tax quotas set by the accounting offices. Second, he could be brought up

---

125 Council order of Engi 14(914)/8/8, *Seiji yōryaku*, KT 28:312–21, cited in Satō, *Heian zenki seijishi josetsu*, pp. 312–16; on Kiyoyuki and his memorial, see note 91, above.

before the Board of Discharge Examiners (*kageyushi*) by his successor, as already described. Finally, he could be impeached on the instance of his subordinate local officers; according to Kiyoyuki, that was a common occurrence. In his memorial, he says:

> The use of inspectors from the capital should be wholly discontinued in this kind of impeachment procedure and the case left entirely to the newly appointed officer, unless it is a matter of treason or sedition. If there are real offenses, the charges can be set forth in a statement of nondischarge, and after a finding by the Discharge Examiners, they can be submitted to the original authorities for determination of crime and penalty.

Kiyoyuki, like Michizane, had experienced difficulties as a provincial governor. Both argued that good officials (*ryōri*) were the only guarantors of good provincial administration, that the governor with Confucian virtue should be allowed broad discretionary authority as the emperor's representative, and that continuous scrutiny from above, as well as insubordination from below, could impair his effectiveness. Beneath the righteous Confucian tone of Kiyoyuki's recommendations lay the realization that the *ritsuryō* system of finance could never be restored. His reliance on discharge proceedings as the chief means of restraint on governors placed supreme importance on a single final accounting at the end of a gubernatorial term and demonstrated his acceptance of the office of the accountable custodial governor as the principal institution mediating between capital and countryside.

The sealed memorial also showed its author's acquiescence in the decline of the *ritsuryō* land system in at least two other ways. First, it seems intentionally to minimize the problem of landholding by capital nobles, declaring the problem solved. According to Kiyoyuki, the orders issued by the Council limiting the extent and development of *shōen* more than ten years earlier had ended the difficulties for both governors and people. Second, the memorial's attitude toward the failed land allotment system was frankly acquiescent. In discussing the subject, Kiyoyuki repeated the familiar complaint that many of the taxable peasants listed in the annual major accounting report were in fact dead or missing. He declared:

> Over half of the peasants listed in the major reports from the various provinces are fictitious. But the provincial administration, solely in accord with the population report, assigns allotment fields and then parcels out loan rice and imposes tribute and labor-commutation taxes. Where the field allottee is an actual person, he cultivates a meager field and pays excessive land and labor-commutation taxes. Where the allottee is dead or missing,

one of the household will privately lease the field, never tilling it himself, and he succeeds in avoiding payment of the field tax, the loan-rice levy, and the tribute- and labor-commutation taxes. Having inquired into this, I respectfully opine that the reason the court distributes allotment fields is to collect tribute and labor-commutation taxes and to lend out tax-grain, but now the fields have been misused, leading at last to deficiencies in the revenue offerings. Provincial governors vainly cling to useless land registers, and the rich and powerful increasingly gather the profits of their accumulated land. This is not simply an injury to the government fisc but also an obstruction to the conduct of administration. Now the various provinces should make field allotments only to persons found to be actually present. As for the remaining land, the provincial administration should take it back and lease it out as public fields at will. If land rent were collected, it could be applied to the tax liabilities of the fictitious allottees.

Kiyoyuki clearly believed that land-leasing by the province was a more reliable means of collecting revenue than the allotment of land. He was apparently quite willing to eliminate about half the total allotment fields carried on provincial registers and convert them to field-manager leaseholdings. In his informed judgment, improved knowledge of who actually controlled the "profits of the land" and a more equitable distribution of tax burdens would result, and actual revenues would not be reduced because rents from confiscated allotment fields could be used to purchase the equivalent of the tax articles.

The problem of fictitious household registers and misappropriated allotment fields had been addressed by the Council of State as early as 864 when it accused governors of fraudulently increasing the census population but not the taxable population in order to take credit for population increases while minimizing their obligations to produce revenue. In 875 the Council complained that failure to strike dead persons from the registers had allowed some individuals to control the allotment fields of more than five hundred households. Kiyoyuki added a new dimension to the issue by blaming not the governors, but the central government itself. The local rich and powerful could easily acquire immunities to personal tax liabilities from various authorities in the capital, he maintained, so that the governors were constrained to "excuse the tax duties of actual able-bodied subjects who are rich and powerful and enter fictitious taxable subjects on the accounting report." The rich and powerful, in other words, did pay taxes, including some rice-loan interest, but what they paid was attributed to allotment peasants whose liabilities they had assumed long before, and now the accounting report was being manipulated in their favor. Taxation, then, was sometimes a matter of unpleasant negotiations with the unofficial holders of supposedly allotted land. False reporting was often the official's best course, despite repeated threats from the capital. In 876, for example, provincial governors had to be cautioned against describing allotment fields as being cultivated by the allottees, when in fact they had absconded, leaving the land in the hands of "conniving migrants."[126]

By the third decade of the tenth century, the allotment system had been tacitly, but clearly, abandoned forever. Some of the fields still carried on official surveys as allotment land had been retaken by the provincial governments and leased out as public fields. Under the statutory code, unallotted surplus fields (*jōden*), regarded as public land, were to be leased out for the direct use of the Council of State, and by the late ninth century, the Council had established local stations throughout the country, called *chūka* (literally, "kitchen-garden houses"), to collect the income. When households holding allotment land became, at least for accounting purposes, "extinct" the land reverted to government control and was let out for rental (*chishi*), it did not become part of the *chūka* system. The rice revenues were added instead to the provincial stored tax-grain, and used to purchase the dues or labor that actual allotment farmers would have paid.[127]

Under the leadership of Fujiwara no Tadahira (880–949), the central government commenced more realistic efforts to prevent lapsed allotment fields from escaping systematic taxation. In 925 the government acted on Kiyoyuki's recommendation by ordering that allotment fields registered to peasants who had died or moved away be rented out and that the tribute- and labor-commutation tax quotas for the absent peasants be met by applying the grain realized from the rents to the purchase of the tax commodities.[128] But Kiyoyuki's advice on curbing the rich and powerful could not be taken. His own experience as a governor had illustrated the difficulties of that.

The rich and powerful could menace and threaten provincial governors, Kiyoyuki noted, and it is very likely that he himself and his

---

126 Council order of Jōgan 18(876)/6/3, *Seiji yōryaku*, KT 28:295.
127 See Abe, "Sekkanki ni okeru chōzei taikei to kokuga," pp. 29–55, at p. 39; Murai, *Kodai kokka*, pp. 339–48; on Dajōkan chūka, see Hashimoto, *Heian kizoku shakai no kenkyū*, pp. 119–20.
128 Council order of Enchō 3(925)/12/14, *Seiji yōryaku*, KT 27:503; Nakano, *Ritsuryōsei shakai kaitai katei no kenkyū*, p. 163; Satō, *Heian zenki seijishi josetsu*, pp. 295–319; Kuroita Nobuo, "Fujiwara no Tadahira seiken ni taisuru ichikōsatsu," in Kodaigaku kyōkai, ed., *Engi Tenryaku jidai no kenkyū*, pp. 123–47.

personal attendants had been subjected to such intimidation while he was chief officer of Bitchū from 892 to 896. In any case, his biography indicates a confrontation of some sort with the Kaya family, whose head was then chief magistrate of Kaya *gun*, where the provincial capital was located. The magistrate's brothers included another *gun* magistrate, a priest of the Kibitsu Shrine, the chief Shinto shrine in the region, and a man who had purchased the office of Junior Secretary in the neighboring province of Bizen. There was, furthermore, a nephew of the chief magistrate who held a junior post in the palace guards, and it is surely no coincidence that palace guards (who were periodically on duty in the capital) and local priests were so bitterly criticized in Kiyoyuki's sealed memorial. The memorial's complaints about such guards and the local constabulary plainly reveal the limited ability of the governors to control the use of local military force.

Kiyoyuki's memorial also castigated unlicensed Buddhist monks and noted how, except for shaving their heads, they behaved like other rich and powerful figures, controlling private wealth and even attacking provincial offices. Such persons appear often in documents of the period, sometimes as field managers. In 924, for example, a communication from the Tōji Temple in Kyoto to the provincial administration of Tamba demanding exemption from extraordinary irregular levies for the cultivators of the Ōyama *shōen* lists a Priest Heishū as superintendent of the *shōen* and three field managers with monks' names.[129] In 932 the provincial headquarters of Tamba complained to Tōji about these individuals, referring to one of them as a *shōen* custodian (*shō azukari*). Two were accused of withholding tribute silk, for which *gun* authorities had distrained their rice holdings. A probable reference to these and other *tato* of Ōyama-no-shō as officially "unlisted migrants" is one of the earliest acknowledgments of corvée and produce dues as charges on landholding. Unlisted *rōnin* were off the books, their names officially withdrawn from the rolls of those liable for corvée and commodity-tax duties. Their licensed presence on Ōyama-no-shō was seen as an official endowment to the proprietary temple, and to the Ōyama estate in particular, of the corvée services and produce normally at the command of the state. Their argument was that since they had, with approval from the cap-

---

129 Communication of Tōji of Shōhei 5(935)/10/25, *HIB* 1:360, doc. 245; on the role of the *gun* here, see Abe, "Sekkanki ni okeru chōzei taikei to kokuga," pp. 29–55.

ital, been exempted from tax liability to the central government, they should also be freed from the locally imposed burden of *rinji zōyaku*.¹³⁰

The document of 932, one of the earliest to show the assumption of peasant tax liabilities by the rich and powerful, reads in part:

The inspector responsible for the village of Amaribe, Heki no Sadayoshi, has reported, saying:

> The aforesaid village has always been without land, its peasant allotment grants being in other villages of the region. Accordingly, the tribute silk for the village has by custom been levied on listed capable farmers of those villages [where the allotment grants were located]. At present, Heishū and [Seihō] are of the same capable status as laymen, and moreover in years past they have submitted the said tribute silk. The names of Heishū and Seihō have then been entered on the original report for two *jō* [6 m.] of silk each.

I went to the personal residences of Heishū and the others in order to make them pay the said silk, but they ran away into the mountains and did not pay. Accordingly, I have impounded two hundred sheaves of rice from each man for the payment of the silk. After the silk has been forwarded, the rice will be released.

"Capable farmers," *kambyakushō*, were those able to guarantee the tax obligations of allotment-field peasants, whether the latter actually existed or not. They were, after the order of 925, the government's principal means of acquiring commodity taxes. The lists of capable farmers alluded to in the document were far more important in revenue raising than the population-based tax-accounting reports, which were gradually losing all real fiscal significance, although they continued to be made until the century's end.¹³¹ The old head taxes were, in effect, being farmed out to the more prosperous field managers.

In the meantime, Kiyoyuki's hopes to restore the *ritsuryō* census and household taxing system had been totally abandoned under Tadahira's new policy, which was aimed at preventing further erosion of the rural tax base, even if some concessions to the rich and powerful had to be made. Judgments by the Board of Discharge Examiners in 933 and 941 made it clear that the provincial governor was himself responsible for the production of revenue from aban-

---

130 Communication of Tamba Province of Shōhei 2(932)/9/22, *HIB* 1:354–55, doc. 240. See also communication of Tōji of Shōhei 5(935)/10/25, *HIB* 1:360, doc. 245, listing the same *tato* as cultivators of Ōyama-no-shō.
131 Abe, "Sekkanki ni okeru chōzei taikei to kokuga," pp. 29–55; Izumiya, "Chōyōsei no henshitsu ni tsuite," pp. 175–308.

doned allotment fields and other such land, holding that a lack of capable farmers to tax was not a valid excuse for revenue shortages. Recruiting and enrolling the necessary cultivators was ultimately part of the governor's duty, and as the tenth century progressed, *kokushi* and district officers (*gunji*) were held increasingly responsible for the desertion of public rice fields. In 933, for example, the Board of Discharge Examiners refused to accept an alleged shortage of capable cultivators as a justification for reporting an unacceptably large area of land as not being worked.[132]

In the *ritsuryō* scheme, all arable paddy had to be registered and all failures to cultivate it reported to the central government. One standard exception to those requirements was damage to land or crops resulting from storms, floods, insects, or other disasters, an exception that applied, however, only to fields in which a crop had already been planted. If no crop at all had been planted for three or more years, the field was designated abandoned (*kōhai*) or permanently out of cultivation (*jōkō*). If, on the other hand, cultivation had been discontinued more recently, the field was called uncultivatable (*fukanden*). Fields could fall into that category for natural reasons like flooding or infertility, but also for social reasons, such as the flight of their assigned cultivators from the district or simply the inability of the cultivators to provide seed grain.

Provincial governors were required to report the extent of uncultivatable fields annually, the central government depending heavily on such reports to assess the state of agriculture nationwide and also to determine how much field tax (*so*) could be collected in each province. Reported acreage totals of uncultivatable fields had a pronounced tendency to increase, not simply because of cupidity on the part of the governors, who could pocket the revenues from uncultivatable fields that were in fact under cultivation, but also because local communities abandoned registered fields of poor quality in favor of unreported newly reclaimed lands. Governors were admonished to carry out inspections in person to detect undocumented reclamation, and when uncultivatable-field and damage totals seemed too high, special inspectors were dispatched from the capital to check the accuracy of the governors' reports.[133] Ever since Nara times, provincial authorities had tended to overstate field damage

---

132 *Kageyushi* decision of Shōhei 3(933)/11/21, *Seiji yōryaku*, KT 28:328; see also decision of Tengyō 4(941), *Seiji yōryaku*, KT 28:327–28.

133 On the meaning of the term *fukandenden*, see Satō, *Heian zenki seijishi josetsu*, pp. 321–35.

and crop losses. This allowed them to take advantage of a legal provision that excused households that had suffered over 50 percent crop damage from flood, drought, insects, or hail from the *so*, and additionally canceled the tribute tax (*chō*) for households with 70 percent crop damage and both tribute and labor-commutation (*yō*) taxes for those with 80 percent or more damage.[134]

The policies instituted by Tadahira were particularly concerned with curbing, rather than preventing, falsification of fiscal reports by accountable governors. Under his guidance, the Council of State elaborated on the earlier measures of "standard damage" (*reison*), all of which, it may be remarked, originated from administrative custom rather than *ritsuryō* rules. The code rules regarding tax exemptions and evasions were, after all, originally aimed at taxable subject households, not governors. Government legal technicians were nonetheless hard at work reinterpreting the old codes to make them apply to the emergent real taxpayers, that is, the *zuryō* governors themselves. Implicit recognition of this may be seen in a ruling of 915, giving the Board of Discharge Examiners, which was exceptionally well staffed with legal experts, authority to recommend rewards or penalties for *zuryō*, and to pronounce on their evaluation generally.[135] In 926 the Council ruled that whenever a province petitioned for tax remission on account of land damage, no more than one-third of allegedly damaged households could be listed as over the 50 percent damage bracket, and thereby eligible for remission of taxes other than *so*. By the middle of the century each province had its "standard damage" allotment, a kind of legal fiction that was beyond challenge. Similarly, uncultivatable fields became a kind of tax deduction on the provincial account, having little relation to actual conditions of arability.[136]

Tadahira's policies regarding damage reports also resulted in a revision of the system of accounting for public fields yielding rent. The established practice of grading such fields into upper, middle, lower, and lower-lower assessment categories was all but abandoned. The rule had been that when damage to public fields under Council supervision was reported, only one-seventh could be upper field, while

---

134 Murao, *Ritsuryō zaiseishi no kenkyū*, pp. 87–101; Nagayama, *Ritsuryō futan taikei no kenkyū*, pp. 219–45; *Buyaku ryō, Suikan no jō, Ryō no gige, KT* 22B:119, *Ryō no shūge, KT* 23: 392–403.
135 Ruling of Engi 15(915)/12/8, quoted in ruling of Tentoku 3(959)/12/4, *Seiji yōryaku, KT* 28:182.
136 Ruling of Enchō 4(926)/12/5, *Seiji yōryaku, KT* 28:504–5; Nakano, *Ritsuryōsei shakai kaitai katei no kenkyū*, pp. 99–107.

two-sevenths were to be in each of the three other categories. The "rule of sevenths" was the standard for delivery of land rents to the Council's provincial collection stations until 928, when a "rule of thirds" (*sambumpō*) was imposed. That rule completely eliminated the "upper" category of land from damage reports and required that for tax- and damage-estimation purposes public fields be presumed to consist of equal parts of the three lower categories.[137] The rule of thirds meant for central government purposes that the land-grading system was largely inoperative, since the average putative yield of about three hundred sheaves per *chō* for the three lower assessment categories eliminated all distinctions.

The virtual disappearance of the grading of fields as a topic of concern in relations between the central and provincial governments did not mean, however, that the subject ceased to be an important issue in relations between the provincial governments and local cultivators. As Empō's land survey of the Echi *shōen* shows, although the grading of fields was the prerogative of the provincial headquarters, it was also subject to informal negotiation with field-manager cultivators, and Tadahira's policies merely defined the area left open to negotiation while making even more obvious the tax-farming aspect of the administrations of accountable governors. The use of mechanical formulas instead of factual surveys as a basis for taxation was clearly an attempt to check the increased bargaining costs that the enforcement of the old taxation rules against the governors had entailed. It illustrates the sort of adversary situations in which legal fictions develop within a context of formally codified law.

The administrative code provided that if paddy in a district increased by one-fifth or more during the term of a local officer of a province or *gun,* his personnel evaluation was to be raised one grade for every one-fifth increase; if the field area declined, the evaluation was to be lowered one grade for every 10 percent lost. In an official promotion system stressing Confucian values of character, diligence, and talent, this mechanical, achievement-oriented standard was somewhat incongruous, as contemporary legal commentators noted, but conditions in the tenth century gave it heightened significance. Renewed stress was also placed on an article of the criminal code that provided similarly graded levels of punishment for officials who allowed fields to drop out of cultivation. Allowing cultivated fields in a district to decrease rated forth blows of the stick for the first one-

---

137 See note 124, above.

tenth and an additional increment in the penalty for each further tenth, up to a maximum of one year's imprisonment.[138] Those draconian penalties were not intended to be carried out in fact, however, since the criminal code made a number of substitute punishments available to the official classes. Loss of an office of Fifth-Rank status, for example, was the equivalent of two years of penal servitude, and loss of a lesser office, the equivalent of one year.[139] Even the substitute penalties could be catastrophic for an accountable governor, however, and the central government was usually reluctant to impose criminal sanctions at all.

The rules rewarding local officials for increasing land under cultivation and punishing them for reductions reflected a major explicit concern of the *ritsuryō* state: the promotion of agriculture, originally regarded as more basic to regional administration than collecting taxes. Misreporting of uncultivatable fields was not only a crime under the penal code but also a violation of this basic policy, and yet despite threats of dire sanctions, provincial and *gun* officers continued to falsify acreages, partly because the sanctions were not consistently applied. Tadahira's Council of State was the last seriously to insist on accuracy. In an order of 918, the Council declared:

The penal code states:

> When within a district damage occurs from drought, flood, frost, sleet, worms, or locusts, and the chief official makes an exaggerated report, the penalty is seventy blows of the heavy rod. Reexaminers who report falsely are liable to the same penalty. If taxes are collected or excused in violation of the law, the crime is that of illicitly acquired goods, meriting an additional seventy blows of the heavy rod. In assessing the penalty for illicitly acquired goods [which increases in proportion to the value of the goods misappropriated], the maximum punishment is three years penal servitude. As for improperly taken goods, the case is one of illicitly acquired goods if the goods have gone into government possession. If the goods fall into private hands, the case is one of official extortion; in sentencing for that, if the amount extorted merits death, the actual sentence will be life at forced labor in exile.

Now, however, when the various provinces send up pleas of crop damage or uncultivatable fields, they regularly ignore actual facts, and when reexamination is made, the discrepancies are found to be excessive. In recent

---

138 *Kōka ryō, Kokugunji no jō, Ryō no gige*, KT 22B:157–58, *Ryō no shūge*, KT 23:591–595; *Kokon ritsu, Bunai denchū kōhai no jō*, Kuroita Katsumi and Kokushi taikei henshūkai, comps., *Ritsu*, KT 22A:115.

139 Ishii Ryōsuke, *Nihon hōseishi gaisetsu*, 2nd ed. (Tokyo: Sōbunsha, 1960), pp. 144–46; Wallace Johnson, *The T'ang Code; General Principles* (Princeton, N.J.: Princeton University Press, 1979).

years, nevertheless, offenders are merely made to restore the tax goods required, and the laws of criminal responsibility are never applied. Deception has become the established rule by the growth of accumulated custom. Now then, as ordinances have pointed out, the established penalties are severe, but forbearance has led to nonenforcement of the law.

The Great Minister of the Right [Tadahira] proclaims, announcing an imperial edict:

> Governance requires adapting to change, and its acts may be strict or lenient. From now on, on the day a reexamination is reported, the examining officer in his report shall divide the area of fields he finds unproductive by ten, and where the misrepresented area is not more than one-tenth greater, criminal penalties will be specially remitted and the official ordered to restore the tax goods. If the limit is exceeded, let the crime be punished according to the law, depending on whether the goods have passed into public or private possession. If a reexaminer in his survey misrepresents the facts, he is always to be punished in accordance with the law. Also, as for matters such as peasants dead from epidemic disease, people requiring famine relief, or damage to official buildings or dikes, when the report is within one-tenth of the actuality, punishment is to be remitted and restitution only ordered.[140]

The allowance of a one-tenth margin of error in exaggerated uncultivatable-field reports and in various other certifications of provincial loss reveals a basic weakness of the *ritsuryō* system. The accountable governors were subject to forces far more compelling than the incentives and sanctions of the codes. Those codes presumed that promoting agriculture was primarily the responsibility of the local administrators and that their direction of the agricultural enterprise, if properly conducted, would be unreservedly welcomed by the populace at large. The fundamental assumption was that the rulers would be in total control of basic resources and in no way dependent on the assets of the subject population. As the numerous irregular officers in each province, the more prosperous field managers, and other such local elites tightened their hold on granaries and peasant labor, the accountable governors found it increasingly difficult to carry out the letter of the law and meet their tax quotas as well. As Miyoshi Kiyoyuki's memorial pointed out, such performance could not be expected of even the most scrupulous governor, and he accordingly opposed direct government reexamination of gubernatorial accounts. To function economically, the governors needed more latitude than the organic code permitted, and the

---

[140] Ruling of Engi 18(918)/6/20, *Seiji yōryaku*, KT 28:493–94; Satō, *Heian zenki seijishi josetsu*, pp. 326–33.

Council of State was forced to acknowledge the use of extralegal discretion in the performance of their duties. The 10 percent margin permitted in the quoted document, however, proved to be an inadequate concession.

In 927 the Council tried once more to pressure the governors into reducing reported losses of cultivatable fields. It imposed on newly appointed governors a positive duty to reclaim lands vacated under their predecessors, to increase the total area of land in production, and to submit annual progress reports on gains made. Any further net loss of arable land in a governor's jurisdiction was to be an absolute bar to future reappointment or promotion.[141] The Council of State seems by those actions to have tacitly acknowledged the difficulty of reasserting total power over reclamation policy, opting instead to establish a compulsory minimum amount of paddy under cultivation to be reported from each province.

The measures taken in 927 failed to prevent further decline in officially registered paddy under cultivation, however, and the Council of State decided in 946 to resort once more to the criminal sanctions imposed in 916, which were still in force. Fourteen provincial governors were impeached for presenting reports exaggerating by more than 10 percent the area of uncultivated paddy in their provinces.[142] One surviving case report deals with the governor of Ise, Tachibana no Korekaze, and two provincial clerks who cosigned a false acreage report.[143] Korekaze had reported about 2,070 *chō* of uncultivatable fields for his province, or about 12 percent of the 18,000 *chō* of registered paddy that other sources show for the province. The inspector from the capital found only about 1,450 *chō* of land actually out of cultivation, and, following the established rule, recommended the signatories of the original report for criminal punishment. The 620 *chō* falsely reported out of cultivation was more than 30 percent above the maximum allowable error of 10 percent.

Asked to determine the proper legal penalty for the crime, the law doctor Koremune no Kinkata responded that final dispensation required further inquiry into the facts. In the case of misappropriation by provincial authorities of taxes from unreported fields under cultivation, the ruling of 918 and the criminal law both specified penal-

---

141 Dajōkan order of Enchō 5(927)/12/13, quoted in the ruling of Tenryaku 1(947)/int. 7/23, *Seiji yōryaku*, KT 28:271–72; see Abe, "Sekkanki ni okeru chōzei taikei to kokuga," pp. 29–55; Satō, *Heian zenki seijishi josetsu*, pp. 330–38.
142 Dajōkan order of Tenryaku 1(947)/int. 7/23, *Seiji yōryaku*, KT 28:271–72. One of these adjudications is that of Tenryaku 1(947)/int. 7/16, *Seiji yōryaku*, KT 28:278–80.
143 The case of Korekaze is outlined in *Seiji yōryaku*, KT 27:496–98.

ties that differed depending on the use of the taxes. In the present instance, Kinkata said, a finding on the matter of use was required before a penalty could be assessed. If the revenues had gone to official agencies such as the provincial headquarters, the culprits were to be sentenced for the crime of illicitly acquired goods, but if they had been converted to the personal use of the provincial officials, the much severer penalties prescribed for extortion were appropriate. The authorities then discovered that taxes on the fields in question had not been collected at all, and that there had therefore been no misappropriation of revenues. The offense was found to be that of illicitly acquired goods, as if the tax-grain had gone to an inappropriate office. Although a general amnesty proclaimed late in the year 947 absolved Korekaze and his subordinates from criminal penalties connected with the case, they were still required to make restitution of the uncollected taxes.

The discovery that no taxes had been collected on the uncultivatable fields falsely reported by Korekaze cannot be interpreted to mean that he was unaware of the cultivation of the fields or remiss in the exercise of his duties. The absence of revenues from those lands was the result more likely of the growing political power of the local elite and the corresponding growth in its ability to resist tax collection by provincial authorities. The adversarial relationship between accountable governors and provincials is as well established in the sources for the period as the well-known ability of accountable governors to use their office for personal gain. The strained legal reasoning in this case illustrates the need of the early Heian officials to maintain the rhetoric of the *ritsuryō* order even as the command economy embodied in it deteriorated.

Seeking to maintain the facade of the authority-intensive *ritsuryō* system, the central government could not officially acknowledge participation of the local elites in its control of the provinces, and it was forced to resort to increasing use of legal fictions in order to cope with them. The decision in Korekaze's case that the crime was an instance of illicitly acquired goods, in other words, the misdirecting of revenue, rather than a failure to collect taxes or personal misappropriation of them, was in fact an indirect accommodation to the power of the local elite through a fictionalized interpretation of penal law. The imperial court was relinquishing its control over agriculture and land use to other hands.

Although the reporting of uncultivatable fields continued for some centuries, the system steadily weakened during the tenth century, eventually becoming simply a heavily ritualized routine of the central bureaucracy. The decline in the practical meaning of the reporting was marked by the discontinuance of the practice of canceling expensive court rituals in years when the area of uncultivatable fields reported was unusually high, by the cessation of the dispatch of special field investigators to determine actual acreages of uncultivatable fields, and by the establishment of reporting quotas of uncultivatable-field acreages for each province (typically pegged at 10 percent of the province's arable), observance of which exempted a province's report from further scrutiny (the quotas, similar to the standard damage allowances mentioned earlier, were called the "standard uncultivatable," *reifukan*). The result was the complete fictionalization of the uncultivatable-field reports and the abandonment by the central government of an important device for overseeing its own tax base.

In the face of the growing power of rural elites and their increasingly successful quest for control over land and peasant labor, the government had little choice but to relinquish authority over rural production. The *ritsuryō* presumption of total peasant dependency on the state could not be maintained against the interests of the rural elites, and the central government's reins on the accountable governors themselves were slipping. The governors required not only more freedom in their attempts to control their refractory populations but also their own private military and civil auxiliaries, paid for from local revenues. Alarmed by the rebellious potential exhibited by its subjects, most notably in the revolt of Taira no Masakado (d. 940), the central government was obliged to recognize the right of governors to military escorts. It stopped short in this period, however, of recognizing the use of private retainers for that purpose.

Condoning greater scope for gubernatorial discretion and giving less scrutiny to local land administration did not mean total loss of control by the noble regime over the countryside, and revenues continued to flow in. The imperial court was, in part, merely confirming concessions already made over the years to the rich and powerful by the governors, concessions that had given local elites an unofficial but profitable role in the revenue system. Perhaps the clearest example of that trend was the system of tax-grain fund exchange (*shōzei kōeki*), on which the government became increasingly dependent during the ninth century. Exchange of tax-grain, for example, had been an important element of the scheme for publicly operated fields proposed for Kyushu in 823. The exchange system was expanded to all taxable lands in the tenth century. Provincial authorities used stored tax-grain funds to purchase the commodities that *ritsuryō* law had required, with growing lack of success, of each taxable household as tribute and labor commutation taxes.

The fiscal authority of provincial governments had never been limited to control over land use and corvée labor. Provinces were required to supervise the manufacture of fine silks and other luxury items, mining, and the gathering of natural food items for the court, and the production of these rare or precious items was the responsibility of the provincial unit itself. In the distributive economy presumed by the *ritsuryō*, the *kokuga* stood directly below the capital in the exchange system. By the tenth century most such activity was reduced to a system of official procurement, the purchase of the required goods with stored tax-grain. For example, the province of Owari was required to provide the sovereign's Chamberlains' Office (*kurōdodokoro*) with an annual supply of lacquer, almost certainly purchased from local growers with tax-grain funds,[144] and the province also bought silk, hemp fabric, *karamushi* fabric, vegetable oil, paper bark, and a variety of other items demanded by the capital. Disputes over prices and quotas could break out between provincial authorities and local suppliers as each side attempted to maximize its own share of the proceeds, and there was a similar area of friction between the provinces and the central government.[145]

As the *ritsuryō* system of taxes became ever more fictionalized and divorced from the actual productive yield of the countryside, the central government began tapping into the provincial system of extraordinary irregular levies (*rinji zōyaku*), at first justifying its new demands by particular exigencies like the need to reconstruct capital buildings after fires or earthquakes. During the eleventh century, the term *rinji zōyaku* acquired a different, far more general meaning. It was applied to any of the various forms of corvée defined by the old *ritsuryō* rules and, at times, to tribute and labor commutation taxes. By the early twelfth century, it meant all taxes not perceived as a direct charge on grain revenues, like *so* and *suiko* payments. Taxes of this latter kind, by contrast, merged into a second major category, *kammotsu*, a term formerly used for "official goods."[146]

Just how and why this transition occurred remains uncertain, and

---

[144] Abe, *Owari no kuni gebumi no kenkyū*, pp. 156–60.
[145] Nagayama, *Ritsuryō futan taikei no kenkyū*, pp. 219–45.
[146] Abe, *Heian zenki seijishi no kenkyū*, pp. 309–10; Nagayama, *Ritsuryō futan taikei no kenkyū*, pp. 285–319; Nakano, *Ritsuryōsei shakai kaitai katei no kenkyū*, pp. 199–299.

there is no exact agreement on which of the old *ritsuryō* taxes became *rinji zōyaku* and which *kammotsu*. Nevertheless, some aspects of this long transition are clear. Most important was the steady advance of the *tato* as the major source of provincial revenues and the chief consignee of resources, including labor resources, in every province. The gradual sorting out of taxes into *rinji zōyaku* and *kammotsu* almost certainly reflected a distinction between labor and land resources, in which control over labor power was, to an increasingly greater extent, a function of control over land. The disposition of stored grain, a major element in the exercise of governmental authority during the ninth century, gradually became a prerogative of the local rich. During the ninth century, the government shifted the burden of the imposts to the stored tax-grain of the provincial governments and used the revenue thus produced for purposes that had once been met from the central treasury. This was an added burden on the stored tax-grain, already strained by its use to purchase the goods for commodity taxes owed the central government and by its misuse on the part of provincial officials. The result was sequestration and hoarding of the stores, and the fictionalization of the *suiko* loan system based on them.

The stored tax-grain on which so much depended was divided into three parts: (1) official government grain funds, the "main fund," or *shōzei* in the narrow sense of the term; (2) public-allowance rice (*kugetō*), reserved for the income of regular provincial officials, including numbers of titular appointees; and (3) "miscellaneous rice" (*zōtō*), for the upkeep of official buildings, religious institutions, and irrigation facilities, and the benefices of irregular officials, local priests, and other rich and powerful provincials. Roughly speaking, each fraction represented one of the three groups most interested in provincial revenues: the nobles in the capital, the accountable governors and their retinues, and the rural elite.[147]

The first component of the stored tax-grain, the official government grain, was regularly tapped by the court during the tenth century as a source of rank- and support-stipends for the middle-ranking nobility. Instead of receiving his stipend in silk and other commodities through the general treasury, a holder of court rank might be told to collect the rice equivalent of the allowance from the stored tax-grain of a specific province, which was by rule always fairly distant from the capital. Those "remote awards" (*yōju*) were frequently diffi-

---

147 See note 61, above.

TABLE 4.3
Stipend grants from stored rice in Izumo

Year	Number of stipendiaries	Total stipends (*in sheaves*)
939	4	1,005
957	12	1,835
1003	15	3,142

cult for a grantee to collect. It was his own responsibility to convert the rice to shippable commodities and transport them to the capital, and for that he was obliged at significant cost to employ the local accountable governor as his agent.[148] The growth in the use of remote awards during the tenth century may be illustrated by data available from the province of Izumo for three different years.[149]

As the administrative and fiscal separation between the capital and countryside became more pronounced, the difficulty of collecting such stipends forced middle-ranking nobles to seek help and protection from individuals of the highest ranks, increasing the trend toward clientage and estate partitioning.

The miscellaneous rice component of provincial stored tax-grain had grown very rapidly during the ninth century, but the government in the tenth century, considerably less solicitous of local interests than its predecessors had been, sought to check that growth, insisting that official government rice was of prime importance and that the miscellaneous rice account was of lowest priority. The government was understandably concerned that the governors might conspire with local officials to accumulate hidden stores of unreported tax-grain under the guise of miscellaneous rice.[150]

The Heian government's policy toward provincial administration during the ninth and tenth centuries may best be seen as one of accommodation to changes beyond its power to control, especially the reorganization of local resources by the regional elite. Direct taxation of land and peasant had to be replaced by a more indirect method, in which a major object of taxation was the product that resulted from the power of the field-manager gentry over the peasants.

---

148 Murai, *Kodai kokka*, pp. 146–50; Yoshimura, *Kokushi seido*, pp. 362–64.
149 Murai Yasuhiko, *Heian kizoku no sekai* (Tokyo: Tokuma shoten, 1972), p. 44; Murai, *Kodai kokka*, pp. 146–74.
150 Abe, *Owari no kuni gebumi no kenkyū*, pp. 69–70; Murai, *Kodai kokka*, pp. 37–59.

Close inspection of land and population resources had to give way to a more flexible system within which the locally recruited resident officials of the provincial headquarters were allowed a considerable degree of autonomy, and it became necessary at the same time to grant accountable governors broader discretionary authority in the performance of their duties. In response to those developments, the more powerful noble households and political bureaus of the capital sought direct links with field-manager cultivators to gain independence of the gubernatorial stratum, as with the directly operated office fields. First established in 879 to provide stipends for central-government officials, they were later parceled out among the central ministries for their individual support.[151]

The ninth- and tenth-century restructuring of the provincial revenue system, with its heavy reliance on tax-grain accounts, remained like the earlier tax system in that it was ultimately based on income from land. But the emergence of a well-differentiated field-manager stratum among the peasantry radically changed the system of linkage between the administration of taxes and the administration of land that had been intended by the original *ritsuryō* planners. Standing between the economies of capital and province, the accountable governors had to extract as much grain as possible from the field managers in order to meet their legal tax obligations, but their success in that respect depended on collaboration with the resident officials in the evasion of *ritsuryō* law regarding the state's power to dispose of land and supervise agriculture. They were, in brief, forced to resort to illegal actions in order to meet their legal obligations.

That development was an essential step in the formation of the Heian period *shōen*. By the mid-tenth century, the various enclaves of *shōen* and publicly operated fields constituted the only arable fields that the capital nobility controlled directly. As the autonomy of the provincial headquarters increased, and as provincial impositions of irregular grain and commodity taxes on *shōen* grew heavier, conflict between the headquarters and *shōen* owners in the capital became inevitable. The conflict was reflected in the policies of Tadahira, apparently forcing even him, a staunch defender of public lands against private encroachment, to retreat somewhat from the strict policies of his predecessors regarding *shōen*.

Tadahira's retreat can be inferred from a "communication" (*chō*)

---

151 Sakamoto, *Nihon ōchō kokka taisei ron*, pp. 127–94. See also, however, Morita, *Heian jidai seijishi kenkyū*, pp. 32–233.

issued in 920 by his household chancery to the governor of Tamba instructing him to respect the tax immunities of the Ōyama *shōen,* a holding of Tōji. One of Kyoto's most powerful temples, Tōji had acquired the land by purchase early in the ninth century. In 845 the temple was awarded certificates by the Council of State and the Ministry of Popular Affairs completely exempting the holding, as it then was, from land taxes. The Popular Affairs certificate defined the *shōen* as consisting of slightly over nine *chō* of privately reclaimed paddy scattered over thirty-six grid squares, thirty-five *chō* of woodland, and a large pond that may in fact have included some rice land. The boundaries of the village-site area were noted, and there was some "public field" within them. In 915 the provincial headquarters of Tamba had recognized Tōji's ownership of about sixteen *chō* of additional paddy reclaimed within an already existing irrigation system.[152] But soon thereafter the headquarters began to challenge Tōji's claims, in two different ways. First, it refused to certify new paddy opened within the area as tax-exempt temple land. Then, it refused to excuse the *tato* in charge from the various irregular and extraordinary levies just then being instituted throughout the countryside.

The questions were referred to Tadahira's private household chancery rather than to the Council of State, presumably because in addition to being the senior minister in the Council, he was also official overseer of Tōji. The first complaint was resolved in the temple's favor, at least for a time, by the communication of 920. The document repeats the complaint received from Tōji, stating in part:

As for the woodland, additional rice fields have been reclaimed [from it] with each passing year. However, after the *shōen* buildings have been erected and the fields reclaimed, the provincial and *gun* officers have confiscated them and made them unallotted public land.

The chancery responded with a request to the provincial headquarters to look into the charge, and if it was true, to return the lands to the temple's possession. Control over land use within the boundaries established in the *shōen* certificates, the communication implied, should rest with the temple rather than with the province or *gun.*

[152] The "communication" (*chō*) of Engi 15(915)/10/23, recognizing temple proprietorship over specified additional fields appears as *HIB* 1:322, doc. 213. For the incident of 920, see Tōji petition of Engi 20(920)/9/7, *HIB* 9.3473, doc. 4555, and Udaijin *kechō* of Engi 20/9/21, *HIB* 1:325–26, doc. 217; Satō, *Heian zenki seijishi josetsu,* pp. 270–83. On the history of Ōyama-no-shō, see Miyagawa, *Ōyama sonshi, Hommon hen,* pp. 69–76. For a good account of this estate in middle and late Heian, see Elizabeth Sato, "Ōyama Estate and *Insei* Land Policies," *Monumenta Nipponica* 34 (Spring 1979): 73–99.

Despite the ambiguities of the document, it seems likely that the action of the local authorities in confiscating the reclaimed fields was not illegal. The term "confiscate" as employed here, it must be noted, did not indicate the extinction of Tōji's proprietary rights. It merely meant that the land in question, although unquestionably a part of Tōji's Ōyama estate, was adjudged subject to all regular charges of grain dues (*kammotsu*). Its cultivators, like all cultivators of public fields, would also be subject to the newly established *rinji zōyaku* imposts. Official maps, kept in the provincial headquarters, designated specific areas in specific grid squares as exempt from *kammotsu*. The governor had the power to confiscate the excess, and would ordinarily do so except in grid squares where some exempt cultivation was already established. Tadahira, through his chancery, here preempted the largely discretionary power of the local authorities. The Tōji complaint makes no claim that the affected land belonged to it by the well-established right of wasteland reclamation, probably because it did not consist of reclaimed fields (*konden*) in the legal sense of that term. It was very likely abandoned public-field land that had been returned to production, a type of reclamation that did not entitle the reclaimer to permanent ownership. If that was the case, the local authorities would have been completely justified in seizing the fields as they did and returning them to public-field status, which would have required that the land rent on them be paid to the government, rather than to the temple.

In confiscating reclaimed land in the Ōyama *shōen*, the Tamba authorities may have been acting in response to some now lost government order, but it is clear that the legal right to confiscate the land did in fact rest with the governor. The registration and classification of land had always been primarily the function of provincial governments. This power had been exercised earlier in the case of the Ōyama *shōen* when, as already noted, sixteen *chō* of newly reclaimed paddy were confirmed in Tōji's ownership. Tadahira through his chancery clearly preempted the discretionary power of the governor of the province to confirm an addition to the tax-exempt *shōen* land.

More important, however, is the gap seen here between the land and taxation system mandated by official regulations and the actual conduct of provincial governors responsible for collecting taxes. The government was doing its best to allow the governors broad discretionary powers in dealing with local notables and *shōen* lords, while at the same time maintaining full taxing authority over all land legally specified as taxable. The result was the development of new categories of taxation, like *rinji zōyaku,* permitting uneven application of the established rules. Acquiescence in gubernatorial discretion, furthermore, facilitated increased participation by local gentry in the tax assessment process.

Land within the boundaries of a *shōen* newly brought under cultivation by the proprietor was subject to annual survey by local authorities whose recommendations reached the governor in the form of an assessment by the "land office" (*tadokoro*). Tax exemptions were, in effect, subject to ratification by the irregular officers of the area concerned, as well as the governor. The assessment of *shōen* land developed into a formalized process involving joint participation by local elites, agents of *zuryō* governors, and agents of estate proprietors like Tōji.

A document of 935 relating to Ōyama-no-shō contains the earliest specific information about *rinji zōyaku,* and illustrates the basically routine nature of this tax. It is also clear from this text that the gentry managers of the estate and its *tato* cultivators were the principal targets of tax gatherers. This document, a communication from Tōji to the *kokuga* of Tamba, expresses the temple's attempt to protect them. It reads in part:

> The said *shō* fields, in accordance with the certificate of the Council of State and the Ministry of Popular Affairs, of Jōwa 12th year [845], 9th month, 10th day, are fields for the support of transmitting Buddhist law, and the use of their rice rent for teaching the law and copying the sutras has been established long since. The prospering of Buddhist law indeed rests on this *shō*.
> Accordingly, from the beginning the field tax (*denso*) and tax-grain funds (*shōzei*) were not assessed, and there were no impositions of extraordinary irregular levies (*rinji zōyaku*). However, we have received a petition from this *shō* saying:
>> The *gun* magistrates order us saying, and the *kokuga* orders us saying:
>> The irregular levy of official exchange silk thread, tribute tax sale silk, rice in ear from provincially cultivated fields, cedar bark for the repair of official buildings, and the [levy of] labor and horses, you are ordered to render.
>
> Because of this, we cannot rest at all either night or day. How can we perform our customary service to the *shō?* We respectfully pray that a communication be sent to the *kokuga* that we be exempted from special irregular levies.
> Our communication is as aforesaid. We pray the *kokuga* to examine the matter and desire that, in accord with precedent, our *shō* custodians (*shō azukari*) and *shō* retainers (*shōshi,* i.e., *tato*) be exempted from special irregular duties. Let the matter be in accord with goodwill, and without con-

cealment. Accordingly, we append a copy of the former governor's order granting exemption from special irregular duties.[153]

Rinji zōyaku, and immunity from it, were mentioned as early as 895 in a declaration made by the Usa Hachiman Shrine, and a petition from Ōyama-no-shō dated 924 requested exemption from the tax, but both documents fail to state what the levy actually was.[154] As the document here implies, *rinji zōyaku* simply did not exist when the *shō* was established in the mid-ninth century, and the former governor's exemption of the *shō* from the levy was almost certainly a discretionary act. Especially noteworthy is the way ordinary provincial taxes on *tato* cultivation are divided into (1) *denso*, the *ritsuryō* tax on riceland; (2) *shōzei*, a grain tax originally paid as interest on rice loans from the fund called *shōzei* but now assessed directly on management of riceland; and (3) *rinji zōyaku*. The five particular types of *rinji zōyaku* enumerated in the document here can be divided into two categories: (1) revenue items procured by local purchase but destined for the capital, represented by "official exchange silk thread" and tribute tax sale silk; and (2) revenue for purely provincial use, here to be collected in such forms as cedar bark for roofing, horses and men for the transport of goods, and, notably, an impost of rice in ear presumably produced on provincially cultivated fields.

"Provincially cultivated fields" were, originally, maintained by corvée labor for the benefit of the governor and other regular provincial officers.[155] It is very possible that the fields of Ōyama-no-*shō* had been provincial fields of this kind before acquisition by Tōji, but in any case, the location of the fields supposedly dedicated to administrative expenses may not have been a major consideration. As we have seen earlier, official direct cultivation of fields was by now a virtual impossibility. The cultivation of provincial fields had always been a labor charge on the populace for the upkeep of official institutions (including the officials themselves). By the early tenth century, the rendering of such produce rice had to be mediated through the local gentry, as did the cedar bark and transport power, human and animal, also mentioned here. All these contributions to the ad-

---

153 Communication of Tōji of Shōhei 5(935)/10/25, *HIB* 1:360, doc. 245, discussed in Murai, *Kodai kokka*, pp. 97–110; Nakano, *Ritsuryōsei shakai kaitai katei no kenkyū*, pp. 210–7; Satō, *Heian zenki seijishi josetsu*, pp. 284–94.
154 Declaration of Usa Hachiman Shrine of Kampyō 7(895)/11/17, *HIB* 9:3464–70, doc. 4549; Tōji communication of Enchō 2(924)/8/7, *HIB* 1:328, doc. 219.
155 On provincially managed fields, see Abe, *Heian zenki seijishi no kenkyū*, pp. 43–46, 134–40; Abe, *Owari no kuni gebumi no kenkyū*, pp. 212–13; Murai, *Kodai kokka*, pp. 271–80; Nagayama, *Ritsuryō futan taikei no kenkyū*, pp. 288–89.

ministrative overhead of the province that originally came under the heading of "irregular corvée" (or *zōyō*) were now, when imposed on the *tato* gentry, *rinji zōyaku*.

Rinji zōyaku, here as in all other documents of the period, was treated as categorically distinct from imposts like *denso* and *shōzei*, grain taxes for which the *kokuga* was directly accountable to the central government. But *rinji zōyaku* was not simply a reconstituted form of provincial corvée. As illustrated by the "official exchange silk thread" and "tribute tax sale silk" mentioned in the document, it also included the forced procurement of tax commodities for the central government. This was the system of "exchange," the official purchase of tax commodities at rates fixed by the *kokuga*. The local elite had become crucial agents of procurement in an area where local and capital budgets intersected.

The use of provincial rice revenues for commodity purchases was a long-established practice, and the government regularly stipulated conversion values for each item demanded. These evaluations were controlling, however, only in transactions between *kokuga* and central government, and the *zuryō* governors had, within limits established by provincial precedent, the opportunity to purchase tax commodities from provincial grain at lower rates, and, in at least some cases, to enrich themselves in the process. A petition lodged against the governor of Owari Province in 988, in complaining about his abuses of the official exchange system, reveals the existence of an unofficial exchange network in which the grain value of silk was much higher.

This system of "exchange" (*kōeki*) often caused conflict between governors and local elites. Forced purchases financed by *suiko* payments and land rents (*chishi*) from "surplus unallotted" fields, had begun in Nara times. By the tenth century, each province had fixed exchange quotas, and *kōeki* had become a major source of tax commodities. The steady decline in directly collected commodity taxes, *chō* and *yō*, prompted the central government to permit larger and larger amounts of provincial grain to be used for exchange, and the system sometimes faltered when *zuryō* governors pleaded that grain reserves were insufficient to meet procurement quotas. In such cases, the governors, with tacit acquiescence from the capital, procured the tax items at a forcibly reduced price (*genjiki*).[156] The

---

[156] On the "exchange" system, see Murai, *Kodai kokka*, pp. 80–116; Murao, *Ritsuryō zaiseishi no kenkyū*, pp. 331–51, 199–239; Nagayama, *Ritsuryō futan taikei no kenkyū*, pp. 288–90; Nakano, *Ritsuryōsei shakai kaitai katei no kenkyū*, pp. 199–239.

growth of the exchange-procurement system probably contributed substantially to the growth of gentry power in the countryside. "Exchange" was essentially a tax limited to the rich and powerful, the only group that could provide the required commodities, and the expansion of the procurement system increased the *kokuga*'s dependence on them. By the middle of the tenth century, this system of procurement was often viewed by the increasingly vocal local elites as a kind of illegitimate commandeering. Their growing command of provincial wealth, confronted by the increasingly discretionary powers of the *zuryō*, led to an escalation of accusations and recriminations that the high nobility of Kyoto could not afford to ignore.

Even under the *ritsuryō*, provincial officials had considerable discretionary taxing authority. The code permitted them to demand up to sixty days of extra labor annually from every able-bodied male in their districts for work not explicitly required by the provision of law. One consequence of this definition was, for example, that repairs or maintenance of existing irrigation works, explicitly required by the codes, were not counted as extra labor, while construction of new facilities was. This onerous requirement was the "irregular corvée," *zōyō*, already mentioned. Although reduced to thirty days during the eighth century, it seems to have been regularly abused by provincial officers. *Zōyō*, along with the obligations of the peasantry to provide transport labor to and from the capital, accounted for a major fraction of provincial revenues. It is therefore reasonable to conclude that *rinji zōyaku* was an outgrowth of this discretionary taxing authority. A further indication of this is that "households of the gods" (*kambe*), originally exempt from *zōyō*, were also held exempt from *rinji zōyaku*.[157] Even in the eighth century, it should be noted, demands for materials as well as labor could be defined as *zōyō*, as was the commandeering of pack horses.[158]

The fraction of special irregular duties paid to the central government, usually in response to orders issued annually to each province, became increasingly important later in the tenth century. Shortages in standard *shōzei* funds and the consequent difficulty in procuring exchange items was one reason why the government in the capital relied increasingly on emergency demands. Underlying the changing relationships between capital and provinces were changes in the *zuryō* governor's position vis-à-vis the local elite.

[157] Nakano, *Ritsuryōsei shakai kaitai katei no kenkyū*, pp. 212–16.
[158] Nagayama, *Ritsuryō futan taikei no kenkyū*, pp. 82–113; Yoshida, "Ritsuryō ni okeru zōyō no kitei to sono kaishaku," pp. 233–62.

It is clear that, by the early tenth century, "capable farmers" (*kambyakushō*) like the Ōyama *tato* Heishū and Seihō, were routinely assuming the tax burdens of the peasantry under their economic domination. Heishū and Seihō paid these redefined obligations to *gun*-based collection agents, like the "responsible inspector" for the village of Amaribe in Tamba who, in 932, confiscated grain from their residences when the required commodities were not forthcoming. The authority of such collection agents, too, was becoming a kind of estate prerogative, and a higher order of gentry was taking shape on the *gun* level.[159]

Heishū and Seihō were, the sources indicate, in control of fields beyond Ōyama-no-shō. Such capable farmers were in a sense purchasing the labor of state subjects by guaranteeing tax payment on their behalf, or, more realistically, paying in taxes for the power they had acquired over peasant labor. Moreover, the report that when presented with the collection agent's demands, Heishū and Seihō fled the district, cannot be taken too literally. In fact, their absence was quite temporary, and the sources show that they were back a few years later, in the same position as before. Such *tato* were indispensable to the operation of tenth-century provincial taxation. According to a document of 988, for example, each official village of Owari Province had four or five *tato* responsible for land dues, an estimate suggesting that the entire province, of perhaps 55,000 souls, had about 300 of this type of tax provider.[160]

Not coincidentally, *rinji zōyaku* came into being just at the time when the *kokuga* was coming to rely on a limited number of tax providers, at least some of whom produced goods and forced labor as surrogates for the original peasant taxpayers. Taxes of the special irregular type, listed together with *denso* and *shōzei* by the Ōyama-no-shō custodians as potential encumbrances on *shōen* revenues, would in this context appear to be a land tax, but the documentary history of Ōyama and other holdings of the time does not support this conclusion entirely. In the case of Ōyama-no-shō, the arguments for exemption from special irregular duties did not rest on the character of the land as such, but on the immunity of its *tato* from *chō* and *yō*, collectively termed *kaeki*. Earlier, in 924, Tōji had requested the Tamba provincial headquarters to exempt the *shō* custodians and *tato* from *rinji zōyaku*.[161] The principal arguments advanced in that

---

159 Abe, "Sekkanki ni okeru chōzei taikei to kokuga," pp. 29–55.
160 Abe, *Owari no kuni gebumi no kenkyū*, pp. 145–53.
161 Tōji communication of Enchō 2(924)/8/7, *HIB* 1:328, doc. 219.

communication were: (1) that the *shō* was certified as exempt temple land by the Council of State and the Ministry of Popular Affairs; (2) that in 920 Tadahira had caused the then incumbent governor to recognize "ten unlisted migrants" for the benefit of the estate, thus immunizing the *tato* involved from *chō* and *yō;* and that (3) all previous governors had acknowledged the holding's immunity, as set forth in the prior governor's certificate exempting the custodians and *tato* from *rinji zōyaku.* The term "unlisted migrants" (*chōgai rōnin*) refers to *rōnin* deliberately taken off the *rōnin* register (but undoubtedly listed elsewhere) and thus made exempt from all formal head taxes (*kaeki*) otherwise due to the central government.[162] The sequence of arguments strongly suggests that the nonlisted *rōnin* were in fact the *tato* themselves, and that their immunities were predicated on their services to Tōji on its Ōyama estate. This linkage to the estate exonerated them from liability for what were in origin personal obligations to the state. But for most gentry, who lacked such advantages, the obligations were probably as much based on command over labor power and grain as on occupation of land. The Ōyama documents also illustrate how migrants, anomalous and illegal under the original *ritsuryō* system, had become an integral element in local tax gathering structures.

The authority to impose *rinji zōyaku,* or to grant exemptions from it, was a discretionary power of the incumbent *zuryō* governor. In this respect, the tax was exactly like the old provincial corvée, *zōyō,* and fundamentally different from *chō* and *yō,* imposts under the control of the central government. Conversely, governmentally sanctioned exemptions from *chō* and *yō,* such as those enjoyed by the *tato* of the Ōyama estate, were no guarantee of exemption from *rinji zōyaku.* The records show that each successive governor had to be asked for the exemption, and, as in the case cited here, the *tato* could often expect help from the proprietary temple in procuring a central government order commanding the governor to desist.

The series of taxes collectively regarded as special irregular duties could, most probably, be demanded of any nonexempt person, but the principal objects of the levies were inevitably those rich and powerful who were able to bear the burden. These heterogenous imposts, imposed by the *kokuga* without the aid of elaborate census reports, were simply collected from those listed as able to pay. This system of subscribed taxes, consisting of local arrangements made

---

162 Nakano, *Ritsuryōsei shakai kaitai katei no kenkyū*, pp. 201–7.

without monitoring from the capital, demonstrates the growing autonomy of the *kokuga* and its by now self-perpetuating stratum of resident officials.

By the end of the tenth century, special irregular duties had become a major revenue source for the central government, particularly, as already noted, for occasional expenses such as court festivals or palace construction. The court was thus taking a share in the governor's discretionary power to tap into free floating resources. Increasing reliance on "occasional" demands, and on the *zuryō* governors' ability to extract extraordinary revenues, contributed substantially in the eleventh century to the granting of *zuryō* appointments for the purpose of accomplishing special projects.[163]

The position of the listed, or "named," tax subscribers most certainly permitted some considerable degree of informal authority over peasant labor, and was undoubtedly a manifestation of the growth of patrimonial authority on the local level. The tax providers' economic base was concentrated in stored rice holdings as much as in land, and their personal power over their clients was not truly that of a domanial landlord. Their power, however, was domanial in a very special sense. The grain storehouses of the powerful *tato* were located in his residential compound, and his dependents, reduced to clientage, were considered to belong to his menage. This was the sort of establishment referred to as *shō* houses in the reformist edicts cited earlier, and was to develop into the local lordship (usually justified by assertions of reclamation) of the twelfth century.[164] The Ōyama estate did not in fact obtain unconditional immunity against *rinji zōyaku* from Kyoto until the early twelfth century.[165] This power of the *kokuga* was most important for the later development of the *shōen*, as it enabled the governors to establish partially immune holdings in their provinces without permission from Kyoto.[166]

Despite the conflicts over *fukandenden* (uncultivatable fields) and damage reports that so preoccupied the officials of the early Heian era, rice land continued to be a most important object of taxation, and the early tenth century regime quickly evolved a new method of securing its share, while at the same time condoning expanded discretionary powers for the governors. With the allotment system aban-

---

163 Takeuchi Rizō, *Jiryō shōen no kenkyū* (Tokyo: Yoshikawa kōbunkan, 1983 reprint), pp. 1–77.
164 Toda, *Ryōshusei*, pp. 5–8, 73–113.
165 Order of Eikyū 2(1114)/11/6, *HIB* 5:1637–39, doc. 1181. See Abe, "Sekkanki ni okeru chōzei taikei to kokuga," pp. 29–55; Miyagawa, *Ōyama sonshi, Hombun hen*, pp. 96–99.
166 On the so-called *zōyakumen shōen*, see Murai, *Kodai kokka*, pp. 351–72.

doned, and periodic compilations of allotment maps and registers discontinued, the central government instead maintained a permanent set of standard land maps for every province, on which exempt temple and *shō* fields were noted by grid square location. All other rice paddy under cultivation, whether within formal *shōen* boundaries or not, was, if under cultivation, to be considered taxable. This was the system applied to newly opened fields of Ōyama-no-shō, as seen above. Governors, or, more accurately, their surrogates, made a complete survey of cultivated fields once during each new gubernatorial term, and the *tokoro* in charge of the actual assessment came to be an important organ of negotiation between *zuryō* and local gentry. The governor's agents, with the participation of the local cultivators and resident officialdom, decided, within the quotas established by map registration and damage allowances, how much *kammotsu* was due from each holding.[167] By the late tenth century, in fact, *tato*-managed rice fields were being taxed at higher rates than ever before, compensating the government, at least partly, for the loss of immediate power over peasant labor.

LOCAL ELITES AS A POLITICAL FORCE

The trend toward discretionary taxes negotiated with the local gentry led to marked increase of political activity on their part. A striking example of this may be seen in the "Petition of the *Gun* Magistrates and Farmers of Owari Province," an impeachment of the incumbent *zuryō* governor presented to the Council of State in 988. By this time, a regularized procedure for the presentation of such complaints in the capital had been established. Meanwhile, direct allusions to the general population, "the people," had disappeared from official documents since about 950, to be replaced by phrases such as "*gun* magistrates and farmers (*hyakushō*)," unambiguous references to the local elite.

The appearance of a hundred or more demonstrators in front of the Yōmei palace gate, bearing a petition for reappointment of a locally esteemed governor, or the dismissal of an unpopular one, was a commonplace event in Kyoto during the tenth and early eleventh centuries. Usually but not always peaceful, this petitioning fre-

---

167 Abe, *Heian zenki seijishi no kenkyū*, pp. 305–13; Inagaki, "Ritsuryōseiteki tochi seido no kaitai," pp. 139–72; Sakamoto, *Nihon ōchō kokka taisei ron*, pp. 1–137; Toda, *Ryōshusei*, p. 96.

quently brought about the desired result. Confrontational negotiation could be effective because officials in the capital were mindful of the increasing incidence of violence against governors in the countryside. Demonstrators were not unequivocally hostile, but they could be impressively tough-looking. On at least two such occasions, in 987 and 1019, certain courtiers considered recruiting the more menacing of the visiting provincials as *sumō* wrestlers.[168]

Owari was probably seen as an especially troublesome province in 988. An earlier governor had been impeached in 974, and, in 939, another had been murdered. The detailed, and floridly written, thirty-one-part accusation of 988 stresses the illegality, only occasionally defined in *ritsuryō* terms, of the governor's behavior, especially his confiscatory tax policies. It asserts that the *tato* had been required to pay a total of 13.2 sheaves per *tan* of paddy, in the following components:

Official goods (*kammotsu*)	1 to 6 *shō*
Field-tax grain (*sokoku*)	3 to 6 *shō*
Tax fund dues (*shōzei*)	1 to 4 *shō* (2.8 sheaves)
Total tax per *tan*	6 to 6 *shō* (13.2 sheaves)

If, as the document clearly states, the governor collected 13.2 sheaves per *tan,* he had surpassed the highest land rent (*chishi*) permitted by the *ritsuryō* for government leasing of surplus unallotted land. That was only 10 sheaves, payable for a year's cultivation of one *tan* of upper-grade paddy, having an assessed yield of 50 sheaves (25 *to* of threshed grain). Although this rate of taxation was protested by the petitioners as illegally high, the somewhat lower levels attributed to prior governors was still far higher than those of the ninth century. Article Five of the petition estimates total land-tax returns at 1 million sheaves, which, taken at the rate 132 sheaves per *chō*, would indicate a total paddy area of about 7,576 *chō* for the province, somewhat more than the 6,280 given by another source, but not implausible, particularly in the light of the petition's further charge that the governor had deliberately overestimated rice land under cultivation.[169]

Of the three categories of tax on rice fields listed in the petition,

---

[168] General discussions of this document, and the whole process of petition and protest, can be found in Abe, *Owari no kuni gebumi no kenkyū;* Morita, *Heian jidai seijishi kenkyū*, pp. 227–60; Nakano, *Ritsuryōsei shakai kaitai katei no kenkyū*, pp. 247–71; Sakamoto, *Nihon ōchō kokka taisei ron*, pp. 203–22; Satō, *Heian zenki seijishi josetsu*, pp. 339–59.
[169] Abe, *Owari no kuni gebumi no kenkyū*, p. 94.

tax fund dues (*shōzei*) appears to have been a kind of ad hoc surtax imposed in addition to normal *shōzei* quotas and without any distribution of principal, "without passing through any special demand for court expenditures, but simply applied to his [the governor's] privately planned uses, either to be used up in trading or hulled and transported to his house in the capital." The second listed category, field-tax grain (*sokoku*), was treated as not totally outrageous but merely excessive. The *ritsuryō* rate for *so* was a modest 1.5 sheaves per *tan*, or, in grain, 7 *shō* 5 *gō*, while the 3 to 6 *shō* mentioned in the complaint is nearly five times that amount. The text expressing this complaint shows that the *ritsuryō* rule governing *so* was, as a practical matter, a dead letter:

> As for field tax grain, the official law has set limits. That being the case, successive governors, although they plead standard damage (*reison*), nonetheless assess the full amount. Some provincial governors exact one *to* five *shō*, and some demand two *to* or less, but the incumbent Motonaga no Ason [Fujiwara no Motonaga, fl. 985–98] has increased the impost to three *to* six *shō*. Never has there been such an example before.

Although the "official law" or Council of State decree (*kampō*) said to regulate *so* rates cannot now be identified, it is clear from the text as a whole that the actual rate was established, within limits, by the discretion of the governors. That would have been unthinkable by *ritsuryō* standards, and the two *to* per *tan* given as a maximum was still nearly three times the amount prescribed by the *ryō*. The governor's use of "standard damage" claims to divert *so* revenues further demonstrates the increasing latitude the *zuryō* could exercise in dealing with local resources.

The protest about the third category, official goods (*kammotsu*), centered on the *ritsuryō* distinction between unallotted rice fields rented out on a yearly basis (*chishiden*) and fields that had been distributed to subjects, including both *kubunden* and *konden*. In *ritsuryō* parlance the latter type had been considered "private," that is, distributed by the government to its subjects for their private welfare. Such fields, as they were subject to *so*, were also called "taxable fields" (*sozeiden*). *Chishiden* was, in theory, land still in the hands of the state, "public" land awaiting redistribution and let out for rental in the meantime. As *tato* agriculture had become the general rule, and allotment was no longer a possibility, this distinction had lost much of its original force. Nevertheless, a difference in tax costs persisted. *Chishiden*, being in theory "public," was free of "tax," yielding only *chishi* rent. While *chishi* rates remained stable, however, taxes imposed on *sozeiden* had increased, and *chishiden* had now become the more advantageous tenure.[170]

In the words of the complaint, "Both types of field should be taxed in accordance with the order of the Ministry of Popular Affairs, but, committing an abuse of law [*ōbō*], he increases taxes as if all were *sozeiden* and thus, for the *tato* farmers, there is no little distress." Although the Ministry of Popular Affairs order mentioned here has not been found, it seems, at least in the minds of the protesters, to have precluded discretionary tax increments on *chishi*-paying fields. The use of the technical *ritsu* term "abuse of law," besides accentuating the general tone of impeachment, implies wrongful conversion of revenue.

In the *ritsuryō* order, allotment fields had been the typical form of *sozeiden*. They were regarded as providing the peasant household with a financial basis for the payment of produce and labor exacted as head taxes. *Chishiden* was free, originally, from all association with personal taxes, but in the tenth century it became ever move closely integrated with the general revenue system. In 925, as we have seen, the Council of State ruled that *kubunden* abandoned because of flight or pestilence should be rented out for *chishi* and the proceeds used to purchase *chō* and *yō* articles.[171] This illustrates a more general shift away from taxation of households to taxation of grain revenues and the administration of land. As the management of agriculture, presumed under the *ritsuryō* system to be an official monopoly, passed to the *tato*, all land so managed became the same. Motonaga's imposition of the added tax on *chishiden* was, in the light of these developments, far from illogical, and anticipated the eleventh century abandonment of the old legal distinction between public and private fields.

This distinction between *chishiden* and *sozeiden*, no longer grounded on the fiscal requirements of the *ritsuryō* state, embodied yet another growing incongruity. The *ritsuryō* assumption was that a landholder had to choose between transfer of possession for a promised rental of about one-fifth the yield, or retention of possession and cultivation with the aid of paid or household labor ("direct cultivation"), even when the owner was the government or a government agency. That assumption was not at all consistent with local practice. As we have already seen, government landholding inevitably involved gentry cultivators with whom the product had to be shared. The *ritsuryō* rules were not intended to accommodate for domanial possession.

170 Abe, *Owari no kuni gebumi no kenkyū*, pp. 77–78.   171 See note 94, above.

Article Twenty-nine of the 988 Owari petition charges Motonaga's "kindred and retainers" with "forcing all the *gun* magistrates and farmers to cultivate possessory fields (*tsukuda*)," and then taking the yield. While demonstrating the surprisingly large amounts of rice land potentially available for immediate appropriation by incoming governors and their personal staffs, the passage shows that these fields remained under gentry management. The principal complaint of this passage concerns the cultivation charges imposed on the local gentry, and the failure to reimburse them from the yield. The operative portion of the complaint states:

> No sooner did his kin and retainers arrive, on the day office was transferred, their possessory fields filled the province and not a single household was overlooked in assigning them for cultivation. Especially the possessory fields of his son Yorikata, four or five *chō* in some *gun* and seven or eight *chō* in some villages, distributed for cultivation throughout the eight *gun*, are extremely numerous. On the day for granting loan rice (*suiko*), management provisions are not assigned to those ordered to work the possessory fields, but when the time for collection comes, with no regard for consent or protest, the rice is taken. This is in fact a seizure of paid-in official goods in the form of harvest rice from forced cultivation. This is to say nothing of the four or five *to* of rice per *tan* taken by the collection agents as local produce [taxes]. When these accumulations are added up, they reach twice the amount of legitimate official tax goods.

The authors of this text seem to have felt no need to explain the legal basis for this expropriation of land. Perhaps, as some have suggested, the land was deserted *kubunden,* or, perhaps, land falling within standardized *fukandenden* exemptions.[172] In any case, it is most probable that Motonaga's kin and retainers were exercising usufruct powers over lands already under the management of the several households mentioned, and that the language implying direct cultivation should not be taken too literally. Especially noteworthy in this connection is the dispersal of Yorikata's "possessory fields" throughout the province. There is, furthermore, another reference to Motonaga's efforts to provide for his retainers asserting that "he seizes the customary tillages (*reisaku*) of the *gunji* and makes them tillages of his retainers." "Customary tillages" were abandoned fields that these magistrates had been allowed to take over for an indefinite period.

Unlike the private acquisitions of *zuryō* class nobles, however, the *tsukuda* distributed by Motonaga was unquestionably a holding of the *kokuga* dedicated to the support of provincial officers. Since

---

172 Abe, *Owari no kuni gebumi no kenkyū,* pp. 210–13.

other articles in the petition accuse Motonaga of failure to distribute stipends due the other regular appointees, the issue of inequitable distribution was clearly significant, but the main burden of this particular accusation is the grievance of the *gun* magistrates and "farmers" (meaning tax-providing farmers as elsewhere throughout the petition) assigned to carry out the cultivation of so-called possessory fields.[173] The lands controlled by each *tato* household fell within a variety of administrative categories, including "provincially managed fields," that were vulnerable to expropriation by the governors.

The expropriations complained of here, however, could not have entailed any wholesale shifts in actual management. Basically, the *tato* managing this *tsukuda* were complaining of an insufficient share in the proceeds. Providing management and labor costs theoretically entitled the holder to take the entire harvest, but "management provisions" had become quite generous and, at least in the case given here, the "possessor" was not expected to take all that was harvested. Otherwise, how could Motonaga's kin take an *additional* "four or five *to* per *tan*"? The "management provisions" (*eiryō*) in this case were unquestionably distributed out of provincial *shōzei* funds. This is clear from the statements that *eiryō* was awarded in conjunction with *suiko* loan rice and that seizure of harvested rice without deducting the *eiryō* portion was in effect the theft of official tax goods (*kammotsu*). The *gun* magistrates and farmers, or at least some of them, seem to have found, under more relaxed circumstances, the management of provincial lands quite profitable, even though the legal system failed to account for the profits. Viewed from this perspective, Motonaga was attempting to reassert control over sources of wealth that were gradually being removed from the oversight of the capital.

Possessory lands, as indicated by the quoted passage, were benefice fields assigned by the *kokuga* to the upkeep of regular and irregular local officials, without close regard for *ritsuryō* quotas for stipendary fields. The added complaint that Motonaga's followers had usurped fields privately administered by *gun* magistrates points up the conflicting interests of *gunji*, irregular *kokuga* officers, and *zuryō* in the disposition of local land revenues. By the middle of the eleventh century, clearly stipulated benefice fields were a prominent feature of every provincial regime, constituting a kind of *shōen* administered by the *kokuga* for the benefit of its officials.[174]

---

173 Abe, *Owari no kuni gebumi no kenkyū*, pp. 142–43.
174 Morita, "Heian chūki gunji ni tsuite no ichikōsatsu," pp. 208–17.

The growing, but as yet imprecisely defined, authority of the *kokuga* to control the distribution of free-floating resources such as these benefices was a major factor in the repeated conflicts between *zuryō* and provincials. One important effect of this was a gradual consolidation of *kokuga* and *gun* networks into a consolidated whole. The Owari petition alleges that provincial benefices and *gunji* fields were appropriated by Motonaga's private staff, who then encroached on the authority of the *gun* magistrates and local officers to preside over land surveys. Surveying and tax gathering were becoming estate prerogatives of the "resident officials" of the *kokuga*'s "offices" (*tokoro*).[175]

Conflicts between *zuryō* and provincial elites over provincial resources of this type, removed as they were from the capital's immediate distributive power, were not direct challenges to the Kyoto court's authority. The struggle between capital and countryside was buffered by the *zuryō* and the opportunities he had for extralegal gain. There was nevertheless considerable potential for future conflict, as the court tapped into the governor's discretionary prerogatives in the form of *rinji zōyaku,* the extraordinary irregular levies already discussed.

Even when acting on behalf of the state's proprietary interest in official goods, the *zuryō* was in an equivocal position. The 988 Owari petition's most striking illustration of this is undoubtedly in its eighth article. This reveals that quantities of tax cloth, grain, and other forms of official goods were

> seized from the persons of the *gunji* on the claim that it is the accumulated liability of their districts, and from the homesteads of the people. On the rationale that it is their proportionate dues, they seize things fraudulently and without cause. When one or two houses are broken into, devastation reaches ten or twenty places....

One of the more significant features of this item of complaint is that, once again, despite its indignant tone, the actions it described were not all violations of *ritsuryō* rules. *Gun* authorities, for example, had often been held personally responsible for taxes not collected in their districts. Complaints elsewhere in the petition that the governor "illegally" increased grain taxes or reduced the exchange price for tribute silk and other tax commodities describe actions that, however unfair they may have been, did not actually violate the written law. On the contrary, such measures can be seen as perfectly proper

---

175 Morita, *Heian jidai seijishi kenkyū*, pp. 239–41; Toda, *Ryōshusei*, pp. 360–61.

means of achieving the revenue goals of the *ritsuryō* state, and, a century or so earlier, would probably have evoked little comment.[176] But the rise of local gentry to controlling positions in the *kokuga* and *gun* meant the displacement of administrative regulation by estate-oriented customary law.

The *gunji* and farmers, in asserting legal norms appropriate to their position, cited provincial precedent in four instances, all of them prescribing limitations on the quantity of items that could be taken as tax, setting new boundaries that, in the eleventh century, would be formalized in rules like "the rule of *kammotsu* apportionment," setting limits on the dues the landholder had to pay.[177] The property interests of the provincial rich and powerful of the provinces were thus awarded a much greater degree of legal protection than the Owari gentry could have hoped for.[178]

In terms of legitimate authority, the most powerful of the local elite before the eleventh century were probably still the *gunji*. Although new kinds of tax-gathering agents, with new titles, were appointed by the *kokuga* in the late tenth century, these seem mostly to have been centered on the *gun* headquarters rather than the provincial capital. The *gun* and its officials survived in somewhat altered form, and appointments were made largely in recognition of the power they already possessed.[179] *Gunji* were leading figures in uprisings like Masakado's rebellion and numerous other less spectacular acts of armed resistance to the authority of provincial governors. Ninth-century *gunji* sometimes exhibited truly impressive power. In 856, Kagami no Yoshio, chief magistrate of Kagami *gun* in Mino Province, and Kagami no Yoshimune, chief magistrate of neighboring Atsumi *gun* in the same province, led a force of "over seven hundred men" in an attack on a government-approved water project. The Kiso (then called the Hirono) River, flowing between the provinces of Mino and Owari over a marshy, flood-prone plain, had changed its course, inundating land on the Owari side, and the Owari governor had received permission to return it to its original course, probably by digging out the blocked channel. Thus began a short inter-provincial war, to which the Kyoto authorities seem to have reacted rather mildly. The Mino governor, who shared legal responsibility for *gunji* misconduct, was simply transferred to another

---

176 Nakano, *Ritsuryōsei shakai kaitai katei no kenkyū*, pp. 247–71. 177 See note 12, above.
178 Ishimoda Shō, "Kodai hō," in *Kodai, IK*, vol. 4, pp. 291–333.
179 Morita, "Heian chūki gunji ni tsuite no ichikōsatsu," pp. 208–17.

province, as was the governor of Owari. What, if anything, actually happened to the offending *gunji* has escaped the records.[180]

The power to marshal such a numerous force, probably including some resident palace guardsmen, could not have depended merely on accumulated wealth, and was surely linked to the *gunji*'s central role in the collection and exchange of tax goods and particularly the holding and distribution of *shōzei* tax rice. *Gunji*, the immediate superiors of a large staff of "irregular officials," certified all land transfers for the *kokuga*'s approval. They were also, by law, jointly responsible with the governor for conducting land surveys, a duty, as we have seen, with considerable potential for conflict.

In addition to their official stipendary fields (six *chō* for the chief magistrate) and possibly other possessory lands, higher-level *gun* officers occupied one or more parcels of land that constituted, as we have seen, a mixed portfolio of private and public holdings. Such parcels were made up of irrigated paddy of various kinds, often including proprietary reclaimed rice fields (*konden*) and unirrigated grain or garden plots scattered piecemeal around a central "house." The house, from which cultivation was directed, was comparable to the "*shō* houses" on lands of nobles and temples, and included granaries and storage facilities. Hata no Tametatsu, the *kaihatsu ryōshu* of the late eleventh century mentioned earlier, held *gunji* office.[181]

The Owari petition provides good evidence that agricultural administration from houses or homesteads, typical of *tato* cultivation in general, had saturated the entire province. It also shows that the scale of agricultural management was usually small, a fact reflected by the establishment of official branch granaries in local areas, partially replacing storage facilities concentrated at the *gun* headquarters. A prosperous house with its own granary, or a granary holding consigned government rice, could extend its influence to neighboring lands through rice loans or assumption of commodity tax obligations. The *gunji* retained much of their importance in the tax exchange and distribution system well into the eleventh century, as well as constabulary and land-surveying powers.

In Atsumi *gun* of Mino Province, the scene of the 856 disturbance just outlined, the *gunji* remained as the major local power right into the twelfth century. Opposition of the *gunji* and his "sycophant

---

180 Entries for Jōgan 7(865)/12/27, *Sandai jitsuroku, KT* 4:169; Jōgan 8(866)/7/9, *Sandai jitsuroku, KT* 4:191; Jōgan 8(866)/7/26, *Sandai jitsuroku, KT* 4:192; Satō, *Heian zenki seijishi josetsu*, pp. 159–67.
181 Toda, *Ryōshusei*, pp. 116–32.

party" was effective against attempts by Tōdaiji to expand Akanabe-no-shō there, and the documents generated by the conflict indicate that land surveys and maps were very largely under *gunji* control. Although the *ritsuryō* titles for *gun* offices had nearly disappeared in favor of *tokoro*-like functional designations, *gun*-based authorities were clearly the major powers to be reckoned with by outsiders.[182] The loss of the old custodial monopoly over official goods in the ninth century, and the later growth of domains within their territories, did not mean their extinction.[183]

Gunji power did not, of course, always go unchallenged. As revenues received in the capital steadily decreased and a combination of factionalism and hereditary prerogative restricted access to office there, resettlement in the provinces became an attractive option for the middle nobility. Transplanted nobility, very often the descendants of former governors, could sometimes rival longer-established elites, and rivalry of this kind was an important factor in Masakado's rebellion. Cooperation from *zuryō* governors, continuing patronage from high noble households, and intermarriage with *gunji* families were major elements in the establishment of immigrant nobles in the countryside. During the ninth century, and especially during the last decade when the Kyoto government was beginning its last serious attempt to revive the old *ritsuryō* order, the Council of State did its best to prohibit the resettlement of nobles as an unwarranted burden on provincial administration. By the middle of the tenth century, on the other hand, the court was sufficiently reconciled to this new group to grant some of them regular appointments as vice-governors or lower in their provinces of residence. As a consequence of this new deviation from Chinese bureaucratic norms of avoidance, a new class of resident official, holding regular rather than irregular provincial office, appeared in the *kokuga* structure. The Owari petition reveals that the commissioned (*nin'yō*) officers, now almost entirely powerless, had the right to participate in land surveys and, denied this by the governor's personal retinue, sided with the resident officials against him.

The challenge to *zuryō* authority by local officers was strongest in the frontier provinces of the northeast. Even during Miyoshi Kiyoyuki's tenure as governor of Bitchū, a few of the local notables he found intimidating held posts on the lowest level of regular provin-

---

182 Koizumi, "Tōdaijiryō Akanabe-no-shō," pp. 430–548.
183 Murai, *Kodai kokka*, pp. 43–58, 347–50; Abe, *Heian zenki seijishi no kenkyū*, pp. 30–32.

cial office,[184] but the preemption of *kokuga* posts by transplanted nobility, besides adding new tensions to an already volatile situation in the outlying provinces, was a particularly ominous sign for the future of court authority.

Yet the Owari petition and numerous other sources demonstrate that control over provincial wealth was largely in the hands of the rich and powerful. Of these "capable farmers," some, especially those on the *gunji* level, were far more powerful than others, and were, like Hata no Tametatsu, destined to become the *shiki*-holding regional lords of the twelfth and thirteenth centuries. Their local, and largely unofficial, control of peasant labor and land, justified by their role as tax subscribers, constituted the chief guarantee of revenue for the *zuryō* governors and, ultimately, the court in the Heian capital.[185] While the *shōen* prohibitions of the late ninth and early tenth centuries pointed up the court's hostility toward the rich and powerful and condemned their efforts to seek protection from the nobility, the government of the late ninth century was more inclined to compromise with the rural elites who constituted its new tax base. The *gunji* and farmers of the 988 Owari petition could express their grievances in an indignant, self-confident tone.

The role of land in the newly developing system of taxation reinforced the importance of the grain-holding elite, who, as capable farmers, paid taxes on land they dominated but did not technically own. Taxes levied directly on irrigated rice fields were, as the 988 petition attests, higher than those prescribed by the *ritsuryō*, but there were limits established by custom. In the early eleventh century these limits were very precisely defined in each province. In Iga Province, for example, the rate per *tan* was:[186]

Actual rice: up to 3 *to* (1 *to* delivered to capital granaries)
Oil 1 *gō*
Rice equivalent: 1 *to* 7 *shō* 2 *gō*
Actual rice in ear: 1 sheaf
Rice in ear: 2 sheaves

This formula, specifying exactly what the *tato* should pay, including how much rice should be threshed and where it should be delivered,

---

184 Abe, *Heian zenki seijishi no kenkyū*, pp. 28–248; Tokoro, *Miyoshi no Kiyoyuki*, pp. 41–70.
185 Takada, "Chūsei shoki no kokka kenryoku to sonraku," pp. 6–25.
186 Petition of resident officials of Iga, Hōan 3(1122)/2, *HIB* 5:171–72 doc. 1958; see also tax assessment of Ōta-inumaru myō, Eishō 1(1046), *HIB* 3:774–75, doc. 639, and Katsuyama, "Kōden kammotsu rippō no seiritsu to sono zentei," pp. 1–43; Murai, *Kodai kokka*, pp. 320–27.

expressed a kind of compact between the capital and the provincials, eliminating some of the uncertainties that had occasioned complaints against *zuryō* governors, although the imposition of extraordinary levies continued under various guises. More important than the precision of the formula, however, was the generality with which it was applied. These were the dues to be paid on all rice lands in the disposal or taxing power of the *kokuga*. The older distinction between *chishiden* and *sozeiden* no longer mattered, as all such land was regarded as public field (*kōden*), as distinguished from fields enjoying some sort of exemption. Of equal importance is the way these rules provided special rates for specific areas called *betsumyō*, literally, "special names." Like the settlement established by Hata no Tametatsu in the late eleventh century, these entities may be regarded as embryonic forms of the medieval *shōen*. Provincial certification of *betsumyō*, sometimes headed by more than one proprietor, was one way the governors could come to terms with the more eminent of the rural gentry.

The definition of the term "public fields" changed accordingly. Public fields were now fields within the provincial domain, whether leased to *tato* from year to year or held as absolute property under the rule of reclamation. The emergence of the provincial domain, and the evolution of the *kokuga* into a kind of estate management agency, was largely the result of the rise of the *tato* class.

The dichotomy between providing tax-rice and cultivating land is one clue as to why local lordships were so slow to develop. *Fumyō* owed their position in the first instance to their control over movable wealth, official rice consignments, rather than land. This wealth enabled them to finance agriculture beyond their own households, giving them de facto control over land owned or occupied by others. As the Owari petition put it, by despoiling one household, a rapacious official could ruin several others. The distinction between *fumyō* and *tato*, fundamentally a distinction based on the kind of assets being administered, broke down in the late eleventh and early twelfth centuries, the same time that term *myō* ("name") came to be applied to a landholding and the cultivators on it, viewed as a single unit. Only then had the power of the tax providers over their clients matured into dominion over the land they cultivated, and the exploitation of people become, in the emerging system of customary law, the exploitation of land. While showing how different the rural societies of the tenth and twelfth centuries were, the Owari petition marks a crucial stage in the transition from autocratic bureaucracy to estatist polity.

APPENDIX: NOTE ON HEIAN MEASURES

Area

1 *bu* = 3.3 sq. meters, a square, 1.8 meters to a side
1 *tan* = 360 *bu* = 1,190 sq. meters, always a rectangular area, typically 54 × 21.6 meters (30 × 12 *bu*)
1 *chō* = 10 *tan* = 11,900 sq. meters, a square, 108 meters (60 *bu*) to a side

Length (land or distance measures)

1 *shaku* = 10 *sun* = 29.7 cm
1 *bu* = 6 *shaku* = 1.8 meters
1 *chō* = 60 *bu* = 108 meters

Volume

For the measure of grain or metal, the codes mandated a standard *shō* measure called a "large *shō*."

1 *shaku* = 7.2 cc
1 *gō* = 10 *shaku* = 72 cc
1 *shō* (the "large *shō*") = 10 *gō* = .72 liters
1 *to* = 10 *shō* = 7.2 liters
1 *koku* = 10 *to* = 72 liters

For measuring other commodities, the code required the use of the "small *shō*," which was exactly one-third the volume of the standard "large *shō*" used for grain.

Sheaf measure

1 grip, *ha*, yields approx. 5 *gō* of hulled rice
1 sheaf, *soku* = 10 *ha*, yields approx. 5 *shō* of hulled rice

The most fundamental unit of volume applied to grain was the *shō*, officially standardized by a measuring box, *masu*. During the eighth century, when the *ritsuryō* system was at its height, one *shō* was about 720 cc. During the ensuing three centuries, volume measure was far from uniform, and it is not often possible to give absolute equivalents for the units of volume that appear in the sources. It is clear that from the tenth century onward, units of volume grew larger. One famous attempt at restandardization, the *senji masu*, or "decree measure" promulgated by the court of Emperor Go-Sanjō in 1072, set one *shō* at approximately 1.2 liters (one of the very few figures still available), but by that time, both local authorities and estate proprietors had established their own standard measures.

The *ritsuryō* text gives the *so* tax rate as 2.2 sheaves per *tan*. This misleading number represents an unsuccessful attempt to redefine grain quantities at the time the Taihō codes were promulgated (702) and does not reflect any deviation from established practice.

In the old system of the seventh century, it was assumed (very optimistically) that one *shiro*, a rectangular area of approx. 23.8 sq. meters, and made up of five square segments called *bu*, could yield one *soku*, or "sheaf" (actually a bundle of rice ears cut from the top of the stalk). Three *soku* of rice in ear per 100 *shiro* of paddy, or 3% of the putative harvest, regardless of actual yield, were payable as *so*. Notwithstanding other changes, this was the actual rate maintained throughout the *ritsuryō* period.

One *soku* was supposed to yield a volume of 1 *to* of unhulled rice, *momi*, or half that volume, 5 *shō*, of hulled rice, *kome*. One *bu* was accordingly presumed sufficient to produce one *shō* (about 104 cc) of hulled rice. When the rules of the Taihō codes required a reduction in the area of the *bu*, units of grain measure were reduced proportionately in order to maintain this equivalency of *bu* and *shō*.

The new codes discarded the *shiro* but retained the *tan*, a much larger rectangle, typically 10 by 25 pre-code *bu*, 119 square meters in area and the equivalent of 50 of the old *shiro*, or 250 of the old *bu*. Measured by previous standards, the *so* rate for this unit area would have been 1 *soku* 5 *ha*, that is, 1.5 sheaves. The Taihō and Yōrō codes, however, subdivided the *tan* into 360 *bu* rather than 250 as before. A *tan* rectangle of 25 by 10 *bu* was now, under this new surveying standard, 30 by 12. The compilers of the code reduced *soku* and *shō* quantities to correspond with the newly reduced *bu*. One sheaf, or *soku*, in the old system became 1.44 *soku* (36/25) in the new. The amount of *so* due from one *tan*, 1.5 *soku* by the old measure, became, precisely calculated, 2.16 *soku* (1.44 × 1.5). The *Taihō ryō* text, rounding out this amount at the first decimal place, called for the payment of 2 *soku* 2 *ha*, i.e., 2.2 sheaves per *tan*. In explaining these recalculations, commentaries to the codes show that there was never any intention in the codes to change the actual amount of *so* to be collected per unit area.

The older, larger *soku* and *shō* units, abolished in law but not, apparently, in fact, were officially restored in 706, only four years after the Taihō code went into force. The official formula for the *so* rate was accordingly reestablished at 1 *soku* 5 *ha* per *tan,* and remained so thereafter. The newly mandated *bu* unit, linked as it was to surveying and land allotment, became standard.

CHAPTER 5

CHINESE LEARNING AND INTELLECTUAL LIFE

INTRODUCTION AND ASSIMILATION OF CHINESE LEARNING

The subject of this chapter is the learning of the Heian upper class – not all of it, by any means, but that portion of it which was regarded as fundamental in the education of males and which, even in times of decline, enjoyed the highest formal prestige. "Chinese learning," for our purposes, can be defined as the reading and writing of Chinese and those kinds of knowledge most directly dependent on learned traditions which boasted Chinese roots. Our focus will be on government, Confucian study, and belles lettres – overlapping categories in the Heian context. We will touch on those aspects of law mostly directly related to Chinese learning and its exponents, but we will largely leave aside some other forms of Chinese knowledge such as medicine, various kinds of divination, the calendar, and explication of the sutras. Mathematics, though important to the practice of government and included among the curricula of the state Academy (*Daigaku-ryō*), ceased to prosper as a field of study very early in the period. We will leave aside also the important topic of the influence of Chinese learning on such native forms of literature as *waka* and *monogatari*,[1] and on painting, music, and dance.

A view that is fortunately losing currency among Western students of Japan holds that to the Japanese the Chinese language remained permanently alien: if Heian males failed to produce masterpieces of imaginative prose paralleling those of their womenfolk, it was owing to the burden of having to compose in a medium in which they were ill at ease; and if, for example, a Japanese literatus chose to write of Taoist immortals in the belief that such beings also existed in his

---

1 See e.g., Jin'ichi Konishi, *A History of Japanese Literature*, vol. 2: *The Early Middle Ages*, trans. Aileen Gatten (Princeton, N.J.: Princeton University Press, 1986); Helen Craig McCullough, *Brocade by Night: "Kokin wakashū" and the Court Style in Japanese Classical Poetry* (Stanford, Calif.: Stanford University Press, 1985); David Pollack, *The Fracture of Meaning* (Princeton, N.J.: Princeton University Press, 1986).

own land, he must have been playing with "exotic" ideas.[2] It is true that a note of something exotic and foreign clings to the idea of China as it appears in the vernacular literature of the time, with China as a place and the Chinese populace presenting the ultimate challenge to Japanese self-esteem – a challenge that the hero of the narrative always surmounts[3] – and with certain types of Chinese goods enjoying almost a magical cachet. But to the Heian Japanese, Chinese culture and its products existed apart from national boundaries as requisite tools of civilization and, to a very high degree, as the marks of civilization itself.

No precise date can be assigned to the beginnings of Chinese learning in Japan. From the fifth century on, however, the importation of Chinese ideas and techniques expanded rapidly. The process contributed to the growth in authority of the central government in a variety of essential ways, from reinforcing the primacy of the emperor (*tennō*) to providing means of record-keeping for his tax gatherers. Until the arrival of Chinese learning, Japanese society had been unlettered, apparently lacking elaborated theories of government or social ethics, with no formal system of law, and without recorded history or a religious canon. To say that Chinese learning filled a vacuum would, of course, do injustice to the resources of oral tradition, but whatever the power of native tradition, the importations often dealt with categories of thought and practice that had not previously existed in Japan and for which the indigenous language lacked words.

Chinese was the basis of government, both ideal and practical. A bureaucratic system carefully modeled after that of the T'ang and referred to by historians as the "statutory" (*ritsuryō*) regime had reached its apogee in the eighth century. By the beginning of the Heian era, the system had already begun to evolve in new directions; by the beginning of the tenth century, although the conception and rhetoric of Confucian government remained, as did its forms and usages, many of its functions were being carried out by other means. Aristocrats and their clients competed for office, empty or not, within its bureaucracy. Chinese provided the medium for the memorials, decrees, codes, administrative regulations, ordinances, com-

---

2 See, e.g., Michele Marra, review of *Il Dio incatenato: Honchō shinsenden di Ōe no Masafusa*, trans. Silvio Calzolari, *Monumenta Nipponica* 41 (1986): 495–97, quoting a passage from that book.
3 See, e.g., Thomas H. Rohlich, trans., *A Tale of Eleventh-Century Japan: Hamamatsu Chūnagon monogatari* (Princeton, N.J.: Princeton University Press, 1983).

mands, communications, and certificates by which the government functioned. Chinese precedents governed the vocabulary and form of these official writings. Chinese exempla and ethical teachings were invoked to justify decisions of state. Above all, the ritual persona of the ruler, whether emperor or regent, was fashioned according to Confucian patterns.

The earliest bearers of Chinese culture in Japan were continental immigrants (*kikajin*) and their descendants. According to the account in the *Nihon shoki*,[4] Chinese learning began about 400 in the reign of Emperor Ōjin with the coming of an emissary from Paekche named Achiki, who was able to read the classics and who gave instruction to the crown prince. Achiki recommended that a more learned man, Wani, be invited to Japan, and he arrived a year later. Tradition says that Wani presented to the court the *Analects of Confucius* and the *Thousand-Character Classic*. Such accounts reflect the prestige of the two works, not historical fact, if for no other reason than that the *Thousand-Character Classic* was not composed until the sixth century. Wani was said to have been the ancestor of a line of scribes, the Kawachi no Fumi no Obito. A certain Achi no Omi, who claimed to be a descendant of Emperor Ling (r. 168–89) of the Later Han, came a few years later, accompanied by "the people of seventeen *hsien* (districts)," and became the ancestor of the Yamato no Aya no Atae, a large hereditary group of scribes and craftsmen who were followers of the Soga. It was members of such groups, some recently arrived, all with strong memories of their continental past, who carried on the profession of reading and writing.

Not until the beginning of the seventh century with Shōtoku Taishi did there appear the first writings of any length in Chinese composed by a Japanese. By the early Heian, however, the *kikajin* had largely been assimilated among the Japanese population, and their skills had been acquired by Japanese. Although some families still boasted of their continental ancestry, the government no longer felt obliged to make special provision for employing them or educating their sons. The ninth century in particular was a time when Chinese learning thrived in Japan, and books in Chinese by Japanese authors included histories, legal compendia and commentaries, manuals of court procedure, dictionaries, encyclopedias, religious tracts, travel diaries, treatises on a variety of subjects, and poetic anthologies.

---

4 W. G. Aston, trans., *Nihongi* (Rutland, Vt., and Tokyo: Charles E. Tuttle, 1972 reprint), vol. 1, pp. 261–62.

During the two hundred years that preceded the Heian era, the Japanese actively sought Chinese knowledge through repeated embassies: ten such missions to Sui and T'ang are known to have taken place or been attempted during the seventh century, and nine more were begun between 702 and 779, of which seven were completed. The cost was great, both in goods and in human lives. Many of the Japanese who went abroad to study died before they could return home; others, such as Buddhist monks, remained in China for decades. Some – including monks who returned to secular life – married Chinese wives and had children who aided in subsequent missions. Of the men, ranging in number from about a hundred to six hundred per mission, who embarked on the fragile ships, sometimes fewer than half would make their way back. Those who did brought not only books but their personal experiences to shape the statutory regime. The ambassadors themselves were usually of the Fourth Rank, the top of the middle aristocracy, and their immediate subordinates were also men of prominent families. Though none rose to be minister, a substantial proportion subsequently achieved the office of Counselor or Consultant or became professors at the state Academy. Accompanying them to China as students were doctors of medicine, *yin-yang* masters, painters, sculptors, musicians, jewelers, metal casters, and other craftsmen.

Only two more embassies to China took place after 800. The first set sail from Japan in 804 and returned in 806. The second departed in 838, and the last of its four boats came back in 840. A final one planned for 894 was abandoned under the urgings of the prospective ambassador, Sugawara no Michizane (845–903), who cited reports of civil disorder on the continent. The underlying reasons for the cessation of the embassies are still a matter of debate. The government's declining ability to support expenditure on such a scale was undoubtedly a factor, as was the growth of private commerce conducted by Chinese and Koreans, which, together with the frequent arrival of embassies from the Manchurian kingdom of Po-hai, provided a safe and less costly means of maintaining contact.[5]

Japanese monks wishing to travel to China for study could do so privately, while aristocrats were able to obtain through trade the luxury goods they prized. And the Japanese now believed that they had acquired the essentials of Chinese knowledge. They had been seek-

---

5 Robert Borgen, *Sugawara no Michizane and the Early Heian Court*, Harvard East Asian Monographs, 120 (Cambridge, Mass.: Council on East Asian Studies, Harvard University, 1986), pp. 246–50.

ing selectively in China to serve Japanese needs and tastes. One of the chief purposes of the pre-Heian embassies had been to deliver and bring back long-term students (*ryūgakushō*) and monks (*ryūgakusō*). In contrast, those who went abroad in the two ninth-century embassies were *shōyakushō* ("students seeking to gain"), specialists sent for a few months to resolve doubtful points of interpretation (e.g., of law) or have specific questions answered; if monks (*shōyakusō*), to bring back doctrinal tracts lacking in Japan, receive initiation into orthodox lineages, and copy holy images.[6] The selectivity of the Japanese borrowings, whether of law or of styles in Chinese poetry, is a theme that must be constantly kept in mind in any study of Japan's cultural relations with the continent.

To what extent Chinese learning had been imported into Japan by the end of the ninth century, as well as which aspects enjoyed the most prestige, is suggested by a bibliography, *Nihonkoku genzai shomokuroku,* compiled in 891 upon imperial order, to inventory the books remaining in the country after the Reizeiin, a former imperial mansion that housed a library collected over generations, was destroyed by fire in 875. The books listed in it totaled almost 19,000 scrolls (*maki*); and although the titles of native works are mixed in among them, the number of books brought from China – most of them as a result of the embassies – is impressive. The compiler, Fujiwara no Sukeyo (847–97), was a prominent literatus who enjoyed the patronage of the regent Fujiwara no Mototsune (836–91).[7] Sukeyo modeled his catalogue after the bibliographical essay in the *Sui shu,* the official history of the Sui dynasty (581–618). Its forty categories begin with the Confucian classics and include law, medicine, agriculture, warfare, astronomy, the calendar, the "five elements," and the works of the various philosophical schools. Especially large categories were those having to do with ritual and with various kinds of historical writing. The extant catalogue lists almost 1,400 scrolls of Chinese dynastic histories and almost 2,000 scrolls of books on rites and ceremonies. More emphasis is given to belles lettres than to the classics – reflecting a T'ang taste that was especially

---

6 Charlotte von Verschuer, *Les Relations officielles du Japon avec la Chine aux viiie et ixe siècles* (Paris: Librairie Droz, 1985); Edwin O. Reischauer, *Ennin's Travels in T'ang China* (New York: Ronald Press, 1955); Robert Borgen, "The Case of the Plagiaristic Journal: A Curious Passage from *Jōjin's Diary*," in Aileen Gatten and Anthony Hood Chambers, eds., *New Leaves: Studies and Translations of Japanese Literature in Honor of Edward G. Seidensticker* (Ann Arbor: Center for Japanese Studies, University of Michigan, 1993), pp. 63–88.
7 Ohase Keikichi, *Nihonkoku genzai shomokuroku kaisetsu kō* (Tokyo: Komiyama shuppan, 1976). For Sukeyo, see Marian Ury, "The Ōe Conversations," *Monumenta Nipponica* 48 (1993): 370.

congenial to the Japanese – and a number of books by Chinese authors appear in it that are not listed in continental bibliographies, several of which have been discovered at Tun-huang. And probably there were other books not deemed worthy of being entered into an official bibliography: handbooks, practical books of various sorts, and volumes to amuse and instruct the less educated, women, and children.[8]

Chinese learning was both assimilated and appropriated into the indigenous culture. As a separate cultural tradition or gathering of traditions, however, Chinese learning became itself a Japanese tradition. Reified, it was possessed, transmitted, hoarded, honored, displayed, boasted of, cultivated, and lamented when it failed to flourish. It came to have its own patriarchs, a history, and curiosities. The most appropriate metaphor might be that of a fund of intellectual capital, consisting of the segment of Heian Japan's intellectual inheritance that depended directly on the use of the Chinese language and education in Chinese books. Originally brought in from abroad, it still received supplements from abroad, though in reduced number, but during the Heian era it can also be seen replenishing itself from its own resources. The intent of this chapter is to describe this Chinese intellectual capital, to portray those who made particular claim to ownership of it, the ways in which they acquired it and the environments in which they utilized it, and to suggest something of its evolution during the first three centuries of the Heian period. The texts it produced are very much more difficult than those of the vernacular traditions, while the aesthetic, spiritual, and moral needs it served are generally alien to contemporaries, Japanese as well as Westerners, in contrast with the more ingratiating and – perhaps only superficially – more accessible intellectuality of the salons that produced the vernacular literature, much of it written by women. The study of the *bunjin* (literati) – virtually all of them men – and their world has suffered comparative neglect, but acquaintance with the subject suggests that the fund of Chinese learning supported a weighty and on occasion lively intellectual life.

Whether or not he was destined to become a professional literatus, a little boy of the Heian upper class would typically begin to learn written characters in his sixth or seventh year – about age five by Western count. First would come the matriculation ceremony: the child's teacher would read aloud the first few characters of the *Clas-*

---

8 Kawaguchi Hisao, *Heianchō no kambungaku* (Tokyo: Yoshikawa kōbunkan, 1981), pp. 71–74.

sic of Filial Piety (*Hsiao ching*) as annotated by the T'ang emperor Hsüan-tsung (r. 712–56), and the child would pronounce them several times after him before the lesson was adjourned for the serious business of congratulations and feasting. In learned families, the teacher was likely to be some senior relative; among the highest nobility, an eminent literatus client. Crown princes were provided with two Confucian tutors, and the post was a great honor. No one thought it odd when a tutor was appointed for a crown prince who was only six months old; as with many other Heian institutions, the ceremonial function was considered to be of absolute value even in the absence of practical activities. In addition to the *Classic of Filial Piety*, beginners were taught the *Thousand-Character Classic*, *Meng ch'iu*, and extracts from the poets.

Meng ch'iu consists of 592 four-character phrases, each recounting the name and salient characteristic or deed of some famous person, the phrases arranged into rhymed couplets for easy memorization.[9] Commentaries, and presumably also the teacher, helped explain the often cryptic text. Learning was by memorization, and memorization meant repeating aloud; students preparing for Academy examinations were expected to memorize commentaries as well as the texts themselves. The student would be expected to be able to recite the Chinese reading for each character, its equivalent in Japanese, and the interpretation. Heian scholars had not yet devised the standardized method of reading Chinese texts known as *kundoku*, in which words are rearranged and grammatical features added in order to convert the Chinese original into pseudo-Japanese. Texts were read aloud word by word as they appeared in the Chinese and then read a second time rendered into Japanese, in a manner which would have seemed free by later standards. Different schools, moreover, had different traditions for Japanizing their texts: that of the Ōe, for example, was freer and more Japanese-sounding than that of the conservative Sugawara.

Chinese was not taught as a spoken language. At the beginning of the Heian period there were Japanese – many of them of recent continental descent – who had facility in spoken Chinese, but the ability had all but disappeared by Michizane's time, so that by the end of the period for a Japanese to be able to speak in Chinese at all was cause for amazement. But the student's education would not have

---

9 Burton Watson, trans., *Meng ch'iu: Famous Episodes from Chinese History and Legend* (Tokyo: Kodansha International, 1986).

proceeded without reference to the sounds of Chinese. There were teachers of pronunciation, of Chinese descent, at the Academy, at least during its prosperous early days. A sign of the lack of contact with oral Chinese was that in composing Chinese verse, the Japanese generally simplified the prosodic rules having to do with tone, while observing those for rhyme.[10] Both rhymes and tones might be dealt with through the aid of handbooks and dictionaries. But the Japanese were not themselves quite deaf to tone: Japanese lexicographers of the period recorded the pitch patterns of native words by a method developed from that used for the notation of Chinese tones.[11]

Works such as *Meng ch'iu* provided Japanese learners with a fund of historical and exemplary lore, a mainstay of elegant discourse. *Meng ch'iu*, moreover, drew its material from a wide variety of canonical Chinese works, with which its male (or sometimes, as in the case of Sei Shōnagon, female) user could therefore become acquainted at second hand. In addition to primers from China, the Heian beginner would also be given compendia of fundamental knowledge written in the Chinese language by Japanese authors. Such a work was *Kuchizusami* (the title might be loosely translated "Fun with Recitation," or just "Fun with Learning"), written in 970 by Minamoto no Tamenori (d. 1011) for Matsuo-gimi, Fujiwara no Tamemitsu's oldest son, then in his seventh year. Tamenori was also the author of a collection of maxims, of a handbook of government offices, and of *Sambō ekotoba*, a collection of pious anecdotes to provide seemly amusement for a young princess turned nun.[12] As a nonpareil beginner's book, *Kuchizusami* was probably inspired by *Wamyō ruijū shō* (comp. 935), a dictionary-encyclopedia of Japanese words arranged by category of meaning, compiled (at the order of a scholarly princess) by Tamenori's teacher Minamoto no Shitagō (911–83). (The categories in *Wamyō ruiū shō*, in turn, were inspired by those of a Chinese encyclopedia compiled by the T'ang poet Po Chü-i). The work became highly popular almost immediately after its compilation and continued to be widely used, serving also as the basis for late-Heian educational compendia.[13] One of its virtues was its accuracy: Ōe no Masafusa (1041–1111), who admired Tamenori,

---

10 Konishi, *A History of Japanese Literature*, vol. 2, p. 49.
11 Oka Kazuo, ed., *Heianchō bungaku jiten* (Tokyo: Tōyōdō, 1972), p. 332.
12 Translated by Edward Kamens in his *The Three Jewels: A Study and Translation of Minamoto Tamenori's Sanbōe* (Ann Arbor: Center for Japanese Studies, University of Michigan, 1988).
13 Kawase Kazuma, *Kojisho no kenkyū* (Tokyo: Kōdansha, 1955), pp. 155–60.

found only two lapses in it, each involving a single character.¹⁴ Tamenori's purpose of supplementing *Meng ch'iu* with material that is "near" is mentioned in the preface in which he speaks of his young charge, naturally endowed with intelligence but not yet used to memorizing, fond of play and fond of singing. Now, if he will sing these words out he will commit them to memory; he must constantly keep this book in his hand as a plaything. . . .¹⁵ The teacher's affection for the boy, easy to read between the lines, suggests a human dimension that historians too often overlook.

As a guide to what was considered essential knowledge for the young Heian aristocrat, *Kuchizusami* well repays attention. The work, about twenty-five pages in modern type with no commentary except its author's own, presents its information under nineteen categories ("gates," *mon*), subdivided into "stanzas" (*kyoku*), here denoting memorizable units of various lengths. Many – almost certainly the majority – are lists of things and enumerations: the three luminaries, the seven stars, the three great edifices, the twenty-five great monasteries, the five tones, the seven tones, the eight tones, the days of Buddhist observance, the gates of the palace, the bureaus of the Ministry of Ceremonial. Under the category of "Geography" are listed the three passes, the seven high mountains, the nine tumuli, and the three bridges. The knowledge that is taught is of two principal kinds: that which is needed in public life, and that which will most directly concern the personal well-being of the learner.

Science for its own sake does not exist, nor do abstractions. The Heian mind was quite incurious about the natural world. Here and there are mentioned some facts of Japanese history, but there is rather more of Chinese. Much emphasis is placed on magical observances and recitations: the commentary in the opening section, "Heavenly Phenomena," informs the learner of the locations of the star deities – important because these were taboo directions¹⁶ – and the category following, "Periods Within the Year," includes formulas to be said to the deities of the four quarters and on *Kōshin* night so as to avoid contracting illness. *Ommyōdō*, the Taoist divinatory science, is a major category, while the category of "Medicines," which, significantly, immediately follows it, is largely concerned with lucky

---

14 Kawaguchi Hisao and Nara Shōichi, *Gōdanshō chū* (Tokyo: Benseisha, 1984), pp. 1277–81; for an introduction and partial translation of this important source, see Ury, "The Ōe Conversations," pp. 359–80.
15 *Zoku Gunsho ruijū* (Tokyo: Keizai zasshi sha, 1960 reprint), vol. 32.1, p. 61 (doc. 930).
16 Bernard Frank, *Kata-imi et Kata-tagae: Étude sur les interdits de direction à l'époque Heian*, Bulletin de la Maison Franco-Japonaise, n.s., 5:2–4 (1958), passim.

and unlucky days on which to dose oneself. The book includes a rather thorough primer of Buddhism, emphasizing praxis and with a number of hymns and gāthas to memorize. Among "Animals" are hawks (giving the dates when various provinces offer them as tribute to the court), horses (including a charm to recite that will cure diseases of horses' bellies), the *shishimushi*, a cicada-like insect whose cry was thought to foretell death, and the *nue*, a thrush whose sad song was associated with unrequited love. Units of measurement are of the greatest importance to the future official as he is likely to be concerned with tax assessments and tax collections, and thus appear throughout the book under various categories, enumerated in great detail and what seems to be every possible variation: two sets of names for units of houses, from 5 to 2,500 (under "Dwellings"); measurements of length, area, and capacity (under "Agricultural Land and Buildings"); how many years constitute a generation (under "Periods of Years"). The final category in the book, headed simply "Miscellaneous," consists of yet more terms of weight and measurement and ends with a multiplication table, starting with 9×9 and going downward 1×1, followed by a list of characters for powers of ten; fourteen are given.

The activities of civilization, in the Heian scheme, had their focus within the imperial compound. It is not surprising, then, that the lengthiest category in the text, at least in its extant form, lists the structures of the palace; it also describes the divisions of the capital city, which would be viewed logically as an extension of the palace. Another lengthy category lists government offices. The category headed "Human Beings" typifies in miniature the mode of Heian learning: it brings together lists of the five emperors of Chinese high antiquity; the three dynasties of Hsia, Yin, and Chou; the eleven emperors of the Former and the twelve of the Later Han; the nine lesser disciples of Confucius, and other lists of worthies of ancient and legendary antiquity; the names for the barbarians of the four directions; the six kinds of portentous dreams; the three conditions under which a man cannot spurn his wife; the seven grounds for divorcing her; the three kinds of subordination which she owes ("to her father before marriage, to her husband upon marriage, and to her son after her husband's death"); the three persons to whom a man owes loyalty ("Father, teacher, and lord"); the organs and cavities of the body; words for various degrees of direct ancestor and direct descendant; kinds of persons and transgressions to be forgiven; the dangerous years in human life ("13, 25, 37, 49, 61, 73, 85, 91"); a charm to protect against a bad dream or make a good dream come true, to be recited under a mulberry tree three times; and a verse to chant should one come across a dead man in the road at night.

Readers of *The Tale of Genji* will remember the skill with which the hero, a paragon at least in his public behavior, dances and plays a number of musical instruments. The lengthy section devoted to "Music" accurately reflects the esteem that was accorded musical performance in public and private life. The most essential of all fields of knowledge, however, was surely that represented by the category of "Writings" (*shoseki*). Heading its lists are those of the five, seven, and eleven classics, the three histories (the *Records of the Historian* [*Shih chi*] and the two *Histories of the Han* [*Han shu* and *Hou Han shu*]), the eight dynastic histories from Wei through T'ang, the forms of verse (*bun*) and the forms of literary prose (*hitsu*). Tamenori's commentary supplies a succinct definition: "If it rhymes, it is *bun;* if it lacks rhyme, it is *hitsu. Bun* is put together in units of two phrases (*ku*); *hitsu* is made up of units of four phrases." There follow some simple rules of prosody: a pattern each for five-syllable and seven-syllable regulated verse (Chinese, *lü-shih*); the seven "sicknesses" of poetry; the seven kinds of antithesis to be used in the central couplets of regulated verse; the six kinds of poetry and principles of poetic rhetoric (those enunciated in the *Greater Preface* to the *Book of Odes* [*Shih ching*]); the system of recording pronunciation of Chinese words, known as *fan-ch'ieh*, used in Chinese dictionaries; the names of the four tones; and the long lists of rhyme-word categories divided by tone that one needed to know in order to consult a Chinese dictionary generally as well as, specifically, to compose Chinese verse. It is interesting to note that Tamenori mixes current with antiquated information. When he compiled his textbook, the T'ang history was only twenty-five years old, a recent work by leisurely Heian standards. In the terms he uses to distinguish prose from poetry, however, he follows Six Dynasties usage; by the T'ang, *bun* had come to mean prose (poetry was *shi*).

The remainder of Tamenori's category of "Writings" is given over to Japanese; but whereas the Chinese items felt to be pertinent were the classics and histories, along with aspects of Chinese rhetoric useful to Japanese who would have to compose in that language or at least demonstrate discrimination in regard to the compositions of others, Japanese books are of only two kinds, both, of course, following Chinese models, both written in the Chinese language, and both equally, from the Heian way of thinking, essential to civilization. These are the Six National Histories (*Rikkokushi*) and the legal codes (writings to be discussed later in this chapter). The compilation of the codes is of some interest to Tamenori: one of his commentaries gives the dates over which this work took place, and a second commentary gives a brief history of the interest of the emperor in legal compilation, beginning with the Seventeen Articles of Shōtoku Taishi. The major divisions within the administrative code (*ryō*) and the criminal code (*ritsu*) are enumerated, and this is followed by an abbreviated list of the eight kinds of oppression and six of the eight "deliberations" as to personal status of the criminal that require amelioration of punishment, a prominent feature of Chinese law.[17] Following, Tamenori offers a verse to help in remembering the Japanese syllabary. Using the forty-seven syllables once each, it is written in the full forms of Chinese characters in the manner of the *Man'yōshū*. Tamenori comments that most people recite the more familiar one that goes "*Ame tsuchi* . . . ," but that his is better.

As an adult, Tamenori's young pupil would have been expected to be able to compose a passable Chinese verse, with correct rhyme words, in one of the Chinese *shih* patterns for arranging tones. That might be as part of the entertainment of a particularly elegant banquet, with everyone pleasantly tipsy, or a formal outing. On more ceremonious occasions, unless he were of a particularly scholarly bent, and quite likely even then, he would present a poem composed on his behalf by a professional literatus. If a composition in parallel prose, the ornate Chinese style that later would come to be known as *p'ien wen*, was required – such as the dedication (*gammon*) that would accompany a gift to a Buddhist temple – he would almost certainly rely on the services of an eminent literatus, in whose personal anthology it would later appear. Such writing was fraught with difficulty, and literati themselves would on occasion commission these documents from colleagues of especial talent and reputation. In his informal writing, the official would ordinarily use less formal Chinese with an admixture in various degrees of Japanese usages, the style varying with the topic and the purpose of the document, as well as the aptitude and education of the writer.

The advanced learner could also rely on compendia. Compiled in

---

17 See Wallace Johnson, trans., *The T'ang Code*, vol. 1: *General Principles* (Princeton, N.J.: Princeton University Press, 1979), pp. 88–104.

the year of its author's death for the youthful Fujiwara no Yorimichi (992–1074), Tamenori's *Sezoku gembun,* the volume of maxims previously mentioned, is an assemblage of useful quotations from Chinese books, arranged by category. Only one of its three original scrolls survives, but it is noteworthy for the range of its sources, quoting no fewer than fifty-three different Chinese books, each meticulously noted by the author.[18] They include the *Analects,* the *Odes,* the *Spring and Autumn Annals* with its commentaries, the *Documents (Shu),* the *Rites (Li chi),* the *Classic of Filial Piety* – all belonging to the Confucian canon – the *Records of the Historian* and the two *Histories of the Han,* and to a lesser degree the histories of the Wei and the Chin, and *A New Account of Tales of the World (Shih shuo hsin yü,* a fifth-century collection of witty anecdotes about intellectuals of the centuries preceding). Works associated with the Taoist tradition, in some cases tangentially, are also cited. *Chuang tzu, Lao tzu, Lieh tzu, Huai-nan tzu, Pao-p'u tzu,* the fantastic geography *Shan-hai ching,* and the legends of the Taoist immortals are quoted. Study of such texts, the *Chuang tzu* especially, was popular with the literati, even though these books were not included in the curricula of the Academy. The Ōe in particular interested themselves in the Taoist sciences, several of them winning reputations as accomplished physiognomists. Of books composed in Japan, only the *Nihon shoki,* first of the National Histories, and the *ryō,* the administrative code, are represented here.

Owing to the nature of the compendium, some other books that figure prominently in Heian education are omitted. Missing are two works that had to be memorized for one of the civil service examinations: the dictionary *Erh ya,* part of the Confucian canon, and the literary anthology *Wen hsüan,* which supplies numerous quotations throughout Heian writing in Chinese. The poems of the beloved Po Chü-i (772–846) and his friend Yüan Chen (779–831), popular sources of couplets for decorating painted screens and singing in the elegant style called *rōei,* are also missing. *Sezoku gembun* falls short of being fully representative of the learned culture of its time in its omission too of the belletristic works in Chinese of the Japanese themselves. Those of Sugawara no Michizane (or rather, the most successful couplets from them) enjoyed great esteem. Japanese literati in general took a lively interest in one another's works, so that the author of an outstanding composition (which is to say, one that

18 Described in Kawase, *Kojisho,* pp. 164–66.

contained a particularly fine couplet) might find that news of it had traveled even to colleagues serving in the provinces.[19]

In a world in which a quotation from a Chinese classic constituted the proof that would clinch any argument and in which the ascertainment of precedent was the first concern in matters ranging from literary judgment to government edict, a collection such as that just described fulfilled very practical needs. Serious scholars, of course, would also study the texts in their entirety. One of the emperor's prescribed activities was to hear lectures on the Chinese classics, histories, and poetic anthologies; the occasions of such lectures, given by the most eminent literati, are recorded in the National Histories. Lectures and debates were part of the *sekiten,* the ceremony to Confucius performed twice annually at the Academy, in the second and eighth months. Lectures were also held in the regent's mansion; their occurrence often indicates genuine interest in the work itself, as well as affirmation through ceremony, of the patron's status. On six known occasions before 965, the court sponsored series of lectures on the *Nihon shoki,* although – as Tamenori's selection suggests – no such attention was given the subsequent histories of Japan. Among popular texts for lectures were books that combined moral instruction with pragmatic advice on the conduct of life. *Shuo yüan* (late first century B.C.E.), a collection of anecdotes teaching the behavior proper to persons in various stations in life, and *Yen-shih chia-hsüu* (late sixth century), written to provide guidance to its author's sons and grandsons on personal decorum and conduct within the family, were much studied. Both works are quoted in *Sezoku gembun.* Especially valued by the Japanese rulers was *Chen-kuan cheng-yao,* a collection of the conversations of the second emperor of the T'ang with his ministers about the art of government. This text too was frequently lectured upon. Heian Japanese themselves, it might be added, also wrote advice to their successors and descendants, among the earliest and best-known examples of works of this genre being *Kampyō goyuikai,* composed in 879 by Emperor Uda upon ceding the throne, and *Kujō Ushōjō yuikai,* by the Minister of the Right Fujiwara no Morosuke (908–60);[20] both of these works, which

---

19 Ōe no Masafusa, "Bonen no ki," collected in Yamagishi Tokuhei, Takeuchi Rizō, Ienaga Saburō, Ōsone Shōsuke, eds., *Kodai seiji shakai shisō,* vol. 8 of *Nihon shisō taikei* (Tokyo: Iwanami shoten, 1979), pp. 161–64. My translation of this work appears in "Ōe no Masafusa and the Practice of Heian Autobiography," *Monumenta Nipponica* 51 (1996): 143–51.
20 In *Kodai seiji shakai shisō,* pp. 103–14, 115–22. For the former, see Borgen, *Sugawara no Michizane,* pp. 213–15; translation of the latter is in Inge-Lore Kluge, "Fujiwara Morosuke und seine 'Hinterlassene Lehre'," *Mitteilungen des Instituts für Orientforschung* 1 (1953): 178–87.

served as models for later ones, are of extremely practical bent, the emperor commenting on the talents of certain individuals at court, and the Minister of the Right even on such specific matters as the lucky days for cutting finger- and toenails.

IDEAL OF THE SAGE-KING

At the center of Chinese learning and Confucian teaching in the Heian scheme was an idea of the Chinese sage-king, superimposed on the original sacerdotal and tribal role of the Japanese *tennō*. The sage-king should be puissant but, as the ideal imagined him, able to rule through moral force alone. The emperor could give evidence of his Confucian sagehood by meticulous attention to court ceremonies and by selecting and rewarding good men. He should request men of outstanding talent and rectitude to advise and admonish him. Whether or not the advice of these ministers had substantive content, the process of requesting and receiving the memorials remained of value as ritual. The degree to which government was seen to inhere in observance of ritual proprieties cannot be overstated. They were simultaneously an essential element in the processes of the state and the essential emblem of all civil order.

According to the ideal, the emperor should conduct himself at all times in the knowledge that Confucian histories, written by impartial observers, would hold him accountable for his actions, and he should command the compilation of such histories of the reigns of his predecessors as mirrors for future generations. He should honor the aged and virtuous throughout the kingdom and exemplify filial piety in his reverence toward his own parents. He should pay due attention to omens and portents reported to him and alleviate the lot of the poor in time of drought or disaster by remission of their taxes, himself setting examples of frugality and admonishing his courtiers against luxury. He should encourage Confucian education and show honor to learned men: if aged as well as learned, so much the better. He should promote Chinese literature. This last was one of the most conspicuous activities of the sinified Japanese courts of the first century and a half of the Heian period. Adult emperors and ex-emperors, whether in possession of some power to rule as well as reign or, like Uda (r. 887–97) after his abdication, largely impotent in the political arena, presided over banquets at which high- and middle-ranking courtiers assembled with professors from the Academy, who generally held more modest ranks, to compose verse in Chinese on conventional subjects. The emperors themselves were usually practicing poets, and the banquets were conducted in an atmosphere of great elegance.

Whether a given Japanese emperor was able to exercise the actual powers of a ruler was largely beyond his control. The monarch whose powers to govern were most like those of his Chinese counterparts was Kammu (r. 781–806). His court was hospitable to literati, and he himself, before his accession, had held the post of Head of the Academy. But he was too much occupied with practical affairs to cultivate the literary graces himself, and the cost of his removal of the capital from Nara, first to Nagaoka and later to Heian-kyō, was regarded by Confucians as extravagant. It was one of his sons, Saga (r. 809–23), who most assiduously acted out the myth of the Confucian sage-king guiding a Confucian state. From the time of his abdication until his death in 842, Saga continued to dominate the affairs of the court, and the tone that he set persisted through the reigns of his successors, his brother Junna (r. 823–33) and his own son Nimmyō (r. 833–50). Kōnin, the era name (nengō) of Saga's reign often made the designation for the reigns of all three, is viewed as a distinctive period in Japanese cultural history. It has been suggested that what finally ended the enthusiasms of the Kōnin court was not intentional change of policy but rather the ill health of Nimmyō's successor, Montoku (r. 850–58).

Saga and his ministers attempted practical measures to shore up the statutory regime, ordering the reallotment of fields and, with more success, the compilation of laws enacted since the promulgation of the original codes (the *Kōnin kyaku* and *Kōnin shiki*, discussed in a later section). He revived annual ceremonies allowed to lapse by his predecessor Heizei and inaugurated others. He commanded the compilation of a manual of court ceremonial, the *Dairi shiki*.[21] He was a determined sinifier of the manners and customs of his people. In 819 he issued a decree directing that the ceremonies of the realm accord with those of T'ang, that men and women wear T'ang costume, and that diplomas of rank for men of the Fifth Rank and above follow T'ang usage. He decreed also that palace buildings, cloisters, and gates were to bear tablets displaying names in Chinese style. To these measures he was urged by a favorite Confucian, Suga-

---

21 Translated in Michael Charlier, *Das Dairi-shiki: Eine Studie zu seiner Entstehung und Wirkung* (Wiesbaden: Otto Harrassowitz, 1975).

wara no Kiyokimi (770–842), a veteran of the embassy of 804 and grandfather of the celebrated Michizane.

Under Saga, the Academy flourished as never before. As its history will show, however, the age was fascinated more by Chinese belles lettres than by the classics. Frugality, one of the attributes of the ideal sage-king, was neglected by Saga as it was by actual Chinese monarchs; personal rule was combined with a fondness for elegant amusement. The Shinsen'en ("Park of the Divine Spring"), a then spacious garden immediately south of the Greater Imperial Palace enclosure, was the site of many of his poetry banquets. Others were held at the Reizeiin, where Saga inaugurated a new style in luxurious living for retired emperors and installed his library. Characteristically, literature – which is to say, poetry – in Japanese was eclipsed by Chinese in his court. Two of three anthologies of literature in Chinese compiled by imperial command (*chokusenshū*) were produced in his reign: *Ryōunshū* (814), containing 90 poems, was compiled chiefly by Ono no Minemori (778–830), himself a classic exemplar of the Confucian "virtuous official" as well as a man of literary ability; *Bunka shūreishū* (818), with 140 poems, was compiled by a committee headed by Fujiwara no Fuyutsugu (775–826), the leading Fujiwara minister. The third, *Keikokushū* (827), produced under Junna, included prose pieces as well as verse; those heading the committee in charge included the future emperor Nimmyō and one of Saga's half brothers, Yoshimine no Yasuyo. Poems by Sage himself, or written by his courtiers to "harmonize" with his poems, are dominant in all three. His sons, whose education he personally supervised, and at least one of his daughters, shared his enthusiasm for writing Chinese poetry. It is significant that those closest to him in the work of governing – whether aristocrats or bureaucrats – were members of his poetic circle.

Saga and his adherents took their cue from a phrase in the critical treatise *Lun wen* by the Wei emperor Ts'ao P'i (187–226): "Literary composition is a vital force in governing the state." This maxim they interpreted in a more literal sense than could ever have been intended by its author. It is quoted in the preface to *Ryōunshū* and supplies the title of *Keikokushū*, literally, "the anthology for governing the state." In fact, the interests addressed in Saga's own poetry were increasingly aesthetic rather than related to government. Some orthodox Confucians did protest the expenditure involved in the poetic gatherings and revived ceremonies, but their voices were ignored.[22]

22 Gotō Akio, *Heianchō kambungaku ronkō* (Tokyo: Ōfūsha, 1981), pp. 7–53.

It was not the time of Saga that was looked back upon in later years as one of sage-reign but those of Daigo (r. 897–930) and Murakami (r. 946–67); together, their era names, Engi (901–23) and Tenryaku (947–57), came to evoke visions of a golden age. But the reputation of these two emperors is based less on accomplishment than on the fact that each ruled without the aid of a Fujiwara regent. This freedom from Fujiwara control was little more than nominal, however, as Daigo dashed his father Uda's hopes for maintaining some independence when Fujiwara leaders persuaded him to exile Michizane, Uda's protégé and the Fujiwara's presumed rival at court. Daigo exerted his power as Confucian monarch with energy in those spheres that remained open to it, while his ministers for the final time attempted to revive the allotment system. The last of the Confucian histories of Japan to be completed and the last, and definitive, collection of administrative statutes, the *Engi shiki,* were compiled under him. But – again, it is thought, in reaction to their actual powerlessness – Daigo and Uda (at least during his long years in retirement) devoted the major portion of their energy to the refined pleasures. In contrast to the Kōnin era, however, Engi saw a revival of native Japanese styles in the arts. Anthologies of poetry in Chinese would continue to be compiled, but no longer by imperial order; in their place were anthologies of poetry in Japanese, beginning with the classic *Kokinshū* in 905.

The reign of Murakami (946–67) looked back to Engi. Murakami greatly admired his father, Daigo, and, at a time when central and imperial authority had suffered even greater erosion, aspired to reign in his style. In company with his elder brother the ex-emperor Suzaku (r. 930–46), he too engaged in a full program of elegant pleasure. He revived the Chinese poetry banquets, which had been less popular than Japanese ones under Daigo and more recently had been allowed to lapse in favor of cockfights, and he inaugurated contests in Chinese poetry to match those in Japanese begun in the previous century. Such meetings were conducted in luxurious style; on the occasion of the first Chinese poetry contest, for example, the verses composed by both sides were written out by the eminent calligrapher Ono no Michikaze (Tōfū) (894–966). But whereas the Chinese poets who gathered around Saga had been his close advisers and those around Daigo included men whose opinions on practical matters of government might still be solicited by the emperor, the academicians whom Murakami summoned were elderly survivors of his father's time, none of whom occupied a position of importance in his government.

The men of Murakami's time felt tradtional rituals to be in danger of slipping out of use, and thus his court gloried in the production of manuals of ceremonies and court procedures. A handbook of annual ceremonies was written by the Fujiwara regent Morosuke, and Morosuke's successor Saneyori (900–70) was looked upon by later times as the founder of a school of *yūsoku kojitsu,* the study of customs and precedents. But in the actual work of governing Murakami took little interest. His successor was mentally unbalanced and was followed in turn by a child and then by a youth who reigned only two years. Confucian teachings continued to be honored at court; there were still learned men. The age of the sage-king, however, was over; it could not, in any event, have long survived the changes in the statutory system and the weakening of its Confucian-trained bureaucracy.

SIX NATIONAL HISTORIES

The sage-king myth was cultivated in part through the writing of histories in the Chinese manner, or at least in what Japanese had come to regard as the Chinese manner. The Japanese already had completed two such chronicles – *Nihon shoki* (720) and *Shoku Nihongi* (797) – and in the early Heian period added four more to make up what came to be known as the "Six National Histories." Prepared over a period of a little more than eighty years were *Nihon kōki,* commanded by Saga in 819, presented in 840; *Shoku Nihon kōki,* commanded by Montoku in 855, presented in 869; *Nihon Montoku jitsuroku,* commanded by Seiwa in 871 and presented in 879; and *Nihon Sandai jitsuroku,* commanded by Uda in 892 and presented in 901. The sage-king was not to rule alone, but with the guidance and support of wise ministers, whom he rewarded; the writing of history was an enterprise involving both aristocrats and professional literati, requiring energy and expertise, and serving the self-esteem of the compilers as well as those who commissioned it. According to a tenth-century protocol, the committee for compilation of a National History should consist of the highest minister of state, a Consultant to take practical charge, one of the two Major Secretaries (*daigeki*) in the Council of State, and four or five learned men selected from among the officials of the various bureaus.[23] Thus, the original head of the *Nihon kōki* committee was Fujiwara no Fuyutsugu, that for *Shoku Nihon kōki* Fujiwara no Yoshifusa, and for *Montoku jitsuroku,* Fujiwara no Mototsune. Fuyutsugu, with some justification, enjoyed a reputation for Chinese learning, and Yoshifusa seems to have participated actively in the work of his committee. Since the committees also included members too old or too young to be major contributors, it may be assumed that they too were named to lend – or be lent – prestige.

Chinese histories were intended to promote wise government by functioning as impartial mirrors of the successes, failures, virtues, and vices of the successive emperors of a dynasty. If the activity of writing orthodox history was based on the Chinese model, its products deviated from it in some significant ways. In form, Chinese dynastic histories contain tables, biographies, and treatises of various kinds, as well as "basic annals" (*pen-chi*), whereas the extant versions of the Japanese National Histories consist of annals only (*Nihon shoki* originally included an imperial genealogy, now lost). Educated Japanese were well acquainted with Chinese historical writing; in the Academy, the study of the histories (*kidendō*) was a popular subject that came to be amalgamated with the older literature curriculum. The choice of a chronological arrangement was not made either from ignorance or necessarily merely from a preference for simplicity. There are precedents in Chinese usage for such an arrangement, most notably in the *Spring and Autumn Annals.* The Chinese genre that the Japanese histories most resemble, however, is the *shih-lu* (*jitsuroku,* "veritable records"), as the titles of the two last examples acknowledge. *Shih-lu* were compiled after the death of an emperor on the basis of diaries kept by his officials and constituted the stage in the preparation of orthodox history immediately preceding the final one of the dynastic history itself. They departed from strict chronological form only in order to include biographies of notable subjects following the announcement of their deaths, a practice also followed by the Japanese starting with *Shoku Nihongi.* Essentially full drafts, the *shih-lu* awaited the demise of the dynasty to be transformed through supplementation and revision into dynastic histories. Other considerations aside, it was appropriate for the Japanese, already proud of their dynastic continuity, to stop at the *shih-lu* level, as fuller histories might have been taken to imply a break in the imperial line.

23 Sakamoto, Tarō, *The Six National Histories of Japan,* trans. John S. Brownlee (Vancouver: University of British Columbia Press, 1991), p. 97, quoting *Shin gishiki.*

It has been claimed that the Japanese had little understanding of the monitory function that history was supposed to serve. Some of the later National Histories do in fact venture criticism of such safe imperial targets as the scapegrace Heizei and mention in their prefaces that praise and blame are to be impartially bestowed. Nevertheless, the purpose of the Japanese histories lay elsewhere: celebration of the imperial house, glorification of its ministers, and promotion of the image of Japan as a Confucian state. To the last of these ends they present examples of the practice by humble persons of Confucian virtue on a heroic scale, inventing them, one suspects, if necessary. *Montoku jitsuroku*, for example, records the award of the lowest court rank to a woman who had spent thirty years in mourning her deceased husband; the same reward was given as well to a woman who had mourned her husband, raised his children (presumably, though it is not stated, by another wife), and performed works of Buddhist piety. Such exemplary instances, described in admiring detail, are included to suggest that they had been the result of imperial virtue. Auspicious events too might be revered as the consequence of beneficent rule. Upon discovery of a sweet spring in Iwami province, the priests of the emperor's ancestral shrine at Ise, as well as the owner of the property where the spring was found and all officials of the district, were advanced in rank; and gifts of grain were made to the aged (those over a hundred years of age got three *koku* each; those over ninety, two; those over eighty, one) and the era name changed.[24]

The compilers of the histories could draw on the archives of the Bureau of Drawings and Books (*Zushoryō*) and the Ministry of Ceremonial (*Shikibushō*), which collected biographies of meritorious subjects. The deaths of persons of the Fourth Rank and above were supposed to be recorded, and biographies appended if the deceased was of Third Rank or higher. Occasionally biographies also appear even though the deceased was of lower rank, if only to explain why the death of a person of humble station should be worth recording. The largest proportion of such biographies are found in the last two histories, which tend toward the anecdotal. Not all biographies are hagiographical: *Nihon kōki*, in particular, is distinguished by the acuity and occasionally the asperity of its biographies.

It is often possible to trace the influence of individual compilers.

---

24 Osamu Shimizu, "Nihon Montoku Tennō jitsuroku: An Annotated Translation, with a Survey of the Early Ninth Century in Japan," Ph.D. diss., Columbia University, 1951, Saikō 1 (854)/3/9, Saikō 1/5/26, and Saikō 1/11/30.

Haruzumi no Yoshitada (797–870) was the most renowned Confucian of his day, tutor to Crown Prince Tsunesada, afterward professor (*hakase*) at the Academy, ultimately Consultant. He owed his success to the patronage of Yoshifusa, whose chief collaborator he was on *Shoku Nihon kōki*. His hand is seen not least in the frequency with which Yoshifusa's name appears there, even where it need not. *Shoku Nihon kōki*, like *Montoku jitsuroku* after it, covers only one reign, so that it comes even closer in form and spirit to the *shih-lu* than do its predecessors. Nimmyō, its subject, is depicted as the perfect Confucian monarch, with special mention made of his filial respect toward his mother, while imperial children are praised for a preternatural mastery of ceremonial deportment. This emphasis on Confucian etiquette perhaps is also due to Yoshitada, as is the inclusion of many anecdotes of the supernatural, in which he was said to take a keen interest. Miyako no Yoshika (834–79), who was probably the chief contributor to *Montoku jitsuroku*, is thought responsible for including in that work an exceptionally large number of biographies of members of the middle aristocracy; he himself achieved only Junior Fifth Rank Lower Grade.

When Uda commanded the compilation of *Nihon sandai jitsuroku*, he appointed a committee that included his Ministers of the Right and Left, Michizane and Fujiwara no Tokihira, and in the spirit of opposition to Fujiwara power he made head of the committee Minamoto no Yoshiari (845–97), a son of Montoku and the highest-ranking Minamoto who was not too old for the task. When Daigo came to the throne a few months after Yoshiari's death, no new members were added. Michizane (also the author of the preface to *Montoku jitsuroku*) was exiled early in 901, and the work was not completed until mid-autumn. It was Ōkura no Yoshiyuki whom the late-thirteenth-century bibliography *Honchō shojaku mokuroku* lists as the chief author. The aged Yoshiyuki was a particular favorite of Tokihira in the latter's role as Confucian patron. (Tokihira's chief achievement in Chinese belles lettres is represented by *Suisekitei shikan*, the record of a poetry party held, also in 901, to celebrate Yoshiyuki's seventieth year.) With the aid of a disciple, Mimune no Masahira, who was twenty-eight years younger, Yoshiyuki devoted a good part of his energies not only to his patron's but to his own glorification. Although not even of the Fifth Rank, he caused his own name to appear in the text a number of times. The committee itself, the processes by which it was constituted and reconstituted, exemplified the relations between literatus and noble, of which more will be said.

Sandai jitsuroku is the most detailed of all the histories; the goal of the compilers, as stated in its preface, was comprehensiveness. Like its two predecessors it focuses narrowly on the court, recording in detail all imperial rites of passage and also Tokihira's *gempuku* (coming-of-age) ceremony. All of the histories chronicle special rites and festivals, but in addition, *Sandai jitsuroku* also records all of the ordinary seasonal festivals. Texts of decrees and memorials are reproduced in full. The compilers take great interest in Shinto shrines; the new awareness of Japanese roots that in poetry produced the anthology *Kokinshū* is manifested here. Portents are recorded in detail – again, one may perceive a native fondness for anecdote. On the thirtieth day of the fifth month of the fourteenth year of Jōgan (872), a great serpent appeared in one of the halls of the official provincial Buddhist temple in Suruga. There were thirty-one copies of the Heart Sutra wrapped around a single roller, and it ate them. The monks who witnessed this tied a rope around its tail and hung it upside down from a tree. Shortly afterward, it disgorged the sacred books and fell on the ground half dead, but then suddenly revived. Again, on the twenty-ninth day of the seventh month of the second year of Ninna (886), at the hour of the boar (roughly 9–11 P.M.), a giant was seen strolling back and forth within the imperial enclosure, in front of the Shishinden. A page boy posting summonses saw him and fainted from fright, and he was also glimpsed by a man who was lighting torches in front of the station of the Right Bodyguards. Subsequently, in the vicinity of the station of the Left Bodyguards a cry was heard, as of a man strangling. People called the apparition the "strangling ghost."[25]

Sandai jitsuroku was the last of the National Histories to be completed and the last to be preserved, but one more was attempted. In 936, the sixth year of his reign, Daigo's successor Suzaku appointed officers to the History Compilation Bureau (*Senkokushisho*), which had been set up in 880 to take charge of the daily records on which histories were to be based. The first pair of Superintendents were a Fujiwara Major Counselor and a Middle Counselor, with two men of the scholarly Ōe family their nominal assistants. Notices of appointments to the bureau appear in various sources over the next thirty years, from the reign of Suzaku through Murakami's and into Reizei's, but what exactly was produced is unclear. Possibly there was some sort of draft, but it cannot have been more than that, and

---

25 Sakamoto, *Six National Histories*, pp. 178–79.

only a few putative fragments remain. One specific reason for the project's lack of success may have been the age and isolation of the directors, so characteristic of the literati of Murakami's court. Ōe no Asatsuna was sixty-nine when finally made Superintendent in 954, his brother Koretoki even older when he in turn became Superintendent in 957, and they lacked competent helpers.

The cessation of the National Histories was one aspect of the general weakening of all the institutions of the statutory system. Education of the literary technicians who staffed the bureaucracy became formalized and impoverished, as will be seen, and standards of written Chinese declined, except among a devoted few. The bureaucracy itself was becoming an empty shell. There was little financial support for writing history, and the bureaucratic archives on which historians depended for their material were no longer maintained. The record-keeping function of the *Senkokushisho* was inherited by the Secretariat (*Geki no chō*) within the Council of State, and for a time *geki nikki*, secretaries' diaries, were thought to furnish possibilities for the revival of national histories. In 1010, for instance, the *Geki no chō* was ordered to search precedents and report to the throne, but the report must not have been encouraging.[26]

COMPILATION OF STATUTES

If the Six National Histories helped enact as well as record the fiction of a harmonious Confucian state, the compiling of official statutes may well be the one substantive achievement of that state. Initially, legal scholarship had consisted of compiling whole new codes, culminating in the *Yōrō ritsuryō*, drafted in 718 but not promulgated until 757. Attention then turned to explication and two important commentaries were compiled early in the Heian period. The first, *Ryō no gige,* written by an officially appointed committee of twelve, was completed in 833 and authorized the following year; the second, *Ryō no shūge,* was the private work of a single legal scholar, Koremune no Naomoto, who completed it during the Jōgan era (859–77). It is only in these commentaries that the texts of the original codes are preserved. The codes themselves, however, were not the only basis of early Japanese law. Over the years, many new regulations were issued either modifying the codes or detailing how they should be enforced. These were promulgated as various forms

26 Sakamoto, *Histories,* p. 191.

of imperial edicts or proclamations by the Council of State, and together they came to be known as *kyaku* and *shiki*. Although the precise distinction is unclear, the *kyaku* usually concerned modifications of the original codes and *shiki*, rules for their enforcement. These statutes were the means by which Japanese court government refined the codes, worked out details for their implementation, and responded to changing circumstances. In the Heian, focus gradually turned to the *kyaku* and *shiki*, which were collected and classified in the Kōnin, Jōgan, and Engi eras – the reigns of Sage, Seiwa, and Daigo. Significantly, although in each case the compilation committee included legal specialists, many of its members were also members of the committees charged with preparation of the National Histories; for example, of the eight men who received the imperial command to revise and expand the Kōnin *kyaku* and *shiki* in the Jōgan era, three were eminent literati who were also compilers of *Montoku jitsuroku*. Heian literati were generalists.

The *Engi shiki* is the major monument of Heian law as well as the most notable achievement of the reign of Emperor Daigo – an expression, moreover, of the belief of his Fujiwara ministers that they were repairing rather than undermining the foundations of the statutory system. Daigo's intention was that Japan be provided with a complete code of *ritsu, ryō, kyaku,* and *shiki*. The command to compile *kyaku* and *shiki* was received in 905 by Tokihira. Among the eleven other members of the original committee were three other nobles, including Ki no Haseo (845–912), Michizane's friend and follower who had managed to remain at peace with Michizane's enemies and been made Consultant in 902, and a certain elderly Taira no Korenori, whom history records also as recipient of a command from Emperor Uda to compile an anthology of Chinese verse composed since the Kōnin era. Below them were eight literati who are surmised to have done the actual work. Among them were the venerable Ōkura no Yoshiyuki and Miyoshi Kiyoyuki (847–918).[27] The lowest ranking member was Koremune no Yoshitsune, a former Professor of Law (*myōbō hakase*). All of the literati were loyal to Tokihira, and most were Yoshiyuki's disciples.

The *kyaku*, in twelve volumes, were completed first, in 907, and authorized in 908. The compilation of the *shiki*, however, dragged on through Daigo's reign and was not finished until 927, after the

---

27 Torao Toshiya, *Engi shiki* (Tokyo: Yoshikawa kōbunkan, 1964), p. 58; see also Tokoro Isao, *Miyoshi Kiyoyuki* (Yoshikawa kōbunkan, 1970), pp. 111–12.

deaths of several members of the original committee, including its head. One reason for the delay was surely the dimensions of the project, since the compilers incorporated the two previous collections of *shiki* into their unified system, along with the great number of individual ordinances that had been issued since the Jōgan period. The resulting work, in fifty *kan*, consists of 3,300 individual articles. But despite its apparent comprehensiveness, the code does not contain *shiki* for such newly created government organs as the Chamberlains' Office (*kurōdodokoro*) and Imperial Police (*kebiishi*). The criterion for inclusion was not whether the office had existed in the original bureaucratic scheme of the statutory system; rather, it seems to have been whether *shiki* for the office in question had appeared in the two previous collections. The *Engi shiki* was therefore a summation of existing and well-established administrative theory and practice, not in any way an attempt to open up new ground, the final stage in the systematization of past forms.

The *Engi shiki* was not authorized until 967, forty years after it was first presented to the throne. Among the reasons for this added delay was the lack of any real need to promulgate it: it merely systematized edicts already in force. Another was that, increasingly, the governmental structure it was supposed to regulate functioned in name only. Yet another, it has been suggested, was that as presented to Daigo it was still incomplete and in need of revision. At least three drafts were made, perhaps four. There is much evidence that Daigo himself was consulted in regard to the second draft. Murakami, too, was personally involved in revision. His aspiration to imitate Daigo's style of rule has already been noted, and most likely it was his interest that caused work on the *Engi shiki* to be resumed. Even though the decree enacting the code was formally issued by his successor, Murakami had set the process in motion. As it had been for Daigo, the *Engi shiki* was Murakami's one genuine claim to the reputation of Confucian sage-king.

What parts of the *Engi shiki* were actually put into practice? Clearly, regulations for the conduct of offices that no longer had real functions to perform were of symbolic rather than practical importance. But its prescriptions continued to be followed in the activities of the court itself and in a variety of religious observances and festivals. It was consulted as authoritative by the authors of manuals prescribing annual events in the court ritual calendar. Preserving correct ceremonial observance was to be a major concern of mid- and late-Heian literati.

STATE ACADEMY

The institution that shaped the men who staffed the statutory system's bureaucracy, wrote the sage-kings' histories, and compiled their laws was the Academy. Properly called the *Daigaku-ryō* (literally, "Bureau of the Great Learning"), the Academy was attached to the Ministry of Ceremonial, the branch of government in charge of evaluating candidates for office. It occupied spacious grounds immediately to the south of the imperial palace and west of the Park of the Divine Spring. Like the civil service examination for which it prepared its students, it was a simplified copy of a Chinese model. T'ang China maintained six schools in its capital, all preparing students to take the civil service examination; the *Daigaku*, by contrast, stood alone in the Heian capital and was much smaller.

The history of the Heian Academy is instructive for a number of reasons. The changes within it illustrate the further Japanizing of a Chinese ideal, first in its intellectual content, then in its institutional and social forms. From one point of view, the commonsensical one, it must be judged to have gone into terminal decline by the beginning of the tenth century; from another, it was being transformed, like *Chuang tzu*'s dying man, into something "all crookedy," assuming a new and in its own way equally valid shape in the course of disintegration. The early tenth century may be seen as a kind of watershed in the function, activities, and morale of the professional men of learning. A description of the Academy is an essential preliminary to that of its graduates before and after, and their place in society.[28]

The Academy at the beginning of the Heian period had already undergone more than a century of development; it is thought to have originated in the first official Confucian school, founded at Ōtsu in the time of Emperor Tenji (r. 662–71). Nothing is known of its structure at this early time, but under the eighth-century civil code it had an administrative staff consisting of a Head (*kami*), an Assistant (*suke*), two secretaries (*jō*), and a small complement of clerks and watchmen; a little later it also acquired a Superintendent (*bettō*) to supervise practical affairs. The faculty at the start of the eighth century consisted of a Professor (*hakase*) with two Assistant Professors (*suke hakase*) who together provided instruction in the Chinese clas-

---

[28] Standard sources for the Heian academic world include Momo Hiroyuki, *Jōdai gakusei no kenkyū* (Tokyo: Meguro shoten, 1947), and Hisaki Yukio, *Nihon kodai gakkō no kenkyū* (Tokyo: Tamagawa Daigaku shuppambu, 1990). See Borgen, *Sugawara no Michizane*, pp. 69–112, 124–40.

sics. In addition, there were two Professors of Chinese Pronunciation (*on hakase*), two Professors of Calligraphy (*fumi no hakase*), and also a Professor of Mathematics (*san no hakase*), whose status was slightly below that of the others and who was in charge of a separate, less highly regarded curriculum. In addition, positions for two Professors of Law (*myōbō hakase*), one Professor of Literature (*monjō hakase*), and three lecturers (*chokkō*) in classics were created in 728. Study of the Chinese classics (later called *myōgyōdō*) was the central curriculum, and its Professor stood above the others. His rank, however, was only Senior Sixth Lower – below the line of aristocratic privilege. His assistants and, after them, the other Professors were ranged in various degrees of the Seventh Rank. Like other low-ranking functionaries, these teachers received their income from the seasonal stipends appropriate to their rank, and they also received fees from their students. The statutes set the number of students at four hundred, with an additional thirty in the mathematics course, and they too were to receive stipends. From 757 on, the revenues of certain lands, known as *kangakuden* ("fields for the promotion of learning"), were set aside for support of the Academy; in the early Heian their number was increased, but by the tenth century almost all had been reappropriated.

If this was the matrix provided by the codes, the school as it emerged in the Heian period, briefly flourished, and then declined into a ceremonial, hereditary institution of peculiarly Japanese aspect that was in actuality much different. The ninth century saw the rise of the curriculum in letters (*monjōdō*) to the highest status and prosperity. The subject of this curriculum was the art of elegant literary composition, its textbooks *Wen hsüan* and three histories – those of the Records of the Historian and of the Former and Later Han. Originally, it had been of distinctly inferior status, its Professor holding the same modest rank as the Assistant Professor of Classics. In 730, when places were created at the Academy for students of literature (and law), they were to be selected from among men holding the lowest, nonaristocratic, positions in the government or true commoners. By the early Heian, this had all changed, and literature came to be the most esteemed subject at the Academy. The prestige of this curriculum corresponded not only to Saga's convictions but to the demands of a mode of government that required preparation of memorials and edicts in a refined style. So elegant indeed was the parallel prose of memorials that many were prized for their beauty and even included in literary anthologies, quite apart from any relationship to their original context. In 813 Saga formally placed the curriculum in letters at the head of the others. Its twenty students constituted an elite group who were trained for the most challenging of the civil service examinations. A decree issued by Saga in 820 gave its Professor – then Sugawara no Kiyokimi – Fifth Rank Junior Grade, thus making him a member of the middle aristocracy. When the separate curriculum in the histories, created in 808, was abolished in 834, a second professorship of letters was created. Only a *monjō hakase* would be given the post of Head of the Academy, an appointment of great honor.

Whereas China had the ideal of universal education, however imperfectly realized, in Japan not until the Edo period did Confucian education become available to members of diverse classes of society. Provincial academies (*kokugaku*), greatly simplified analogues to the academies in the Chinese provinces, were intended to educate the sons of district officials, but they foundered early, with the exception of the school in Dazaifu. Admission to the Academy in the capital was originally based on rank. The earliest rule guaranteed places for sons and grandsons of men of the Fifth Rank and above and accepted the sons of men of the Six through Eighth on special petition. Another group eligible was the sons and grandsons of government scribes descended from Korean immigrants, although by the early Heian they no longer appear among the extant scattered references to students of the Academy. Although students of both literature and law originally were supposed to be of more humble background, in practice, commoners were few at the Academy. One family, the Nakahara, which came to share dominance in the classics curriculum with the Kiyohara, is thought to have been of common origin despite its claim of descent from an ancient and surely legendary emperor.[29] It, however, was the exception.

A decree by Emperor Heizei set the lower age for enrollment, formerly thirteen, at ten; in 824 the upper, formerly sixteen, was set at twenty. The celebrated monk Kūkai was in his eighteenth year when he entered, and Miyoshi Kiyoyuki was most likely in his seventeenth. There was no division of students by age or grade. As in China, a student might remain as long as nine years; after that he would be expelled if he had failed to pass the Ministry's examination. Within the Academy, students were examined annually and also every ten days, those who did poorly being expelled. The Professors lectured

---

29 Hisaki, *Nihon kodai gakkō*, pp. 290–92.

on a text from beginning to end – lecturing, it may be surmised, consisting of reading the text aloud and explicating the words and phrases. The *Engi shiki* stipulates the number of days allotted to the exegesis of each book: the *Li chi* and *Tso chuan* at 770 days each, *Shih ching* at 480 days, and so on.[30] There was a holiday following each examination day, and there were two vacations, a month each, during the year. Students were enjoined to be serious and forbidden such amusements as archery and playing the *koto* (zither).

As literary studies became increasingly popular in the ninth century, an elaborate system for screening students evolved. In its final form, a student who wished to enter the curriculum in literature would first have to study the classics. If judged outstanding, he would be allowed to take an examination administered by the *Daigaku-ryō*, the *ryōshi* (bureau examination), and if he passed, he would become a Provisional Scholar of Letters (*gimonjōshō*). The next step for the aspirant was an examination administered by the Ministry of Ceremonial, the *shōshi* (ministry examination); by passing this, he became a Scholar of Letters (*monjōshō*) and bore the honorary title of *shinshi*, which, strictly speaking, was supposed to be awarded to those who had passed the civil service examination modeled on China's *chin shih* civil service examination but lacking the prestige of the original and hence rarely taken. The stages in this progress could be long or short: Michizane became a *monjōshō* at eighteen, Haruzumi no Yoshitada at twenty-eight. Michizane preserved his ministry examination. It consists of six short (sixteen-character) verses praising recent auspicious portents.

The two best *monjōshō* were selected by recommendation or occasionally by examination to become Distinguished Scholars of Letters (*monjō tokugōshō*) and receive a special stipend; they bore the title *shūsai* (Chinese, *hsiu-ts'ai*), which again was supposed to indicate success on a civil service examination, in this case the most challenging one. *Tokugōshō* were also given nominal provincial offices; and some did, in fact, become provincial officials and cease for a time to be students before returning for their examinations. There was, again, no set period of preparation; Kiyoyuki remained a *tokugōshō* for seven years. The highest examination, the one that had originally qualified candidates for the title *shūsai*, was the *hōryakushi*, administered by imperial command and of such difficulty that in the

---

30 Felicia G. Bock, *Classical Learning and Taoist Practices in Early Japan: With a Translation of Books XVI and XX of the Engi-shiki* (Tempe: Arizona State University Center for Asian Studies, Occasional Paper No. 17, 1985), p. 70.

more than two hundred years from 704 to 931, only sixty-five men passed it. The candidate was obliged to compose two essays in ornate Chinese parallel prose treating problems in such areas as morality, philosophy, and Chinese history. The answers, called *taisaku*, were included in Heian anthologies of Chinese belles lettres, their outstanding couplets much praised. According to later anecdotes, any means was thought justified in passing this examination: Miyako no Yoshika, who in his turn was to be Michizane's examiner, was reputed to have obtained the discarded draft of an examination question by seducing a maid of Yoshitada, his examiner; the answer that he then composed included a passage describing the islands of the immortals later anthologized in *Wakan rōei shū*, that lovers of the arts might sing them or use them in the decoration of screens. Although the anecdote mentions only one passage, *Wakan rōei shū* actually contains two from Yoshika's examination. Michizane himself refused to stay shut up in his examination shed, rambled about the Ministry grounds, and when puzzled for an answer at one point sent a friend galloping off to a certain mysterious "Recluse Gentleman of Saga" for advice.[31]

The rewards of passing the examinations were nevertheless too low to make the Academy attractive to those who had other means of attaining advancement. First in 739, the Council of State ordered all aristocratic youths to study at the Academy. Again, in 806, Heizei attempted to make enrollment compulsory for all imperial princes as well as for the children and grandchildren of aristocrats, but the attempt failed and six years later the edict was rescinded on the grounds that ignorant minds are not easily improved and some had wasted many years without mastering a single subject; better to leave academic work to those who were interested. Readers of the *Tale of Genji* will remember the young Yūgiri's misery at being singled out from his companions to be made a student. Sons of men holding the Fifth Rank and above and grandsons of men holding the Third and above automatically received rank upon reaching their twenty-first year. By this system of "shadow ranks" (*on'i*), the heir of a man who held Third Rank, for example, would receive Junior Sixth Rank Lower Grade, while a younger son of a man who held Junior Fifth Rank, at the bottom of the scale of those eligible, would receive Junior Eighth Rank Lower Grade. By comparison, a candidate who

---

31 Ozawa Masao, Gotō Shigeo, Shimazu Tadao, and Higuchi Yoshimaro, *Fukuro sōshi chūshaku*, vol. 1 (Tokyo: Hanawa shobō, 1974), pp. 298–303; Kawaguchi and Nara, *Gōdanshō chū*, pp. 1117–23.

was not entitled to shadow rank could obtain no better than Senior Eighth Rank Upper Grade by passing the highest examination, no matter how brilliant his performance. And if he possessed shadow rank, passing the examination would raise his rank only one step. The gains from the other examinations were even smaller. Those who aspired to them were youths from modestly placed, ambitious families to whom success on the examinations offered the possibility of rising in the world or, increasingly as time passed, scions of families whose hereditary profession was Chinese letters. In the eighth century one hears of provincial families exhausting their resources to send a promising son to the Academy, but all those who passed the highest examination after 889 were sons or grandsons of Confucian officials.

By Michizane's day, the academic profession was gradually becoming the exclusive possession of certain families who guarded their prerogatives as jealously as the regental Fujiwara did theirs. Eventually, the *monjōdō* would belong to the Sugawara, the Ōe, and the Hino, Ceremonial, and Southern branches of the Fujiwara – comparative newcomers whose entry, achieved with the support of their influential relations, was resented – while only members of the Nakahara and Kiyohara might become *myōgyō hakase*. The Monjōin, a collegium founded by Ōe no Otondo (811–77) and Sugawara no Kiyokimi to minister to the needs of students in the belles-lettres curriculum, was divided into an East House and a West House. The East was dominated by the Ōe, Ki, and Takashina; the West by the Sugawara, Tachibana, and Fujiwara, and the spirit of rivalry between their adherents was often intense. One of the complaints against Michizane, and according to some reckonings a major factor in his ultimate fall, was his relentless promotion of his own disciples, pupils or former pupils of the Sugawara family private school, Kanke Rōka, to the exclusion of others.

If the first part of the ninth century, and in particular the Kōnin era, was a period of prosperity for the Academy, the abandonment of embassies was followed by a rapid and irreversible decline in its fortunes. An early-tenth-century document complains of favoritism in examinations, the decrepitude of the buildings, and the skimpiness of the students' rations. Some students might be able and industrious, but a majority were not, and many of these stayed on year after year, into destitute middle age.[32] To forestall favoritism, examinations were

---

[32] David John Lu, *Sources of Japanese History*, vol. 1 (New York: McGraw-Hill, 1974), pp. 63–65.

supposed to be administered by a professor from the house other than the candidate's, but as degree-taking became increasingly a matter of hereditary privilege, factional resentments became ever more conspicuous. In 997 a factional dispute over the grading of an examination provoked a scandal. Soon, however, the examination of candidates from influential families became an almost purely ceremonial undertaking, a form of high-toned entertainment. In 1090, for instance, ex-emperor Shirakawa and Emperor Horikawa summoned literati for a *gimonjōshō* "examination" which was in reality a Chinese poetry competition on the topic "The clothes of the dancers flutter in the palace garden."[33] Within the actual Academy, fathers would often resign their posts to their sons as soon as the latter reached majority. Since the new Professor would have undergone an examination that was a formality only and had little inclination to memorize the books on which he was to lecture, it became customary to note down the readings and interpretations traditionally taught by each house in copies of the texts passed down from father to son. This was the origin of *o-koto ten*, an early system for recording Japanese readings of Chinese texts and a precursor of the marks used in modern *kundoku*. To that extent, if no other, *kagaku* ("the learning of the houses") ultimately contributed to the spread of education. Physically, too, the Academy fell into ruins. There were frequent fires. After a fire in 960, the buildings were reconstructed, but in 1135 a petition bemoans the fact that where lecture halls once stood weeds now grow. What remained of the halls was destroyed in the great fire of 1177 and no attempt was made to rebuild.

As was the case with other organs of the statutory system, the relevant functions of the Academy were taken over by extrastatutory institutions. Attached to the Academy and gradually eclipsing it in importance were a number of institutions known as *bessō*, established and supported by the individual clans. The best-known and most prosperous was the Kangakuin, founded by Fujiwara no Fuyutsugu in 821. The Kangakuin is often inaccurately described as the private school of the Fujiwara. Rather than an independent school, however, it is argued to have been originally a combination dormitory and research institute, providing housing for poor Fujiwara boys while they attended the *Daigaku* – in Western terms, a collegium rather than a college.[34] Just as the *Daigaku-ryō* itself was charged equally with

[33] Kawaguchi Hisao, *Ōe no Masafusa* (Tokyo: Yoshikawa kōbunkan, 1968), p. 153.
[34] Ōmori Kingorō, "Ōchō jidai no shigakkō ni tsuite," *Rekishi chiri*, 53 (1929): 330–37; for an opposing view, see Takahashi Toshinori, *Nihon kyōiku bunka shi*, vol. 1 (Tokyo: Kōdansha [1933], 1978), pp. 97–99.

conducting the semiannual ceremonies to Confucius and with instructing students, so the Kangakuin also served diverse needs. An obligation of its students was to go in procession to offer their respects upon the birth of a prince to a Fujiwara imperial consort. The Kangakuin also served administrative functions for the Fujiwara family temple, Kōfukuji. After the fire of 1177, it was rebuilt; by that time there were lecture halls in it, proof that it had undergone the transition to college.

Other important *bessō* were the Gakkan'in, founded in the Jōwa era (834–47) by Saga's Tachibana empress on behalf of her clan; and the Kōbun'in, founded ca. 820 on behalf of the Wake clan by the then Superintendent of the Academy, the renowned literatus and physician Wake no Hiroyo, and noteworthy for housing the library of a thousand volumes that had belonged to the founder's father, Kiyomaro. In the Monjōin, the East and West houses came to function as *bessō* for the Ōe and Sugawara clans respectively. The Shōgakuin, founded in 881 by Ariwara no Yukihira for the education of princes and located in the southern part of the Academy grounds, had an interesting fate: it declined as an educational institution during the late Heian, but its superintendency became hereditary in a branch of the Minamoto clan and, ultimately, in the house of the Tokugawa shogun, persisting as a title until the Meiji Restoration.

In the late Heian, the main locus of education changed from these *bessō* to the private academies of individual literati. There is evidence that private schools had existed as early as the seventh century, and it can easily be surmised that at all times they played an important role. For example, the Sugawara school at its peak under Michizane is said to have had several hundred students and of them, Michizane boasted, nearly a hundred had gained admission to the Academy. The structure of such schools must have been extremely simple, consisting in the main of a teacher – typically a Professor at the Academy – who lectured, aided perhaps by a chief disciple who was likely to be his own son or grandson. The student who was also enrolled at the Academy could expect the advantage of his master's favor in his career at the official institution. Those of the nobility who wished to acquire learning studied, as they always had, with private tutors, generally senior relatives or literati clients.

The subject of schooling cannot be left without some mention of Kūkai's Shugei Shuchiin ("Academy of Arts and Sciences"), typical of an idealism found only at the beginning of the Heian period. Kūkai's intention was to establish a school that would make education available to poor boys as well as the well-to-do, and the comprehensive curriculum he envisioned was to combine instruction in Exoteric and Esoteric Buddhism with Confucian teaching. The protocols of the school were written in 828, and construction was started at a site near the Tōji, but the school lasted – if it was ever properly in operation – no more than seven years. After Kūkai's death in 835, it fell under the supervision of his disciple Jitsue (786–847), who was not a powerful man. There were financial troubles, and such buildings as had come into existence already needed repair. The site was soon sold to obtain money to expand the Tōji's estates in Tamba, and by mid-century only Kūkai's eloquent proposal remained of this visionary scheme.[35]

SCHOLARS AND THEIR ACCOMPLISHMENTS

Even a cursory acquaintance with the lives of the most prominent literati leaves an impression of their individuality; familiarity makes it hard to credit the lack of a sense of "selfhood" said to be common to Japanese. Perhaps the great difficulty of the course of study, the encountering and surmounting of disappointments, praise – or the hope of it – for possessing "talent" (a key word in traditional biographies), and a conviction of the centrality of the knowledge acquired, together with pride at the ranks and offices attained or, in the vast majority of cases, years of resentment over the paltriness of the official reward, all contributed toward making men of distinctive character. Literati of Murakami's time and onward tended to exceptional piety; those active from the middle of the eleventh century were likely to see themselves as isolated or as members of a small fraternity, each member of which was to be valued. None of the men whose work or character is discussed below is fully representative of the others of his time, but each is of interest in representing some of the currents of his age and class, and some of the possibilities of temperament. Behind each one may be seen the figures of other literati, some of them equally or almost equally eminent in the eyes of their colleagues, and perhaps others, less successful, even more humbly employed, whose identities are lost to history.

If there are traits common to many of the prominent literati, they

---

35 Wm. Theodore de Bary, ed., *The Buddhist Tradition: In China, India and Japan* (New York: The Modern Library, 1969), pp. 309–13; Yoshito S. Hakeda: *Kūkai: Major Works* (New York: Columbia University Press, 1972), pp. 56–58. Kūkai's Shingon sect alluded to its patriarch's school when it gave the name Shuchiin Daigaku to its Kyoto seminary in 1949.

are energy and the sense of a mission to educate, expressed in the voluminous production of works intended to supply the practical needs, as the Heian period defined them, of cultivated people. Kūkai, discussed at length in Chapter 7, deserves further mention here. In his youth a student at the Academy (before the removal of the capital to Heian-kyō), he brought new secular as well as religious learning with him on his return from China. He owed Saga's favor more to the emperor's appreciation of his artistic gifts than to his religious eminence. He was ranked as one of the three great calligraphers of his day, along with another former visitor to China, Tachibana no Hayanari (d. 842), and Saga himself. He was a frequent partner in the emperor's poetic exchanges, accompanying him on his outings to the Park of the Divine Spring, composing verses to be copied on screens in the palace and inscribing characters on tablets for the palace gates. He wrote dedications on behalf of Saga's nobles – a task, despite the religious content of the compositions, more typical of literati than of monks. His most celebrated secular work, however, is *Bunkyō hifu ron*, a digest of a number of Six Dynasties and T'ang treatises on the rules for poetic composition, presented to the throne in 819, its subjects ranging from rhyme, tone, and diction to the sources of poetic inspiration. Many of the works that he excerpted are no longer extant and are now known only because he quotes them. If none of *Bunkyō hifu ron* represents Kūkai's original thinking – as would scarcely have been expected – Japanese scholars have nevertheless found occasion to note his independence of judgment in selecting and arranging his sources.[36] The demand for such a work is testified to by the fact that, a year later, he prepared an abridged version, under the title of *Bumpitsu ganshin shō*. Kūkai was also responsible for *Tenrei banshō myōgi*, an edition of the popular Six Dynasties character dictionary *Yü p'ien*. The work boasts some special annotation for Japanese users and is the oldest surviving (though not the oldest) character dictionary produced in Japan. The Heian period in general was fertile in dictionaries and glossaries of many kinds compiled to serve religious as well as secular needs.

Whereas Kūkai, born in Shikoku, was the scion of a branch of the ancient Ōtomo clan, Sugawara no Michizane was the fourth in a line of professional scholars ennobled by Kammu. His father Koreyoshi (812–80) had a career typical of the successful literatus, occupying,

---

36 Abe Akio, *Chūko Nihon bungaku gaisetsu* (Tokyo: Shūei shuppan, 1977), p. 23.

among other posts, those of tutor to the crown prince, Head of the Academy, and provincial governor, lecturing at court, becoming a senior noble in his old age, and leaving behind him a great quantity of writings, which included a thesaurus, *Tōgū setsuin*, based on thirteen Chinese rhyming dictionaries, and an anthology of his own Chinese poems in the usual form of six chapters.

Michizane himself was the most admired of all classical Japanese poets in Chinese. The quantity of his productions and the number and nature of those that he produced on behalf of others deserve to be noted, as a suggestion of what was expected of the court scholar; he was prolific, but perhaps not very exceptionally so. Michizane composed his first Chinese poem in his eleventh year, his first couplet worthy of being quoted in an anthology in his fourteenth, his first prose work on behalf of a patron in his fifteenth. He completed his Academy studies in 870, his twenty-sixth year – an early age at the time. The following year, his compositions included a dedication to accompany a donation by an imperial consort and a series of three memorials submitted to the throne by the regent Yoshifusa, in which, as etiquette demanded, the regent attempted to decline an addition to his emoluments. The year after that, he was assigned to the entertainment of an embassy from Po-hai. A major part of the entertainment consisted of exchanges of Chinese poems with the foreign visitors. (In this instance, Michizane's activities were cut short by his mother's death, but he was to officiate in receiving two subsequent embassies.)[37] His compositions on behalf of others this year included a resignation proffered by an Assistant Professor at the Academy and a memorial from the new Minister of the Right, Fujiwara no Mototsune, giving thanks for his appointment, as well as a letter in parallel prose from Emperor Seiwa to the king of Po-hai. In the next year, 873, he wrote a dedication for an official of the Treasury Ministry, presenting house and lands to the temple Urin'in, and a dedication for Mototsune to accompany a gift of rice fields to the Fujiwara clan temple Kōfukuji.

These writings represent only a portion of his output during a few typical years early in his career: *Kanke bunsō*, the principal collection of Michizane's belles lettres, records eleven prose pieces attributed to the two years 872–73, and there must have been other works, thought not worth preserving. In all, the anthology contains more than 150 compositions in formal prose, including rhyme-prose (*fu*),

---

37 Borgen, *Sugawara no Michizane*, pp. 231–40.

funeral inscriptions and eulogies, prefaces (*jo*), examination questions and answers, edicts written on behalf of emperors, and a variety of memorials. Of more interest to present-day readers are the more than 500 Chinese poems in the anthology. Many are conventional verses composed for banquets, but the best are expressions of their author's deepest feelings. The turning point in his evolution as a poet came with his unwilling posting as governor to the province of Sanuki in Shikoku, in 886. The poems written after Michizane's exile to Kyushu in 901 (preserved in a supplementary anthology) are especially prized for their poignancy.[38]

Among Michizane's compositions from the year 873 is a formal preface to *Chiyō shakuen*, a handbook of government he was compiling to aid students preparing for their civil service examinations. The handbook itself was intended to be of monumental dimensions. Although it remained unfinished, it prepared the way for his later major historical work, *Ruijū kokushi*, in which the contents of the Six National Histories are rearranged by topic. *Ruijū kokushi* was begun at the command of Emperor Uda and presented to the throne in 892. (How exactly it came to include the contents of *Sandai jitsuroku* is not known.) The thoughtfulness of its arrangement is noteworthy, for it makes use of a kind of cross-referencing, and it deals meticulously with its sources, unlike the histories compiled privately later in the Heian period. The categories were devised by Michizane on the general model of the Chinese *lei-shu* but conforming to Japanese priorities. They tell us a good deal about the concerns of the court. First is the Way of the Gods, followed by emperors, imperial women, and the rest of humanity; then "Calendar," "Music," "Banquets," "Memorials," "Government Bureaus," "Literature" (*bun*, i.e., literature in Chinese), "Agriculture," "Felicitous Omens," "Disasters." The relegation of Buddhism to a place near the end of the list is due to a sense of the proprieties of Confucian history, not a lack of piety. Unfortunately, less than a third of the 200-chapter original is extant.

Michizane's rise to power and sudden fall belong to political history and are discussed in Chapter 1, but a few additional points are relevant to the concerns of the present chapter. One has to do with the lineaments, discerned in later anecdotes about him, of a strong but unstable character. He inspired devotion, but he was also arrogant and had violent outbursts of temper. Another is the suggestion

---

38 Burton Watson, trans., *Japanese Literature in Chinese*, vol. 1: *Poetry and Prose in Chinese by Japanese Writers of the Early Period* (New York: Columbia University Press, 1975), pp. 73–130.

that the coup against him was brought about through the animosity of rival literati. This cannot be the whole story, but there may be much truth in it, as one act can serve a number of motives. Not only all desirable Academy posts but half or more of all bureaucratic positions were said to be held by Sugawara disciples, so that his exile might have been expected to open the way to literati clients of the rival party. Michizane was habitually outspoken in his scorn of those he considered his intellectual inferiors. One who had good reason to resent him was Miyoshi Kiyoyuki, of whom he was intemperately contemptuous and whom he initially failed in the doctoral examination. Perhaps with reason, traditional accounts of Michizane's fall make Kiyoyuki one of the chief villains of the affair.

Kiyoyuki's rise was more gradual than Michizane's; his final rank, Junior Fourth Lower Grade, still left him below the senior nobility, and his highest post, that of Consultant, though a considerable prize, was achieved only when he was past seventy. Michizane, by contrast, became Consultant in his forty-ninth year. Rather than descending from a family of scholars, he was the son of an obscure provincial governor. He seems to have owed his success at the Academy, over Michizane's opposition, to Kose no Fumio (824–92), whose disciple he was; his promotion to *monjōshō* coincided with the elevation of his teacher to Head of the Academy. In 883, two years after the original examination, Michizane changed his grade to a passing one and Kiyoyuki was appointed Assistant Professor under Fumio. In the Akō Controversy, Kiyoyuki ranged himself with the regent's party against Emperor Uda, and just as Michizane was rewarded for his loyalty to the emperor after the regent's death, Kiyoyuki, among others of Mototsune's clients, found himself rusticated in an unwanted provincial governorship. Even after his return in 897, his way to further advancement was blocked, for not only did Michizane's followers occupy all available academic posts, but in 897 Michizane's son Takami was Head of the Academy. Kiyoyuki did succeed in being named Professor of Literature in 900 – after Uda, by taking the tonsure, had effectively eliminated himself as Michizane's protector. Following the exile of Michizane and his sons, Kiyoyuki became Head of the Academy as well, a triumph soon compounded with the addition of the office of Vice-Minister of the Ministry of Ceremonial.

Factions were rife among Heian literati. Personal loyalties, of course, were an important consideration, but in addition, temperament, talent, and ideology distinguished the pragmatists among them from those of more purely literary and scholarly inclinations.[39] If Michizane was an example of the latter, Kiyoyuki is an example of the former. Scarcely the poet that Michizane was (although he accumulated enough verses to form a six-chapter collection), Kiyoyuki was an outstanding writer of ordinary expository prose. His work is noted for breadth of subject matter and clarity of expression – the latter a quality neither common in Heian Chinese nor admired by writers of the age. Like many other Heian literati – for example, Haruzumi no Yoshitada and Ōe no Otondo before him and Ōe no Masafusa after him – Kiyoyuki was strongly interested in the Taoist art of prolonging life and in the occult. For men of the Heian era, the occult was an aspect of reality, and it was the man of inquiring mind who garnered anecdotes about it, as Kiyoyuki and Masafusa both did. Kiyoyuki was especially devoted to the study of Chinese calendrical lore. A learned memorial, the *Kakumei kammon,* which he submitted in 900, stressed that the following year, the fifty-eighth in the cycle of sixty and a fateful year in the larger cycles as well, would be unlucky and bound to bring "revolution" (in the sense of change in leadership) unless a new era name was adopted. This may have been intended as part of his campaign against Michizane. His argument is marred by some faulty arithmetic, but there is no reason to believe that he was insincere in the science that he invoked. The court was indeed persuaded to change the era name in 901, and the memorial enjoys independent fame for having originated a custom followed through subsequent sixty-year cycles as well as providing the model for the compositions appropriate to such occasions.

Where Michizane's unwelcome posting to a provincial office brought about his maturation as a poet, Kiyoyuki's undoubtedly deepened his appreciation of the practical difficulties of governing. The fruits of his experience are recorded in a celebrated document, the *Iken fūji* submitted in 914 in response to a request made by Daigo in 909. (*Iken fūji* were statements of opinion on the successes and failures of government, prepared after a call was issued by the emperor.) The document noted real problems and expounded concrete remedies. It can be read not only as evidence of general conditions at the time but as a sign of the sympathies and anxieties of Kiyoyuki's class. The introduction deplores past extravagances, praises Kiyoyuki's patron, the late regent Mototsune, and depicts a depop-

---

39 Gotō, *Heianchō kambungaku,* pp. 79–93; Hayashi Rokurō, *Jōdai seiji shakai no kenkyū* (Yoshikawa kōbunkan, 1969), pp. 381–509.

ulated, impoverished countryside. The topics of the individual articles are as follows:

1. Preventing floods and droughts and obtaining rich harvests: Kiyoyuki blames unsatisfactory conditions on the fact that priests who carry out the great national rituals are not men of pure conduct.
2. Luxury should be forbidden.
3. Redistribution of government allocation fields should be carried out in the provinces in proportion to the actual population. (A redistribution had been ordered in 902. Kiyoyuki's motive is less fairness to the peasantry than the hope of increasing revenues through confiscation of excess land.)
4. Funds allotted for support of students at the Academy should be increased.
5. The number of dancers at the Gosechi Festival should be reduced; at present, Kiyoyuki says, parents of the dancers compete in expenditure.
6. The number of judges should be increased to that of former times. Provincial governors should be exempt from punishment for minor crimes or because of unfounded accusations.
7. All officials should be paid their half-yearly stipends without exception; in recent years, only the senior nobles have received them regularly.
8. There must be an end to the practice of discharging provincial officials upon accusation by the local gentry and under-officials.
9. A limit should be placed on the number of men in the provinces exempt from taxation as nominal officials of the lowest class.
10. Sale of appointments to the Imperial Police and Guards should be stopped. Soldiers should be trained in the use of the catapult.
11. The disorderliness of imperial guards and monks in the provinces must be forbidden. Over half of the two to three hundred men who become monks each year are rascals. Provincial householders take the tonsure to avoid taxation but do not abandon secular ways; some even join gangs of thieves. Guards sent to the provinces do not return to the capital but stay and terrorize the populace.
12. A renewed plea that the port of Uozumi in Harima Province be reopened.[40]

---

[40] Complete German translation in Inge-Lore Kluge, *Miyoshi Kiyoyuki: sein Leben und seine Zeit* (Berlin: Institut für Orientforschung, 1958), pp. 40–70; partial English translation in Lu, *Sources of Japanese History*, vol. 1, pp. 60–65.

Kiyoyuki believed strongly in the Confucian ideal of the provincial governor who was frugal, compassionate, loyal, and honest to the point of impoverishing himself. When he argues that provincial governors should be excused their failings, his assumption is not that the men are invariably upright but that to some degree corruption, quarrels with local magnates, and failure to meet the central government's expectations are inevitable. He is keenly aware also of the chronic dissatisfactions of students and lesser officials, which he no doubt shared. Where he complains against the evils of luxury, his modern biographer sees, besides Confucian idealism, the resentment of the literati, as a class, against the senior nobles.[41] Kiyoyuki's memorial contains eloquent testimony to hard times.

In 954 Murakami issued another call for *Iken fūji*. Three and a half years later, Michizane's eminent grandson Sugawara no Fumitoki (899–981), known especially as a master of poetic rhetoric, responded by producing a memorial in three articles. He urged (1) the prohibition of luxury, (2) stopping the sale of offices, (3) supporting the Academy and the literati. Not only was Fumitoki's *fūji* shorter, but it represented the viewpoint of aristocrats and officials in the capital and was extremely abstract. Each of its articles is related to one of Kiyoyuki's and includes expressions that may be adaptations of Kiyoyuki's.[42] Following the correct model for composition was more important for Fumitoki than giving advice wrought out of his personal experience – advice that in any event the emperor could scarcely have implemented. By his day, most of the central government offices that literati had been trained to fill existed in name only; the primary relationship of the literatus was with the nobleman who was his patron. The literatus was a specialist from whom the noble received such instruction as he desired but whose professional skills he need not personally aspire to – except in the way that, through some quirk of talent or circumstance, he might aspire to mastery of a particular musical instrument. He demonstrated his Confucian commitment by his beneficence to his literati clients, entertaining them suitably and sponsoring them for court appointments and provincial governorships. They were of use to him also as stewards (*keishi*) in his household office and administrators of his provincial estates. When the court held Chinese poetry competitions, each team would consist of literati who composed the poems offered for judgment and nobles who presented the poems with due

---

41 Tokoro, *Miyoshi Kiyoyuki*, pp. 168–69. 42 Tokoro, *Miyoshi Kiyoyuki*, pp. 182–83.

ceremony and defrayed the often considerable expenses of the trappings and refreshments.

When a mid-Heian noble of high rank was himself learned in Chinese things it was often because he was an artistic polymath. An example is Fujiwara no Kintō (966–1041), a second cousin of Michinaga and brother of one of Emperor En'yū's consorts, a man skilled not only in Chinese poetry but in Japanese *waka* and in calligraphy and music and an authority, characteristically, on ceremonial customs and precedents. Tastes in Chinese learning were also cultivated by persons who might have been in power but were not. Daigo's sixteenth son, Kaneakira (914–98), a distinguished poet known as the *Saki no chūsho-ō* ("Former Archivist Prince"), and Murakami's seventh son, Tomohira (964–1009), the *Nochi no chūsho-ō* ("Later Archivist Prince"), presided over literary salons. Another active patron was Fujiwara no Michinaga's unfortunate nephew Korechika, who was remembered by later literati as a poetic arbiter worthy of respect, although he composed no Chinese poems after returning from exile. The role of Confucian patron was also flattering to the grandiose style of Fujiwara no Michinaga. He amassed a large Chinese library, and Chinese learning as a whole underwent a modest revival (which seemed a great one a generation later), thanks to the encouragement he gave it. But all of the Fujiwara regents were Confucian patrons, if only because their position as *uji no chōja* (clan chief) of the Fujiwara made it incumbent upon them to promote the moral well-being of their clan and descendants.

There was no slackening at court of Confucian ceremonies, nor of Chinese poetic entertainments. In the fifth month of 1003, for example, on the sixth day, there was a poetic gathering in the palace. Among those attending, in addition to Michinaga, were such aristocratic literary lights as Kintō, Fujiwara no Arikuni (943–1011), and Fujiwara no Tadanobu (967–1035). The topic (*dai*) given the versifiers was "the thin, solitary voice of the first cicada." On the twenty-seventh day, Michinaga held an entertainment at Uji, with Chinese and Japanese poetry and instrumental music. The topic for Chinese poems was "the freshness of mountains and streams after the sky has cleared." It was typical of the age that men with talent for composing Chinese poetry were unlikely to confine themselves to that language; many of those who distinguished themselves at these gatherings, like Tadanobu, are better known for their work in Japanese.

Among those who frequented the literary gatherings at Prince Tomohira's mansion were two disciples of Fumitoki who, though men of ability, had to be content with modest rewards in their official careers. Fujiwara no Tametoki (947?–1021?), father of the great writer Murasaki Shikibu, owed his initial progress in office to a roundabout marital connection with the fifth son of a former regent. With the abdication of Kazan, he lost his posts and, except for a brief term as provincial governor, went many years without official employment. Yoshishige no Yasutane (d. 1002) exemplifies the difficulties encountered by the literatus who was not of a family of hereditary scholars. That he would pass the highest civil service examination was not expected, and after he did so, for all his brilliance, he was unable to obtain any significant promotion. He ended his career almost at the rank at which be began. His notable works include *Chiteiki*[43] – modeled in part on a work of Po Chü-i and itself a predecessor in Chinese of Kamo no Chōmei's classic *Hōjōki* – and *Nihon ōjō gokuraku ki,* which inaugurates a genre of hagiographical collections in Chinese, celebrating the lives of Japanese Buddhist holy men, monks and laymen alike, the humble as well as the highly placed. A follower of Kūya, revered in turn by Genshin (who saw to it that his devotional poetry was sent to China),[44] he was the founder of a characteristic Heian religious institution, the *kangaku-e,* a two-day semi-annual gathering at which twenty Tendai monks and twenty literati laymen would hear lectures on the Lotus Sutra and compose Chinese poems on topics chosen from the sutra. When Yasutane formally entered religion he took the name Jakushin, and as a monk, his deeply felt, literal-minded piety, which took the Buddhist doctrine of compassion for all living beings to an extreme, became the subject of legend. A number of Ōe literati became his disciples in religion and, like their master, are themselves commemorated in the hagiographical literature; one went to China and died there.[45]

Other names might be mentioned: enumerating in admiration the eminent men – from ministers to warriors – who added luster to the court of Emperor Ichijō (r. 986–1011), Ōe no Masafusa listed ten names of literati, and placed his great-grandfather Ōe no Masahira (952–1012) at the head.[46] Masahira, tutor to the crown prince and lecturer to Ichijō and Sanjō, had the advantages of his ancestry, his

---

43 Translation in Watson, *Japanese Literature in Chinese,* pp. 57–64.
44 Kawasaki Tsuneyuki, *Jimbutsu Nihon no rekishi,* vol. 3. *Ochō no rakujitsu* (Tokyo: Yomiuri shimbunsha, 1966), pp. 112–15.
45 "Zoku honchō ōjōden," in Inoue Mitsusada and Ōsone Shōsuke, eds., *Ōjōden, Hokke genki, Nihon shisō taikei,* vol. 7 (Tokyo: Iwanami shoten, 1974), pp. 247–48.
46 Inoue and Ōsone, eds., *Ōjōden,* p. 224.

skill in poetic rhetoric, and the patronage of Michinaga in achieving a highly respectable, though not exalted, Fourth Rank. He too was a pious man. He remained throughout his life a subordinate, as a modern biographer has pointed out, with neither influence nor aspirations to influence in the practical conduct of government. The same biographer also notes the extent to which he was professionally occupied with words: criticizing the use of two characters in an edict, proposing era names (two of those he recommended were adopted), and advising Michinaga on names for imperial princes.[47] A similar observation, of course, might be made about almost any other literatus serving at court throughout the period.

The most elegant of the writings of these men were collected by a Professor of Literature, Fujiwara no Akihira (989–1066). His *Honchō monzui*, in fourteen chapters, took its name from a Chinese anthology, *T'ang wen-ts'ui*, and its form and ambitions from *Wen hsüan*. He is thought to have completed it during the Kōhei era (1058–65). Again, as with Tamenori's inclusion of the T'ang history in his *Kuchizusami*, Akihira's choice of title demonstrates that books from China continued to appear in Japan, for *T'ang wen-ts'ui* was completed in 1011 and first printed in 1039. Although there were a number of other privately compiled anthologies of belles lettres, *Honchō monzui* became the most prestigious, providing models for later writers. The work seems to have been conceived as a successor to the three imperial anthologies compiled in Saga's time. The periods most represented in it are those of Daigo and Murakami, but the individual writer whose compositions appear most often is Masahira.

Akihira succeeded to Masahira's eminence and honors, and he came to regard himself, no doubt with justice, as the sole preserver of the glories of Masahira's time. He was additionally, however, a man of independent and original mind, with a keen eye for the contemporary scene. He wrote to educate, and his *Shin sarugaku ki* and *Unshū shōsoku* are as remarkable for their liveliness as for their informativeness. Both works are accounted ancestors of the later genre of textbooks called *ōrai mono*.

Shin sarugaku ki presents the principal occupations of the time and their vocabulary with encyclopedic thoroughness. The work is a kind of fiction: to a performance of the entertainment called *sarugaku* come a captain of the Gate Guards, his three wives – one old

---

47 Francine Hérail, "Un lettre à la cour de l'empereur Ichijō: Ōe no Masahira (953–1012)," in *Mélanges offert à M. Charles Haguenauer en l'honneur de son quatre-vingtième anniversaire. Etudes japonaises* (Paris: L'Asiatique, 1980), pp. 369–87, esp. 383–84.

and jealous, one housewifely and maternal, one young and adored – his sixteen daughters and nine sons. Each of his daughters' husbands, some of his daughters, and each of his sons is a paragon of a different occupation or example of a social type, with the symmetries and hyperbole of Chinese rhetoric contributing to the reader's education. There is a master gambler, a bowman, an exemplary provincial official skilled in agriculture, a metalsmith, a *sumō* wrestler, a teamster, a physician and acupuncturist, a *yin-yang* master, a painter, a calligrapher, a maker of Buddhist images, a *yamabushi*, and a Tendai monk as impressive in appearance as he is learned. One daughter is a courtesan, another a pious widow, yet another, extremely rich, a shamaness. One daughter is a beauty "not inferior to Yang Kuei-fei," while an ugly sister, whose defects are described, has formed a liaison with a charcoal burner. Another ugly sister is married to a criminal the list of whose transgressions enriches the reader's vocabulary. There are suitors: a Japanese poet much fancied by the nobility, and a boy musician beloved by all the monks. Perhaps of greatest interest in the present context are a trader who deals in Chinese imports as well as native goods and a scholar learned in all four curricula of the Academy, who has read *Wen hsüan, Shih chi, Han shu*, and all the classics; the *ritsu* and the *ryō*, the *kyaku* and the *shiki;* has mastered the varieties of calculation; and is skilled in the composition of Chinese verse and rhyme prose, prefaces, edicts of all sorts, commands, memorials, dedications, prayers, letters and responses, interbureaucratic memos, requests, and diaries. Akihira gives him the evenhandedly concocted name of "Sugawara no Masafumi," the "masa" suggesting Masahira, and the "fumi," Fumitoki; the two words in combination meaning "correct writing."

Unshū shōsoku is a collection of more than two hundred model letters, many of them, it is thought, supplied from Akihira's personal and official correspondence. As with *Shin sarugaku ki*, its Chinese is notably influenced by Japanese usage.[48] Written very much from the point of view of Akihira's own class, the work gives invaluable insight into the activities, mores, and needs of the middle-ranking official, as well as into the etiquette of polite address. There are invitations – to poetry parties, athletic contests, scenic excursions, a moon-viewing party – congratulations, and requests for information. A complaint about the slow receipt of tax revenues is accompanied by a hint that the writer would like to be promoted. There are com-

---

[48] Konishi, *A History of Japanese Literature*, vol. 2, pp. 185–86.

plaints about the difficulty of promotion, which can best be accomplished if the aspirants will donate a building to their lordships. A writer protests that he is unable to provide a feast requested for an observance at the regent's mansion. A former governor writes to a monastic official asking for instruction on dyeing priests' garments and preparing offerings. Someone who is housebound because of a directional taboo is given a description of a festival he has missed; a near riot, mountebanks cavorting obscenely – great fun in the letter writer's opinion. An Academy student facing an examination is advised to borrow a certain crib book. There is a great deal about borrowing and lending, suggesting to a modern commentator that middle officials were evidently obliged to live beyond their means. A series of dunning letters is also provided. Akihira, who served as governor of Izumo, offers a number of letters dealing with provincial affairs. It has been suggested that the work was intended as a textbook for an advanced course for students of present-day middle-school age, and that its contents grew in response to very specific needs.[49] Its provision of polished phrases with which the individual could meet the exigencies of his economic and social life makes it an interesting complement to Tamenori's primer.

Ōe no Masafusa (1041–1111), in his twenty-sixth year when Akihira died, succeeded to his lonely eminence. A child prodigy (precocity is a common element in Chinese literary hagiography, both Japanese and continental), in old age he composed a brief memoir reciting the names of the great men, now long dead, who had petted and praised him; the memoir is no less poignant for following, phrase by phrase, a poetic preface composed by Michizane's disciple Ki no Haseo for the rather different purpose of bemoaning the factionalism of his day.[50] It is characteristic of the Japanese literati to have modeled their compositions on the admired examples of Japanese predecessors. Masafusa is an intriguing figure for a number of reasons, one being that he sums up so many of the qualities and tendencies of his class. He was both a conservative and something of a new man. The proceeds of a term as governor of Mimasaka Province enabled him to construct a building to house the extensive Ōe family library; his most important work is a monumental ceremonial compendium, *Gōke shidai*. He achieved some distinction as a poet in

---

49 Miho Tadao and Miho Satoko, eds., *Unshū ōrai* (Osaka: Izumi shoin, 1982), p. 480. Partial translation of the text in Clemens Scharschmidt, "*Unshū ōrai* oder die Briefsammlung des Unshū," *Ostasiatische Studien* 20 (1917): 20–114.
50 Gotō, *Heianchō kambungaku*, pp. 282–309.

Japanese as well as Chinese and was wont to stress the value of Japaneseness, on one notable occasion instructing a regent that *yamato-damashii* (Japanese spirit) was more important for the regent's young son than Chinese book-learning. Like Akihira, he wrote about the lively scene, taking as his subjects itinerant entertainers, the prostitutes of Eguchi and Kanzaki, and the dancing mania of 1096 – although it is impossible for the modern reader of the compositions in question not to feel the pressure of his learned Chinese style against the accurate expression of what he saw. He was a pious Buddhist, compiling a continuation of Yasutane's *Nihon ōjō gokuraku ki;* unlike its predecessor, however, Masafusa's collection combines political with religious concerns, in keeping with its author's own character. As was traditional among the Ōe, he was adept in Taoist lore, and he also compiled a collection of lives of Japanese Taoist "immortals," beginning with the legendary Yamato Takeru and Prince Shōtoku. He had a reputation as a polymath – although the story that he gave instruction in the art of warfare to Minamoto no Yoshiie is almost certainly apocryphal. His reputation as a greedy and dishonest governor is more likely well deserved. His fondness for collecting anecdotes in his old age provoked the disapproval of more dignified contemporaries. He took great pride in inheriting the traditions of the Ōe and pride also in surpassing his forefathers in attaining Second Rank (Junior, 1094; Senior, 1102).

In his pragmatic and inquisitive temperament, accompanied by his fascination with the magical and supernatural, Masafusa resembles Kiyoyuki, but his attainment of high position suggests a comparison with Michizane, for whom Masafusa's own reverence went deep.[51] Masafusa owed his success to the determination of emperors Go-Sanjō (r. 1068–73) and Shirakawa (r. 1073–87) to rule for themselves, but whereas Michizane in power was isolated, Masafusa was one of a number of Confucian advisers to the emperor, appointed to relatively inconspicuous posts that kept him in close contact with his master. His association with Go-Sanjō began while the future emperor was crown prince. Appointed tutor to the crown prince in 1067, the final year before Go-Sanjō's succession, he remained tutor to successive crown princes until 1085. Confucianism was the storehouse to which every aspiring ruler would go for his intellectual and ideological stock, the more conspicuously the better, and Go-Sanjō

---

51 Robert Borgen, "Ōe no Masafusa and the Spirit of Michizane," *Monumenta Nipponica* 50 (1995): 357–84.

was an attentive student. Asked about his abilities, Masafusa replied enthusiastically that the emperor was "as good a scholar as Ōe no Sukekuni."[52] Sukekuni, an older contemporary and a great-grandson of the famed Ōe no Asatsuna (886–957), was one of the most distinguished literati of the time. Go-Sanjō was said to have taken Masafusa's advice on appointments, and Masafusa is credited with having been the architect of one of Go-Sanjō dearest projects, that of regulating the *shōen*. Masafusa was also a confidant of Shirakawa; when Shirakawa abdicated, he was one of the five inaugural superintendents (*bettō*) of the new ex-emperor's household office. Another of Masafusa's patrons was the Fujiwara regent Moromichi (1062–99), who disapproved of Shirakawa's activity as ex-emperor, and it may well have been the tension between the two, as well as the desire to enrich himself, that prompted Masafusa's ready absence from the capital for a term as governor general of Kyushu. In Kyushu, Masafusa endowed shrines and instituted additional ceremonies to Michizane.

Masafusa, both as individual and as representative of the interests of his class, is revealed most fully in *Gōdan* ("The Ōe Conversations"; also, *Gōdanshō*), a record of his talks transcribed by a youthful disciple along with, perhaps, some of the anecdotes he himself had recorded. Masafusa's subjects in it are men, Chinese poetry, public affairs – meaning ceremonial, not economics or the science of governing, despite his actual activities – the supernatural, and learning as a virtuoso accomplishment. The men are those of the Japanese literati past, and he is interested in them as individuals. He portrays them as cantankerous and competitive. In poetry, he is interested in words and phrases. A particularly fine couplet may be the achievement that justifies a life – as he said of himself.[53] The tone of a particular Chinese word may be the subject of a lengthy discussion. An occasion on which an allusion has been identified as inappropriate is worthy of note, in part because it suggests the superior subtlety of the literatus who has so identified it. China itself is mentioned as the source of accolades: the works of a poet are said to be worthy to be sent to China. But Masafusa is not interested in the Chinese poets as individuals, nor in their poetry for its own sake. Chinese learning in Japan has become a self-contained tradition, with its roots and objects in its own past.

---

52 Takeuchi Rizō, *Bushi no tōjō*, vol. 6 of *Nihon no rekishi* (Tokyo: Chūō kōron sha, 1972), pp. 144–45, from *Zoku kojidan*.   53 Kawaguchi and Nara, *Gōdanshō chū*, pp. 1154–60.

CHAPTER 6

ARISTOCRATIC CULTURE

The term aristocratic culture is here used to mean a style of social and artistic expression characteristic of the Japanese court at Heian-kyō and limited primarily to its members. The small, isolated, tightly knit court community shared traits that conditioned the development of the culture: a strong sense of status and a firm subordination of the individual; an emphasis on order, decorum, and conformity; a greater interest in immediate solutions to practical problems than in ethical questions, philosophical speculation, or scientific inquiry; a general tendency toward emotionalism in preference to intellectualism; a pervasive, melancholy concern with the changes wrought by the passing of time; a high esteem for literature, calligraphy, and music; an acute sensitivity to beauty and to the moods of nature; and an unwavering belief in the importance of taste as an index of character and breeding. As a group, those characteristics seem to have crystallized during the last decades of the ninth century and the first half of the tenth – a period, symbolized by the cancellation in 894 of the court's last projected official mission to China, during which the Japanese repudiated earlier efforts to make their court a mirror image of the one at Ch'ang-an, and moved instead toward the amalgamation of foreign and native elements into a civilization distinctively their own.

The preoccupation with beauty, one of the most conspicuous aspects of the new culture, influenced attitudes toward nature, standards of judgment in the arts, appraisals of human worth, and norms of social behavior. It also powerfully affected almost every facet of ordinary life, both public and private, as may be seen from a survey of upper-class living accommodations, dress, and dietary customs.

DOMESTIC ARCHITECTURE AND FURNISHINGS

From around 950 on, the typical aristocratic residence consisted of a group of buildings situated in a large urban estate, its stands of pine and maple trees, artificial hills and streams, and island-studded lake imitating the natural landscape of the Kyoto basin, or echoing the features of a famous scenic spot in the provinces. In architecture of this type, known as *shindenzukuri* (main hall construction), the buildings were carefully designed to harmonize with the setting. The main hall (*shinden*) was a simple, graceful, rectangular one-story structure made of unpainted wood, with a gabled, shingled roof and a wooden floor raised a few feet off the ground on posts. Its large central room (*moya*) was divisible into smaller areas by movable curtains and screens. Secondary rooms, known as eave chambers (*hisashi no ma*), gave onto open verandas, from which they were separated by removable wooden shutters (*shitomi*) and bamboo or reed blinds (*sudare*). Well suited to the hot, humid summers of the region, the dark, drafty, high-ceilinged rooms offered little comfort in winter, when they were heated only by inefficient charcoal braziers.

Since the *shinden* was ordinarily used as a residence by the master or mistress of the establishment, it commanded the best view of the main sanded courtyard, the lake, and the gardens with their rocks, shrubs, and seasonal displays of flowering plum, cherry, wisteria, *yamabuki* (Japan globeflower), white chrysanthemums, autumn leaves, and plume grass (*susuki*), all of which adjoined it on the south. It was connected by covered galleries to lesser buildings of similar architecture, which varied in size and number according to the owner's wealth and social importance, but which normally included at least one or two wings (*tai*) assigned to the reception of callers, the accommodation of family members and attendants, and other uses. Great estates were provided with libraries, Buddhist chapels, racetracks, dance platforms, and fishing pavilions; and the waters, hills, trees, and flowering plants of their extensive gardens were among the happiest expressions of Heian sensitivity to visual beauty.[1]

The simplicity of the architecture was complemented by the deliberate sparseness of the interior furnishings. Even the best-equipped room seldom contained more than screens and curtains; one or two double-tiered cabinets or chests; boxes for writing equipment, poetic anthologies, small toilet articles and mirrors; an incense burner; an armrest; a lampstand; some mats and cushions; and a small curtained alcove, the *chōdai* (curtain-dais), which did double duty as bedchamber and sitting room.

---

1 For an exhaustive study of the *shindenzukuri* style, see Ōta Seiroku, *Shindenzukuri no kenkyū* (Tokyo: Yoshikawa kōbunkan, 1987).

Wood, lacquered for decorative purposes and as a protection against insects and rot, was the preferred material for furniture and articles of everyday use. The many lacquer techniques and designs introduced from China in the eighth century continued to be employed to some extent in the ninth and early tenth, but thereafter they were supplanted by a new, purely native style. The technique on which the style was based, known as *makie*, consisted in applying metal powder to a drawing traced in the lacquer base, or directly onto the wet lacquer. Motifs, usually inspired by the natural surroundings, included flowers, trees, birds, butterflies, and stylized waves. By the end of the period, superbly decorative romanticized landscapes had appeared, such as the one on a small Chinese-type chest for Buddhist objects, a national treasure preserved at Mount Kōya, where the artist has depicted marsh irises and plovers in a setting reminiscent of a famous episode from *Ise monogatari* (*Tales of Ise*), a tenth-century book of tales about poems. The perfectly balanced use of mother-of-pearl inlay, gold, silver, and pale gold (a mixture of gold and silver powders) complements the chest's rounded lines, producing an effect of quiet opulence and soft, delicate beauty that can be said to typify Heian aristocratic taste at its best.[2]

Metals and ceramics figured less prominently than lacquer in the Heian house – in part, it seems, because it was difficult to achieve the desired effect of softness when working with those materials. As in earlier periods, bronze was the principal metal used, although silver also became popular for dinnerware, boxes, and other articles. Instead of attempting to develop new metalworking techniques, craftsmen concentrated on creating simple, elegant forms and flowing designs using natural motifs. The heavy octagonal Chinese-style mirrors of the eighth century, for example, were replaced by thin, plain circular forms, with stylized flowers for knobs and delicate decorative designs of cranes, pine branches, butterflies, and autumn grasses.

T'ang-style three-color ceramics (*sansai*), a notable development of the Nara period, were no longer produced, probably because they lacked the subtlety demanded by the new era. The traditional unglazed *sueki*, a grey, wheel-turned pottery that had been introduced from Korea around 400 C.E., continued in production, as did a new off-white variant of the same ware, which was often glazed in pale green and incised with graceful floral designs. But aristocratic

---

2 For an illustration, see Yamanobe Tomoyuki, Okada Jō, and Kurata Osamu, *Senshoku shikkō, kinkō*, vol. 20 of *Genshoku Nihon no bijutsu* (Tokyo: Shōgakukan, 1969), p. 63.

taste preferred lacquered wood for objects of everyday use and imported Sung porcelains for special treasures; and the Heian period was consequently one of general decline in the ceramic arts.

The largest, most conspicuous furnishings of a room were blinds, screens (both folding and rigid), and curtains (both fixed and portable), which were used to partition spaces, prevent drafts, and guard privacy. *Eiga monogatari* (*A Tale of Flowering Fortunes*), an anonymous eleventh-century chronicle, describes articles of this type assembled in 1023 for the coming-of-age ceremony of Princess Teishi (1013–94), Fujiwara no Michinaga's granddaughter.

> The bombycine[3] lavender curtains, shading to purple toward the bottom, were decorated with embroidered branch designs, and their Chinese-braided streamers were cluster-dyed in purple. The curtain-dais was decorated in the same manner.... The curtain-stands and folding-screen frames were inlaid with mother-of-pearl and gold lacquer. On the five-foot screens there were quotations from Chinese works, inscribed in elegant Chinese characters by Major Counselor Yukinari; and on the four-foot Chinese damask screens, their colored-paper sections lightly tinged with purple, there were texts in Yukinari's cursive Japanese script, the calligraphy and underlying designs together producing an effect of indescribable brilliance and taste. The edgings were of Chinese brocade.... The blinds were edged in green bombycine with a large figure.[4]

This passage bears witness to the care with which colors and designs were coordinated, and to the continuing attraction of Chinese material culture. It also reflects the importance attached to literature and calligraphy, the two arts which – together with music and its handmaid, dance – had traditionally been esteemed by Chinese Confucianists as instruments of self-cultivation and government, and which were regarded by Heian Japanese as supremely desirable social accomplishments. Ladies and gentlemen were expected to write a good hand, recognize a literary allusion, compose a creditable poem when called on, perform with skill on one or more musical instruments, be enough of a connoisseur to judge the efforts of others, and, in the case of men, master the steps of certain dances and sing familiar songs in a subtly original manner. So seriously were the requirements taken – so great was the prestige of Chinese example and so active the sponsorship in high circles – that the arts

---

3 *Orimono*, a term thought to have designated a luxurious silk fabric, possibly a changeable damask. See William H. and Helen Craig McCullough, *A Tale of Flowering Fortunes*, 2 vols. (Stanford, Calif.: Stanford University Press, 1980), p. 140, n. 26.

4 Matsumura Hiroji and Yamanaka Yutaka, eds., *Eiga monogatari*, vols. 75–76 of *Nihon koten bungaku taikei* (Tokyo: Iwanami shoten, 1964–65), vol. 2, pp. 104–5; translation after McCullough and McCullough, *Flowering Fortunes*, p. 584.

permeated everyday life to an extent seldom, if ever, matched elsewhere. Little Princess Teishi's domestic furniture, with its inscriptions in the hand of one of the world's greatest calligraphers, may indeed be said to call into question the utility of attempting to distinguish between the fine and the applied arts for the Heian period. We do so primarily for convenience.

TEXTILES AND COSTUMES

Damasks, brocades, and bombycines, mentioned in the description of Princess Teishi's screens and curtains, were among the principal fabrics worn by members of the upper classes, who dressed almost exclusively in silks. Except for a brief early period, Heian weaving and dyeing techniques were less varied than those of the eighth century, during which the Japanese had mastered tie-dyeing, stenciling, and batik techniques and skillfully imitated a wide assortment of continental weaves, including rich damasks, many types of brocades with striking designs, and intricately woven chiffon-like gauzes. Heian brocades employed fewer colors and smaller designs, the gauzes were less elaborate, and the damasks fell below Nara standards. Throughout the Heian period, long after the cessation of official intercourse, Chinese fabrics were imported by the wealthy because of their superior quality. But it would be a mistake to infer that Heian craftsmen were incapable of first-class work, or that their patrons were less interested in dress than their Nara-period predecessors. The changes represented, rather, a response to a changing aesthetic – a new interest in subdued effects, achieved not by flamboyant polychromes but by the graceful, flowing lines and subtle monochromes of wide-sleeved robes, woven of luxurious but unassertive fabrics and worn in voluminous layers. The demand was for large-scale production, and the weavers consequently avoided difficult, time-consuming methods.

Far from dismissing personal attire as unimportant, society regarded it as a major indicator of taste. Much anxious thought was devoted to the subject, especially by women, whose beauty was judged primarily by their dress and by the length, thickness, and lustre of their hair, rather than by their faces, which were made up according to a convention calling for chalky skin, rouged cheeks and lips, thick painted eyebrows, and blackened teeth.[5] Interest could be

---

5 For short discussions of Heian cosmetics, see Ivan Morris, *The World of the Shining Prince* (New York: Alfred A. Knopf, 1964), pp. 203–4, and Ema Tsutomu, *Yūsoku kojitsu* (Kyoto: Kawara shoten, 1965), pp. 75–77.

lent to a garment by artful shading of a color, or by the combination of robe and lining in such a way as to suggest an aspect of nature appropriate to the season. There were, for example, wisteria robes of pale purple lined with green, and fallen-leaf robes of yellowish brown lined with yellow. Another alternative was to use discreet woven or embroidered designs, such as lozenges and stylized birds and animals; another was to accentuate texture, as with the redplum robe, in which the warp thread was purple and the woof red, or the grape robe, which had a warp thread of pale red and a woof of pale purple.

In each such choice, the wearer's sensitivity was at stake, but the supreme test came when a complete costume was assembled – an ensemble that might include, in addition to the short outer jacket and long train prescribed for women on formal occasions, as many as twenty or more identically cut robes, their softly blending colors visible at the collar, sleeve openings, and hemline. As with individual lined garments, layers were expected to harmonize with the season. *Eiga monogatari* describes spring combinations worn by both sexes at a New Year banquet held in 1025 by Grand Empress Kenshi, Michinaga's second daughter.

After the ceremonial obeisances, Yorimichi, as Minister of the Left, led a stately procession up the east steps of the main hall. He occupied the seat of honor east of the south steps. The Ononomiya Minister of the Right was next to him, and then came Tadanobu and all the others. They sat on square cushions facing north, with the tails of their under-jackets draped over the balustrades behind them. The color combinations of the jackets were [red] glossed silk, willow, cherry, grape, and, in the case of the younger men, red plum – a most delightful and glittering array.

Once seated, the gentlemen inspected the edges of the rows of blinds in front of them. By mutual consent, each of the ladies on the other side was wearing three of the same five color combinations – willow, cherry, yellow, red plum, and yellowish green. Some had on five robes in each of their three combinations, a total of fifteen; others, six or seven, amounting to eighteen or twenty-one in all. Some were wearing Chinese damasks; others seemed to have on bombycines that were either bound- or float-patterned, the difference being determined by the color combination. Some of the mantles were five-layered; others seemed to be glossed unlined garments dyed pale green and other such colors. The jacket colors were chosen from among the same five combinations, and the trains were decorated with seashore patterns. The stand curtains were in red plum, yellowish green, and cherry colors, deepening toward the bottom, and were decorated with paintings and brilliant green streamers.[6]

---

6 Matsumura and Yamanaka, *Eiga*, vol. 2, pp. 177–78; translation from McCullough and McCullough, *Flowering Fortunes*, pp. 651–52.

As this passage intimates, the wearer's freedom of choice was circumscribed by the necessity of dressing in a manner recognized as appropriate to his or her age. There were also official regulations correlating colors and fabrics with court rank. Speaking earlier of Kenshi's appointment as empress in 1012, *Eiga monogatari* comments:

> In the past, it had been almost impossible to distinguish the various ranks of Kenshi's attendants, who had all dressed as they pleased. Some of them had disapproved of such laxity, but many of those very ladies found their prescribed costumes a source of embarrassment on the day of their mistress's elevation. The timid and conservative were obliged by the regulations to put on bombycine jackets, whereas others who had prided themselves on their elegance were suddenly confronted by the devastating necessity of appearing in plain silk.[7]

Similarly, in *Genji monogatari* (*The Tale of Genji*), the fiction writer Murasaki Shikibu describes the plight of Genji's young son, Yūgiri, who continues to wear the ignominious blue of the Sixth Rank after his contemporaries have moved up to more prestigious colors.[8] Such regulations are further evidence of the great importance attached to dress, as are the sumptuary edicts that were repeatedly promulgated during the Heian period in a vain effort to curb extravagant displays of the type just described.

Incense

To complete a costume successfully, it was necessary to scent the garments. Incense for the purpose was compounded from aromatic substances such as spikenard, sandalwood, musk, herbs, and cloves, which were pulverized, bound together with honey or some other sweet agent, and kneaded into hard balls. Incense making was considered an art, and one of the marks of taste was the ability to discriminate between traditional blends (which bore such names as fragrant-robe, gentleman-in-waiting, and plum-blossom), to create original variations, and to judge the products of others.

Fans

Careful attention was also devoted to the costume's principal accessory, the folding fan, a Japanese invention dating from around the

---

7 Matsumura and Yamanaka, *Eiga*, vol. 1, p. 324; translation from McCullough and McCullough, *Flowering Fortunes*, p. 332.
8 Yamagishi Tokuhei, ed., *Genji monogatari*, vols. 14–18 of *Nihon koten bungaku taikei* (1958–63), vol. 2, p. 277; Edward G. Seidensticker, trans., *The Tale of Genji*, 2 vols. (New York: Alfred A. Knopf, 1976), pp. 361–62.

tenth century. As was recognized by the Chinese, who were already importing them in the Northern Sung period (960–1126), many of these objects were works of art. They were of two types, one for winter use and one for summer. The former was made of joined strips of wood, the material, color, and decoration of which were determined by the user's sex, age, and social status; the latter had paper on one side and exposed ribs on the other, and was bound by no restrictions as to style or use. Most contemporaneous descriptions are of the summer variety, like the one below, which appears in *Ōkagami* (*The Great Mirror*), a historical tale dating from around the beginning of the twelfth century.

Most of their creations had ribs of gold lacquer, or of carved or inlaid silver, gold, aloeswood, or sandalwood; and their gorgeous paper surfaces were inscribed with unfamiliar Chinese and Japanese poems, or adorned with pictures of famous places mentioned in poetic handbooks. But Yukinari, with his usual flair, chose plain, tasteful lacquered ribs and yellow Chinese paper decorated with intriguingly faint pictures. On the front he wrote a Chinese song in elegant formal script, and on the back a few graceful cursive lines. The emperor examined the fan many times and then treasured it carefully in his handbox. The others he forgot after a brief show of interest. Say what you will, nothing is better than a sovereign's approbation.[9]

This author's bias in favor of elegant simplicity, in support of which he musters the highest possible social authority, reminds us that luxurious ornamentation and elaborate conceits were not sufficient in themselves to meet the standards of exacting connoisseurs. It can perhaps be said, by way of conclusion to the foregoing discussion of the major applied arts, that in this sphere, as in others, fastidiousness and restraint played a fundamental role in shaping taste, and, further, that those traits fostered a concern with total effect – with the achievement and appreciation of a sophisticated balance between the rich, glowing beauty of gold-lacquered cabinets, crimson fulled robes, and purple gossamer curtains, on the one hand, and, on the other, the spartan bareness, clean lines, and cool, dim interiors of the rooms in which they were displayed. A sure sense of visual effect produced sumptuousness without vulgarity; and fresh, original designs attest to the fact that in this realm, at least, the individual enjoyed considerable freedom of expression.

---

9 Matsumura Hiroji, ed., *Ōkagami*, vol. 21 of *Nihon koten bungaku taikei* (1960), pp. 144–45; translation from Helen Craig McCullough, *Ōkagami, The Great Mirror* (Princeton, N.J.: Princeton University Press, 1980), p. 147.

DIET

Surrounded though they were by extraordinary natural and manmade beauty, Heian aristocrats lived far from sybaritic lives. Caftanlike robes with huge sleeves provided inadequate protection against the winter cold of unheated houses; sanitary facilities were primitive; and mosquitoes, fleas, lice, and other insects were no respecters of rank. Members of society sat or reclined on the floor during the daytime and lay on the floor at night, covered by a robe or two. Worst of all was the poverty of their diet, which caused boils and other medical problems stemming from malnutrition, and which, in the view of some writers, may have been at least partially responsible for the passivity and pessimism that bulk so large in Heian history and literature.[10]

The upper classes consumed two main meals a day, probably around ten A.M. and four P.M., supplementing them with occasional snacks. After brief experimentation with Chinese cuisine at the beginning of the ninth century, court society had returned almost entirely to native foods and native methods of preparation. Most of the calories in the diet came from polished rice, which was served in a number of ways – boiled with water, steamed and dried for travel fare, combined with other grains and vegetables in cakes, or thinned with water to produce a gruel, which was sometimes mixed with red beans, chestnuts, or the like. A standard banquet dish, sweet potato gruel, consisted of rice cooked with thin slices of sweet potato and flavored with *amazura,* a sweet liquid obtained from a vine.

The principal source of vitamins was a fairly wide variety of vegetables – eggplant, bamboo shoots, cucumbers, miscellaneous greens, burdock, onions, long scallions, daikon radishes, various legumes, and so on – which seem to have been consumed chiefly in pickled, boiled, or steamed form. Ample iodine was supplied by several kinds of seaweed.

Protein came primarily from such fish and shellfish as bonito, sea bream, eel, carp, sea bass, mackerel, sardines, trout, whitebait, prawns, squid, jellyfish, crabs, and clams. Because of transportation and storage difficulties, most fish had to be dried unless they were

---

10 See Ishimura Teikichi, *Yūsoku kojitsu kenkyū,* 3 vols. (Tokyo: Yūsoku kojitsu kenkyū kankōkai, 1958), vol. 2, p. 353; Watanabe Minoru, *Nihon shokuseikatsu shi* (Tokyo: Yoshikawa kōbunkan, 1964), pp. 109, 113.

obtained from local waters. Buddhist-inspired official edicts prohibited consumption of the flesh of such animals as dogs, monkeys, horses, and oxen, but custom sanctioned the use of boar meat and venison, as well as pheasants (a particular favorite) and other game birds and their eggs. By the end of the twelfth century, however, most members of the nobility seem to have been subsisting on largely vegetable and grain diets, supplemented by inadequate amounts of fish. Supply problems had long since ended the early Heian consumption of milk and two butter-like dairy products, with the result that the average diet lacked sufficient fat.

This simple fare was rendered more palatable by the use of such condiments and seasonings as salt, onion salt, ginger, garlic, vinegar, *miso*, and fish broth, and of three sweeteners – honey, *amazura*, and glutinous rice jelly. Imported sugar, when obtainable, served almost exclusively as a drug. For special occasions, there were a number of kinds of elaborately shaped "Chinese cakes" (*karagashi*), made of one or more types of flour, often stuffed with bean jam, rice jelly, bits of vegetable, or duck egg, and fried in sesame or walnut oil. Pears, tangerines, persimmons, loquats, plums, pomegranates, peaches, apples, strawberries, pine nuts, chestnuts, and other fruits and nuts were special delicacies, used, for example, to tempt the appetites of invalids. Another rare treat was shaved ice, obtained from blocks kept in storage chambers during the summer.

Tea, the seeds of which had been brought to Japan in 805, was grown in and around the capital, but almost entirely for medicinal purposes. (It was prepared for drinking by pounding the leaves, combining them with *amazura* or ginger in a ball, and steeping in hot water.) The only common beverage other than water was rice wine (*sake*), which was produced in a number of unrefined varieties. Although its alcohol content was relatively low, the wine seems to have been highly intoxicating, possibly because of the absence of fat in the diet; and we may assume, on the basis of much contemporary evidence, that it and the host's presents constituted the two main attractions of the many formal banquets on the official calendar – affairs at which dishes of negligible gastronomic interest, presented with exquisite attention to visual effect, were eaten in ceremonious silence by richly attired gentlemen, each of whom consciously contributed to the elegance of the scene by his appearance and behavior, relaxing into informality only after the red lacquered plates and silver cups had disappeared and the festive bowl had begun to circulate freely.

ARISTOCRATIC OCCUPATIONS AND PASTIMES

Although works like *The Tale of Genji* may convey a different impression, it is probably safe to say that the overriding concern of most male Heian aristocrats was the maintenance and enhancement of status. In economic terms, that aim meant securing a generous patron, seeking lucrative provincial governorships, and/or husbanding and increasing private sources of income, such as *shōen* (rural estates), in order that the individual might house and clothe himself and his many dependents in the discreetly luxurious manner already described. Politically, it meant using talents and connections in an unceasing effort to rise in the bureaucracy, and, in particular, to achieve multiple offices of high ceremonial visibility. Socially, it meant actively pursuing advantageous alliances with other families and exhibiting such esteemed personal qualities as beauty, skill in poetry, music, and calligraphy, and the ability to rise to an occasion with a witticism or a comment showing sensitivity to the evanescence of worldly things.

Members of minor court families, barred by birth from high position, clung to modest official niches by developing expertise in, and hereditary claims to, such specialities as precedents, ceremonies, law, mathematics, the preparation and processing of documents, and the rudiments of astronomy and medicine, and by assuming responsibility for routine governmental operations. It was they who kept the bureaucracy running – and, as will be seen later, it was from their ranks that many quasi-professional poets emerged to achieve a degree of recognition that would otherwise have been unthinkable. In the status-bound world of the Heian court, outstanding literary ability was virtually the only avenue to relative prominence for men whose ambitions were frustrated by the accident of birth, or by the superior manipulative skills of their peers, but it was not a substitute for rank and office, as can be seen by the regularity with which low-ranking poets lamented their inability to climb the official ladder. As a class, men from minor families lacked prestige. It was their superiors who set the tone of Heian culture.

For the highborn noble, whose success in life depended on circumstances only tangentially connected to his competence and diligence in office, the pursuit of status assumed forms not always readily distinguishable from the pursuit of pleasure, with the result that he is sometimes portrayed as a carefree dilettante, enjoying himself with whatever came to hand in the daytime, and flitting from flower to flower at night. Such descriptions overlook the demands and restrictions imposed on the individual by his censorious, gossipy peers, who expected him above all to function as a smooth cog in the social machinery, and who had a correspondingly low tolerance for unorthodoxy. The line between public and private behavior was ambiguous – or perhaps it would be more accurate to say that very little of a man's behavior was private in the sense of being outside the purview of rules, whether explicit or unwritten. It was, of course, of the utmost importance that he contribute by his attire, demeanor, and knowledge of protocol to the successful execution of the annual ceremonies (*nenjū gyōji*) around which court life revolved – those great Chinese-inspired civil pageants, themselves a supreme affirmation of status, which symbolized the values and preoccupations of the pacific Heian court as surely as tournaments of arms represented those of its medieval Western counterparts. But the scrutiny of society was equally intense, and the demand for conformity equally insistent, on lesser occasions, including those that might impress an observer as having been designed purely for amusement.

Excursions

Participation in the quasi-official pleasure excursions of imperial personages and Fujiwara leaders was both an honor and an obligation, both an occasion for enjoyment and an opportunity for a man to distinguish himself by his appearance, horsemanship, knowledge of precedent, wit, or literary proficiency. Such events were usually linked to the seasons, focusing in the spring on blossom-viewing at suburban sites like Kitano and the Urin'in cloister, or in autumn on enjoyment of the foliage at Arashiyama or some other favorite spot. The Ōi River, at the base of Arashiyama in what is now Ukyō-ku, Kyoto, was the scene of many elegant entertainments, including an autumn river excursion arranged by Michinaga, at which the talented Kintō (966–1041) received the signal honor of being invited to choose from among the three boats – "one for guests who were skilled in the composition of Chinese verse, another for expert musicians, and a third for outstanding *waka* [Japanese verse] poets."[11]

The usual winter objective was falconry, the only form of hunting sanctioned by the court, which was apparently prompted by the sport's popularity to disregard the Buddhist prohibition against the

---

11 Matsumura, *Ōkagami*, p. 94; translation from McCullough, *Ōkagami*, p. 113.

taking of life. Falconry was a favorite pastime of at least eleven emperors, from Kammu in the ninth century to Shirakawa in the twelfth; and there are many records of festive outings at which royal spectators and their courtiers watched the activities of falconers and dog handlers, who gradually came to be members of specialist families, versed in secret traditions and masters of elaborately ritualized techniques. Whatever the occasion, the excursions of leading court figures usually began with a procession through the city streets and ended with food, wine, music, poetry, and gifts from the host. Smaller, more private outings for similar purposes were somewhat less formal but followed the same general pattern.

Horsemanship

Most of the retinue traveled on horseback during such pleasure jaunts, which sometimes extended over several days but more typically were arranged so as to avoid spending the night away from the capital. The ability to ride was also necessary if a man was to play his assigned role in great state events like the Imperial Purification, held on the Kamo River beach at the beginning of a new reign, or the Kamo Festival, which was preceded by the most magnificent procession of the year. In earlier periods, riding had been closely associated with military prowess, a tradition that persisted in the warrior class throughout the Heian centuries. Numerous members of the upper aristocracy are also praised for their horsemanship in contemporary records – for example, Minamoto no Makoto (810–69), who met his death in a racing accident, and such prominent Fujiwara nobles as Uchimaro (756–812), Michinaga, Tadazane (1078–1162), and Tadamichi (1097–1164). But the connection with warlike activities is seldom, if ever, made in such cases. Rather, there is increasing emphasis on the individual's contribution to a total visual effect, a task requiring not only skillful horsemanship but also careful attention to the horse's appearance, to the rider's costume, and to the burgeoning rules that prescribed the manner in which the bridle was to be held, the angle at which the whip was to be applied, and the like.[12]

Racing, which had claimed Makoto's life in the ninth century,

---

12 See Matsumura, Ōkagami, p. 221 (McCullough, Ōkagami, p. 196); Yamada Yoshio, Yamada Tadao, Yamada Hideo, and Yamada Toshio, eds., Konjaku monogatari shū, vols. 22–26 of Nihon koten bungaku taikei (1959–63), vol. 4, pp. 271–72; Bernard Frank, Histoires qui sont maintenant du passé (Paris: Gallimard, 1968), pp. 156–57.

continued in favor, partly because it was associated with gambling, but, like hawking, it became primarily a spectator sport for the upper classes. The main races of the year were offical functions, held on the fifth and sixth of the fifth month. Two teams of men from the guards divisions competed on mounts provided by princes and other notables, the winners presented a musical program, and in the evening there was feasting, with music and imperial gifts. A similar pattern was followed on private occasions, as when an emperor or retired emperor visited the home of a minister of state.[13]

Archery

Archery, another sport with strong roots in the martial past, retained its popularity throughout the Heian period. Participation in the mounted variety was left primarily to warriors and members of the lower nobility, although emperors and regents demonstrated their interest by rewarding proficiency. Foot archery, which claimed the prestige of Chinese endorsement, was considered an appropriate exercise for a gentleman. (It was one of only two forms of recreation sanctioned for university students, the other being playing the *koto*.) Numerous ninth-century princes and other personages were renowned for their marksmanship, and the sport was further recognized by the inclusion of an official contest, the Archery Ceremony (*jarai*), in the court calendar. Men of every rank were expected to make themselves available for the two competing Archery Ceremony teams, which performed on the seventeenth of the first month. As time went on, however, senior nobles showed themselves reluctant to participate, and a subsidiary contest on the eighteenth, the Bowman's Wager (*noriyumi*), established itself as the focal point of attention, apparently because the higher nobles were able to watch guardsman teams compete without being obliged to demonstrate their own skill. There were also less formal matches, both at court and in private circles, between teams of wellborn young men. On the lighter side, such events furnished an excuse for drinking and betting, but they were also serious matters for the families involved, because they offered a youth an opportunity to attract favorable notice by his dress, mastery of techniques (and of a growing number of complicated rules), and performance in the later musical entertainment.

13 See "An Imperial Visit to the Horse Races," McCullough and McCullough, *Flowering Fortunes*, pp. 631–39.

Wrestling

Another type of physical prowess was celebrated in the seventh-month wrestling (*sumai*), a lavish summer spectacle featuring competition between two teams of champions, recruited from the provinces and trained by members of the imperial bodyguards. After the ninth century, wrestling was almost entirely a spectator sport, but the official matches were one of the highlights of the year, and it was probably economic difficulties, rather than flagging interest, that led to their disappearance from the court calendar in 1174.[14]

Kemari

The tendency to shun participation in strenuous sports may have stemmed in part from the inadequacy of the upper-class diet, but the principal explanation is doubtless to be sought in Chinese-inspired notions of decorum, and in the increasing disposition to treat sport as tableau. The strong emphasis on social harmony seems to have played a role in the preference for team competition. It is significant that the element of competition was almost completely lacking in *kemari* (kickball), the one notably active sport in which male aristocrats consistently indulged. *Kemari* was a game played with a small deerskin ball on a hard-surfaced square court, approximately seven meters long on each side. Eight men, of whom two were stationed under each of four trees at the court's corners, attempted to keep the ball in the air for as many counts as possible, using only their feet. Counting, which began after the fiftieth kick, continued in theory to 1,000, the perfect score, but the usual score seems to have been below 300. Every noble family had its *kemari* court, and the game's enthusiasts included such prominent figures as Emperor Go-Toba (1180–1239), the poet Saigyō (1118–90), and Saigyō's teacher, Fujiwara no Narimichi (1097–1159), the greatest of all *kemari* masters, who held the high court rank of Major Counselor. Even this innocuous pastime, however, was censured by Murasaki Shikibu and Sei Shōnagon, those supremely articulate spokeswomen for naturalized Chinese values (see section entitled "Literature: Narrative Prose"), who found it indecorous and inelegant for gentlemen to rush around in pursuit of a ball. Given the strength of the attitude

---

14 For a description of the *sumai* festivities, see McCullough and McCullough, *Flowering Fortunes*, pp. 391–92.

the two represented, it is not surprising that upper-class amusements tended to be sedentary, and that we hear nothing of such highly competitive activities as swordsmanship.

Feminine occupations

Most aristocratic women had little contact with, or knowledge of, the official activities of men, or of such masculine recreations as hawking, archery, and wrestling. They led quiet, very private lives at home, practicing calligraphy, studying the poetic anthologies, improving their musicianship, reading or listening to stories, assembling costumes, caring for children, and keeping up a poetic correspondence with men and others in the outside world. The monotony of their existence was broken by the companionship (often chiefly nocturnal) of husbands or lovers, by domestic ceremonies and religious activities, and by occasional pilgrimages and sightseeing excursions, made behind the curtains of ox-drawn carriages – vehicles used by both men and women, which accurately reflected the wealth and social status of their owners in their size, construction, fittings, and ornamentation.

Members of both sexes played *go*, character guessing, backgammon (*sugoroku*), and other parlor games, among which backgammon seems to have been a particular masculine favorite. "Whenever Michinaga and Korechika settled down to gamble [at backgammon]," *Ōkagami* says, describing what may have been a fairly typical case, "they bared their torsos, bundled up their robes around their waists, and kept at it until midnight or beyond.... Some remarkable and very tasteful stakes changed hands."[15]

Monoawase

Much more to the liking of fastidious feminine writers – and of women in general, we may suppose – were "matchings of things" (*monoawase*), of which Sei Shōnagon wrote in "Things That Bring Happiness," "How could anyone help feeling happy after winning one of those contests in which various things are compared?"[16]

The *monoawase*, ranked by a modern authority as one of the three

---

15 Matsumura, *Ōkagami*, p. 184; translation from McCullough, *Ōkagami*, p. 173.
16 Ikeda Kikan, Kishigami Shinji, and Akiyama Ken, eds., *Makura no sōshi, Murasaki Shikibu nikki*, vol. 19 of *Nihon koten bungaku taikei* (1958), p. 281.

favorite Heian pastimes (the others being falconry and *kemari*),[17] was in many respects the amusement most characteristic of the period and the society. With the exception of the ancient sport of cockfighting, which might be called a special case, such contests were group enterprises, in which the victory earned by one of the two sides – identified as the Left (the socially superior) and the Right – was scarcely more important than the preparation of costumes and accessories, the scene when the entries were presented, the attendant music, poetry, drinking, and other festivities, and the general opportunity to display taste, ingenuity, and wealth in an atmosphere of well-bred harmony. Sometimes these elegant battles were fought with man-made weapons, such as fans, incense balls, small boxes, musical instruments, pictures, poems, and romances. On other occasions, the combatants turned to nature, comparing the plaintive cries of insects displayed in dainty bamboo cages; matching the plumage or songs of ducks, quail, warblers, or doves; arranging sprays of spring blossoms along the borders of a garden stream or pond; or presenting autumn plants, such as chrysanthemums or colored leaves, on "sandbar-beach tables" (*suhama*), so called because of their gracefully curving tops, and because the entries were often incorporated in a seacoast setting.

The account below conveys some of the flavor of such occasions: the attention to symbolism and visual effect, the prominence assigned to music and poetry, and the preoccupation with status, shown in the care with which ranks and titles were recorded and seating arrangements noted. It describes a sweet-flag root contest held in the middle of the eleventh century – that is, during the heyday of Fujiwara opulence and splendor, which coincided with the regency of Michinaga's son Yorimichi (992–1074; regent 1017–67). Yorimichi was the moving spirit behind a succession of extravagant contests, many of them nominally sponsored by one or another of the regent's female relatives or, as here, by the emperor. The leaves and roots of the sweet flag, or calamus, were considered to possess medicinal properties. They figured in a number of customs associated with the Sweet-Flag Festival, held on the fifth of the fifth month as a protection against summer diseases; and it was therefore appropriate to associate them, as the Left did, with pines, cranes, and tortoises, all symbols of longevity. Of the two empresses mentioned, Kanshi was Yorimichi's daughter and Shōshi the daughter of his

---

17 Ishimura, *Yūsoku kojitsu kenkyū*, vol. 2, p. 487.

nephew, the late emperor Go-Ichijō. We learn from another source that Kanshi's ladies-in-waiting were "brilliantly attired in sweet-flag, China-tree, wild pink, and azalea combinations, with bordered sleeves and gold and silver flower and bird designs," and that Shōshi's wore identical glossed silk sweet-flag robes, wild pink bombycine cloaks, mugwort Chinese jackets, and China-tea trains.[18]

There was a sweet-flag root contest in the imperial palace on the fifth of the fifth month in the sixth year of Eishō [1051]. His Majesty had summoned one or two proficient senior nobles and a number of other courtiers for an archery contest on the last day of the third month, and there had also been cockfights, but no clearcut victory had been won, and so it had been determined that the decision should rest on the outcome of a sweet-flag contest.

The preparations in the apartments and grounds were the same as for the poetry contest in the tenth month of the fourth year of Eishō [1049]. Both empresses were present. Among those who attended were the Palace Minister Yorimune, the Minister of Popular Affairs Nagaie, the Inspector Major Counselor Nobuie, the Onoomiya Middle Counselor Kaneyori, the Commander of the Left Gate Guards Takakuni, the Chamberlain Middle Counselor Nobunaga, the Nijō Middle Counselor Toshiie, the Master of the Empress's Household Tsunesuke, the Consultant Middle Captain of the Left Yoshinaga, the Middle Captain of Third Rank Toshifusa, and the Lesser Captain of Third Rank Tadaie. The members of the Left and Right teams arrived in the evening.

First, oil was provided. Then it was time to produce the *suhama* prepared by the Left and the Right. The *suhama* of the Left, which was four feet high, was carried in and deposited east of the door leading to the east bay of the south eavechamber. It depicted a seaside scene, with silver pine trees, silver cranes and tortoises, and a silver stream flowing among aloeswood rocks. There was a scroll on a stand in front. On the scroll paper, which was decorated with delicately edged designs, there were five colored squares, each containing a poem. The green wrapper was decorated with silver, the roller was of amber, and the cord was of silver. There was a green gossamer cloth with a wave design to go under the *suhama*. Five long roots, twisted into circles, were arranged on the pine trees and beside the shore.... Five medicinal balls with long multicolored streamers were arranged in circles on the beach.

The members of the side seated themselves on the east veranda. Next, the scorekeeper's *suhama* was presented by chamberlains, who carried it in and put it down east of the principal *suhama*. It contained rocks and tiny pine trees, and there were artificial sweet flags to be used as tallies.

Next, other chamberlains carried in the *suhama* of the Right, which held a drumstand on a pedestal about two feet square, surmounted by a drum. In front of the drum there were dolls, representing children performing the

---

18 Matsumura and Yamanaka, *Eiga*, vol. 2, p. 449. For the Sweet-Flag Festival, see McCullough and McCullough, *Flowering Fortunes*, p. 412.

butterfly dance; and on each root a poem had been inscribed. Everything was made of silver. The long streamers of the gold and silver medicinal balls were arranged in circles near the shore.

The members of the side seated themselves on the west veranda. Next, the scorekeeper's *suhama* was presented. A single Chamberlain carried it in and put it down west of the principal *suhama*. It held an imitation of one of the bamboo clumps outside the imperial residence, and its tallies were bamboo stalks.

Next, in compliance with an imperial command, the senior nobles divided up into Left and Right sides. The senior nobles of the Left withdrew from their places, crossed to the east by way of the veranda in front of the emperor, and seated themselves. They were the Palace Minister, Lord Morokata, Lord Kaneyori, Lord Nobunaga, Lord Tsunesuke, and Lord Toshifusa. The captains of the Left and Right, Head Chamberlain Controller Tsuneie and Head Chamberlain Middle Captain Suketsuna, came forward and took their places below their *suhama*. Meanwhile, two child scorekeepers took their places, one for each side. They were sons of Lord Takakuni who were in service at the Courtiers' Hall.

Tsuneie summoned Yoshimoto and Suketsuna summoned Motoie. . . . Tsuneie picked up a long root and handed it to Yoshimoto, who stretched it out under the south eaves. The Right followed the same procedure, and then the lengths were compared. The Left's root was eleven feet long and the Right's twelve; hence the Right won. A second and a third round followed. In each, both roots measured ten feet, but the Right's was slightly longer, so the Right was adjudged the winner. It was decided that the contest would end with the third round.

Next, the five poems [of the Left and the five of the Right] were read. The reciters and their assistants were Nagakata and Tsuneie for the Left, and Takatoshi and Suketsuna for the Right. The Palace Minister was the judge. The topics were "Sweet Flags," "The Cuckoo," "Rice Seedlings," "Love," and "Felicitations." Everyone returned to his original seat after the readings.

Next, his Majesty gave the command for music. The Japanese *koto* was played by the Minister of Popular Affairs, the thirteen-stringed *koto* by the Middle Counselor of Second Rank, the lute by Tsunenobu, the mouth organ by Sadanaga, the flute by [missing], and the oboe by Takatoshi. The singer was Sukenaka. After an oboe solo, the Palace Minister . . . presented a flute to the emperor. His Majesty took it and told the Minister to use the clappers. The Minister assented and returned to his seat. Then the song "Ah! How August!" was sung. At the end of the song in the *ritsu* scale, His Majesty presented gift robes to the senior nobles, who then withdrew. I believe I have heard that there were no imperial gifts for the other courtiers on that occasion.[19]

Murasaki Shikibu, in *The Tale of Genji*, devotes a chapter to a contest in which two teams of ladies, representing rival imperial con-

---

19 Nagazumi Yasuaki and Shimada Isao, eds., *Kokon chomonjū*, vol. 84 of *Nihon koten bungaku taikei* (1966), pp. 498–500.

sorts, offered paintings for judgment in the emperor's presence. The preliminary maneuverings of the consorts' supporters as they sought to outwit the competition, and the anxious attention devoted to costumes, boxes, mountings, and cords, remind us that the winner of such a contest was considered to have gained a significant advantage in the incessant jockeying for favor that went on among powerful families with daughters in the palace harem. It was not only Prince Genji's enthusiasm for art, but also his desire to protect the interests of his protégée, Akikonomu, that impelled him to the exertions Murasaki describes.[20] Even when the stakes were lower, any *monoawase* – and particularly any public one – had its serious side, because it exposed the taste and sensitivity of the participants to exacting scrutiny. Like the other major pastimes we have reviewed, this one was seldom taken lightly.

SECULAR PAINTING

Toward the end of Murasaki Shikibu's "Picture Competition" chapter, Prince Hotaru remarks to his brother, Prince Genji, "Our father used to say, 'It goes without saying that Genji has mastered the art of poetic composition. As regards the other major accomplishments, he is best at playing the seven-stringed *koto;* then come the flute, lute, and thirteen-stringed *koto*.' Everyone else thought the same, so I assumed painting was merely something you did for amusement."[21]

That rather ambiguous comment might imply that painting was regarded as an important aristocratic accomplishment – a proposition for which there would appear to be support in *The Tale of Genji* itself, where members of the imperial family are depicted as zealous wielders of the brush; and also in other works, such as *Ōkagami* and *Eiga monogatari,* which describe the proficiency of leading court personages. We will probably be closer to the truth, however, if we assume that painting was acknowledged to be a skill requiring native ability (a point Prince Hotaru makes elsewhere in the same *Genji* passage), and that members of society were under no compulsion to try to master it. It seems to have been viewed in somewhat the same light as cooking, another hobby in which eminent gentlemen often dabbled. Like the applied arts, it was essentially the province of professionals – men

---

20 See H. Richard Okada, *Figures of Resistance: Language, Poetry, and Narrating in 'The Tale of Genji' and Other Mid-Heian Texts* (Durham, N.C.: Duke University Press, 1991), pp. 232–38, for a discussion of the interplay between politics and aesthetics on this occasion.
21 Yamagishi, *Genji,* vol. 2, p. 186.

of low social status who worked in the court Painting Office, or in private or temple ateliers. Although there was some overlapping, secular art was produced primarily by court and other lay painters; Buddhist art, by painter-monks associated with the big temples.

Only a few Heian painters' names have survived. Their Nara-period predecessors had been anonymous artisans, and the status of the profession remained much the same, even after the ninth-century rise of secular painting had brought new opportunities for the display of individual talent. Those of whom we hear remain shadowy figures, like Kudara no Kawanari (782–853), the first artist to enter the historical record, who was celebrated for his realism, and Kose no Kanaoka (fl. ca. 980), an expert painter of horses and the founder of the long-lived Kose school. Mentions of Kawanari, Kanaoka, and others recur from time to time in Heian texts, but we get little sense of their accomplishments, because their work, unlike that of the professional poets, no longer survives. Of the handful of extant Heian secular paintings, none can be attributed with confidence to a known artist.

We must likewise rely almost exclusively on literary sources for the history of Heian secular art. A great many paintings are known to have been executed on screens and panels (which were needed in large numbers after the adoption of *shindenzukuri* architecture), and also in small picture books and scrolls, designed primarily for feminine enjoyment. During the early ninth century, when Chinese influence was all-pervasive, styles and subjects were usually Chinese, but Japanese themes became increasingly popular by the tenth century, and a distinction was then made between *karae* (pictures with Chinese subjects) and *yamatoe* (pictures with Japanese subjects). As the Heian period advanced, *karae* continued to be produced. The only extant Heian landscape screen, for example, a work dating from around 1050, is a *karae* preserved at the Tōji Temple, depicting a young court noble visiting an elderly recluse who is probably to be identified with the Chinese poet Po Chü-i (772–846).[22] But the *yamatoe* became the predominant form, evolving from the *karae* – through a process that cannot be traced with certainty – into the mature Japanese style we find in the oldest remaining examples, most of which date from the twelfth century.

---

22 Illustrated in Saburo Ienaga, *Painting in the Yamato Style* (New York and Tokyo: John Weatherhill and Heibonsha, 1973), plate 26; also in Akiyama Terukazu, *Emakimono*, vol. 8 of *Genshoku Nihon no bijutsu* (1968), p. 164.

Rise of Yamatoe

In the second half of the ninth century, the Japanese were actively naturalizing or discarding many of the imported elements in their everyday life, in areas ranging from food and dress to music, art, and literature. The pivotal event of those decades was the emergence of a workable native syllabary (*kana*). By freeing the Japanese language from total dependence on an alien logographic writing system, *kana* paved the way for the remarkable social rise of Japanese poetry – that is, of the thirty-one-syllable *waka*, which can be said to have constituted the dominant element in aristocratic culture from the tenth century on. Paradoxically, this seeming move away from China proved to be a major step toward a truly Chinese-style society, because it made poetic expression an integral part of upper-class existence, instead of a self-conscious exercise in a foreign tongue. The evolution of *kana* also resulted in the development of narrative prose fiction, which, if it lacked Confucian sanction, nevertheless contributed to the literary atmosphere at court. As we shall see, it also influenced the direction taken by Japanese calligraphy. And it profoundly affected the content and form of the *yamatoe*.

Screen and panel pictures, the earliest form assumed by the *yamatoe*, were not regarded as independent works of art, but, rather, as companions to poems and as vehicles for the evocation of bittersweet emotion. The overwhelming majority were landscape paintings with added genre elements. They focused on the passing of time, as illustrated by the natural phenomena and human activities conventionally associated with the four seasons. Figures gathering young greens indicated spring, as did hazy hills dotted with flowering trees; a cuckoo pointed unmistakably to summer; deer or colored leaves to autumn; snow or falconry to winter. Colored-paper squares, positioned to enhance the total design, contained graceful poems (or, less frequently, prose), inscribed in flowing script, which endowed the pictures with specific connotations.

Although the pictures have long since vanished, many of the poems remain, helping us to visualize the content of the paintings and to understand the manner in which man and nature were linked. The five *waka* below, which may be considered typical, were all composed in 875 for a screen behind the guest of honor at a longevity celebration.

kasugano ni	The gods must know well
wakana tsumitsutsu	The feelings with which I pray,
yorozuyo o	"Ten thousand years"
iwau kokoro wa	As I pluck the tender shoots
kami zo shiruran	On the plain of Kasuga.

yama takami	So high the mountains
kumoi ni miyuru	They seem to float in the sky –
sakurabana	Those cherry blossoms
kokoro no yukite	My spirit visits daily,
oranu hi zo naki	Longing to break off a bough.

mezurashiki	Yours is not, cuckoo,
koe naranaku ni	A song we hear but rarely –
hototogisu	Why, then, should it be
kokora no toshi o	That listening through the years,
akazu mo aru ka na	We never weary of you?

chidori naku	Mists must be hovering
sao no kawagiri	Above the Sao River
tachinurashi	Where plovers call out,
yama no ko no ha mo	For now the mountain foliage
iro masariyuku	Takes on ever deeper hues.

shirayuki no	When white flakes of snow
furishiku toki wa	Flutter thick and fast toward earth,
miyoshino no	Flowers indeed scatter
yamashitakaze ni	Before the gale sweeping down
hana zo chirikeru	From fair Yoshino's mountains.[23]

In order to form a notion of the actual appearance of these four-seasons screens and panels, we must examine the few scraps of evidence remaining from the Heian period itself, as well as comparable examples of the later *yamatoe* style. Naturalized landscape backgrounds dating from the mid-eleventh century are to be seen in the Tōji *karae* screen and in religious door paintings at the Byōdōin in Uji; and there are numerous small-scale landscapes, including representations of screens and panels, in twelfth-century scrolls. The pictorial designs on lacquer, ceramic, and metal objects also offer useful hints. It seems safe to conclude, after such a review, that most Heian *yamatoe* landscapes modified Chinese techniques in order to achieve soft, delicate, romantic effects, and that the total impression was one of elegant refinement.

---

23 Saeki Umetomo, ed., *Kokin waka shū*, vol. 8 of *Nihon koten bungaku taikei* (1959), nos. 357–59, 361–62. Here and below, *Kokinshū* translations, sometimes slightly altered, are from Helen Craig McCullough, *Kokin Wakashū: With 'Tosa Nikki' and 'Shinsen Waka'* (Stanford, Calif.: Stanford University Press, 1985). Poem numbers in Saeki are identical with those in *Shimpen kokka taikan*.

Emakimono

The appearance of the *yamatoe* coincided with the development of such vernacular narrative prose forms as the romance, the diary, and the poem tale (see section entitled "Literature: Narrative Prose"). It was not long before romances and similar works began to inspire paintings, which sometimes took the form of screen decorations but most often appeared as booklets (*sōshi*) or horizontal, hand scrolls (*emaki*[*mono*]) – small treasures for highborn ladies, who gazed at them while attendants read from related texts or told stories of their own invention. The horizontal scrolls were made of sheets of paper pasted together and attached to a mounting at one end and a roller at the other. Quite apart from the aesthetic value of their paintings, they were objects of art in their own right, with braided silk cords, richly colored mountings, rollers made of jade, crystal, or precious wood, and textual passages inscribed in exquisite calligraphy on paper flecked with silver and gold. That they were favored over the plainer *sōshi* is suggested by the frequency of their mention in works like *The Tale of Genji,* and by the fact that all the principal surviving Heian *yamatoe* are in *emakimono* form.

Two main types of Heian secular narrative *emakimono* exist today, known respectively as *onnae* (feminine pictures) and *otokoe* (masculine pictures). Both probably derive from Chinese antecedents, through a process that cannot be reconstructed, and both are closely associated with native literary genres – *onnae* with romances, *kana* diaries, and poem tales; *otokoe* with an anecdotal, supposedly factual, ultimately oral genre of very short stories called *setsuwa*. The oldest extant set of *onnae* scrolls, the *Genji monogatari emaki* (*The Tale of Genji Picture Scrolls*), is a masterpiece that obviously represents the culmination of a long line of development. There is also ample literary evidence to show that *onnae* were probably being produced by around the middle of the tenth century, and that they were extremely numerous and popular from at least the eleventh century on. No comparable information exists for *otokoe*, but it does not necessarily follow that the *otokoe* was a much later phenomenon, as has sometimes been maintained.[24] Rather, in view of the high artistic

---

24 Tokyo National Museum, *Painting 6th–14th Centuries*, vol. 1 of *Pageant of Japanese Art* (Tokyo: Toto Shuppan, 1957), p. 37; Seidensticker, *Genji*, pp. 307–17; Hideo Okudaira, *Narrative Picture Scrolls* (New York and Tokyo: Weatherhill and Shibundō, 1973), p. 29; Dietrich Seckel, *Emakimono: The Art of the Japanese Painted Hand-Scroll* (London: Jonathan Cape, 1959), p. 25.

level of the oldest known examples, it seems best to postulate an ancestry of considerable antiquity. We may conjecture that the lack of references to *otokoe* in the writings of court women, our best sources in such matters, is due not to their absence from the society but to a feminine preference for pictures illustrating literature of a different kind.

Very soon after the appearance of *The Tale of Genji* in the early eleventh century, that great work of fiction was canonized as the supreme embodiment of the Heian spirit, and as a magisterial exposition, in particular, of the central aesthetic concept known as *mono no aware*, which may be roughly defined as deep but controlled emotional sensitivity, especially to beauty and to the tyranny of time. The book was read, re-read, quoted, imitated, explicated, and illustrated by generations of admirers; and it is surely no coincidence that it furnished the subject matter for what is not only the earliest surviving set of *onnae* scrolls but also, in the view of some scholars, the finest achievement in the history of Japanese painting. As is true of most *emakimono*, the four *Genji monogatari emaki* scrolls contain both pictures and textual passages. Traditionally ascribed to the court painter Fujiwara no Takayoshi (fl. ca. 1147), they are now recognized to have been produced by different painting ateliers and different calligraphers, probably around the 1120s or 1130s. In its present incomplete state, the set includes paintings of nineteen separate scenes, almost all of which are laid in *shindenzukuri* apartments and adjoining verandas. The strong, dramatic parallel lines of railings, partitions, and lintels contrast magnificently with the richly colored robes, screens, curtains, and blinds; and the stylized human figures, with slit eyes and hooks for noses, are represented in static, pensive poses, perfectly attuned to the majestic pace and melancholy tone of Murasaki's work, and to the planes and masses of the total composition. As in the society of which it is a microcosm, there is small place in this romantic, dreamlike world for ill-bred assertions of individuality or violent outpourings of emotion. Prince Genji's face is impassive when he holds his wife's infant son by another man, and only the tilt of his head hints at his feelings.[25]

Two outstanding examples of the *otokoe* technique survive, both dating from around the middle of the twelfth century. The three scrolls of the first, the *Shigisan engi emaki* (Shigisan Legend Picture

---

25 Akiyama, *Emakimono*, plate 2; also Ivan Morris, *The Tale of Genji Scroll* (Tokyo: Kodansha International, 1971), facing p. 54.

Scrolls), depict miraculous events associated with the monk Myōren (fl. tenth century); the subject of the second, the *Ban dainagon emaki* (Ban Major Counselor Picture Scrolls, 3 scrolls), is the Ōtemmon palace gate fire of 866, said to have been set by the court noble Tomo (or Ban) no Yoshio (809–68) in an attempt to discredit a political rival. The *Shigisan engi emaki* stories unfold in a swift, cinematic style, characterized by robust realism and freely flowing brushwork. Colors appear only in thin washes, and the human figures are almost all members of the lower classes, who reveal their feelings of alarm, amazement, or joy through exaggerated facial expressions and hand and foot movements. Most of the action takes place outdoors. The *Ban dainagon emaki* makes more conspicuous use of color and devotes more attention to the upper classes, but its vigorous realism, boisterous crowds of uninhibited commoners, and arson and fisticuffs remove it, too, very far from the feminine milieu of the *Genji monogatari emaki*.[26]

Of other *emakimono* remaining from the late Heian period, the most important are the first two scrolls of the *Chōjū jimbutsu giga* (Bird, Animal, and Human Caricatures), a work consisting of four scrolls in all. The two Heian scrolls (mid-twelfth century?), which may be from a single hand, contain drawings of monkeys, rabbits, and frogs mimicking humans (scroll 1) and sketches of horses, oxen, roosters, lions, dragons, and other real and imaginary creatures (scroll 2); the other two (early thirteenth century) repeat the subject-matter of scroll 1, with additional scenes of monks and laymen gambling (scroll 3), and depict monks and laymen engaged in frequently enigmatic activities (scroll 4). The symbolic intent, if any, is not understood. All four are executed almost exclusively in ink, using a technique derived from Buddhist copybooks; and the first and second are particularly noteworthy for their skillful composition, lively realism, and fluent, powerful brushwork.[27]

CALLIGRAPHY AND PAPER

The *Chōjū jimbutsu giga* scrolls, unusual in so many other respects, are also among the few Heian *emakimono* without calligraphic sections. All the other major narrative scroll sets contain brief textual passages, which were probably intended not so much to inform the

---

26 For illustrations, see Akiyama, *Emakimono*, plates 22–30 (*Shigisan engi emaki*) and plates 31–35 (*Ban dainagon emaki*).
27 Illustrated in Akiyama, *Emakimono*, plates 36–40.

viewer, who could have been expected to know the stories, as to enhance the visual effect and reinforce the connection between painting and the prestigious arts of literature and calligraphy.

Although Chinese writing styles had been competently copied earlier, Japanese study of calligraphy as an art began with the great religious leader Kūkai (or Kōbō Daishi, 774–835), who absorbed the major T'ang styles during his fourteen months in China. The square (*kaisho*), running (*gyōsho*), grass (*sōsho*), and other styles sponsored or introduced by Kūkai after his return were essentially those perfected by the legendary Wang Hsi-chih (321?–71?) and his son Wang Hsien-chih (344–88). They provided the foundation for what was later known as the Chinese style (*karayō*); and Kūkai and two of his contemporaries, Emperor Saga (786–842) and Tachibana no Hayanari (d. 842) – the so-called Three Brushes (*sampitsu*) – were recognized as the style's best early practitioners.

Meanwhile, the Japanese were continuing the experimentation that was to lead ultimately to the modern *hiragana* syllabary. Their first step had been to adopt a bewildering variety of Chinese characters for the phonetic rendering of proper nouns, poems, and the like. Such characters, called *man'yōgana* because of their prominence in the eighth-century poetic anthology *Man'yōshū* (*Collection of Ten Thousand Generations*), continued to be used by early Heian writers, who often set them down in the grass style, producing a form called *sōgana*. By around the second half of the ninth century, a relatively small number of *sōgana* were being further streamlined, a process that led to the creation, by the early eleventh century if not before, of a syllabary (*kana*) similar to the modern one except for the survival of numerous alternative forms for most sounds. It was primarily in that syllabary, known also as the woman's hand (*onnade*), that poetry, romances, and women's diaries were written. (*Katakana*, the other modern syllabary, which dates from the same general period, developed as a utilitarian system of notation outside the mainstream of Heian culture.)

There is evidence that *kana* were used to some extent by men during the period of gestation, but most scholars assume that the lead was taken by women, for whom the study of Chinese characters was considered unsuitable, and who consequently needed a script for the letters and poems that bulked so large in their daily lives. It would be a mistake, however, to conclude that the suppleness and elegance of the script thus developed were qualities that appealed only to feminine taste. The first great calligrapher of the tenth century, Ono no

Michikaze (or Tōfū, 894–966), wrote Chinese characters in a graceful, simple manner that was already significantly different from the dignity and vigor of the orthodox style followed by the Three Brushes. The naturalization process was carried further by Fujiwara no Sukemasa (944–98), who was born about fifty years after Michikaze; and it reached maturity a generation later with Fujiwara no Yukinari (972–1027). Although Yukinari is bracketed with his two predecessors as one of the Three Calligraphers (*sanseki*) in the Japanese style (*wayō*), he is by far the most notable figure of the three, because it was his gentle, smooth brushwork that became the classic model, transmitted for generations by the immensely influential Sesonji school.

Yukinari's name is also associated with the classic *kana* style, which achieves an effect of great fluidity and elegance by linking individual *kana* in a long series of graceful loops and curves. The best examples of *kana* calligraphy in its golden age are the *Kōyagire* (Kōya fragments, ca. 1100?), a group of scrolls and fragments containing portions of the first imperial poetic anthology, *Kokinshū* (*Collection of Early and Modern Times*).[28] Two later works, the *Genji monogatari emaki* and *Sanjūrokunin shū* (*Collection of Thirty-Six Poets*, ca. 1110–20?), are celebrated for the superbly decorative manner in which they combine the arts of calligraphy, literature, painting, and paper making.

Sanjūrokunin shū, in particular, utilizes many different kinds of fine paper – heavy, white domestic *michinoku*; Chinese *rōsen*, decorated with wax designs; numerous kinds of domestic and imported *karakami* (Chinese paper), the *kana* paper par excellence, decorated with mica paste designs and gold and silver dust – juxtaposing different colors and textures with great verve and originality. One white sheet, for example, is decorated with an overall silver wave pattern and a picture showing an island, a boat, and wild geese in flight. An irregular brown band of differently textured paper has been added in the approximate center, with its own design of gold dust and plume grass, and there is a dark brown accent at the bottom of the page, studded with bits of gold leaf.[29]

Similarly opulent paper was used for religious purposes, as in the case of the well-known *Heike nōkyō* (*Taira Family Dedicatory Sutra*).

---

28 Illustrated in Ozawa Masao, ed., *Kokin waka shū*, vol. 7 of *Nihon koten bungaku zenshū* (Tokyo: Shōgakukan, 1971), p. 6.
29 For illustrations of *Genji monogatari emaki* and *Sanjūrokunin shū* paper and calligraphy, see Ienaga, *Painting*, plates 95–97; also Morris, *Genji Scroll*, passim.

The thirty-three scrolls in this set of the *Lotus Sutra*, presented to Itsukushima Shrine in 1164 by the powerful Taira family, are inscribed on paper lavishly decorated with gold and silver, dainty floral patterns, and under-paintings; and the *karae* and *yamatoe* illustrations, gold and silver fittings, mother-of-pearl inlays, and crystal rollers make the viewer feel that "their splendor and sumptuousness [suggest] collections of elegant verses rather than sutras," as *Eiga monogatari* comments of a similar set.[30]

It is not surprising that Heian aristocrats should have copied sutras in much the same spirit as poems, with equal attention to calligraphy, paper, and general artistic effect. To a considerable extent, religion itself was regarded as an aesthetic experience – a source of material and spiritual benefits, to be sure, but also an opportunity to delight the senses with the gorgeous ecclesiastical vestments, the solemn massed chants, the clouds of fragrant incense, and the pageantry that were associated with esoteric rituals, in particular. Sei Shōnagon expressed what must have been a common opinion when she said, "A preacher ought to be handsome. Otherwise, his ugliness leads us into sin by encouraging us to let our attention wander."[31] And since members of court society were the principal patrons of the great temples, their tastes inevitably affected the development of Buddhist painting and sculpture.

BUDDHIST ART

As with secular screen paintings and *emakimono*, we know from literary sources that Buddhist art was produced in huge quantities during the Heian period. The two esoteric sects, Shingon and Tendai, which dominated the early religious scene, required at least one new icon for each of the innumerable special rituals their monks performed day in and day out for aristocratic patrons; and groups of as many as a thousand paintings or statues were commissioned repeatedly by wealthy believers, especially in the eleventh and twelfth centuries.

Most of those works are gone, but a substantial number remains – fifty or sixty statues from the ninth century alone. Often pre-

---

30 Matsumura and Yamanaka, *Eiga*, vol. 2, pp. 43–44; McCullough and McCullough, *Flowering Fortunes*, p. 532. For *Heike nōkyō* illustrations, see Ienaga, *Painting*, plate 98; also Robert Treat Paine and Alexander Soper, *The Art and Architecture of Japan*, Pelican History of Art (Baltimore: Penguin Books, 1955), plate 57; and H. Minamoto, *An Illustrated History of Japanese Art* (Kyoto: K. Hoshino, 1935), plate 79.
31 Paraphrased from Ikeda, *Makura no sōshi*, pp. 73–74.

served in isolated temples, where they were relatively safe from spreading fires, warfare, and other dangers, such statues and paintings enable us to trace broad stylistic developments with comparative assurance. Art historians have usually treated them in terms of two periods, Jōgan (or Kōnin, or Kōnin Jōgan, after ninth-century era names) and Fujiwara, with Fujiwara representing the kind of courtly taste we have been discussing. In the view of some scholars, the Fujiwara period begins as early as 894; in that of others, as late as 980. To avoid ambiguity, we shall speak here of centuries, or of early Heian (ninth century), mid-Heian (tenth and eleventh centuries), and late Heian (twelfth century).

Sculpture

For Buddhist art, as for other aspects of Heian culture, Chinese influence predominated at the beginning of the ninth century. Sculpture imitated mid- and late-T'ang models, and through them the art of southern India, continuing a late eighth-century trend away from the realism and classic repose of the Nara masterpieces. The material was almost invariably a single block of wood, frequently embellished with polychrome decoration. The style, copied from imported statues and pattern books, was characterized by somber facial expressions; stout, almost corpulent bodies; formal, stylized poses; powerfully carved drapery swirling in abstract designs; and a suggestion of sensuous languor, imparted by half-closed eyes, full lips, and swelling flesh.

Although it is possible to detect a certain degree of naturalization well before the end of the ninth century, all of the above traits are present not only in the Jingoji Yakushi Nyorai, which probably dates from around 800, but also in works attributed to the mid- and late-ninth century, such as the Kanshinji Nyoirin Kannon and the Hokkeji Eleven-Headed Kannon.[32] Moreover, they are still to be found in statues of the early eleventh century. This continental style persisted, in short, well after the eclipse of Chinese poetry and Chinese fashions in calligraphy and secular art – partly because glowering faces and powerful torsos were suitable attributes for the Mystic Kings and other fierce deities who figured prominently in esoteric

---

32 For the Jingoji Yakushi Nyorai, see Minamoto, *Japanese Art*, plate 41, and Kurata Bunsaku, *Mikkyō jiin to Jōgan chōkoku*, vol. 5 of *Genshoku Nihon no bijutsu* (1967), plate 27; for the Kanshinji Nyoirin Kannon, Kurata, *Mikkyō*, plates 63–64; for the Hokkeji Eleven-Headed Kannon, Minamoto, *Japanese Art*, plate 48, and Kurata, *Mikkyō*, plates 72–73.

rituals; partly because of the conservatism nurtured by iconographic pattern-books and by the strictly formulaic approach of the Shingon sect. In the end, however, it failed to withstand the challenge of innovations catering to the aristocratic preference for refinement, mildness, and luxurious decorative effects.

When members of the court circle were in need of immediate divine assistance – for example, to secure a promotion, ensure a safe journey or an uneventful childbirth, resolve a land dispute, or recover from an illness – they turned to the esoteric sects, the native gods, the *yin-yang* prognosticators, and their own special protective buddhas and bodhisattvas. When they contemplated the afterlife (a frequent practice in a society preoccupied with ephemerality), they found solace chiefly in the hope of rebirth in Amida's Pure Land paradise. Worship of Amida, designed to secure forgiveness for sins and assistance for the dead, had existed in Japan for centuries, leaving its artistic mark most notably in the Golden Hall frescoes at the Hōryūji, where Amida's Pure Land, among others, was depicted in a style whose Chinese antecedents can be seen at Tun-huang.

In 985, the Tendai monk Genshin (942–1017) gave new prominence to Amidism with a treatise, *Ōjō yōshū* (*Anthology on Rebirth in Pure Land*), which made the cult an alternative, rather than an adjunct, to other forms of Buddhism; and which contained vivid descriptions of the beauty and compassion of the Buddha and his attendants, and of the pleasures of the Pure Land.[33] As depicted in *Ōjō yōshū*, the Pure Land was a place where the ear was delighted with music, the nose with fragrance, and the eye with drifting blossoms, crystal pools, golden palaces, and exquisite raiment – an idealized counterpart, we might say, of the Heian capital.

Around the beginning of the eleventh century, thanks in large part to Genshin, Amidism began to move religious art and architecture in a new direction. The esoteric and other sects continued to produce works to meet their own needs, but lay believers increasingly commissioned serenely benevolent images of Amida and his bodhisattvas, which they installed in tile-roofed halls decorated with gold, jewels, lacquer, and mother-of-pearl. The most magnificent of many such undertakings was Michinaga's Hōjōji Temple, where the grounds and buildings were consciously designed to suggest the glories of the Pure Land, and where the central icon, a sixteen-foot

---

33 For a partial translation, see A. K. Reischauer, "Genshin's Ojo Yoshu: Collected Essays on Birth into Paradise," *Transactions of the Asiatic Society of Japan*, second series, 7 (1930): 16–97.

statue of Amida, "shining with peerless holy radiance," conformed in every feasible respect to the glittering description of the Buddha in *Ōjō yōshū*.[34] Another was the Byōdōin at Uji, founded by Michinaga's son Yorimichi, where the main image, seated Amida, still survives in the original airy, elegant Phoenix Hall (Hōōdō), a building that combines *shindenzukuri* architectural features with those of edifices in Tun-huang Pure Land paintings. Executed in 1053 by Jōchō (d. 1057), a sculptor who had won acclaim earlier for his contributions to the Hōjōji, the statue is a noble work, its graceful, well-proportioned body, soft drapery, and tranquil, dignified face combining with a sumptuously decorated golden halo to produce an effect of the utmost beauty and refinement.[35]

As we might expect, the Phoenix Hall Amida did not spring fullblown from Jōchō's inventive genius. Its ancestry can be traced back through at least one hundred years of evolution. Nor can we assume that it was hailed as the outstanding masterpiece of its day, since we hear much more about the vanished splendors of the Hōjōji from contemporaneous writers. Nevertheless, it is a work of unique importance, not only for its intrinsic quality, but also for its effect on the subsequent course of Heian sculpture. Admiration assumed the form of imitation, with the result that the last hundred and fifty years of the Heian period witnessed no new developments, but merely the gradual debasement of Jōchō's style into weak conventionalism. There was mass production of bland images, assembled from many small wooden parts (a technique Jōchō had perfected), and decorated with bright colors, intricate patterns, and cut gold in a manner that occasionally bordered on vulgarity, as in the Jōruriji Kichijōten, with its elaborately simulated textile designs and its multifarious streamers, bangles, and hair ornaments.[36]

Painting

Before the rise of Amidism, there were two main categories of Heian Buddhist painting, both intimately associated with the Shingon and Tendai sects. One was the mandala, a symbolic representation of the

---

34 Quotation from McCullough and McCullough, *Flowering Fortunes*, p. 567. For the *Ōjō yōshū* description, see Allan A. Andrews, *The Teachings Essential for Rebirth: A Study of Genshin's Ōjōyōshū* (Tokyo: Sophia University, 1973), pp. 13–14.
35 Illustrated in Paine and Soper, *Art and Architecture*, plate 37; also in Kudō Yoshiaki and Nishikawa Shinji, *Amidadō to Fujiwara chōkoku*, vol. 6 of *Genshoku Nihon no bijutsu* (1969), plates 1, 4–5.
36 Illustrated in Paine and Soper, *Art and Architecture*, plate 35B.

universe. In the most common type of mandala, scores of miniature divinities were grouped hierarchically in geometric patterns around a central image of Vairocana (Dainichi), of whom they were regarded as manifestations. A variety of decorative effects was achieved by executing the figures in fine gold or silver lines on dark blue paper, or in red outlines complemented by a palette of bright colors; and there were also variations in the types of circles and rectangles employed to make up the total composition. But a basic uniformity, the result both of the tiny sizes of the figures and of detailed iconographic regulations, may be said to limit the aesthetic interest of the mandala.[37]

Awesomely energetic fierce deities are the representative subjects of paintings belonging to the other category, which is characterized by an iconic, expansive, forbidding style paralleling that of contemporaneous sculpture. With the possible exception of the massive Myōōin Red Fudō (which art historians classify merely as "early"), no major ninth-century work in this vein survives, but excellent examples remain from the next century and a half – for example, the Boston Museum's Daiitoku and the Shōren'in Blue Fudō – showing that the style, protected by strong conservative forces, was able to maintain its integrity until well after the first manifestations of heightened interest in Amida and the Pure Land.[38]

Meanwhile, at temples like the Hōjōji and the Byōdōin, painters were exploring a new subject, the descent of Amida and his heavenly host to escort the dying believer to paradise. Pictures of this kind, called *raigō* ("coming to welcome"), were not unknown in China, but it was in Japan that they became a major element in Pure Land art. Relatively unencumbered by iconographic considerations, painters created compositions reflecting aristocratic taste: richly attired bodhisattva musicians riding on purple clouds, with a golden Amida in the central position and a *yamatoe* landscape at the bottom. The oldest extant *raigō* paintings, a group executed in 1053 on walls and doors at the Byōdōin, are now badly worn and faded, but protected sections, uncovered in the course of twentieth-century repairs, have revealed bright yellows, oranges, reds, blues, purples, and

---

37 For a short discussion of mandalas, see Akiyama Terukazu, *Japanese Painting* (New York: Rizzoli International Publications, 1977), pp. 37–40; for illustrations, Takada Osamu and Yanagisawa Taka, *Butsuga*, vol. 7 of *Genshoku Nihon no bijutsu* (1969), plates 38–42, 45–53.
38 For the Myōōin Red Fudō, see Takada and Yanagisawa, *Butsuga*, plate 59; for the Boston Museum Daiitoku, Takada and Yanagisawa, *Butsuga*, plate 68, and Akiyama, *Japanese Painting*, p. 54; for the Shōren'in Blue Fudō, Takada and Yanagisawa, *Butsuga*, plates 56–57, and Akiyama, *Japanese Painting*, p. 55.

greens, as well as ornamental designs produced by the application of cut gold leaf (*kirikane*), a new technique that was to assume increasing prominence during the remainder of the Heian period. As noted earlier, the pines and hills in the Byōdōin *raigō* are among the oldest extant fragments of *yamatoe* landscape painting.[39]

The greatest Heian *raigō*, known as the Kōyasan triptych, consists of three hanging scrolls, which appear to have originated as a single painting. Brownish clouds, believed to have been lavender, shape the composition into an ellipse, indented at the lower left to admit an autumnal mountain scene. The bodhisattvas, outlined in clean red lines, have skins delicately flushed with pink or tan, and their graceful white streamers repeat the undulating motions of the clouds, as do the bands of red, blue, green, orange, and purple formed by their patterned robes. Extensive and extremely sophisticated use of gold, especially for the central figure and its halo, supports the attribution of this work to the late Heian period.[40]

Mildness, delicacy, grace, and decorativeness, qualities ideally suited to the content of *raigō* paintings, played an increasing role in Buddhist art as a whole during the last hundred and fifty Heian years. One of the finest works of the late mid-period is a hanging scroll at Mount Kōya, dating from 1086, which represents the death of Śākyamuni, the historical Buddha. The background is occupied by hills and water in the *yamatoe* style. In the center, the Buddha lies in tranquil grandeur, many times life-size, framed by graceful śāla trees in full bloom, and surrounded by mourners, who spill over into the foreground. Like the aristocrats in *onnae emakimono*, the divine personages show their grief only through slight gestures, if at all; like the commoners in *otokoe*, the human figures shriek and weep without inhibition. A sorrowing lion writhes in the lower right-hand corner; a calm Queen Māyā, the Buddha's beautiful mother, hovers in the upper right. Painstaking attention has been devoted to color contrasts and harmonies, and to the patterns in the mourners' luxurious robes, which closely resemble mid-Heian descriptions of upper-class attire, but the commanding presence of the Buddha and the grief of the mourners serve as a counterpoise to the decorative elements, and the total effect is one of great vitality and textural richness.[41]

---

39 Illustrated in Kudō and Nishikawa, *Amidadō*, plate 7.
40 Illustrated in Akiyama, *Japanese Painting*, pp. 46–47; also in Takada and Yanagisawa, *Butsuga*, plates 115, 118.
41 Illustrated in Takada and Yanagisawa, *Butsuga*, plates 1–5; see also the discussion in Akiyama, *Japanese Painting*, p. 49.

In many other cases, the modern viewer feels that dignity, compositional strength, and religious feeling have been sacrificed to surface glitter and fussy detail. Images of the bodhisattva Fugen, a cult figure worshiped particularly by women, appear against a background of falling blossoms, wear elaborate polychrome costumes and innumerable bracelets, necklaces, and pendants, and ride elephants whose saddles are embellished with designs resembling the intricate patterning of Persian miniatures.[42] The once powerful bodies of fierce deities are swallowed up in near-abstract designs, where the focus is on *kirikane,* tiny patterns, and the interplay of planes of reds and browns.[43] The Peacock King, another esoteric divinity, is festooned with dozens of green and gold loops, and the feathers of his mount become layers of contrasting colors, each with its own complex pattern traced in gold.[44]

If we are tempted to accuse some of these paintings of excessive ornamentation, or even of garishness, we may remind ourselves that they were intended to be seen in dusky surroundings, not in brightly lit museums or on the glossy pages of art books. But impressions of insipidity and sentimentality are harder to dismiss. Without wishing to deny the many attractive qualities of late Buddhist painting, we must agree with those who find that here, as in the sculpture of the same period, conservatism and overrefinement have resulted in decadence. It is not to the temples that we can profitably turn for the best in twelfth-century Japanese art.

MUSIC

In the four centuries immediately preceding the Heian period, the introduction of many kinds of foreign instrumental music and dance brought revolutionary new aesthetic experiences to the Japanese upper classes, for whom music had previously meant simple vocal performances and dances, with or without flutes, bells, drums, and six-stringed *kotos* by way of accompaniment. The native tradition survived, thanks to an intimate association with tenacious magico-religious beliefs and practices, but it was the importations that bulked largest in the official and private lives of the nobility by the start of the ninth century.

The earliest arrivals had been *sankangaku* (music of the three Ko-

---

42 See Takada and Yanagisawa, *Butsuga,* plates 14–16.
43 Takada and Yanagisawa, *Butsuga,* plate 29.
44 Takada and Yanagisawa, *Butsuga,* plates 73–74.

reas), mixed Chinese and Korean styles from the Korean states of the Three Kingdoms period (313–668). Then came *gigaku,* introduced in 612, which seems to have consisted mainly of satirical dances, performed with masks suggestive of a Central Asian or Western origin. *Dora-gaku* and *rin'yūgaku,* from short-lived unidentified countries that may have been located in Southeast Asia, appeared in the eighth century, as did *Bokkai-gaku,* the music of the Tungusic state of Po-hai, which occupied parts of eastern Manchuria, the Russian Maritime Province, and northern Korea between 700 and 926. And from around 685 on, there was piecemeal importation of *tōgaku,* the flourishing, cosmopolitan music and dance of T'ang China.

Gagaku

Of three principal types of T'ang music, two found their way to Japan. One was *yen-yüeh* (Japanese, *engaku*), "banquet music," a formal, dignified amalgam of many elements, including folk songs and dances and the music of Central Asia, India, and other areas, which the Chinese used for court entertainments. The other was *san-yüeh* (Japanese, *sangaku*), "scattered music," a popular, relaxed form of entertainment, which was accompanied by juggling, acrobatics, stilt-walking, and the like.[45] The third, *ya-yüeh* (Japanese, *gagaku*), "elegant music" used at rituals and ceremonies to ensure the harmonious functioning of the Confucian state, was not imported – it being felt, apparently, that sufficient resources for such purposes existed – but it gave its name to the Gagakuryō (Bureau of Elegant Music), a government office established in 701. Although the original mandate of the Gagakuryō covered all forms of court music, native music was transferred to a new office, the Outadokoro (Folk Music Office), around the end of the eighth century; and we shall therefore use the common but ill-defined term *gagaku* to designate only foreign or foreign-style music and dance of the type supervised and performed by the Gagakuryō after the separation.

By the beginning of the ninth century, the Chinese *engaku* (usually called *tōgaku,* "T'ang music") had become by far the most important of the *gagaku* genres. *Rin'yūgaku,* which was prized as representative of Indian music, occupied second place; the music of the three Koreas and Po-hai followed at a considerable distance; and *gi*-

---

[45] For details, see James T. Araki, *The Ballad-Drama of Medieval Japan* (Berkeley and Los Angeles: University of California Press, 1964), pp. 50–54.

gaku, doragaku, and *sangaku* were well on the way to their subsequent disappearance from court life. The native music was still flourishing because of its unique acceptability to the Shinto gods.

Around 835 the sinophile court, dissatisfied with the chaotic state of the *gagaku* corpus, set out to make music and dance more "correct." Retired Emperor Saga, an enthusiastic amateur who is said to have been an expert at several Chinese instruments, supplied the initial leadership in what became one of the major musical developments of the Heian period, a process of gradual consolidation and reorganization lasting for more than a century. Non-Chinese pieces were recast in the Chinese mold; fragmentary compositions were fleshed out; large numbers of exotic instruments were discarded; scores were rewritten to eliminate all but two structural types and six main modes; and new works were composed, both by professionals and by prominent members of the court.

As the decades passed, systematization shaded imperceptibly into naturalization. We can seldom be sure when a given change took place, but it is apparent that *gagaku* was much more reflective of Heian aristocratic taste in the late tenth century, at the end of the reorganization process, than it had been in 800. By that time, in addition to the changes just mentioned, the *gagaku* repertoire, including the dance repertoire (*bugaku*), had been divided into two paired categories. The first, *tōgaku* or *sagaku* (Music of the Left), consisted of the old *tōgaku* and *rin'yūgaku* pieces, plus Japanese compositions in the Chinese vein; the second, *komagaku* (Korean music) or *ugaku* (Music of the Right), of drastically revised pieces from Korea and Manchuria. The categories were the provinces of two troupes of professional musicians, who played approximately the same kinds and numbers of instruments – the transverse flute, oboe, mouth organ, lute, thirteen-stringed *koto,* and drums for the Left; Korean flute, oboe, and drums for the Right – and who dressed in sumptuous harmonizing costumes, red for the Left and green for the Right. Dances were performed in pairs, with, for example, a Left bird dance matching a Right butterfly dance, or a Left masked warrior a Right masked warrior.

Another aspect of the reorganization was the establishment of regulations assigning music an integral role in all the main court ceremonies and rituals. The two orchestras and their dancers also figured prominently in the entertainments accompanying wrestling matches, horse races, poetry contests, and other competitions, in which the contesting sides were likewise designated as Left and Right. And, as noted below, *gagaku* was an essential element in the elaborate Buddhist services sponsored by members of the nobility.

This kind of emphasis, reinforced by the keen personal interest of successive sovereigns, created a musical atmosphere at court and led, early in the ninth century, to the inauguration of the custom of *gyoyū* (or *on-asobi,* "august music"), woodwind and string *gagaku* music played for recreation at the imperial residence by the emperor and other gentlemen of the court. There is much literary evidence to show that the performances of talented amateurs were considered fresher and more elegant than stereotyped renditions of the same compositions by professional musicians, and that musical competence was expected of every member of society. The sons of high nobles, taught by court musicians to dance and play the major *gagaku* instruments, were given ample opportunity to display their skills, both in childhood, when they were the featured performers at longevity celebrations for older members of the family, and on innumerable later formal and informal occasions. Among the lower nobility, musical expertise came to be especially vital for members of the palace guards (*efu*), who found themselves constant participants in *gyoyū* because of their proximity to the imperial person.

Ironically, the popularity of *gyoyū,* a type of performance that permitted at least a degree of spontaneity and originality, seems to have contributed materially to the ultimate fossilization of *gagaku.* In the tenth century, the musical preeminence of the guardsmen was recognized by the creation of a new organ, the Gakuso (or Gakusho, Music Office), staffed with *efu* members, which took over the functions of the Gagakuryō. By the early eleventh century, Gakuso posts were hereditary, and by the twelfth the office was a bastion of conservatism, with each family jealously guarding its secret lore and all alike insisting on the inviolability of tradition and on the status of music as a quasi-mystic Way – an art that sanctioned subtle refinements but strictly prohibited innovations like new compositions. It may be said, in short, that *gagaku,* the principal Heian musical form, followed a course similar to the one we have already traced for Buddhist art: an initial phase of sinitic vigor, an intermediate stage of elegant refinement, and a final period of decline.

Shinto and Secular Vocal Music

At the Heian court, the traditional Japanese preference for vocal music was partially satisfied by the performance of Shinto sacred songs – notably the long cycle known as *mi-kagura,* a carefully structured combination of poetry, music, and dance, perfected at the start of the eleventh century, which focused on the performance of two choruses, singing to welcome, entertain, and send off a divine visitor.[46]

A number of new secular song forms also appeared. One was the *saibara* (a name of uncertain meaning), which entered aristocratic circles around the beginning of the Heian period and enjoyed its greatest vogue in the early eleventh century. Simple Japanese lyrics – often of folk origin, and characterized by the inclusion of meaningless syllables (*hayashikotoba*) to adjust the rhythm – were set to *gagaku* melodies and sung in a drawn-out style to the accompaniment of *gagaku* instruments.

A second genre, the *rōei* (recitation), also flourished around the beginning of the eleventh century. As the name suggests, it was more recitation than song. *Rōei* lyrics usually consisted of a pair of seven-word lines from a familiar Chinese poem, rendered in a combination of Chinese and Japanese; and the performance style, which resembled round singing (with or without musical accompaniment), made the form particularly appropriate for social occasions. Two well-known collections of lyrics attest to the popularity of the *rōei: Wakan rōei shū* (*Collection of Japanese and Chinese Rōei,* ca. 1011?), by Fujiwara no Kintō, and *Shinsen rōei shū* (*Newly Selected Collection of Rōei,* ca. 1107–23?), by Fujiwara no Mototoshi (1056–1142).

The last major secular vocal genre to appear was the *imayō*[*uta*] (modern style [song]), which seems to have originated around the last quarter of the tenth century, and to have been fairly well known by the early eleventh. The melodies were taken from a few favorite *gagaku* compositions, and many of the lyrics were adaptations of simple Japanese Buddhist liturgical pieces (*wasan*). The heyday of the *imayō* was the second half of the twelfth century, when the songs were sung both by courtiers and by female professional entertainers, such as dancers, puppeteers, and courtesans, who sometimes served as music teachers to high-born students. The greatest aristocratic aficionado was Retired Emperor Go-Shirakawa (1127–92; r. 1155–58), who compiled an *imayō* collection, *Ryōjin hishō* (*Secret Selection of Songs*), held *imayō* contests, including one that lasted for fifteen nights, and personally consoled an ailing eighty-three-year-old entertainer by singing *imayō* and reciting the *Lotus Sutra* at her bedside.

---

46 For details, see McCullough and McCullough, *Flowering Fortunes,* pp. 410–11.

Buddhist Music

The recognition achieved by female *imayō* singers presaged the approach of the medieval era, when Japanese culture and aristocratic culture would no longer be virtually synonymous terms. Among the many factors responsible for the new order, the most conspicuous were the decline of the nobility and the ascension of the military, but an almost equally important part was played by Buddhism, which, throughout the Heian centuries, quietly lent its support to types of popular entertainment that were destined to exert a profound influence on the mainstream of medieval music and literature. For example, temple patronage helped to preserve *sangaku*, one of the ancestors of the *nō* drama, after its banishment from court; and it also sustained the itinerant blind reciters known as *biwa hōshi* (lute monks), who developed the great body of medieval oral literature known to us today as *Heike monogatari* (*The Tale of the Heike*). Since the *biwa hōshi* remained a subterranean plebeian element in Heian culture, they do not fall within the purview of this chapter, but it may be noted that they, like the *imayō* performers, were harbingers of the medieval renaissance of vocal music (and the concomitant eclipse of *gagaku*), and that their chanting style was deeply indebted to Buddhist vocal forms, which, like Buddhist art, constituted one aspect of aristocratic culture.

Heian Buddhist vocal music, known as *shōmyō*, consisted primarily of liturgical music, sacred texts, and eulogies, all of which were sung or chanted by monks – at first in Chinese styles introduced by the patriarchs of the esoteric sects, and later in naturalized styles, perfected especially by the Pure Land monk Genshin. The chanted forms, which influenced the later *Heike* recitations and *nō*, were relatively simple; the songs, like the secular *saibara*, decorated a single syllable with many notes. Both were complemented by instrumental music and dances from the *gagaku* repertoire, performed as an integral part of the services and also afterward as entertainment.

Contemporaneous writers have little to say about the musical aspects of Buddhist rituals before the last quarter of the tenth century, but the rise of Amidism seems to have nurtured a new interest in the relationship between music and salvation. It became common practice to call in small groups of musicians to perform compositions of the kind the believer expected to hear in the Pure Land; and also to send off the dying with woodwinds, strings, and song – partly, perhaps, in the hope of summoning Amida and his attendants, as the shaman's *koto* had summoned the gods in ancient times.[47] The intimate connection perceived by the middle and late Heian mind between music and the Pure Land is further apparent in the prominence assigned to musicians and their instruments in *raigō* paintings, and in the comments of writers like Murasaki Shikibu, who compares Prince Genji's singing voice (on a purely secular occasion) to the warbling of a kalaviṅka bird in paradise.[48] We have already noticed that the layouts, architectural features, images, and furnishings of temple compounds like Michinaga's Hōjōji were intended as earthly replicas of sights to be seen in the Pure Land; and the same spirit is discernible in the magnificent rituals staged at such religious institutions, in which music played a central role. The point is made quite explicitly in the famous seventeenth chapter of *Eiga monogatari*, an account of the Hōjōji Golden Hall dedication, which bears the title "Music":

> Five or six imposing monks, dressed in red and green robes and surplices, began to clear people out of the way with a great show of vigor. Marshals arrived, and then came the Lecturer and Reader riding in litters, with Censors, officers of the Bureau of Buddhism and Aliens, and others from the two ministries walking before them on the left and right, as though for a *Golden Light Sutra* lecture. Heralded by a tremendous burst of fast music from the Music Office [Gakusho] orchestra, a lion danced out leading a cub. The spectacle as all awaited the Emperor seemed part of another world.
>
> Next the monks filed in from the south gallery, forming lines on the left and right; and tears came to the eyes of the speechless spectators at the sight of that great multitude of holy men moving forward in unison, each group headed by a marshal. The monks' costumes varied in accordance with their offices – Clear-tone Singers, Tin-staff Chanters, and the like. Those who wore patchwork surplices had imported them from China especially for the dedication, and the colors shone with all the vivid freshness of ropes of gems, creating an effect of great dignity and splendor. Incense smoldered in silver and gold censers, filling the compound with the scents of sandalwood and aloeswood, and blossoms of many hues scattered from the sky. . . .
>
> Innumerable bodhisattva dances were presented on the platform, and children performed butterfly and bird dances so beautifully that one could only suppose paradise to be little different – a reflection that added to the auspiciousness of the occasion by evoking mental images of the Pure Land. There were peacocks, parrots, mandarin ducks, and kalaviṅka birds, and the harmonies produced by the Music Office were utterly delightful – true voices of the dharma. Those who listened felt as though the singers were

---

47 Ogi Mitsuo, *Nihon kodai ongaku shiron* (Tokyo: Yoshikawa kōbunkan, 1977), pp. 144–45.
48 Seidensticker, *Genji*, p. 132.

the celestial beings and the holy multitude, lifting their voices in praise of the Buddha's teachings.[49]

(On the construction and dedication of the Hōjōji, see the section "New Imperial and Fujiwara Buildings" in Chapter 2.)

The collapse of court power in the late twelfth century ended aristocratic sponsorship of such lavish religious spectacles. It also radically altered the way of life in which music had figured so prominently. Of all the major Heian musical forms, the Buddhist *shōmyō* alone weathered the passage into the new era, surviving to become the ancestor of almost every new native secular vocal genre. The others, vocal and instrumental alike, receded into obscurity.

LITERATURE: POETRY

In poetry, as in other aspects of court life, the first half of the ninth century was a period of direct imitation of Chinese models.[50] The composition of Chinese poems (*kanshi*) was an integral part of many official functions, symbolizing the authors' cultivation and the emperor's status as foremost patron of the arts; and three imperial *kanshi* anthologies, compiled between 814 and 827, attest to the importance attached to such activities. Meanwhile, Japanese poetry disappeared almost completely from public life. If there were gifted *waka* poets in the first Heian decades, their names have not been preserved. We know, however, that the *waka* was undergoing significant changes behind the scenes.

During the seventh and eighth centuries, native poets had produced impressive long compositions (*chōka*) of great lyric intensity and technical complexity, notably the elegies and encomiums of Kakinomoto no Hitomaro (fl. late seventh century), who seems to have served as an official bard. But there was no longer a demand for the services of a Hitomaro by the beginning of the ninth century. Moreover, although the *waka* survived in private – protected by the inertia of custom and, we may conjecture, by the desire of women to demonstrate at least one type of literary competence – it tended to degenerate into little more than a pawn in the half-joking game of romantic intrigue, "nothing but empty verses and empty words . . . the province of the amorous," as the poet Ki no Tsurayuki (873?–945?)

---

[49] Matsumura and Yamanaka, *Eiga*, vol. 2, pp. 71–72; translation from McCullough and McCullough, *Flowering Fortunes*, pp. 556–57.
[50] See Helen Craig McCullough, *Brocade by Night: 'Kokin Wakashū' and the Court Style in Japanese Classical Poetry* (Stanford, Calif.: Stanford University Press, 1985), chap. 3.

complained.⁵¹ With the development of *kana,* it also became an instrument of casual social intercourse, functioning as the main element in a note of invitation, thanks, or condolence, or as a well-bred response to a moving incident, or as a witty escape from an awkward situation. And because the *chōka* was obviously less well adapted to such uses than the thirty-one-syllable *tanka* (short poem), the *tanka* became the standard *waka* form.

When the *waka* reemerged after its so-called dark age, therefore, serious writers like Tsurayuki confronted difficulties unknown to Hitomaro and his contemporaries. The *tanka* was, in effect, the sole approved form, and the frivolous function of poetry as social grace and pastime was firmly established. As will be shown, there were other formidable handicaps as well. It is easy to perceive ways in which Heian poets fell short of their *Man'yōshū* predecessors; less easy, perhaps, to appreciate the skill, ingenuity, and dedication with which the best of them met the challenge of a new era, or to do full justice to the remarkable edifice they erected on an unprepossessing foundation.

The *waka* began to reappear in public around the middle of the ninth century.⁵² Its return was associated with a number of other developments, among them the general revival and refinement of traditional interests and values; the resurgence of the hereditary principle, which diminished the utility of a Chinese education; the perfection of *kana;* and the increasing tendency of the great families to seek power through their feminine representatives in the imperial harem, each of whom was the potential mother of a malleable child sovereign. In particular, the buildings where the consorts lived, known collectively as the rear palace (*kōkyū*), were becoming centers of musical, artistic, and literary activity. It seems to have been from their luxuriously furnished apartments that folding screens decorated with Japanese poems spread to the public parts of the palace (ca. 850–900), and it was their mistresses' interest in elegant competitions, noted earlier, that probably contributed most significantly to the birth of the poetry contest, one of the major cultural phenomena of the Heian period.

There was a sharp spurt in the demand for formal *waka* during the last fifteen years of the ninth century. The Japanese screen poem (*byōbu uta*) entered its century-long heyday, poetry contests were held

---

51 Saeki, *Kokin waka shū,* p. 97; McCullough, *Kokin Wakashū,* p. 5.
52 McCullough, *Brocade by Night,* chap. 4.

with increasing frequency, and the *waka* began to supplant the *kanshi* at banquets and other official functions. Quasi-professional poets, of whom Tsurayuki became the most highly esteemed, arose from the ranks of the lesser nobility, using their literary prowess to forge ties with the great, and working in many ways to elevate the status of native verse. Early in the tenth century, this activity culminated in the compilation of the first imperial *waka* anthology, *Kokin[waka]shū*, which was edited by Tsurayuki and three other minor-bureaucrat poets and submitted to the throne in or around 905.

Tsurayuki supplied the anthology with a preface that compared the *waka* to a plant "with the human heart as its seed and innumerable words as its leaves," reviewed the form's illustrious history, discussed its social and political virtues, and otherwise sought to establish it on an equal footing with Chinese poetry.[53] "Thanks to this collection," he ended in a burst of rhetoric, "poetry will survive as eternally as water flows at the foot of a mountain; thanks to the assembling of these poems in numbers rivalling the sands of a beach, there will be no complaints of the art's declining as pools in the Asuka River dwindle into shallows; there will be rejoicing for as long as it takes a pebble to grow into a mighty boulder."[54] His predictions erred on the side of optimism, but the basic aims of the compilers were more fully realized than they could have dared to hope. The exalted sponsorship of *Kokinshū*, together with its precedent-setting status, made the *waka* the nation's supreme literary form and established compositional norms that endured well into the nineteenth century. The occasional radical challenge was turned back, and other new developments remained little more than variations on a theme. The *Kokinshū* style became the orthodox style in a society where orthodoxy was almost all.

Some of the 1,111 *Kokinshū* poems, like the anonymous composition below, are simple, straightforward expressions of emotion, similar in construction and tone to the many folk-influenced *tanka* preserved in *Man'yōshū*.

<blockquote>

sugaru naku　　　　　How long must I wait
aki no hagihara　　　　To see again the traveler
asa tachite　　　　　　Who leaves this morning,
tabi yuku hito o　　　Journeying where wild bees hum
itsu to ka matan　　　In autumn bush-clover fields?[55]

</blockquote>

---

53 Saeki, *Kokin waka shū*, p. 93; McCullough, *Kokin Wakashū*, p. 3.
54 Saeki, *Kokin waka shū*, p. 103; McCullough, *Kokin Wakashū*, p. 8.
55 Saeki, *Kokin waka shū*, no. 366.

The style usually identified with the anthology's name is more complex, however, and much more aristocratic in tone. As modern scholarship has shown, it reveals strong influence from the ninth-century *kanshi*, and from the *kanshi*'s Chinese models.[56] It is natural to suppose that masculine members of the court circle, who were constantly endeavoring to compose *kanshi*, would have begun to use continental conceits and techniques in the *waka* they exchanged with women, and that the women would have responded in kind – particularly because the *kanshi* style in favor was a witty, indirect one, suited to "the fencing about the truth that characterized the romantic intrigues of the day."[57]

Early-ninth-century *kanshi* were imitations of sixth-century Chinese southern-court poetry – that is, of the style of the latter part of the Six Dynasties period (220–589), which feigned inability to distinguish between such natural phenomena as plum blossoms and snow, made extensive use of figurative language, and delighted in drawing rational conclusions, which were often based on cause-and-effect relationships. The examples below are from two typical poems by Yü Hsin (513–81), "In a Boat, Gazing at the Moon" and "The Mirror."[58]

> The mountains are bright; one wonders if snow might have fallen.
> The shore is white, but not because of sand.
>
> A moon appears in which there is no cinnamon tree;
> A flower opens, but it will not follow spring.

Many compositions of the same kind appear in Japanese *kanshi* collections dating from the early ninth century, and there is evidence to show that the *waka* was developing along similar lines. Just as Yü Hsin pretends to confuse moonlight with snow and sand, so Ono no Takamura (802–53), who, significantly, is best known as a *kanshi* poet, professes himself at a loss to tell plum blossoms from snow:

> hana no iro wa   Although your blossoms
> yuki ni majirite   Elude our gaze, their color lost
> miezu tomo   Amid flakes of snow,
> ka o dani nioe   Send forth, at least, your fragrance,
> hito no shirubeku   That men may know you are here.[59]

And just as Yü Hsin makes moon and flower metaphors for a beautiful woman, so Ariwara no Narihira (825–80) uses flowers (meaning cherry blossoms) in an indirect accusation of fickleness:

---

56 The definitive study is Jin'ichi Konishi, "The Genesis of the *Kokinshū* Style," trans. Helen C. McCullough, *Harvard Journal of Asiatic Studies* 38, 1 (June 1978): 61–170.
57 Konishi, "Genesis," p. 164.   58 Konishi, "Genesis," pp. 85, 102.
59 Saeki, *Kokin waka shū*, no. 335.

kyō kozu wa	Had I not come today
asu wa yuki to zo	They would have fallen tomorrow
furinamashi	Like drifting snowflakes.
kiezu wa ari tomo	Though they have not yet melted,
hana to mimashi ya	They are scarcely true flowers.[60]

Six Dynasties techniques are omnipresent in the *Kokinshū* "Spring," "Summer," "Autumn," and "Winter" books, a large sub-collection in which the natural phenomena of the four seasons are closely associated with human emotion – especially with the feeling of sadness evoked by the passing of time. Such seasonal poems, which tended to be formal and public in nature, must have been available to the compilers in comparatively large numbers, and preference was no doubt given to compositions with an up-to-date Chinese tone. But it should be noticed, in order to view the Chinese contribution in perspective, that the influence of the imported style is weaker in "Love," the second of the two major categories in the anthology. We may surmise that authentic love poems of the kind we have postulated, which were private in nature, were harder to come by than seasonal verses, and, further, that many of them were too personal for inclusion in a public anthology, where individualism and strong expressions of emotion were no more permissible than in an *onnae* painting. Like the examples that follow, most "Love" compositions are elegant, gracefully subdued statements of longing, with the speaker's feelings closely linked to nature, as in seasonal poems, but with the "reasoning" style less apparent, if it is present at all.

michinoku no	Shall I always love
asaka no numa no	Someone I have scarcely met –
hanakatsumi	A girl as pretty
katsu miru hito ni	As an Asaka marsh iris
koi ya wataran	Blooming in Michinoku?[61]
awanu yo no	If, like these snowflakes,
furu shirayuki to	The nights when we fail to meet
tsumorinaba	Should accumulate,
ware sae tomo ni	I, too, must surely perish
kenubeki mono o	Along with the melting drifts.[62]

Although the source of these two compositions is unknown, their plaintive, passive, somewhat impersonal quality is duplicated in many others that can be shown to have originated as screen poems – verses in which the sentiments belong not to the authors but to fig-

---

60 Saeki, *Kokin waka shū*, no. 63. 61 Saeki, *Kokin waka shū*, no. 677.
62 Saeki, *Kokin waka shū*, no. 621.

ures in the paintings, and where the intent is not to intrigue the reader with clever reasoning but to hint at a romantic situation. A screen poem serves, in effect, as a clarification of the picture it accompanies, a reversal of the process by which an *emakimono* amplifies a tale (*monogatari*). *Kokinshū* poems of the *byōbu uta* type, closely associated with women and their interests, are among the least public in the anthology. Nevertheless, they are clearly formal in nature, adhering to the conventions of a genre that discouraged originality and circumscribed artistic freedom by predetermining topics, themes, and imagery, and by requiring a tone of quiet harmony and moderation, in keeping with the idealized beauty of the pictures and the tastes of the screens' owners.

There is also a strong resemblance between *Kokinshū* poems and compositions preserved in the more than 470 surviving Heian contest records. From its inception around 885 until the late eleventh century, the poetry contest (*uta awase*) was not a literary event but a social function, comparable in structure and emphasis to the *monoawase* described earlier, in which the aim was to spend a pleasant evening in an atmosphere of opulence, taste, and friendly rivalry. The judge's comments were bland, inoffensive, and as objective as possible. The first poem of the Left, the side of superior status, was invariably the winner. Neither side ever lost by an embarrasing margin, and the contest never ended in a tie, which would have made it impossible for winners and losers to present appropriate musical entertainments. A poem mentioning the gods was assured of a win, as was one into which the poet had managed to introduce an auspicious sentiment. Unconventional or inadequate treatment of the assigned topic constituted grounds for defeat, as did illogicalities, flights of fancy, unorthodox imagery, and indecorous, inelegant, or inauspicious language. Personalism was so assiduously avoided that even phrases like *waga yado*, "my dwelling," came to be proscribed. From around 960 on, if not before, acceptable precedents were required for departures from customary practice – for example, the use of archaic or unfamiliar diction, or the failure to include a word like "water" or "bank" in the same context with *fujinami*, "wisteria wave," a term for cascading clusters of wisteria blossoms.

It is natural that the conception of poetry as game should have made its influence felt with particular strength in the area of contest rules. What may seem less understandable is that Tsurayuki, the first Heian writer to advocate the reinstatement of the *waka* as serious literature, should have given tacit approval to essentially the same criteria. There is no discernible difference in tone, subject matter, or form between the ninety-five known contest poems in *Kokinshū*, which are representative of their genre, and the remaining 1,016. The contest judges, it appears, were merely expressing a consensus about the nature of the public poem. Just as a screen poem was required to harmonize in topic and sentiment with the delicate beauty of a *yamatoe* painting, so a contest poem struck the right note at a well-bred gathering only if it was graceful, conventional, and readily comprehensible.

If a high price was paid for the public rehabilitation of the *waka*, the many admirable poems in *Kokinshū* and later anthologies show how much of value was obtained in return.[63] Moreover, literary considerations were never ignored altogether, even by the social contest judges, who commented regularly on diction, conception, freshness, and similar matters, often with considerable acumen. Particular weight was attached to auditory effect, because contest poems were apprehended through the recitations of the competing spokesmen. Compositions were criticized for sounding awkward, crabbed, unpolished, and "unintelligible" (*iishirenu*, used of archaisms, colloquialisms, and complicated word plays, all of which were also said to "grate on the ears"); they were praised for elegant cadences, refined, flowing effects, and clear, serene, rhythmic beauty. That the same considerations were present in the minds of Tsurayuki and his colleagues is apparent from the melodic flow and intricate sound patterns of *Kokinshū* compositions like the two below – attributes that unfortunately disappear in translation.

    yo no naka ni   If ours were a world
   taete sakura no   Where blossoming cherry trees
     nakariseba   Were not to be found,
  haru no kokoro wa   What tranquillity would bless
 nodokekaramashi   The human heart in springtime![64]

     hisakata no   On this springtime day
   hikari nodokeki   When the celestial orb
    haru no hi ni   Diffuses mild light,
 shizugokoro naku   Why should the cherry blossoms
 hana no chiruramu   Scatter with unquiet hearts?[65]

There are *Kokinshū* poems richer in imagery, more original in conception and treatment, more complex, and more moving than

---

63 The best study in English on this subject is Robert H. Brower and Earl Miner, *Japanese Court Poetry* (Stanford, Calif.: Stanford University Press, 1961).
64 Saeki, *Kokin waka shū*, no. 53.   65 Saeki, *Kokin waka shū*, no. 84.

these two by Ariwara no Narihira and Ki no Tomonori (fl. ca. 890), but none falls on the ear more pleasingly, and none is more representative of the main elements in the style – the intellectualizing, the formal, public authorial stance, the association of man with nature, the expression of elegant conventional sentiments about a topic with strong overtones of romantic beauty, the sensitivity to the passing of time, and the attention to sound.

In all, seven imperial anthologies were compiled in the Heian period: *Kokinshū* (ca. 905), *Gosenshū* (*Later Selection,* ca. 951), *Shūishū* (*Collection of Gleanings,* ca. 1006), *Goshūishū* (*Later Collection of Gleanings,* 1087), *Kin'yōshū* (*Collection of Golden Leaves,* ca. 1126), *Shikashū* (*Collection of Verbal Flowers,* ca. 1151), and *Senzaishū* (*Collection of a Thousand Years,* ca. 1188).

The second and third, *Gosenshū* and *Shūishū*, which closely resemble *Kokinshū* in style, were both commissioned during the high noon of aristocratic culture. The other four, which incorporate some noteworthy innovations, coincided in time with the long twilight of the court, the hundred-year period during which the emperors and their Fujiwara regents struggled with ever diminishing success to maintain the traditional way of life. The principal poetic development of the century was the emergence of a number of gifted writers who regarded composition as a high calling, and who developed independent ideas about the manner in which the potentialities of the *tanka* form could best be realized.

The fourth anthology, *Goshūishū,* departed from tradition by introducing a new style of descriptive lyricism, typically focusing on bleak autumn and winter landscapes, as in this poem:

mishi yori mo	Still more desolate
are zo shinikeru	Than when I saw it of old:
isonokami	Isonokami
aki wa shigure no	Where the rains of late autumn
furimasaritsutsu	Shower and shower again.[66]

Kin'yōshū and *Shikashū* included many poems of the same general type, among them outstanding examples of what was coming to be known as the lofty style, a compositional mode in which the objective was to convey an impression of power and dignity, usually through the presentation of a panoramic scene in which no human presence except that of the poet-observer intruded. The *Kin'yōshū*

---

[66] *Shimpen kokka taikan,* ed. Shimpen kokka taikan henshū iinkai, 10 sections, each composed of text and index volumes (Tokyo: Kadokawa shoten, 1983–92). *Goshūishū,* no. 367.

compiler, Minamoto no Shunrai (or Toshiyori, 1057?–1129), and his father, Tsunenobu (1016–97), were outstanding practitioners of the lofty style, as may be seen from the two poems below, the first by Tsunenobu and the second by Shunrai.[67]

yū sareba	As night settles down
kadota no inaba	There comes a rustling of leaves
otozurete	In home paddy fields
ashi no maroya ni	And the whistling autumn wind
akikaze zo fuku	Visits huts with reed-thatched roofs.
uzura naku	In the autumn dusk
mano-no-irie no	Waves of plume grass come rippling
hamakaze ni	Blown by the shore wind
obana namiyoru	At Mano-no-irie
aki no yūgure	Inlet of quail's plaintive cries.

Tsunenobu and Shunrai were also prominent disputants in hot arguments about poetic practice – controversies pursued with especial vigor at the literary poetry contests by which the old social competitions had been replaced around 1085. Tsunenobu tried to broaden the scope of the *waka*, principally by introducing themes from rural life; Shunrai advocated a closer connection between poetry and everyday experience, as well as enlargement of the tiny *Kokinshū* word hoard (about 2,000 items) through acceptance of colloquialisms and *Man'yōshū* vocabulary. *Kin'yōshū* and *Shikashū* contain numerous poems reflecting their views and those of like thinkers, but the imperial patrons of the two anthologies apparently balked at admitting what is perhaps the most famous "progressive" poem of its type, a "Love" *tanka* in which Shunrai uses two conspicuously crude images – dog and crow, symbolic in popular lore of fidelity and infidelity, respectively. The poem has been preserved in Shunrai's private collection.

iisomeshi	Do your feelings now
kotoba to nochi no	Match the speeches you uttered
kokoro to wa	When our love began?
sore ka aranu ka	Or might they be different?
inu ka karasu ka	Are you a dog or a crow?[68]

Fujiwara no Shunzei (or Toshinari, 1114–1204), the *Senzaishū* compiler, was an outstanding poet and contest judge who wielded tremendous authority during the last decades of his long life. He refused to countenance liberal views like Shunrai's, insisting that the

---

67 *Shimpen kokka taikan, Kin'yōshū*, no. 173 and no. 239.
68 *Shimpen kokka taikan, Samboku kikashū*, no. 1071

abundant overtones and delicate nuances of the traditional vocabulary constituted an indispensable resource for poets seeking to make significant statements in thirty-one syllables. At the same time, he rejected the preciousness, mannerisms, and shallow cleverness that marred the *Kokinshū* legacy, espousing instead the strongest qualities of the evolving descriptive style. In the best *Senzaishū* poems, a melancholy, lonely, austere tone is combined with the use of compression and association to achieve rich complexity and pregnant ambiguity. One of Shunzei's own compositions from the anthology can be said to exemplify what might be called the *Senzaishū* compromise – the blending of "old words and new feeling," as Shunzei put it, which constituted the last great poetic achievement of the Heian period.

> yū sareba As evening falls,
> nobe no akikaze From along the moors the autumn wind
> mi ni shimite Blows chill into the heart,
> uzura naku nari And the quails raise their plaintive cry
> fukakusa no sato In the deep grass of secluded Fukakusa.[69]

Here Shunzei uses familiar diction to express "awareness of mutability" (*mujōkan*), the most familiar of all Japanese poetic sentiments. But the brooding, nostalgic tone of his poem (heightened by the reference to Fukakusa, a place apart from the capital and its life, and known moreover as a burial ground) differs strikingly from the romanticism and facile grace of the two poems by Narihira and Tomonori on the same theme.

Without pretending to explain a complicated literary development in a sentence, we may venture the statement that objective circumstances were far more hospitable to lighthearted poses at the beginning of the tenth century, when not a cloud obscured the brilliance of the court's prosperity, than at the gloomy end of the twelfth. In the same connection, it should be noted that the decline of the court had destroyed the cultural influence of the salons maintained by imperial consorts and princesses during the Fujiwara hegemony – in other words, from around 850 until the last quarter of the eleventh century. The tastes of women like Michinaga's daughters Shōshi, Kenshi, and Ishi, who married three successive sovereigns between 999 and 1018, had helped to shape almost every aspect of the culture we have been reviewing, and thus to nurture an environment to which composition

---

[69] *Shimpen kokka taikan, Senzaishū*, no. 259; translation from Brower and Miner, *Japanese Court Poetry*, p. 17.

in the light, witty, social *Kokinshū* style was peculiarly appropriate. It is unlikely to have been an accident that *Goshūishū,* the first imperial anthology to depart from that style, appeared at just the moment when the salons were fading from the scene.

LITERATURE: NARRATIVE PROSE

The salons made an equally significant contribution to the history of narrative prose, the only other noteworthy Heian belletristic form. One genre, the *setsuwa,* mentioned earlier, remained outside their purview, but all the others were affected in varying degrees: the poem tale, the literary diary, the miscellany, the romance, and the historical tale.

As with secular art, relatively little survives of what must have been a corpus of impressive dimensions. (Some eighty titles of romances have been preserved from the ninth and tenth centuries alone.) The poem tale (*uta monogatari*), a brief, elegant anecdote about aristocratic life, centering on one or more poems, is represented by three short anonymous tenth-century collections, the best of which is the oldest, *Ise monogatari* (*Tales of Ise*) – a classic expression of Heian aesthetic ideals, a poetic handbook, and a compendium of types of courtly love, written in simple, chaste language.[70] All three appear to have been compiled by men.

The author of the oldest extant literary diary, *Tosa nikki* (*Tosa Journal,* 935), was also a man, the poet Ki no Tsurayuki. Perhaps because the usual masculine diary of the day was a nonliterary Chinese record of matters useful for bureaucratic and family reference, Tsurayuki assumed the persona of a woman in setting down his account, which is a brief history of a fifty-five-day journey from Shikoku to the capital, dominated by sixty poems.[71] Of several surviving later Heian works in this rather misleadingly named genre, by far the best is *Kagerō nikki* (*Gossamer Journal,* ca. 982?), by "Michitsuna's mother," a secondary consort of the regent Kaneie (929–90), which describes, with powerful realism and tight thematic unity, the misery and resentment of a neglected wife.[72] *Izumi Shikibu nikki*

---

70 For a translation of *Ise monogatari,* see Helen Craig McCullough, *Tales of Ise: Lyrical Episodes from Tenth-Century Japan* (Stanford, Calif.: Stanford University Press, 1968).
71 *Tosa nikki* is translated in McCullough, *Kokin Wakashū,* pp. 263–91.
72 Translated in Edward Seidensticker, *The Gossamer Years: The Diary of a Noblewoman of Heian Japan* (Rutland, Vt., and Tokyo: Charles E. Tuttle, 1964). See also the partial translation in Helen Craig McCullough, ed., *Classical Japanese Prose: An Anthology* (Stanford, Calif.: Stanford University Press, 1990), pp. 102–55.

(*Diary of Izumi Shikibu,* ca. 1004?), ascribed to the poet Izumi Shikibu (b. 976?), is a lyrical, vaguely melancholy, poem-studded account of the protagonist's love affair with an imperial prince.[73] *Murasaki Shikibu nikki* (*Diary of Murasaki Shikibu,* ca. 1010), a short memoir by the author of *The Tale of Genji,* focuses on the activities surrounding the birth of an heir to the throne.[74] *Sarashina nikki* (*Sarashina Diary,* ca. 1060?), by "Sugawara no Takasue's daughter," portrays the uneventful life of a romantic, religious woman.[75]

As a group, works in these two genres – and also *Eiga monogatari,* the first historical tale, and Sei Shōnagon's *Makura no sōshi* (*Pillow Book,* ca. 993–1001?), the sole miscellany, discussed below – contained material of obvious interest to women: poetry, gossipy stories about well-known people, courtly anecdotes, talk of dress and babies and domestic problems, and, above all, accounts of relations between the sexes. Romances ([*tsukuri-*]*monogatari*) offered most of the same features, and, in addition, were often considerably longer. Whereas the typical *Ise monogatari* story occupies less than a page in a modern Japanese printing, even the shortest extant Heian romance, *Taketori monogatari* (*The Tale of the Bamboo Cutter,* ca. 900?), uses thirty-nine, and three volumes are required to accommodate the longest, *Utsuho monogatari* (*The Tale of the Hollow Tree,* ca. 970–1000?). For women with time on their hands, such works must have been especially attractive. Sei Shōnagon brackets romances with *go* and backgammon as among the three best cures for boredom, and Takasue's daughter tells us how eagerly they were sought – and how hard they were for the ordinary woman to come by, even though hundreds appear to have been committed to writing.[76]

The scarcity of paper, a luxury item reserved for the wealthy, was chiefly responsible for the difficulties encountered by would-be readers, and by putative authors as well. Sei Shōnagon, a member of

---

73 Translated in Edwin A. Cranston, *The Izumi Shikibu Diary: A Romance of the Heian Court* (Cambridge, Mass.: Harvard University Press, 1969).
74 Translated in Richard Bowring, *Murasaki Shikibu: Her Diary and Poetic Memoirs* (Princeton, N.J.: Princeton University Press, 1982); see also Edward Seidensticker, "Murasaki Shikibu and Her Diary and Her Other Writings," *Literature East and West* 18, 1 (March 1974): 1–7.
75 Translated in Ivan Morris, *As I Crossed a Bridge of Dreams: Recollections of a Woman in Eleventh-Century Japan* (New York: Dial Press, 1971).
76 For Sei Shōnagon's comment, see Ikeda, *Makura no sōshi,* p. 195; and Ivan Morris, trans., *The Pillow Book of Sei Shōnagon,* 2 vols. (New York: Columbia University Press, 1967), vol. 1, p. 145. For Takasue's daughter, see Suzuki Tomotarō, Kawaguchi Hisao, Endō Yoshimoto, and Nishishita Kyōichi, eds., *Tosa nikki, Kagerō nikki, Izumi Shikibu nikki, Sarashina nikki,* vol. 20 of *Nihon koten bungaku taikei* (1957), pp. 490–93, and Morris, *Bridge of Dreams,* pp. 53–55.

the middling aristocracy like most of her fellow writers, explains that she wrote *Makura no sōshi* because her mistress happened to make her a present of a large quantity of paper; otherwise, presumably, she could not have afforded to do so.[77] Similarly, the average noble lady must have had to while away innumerable hours with her attendants' gossip, anecdotes, and oral tales for every one spent with a written *monogatari*. But imperial consorts and princesses were able to make use of their social and economic advantages to collect, reproduce, and order literary works with relative freedom. Manuscript copying was one of their attendants' tasks, and women with literary gifts were regularly brought into their entourages, both to add luster to the social life centering on their salons, as Sei Shōnagon did for Empress Teishi, and to increase their store of romances.

So few romances remain today that it is easy to underestimate the scope of such activities. The major poetry of the period has survived, thanks to its brevity, public nature, and imperial sponsorship, but most of the romances, like the paintings that illustrated them, vanished with the old life. Examination of the ones still available suggests that standards were not exacting, and might lead to the conclusion that the salons were of dubious literary significance. Of the three known early works in the genre, the first, *Taketori monogatari*, is a charming fairy tale about a moon maiden and her earthly suitors; the second, *Utsuho monogatari*, is a rambling story of upper-class life, unified to some extent by recurrent illustrations of the miraculous power of music; and the third, *Ochikubo monogatari* (*Tale of the Sunken Room*, ca. 985?), presents a Japanese version of the worldwide Cinderella theme, told with realistic detail and occasional earthy humor.[78] A handful of others, all from the late period, vary in length and quality, the longer ones tending to indulge in improbabilities while attempting unsuccessfully to imitate *The Tale of Genji*.[79]

---

77 Ikeda, *Makura no sōshi*, p. 331; Morris, *Pillow Book*, vol. 1, p. 267. Morris's book contains a full translation of Sei Shōnagon's miscellany; McCullough, *Classical Japanese Prose*, translates extended excerpts (pp. 158–99).

78 *Taketori monogatari* has been translated by Donald Keene in J. Thomas Rimer, *Modern Japanese Fiction and Its Tradition* (Princeton, N.J.: Princeton University Press, 1978), pp. 275–301; *Ochikubo monogatari*, translated by Wilfred Whitehouse and Eizo Yanagisawa in *Ochikubo Monogatari or The Tale of the Lady Ochikubo: A Tenth Century Japanese Novel* (Tokyo: Hokuseido Press, rev. ed. 1965). For partial translations of *Utsubh monogatari*, see Edwin A. Cranston, "*Atemiya*: A Translation from the *Utsubo Monogatari*," *Monumenta Nipponica* 24, 3 (1969): 289–314; Wayne P. Lammers, "The Succession (*Kuniyuzuri*): A Translation from *Utsubo Monogatari*," *Monumenta Nipponica* 37, 2 (1982): 139–78; and Ziro Uraki, *The Tale of the Cavern* (Tokyo: Shinozaki Shorin, 1984).

79 For translations of post-*Genji* romances, see Robert L. Backus, *The Riverside Counselor's Stories: Vernacular Fiction of Late Heian Japan* (Stanford, Calif.: Stanford University Press,

More important than the general level of quality that may have prevailed, however, are certain other considerations. There were, in effect, two kinds of literature at the Heian court: poetry, which was the recognized public genre, suitable for both masculine and feminine attention; and narrative prose, which was largely relegated to the rear palace (unless, like *Ise monogatari*, the work functioned as a poetic manual). The imperial ladies thus presided over the only catholic literary centers of the day, embracing both poetry and prose in their interests, and encouraging literary activity both indirectly, by setting a prestigious example, and directly, by patronizing individual writers. The antecedents of the literary diary, for example – the genre exploited so brilliantly by Michitsuna's mother – can be traced to the tenth-century salon of Empress Onshi (885–954). Michitsuna's mother herself never served at court, but every other known major diary author except Tsurayuki was a lady-in-waiting to a consort or princess at some time in her life. It may well be, indeed, that we would not possess either *Kagerō nikki* or any of the others if it had not been for the custodial function assumed by the salons.

Feminine sponsorship at court also helped *Ise monogatari* to win recognition as a classic, and feminine interest in the romance paved the way for the single most impressive accomplishment of Heian civilization, Murasaki Shikibu's *The Tale of Genji* (*Genji monogatari*, early eleventh century). In that magnificent work, which must rank high on any list of the world's great psychological novels, Murasaki echoes the concerns and adopts some of the techniques of the *waka* poet, developing two major themes – the tyranny of time and the inescapable sorrow of romantic love – within the context of man's relationship to nature. But whereas the poet seeks to distill *mono no aware* into the briefest of lyric expressions, Murasaki uses both poetry and prose to explore the concept in evocative, leisurely detail, weaving a fabric of infinite richness and complexity. Whereas the anthology poet avoids indecorous personalism, Murasaki fills her stage with more than five hundred characters, each a recognizable individual, and makes her long story develop logically from their thoughts and feelings, and from the interplay of their personalities.

1985); Carol Hochstedler, *The Tale of Nezame: Part Three of Yowa no Nezame Monogatari* (Ithaca, N.Y.: Cornell University East Asia Papers 22, 1979); Thomas H. Rohlich, *A Tale of Eleventh-Century Japan: Hamamatsu Chūnagon Monogatari* (Princeton, N.J.: Princeton University Press, 1983); Rosette E. Willig, *The Changelings: A Classical Japanese Court Tale* (Stanford, Calif.: Stanford University Press, 1983); and Wayne P. Lammers, *The Tale of Matsura: Fujiwara Teika's Experiment in Fiction* (Ann Arbor: Center for Japanese Studies, University of Michigan, 1992).

She is both the quintessential representative of a unique society and a writer who speaks to universal human concerns with a timeless voice. Japan has not seen another such genius.[80]

Murasaki appears to have written the oldest parts of *The Tale of Genji* away from court around the beginning of the eleventh century (possibly for a private patron), to have been taken into Empress Shōshi's service after word of the work spread, and to have completed it during the next decade or so. Her celebrated older contemporary, Sei Shōnagon, who became a lady-in-waiting to Shōshi's rival, Empress Teishi (976?–1001), around 993, probably finished *Makura no sōshi* shortly after Teishi's death in 1001. *Makura no sōshi*, classified by Japanese scholars as a miscellany (*zuihitsu*), is a jumble of reminiscences about the author's days at court, random observations on people, nature, and life in general, and innumerable lists of things – waterfalls, mountains, bridges, musical instruments, games, "Adorable Things," "Things That Make One Impatient," "Things That Give a Vulgar Impression" – all set down in a sparkling, witty style with fastidious sensitivity and small tolerance for human shortcomings. Under "Things That Are Unpleasant to See," she lists "a lean, hirsute man taking a nap in the daytime. Does it occur to him what a spectacle he is making of himself? Ugly men should sleep only at night, for they cannot be seen in the dark and, besides, most people are in bed themselves. But they should get up at the crack of dawn, so that no one has to see them lying down."[81]

Sei Shōnagon has a trenchant wit and a marvelously observant eye. If her gaze is less serious and penetrating than Murasaki Shikibu's, she does us the service of calling attention to the gay, high-spirited, somewhat feckless side of court life, which Murasaki's preoccupation with weightier matters tends to obscure. We must read both if we are to capture the flavor of aristocratic society, just as we must

---

80 Seidensticker, *Genji*, contains a complete translation of Murasaki's work. There is also a virtually complete translation in Arthur Waley, *The Tale of Genji: A Novel in Six Parts*, 2 vols. (Boston and New York: Houghton Mifflin, 1935). Helen Craig McCullough, *Genji and Heike* (Stanford, Calif.: Stanford University Press, 1994), pp. 25–242, translates many of the chapters dealing with Prince Genji. For studies and bibliographies, see Haruo Shirane, *The Bridge of Dreams: A Poetics of 'The Tale of Genji'* (Stanford, Calif.: Stanford University Press, 1987); Norma Field, *The Splendor of Longing in The Tale of Genji* (Princeton, N.J.: Princeton University Press, 1987); Richard Bowring, *Murasaki Shikibu: The Tale of Genji* (Cambridge: Cambridge University Press, 1988); Okada, *Figures of Resistance;* and Andrew Pekarik, ed., *Ukifune: Love in The Tale of Genji* (New York: Columbia University Press, 1982). See also the discussions in Donald Keene, *Seeds in the Heart* (New York: Henry Holt, 1993), pp. 477–513; and Jin'ichi Konishi, *A History of Japanese Literature*, vol. 2 (Princeton, N.J.: Princeton University Press, 1986), pp. 317–46.
81 Ikeda, *Makura no sōshi*, pp. 168–69; translation from Morris, *Pillow Book*, vol. 1, p. 266.

take both Six Dynasties obliquity and screen-poem romanticism into account when we seek to understand the *Kokinshū* style.

However favorable the circumstances, a tiny court circle, isolated from outside influences, is unlikely to produce a steady stream of important writers. Only one other woman need be noticed here: the anonymous author – probably Akazome Emon (b. ca. 960?), a poet in the service of Michinaga's wife – who created the historical tale (*rekishi monogatari*) genre by writing *Eiga monogatari* (*A Tale of Flowering Fortunes*, started ca. 1030?).[82] Akazome, as we may identify her for convenience, was her country's first vernacular historian, and the first Japanese to treat historical materials in the *monogatari* style. Her book is a naively enthusiastic celebration of Michinaga, his family, and his times. As literature, it falls far short of *The Tale of Genji*, its apparent model, but its detailed descriptions of everyday aristocratic life make it an invaluable source for the social historian. We are also indebted to Akazome for inspiring another writer to produce *Ōkagami* (*The Great Mirror*, ca. 1086–1125?), the second and most important work in the genre she invented.[83]

We return to the world of masculine letters with *Ōkagami*, a book written by a man for what must have been primarily a male readership, judging from its contents. The anonymous author had had a number of male predecessors in the general area of narrative prose. Strangely, all three of the surviving tenth-century romances and at least one from the eleventh century appear to have been written by men; and Tsurayuki was not quite the only male diarist. Men also monopolized the tenth-century poem tale genre, probably because it was, in effect, a special type of *setsuwa* collection.

The compilation of anecdotes and short factual tales, which enjoyed the prestige of Chinese example, seems to have been a fairly common occupation for educated men throughout the Heian period.[84] Many collections were put together for utilitarian purposes. Of the ones that survive, the bulk are Buddhist, assembled by monks to enliven sermons; and most of the others are twelfth-century compendiums of scraps of information about musical instruments, poetry, official ceremonies, and the like – further evidence of the late Heian desire to embalm the golden past. Nostalgia probably also played a part in the compilation of the greatest monument of *setsuwa* literature, *Konjaku monogatari*[*shū*] ([*A Collection of*] *Tales of Times*

---

82 Major portion translated in McCullough and McCullough, *Flowering Fortunes*.
83 Translated in McCullough, *Ōkagami*.   84 See McCullough, *Ōkagami*, pp. 1–14.

Now Past, ca. 1120?), an anonymous collection of more than a thousand tales, dealing with a great variety of Buddhist and secular subjects, and with many social classes.[85] Certainly, the conservatorial spirit was in the air. But the inelegant concerns of *Konjaku monogatari* are a far cry from the world of Genji, the Shining Prince, and it may be best to think of the collection as primarily a preachers' manual – and as a forerunner, like the *imayō* and the *biwa hōshi*, of the medieval rise of new elements in the Japanese cultural mix.

Ōkagami, like *Ise monogatari*, can be considered a special kind of *setsuwa* collection. The author, looking back on Michinaga's spectacular career, finds himself dissatisfied with Akazome's treatment of it, and determines, as he tells us at the outset, not only to describe but also to explain.[86] He retells Akazome's story, forsaking the chronological approach for the anecdotal, and selecting his materials to support the argument that Michinaga's success arose from a combination of luck, family connections, and favorable personal qualities. To readers of *The Tale of Genji* and *Makura no sōshi*, it comes as no surprise that Michinaga is praised for physical beauty, taste in dress, and poetic ability, and that he is depicted as sponsoring literary entertainments like the Ōi River excursion described earlier in this chapter. But nothing in the works of feminine authors prepares us for the discovery that equal space is devoted to his prowess as an archer and a horseman. Even more unexpected is the extensive documentation, in story after story, of his courage, coolness, prudence, and resourcefulness in public life – characteristics, noted approvingly in comments on other men as well, of which we hear virtually nothing from women writers (whose concerns, as has been seen, are basically private), but which are also singled out for praise in *Konjaku monogatari* and other collections of anecdotes.[87]

Ōkagami provides an important corrective to the notion that the Heian court produced remarkable aesthetes but bestowed little esteem on practical men of affairs. The truth is surely that the virtues

---

85 For partial translations, see Robert Hopkins Brower, "The *Konzyaku monogatarisyū*: An Historical and Critical Introduction, with Annotated Translations of Seventy-Eight Tales," Ph.D. diss., University of Michigan, Ann Arbor, 1952; Frank, *Histoires;* Marian Ury, *Tales of Times Now Past: Sixty-Two Stories from a Medieval Japanese Collection* (Berkeley and Los Angeles: University of California Press, 1979); William Ritchie Wilson, "The Way of the Bow and Arrow: The Japanese Warrior in *Konjaku monogatari*," *Monumenta Nipponica* 28, 2 (Summer 1973): 177–233.
86 McCullough, *Ōkagami*, p. 68.
87 McCullough, *Ōkagami*, pp. 48–53; Ury, *Tales*, p. 17; Hiroko Kobayashi, *The Human Comedy of Heian Japan: A Study of the Secular Stories in the Twelfth-Century Collection of Tales, Konjaku Monogatarishū* (Tokyo: Centre for East Asian Cultural Studies, 1979), pp. 159–60.

of both were recognized. Living as they did in a stable society almost devoid of foreign or internal threats, Heian aristocrats were under no compulsion to practice the martial arts as their ancestors had done, but they did not wholly reject the heritage of the turbulent era before the advent of Chinese culture. Rather, they performed the exceptional feat of reconciling the most useful virtues of their barbaric forebears with a revolutionary new conception of civilized behavior; and the synthesis proved enduring enough to gratify the most conservative of Heian hearts. Although the establishment of the Kamakura shogunate brought ancient attitudes into renewed prominence, the Japanese never turned their backs on the ideals represented by the lacquerer of the Kōyasan marsh-iris chest, the *Genji monogatari emaki* painters, the calligrapher Yukinari, the sculptor Jōchō, the poet Shunzei, and the novelist Murasaki Shikibu. Remote as Heian society may seem to us today, many of its essential characteristics survive in modern Japan. Practical ability continues to be highly valued. Great importance is still attached to status within a hierarchy, to group solidarity, to decision by consensus, and to peer approval. There is less individual freedom than in Western countries of comparable international stature. And there remains a persistent feeling that a true Japanese, whatever his walk in life, ought to be able to compose a verse, judge a specimen of calligraphy or an artistic performance, and savor beauty with a proper appreciation of its ephemerality.

CHAPTER 7

ARISTOCRATIC BUDDHISM

THE PRELUDE TO HEIAN BUDDHISM

Since its introduction into Japan in the middle of the sixth century, the Buddhist religion experienced steady growth under the patronage of the imperial family and powerful clans who sponsored the founding of magnificent temples and monasteries, which they generously endowed with gifts of agricultural land to provide an economic base for the upkeep of these institutions. The rapid expansion of the church is evident in the following figures taken from eighth-century sources. A census conducted in the year 624 – less than a century after Buddhism made its appearance at the court – revealed that there were forty-six functioning monasteries in Japan that accommodated a total of 816 monks and 569 nuns.[1] By the year 681 the number of monasteries in the capital region alone had grown to twenty-four.[2] Larger monasteries capable of accommodating hundreds of monks appeared during the course of the seventh century. Thus an entry in the *Nihon shoki* for the year 690 notes that gifts of cloth were presented to some 3,363 monks residing in seven monasteries.[3]

Although we lack reliable figures for the total number of monasteries in Japan at this time, it is possible to confirm on the basis of archaeological evidence, mainly tiles and foundation stones, the existence of at least two hundred temple sites dating from the Asuka-Hakuhō period (593–710).[4] As might be expected, most of these sites

---

1 *Nihon shoki* (720), kan 22, in Sakamoto Tarō, Ienaga Saburō, Inoue Mitsusada, and Ōno Susumu, eds., *Nihon shoki*, vols. 67–68 of *Nihon koten bungaku taikei* (hereafter *NKBT*), 100 vols. (Tokyo: Iwanami shoten, 1957–67), vol. 68, p. 210. Other abbreviations used in this chapter are: *BZ* for *Dai Nihon Bukkyō zensho*, 151 vols. (Tokyo: Bussho kankōkai, 1912–22); *DDZ* for *Dengyō Daishi zenshū*, 5 vols. (Sakamoto: Hieizan tosho kankōsho, 1926–27); *KT* for Kuroita Katsumi, ed., *Shintei zōho: kokushi taikei*, 62 vols. in 66 (Tokyo: Yoshikawa kōbunkan, 1929–64); *T* for Takakusu Junjirō, ed., *Taishō shinshū daizōkyō*, 100 vols. (Tokyo: Taishō issaikyō kankōkai, 1924–34).
2 *Nihon shoki*, kan 29, Temmu 9 (680)/5/1, *NKBT*, vol. 68, p. 440.
3 *Nihon shoki*, kan 30, Jitō 4 (690)/7/14, *NKBT*, vol. 68, p. 504.
4 Summary of two studies by Ishida Mosaku, cited in note in *Nihon shoki*, *NKBT*, vol. 68, p. 563, note 9.

are in Yamato Province, although a few are found as far west as Bitchū and as far east as Owari, which gives some indication of the diffusion of Buddhism in this early period. Although the government supported the Buddhist religion in the expectation that its rituals would provide protection for the state, the authorities became increasingly concerned about the unrelenting growth in the size of the monastic establishments and the tax-exempt agricultural lands that they held.

The position that the church was to occupy in the new centralized state was made abundantly clear by the *Taihō ritsuryō*, the legal code that was promulgated in 702, and the *Yōrō ritsuryō*, which replaced the former in 757. Both the *Taihō ritsuryō* and *Yōrō ritsuryō* contained a section entitled *Sōniryō* (Administrative Laws Pertaining to Monks and Nuns) that consisted of twenty-seven articles regulating the behavior of the Buddhist clergy.[5] While some articles basically restated prohibitions already enunciated either in the *Vinaya* (the section of the Buddhist canon containing ecclesiastical law) or in certain sutras – namely, the prohibitions against murder, fornication, theft, gambling, the consumption of meat and wine – the majority of the articles sought to define the position, responsibilities, and scope of the activities of the clergy within Japanese society.

A primary concern of the *Sōniryō* was to prevent monks and nuns from taking advantage of their respected religious status to interfere in political affairs, as can be seen from the first article, which specifically forbids clerics to "speak falsely about misfortunes or blessings based on interpretations of mysterious natural phenomena, discuss matters relating to the state, delude the common people, or read military books."[6] Fearing that monks and nuns might exploit their charisma to gain a large personal following, the *Sōniryō* banned the establishment of private chapels (*dōjō*), proselytizing among the masses, itinerant begging without a permit (Art. 5), religious training in the mountains (Art. 13), the practice of divination, and the use of magic to cure illness (Art. 2). There was also a prohibition against wearing clerical garb while pleading a case in civil court (Art. 17).

It is apparent from the *Sōniryō* that the government was much troubled by the abuse of the privileges accorded the clergy, the foremost being the exemption from all taxes. Members of the clergy

---

5 For the reconstructed texts of the *Taihō ritsuryō sōniryō* and the *Yōrō ritsuryō sōniryō*, see Futaba Kenkō, *Kodai Bukkyō shisō-shi kenkyū* (Kyoto: Nagata bunshōdō, 1962), pp. 167–76.
6 Futaba, *Kodai Bukkyō* p. 167.

were forbidden to "lend their names" to others (Art. 16), which was a technique commonly employed in tax evasion. Although monks were free to accept devout young boys as their personal attendants, the law stipulated that these boys must be sent back to their homes before reaching the age of seventeen so that their names could be entered in the tax registers (Art. 6). Monastic officers were required to notify the authorities whenever a monk died so that his identity could not be assumed by another (Art. 20). It was further decreed that persons privately ordained (*shido*), that is, ordained without official authorization, could not be accorded clerical status even though they might have received all the formal training expected of a monk (Art. 24). Finally, members of the clergy were denied the right to private ownership of land, buildings, and valuables, or to engage in trade or collect interest on loans (Art. 18). In addition, monks and nuns were prohibited from accepting personal gifts of slaves, cattle, or weapons (Art. 26).

Although it is clear that some attempt was made during the early years of the Nara period to enforce the *Sōniryō*, the clergy became increasingly independent of state control after the accession of the strongly pro-Buddhist emperor Shōmu (r. 724–49). The chronicles covering the latter half of Shōmu's reign abound in references to the illegal acquisition of land by monasteries, faulty record-keeping by temple officers, and fraudulent practices by monks.[7] In open defiance of the *Sōniryō*, not to mention the *Vinaya*, some monks took wives and engaged in usury. Monasteries practiced pawnbroking to augment their income, charging rates as high as 180 percent per annum.[8]

Efforts to limit the growth of the Buddhist church in the Nara period proved largely unsuccessful because of the enthusiastic patronage it received from Shōmu and his daughter Kōken (reigned 749–58 and again, under the name of Shōtoku, 764–70), who succeeded him on the throne. When the imperial court moved to Nara in 710, major monasteries such as the Daikan daiji (renamed Daianji in 729), Yakushiji, Gangōji, and Kōfukuji that had been scattered throughout the Asuka region were dismantled and reconstructed in the newly established capital on an even grander scale. In addition to these older transplanted Asuka monasteries, magnificent new ones such as

---

[7] *Shoku Nihongi* (797), kan 16, Tempyō 18 (746)/3/16, *KT*, vol. 2, p. 186; Tempyō 18/5/9, *KT*, vol. 2, pp. 187–88; kan 22, Tempyō hōji 3 (759)/6/22, *KT*, vol. 2, p. 264.
[8] See the Shōsōin documents dated Hōki 4–6 (773–75) in Takeuchi Rizō, *Nara-chō jidai ni okeru jiin keizai no kenkyū* (Tokyo: Ōokayama shoten, 1932), pp. 205–6.

the Tōdaiji, Tōshōdaiji, and Saidaiji were built in Nara throughout the course of the eighth century.

Just as the government failed in its effort to restrict the number and size of monastic establishments, so too was it unsuccessful in limiting the flow of people joining the clergy. In 696 a decree was issued stipulating that henceforth ten monks should be ordained on the last day of each year.[9] The authorities, however, were unable to keep the annual ordinations at this modest level for long. An early-ninth-century document reveals, for example, that 773 monks were admitted to the priesthood in the annual ordination ceremony held at the imperial palace in the twelfth month of 741.[10] In a similar ceremony conducted in 747 at Emperor Shōmu's palace at Naniwa, 6,563 monks were ordained.[11] A tabulation of the various records shows that at least twenty-seven separate ordination ceremonies were conducted during the Nara period, at which a total of 18,520 persons were granted clerical status.[12] Individual monasteries by this time were housing large numbers of monks: the Hōryūji had 176 resident monks and 87 novices in the year 747;[13] the Daianji during the same year accommodated 473 monks and 414 novices.[14]

With the rapid expansion of the Buddhist church in Nara and the great respect accorded to learned or charismatic clerics, it was perhaps inevitable that monks would become deeply involved in the affairs of state, the strictures of the *Sōniryō* notwithstanding. Typical of such political monks was Gembō, who had spent seventeen years in China, where, in recognition of his scholarship, he was appointed by Emperor Hsüan-tsung to the Third Rank (*san-p'in*) and granted the purple robe, the highest honor that can be bestowed on a monk. Upon his return to Japan in 734, Gembō presented the court with a precious gift – a complete set of the Buddhist scripture in some five thousand fascicles. In 736 one hundred households and ten *chō* of land were assigned for his support. The following year he was appointed to the office of *sōjō* (bishop), the highest ecclesiastical rank, and at the same time was designated a court chaplain (*naigubu sō*). Immediately putting his faith-healing skills to work, he succeeded in curing the empress dowager of her chronic depression, which greatly enhanced his standing with the imperial family. Gembō used his

---

9 *Nihon shoki*, kan 30, Jitō 10 (696)/12/1, *NKBT*, vol. 68, p. 532.
10 Saichō, *Naishō Buppō sōjō kechimyaku fu* (819), *DDZ*, vol. 1, p. 213.
11 Takeuchi Rizō ed., *Nara ibun*, 3 vols., rev. ed. (Tokyo: Tōkyō-dō, 1962), vol. 2, p. 522.
12 Takeuchi, *Nara-chō jidai ni okeru jiin keizai no kenkyū*, p. 26.
13 *Hōryūji garan engi narabi ni ruki shizai chō* (747), *BZ*, vol. 97, p. 3b.
14 *Daianji garan engi narabi ni ruki shizai chō* (747), *BZ*, vol. 28, p. 117b.

newly acquired influence to promote the fortunes of the scholar Kibi no Makibi, who had been his fellow student in China, and collaborated with Tachibana no Moroe, who was attempting to loosen the Fujiwara stranglehold on the court. So strong was Fujiwara resentment against the meddling of Gembō that a leading member of the Fujiwara family, Hirotsugu, began an insurrection in the hope of driving him from the court. Although the insurrection failed and Hirotsugu was put to death, the Fujiwara managed to regain their ascendancy and arranged, in 745, to have Gembō sent to Kyushu to oversee the construction of the Kanzeonji. Once he was out of the capital, an order was issued stripping him of his property. Gembō died in Kyushu the following year, possibly at the hands of Hirotsugu's partisans.

An even greater threat to the government was posed by the monk Dōkyō, whose apparently intimate relationship with Empress Kōken became one of the most scandalous episodes in Japanese history. Trained in the mountains where he had mastered various esoteric rites, Dōkyō had already acquired a reputation as thaumaturge when he was summoned to the court by Empress Kōken in 752. He grew particularly close to Kōken after her abdication in 758 and was credited, in 761, with having brought about her recovery from a serious illness. After the eminent monk Jikun was summarily dismissed from his position as *shōsōzu* in the Buddhist hierarchy in 763 to create a vacancy the Dōkyō might fill, resentment against Dōkyō began to grow. The following year the Chancellor, Fujiwara no Nakamaro, who eighteen years earlier had forced the banishment of Gembō, attempted to remove Dōkyō by a coup, which soon collapsed. Nakamaro was captured and ignominiously executed along with his wife and children.

Two days after the death of Nakamaro, Dōkyō was appointed his de facto successor and given the newly created title *Daijin Zenji* (The Meditation-Master Who Ranks as Minister of State). The incumbent emperor Junnin, who had been a protégé of Nakamaro, was forced to abdicate in favor of Kōken, who reassumed the throne under the new name of Shōtoku. Following a visit by the empress in 765 to Yuge to worship at Dōkyō's clan temple, Dōkyō was honored with yet another newly coined title, *Daijō Daijin Zenji* (The Meditation-Master Who Ranks as Chancellor), indicating that he now occupied the highest office in the government. A year later Dōkyō was granted the title *Hōō* (King of the Buddhist Faith) to signify his supremacy in the religious world as well. Honors, unprecedented in the case of a layman, were heaped on him: ministers of state were required to do obeisance; the imperial carriage was made available for his personal use; all ordinations had to have his approval, indicated by the imprint of his personal seal. Not content with having concentrated both political and ecclesiastical power in his hands, Dōkyō contrived, in 769, to have an oracle delivered to the court from the Hachiman Shrine in Usa that promised peace for the nation if Dōkyō became emperor. Owing to the opposition of loyalists, particularly the highly respected Wake no Kiyomaro, the oracle was rejected in favor of a new oracle that affirmed that only members of the imperial family might occupy the throne. Dōkyō's secular and ecclesiastical powers were ultimately based solely on his close personal relationship with the empress. For the aristocratic families and Buddhist clergy, he was an object of contempt. Less than a month after the death of Empress Shōtoku in 770, Fujiwara no Nagate, who held the office of Minister of the Left and who had long chafed under Dōkyō's arrogant rule, succeeded in having him banished to Shimotsuke, where he lived in obscurity as superintendent (*bettō*) of the Yakushiji, a local temple, until his death there two years later.

THE ASSERTION OF GOVERNMENT CONTROL OVER THE BUDDHIST CHURCH

The Gembō and Dōkyō affairs dramatically illustrated the dangers that an unchecked clergy posed to the powerful aristocratic clans and even to the hitherto sacrosanct imperial family. Within the short span of twenty years two monks, Gembō and Dōkyō, had managed to exercise control over the government by using their religious charisma to win favor with ex-empresses. Their extraordinary hold on political power is evident from the crushing military defeats suffered by the two Fujiwara chieftains who sought to expel the clerics from court. It is important to remember, however, that neither Gembō nor Dōkyō achieved power through the church itself. While Gembō at least might have commanded respect within the clerical community on the basis of his scholarly credentials, Dōkyō could be viewed only as an unscrupulous cleric who rode roughshod over the established ecclesiastical hierarchy (*sōgō*), countenancing the dismissal of some of its most distinguished members simply to fulfill his own personal ambitions.

Although the church as a whole may not have been responsible for the success of such political monks as Gembō and Dōkyō, the imperial family as well as the Fujiwara could not have failed to see the perils of having the affairs of state conducted in a city like Nara, where the offices of government were overshadowed by imposing monasteries accommodating thousands of monks. The desire to escape interference by the church no doubt was a major factor in the decision by Emperor Kammu, who ascended the throne in the fourth month of 781, to abandon Nara in favor of a new administrative center. Yet it should be remembered that aside from the fear of clerical domination there were other reasons for relocating the capital. For one thing, the location of Nara, surrounded by hilly terrain to the north, east, and west, did not allow easy access to the port of Naniwa, which had assumed increasing importance with the emergence of a centralized state in the eighth century. Another consideration may have been the lack of an adequate supply of water to sustain Nara's burgeoning population.[15]

Pressure to establish a new capital from which the country could be more easily governed intensified after 780 when news of the rout of government forces by the Emishi aborigines in Mutsu created great unrest in Nara. The following year the aging Emperor Kōnin, who had succeeded Empress Shōtoku in 770, relinquished the throne to his energetic eldest son, Prince Yamabe, then forty-four years of age. The new emperor, known as Kammu (r. 781–806), immediately undertook a series of economic reforms designed to strengthen the central government. In the fifth month of 784, Fujiwara no Oguromaro, who had three years earlier won an impressive victory over the Ezo, was ordered to inspect the Nagaoka region in Yamashiro Province and report on its suitability as the site for a new seat of government. Construction of the new capital at Nagaoka, which bordered on the Katsura River, a tributary of the Yodo River that passed through Naniwa, was begun the following month. By the end of the year the emperor formally took up residence in a temporary palace at Nagaoka. Despite an enormous expenditure of tax revenue and labor, construction of the Nagaoka capital did not progress satisfactorily, partly owing to the belief that the area was haunted by the vengeful spirits of Fujiwara no Tanetsugu and Prince Sawara, who lost their lives in 785 because of intrigues relating to the establishment of the new capital. In 793 the government finally abandoned Nagaoka and announced its intention of relocating at

---

15 Kuroita Katsumi, *Kōtei kokushi no kenkyū* (Tokyo: Iwanami shoten, 1936), vol. 2, pp. 197–98.

Uta to the northeast of Nagaoka. Kammu, who moved here during the following year, renamed the new city Heian-kyō (The Capital of Peace and Tranquillity), which later came to be called simply Kyoto (The Capital).

As descendants of Emperor Tenji (r. 661–72), Kōnin and his son Kammu did not feel themselves bound to continue the unrestrained pro-Buddhist policies pursued by the Nara rulers Genshō, Shōmu, and Kōken, who all belonged to the rival lineage of Emperor Temmu (r. 673–86). Determined to bring the northern aborigines under imperial control and to alleviate the hardships suffered by the peasantry, Kōnin, unlike his predecessors, concerned himself primarily with military and economic problems. It was only in the last two years of his reign that Kōnin began to consider the consequences of a church functioning free from government supervision.

In 779 the Civil Affairs Ministry (*Jibushō*) issued two directives designed to curb the illegal activities of monks. One stipulated that a nationwide census of the clergy be taken to identify "official monks" (*kansō*).[16] By compiling such a register, the authorities hoped to weed out those monks who had been ordained without government sanction. A second directive sought to send back to their home provinces all monks affiliated with the *kokubunji* (the government-supported monasteries established in each province after 741) who were illegally residing in the capital.[17] Emperor Kōnin's critical attitude toward the Buddhist clergy was revealed in a remarkable edict written on the twentieth day of the first month of 780, just six days after the pagodas of the Yakushiji and Katsuragidera had been struck by lightning and destroyed in the ensuing fire.[18] Citing the widely held Chinese belief that unusual natural phenomena reflected the judgment of Heaven, Kōnin declared that the destruction of the pagodas signified such divine censure. While acknowledging in stereotyped language his own lack of virtue, he asked how the clergy could not but be ashamed of its conduct, which was no different from that of laymen, and accused the church of violating both the teachings of the Buddha and the laws of the land. It can be regarded only as an irony that the Buddhist clergy, which since Asuka times had been thought to provide protection for the state, was seen by the end of the Nara period as the very cause of the natural disasters that it was supposed to prevent.

16 *Shoku Nihongi*, kan 35, Hōki 10 (779)/8/19, *KT*, vol. 2, p. 451.
17 *Shoku Nihongi*, kan 35, Hōki 10/8/26, *KT*, vol. 2, p. 451.
18 *Shoku Nihongi*, kan 36, Hōki 11 (780)/1/20, *KT*, vol. 2, p. 456.

Sharing his father's fear of an unrestrained church, Emperor Kammu, or his Council of State, in the course of his twenty-five-year reign issued more than thirty directives that sought to correct abuses by the clergy and reduce the threat that temples and monasteries posed to the national economy. The various strictures applied by Kammu were not intended to humiliate the clergy or denigrate Buddhist doctrine, for he always saw himself as a devout follower of Buddhism who founded monasteries, sponsored religious services at court, and periodically ordered moratoriums on the slaughter of animals, albeit to a lesser extent than his predecessors in the Temmu lineage. Kammu's political goal was to revitalize the *ritsuryō* state and create a strong and fiscally sound government. It is not surprising, therefore, that many of the measures that he adopted reflected prohibitions already found in the *Sōniryō*, which, like the laws in the *ritsuryō* itself, had been increasingly ignored during the second half of the Nara period.

The underlying theme of Kammu's reign was sounded in a rescript issued in 782, just one year after he ascended the throne, in which he declared that only by bringing an end to the various construction projects, by developing agriculture, and by the practice of frugality on the part of government, could the nation become prosperous.[19] Specifically linking the decline in the price of silver to the decision to put a stop to temple construction, Kammu ordered the disbanding of the Office for the Construction of the Hokkeji, which was supervising work on the still uncompleted Hokkeji, a major convent in Nara founded by Empress Kōmyō, who was the consort of Emperor Shōmu.

Another of Kammu's major concerns was the widespread practice of acquiring tax-exempt land through the creation of privately controlled temples. In the years following the move of the capital to Nara, the government permitted a limited number of powerful families to found temples that would essentially be under their own control. Since such temples were expected to offer prayers for the wellbeing of the country and to conduct services for the benefit of their lay sponsors, they received annual payments of rice from the government as an indication of their quasi-official status. The lay sponsors (*dan'otsu*) and their heirs held in perpetuity the right to appoint the clerical officers (*sangō*) who administered these temples, which were officially designated *jōgakuji* (temples within the set limit). According to a decree issued in 749, *jōgakuji* were prohibited from own-

---

[19] *Shoku Nihongi*, kan 37, Enryaku 1 (782)/4/11, *KT*, vol. 2, pp. 483–84.

ing more than 100 *chō* of cultivated land, which was a mere 10 percent of the amount allowed for the "great monasteries" (*daiji*) such as Daianji, Yakushiji, Kōfukuji, Hokkeji, and the provincial *kokubunji*.[20] Nevertheless *jōgakuji* continued to expand their landholdings, thereby enriching their sponsors who exercised de facto control over the temples through their handpicked clerical officers.[21]

To cope with this problem Kammu issued an edict in 783 chastising officials for their laxity in enforcing earlier prohibitions against unsanctioned private temples, which, he said, if left unchecked would in time acquire every square inch of land in the country.[22] Not only were both private temples that had not been accorded status as *jōgakuji* and "chapels" (*dōjō*) to be banned, but even unauthorized donations of land or other property to established monasteries were forbidden. Violators were subject to severe punishment: immediate dismissal for officials, eighty lashes of the whip for others. Kammu's predecessor, Kōnin, likewise troubled by donations to monasteries, had declared three years earlier, in 780, on the occasion of his gift "in perpetuity" of one hundred households to the Akishinodera in Nara, that the term "in perpetuity" must henceforth be interpreted in all cases to mean "for one generation only."[23] In 795, one year after the capital was moved to Kyoto, the injunction against donations of land or property to monasteries was repeated, with a new stipulation requiring registration with the central government of all land previously donated.[24] Monasteries were also warned, as were families of ranking ministers, in 784, immediately after the capital was moved to Nagaoka, and again in 798, after the move to Kyoto, to cease acquiring plots of land in a pattern that effectively blocked access of the common people to mountains, rivers, and marshes, which were all in the public domain.[25] By monopolizing such areas, which had previously been open for hunting, fishing, and certain types of specialized agriculture, the powerful families and monasteries increased their wealth but, as the edict of 784 pointed out, only at the cost of great hardship to the people.

Even the legitimate property of recognized monasteries was

---

20 *Shoku Nihongi*, kan 17, Tempyō shōhō 1 (749)/7/13, *KT*, vol. 2, p. 204.
21 See, for example, the directive of the Council of State (*Daijō kampu*) Enryaku 24 (805)/1/3 in *Ruijū sandai kyaku* (mid-eleventh century): *zempen*, kan 3, *KT*, vol. 25, p. 116.
22 *Shoku Nihongi*, kan 37, Enryaku 2 (783)/6/10, *KT*, vol. 2, pp. 493–94.
23 *Shoku Nihongi*, kan 36, Hōki 11 (780)/11/6/5, *KT*, vol. 2, p. 461.
24 *Ruijū kokushi* (892): *zempen*, kan 182, Enryaku 14 (795)/4/20, *KT*, vol. 6, p. 279.
25 *Shoku Nihongi*, kan 38, Enryaku 3 (784)/12/13, *KT*, vol. 2, p. 503; *Ruijū sandai kyaku: kōhen*, kan 16, directive of the Council of State dated Enryaku 17 (798)/12/8, *KT*, vol. 25, p. 497.

henceforth to be subjected to careful scrutiny. A directive issued in 796 empowered the provincial governor, along with the temple officers (*sangō*), to audit temple property, which was now subject to confiscation if some illegality was discovered in the course of the investigation.[26] While this directive affirmed the right of the lay patron, in consultation with the monks of the temple, to appoint the temple officers, such appointments also required the approval of the provincial governor, who could subsequently press charges against the lay patron in the event that the temple officers were guilty of any illegal acts.

Each recognized temple was required to submit annually to the central government an inventory of its property (*shizai chō*). Such records, however, could be easily falsified since it was often not possible to check their accuracy if the temple was far from the capital. The Council of State therefore decided in 798, at the behest of Kammu, to replace these annual reports with an on-the-spot verification by each newly appointed provincial governor.[27]

Since a major reason for the decision to remove the capital from Nara was the venality of many clerics in the great monasteries, it is not surprising that Kammu should have singled out the monasteries of Nara and their clergy for particular condemnation. As early as 783 he issued a sharply worded edict denouncing specifically the Nara monasteries for charging usurious interest rates on loans (*suiko*) that inevitably led to the forfeiture of mortgaged lands and property, depriving farmers of their livelihood.[28] Such practices, it was pointed out, not only contravened the laws of the state but also signified the secularization of the church. While the edict did not prohibit monasteries from making loans, it limited the interest they could charge, regardless of the length of the loan, to 10 percent. This was well below the current rate for private loans, which fluctuated between 50 percent and 100 percent per annum.

In 795, one year after the court had moved to Kyoto, Kammu was informed by his ministers that the seven great monasteries of Nara were still making loans at exorbitant interest rates, which had so impoverished the peasantry that they could no longer pay their taxes or sustain their families.[29] Although the ministers' proposal to restrict

---

26 *Ruijū sandai kyaku: zempen*, kan 3, directive dated Enryaku 15 (796)/3/25, *KT*, vol. 25, pp. 115–16.
27 Directive dated Enryaku 17 (798)/1/20, in *KT*, vol. 25, p. 116.
28 *Shoku Nihongi*, kan 37, Enryaku 2 (783)/12/2, *KT*, vol. 2, p. 496.
29 *Ruijū kokushi: kōhen*, kan 182, memorial dated Enryaku 14 (795)/11/22, *KT*, vol. 6, p. 279.

the frequency of temple loans was readily accepted by the emperor, it proved difficult to enforce. Kammu made no secret of his dislike for the Nara clergy. No sooner had he moved to Kyoto than he dispatched a commissioner to Nara to investigate the clergy of the seven great monasteries.[30] In an edict issued in 798, Kammu again lashed out at the Nara clergy, accusing them of licentious behavior, and appointed the governor of Yamato Province, Fujiwara no Sonohito, to carry out an investigation.[31]

By Heian times clerical misconduct was no longer a phenomenon limited to the Nara monasteries. Although the *Sōniryō*, which in theory defined the standards of behavior of the clergy, remained in force after Nara was abandoned as the capital, it became increasingly apparent that many monks and nuns were openly flouting its provisions. To bring the wayward clergy under greater control of the authorities, Kammu issued within the short span of fifteen years an unprecedented number of directives aimed at correcting specific abuses. A list of the principal decrees follows:

784: Edict deploring corrupt provincial bishops (*kokushi*) who expect to be received with ceremonies appropriate for lay officials. Such persons, who cause much hardship to the people, must be replaced.[32]

785 (and again in 798): Edict deploring the failure of the authorities to arrest corrupt monks who choose their own lay patrons or who tour villages claiming to be able to work miracles and thus delude the ignorant masses. Such monks should be exiled to a distant province and required to stay in a recognized temple.[33]

785: Edict ordering that a roster of "virtuous monks" be compiled and sent to the central government so that such monks might be commended as models for the clergy.[34]

785 (and again in 799): Decrees prohibiting monks, nuns, or lay persons from practicing black magic in the mountains with the aim of harming their enemies.[35]

797: Edict instructing the provincial bishops (*kōji*) to scrutinize internal temple affairs and correct any abuses by the clergy within their jurisdiction.[36]

30 *Ruijū kokushi: kōhen*, kan 180, Enryaku 14 (795)/7/18, *KT,* vol. 6, p. 257.
31 *Ruijū kokushi: kōhen*, kan 186, edict dated Enryaku 17 (798)/7/28, *KT,* vol. 6, p. 300. Kammu decried the immorality of the clergy in at least two other edicts issued in the course of this year. See entries for Enryaku 17/4/15 and 10/17 in *Ruijū kokushi: kōhen, KT,* vol. 6, p. 300.
32 *Shoku Nihongi*, kan 38, Enryaku 3 (784)/5/1, *KT,* vol. 2, p. 499.
33 *Shoku Nihongi*, edict dated Enryaku 4 (785)/5/25, *KT,* vol. 2, p. 508; *Ruijū kokushi: kōhen*, kan 186, edict dated Enryaku 17 (798)/4/15, *KT,* vol. 6, p. 300.
34 *Shoku Nihongi*, kan 38, edict dated Enryaku 4 (785)/7/11, *KT,* vol. 2, p. 511.
35 *Ruijū sandai kyaku*, kan 2, directive of the Council of State dated Shōtai (901)/2/14, citing an earlier directive dated Enryaku 4 (785)/10/5, *KT,* vol. 25, p. 74; *Nihon kōki* (840), kan 8, Enryaku 18 (799)/6/12, *KT,* vol. 3, p. 22.
36 *Ruijū kokushi*, kan 186, edict dated Enryaku 16 (797)/8/11, *KT,* vol. 6, p. 300.

798, 4th month: Edict deploring the lack of proper training of the annual ordinands (*nembun dosha*), who are described as resembling monks only in appearance but whose behavior is like that of laymen. Henceforth only people of good character and learning, over thirty-five years of age, will be eligible for ordination. The edict further prohibits those monks who engage in commerce and "tour the villages like ordinary people" from residing in monasteries.[37]

798, 9th month: Edict ordering all monks who have fathered offspring to be returned to lay life.[38]

799: Directive ordering provincial governors and bishops to purge the *kokubunji* of corrupt monks.[39]

An attempt was also made to raise the intellectual level of the clergy. According to a directive issued by the Council of State in 734, the minimum requirements that a novice had to fulfill in order to be ordained were (1) that he be able to recite from memory passages from either the *Hokekyō* (Lotus Sutra) or the *Konkōmyōkyō* (Sutra of Golden Light) – the two scriptures chanted regularly at the *kokubunji* for the protection of the state; (2) that he know the rules for proper worship; and (3) that he have completed three years of service as a novice.[40] While such training might suffice for a monk whose primary duty was to conduct routine services at a *kokubunji*, it did not guarantee that a monk had any real understanding of Buddhist doctrine. Consequently, Kammu ordered in 798 that a candidate for admission to the clergy must take a qualifying examination (*kanshi*) in which he successfully answers five out of ten questions on doctrine as expounded in the scriptures before he can be granted the status of a full-fledged novice.[41] On the day of the ordination proper, the candidate was required to pass a second, more detailed examination (*shinshi*) in which he was expected to answer eight of ten questions. It was further stipulated that only those who had learned the *kan'on* pronunciation of Chinese, which had recently been introduced from Ch'ang-an, would be eligible for ordination. The requirement for the second examination, administered on the day of ordination, was dropped in 801, apparently because the scope of the first qualifying examination

---

37 *Ruijū kokushi*, kan 187, edict dated Enryaku 17 (798)/4/15, *KT*, vol. 6, p. 313. See also the edict dated Enryaku 20 (801)/4/15 in *KT*, vol. 6, p. 314, which lowers the minimum age for ordination to twenty.
38 *Ruijū sandai kyaku: kōhen*, kan 19, Enryaku 17 (798)/9/17, *KT*, vol. 25, p. 621.
39 *Nihon kōki*, kan 8, directive dated Enryaku 18 (799)/5/19, *KT*, vol. 3, p. 21.
40 *Shoku Nihongi*, kan 11, directive dated Tempyō 6 (734)/11/21, *KT*, vol. 2, p. 135.
41 *Ruijū kokushi*, kan 187, edict dated Enryaku 17 (798)/4/15, *KT*, vol. 6, pp. 313–14.

was expanded to include questions on the complex doctrines of the Sanron and Hossō schools.⁴²

SAICHŌ

The Heian period was dominated by two schools, Tendai and Shingon, the former established by Saichō and the latter by Kūkai, two of the most important figures in the history of Japanese Buddhism. Although both Tendai and Shingon were originally introduced from China, they were transformed by their Japanese protagonists into uniquely Japanese schools of Buddhism.

Saichō was born in 767 in Furuchi-gō (part of the present-day Ōtsu city) in Ōmi Province.⁴³ At the age of eleven he "left his family" (*shukke*) to enter the Ōmi Kokubunji, where he came under the tutelage of Gyōhyō, the provincial bishop of Ōmi. Two years later Saichō received his *tokudo* (initiation as a *shami*, "novice"). His full ordination (*jukai*, "accepting the [250] precepts") raising him to the status of monk (*sō*) took place at Tōdaiji in 785. Immediately thereafter Saichō moved to Mount Hiei, where he devoted himself to meditation, worship, and especially the study of scripture. His abrupt move to Hiei was in keeping with the practice of many monks of the time, who sought to purify themselves and perhaps even acquire supernatural powers by undergoing austerities in the mountains. In Saichō's case, as the five vows he made at the time suggest, the move to Hiei reflected disenchantment with the corruption that was infecting the great monasteries of Nara.

Saichō probably first heard of Tendai from his master Gyōhyō, who had been a disciple of Tao-hsüan (Japanese, Dōsen), a learned Chinese monk who was said to have been versed in the doctrines of

---

42 *Ruijū kokushi*, kan 187, edict dated Enryaku 20 (801)/4/15, *KT*, vol. 6, p. 314.
43 The earliest and most reliable source for the biography of Saichō is the *Eizan Daishi den* compiled by his disciple Ninchū and included in *DDZ*, vol. 5, *furoku*, pp. 1–48. Another important primary source providing valuable information regarding Siachō's date and place of birth, family background, service as a novice, and various ordinations is the collection of ordination certificates included in the same volume on pp. 101–5. For critical modern biographies of the life of Saichō, see Paul Groner, *Saichō: The Establishment of the Japanese Tendai School* (Berkeley, Calif.: Berkeley Buddhist Studies Series, 1984); Katsuno Ryūshin, *Hieizan to Kōyasan* (Tokyo: Shibundō, 1959); Kiuchi Hiroshi, *Dengyō Daishi no shōgai to shisō*, *Regurusu bunko*, vol. 56 (Tokyo: Daisan bummeisha, 1976); Nakao Shumpaku, *Dengyō Daishi Saichō no kenkyū* (Kyoto: Nagata bunshōdō, 1987); Saeki Arikiyo, *Dengyō Daishi den no kenkyū* (Tokyo: Yoshikawa kōbunkan, 1992); Shioiri Ryōdō and Kiuchi Gyōō eds., *Saichō*, vol. 2 of *Nihon meisō ronshū* (Tokyo: Yoshikawa kōbunkan, 1982); Tamura Kōyū, *Saichō, Jimbutsu sōsho*, vol. 193 (Tokyo: Yoshikawa kōbunkan, 1988).

the Kegon, Ritsu, and Zen schools, in addition to those of Tendai.[44] It was only after Saichō had settled on Hiei, however, that he was able to acquire a set of the major Tendai treatises, which he then studied with great enthusiasm. Gradually a small group of followers, which included monks such as Gishin and Enchō who were destined to become major disciples, gathered around him. Official recognition of his learning came twelve years after his move to Hiei, when, in 797, he was named one of the ten court chaplains (*naigubu jū zenji*) whose responsibility was to pray for the well-being of the emperor. This appointment entitled his small temple on Hiei to receive a subsidy paid from the Ōmi tax revenues.

The following year Saichō invited ten monks from Nara to hear a series of lectures on the *Hokekyō* and two related sutras, which together constitute the basic scriptures of Tendai. These lectures, designed by Saichō to commemorate the anniversary of the death of Chih-i, the Chinese systematizer of Tendai, provided him with an opportunity to expound to the scholar-monks of Nara Tendai doctrine, which had been only briefly introduced by the *Vinaya* master Chien-chen (Japanese, Ganjin), who had arrived in Japan in 754 carrying the major treatises of this school.[45] Known as the *Hokke jikkō* (The Ten Lectures on the Lotus), these memorial lectures held annually on Hiei in the eleventh month subsequently became a major event on the Tendai calendar.

In 802, Emperor Kammu, who was troubled by the frequent wrangling between the Nara schools, particularly between Hossō and Sanron, ordered Wake no Hiroyo, the head of the state Academy (*Daigaku*) and eldest son of the loyalist Kiyomaro, and Hiroyo's brother, the renowned scholar Matsuna, to arrange for lectures on Tendai at the Wake clan temple Takaosanji (the predecessor to present-day Jingoji in Kyoto). Kammu promoted Tendai, apparently hoping to provide some common ground for a resolution of the disputes between the Sanron and Hossō schools, since Tendai teachings included the concept of progressive revelation, according to which each of the major groups of scriptures had its own place in a grand design devised by Śākyamuni Buddha to lead his followers to accept

---

44 Gyōnen (1240–1321), *Sangoku Buppō denzū engi, kan* 2, BZ, vol. 101, p. 115a. In the same work Gyōnen quotes the now lost *Tendai fuhō engi*, which is attributed to Saichō, as saying that the Chinese monks Tao-hsüan, Chien-chen, and Fa-chin all disseminated the Tendai teachings in Japan (pp. 126b–27a).
45 Genkai, *Tō Daiwajō tōsei den* (779), BZ, vol. 113, p. 120a.

the *Hokekyō* as his final and highest teaching.[46] Kammu's plan to use Tendai as a unifying ideology for Japanese Buddhism was not unreasonable since Chi-tsang and Tz'u-en, the two most prominent scholar-monks of the Chinese Sanron and Hossō schools respectively, had written major commentaries on the *Hokekyō*.

In the course of the Takaosanji lecture, in which Saichō played the leading role, Kammu expressed his desire to see Tendai established as a full-fledged Buddhist school in Japan. Saichō immediately responded, in a message relayed to the emperor by Hiroyo, that this could be accomplished only if a mission was sent to China to create a formal link with the Chinese patriarchate in the T'ien-t'ai mountains, where the school originated and maintained its head monastery. Without such a formal transmission of doctrine, Saichō insisted, Tendai would carry little authority in Japan. He also made clear to Kammu his own conviction that Tendai was inherently superior to both Sanron and Hossō because the latter two schools were based on treatises written by Indian scholiasts, whereas Tendai was rooted in the *Hokekyō*, a scripture preached by Śākyamuni Buddha himself. Saichō's proposal to undertake a mission to China was promptly accepted, and he was granted permission to make a short visit to the T'ien-t'ai mountains accompanied by his disciple Gishin, who was to serve as his interpreter.

Sailing on one of the four ships that transported the Japanese embassy to the T'ang court, Saichō arrived at Ming-chou (the present-day Ning-p'o) in the ninth month of 804. En route to the T'ien-t'ai mountains he stopped briefly at T'ai-chou (present-day Lin-hai), where he met Tao-sui, the then patriarch of the Chinese Tendai school. By the tenth month Saichō had reached T'ien-t'ai, where he visited the holy sites and had a chance to study Tendai doctrine at its source. A totally unexpected reward from his visit to T'ien-t'ai was an encounter with a monk named Hsiao-jan, who initiated him into the Gozu (Chinese, Niu-t'ou, "Ox Head") lineage of Zen (Chinese, Ch'an).[47] The following month Saichō returned to T'ai-chou for further instruction in Tendai doctrine from Tao-sui, and, in the third month of 805, on the eve of his return to the embarkation point of

---

46 For a brief account of Chih-i's classification of the major groups of sutras, see my "Imperial Patronage in T'ang Buddhism," in *Perspectives on the T'ang*, ed. Arthur F. Wright and Denis Twitchett (New Haven, Conn.: Yale University Press, 1973), pp. 284–87.

47 In addition to the Gozu lineage of Zen, Saichō claimed to have received the transmission of the Northern School (Hokushū) through both Gyōhyō and Tao-hsüan. The latter had been a pupil of P'u-chi, the Dharma-heir to the famous (Northern) Sixth Patriarch, Shen-hsiu. See Saichō, *Naishō Buppō sōjō kechimyaku fu*, *DDZ*, vol. 1, pp. 210–15.

Ming-chou, received from Tao-sui the *endonkai* (perfect and immediate precepts), which was a Tendai ordination based on the fifty-eight bodhisattva precepts (*bosatsukai*) taught in the *Bommōkyō*.

Upon learning after his arrival in Ming-chou that the embassy's departure for Japan was to be delayed, Saichō decided to use the extra time allowed him in China to visit Yüeh-chou (present-day Shao-hsing), where he hoped to find additional Tendai manuscripts and, perhaps, also to acquire texts belonging to the Mikkyō (Esoteric Buddhist) tradition. During his stay in Yüeh-chou, which occupied most of the fourth month of 805, Saichō managed to receive an esoteric initiation (*kanjō*, "sprinkling of consecrated water on the head") from one Shun-hsiao, who also provided him with many esoteric texts and several implements for use in esoteric rituals. In all, Saichō collected 120 manuscripts in T'ai-chou and 102 manuscripts in Yüeh-chou, most of the latter being Mikkyō works.[48]

Saichō sailed from Ming-chou on an embassy ship in the fifth month and reached Kyushu in the middle of the sixth month. He was immediately summoned to the court, where he personally presented Kammu with the manuscripts and ritual implements that he had acquired in China. Not surprisingly, the emperor ordered that copies of the Tendai texts be distributed to each of the seven great monasteries of Nara. But what impressed Kammu, whose health was now failing, even more than the precious Tendai manuscripts was Saichō's newly acquired status as a practitioner of Mikkyō, in which interest had been steadily growing since Nara times because of its practical value for curing illnesses, preventing misfortunes, and producing various benefits. It might well have struck Saichō as ironic that the first service that Kammu ordered him to perform after his return to Japan was not related to Tendai, which he had gone to China specifically to study, but rather to the Mikkyō, which was at best only of secondary interest to him. By imperial decree a platform-altar for esoteric initiations (*kanjōdan*) was constructed at Takaosanji, where, in the ninth month of 805, Saichō performed for eight monks from Nara the first esoteric initiation rites ever held in Japan. Later the same month Saichō was summoned to the palace to conduct an esoteric ritual that would bring about the recovery of the ailing emperor.[49]

---

48 For a list of the titles of the manuscripts acquired in T'ai-chou and Yüeh-chou, see *Dengyō Daishi shōrai Taishū roku* and *Dengyō Daishi shōrai Esshū roku*, both compiled by Saichō (*T*, vol. 55, pp. 1055a–58a and pp. 1058b–60b).

49 *Eizan Daishi den, DDZ*, vol. 5, *furoku*, pp. 21–24. Kammu's faith in the esoteric Buddhism transmitted by Saichō is attested in a proclamation issued by Kammu included in Saichō's *Kenkairon engi* (821), *DDZ*, vol. 1, pp. 283–84.

In the first month of 806, Saichō sent a petition to Kammu requesting that Tendai be formally accorded status as one of the recognized Buddhist schools.[50] To accomplish this, Saichō proposed that the traditional system of ordaining ten monks at the beginning of the new year to pray for the well-being of the nation be restructured and expanded to include representatives of each of the officially recognized schools.[51] The Kegon, Tendai, and Ritsu schools were to be allocated two novices each; the Sanron, to which the Hīnayānist Jōjitsu school was attached, and the Hossō, to which the Hīnayānist Kusha school was appended, were to be assigned three novices each, for a total of twelve annual ordinands (*nembun dosha*). The government promptly accepted Saichō's proposal, which had won immediate backing from the hierarchy (*sōgō*), but stipulated that of the two ordinands allotted annually to the Tendai school only one should devote himself solely to the study of classical Tendai doctrine. The other candidate was to study and become a specialist in Mikkyō. Thus from its inception the Japanese Tendai school, unlike its Chinese parent, had Mikkyō as one of its major components. The reconciliation of Mikkyō with classical Tendai thought was to become one of the principal tasks for future generations of Tendai scholars.

With the death of Kammu in the third month of 806 Saichō lost a strong supporter. The new emperor, Heizei (reigned 806–9), seeking to reduce government expenditures, placed restrictions on the construction of new temples and the use of state revenues for religious purposes. Because of this new policy no Tendai monks were ordained until 810, when Heizei's successor, Saga, allowed eight Tendai novices to be tonsured at the court, thus compensating for Heizei's failure to honor Kammu's promise to Saichō. Saga's decision to carry out the ordinations created practical difficulties for Saichō, since one of the two annual Tendai ordinands had to be trained in Mikkyō, which Saichō himself had not had the opportunity to study properly in China. Another problem was that Saichō's library on Hiei was lacking many important Mikkyō texts. To acquire copies of these texts and also to supplement his obviously deficient knowledge of Mikkyō, Saichō turned to Kūkai, a monk seven years his junior, whose understanding of Mikkyō was without equal in Japan.

---

50 For Saichō's proposal, the statement by the hierarchs, and the official response by the government, see *Kenkairon engi, DDZ*, vol. 1, pp. 292–96.

51 The practice of ordaining ten monks at the court on the last day of the year or at the beginning of the new year was begun in 696. See *Nihon shoki, kan* 30, Jitō 10 (696)/12/1, *NKBT*, vol. 68, p. 532, and Saichō's *Kenkairon* (819), *kan* 3, *DDZ*, vol. 1, p. 150.

Unlike Saichō, who went to China to study Tendai but by chance happened to encounter Mikkyō adepts who conferred on him low-level initiations, Kūkai visited China with the specific objective of mastering the doctrines and rituals of Mikkyō and received its highest initiations. Although both men sailed in the same flotilla, they traveled on different ships and probably became acquainted with each other only after their return to Japan. Saichō's ship, as we have noted, landed in Ming-chou, whereas the ship carrying Kūkai entered the port of Fu-chou, whence Kūkai proceeded in the entourage of the Japanese ambassador directly to Ch'ang-an, where he intensively studied Mikkyō for more than a year. When Kūkai returned to Kyushu in the tenth month of 806, he had in his possession a priceless collection of esoteric texts, ritual implements, paintings, and mandalas (graphic representations of various divinities, often portrayed through mystical symbols and arranged according to a pattern that emanates outward from a central point).[52]

In the eighth month of 809, Saichō sent a disciple to Kūkai, who had taken up residence at Takaosanji a month earlier, bearing a letter requesting the loan of twelve esoteric texts. Over the next six years Saichō wrote almost thirty such letters, often signing them "your disciple Saichō," even though Kūkai was seven years his junior.[53] Although Saichō himself had received several esoteric initiations while in China and had performed such an initiation at Takaosanji in 805, he openly acknowledged Kūkai's superior understanding of Mikkyō. Toward the end of 812 Saichō visited Kūkai at Takaosanji to request the initiation based on the *kongōkai* (diamond realm) and *taizōkai* (embryo realm) mandalas, which are the two principal mandalas of the line of Mikkyō transmitted by Kūkai that subsequently came to be known in Japan as Shingon Mikkyō. Kūkai readily assented, but conferred on Saichō only a *kechien kanjō* (an initiation establishing a link), which is the most elementary of the various levels of initiation.[54] Despite Saichō's eminence as a Tendai monk, his previous esoteric initiations in China, and his subsequent

---

52 Kūkai's catalogue, the *Go-shōrai mokuroku* (*T,* vol. 55, pp. 1060a–66a) lists the titles of 216 works that he brought back to Japan.
53 Saichō's letters to Kūkai are included in the *Rankei yuionshū,* Mikkyō bunka kenkyūjo, ed., *Kōbō Daishi zenshū,* 3rd ed., revised and enlarged (*zōho*), 8 vols. (Kōyasan: Mikkyō bunka kenkyūjo, 1965–68), vol. 5, pp. 353–86.
54 Although virtually all Shingon scholars hold that Saichō received only the introductory initiation, there is a tradition within the Tendai school, based on a letter Saichō's disciple Enchō wrote to Kūkai in 831, that Kūkai conferred an intermediate level ordination on Saichō. See my "Beginnings of Esoteric Buddhism in Japan: The Neglected Tendai Tradition," *Journal of Asian Studies* 34, 1 (1974): 188.

self-study of esoteric texts, he was in Kūkai's eyes still an amateur in Mikkyō, a point that was driven home when Kūkai granted Saichō only the lowest level of initiation at a ceremony in which laymen also participated.

Saichō and Kūkai each viewed Mikkyō differently. For Saichō, Mikkyō and classical Tendai formed the two wings of the newly established Tendai school, a unique amalgam not found in China.[55] To Kūkai, however, Mikkyō was the ultimate teaching of Buddhism and fully constituted a school in its own right. It is not surprising, therefore, that the two men would inevitably part company. The first indication of serious difficulty was Kūkai's refusal, in 814, to lend Saichō an esoteric manuscript that he had requested. Kūkai sharply rebuked Saichō for trying to understand Mikkyō through texts alone, which, Kūkai asserted in a letter to Saichō, were no more than the "dregs of Buddhism." Truth, in other words, Mikkyō, could be transmitted only "from mind to mind." To teach Mikkyō without having received a proper transmission, Kūkai warned, was tantamount to "stealing the doctrine."[56] The relationship between Saichō and Kūkai ended on a bitter note in 816, when Saichō's disciple, Taihan, who at Saichō's urging had gone to study Mikkyō with Kūkai four years earlier, refused Saichō's request that he return to Hiei.

The break with Kūkai marked the end of Saichō's period of docility, as was indicated by his decision to circulate publicly his *Ehyō Tendai shū*, a polemical work written in 813 that sought to document the superiority of Tendai over all other schools. Once the rupture became final in 816, Saichō embarked on a tour of the Kanto region, where he laid the basis for a future Tendai stronghold by lecturing on the *Hokekyō*, establishing pagodas enshrining this sutra and proclaiming before large groups of rural people the Tendai/*Hokekyō* doctrine of One Vehicle (*ichijō*), namely, that the three traditional divisions of Buddhism known as the Three Vehicles (*sanjō*) were no more than an expedient device created by Śākyamuni, the historical Buddha, to lead people of different intellectual and spiritual capacities to the One Vehicle that will ultimately carry each and every sentient being to Buddhahood.

By publicly proclaiming the Tendai doctrine of universal enlightenment, Saichō openly challenged the influential and aristocratic Hossō

---

55 See, for example, Saichō's letter to Taihan (in *DDZ*, vol. 5, p. 469), written in 816, in which Saichō declares that the teachings of the *Hokekyō* and those of Shingon are equally true.
56 The letter is included in the anthology of Kūkai's writings entitled *Henjō hakki Seirei shū*, in *Sangō shiiki, Seirei shū*, vol. 71 of *NKBT*, pp. 442–50. The passage cited occurs on p. 447.

school, which took the opposite view – namely, that the doctrine of One Vehicle taught in the *Hokekyō* was merely an expedient teaching intended to encourage simpleminded people to put their faith in Buddhism and uphold its basic moral code. For the Hossō school, the ultimate teaching of Buddhism was to be found in the *Gejimmikkyō* (Sutra Explaining the Profound Doctrine), its principal scripture, which not only accepted the concept of three real, distinct vehicles, but also held that sentient beings were inherently divided into five groups (*goshō*), the lowest consisting of the luckless *mushō* (those lacking the Buddha-nature), who, strive as they might, were destined to wander eternally through the cycle of birth and death. Saichō's popular gospel of universal salvation was immediately denounced by the well-known Hossō scholar Tokuitsu, who likewise was active in the Kanto area. Over the next five years the two men produced a total of eight works in an effort to refute each other's positions.

Having severed relations with Kūkai and having become involved in a protracted doctrinal dispute with Tokuitsu, Saichō was now ready to dissociate himself completely from the traditional Buddhism that centered around the six Nara schools. It was Saichō's view, but not that of Chinese Tendai, that the *Shibunritsu* – the disciplinary code used in both China and Japan to ordain monks and nuns – was essentially a Hīnayānist work and hence not suitable for Mahāyānist ordinations. In the third month of 818 Saichō took the unprecedented step of formally renouncing the 250 precepts of the *Shibunritsu* that he had taken at the time of his ordination at Tōdaiji. Two months later Saichō requested approval from the throne for a set of six regulations that he had formulated and wished to make binding on all future Tendai ordinands.

Formally known as the *Tendai Hokke-shū nembun gakushō shiki* (Bylaws for the Annual Ordinands of the Tendai Hokke School), the new regulations had far-reaching implications for the future course of Japanese Buddhism.[57] Particularly significant were the following proposals: (1) The names of candidates for ordination should not be removed from family registers, as was the custom, but retained with the added notation "son of the Buddha" (*Busshi*). Under the prevailing law, when someone was accepted as a novice his name was deleted from the family register, which was under the control of the secular authorities, and entered into a clerical register (*sōseki*), which placed him directly under the supervision of the Nara hierarchs

---

57 The text is included in Saichō's *Sange gakushō shiki*, *T*, vol. 74, pp. 623c–24b.

(*sōgō*). (2) The *tokudo* (initiation as a novice) and *jukai* (full ordination as a monk) should take place in the same year. It had been the practice to receive the *tokudo* from a monk at one's "home temple" and the full ordination several years later from preceptors belonging to the Ritsu school at one of the three monasteries authorized to have ordination platforms (*kaidan*): Tōdaiji in Nara, Yakushiji in Shimotsuke, and Kanzeonji in Chikuzen. By linking the *jukai* with the *tokudo*, Saichō hoped to keep Tendai novices out of the hands of the Ritsu preceptors. (3) Ordinations should be based on the *Busshi kai* (precepts for sons of the Buddha), an ambiguous term coined by Saichō suggestive of the *bosatsukai* (bodhisattva precepts) in the *Bommōkyō*. (4) Newly ordained monks should be required to reside on Hiei for an uninterrupted period of twelve years. As Saichō was to point out later, only ten of the twenty-four annual ordinands selected between 807 and 818 remained on Hiei, the others having been "stolen" (his word) by the Hossō (six monks) and Shingon (one monk) schools or else having left for reasons of their own.[58] (5) Tendai monks, regardless of whether they specialized in esoteric rituals (*shanagō*) or traditional Chinese Tendai meditation (*shikangō*), should view the protection of the state (*gokoku*) as their primary concern. (6) Those monks who exhibit special talents after completing their twelve-year training period should be appointed to serve as proselytizers or provincial bishops. In addition to their religious tasks, these monks should also actively promote the public welfare by sponsoring the construction of irrigation ditches, the reclamation of farmland, the building of bridges, and other such projects.

The court forwarded Saichō's proposals to the Office of Hierarchs (*Sōgō-sho*), which did not comment on them, perhaps because Saichō's occasionally vague language left the hierarchs uncertain about how far he was prepared to go in establishing Tendai as a school completely independent of the established church. In the eighth month of 818, Saichō submitted to the court another document containing eight proposed bylaws regarding the administration of Hiei and the training of its monks.[59] Again, the Office of Hierarchs, to which the document was referred, remained silent.

Any doubts regarding Saichō's ultimate intentions were dispelled when, in the third month of 819, he presented a third set of bylaws

---

58 For a list of the students, with notations indicating their reasons for leaving Hieizan and the names of the schools to which they defected, see Saichō, *Tendai Hokke-shū nembun tokudo gakushō myōchō*, DDZ, vol. 1, pp. 250–53.

59 The document, entitled *Kanshō Tendai-shū nembun gakushō shiki*, is included in *Sange gakushō shiki*, p. 624b–c.

to the court for consideration. Reflecting his increasing impatience with the court's failure to act on his earlier proposals for a truly independent Tendai school that he believed had been sanctioned by his imperial patron Kammu, Saichō provocatively entitled his new set of regulations *Tendai Hokke-shū nembun dosha eshō kōdai shiki* (Bylaws for the Conversion of the Annual Ordinands of the Tendai Hokke School from Hīnayāna to Mahāyāna).[60] The three chief points made in this final set of new regulations were: (1) There are three categories of monasteries: (a) those exclusively Mahāyānist, (b) those exclusively Hīnayānist, and (c) those in which Mahāyāna and Hīnayāna coexist. Tendai ordinands and "those who converted to Mahāyāna," that is, monks originally belonging to one of the Nara schools who had subsequently joined Tendai, should be required to spend twelve years on Hiei, which in Saichō's view would become the only truly Mahāyānist monastery in Japan. (2) There are two types of precepts: (a) the fifty-eight Mahāyānist ones of the *Bommōkyō* and (b) the 250 Hīnayānist ones of the *Shibunritsu*. (3) There are two types of ordinations: (a) the Mahāyānist one based on the *Kanfugengyō*, in which the Buddha and two bodhisattvas act as preceptors and (b) the Hīnayānist one based on the *Shibunritsu*, in which three senior monks serve as the preceptors. Tendai novices should, of course, receive the Mahāyānist type of ordination using Mahāyānist precepts.

This last set of proposals signaled the beginning of a reform unprecedented in the history of East Asian Buddhism. First, Saichō's insistence that Tendai monks live in an "exclusively Mahāyānist monastery" marked the emergence in Japan of the sectarian monastery, which subsequently became one of the hallmarks of Japanese Buddhism. Hōryūji, Daianji, Gangōji, and other large Nara monasteries each accommodated groups of monks belonging to different schools. It was only after the time of Saichō that the idea of an exclusive sectarian monastery or temple took root and became the norm.

Second, Saichō broke completely with previous East Asian Buddhist practice when he replaced the *Shibunritsu* precepts with those of the *Bommōkyō*. This latter set of precepts, which lays particular stress on the social responsibility of the individual, had been traditionally viewed as precepts intended primarily for the bodhisattva (*bosatsukai*), that is, precepts for laymen, which monks might also voluntarily choose to accept, as Saichō himself had done in China. Monks had always been minutely regulated in their monastic life by

---

60 *Sange gakushō shiki, T,* vol. 74, pp. 624c–25b.

the 250 precepts of the *Shibunritsu,* which were thought to transcend such relativistic categories as Hīnayāna or Mahāyāna. By labeling as Hīnayānist the *Shibunritsu* precepts, which had hitherto formed the basis of all ordinations, Saichō was implying that there were no true Mahāyāna monks in Japan.

Third, Saichō repudiated the ordination system prevailing in East Asia when he categorized as Hīnayānist the traditional ordination ceremony in which three monks administer the precepts to the ordinands, as prescribed in the *Shibunritsu.* By proposing to substitute the *Kanfugengyō,* a sutra linked to the *Hokekyō* and particularly esteemed in Tendai, for the *Shibunritsu,* Saichō was creating an entirely new ordination system peculiar to Tendai, the practical effect of which was to make Tendai a completely independent school, no longer dependent on the Ritsu monasteries for the ordination of its clergy. To accomplish this, Saichō sought permission to establish his own ordination platform on Hiei, beyond the jurisdiction of the Nara hierarchs, where he could perform his own ordinations.[61]

Outraged by Saichō's third set of proposed bylaws for Tendai ordinands, the Office of Hierarchs sent a sharply worded memorial to Saga in the fifth month of 819 denouncing Saichō's views on precepts, ordination, and the training of monks and urged the government to reject Saichō's proposals. Saichō responded some ten months later with his famous *Kenkairon* (Treatise on the Precepts), which refuted in fifty-eight articles the arguments against him put forward by the hierarchs. Along with the *Kenkairon* he submitted another important work, the *Naishō Buppō sōjō kechimyaku fu,* in which he sought to demonstrate that he – and hence the Japanese Tendai school – was the legitimate heir to four distinct traditions: (1) Tendai proper through his study in China under Tao-sui and Hsing-man; (2) Zen through his master Gyōhyō and the transmission that he received later in China from Hsiao-jan; (3) the Bodhisattva (that is, Mahāyānist) Precepts through the ordination he received at T'ien-t'ai shan based on the *Bommōkyō;* and (4) Mikkyō through the initiations by Shun-hsiao and Wei-hsiang.

The *Kenkairon* was forwarded by the court to the hierarchs, who

---

61 The full text of Saichō's petition to the throne for permission to conduct ordinations is given in *Eizan Daishi den, DDZ,* vol. 5, *furoku,* pp. 33–34. Although ninth-century records do not specifically report that he sought the approval of the emperor to build a *kaidan,* it is likely that he did so, since it had been the custom for ordinations to be performed on a *kaidan.* Saichō's biography in Kokan Shiren, *Genkō Shakusho* (1322), states unambiguously that in the third month of 819, Saichō requested permission for the construction of a *kaidan* (*BZ,* vol. 101, p. 149b).

declined to respond. In 821 Saichō presented the court with yet another work, the *Kenkairon engi*, defending the principle of independent Tendai ordinations, but again was met with silence from the hierarchs and consequently from the throne. Frustrated by his failure to get permission from the government to conduct his own ordinations, Saichō spent the final year of his life quietly managing the affairs of Hiei. In response to a personal appeal from one of Saichō's disciples, Emperor Saga on his own authority promoted Saichō to the highest ecclesiastical rank, *dai hōshii*, an honor that had already been granted to Saichō's junior, Kūkai, two years earlier. Less than four months later, on the fourth day of the sixth month of 822, Saichō died on Hiei, without having gained the permission he so fervently sought to construct a Tendai ordination hall. Seven days after Saichō's death, Saga, without consulting the hierarchs whose opposition was well known, agreed to a petition signed by four of Saichō's prominent lay supporters, including Fujiwara no Fuyutsugu, who was the Minister of the Right, and Yoshimine no Yasuyo, a son of Kammu and half brother of Saga, to allow ordinations on Hiei. The following year an imperial decree was issued granting the name Enryakuji to Saichō's monastery on Hiei in memory of Kammu whose reign was known as Enryaku. Two months later the first Tendai ordinands, fourteen in all, received the *Bommōkyō* precepts from Gishin, who had succeeded Saichō as abbot of Hiei. The long-awaited ordination hall (*kaidan'in*) was completed in 827 with a grant of 90,000 sheaves of rice to defray construction costs.[62]

KŪKAI

Kūkai, the founder of the Japanese Shingon school, was born in 774 in Sanuki Province (present-day Kagawa Prefecture in Shikoku), where his family, surnamed Saeki, exercised considerable influence.[63] At the age of fourteen he was brought to the capital by his maternal uncle, Ato no Ōtari, who was the Confucian tutor to Prince Iyo, the third son of Emperor Kammu. After three years of intensive study of the Chinese classics under the tutelage of his uncle, Kūkai entered the state Academy with the intention of eventually establishing himself as a scholar of Chinese. Shortly thereafter, however,

---

62 *Denjutsu isshinkai mon, kan* 2, *DDZ*, vol. 1, pp. 588–90.
63 For critical modern biographies, see Katsuno, *Hieizan to Kōyasan;* Kushida Ryōkō, *Kūkai no kenkyū* (Tokyo: Sankibō Busshorin, 1981), and Watanabe Shōkō and Miyasaka Yūshō, *Shamon Kūkai, Chikuma sōsho*, vol. 84 (Tokyo: Chikuma Shobō, 1967).

he encountered a monk who taught him the esoteric ritual known as *Kokūzō gumonjihō*, the purpose of which is to increase the powers of memory through incessant repetition of a mystical incantation.[64] After beginning the *gumonjihō*, Kūkai had some sort of deep religious experience, which led him to withdraw from the Academy and retreat to the mountains where he undertook austerities.

According to the traditional accounts dating from late Heian times, Kūkai entered Makiosanji in Izumi at the age of nineteen to start his training as a novice under Gonzō, an influential Sanron monk, and was ordained two years later at Tōdaiji.[65] However, in his first book, the *Sangō shiiki*, written in 797 when he was twenty-three, Kūkai gives no indication of being an ordained monk. On the contrary, it is apparent from the *Sangō shiiki*, a semiautobiographical work that seeks to demonstrate the superiority of Buddhism over Taoism and Confucianism, that Kūkai had an aversion to the formalistic and often corrupt Buddhism of the great monasteries. His sympathies clearly lay with the itinerant holy man (*hijiri*) who, although often lacking a proper ordination, spends his life searching for truth while bringing the word of the Buddha to the common people. In all likelihood such was the life led by Kūkai between 791 when he retreated to the mountains and 804, when, according to the *Shoku Nihon kōki* (compiled in 869), a more reliable source than the late Heian biographies, he first became a novice, presumably in order to be eligible for study in China.[66] His full ordination took place at Tōdaiji in the fourth month of the same year.[67]

Virtually nothing definite is known about Kūkai's study of Mikkyō before his visit to China. The traditional biographies claim that Kūkai first learned of the *Dainichikyō*, one of the basic Mikkyō scriptures, in a dream.[68] After locating a copy of this text beneath a

---

64 Most biographies of Kūkai, dating from the end of the Heian period or later, identify the unnamed monk as Gonzō, a respected cleric who stood in the Sanron lineage. This view has been challenged by some contemporary scholars. For a summary of their arguments, see Shimode Sekiyo, "Kūkai to Shingon-shū," in *Nihon hen*, vol. 2 of Nakamura Hajime, Kasahara Kazuo, and Kanaoka Shūyū, eds., *Ajia Bukkyō shi* (Tokyo: Kōsei shuppansha, 1974), pp. 134–38, and Watanabe and Miyasaka, *Shamon Kūkai*, pp. 34–39.
65 See, for example, Kyōhan, *Daishi on-gyōjō shūki* (1089), in *Zoku gunsho ruijū*, vol. 8 (Tokyo: Keizai zasshisha, 1904), pp. 495–96, and Ken'i, *Kōbō Daishi go-den* (first half of the 12th century) in *Zoku gunsho ruijū*, vol. 8, p. 526.
66 *Shoku Nihon kōki* (869), kan 4, Jōwa 2 (835)/3/25, *KT*, vol. 3, p. 38.
67 *Zō Daisōjō Kūkai Wajō denki* (895), *Kōbō Daishi zenshū*, shukan, p. 9.
68 The earliest reference to this well-known legend occurs in the *Go-yuigō* (*T*, vol. 77, p. 408c), which purports to have been written by Kūkai on his deathbed. Although it is no longer generally recognized as an authentic work of Kūkai's, it was accepted as such since Heian times and hence served as a source for many of the biographies of Kūkai.

pagoda at Kumedera in Yamato, these accounts relate, Kūkai resolved to travel to China, where he could receive proper instruction from Mikkyō masters regarding the meaning of this difficult scripture. Although the traditional biographies make Kūkai's encounter with the *Dainichikyō* appear miraculous, the simple fact is that esoteric texts were in use in Japan long before Kūkai's birth. By the end of the Nara period more than 130 such texts, including the *Dainichikyō* and the *Kongōchōkyō*, the other principal scripture of Shingon Mikkyō, had been brought to Japan.[69] More than one quarter of the 150 surviving images from the eighth century are representations of Mikkyō divinities, which is another indication of the inroads that Mikkyō had already made in Japan.[70] Although not yet recognized as an independent school in Nara times, iconographic and textual evidence shows that Mikkyō was widely known and practiced even before Kūkai undertook his journey to China.

We have no reliable information about how Kūkai managed to get permission from the Japanese government to study in China. Traveling in the company of the ambassador, Fujiwara no Kadonomaro, on whose behalf he drafted letters to the Chinese authorities, Kūkai reached Ch'ang-an at the end of 804. In the sixth month of 805 he was accepted as a disciple by Hui-kuo, who was recognized as the foremost master of esoteric Buddhism in China. According to Kūkai's account, Hui-kuo, who was then ailing, declared at their first encounter that he had been long awaiting the arrival of Kūkai, whom he formally designated as his successor.[71] After receiving the initiations based on the *kongōkai* and *taizōkai* mandalas, Kūkai was granted the *dembō kanjō* (the initiation for transmitting the Dharma), which is the highest of the three levels of esoteric initiations and signifies that its recipient has become a *dembō ajari*, that is, an esoteric master (*ajari*) who is himself empowered to transmit the teachings. Before Hui-kuo's death in the twelfth month of 805 he passed on to Kūkai a reputed relic of the Buddha, various paintings, images, ritual implements, texts, and mandalas. Although Kūkai had originally planned to spend twenty years in China, he decided to return to Japan immediately after Hui-kuo's death so that he could disseminate the "orthodox" Mikkyō that he had learned from Hui-kuo.

Kūkai traveled back to Japan with the embassy of Takashina no

69 Ishida Mosaku, *Shakyō yori mitaru Nara-chō Bukkyō no kenkyū* (Tokyo: Tōyō bunko, 1930), p. 146.
70 Katsumata Shunkyō, *Mikkyō no Nihon-teki tenkai* (Tokyo: Shunjūsha, 1970), p. 10.
71 *Go-shōrai mokuroku, T,* vol. 55, p. 1065b–c.

Tōnari, reaching Kyushu in the tenth month of 806. Through the ambassador he submitted to the court a catalogue of the precious esoteric manuscripts and religious objects that he had acquired in China, hoping to be summoned to the capital to transmit the Mikkyō teachings. Although later biographies claim that he moved to Makiosanji the following year, it is clear from earlier records that despite his unique training in China, no warm welcome awaited Kūkai in Kyoto.[72] His exclusion from the capital was almost certainly due to political happenstance. In 807, one year after ascending the throne, Heizei sent his half-brother, Prince Iyo, into exile on suspicion of plotting mutiny, ultimately forcing him to commit suicide. Kūkai, through his uncle Ōtari, who had been Prince Iyo's tutor, had had a long-standing friendship with the Prince, which, no doubt tainted Kūkai in the eyes of Heizei.

Kūkai's fortunes abruptly changed when Saga became emperor in the fourth month of 809. The new emperor had a deep interest in Chinese culture, particularly literature, poetry, and calligraphy – areas in which Kūkai excelled. In the seventh month of 809, Saga invited Kūkai to take up residence in Takaosanji, where four years earlier Saichō had erected an altar for esoteric initiations (*kanjōdan*) at the behest of Saga's father, Kammu. A close relationship immediately developed between Saga and Kūkai through frequent exchanges of poetry and calligraphy. Saga, who was not especially concerned with religion, esteemed Kūkai primarily for his profound knowledge of Chinese culture. For Kūkai the strong personal bond with Saga provided entree to the court and aristocracy and gave him the opportunity to lay a solid foundation for Shingon Mikkyō.

Kūkai lost no time in trying to convince the court of the practical value of Shingon. In the wake of an unsuccessful coup to restore Retired Emperor Heizei to the throne in 810, Kūkai successfully petitioned Saga for permission to hold an esoteric rite at Takaosanji to ensure the tranquillity of the country, using the occasion to remind Saga of the prevailing Chinese custom of maintaining a permanent palace chapel (*naidōjō*) staffed by monks who were expert practitioners of esoteric ritual.[73] Kūkai's preeminence as a Mikkyō master

---

72 The three earliest biographies of Kūkai – the *Kūkai Sōzu den* attributed to his disciple Shinzei, the *Daisōzu Kūkai den* compiled by Fujiwara no Yoshifusa (804–72) et al., and the *Zō Daisōjō Kūkai Wajō denki* – make no mention of Kūkai's whereabouts between his arrival in Tsukushi in Kyushu in 806 and his move to Kyoto in 809.

73 Kūkai's petition, entitled *Kokke no on-tame ni shuhō sen to kou hyō* (A Memorial Requesting Buddhist Services for the Benefit of the Nation), is contained in the *Seirei shū, kan 4, NKBT*, vol. 71, pp. 228–30.

was acknowledged by everyone, including his future rival Saichō. When Kūkai acceded to Saichō's request in 812 to conduct *kongōkai* and *taizōkai* initiations, close to two hundred people flocked to Takaosanji to take part.[74] Among those receiving initiations from Kūkai were not only Saichō and his disciples, but also twenty-two monks from the major Nara monasteries, thirty-eight novices, and more than forty laymen, including the influential Wake brothers, Matsuna and Nakayo, who effectively controlled Takaosanji. In recognition of Kūkai's status as a Mikkyō master, Saichō instructed five of his leading disciples to remain with Kūkai until the following year so that they might receive the highest level of initiation, the *dembō kanjō*, from him. After receiving their esoteric initiations from Kūkai in the twelfth month of 812, the Wake brothers entrusted the administration of Takaosanji to Kūkai, allowing him to appoint his own disciples as the ranking temple officers (*sangō*). In 829 the Wake brothers formally vested Kūkai and his successors with irrevocable authority to manage Takaosanji, which had been made an officially sanctioned Shingon temple five years earlier.

At the very time that Saichō had embarked on a course of confrontation with the older schools, Kūkai, following a conciliatory policy, was winning acceptance for Shingon at the court and among the Nara hierarchs. In 816 Saga approved a request from Kūkai that he be given exclusive proprietary rights to Mount Kōya, on which he sought to establish a retreat for meditation and a monastery for the training of Shingon monks. Two years later Kūkai moved to Kōya, where two of his disciples were already laying foundations for the future Kongōbuji monastic complex. Despite his strong desire to remain on Kōya, Kūkai was summoned back to Kyoto in 819, his presence in the capital being deemed indispensable. Kūkai strengthened his links with Nara by establishing in 822 a hall for esoteric initiations (*kanjō dōjō*) within the precincts of Tōdaiji. This hall, later known as Shingon'in, which remained under the control of Shingon monks, played a key role in the dissemination of Mikkyō among the Nara clergy.

In the first month of 823, three months before his abdication, Saga ordered that Kūkai be put in charge of Tōji, the chief state-supported temple in Kyoto. Saga's successor, Junna, stipulated later in the same year that henceforth only Shingon monks would be permitted to reside at Tōji, fixing their number at fifty. In 824, Junna further decreed that control of Tōji would be permanently vested in Kūkai and monks of his lineage. The conversion of Tōji into an exclusive Shin-

---

74 For a list of participants, see Kūkai's *Takao kanjō ki, Kōbō Daishi zenshū*, vol. 3, pp. 620–29.

gon temple was a clear indication that Kūkai's Shingon Mikkyō had become the officially sanctioned religion of the court.

Unlike Saichō, who after 816 was continually at odds with the older schools, Kūkai always remained on good terms with the Nara clergy in the hope of persuading it to accept Shingon as a supersectarian system of esoteric ritual that would bring an infinite variety of benefits to both the individual and the state. Thus, while Saichō encountered stiff opposition in his efforts to build an independent ordination platform on Hiei, Kūkai succeeded in establishing a hall for Shingon services in the very heart of Nara. Even the Hossō scholar Gomyō, who as the ranking hierarch had denounced Saichō's proposal for an independent ordination platform, felt no contradiction in accepting an administrative position at Tōji after it was designated a Shingon temple. Nor was it unusual for Shingon monks to be named to the superintendency (*bettō*) of Tōdaiji, which was nominally a Kegon monastery. So completely had Kūkai succeeded in winning acceptance from the hierarchs that when he submitted to the throne in 830 his *Jūjūshin ron*, a treatise in which he proclaimed the superiority of Shingon over all other schools of Buddhism as well as over the secular philosophies, not a word of protest was heard from Nara.

Kūkai finally received permission to return to Kōya in 832. Two years later the court granted his petition to establish within the palace precincts a Shingon'in (Shingon Chapel), where an annual esoteric rite known as *go-shichinichi mi-shiho* was to be performed from the eighth to the fourteenth day of the first month by Shingon monks from Tōji. The purpose of the rite was to ensure the well-being of the emperor and the prosperity of the nation. In the first month of 835, the Shingon school was officially admitted to the annual ordinand (*nembun dosha*) system and was allotted a yearly quota of three state-supported novices, which exceeded by one the number allowed the Tendai school. The following month Kongōbuji was accorded the status of a recognized temple (*jōgakuji*). Thus by the time of Kūkai's death in the third month of 835, Shingon was firmly established within the imperial court, a position it was to hold until the first years of Meiji.

THE TENDAI SCHOOL AFTER SAICHŌ

Although the Tendai school gained independence from the Nara hierarchy when it was granted the right to conduct its own ordinations in 822, it nevertheless fared poorly in the first decades after Saichō's death. By the 820s the Japanese aristocracy had become intoxicated with Mikkyō rituals, which were performed to achieve specific material or spiritual ends. Saichō's disciples and followers on Hiei had been completely overshadowed by Kūkai, who had established himself in Tōji, where he performed various esoteric rites commissioned by the government. The plight of the monks on Hiei after the death of Saichō was graphically illustrated in a letter sent in 825 by its lay superintendent (*zoku bettō*), Tomo no Kunimichi, to an official who was an influential patron of Hōryūji, requesting the latter to use his good offices to find a place for the "foodless monks of Hiei" at Hōryūji and Shitennōji so that they could continue to transmit the teachings of Tendai.[75]

It was clear to the Hiei community that in order to enhance its standing with the aristocracy, which was more interested in the material rewards accruing from esoteric rites than in the lofty but impractical philosophy of classical Tendai, it would have to prove its competence in Mikkyō, which, as we have seen, had been viewed by Saichō as one of the two wings of the Japanese Tendai school. This need to acquire additional training in Mikkyō forced Enchō, one of Saichō's disciples and a future abbot of Enryakuji, to swallow his pride and appeal, in 831, to Kūkai for further instruction in the doctrines of Mikkyō, for which, he frankly admitted, he had as yet not been able to find a suitable teacher.[76] Obviously, such appeals were humiliating and, worse still, tended to confirm the view that Kūkai's Shingon school was the ultimate authority in matters of Mikkyō.

Ennin, Enchin, and Annen

In 835, Ennin, a relatively obscure monk who had become a disciple of Saichō in 808 at the age of fourteen, was granted permission to travel to China with Fujiwara no Tsunetsugu, the newly appointed envoy to the T'ang court. Although the purpose of Ennin's mission was ostensibly to visit T'ien-t'ai shan in order to receive further training in Tendai doctrine, it is apparent that Ennin planned from the outset to take advantage of his stay in China to learn as much as possible about Mikkyō.

After several false starts, the ship carrying Ennin arrived at Yang-

---

75 *Denjutsu isshinkai mon*, kan 2, DDZ, vol. 1, pp. 592–93.
76 Enchō's letter, which was also signed by nine other monks from Hiei, is included in *Chōya gunsai*, kan 16, KT, vol. 29A, pp. 397–98.

chou in the seventh month of 838.⁷⁷ While awaiting permission from the Chinese authorities to travel to T'ien-t'ai shan, Ennin sought out two Mikkyō adepts in Yang-chou, who gave him instruction in *shittan*, the peculiar Indic script used to write esoteric formulas, and allowed him to make copies of manuals explaining esoteric rituals. Ennin lost no time in securing an initiation (*kanjō*) from one of these adepts, Ch'üan-ya, who was a third-generation disciple of Kūkai's master Hui-kuo.

In the second month of 839 Ennin was told by local officials that there was not sufficient time for him to visit T'ien-t'ai shan since he was, strictly speaking, not a student-monk (*rugakusō*) but a scholar attached to the embassy and hence had to leave China with the embassy, which was due to sail later that month. By the time Ennin's ship reached Wen-teng at the tip of the Shantung peninsula, the last anchorage before crossing the Yellow Sea, Ennin had resolved to remain behind in China even though he lacked permission from the authorities. After spending the winter at a monastery in Shantung run by Korean monks, Ennin set out in the second month of 840 for Wu-t'ai shan, a major place of pilgrimage in Shansi, in order to consult with Chih-yüan and several other learned Tendai monks who resided in one of the many temples dotting the mountain. While there is no reason to doubt that the opportunity to meet Tendai scholars was a principal factor in Ennin's decision to travel to Wu-t'ai, it should also be noted that Wu-t'ai was renowned as a center for popular Mikkyō cults, one of its most prominent temples, Chin-ko ssu, having been founded by the great esoteric master Pu-k'ung (Amoghavajra), who was the teacher of Kūkai's mentor, Hui-kuo. During his fifty-day stay on Wu-t'ai, Ennin spent about two weeks at the Chu-lin ssu, where he learned the *goe nembutsu*, a rhythmical chanting of the name of Amida Buddha using five different intonations. As we shall see, this *nembutsu* practice was later to have a profound influence on the development of Pure Land Buddhism in Japan.

In the eighth month of 840, Ennin arrived in Ch'ang-an, where he was to spend almost five years engaged in the study of Mikkyō while systematically acquiring esoteric texts, formulas written in the *shittan* script, and copies of mandalas. He received instruction and esoteric initiations from three Mikkyō masters, each a second-generation dis-

77 The primary source for Ennin's stay in China is his very rich diary entitled *Nittō guhō junrai kōki*. For a critical edition with full annotation, see Ono Katsutoshi, *Nittō guhō junrai kōki no kenkyū*, 4 vols. (Tokyo: Suzuki gakujutsu zaidan, 1964–69). The diary has been translated into English by Edwin O. Reischauer under the title *Ennin's Diary: The Record of a Pilgrimage to China in Search of the Law* (New York: Ronald Press, 1955).

ciple of the illustrious Hui-kuo, who had administered the *taizōkai* and *kongōkai* initiations to Kūkai. Not only did Ennin likewise receive both these initiations, but he was also granted a third type of initiation known as the *soshitsuji kanjō* (initiation according to the *Soshitsuji* Sutra), which symbolically integrated the *taizōkai* and *kongōkai* initiations. Ennin took particular pride in having been admitted to this third level of initiation, since it had not been offered to Kūkai even though it was evidently transmitted within Hui-kuo's lineage.

Life in Ch'ang-an became increasingly difficult for Ennin after the fanatically anti-Buddhist emperor Wu-tsung began the persecution of the clergy in 842. In the fifth month of 845, Ennin was defrocked and ordered to return to Japan. He immediately left Ch'ang-an for the port of Teng-chou in Shantung, which he reached three months later. After an agonizing delay of two years, he finally found passage on a Korean merchant ship bound for Japan. Ennin landed in Kyushu in the ninth month of 847 carrying 584 texts, mostly esoteric, in 802 fascicles, 21 ritual implements, and a collection of religious paintings, and mandalas.[78] Still more important, he had spent five years in Ch'ang-an studying with the leading esoteric masters of the day, whereas Kūkai had been under the tutelage of Hui-kuo for only half a year before the latter's death. Having received a total of thirteen different initiations in China,[79] Ennin was now in a position to challenge the Shingon monopoly of Mikkyō.

Ennin's extraordinary command of Mikkyō, which was promptly recognized by the court, was instrumental in reversing the decline of Hiei. In the sixth month of 848, a mere three months after his arrival in Kyoto, the court accepted Ennin's proposal that it sponsor annual esoteric initiation rites "for the enhancement of the imperial cause and the protection of the state."[80] These rites, popularly known as *Hiei kanjō*, were first performed at Enryakuji in 849, the government providing support for more than a thousand monks who participated in the ceremony.[81] Until Ennin's return from China Shingon

---

78 Ennin, *Nittō shingu shōgyō mokuroku, T,* vol. 55, p. 1078c.
79 This figure appears in the *Jūsan-jū kanjō hiroku*, a record claiming to have been compiled by Ennin and transmitted to his disciple Shōun. See *Tendai kahyō, kan* 5, part 1, *BZ,* vol. 126, pp. 526b–27b.
80 The text is included in *Ruijū sandai kyaku: zempen, kan* 2, Kashō 1 (848)/6/15, *KT,* vol. 25, pp. 69–71.
81 *Nihon sandai jitsuroku: zempen* (901), *kan* 8, Jōgan 6 (864)/1/14, *KT,* vol. 4, p. 126. For an early description of the *Hiei kanjō*, see Minamoto no Tamenori, *Sambō ekotoba*, written in 984, *kan* 3, *BZ,* vol. 111, pp. 469a–70a; English translation by Edward Kamens, *The Three Jewels: A Study and Translation of Minamoto Tamenori's* Sambōe (Ann Arbor, Mich.: Center for Japanese Studies, 1988), pp. 349–52.

monks had complete responsibility for the various esoteric rites that were performed at the court. This exclusive control of Mikkyō ritual by Kūkai's disciples was brought to an end by Ennin, who easily forged close links with the imperial family and aristocracy thanks to the exceptional prestige that accrued to him as a result of his lengthy studies and religious training in Ch'ang-an. From 850 on Ennin was repeatedly invited to the imperial palace to conduct esoteric rites or administer lay precepts to members of the imperial family. His influence with the aristocracy reached its pinnacle in 856 when he performed the twofold initiation (*ryōbu kanjō*) for Emperor Montoku, the Crown Prince, Minister of the Right Fujiwara no Yoshifusa, the latter's adopted son Mototsune, and Major Counselor Fujiwara no Yoshisuke.

Ennin's standing at the court brought immediate gains to Hiei. In 850 Emperor Montoku, at the urging of Ennin, ordered the construction of Sōjiin, an imperially endowed cloister on Hiei accommodating fourteen monks, which was to serve as a *hommyō dōjō*, a chapel in which prayers for the tranquillity of the nation were offered to the star governing the year of the emperor's birth.[82] During the same year the Tendai school was authorized two additional annual ordinands, one to specialize in the *Kongōchōkyō* and the other in the *Soshitsujikyō*, thereby giving formal recognition to the particular version of Mikkyō transmitted by Ennin from China. In 854 the court appointed Ennin abbot of Enryakuji, formally designating his office *zasu* (head of the community), a title subsequently held by all succeeding abbots, indicating that the incumbent was not under the jurisdiction of the Nara hierarchy.[83] Ennin's success in establishing Tendai Mikkyō as the predominant form of Buddhism at the court was clearly demonstrated in 866, two years after his death, when the government conferred the honorary posthumous names Dengyō Daishi and Jikaku Daishi on Saichō and Ennin respectively.[84] By contrast, Kūkai was not granted the posthumous name Kōbō Daishi until half a century later, in 921.[85]

It was the good fortune of the Tendai school that Ennin was followed on Hiei by a line of eminent monks who could further consolidate the close relationship he had established with the imperial

---

82 *Nihon sandai jitsuroku: zempen, kan* 8, Jōgan 6/1/14, *KT*, vol. 4, p. 126.
83 The two abbots preceding Ennin, namely, Gishin and Enchō, were officially designated Dembōshi, "Master Who Transmit the Dharma." See Shibuya Ryōtai ed., *Kōtei zōho Tendai zasu ki* (Tokyo: Daiichi shobō, 1973), *kan* 1, p. 8.
84 *Chōya gunsai, kan* 17, *KT*, vol. 29A, pp. 424–25.
85 *Nihon kiryaku* (ca. 12th century): *kōhen, kan* 1, Engi 21 (921)/10/18, *KT*, vol. 11, p. 24.

family and Fujiwara. Four years after Ennin's death, the scholar-monk Enchin was installed as abbot of Enryakuji. Like Ennin, Enchin had spent five years in China studying Mikkyō in Ch'ang-an and Tendai doctrine at T'ien-t'ai shan, which Ennin had not been able to visit. In 859, the year after his return to Japan, Enchin accepted an invitation to become abbot (*chōri,* "head officer") of Onjōji (also called Miidera), in Ōtsu, a temple belonging to the Ōtomo clan. Enchin, who had not been a disciple of Ennin's, seemed to have thought it prudent to keep a respectable distance from Hiei during the incumbency of Ennin in order not to detract from this senior monk by appearing as a competitor.

Immediately after Ennin's death, Enchin was summoned to the imperial palace to administer esoteric initiations to Emperor Seiwa, Fujiwara no Yoshifusa, and other eminent figures. In 868, Enchin was named abbot of Enryakuji, succeeding Ennin's disciple Anne, who had died that year. In time of drought or illness, or when a new emperor ascended the throne, the court invariably turned to Enchin for the appropriate prayers and rituals. By the time of his death in 891, Enchin is said to have conferred the exalted esoteric rank of *ajari* on over 100 individuals, personally tonsured more than 500 monks and administered the precepts to some 3,000 persons.[86] Moreover, he had secured a decree guaranteeing that future abbots of Onjōji would be chosen exclusively from monks belonging to his own lineage.

Owing to the efforts of Ennin and Enchin, Japanese Tendai was transformed into a thoroughly esoteric school, with scant attention being given to the teachings of traditional Chinese Tendai doctrine. In addition to the frequent esoteric rituals and initiations they performed in the palace or on Hiei to enhance the standing of the Tendai school, Ennin and Enchin also sought to provide a solid theoretical foundation for Tendai Mikkyō (also known as Taimitsu, as opposed to Kūkai's Shingon Mikkyō, also called Tōmitsu) by writing a number of doctrinal works defining the relationship of the *Hokekyō* to the Mikkyō scriptures. Saichō, preoccupied with his struggle to win approval for an independent ordination platform and his polemics against his Hossō rival, Tokuitsu, never adequately addressed this question. His view, as indicated in a letter to his ex-disciple Taihan, was that the revealed teachings of the *Hokekyō* and the secret teachings of the Mikkyō scriptures were equally true since

---

86 Sontsū, *Chishō Daishi nempu* (1467), *BZ,* vol. 28, p. 1395b.

both these scriptures took the position that there was ultimately only the One Vehicle (*ichijō*) that would lead all beings to Buddhahood. Saichō believed that both the *Hokekyō* and the esoteric scriptures rejected the notion that the Hīnayāna constituted a separate vehicle for enlightenment and hence stood in opposition to Mahāyāna. Rather, Hīnayāna was seen as an expedient device established by Śākyamuni to lead the ignorant gradually to an appreciation of Mahāyāna and through that to the attainment of Buddhahood itself.

Contrary to the position of Saichō and Chinese Tendai, Ennin asserted that the *Hokekyō* was in fact an esoteric scripture.[87] He gave two reasons for this view. First, the *Hokekyō* teaches the doctrine of One Vehicle, which, according to Ennin's unique interpretation, was the principal criterion for defining Mikkyō. Second, the earthly Buddha Śākyamuni who preached the *Hokekyō* revealed himself in the second half of the sutra to be an eternal Buddha and therefore must be identified with Dainichi Nyorai, the Buddha who expounded the esoteric scriptures. Thus, with respect to doctrine, Ennin viewed the *Hokekyō* as being on par with the "pure" esoteric scriptures such as the *Dainichikyō* and *Kongōchōkyō*. But as Ennin admitted, Mikkyō also stresses various secret practices – incantations, hand signs, mandala initiations, and so on – which are not mentioned in the *Hokekyō* but figure prominently in esoteric scriptures. Ennin concluded, therefore, that although the *Hokekyō* could be characterized as "esoteric in doctrine" (*rimitsu*), it ranked below the "pure" Mikkyō scriptures, since the latter were esoteric in both the doctrines and rituals that they taught (*jiri gumitsu*).

Enchin saw an even wider gap between the *Hokekyō* and the "pure" Mikkyō scriptures. While recognizing in principle that the *Hokekyō* could be deemed an esoteric scripture, Enchin nevertheless included it among the exoteric scriptures on the grounds that it had been openly preached by the Buddha. Since the *Hokekyō* did not teach the secret practices of Mikkyō, Enchin held that it was inferior to the "pure" esoteric scriptures, which he collectively designated "the king of Mahāyāna, the most secret of the secret" (*Daijō-chū no ō, hi-chū no saihi*).[88] This tendency to upgrade steadily the status of Mikkyō within the Tendai school culminated in the extra-

---

87 For a succinct account of the teachings of Ennin, Enchin, and Annen, see Katsumata, *Mikkyō no Nihon-teki tenkai*, pp. 275–91.
88 *Daibirushanakyō shiki, T*, vol. 58, p. 19b.

ordinary ranking of the various Buddhist doctrines by the great scholar Annen (841–ca. 895), who devised an elaborate systematization of Tendai Mikkyō. According to Annen, who was a junior contemporary of Enchin, Mikkyō, as revealed in the "pure" esoteric scripture, represented the ultimate teachings of Buddhism. Despite his own Tendai affiliation – he actually belonged to the lineages of both Ennin and Enchin – Annen held that classical Tendai ranked below both Mikkyō and Zen, the latter, in his view, being a nonverbal – hence "secret" – transmission of the Buddha's enlightenment. Taking the view that Mikkyō was the highest teaching within Buddhism to its logical conclusion, Annen referred to his school not as Tendai but as Eizan Shingonshū (the Shingon School of Hiei), as opposed to the Shingon school of Kūkai.

Hiei prospered as a result of the close contacts that Ennin, Enchin, and subsequent abbots of Enryakuji had established with the imperial family. Successive emperors founded cloisters on Hiei: Montoku built the Sōjiin and Shiōin; Suzaku, the Emmyōin; Kazan, the Jōryoin; and Go-Reizei, the Jissōin. Gifts of land by ex-emperors and princes for the general upkeep of Hiei or for the endowment of specific annual rituals became commonplace after the 860s. The first such major grant was made in 863 by Emperor Nimmyō's sons, Saneyasu and Tsuneyasu, whose households together contributed 224 *chō* of tax-exempt land.[89] In addition, substantial amounts of tax-rice were allocated for the support of specific cloisters such as Shakadō, Jōshin'in, Sōjiin, and Shiōdō. By 972, Hiei controlled estates in Ōmi, Wakasa, and Yamashiro in central Honshu and Izumi in the west.[90] In the hope of expanding its influence in the countryside, Hiei persuaded the government to designate many of the recognized temples (*jōgakuji*) that were located in the provinces "Tendai betsuin" (Tendai branch temple), which signified that these temples would henceforth be administered only by monks ordained at Enryakuji. By the end of the ninth century Tendai *betsuin* were found in such diverse regions as Mutsu, Kōzuke, Harima, Shinano, and Kaga.[91]

---

89 *Nihon sandai jitsuroku: zempen, kan* 7, Jōgan 5 (863)/4/10, *KT,* vol. 4, p. 110.
90 For a list of the donations made by the imperial family and the aristocracy to Hiei in the ninth and tenth centuries, see Murayama Shūichi, "Heian Bukkyō no tenkai," in Ienaga Saburō, ed., *Kodai hen,* vol. 1 of *Nihon Bukkyō-shi* (Kyoto: Hōzōkan, 1967), pp. 244–45.
91 For a list of Tendai *betsuin,* see Sonoda Kōyū, "Saichō to Tendai-shū," in *Ajia Bukkyō-shi: Nihon hen,* vol. 2, p. 131.

Ryōgen

The appointment of Ryōgen as abbot of Enryakuji ushered in a period of increased grandeur and power for Hiei.[92] In 937, at the relatively young age of twenty-five, Ryōgen won acclaim for his skill in outwitting the learned monks of the Nara monasteries in the annual debate on the *Yuimagyō* (the so-called *Yuima-e*) held at Kōfukuji. Word of this extraordinary achievement soon reached the Chancellor, Fujiwara no Tadahira, who, together with his influential son, Morosuke, and grandsons, Koretada and Kaneie, subsequently became devoted patrons of Ryōgen. In 964 Ryōgen was named a court chaplain (*naigubu*) and the following year, at the age of fifty-three, became the youngest monk to be admitted to the hierarchy (*sōgō*) since its creation in the seventh century.

Three months after Ryōgen's appointment as abbot of Enryakuji in 966, Hiei was ravaged by a fire that destroyed thirty buildings, including such important structures as the Sōjiin, Lecture Hall (Kōdō), Shiōin, Emmyōin, and Jōgyōdō.[93] The devastation of Hiei was now almost complete, since Hiei had not yet fully recovered from an earlier fire that occurred in 935 and claimed many buildings, including Kompon Chūdō, the main hall of Enryakuji.[94] Undaunted by the magnitude of the task, Ryōgen vowed to rebuild Hiei during his own lifetime. Besides the support that he could count on from the imperial family, whose endowed cloisters such as Sōjiin, Shiōin, and Emmyōin had been lost in the conflagration, Ryōgen could also draw upon the income from eleven estates that Morosuke had bequeathed to his son, Jinzen,[95] who at Morosuke's urging had become Ryōgen's disciple in 958, two years before his father's death.

Ryōgen mobilized all the resources at his command to carry out the reconstruction of Hiei. In 967 the Hokkedō and Jōgyōdō were completed; in 972 ceremonies were held marking the reconstruction of the Lecture Hall and four other buildings; in 979 the Shakadō, the Sutra Repository for the Hōdōin, and the Jeweled Pagoda (Hōtō) were finished, and in 984 the ornate Hōdōin was completed, the gold for the temple fittings having been supplied by Fujiwara no Tame-

---

92 For critical studies of the life of Ryōgen and his contributions to the Tendai school, see Hirabayashi Moritoku, *Ryōgen, Jimbutsu sōsho*, vol. 173 (Tokyo: Yoshikawa kōbunkan, 1976), and Eizan Gakuin, ed., *Ganzan Jie Daishi no kenkyū* (Kyoto: Dōbōsha, 1984).
93 *Nihon kiryaku:kōhen, kan* 4, Kōhō 3 (966)/10/28, *KT*, vol. 11, p. 99.
94 Ryōgen, *Tengen sannen Chūdō kuyō gammon* (980), reprinted in *Koji ruien*, 51 vols. (Tokyo: Yoshikawa kōbunkan, 1967–71), vol. 12 (*shūkyō bu* 4), p. 563.
95 Hirabayashi, *Ryōgen*, p. 58.

naga, governor of Mutsu. But the high point in the restoration of Hiei was reached in 980, when Kompon Chūdō was formally consecrated in a service conducted by Ryōgen in which Emperor En'yū, Regent Fujiwara no Yoritada, Minister of the Left Minamoto no Masanobu, and Minister of the Right Fujiwara no Kaneie participated.

During the rebuilding of Enryakuji, Ryōgen paid special attention to Yokawa, which together with Tōtō (Eastern Pagoda) and Saitō (Western Pagoda) comprise the Santō (Three Pagodas), that is, the geographical areas into which Hiei has been traditionally divided. The Tōtō area, in which Kompon Chūdō, the Lecture Hall, and the Ordination Hall are situated, was originally developed by Saichō. Saitō, which is to the west of Tōtō, centers around Shakadō built by Saichō's disciple Enchō. Yokawa, which lies to the north of Tōtō and Saitō, was first settled by Ennin, who withdrew to this desolate part of Hiei in 831 in order to undertake spiritual exercises in preparation for his death, which he believed to be imminent. After his recovery Ennin established Shuryōgon'in, which became the central cloister of Yokawa.

Following Ennin's appointment as abbot of Enryakuji, he moved to Zentōin in Tōtō, entrusting the management of Yokawa to his disciples. Although Yokawa continued to be administered by monks belonging to Ennin's lineage, its fortunes declined rapidly after Enchin assumed the abbotship of Enryakuji. When Ryōgen's patron, Tadahira, died in 949, Ryōgen, who stood in Ennin's lineage, retreated to Yokawa where he offered prayers for the repose of the deceased Tadahira. At Morosuke's request, he also beseeched the divinities to grant Morosuke's daughter, who was the consort of Emperor Murakami, a male child, which would put Morosuke in the position of being the grandfather of a potential successor to the throne. The birth of a boy, Prince Norihira (the future Emperor Reizei), in 950 convinced Morosuke of Ryōgen's supernatural powers. He immediately had Ryōgen appointed "protector-priest" (*gojisō*) for his grandson and announced his intention of restoring Yokawa, where the prayers had been offered. In 954 Morosuke, accompanied by his eldest son Koretada, visited Yokawa to dedicate the nearly completed Hokke zammai'in, which was to function primarily as a prayer cloister for Morosuke's branch of the Fujiwara clan. Morosuke felt a particular attachment to the Yokawa community, which he expressed in a vow promising support to the lineage of Ennin. Kaneie, the third son of Morosuke, continued to promote the expansion of Yokawa, building Yakushidō and Eshin'in in 983. The number of monks resident in Yokawa increased from the two or three that Ryōgen found there in 949 to more than two hundred by the time of his death.[96]

Although Ryōgen, like his predecessors, regularly performed esoteric rituals for his imperial and aristocratic patrons and wrote several treatises on Mikkyō, he deplored the decline in classical Tendai learning on Hiei, which became particularly acute after the death of Enchin. As a way to stimulate Tendai scholarship, Ryōgen proposed, upon his appointment as abbot, that the annual services commemorating Saichō's death include a formal five-day debate on the Tendai interpretation of the *Hokekyō*. The format of the debate called for an examinee (*rissha*) to lecture on ten doctrinal problems (*dai*) put to him by five questioners (*monja*), who would then challenge his explanation. If the monk who acted as a judge (*tandai*) determined that the examinee had successfully withstood the challenges, the examinee would be accorded the much coveted academic rank of *tokugō* (scholar). These debates, formally known as *kōgaku ryūgi* (erudite disputations) or, more popularly, *yama no rongi* (the [Hiei] mountain debates), subsequently played an important role in reviving Tendai scholarship.

In addition to encouraging formal Tendai learning, Ryōgen sought to tighten discipline on Hiei. Four years after becoming abbot, he issued a code in twenty-six articles, called *Nijūrokka jō kishō*, which was intended to curb widespread abuses by the Hiei clergy.[97] Several articles prohibit offerings of food or gifts to priests officiating at services; monks are told that they should rehearse and be thoroughly familiar with the various rituals they are expected to perform, that they should attend all services, that they should not leave the mountain during their twelve-year period of training, that they must not wear elegant garb, and that they must not keep horses on Hiei. While some of these regulations restate proscriptions issued by Saichō in 818 and Ennin in 866, other articles in Ryōgen's code clearly bespeak the secularization of the clergy that was beginning to occur in the powerful monasteries. In this category are the regulations calling for the expulsion of monks who conceal their faces (*katō*), carry weapons, inflict corporal punishment, or violently disrupt religious services – behavior suggestive of the *akusō* (wicked monks), later

---

96 Shimaji Daitō, *Tendai kyōgaku shi* (Tokyo: Meiji shoin, 1929), p. 353.
97 The text of the *Nijūrokka jō kishō* has been published in Takeuchi Rizō, ed., *Heian ibun*, 15 vols. (Tokyo: Tōkyō-dō, 1947–80), vol. 2, pp. 431a–440a. For a critical study of this important document, see Hori Daiji, "Ryōgen no *Nijūrokkajō kishō* seitei no igi," *Shisō*, 25 (March 1967): 12–39.

popularly known as *sōhei* (monk warriors). During his nineteen-year incumbency Ryōgen ordered that the names of seven hundred wayward monks who did not participate in services be expunged from the Hiei registers.[98]

Ryōgen was honored for the successful prayers that he offered for his imperial and aristocratic patrons and was eventually deified for his restoration of Enryakuji. In recognition of his having brought about the recovery of Emperor En'yū in 981, he was granted the privilege of being allowed to enter the palace grounds in a palanquin and was awarded the supreme ecclesiastical rank of *daisōjō* (archbishop), the first time that this rank had been conferred since the eighth century. In 987, two years after Ryōgen's death, the honorary posthumous name Jie Daishi was conferred on him.[99] By the end of the Heian period, Ryōgen, popularly known as Ganzan Daishi (The Great Master Who Passed Away on the Third Day of the New Year), was variously viewed as a reincarnation of Saichō, Ennin, or even Kannon. It was widely believed that Ryōgen, instead of departing for Pure Land on his death, remained on Hiei as its protector. Rubbings containing his likeness were widely used in Kamakura times as amulets to ward off malevolent spirits, cure illness, and avert natural disasters.[100]

The Schism within the Tendai school

The origin of the conflict that ultimately split the Tendai school into opposing Sammon (Hiei) and Jimon (Onjōji) factions in the late tenth century can be traced back to successional disputes among Saichō's disciples. When Saichō fell ill in 812, he designated Enchō, his disciple of longest standing, to be his successor. On his deathbed ten years later, however, Saichō indicated that the leadership of the Hiei community should be entrusted to Gishin, who had traveled with Saichō to China, where he received ordinations identical to those of Saichō's. After their return from China in 805, Gishin did not remain on Hiei, but went back to his native Kanto to proselytize. It was only in 813, a year after Saichō's illness, that Gishin took up permanent residence on Hiei.

---

98 Sonoda Kōyū, "Heian Bukkyō," in *Kodai*, vol. 4 of Ienaga Saburō, Ishimoda Shō, Inoue Kiyoshi et al., eds., *Iwanami kōza: Nihon rekishi* (23 vols.) (Tokyo: Iwanami shoten, 1962), p. 194.
99 *Nihon kiryaku: kōhen*, kan 9, Eien 1 (987)/2/16, *KT*, vol. 11, p. 161.
100 Hazama Jikō, *Tendai shūshi gaisetsu* (Tokyo: Daizō shuppan, 1969; rev. by Ōkubo Ryōjun), p. 124. For an up-to-date list of temples containing halls or chapels dedicated to the worship of Ryōgen, see *Ganzan Jie Daishi no kenkyū*, pp. 299–316.

Although regarded as something of an outsider by Saichō's immediate disciples, Gishin was nevertheless accepted by them as the first abbot of Enryakuji in accordance with Saichō's last request. However, when Gishin, on his deathbed, ordered in 833 that the abbotship be passed on to his own disciple Enshu, who had only recently moved to Hiei, Saichō's leading disciples protested to the lay superintendent of Hiei that Gishin was attempting to replace Saichō's lineage with his own. After eight months of wrangling the authorities finally agreed to dismiss Enshu from the office of abbot and appoint Enchō in his place.[101]

Gishin's lineage on Hiei, however, did not come to an end with Enshu's departure. On the contrary, the appointment of Enchin, a disciple of Gishin, as abbot of Enryakuji in 868 assured it a prominent position within the Tendai school. During Enchin's incumbency, which spanned twenty-three years, his followers came to overshadow those of the equally prestigious Ennin, who had been a direct disciple of Saichō. While Enchin himself had no quarrel with his predecessor Ennin – indeed, he held him in high regard – he was aware of the possibility of future trouble between their respective groups of followers and hence before his death specifically urged his own disciples to honor the memory of Ennin.[102]

Monks of the two lineages – Ennin's and Enchin's – managed to avoid an open breach until 980 when Ryōgen, who belonged to the Ennin lineage, failed to invite a representative of the Enchin lineage to participate in the lavish ceremonies dedicating the newly rebuilt Kompon Chūdō.[103] The Enchin faction, taking this as a deliberate affront since representatives of other schools had been asked to take part in the services, appealed to the court, which ordered Ryōgen to include Yokei, who, as abbot of Onjōji, was the head of the Enchin faction.

The first violent confrontation between the two factions occurred the following year, when Yokei was named tenth abbot of Hosshōji, a temple founded in 925 by Ryōgen's future benefactor, Tadahira. The nomination of Yokei infuriated the Ennin faction, which petitioned the court to remove Yokei's name on the grounds that all previous abbots had been selected from their own faction. When the

---

101 The relevant documents are included in *Denjutsu isshinkai mon*, DDZ, vol. 1, pp. 640–45. See also *Kōtei zōho Tendai zasu ki*, p. 8.
102 Enchin, *Yuisei*, BZ, vol. 28, pp. 1349b–50b, and also his *Seikai mon*, cited in Tsuji Zennosuke, *Nihon Bukkyō-shi: jōsei hen* (Tokyo: Iwanami shoten, 1944), p. 827.
103 For a discussion of the major events leading to the split between the Ennin and Enchin lineages, see Takagi Yutaka, "Tendai-shū no tenkai," in *Ajia Bukkyō-shi: Nihon hen*, vol. 2, pp. 182b–85a.

court refused to do so, asserting that spiritual attainment and high intellect were the only proper criteria for nominating an abbot, more than two hundred monks belonging to the Ennin lineage on Hiei, including several holding high office, carried out a violent demonstration at the residence of Fujiwara no Yoritada, the Chancellor and lay superintendent of Enryakuji. The willingness of the Ennin faction to resort to force was sufficient to intimidate Yokei and several hundred other monks of the Enchin faction, forcing them to quit Hiei and seek refuge in nearby temples. Meanwhile, a stalwart band of three hundred monks of the Enchin faction held fast at Senjuin atop Hiei, which had been Enchin's residence and was the repository for his manuscripts. It was so widely rumored that Ryōgen was planning to order an assault on all temples sympathetic to the Enchin faction, including Senjuin, that he was compelled to issue a denial.[104] Calm returned to Hiei only when Yokei yielded to his opponents and resigned the abbotship of Hosshōji.

After the Hosshōji incident the Ennin faction was even more determined to maintain its preeminent position on Hiei, which had been firmly established during the nineteen-year incumbency of Ryōgen. When word reached Hiei in 989 that Yokei had been nominated by the court to be the new abbot of Enryakuji, replacing Ryōgen's disciple Jinzen, who had just retired, the Ennin faction protested vigorously, declaring that they would seal the halls of Enryakuji rather than admit an abbot from the Enchin lineage. The imperial envoy carrying the official notification found his path blocked by irate clerics. When a second envoy was dispatched several days later accompanied by the police officials, angry monks snatched the court order from his hand as he attempted to read it. After an interval of several weeks the court made a third attempt, this time sending a ranking official, Fujiwara no Arikuni, backed by a large detachment of police, directly to Zentōin, where Ennin was enshrined, in the hope that the monks would refrain from violence at so holy a place. The court order was read aloud before Ennin's spirit tablet, along with an indictment of the Hiei monks for their unruly behavior. But all to no avail, for when Yokei arrived on Hiei, the monks refused to perform any services under his direction. Faced with such intransigence, Yokei had no choice but to resign as abbot, a mere three months after his appointment.[105]

---

104 *Fusō ryakki* (ca. 1150), kan 27, *KT*, vol. 12, pp. 250–51.
105 *Nihon kiryaku: kōhen*, kan 9, Eiso 1 (989)/9/29 and Eiso 1/12/27, *KT*, vol. 11, pp. 167–68.

In 993 Yokei's disciple Jōsan, smarting from the humiliation suffered by his mentor, who had died two years earlier, assembled a group of monks at Kannon'in in Kita Iwakura (in present-day Kyoto), a stronghold of the Enchin faction, from which he carried out a raid on Sekisan Zen'in, the cloister on Hiei where Ennin had lived, reportedly damaging many artifacts that had belonged to Ennin.[106] The Ennin faction retaliated by destroying more than forty buildings on Hiei affiliated with the Enchin faction and putting to flight more than a thousand of its monks, most of whom subsequently settled at Onjōji. This temple thus became the headquarters of the Enchin lineage, which subsequently was known as the Jimonha (Temple Branch) of the Tendai school, as opposed to the Sammonha (Mountain Branch), in other words, the temples of Hiei that were under the permanent control of monks in the Ennin lineage. Although the monks who had fled to Onjōji made no attempt to return en masse to Hiei – to do so would clearly have invited more violence – they asserted that members of their own faction should be considered eligible for appointment to the abbotship of Enryakuji since, in their view, the abbot of Enryakuji was the head of the entire Tendai school and not merely the chief administrator of the temples on Hiei.

This principle was first put to the test in 1038, when Myōson, the learned abbot of Onjōji, was nominated by his lay patron, Regent Fujiwara no Yorimichi, to fill the vacant abbotship of Enryakuji.[107] Hiei responded with an enormous show of force: three thousand monks descended on Yorimichi's residence demanding that he choose a monk from Hiei. When he refused, citing Myōson's great attainments, the outraged mob began dismantling the locked gates of Yorimichi's residence. Troops were summoned, and a bloody melee ensued. Several weeks later Yorimichi agreed to appoint Kyōen, the candidate of the Hiei monks. When Kyōen died in 1047, Yorimichi, ignoring the outcry from Hiei, managed to force through the appointment of Myōson as Kyōen's successor, but owing to the fierce opposition on Hiei the seventy-seven-year-old Myōson was compelled to resign after only three days in office. By the end of the twelfth century, seven other monks from Onjōji had succeeded in securing appointments to the abbotship of Enryakuji, but none was able to hold office for more than a few days.

106 *Fusō ryakki*, kan 27, pp. 260–61.
107 For a detailed account of this episode, see Shikō, *Jimon denki horoku* (1397), kan 19, *BZ*, vol. 127, pp. 426a–27b.

The militarization of the clergy

As their secular power and wealth grew, the larger monasteries – particularly Kōfukuji, Tōdaiji, Enryakuji, and Onjōji – increasingly resorted to force when they felt their interests threatened. Although some of their fighting men fell into the category of servitors who were recruited from monastic estates, the majority came from the large body of minimally educated monks and temple hangers-on, who seem to have been more at home with weapons than with Buddhist scripture. The employment of monks in a military capacity was striking proof of the debased character of large segments of the clergy, since the Mahāyānist disciplinary code used in China and Japan specifically forbade monks to carry weapons or engage in any form of belligerent activity.[108]

The first major incident involving violence by clerics occurred in 949, when fifty-six monks from Tōdaiji gathered at the residence of an official in Kyoto to protest an appointment that displeased them.[109] A brawl ensued, claiming the lives of several of the participants. In 969 a dispute over conflicting claims to temple land resulted in the death of several Kōfukuji monks at the hands of monks from Tōdaiji.

While such violent clashes became commonplace in the eleventh and twelfth centuries, monasteries generally tried to achieve their objectives through intimidation rather than brute force. Typically, thousands of protesting monks would surround an important government building or the residence of a high official and refuse to disperse until their demands had been met. Because of their clerical status and the sanctity of the religious implements they carried, these monks were not often subjected to rough treatment by the secular authorities. After 968, Kōfukuji clerics repeatedly terrorized the Fujiwara by storming into Kyoto carrying branches of the sacred *sakaki* tree especially consecrated for the occasion by Kasuga Shrine, which was under the control of Kōfukuji. Since Kasuga was the clan shrine of the Fujiwara, the latter were compelled to seclude themselves in their residences (*rōkyo*) whenever such a demonstration took place. Another device used by Kōfukuji in dealing with ob-

---

108 See *Bommōkyō, kan* 2, *T*, vol. 24, p. 1005c, which forbids the possession of "swords, clubs, bows, arrows, halberds, axes, and implements of combat."
109 For a detailed chronology of the major events involving warrior-monks, see Katsuno Ryūshin, *Sōhei* (Tokyo: Shibundō, 1955), pp. 156–99, which provides a wealth of information on the use of warrior-monks in the conflicts between monasteries.

stinate Fujiwara was to threaten expulsion from the clan (*hōshi*), which was done by denouncing the offender at the Kasuga Shrine. The first instance of this occurred in 1163, when Shijō Takasue was ousted for criticizing Kōfukuji.

By the end of the eleventh century Hiei monks had developed their own unique method of intimidating recalcitrant officials. Protesting monks would descend upon Kyoto carrying sacred palanquins (*mikoshi*) from the seven major shrines on Hiei that were believed to protect the capital from natural disasters and epidemics. The simple act of transporting the sacred palanquins through the city streets was usually sufficient to strike terror in the hearts of the people, who feared that they might incur the wrath of the deities if the Hiei monks were mistreated. A favorite tactic employed by Hiei monks when their protests were ignored was to abandon the palanquin at a palace building, a residence of a high official, or the Kangakuin (the office overseeing Fujiwara affairs), which would create turmoil since laymen did not know how to dispose of so sacred an object.

The clerical violence that frequently erupted during the second half of the Heian period was generally provoked by conflicting claims to temple lands, attempts by a particular monastery to establish jurisdiction over lesser temples and shrines, real or imagined slights of one monastery by another, and dissatisfaction with ecclesiastical appointments. Doctrinal disputes between different schools, on the other hand, rarely led to armed confrontations. Thus Tōdaiji and Kōfukuji most often wrangled over land. Hiei and Kōfukuji clashed repeatedly because of Hiei's success in extending its influence and control over such previously Kōfukuji-dominated religious establishments as Gion and Tōnomine. Acts of great violence were often precipitated by trivial incidents. Hiei monks burned Kiyomizudera to the ground in 1165 because monks from Kōfukuji, with which Kiyomizudera was allied, had damaged a plaque bearing the name of Enryakuji during a memorial service for Emperor Rokujō at Ninnaji. The following day, Kōfukuji monks, bent on revenge, rampaged through Kyoto in an attempt to burn to the ground all temples and shrines connected with Hiei.

Onjōji's request for permission to establish its own ordination platform

An extraordinary degree of enmity existed between Enryakuji and Onjōji, the two major Tendai monasteries after the expulsion from

Hiei of monks of the Enchin lineage in 993. Enryakuji was angered by Onjōji's persistent demand that it be accorded equal treatment with Enryakuji itself and not be viewed merely as a branch temple of Enryakuji. It suspected, not without reason, that Onjōji was scheming to reestablish the dominance of the Enchin lineage on Hiei by insisting that its leading monks be appointed to the abbotship of Enryakuji.

Hiei's distrust of Onjōji was further intensified in 1039 when Myōson, after having been denied appointment as abbot of Enryakuji because of the intense opposition of the Hiei monks, sought permission from the court for Onjōji to construct its own ordination platform.[110] This was an understandable request since novices from Onjōji found it increasingly difficult to receive proper ordinations owing to the hostility between their temple and Hiei, which controlled the only Tendai ordination hall in Japan. Onjōji openly challenged the validity of the Hiei ordinations by asserting that the fifty-eight bodhisattva precepts constituting the core of a Tendai ordination had been transmitted properly only within its own lineage, which traced its origin back to Gishin, who had received these precepts directly from Tao-sui, the seventh Chinese patriarch of Tendai. Onjōji recognized, of course, that Saichō had also received these precepts along with Gishin in the same ceremony, but maintained with some justification that Saichō had never transmitted them to Ennin because Saichō had not been granted permission by the court to conduct ordinations. Since authorization to build an ordination hall on Hiei was given only after Saichō's death, the first true Tendai ordinations, Onjōji argued, were performed by Gishin, when he administered the precepts to his disciple Enchin.

Enryakuji vigorously opposed Myōson's petition, arguing that the existence of two separate ordination platforms within a single school would only create dissension. Enryakuji's real fear was that it would not be able to maintain its primacy within the Tendai school if Onjōji could carry out its own ordinations. Onjōji, not surprisingly, was supported in this dispute by the Nara temples, especially Kōfukuji, which saw this as a chance to weaken Enryakuji. In the face of Enryakuji's unwavering opposition, the court, after much deliberation,

---

110 *Jimon denki horoku, kan* 19, *BZ*, vol. 127, pp. 426a–27b; *Shunki* (the diary of Fujiwara no Sukefusa, covering the years 1038–52, with lacunae), *Tankaku sōsho* (Tokyo: Kokusho kankōkai, 1912), vol. 1, pp. 150–51; *Gempei seisuiki, kan* 10, vol. 1, pp. 325–27, in Tsukamoto Tetsuzō, ed., *Yūhōdō bunko* (121 vols.) (Tokyo: Yūhōdō shoten, 1914–18). For the dispute regarding the establishment of an ordination platform at Onjōji, see Tsuji, *Nihon Bukkyō-shi: jōsei hen*, pp. 835–38, and Katsuno, *Sōhei*, pp. 92–95.

rejected Myōson's petition, but sought to mollify Onjōji by appointing him abbot of Enryakuji, a position, as we have already noted, that he was able to retain only for three days. The question of whether Onjōji should be allowed to have its own ordination platform was discussed again by the court in 1070, but still no decision was reached. The issue was raised once more in 1074 when Raigō, a monk of Onjōji who was asked by Emperor Shirakawa to offer prayers for the birth of a crown prince, declared that if the court wished to reward him for his services, it should grant Onjōji's longstanding petition for an ordination platform. This provoked a violent demonstration by Hiei partisans, who set fire to Onjōji.

Relations between the two Tendai monasteries had so deteriorated by 1081 that a minor altercation at a shrine festival between underlings from Onjōji and Hiei sparked a series of increasingly serious incidents, which finally culminated in an attack on Onjōji by a force of several thousand armed monks and laymen assembled by Hiei from its subordinate temples and shrines.[111] Although Onjōji, which at the time consisted of fifteen imperially sponsored temples, seventy-nine halls, fifteen sutra repositories, and dozens of other structures, was totally devastated by fire, its abbot, as an indication of the importance Onjōji attached to the right to conduct its own ordinations, did not seek any restitution from Hiei, but instead requested permission to establish an ordination hall once Onjōji was rebuilt. But fear of the *yama-hōshi* (monks from the mountain), as the Hiei clergy were known, was sufficient to deter the court from granting even this seemingly modest request.

Enryakuji continued to show profound hostility toward Onjōji after its reconstruction in 1092. On the flimsiest of pretexts monks from Enryakuji, in 1121 and again in 1140, put the torch to Onjōji, which consequently prohibited its novices from receiving ordinations on Hiei, thus further strengthening Onjōji's case for an independent ordination hall. In 1163, Enryakuji obtained an order from the court requiring that Onjōji novices henceforth be ordained on Hiei and not in the ordination hall of Tōdaiji, which, although denounced as Hīnayānist by Saichō, was the only ordination procedure available to them if they declined to go to Hiei.[112] Kōfujuki joined Onjōji in protesting the court ban on Nara ordinations for Tendai monks and, with support from Onjōji, proposed that Enryakuji be

---

111 *Fusō ryakki, kan* 30, pp. 322–23; Tsuji, *Nihon Bukkyō-shi*, pp. 840–42.
112 *Jinten ainōshō* (1532), *kan* 18, *BZ*, vol. 150, p. 443a. See also Katsuno, *Sōhei*, pp. 99–103, and Tsuji, *Nihon Bukkyō-shi*, pp. 888–91.

made a subsidiary temple of Kōfukuji on the grounds that Saichō, Gishin, Ennin, and Enchin had been ordained in Nara. Outraged at the audacity of Kōfukuji, Hiei vented its anger by burning down Onjōji for a fourth time in less than a century. By the end of the Heian period neither side could claim a victory: Onjōji failed to receive approval for its own ordination hall, but Hiei was unable to enforce the decree requiring Onjōji novices to be ordained on Hiei.

THE SHINGON SCHOOL AFTER KŪKAI

Unlike Tendai, which was temporarily eclipsed when Saichō passed from the scene, Shingon continued to enjoy unwavering support from the imperial family and aristocracy even after Kūkai's death.[113] Shingon monks were regularly summoned to the court to pray for rain or to perform rites of exorcism. Shingon services likewise became an integral part of the annual imperial calendar, the two most important rituals being the previously mentioned *go-shichinichi mishiho* performed in the Shingon'in (Shingon Chapel) within the palace precincts, and the *taigenhō* held at the same time as the *mishiho* in the Jōneiden (Jōnei Hall), which was part of the imperial residence. Introduced from China by Kūkai's disciple Jōgyō, the *taigenhō*, which became an annual observance in 851, was a complex ritual in which various weapons were laid out at an elaborately appointed, multitiered altar in the expectation that these implements would vanquish all enemies of the emperor and protect his person.

Kūkai's disciples

The major institutional problem confronting Kūkai's successors in the ninth century was the lack of a universally recognized Shingon center comparable to Hiei. Before his death Kūkai entrusted the administration of each of the four major Shingon establishments to a different disciple: Jitsue, the most senior disciple, was appointed abbot of Tōji; Shinzei was given responsibility for Takaosanji; Shinga, Kūkai's younger brother and confidant, was put in charge of the Shingon'in at Tōdaiji, and Shinzen, Kūkai's nephew, was made abbot of Kongōbuji on Kōya, where Kūkai had chosen to be interred.

---

113 Three sources that were particularly helpful to me when I was writing this section are Shimode Sekiyo, "Shingon-shū no tenkai," in *Ajia Bukkyō-shi: Nihon hen*, vol. 2, pp. 205–22; Sonoda Kōyū, "Heian Bukkyō no seiritsu," in *Nihon Bukkyō-shi*, vol. 1, pp. 226–33; Katsuno, *Hieizan to Kōyasan*, pp. 197–242.

Although there is no evidence to suggest that the disciples bore any personal animosity toward each other, this arrangement could not but create serious difficulties given their different personalities, interests, and family backgrounds.

Eager to secure the patronage of the powerful families, Kūkai's disciples sometimes found themselves on opposing sides in political conflicts. In 850, Shinzei, who was then abbot of both Takaosanji and Tōji, agreed to a request by Emperor Montoku to pray that the latter's eldest son, six-year-old Prince Koretaka, be chosen heir to the throne. Koretaka's mother was a member of the Ki clan, as was Shinzei.[114] This attempt to secure the right of succession for a member of the Ki clan was strongly opposed by the Minister of the Right, Fujiwara no Yoshifusa, whose daughter, Meishi, also a consort of Montoku's, had likewise given birth to a son, Prince Korehito (the future Emperor Seiwa). To counter Shinzei's efforts on behalf of Koretaka, Yoshifusa turned to Shinga, whose prayers for Korehito's succession eventually proved successful. Shinga was rewarded with the abbotship of Tōji in 860, even though this necessitated bypassing the *dembō ajari* Shinshō, who was his senior with respect to ordination. So great was the esteem for Shinga that he became the first monk permitted to enter the palace grounds in a carriage.

Rivalry among the major Shingon temples

Even more divisive than the personal alliances between Shingon monks and opposing factions of the aristocracy was the rivalry between Tōji, which performed a vast array of esoteric rites for the court, and Kōyasan, where Shingon novices underwent rigorous training. In 853, Shinzei, then abbot of Tōji, persuaded the court to decree that in view of Kōya's remoteness the annual examination of candidates for ordination as Shingon monks, whose number had been increased from three to six that year, should no longer be conducted at Kōya, which had been the rule since 835, but at Tōji.[115] Only three of the successful candidates would be permitted to proceed to Kōya for the actual ordination; the remaining three were to be ordained at Takaosanji. Several years later, however, it became the practice for all ordinations to be done at Tōji. Resentful of its loss of

---

114 Ōe no Masafusa, *Gōdanshō* (ca. 1107), *kan* 2, *Gunsho ruijū* (Tokyo: Keizai zasshisha, 1905), vol. 17, p. 568.
115 For the dispute regarding the proper site for Shingon ordinations, Katsuno, *Hieizan to Kōyasan*, pp. 209–12.

control over ordinations, Kōya was able to have the offending decree rescinded in 885, after its abbot, Shinzen, who a year earlier had been asked to serve concurrently as abbot of Tōji, protested vigorously. Shinzen's successor at Tōji, Yakushin, who belonged to the Tōji lineage proper emanating from Jitsue and who also enjoyed the strong support of Emperor Uda, succeeded in convincing the court in 897 to return to the arrangement of 853, arguing that Kōya, "a branch temple located in the mountains," had usurped the prerogatives of Tōji.[116] The wrangling over the right to ordain continued for another ten years when the government forced a compromise. The number of annual ordinands was increased from six to ten, four to be examined at Tōji, three at Kōya, and three at Takaosanji.

The cause of Kōya was championed primarily by Shinzen, who as a nephew of Kūkai was determined not to permit Kōya, Kūkai's retreat and place of burial, to be overshadowed by Tōji, which was benefiting enormously from its proximity to the center of secular power. While Kūkai's other disciples were busily engaged in performing rituals for the aristocracy in the capital, Shinzen devoted himself singlemindedly to expanding Kongōbuji and codifying its basic rituals. When he moved to Kyoto to become abbot of Tōji in 884, Shinzen left the administration of Kongōbuji to his disciple Juchō, who had no ties to the rival Tōji. In 889, at the urging of Shinzen, the court awarded Juchō the prestigious title of *zasu*,[117] to be passed on in perpetuity to succeeding abbots of Kongōbuji, who would now enjoy equal status with the abbots of Enryakuji. Shinzen entrusted to Juchō, as a token of the authority of the office of the Kongōbuji *zasu*, a highly treasured collection of manuscripts known as the *Sanjūjō sakushi*, mostly in Kūkai's hand, which Shinzen had borrowed from Tōji in 881, while Shinga, his master and uncle, was still its abbot.

Shinzen's efforts notwithstanding, Kōya was hard-pressed to maintain its independence from Tōji, especially after 901 when Retired Emperor Uda received the *dembō kanjō* from the Tōji abbot Yakushin. The relationship between the two Shingon centers became increasingly strained because of Kōya's persistent refusal to return the *Sanjūjō sakushi* to Tōji.[118] In 915, Kangen, the powerful abbot of Tōji, obtained from Uda a decree instructing Mukū, the then abbot

---

116 Kōhō, *Tōbōki* (1352), kan 8, *Zokuzoku gunsho ruijū* (Tokyo: Kokusho kankōkai, 1907), vol. 12, p. 156.
117 Kaiei, *Kōya shunjū hennen shūroku* (1719), kan 3, BZ, vol. 131, p. 36.
118 For the dispute regarding the *Sanjūjō sakushi*, see Tsuji, *Nihon Bukkyō-shi: jōsei hen*, pp. 409–10.

of Kongōbuji, to surrender the manuscripts. Refusing to do so, Mukū resigned his office and accompanied by a few disciples fled with the *Sanjūjō sakushi* to Iga, where he died three years later. Only after being presented with yet another decree from Uda did Mukū's disciples agree to hand over the manuscripts to Kangen, who, after a triumphant display at the imperial palace, deposited them in the Tōji treasure-house. In 919, the year after the return of the *Sanjūjō sakushi,* the court formally recognized the primacy of Tōji by decreeing that its abbot (traditionally called *chōja,* "elder") would henceforth also serve concurrently as overseer (*kengyō*) of Kongōbuji.[119] By combining the abbotships of the two major Shingon centers, the government was able to avoid the sort of schism that plagued the Tendai school and resulted in the almost continuous warfare between its Enryakuji and Onjōji factions. The Shingon school achieved full parity with Tendai in 921, when the court, acting on a petition by Kangen, gave Kūkai the posthumous name Kōbō Daishi, thereby according him the same honorary status that it had granted Saichō and Ennin in 866.

Ninnaji and Daigoji

Beginning with the reign of Uda (887–97) the imperial family developed a particularly warm relationship with the Shingon school, probably as a reaction to the domination of Enryakuji by tonsured members of the Fujiwara clan. Ninnaji and Daigoji were the two Shingon temples most directly linked with the imperial family. Situated to the west of the palace, Ninnaji was originally established in 888 as a Tendai temple by Emperor Uda in memory of his father, Kōkō, whose reign had been known as Ninna. In 899, two years after abdicating in favor of his son Daigo, Uda was tonsured at Ninnaji by Yakushin, the learned abbot of Tōji. The following year Uda appointed Kangen superintendent (*bettō*) of Ninnaji, thereby transforming it into a Shingon temple. In 904, Uda moved to the newly constructed Omuro (Imperial Chamber) adjacent to Ninnaji, to become its first *monzeki* (abbot of imperial or aristocratic lineage). Uda occupies a unique position in the history of Japanese Buddhism as the only emperor to have carried out, as a *dembō ajari,* the formal transmission of the Dharma to his successors. His major disciple and spiritual heir, Kangū, became abbot of Tōji in 949, and his

---

119 *Tōji chōja bunin* (ca. 1634), kan 1, *Zokuzoku gunsho ruijū,* vol. 2, p. 491a.

grandson, Kanchō, who had studied under both Uda and Kangū, was named abbot of Tōji in 981.

Throughout its history Ninnaji retained extremely close ties to the imperial family, no less than twenty-two of its abbots having been *hōshinnō* (ordained imperial princes of the first generation), eight of them in the Heian period alone. Ninnaji reached the pinnacle of its influence during the incumbency of its sixth *monzeki*, Shukaku, who was the second son of Emperor Go-Shirakawa. A learned monk with a reputation as a skilled practitioner of esoteric rites, Shukaku eventually became abbot of nine temples in the Kyoto area, bringing them under the sway of Ninnaji. So great had the prestige of Shukaku become that when he requested Tōji, in 1186, to "lend" Ninnaji the precious *Sanjūjō sakushi* and two mandalas attributed to Kūkai, Shunshō, the abbot of Tōji, was unable to refuse. The *Sanjūjō sakushi* has remained "on loan" at Ninnaji ever since.

The other Shingon temple to receive comparable support from the imperial family was Daigoji, located in the southeastern suburbs of Kyoto. Originally built in 874 as a hermitage for Shōbō, an eminent Shingon monk of imperial descent, Daigoji was richly supported by Shōbō's devoted patron, Emperor Daigo, who sponsored the construction of the Shakadō, Yakushidō, and Godaidō, which are three major halls of Daigoji, between 904 and 907. Daigo decreed in 919, on the tenth anniversary of the death of Shōbō, that henceforth only monks belonging to Shōbō's lineage could serve as abbot of Daigoji and that they would have the rank of *zasu*, the same title used for the abbots of Enryakuji and Kongōbuji. Kangen, who was Shōbō's foremost disciple and successor, was named the first abbot of Daigoji. Since Kangen already held the abbotship of Tōji and Kongōbuji and was also superintendent of Ninnaji, the practical effect of Daigo's decree of 919 was to bring all the principal Shingon centers in Japan under the nominal control of a single monk.

Daigo's sons, the emperors Suzaku and Murakami, whose births were attributed to prayers offered at Daigoji by Kangen, further enlarged the temple by constructing new halls and making periodic donations of land and tax revenue. In 952 a five-storied pagoda, which still stands, was consecrated in memory of Daigo, whose grave was placed adjacent to the temple. Suzaku and Murakami were likewise buried at Daigoji, as were the consorts of emperors Shirakawa and Go-Toba, as well as numerous other women of the imperial family. Daigoji became a frequent place of pilgrimage for members of the imperial family, particularly if they were seeking offspring, since it was widely believed that the bodhisattva Jundei Kannon, who was enshrined in Daigoji, would intercede in such matters.

Because of its extraordinarily close ties with the imperial family, Daigoji, like Ninnaji, was able to become a virtually autonomous Shingon temple. In 1018 it was decreed that henceforth only monks of Shōbō's lineage who had actually been trained at Daigoji could occupy the office of abbot. The specific intent of the decree was to exclude the appointment of monks from Tōdaiji, where Shōbō, who was also a Sanron scholar of note, had established in 904 Tōnan'in, a major subtemple for Sanron and Shingon studies. Since the monks at Tōnan'in constituted one branch of Shōbō's lineage, they had, on occasion, been selected by the court to serve as abbots at Tōji and Daigoji. Ever anxious to expand its influence, Tōdaiji used this as a pretext for asserting its supremacy over the Shingon temples in Kyoto by arguing that since abbots of both Tōji and Daigoji had come from Tōdaiji, Tōji should be regarded as a branch temple (*betsuin*) of Tōdaiji and Daigoji as a subordinate temple (*matsuji*). The decree of 1018 thus guaranteed the independence of Daigoji from Tōdaiji.

After the declaration that monks belonging to Shōbō's Tōdaiji lineage would no longer be eligible to occupy the highest office of Daigoji, its abbotship passed firmly into the hands of descendants of Emperor Daigo: the twelfth *zasu*, Kakugen, was the son of Emperor Kazan (Daigo's great-grandson); the thirteenth *zasu*, Jōken, was the son of Minamoto no Takakuni (another great-grandson of Daigo); the fourteenth *zasu*, Shōkaku, was the son of Minamoto no Toshifusa (a fourth-generation descendant of Daigo); the fifteenth *zasu*, Jōkai, was the son of Minamoto no Akifusa (another fourth-generation descendant of Daigo), and so on.

A new round of temple construction around Daigoji was begun in 1115, when Shōkaku built Sambōin, which was soon recognized as a major center of Shingon learning. Sambōin was the first of five subtemples erected in the vicinity of Daigoji during the twelfth and early thirteenth centuries to be headed by abbots of imperial or aristocratic ancestry (*monzeki*). Toward the end of the Heian period it had become customary to choose the abbot of Daigoji from one of these five subtemples, collectively referred to as the Daigoji gomonzeki (The Five Aristocratic Temples of Daigoji). By 1155 the Daigoji complex consisted of 42 main halls (*dō*), 4 pagodas, 3 imperial villas (*gosho*), 4 sutra repositories, and 183 dormitories to accommodate monks.

The Ono and Hirosawa branches of Shingon

The growing complexity of Shingon rites led during the twelfth century to the emergence of twelve subschools (*ryū*), each based in a different temple. These subschools, which differed from one another not so much in matters of doctrine as in the minutiae of ritual, were divided into two groups, the Ono ryū and the Hirosawa ryū, each in turn consisting of six subschools.

The Ono ryū, which traced its lineage back to Shōbō, took its name from the Ono district of Kyoto, where the great Shingon scholar Ningai, who was a fourth-generation disciple of Shōbō and the de facto founder of the Ono ryū, established Zuishin'in in 991. The Ono ryū subsequently split into the two groups: (1) the Three Daigoji Subschools (*Daigo sanryū*) based in the Sambōin, Rishōin, and Kongōōin, which were part of the Daigoji complex; and (2) the Three Kanjuji Subschools (*Kanjuji sanryū*) located in Kanjuji, Anjōji, and Zuishin'in in Yamashina to the north of Daigoji.

The rival Hirosawa ryū traced its origins back to Yakushin, the seventh abbot of Tōji, through his disciple, the tonsured retired emperor Uda. Named after Hirosawa Pond in northwest Kyoto, where Kanchō, Yakushin's disciple in the third generation, founded Henjōji in 989, the Hirosawa ryū subdivided around the beginning of the twelfth century into six subschools, four of which were based in subtemples within the Ninnaji complex. The two remaining Hirosawa subschools, the Ninnikusen ryū and the very important Daidembōin ryū, evolved in temples in Yamato and Kii provinces respectively.

The restoration of Kōya

After it was decided in 919 to have the abbot of Tōji serve concurrently as abbot of Kongōbuji, it soon became apparent that the interests of the Kongōbuji could not be adequately represented in such an arrangement, since the abbot of Tōji was required to reside permanently in Kyoto. In 928, Saikō, the twelfth abbot of Tōji, sent an appeal to the court in which he deplored the impoverished condition of Kongōbuji and requested funds for its renovation.[120] In response to Saikō's petition the court agreed to the appointment of a resident "executor" (*shigyō*) on Kōya whose primary function would be to promote the restoration of Kongōbuji. The executor, while techni-

---

120 For the rebuilding of Kōyasan, see Katsuno, *Hieizan to Kōyasan*, p. 216.

cally subordinate to the *zasu*, who resided in Kyoto, was the highest-ranking monk in Kōya and hence became its de facto abbot. In 983, with the renovation and expansion of Kongōbuji almost completed, the designation "executor" was changed to "overseer" (*kengyō*), a title that remained in use until 1875, when the original title *zasu* was reinstituted to designate the head monk of Kōya.

The Kongōbuji was almost completely destroyed in 994 by a fire that started when lightning struck its main pagoda. Although Kanchō, the influential nineteenth abbot of Tōji, was immediately able to secure a decree ordering the reconstruction of Kongōbuji, the project made little headway because of a lack of funds. The situation was further aggravated when the governor of Kii, who had been charged with the responsibility for rebuilding the Kondō (Golden Hall), seized the Kōya estates after Kanchō's death in 998, allegedly to meet construction costs. Deprived of their sole source of income, the few remaining monks on Kōya were compelled to quit the mountain completely.

The reconstruction of Kongōbuji and its subsequent popularity as a place of pilgrimage were ultimately brought about by the unflagging efforts of two monks, Kishin (also known as Jōyo) and Ningai. Kishin moved to Kōya in 1016 at the relatively advanced age of fifty-eight in response to a command received in a dream that he had after imploring the bodhisattva Kannon to inform him of the whereabouts of his deceased parents.[121] When he reached Kōya, it is said, his spiritual eye was suddenly opened, enabling him to see that Kongōbuji was none other than the Inner Palace of Tosotsu (Tuṣita) Heaven, the celestial realm in which Miroku (Maitreya), the Future Buddha, is believed to reside until the time is ripe for his descent into this world. Here Kishin discovered his parents, transformed into bodhisattvas, seated on lotus thrones. After making his way to the tomb of Kūkai, which was almost inaccessible because of the dense overgrowth after years of neglect, Kishin made a solemn vow to devote the remainder of his life to the restoration of Kōya. Kishin's efforts bore fruit, and by the time of his death in 1047 Kongōbuji enjoyed a greater degree of prosperity than ever before.

The perception of Kōya as a sacred mountain was also widely promoted by the prestigious monk Ningai, whose power to summon rain in times of drought assured him a large following at the court. Known popularly as the "Rain Bishop" (Ame Sōjō), this exception-

---

[121] This story is recounted in Tsuji, *Nihon Bukkyō-shi*, pp. 413–14.

ally learned monk, who, as already noted, is regarded as the founder of the Ono branch of Shingon, felt a particular attachment to Kōya, where, in 957, at the age of six he had been tonsured by Gashin, who later became the first monk to hold the office of overseer of Kongōbuji.

In 1023, Ningai persuaded the former regent, Fujiwara no Michinaga, then fifty-seven years of age, to undertake the arduous journey to Kōya.[122] Ningai convinced Michinaga that by making a pilgrimage to Kōya, he would not only be sure to escape an unpleasant rebirth but would also be present when Miroku makes his descent into this world from Tosotsu Heaven. Accompanied by an entourage of sixteen high-ranking monks and laymen, Michinaga spent some five days on the road before reaching the Inner Sanctum (Okunoin) of Kōya, where Kūkai was entombed. In an emotional declaration of his faith, he pledged the rebuilding of Kūkai's mausoleum and the donation of land for the upkeep of Kōya.

It subsequently became a regular practice for Fujiwara regents and retired emperors to undertake such a pilgrimage to Kōya.[123] In 1048 Yorimichi visited Kōya, followed by Morozane in 1081, Moromichi in 1108, Tadazane in 1144, and Yorinaga in 1148. The retired emperors Shirakawa and Toba made three visits each to Kōya (Shirakawa in 1088, 1091, and 1127; Toba in 1124, 1127, and 1132).[124] As might be expected, the pilgrimages by the retired emperors, like those by the Fujiwara regents, were lavish affairs, the entourage usually including ministers of state, leading clerics from the main Shingon monasteries in Kyoto, and a military escort, which accompanied the procession only as far as the Administrative Office (*mandokoro*) of Kongōbuji. These aristocratic and imperial pilgrims contributed generously to the reconstruction and expansion of Kongōbuji. On the occasion of his first visit, Shirakawa formally ordered the rebuilding of the Great Pagoda (Daitō), donating an estate in Bingo for its permanent upkeep. On his second visit, he presented Kōya with an estate located in Aki. In 1124, Toba sponsored the construction of the Western Pagoda, which he subsequently endowed. After the construction of Daidembōin in 1132, Toba donated seven estates specifically for the training of its monks.

---

122 *Fusō ryakki, kan* 28, *KT*, vol. 12, pp. 276–77; *Kōya shunjū hennen shūroku, kan* 4, *BZ*, vol. 131, p. 66.
123 On the pilgrimages to Kōya by the Fujiwara, see Katsuno, *Hieizan to Kōyasan*, pp. 218–20.
124 The imperial visits to Kōyasan at this time are chronicled in Kongōbuji, ed., *Kōyasan sen hyakunen shi* (Kōyasan: Kongōbuji, 1942), pp. 76–83.

The enormous popularity of Kōya as a pilgrimage site after the eleventh century indicates the profound esteem in which Kūkai was held.[125] By the end of the tenth century it was believed that Kūkai had not actually died at Kōya in 835 but rather had entered into a deep trance (*nyūjō*), from which he would emerge upon Miroku's descent from Tosotsu Heaven. According to a widely held belief, when Kangen opened Kūkai's tomb in 921 to read the court decree granting Kūkai the posthumous name Kōbō Daishi, he discovered that Kūkai's body was intact: his facial color was normal, his skin was warm, and his hair had grown longer – all indications that he was indeed still alive. Since Kūkai had been a devotee of Miroku, he soon was identified with him. If Kūkai was the earthly incarnation (*keshin*) of Miroku, it was only natural to view Kōya, Kūkai's abode, as a terrestrial manifestation of Tosotsu Heaven.

By the late eleventh century the deification of Kūkai had progressed to the point that he was being equated with the great cosmic Buddha Dainichi, the supreme deity of Shingon. When Shirakawa, in 1088, expressed a wish to visit Vultures' Peak in India where Śākyamuni was believed to have preached many of the Mahāyāna sutras, he was urged by the court scholar, Ōe no Masafusa, to make a pilgrimage to Kōya instead, since Kōya, Masafusa declared, was none other than the eternal Pure Land of Dainichi Nyorai (Mitsugon Jōdo) and hence vastly superior to Vultures' Peak in India.[126] So highly was Kūkai revered that when a lock of hair belonging to the deceased emperor Horikawa was discovered in 1108, the court decided to inter it alongside Kūkai's tomb in the hope of establishing a spiritual link (*kechien*) between the deceased emperor and the deified Kūkai. In 1165 a lock of hair belonging to the deceased emperor Nijō was sent to Kōya for the same purpose.

The first instance of the burial of a lay person on Kōya, which was to become a common practice – Kōya now has more than 100,000 graves – occurred in 1160, when Mifukumon-in, the consort of Emperor Toba, was interred there. A devout believer in Kūkai, Mifukumon-in had not been allowed to make the pilgrimage to Kōya in her lifetime because of the ban against visits to the mountain by women. In the final years of her life, she erected a hermitage at Arakawa, about twenty kilometers west of Kōya, from which she worshiped daily in the direction of Kūkai's tomb. In accordance with her will,

---

125 The following account is largely based on Shimode, "Shingon-shū no tenkai," in *Ajia Bukkyō-shi: Nihon hen*, vol. 2, pp. 210b–14a.
126 Washio Junkyō, *Kōshitsu to Bukkyō* (Tokyo: Daitō shuppansha, 1939), pp. 265–66.

her cremated remains were brought to Kōya for burial near the main hall of Kongōbuji, where her tomb still remains.

THE GROWTH OF PURE LAND BUDDHISM

Amida (Sanskrit, Amitābha or Amitāyus) Buddha, the central figure of the Pure Land faith, is one of the most popular divinities in the Buddhist pantheon, his name or that of his Pure Land appearing in more than 270 scriptures, roughly one out of every three works in the Mahāyānist canon.[127] At a very early stage in the development of Indian Mahāyāna there emerged a cult centering on Amida, that viewed him as a sort of savior who had, through his own boundless merit, created a Pure Land, or haven, offering shelter to all beings who demonstrated their faith in him by certain devotional acts. In China the Amida cult grew steadily after the year 402, when the monk Hui-yüan founded the first Pure Land association of lay and clerical devotees. Faith in Amida and his vow to deliver all beings to Pure Land became one of the dominant themes in Chinese Buddhism and was recognized as an ancillary teaching by the various Buddhist schools, whose masters often produced commentaries on the Pure Land scriptures and advocated the Pure Land faith, but always in such a way that it was subordinate to the principal tenets of their own school. In addition to these sectarian interpretations of Pure Land, however, an independent cult, which viewed Pure Land Buddhism as the only valid type of religious practice for the present age, began to take shape in the sixth century under the guiding hand of T'an-luan. This cult, known later in China and Japan as the Pure Land school, culminated in the work of Shan-tao, who, while recognizing the necessity of such traditional practices as sutra chanting, meditations, image worship, and the presentation of offerings, asserted that the vocal recitation of Amida's name was the primary devotional act leading to rebirth in Pure Land.

Although Pure Land scriptures had already been copied and studied in the Nara period and images of Amida could be found in Nara temples, it was only in Heian times that the Pure Land faith emerged as a major movement within Japanese Buddhism. In seventh- and eighth-century Japan, Amida was viewed primarily as a Buddha who could deliver the souls of the dead to his Pure Land, commonly

---

[127] Yabuki Keiki, *Amida Butsu no kenkyū*, rev. and enlarged ed. (Tokyo: Meiji shoin, 1937), p. 449.

called Paradise (Gokuraku).[128] As the inscriptions on his images indicate, Amida was worshiped most frequently by laymen seeking to ensure the rebirth of a deceased relative in Pure Land. Relatively few instances are recorded of individuals commissioning statues of Amida in the hope that they themselves might be able to enter his Pure Land after death.[129]

Pure Land observances on Hiei

The systematic practice of chanting the name of Amida in the hope of attaining rebirth in his Pure Land was introduced into Japan by Ennin, who, as we have already noted, first became acquainted with the *goe nembutsu* service during his brief stay at the Chu-lin ssu in Wu-t'ai in 840. The founder of this monastery was the Pure Land devotee Fa-chao (died c. 820), who had himself devised the *goe nembutsu*, which combined the traditional meditations on Amida with the fervent invocation of his name as taught by Shan-tao. Ennin encountered the *goe nembutsu* again at the Tzu-sheng ssu, the monastery in Ch'ang-an at which he resided for almost five years. The melodious chanting of Amida's name constituted an important part of the liturgy used at the Tzu-sheng ssu.

In 848, the very year that Ennin returned from China, he built a Jōgyō zammai-dō (frequently abridged to Jōgyōdō) in the Tōtō (Eastern Pagoda) temple complex on Hiei. The Jōgyōdō, as its name indicates, was a hall exclusively devoted to the practice of the *jōgyō zammai*, a meditation lasting ninety days in which one concentrated one's thoughts on Amida while invoking his name and circumambulating his image.[130] The *jōgyō zammai*, which was one of the four basic types of meditation taught by the Tendai school, was practiced not primarily to bring about rebirth in Pure Land but, rather, to enhance the powers of concentration of the devotee by enabling him to focus his mental and physical activities on Amida. But for Ennin, who had been greatly influenced during his stay in China by the intense piety of Fa-chao, the *jōgyō zammai* was not simply a meditative exercise but an act of devotion to Amida that facilitated entry into his Pure Land. So strongly did Ennin feel about Amida worship that,

---

128 Although Buddhism does not technically recognize the existence of a soul (Sanskrit, *ātman*; Japanese, *ga*), the notion of a soul, commonly referred to as *rei* or *ryō*, is widespread in popular Japanese Buddhism.

129 Inoue Mitsusada, *Nihon Jōdo-kyō seiritsu-shi no kenkyū* (Tokyo: Yamakawa shuppansha, 1956), pp. 15–26.

130 *Eigaku yōki* (ca. 1267), kan 1, *Gunsho ruijū*, vol. 15, p. 542a.

in his will, he instructed his disciples to begin the practice of *fudan nembutsu*, "uninterrupted contemplation of [Amida] Buddha."[131]

First performed in 865, the year after Ennin's death, the *fudan nembutsu* played a crucial role in the dissemination of the Pure Land faith among the Hiei clergy and their aristocratic lay supporters. The *fudan nembutsu* was held annually at the Jōgyōdō from the morning of the eleventh day of the eighth month through the night of the seventeenth day. The goal of the participants was to achieve rebirth in Pure Land through the practice of the *fudan nembutsu*, which it was believed had the power to destroy the effects of accumulated evil karma. The *fudan nembutsu* had three components, each signifying a different realm of human activity: (1) the continuous invocation of Amida's name, occasionally interrupted by the chanting of passages from the *Amidakyō* extolling the merit embodied in the name; (2) the circumambulation of an Amida's image; and (3) the concentration of one's thoughts on Amida. These three components represented respectively the verbal, physical, and mental activities of the person, in short, the totality of human actions. By dedicating his verbal utterances, physical movement, and mental processes to Amida in this fashion, the devotee immersed himself completely in Amida, which guaranteed his rebirth in Pure Land.[132]

The popularity of the *fudan nembutsu* grew steadily: in 893 a second Jōgyōdō was built with imperial sponsorship in the Saitō (Western Pagoda) complex on Hiei and in 968 a third Jōgyōdō was established by Ryōgen at Yokawa, the third major temple complex, thus enabling the two thousand or so monks on Hiei to take part in the annual *fudan nembutsu*. It was not long before provincial clerics who came to Hiei for training also became devotees of the *yama no nembutsu* (Amida-contemplations of [Hiei] mountain), as the *fudan nembutsu* came to be popularly called, and erected Jōgyōdō in their home regions. By the end of the tenth century Jōgyōdō could be found in such diverse places as Kyoto, Ōtsu (as an adjunct of Onjōji), Tōnomine, and as far east as the Izu peninsula. The predominance of Amida pietism on Hiei is attested in a document dated 970, which wryly observes that although novices had been expected to spend twelve years learning all four types of Tendai meditations, they now limit themselves to the practice of *jōgyō zammai* alone.[133]

131 *Sammon dōsha ki* (early 14th century), *Gunsho ruijū*, vol. 15, p. 488a.
132 For a description of the *fudan nembutsu*, see *Sambō ekotoba, BZ*, vol. 111, p. 467; English translation, Kamens, pp. 342–44.
133 *Nijūrokka jō kishō, Heian ibun: komonjo hen*, vol. 2, p. 435a.

The Ōjō yōshū and the dissemination of the Pure Land faith among the aristocracy

The appearance of Genshin's *Ōjō yōshū* (*Anthology on Rebirth in Pure Land*) in 985 marked the beginning of a new phase in the development of Japanese Pure Land Buddhism. Its author, Genshin (942–1017), who had been a disciple of Ryōgen, won recognition early in his career for his great learning. Instead of pursuing high ecclesiastical office, as was the custom of the Hiei elite, Genshin chose to go into seclusion at Eshin'in in Yokawa, where he devoted himself to meditation and scholarship. With more than eighty extant works attributed to him, Genshin was one of the most prolific monks of the Heian period, his writing covering such diverse topics as Tendai doctrine, Hīnayāna philosophy, logic, esoteric ritual, and Pure Land teachings. Although Genshin always remained within the Tendai tradition, his interpretation of Pure Land doctrine, particularly as he presented it in his *Ōjō yōshū*, provided the impetus for the Pure Land faith that swept Japan in the eleventh and twelfth centuries resulting in the rise of the Jōdo, Jōdo Shin, and Ji schools of the Kamakura period.

What distinguished Genshin's approach to Pure Land doctrine from those of his Tendai predecessors was his belief that the world was on the verge of entering the *mappō* age, that is, a period of irreversible spiritual decline that called for less demanding religious exercises. Whereas in earlier periods it was possible to attain enlightenment through meditation, adherence to precepts, and cultivation of wisdom, in the *mappō* age, which Genshin believed was about to commence, these practices were exceedingly difficult, if not impossible, for most people.[134] The most appropriate teaching for the *mappō* age, in Genshin's view, was that of Pure Land, which Amida Buddha had created as a refuge for all beings, both good and evil, who sought rebirth there. Although Ennin established Pure Land as a devotional practice on Hiei, he did not attempt to provide a doctrinal justification for it in any of his numerous writings. That task fell to Genshin, who, in order to lay a firm theoretical foundation for the practice of Pure Land within the Tendai school, undertook an extensive study of the Buddhist scripture as well as of the various treatises on Pure Land by Chinese scholars, as is attested in his *Ōjō yōshū*, which quotes from more than 160 different works.[135] It is par-

---

134 See the opening lines of his *Ōjō yōshū*, kan 1, *T*, vol. 84, p. 33a.
135 Hanayama Shinshō, trans., *Ōjō yōshū*, *Iwanami bunko*, vol. 2992–96 (Tokyo: Iwanami shoten, 1942), p. 3.

ticularly significant that among the Pure Land treatises most frequently cited are those of Shan-tao and his master, Tao-ch'o, who laid the foundation for an independent Pure Land faith in China.

Running through the *Ōjō yōshū* was a simple theme: our present world is one of defilement and pain in contrast to the Pure Land of Amida, which is a blissful realm free from taint or suffering. By using copious quotations from the scripture that provided graphic accounts of the suffering of beings trapped in the cycle of transmigration contrasted with the ecstatic existence of the inhabitants of Pure Land, Genshin sought to warn his contemporaries about attachment to the transitory pleasures of this life and awaken within them a yearning for Amida's Pure Land. While Genshin in theory accepted the traditional Tendai emphasis on the importance of meditation on Amida as a means to achieve rebirth in Pure Land, he also recognized that in the *mappō* age such practices were difficult for most people, who could not sustain for long periods of time the demanding meditations in which one contemplated each of the thirty-two physical signs of Amida's Buddhahood, not to mention the more abstract ones in which Amida's radiant form is viewed as a manifestation of absolute truth.

For such spiritually weak people – and Genshin included himself in this group – Genshin advocated, as a last resort, *isshin shōnen,* "wholehearted invocation of Amida's name (*shō*) combined with contemplation (*nen*)," the latter referring specifically to contemplating the act of submitting oneself to Amida or to visualizing the deathbed scene in which Amida, accompanied by a host of bodhisattvas, descends from the sky to lead the dying person to Pure Land. The single most important religious practice for the Pure Land devotee was *nembutsu,* which signified not simply the repetition of the name of Amida as it did in Kamakura times and later, but also included the notion of meditating on Amida as well. To Genshin, the highest expression of Pure Land faith was *jinjō nembutsu,* in other words, the continuous practice of *nembutsu* in one's daily life. Since Genshin believed, however, that the world was about to enter the *mappō* age, he acknowledged that *jinjō nembutsu* remained more of an ideal than a practical course of action. He therefore attached particular importance to *rinjū gyōgi,* "deathbed rites," in which the dying person, surrounded by friends and relatives urging him to think of Amida's imminent arrival, repeatedly invokes Amida's name while holding a cord attached to the hand of an image of Amida.

It seems likely that Genshin intended the *Ōjō yōshū* to be a practical guide for the Nijūgo zammai-e, a spiritual mutual-help society formed in 986 by twenty-five monks from the Shuryōgon'in in Yokawa who vowed to assist one another in attaining rebirth in Pure Land.[136] The monks agreed to meet on the fifteenth day of each month for a service that opened in the early afternoon with a lecture on the *Hokekyō*, after which the group began meditations on Amida, while invoking his name and chanting the *Amidakyō*. If any member of the society became ill, he would be cared for by the others, and if it seemed that he was dying, he would be brought to the Ōjōin (Chapel for Rebirth), which was a hall enshrining an image of Amida, where his colleagues would encourage him to chant Amida's name while envisioning the arrival of Amida with his retinue of bodhisattvas. In return, the dying person promised that after reaching Pure Land he would reappear in the dreams of his colleagues to describe Pure Land and strengthen their determination to reach it.

The rules of the Nijūgo zammai-e were drafted by Yoshishige no Yasutane, a devout Pure Land believer who had taken the tonsure just before the Nijūgo zammai-e was established. Earlier, in 964, Yasutane had founded the Kangaku-e (Society for the Promotion of Learning)[137] which was a Pure Land society consisting of twenty monks from Hiei and twenty laymen, most of whom had aristocratic or literary backgrounds. The Kangaku-e, which met twice yearly at temples around Hiei, contributed to the spread of the Pure Land faith among the upper classes and helped pave the way for the all-clerical Nijūgo zammai-e, whose membership soon expanded to include Genshin himself and Emperor Kazan, who had renounced his throne and taken holy orders a month after the founding of the Nijūgo zammai-e.

The *Ōjō yōshū* was well received by the aristocracy, who were deeply moved by its profound religious message and enthralled by its detailed description of the palaces, lakes, and gardens of Pure Land. The most powerful aristocrat of the day, Fujiwara no Michinaga, was an avid reader of the *Ōjō yōshū* and an admirer of Genshin, to whom he twice sent emissaries after becoming ill in 1004.[138] A de-

---

136 For the Nijūgo zammai-e, see Inoue Mitsusada, *Nihon kodai no kokka to Bukkyō* (Tokyo: Iwanami shoten, 1971), pp. 162–64, and the same author's *Nihon Jōdo-kyō seiritsu-shi no kenkyū*, pp. 148–49.

137 The origins and practices of the Kangaku-e are discussed in Inoue Mitsusada, *Nihon Jōdo-kyō seiritsu-shi no kenkyū*, pp. 150–52. For an early account see *Sambō ekotoba, BZ*, vol. 111, pp. 450b–51b; English translation, pp. 295–98; see also the valuable notes in Yamada Yoshio, *Sambōe ryakuchū* (Tokyo: Hōbunkan, 1951), pp. 288–92.

138 For Michinaga's involvement with Pure Land Buddhism, see Inoue, *Nihon kodai no kokka to Bukkyō*, pp. 165–70, and Tsuji, *Nihon Bukkyō-shi: jōsei hen*, pp. 572–73.

vout Pure Land believer, Michinaga took the tonsure in 1019 and the following year built an Amida Hall (also known as Midō or Muryōjuin), in which he installed nine 16-feet-tall gilded images of Amida, each representing this Buddha in one of the nine traditional divisions of Pure Land. Michinaga died at his Amida Hall, in the manner of Genshin, clutching a silk cord that linked him to the nine images of Amida. Michinaga's son and successor, Yorimichi, likewise built an Amida Hall, the famous Hōōdō at Byōdōin in Uji, which when viewed with its surrounding landscape was intended to be a re-creation of Pure Land in this world. The great popularity that the Pure Land faith enjoyed among the aristocracy and the powerful clans is attested by the large number of Amida Halls built in the eleventh and twelfth centuries. Documents of the period indicate that at least ninety-five Amida Halls were established between 1020, when Michinaga dedicated his Midō, and 1192, when Minamoto no Yoritomo built Nikaidō with its nine images of Amida at Eifukuji in Kamakura.[139]

The popularization of the Pure Land faith

The Amida Halls with their resplendent images and elegant gardens suggestive of the topography of Pure Land, the meditations on Amida, and the elaborate ceremonies called *mukae-kō* (welcoming services) in which young monks wearing jeweled crowns, golden masks and the raiments of bodhisattvas pretend to welcome their prestigious patrons in to Amida's Paradise had little to do with the Pure Land faith of the common man, who could neither read the Chinese in which the *Ōjō yōshū* was written nor participate in the rituals of the aristocratic Amida Halls.[140] His faith in Pure Land was inspired not so much by the monks of the great monasteries as by the *hijiri*, "holy men," who were typically clerics who had chosen to pursue the religious calling away from the main monasteries.[141] Some of the *hijiri* were eccentrics who shunned clerical garb in favor of deerskins; others spent long periods in remote mountain retreats practicing austerities while chanting the *Hokekyō;* still others lived in her-

139 Inoue, in his *Nihon kodai no kokka to Bukkyō*, pp. 171–78, provides a detailed list of the Amida Halls of this period giving the date of construction, the name of the hall, its sponsor, and the primary sources in which the hall is mentioned.
140 On *mukae-kō*, see Ishida Mizumaro, *Jōdo-kyō no tendai* (Tokyo: Shunjūsha, 1967), pp. 130–32.
141 For a comprehensive study of the *hijiri*, see Hori Ichirō, "On the Concept of *Hijiri* (Holy-Man)," *Numen* 5, 2 (April 1958): 128–60; 5, 3 (September 1958): 199–232.

mitages known as *bessho,* "places apart," which were located on the fringes of the precincts of larger monasteries; some others such as the *yugyō hijiri,* "wandering *hijiri,*" roamed the countryside preaching to the common people and soliciting small contributions from them for religious projects – a practice known as *kanjin* – which appealed greatly to members of the lower classes for it enabled them to "establish affinity" (*kechien*) with a *hijiri* and partake of his great merit.

Although *hijiri* appear in Buddhist sources as early as the Nara period, it was only after the middle of the tenth century that they became a prominent feature of Japanese Buddhism. Their religious faith, for all its intensity, was usually an amalgam of esoteric rites that were simple enough to be performed by the individual, devotion to the *Hokekyō,* and belief in Amida as a savior, coupled with a yearning for rebirth in his Pure Land. The first *hijiri* to play a major role in the dissemination of the Pure Land faith was Kūya (903–72), also known as Kōya, who had spent his early years undertaking spiritual exercises in the mountains.[142] After tonsuring himself in his twenties at the Owari Kokubunji, Kūya became an itinerant proselytizer, carrying scriptures and holy images in his backpack. Like the famous Gyōki of the Nara period, he is said to have built roads, erected bridges, dug wells, and collected abandoned corpses for cremation, all activities that brought him close to the common people. Known as *Amida hijiri* because of his continuous chanting of the name of Amida – even the wells he dug came to be called "Amida wells" – Kūya settled in Kyoto in 938, spreading the Amida faith among its inhabitants and earning the appellation *ichi hijiri,* "the *hijiri* of the marketplace." Kūya's alienation from the established church, which was common to many *hijiri,* is evidenced by his failure to seek formal ordination on Hiei until he had reached the relatively advanced age of forty-five. Commenting on his achievements, the *Nihon ōjō gokuraku ki,* which is a late-tenth-century collection of biographies of people who have attained rebirth in Pure Land, observes that before the Tengyō era (938–47) few of the simple folk practiced Amida devotions, but thanks to the efforts of Kūya, "who invoked the name himself and made others invoke the name," the whole of Japan came to devote itself to *nembutsu.*[143]

---

142 The most reliable treatment of Kūya's life is to be found in Hori Ichirō, *Kūya, Jimbutsu sōsho,* vol. 106 (Tokyo: Yoshikawa kōbunkan, 1963).
143 Yoshishige no Yasutane, *Nihon ōjō gokuraku ki* (985), in Inoue Mitsusada and Ōsone Shōsuke, eds., *Ōjō den, Hokke genki,* vol. 7 of *Nihon shisō taikei* (Tokyo: Iwanami shoten, 1974), p. 9.

By the eleventh century, warriors, farmers, fishermen, and others whose occupations brought them into conflict with the Buddhist precepts increasingly viewed the practice of *nembutsu* as the principal method for achieving rebirth in Pure Land. The five *ōjō den* (biographies of people who have attained rebirth in Pure Land), written in the twelfth century, contain numerous stories of such individuals – not to mention rapacious officials, monks who had fathered children, and other assorted miscreants – who were saved through the power of the *nembutsu*. Typical is the biography of Kiyohara no Masakuni in the *Shūi ōjō den,* which claims that although "there was not an evil act that he did not commit," he nevertheless attained rebirth in Pure Land after taking up the practice of *nembutsu* at age sixty, reciting the name 100,000 times daily.[144] Similarly the learned monk Jungen, "who turned his daughter into his wife," began the practice of *nembutsu* only on his deathbed and yet was received into Pure Land.[145]

Although in most cases the *nembutsu* was practiced in conjunction with other devotional acts not intrinsically connected with the Pure Land faith, such as chanting the *Hokekyō* or performing simple esoteric rites, the *ōjō den* indicate that some laymen and monks performed *nembutsu* alone, to the exclusion of all other types of Buddhist devotional practice. The *Go-shūi ōjō den* reports, for example, that a Hiei monk named Ryūsen (1047–1116) renounced the study of Tendai and Mikkyō early in his career to devote himself exclusively to *nembutsu,* uttering the name of Amida 120,000 times daily for thirty years.[146] The same work tells of an impoverished farmer from Ōmi who was too poor to make offerings, but instead continuously recited the name of Amida both when doing his daily devotions as well as when working in the fields.[147] As the *Konjaku monogatari* attests by its frequent use of such phrases as *nembutsu wo tonau,* "to recite the *nembutsu,*" the term *nembutsu* by the twelfth century had come to signify for many laymen and nonelite monks simply the recitation of Amida's name without any reference to meditation.[148]

The concept that even evil men could attain rebirth in Pure Land, the belief that practice of *nembutsu* alone was sufficient to bring about rebirth there, and the emergence of the view that the *nembutsu*

---

144 Miyoshi Tameyasu, *Shūi ōjō den* (ca. 1111), kan 2, *Ōjō den, Hokke genki,* p. 339.
145 *Shūi ōjō den,* kan 3, pp. 363–64.
146 Miyoshi Tameyasu, *Go-shūi ōjō den* (1139), kan 1, *Ōjō-den, Hokke genki,* p. 649.
147 *Go-shūi ōjō den,* kan 1, p. 651.
148 *Konjaku monogatari shū* (ca. 1120), kan 15, *NKBT,* vol. 24, p. 382.

consisted primarily of reciting the name of Amida laid the foundation for the Pure Land schools that were established in the Kamakura period and that came to figure so prominently throughout Japanese religious history. Shinran (1173–1262), the founder of the Jōdo Shin school, openly acknowledged his debt to the lay tradition of Pure Land Buddhism that emerged in the Heian period by declaring that he modeled himself after Kyōshin (d. 866), a tonsured but married layman (*shami*) who expressed his deep faith in Pure Land simply by reciting Amida's name as often as possible in his everyday life.[149]

[149] Kakunyo, *Gaijashō* (1335), *Shinshū shōgyō zensho*, vol. 3 (Kyoto: Ōyagi kōbundō, 1964), pp. 67–68. For examples of Kyōshin's piety, see Yōkan's *Ōjō jū in* (1103), *Jōdo-shū zensho*, vol. 15 (Tokyo: Sankibō Busshorin, 1971), pp. 375b–77a.

CHAPTER 8

RELIGIOUS PRACTICES

Upon arising, first of all repeat seven times in a low voice the name of the star of the year. Take up a mirror and look at your face, to scrutinize changes in your appearance. Then look at the calendar and see whether the day is one of good or evil omen. Next use your toothbrush and then, facing West, wash your hands. Chant the name of the Buddha and invoke those gods and divinities whom we ought always to revere and worship. Next make a record of the events of the previous day. Now break your fast with rice gruel. Comb your hair once every three days, not every day. Cut your fingernails on a day of the Ox, your toenails on a day of the Tiger. If the day is auspicious, now bathe, but only once every fifth day.[1]

As these Testamentary Admonitions of Fujiwara no Morosuke (908–60) indicate, the life of aristocrats during the Heian period was punctuated by a plethora of practices and precautions of a ritual character. What appear on the surface to be common practices, such as washing one's hands or brushing one's teeth, were directly related to the daily performance of specific rites dedicated to various *kami* and buddhas and bodhisattvas. These rites were related to Taoist practices, to various ritual elements of Buddhism, or to beliefs and practices subsumed under the category of *yin* and *yang*. Yet other ritual practices were of a political character, or appear to be outside any immediately identifiable framework. This complexity of the ritual and liturgical world was part and parcel of life among aristocrats during the Heian period.

The short quotation from Morosuke's admonitions informs us that the human body was treated with great ritual care. This notion might be related to the highest levels of the doctrine of Esoteric Buddhism which stated that Buddhahood could be achieved in this lifetime and in this very body, while it might also be related to more ancient, autochthonous views concerning purification. No matter

---

[1] *Kujō-den no Goyuikai*, translated in George Sansom, *A History of Japan*, vol. 1 (Stanford, Calif.: Stanford University Press, 1958), p. 180.

what those preceding views and practices might have been, there is little doubt that Esoteric Buddhism redefined the ontological position of the human body in radical terms, and may have been an important factor in the centrality of ritual concerns with the body throughout the Heian period.[2] Furthermore, Morosuke's admonitions tell us that attention was given to the cosmic context of space and time, thus suggesting a particular conceptualization of the body within larger parameters. The same admonitions also indicate that daily rituals were dedicated to autochthonous *kami* as well as to buddhas or bodhisattvas, thereby leaving the impression that such acts of reverence were of an inclusive character in which both indigenous and imported cultural and ritual practices and notions were in contact, if not in interaction. As will be seen presently, such was indeed the case: the majority of ritual and liturgical practices of the Heian period were cast within a vast congruity consisting of specific notions of reality laid out in a number of documents, of particular economic behavior, and of elaborate concepts of time and of space, all of which were in turn directly related to (Shinto) shrines and to (Buddhist) temples set in a distinctive sociopolitical framework.

Generally speaking, in their study of the overall establishment of religion in Japan, scholars have laid emphasis on the development of Buddhism through the support of the imperial house, and have analyzed the doctrinal aspects of Buddhism through the elaboration of sects or schools of thought; in contradistinction, little has been said about the presence or concurrent establishment of shrines in the immediate vicinity of temples, or about the growth and status of ritual practices in both shrines and temples. However, this concurrence was structurally responsible for specific practices and beliefs such as those mentioned by Fujiwara no Morosuke.

Government as it had been set up under the *ritsuryō* (statutory system) at the end of the seventh century and at the beginning of the eighth century had established a Department of Shrines (*Jingikan*), one of the duties of which was to formalize rituals performed by various sacerdotal lineages in the name of private families or of the state, and to regulate the "worship of the *kami* of Heaven and Earth" (*jingi sūhai*) in shrines. The Bureau continued to exist during the Heian period and exercised much influence on the beliefs, rites, and practices of sacerdotal lineages, of the aristocracy at large and, be-

---

[2] The text positing the centrality of the body is Kūkai's *Sokushin jōbutsu-gi;* see Yoshito Hakeda, *Kūkai: Major Works* (New York: Columbia University Press, 1972), pp. 225–34.

yond those privileged groups, of the populace in the geographical areas under the direct control of the government.

One of the more significant developments of the one hundred and fifty years before the beginning of the Heian period was the creation of capital cities designed on a Chinese model.[3] That development was significant for two major reasons. First, it suggests that the state was conceived of in a radically different way than it had been in the past; second, it brings to light a new type of relationship between the center and the periphery, and between the imperial lineage and its surrounding houses and clans. In the realm of ritual and liturgical organization this meant, consequently, that centralized ritual practices would play a strategic role in the formulation of imperial legitimacy.

With regard to the new conception of that state, the compilation of the *Kojiki* and *Nihon shoki* fixed the myths and symbols that became central to the definition and to the legitimation of the state. With regard to the new relationship between center and periphery, the creation of temples and the erection of shrines in the capital as well as in the provinces show a new type of institutional organization and cultic emphasis. Their establishment reveals, for example, the delineation of geopolitical spheres of influence and an attempt to unify ritual and liturgical notions and practices. The appearance of those texts and institutions expresses forcefully that the cults dedicated to the *kami* of Heaven and Earth were being unified at the level of the state. The need for such unification might be explained according to the following three hypotheses. First, in maintaining a single realm of symbols, ritual, and protocol, the state was hoping to institutionalize its control over houses and lineages surrounding the imperial family. Second, the control over shrines was accompanied by an equal increase of control over Buddhist temples (although such control was evident by the mid-Nara period, as is manifest in the establishment of the provincial monasteries and nunneries [*kokubunji, kokubunniji*] in 741, it had become necessary by the end of that period). And third, there arose a need to ground the definition and legitimacy of the centralized state in a symbolic and ritual realm pertaining to both shrines and temples.

Many of the ritual practices of the Heian period can be explored and explained in terms of these three hypotheses.

---

3 See Paul Wheatley and Thomas See, *From Court to Capital* (Chicago: University of Chicago Press, 1978).

THE ASSOCIATION OF SHINTO SHRINES WITH BUDDHIST TEMPLES

The need for unification of ritual in shrines

The existence of specialists in liturgical and ritual matters is attested in documents from the fourth century C.E. on.[4] When those specialists came to form social units in which liturgical functions were transmitted hereditarily is not altogether clear, but it seems that some of these units have a long history. Japanese scholars refer to ritual specialists of pre-Nara periods by the word *shūkyō-teki bemin*, literally, religious professional corps. The term *be* denotes, in pre-Taika (645) society, a number of professional groups controlled or owned by the emerging court or by influential houses. Even though the Taika Reforms engineered by Prince Naka no Ōe and his adviser Nakatomi no Kamatari eliminated the term, the social reality remained in one form or another, especially in the case of sacerdotal houses, whose name often contains the term *be,* such as Imbe, or Urabe, and others. The term *shake* (literally, "shrine-house"), used today to refer to social units charged with liturgical matters, appears in texts only from the medieval period onward. These specialists in ritual and liturgical matters carried separate traditions of practice and interpretation, which the government tried to unify during the eighth century, as is evidenced by the *Kojiki,* the *Nihon shoki,* and the *Fudoki,* in the compilation of which some of the sacerdotal lineages closely related to the dominant houses cooperated. For example, one notices that the Nakatomi sacerdotal lineage (out of which the Fujiwara house emerged at the end of the seventh century) took some part in compiling those documents. That sacerdotal houses did not agree on all points of liturgy, ritual, and mythology is illustrated by the compilation of the *Kogoshūi* in 807, in which the Imbe sacerdotal house expressed its own views. It was certainly not by chance that the sacerdotal lineage governing shrines symbolizing the imperial state (such as Ise or Kasuga) was the Nakatomi lineage related to the Fujiwara house.

The Taika Reforms conceived of the structure of government in terms of a separation (and, at the same time, of an interdependence) of cultic and policy-making duties; the Department of Shrines (*Jingikan*) was set above the Council of State (*Daijōkan*), even though the

---

4 See Inoue Tatsuo, *Kodai ōken to shūkyō-teki bemin* (Tokyo: Kashiwa shobō, 1980).

rank of its members was inferior to that of the members of the *Daijōkan*. The *Jingikan* determined ritual practice pertaining to the conduct of political affairs and of social matters within the court, but it also functioned as an apparatus of control of the main sacerdotal lineages of the time. Of great importance is that the *Jingikan* was thought to be above the purely policy-making organs of government; this does not mean that ritual matters took precedence over policy making, but implies that ritual matters were central to the definition of the state and of its social construct, and to the legitimation process of some decisions made by the government. A corollary of this implication is that the social construct, the imperial state, and the policies made by the government were not only legitimized, but colored by, and grounded in, ritual considerations. Since this principle determines in part our understanding of ritual practices and retained some of its validity throughout the Heian period and beyond, it needs some elaboration. One objective of the compilation of the *Kojiki* and *Nihon shoki* had been to establish the supremacy of certain clans (*uji*) by postulating their direct descent from specific divinities (*kami*) which played an important role in the myths described in those texts. This postulation not only created a definite prestige for the houses, it also determined their position vis-à-vis the imperial lineage by virtue of what were considered to be historical events. Furthermore, this postulation suggested that the structure of society was a mirror reflection of the structure of the *kami* pantheon, by virtue of which rituals that were dedicated to the *kami* had sociogenic characteristics. These rituals dedicated to the *kami* of Heaven and Earth served to reinforce the existing political power structure, especially since the *kami* of Heaven were related to the sociocosmic construct of the state and to its main houses, while the *kami* of Earth were related to other matters: as a general rule, few of those are the ancestral *kami* of the main aristocratic houses. In other words, the world of shrines dedicated to those *kami* which played an important role in the imperial mythology was intensely sociopolitical; this is what accounts, in part, for the dominantly protocolar character of ritual in shrines. When Buddhism appeared, it was sponsored by precisely those houses and lineages immediately surrounding the imperial lineage; this means that it was expected to play, at the level of aristocratic houses and of the state, the role played by the main shrines, and that the Buddhist clergy would play a role similar to that of sacerdotal lineages. That is one of the reasons why shrines and temples came to be associated with each other early in history, and why those associations retained strong sociopolitical overtones through much of Japanese history. If we keep in mind the sociopolitical roles of the shrines and temples, we understand much better the types of practices of a ritual or liturgical character that flourished during the Heian period, and achieve a better insight into the combinatory nature of those practices and of their related creeds.

Many of the most important temples of the Nara period were dedicated to the welfare of the spirits of departed leaders of the main lineages, while a number of shrines were dedicated to the ancestral and tutelary *kami* of the very same lineages. Concerned perhaps that the private character of these institutions might lead to an excessive fragmentation of society, the government transformed many such temples into state-sponsored operations, and gave a new and unified structure to the cult in the main shrines to ensure that it was directed toward the state rather than toward private interest. The government did not completely succeed in this attempt.

The Heian period is distinguished in part by the introduction and remarkably swift acceptance of Esoteric Buddhism, symbolized by the creation of the Enryakuji on Mount Hiei by Saichō (Dengyō Daishi, 767–822) to house the Tendai school of Buddhism,[5] and by the creation of the Tōji (Kyōō-gokokuji) in Kyoto and of the Kongōbuji on Mount Kōya by Kūkai (Kōbō Daishi, 774–835) to house the Shingon school.[6] Even though the Tendai school was based on the Lotus Sutra, esoteric practices of Shingon character and of Taoist origins crept in during Saichō's lifetime and became the main praxis of the school under the direction of Ennin (794–864) and Enchin (814–91), to the point that one refers to Shingon esotericism as *Tōmitsu* (i.e., esotericism [*mitsu*] of the Tōji [*tō*] Temple), and to Tendai esotericism as *Taimitsu* (i.e., esotericism of Tendai, here referred to as *Tai*). These were separated on the institutional level and by different emphases on certain rituals which are discussed later in this chapter. These forms of esotericism tended to be highly inclusivistic and eclectic, and became the main vehicle for the assimilation by Buddhism of all kinds of ritual practices whose origins were not Buddhist or which belonged either to Chinese and Korean traditions or to Japanese indigenous practices. Thus, the

---

[5] See Paul Groner, *Saichō* (Berkeley, Calif.: Asian Humanities Press, Buddhist Studies Series, 1985).

[6] See Hakeda, *Kūkai: Major Works*. On the relationship between Kūkai and Saichō, see Allan Grapard, "Patriarchs of Heian Buddhism Kūkai and Saichō," in *Great Historical Figures of Japan* (Tokyo: Japan Culture Institute, 1978), pp. 39–48.

main aspect of Buddhist practices throughout the Heian period was esoteric and combinatory. This point cannot be emphasized enough, for much of the ritual world of Heian evolved as the result of systematic combinations between Esoteric Buddhism and the ritual world of the shrines that, for convenience's sake, even though inadequately, has been named Shinto.[7] However, as we shall see, the ritual world of the shrines was heavily laden with Taoist notions and practices, as was, in fact, the Buddhist world. The cultic realm of all classes of Heian society was combinatory, by which is meant that it consisted of intermeshed forms of Esoteric Buddhism, Exoteric Buddhism, Taoism (though not of the institutionalized form such as was then found in China), and various practices taking place in shrines. I will approach this combinatory world by separating its main components, first at the institutional level, and then at the level of practices.

Institutional considerations

Ritual and liturgical practices of the Heian period are marked by the creation or enlargement of shrines (*jinja*) and temples (*tera*) supported by the government, by the codification of rituals performed therein, by the emergence of new schools of Buddhism, by the appearance of a preeminence of practice over theory, and by the association of *kami* with buddhas and bodhisattvas worshiped in adjacent Buddhist temples. These associations resulted in the emergence of specific cults of great importance, the analysis of which yields an adequate understanding of varied but distinctly related dimensions of Heian cultic life.

The various processes outlined in the paragraphs above continued to evolve after the move of the capital to Kyoto, and came to fruition toward the middle of the Heian period. Furthermore, the gradual association of some temples with shrines seems to have been related to the formulation of the protection of the state (*chingo kokka*), to the creation of the ideology of mutual support between the state and Buddhism (*ōbō buppō*), and to the evolution of Heian culture in general. This is most conspicuous in the phenomena known as the "shrine-temples" (*jingūji*), and the "Twenty-two Shrines" (*nijūnisha*).

---

[7] On this topic of importance, see Kuroda Toshio, "Shinto in the History of Japanese Religions," *Journal of Japanese Studies* 7 (1981): 1–21.

Shrine-temples: the jingūji

Japanese Buddhist monks backed by private support began to build temples on the grounds of shrines by the middle of the Nara period; such temples are known as *jingūji*. Even though it is most probable that this phenomenon originated in Kyushu around the Usa Shrines dedicated to Hachiman (where the Mirokuji was begun in 739 and completed in 779),[8] the earliest documented case occurred in Kashima in Hitachi Province (present Ibaraki Prefecture), where a certain Mangan erected a temple next to the shrine in 749. This is an interesting matter, for the shrine in question was an important one located in the easternmost part of the country controlled at the time by the Yamato government; in point of fact, it was so important that the *kami* enshrined there, Takemikatsuchi no mikoto, was taken around that time by the Fujiwara clan as its tutelary *kami* (*ujigami*) and was subsequently enshrined in the Kasuga Shrine in Nara. The other main tutelary *kami* of the Fujiwara house is Futsunushi no mikoto, which was enshrined in Katori, located a few miles west of Kashima. A *jingūji* was erected in Katori also, but the date is unclear.[9] Other *jingūji* were built during the Nara period in shrines that were distant from the center of government, by monks who appear to have been associated with the Kōfukuji, the main clan-temple (*ujidera*) of the Fujiwara. One thus notes the creation of the *jingūji* of Tado in 763 (Ise Province, present Mie Prefecture), and of those of Kehi (Echizen Province, present Fukui Prefecture), Taga (Ōmi Province, present Shiga Prefecture), Okutsushima (Ōmi Province), Usa (Buzen Province, present Oita Prefecture), and Utagahama (Shimotsuke Province, present Tochigi Prefecture) in the following decades. This last one was created by Shōdō (735–817) in 784; a detailed document showing the processes which led to its creation was written in 814 by Kūkai.[10] This document indicates that Shōdō made the ascent of Mount Futara (today called Nantaizan, in Nikkō), in order to worship local *kami* and to achieve enlightenment, and that this ascent was a religious experience in which he visualized the

---

8 See Nakano Hatayoshi, *Hachiman shinkō-shi no kenkyū* (Tokyo: Yoshikawa kōbunkan, 1975).
9 On the topic of the Kashima and Katori Shrines, see the primary sources contained in Shintō taikei hensankai, ed., *Shintō taikei*, vol. 22 (Tokyo: Seikōsha, 1984). For a study of the shrines, see Miyai Yoshio, *Fujiwara-shi no ujigami-ujidera shinkō to sobyō saishi* (Tokyo: Seikō shobō, 1978).
10 See the translation of this text by Allan Grapard, "Kūkai: Stone Inscription for the śramana Shōdō, who Crossed Mountains and Streams in His Search for Awakening," in Michael Tobias and Harold Drasdo, eds., *The Mountain Spirit* (New York: Overlook Press, 1978), pp. 50–59.

Bodhisattva of Compassion (Kannon) and saw Mount Futara as its transcendental abode on earth. He then erected on the shores of the lake (called today Chūzenji-ko) a *jinguji*. Besides being the first complete text documenting the ascent of mountains for religious purposes in Japan, this text reveals that, at least in Kūkai's eyes, the combined worship of *kami* and buddhas and bodhisattvas posed no problem.

The *jinguji*, then, were institutions symbolizing early trends of nonexclusive attitude toward autochthonous and imported creeds and practices, while they were at the same time institutions expressing the power of houses concerned with controlling cultic matters, such as the Fujiwara house. The Buddhist clergy administering those shrine-temples performed Buddhist rites in front of the *kami*, chanting Buddhist scriptures with the avowed goal of releasing the *kami* from their unenlightened state of being and guiding them toward the Buddhist goal of awakening. This was probably one of the strategies used by Buddhism to gain converts in remote areas, but it was also a strategy aimed at installing, in distant places, cult representatives of the government. Indeed, government provisions concerning the number of monks that could be ordained by temples under government supervision stipulated that a certain number would specialize in shrines; they were called *shimbun dosha*, "monks ordained for the worship of the *kami*." The Heian period saw the creation of temples on the grounds of shrines on a massive scale, but the term *jinguji* tended to be abandoned. This suggests that the function of temples vis-à-vis shrines evolved toward increasing control (if not domination), as is shown by the following analysis of the system of state-sponsored shrines and temples called traditionally, though improperly, *nijūnisha*, the "Twenty-two Shrines."

The Twenty-two Shrines system

The term *nijūnisha* indicates twenty-two shrines that became the object of imperial support during the first part of the Heian period and thus became major institutions symbolizing what might be called the cultic system of the imperial lineage. By the middle of the ninth century this system showed a trend toward the unification of ritual modes and the stabilization of a government ideology concerning the relations between shrines and temples. At the time of ritual performance, which followed the seasonal cycle overlaid with calendrical principles originating in India and China, the emperor or some of his representatives would participate in rites according to strict standards laid down by the government, make offerings the value of which was set forth in decrees, and provide economic support of the sites of cult. The appearance of that system heralded a significant step in the evolution of cultic and policy-making institutions and practices, as well as a major increase in state control. This evolution led to the systematic institutionalization of the dominant Heian government ideology, namely, the "protection of the imperial state (by shrine-temple multiplexes)" (*chingo kokka,* a term that will be discussed later), and the mutual support between the state and the combined exoteric–esoteric system (*kemmitsu taisei*) of shrines and temples, also discussed later in this chapter.

The shrines under consideration were located, for the most part, in the Kinai area (the five provinces immediately surrounding the capital), and most were included in the list of major shrines established by the *Engi shiki* in 927 because they were related to the central lineages supporting the imperial house, or to some lineages of great historical importance.[11] Those shrines included in the list of twenty-two, but not in the *Engi shiki,* are sites of cults that gained popular significance thereafter, or that were created at the time to accommodate the court. The origin of the majority of these shrines goes back to antiquity, when they already represented specific connections between cultic and sociopolitical concerns. It is those concerns that came to be expressed and reinforced by the creation of the system and its accompanying ideology.

The process of quasi unification of those shrines may have begun at the onset of the Heian period for, when the list appears for the first time in documents in 966, sixteen shrines were included that had long been the object of imperial offerings. These were separated into an Upper Group of seven shrines, a Middle Group of seven, and a Lower Group of two to which were added three shrines in 991, one in 994, and two in 1039.

A study of these shrines brings to light two major characteristics: a very specific relationship of those institutions to the Fujiwara house and the presence of Buddhist institutions at most of the twenty-two shrines.

Indeed, the classification of the twenty-two shrines into three groups exhibits two rationales: one geopolitical, and one political. In the first case, five of the first seven shrines are located in the province

---

11 See Felicia Bock, trans., *Engi-shiki: The Procedures of the Engi Era,* 2 vols. (Tokyo: Sophia University Press, 1970–72).

TABLE 8.1
The Twenty-two Shrine-temples sponsored by the imperial government

Upper seven	Middle seven	Lower eight
Ise	Ōharano	Hie
Iwashimizu	Ōmiwa	Umenomiya
Kamo	Isonokami	Yoshida
Matsunoo	Yamato	Hirota
Hirano	Hirose	Gion
Inari	Tatsuta	Kitano
Kasuga	Sumiyoshi	Nibunokawakami
		Kibune

of Yamashiro, where the capital Heian-kyō is located; the two other shrines are Ise (in Ise Province) and Kasuga (in Yamato Province), dedicated respectively to the ancestral and tutelary *kami* of the imperial lineage and of the Fujiwara house. The second seven shrines are located in the Yamato region, with the exception of the Ōharano and Sumiyoshi Shrines; the Ōharano Shrine (in Yamashiro Province) is the Kasuga Shrine that had been duplicated in the Nagaoka capital, while the Sumiyoshi Shrine (in Settsu Province) was directly related to imperial mythology and imperial enthronement ceremonies, particularly during the Heian period. The last group of eight shrines consists of shrines and temples located in the Kinai provinces and specializing in placating droughts or various nocive forces that made themselves evident during the period. In other words, the first group is close to the capital, the second group represents the past history of the lineages in Yamato, and the third group represents a larger concern with the periphery.

In the case of political rationale, it must be pointed out that the Fujiwara house made sure that its major shrines would be represented in the three classes of shrines: Kasuga in the first, Ōharano in the second, and Yoshida (the Kasuga Shrine of Kyoto), in the third. This indicates that the Fujiwara house emphasized its presence at the three levels of organization. Furthermore, one might emphasize that shrines related to Kyushu are found in the three classes: Iwashimizu (Hachiman) in the first, Sumiyoshi in the second, and Hirota in the third. This suggests that certain aspects of mythology remained important during the Heian period.

Equally important is the often ignored fact that the Twenty-two Shrines were associated with Buddhist temples located on or near their precincts. By the middle of the Heian period the Twenty-two "Shrines" had become major shrine-temple multiplexes (*jisha*) consisting of complex combinations and interactions between autochthonous (or foreign) *kami* and imported buddhas and bodhisattvas, between sacerdotal lineages in the shrines and Buddhist lineages in the temples, between administrative and economic structures of the two types of institutions, and between modes of cult, all under the aegis of the state symbolized by the overwhelming presence of members of the Fujiwara house as the leading prelates of those institutions. Many of the shrines and temples had been created by the Fujiwara house, or were restored by members of the house during the Heian period. This indicates that the Fujiwara house consolidated its grip over the country in part through the formation and administration of shrine-temple multiplexes to which the imperial house made offerings and from which it requested the performance of sumptuous rites for the protection of the realm under its governance. The soon dominant modality of relationship between cultic and policy issues, which took the name of mutual support between these institutions and the state (*ōbō-buppō*), was thus institutionalized in the system (*taisei*) of shrines and temples of exoteric (*ken*) and esoteric (*mitsu*) Buddhism (that is, *kemmitsu taisei*).[12]

Of particular fame and importance were the shrine-temple multiplexes of Hie-Enryakuji (Mount Hiei),[13] of Kasuga-Kōfukuji,[14] of Iwashimizu Hachiman-Gokokuji,[15] of Sumiyoshi-Shiragidera,[16] of Gion-Kankeiji (Kanshin'in), and of Kitano-Kannonji. All these played a central role in the evolution of Heian cultic life and its political components, and continued to be major sites of cult throughout Japanese history.

Chingo kokka *theories and practices*

In its narrow meaning the term *kokka* refers to the imperial lineage and supporting houses (*ka*) which govern the realm of the country

---

12 These issues have been studied in detail in Kuroda Toshio, *Jisha seiryoku* (Tokyo: Iwanami, 1980), and *Ōbō to buppō* (Kyoto: Kōzōkan, 1983).
13 See Murayama Shūichi and Kageyama Haruki, *Hiei-zan* (Tokyo: NHK Bukkusu, 1970).
14 See Allan Grapard, *The Protocol of the Gods* (Berkeley: University of California Press, 1992); and Royall Tyler, *The Miracles of the Kasuga Deity* (Princeton, N.J.: Princeton University Press, 1990).
15 See Nakano Hatayoshi, *Usa-gū* (Tokyo: Yoshikawa kōbunkan, 1985); *Hachiman shinkō-shi no kenkyū*, 2 vols. (Tokyo: Yoshikawa kōbunkan, 1975); Allan Grapard, *The Religion of Space and the Limits of Religion* (forthcoming).
16 See Nishimoto Yutaka, *Sumiyoshi taisha* (Tokyo: Gakuseisha, 1977); see also Ueda Masaaki, ed., *Sumiyoshi to Munakata no kami* (Tokyo: Chikuma shobō, 1988).

(*koku*); in its larger meaning, however, it denotes the state at large, with an emphasis on its geopolitical domain or territory. As such, the term *chingo kokka* refers to a government ideology legitimated by rituals performed by both sacerdotal lineages in specific shrines and Buddhist lineages in specific temples, in the name of the imperial lineage and its satellite households, particularly the Fujiwara. Although the term is of Sino-Japanese origin, the concept of protection of a state was also present in Buddhism in India. It was developed to a great extent in China (one of the scriptures on which Buddhism relied for those rituals, the *Ninnō-kyō*, is actually an apocryph conceived in China),[17] and made its way into Japanese theory and practice as early as the Nara period, to blossom during the Heian period in the Twenty-two Shrine-temple multiplexes as well as in other sites of cult located in various parts of the country. Thus, what is covered by the term *chingo kokka* is in reality a complex assortment of Indian and Chinese concepts and practices adapted to Japanese needs and within the parameter of the political submission of various Buddhist communities to the state.

It had been noted above that the term *kokka* may have meant originally the imperial lineage and the realm under its rule. One of the basic notions related to that meaning was that the realm in question was seen as literally embodied in the person of the emperor, who was considered to be descended from *kami* such as Izanami, Izanagi, and Amaterasu. These central figures of the pantheon exhibited in their symbolic body the very structures and functions of the ideal classical society; therefore, the emperor's body symbolized the same structures and functions, and that body came to be seen as the "body of the imperial state" (*kokutai*). A primary consequence of this view was that some of the major rites of protection of the state were in fact rites of protection of the emperor's body. Thus, when the emperor fell ill, rituals were requested from shrines and temples in the name of the protection of the state; and a majority of rites for the protection of the state tended to be related, in one way or another, to the body of the emperor. The two were inseparable. A rite such as that dedicated to the peacock (*Kujaku-hō;* Sanskrit, Mahāmāyūri) in Esoteric Buddhism came to be used, in Japan, for the protection of the state: that ritual was originally related to snake bites, poison, and

---

17 *Ninnō-kyō*, properly, *Ninnō haramitsu-kyō*, in Takakusu Junjirō, Watanabe Kaigyoku, Ono Gemmyō, eds., *Taishō shinshū daizōkyō* (hereafter abbreviated as *T*), 100 vols. (Tokyo: Taishō issaikyō kankōkai, 1924–34), vol. 8, no. 245 (in Kumārajīva's translation), and no. 246 (in Amoghavajra's translation).

disease, and was not, at the time of its inception in India, connected to the notion of realm or to the political power of a ruler.

The tradition conceiving of the body of the emperor as a symbol of the state can be explained from several perspectives in the Indian and Sino-Japanese contexts. In the case of India, it is well known that enthronement rites were related to speculations concerning the microcosmic nature of the human body in relation to the macrocosm. In the case of China, Taoism conceived of the body of the ruler as a cosmic body as when, for example, the Yellow Emperor was thought to be a manifestation on earth of Lao-Tzu, himself a cosmic body.[18] In Japan, the *Kojiki* and the *Nihon shoki* offer several indications to the effect that threats to the imperial body were threats to the structure of society, and that death of the imperial person needed to be treated by rituals protecting the realm at large. That is how one might look at the *tama-shizume* (*chinkonsai*) rituals aiming at restoring longevity to the imperial figure, and it is not by chance that the term *shizume* ("to pacify") is found in the term *chingo kokka* (in which it is pronounced *chin*). Therefore, when we find in the language of rituals dedicated to the protection of the state, even within a Buddhist context, that the object of those rituals is the body of the emperor, we must understand that what is meant is both the physical and symbolic body of the emperor/realm. Since both the realm and the imperial body were conceived of as symbolic entities, ritual was the appropriate solution to any type of "disease" affecting them. And in that ritual cure, shrines and temples played a structurally similar role in which they were partly competing, and partly cooperating. Indeed, the emperor came to be represented, at the ideal level, as a bodhisattva (as opposed to India, where the bodhisattva was described as a ruler).

Since the Twenty-two Shrine-temple multiplexes were those from which rituals for the protection of the realm were requested, and since the appearance of the system seemed to herald a unification process, one might expect that the unification would have occurred, and that a single administrative body governing the system might have emerged. This was not the case, however, and the reason might

---

18 On the topic of the Yellow Emperor, see Anna Seidel, "La Divinisation de Lao-tseu dans le Taoisme des Han," Publications de l'Ecole Française d'Extrême-Orient, vol. 71 (Paris: Ecole Française d'Extrême-Orient, 1969). On the subject of the body in Chinese religious thought in general, see Christofer Schipper, "The Taoist Body," *History of Religions* 17 (1978): 325–51. And for views of the body in India, see Frits Staal, "Indian Concepts of the Body," *Somatics* (Autumn/Winter 1983–84): 31–41.

be that the unification process was true only at the level of the ritual and legitimacy needs of the imperial house and its satellite lineages. The system of multiplexes never did develop into a single unified body of practice or theory, or into anything close to what might be termed religious orthodoxy. If there was any orthodoxy in Heian Japan, it was of a sociopolitical nature, and was embedded in rituals performed in discrete and semiautonomous sites of cult governed by distinct sacerdotal lineages under the direction of powerful houses, and by ecclesiastic elites issued from aristocratic lineages. For example, starting in the late tenth century, shrine-temple multiplexes came to be governed by aristocracy-born ecclesiasts (the *monzeki* governed by *kishu*, "noble seeds," from main lineages, and by *ryōke*, "members of good households," from lesser aristocratic birth).[19] This means that multiplexes represented house-oriented private interests, even when their public rhetoric was geared to the state. A second reason is connected with the decline of the statutory (*ritsuryō*) system during the Heian period. Shrine-temple multiplexes garnered vast land estates free from taxation, and thus developed into major economic and ideological units that, by the end of the Heian period, came into various conflicts either with the imperial government or with warrior houses, or with each other. Indeed, during the period a few emperors attempted to curb the growing political, economic, and military power of those sites of cult, but the private interests of specific sites of cult overrode any other interest, so that violent conflict erupted between multiplexes that should have been unified at least at the doctrinal level.[20] However, these shrine-temple multiplexes represented the cultic orthodoxy of the imperial state, and most of them were closed, during the Heian period, to people who did not belong to the main houses that formed the court. The theory and practice of the protection of the state that they evolved during the course of the Heian period were thus restricted to the imperial house and its satellite lineages. Such theory and practice continued to survive centuries after the end of the Heian period and were revived at the time of foreign invasions or at the time of imperial succession crises.

19 Not surprisingly, the first *monzeki* was the Ichijō-in (created between 978 and 983) of the Kōfukuji, whose abbot was Jōshō, grandson of Fujiwara no Moroyasu, then Minister of the Left.
20 See Gaston Renondeau, *Les Moines Guerriers du Japon* (Paris: Imprimerie Nationale, 1965). See also Kuroda, *Jisha seiryoku*.

RITUALIZED AND RITUALIZING ACTIVITIES

Rituals performed in shrine-temple multiplexes

During the Nara period, rituals of protection of the state had been performed in shrines and temples in order to placate various forces responsible for earthquakes, droughts, epidemics, and disease striking the imperial person or leading aristocrats, or the country at large. Buddhist statues were commissioned and copying of scriptures (*shakyō*) took place as preventive measures. The scriptures in question belonged to the literature of the Perfection of Wisdom (*daihannya*; Sanskrit, *mahā-prajñā pāramitā*). Furthermore, the erection by the government of monasteries and nunneries in the various provinces (the *kokubunji* system created in 741) had been undertaken with the avowed purpose of protecting the realm at two levels: those of ritual and education. Specific members of the pantheon enshrined in shrines and temples were regarded as active protectors of the state in this context, and were therefore the object of ritual and devotion; preeminent among those in the Buddhist context were Kannon (Avalokiteśvara), whose sculptures were made at the time of major political or military unrest threatening the texture of society and, among many more, the Four Heavenly Kings (Shitennō), guardians of the four directions. These rituals belonged to the unorganized tradition of "mixed esotericism" (*zōmitsu*), which was spread widely in the western part of Japan and did not have allegiance to particular schools of Buddhism.

However, Kūkai and Saichō came back from China at the beginning of the ninth century and created new schools of Buddhism that were to have a tremendous impact on the ritual and philosophical world of Heian. Both introduced to Japan new rituals of protection of the state.

Saichō had learned during his stay in China a number of rites to this effect: the *Birushana-hō* (ritual of Vairocana), which he eventually performed in the imperial palace; the *Gundari-dampō* (ritual of Kundalī), which is essentially martial; the *Fugen-e dampō* (ritual of Samantabhadra), the *Nyoirin-dampō* (ritual of Cintāmani), and the *Gobutchō-hō* (ritual of the Five Buddhas emanated from Śākyamuni's cranial protuberance). But the full-fledged development and performance of rituals by the Tendai lineage did not occur until Saichō's disciples Ennin and Enchin returned from China with the latest developments in the field, and thoroughly transformed

Tendai into an esoteric ritual tradition geared to the protection of the state.[21]

When Kūkai returned from China in 806, his expertise was immediately sought after by the government. He set to the task of reproducing mandalas and altars for these protective rituals and performed initiatory unctions (*kanjō*), allowing monks and aristocrats alike to be participants in the esoteric doctrine and the rituals connected to it. The government requested in 816 that he build an Initiation Hall within the compounds of the Tōdaiji in Nara for the protection of the state. In 834, one year before his death, Kūkai saw to it that a special building designed for the performance of those rites was built within the imperial palace. That is the Shingon'in, in which Shingon's major rite for the protection for the imperial house, the *go-shichinichi mi-shiho*, was performed during the second week of the first month.

The Shingon tradition and rituals for the state

The first ritual Kūkai performed for the protection of the state was in 810, the year after the rebellion of Fujiwara no Kusuko which signaled the decline of the Shiki branch and the surge to power of the Northern branch of the Fujiwara house. Kūkai obviously sided with the Northern branch, since it is reported that he performed in 814 the rituals for the opening of the Nan'en-dō at the Kōfukuji in Nara, which remained for centuries one of the salient symbols of dominance of the Northern branch of the Fujiwara house. As Kūkai wrote in a document asking for permission to perform this ritual, he needed to teach correct procedure to his disciples; he admitted that even though he had been initiated by his master in China and was thus qualified to perform the rite, he still needed to train. He also stated that past rituals for the protection of the state had emphasized the chanting of scriptures, but he emphasized that rituals would be far more effective if they were based on esoteric doctrine and on the adequate formulation of potent formulas and charms (*darani*), which he equated with the proper intake of medicine.[22] The aristocrats of the time welcomed Kūkai's stance because it fit perfectly

---

21 The best treatment of the variegated aspects of Tendai esoteric practices and ideas is in Misaki Ryōshū, *Taimitsu no kenkyū* (Tokyo: Sōbunsha, 1988); *Mikkyō to jingi shisō* (Tokyo: Sōbunsha, 1992); *Taimitsu no riron to jissen* (Tokyo: Sōbunsha, 1994); and *Nihon. Chūgoku Bukkyō shisō to sono tenkai* (Tokyo: Sankibō, 1993).
22 Hayami Tasuku, *Heian jidai kizoku-shakai to bukkyō* (Tokyo: Yoshikawa kōbunkan, 1975).

their concern with magic, manipulation of symbols, and medicine. Indeed, Kūkai insisted in many of his writings on the therapeutic quality of the teachings of the Buddha and, more specifically, of the rituals of esotericism.[23] To cure the body and the mind stood, in the early Heian period, as the prime metaphor for the protection of the state. If the cosmos was seen as a body, and the human body as a microcosm thereof, then cosmic disasters were to be treated like a disease in the body. That is why Kūkai and his contemporaries had a strong personal devotion to the Buddha of Medicine, and why that Buddha became a central figure in rituals of protection of the state.

The scriptures used for those rituals were already used during the Nara period: they were the *Konkōmyōkyō*,[24] the *Daihannya-kyō*,[25] and the *Kongōhannyakyō*,[26] on which Kūkai wrote several interpretive documents (*kaidai*).[27] In the time of Kūkai, aristocrats requested the performance of those rituals for themselves or members of their family; several such requests are mentioned in Kūkai's works, accompanied by the petitions he wrote for those rites.[28] Another trend, known as "day chanting of scriptures, and evening rites of penitence," surfaces as early as 833 in court orders to perform such rites against epidemics, and in 834 against threats to crops; in both cases the court ordered that various temples dedicate three days to readings of the *Kongōhannyakyō*, and three evenings to rites of penitence. Penitence was the most fundamental aspect of Mahāyāna ritual; it consisted mainly in reciting lists of sins in order to purify the organs of perception. Once accomplished, this allowed a direct and undefiled perception of the universe, which took the form of visions to which a therapeutic character was assigned. It is clear that Kūkai, and others with him, considered natural events such as epidemics and droughts to be caused by unethical behavior grounded in misperceptions of reality, and therefore countered them by acts of penitence leading to a more adequate perception of the natural world and of one's place in it. The rites of penitence in question were those associated with the scriptures dedicated to the Buddha of Medicine,

---

23 See, for instance, the introduction to his *Himitsu mandara jūjūshinron* in Katsumata Shunkyō, ed., *Kōbō Daishi zenshū*, vol. 1 (Tokyo: Sankibō, 1968), p. 210.
24 *Konkōmyō-kyō*, *T*, vol. 16, no. 663.
25 *Daihannya-kyō* (properly, *Maka hannya haramitsu-kyō*), *T*, vol. 8, no. 223.
26 *Kongōhannya-kyō* (properly, *Kongō hannya haramitsu-kyō*), *T*, vol. 8, no. 235.
27 See, for instance, his *Ninnō-kyō kaidai*, in *Kōbō Daishi zenshū*, vol. 1, p. 329, and his *Kongō hannya-kyō kaidai*, in *Kōbō Daishi zenshū*, vol. 1, p. 489.
28 See examples of these petitions in Watanabe Shōkō and Miyasaka Yūshō, eds., *Sangō-shiiki, Seireishū* (Tokyo: Iwanami, 1965): *Seireishū*, *kan* 4, no. 20, for a petition for a ritual for the imperium; for rituals for aristocrats, see *kan* 6, no. 46, no. 50, no. 52, no. 55, and others.

and were known as *Yakushi keka*. Whereas in Chinese practice rites of penitence tended to be individual matters (even though that was not the case in the early Taoist context), the Japanese required group penitence for the sake of the state, aiming at the removal of baleful omens concerning whatever might threaten the human representatives of that state. By the second half of the ninth century, however, the evening sessions tended to be devoted to the recitation of charms and spells dedicated to the Buddha of Medicine or to the Bodhisattva of Compassion, and were followed by the recitation of mantras known as *kōmyō shingon* and *Shaka butsugen shingon*.

Beyond those rites, Esoteric Buddhism initiated the performance of specific rites dedicated to individual members of the pantheon. Among these were two major rites for the protection of the imperial state, performed in competition by Shingon and Tendai. The major Shingon rite, still performed in the modern period, is known as *Daigen(sui)-hō*. The main Tendai ritual performed over the centuries for the protection of the state is the *Shijōkō-hō*. Various Shingon lineages also specialized in the performance of rainmaking rituals, which were important matters of state.

The Ritual of Daigen(sui)

The first of these rites concerned the pantheon figure Daigensui, one of the important "Kings of Science" (*myōō*) of Japanese esotericism.[29] In India Daigensui's name was Āṭavaka, an ogre who converted to Buddhism and became one of the eight attendants of Vaiśravana (Japanese, Bishamon), the guardian of the northern direction (itself the object of important rites of protection of the realm in China as well as in Japan). In China, however, the term Daigensui designated the supreme commander of military forces; later it came to designate in both China and Japan the emperor as commander in chief of all forces (in Japan, from the Meiji period). Because Daigensui was the commander in chief of all spirits and demons protecting the land, his cult developed with a focus on the protection of the state; it penetrated the court in China during the T'ang dynasty, and was introduced to Japan by Kūkai and his disciple Jōgyō (d. 866), where it became one of the most important national rituals kept in the highest degree of secrecy.

---

29 See Robert Duquenne, "Daigensui," *Hōbōgirin*, 6 (1983): 610–40. (Usually, within the Shingon tradition, the graphs *dai*, *gen*, and *sui* are written, but *sui* is not pronounced.)

In Japan, various altars and purified areas were constructed for the performance of the rituals dedicated to Daigensui; the rites involved preliminary purification, the chanting of incantations, various offerings, and the layout of military attributes symbolizing the deity, such as swords, bows, and arrows. The ritual was performed for the first time in 840 in the Jōneiden within the imperial palace. In 850 Jōgyō requested that the rite be performed by fifteen monks, as in the case of the other main Shingon ritual performed in the Shingon chapel of the imperial palace. The Daigensui ritual was performed in the imperial palace every year, with even more regularity than the *goshichinichi mi-shiho*, but it was abandoned in early Meiji at the time of anti-Buddhist movements.[30]

Rainmaking rituals

Rituals performed to cause rain to fall were, in Japan, important matters of state directly related to the emperor, and were requested from both shrines and temples. The *Engi shiki*, for instance, mentions the existence of as many as forty-nine shrines (of the *yamaguchi* and *mikumari* types) specializing in such rituals in the Kinai area alone. On the Buddhist side, Shingon specialized in the performance of such rituals, but there are few records showing that Tendai monks did them. Two major types of "Buddhist" rain rituals existed during the Heian period: the *Kujaku-hō* (Rite of the Peacock),[31] which became the specialty of the Hirosawa lineage of Shingon, and the *Shōu-kyō-hō* (based on the scripture of the same name),[32] in which the Ono lineage of Shingon specialized. Such rites were already performed during the Nara period, but in the Heian eminent thaumaturgists were called upon. A famous case is that of the Ono lineage thaumaturgist Ninkai (b. 951), who came to be known as *ame sōjō*, literally, the "Monacal Rector of Rain." He performed the ritual successfully nine times between 1028 and 1044.

Tradition claimed that Kūkai performed the first ritual for rain at the Shinsen'en garden in the capital in 824, though there is no proof. But the text he is said to have authored in the wake of his success is

---

30 The ritual was subsequently reinstated with the provision that it be performed only once during the reign of an emperor. It was last performed, officially, in 1928; however, extraordinary performances took place during World War II.
31 The peacock ritual is in the *Dai kujaku myōō gazō danjō giki*, T, vol. 19, no. 983 [a].
32 *Shōu-kyō* (properly, *Daiunrin shōu-kyō*), T, vol. 19, no. 989. The ritual is *Daiun-gyō kiu dampō*, T, vol. 19, no. 990.

so filled with information related to the preceding discussion of the "body of the state" that it deserves full presentation.

How pitiful we are! Poor people living in the age of decadence of the *dharma*, deaf and blind who fail to pay heed to the words of the Buddha. Forever submerged in the drowsiness caused by the alcohol of ignorance, unaware of the source of Innate Awakening. Eternally lost in slumber while dreaming up the Triple World, and creating a foolish attachment to this body composed of four elements! We perpetrate the ten evils with body, speech, and mental activities. Ignoring filial piety or loyalty, we let the thicket of sins grow wild and, discarding the law of cause to effect, we fail to realize the distinction between well-being and misery. Lost in the dark of illusion we follow wit and greed and thus strain the function of mouth and belly. Laughing while alive, and crying upon death. Losing control we find ourselves struck now to the east, now to the north. But the retribution of evil acts is heavy, while that of good acts is light. That is why one day we will see fire instead of water in rivers. We find hell in what is in fact our Buddha-body, and fail to see the value of the seven jewels with which we are adorned. And thus even though it is time for rain to fall, the four horizons are blazing with heat: the sun burns everything, and rice and millet ears are all dry. The entire natural world dries up and hardens, and animals of fur and scale perish. With nothing to see but aridity in the land, court and peasants alike pour tears ceaselessly.

That is the moment our emperor chose to express a vow and, for the sake of the people, to leave his palace. Filled now with wisdom, now with humaneness, he surveyed the Eight Islands. Holding in mind the Three Teachings and the Nine Sciences, he remained set in his practice of the Four Incommensurable Concentrations and of the Six Perfections. Taking responsibility for the drought upon his own person he left his palace and, for the benefit of all living things, has reduced his food and sits day and night in pain. At this juncture he has requested monks in all temples to perform rituals and has sent emissaries to all mountains to ask thaumaturgists to enter ascetic concentrations.

As the venerable monks chant the sacred scriptures, light clouds appear in the sky, and as the practitioners of meditation hold firm to their concentration, rain clouds gather on the horizon. Then, sweet nectar of rain, that sublime ghee obscures the skies and comes to wash mountains and valleys. Waterfalls gush forth from high peaks and soak wild animals, while rain fills the fields enough to drown water buffaloes. Green trees are as if decorated with gems at the tips of their leaves, and the wide dams now overflow with water green as lapis lazuli.

Peasants, do not lament anymore! Go look and see whether early and mature rice are dead or alive. The southern fields abound with seedlings turning green. The eastern fields echo with the beat of the drums; songs and rhythms fill the air all around. See the storehouses, where grain piles up like islands, like mountains. How marvelous it is that the efficiency of the *dharma* need not be explained. How felicitous it is that the power of the emperor cannot be measured. A bodhisattva's single spit can extinguish the fires of a hundred realms, and in a moment end the laments of all subjects.

I, Kūkai, herewith give teachings to those who peregrinate through the six destinations; using the words of the Buddha, I let you know of the Buddha within you. Men and women! While holding firm to the single letter *a*, envision the inner palace of your own heart-mind! It is the very ground of the Triple Body of the Buddha, adorned from the origins with the Five Wisdoms. Should you wish to discover this Original Source, undergo the rite of Initiation. By doing so and holding firmly to it, you will immediately reach the level of the Awakened One. As rain falls from Heaven, so will food and clothing. And since you will not interfere with nature and will be without cause to worry, you will forget even the virtue of the emperor.[33]

Whether written by Kūkai or not, this document does indicate that the emperor was seen as symbolizing in his body the entirety of the realm; it was as carrier of everyone else's deeds that he performed the rituals. And it was through ascetic practices in his body that he caused the rain to fall. Naturally, Kūkai was the performer of the austerities and rites, and much more than "in the name" of the emperor: he was the emperor's ritual body. Another interesting aspect of this text is that it indicates that the rites of rainmaking were somehow grounded in penitence, which implies a relatedness between ignorance and natural calamities. This relatedness is inscribed within the larger framework of a dialectic between nature and culture, one of the results of which suggests that the natural world is sensitive to unethical human behavior, in which case it goes awry, and that it is also sensitive to ethical action, in which case it goes back to its ideal workings. That is the reason why meditation and ethics were a central part of rainmaking rituals.

The first credible record of the performance of this rite at the Shinsen'en appears in 875 with the name of Shōbō (832–909), the Shingon organizer of mountain asceticism (Shugendō). After 915, rain rituals were usually accompanied by the rite of the Five Dragons (*Goryūsai*), of Chinese origin.

The Tendai tradition and state rituals

As discussed earlier, Saichō did bring back to Japan a number of rites and made sure that they were performed in the name of the imperial state, because this meant sponsorship by the government and the leading aristocratic lineages. However, it became quickly evident

---

33 Kūkai, *Shōryōshū*, kan 1, no. 4, in *Sangō shiiki: Shōryōshū*, p. 168. There is yet another petition for rain written by Kūkai in 827, in *Shōryōshū*, kan 6, no. 47, p. 292.

that Shingon esotericism was superior because it provided a complex ritual framework backed by a doctrine that appealed to the aristocracy, and Tendai henceforth competed with Shingon by sending its monks to China to bring back even more rituals. Thus, Ennin, who went to China in 838 and stayed there for nine years, brought back a number of rituals of importance, among which were rites for the protection of the state: the *Emmyō-hō* (to prolong life); the *Shichibutsu Yakushi-hō* (a grand rite in front of seven sculpted representations of the Buddha of Medicine); and the *Monju hachiji-hō*, dedicated to the Bodhisattva of Wisdom and based on the *Monjushiri bosatsu hachiji sammai-hō* translated into Chinese by Bodhiruci.[34] But the most important ritual introduced by Ennin was the *Shijōkō-hō*, which became the central Tendai rite for the protection of the state.

The ritual of Shijōkō

The word *Shijōkō*, which means "radiance of a vivid fire," is the name of one of several personified emanations that sprang from the cranial protuberance of the Buddha, five of which gradually achieved a single status in doctrine and ritual, while the others remained in groups of five, eight, or ten.[35] Even though the ritual of Shijōkō had been brought back from China by Kūkai, it was never emphasized within the Shingon tradition; it became instead the central ritual for the protection of the state in the Tendai lineage within the Sammon (Enryakuji) tradition, in which it served as a balance to the ritual of Daigensui of Shingon.

Ennin's first performance of the ritual took place either in 849 or 850 on Mount Hiei. The principal object of the ritual was the annihilation of natural catastrophes, but it came to be associated with the emperor in a direct way, and was requested by the government whenever military danger faced the court. Originally performed by fourteen monks in the Sōjiin of Mount Hiei, which had been created by Emperor Montoku for that purpose, it came to be performed from the tenth century on more often and for different reasons. In

---

34 The original title of this scripture is *Monjushiri hōbōzō darani-kyō*, *T*, vol. 20, no. 1185; the current title was dictated by common usage over time.

35 The Japanese generic term used to refer to those emanations in *Butchō* (Sanskrit, Buddhoṣṇīsa, or Uṣṇīṣarāja). The *Shijōkō* emanation under discussion here is the object of the *Shijōkō daiitoku shōsai kichijō darani-kyō*, *T*, vol. 19, no. 963; and the *Daiitoku kinrin butchō shijōkō nyorai shōjo issai sainan darani-kyō*, more commonly called *Shōjosainan-gyō*, *T*, vol. 19, no. 964. The oldest extant ritual text, *Shijōkō dōjō nenju-gi*, *T*, vol. 46, no. 1951, was compiled by Fa-bao Ta-shi (946–1032).

905 the number of monks was changed from fourteen to forty, and in 911 the ritual was performed within the imperial palace after there had been an ominous occurrence involving a heron. A new accompanying scripture was given by a T'ang merchant to no less than Fujiwara no Tokihira (871–909). Because that ritual was shrouded in secrecy, it did not involve the establishment of a specific mandala; however, paintings representing the Buddha Shijōkō do exist.[36]

How did a ritual aimed at preventing natural calamities come to be associated with military threats to the court? People of the time believed that disturbances in the world of nature were advance warnings of impending military rebellions. This was not a specifically Buddhist phenomenon, for we read in the *Fudoki* that the rumbling and shaking of a mountain in Kyushu was thought to mean that an army was on the march.[37] In a similar vein, the cult dedicated to Nakatomi no Kamatari (the ancestor of the Fujiwara house) on Mount Tōnomine in the province of Yamato was partly based on ritual counteractions to tremors that shook the mountain or cracked Kamatari's statue.[38] In that case it was believed that the direction of the epicenter of the quake indicated specific realms of governance by the Fujiwara house. Thus, any sudden and frightening occurrence in the realm of nature was thought to be an omen concerning political affairs and the security of the imperial lineage. This was also part of the nature–culture dialectic that so profoundly impacted Heian culture and that was central to cults such as those which evolved in the Gion and Kitano multiplexes. This, then, was the main reason why the ritual of Shijōkō was performed for the protection of the state, in contradistinction to the ritual of Daigensui, which was geared toward military affairs from the outset.

Doctrinally, Ennin held the view that the esoteric tradition of Shingon was equal to the exoteric tradition of Tendai, and that theory and praxis were also equal. But his successor Enchin caused an important shift in the Tendai tradition by insisting that the esoteric tradition was superior and that praxis was far more important than theory. Thus, from Enchin's time on, esoteric practices and rituals became the chief concern of the Tendai tradition. This developed to such an extent, in fact, that Annen (b. 841?) claimed that Tendai es-

---

36 See, for instance, Hamada Takashi, *Zuzō* (Tokyo: Shibundō, 1969), p. 39, fig. 54.
37 *Hizen no kuni itsubun*, in Akimoto Kichirō, ed., *Fudoki* (Tokyo: Iwanami shoten, 1958), p. 515.
38 See Allan Grapard, "Japan's Ignored Cultural Revolution: the Separation of Shinto-Buddhist Divinities and a Case-study: Tōnomine," *History of Religions* 23, 3 (1984): 240–65.

otericism should be called Shingon. From that point on the court looked to the shrine-temple multiplexes it sponsored for Taimitsu and Tōmitsu rituals; by the tenth century it was also asking for help from thaumaturgists who had trained in mountains in order to gain supernatural forces and who were reputed for the efficacy of their rites and incantations. One began to see an increasing number of mountain ascetics (*yamabushi*) at court.

The privatization of ritual activity

The position of the emperor declined while the power of the Fujiwara house grew; by the tenth century, as government came under the control of Fujiwara regents, rituals that had been performed in the name of the emperor came to be requested by individual aristocrats for their own welfare. The government forbade, after the exile of Sugawara no Michizane in 901, the performance of such rituals for private purposes. But the practice resurfaced with increased vigor, in connection, perhaps, with the disintegration of the social system based on the statutes, and the emergence of private concern and individual competition within given lineages. This trend toward individualization of cultic and political concerns accelerated throughout the rest of the Heian era and was partly responsible for the acceptance of Pure Land beliefs. Indeed, most rites performed on a private basis by aristocrats in the second half of the Heian period concerned their private fate; eschatological concerns increased among the elite, and private temples that would take care of individuals after their death (*bodaiji*) were built at a fast pace. Other aristocrats, alienated by the growing power of the Fujiwara regency, performed rituals to solve public problems through private observances, while the leaders of the Fujiwara house sponsored extravagant renditions of the Pure Land in their private temples. This background, while providing a fertile soil for the development of Pure Land beliefs, fostered increased interest in magical and ritual practices that would protect the individual.[39]

Indeed, it came to be widely accepted that specific forces determined the fate of an individual, both from within and without as, for example, in astrology. Therefore, aristocrats paid great attention to the decimal and duodecimal signs corresponding to the date of their

---

[39] See a wide-ranging discussion of these issues in Miyai Yoshio, *Jōdai no shimbutsu shūgō to Jōdo-kyō* (Tokyo: Seikō shobō, 1980).

birth, and believed that by performing rites of devotion to planets and stars related to those signs, they might attract benefits of a this-worldly character (*genze riyaku*) and thus engineer a better existential situation. The study of those rites impresses upon the observer the centrality of systematic combinations between "Shinto," Buddhism, *yin-yang* philosophy and practices, and Taoism. All these aspects merged in a rather rigorous manner and in a vast coherence in which one can read the main concerns of the people of the time, but they also resulted in an impressive network of limitations and censorship of the body and mind, which came to be increasingly ritualized.

The most widely performed rituals at an individual level for the aristocrats were the *Fugen emmyō-hō*, dedicated to the bodhisattva Samantabhadra to request an enhanced longevity,[40] and the *Fudō-hō*, ritual of Acala, performed in a wide variety of contexts.[41] Tendai esotericism performed the Samantabhadra ritual in order to remove the fear of death; this ritual was originally reserved for the emperor (as a kind of *chinkonsai*) but, from 950 on, it was performed for aristocrats who were considered to represent the imperial state. Indeed, the first aristocrat for whom this ritual was performed was no less than Fujiwara no Morosuke, then chieftain of the Fujiwara house, whose Testamentary Admonitions were quoted at the beginning of this chapter.

The *Fudō-hō*, less complicated in scale, was even more widely appropriated by the nobility since it required less lengthy preparations. It seems that Fujiwara no Tokihira, Mototsune's son, was the first to request its performance to cure a personal disease, and then to ensure the safe birth of one of his children in 903.

Yet another rite of importance throughout the Heian period at the state level as well as at the personal level was the *Daiitoku-hō*, dedicated to the powerful and frightening Yamāntaka.[42] This important divinity of the esoteric pantheon, one of the "Five Powerful Ones" (*godairiki*) in a wrathful appearance (*funnu*), was a manifestation of the Bodhisattva of Wisdom, Mañjuśrī. Symbolized by the number six (it has six arms and six feet), it was conceived to be more powerful than Yama (Emma, in Japanese), the King of Hells.

40 This ritual was based on the *Kongō jumyō darani-kyō*, *T*, vol. 20, no. 1134 [b], and is described in the *Kongō jumyō darani-kyōhō*, *T*, vol. 20, no. 1134 [a].
41 There were several forms of Fudō rituals, variously emphasized in Shingon and Tendai lineages. The main texts on the topic are contained in *T*, vol. 21.
42 *Daiitoku-hō*. There are several texts describing varied rites dedicated to Daiitoku; of central importance are those contained in *T*, vol. 21, no. 1214 and no. 1216. See Robert Duquenne, "Daiitoku myōō," *Hōbōgirin* 6 (1983): 652–70.

In the esoteric tradition each of the Five Powerful Ones was thought to protect one of the five directions; Daiitoku protected the west, long considered to be a dangerous direction (the whole complex of Mount Atago, just west of the capital, had been erected to ward off evil from that direction). Hence, he came to be seen not only as the manifestation of Mañjuśrī but also of Amitābha/Amitāyus. Like all major deities of the esoteric pantheon, Daiitoku was represented in a mandala for ritual purposes, either in painting or sculpture, in which each iconographic detail was related to a doctrinal aspect and was therefore subjected to great attention. In terms of esoteric doctrine, the Buddha possessed five wisdoms conceived of under three aspects: Self-nature, symbolized by a buddha; Correct Law, symbolized by a bodhisattva; and Injunction, symbolized by a wrathful manifestation of either, and whose function was to forcefully inculcate the teachings to reticent beings, and to transform relative cognitions into a corresponding wisdom. Thus, the five wisdoms of the Buddha were symbolized by five buddhas, five bodhisattvas, and five wrathful manifestations, each corresponding to the other and represented in spatially oriented mandalas. This was propagated in scholastic milieus of Heian esoteric Buddhism by a new version of the apocryphal *Ninnō-kyō*, and by the ideology sustaining the protection of the state through rituals involving spatially oriented mandalas that came to represent the land under its control. The most common rite seems to have been that of fire oblation (*goma*) accomplished over a triangular altar (*abisharoka*), the summit of which was occupied by Daiitoku, and faced north. The officiant, dressed in black and positioned to the south, drew an image or inscribed on the ash at the bottom of the hearth the name of the agent to be vanquished by the ritual.

The most important texts describing those rituals date back to the end of the Heian period or the beginning of the Kamakura period. Documents of the time show that these rites were used for different purposes: to separate a wife from her husband so that she became available for the amorous ardor of a prince or emperor, or to cause two persons to fall in love. More generally, however, the Daiitoku rites were used to bring success in military endeavors.

The ritual world of shrines

A salient feature of the world of shrines during the Heian period was the reformulation and codification of ritual practices under the aegis of the government and the dominant sacerdotal lineages. This reformulation appears in the Procedures of the Jōgan Era (*Jōgan gishiki*) promulgated in 869–71, and in the Procedures of the Engi Era (*Engi shiki*), completed in 927 but promulgated in 967, which unified the preceding procedures. These documents indicate that the "worship of the *kami* of Heaven and Earth" was redefined during the Heian period according to specific notions held by the government. Indeed, although little information is available on ritual conduct before the Heian period, it is probable, and in some cases evident, that most of the rituals classified and determined in great detail in those Procedures were substantially different in the Nara period.

It must be noted that most shrines that came to be supported by the imperial state in Heian had been either maintained or built privately by the major social lineages and clans (*uji*), even though some (if not most) were subtle indicators of those lineages' claim to a privileged relationship to the imperial lineage and thereby to the state. What changed during the Heian period was that the government, even while recognizing the private character of those shrines, began to acknowledge them as its own symbols, and therefore made offerings of food and various products and in some cases set up government representatives to oversee the architectural development of shrines with funds given by the state. In the case of the Twenty-two Shrines, such as the Kasuga Shrine dedicated to the ancestral and tutelary *kami* of the Fujiwara house, the imperial lineage would send messengers at the time of major rites; these messengers were charged with reading a *supplique* in the name of the emperor to the *kami* and making predetermined offerings. The promulgation of these procedures coincided in time with the rapprochement of Buddhist temples to the newly enlarged shrines. Several hypotheses can be offered to interpret the meaning of those developments.

First, it is evident that those rules of the *Engi shiki* which concerned ritual and liturgy were applicable not only to the Department of Shrines but also to the conduct of ritual at court, and that they had a triple interrelated character: they attempted to determine expenditures (of money and offerings) in relation to certain practices inscribed in space (the protocol of ritual and alliances with the periphery), and in time (the determination of ritual performance according to seasonal rhythm and within a complex framework of control of time). Money, time, and space are therefore three of the fundamental categories from which ritual practices in shrines, temples, and at court, might be approached.

Second, the formulation of ritual conduct in the *Engi shiki* was parallel to the establishment of the system of Twenty-two Shrines described earlier in this chapter, and therefore represents a concerted effort to unify practices in shrines, but within the context of shrines and temples. While this formulation of ritual represents concerns of the government, it perhaps also expresses concern on the part of sacerdotal lineages worried by the wide acceptance of Buddhist ritual. One notes in those codes, for example, that Buddhist prelates were no longer allowed at enthronement rituals.

Third, the developments just outlined determined aspects of the relationships between the worlds of shrines and temples: clear demarcations prevented chaotic syncretism from occurring, and called instead for combinations whose elements retained some of their integrity. Had it been otherwise, it is probable that one discourse, grounded either in shrines or in temples, would have become dominant and would have reduced the other to a meaningless amorphousness. The discourse issued from temples attempted to be dominant, but it never succeeded in replacing the realm of the shrines, and even took second place in later periods. The world of combinations exhibited by shrine-temple multiplexes during the Heian period became a central part of the cultic world during the medieval period.

Yet another element must be mentioned at this point: the fact that the temples related to the Twenty-two Shrines were closely connected to the leading houses of the Heian period means that Buddhism was restrained and confined within those limits of sociopolitical order. In any other situation, freethinkers and heterodox figures would have taken Buddhism to other parts of Japanese society, with radically different messages – which is precisely what happened toward the end of the Heian period.

Expenditures, time, and space in ritual

Even a cursory reading of the *Engi shiki* impresses upon the reader the fundamental features of ritual in shrines during the Heian period: the performance of codified behavior on the part of a strictly defined social body within the confines of particular spatial arrangements at strictly defined times of the year, month, and day, and focusing on a specific relationship to a divine entity, expressed by purification and by various offerings among which the offering and sharing of food took precedence.

The literature of the Heian period is striking in the total absence of the word "Shinto." This does not mean that cultic aspects of what came later to be called Shinto were not a significant part of the cultic and political world of the times; it simply means that the cultic world of Heian was not conceived of according to the tentative distinctions made today on the basis of more recent history. What we find instead is a marked emphasis on sites of cult which were, for the duration of the period and beyond, a conglomerate of shrines and temples, and we also find an emphasis on the observance of protocol both at court and in those multiplexes. Thus, the first striking aspect of cultic life in Heian is its relation to place within the context of combinations between imported and autochthonous cultic systems, all subsumed under a sociopolitical ideology.

A second striking characteristic concerns the strict regulation of expenditures by the government at the time of ritual observances; this means that private houses were probably competing in prestige through outlays of wealth ranging from amounts of rice offerings to ceremonial clothing and horses. This competition, which had been brought under control by the stipulations of the *Engi shiki*, returned to the fore when the government began to cede land to centers of cult as a reward for success in rituals. Furthermore, since many of these land holdings were partly free from taxation, a number of people began to grant parts of their land to centers of cult for "spiritual protection," in order to avoid taxation. That land was granted to specific shrines and/or temples, not to "Shinto" or to "Buddhism." Hence, ritual came to be ever more connected to economics.

A third notable characteristic of ritual in Heian was the emphasis on hierarchy and code and on the observance of protocol. This emphasis can be understood from two related perspectives: a sociological concern and a concern with purity and pollution. One way to focus on the relation between these two concerns is to observe that many of the multiplexes of the Heian period were dedicated to ancestor worship and to the cult of ancestral *kami* (associated yet different phenomena). In the temples, ancestors were worshiped in part through the performance of rites of penitence which, as seen earlier, were for the most part rites of purification of the sense organs; and in the shrines, ancestral *kami* were worshiped in the context of a triple type of ritual purification (*ōharae*, ethical purification; *omisogi*, physical purification; and the use of special individuals related to the observance of taboo, *mono-imi*), all in the context of ritually prepared food offerings involving a high level of precautionary measures against any type of pollution. At the sociological level, it must be emphasized that many of those rituals were used to reinforce social bonds within clear contexts of time and space, and within frameworks of exclusion and inclusion: included were the social group whose personal *kami* were worshiped, as well as the social group charged with the governance of shrines and ritual observances before, during, and after the main rites. Excluded was any social group that, by definition, did not worship ancestors or ancestral *kami* of others. That is one of the reasons why cultic practices in Heian times were greatly hierarchized and related to specific places. In the case of the neighboring temples, although Buddhism was not geared toward the exclusion of any member of the social body (with the significant exception of the almost systematic exclusion of women), in fact the higher echelons of the priestly hierarchy came to be reserved for leading ecclesiasts born from those noble lineages which had dedicated or created the temples in the first place. Thus, principles of exclusion tended to remain important aspects of the social construct of "monastic" communities, ideology notwithstanding.

A fourth and final characteristic of cultic life in Heian was the emphasis on the performance of dances, songs, and music at the time of grand rites in shrines, and later in temples as well. Much of the culture of the Heian period was transmitted to the present day through the medium of those rites, which show that cult and culture were intrinsically related phenomena, and that both were related to performance and grounded in aesthetic concerns.[43]

DEALING WITH THE FORCES OF NATURE

*The Bureau of Yin and Yang (*Ommyōryō*)*

The Bureau of Yin and Yang was reorganized by promulgation of the Yōrō code in 718 by Fujiwara no Fuhito and others.[44] Although it was conceived on the model of its counterpart established by the T'ang dynasty, it was different in scope and partly different in structure. The Bureau was governed by a director under whom four ad-

---

43 For discussions of these issues, see Yamagami Izumo, *Nihon geinō no kigen* (Tokyo: Yamato shobō, 1977).
44 The following discussion is based in part on Murayama Shūichi, *Nihon ommyōdō-shi sōsetsu* (Tokyo: Hanawa shobō, 1981). The reader may also refer to Saitō Tsutomu, *Ōchō-jidai no ommyōdō* (Tokyo: Sōgensha, 1947), and Felicia Bock, *Classical Learning and Taoist Practices in Early Japan* (Center for Asian Studies Occasional Paper, Tucson: University of Arizona Press, 1985).

ministrators oversaw the activities of specialists in four major fields. The director himself was responsible for astronomy and the calendar, while he also observed and interpreted climatic phenomena. In the advent of any abnormalities (*i*) in the natural cycles, he reported secretly to the emperor. Under the four administrative aides to the director were six Masters of Yin and Yang (*ommyōji*) who specialized in divination (*uranai*) and in geomancy (*fūsui*). The four major fields of investigation were, in descending order of importance: Yin and Yang, Calendar, Astronomy, and Time. Each of these fields was under the supervision of a scholar (*hakase*), who taught his skills to ten students in each of the first three fields, while two scholars taught twenty students in the field of time measurement. These two scholars were helped by twenty-three assistants who, in all probability, worked in shifts. Murayama Shūichi notes that by the year 720 the Bureau of Yin and Yang employed a total of eighty-nine officers instructed by four scholars who were all either of Chinese or Korean origin, and who were all in their fifties. By comparison, the same bureau in China employed a grand total of 1,413 people whose functions were roughly divided between astronomy and the calendar on the one hand, and divination on the other. The preeminence of these fields was reversed in Japan. A final distinction between the Chinese and Japanese systems must be added: divination by turtle shell was not assigned to the Bureau of Yin and Yang in Japan, but to the Department of Shrines, where it was performed by the Nakatomi and Urabe sacerdotal lineages.

Many of the practices related to *yin* and *yang* were of Taoist origin and were associated with medicine. The Chinese organs of government included an office of medicine, part of which specialized in the "magical" cure of disease; the same was true of Japan in the Nara period, for there was a Bureau of Medicine, parts of which were staffed by one *hakase* ("doctor"), two masters, and six disciples, all specializing in exorcism. The Bureau continued to exist during the early Heian period, but did not develop because of the combined influences of Esoteric Buddhism (within which there evolved specific practices of medicine related to magic and exorcism), and of the "Way of Lodgings and Planetoids" (*Sukuyōdō*) and mountain asceticism (Shugendō), in which various strains of *yin* and *yang* practices and notions (*ommyōdō*) evolved. Furthermore, the exorcists of the Bureau of Medicine were originally almost all of foreign descent (*kikajin*): Hirotari, the infamous disciple of En no Gyōja (the putative founder of Shugendō), was of Korean origin and a member of that Bureau.

The Nara aristocracy and common people were a fertile ground for the growth of magical practices; the government issued several decrees prohibiting them during the course of the eighth century. It is possible that the use of magic was thought by the authorities to be potentially nefarious to the ideals of the state if it was engaged in by enemies of the state; for example, the case of the Buddhist prelate Dōkyō, whose claim to the throne during the Nara period was based on his access to oracles from Hachiman, suggests that some ritual activities were viewed as potent forces acting on the symbols upon which the state rested. Another reason to prohibit such practices was medicine: the government claimed that magic "treatment" was ineffective and led people astray with false hopes. By and large, however, the treatment of disease remained the favorite domain of mountain anchorites (*yamabushi*), and other thaumaturgists.

The case might be offered that Buddhism presented itself as a social body mainly interested in doctrinal exchange within the institutional context of a school of thought. But reality was otherwise, for there was a need for dialectical exchange between society and the monastic community; in this exchange, lay society was concerned more with magic and cure of disease than it was with metaphysical speculation, and the monastic community did need some popular support in order to attract the masses to its teachings. And so it was that Buddhist monks, especially those who had been to China, used magic and charms for a variety of purposes ranging from curing disease to fighting off zealous government officials checking on their credentials. But, all in all, the main interest of the people and of the court was the cure of disease; this remained a central element of many cults throughout history.

In yet another realm of practical concern, Buddhists used geomantic knowledge acquired in China to decide on sites for the construction of temples, or used their knowledge of astronomy and astrology to determine the proper placement of the body of ecclesiasts and aristocrats in space and time. Many practices related to those issues were not looked upon favorably by the authorities, perhaps because some of them were too closely related to Taoist notions the government did not condone. This was true also of rites related to the Polar Star, which focused on Ursa Major; these rites in China had long involved sexual promiscuity. The government prohibited sacrifices of bulls in rites dedicated to fertility. But some prohibitions were ineffective, and many rites were soon coopted by Esoteric Buddhism, which developed combinations between the Polar Star cult and a cult to the bodhisattva called in Japanese Myōken, or Sonshō-ō. The main scripture on which this ritual was based was the *Hokuto shichishō emmyō-kyō*, which promised accrued longevity to those who requested its performance.[45] Yet another example of Taoist practices which developed in Esoteric Buddhism is the *Kōshin* belief, also related to longevity, which involved spending a sleepless night every sixty days on the day of the Monkey in order to prevent demonic inhabitants of the body from leaving it to report to the heavenly bureaucracy on one's evil deeds. The name of the divinity in Esoteric Buddhism was *Shōmen kongō*. The cult developed in Tendai esoteric circles and quickly spread to the populace. (It is still extant today.)[46]

Practices based on *yin* and *yang* notions infiltrated the ritual world of shrines as well, particularly in the evolution of practices of purification. The Nakatomi, Urabe, Abe, and Kamo sacerdotal lineages were responsible for these rituals intended to protect the body, the imperial city, and the country against epidemics. An excellent example is provided by the *michi-ae* rites, of which we have some record in the *Engi shiki*.[47] These rites were performed at crossroads and at the various entrances to the capital at the time of epidemics, but in particular also at the time of the approach of foreign missions. This can be explained by the belief that disease came from afar along various paths, and that visitors from foreign countries were apt to bring it, as history amply demonstrated. These *michi-ae* rites consisted of offering food and of formulating incantations, probably of Chinese origin. In this manner a large number of notions, concepts, and practices belonging to the world of *yin* and *yang* in China found their way into Buddhism and into the ritual world of shrines.

For reasons that are yet to be determined, the early Heian government did not support the activities of the Bureau of Yin and Yang; it was disbanded in 820. Instead, the government relied on both Shingon and Tendai traditions of esotericism to perform a number of rites that in earlier years would have been the domain of the *ommyōryō*. At the time of the Jōwa Incident of 842, in which the Fujiwara house began to assert its centrality in decisions concerning the choice of emperors, the government requested the performance of rituals by one hundred Buddhist monks within the imperial

---

45 *Hokuto shichishō emmyō-kyō, T,* vol. 21, no. 1307.
46 On this topic, see Hirano Minoru, *Kōshin shinkō* (Tokyo: Kadokawa shoten, 1969). See also Tsubo Noritada: *Kōshin shinkō* (Tokyo: Yamakawa, 1956), and *Kōshin shinkō no kenkyū* (Tokyo: Nihon Gakujutsu shinkōkai, 1961).
47 See Felicia Bock, *Engi-shiki*, vol. 1, p. 86, and vol. 2, pp. 90–92.

palace, and asked them to read the Sutra of the Buddha of Medicine, to perform rites dedicated to that Buddha, and further requested readings of the *Daihannya-kyō* within the imperial palace. The Jōwa Incident was the first in a series of coups engineered over a period of one hundred years by the Fujiwara house to ensure that emperors were chosen exclusively among children born of a union between a reigning emperor and a woman of Fujiwara birth; this enabled the Fujiwara ministers to govern in the name of their grandchildren and thus control the imperial lineage. Cultic activity was an essential feature of their claims to legitimacy in that context.

The frequency with which both ominous and auspicious natural events occurred during the Heian period indicates most clearly the mood of the times. From Emperor Heizei (r. 806–9) to Emperor Go-Sanjō (r. 1068–73), as many as 1,686 natural occurrences of an ominous nature were officially recorded: 653 earthquakes, 134 fires, 89 instances of damage to the crops, 91 outbreaks of epidemics, 356 calamitous occurrences of a heavenly nature (volcanic eruptions, comets, eclipses, thunder in clear skies), and 367 ghostly events. In contradistinction, the same documents record a grand total of only 185 auspicious occurrences during the same period. The reign of Emperor Yōzei (876–84) seems to have been plagued by the largest number of calamities (as many as 133 in the course of seven years), and to have been visited by the largest number of auspicious signs as well: as many as 31, the largest number for any single reign. This period corresponds exactly to the rise to ascendancy of the Fujiwara house and to the regency of Fujiwara no Mototsune, a fact which reveals that political worries in Heian Japan were as if symbolically manifested in an increased consciousness of the course of nature in relation to human affairs, well within the framework of the nature–culture dialectic mentioned earlier in this discussion. The notable increase in records of natural occurrences interpreted as heavenly warnings or blessings is related to the evolution of the *goryō* belief system (discussed later), and might be viewed as a manifestation of popular criticism of governmental policies and of the internecine struggles that took place within the aristocracy. It was just a few years after the reign of Emperor Yōzei that the exile of Sugawara no Michizane caused the people to interpret fires in the imperial palace as heavenly reprimands by the angry spirit of the wronged statesman.

In other words, when the government began to applaud the miraculous appearance of a white turtle in 715, 724, and 770, and interpreted it to be a manifestation of heavenly pleasure with its rule, little did it know that a few years later the reasoning would be reversed, and that people would pay great attention to ominous occurrences in order to criticize the government.[48] In both cases, the court turned to liturgical and ritual behavior: when an auspicious sign appeared, emissaries were sent to make announcements to the major shrine-temple multiplexes of the realm and to as many as twelve imperial mausolea; and when ominous signs appeared, rituals to placate the wrath of cosmic powers were requested from the same multiplexes. This may have been one reason why thaumaturgists came to play a role in Fujiwara politics, and it shows that policy making was rarely if ever separated from cultic concerns: the more unstable the political world, the more active the multiplexes. As time passed and political concerns grew, ritual activity increased accordingly at all levels of society, and cultic procedure became complex and cumbersome. Such was the price to pay for grounding a rule in symbol and rite.

The reformulation of ritual and liturgy exemplified in the *Jōgan gishiki* and in the *Engi shiki* compilations marked a definite impact of *yin* and *yang* practices on ritual procedures within the world of shrines and temples. Precisely at the same time, the practices of directional taboos originated,[49] concurrently with the practice of devotional respect to the four directions (*shihōhai*), which was performed by the emperor for the first time in 860.[50]

The practices related to directional taboos (*kata-imi*) concerned travel or, in other words, movements of the human body through space. It was thought that certain celestial forces and bodies, whose movement was carefully followed, determined spatial zones that should not be crossed by people at certain times and in certain directions. Thus, when aristocrats planned to travel (or build a house, or break the earth for other purposes), they consulted specialists who determined whether the time and space correlations were favorable or ominous. Such restrictions on the movement of the body came to be so pervasive that palliative measures were devised, to which the name of "directional alternatives" (*kata-tagae*) was given.

---

48 Murayama Shūichi, *Nihon ommyōdō-shi sōsetsu*, pp. 50–69.
49 See Bernard Frank, *Kata-imi et kata-tagae: Etude sur les interdits de direction à l'époque Heian*, Bulletin de la Maison Franco-Japonaise, Nouvelle Série, Tome 5, 2–4 (Tokyo and Paris, 1958).
50 See Fukuyama Toshio, *Chūsei no jinja kenchiku* (Tokyo: Shibundō, 1977), pp. 95–96: "Chūseijin no shinkō to jinja," in which the author discusses the history and conduct of the *shihōhai* ritual.

This involved moving for one day in a direction other than planned, spending the night there, and reaching one's intended destination the following day. As time passed, aristocrats transformed these cumbersome practices into a kind of game that involved plans to spend a night at the home of some relative or acquaintance in order to be entertained. The system gradually degenerated and was more or less abandoned toward the end of the Heian period. However, the notion of the body as a cosmic entity submitted to powers in space and time remained of importance in various Japanese cultic traditions, and a number of practices associated with the *kata-imi* phenomenon have survived up to the present.

Celestial irregularities

The world of *yin* and *yang* beliefs and practices evolved as part and parcel of Chinese studies during the Nara and Heian periods and centered on the definition of the position of man within the cosmos. It provided a framework of interpretation according to which the natural world was thought to impact the destiny of man, and, conversely, according to which human activity was thought to impact the processes of nature. In other words, man was thought to be an agent of cosmic (but not historical) change, at the same time he was considered to be under strong cosmic influences, as is evidenced in astrology. A primary aspect of those beliefs and attitudes is found in the *Sukuyōdō*, "Way of Lodgings and Planetoids," a complex system resulting from a crossing of astronomy with astrology that had occurred in India, but that had been enriched in China before it reached Japan.[51] Almost all Indian science reaching Japan was brought by Buddhist monks, so that astronomy became a primarily Buddhist matter. Monks were not only specialists of metaphysics and philosophy, they also tended to be healers, thaumaturgists, diviners, and astrologers. During the Heian period almost all astronomy and astrology developments that had taken place in various milieus in China were transmitted to Japan by monks of Shingon and Tendai Esoteric Buddhism, so that that form of Buddhism was heavily laden with notions and rituals that belonged originally either to

---

51 Little has been published on the topic of *Sukuyōdō*. There is a popular treatment of the subject by Yoshida Mitsukuni, *Hoshi no shūkyō* (Kyoto: Tankōsha, 1970). A more detailed analysis of the topic in direct reference to esotericism is provided by Manabe Shunshō, *Kobijutsu*, 35 (1971): 1–48. Other indications can be found in Murayama, *Nihon ommyōdō-shi sōsetsu*, and Hayami, *Heian jidai kizoku-shakai to bukkyō*.

Indian ritual science or to Chinese Taoist and other practices. The Japanese did not use the term "Taoism"; instead, Taoist practices became part and parcel of the praxis of Esoteric Buddhism and Shugendō, and of the ritual world of shrines.[52] This is evident in the history of the practice of astrology and related matters such as the system of beliefs surrounding epidemics, the realms of combinations between shrine and temple deities, and the cults to vengeful spirits and ghosts.

From about the middle of the ninth century documents indicate a formidable interest in astrology on the part of the government and aristocrats. Official documents also indicate an alarming increase of strange movements on the part of planets and constellations. Such occurrences were seen as signs of impending calamities at the level of the state; rituals to counteract these events were therefore in great demand and were proposed mostly by the Tendai and Shingon lineages. First, changes of era names were used to deflect those celestial threats.

It was thought that the name of a year era (*nengō*) was closely associated with the character of life during that era. If a catastrophic event occurred, one of the ways of dealing with it was symbolic and entailed changing the name of the era. There were two types of changes: the first one was positive and occurred when favorable portents appeared in the world of nature; the other was negative and occurred whenever a foreboding calamity took place. The latter case of name change was a protective or defensive measure aimed at appeasing the worries of the leading politicians, while reinforcing their notion that the power of naming was effective. The rituals protected the state, which means that they kept the Fujiwara regents in control; but it also meant that the thaumaturgists in some way con-

---

52 On the place of Taoism in Japan, see Murayama, *Nihon ommyōdō-shi sōsetsu;* Saitō, *Ochōjidai no ommyōdō;* Shimode Sekiyo, *Dōkyō to Nihonjin* (Tokyo: Kōdansha, 1975); Fukunaga Mitsuji, *Dōkyō to Nihon bunka* (Kyoto: Jimbun shoin, 1982); Shimode Sekiyo, *Nihon kodai no jingi to Dōkyō* (Tokyo: Yoshikawa kōbunkan, 1972); Fukunaga Mitsuji et al., eds., *Dōkyō to kodai no tennōsei* (Tokyo: Tokuma, 1978); and Felicia Bock, *Classical Learning and Taoist Practices in Early Japan*. The reader may also refer to Osabe Kazuo, *Ichigyō zenji no kenkyū* (Kobe: Kōbe Shōka Daigaku, 1963).

On the topic of Shugendō, see Murayama Shūichi, *Yamabushi no rekishi* (Tokyo: Hanawa, 1970); Wakamori Tarō, *Shugendō-shi kenkyū* (Tokyo: Tōyō bunko, 1972); and Wakamori Tarō et al., eds., *Sangaku shūkyō-shi kenkyū sōsho*, 18 vols. (Tokyo: Meicho shuppan, 1977). See also Gaston Renondeau, *Le Shugendō: Histoire, Doctrines et Rites des Anachorètes Dits Yamabushi* (Paris: Imprimerie Nationale, 1965); Hartmut O. Rotermund, *Die Yamabushi: Aspekte Ihres Glaubens, Lebens und Ihrer Sozialen Funktion im Japanischen Mittelalter* (Hamburg: Kommissionsverlag Cram, De Gruyter, 1968); and Byron Earhart, *A Religious Study of the Haguro Sect of Shugendō* (Tokyo: Sophia University, 1970).

trolled the aristocrats. These changes in names of eras went hand in hand with the performance of rituals such as the *Daigen(sui)-hō*, the *Daiitoku-hō*, the *Shitennō-hō*, the *Shijōkō-hō*, the *Kujaku-ō-hō*, and the *Shōu-kyō-hō*, in which Shingon and Tendai thaumaturgists competed for rewards. The competition was fierce and the claims of success important, for success meant the granting of land, limelight for the ritualists, and the attention of the court. The stakes grew throughout the Heian period, especially as political and military unrest shook the provinces and moved closer to the capital. Aristocrats responded to an upheaval not only by sending militias to quell it, but also by asking the multiplexes to perform rituals to ensure the victory of the court and pray for an end to such upheavals. The *Engi shiki* states that the *Daigen(sui)-hō* must be performed every year during the second week of the first month, "to protect from armed upheavals." This was the case at the time of the rebellion of Taira no Masakado in 939.[53] In 941, the *Daiitoku-hō* was performed by Gikai (the abbot of Tendai) on Mount Hiei when it was learned that Korean pirates were sighted off Kyushu; at the same time, the *ajari* Enshō performed the *Fudō-hō* at the Hosshōji, one of the great Fujiwara temples in Kyoto. Some of those rites bear traces of *yin* and *yang* practices; all involved some combined aspects of Buddhist, Taoist, or "native" rituals.

An early response to celestial irregularities had been the reading of scriptures, which was the main original palliative in Japan. From the tenth century onward, thaumaturgists were most sought after. They performed what is known as *tenku* (service dedicated to the *devas*), or *seiku* (*shōku*, service for the stars). Such rites were not held exclusively for the welfare of the state, since the scriptures on which they were based (the *Kujaku-kyō* and *Hokuto shichishō emmyō-kyō*) recommended that these rites be performed on a personal basis as well.

Among the many stellar rituals, by far the most popular throughout East Asia were those dedicated to the Polar Star. Called in Japanese *hokuto*, Ursa Major was the focus of rites that the government prohibited as early as 796 for various reasons. But these rites came again to the fore during the Heian period, so much so that almost all aristocrats performed them at one time or another. The first performance of a major stellar ritual for the state on the part of Buddhist prelates was by Gikai in 945, at the time of the passage of a comet. Such rites were performed regularly thereafter upon the pas-

---

53 Murayama Shūichi, *Nihon ommyōdō-shi sōsetsu*, pp. 102–10.

sage of comets or the determination of eclipses, and with increasing frequency during the eleventh century.

Another major practice of Buddhist prelates and, thereafter, of the nobility, was related to what is called *hommyōshō*. The term *hommyō* (Chinese: *p'eng-ming*, meaning personal fate) was drawn from Taoist terminology and was assimilated by Buddhism in China before being introduced to Japan sometime during the early Heian period, where it designated the notion that certain celestial bodies (*shō*) held sway over the destiny of individuals. There was some question as to exactly what was to be designated as the *hommyō* celestial body of a person, and whether some days were to be considered as times when specific rites should be performed. There was also some question as to whether it was to be determined in relation to the decimal and duodecimal signs of the day of birth or of the year of birth. Originally, the observance of such rites was limited to the emperor, but it spread to all parts of society. Minamoto Counselors argued in 943 against the observance of the *hommyō* rite by the emperor, but were overruled by Fujiwara no Yoshifusa. Discussions concerning the day or the year of birth as a deciding factor for the identification of the *hommyōshō* took place in 961: on the side of the day of birth was the monk Hōzō, and on the side of the year was the *yin-yang* specialist Kamo no Yasunori. The decision to follow Kamo no Yasunori's theory was taken by Nichizō, the famous Yoshino thaumaturgist. Which celestial body could be chosen as *hommyōshō* was based upon a document entitled *Zokushō hihō*, written by Yi-hsing, in which it was stipulated that the decimal and duodecimal signs of the time of birth were to be inscribed on a diagram representing the five planets: Mars, Mercury, Jupiter, Venus, and Saturn. However, from the time of Ninkai (953–1046) on, the planets were abandoned and replaced by the seven stars composing Ursa Major, which were thought to be hypostatic forms of the planets. Thus, the rites connected to one's "planet" consisted in worshiping one of the stars of Ursa Major on one's birthday. Such practices became quite popular and continued in cultic circles for centuries.

Upon the occurrence of a baleful sign (*yō*), the Masters of Yin and Yang (*ommyōji*) decreed a number of taboos, restrictions, and restraints (*kinki*). Baleful signs came to be seen in each and every aspect of life; for instance, after a fire destroyed a large part of Kyoto, wearing red clothes was forbidden. From 960 onward, the Masters of Yin and Yang began to perform rites to placate calamitous forces; these were known as *kasai matsuri*, "calamity rites," and were related to the fire that had engulfed the imperial palace that year for the first time since the creation of the capital. This fire caused great anxiety among the aristocracy, and the government ordered that offerings be made immediately to Ise and other shrines, and that the fire be reported to the mausolea of emperors Tenji, Kammu, and Daigo. The following year the first *kasai matsuri* was held within the compounds of the imperial palace. Although we do not have detailed information on the conduct of the rite, documents left by the Abe sacerdotal lineage indicate that the pillars of various buildings of the imperial palace were decorated with swords on which inscriptions were engraved. These inscriptions show that Taoism was an aspect of the protection of imperial buildings in Heian Japan. Some of the swords had been offered by Korea: one was called "sword to protect from enemies," and another was called "sword to protect the body." These swords were inscribed with the symbols of the three kings and five emperors of China, with the Polar Star of the south, emblems of the dragon, magic charms used by the guardians of Hsi-wang Mu (all these on the left side of the sword), while the right side of the sword bore inscriptions of the five stars of the north pole, the seven stars of Ursa Major, emblems of the tiger, and magic charms "of Lao-tzu" to vanquish enemies. To these were added inscriptions asking for protection from the four directional emblems and for the realization of all wishes, protection from calamities, and achievement of longevity. The document of Abe no Haruaki (Abe no Seimei) written for the occasion indicates that these inscriptions had disappeared in the fire, and that new swords bearing them ought to be ordered. A further notice indicates that these swords were to be made on the auspicious day of the Monkey, in typical Taoist fashion: swords made on those days were more potent than others.

Thus we realize that within the imperial palace alone absolutely all available forms of cultic practice were used: *yin* and *yang* practices, Taoism, "Shinto" rituals colored by Korean shamanism, and the entire panoply of rituals offered by the Taimitsu and Tōmitsu forms of Esoteric Buddhism, be they performed by the main leaders of various branches of Tendai and Shingon or by powerful thaumaturgists who had gained their supernatural powers in the wilderness of mountains.

Some of these ritual forms were also present among the general populace, and may even have originated there and gradually pervaded aristocratic consciousness, as is suggested by an analysis of oracular practice.

Oracular practice

Oracular practice was certainly one of the prevalent aspects of cultic life during the Nara period, but it took on even more importance during the Heian period at all levels of society. Entire cults that developed in some of the Twenty-two Shrine-temple multiplexes described earlier, such as the Hachiman, Kitano, and Gion cults, rested upon the practice of asking specific deities for their will, by divination, or of being granted an oracle (*takusen*) in which the deity gave its indications. The Urabe sacerdotal lineage specialized in plastromancy (divination on sea turtle shells), while the Nakatomi sacerdotal lineage specialized in scapulimancy (divination on deer shoulder blades); both types of divination were regularly performed in specific shrines, usually by request, and the results were transmitted to the emperor.

Oracular practice during the Heian period can be classified as three types: the *jingūji* phenomenon discussed earlier in this chapter, in which oracles played a central part, the *goryō* phenomenon, and the *onryō* phenomenon. The most important *jingūji* in this respect was the Mirokuji of the Usa Hachiman Shrine in Kyushu; the Hachiman cult originated as an oracular cult in which female officiants, under possession, uttered sounds that were then interpreted by a male officiant called *saniwa*. The Hachiman cult may have been in the early eighth century no more than a local oracular cult, but it came to the attention of the court in 764, when the Hossō monk Dōkyō claimed that an Usa Hachiman oracle stipulated that he should become *hōō*, "*dharma*-king," of Japan. Shocked by the announcement, the court sent one of its representatives, Wake no Kiyomaro, to Usa, where he received an oracle declaring that Dōkyō was an impostor and that only members of the imperial lineage were entitled to rule the realm. Dōkyō was subsequently exiled, and Hachiman was enshrined in the Tamuke Hachiman Shrine as the *chinju* (protector) of the Tōdaiji imperial temple in Nara. A few years later, Hachiman came to be regarded as an incarnation of "Emperor" Ōjin, and his cult was sponsored directly by the state; indeed, a major multiplex dedicated to Hachiman was erected in 859 at Iwashimizu, south of Heian-kyō, in honor of Emperor Seiwa's enthronement. Hachiman, however, was conceived of as a bodhisattva, not as a *kami*, and this might explain why after the year 839 oracles were revealed, not to female officiants of Hachiman shrines as they used to be, but to male Buddhist monks who gradually took over their oracular functions. The Hachiman oracles became in the fourteenth century the object of a compilation and interpretation by Jin'un, a Buddhist prelate born in an Usa Shrine sacerdotal house, that is, the *Hachiman Usa-gū gotakusenshū,* "Compendium of Usa Hachiman Oracles," one of the most important medieval documents of the Hachiman cult and a key source for understanding oracular practice.[54] Oracular practice thus survived predominantly among Buddhist prelates, but also among some women who tended to be wives of *yamabushi.*

The goryō *and* onryō *cultic systems*

The term *goryō* originally denoted the spirit of a departed person, but it came to be applied to the notion that either the spirit of departed aristocrats forced into unjust and politically motivated death, or some cosmic power, were responsible for epidemics. The most famous case of a *goryō* was at the basis of a complex cult which originated under the name of *Gozu tennō* ("Bull-headed king of the *devas*") at the Gion shrine-temple multiplex in 876. Festive rituals aimed at pacifying those disruptive forces took place generally in summer, a season in which epidemics were prone to occur. These rituals were performed during daytime, in contrast to spring and autumn rituals which tended to be performed at night. They became popular especially in the major cities, and included prominently the performance of popular dances, the formation of impressive processions in which floats were lavishly decorated, and the performance of popular songs and music, as early as the year 1013 in the case of the famous Gion Festival of Kyoto.[55]

Another type of cult that developed at about the same time was known as *onryō* ("wrathful spirit"). It concerned the spirit of an aristocrat forced to an unjust death that remained unpacified and resided in limbo, whence it manifested its wrath (*tatari*) in the form of disease, earthquakes, droughts, and the like. This belief originated during the Nara period around several cases mentioned below, and culminated in the cult dedicated to the wrathful spirit of Sugawara no Michizane. The main distinction between the two cults is that an *onryō* is always the vengeful spirit of a deceased person, whereas a

---

54 See Shigematsu Akihisa, *Hachiman Usa-gū gotakusen-shū* (Tokyo: Gendai Shichōsha, 1986); see also Nakano, *Usa-gū;* Kagawa Mitsuo and Fujita Seiichi, eds., *Usa* (Tokyo: Mokujisha, 1976).
55 Shibata Minoru, *Chūsei shomin shinkō no kenkyū* (Tokyo: Kadokawa, 1966). On the Gion cult, see Yoneyama Toshinao, *Dokyumento Gion matsuri – toshi to matsuri to minshū to* (Tokyo: NHK bukkusu, 1986).

goryō may be a force of another nature. The *onryō* phenomenon was accompanied by the belief that spirits could be pacified even after the death of the person: rituals of exorcism (*chōbuku-hō*, literally, "rite to control and vanquish") manipulated and pacified spirits that were forced by the power of their passion to remain in limbo and were thus prevented from what might be an almost mechanical rebirth into any of the six destinations provided for in classical Buddhist cosmology. The thaumaturgists dealing with these spirits were regarded with awe, for they had firsthand knowledge of the realms of death gained through their austerities in mountains and even through their cataleptic experiences of hell described in various texts of the Heian period.

The main *onryō* cults originated with the case of Imperial Prince Nagaya in 729, and developed thereafter for Fujiwara no Hirotsugu in 740, and Imperial Prince Sawara ("Emperor" Sudō) in 785. During the Heian period, there were the cases of Imperial Prince Iyo in 807, Tachibana no Hayanari in 842, and finally of Sugawara no Michizane in 903.

Sugawara no Michizane: the Kitano cult

The spirit of Sugawara no Michizane became the most famous and important in the entire tradition of wrathful spirits. It became the object of a major cult that left a remarkable imprint on Japanese culture.[56]

Sugawara no Michizane (845–903), who came to hold the position of Minister of the Right, was regarded by Fujiwara leaders as a major threat to their monopoly of power. To discredit him, they accused him of plotting against the throne. He was swiftly exiled to Kyushu, where he died two years later, in 903. One of his attendants established an altar in 905 near his gravesite, which was transformed into the Anrakuji in 919 by Fujiwara no Tokihira's cadet, Nakahira; this shrine-temple multiplex came to be governed by members of the Sugawara lineage. The men who had falsely accused the statesman of wrongdoing died in sudden or mysterious circumstances in the years after Michizane's death: Tokihira died in 909; his nephew Ya-

---

[56] On the topic of the *goryō* and *onryō* phenomena, see Murayama Shūichi, *Honji suijaku* (Tokyo: Yoshikawa Kōbunkan, 1974); Kuroda Toshio, "Chinkon no keifu," in Kuroda Toshio, *Nihon chūsei shakai to shūkyō* (Tokyo: Iwanami shoten, 1990), pp. 127–56. On the deification of Sugawara no Michizane, see Robert Borgen, *Sugawara no Michizane and the Early Heian Court* (Cambridge, Mass.: Harvard University Press, 1986), pp. 307–36.

suakira, who had been made crown prince, died in his youth in 923. At this point the court pardoned Michizane, struck from the record the decree of exile, and reinstated him to his rank and position, hoping to quell his wrath. But matters continued to worsen; in 930 a lightning bolt struck the imperial palace and killed the man who had reported Michizane's "admission of guilt" and three other members of the court. Emperor Daigo became despondent over the string of crises and died. By that time, the vengeful spirit of Michizane had assumed the divinized form of lightning, a fact that precipitated the popularization of the cult because of the thunder-lightning cults that had been a part of ancient agricultural practices. The thaumaturgist Nichizō claimed in 941 that, after falling into catalepsy, he had visited the hells and encountered there the spirit of Michizane surrounded by thousands of irate demons claiming vengeance. Michizane would have then told Nichizō that, if his spirit was given a proper cult, he would protect the state. In that document Michizane was said to have called himself *Nihon Dajō Itoku-ten*, a name that might indicate an association of Daiitoku (Yamāntaka, discussed earlier) and *daijō-daijin* (Chancellor).[57] This must be linked with the fact that Daiitoku used the bull as his mount and with the popular rites of propitiation of rain and lightning in which bulls were sacrificed. Indeed, the spirit of Michizane came to be associated with the bull.

Furthermore, in 942 a woman of lower extraction claimed to have been possessed by the spirit of Michizane; in the oracle she uttered, the vengeful spirit requested the erection of a shrine; that is the Ayako Temmangū located in the southern part of the capital. The woman was Tajihi no Ayako, whose forebears were known for their worship of thunder. In 946 a certain Miwa no Tarōmaru, then only seven years old and born in the sacerdotal house of the Hira Shrine, was also possessed by Michizane's spirit and rendered an oracle that has been recorded in full, in which Michizane requested the transfer of the shrine. The next year a new shrine-temple was dedicated to Michizane's spirit on a site that had been used for the propitiation of the *kami* of Heaven and Earth; that is the Kitano "Shrine," located on what was then the northern edge of the capital. In that multiplex, and in the Anrakuji of Dazaifu, Michizane came to be worshiped under the name Temman Daijizai Tenjin, a compound in which the term Daijizai must be associated with Daijizaiten, the

---

57 See Iyanaga Nobumi, "Daijizaiten," *Hōbōgirin* 6 (1983): 713–65.

Maheśvara (Supreme Lord) which plays an important role in the Buddhist pantheon and which is also associated with the bull.

Finally, there must be a relation between that name and the cult that was dedicated to Shidara in the middle of the tenth century, a cult so popular that thousands of people participated in it, carrying portable shrines in which one of the deities was named Ayae Jizai Tenjin.[58]

By 987 the Kitano shrine-temple multiplex came under the control of the court and Mount Hiei. Leading thaumaturgists of the time performed rituals of exorcism and attempted to bring peace to the spirit and to the political realm. It is possible that the sudden growth of this cult indicates moral concerns on the part of the aristocracy as well as political consciousness on the part of the populace of Kyoto; there is little doubt that the thaumaturgists responsible for the institutionalization of the cult were mediators between these two classes of interest, because what needed to be pacified were not only the spirit of Michizane but also the worries of the aristocrats and the fears of the populace as well. The aristocratic pangs of conscience, if there were any, might have been laid to rest by individualized ritual, but the fears of the populace were less easy to quell because they were multifaceted: they arose from the belief that the natural world was ethically reactive to human behavior, as well as from what might have been a kind of obscure suspicion that the political manipulations of the court were not in accord with its stated ideology. Because overt criticism of politics on the part of the general populace was not possible, only cultic behavior provided an outlet for political and, therefore, ritual concerns. The Shidara cult, the early stages of the Kitano cult, and other structurally related cults are good examples of such symbolic action whereby some sense of popular participation was achieved.

It is often said that the Shidara cult is popular in nature; but its roots are continental and it is not clear how this type of cult came to exercise such a fascination among the less educated. It might be appropriate to suggest that this type of cult is related to one of the frameworks of interpretation of the existential situation that marked the Heian period and that has been mentioned earlier, namely, the dialectic between nature and culture. This dialectic surrounds notions according to which human ethical behavior is an agent of cosmic change. Born in China among communities that were critical of

---

[58] In reference to the Shidara cult, see Murayama Shūichi, *Honji suijaku,* chap. 8.

imperial rule, these notions were carried to Japan and in time interacted with notions held by the common people, according to which natural disasters were caused by forces that came to be linked to the vengeful spirits of wronged statesmen. These forces therefore needed to be propitiated in such manner that the political manipulators responsible for unjust deaths be punished so that the natural world might return to its ideal smooth rhythm.

A document from China and its interpretation by Joseph Needham offer insight into the nature of the problematic. The first-century skeptic philosopher Wang Ch'ung wrote diatribes against what he called the "phenomenalists," in which he says:

Ceremonies originate from want of loyalty and good faith, and were the beginning of confusion. On this score people find fault with one another, which leads to mutual reproof (of superiors and inferiors). At the time of the Three Rulers people sat down informally (without attending to precedence) and walked about at their ease. They worked themselves instead of using horses and oxen. Simple virtue was the order of the day, and the people were unsophisticated and ignorant (of social distinctions). Minds acquainted with "knowledge" and "cleverness" had not then developed. Originally there were no calamities or omens, or if there were, they were not considered as reprimands (from Heaven). Why? Because at that time people were simple and unsophisticated, and did not restrain or reproach one another. Later ages have gradually declined – superiors and inferiors contradict one another, and calamities and omens constantly occur. Hence the hypothesis of reprimands from Heaven has been invented.

Wang Ch'ung offered us a clue when he stated, at the peak of his attacks against the phenomenalists:

Decaying generations cherish a belief in ghosts. Foolish men seek relief in exorcism. . . . The conclusion is that man has his happiness in his own hands, and that the spirits have nothing to do with it. It depends on his virtues and not on sacrifices.[59]

Needham comments that governmental bureaucratic circles frowned upon the beliefs, and that "the government felt it inexpedient that the common people should engage in arguments about the relations between the emperor and Heaven." This means that, at the time, some people felt that natural calamities were caused by ghosts or spirits that could be propitiated through the performance of rituals and ceremonies, and that some people also believed that the destructive activities of those ghosts and spirits had been caused by political acts of questionable character. We thus have here two related

---

59 Joseph Needham, *Science and Civilization in China*, vol. 2: *History of Scientific Thought* (Cambridge: Cambridge University Press, 1962), pp. 376–78.

issues, one concerning a dialectic between nature and culture, and the other one concerning political relations between structure (the establishment), and communitas (the common people).

The *goryō* and *onryō* beliefs of Nara and Heian Japan seem to be related to those Chinese practices and beliefs which date back to the Han dynasties, if not earlier. In Japan, they might be characterized as being the result of structural interactions between Buddhism and the worship of *kami,* between nature and culture, and between structure and communitas. These interactions evolved at several levels of society and came to rest in the shrine-temple multiplexes, where they were sustained by a variety of rites originating in shamanic possession and oracular religion, as well as in the esoteric Buddhist traditions; new Buddhist elements appearing in history were grafted onto the cult: elements of Pure Land and Zen became in time integral parts of the evolution of the Kitano cult.

One understands perhaps better now what caused the Kitano phenomenon and its solution. Aristocrats were confronted with the reverse side of the coin they had so successfully played earlier in claiming that their rule enjoyed the backing of "Heaven," since, after Michizane's demise, people claimed that natural disasters impacting their own lives were a manifestation of discontent on the part of the very same Heaven. And between the people and the aristocrats the thaumaturgists stood, equally pressured by both groups to pacify all concerned. Sugawara no Michizane was eventually deified as the patron saint of poetry and learning, and his cult has continued to develop up to the present day.

THE ASSOCIATION OF *KAMI* WITH BUDDHAS

The associations between kami and buddhas/bodhisattvas

The creation of shrines and temples was discussed earlier in political and ritual contexts, but we must now consider a closely related topic: the cultic associations between various *kami* and buddhas and bodhisattvas. These associations are often but inadequately referred to as a syncretism between Shinto and Buddhism.[60]

It should be noted that the Japanese of the Heian period never spoke of Shinto versus Buddhism, and this for several reasons. First,

---

60 See Murayama Shūichi, *Shimbutsu shūgō shichō* (Kyoto: Heirakuji, 1957), and *Honji suijaku;* Ōyama Kōjun, *Shimbutsu kōshō-shi* (Kyoto: Rinsen shoten, 1975); and Kubota Osamu, *Chūsei Shintō no kenkyū* (Kyoto: Shintō-shi gakkai, 1959).

there is a question concerning the definition of phenomena to which the tradition itself gave the name Shinto. When the term appears during the medieval period, it refers to specific ritual and doctrinal systems related to particular shrine-temple multiplexes, never to an overarching, nationally accepted body of doctrine and ritual. "Shinto" as a system of belief totally independent from Buddhism did not exist before the Edo period, and even then the term denoted a system heavily impacted by Neo-Confucianism, Taoism, and *yin-yang* notions and practices. In the Heian period the realm of shrines exhibited indigenous and imported creeds, practices, and institutions; these were rarely at odds with the world of temples. The overall unifier of the world of shrines and temples was, as we have seen several times in the course of this chapter, the conglomerate of governing lineages, from whose point of view the sole difference between shrines and temples was a matter of social, cosmological, and ritual considerations. Second, the Japanese cultic traditions emphasize, more than syncretism between Shinto and Buddhism as bodies of doctrine and practice, locale-specific associations between the particular *kami* of a shrine and the particular buddhas and bodhisattvas of the temple with which that shrine was associated throughout the Heian period and, indeed, for the most part, until the nineteenth century.

The term for the phenomenon is *shimbutsu shūgō*, which means, literally, combinations (*shūgō*) between *kami* (*shin*) and buddhas and bodhisattvas (*butsu*). Thus what we are confronting here is not syncretism between "Buddhism" and "Shinto," but specific relations between shrines and temples where those divinities were enshrined. It is, however, true that in most cases the combinations were grounded in a framework of interpretation issued either from the Tendai or Shingon philosophical systems; the Japanese themselves, during the medieval period, believed that most combinatory rationales had been authored by Kūkai and Saichō, the founders of Shingon and Tendai schools. This means that, during the medieval period, the most widely circulated rationales were grounded in esotericism. There was some syncretism in Japan; but the phenomenon under consideration at the present is structurally different, since we are looking at systems of combinations located in clear spatial and temporal areas, and generally placed against the background of the *chingo kokka* theories.[61]

61 On the topic of syncretism as an altogether different issue, see, for example, Birger A. Pearson, ed., *Religious Syncretism in Antiquity* (Missoula, Mont.: Scholars Press, 1975).

The *jingūji* and the Twenty-two Shrines being institutions politically related to the evolution of Buddhism in Nara and Heian Japan, it is not surprising that shrines and temples developed interactions at the ritual and philosophical levels as well. In these interactions, Buddhism tended to represent the dominant discourse by virtue of the fact that temples developed an institutional supremacy over the shrines which they came to govern, and because the definition of the *kami* was apparently left to Buddhist prelates. The interactions focused on different aspects of the symbolic realms embodied by shrines and temples.

It is important to emphasize that during the Heian period one rarely finds anyone of whom it can be said with absolute confidence that he was purely Buddhist or that his life was exclusively determined by the realm of shrines. This was true for members of sacerdotal lineages and for prelates governing the temples. Just by looking at the calendar of festive ceremonies and rituals of the Heian period (the *nenjū gyōji*), we must conclude that cultic life was also political, and that it involved the members of the court in shrines and temples, sometimes separately and sometimes concurrently. People did not reflect on these matters in an abstract manner. The separation was not doctrinal: it was mostly social and sometimes ritual.

We thus see "Buddhist" prelates going on pilgrimage to shrines in order to ask for the protection of the *kami* in their endeavor to achieve awakening. Some even spent long periods in ascetic seclusion on the grounds of shrines, where they had erected various buildings to house scriptures and to perform rites such as the famed *Hokke-hakkō*.[62] Conversely, the powerful Nakatomi sacerdotal lineage, for instance, wrote texts proposing Buddhist interpretations of purification, one of the most important "Shinto" rituals. These systematic interactions profoundly marked the Heian period at all levels of life. The Taira house built the Sanjūsangendō in Kyoto and the Itsukushima shrine-temple multiplex on Miyajima. The Fujiwara house developed a large framework of shrines and temples throughout the country, and the Minamoto house (the Seiwa Genji) developed the Futara shrine-temple multiplex, all the while taking Hachiman as tutelary deity, and later enshrining him at Tsurugaoka in Kamakura.

It was in this context that Buddhist prelates began to explain the

---

[62] See Willa Tanabe, "The Lotus Lectures: *Hokke hakkō* in the Heian Period," *Monumenta Nipponica* 39, 4 (1984): 393–407.

existence and the power of indigenous *kami* in terms of Buddhist doctrine, with special reference to the theory known as *honji suijaku* and traditionally associated with the Lotus Sutra. According to this theory the Body of Essence of the Buddha used expedient devices (*hōben*) to manifest itself in various guises in the world in order to guide it toward salvation. One of the many guises it would take was as a *kami*. It thus became customary to identify specific *kami* of shrines as hypostases of the specific members of the Buddhist pantheon worshiped in their adjacent temples. *Kami* and buddhas were associated to each other according to various rationalizations usually couched in an atmosphere of mystical union expressed by linguistic associations and metaphors. For example, the main *kami* of the Kasuga Shrine – whose theriomorphic emblem was the deer – was said to be a hypostasis of Fukūkensaku Kannon because the iconography of that Kannon called for a deer hide on its shoulder. People looked at the presence of the deer in the shrine, then in the temple, saw it as a subtle and mysterious indication of the essential identity of the *kami* and of the bodhisattva, and thus combined them. This type of rationalization pervaded the world of associated shrines and temples, and spread among the aristocracy as well as other strata of society.

Furthermore, it might be useful to suggest that if at the individual level, people thought that destinies were decided upon by higher forces such as planets and the like, at the state level it was believed that much of the destiny of the state rested in those forces and deities, and that this was one of the reasons for the importance of ritual. These notions paved the way for the belief that history was the result of the divine will of *kami* and buddhas or bodhisattvas revealed through the medium of divination and oracles, and propitiated through the medium of rites, be those preventive or curative.[63] In this specific context the associations between shrines and temples played a central role: the realm of shrines insisted upon regular ritual return to the origins and expounded on the views of the *Kojiki* and *Nihon shoki* concerning myth and history, while the realm of temples expressed the notion that reality was the result of complex

[63] The processes leading to certain types of historical consciousness in medieval Japan have been studied by Kuroda Toshio in "Kemmitsu bukkyō ni okeru rekishi ishiki," in Kitanishi Hiromu sensei kanreki kinenkai, ed., *Chūsei shakai to ikkō ikki* (Tokyo: Yoshikawa kōbunkan, 1985), pp. 505–23. See also Kuroda Toshio, "Historical Consciousness and *Honjaku* Philosophy in the Medieval Period on Mt. Hiei," translated by Allan Grapard in George Tanabe and Willa Tanabe, eds., *The Lotus Sutra in Japanese Culture* (Honolulu: University of Hawaii Press, 1989), pp. 143–58.

networks of mutual causation (*engi*) over which individuals had little control.

These views were then projected at the popular level by the didactic literature of *setsuwa*, in which people were told that their affairs were mediated partly by personal responsibility, but mostly by the will of entities that were the object of cults in shrines and temples to which they were invited to go on pilgrimage in order to beseech them. In what other way could they have explained the sudden intrusion of buddhas and bodhisattvas into their lives, be that intrusion the manifestation of compassion or of supernatural wrath?

Combinations between *kami* and buddhas or bodhisattvas were a central part of edifying tales such as those found in the *Konjaku monogatari-shū*. The practice of Buddhism to the exclusion of the realm of shrines did not exist in Japan before at least the Edo period; on the other hand, the elaboration of "Shinto theses" that took place in the Kamakura and Muromachi periods in fact owed a great deal to Buddhist interpretations. These were not dominant issues during the Heian period.

The combinations in Kunisaki

The Kunisaki peninsula in Kyushu exemplifies the general principles advanced in the present chapter. Kunisaki was a discrete geographical area governed by mountain ascetics who, within a complex epistemological framework and under Tendai institutional direction, organized a cult dedicated to the Lotus Sutra and to Hachiman with the avowed purpose of protecting the state. The religious world of Kunisaki was a system of ritual and philosophical interactions between elements issuing from local creeds, from continental shamanistic practices, from Tendai and Shingon esoteric rites, and from Taoist themes and rites. These interactions caused an evolution in the concept of sacred nation (*shinkoku*) that was sustained through the performance of major rituals for the protection of the state, and a host of related creeds, practices, and rituals. This system evolved and came to fruition during the Heian period.

The Hachiman cult is of distant and most unclear origins, and its structure has been reorganized several times in the course of history.[64] It is probable that its source is to be found in Korea, and per-

---

[64] On the Kunisaki peninsula, see Allan Grapard, "Lotus in the Mountain, Mountain in the Lotus," *Monumenta Nipponica* 14, 1 (1986): 21–50, and "Enmountained Text, Textualized Mountain: The Lotus Sutra in the Kunisaki Peninsula," in George Tanabe and Willa Tana-

haps even farther on the continent; in Japan, its original site is in the northeastern part of Kyushu, an island that literally fell under its economic control during the Heian period. Originally related to litholatry, to solar worship, and to sword worship, this combination of local cults attached itself to the mythology of the state when it was stated in the early ninth century that Hachiman was the deified form of the fourth-century king Homuda Wake ("Emperor Ōjin") and of his mother, Tarashi Hime ("Consort Jingū"), who became an important figure in the formation of the concept of Japanese territory when it was claimed (in the *Kojiki* and *Nihon shoki*) that she had conquered Korea.

The main center of the Hachiman cult came to be located in Usa for reasons that are most unclear, and the Mirokuji Buddhist temple was built next to the shrines during the eighth century. The sacerdotal lineage that first governed the shrines was named Ōga (Ōmiwa), but it was replaced some time in the course of the eighth century by the Usa sacerdotal lineage, members of which administered the shrines, while other members (of both lineages) became Buddhist prelates and administered the temples. It appears that the Nara prelates of Usa were thaumaturgists (*fusō*), that is, shaman-like monks who were well versed in Chinese religious practices, engaged in cults dedicated to various *kami*, and used a predominantly Buddhist conception of the world. The role of the oracles of Usa Hachiman became intensely political at the time of the Dōkyō incident in 769, when an oracle recommending Dōkyō's accession to the throne was questioned in some governmental circles and another oracle was requested. That second oracle stipulated that only members of the imperial lineage could rule Japan, and ordered that Dōkyō be removed from government. As was seen earlier, Hachiman was subsequently brought to Nara to become the protector (*chinju*) of the Tōdaiji. The Hachiman cult developed an even more intense relation to the state when Fujiwara no Yoshifusa created the Iwashimizu shrine-temple multiplex south of Kyoto in 859 to celebrate the accession to the throne of his grandson, Emperor Seiwa, the preceding year. In time Iwashimizu came to administer the Usa Hachiman site of cult.

When mountain asceticism developed in the Kinai area at the beginning of the tenth century, and especially so in the Kumano re-

---

be, eds., *The Lotus Sutra in Japanese Culture*, pp. 159–89. See also Nakano Hatayoshi, *Hachiman shinkō-shi no kenkyū*.

gion, it also developed in Kyushu on Mount Hiko near Usa. As a result, the evolution of mountain asceticism in Kyushu went hand in hand with the development of the Usa Hachiman cult. It was under the combined influences of Kyushu Tendai Buddhism, mountain asceticism, and Hachiman that the Kunisaki peninsula religious system developed during the second part of the Heian period. The various monks who developed that elaborate institutional and ritual framework were seen as a single bodhisattva named Nimmon, who was in turn seen as the Buddhist aspect of Hachiman in that part of Japan.

A number of temples were built on the slopes of the volcanic peninsula and were put under the administration of Tendai-controlled institutions, which attempted to gain control of the Hachiman cult in the Usa shrine-temple complex. The Tendai school is based on the Lotus Sutra, traditionally referred to as the "Scripture in Eight Scrolls" or "Twenty-eight Chapters," further subdivided by scholarly commentary into three distinct parts. As a consequence, the people administering the land domains that were located in the Kunisaki peninsula and belonged to the Mirokuji Temple of Usa built as many temples as there are chapters in the Lotus Sutra, and separated them into three administrative and ritual categories that would correspond to the scholarly tripartite distinction of the Lotus Sutra. Furthermore, it was suggested (at a time that is unclear) that there should be as many representations of buddhas and bodhisattvas on the slopes of the volcano as there are graphs in the Chinese version of the scripture. The result of these decisions was that the entire peninsula was regarded as if it were a natural and cultural embodiment of the Lotus Sutra itself. Metaphorical associations between elements of the Lotus Sutra and elements of the Hachiman cult were subsequently established so that the peninsula came to be seen as the Japanese form of the Peak of the Numinous Eagle on which the Buddha preached the Lotus Sutra, and as the area of manifestation of the golden radiance of Hachiman in its theriomorphic appearance as an eagle or falcon (later seen as a dove). The major rituals performed in Kunisaki were rituals for the protection of the state against foreign invasions.

It is clear that the Kunisaki system cannot be understood from the perspective of Buddhism only, or from the sole perspective of the realm of shrines. Kunisaki, like most other cultic sites which developed in Heian Japan, was a combinatory phenomenon.

The combinations in Kumano

Located at the southernmost tip of the Kii peninsula directly to the south of Kyoto, the Kumano region is one of the most important cultic areas of Japan. It is home to three major shrines: Kumano-hayatama (Hongū), Kumano-nimasu (Shingū), and Nachi, which, over the centuries, developed complex associations with the temples that came to be built near them. Kumano appears in documents first in the *Kojiki*, in which it is purported to be the burial site of the cosmogonic deity Izanami. But it soon gained recognition on the part of anchorites during the Nara period for it was considered to be an ideal site for withdrawal from the world. The *Nihon ryōiki*, Japan's first compilation of didactic stories written by the monk Kyōkai around 820, mentions the place in this respect.[65] The exquisite beauty of Kumano's natural environment quickly drew the attention of the imperial court, and the shrines of Hongū and Shingū were awarded higher ranking in 859, precisely at the time of the Jōgan era major reformulations of ritual discussed earlier; this indicates direct Fujiwara control. In fact, members of the court were so attracted to the region's beauty and celebrated hotsprings that Retired Emperor Uda made a pilgrimage to Kumano as early as 907, starting what was to become a tradition among emperors. At the end of the Heian period, the tonsured emperor Go-Shirakawa made the journey thirty-four times, while Emperor Go-Toba went thirty times. Aristocrats followed close behind: Jōzō, the son of Miyoshi Kiyoyuki (847–918), took the orders and spent three years in ascetic seclusion at the foot of Nachi waterfall; Fujiwara no Tamefusa went on pilgrimage in 1081, and thereafter the desirable position of abbot of Kumano tended to remain within the lineage of the Ichijō branch of the Fujiwara house.

Almost the entirety of the Kii peninsula then developed as a major center of practice for the mountain ascetics of both Shingon and Tendai lineages, and became the nexus of a particular mode of mountain asceticism with a great formative influence on almost all other mountain cultic centers of Japan. The cosmology of Buddhism and the cosmography of the Pure Land, combined with the native emphases on purification and on eschatology also had a great effect

---

[65] On the Kumano cult, see Kumano Nachi Taisha, ed., *Kumano Sanzan to sono shinkō*, 3 vols. (Tokyo: Meicho shuppan, 1984). The reference to Kumano in the *Nihon ryōiki* is in *kan* 3, no. 1. See Endō Yoshimoto and Kasuga Kazuo, eds., *Nihon ryōiki* vol. 70 of *Nihon koten bungaku taikei* (Tokyo: Iwanami shoten, 1967), pp. 316–21.

on the evolution of Kumano as a cultic site without equal in the rest of the country. Kumano came to be seen as a physical gate to the transcendental space of the Pure Land, and then as a Pure Land in this world. It remained one of the most important foci for the development of mountain cults throughout Japanese history.

LATE HEIAN DEVELOPMENTS

Personal practices in the late Heian period

As suggested earlier, rituals tended to leave the exclusive domain of the emperor at the same time the emperor came to be less and less regarded as the true body of the state, or the nation as his embodiment, and as those rites were widely adopted by aristocrats on an individual basis.

These developments accompanied the appearance of individual concerns for salvation, and it is in this context that the Japanese of the latter half of the Heian period did not find any contradiction in worshiping at the same time divinities related to the esoteric traditions of Tendai and Shingon, or colored by Taoism or indigenous associations and accretions, together with Pure Land beliefs and practices. An element common to all these was the reference to the individual as the locus of cultic belief and practice within a sociocosmic framework. This is best illustrated, perhaps, by the popularization of the *nembutsu,* or chanted invocation to the Buddha Amitābha (Japanese, *Amida*), a movement that appeared against the background of political troubles and natural calamities. When massive esoteric ritual counteraction on the part of the state proved to be ineffective or was perceived to be geared exclusively to the protection of aristocrats in positions of power, personal salvation came to be emphasized. Furthermore, a Buddhist doctrine of time and history gained wide acceptance around the eleventh century: in its framework of reference, history was not seen anymore as the symbolic manifestation of the will of the *kami* and their associated buddhas and bodhisattvas, but as a devolutionary process over which human beings had little or no power. Time was conceived of as an inexorable process leading to the final conflagration of all worlds, an event whose date was proposed in several scriptural sources; the final period of history (*mappō*) leading to the ultimate conflagration was believed in Japan to begin in the year 1052. It was thought that one of the marks of such a period was political and social unrest, which was precisely the case in Japan at the time. In that context, salvation was proposed as residing mainly in a total surrender to the saving grace of Amida, through the medium of chanting his name. It was said that the Buddha would remember those who called on him, and would therefore allow them rebirth into his Pure Land, an ideal space of residence where the practice of Buddhism would be much easier than in the troubled human world. An important corollary was that it was claimed that sole reliance on the Buddha Amida ensured rebirth into the Pure Land, and that therefore the worship of autochthonous *kami* was not necessary. This caused immediate divisions, whose nature was obviously political, because the rejected *kami* were in fact those that represented the ideology of the state in the shrine-temple multiplexes. Indeed, it was from such multiplexes that massive opposition to Pure Land ideology stemmed.

The late Heian period was thus pulled between opposing tendencies of a cultic and political character, each tendency being echoed in ritual or practice. On the one hand were rituals for the protection of the state; and on the other hand were personal devotions within the context of grace. In an almost direct cause-to-effect relation, when leading Fujiwara figures lost their grip on political affairs they "converted" to personal surrender to the grace of Amida and hoped to be reborn into a better world.

The last part of the Heian period saw a frenzy of ritual activity. The Insei period, which began in 1086 and during which emperors took the tonsure in the expectation of wielding administrative power more effectively, was marked by stately rituals that had one major goal: the reestablishment of imperial authority through the use and manipulation of symbols. One might say that, in the process, the emperor was drowned in a mass of ritual activity. Most of the practices described up to the present point were aspects of the discourse of political power in classical Japan where, as usual, the delimitation of purely political power as different from cultic power was fundamentally ambiguous. One can propose that the more intense the political conflicts were, the more intensified the ritual activity. Legitimacy being a symbolic phenomenon, ritual manipulation was an important tool of both politicians and thaumaturgists.

Ecstatic mass movements

If the Heian period saw the systematic development of ritual activity on a private level in relation to the world of shrine-temple multiplexes associated with the ideology of the government and its various lineages, it also saw, by contradistinction, the phenomenal rise of antithetic, ecstatic mass movements.

We have seen that the Shidara cult and a number of *goryō*-related cults spread among the Kyoto populace. Other popular cults that developed during the Heian period were related to the spread of Pure Land doctrine and devotional practices. The precursor of such movements of Pure Land Buddhism was Kūya (sometimes called Kōya, 903–72), a man of aristocratic descent who became an itinerant monk (*yūgyōsō*) and who, upon his return to Kyoto in 938, kept popularizing invocation to the Buddha Amida (*nembutsu*) among prisoners, common folks, and courtiers alike. He became famous for adding musical rhythm and dance to public invocations, in which he invited people to join him and dance; this was known as *yūyaku nembutsu* or, more simply, *odori nembutsu*, "danced invocation." Kūya's predilection for public places earned him the title of *ichi hijiri*, "saint of the marketplace."

Further popularization of the devotional practices of the Pure Land was achieved through the work of Genshin (942–1017), more particularly his *Anthology on Rebirth in Pure Land* (*Ojō yōshū*), which generalized a mood of impermanence befitting the troubled times, a strong sense of piety linked to paradise and hell imagery, and a fervent devotion to the Buddha Amida as the sole means to salvation. However, the popularization of the *nembutsu* among the lower classes was further enhanced by Ryōnin (1072–1132), who proposed a magic-oriented, mass recitation of the invocation to Amida, known as *Yūzū-nembutsu*, "universally transferred merit of the invocation."[66]

It might be proposed that the mass devotional movements of the second part of the Heian period indicate the growth of eschatological concerns in a society that was witnessing the gradual erosion of classical rule in the midst of warfare and natural calamities. Such movements have tended to appear in Japanese history in the decades preceding momentous sociopolitical changes, and further investigation of symbolic behavior and popular cults within the context of power relations seems necessary before a complete assessment is offered.

---

66 On Kūya, see Kon Tōkō et al., eds., *Rokuharamitsuji* (Kyoto: Tankōsha, 1969); Hori Ichirō, *Kūya* (Tokyo: Yoshikawa kōbunkan, 1963). On Genshin and Ryōnin, see Ono Tatsunosuke, *Jōdai no Jōdo-kyō* (Tokyo: Yoshikawa kōbunkan, 1972).

Conclusion

The Japanese of the Heian period attempted to establish structural relations between institutions, ideologies, and the rituals that either sustained or developed them. The creation of the Twenty-two Shrine-temple system, coupled with the reformulation of ritual procedures, was a momentous event indicative of what came to be the dominant ideology of the state.

It is quite clear that, overall, the realm of combined shrines and temples was one of the structuring devices of the ritual formulation of the state (and of the state sponsorship of ritual), and that individuals who needed personal salvation out of the framework provided by the state could find it in those multiplexes only with great difficulty; indeed, pilgrimage to those sites of cult seems to have been engaged in by courtiers only. This explains in part the surge of heterodox movements and mass ecstatic movements that characterize the second part of the Heian period.

The "rule of taste" of the classical age of Japan belongs to the Fujiwara dominance and to the combined world of shrines and temples that protected it. The slow demise of the statutory system brought the ideal state and the rule of taste to a dramatic close, as the Heian period ended in warfare and in the emergence of other social, political, and cultic ideals.

CHAPTER 9

INSEI

In late Heian times, the retired sovereigns Shirakawa, Toba, and Go-Shirakawa dominated the court as few former sovereigns, reigning or retired, had done. Later historians referred to this form of political domination as *insei* or "cloister government," a term derived from the fact that abdicated emperors resided in well-appointed villas or religious cloisters (*in*) from which they conducted politics (*sei*). The ex-sovereign's office had numerous subordinate bureaus staffed by courtiers who supported his interests at court and supervised extensive provincial estates. Retired emperors so dominated the Heian court that historians call the period 1086–1185, stretching from late Heian to the beginning of Kamakura times, the Insei period.

Once a person has attained the highest office in the land, it is difficult to revert to the status of a common citizen; the aura of authority remains. In modern times, this is true of former kings, presidents, and prime ministers; however, the more hierarchic the society, the more we should expect the residual authority to remain viable. In Heian Japan, substantial authority remained with a former sovereign. Although rulers everywhere abdicate, nowhere has the practice been as common as it was in Japan. And nowhere else did former sovereigns regularly influence national affairs so significantly. A brief recapitulation of some features of the Japanese dynasty is necessary background for an understanding of this phenomenon.

ABDICATION, REGENCY, AND THE JAPANESE THRONE, 645–1068

Abdication was not peculiar to late Heian times, nor were powerful ex-sovereigns unknown in other eras. The first recorded abdication occurred in 645 when the Empress Kōgyoku stepped down in favor of Emperor Kōtoku and simultaneously confirmed her son Prince Naka no Ōe (future emperor Tenji) as crown prince. From that time until the abdication of Go-Sanjō in 1073 – his abdication marks the prelude to the *insei* – twenty-three of the thirty-four or thirty-five sovereigns abdicated.[1] In fact, abdication became the standard means of transferring the dynastic title.

Japanese sovereigns abdicated for many reasons: ill health, belief in spirits, the pressures of office, pressure from Fujiwara ministers, the desire to enter the monastic life, or because they were female.[2] At the basis of all acts of abdication, however, lay the critical problem of transferring royal succession. Whatever the reasons behind the timing of an abdication, the politics of the act was crucial. The frequency of abdication in Japan seems to be due to the fact that experience proved it the least problematic way of deciding royal succession.[3]

In early Japanese history, indeterminate succession practices often provoked bitter struggles for the throne. During the Asuka and Nara periods (the seventh and eighth centuries), the dynasty that today still reigns in Japan made great efforts to strengthen the imperial position, including experimentation with several methods of imperial succession to avoid armed conflict. Examination of the succession practices of this period reveal the following:

1. The dynasty was becoming gendered: adult males were normally considered to be proper holders of the kingship.
2. The concept of lineal succession in the senior male line was adopted in principle and included in the official codes.
3. The crown prince was designated early in the reign and frequently enjoyed broad powers of co-rulership.
4. Female rulers were frequently enthroned, often in times of dynastic crisis; but after the late Nara period, female rule was abandoned.
5. The practice of abdication was introduced.

These phenomena were of course interrelated. The ancient Japanese dynasty was attempting to deal with the problem of transferring a scarce resource – the kingship – among a large dynastic group with a minimum of conflict. But conflict was prevalent, resulting in armed rebellion and the deaths of a number of claimants to the dy-

---

1 The number of sovereigns differs, depending upon whether or not one accepts Emperor Kōbun's accession. He is included in the "official" Japanese list, but there is great disagreement among Japanese scholars.
2 These are the kinds of reasons listed in the section of *Koji ruien* dealing with ex-emperors; the noted *insei* scholar Kōno Fusao reiterates them in *Heian makki seijishi* (Tokyo: Tōkyōdō, 1979), pp. 7–8.
3 G. Cameron Hurst III, *Insei: Abdicated Sovereigns in the Politics of Late Heian Japan, 1086–1185* (New York: Columbia University Press, 1976), pp. 47–49.

nastic title. The first three practices, in somewhat different form, are part of the dynastic practice in Japan today; however, the latter two features – female rule and abdication – are especially associated with the Asuka and Nara periods, most likely relied upon to curtail conflict. One proved successful and was retained for many years, the other failed and was abandoned. The important point, however, is that they seem linked, as two parts of a process to smooth dynastic transfer.

Eight of the ten or eleven female Japanese sovereigns reigned in the Asuka and Nara periods;[4] no women were enthroned after the death of Empress Shōtoku in 770 until the Tokugawa period a millennium later. Empresses, at first principal consorts of a deceased emperor but later other female members of the dynasty as well, were enthroned in situations of actual or potential conflict over succession until an appropriate male member of the dynasty could be chosen.[5] But when and how to transfer the kingship proved problematic. During Suiko's reign (592–628), her nephew Prince Shōtoku enjoyed broad powers of co-rulership as regent. She was apparently preserving the dynastic title for him, but he predeceased her, provoking yet another dynastic dispute. This precedent may have well been in the mind of Empress Kōgyoku, who was enthroned under somewhat similar circumstances in 645, when she attempted to abdicate early in her reign.

All seven of the female rulers after Suiko abdicated. (Two, however, abdicated and then reascended the throne.) Since these female rulers were essentially enthroned as caretakers – Professor Inoue refers to them as *nakatsugi* ("transitional heirs") – to reign temporarily in lieu of a male sovereign (which by no means implies that they were not fully able to rule in their own right), then abdication

---

4 The counting here is somewhat misleading. There were only six women enthroned (technically) in ancient Japan, but two of them – Kōgyoku/Saimei and Kōken/Shōtoku – ascended the throne twice. And the rule of one woman, Iitoyo, is disputed.

5 Inoue Mitsusada, *Nihon kodai kokka no kenkyū* (Tokyo: Iwanami shoten, 1965), pp. 179–218, passim. Joan Piggott argues persuasively that co-rulership – "gender-complementary chieftain pairs" – were common in the Yayoi and Tomb periods and that that precedent legitimized female rulers in their "participation in the routinization of dynastic succession in the sixth and seventh centuries." Joan Piggott, "Chieftain Pairs and Co-rulers: Female Sovereignty in Early Japan," in Hitomi Tonomura, ed., *Gender in Japanese History,* for Japanese Studies, University of Michigan, forthcoming), p. 2. I also agree with her that they were not "sovereigns-as-usual" (p. 36) but were stand-ins, or stakeholders. Unlike Inoue, however, I do not mean that these female rulers were figureheads. On the contrary, they could and did rule in precisely the same way as male sovereigns. I use these terms solely in consideration of the reasons for their selection as ruler in a dynasty that was in transition to a male-dominated one; they were enthroned in, precisely as Piggott says, "liminal moments, moments of succession crisis" (p. 36).

was the only means to transfer the kingship when conditions were appropriate. Postponing the transfer until death would have caused further complications. Thus, it appears that abdication was intimately linked to female rule in early Japan and developed as part of the process of routinizing dynastic succession during a period of great fluidity.

The first instance of male abdication occurred in the Nara period: Shōmu abdicated in 749. It was soon recognized that this was the safest means of transmitting the kingship to the desired heir. Female rule had not been successful in stemming conflict over the throne, and it was also believed that the Buddhist priest Dōkyō had been able to manipulate Empress Shōtoku's emotions. In early Japanese history crown princes or strong claimants to the throne had often been eliminated; however, during the Nara period there were no depositions of reigning sovereigns until Junnin and perhaps only two cases of regicide. Once a claimant was enthroned, relative security could be assumed, and the safest way to effect that enthronement was to abdicate. Thus pre-mortem royal succession became standard.

During Heian and Kamakura times, dynastic succession practices showed much greater stability than in the Asuka and Nara eras.

1. Only male members of the dynasty could hold the royal position, but it was no longer required that they be adult.
2. Lineal succession remained important in principle, but in practice other forms, especially fraternal succession, occurred frequently.
3. The crown prince was named early in a reign but enjoyed no regency power.
4. Fujiwara clan regency became institutionalized, but it was possible for ex-emperors to wield imperial-house regency powers.
5. Female rule did not occur.
6. Abdication increased in frequency; pre-mortem succession became standard.

Politics in the Asuka and Nara periods was characterized by powerful prince regents and female sovereigns. By contrast, in the Heian period after several strong emperors, imperial regents of the Fujiwara clan and retired emperors enjoyed maximum political power. All these political styles, however, derived from the same source, a dynasty that claimed legitimacy on the basis of descent from the Sun Goddess. With the universal acceptance of this claim, the dynasty had been placed permanently above other groups; no one could duplicate its genealogy.

Kingship was an estate right of the dynasty as a group, although title lay with the person of the emperor.⁶ Other dynastic members had a stake in their common estate right, however; and shared authority, which permitted co-rulership, was a feature of the Japanese dynasty. However, authority and power were normally separated. The emperor was the repository of dynastic authority, but he usually remained outside the daily scramble for political and economic power. Power could be – and usually was – delegated to someone else: a member of the dynasty (prince regent or ex-emperor), another noble (the Fujiwara regent), or a military hegemon (the shogun). In modern times, power has been delegated to the cabinet and the parliament.

The sovereign's primary function was sacerdotal rather than political, but since the imperial institution was buttressed by Chinese Confucian political ideals, the sovereign was never totally powerless. If other political factors permitted, it was possible for an emperor to exercise direct political power (*shinsei*); however, this was unusual. Delegating power ensured the longevity of the Japanese ruling house: competition for power was confined to the right to control royal authority rather than to usurp it. This provided relative security for the dynasty and the possibility for other groups to enjoy political hegemony.

Abdication was standard practice in Heian times; retired emperors were important political figures at court even before *insei* became a regular feature of society. In fact, during the Heian period one can discern an extended competition between the Fujiwara clan and ex-emperors, on behalf of the imperial house, for control over the right to "possess" what the dynasty "owned."

From Kammu's time through the death of Emperor En'yū in 991, eleven of sixteen sovereigns abdicated the throne. After abdication an ex-emperor was given the honorific title *dajō tennō* ("great abdicated emperor"), but was more commonly known by a shortened version, *jōkō*. If he later took the tonsure, the title was *dajō hōō* ("priestly retired sovereign") or in abbreviated form, *hōō*. In courtier diaries, he was often simply referred to as *in* ("cloister"), hence the term *insei*. From early Heian times, ex-sovereigns enjoyed some of the prerogatives of reigning monarchs, although the imperial codes did not stipulate a formal position for them. They appear

---

6 See Cornelius J. Kiley, "Estate and Property in Late Heian Japan," in John W. Hall and Jeffrey P. Mass, eds., *Medieval Japan: Essays in Institutional History* (New Haven, Conn.: Yale University Press, 1975), pp. 109–24, for a discussion of the estate rights of corporate groups.

to have issued edicts through the same channels the emperors used. They were provided with retirement palaces and complete income-producing lands, which became private, heritable assets of the imperial house.

The presence of both former and reigning sovereigns proved disruptive, however. In 809, Emperor Heizei abdicated in favor of his brother Saga. But Heizei did not abdicate of his own volition; he was following a plan prescribed by their late father, Emperor Kammu. Consequently, there was great animosity between the brothers. When some courtiers followed Heizei and settled in the old Nara capital, there were in effect two separate and hostile courts.[7] After an abortive rebellion, Heizei remained in Nara as a monk. His son was demoted and replaced as crown prince by one of Saga's sons. Saga emerged all-powerful, but people at court were obviously confused over the relative degree of authority accruing to the reigning and abdicated sovereigns.

It was Saga who tipped the balance in favor of later ex-emperors. He abdicated in 823 but did not become active in politics until his son Nimmyō became emperor in 833. He issued edicts and determined affairs of state on Nimmyō's behalf, his power and prestige deriving from his position as head of the imperial kin group. This marked a clear departure from earlier periods, when it appears that ex-sovereigns did not exercise this private, familial role. Previously the emperor in his public position of head of state seems to have taken precedence.[8]

But in Saga's time things changed. Clearly the fact that he was Emperor Nimmyō's father determined their respective roles. To initiate the new year the emperor paid Saga formal visits of respect, speaking to him as a subject would address his sovereign. Saga had emerged as the senior figure in the imperial house, and his patriarchal authority gave him the informal power to influence politics. He was more powerful in this essentially co-regent capacity than Asuka period princes had been.

There were retirement palaces and lands allotted specifically for Saga's support. He appointed men who had served him closely when he was emperor to be *inshi,* or ex-emperor's officials. His patriarchal authority extended beyond the strict confines of the dynastic group to include his offspring who had been made Minamoto nobles. The

---

7 *Nihon kōki,* in *Kokushi taikei,* vol. 3 (Tokyo: Yoshikawa kōbunkan, 1965), p. 85, Kōnin 1/9/10.
8 Hurst, *Insei,* pp. 61–62.

practice of dynastic shedding helped to limit claimants to the throne and curtail demands upon the imperial treasury. Saga had fifty-seven children; he gave many of them the surname Minamoto, formally cutting them off from the royal house. Nevertheless, he summoned them to participate with imperial house members in ceremonies at which he presided as patriarch. Saga can perhaps be seen as the prototype of the abdicated emperors of some two and a half centuries later.

After Saga, retired emperors developed separate institutions for issuing documents and administering the needs of a growing retinue of personal retainers. The first extant ex-sovereign decree was issued by Uda in 928.[9] The ex-sovereign's private office (*in-no-chō*), with a complement of subordinate bureaus and officials who could issue decrees in the name of the ex-emperor was in existence at least by the time of En'yū's abdication in 984.[10]

Early Heian period ex-emperors, especially Saga, Uda, and En'yū, were able to assert themselves forcefully in political affairs. As heads of the imperial house, they exercised paternal authority over sons and grandsons to influence decisions favorable to the dynasty. This was especially true at times when the emerging Fujiwara clan regency was weak, or when there was no regent, as during the reign of Daigo when Uda was ex-sovereign. But it was true even when a strong Fujiwara regent was appointed. Kaneie, for example, lamented the fact that ex-emperor En'yū's requests were "weighty and difficult to refuse."[11]

This is a telling statement, striking at the heart of the competition between the imperial house and the Fujiwara regent's line (*sekkanke*). The major development of early and mid-Heian was the establishment of a permanent Fujiwara regency that dominated the throne through marriage relationships. Disparity of status made it impossible for the Fujiwara to aspire to the position of sovereign, but they enjoyed an interest in the dynasty in the form of a permanent regency supported by intermarriage, which over time reduced the solidarity of the imperial house as a cohesive kinship group. Under the marriage customs of the mid-Heian period,[12] an imperial prince

---

9 *Tōdaiji yōroku*, in *Zoku zoku gunsho ruijū* (Tokyo: Gunsho ruijū kankōkai, 1909), vol. 11, pp. 160–61, Enchō 6/8/28.
10 Hurst, *Insei*, pp. 85–87.
11 *Shōyūki*, in Tōkyō daigaku shiryō hensanjo, comp., *Dai Nihon kokiroku* (Tokyo: Iwanami shoten, 1952), series 10, vol. 1, p. 162, Eiso 1/2/21.
12 William McCullough, "Japanese Marriage Institutions in the Heian Period," *Harvard Journal of Asiatic Studies* 27 (1967): 103–67.

born of a Fujiwara woman was reared in the residence of his grandfather or uncle. Strong ties of affection developed. When the child became emperor, it was natural that he would be dominated by his Fujiwara kin. However, Fujiwara clan heads were aware that their regency was different from a royal regency.

After En'yū's death, there were no abdicated sovereigns of any political importance until Go-Sanjō's time. This reduction of the power of retired emperors corresponds to the apogee of Fujiwara regency control, when Michinaga's daughters produced several sons who became emperor. Michinaga's son Yorimichi, however, was not blessed with daughters who produced potential heirs to the throne, and thus faced the distinct possibility of the reemergence of a strong ex-emperor who might exercise familial power over the reigning sovereign. During Yorimichi's long tenure as regent, he never permitted an emperor the opportunity to evolve into a forceful retired sovereign; each abdicated just prior to death.

In effect, two forms of regency developed during early and mid-Heian times. The Fujiwara clan controlled the right to provide imperial consorts and thus aided by the marriage practices of the day, exercised regency power through the maternal side. But an ex-emperor, as head of the royal house, could also exercise a kind of regency power from the paternal side. The marriage connection made the Fujiwara regency innately fragile. Yorimichi (and probably Kaneie and other clan chieftains as well), realizing that a royal regency exercised by an ex-emperor was potentially more powerful than a nonroyal regency, guarded against early abdication.

GO-SANJŌ AND THE PRELUDE TO *INSEI*, 1068–1073

Emperor Go-Sanjō (1034–73) came to the throne in 1068. He was the first emperor since Uda, eleven reigns and 170 years earlier, whose mother was not a Fujiwara. Go-Sanjō, the second son of Emperor Go-Suzaku, was born in 1034 when his father was still crown prince. His mother, Princess Teishi (better known as Yōmeimon-in), was a daughter of the late emperor Sanjō (see Figures 9.1 and 1.1). The possibility of Go-Sanjō's accession threatened Fujiwara domination of the imperial position; Regent Yorimichi (992–1074) tried to prevent it. The primary reason for Yorimichi's worry was the dearth of possible Fujiwara heirs to the throne. His sister Shōshi was mother of both emperors Go-Ichijō and Go-Suzaku, and another sister, Kishi, had borne Go-Reizei. While Yorimichi enjoyed exten-

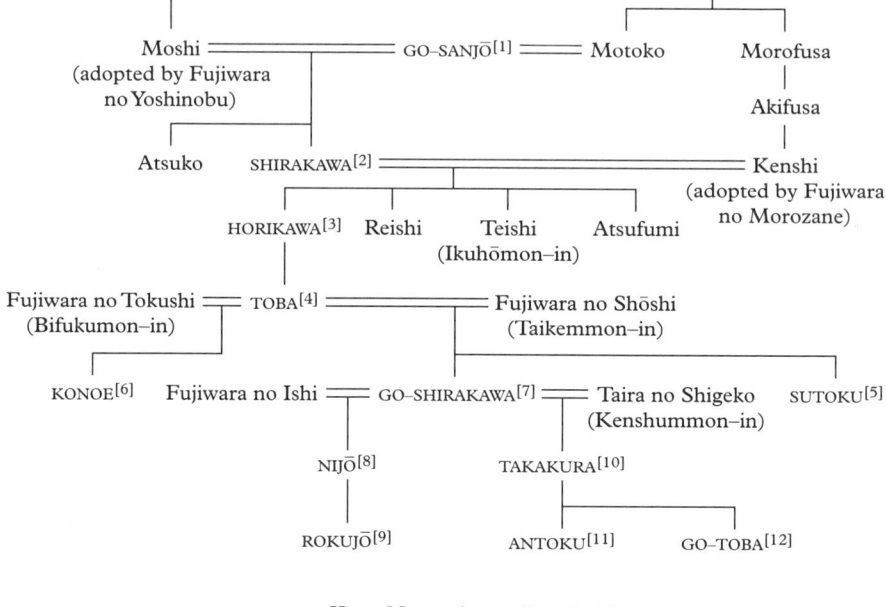

Figure 9.1. Genealogy of emperors during the *Insei* period.

sive power as maternal uncle to several rulers, his position was much less secure than it would have been had his own daughters produced sons. Two of his daughters were married to Go-Reizei, but no princes were born.

In 1044, when Go-Suzaku became seriously ill and desired to abdicate in favor of Go-Reizei, Yorimichi faced a crisis: there was no *sekkanke* heir as candidate for crown prince. It was customary to name a crown prince at the time of accession. Go-Suzaku wanted Go-Sanjō (then Prince Takahito) to be appointed because Go-Reizei had no male children. Having no alternative, and because the wishes of a dying emperor were not easily disregarded, Yorimichi grudgingly consented to this arrangement.

Go-Sanjō was crown prince for an unprecedented twenty-three years, during which time he was the focus of Yorimichi's animosity. There may even have been an attempt upon his life.[13] In the past, sev-

---

13 Kawaguchi Hisao, *Ōe no Masafusa* (Tokyo: Yoshikawa kōbunkan, 1968), p. 62.

eral crown princes had been forced into resignation, victimized by plots that resulted in their removal, or killed. Less than a half-century earlier, for example, Michinaga had forced Go-Sanjō's maternal uncle Prince Atsuakira to step down. Yorimichi stalled Go-Reizei's abdication as long as possible, hoping for the birth of a Fujiwara prince. But when Go-Reizei died in 1068, he could not block the accession of the thirty-three-year-old Go-Sanjō. Yorimichi's frustration is well mirrored in his response: he yielded the regency to his younger brother Norimichi and retired permanently to his villa at Uji.

Thus, the first emperor in almost two centuries not hampered by close Fujiwara relatives began his short, active, and exemplary rule. In their accession edicts emperors since Emperor Mommu, who reigned at the start of the Nara period, had emphasized that they would rule wisely, and that subjects should serve faithfully. But the Japanese preference for indirect rule, with a separation of formal authority and actual power, dictated that sovereigns reigned but only infrequently ruled. The present-day Japanese emperor, like his British counterpart, for example, performs a legitimizing and symbolic role. Unlike his British counterpart, however, the Heizei emperor's reign is in harmony with that of most of his predecessors.

And yet, as we have seen, the Japanese regarded direct imperial rule (*shinsei*) without the intervention of prince regents, imperial regents, ex-emperors, or shoguns, as the ideal pattern. Therefore when the opportunity presented itself, emperors sought to enter into the political arena. There had been few such opportunities, especially since the institution of the Fujiwara regency virtually relegated emperors to a permanent state of minority. But Go-Sanjō was in his prime. He had been educated in the Chinese classical tradition and assiduously prepared for ruling. There was no Fujiwara hindrance to his rule. Norimichi was regent, but, lacking the strong maternal link, he could not restrain a determined emperor. Go-Sanjō was able to exercise a vigorous imperial rule quite unusual by Japanese standards. He was in fact much closer to the Chinese model than emperors Uda and Daigo (who reigned 887–930), who had been especially regarded by later generations as representing a "golden age" of imperial strength.

During the nearly five years of Go-Sanjō's reign, he was actively involved in government. This involvement extended from a deep concern with appointments in the official bureaucracy to attempts to reform the economic woes that plagued Heian society. The *Kojidan*, an early-thirteenth-century compilation, praises his reign as a period of "just rule." Hoping to break the monopoly of the highest-ranking nobles, especially *sekkanke* nobles, over government posts, Go-Sanjō sought the participation of middle-ranking courtiers, provincial governors, and scholars. He also attempted to open the way for imperial offshoot clan members, especially the Murakami and Daigo lineages of the Minamoto, to move into the *kugyō* (nobles of Third Rank and above) council so long dominated by the *sekkanke*. Since Yorimichi had actively attempted to block Go-Sanjō's accession, the thrust of Go-Sanjō's rule was directed toward reducing the power of Yorimichi and the *sekkanke*.

This is obvious from an investigation of the appointment practices during Go-Sanjō's reign.[14] When Yorimichi was regent in the reigns of Go-Ichijō and Go-Suzaku (1016–45), the highest positions in the *kugyō* were dominated by the *sekkanke*. Fujiwara clan members held a virtual stranglehold over *kugyō* membership, never dipping below an 80 percent majority. During Go-Reizei's reign, as the succession problem became acute, Yorimichi's power began to slip. Previously, there had never been more than four or five *kugyō* of the Minamoto clan, particularly the Murakami branch (Murakami Genji, see Figure 9.2); now there were seven or eight. In 1067, Go-Reizei's last year, there were ten Minamoto *kugyō*, more than one-third of the total. (*Kugyō* membership averaged about twenty-eight during the reigns of Go-Ichijō, Go-Suzaku, Go-Reizei, and Go-Sanjō.) Moreover, dissension broke out between Yorimichi and his younger brother Yoshinobu, the house member most closely related to Go-Sanjō, and Yorimichi's ability to control the *sekkanke* began to weaken.[15]

The Council of State gained in importance in the mid- and late Heian periods. No longer restricted to its original statutory role of deliberative council, it was transformed into a decision-making body. At the height of Fujiwara power, the decisions of the Council had been implemented by the regent acting on the sovereign's behalf, but from Go-Sanjō's era, the regent was merely one of the participants in the Council's deliberations. The ex-emperor normally implemented decisions. Despite the power of Fujiwara regents and ex-emperors, however, the noble council had never become a body composed solely of their private officials.[16] It remained the major de-

---

14 Hurst, *Insei*, p. 108, table 2, based on *Kugyō bunin*.
15 Yoshinobu was Michinaga's fifth and last son; since his daughter was maried to Go-Sanjō, he stood to gain by the accession of this emperor.
16 Hashimoto Yoshihiko, "Kizoku seiken no seiji kōzō," in *Iwanami kōza Nihon rekishi, Kodai* vol. 4 (Tokyo: Iwanami shoten, 1975), pp. 26–27.

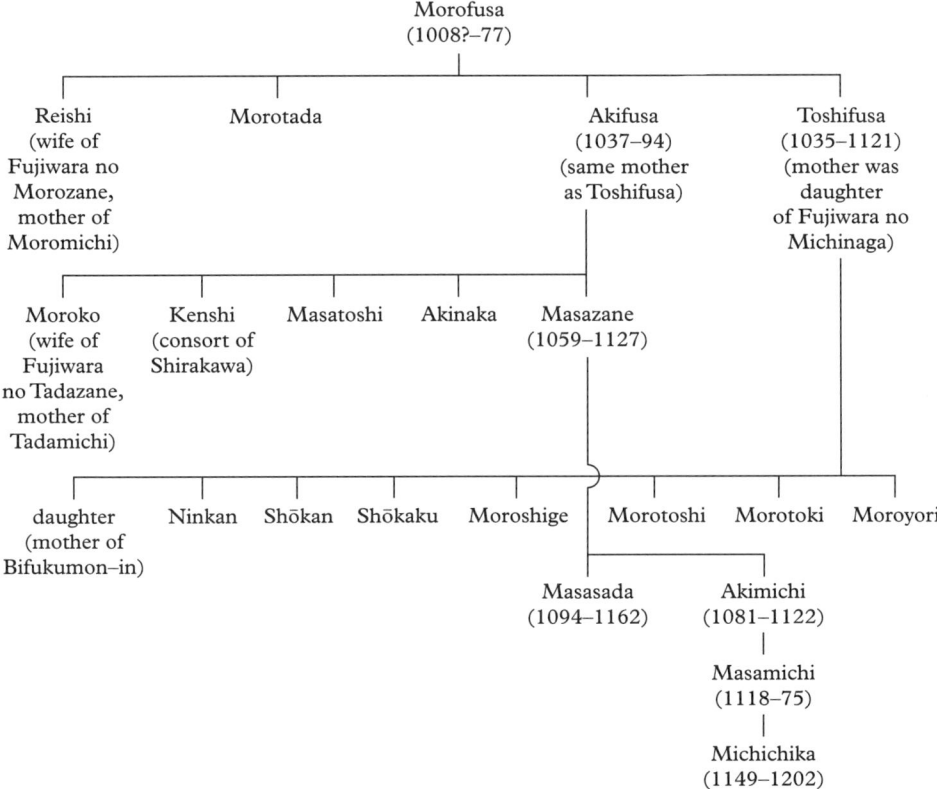

Figure 9.2. Genealogy of the Murakami Genji (Minamoto).

cision-making organ of the state in which consensus decided affairs. Consequently Go-Sanjō and the ex-emperors of the *insei* period attempted to control the noble council by cultivating its members.

The Fujiwara main line became less influential in the noble council when, during Go-Sanjō's reign, Minamoto courtiers not only composed one-third of the *kugyō* membership but also held the most important ministerial positions and the major counselor posts. These courtiers also tended to cooperate closely with Go-Sanjō as an "imperial faction."[17] With the *sekkanke* fragmented and unable to dominate the noble council as in the past, Go-Sanjō was relatively free to carry out policies of his own making with little opposition.

Among the courtiers closest to Go-Sanjō, three in particular are

---

17 Hayashiya Tatsusaburō, *Zusetsu Nihon bunkashi taikei* (Tokyo: Shōgakukan, 1957), vol. 5, *Heian jidai* 2, pp. 63–64.

worthy of mention: Ōe no Masafusa, Fujiwara no Tamefusa, and Fujiwara no Korefusa. These men became known to later historians as the "former three fusas" in contrast to the "latter three fusas" who served Emperor Go-Daigo in the fourteenth century. Although only Korefusa became a *kugyō* during Go-Sanjō's lifetime, these three middle-ranking courtiers served the emperor loyally throughout his life. Their career patterns are instructive because they represent the emergence of a type of courtier who, in the Insei period, would become the founder of a client family of the imperial house.

All three men served in the Chamberlains' office (*Kurōdodokoro*) and were thus intimately involved in governmental affairs. Fujiwara no Sanemasa had been Go-Sanjō's tutor when he was crown prince and was influential as a Confucian adviser; he was also appointed to serve as teacher for Go-Sanjō's son, Prince Sadahito (future Emperor Shirakawa). After Go-Sanjō's abdication, these men became superintendents (*bettō*) in his *in-no-chō*. In sum, they spent their entire career in close service to the sovereign. Go-Sanjō was able to rely on them because none was closely connected with the Fujiwara regent's house. Tamefusa was a member of the Kanjūji branch of the Fujiwara; Korefusa, although of the Northern branch, was not from the *sekkanke;* and Masafusa was from the minor Ōe clan, which traditionally trained its sons as Confucian scholars. Sanemasa, too, was of non-*sekkanke* Fujiwara lineage.

Thus, Go-Sanjō enjoyed an unusual situation. He was an active emperor in the prime of life. There was neither a powerful Fujiwara regent nor a retired sovereign to exercise any "advisory" function. *Sekkanke* control of the noble council was greatly weakened, and there was an "imperial faction" operating there. His closest advisers were non-*sekkanke* courtiers who seem to have been predisposed in favor of a strong emperor. Such a background allowed Go-Sanjō to deal forcefully with political issues.

There is a paucity of source materials for a study of Go-Sanjō's reign, but it appears that he focused mainly on shoring up the declining economic foundations of the imperial state system. He adopted concrete policies of *shōen* regulation, standardization of the official *masu* dry measures used in taxation, price control and market regulation, and quality control of silk and hemp cloth.

Enacted in 1069 (Enkyū 1), Go-Sanjō's *shōen* (estate) regulation is known as the Enkyū *shōen* regulation ordinance. For more than a century there had been criticism of *shōen* policy as well as several attempts at regulation.¹⁸ Earlier attempts had not been noticeably effective, however, as the continued issuance of legislation amply demonstrates. The major obstacle to effective regulation of the growth of these private, tax-exempt landholdings was the lack of an enforcement mechanism. To be fully privatized for long periods of time, *shōen* required certification from the major organs of the central government. In effect, that meant cooperation or collusion with the major nobles in the central government, the people supposedly responsible for maintaining the viability of taxable lands. Tenure over *shōen* holdings could be obtained from provincial governors, but such lands were inherently insecure because governors rotated every four years, and new governors often disregarded their predecessors' arrangements.

Go-Sanjō's estate regulation, though from all evidence the most successful attempt of its kind, did not challenge the existence of estates per se. On the contrary, like all other regulatory attempts, it confirmed the right of persons or institutions to possess private holdings, merely defining more strictly the legal ground rules by which estates could be acquired. The relative success of the Enkyū legislation was due to the establishment in 1069 of a special government commission to handle regulation, the Office for the Investigation of Estate Documents (*Kiroku shōen kenkeijo*). This *kirokusho*, or Records Office, as it is better known, was charged with carrying out the ordinance that stipulated: (1) all estates established after 1045 (the date of Go-Reizei's accession) were to be declared illegal and confiscated; and (2) older estates with improper documentation, or estates that hampered the conduct of provincial administration, would suffer a similar fate.

The main source of information on the Enkyū regulation is a document concerning a subtemple of the Iwashimizu Hachiman Shrine. Of thirty-seven estates belonging to the subtemple Gokokuji for which documents were submitted, twenty-four were recognized as adhering to the legally prescribed form; but thirteen, some 30 percent of the temple's portfolio, were confiscated.¹⁹ A few conclusions can be drawn from this document. First, the Records Office had established more rigorous standards for confiscation of illegal estates;

---

18 See Hurst, *Insei*, pp. 110–14, and Elizabeth Sato, "Ōyama Estate and *Insei* Land Policies," *Monumenta Nipponica*, 34, 1 (1979): 73–99.
19 Takeuchi Rizō, comp., *Heian ibun*, 15 vols. (Tokyo: Tōkyōdō, 1963–74), vol. 3, pp. 1092–1107, doc. 1083, Enkyū 4/9/5.

previous enforcement attempts had been entrusted to individual governors. Second, the primary targets were estates with weak documentation. Third, also targeted were lands for which the conditions of tax liability were unclear, that is, *shōen* whose paddy fields were not clearly fixed (*ukimen no shō,* or "floating field estates") or land on which control of paddy fields and labor was shared or split between estate holder and provincial government. Even estates recognized as legal by the Records Office suffered confiscation of lands that had been added to their original exemption since 1045.[20]

The officials known to have served in the Records Office, men like Ōe no Masafusa, who is regarded as the author of the legislation, Fujiwara no Tamefusa, and Otsuki no Takanobu, were all close associates of the emperor and members of the provincial governor (*zuryō*) class with no connection to the Fujiwara regency line. This suggests it was the *zuryō* who urged estate control and that the *shōen* of the Fujiwara main house, perhaps the largest estate holder, were targets for confiscation.

Provincial governor involvement in the estate process is, however, somewhat puzzling. The Enkyū regulation ordinance did apply to weakly documented *shōen* exempted by *zuryō*, called *kokumen no shō* (provincially exempt estates), that had been established since 1045. On the other hand, a crucial result of the work of the Records Office is that provincially exempt estates with clear documentation were recognized as legal, ranking with estates that possessed central government documents. Thus we have a policy initiated by *zuryō* seeking to limit the growth of estates due to the increased power of the same *zuryō* class, but at the same time increasing the actual power of *zuryō* to exempt estates in their own provinces. This seeming contradiction derives from the dual nature of the *zuryō* as both public official and private courtier: it was in the governor's interest to control estates and increase his public income while in office, and equally in his interest to permit *shōen* establishment at the end of his tenure and reap private benefits. The Enkyū effort represented the attempts of conscientious *zuryō* to restrain the corrupt actions of other *zuryō,* but it was necessarily less than thorough.[21]

It is difficult to document how the Records Office dealt with estates of the Fujiwara main line. It was once believed that Yorimichi's

---

20 Wakita Haruko, *Nihon chūsei shōgyō hattatsushi no kenkyū* (Tokyo: Ochanomizu shobō, 1969), pp. 99–101. See also Yasuda Motohisa, *Insei to Heishi,* vol. 7 of *Nihon no rekishi,* 33 vols. (Tokyo: Shōgakukan, 1973–77), pp. 33–35.
21 Wakita, *Nihon chūsei shōgyō hattatsushi,* pp. 102, 108.

strong objections to the legislation forced Go-Sanjō to exempt the *sekkanke* from the process, but it appears that Yorimichi actually did submit documents to the Records Office, and that the house lost estates. At least one source refers to the confiscation of the Doi-no-shō, an estate belonging to Fujiwara no Morozane.[22] Of course, the major estate owners were unhappy with Go-Sanjō's attempt to increase national finances at the expense of private holdings. The great Tōdaiji temple of Nara, for example, was half a year late in submitting its paperwork to the Records Office.

Although the purpose of regulation was to confiscate lands and return them to a public, that is, tax-paying status, Go-Sanjō seems to have had other intentions for some of these lands. Imperial edict fields and the holdings attached to the *goin*, retirement palaces of abdicated sovereigns, did not provide extensive royal income. With the decline of public revenues, all courtier families experienced a loss of income, but the imperial house suffered most. Unlike the *sekkanke* and other noble houses, it was unable to accumulate much privately held land as a source of income. Just why this was so is not clear. There seems to have been more of an institutional, almost psychological, restraint than a legal stricture. Perhaps it was unseemly for the emperor, as head of a state that expressly rejected private ownership in favor of state-owned taxable lands, to establish *shōen*.

But Go-Sanjō took actions that paved the way for the acquisition of private landed wealth by the imperial house. From among the confiscated estates, Go-Sanjō established new *chokushiden* or "edict fields" (the exact number is unknown) that were virtually indistinguishable from the *shōen* belonging to courtiers and religious institutions.[23] This demonstrates the dual purpose of Go-Sanjō's estate regulation policy: to curtail illegal estates belonging to other proprietors and to acquire private holdings for the imperial house. The effect of Go-Sanjō's regulation of estates was momentous. By establishing a bureaucracy that demanded the submission of *shōen* charters and then ruled on their legitimacy, Go-Sanjō in effect legitimized those estates whose documentation was in order. As Thomas Keirstead has phrased it, the emperor's actions represent an "emblem of the reordering of the realm that produced the *shōen* system." The Records Office – "Go-Sanjō's archive" – went beyond simple

---

22 *Go-Nijō Moromichi-ki*, in *Dai Nihon kokiroku* (Tokyo: Iwanami shoten, 1951) vol. 2, p. 197, Kanji 5/12/12.
23 Okuno Takahiro, "Go-Sanjō tennō goryō," in *Nihon rekishi daijiten* (Tokyo: Kawade shobō, 1956–61), vol. 4, p. 525.

legitimation of estates and, by embedding the estate within a public domain and private land system circumscribed by maps, land surveys, charters and the like, essentially "established a new syntax of landholding . . . [I]n Go-Sanjō's archive we can perceive the first condition of the possibility of the estate system as system."[24]

Go-Sanjō's other economic policies are less well known and certainly not as far-reaching as his *shōen* regulation, but they are related. Not only had imperial control of the country's paddy fields broken down, there was also laxity in the application of uniform standards throughout the country. For example, the size of the *masu*, a measuring unit established in Nara times, was no longer standard but varied from place to place. It sometimes also varied according to purpose: a *shōen* owner might use one size *masu* when measuring payments, and another, somewhat larger, when receiving rents. To overcome the economic problems caused by such inconsistency, Go-Sanjō issued an edict in 1072 that determined the official size of the *masu* to be used throughout the realm. The measure became known as the "imperial edict measuring box of the Enkyū era" (*Enkyū no senji masu*). The *masu* was important as the basis for the system of equal provincial levies (*ikkoku heikin no kayaku*) initiated in Go-Sanjō's era. These levies were made on all lands, public or *shōen*, to pay for such national projects as the reconstruction of the palace or the Ise Shrine.[25] This unit of measure remained in use nationwide through the Kamakura period.

In 1070 there seems to have been another attempt at standardization: an ordinance was issued controlling the quality of silk and hemp cloth. Both materials had long been in use as media of exchange, and most likely this was another attempt to stabilize economic conditions by fixing the rate of exchange between these materials and rice, the official medium of payment. In 1072, another law was issued covering prices and other market matters. Since the establishment of the capital in the late eighth century, commercial activity had been increasing and government ability to regulate the exchange of goods and services had been decreasing. Although the terms of this law are not known, it was probably an attempt to bring the activities of merchants under greater official control.

Early in 1073 Go-Sanjō abdicated in favor of his son Sadahito (Emperor Shirakawa). On the same day, Prince Sanehito, Go-

---

24 Thomas Keirstead, *The Geography of Power in Medieval Japan* (Princeton, N.J.: Princeton University Press, 1992), pp. 18–19.
25 Yasuda, *Insei to Heishi*, pp. 39–40.

Sanjō's second son, was named crown prince. Since the time of the Buddhist priest and historian Jien, writing in the thirteenth century, it was generally assumed that Go-Sanjō's motive for retirement was to set up a system of rule by abdicated emperors (*insei*). No evidence for this theory exists, and recently scholars have come to reject it. A consciously worked out, elaborate, institutional scheme probably never occurred to Go-Sanjō. But to say that Go-Sanjō did not attempt "to establish the *insei*" is not to deny that he fully intended to exercise a guiding influence in government. The history of abdicated sovereigns prior to the heyday of Fujiwara *sekkanke* power must have given him ample expectations for an active postretirement career.

The timing of Go-Sanjō's abdication may have had something to do with the state of his health, although it is hard to judge from the sketchy information available. In a document Go-Sanjō dedicated to the Iwashimizu Hachiman Shrine, which he visited in the second month of 1073, he mentions having been ill during the preceding winter and again in the spring, and seeks the deity's aid in regaining his health.[26] In the third month an amnesty was proclaimed to benefit his health. In the fourth month he took the tonsure; one source gives the reason as sudden illness.[27] One can tentatively conclude that while Go-Sanjō was ill near the end of his reign, it was no chronic illness, and that for his four years on the throne he was relatively healthy. After his abdication, however, at least from the time of the amnesty proclamation, Go-Sanjō was seriously ill. However, illness alone probably does not explain his decision to retire.

The most plausible explanation for Go-Sanjō's abdication is his concern for royal succession. It is instructive to compare the designation of crown princes at the accessions of Go-Sanjō and Shirakawa. Go-Sanjō's enthronement ceremony took place on the twenty-first day of the seventh lunar month in 1068; Shirakawa was not named crown prince until some nine months later, even though he was Go-Sanjō's eldest son and already fifteen years old. By contrast, when Go-Sanjō abdicated in favor of Shirakawa, he appointed his own one-year-old son, Sanehito, as crown prince on the same day. The identity of the mothers of the two princes reveals the reason behind Go-Sanjō's actions (see Figure 9.3).

Shirakawa's mother was Fujiwara no Moshi, the adopted daughter of the *sekkanke* courtier Fujiwara no Yoshinobu. Despite the an-

---

26 *Heian ibun*, vol. 3, pp. 1113–14, doc. 1091, Enkyū 5/2/2.
27 *Fusōryakki*, vol. 12 in *Kokushi taikei* (Tokyo: Yoshikawa kōbunkan, 1965), pp. 315, Enkyū 5/3/18.

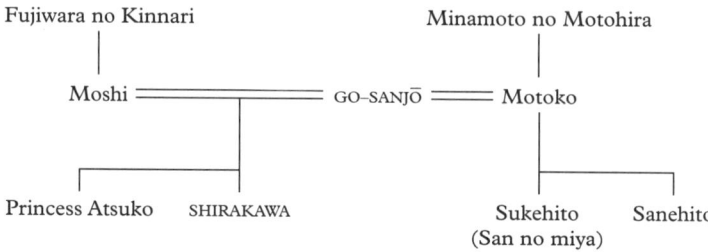

Figure 9.3. Family relations of Go-Sanjō.

imosity between Yoshinobu and Yorimichi's senior line, there remained the inherent danger that an influential Fujiwara regency might reemerge. Sanehito's mother was Motoko, daughter of Minamoto no Motohira. Go-Sanjō also had a consort whose father was Go-Ichijō; he decided to wait almost a year before confirming Shirakawa as crown prince because he hoped one of these non-*sekkanke* consorts might present him with an heir.

When Prince Sanehito was born in 1071, he was named an imperial prince within six months. When his father abdicated in favor of Shirakawa, Sanehito was named crown prince, although he had not yet reached his second birthday. The difference in Go-Sanjō's handling of the succession issue leaves little doubt as to his abdication motive. Furthermore, when Motoko gave birth to a second son, Prince Sukehito, in 1073, Go-Sanjō made it clear that he expected succession to follow in a fraternal line from Sanehito to Sukehito.

Thus it appears that Emperor Go-Sanjō abdicated in order to guarantee the future direction of imperial succession and to protect the imperial house from a possible resurgence of Fujiwara regency power. He was able to enthrone his eldest son, who did have tenuous *sekkanke* connections, but he appointed a Minamoto heir as next successor and indicated another Minamoto offspring to carry on after that. He was laying out a long-term succession plan in which the emperor would be unencumbered by Fujiwara maternal connections. The history of Japanese succession practices had demonstrated that abdication was the surest means to guarantee one's succession plans. As a young retired emperor (Go-Sanjō was only thirty-eight at abdication), he could certainly have expected to exercise familial supervision over his son Shirakawa in the manner of earlier Heian ex-emperors, indeed to participate in his kingship. While we may say the Go-Sanjō did not conjure up the idea of *insei*, it is certainly possible to see in his reign and abdication the prelude to such a development.

SHIRAKAWA AND THE NORMALIZATION OF *INSEI*, 1073–1129

Go-Sanjō's son Shirakawa (1053–1129, r. 1073–87) died at age seventy-six after living one of the most active and involved lives of any Japanese sovereign of the premodern period. It was during Shirakawa's lifetime that the *insei* became an almost formalized political norm, if by *insei* we mean a political situation in which the retired sovereign, operating as the head of the imperial kin group and "borrowing" the legitimacy of the titular sovereign, served as the de facto arbiter of political and economic interests of the court. It is, however, not so easy to say that Shirakawa's abdication was motivated by a desire to establish such a system.

Shirakawa was nineteen years of age when Go-Sanjō abdicated in his favor early in 1073, presenting him with a succession pattern that effectively bypassed his future progeny. But fate gave Shirakawa an opportunity to amend his father's scheme. Shirakawa's abdication in 1087 was not intended to establish a new political system; it had the more limited political goal of bringing about the accession of his own line instead of perpetuating his half-brother's. And yet other factors produced a situation in which Shirakawa emerged as the major political force in the realm. Whether or not he had originally conceived of an *insei*-like arrangement, by his death in 1129, the pattern of an actively ruling retired sovereign was firmly established. Just what was the nature of that system, and how did it develop so extensively during Shirakawa's reign?

Shirakawa reigned for fourteen years in much the same manner as his father had, exercising considerable personal authority because of the weak position of the Fujiwara regency. Morozane served as regent, and although the *sekkanke* remained the most powerful nonroyal house, he was unable directly to affect imperial action. Instead, Shirakawa exercised direct personal rule, employing the same kind of bureaucratic personnel practices as Go-Sanjō had. The "former three fusas" and Fujiwara no Sanemasa were among his chief advisers; all of them moved into the ranks of the *kugyō* noble council.

The Minamoto also continued to increase their influence at the expense of Fujiwara courtiers. This did not escape the attention of Shirakawa's contemporaries Fujiwara (Nakamikado) no Munetada, whose diary *Chūyūki* is one of the major sources of information for the period, comments several times on the advance of the Murakami Genji. In 1069 the ranking Murakami Genji, Morofusa, became Minister of the Right and the next year Minister of the Left, second only to Morozane. By 1083 his sons held both the Left and Right ministerial positions, a rare occurrence indeed. Some eleven years later, Munetada warned the *sekkanke* to be wary, since both ministers and the two major captains were Minamoto, as were three of five counselors, five of six captains of the guard, and four of seven controllers.[28]

Two political matters that seem to have greatly concerned Shirakawa were the continuing problem of *shōen* regulation and the increasing frequency of lawless behavior on the part of soldier monks of the great capital area temples. Shirakawa seems to have inherited his father's desire to limit the illegal acquisition of estate holdings; he issued a regulation edict that affected at least two Tōdaiji estates in Mino.[29] That he was forced to do so indicates that even Go-Sanjō's thorough legislation was insufficient to deal with the problem. Considering the number of *shōen* that were being established, by both legal and illegal means, it seems that Shirakawa was no more successful than his father.

On a number of occasions unruly monks, the so-called *akusō* from Mount Hiei and other great Buddhist establishments, threatened the peace of the capital. In 1079, for example, an ecclesiastical appointment precipitated a disturbance by more than a thousand armed Mount Hiei monks and the court was forced to send warriors against them. In 1081 an old dispute between Mount Hiei and Onjōji broke out again, resulting in considerable fire damage to both temples. (See Chapter 7.) There was such unrest that when Shirakawa visited the Iwashimizu Hachiman shrine south of the capital, he required the protection of an entourage of warriors led by Minamoto no Yoshiie. *Akusō* outrages proliferated, ultimately becoming the nobility's chief cause for concern. Shirakawa and his successor ex-emperors were forced to adopt new forms of military organization to cope with them.

During his reign, Shirakawa's main worry, however, was the poli-

---

28 *Chūyūki*, vols. 9–15 of *Zōho hiryō taisei*, 48 vols. (Kyoto: Rinsen shoten, 1965–89), vol. 1, p. 108, Kanji 7/12/27.
29 *Heian ibun*, vol. 3, pp. 1128–29, doc. 1118, Jōhō 2/8/23.

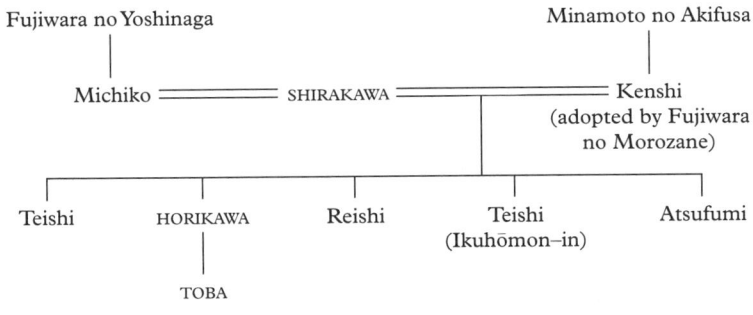

Figure 9.4. Family relations of Shirakawa.

tics of succession. Shirakawa had been presented with a predetermined succession plan, which gave precedence to his half brothers Sanehito and Sukehito, sons of Go-Sanjō's Murakami Genji consort Motoko. When in 1075 his own consort Kenshi gave birth to a prince, Shirakawa could foresee the possibility of royal succession passing to his own offspring; but the boy died a few years later in an epidemic that swept the land. In 1079, Kenshi gave birth to Prince Taruhito, the future Emperor Horikawa, and once again the possibility of altering his father's plan presented itself to Shirakawa (see Figure 9.4). No contemporary records even suggest that Shirakawa originally planned to overturn his father's succession plan. Extrapolation from later actions suggests, however, that succession was much on Shirakawa's mind. Fate also played a hand in the matter when in 1085, at the age of fourteen, Crown Prince Sanehito died of smallpox.

According to Go-Sanjō's instructions, Shirakawa should have immediately invested Prince Sukehito as crown prince, but he made no decision for almost a year. Shirakawa was certainly considering the appointment of his own young son, but there were obstacles. His father's injunction was clear. Furthermore, Go-Sanjō's mother, Yōmei-mon-in, was still alive and not likely to look favorably upon Shirakawa ousting her grandson. So he procrastinated.

By the eleventh month of 1086, Shirakawa finally resolved the dilemma. He made Taruhito crown prince then abdicated in his favor. Shirakawa had chosen to shift succession to his own line, cutting off Prince Sukehito from the throne. He had already constructed a magnificent retirement palace south of Heian. To at least one observer, the movement of men and supplies appeared to resemble the move of the capital. Many historians consider the building of this Toba-dono complex tantamount to establishment of the *insei*.[30]

Given that there was no respectable palace for a retired sovereign to use, however, it is not surprising that Shirakawa constructed one. In the late 1070s and early 1080s there had been numerous fires at the great mansions of the imperial family, the *sekkanke*, and other *kugyō*. Shirakawa was constantly moving between one temporary palace, normally the mansion of the regent or other major noble, and another. If he had intended to dominate politics in retirement, it would have been more logical to build a palace in the city close to the center of activity, as, for example, Saga had. The Toba-dono seems never to have been the center of his activities. He was not even named posthumously for this palace, but rather for the Shirakawa-in, a palace on the eastern fringes of the city. Shirakawa seems to have utilized the Ōi-dono more frequently as a palace; his trips to Toba were always termed "visits." So the establishment of a retirement palace at Toba-dono did not necessarily signal the raising of the curtain on the *insei*.

In fact, for some years after his retirement Shirakawa was not very active politically. His assumption of a major governmental role appears to have been as much the result of circumstance as of a plan. Once he decided to devote himself to rule in abdication, Shirakawa was very willful and powerful, but the evidence does not indicate that he had been that way from the outset. For example, shortly after Shirakawa's abdication, the court was forced to deal with the rising power of Minamoto no Yoshiie (1039–1106). The ex-emperor does not seem to have played an active role. Yoshiie had emerged from the Earlier Nine Years' War (1051–62) as the leading warrior in the land, chieftain of the Seiwa Genji. During Shirakawa's reign, he and his vassals had frequently been employed to guard the emperor on outings. After the Later Three Years' War (1083–87), Yoshiie's reputation spread, and local landholders began to commend *shōen* to him. At this point the nobles began to turn against Yoshiie, and the regents Morozane and Moromichi took the lead, not Shirakawa.

Traditionally the *sekkanke* had relied on the military power of the Seiwa Genji, but now they turned on Yoshiie. The nobility had long regarded the warrior as a samurai ("one who serves"), but Yoshiie

---

[30] Murayama Shūichi, *Heian-kyō* (Tokyo: Shibundō, 1957), pp. 146–76.

was threatening to compete with them on equal terms. Morozane, Moromichi, and the nobles began to support Yoshitsuna against his elder brother Yoshiie and, in 1091, precipitated a quarrel over leadership of the Minamoto warrior league. Afraid that Yoshiie would dispatch troops, the court forbade his men from entering Heian and prohibited local landholders from commending estates to him. Thus in the 1090s the Fujiwara regents Morozane and Moromichi led the court nobility – though Shirakawa may have been in agreement – in taking concrete actions against a threat to their collegial leadership.

Emperor Horikawa reigned from 1087 to 1107 and, according to contemporary documents, took his duties, especially appointments, seriously and was judicious in political matters.[31] Fujiwara no Nagako's description of Horikawa portrays him as a sensitive and tender man, a considerable flautist and poet who was the focus of a poetic circle that included a wide range of people at court, not the least among whom were his Minamoto maternal kinsmen.[32] Though Horikawa was only seven at his succession and passed away at twenty-eight, Shirakawa does not seem to have exercised much, if any, political authority during Horikawa's reign.

As we have seen, the Fujiwara regents Morozane and Moromichi appear to have played major roles in the government, without, however, the kind of dominance earlier regents had attained. Shirakawa was strong enough to prevent that. Also, Horikawa's mother, Kenshi, was Morozane's adopted daughter, which obviated the strong maternal tie necessary for regency domination. (Kenshi was the real daughter of Minamoto no Akifusa, and her Murakami Genji relatives enjoyed considerable influence at this time.) Although the accident of document survival makes any conclusions extremely tenuous, it is interesting to note that there are eleven extant imperial edicts issued by Horikawa. There is only one extant Shirakawa edict and, more important, there are no documents issued by ex-emperor Shirakawa or his office during Horikawa's reign. The first extant *in-no-chō* document is dated Tennin 2 (1110), early in Toba's reign.[33]

Although he had dispossessed Prince Sukehito, Shirakawa continued to feel pressure from that quarter and would not rest secure until Horikawa had produced an heir to the throne. Shirakawa was

---
31 Jien, in his *Gukanshō*, in *Nihon koten bungaku taikei* (Tokyo: Iwanami shoten, 1967), vol. 86, p. 204, makes this claim; other sources, including Munetada, also give high marks to Horikawa.
32 Fujiwara Nagako, *The Emperor Horikawa Diary*, trans. Jennefer Brewster (Honolulu: University of Hawaii Press, 1977), passim.
33 In *Heian ibun*, Horikawa's documents are all collected in vol. 4, except for one in vol. 9.

preoccupied with the problem, but he had himself to blame. In his zeal to avoid the possibility of a reestablished Fujiwara maternal connection, Shirakawa had married Horikawa to his aunt, Princess Atsuko, even though she was twenty-one years his senior (see Figure 9.3). The marriage took place in 1091, when Horikawa was only twelve; it is not surprising that, despite Shirakawa's diligence in offering prayers for the birth of an heir, Atsuko failed to conceive. In 1098, Shirakawa finally arranged a more congenial marriage for his son with Ishi, daughter of Shirakawa's uncle and close associate, Fujiwara no Sanesue. This time he was more fortunate: in 1103 a prince (the future emperor Toba) was born to the couple.

Shirakawa was greatly relieved. Horikawa was twenty-four and had fallen ill; complications would bring his life to an end in four years. Shirakawa had been very worried. Although he had abdicated and become a monk, he had avoided taking the final vows and adopting a Buddhist name so that he would be able to reascend the throne if anything were to happen to Horikawa before he had a son.[34] Horikawa had been without a designated successor for eighteen years. But when Toba was five months old, he was formally named Prince Munehito and in his eighth month was made crown prince. There can be little doubt that Shirakawa had intended to replace Go-Sanjō's Minamoto heirs with his own line.

The birth of Munehito created a rare situation in the history of the Japanese imperial house. Within the house, Shirakawa, Horikawa, and Munehito – grandfather, father, and son – served as abdicated sovereign, emperor, and crown prince. This was the first instance of such imperial continuity since Uda, Daigo, and Suzaku had held similar positions in the early tenth century, and it was interpreted by at least one observer as a great sign, a matter for rejoicing by both the court and the people.[35]

Such imperial unity, unencumbered by stifling *sekkanke* maternal relations, had the potential for providing the basis for a powerful and independent royal house. Although the imperial succession did not follow the course outlined by Go-Sanjō, Shirakawa accomplished the goal his father had envisioned.

But Shirakawa's worries were not over. In 1103, Sukehito had a son, Arihito, a prince with a Minamoto mother. Morotada, chieftain of the Murakami Genji, was aware that his house would prosper even further if this boy were to become emperor. Horikawa died, not unexpectedly, in 1107. Faced with a four-year-old emperor, Toba,

---

34 *Taiki*, vols. 23–25 of *Zōhō shiryō taisei*, vol. 1, pp. 67–68, Kōji 1/5/16.
35 Hurst, *Insei*, p. 137.

and with no desirable crown prince in sight, Shirakawa must have been concerned about the future of his line. Significantly, it was only at this point that he became an active participant in the political process as ex-emperor. He left the position of crown prince unfilled; having expended so much effort, he was not about to yield to his half brother.

Shirakawa's decision to move forcefully into politics adversely affected the fortunes of the Murakami Genji. They had been close allies of the imperial house during the reigns of both Go-Sanjō and Shirakawa; but having reached a position of influence rivaling that of the Fujiwara main line with two powerful candidates for crown prince, they had become more of a threat to Shirakawa than an asset. Ironically, the fate of the Minamoto princes Sukehito and Arihito was sealed by a precipitous act of their own clan members.[36] In 1113 a plot against the life of Emperor Toba was uncovered; it had been engineered by priests of the Daigoji, Shōkaku and Ninkan, both sons of Minamoto no Toshifusa (see Figure 9.2). The noble council, after debating their guilt, exiled several Genji courtiers.

This proved to be a damaging blow to Genji prestige, but strangely, it resulted in Shirakawa's adopting a conciliatory attitude toward Sukehito. The ex-emperor also adopted young Arihito. In 1119, when Toba's consort gave birth to a prince, Shirakawa gave Arihito the Minamoto surname and treated him with extraordinary honors. Nevertheless, Minamoto no Morotoki notes in his diary that although there was an outside possibility of Arihito's ultimate succession, his chances were virtually dead. He also saw that Arihito had more in common with two earlier frustrated Minamoto claimants to the throne, Minamoto no Takaakira and Koichijō-in, than with Emperor Uda, the only sovereign who, being dispossessed as a royal clansman and granted the Minamoto surname, had gone on to become emperor.[37]

Thus, in the decade after 1100, a number of factors combined to prod Shirakawa into action. One was his concern with maintaining imperial succession in his own line and the continued threat from his Minamoto half brother Sukehito, Sukehito's son Arihito, and family. Another factor was misfortune within the *sekkanke*. Moromichi had succeeded his father Morozane as regent for Horikawa, but died prematurely in 1099. Morozane himself died in 1101, leaving Mo-

---

36 Fujiwara no Tadazane records the event fully in his diary *Denryaku*, in *Dai Nihon kokiroku* (Tokyo: Iwanami shoten, 1968), vol. 4, pp. 59–62. Eikyū 1/10/5–22.
37 *Chōshūki, Zōho shiryō taisei*, vol. 1, p. 157. Gen'ei 2/8/7.

romichi's son Tadazane, then only twenty-two, as chieftain of the clan. Minamoto no Toshifusa was the senior court figure at the time and outranked Tadazane. Tadazane did not become regent until 1105 but was still too young to be the major figure at court.

When the young Toba came to the throne in 1107, Shirakawa was faced with the threat of a Minamoto crown prince at a time when he had no candidate of his own. The influential Minamoto clan could be expected to press the candidacy of young Arihito; and the *sekkanke* was at a particularly weak point. Shirakawa was almost forced into taking action. His pre-1100 actions do not accord with later characterizations of him as the embodiment of the despotic *insei* ruler. If we wish to see Shirakawa in that role, we must turn to the post-1100 period.

A perusal of documents and diaries of the quarter century before Shirakawa's death in 1129 leave no doubt that he was the political focus of the Heian court. Most of the personal statements we have about Shirakawa date from this period. Our image of him is thus shaped by these views. The *Heike monogatari* gives perhaps the quintessential depiction of Shirakawa as despotic ruler of the realm, stating that the only things outside Shirakawa's control were the Kamo River floods, *sugoroku* game dice, and the unruly Mount Hiei monks. This statement is strikingly similar to those scattered through the pages of Munetada's *Chūyūki*, which is the most complete record of the Shirakawa era. Munetada remarks that Shirakawa, "yielding to his desires, makes appointments unbound by law" and that "the grandeur of the abdicated sovereign is equal to that of His Majesty, and at the present moment this abdicated sovereign is sole political master."[38]

Shirakawa appears to have been an uncomplicated man who acted decisively on the basis of his own likes and dislikes, caring little for established custom. He lavished favors upon those he liked, and depended heavily on them. He loved and hated in the extreme. His great love for his consort Kenshi colored his feelings for their son, Toba, and daughter, the lady Ikuhōmon-in. The latter, if we are to believe Munetada, had a powerful influence on political decisions.[39] Also, Shirakawa's close relationship with his retainers (*kinshin*) gave them considerable influence over politics; sources cite

---

38 *Chūyūki*, vol. 3, p. 410. Tennin 1/10/28.
39 Takeuchi Rizō, *Bushi no tōjō*, vol. 6 of *Nihon no rekishi*, 31 vols. (Tokyo: Chūō kōronsha, 1965–67), pp. 225–26, quotes Munetada to the effect that Shirakawa loved this lady above all his other offspring, and thus power in the realm accumulated in her alone.

several of them as being of crucial importance to Shirakawa in decision making.

It is, of course, difficult to depend solely upon the diary entries of a few courtiers to reconstruct Shirakawa's personality. In the history of the Japanese imperial house, no one had been as politically active for such a long period; opinions of him must certainly have changed. On certain occasions, Munetada praises Shirakawa: when Shirakawa died, Munetada remarked on the long years of his tenure, concluding "his majesty filled the four seas and subdued the empire – since the time of Emperor Kammu there has been no such example. He should be called a sage ruler, a sovereign for eternity."[40] Conversely, on the death of Emperor Horikawa in 1107, Munetada noted the sadly deteriorating conditions in the Latter Day of the Law and was at pains to point out that the source of the problem was not Horikawa but Shirakawa – "it is because the priestly sovereign [Shirakawa] still lives, and the affairs of the land are split in two."[41]

Enough documents survive to confirm that Shirakawa was a dominating figure dedicated to the pursuit of the good life, that he lavished favors on the Buddhist establishment and reacted with strong personal likes and dislikes to persons and incidents. It seems that his temper flared frequently, and that he did not forgive easily. According to a famous story from the *Kojidan*, on one occasion when there was to be a dedication ceremony for his private temple, the Hosshōji, it rained hard and the ceremony had to be postponed. The next day it was again postponed due to rain, then a third day, and finally a fourth day. The irate Shirakawa became so upset, he ordered that rain be collected in a vessel and thrown into prison.[42]

Perhaps a more famous – and more credible – example is the case of Fujiwara no Tadazane (1078–1162).[43] Once Shirakawa had emerged supreme at court, and the *sekkanke* appeared to pose no great threat to the imperial house, Shirakawa was quite attentive to the *sekkanke* nobles. In 1120 he even suggested that Tadazane's daughter Taishi be admitted to Emperor Toba's women's quarters. Tadazane refused, incurring the wrath of the ex-emperor. Later Tadazane changed his mind and approached Shirakawa. This reversal seems to have enraged Shirakawa so much that he ordered Tadazane stripped of his post as regent; Tadazane went into seclusion until Shirakawa's death

---

40 *Chūyūki*, vol. 6, p. 65, Daiji 4/7/7.   41 *Chūyūki*, vol. 3, p. 231, Kaō 2/7/19.
42 This story is told in detail in Yasuda, *Insei to Heishi*, p. 56.
43 Hurst, *Insei*, p. 149, quoting from the diaries of Munetada and Morotoki.

twelve years later. Taishi was not only immediately prohibited from becoming consort, but Shirakawa wrote in his testament that she should never be made consort. He even dismissed four Hosshōji priests who were observed close to Tadazane.

Shirakawa was the towering figure of his age, political arbiter, imperial family head, and devout Buddhist. With his emergence as the supreme political figure at court we recognize the "*establishment of the insei.*" But we must be careful to define, on the basis of extant materials, precisely what we mean by this. The medieval historian Kitabatake Chikafusa (1293–1354), for example, states in his *Jinnōshōtōki* that from Shirakawa's time the ex-sovereign's documents took precedence over imperial edicts, since the ex-emperor had become the repository of sovereignty. But this does not seem to have been the case.

Sources hint that the *in-no-chō* of various ex-sovereigns issued documents, but there is only one, an *inzen* (decree) of the ex-emperor Uda, extant from before Shirakawa's time. Beginning with Shirakawa's time, however, these documents become more numerous; we find *inzen* and two documents issued by the *in-no-chō* on his behalf, *kudashibumi* (order) and *chō* (communiqué). But there are only six extant from Shirakawa's forty-three years as retired sovereign, three *inzen*, two *kudashibumi*, and one *chō*. By contrast, we can identify at least eleven edicts of Emperor Horikawa, who reigned for twenty of these years, and eight of Emperor Toba, who reigned for only sixteen. Importantly, none of the extant retired emperor documents dates from Horikawa's reign; the first is dated the twenty-second day of the last month of Tennin 2, which in the Western calendar would be early in 1110.[44] Granted, Shirakawa's activities far exceeded those of earlier ex-emperors and extant documents are more numerous, but he did not issue a large number of documents that would become the law of the land.

Like previous Heian ex-emperors, Shirakawa opened an *in-no-chō* upon his reitrement. He staffed it with the same kinds of personnel as had his predecessors: men who had served close to him (and to Go-Sanjō) while he was emperor. But Shirakawa's office was larger than that of earlier ex-emperors, reflecting his great power. Also, we can discern patterns of recruitment that tend to corroborate, with certain qualifications, Jien's claim that the ex-sovereign's officials had become extremely powerful.

[44] These are all contained in *Heian ibun*. Also see note 31, above.

Kurōdodokoro
    (private household office)
Fudono
    (secretariat)
Tsukae-dokoro
    (attendants' office)
Meshitsugi-dokoro
    (servants' office)

Mizuishin-dokoro
    (office of official bodyguards)
Mushadokoro-chō
    (warriors' office)
In-no-hokumen
    (office of ex-sovereign's warriors
    of the northern quarter)

Shimmotsu-sho
    (ex-sovereign's kitchen)
Gofuku-dokoro
    (office of ceremonial dress)
Saiku-sho
    (ex-sovereign's workshop)
Mimaya
    (ex-sovereign's stable)
Bechinō-sho
    (special warehouse)

Figure 9.5. Structure of the *in-no-chō*. Adapted from Hurst, *Insei*, p. 220.

It is difficult to grasp the size of Shirakawa's official *in-no-chō* staff. Organization closely resembled the house organization of the *sekkanke* and other major courtier houses. This is hardly surprising, since the original purpose of the *in-no-chō* was to provide a private organization, the lack of which had put the imperial house at a disadvantage in its political and economic competition with the leading noble families. The *in-no-chō* included among its offices a household office, attendants' office, servants' office, kitchen office, workshop, stable, and several offices for bodyguards and other warriors (see Figure 9.5). At Shirakawa's death, Munetada noted that there were twenty *bettō* (superintendents), five scribes, four secretaries, five assistants, and in excess of eighty warriors in the *in-no-hokumen*, the *in*'s guard unit.[45] This was quite an expansion from the modest beginnings in 1086, when Shirakawa had appointed to the *in-no-chō* five superintendents and six scribes, making only a few more appointments, including ten warriors to a *mushadokoro* (warriors' office), over the next several months.[46]

Most of the men who became retainers of ex-emperor Shirakawa were middle-ranking courtiers and *zuryō*, that is, governors or vice-governors who served in the province of their appointment. These

45 *Chūyūki*, vol. 6, p. 76, Daiji 4/7/15.
46 *Yanagihara-ke kiroku*, in Tokyo daigaku shiryō hensanjo, comp., *Dai Nihon shiryō* (1901–), series 3, vol. 1, pp. 3–10.

men provided the economic foundation for Shirakawa's regime. The expansion of *zuryō* economic power was aided greatly by *shōen* regulation that increased the public lands, which *zuryō* could exploit to enhance their income. Another result of regulation was the accumulation of a large number of imperial estates under the ex-emperor's control. The role of the *zuryō* in the process was crucial.

The importance of the Shirakawa–*zuryō* relationship was evident at the time. When Shirakawa died, Munetada noted seven things that first came to pass during Shirakawa's era. Five of these involved *zuryō*:[47]

1. *Zuryō* made enormous "contributions' (*kō*) to the government.
2. Boys in their teens became *zuryō*.
3. Appointments to more than thirty governorships were fixed.
4. Three or four members of one family served as *zuryō* simultaneously.
5. *Zuryō* failed to pay levies due temples, shrines, and courtiers.

The most obvious way in which *zuryō* aided Shirakawa was through "contributions." This was a kind of institutionalized bribery, known as *jōgō*, that had arisen in Heian times as public revenues decreased. Those who made private contributions toward the construction of public buildings or the expenses of court or religious ceremonies were rewarded with appointment to rank and/or office.

Although Go-Sanjō had attempted to curtail the practice, Shirakawa actively encouraged *zuryō* "contributions." The reward was reappointment or transfer to a more lucrative governorship. During Shirakawa's *insei*, provincial governors contributed toward the construction of major temples and shrines, imperial residences, and especially to new chapels built for the imperial house under Shirakawa's sponsorship. During his hegemony four of six imperial clan temples (*rikushōji*) located in the Shirakawa area east of the Kamo River were built, all by *zuryō* "contributions."

The *zuryō* were in the ideal position to make such contributions since they were little more than tax managers for the central government. As long as they forwarded the required levies to the capital, no one interfered with their attempts to make further exaction on the citizenry. *Zuryō* greed was a fact of life. If several members of a family held provincial governorships, the family could easily make the kind of "contributions" to which Munetada referred.

---

47 Yasuda, *Insei to Heishi*, pp. 77–78, quoting Munetada's diary entry at Shirakawa's death. *Chūyūki*, vol. 6, p. 65, Daiji 4/7/7.

Those serving most closely to Shirakawa were known as *kinshin*, or retainers.[48] While most of them were *zuryō*, they were not all of the same social origin. Some were from traditional *zuryō* families; others held a governorship in addition to their main bureaucratic post in the capital. Some had emerged from the lowest ranks of the nobility, while others had come from the warrior class, become *zuryō* and later served in Shirakawa's *in-no-hokumen*. The term *kinshin-zuryō* appears often in sources.

Shirakawa's retainers established more than a personal patron-client relationship with the ex-emperor. The tie extended to their families over time, so that sons, grandsons, and great-grandsons served the successive ex-sovereigns Shirakawa, Toba, and Go-Shirakawa. They became, in effect, client families of the imperial house. Among Shirakawa's retainers whose descendants became client families were Fujiwara no Tamefusa, Fujiwara no Akisue, Fujiwara no Akitaka, Takashina no Tameaki, and Taira no Masamori.

All but one of Shirakawa's *in-no-chō* offices had analogues in previous *in-no-chō*; the *in-no-hokumen*, or ex-sovereign's warriors of the northern quarter, was his own innovation. The *in-no-hokumen*, named for the location of their quarters in the ex-sovereign's palace, was a personally recruited elite guard, composed of essentially two kinds of warriors. There were small-scale warrior-landholders from the immediate capital region, who had come to Heian to serve as lower-level warriors, and middle-ranking provincial officials able to mobilize *bushidan* organizations through their local connections.[49]

But the *hokumen* was not the only military organization upon which Shirakawa relied for the support of his political power. While these warriors formed a standing military guard, others of greater stature were recruited privately to serve close to him. A good example was the Seiwa Genji chieftain Minamoto no Yoshiie, who, as we have seen, had emerged from the wars in the northeast as the greatest warrior in Japan. Although Shirakawa and the collective noble leadership had been sufficiently wary of Yoshiie that they prohibited landholders from commending estates to him,[50] the ex-emperor did ultimately receive Yoshiie in audience – which was tantamount to es-

---

48 Hurst, *Insei*, chap. 9, pp. 237–53, and appendix 2, pp. 285–311, discusses the *kinshin* in some depth.
49 Ishii Susumu, "Insei jidai," in *Hōken shakai no seiritsu*, vol. 2 of Nihon kenkyūkai, comp., *Kōza Nihonshi*, 10 vols. (Tokyo: Tokyo daigaku shuppankai, 1970–71), pp. 202–3.
50 *Go-Nijō Moromichi-ki*, vol. 1, p. 284, Kanji 3/10/10, contains the record of *kugyō* discussion of the commendations to Yoshiie. The same diary, vol. 2, p. 133, Kanji 5/6/12, mentions the edict.

tablishing a patron-client relationship – and ordered him to serve closely. Later the Ise Heishi rose from Masamori's service in the *hokumen* to become higher-level clients of Shirakawa and his successors; their military service was also of a highly private nature.

This kind of coercive force was needed neither to maintain Shirakawa's hegemony against possible opponents among the collegial leadership of the small circle of court nobles, nor to defend the prerogatives of the nobility as a class against revolution by the peasantry. It seems mainly to have protected the person of the ex-sovereign and the court against the armed monks of the major temples and enforced the widespread *shōen* regulation attempts at the provincial level. In 1118, for example, when the monks of Enryakuji stormed into the city, over one thousand of Shirakawa's *hokumen* and their vassals were mustered out at the Kamo riverbed. The establishment of expanded military forces, however, did nothing to prevent such uprisings. During the Insei period hardly a year passed without several incidents involving the rowdy monks of the great temples either fighting among themselves or demanding some redress from the court.

With the support of *kugyō* in the noble council, where Fujiwara *sekkanke* strength had waned, and with a large private organization including military forces, Shirakawa was able to dominate Heian society as had few other imperial house members before him. It is perhaps his dismissal of Tadazane in 1120 that marks his acquisition of supreme power. His emergence to such a position and the concomitant decline of the Fujiwara regent's house resulted in the formation of the *insei*, which was to remain the dominant political style of courtier rule until Go-Daigo's time in the fourteenth century.

THE HEGEMONY OF TOBA, 1129-1156

When Shirakawa died in 1129, *insei* rule was continued by his grandson Toba (1103–56, r. 1107–23), a man as arbitrary, strong-willed, and domineering as Shirakawa had been. Throughout Toba's reign under Shirakawa's *insei*, the relationship between grandfather and grandson had been antagonistic. As a result, Toba tended toward direct opposition to the policies Shirakawa had adopted.

The seeds of antagonism were sown early in Toba's life. Toba was, of course, the long-awaited heir of Shirakawa's son, Emperor Horikawa; he was made crown prince shortly after his birth. When Toba was four, Horikawa died, and Toba was enthroned. From this

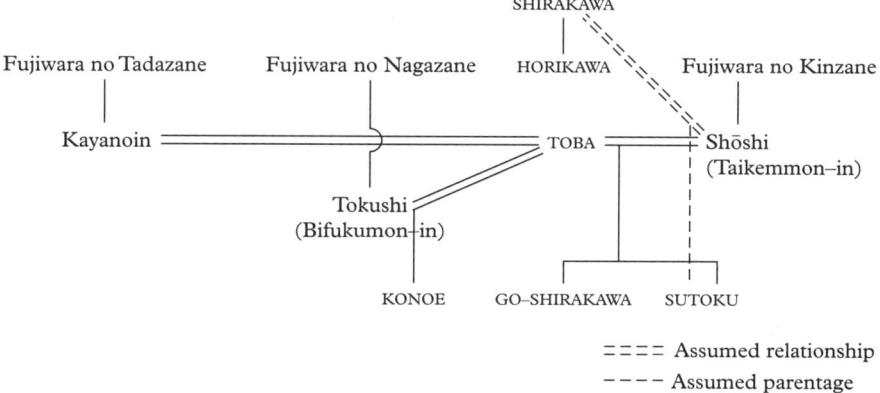

Figure 9.6. Family relations of Toba.

time Shirakawa emerged as the premier power at court, and during his sixteen years on the throne Toba had little opportunity to act as sovereign. Shirakawa chose as Toba's consort Fujiwara no Shōshi, a lady whom Shirakawa had adopted. Shōshi, better known by her honorary title Taikemmon-in, became consort to the fourteen-year-old Toba when she was sixteen and soon gave birth to Prince Akihito, the future emperor Sutoku (1119–64, r. 1123–42). Court gossip suggested that Sutoku was actually Shirakawa's child and not Toba's. Toba apparently was quite aware of the child's paternity. According to one source, Toba referred to Akihito as his "uncle" (*ojigo*).[51] Still, Toba seems to have had affection for Taikemmon-in, who was known as quite a beauty. She bore him four other sons and two daughters (see Figure 9.6).

In 1123, Shirakawa forced Toba to abdicate in favor of Sutoku. For more than six years, during the height of Shirakawa's rule, Toba languished as junior retired sovereign with no political influence at court. Toba must surely have been frustrated with Shirakawa and Sutoku for dominating the two primary positions in the imperial house, while he had sons who were also possible candidates for the throne. The three retired, honored members of the house – Shirakawa, Toba, and Taikemmon-in (the *san'in*, or "three *in*," as they were known) – seem to have made a number of pilgrimages together and enjoyed the wealth and prestige due their station, but considerable enmity brewed beneath the surface.

[51] Yasuda, *Insei to Heishi*, p. 127.

TABLE 9.1
Reigning and retired emperors in the Insei *period*

Reigning emperor	Reign dates	Senior retired emperor	Junior retired emperor
Go-Sanjō	1068–1073		
Shirakawa	1073–1087		
Horikawa	1087–1107	Shirakawa	
Toba	1107–1123	Shirakawa	
Sutoku	1123–1129	Shirakawa	Toba
Sutoku	1129–1142	Toba	–
Konoe	1142–1155	Toba	Sutoku
Go-Shirakawa	1155–1156	Toba	Sutoku
Go-Shirakawa	1156–1158		
Nijō	1158–1165	Go-Shirakawa	
Rokujō	1165–1168	Go-Shirakawa	
Takakura	1168–1180	Go-Shirakawa	Rokujō (to 1176)
Antoku	1180–1185	Go-Shirakawa	Takakura (to 1181)
Go-Toba	1183–1192	Go-Shirakawa	
Go-Toba	1192–1198		

Source: *Kodansha Encyclopedia of Japan* (1983), adapted from George Sansom, *A History of Japan to 1334* (1958).

At his grandfather's death in 1129, Toba moved quickly to inherit the exalted position Shirakawa had carved out for the retired sovereign. He immediately seized control of the numerous wealth-filled storehouses Shirakawa had built in the capital. Although some courtiers grumbled about the inappropriateness of this act, it was logical and necessary for Toba to secure this economic base as he began his tenure as abdicated sovereign. Shirakawa had been a dominant ex-emperor for so long (and the *sekkanke* had sunk so low) that no one seemed seriously to have expected the political scene not to continue in the *insei* form. From the start Toba's approach was different from Shirakawa's, even if his manner was similar. The three main differences involved Toba's attitude towards his retainers, his feelings about *shōen*, and his relationship with the *sekkanke*.

Toba initially dismissed a number of retainers who had been especially loyal to Shirakawa, replacing them with men loyal to himself. This is typical of almost any authoritarian ruler who attempts to impose personal control over the political scene. In Toba's time, there were also changes in the types of people who served the retired sovereign; the importance of *zuryō*, especially, seems to have decreased. This was partially due to *zuryō* advancement in rank and position at court. Furthermore, with the development of the proprietary province (*chigyōkoku*) system, under which high-ranking nobles became provincial proprietors (*chigyō kokushu*) and received the tax revenues from the province, *zuryō* became less important. They could no longer monopolize tax receipts. (Some *zuryō* did advance to become provincial proprietors under the ex-emperor's patronage.) But the main reason for the diminished importance of the *zuryō* under Toba was that he accumulated a large independent economic *shōen* base so that *zuryō* economic support was no longer necessary.[52]

Similarly, his policy of conciliation toward the *sekkanke* was motivated by a desire to undo the precedents set by Shirakawa. In 1120, Shirakawa, in perhaps his greatest exhibition of arbitrary power, had stripped the Fujiwara chieftain Tadazane of his regency. The clash with Tadazane had involved Taikemmon-in, then called Shōshi, who had become consort to Toba. When Shirakawa tried to have Tadazane's daughter Taishi afforded the same honor, the Fujiwara leader had refused, infuriating Shirakawa. Tadazane probably opposed Shirakawa because of Shōshi's rather unsavory reputation. Tadazane found her a "strange and unusual consort";[53] she had had numerous liaisons with other men at court, including an arranged marriage with Tadazane's son Tadamichi, which had been postponed several times, then canceled.

Less than a year and a half after Shirakawa's death, Toba succeeded in luring Tadazane back to court; Munetada, at least, found this reunion of sovereign and subject praiseworthy.[54] Once again, in contrast to Shirakawa's last years the imperial house and the *sekkanke* appeared to be in harmony. But the regent's house was a pale shadow of its former self. Tadazane's return marked the beginning of a new kind of relationship, a clientization or vassalization of the *sekkanke*, as its members, too, became retainers in service to the ex-sovereign. Tadazane regained the clan headship and governmental positions (in fact, if not immediately in name) from his son Tadamichi, widening the breach that already existed between them and further weakening the *sekkanke*. The breach between Tadazane and Tadamichi and, in the imperial house, between Toba and Su-

---

52 Ishii, "Insei jidai," p. 208.
53 *Denryaku*, in *Dai Nihon shiryō*, series 3, vol. 18, pp. 421–23, Eikyū 5/12/13, contains Tadazane's record of the events surrounding Shōshi's entry into the women's quarters. Three times Tadazane uses the phrase *kikai fukashigi* ("strange and unusual") to describe Shōshi. *Kikai* actually conveys a strong sense of "outrageous" or "scandalous." He refers to the whole procedure as the "most scandalous affair in Japan" (*Nihon daiichi kikai na koto*).
54 *Chūyūki*, vol. 6, p. 301, Daiji 6/11/17.

toku, would be major factors in the Hōgen Disturbance, which broke out at Toba's death. Such were the problems brought about by the arbitrary actions of retired emperors.

Perhaps the greatest difference between the policies of Toba and his grandfather was in the area of *shōen* regulation. Whereas Shirakawa inherited from his father the desire to control the acquisition of *shōen*, Toba wholeheartedly backed acquisition. There were a number of *shōen* regulation attempts in Shirakawa's time, but there are none recorded during Toba's years. While there are few documents extant from Shirakawa's era, we find an abundance of the three types of *in* documents in Toba's time, all relating to the matter of estate acquisition and management, demonstrating quite clearly that the main business of the *in-no-chō* was the management of estates belonging to the ex-emperor, other imperial family members, and clients.[55] Even the number of *chō* (documents directed to offices with which there was no superior–subordinate relationship) increased as communication about *shōen* control became more important to the imperial house.

While it is undeniable that Shirakawa was responsible for acquiring vast assets and building many great temple complexes, he did not accumulate many *shōen*. He tended to raise support through court-awarded grants, direct commendation, and contributions from his many provincial official clients. By contrast, Toba actively sought the establishment of new *shōen*. His documents largely concern guarantees of exemption from taxation for landholdings that normally had been commended to one of the numerous imperial Buddhist chapels or to Shinto shrines. Toba's *insei* was an epochal period of *shōen* acquisition for the imperial house.[56] The Anrakujū-in Temple (a complex within the Toba-dono) is a good example: of forty-seven holdings, four date from Shirakawa's time and forty-three from Toba's. This seems to reflect rather well their respective attitudes toward *shōen*.

The Noto Province *ōtabumi* (land register) compiled in 1221 lists public and *shōen* landholdings. It shows that more than 70 percent of cultivated lands were in some form of *shōen* holding. Three-quarters of that land (52 percent of the total landed area) was established in Toba's time.[57] Furthermore, Anrakujū-in documents suggest that

---

55 Hurst, *Insei*, pp. 223–36, passim. Much of the information on documents is gleaned from the unpublished manuscript of the late Suzuki Shigeo, "Inseiki in no chō no kinō ni tsuite: in no chō Hakkyū monjo o tsūjite mitaru."
56 Ishii, "Insei jidai," pp. 210–13.   57 Ishii, "Insei jidai," p. 209.

commendation estates were spread widely throughout Japan, beyond the Kinai region to middle-distant and outlying provinces.

Though Toba engaged in extensive *shōen* acquisition for the imperial house, acquisition was conducted somewhat differently than in other great houses, such as the *sekkanke*. Estates were not held in the name of the retired emperor, nor was he necessarily the highest level *shiki* holder. Virtually all holdings, like those of the Anrakujū-in, were lands for the support of temples or chapels belonging to some member of the imperial house, which was headed by the retired sovereign. This may in part have been a necessary device, disassociating the ex-emperor from a process that, though legal, was thought to run contrary to the spirit of the eighth-century statutory system, to which even the most fiercely independent ex-sovereign remained somewhat deferential.

Toba, like Shirakawa before him, continued to build numerous temples and sponsor construction on behalf of house members, to whom accrued substantial landholdings in the form of *shōen* commendations. Toba also began the process of consolidating these scattered holdings into blocs or portfolios, which he then used as economic resources for distribution to imperial ladies. The purpose evidently was both to make transmission of the holdings more secure and to provide for the ladies. For example, it was Toba who created the massive portfolio of estates known as the Hachijō-in-ryō. Hachijō-in was the palace name (*ingō*) of Princess Shōshi, daughter of Toba and Bifukumon-in. In 1140, Toba gave the princess twelve holdings; when Bifukumon-in died in 1160, Hachijō-in inherited all her mother's lands as well. Together they came to be known as the Hachijō-in-ryō and were handed down in the imperial house as an indivisible bloc. In the Kamakura period, when the house effectively split into two branches, these holdings numbered some 220 separate estates.

Taken together, the evidence suggests that Toba's period as retired emperor represented a high point in the process of *shōen* development and that a considerable portion of these new *shōen* came to endow the Buddhist chapels that formed the basis of the imperial house *shōen* holdings. But this was true not only of chapels sponsored by imperial family members. It seems that while virtually all new estates of the period were of the commendation type (*kishinchikei shōen*), a considerable number were commended to temples and shrines rather than to individual courtiers. Some scholars believe that during Toba's time, and to a lesser extent during Go-Shirakawa's, somewhat loosely controlled temple *shōen*, originally of the *zōyakumen* (miscellaneous post exemption) type, became more fully controlled, physically distinct *shōen*.[58] (*Zōyakumen* estates developed from the tenth century on, when a *portion* of the obligations peasants owed to the provincial government was exempted, that is, ceded to a temple or shrine. The form was literally "miscellaneous": it might mean rice, oil, roof tiles, straw rope, other products, or service labor. Such estates came under the dual control of provincial government officials and the estate holder.)

Politically, Toba was not the outstanding figure his grandfather had been, perhaps because his life was shorter. He continued to manipulate the traditional symbols of authority. The collegial noble council, again staffed increasingly by clients in his service, decided matters of state. But perhaps we can see him intruding more personally into the process and arrogating to himself more of the prerogatives of imperial power; for example, he is reputed to have issued his own *inzen* (not extant) to summon Fujiwara no Tadazane back to court.

During Toba's era, there was also expansion of military organizations under the ex-emperor's control. One very important development was the rise of Taira no Tadamori (1096–1153) as a military hegemon and Toba's reliance upon him. The Ise branch of the Taira had already established a close relationship with ex-emperor Shirakawa. Tadamori's father, Masamori, had commended some twenty *chō* of land in Iga Province to the Rokujō-in, a chapel dedicated to the repose of the soul of Shirakawa's beloved daughter Ikuhōmon-in. For this "contribution," Masamori received Shirakawa's fervent support as well as appointments to lucrative *zuryō* posts. He also continued to serve in the *in-no-hokumen* (see Taira genealogy, Figure 9.7).

Tadamori inherited that military position, but he rose far beyond his father to become one of ex-emperor Toba's major retainers. This was in part due to the unsettled times and Toba's need for a military force to deal with local unrest and *akusō* outbursts, but it was also the result of Tadamori's skillful maneuvering. When he was governor of Bizen in 1132, Tadamori "contributed" to the construction of the Tokuchōjū-in chapel and was admitted to imperial audience. Because of his lowly background and warrior vocation, Tadamori was resented by the rest of the nobility. According to *Heike monogatari*,

[58] Ishii, "Insei jidai," pp. 212–13.

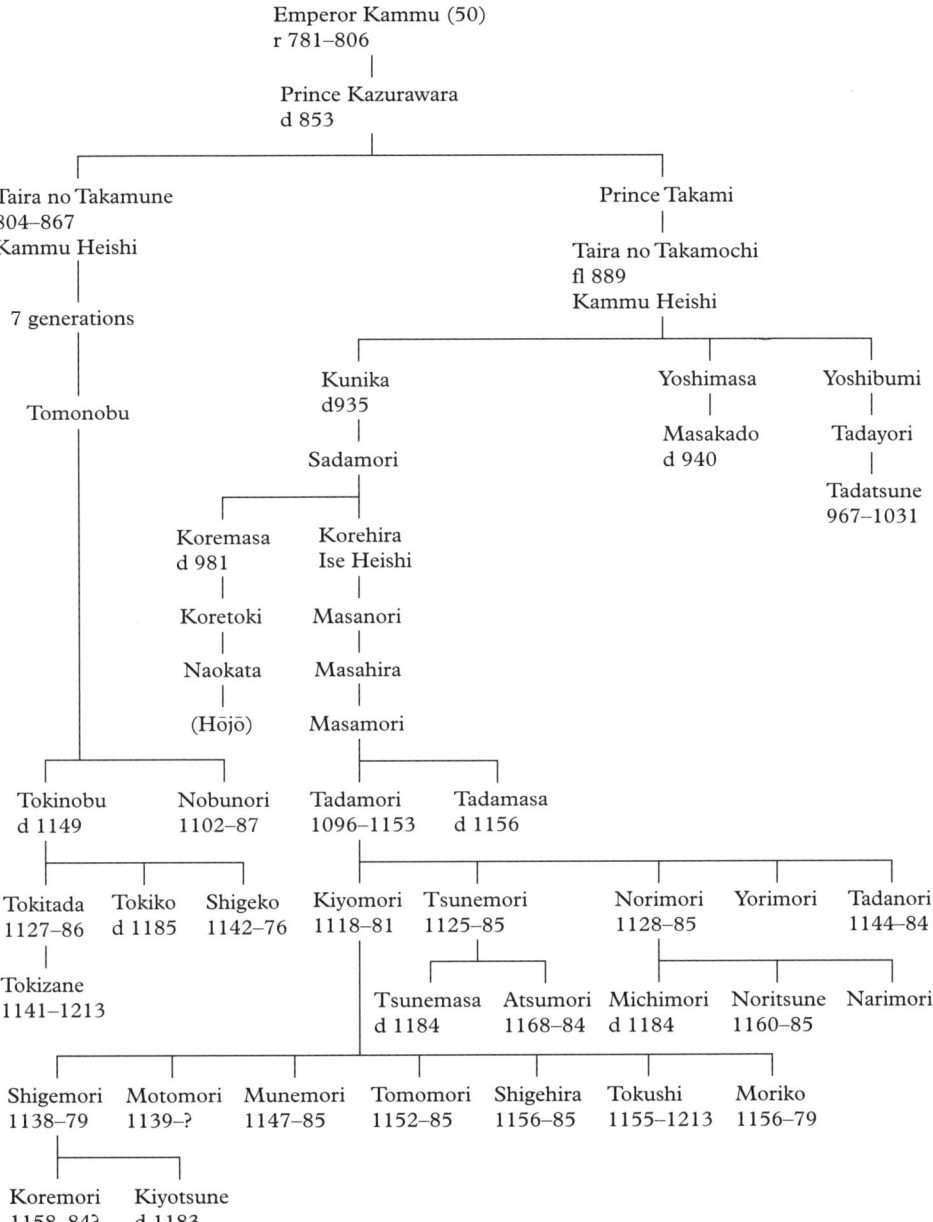

Figure 9.7. Genealogy of the Kammu Heishi (Taira). Adapted from *Kodansha Encyclopedia of Japan*.

they openly ridiculed him, even plotting his murder. But ex-emperor Toba favored Tadamori, and his house prospered.

In his late teens, Tadamori had subdued the bandit Natsuyaki dayū, thus establishing his military reputation; but his greatest exploits were against pirates in the west. He was first dispatched by the court in 1129 on an inconclusive campaign. The court sent him out again in 1135, choosing him over another great warrior hegemon, Minamoto no Tameyoshi. Sources reveal that he was chosen at Toba's recommendation, because the Taira already had a secure power base in the west.[59]

Tadamori soon returned in triumph with the head of the pirate leader Hidaka Zenji and some seventy prisoners, staging an elaborate entry into the capital and dazzling the citizenry. There were widespread rumors that these "pirates" were actually only local warriors who had refused to become Tadamori's vassals, but at least the uprising had been quelled. Whether or not Tadamori had merely engineered a successful public relations campaign, the Taira house was rewarded – Tadamori's son Kiyomori (1118–81) was promoted – and Tadamori's reputation as a warrior was enhanced. Perhaps more important, the expedition enabled Tadamori to solidify his power in the area; he organized local warriors into a vassal band (*bushidan*) with himself as warrior chieftain (*tōryō*).[60]

Toba already had the *in-no-hokumen*, which had been established in Shirakawa's time. The Imperial Police (*kebiishi*) could also be mustered out for protection of the imperial house and defense of the capital. But Tadamori's band was a rather different kind of force; Toba's use of Tadamori can in a sense be regarded as the establishment of a central government mercenary army. After the abandonment of conscript armies in early Heian times, local uprisings (such as Taira no Tadatsune's rebellion and the wars in the northeast in the eleventh century) had been handled by recruiting local warrior bands or troops under the command of the provincial governor.[61] Local uprisings were handled by local means, whether the court appointed a central official as general or not.

But under Toba's hegemony, capital warriors like the *in-no-hokumen* and others in his service were mustered out like mercenaries

---

59 Yasuda, *Insei to Heishi*, pp. 147–48.
60 Yasuda, *Insei to Heishi*, p. 150. *Bushidan* is a later, scholarly term rather than a contemporary one.
61 For a discussion of how the Heian court effectively harnessed local warrior power, see Karl F. Friday, *Hired Swords: The Rise of Private Military Power in Early Japan* (Stanford, Calif.: Stanford University Press, 1992).

and sent to quell local uprisings. Tadamori's *bushidan*, incorporated with other "public" forces, was mobilized to perform "public" functions. At the heart of the force was Tadamori's personal vassal band, a mercenary group organized by Toba, which came to function as a kind of central government army.[62] Tadamori became one of Toba's main sources of support; in this respect, Toba's *insei* had developed beyond Shirakawa's.

Actually, things seemed on the surface to be somewhat less complex under Toba. The *sekkanke* was brought back into the political process more fully, and there appeared to be little question as to where actual power at court lay. But the changing nature of the political situation – the rise to power of the ex-sovereign and the consequent increased power and wealth of other imperial house members, the corresponding decline in the fortunes of the Fujiwara, and the infiltration, through the dyadic contract with Shirakawa and Toba, of middle-ranking courtiers into the previously sacrosanct circles of the *kugyō* – produced a number of personal and factional rivalries that were to surface when Toba was near death.

Tensions were high among members of both the imperial and Fujiwara lineages, largely because of Toba's favoritism. We have already seen that he had called back into service the old patriarch of the family, Tadazane, whom Shirakawa had banished in 1120. Tadazane's return had seriously compromised the position of his son, Tadamichi; matters became worse as Tadazane looked increasingly to his younger son, Yorinaga, as the future *sekkanke* leader.

Both Tadamichi and Yorinaga saw their best chance for future success through the traditional technique of establishing a marital alliance with the royal house, and they engaged in fierce competition to provide consorts to Emperor Konoe, each hoping that a son borne by his daughter might become emperor. Both succeeded in having their daughters appointed consort, but this only intensified the rivalry. In 1150, Tadazane took the symbols of Fujiwara headship from Tadamichi and had them bestowed on Yorinaga. Soon the regency, too, passed to the younger Fujiwara lord; from that time Tadamichi was completely estranged from his father and brother.

The imperial house was not at harmony either, owing to the late Shirakawa's disposition of matters. Toba was senior retired emperor and the acknowledged leader of the Heian nobility, and his son Konoe had been enthroned in 1142 at the age of two. But ex-

---

62 Yasuda, *Insei to Heishi*, pp. 151–53.

emperor Sutoku was still alive and eager to redeem his political position. He had been emperor when Konoe was born to Toba and Bifukumon-in and had been forced off the throne soon thereafter by Toba. Although the two ex-emperors, Toba and Sutoku, were supposedly father and son, Toba had no reason to desire that succession continue in Sutoku's line. Sutoku, however, was waiting in the wings. He had pinned his hopes on the succession of his son, Prince Shigehito.

Besides these rifts in the two most important noble houses, there was a serious split in one of the major warrior leagues of the day, the Seiwa branch of the Minamoto. The Seiwa Genji, along with the newly risen Taira, were heavily relied upon as the military arm of the Heian court. Yoshitomo and his father Tameyoshi were, however, engaged in a dispute over the position of Minamoto warrior hegemon. In Heian society, while certain estate rights, such as the emperorship or the regency position, were the exclusive possession of discrete groups, factional alignments between members of noncompetitive groups could easily band together to further their own particular goals. This kind of factionalism was common and can be seen in the patron–client relationships between people from various levels of society and the *shōen* relationships in *shiki*.[63]

Thus members from all three groups – the imperial house, the *sekkanke*, and the Minamoto warrior league – soon found common ground to form distinct factions. When the young but sickly emperor Konoe died in 1155, followed quickly by Toba's illness and demise, these factional divisions at court erupted into a brief but crucial armed conflict known as the Hōgen Disturbance.

GO-SHIRAKAWA AND THE TAIRA, 1156–1185

It was prophetic that Go-Shirakawa's era was ushered in by the outbreak of the Hōgen Disturbance, for it was during his lifetime that the age of the warrior came to Japan. The clash of arms was precipitated by complex rivalries in the Fujiwara and imperial families focusing on the problem of succession and political control. Although he would succeed to the throne and eventually enjoy more than thirty years of power as ex-emperor, Go-Shirakawa (1127–92) was not a prime candidate for the imperial position in the mid-1150s.

Go-Shirakawa's mother, Taikemmon-in, was no longer close to

---

63 Kiley, "Estate and Property" (see note 6, above).

Toba; and he was some eleven years older than his half brother Konoe. Also, it was his father Toba's opinion that Go-Shirakawa was not qualified to become ruler.[64] Yet events worked in his favor. Tadazane and Yorinaga hoped that Konoe would produce an heir, but the emperor was sickly. Toba's favorite, Bifukumon-in, supported Go-Shirakawa's son, the young prince Morihito. Morihito's mother had died and he had been adopted by Bifukumon-in, who held great hopes for his future. Her collaborator, Tadamichi, also saw in him an opportunity to regain power. When Konoe died in the seventh month of 1155, Bifukumon-in, Tadamichi, and Toba discussed the possibility of enthroning Morihito, but concluded that it would be inappropriate to skip over Go-Shirakawa and enthrone his young son. Thus, Go-Shirakawa became emperor, and Morihito was appointed crown prince. At the age of twenty-seven, Go-Shirakawa had unexpectedly come to the throne, the result of complex factional alignments largely unrelated to his own personal qualities.

Go-Shirakawa's accession further intensified rivalries at court. In the Fujiwara house, it strengthened Tadamichi's position against his father, Tadazane, and younger brother Yorinaga, who were both at the time estranged from Toba; they had no influence on the succession decision. To make matters worse, it was rumored that they had cursed Konoe, causing his early death. The grief-stricken Toba gave credence to the rumors. Yorinaga could not convince Toba of his innocence and dispel the ex-sovereign's increasing hatred. At the end of 1155 his younger sister and Toba's consort, Kaya-no-in, died, cutting his only tie to Toba. Thus the situation at court appeared desperate for Yorinaga and Sutoku, and developments forced them together.

Toba died almost exactly a year after Konoe, on the second day of the seventh month of 1156. Within eight days of his death, the opposing forces were in place for a major confrontation.[65] The Hōgen Disturbance, which broke out on the eleventh, was brief and resulted in a victory for the forces supporting Go-Shirakawa: Yorinaga died of an arrow wound, Sutoku was exiled to Sanuki, and Tameyoshi and many other Minamoto warriors were executed, in the first case of capital punishment in Kyoto in about 350 years. Go-Shirakawa, Tadamichi, Kiyomori, and Yoshitomo were the clear victors.

Another important figure in these events was the lay priest Shin-

---

64 *Taiki*, vol. 2, p. 104. Nimpyō 3/9/23.
65 *Heihanki*, 5 vols. in *Zōho shiryō taisei*, is the most complete primary source for the Hōgen Disturbance; see vol. 2, pp. 112–26.

zei, Fujiwara no Michinori, one of the retainers who had been closest to the late retired emperor Toba. Shinzei, whose wife Kii-no-nii was Go-Shirakawa's wet-nurse, seems to have had a major advisory role in the decision to enthrone Go-Shirakawa, and in the aftermath of Hōgen, he had great influence over the new emperor. He was a leading scholar who worked with Go-Shirakawa to reinvigorate the declining organs of imperial government;[66] but he was also an upstart, a schemer, a man whose political successes were achieved at the expense of others. He engendered considerable animosity among certain entrenched groups at court, which ultimately led to another outbreak of violence and Shinzei's death.

Go-Shirakawa reigned for only three years before abdicating in favor of Prince Morihito. During that time, mainly on Shinzei's advice, efforts were made to reform "evil practices of the degenerate age." For example, a seven-article addendum (*shinsei*) to the imperial codes, issued in late 1156, attempted to curtail some of the illegal activities of the major Buddhist centers that continued to plague the court. The first two articles, however, dealt with continued *shōen* growth, declaring confiscate all improperly documented *shōen* established since Go-Shirakawa's accession in 1155. They also declared that added lands (*kanōden*) incorporated within originally exempted *shōen* boundaries were to be seized immediately. An important exclusion to this general principle, however, affords insight into the relative nature of the power and authority of ex-emperors in this *insei* period.

A stipulation was made that holdings with documents of exemption from ex-sovereigns Shirakawa and Toba should not be immediately confiscated; instead, the owners should forward imperial edicts and *in-no-chō* documents in their possession to the central government for perusal and await imperial decision. Following the example of Go-Sanjō, Go-Shirakawa reestablished the Records Office to carry out the legislation. From this case, one can see that ex-emperor documents were considerably more prestigious than others but not more authoritative than imperial edicts. They did not guarantee clear title to land: formal imperial approval obtained through the issuance of an edict was ultimately most valuable.

Go-Shirakawa and Shinzei also attempted to restore the throne to the center of the political stage, first symbolically by the reconstruc-

---

[66] Michinori was born a Fujiwara but took his wife's family name, Takashina, and was sponsored by the family. The Takashina traditionally produced Confucian scholars. Later, Michinori reverted to the Fujiwara surname, by which his sons were known.

tion of the imperial palace, which had burned so many times during the period. Special levies were made on all public and private lands, and in the third month of 1157 the ceremony for raising the ridgepole was held. Soon the emperor was able to move into the new palace, where court ceremonies could be conducted as in former times. Shinzei was eager to restore all the old practices and ceremonies that had fallen into disuse.

In 1158, however, Go-Shirakawa abdicated in favor of his son Morihito, who ruled for the next seven years as Emperor Nijō (1143–65). Some have argued that Go-Shirakawa's early abdication indicated his lack of interest in politics, evidenced also by his preoccupation with Buddhism and the poetic craze of *imayō*. Actually, Go-Shirakawa abdicated in anticipation of playing a major political role. He knew that his son Morihito was expected to become emperor. Having abdicated in Morihito's favor, it would be entirely in accord with recent precedent for him to enjoy political supremacy as father of the sovereign. This move would also be advantageous to his advisers, Shinzei in particular. Shinzei was of low rank and had become a lay monk, two factors that hindered his operation within the regular bureaucracy. As a *kinshin* of the ex-emperor, however, these were less serious handicaps to the exercise of power.

Like his two predecessors as senior retired sovereign, Go-Shirakawa abdicated fully intending to exercise his powerful influence at court. But for a while, at least, his ability to dominate the court was seriously hampered, and it was some time before he approached the level of dictatorial control that Shirakawa and Toba had enjoyed. This may have been due in part to his own unpreparedness for ruling – he had only reigned for three years after his unexpected accession. However, a more important reason was the presence of a strong and mature emperor in Nijō, who desired to exercise the authority due him as the formal head of state. The *insei* was subject to somewhat the same kind of institutional restraint as the regency power of the Fujiwara main line. Both forms of indirect control by familial authority worked best when the emperor was a minor. Thus, the *insei* tended to perpetuate the tradition of enthroning children.

When there was a more mature emperor, an abdicated emperor was considerably less able to dominate the court, sometimes not making the attempt despite his superior position within the imperial house. At the beginning of the *insei* period, it will be remembered, Shirakawa did not attempt to dominate Emperor Horikawa at all; his real role in government began in the reign of the young Emperor

Toba. When Go-Shirakawa abdicated, he was faced with the strongest emperor to rule during the tenure of an ex-sovereign, his own son, Emperor Nijō (r. 1158–1165). Nijō had been chosen for the imperial position before his father and thus most likely expected to be an active ruler even though he was only fifteen. As soon as Nijō became emperor, there arose several factional alignments, among which Nijō's faction, supporting direct imperial rule, obtained the upper hand. Certainly Heian politics had exhibited factional tendencies before, but it is obvious that the development of two potential foci of imperial authority in the *insei* period exacerbated the situation immensely.

This faction included Fujiwara no Tsunemune, whose younger sister was Nijō's mother, and Fujiwara no Korekata, son of Nijō's wet-nurse. While by no means the traditional *sekkanke* type of maternal connection, these close bonds with the sovereign provided a basis for cooperation. Others were drawn to this group because of their opposition to Shinzei, whose power at court had won him many enemies. Shinzei even made enemies of others among Go-Shirakawa's retainers, such as Fujiwara no Nobuyori. There were also a military faction, the major figures being Taira no Kiyomori and Minamoto no Yoshitomo. Since their emergence in the Hōgen affair, warriors had become a political force with which to reckon. At the outset of Nijō's reign, the imperial faction may have held the upper hand, but relationships between the aspirants for power was fluid: antagonisms flared up not only between factions, but within them as well.

In the last lunar month of 1159, these animosities culminated in the Heiji Disturbance. In this conflict the anti-Shinzei and anti-*insei* faction among the nobles included the Fujiwara courtiers Tsunemune, Nobuyori, and Korekata. When they were joined by the disaffected Minamoto warrior chieftain Yoshitomo, a bitter enemy of his military rival, Taira no Kiyomori, and of Shinzei, the faction had military power sufficient to contemplate a coup to topple Shinzei and Kiyomori.

The details for the Heiji Disturbance as well as for the Hōgen fighting need not concern us here; they are related in Chapter 10. Although the plotters managed to kill Shinzei, the rebellion ended with the victory of Kiyomori's troops. The Genji forces fled in defeat, Yoshitomo and his family and followers attempting to reach the safety of the east, where local warriors might rally to their cause. Many, including Yoshitomo, were killed, but at the behest of the

Taira lady Ike-no-zenni, Kiyomori spared Yoshitomo's thirteen-year-old son, Yoritomo, exiling him to Izu. It was a magnanimous gesture Kiyomori would later regret.

The political situation immediately following the Heiji affair did little to increase Go-Shirakawa's power at court. It was a low point for *insei* power, as the courtiers who had eliminated Go-Shirakawa's key political supporter Shinzei drew closer to Kiyomori in support of direct imperial rule by Nijō. This group included the wily Tsunemune and Korekata, who had shifted sides several times during the era to enhance their positions. Shinzei had once complained to Kujō Kanezane that Go-Shirakawa was the most ignorant sovereign in Japanese and Chinese records for failing to recognize these plotters from the beginning.[67] Go-Shirakawa was primarily an observer in the Heiji affair and enjoyed little political support in its aftermath.

Conflict soon arose between the ex-emperor and his son. In 1158, at the outset of Nijō's reign, both the emperor and his regent Motozane had been only fifteen years of age. Their fathers, Go-Shirakawa and Tadamichi, had acted in advisory capacities for their sons, with considerable influence on policy making.

But by the early 1160s, Nijō and Go-Shirakawa began to clash over the degree of influence the ex-sovereign ought to enjoy. There were several plots by Go-Shirakawa and his retainers against courtiers serving Nijō, which suggests that the relationship was strained. In 1161, Nijō struck back twice at supporters of Go-Shirakawa. On one occasion he exiled Taira no Tokitada and dismissed from office six courtiers, who were also Go-Shirakawa's retainers, for plotting to make Norihito – the infant son of the ex-emperor and Tokitada's sister – crown prince.[68] Within a few years the antagonism between Nijō and Go-Shirakawa was openly acknowledged at court, but clearly Nijō was in control. The man in the middle, the man who was using both sides as much as possible to further the interests of his own house, was Kiyomori.

The *Gukanshō* refers to the post-Hōgen-Heiji eras as the "age of the warrior" (*musha no yo*), and to an extent this was true. Kiyomori's military power overshadowed all others, and his rise in court was rapid. A year after the Heiji affair, he became a *kugyō* and thereafter was a full participant in important state affairs. Because of unsettled conditions in both the capital and the provinces, the court

---

67 Quoted in Takeuchi, *Bushi no tōjō*, p. 375, and Yasuda, *Insei to Heishi*, p. 253.
68 Hurst, *Insei*, pp. 194–97, discusses the incidents.

had to rely on Kiyomori's forces. Yet the 1160s (despite some scholars' arguments) is still too early to postulate the establishment of a "Taira polity."

It is important to note a change in the strategic maneuverings of Kiyomori and his kinsmen. During the Heiji rebellion, Kiyomori acquired control over a number of courtier *shōen* holdings and replaced Yoshitomo as warrior hegemon by incorporating a number of local warrior-proprietors into his military league. But as soon as he became a member of the elite courtier circle, Kiyomori gave up the strategy of organizing local landholders against central authority. Instead, he became a conservative supporter of the political system, adopting the age-old strategies of forging marital alliances with the imperial family and the *sekkanke* and dominating the *kugyō* bureaucratic apparatus. He became a military-courtier and thus missed an opportunity to unify the various frustrated local warrior elements into a powerful revolutionary force to topple the traditional elite. That task had to await Minamoto no Yoritomo.

The key to understanding the political situation at court during the crucial two decades before the 1180–85 war between the Taira and Minamoto lies in following the maneuverings of Go-Shirakawa and Kiyomori. Each used the other to further his own goals, cooperating for a considerable time until Kiyomori became powerful enough to dominate his former patron. In this sense, Go-Shirakawa's *insei*, at least until the outbreak of war, was less dictatorial and less powerful than those of Shirakawa and Toba. Go-Shirakawa could not dominate the court during Nijō's reign, but even after Nijō died in 1165, Go-Shirakawa was unable to dominate his grandson, Emperor Rokujō (1164–76, r. 1165–68). Kiyomori was in the way.

An example of competition, within a larger framework of cooperation, between the ex-sovereign and the Taira leader can be seen in their influence on the direction of succession. Nijō had no heir. As crown prince he had been married to Bifukumon-in's daughter, but after an extended illness, she became a nun. He then shocked the court by taking as his empress, Tashi, consort of the deceased sovereign Konoe, who came to be known as the "empress of two reigns" (*nidai no kisaki*). Nijō had no offspring from these two unions or from his marriage to Tadamichi's daughter Takamatsu-no-in. Consequently, the birth of the Taira prince Norihito threatened the possibility of the imperial line continuing among Nijō's descendants.

In 1164 a palace lady finally bore Nijō a son, and the child was immediately given to Takamatsu-no-in to raise in preparation for succession. Nijō's health was already poor, and he became critically ill shortly after the child's birth. Without even formally making him crown prince, Nijō abdicated in favor of his son. He opened the *in-no-chō* and appointed his officials, but died a month later. Thus the new emperor, known as Rokujō, came to the throne as an infant less than one year old, incredibly young even for a Heian sovereign.

The death of Nijō, and shortly thereafter of his loyal regent Motozane, made Go-Shirakawa the most powerful figure at court and within the imperial house. The exiled Taira no Tokitada was recalled, dismissed courtiers were reinstated, and Norihito was named crown prince only six months after Nijō's death. Go-Shirakawa was in the unusual positions of grandfather of the emperor and father of the crown prince. He was unchallengeable within the imperial house and master of the political situation. The *insei* form of government was firmly intact, but Kiyomori, manipulating the ex-emperor while himself being used, proved a stumbling block to Go-Shirakawa's complete domination of the court.

The rise of the Taira was the major development of the post-Hōgen Heian court. Much of the Taira success can be attributed to the nature of court politics in the *insei* period: the possibility of a bifurcation of authority between two imperial figures could lead to greater factional infighting than in earlier Heian times, and the use of force increasingly became necessary to settle disputes. It is also widely believed that Kiyomori was the illegitimate son of former emperor Shirakawa.[69] But one cannot overlook Kiyomori's skill at political maneuvering. After entering the ranks of the *kugyō* in 1160 as the first warrior-courtier, Kiyomori's rapid rise was due not only to his military power or presumed royal birth but to his ability as well. When his younger sister-in-law, Shigeko, entered Go-Shirakawa's service and caught the attention of the ex-emperor, Kiyomori worked skillfully to serve both factions, but necessarily drew closer to Go-Shirakawa.

By 1162 he had risen to the second rank and in 1164 managed to have his daughter Moriko marry Regent Motozane. The marriage placed him in a close relationship with the Konoe branch of the *sekkanke*, in effect preventing the Fujiwara from becoming an anti-Taira force. When Motozane died in 1166, Kiyomori had control of the greater portion of *sekkanke* property pass to Moriko, under the pretext that Motozane's successor, Motofusa, was too young. This

---

[69] Takeuchi, *Bushi no tōjō*, pp. 388–92; Hurst, *Insei*, pp. 181–82.

gave Kiyomori control over these Fujiwara assets. In 1162, Kiyomori completed the construction of the Rengeō-in Temple complex for Go-Shirakawa, a project that enhanced his relationship with the ex-emperor. His reward for this "contribution" was appointment as governor of the rich Bizen Province.

By early 1167, Kiyomori had progressed through several major court offices to become Chancellor (*daijō daijin*) and held the First Rank. This was all the more astonishing because he had risen this far in only the eight years following the Heiji affair. Much was due to his relationship with Go-Shirakawa, which became even closer with the appointment of Shigeko's son Norihito as crown prince. The two men seem not only to have gravitated toward each other for political reasons; they seem to have been very alike in character as well. It was perhaps this similarity in personality that led them into cooperation for a time and later to confrontation.

Both Go-Shirakawa and Kiyomori seem to have been determined to accomplish their objectives regardless of cost. Shinzei once criticized Go-Shirakawa severely for his stupidity but granted that he did possess two virtues.[70] First, he could not be restrained from accomplishing his goals. Second, he never forgot anything he heard. There are many stories that describe Kiyomori in the same fashion, perfectly willing to break tradition to accomplish an objective. In the Gion Shrine incident of 1146, for example, he shot arrows at the sacred palanquin, showing none of the hesitation that usually crippled the court in dealing with obstreperous monks. Also, despite his basic Buddhist and Shinto faith, Kiyomori put little stock in the efficacy of prayer to cure illness or bring rain during a drought.

By the time Kiyomori had become Chancellor there were several Taira *kugyō*, who provided backing on the noble council. Kiyomori resigned the office after only three months because of illness, but "retirement" did nothing to minimize his power. He was supported by Go-Shirakawa and wielded power as a "former chancellor." He and Go-Shirakawa, ex-chancellor and ex-emperor, were on similar institutional grounds.

Early in 1168, Kiyomori fell ill and became a lay monk.[71] The illness was serious enough that many courtiers, including Go-Shirakawa, were afraid he might die, endangering the security of the realm. Go-Shirakawa ordered prayers for Kiyomori's health and de-

---

70 Kanezane records this statement about Go-Shirakawa made by his close associate Shinzei. Yasuda, *Insei to Heishi*, pp. 266–67.
71 *Gyokuyō* (Tokyo: Meicho kankōkai, 1971), vol. 1, p. 40, Nin'an 3/2/9–11.

clared an amnesty. The ex-emperor was so worried that he hastily arranged for Rokujō to abdicate in favor of Norihito, who became Emperor Takakura (1161–81, r. 1168–80). With Go-Shirakawa's son on the throne, the pro-imperial rule faction would have been unable to work through Rokujō in the event of Kiyomori's death. Go-Shirakawa could thus reasonably hope for the continuation of his *insei* rule. So while Kiyomori was alive, the ex-emperor acted in concert with the Taira chieftain to effect this change.

Kiyomori did not die. During Takakura's reign, he and his clan rose to even greater heights. This was partly because of Shigeko's status as mother of the emperor. She was raised to the position of empress dowager and given the palace name Kenshummon-in. Takakura's accession, however, brought Kiyomori and Go-Shirakawa into competition over the emperor. In form at least, Go-Shirakawa, as father of the emperor and senior figure in the imperial family, continued his *insei* rule; but Kiyomori, with close maternal relations to the emperor and significant military and economic assets, was able to enjoy much more power than Go-Shirakawa desired.

At least until 1175, the relationship between the two appeared cordial, but as Taira power increased unchecked Go-Shirakawa's frustrations grew, especially because, in the face of continued trouble with the major temples, he was dependent on Kiyomori's warriors. (Even though Go-Shirakawa had become a monk in 1169, his ability to deal with the recalcitrant armed monks who demanded both ecclesiastic privileges and material rewards was severely limited.) He solidified his ties to the Taira by adopting Kiyomori's daughter Tokushi and making her consort to Takakura. The birth of a son would put Kiyomori in the enviable position of earlier Fujiwara regents. Taira influence, seemingly with the endorsement of the ex-emperor, continued to expand.

It would have been strange if other courtiers had not resented the Taira, upstarts who had reached the pinnacle of success at court, had married into the *sekkanke* and the imperial house, and held offices that in the past would have been denied them. The Taira were a new phenomenon at court, having started as provincial warriors but risen to become *kugyō* courtiers in the traditional mold. Yet they were distinguishable from other courtiers. They maintained military preparedness and skills that set them apart, though they did not integrate the local warrior populace into a separate authority structure as Yoritomo later did. In Rokuhara, a walled-off Taira suburb outside the borders of the Heian capital, they created family and residence arrangements different from those of other courtiers.

The Rokuhara area was located across the Kamo River, east of the capital proper. There the Taira maintained a cluster of clan houses that combined residential and military functions.[72] In twelfth-century warrior society the nuclear family became a residential unit, with fathers and sons, brothers and sisters, and other members of the extended family building their residences in proximity to form a community of kinsmen. Family residences were surrounded by the houses of retainers. This became possible through the adoption of the *yometori* form of marriage, in which the wife is brought into the husband's family. There was a basic need for self-defense in the warrior's world, and such a residential community, centered around the *sōryō* or clan head, reflected *bushidan* organization.

The warrior Taira had brought this family organization with them to the capital in the time of Kiyomori's grandfather Masamori. As they became more powerful and numerous, Rokuhara expanded accordingly. In giving a figure of more than 5,200 Heike-related houses in Rokuhara, *Heike monogatari* may be exaggerating, but the whole area from present-day Rokujō to Shijō along the east bank of the Kamo River was a Taira suburb including Kiyomori's Izumi-tei, Shigemori's Komatsu-dono, Yorimori's Ike-dono, and other famous mansions. The Taira did not break precedents in organizing their power structure in the 1170s, and they did their best to follow traditional patterns; but they were still a breed apart. The physical separateness of the suburb, the community of family residences, and the military superiority of the Taira made the very name "Rokuhara" threatening to both the nobility and the commoners of the capital.

From 1175, Kiyomori and his clansmen began to clash rather frequently with their longtime patron Go-Shirakawa, and there were several threats to the continuation of the Taira presence at court. In 1177 the friction broke into the open when a number of courtiers close to Go-Shirakawa were discovered plotting against Kiyomori at Shishigatani. Plotters were executed or banished, but no direct action was taken against the retired sovereign. The warning was thought to be sufficient, but Go-Shirakawa continued to plot against the Taira.

In early 1179, Go-Shirakawa took actions that could only be interpreted as a challenge to Kiyomori's position. Kiyomori's daughter

---

72 Yasuda, *Insei to Heishi*, pp. 272–74.

Moriko was the widow of Regent Motozane; at his death in 1166 she had inherited the bulk of the *sekkanke* holdings. When she died in the sixth month of 1179, Go-Shirakawa broke precedent and seized those holdings for his own. Two months later, when Kiyomori's eldest son, Shigemori, died, Go-Shirakawa seized his proprietary province of Echizen. He soon moved to isolate the Konoe line of the Fujiwara, which was related to Kiyomori through Moriko's marriage.

In the eleventh month of 1179, Go-Shirakawa's actions came to naught: Kiyomori staged a coup, demanding a rash of dismissals and new appointments. Thirty-nine courtiers, from the Chancellor on down, were dismissed, most of them *kinshin* of Go-Shirakawa.[73] This time Kiyomori moved against the ex-sovereign as well. Titles to his landholdings were seized for examination, and Go-Shirakawa was placed under house arrest in the Toba-dono. Early the next year, a *goin*, an office that managed imperial finances in anticipation of abdication, was established for Takakura. In the Second Month Takakura was forced to abdicate, and the infant Prince Tokihito came to the throne as Emperor Antoku (1178–85, r. 1180–85). Antoku was the son of Takakura and his Taira empress Tokushi, Kiyomori's daughter. The Taira clan had reached the height of its domination.

Anti-Taira sentiment remained strong, however, and Kiyomori felt it necessary to move Go-Shirakawa to a Taira residence where he could be watched more closely. Kiyomori instituted unusually severe military rule, dispatching more than three hundred of his spies (*kamuro*) throughout the capital to terrify the citizenry into compliance. It was in this kind of military atmosphere that, in the fourth month, Antoku's accession ceremony was held. That year, the Taira held fifteen proprietary provinces (*chigyōkoku*), and a Taira kinsman or adherent served as governor in thirteen provinces.[74] With the coup d'état of 1179, the confiscation of opponents' *shōen* holdings, and a move to dominate local power structures, the Taira had created their own polity.

But it was a transitory one. The Taira had alienated too many groups to enjoy much support. The great temples around Heian became dangerous enemies, partially owing to Go-Shirakawa's machinations. With their military might, they were the only power strong enough to challenge Kiyomori. Ex-emperor Takakura made his first pilgrimage, at Kiyomori's insistence, to the Taira family shrine at Itsukushima in Aki Province, not to one of the traditional shrines

---

73 *Gyokuyō*, vol. 2, p. 310, Chishō 3/11/17.   74 Yasuda, *Insei to Heishi*, pp. 292–93.

like Iwashimizu Hachimangū. At this the Onjōji monks rose up, calling on the Enryakuji to join them. Although they failed in their attempt to rescue the ex-sovereigns Go-Shirakawa and Takakura from Kiyomori's hands, it was the first time these large institutions had cooperated in a common enterprise. Kiyomori was forced to take precautions to guard Go-Shirakawa.

By the time Takakura had returned to the capital, Go-Shirakawa's third son, Prince Mochihito, a frustrated twenty-nine-year-old who had several times been passed over for succession, had issued an edict calling for the Genji and other forces to rally and oust the Taira from their seat of power. His co-conspirator was the aged Minamoto warrior Yorimasa, the lone Genji presence at court during the Taira heyday. The Taira tried to arrest and exile Mochihito, but he fled to the sympathetic Onjōji monks. Several days later, however, Mochihito, Yorimasa, and the Minamoto warriors in their service were killed by Taira forces in a battle at Uji.

To the consternation of the citizenry, Kiyomori then moved the capital from Heian to his family headquarters at Fukuhara (near modern Kobe), but that did not stop the anti-Taira movement. Mochihito's call had reached the eastern provinces, and by the ninth month Kiyomori heard rumors that Minamoto no Yoritomo (1147–99) had rebelled. In the eleventh month, the defeated Taira general Koremori returned with tales of a huge enemy concentration of troops. Kiyomori moved back to the capital in order to be close to the center of activities. The Gempei War had begun.

Go-Shirakawa was kept from political activity until 1181, when both Kiyomori and Takakura died. He reached the height of his power only when the Taira fled the capital in the seventh month of 1183, taking Emperor Antoku with them. Go-Shirakawa enthroned his grandson Go-Toba (1180–1239, r. 1183–98) – even though Antoku was technically still emperor and the Taira courtiers had the imperial regalia in their possession – and proceeded to dominate the Heian political world as he had been unable to do earlier. Go-Shirakawa was the only political figure able to deal with the military factions of the Genji warriors – Yoshinaka, Yoshitsune, and Yoritomo – as well as the Taira. Although later chronicles characterize him as wily and treacherous, Go-Shirakawa was trying to defend the prerogatives of the traditional court society against the onslaught of the warriors. To a great extent, it was because of his efforts that rapprochement was reached at the end of the war, and that the traditional state expanded to incorporate Yoritomo's newly created bakufu as an arm of the government. One can give credit to Go-Shirakawa for helping to effect a courtier-warrior union that would persist through most of the Kamakura period, until the warriors wrested all power from the court.

Go-Shirakawa was abdicated sovereign for thirty-four years, from his abdication in 1158 until his death in 1192, but this was by no means a period of uninterrupted total control. He had initially been kept from exercising dictatorial control by his son, Emperor Nijō, and was later checked by the rising power of the Taira. It was only after the death of Kiyomori and the flight of the Taira that Go-Shirakawa was able to direct politics at will. Because of the complex factional alignments, which were in part a result of the rise of the *insei*, for most of his tenure Go-Shirakawa was unable to act in as dictatorial a fashion as Shirakawa and Toba had.

Like his predecessor Toba, Go-Shirakwa was active in the acquisition of imperial estates, and the huge block of Chōkōdō-ryō estates, put together in his time, became one of the two major landed assets of the imperial house in the medieval era. Go-Shirakawa may appear to have maintained some ambivalence about *shōen* acquisition, for at least twice, as emperor and ex-sovereign, he attempted regulation. But *shōen* were an economic necessity. As Fujiwara no Koremichi, one of ex-emperor Toba's *kinshin*, stated: "Nobles today receive no official allotments at all. Without *shōen* how could they fulfill their public and private (obligations)?"[75] Public stipends for rank and office had disappeared. Nobles, including ex-emperors, could generate income privately through *shōen*, or in a quasi-public way through the proprietary province (*chigyōkoku*) system, which allowed private control of provincial tax revenues. (For imperial house members, they were called allotment provinces, or *bunkoku*, but the system was similar.)

Go-Shirakawa enjoyed extensive income from the far-flung network of *shōen* holdings that supported his religious and secular residences and elaborate lifestyle. Since he had formally become a monk in 1169, he often stayed in Buddhist chapels where all his needs were met. A document survives that lists the specific requisitions made of the various *shōen* for the support of the Chōkōdō chapel.[76] For vir-

---

[75] Murai Yasuhiko, *Kodai kokka kaitai katei no kenkyū* (Tokyo: Iwanami shoten, 1965), p. 337, quoting Koremichi's diary *Taikai hishō*.
[76] Takeuchi, *Bushi no tōjō*, pp. 282–87. For the full document, see Takeuchi, comp., *Kamakura ibun* (Tokyo: Tōkyōdō, 1971–), vol. 1, pp. 426–50, Kenkyū 2/10/no day recorded. The information on Fukiya-no-shō appears on p. 427.

tually every day of the year, different *shōen* provided various goods and services for the support of the ex-emperor and/or the chapel.

One of the Chōkōdō *shōen* was Fukiya-no-shō in Ubara district, Settsu Province, southwest of the Heian capital. Fukiya-no-shō was responsible for certain provisions required during the first three days of the new year (1192): a number of sets of new bamboo blinds (*sudare*), five *tatami* mats of differing types, cloth curtains, and five *ryō* of sand for use in Buddhist ceremonies at the temple. The *shōen* was also required to provide two laborers to serve at the temple during the sixth month and seven warrior guards to be posted during the sixth month at the gate facing Abura-no-kōji Street and during the first ten days of the seventh month at the inner gate.

Many other levies were made on Fukiya-no-shō for the Chōkōdō, from feed for oxen in the twelfth month to *go* boards. The necessities and luxuries for temples and other estate proprietors were provided by their estates; the complex requirements for each *shōen* were carefully spelled out to cover the entire year's needs. Even a glance at such documents confirms the accuracy of Fujiwara no Koremichi's statement about the need for *shōen*.

During the Insei era under Shirakawa, Toba, and Go-Shirakawa, the imperial house established a vast compex of *shōen* holdings, later called the "lands accumulated during the three reigns (*sandai gokishō no chi*)."[77] This powerful economic base helped ex-emperor Go-Shirakawa and his predecessors to dominate the Heian court as few imperial figures had in earlier eras.

By the time of Go-Shirakawa's death, *insei* government was so ingrained that the form would be retained for much of the Kamakura period. The warriors were so used to dealing with ex-emperor Go-Shirakawa that it was no problem for them to shift their allegiance to his successor, Go-Toba. Even after the Jōkyū War (1221), the Hōjō leaders did not abolish the position of ex-emperor; instead they made Go-Takakura "ex-sovereign," although he had never been emperor. This was unprecedented but indicative of how institutionalized the *insei* had become.

FOREIGN RELATIONS, 1070–1185

Another source of Taira power in late Heian times was wealth obtained through control of the China trade. As seen in Chapter 1,

[77] Hurst, *Insei*, pp. 254–74, discusses Insei-period imperial *shōen*.

after the Japanese court ceased formal relations with the Chinese in 838 and with the Po-hai kingdom in 920, it remained basically isolationist. However, the contact with Koryŏ, established in the 1019 attack of the Toi (Jurchen pirates), blossomed into a brisk trading relationship in late Heian times, especially under the sponsorship of Kiyomori.

King Munjŏng (r. 1046–83) ruled during the apogee of dynastic development, when Koryŏ firmly institutionalized the imported Chinese bureaucratic system. Munjŏng took steps to clear up a border dispute with the Khitan in the north, as well as to reestablish trade with the Sung after a lapse of about thirty years. Munjŏng also seems to have been favorably inclined toward Japan, presenting the opportunity for Japanese ships to reopen trade with China, using Koryŏ as middleman.

The first recorded visit of Japanese trade ships to Koryŏ occurred in 1073, when forty-two Japanese traders traveled to Korea and presented King Munjŏng with a number of Japanese specialty products, including bows and arrows, ink stones, and a saddle inlaid with mother-of-pearl.[78] Koryŏ records for the reigns of Munjŏng and his two successors show that Japanese ships made at least twenty-four trips to Koryŏ. Since the Japanese normally bore the title of envoy (*tsukai*) from Japan or Tsushima, it appears that this exchange of goods took the form of tribute and was conducted through Dazaifu channels.[79] In other words, it was public, not private, trade and served as an opening wedge in the reestablishment of quasi-legal trade with the Sung.

The import of Chinese goods through Koryŏ whetted courtiers' appetites, undermining the passively negative official policy against foreign trade. Courtiers and temples with *shōen* interests in Kyushu and rich merchants in the area attempted to escape Daizaifu controls and work out their own trade arrangements. During Toba's *insei*, certain courtier-officials with pro-trade leanings emerged, and a quasi-legal Sung–Japan trade was instituted.

At about the same time, however, the brisk trade with Koryŏ abruptly ended, owing to the rise of a military faction in Koryŏ and the ensuing internal chaos. Koryŏ came to regard Japanese trade ships as pirates; ships were sometimes stopped, the goods confiscated, and the crews executed. Consequently, Japanese traders, de-

---

78 Miura Keiichi, "10 seiki–13 seiki no Higashi Ajia to Nihon," in *Hōken shakai no seiritsu*, vol. 2 of *Kōza Nihonshi*, p. 258.
79 Miura, "10 seiki–13 seiki," p. 257.

nied open access to Koryŏ, began to turn exclusively to piracy, ravaging the Koryŏ ports. These were the earliest of the so-called *wakō*, or freebooters, who were to play a crucial role in Korean–Japanese relations during the medieval period. There had been considerable improvement in navigational techniques since the previous century, so it was no longer necessary for traders to rely on Koryŏ as an intermediary. Sailing directly to China was easier and offered greater profits.[80]

Trade with Sung China began on a private basis, but as Japanese ships ventured into the China trade, profit-seeking courtiers in Toba's retinue began to adopt a more positive attitude toward foreign relations. As relations improved it appears that certain Japanese circles, and especially the more intellectually oriented of the nobles, developed an interest in Sung culture. This made Chinese goods more desirable and moved Japan along a course of receptivity toward continental contact, which had not been seen for several centuries.

Shinzei is an example of the kind of person at Toba's court interested in things Chinese. Far more than just a political figure, he was the author of the historical compilation *Honchō seiki* and, along with Fujiwara no Yorinaga, was considered one of the great scholars of his day. Once during a discussion, Shinzei amazed a visiting Chinese priest with his brilliance. He apparently understood Chinese and expected to be dispatched as an envoy to the Sung court.[81] Such people were responsible for the positive attitude of the court toward foreign trade.

In late Heian times, no one was more interested in Sung trade than the Taira. The base for Taira trade domination seems to have been prepared by Kiyomori's father, Tadamori, during Toba's era. Tadamori's connection with the Sung trade is undocumented, but during the course of his several commissions to chastise pirates in the Inland Sea area, Tadamori established impressive regional bases along the Inland Sea, in both Shikoku and Honshu. These later developed into a network of bases, to which the Taira retreated during the Gempei War of the 1180s. With bases in the west, Tadamori may have begun to participate in the Sung trade, which was then vigorously under way in northern Kyushu.

One incident, noted in *Chōshūki*, the diary of Minamoto no Morotoki, hints at such an involvement.[82] In 1132, Tadamori was serv-

---

80 Yasuda, *Insei to Heishi*, p. 167.   81 Yasuda, *Insei to Heishi*, p. 167.
82 Yasuda, *Insei to Heishi*, pp. 168–69, based on *Chōshūki*.

ing as governor of Bizen. He was also a retainer of retired emperor Toba serving as *azukaridokoro* on the imperial estate Kanzaki-no-shō in the province of Hizen. That year a Chinese merchant vessel landed at Kanzaki-no-shō, and Dazaifu officials, in accordance with precedent, carried out an exchange for the merchandise on board. Tadamori, however, objected, calling this interference. He forged a document, which he claimed was a decree issued by the ex-emperor, giving him – as *azukaridokoro* of the imperially owned estate – authority to deal with the ship. Since the ship had landed on estate property, he claimed that Dazaifu officials did not have jurisdiction. The local officials complained to the court, severely criticizing Tadamori's behavior. It is likely that Toba's support allowed Tadamori to escape censure.

It is Taira no Kiyomori who is best known for having an interest in foreign relations. As governor of Aki, Kiyomori ordered construction of the main hall of Itsukushima Shrine as a display of reverence for the tutelary god of navigation and to serve as a base for maritime activities on the Inland Sea. Kiyomori's concern with the control of the Inland Sea may have been an indication of his desire to monopolize overseas trade. A more important step came with Taira monopoly of the post of *dazai no daini*. Kiyomori was appointed in 1158 and named a kinsman to act for him. But when Yorimori succeeded his brother in the post, he went to Kyushu and was influential in establishing the Taira family base on the island. With control of this influential Daizaifu post secure, the Taira were in an excellent position to monopolize Sung trade.

Although Chinese vessels entered a number of ports along the Japan Sea and East China Sea coasts, the official port of entry was Hakata. For obvious reasons, foreign ships were prohibited from entering the Inland Sea; there was even a watch point at Moji. After Kiyomori became Chancellor in 1167, however, permission was granted for foreign ships to enter the Inland Sea, and a special port was constructed at Ōwada-no-tomari (Kobe) to accommodate them. Thus, the Kyoto nobles had easy access to Chinese goods.[83] Kiyomori's interest in the trade is reflected in his constructing a villa at nearby Fukuhara.

Fortuitously, the period of Kiyomori's political dominance coincided with the reign of the Southern Sung emperor Hsiao Tsung (r. 1163–90), whose domestic policies and interest in stimulating for-

---

83 Yasuda, *Insei to Heishi*, p. 170.

eign trade made him one of the leading figures in the history of the dynasty. He lowered customs rates to encourage visits by foreign merchants, and clarified tariffs and standardized procedures governing commerce to stimulate Chinese traders to go abroad. The purpose behind the revived trade was, of course, to obtain profits for the imperial treasury.

In 1172, Hsiao Tsung requested that the Japanese court send an official envoy to Sung. Naturally, some nobles held to the traditional position that it was outrageous for the Chinese to request, in effect, tribute and use the term *Nihon kokuō*– the "king of Japan" – to refer to their sovereign. But Kiyomori, it seems, chose to meet with the Sung envoy, draft a reply, and send gifts to the Chinese emperor, thus initiating formal trade between the two countries. With Japanese and Chinese vessels plying the waters of the East China Sea, Japan was drawn into the East Asian trading orbit.[84]

The major Japanese trade items were sulfur, mercury, mother-of-pearl, fans, lacquerwork in gold and silver, and swords. Heian courtiers were eager for high-quality medicines, scents, porcelains, fabrics, and books from China. However, as domestic Japanese commerce began to develop, Chinese copper coins came to be the primary object of Japan's trading interests. Coins minted in Japan (the so-called *kōchō jūnisen*) had gone out of circulation by the end of the tenth century and had been replaced by rice, silk, or gold and silver. But the expansion of *shōen* held by capital nobles and monasteries led to an increase in the exchange of goods between province and capital, and by the twelfth century there was a demand for a circulating currency. The Japanese turned to Sung coins.

These coins were accepted for the purchase of residential land and paddy fields and the payment of *shōen* rents; soon they were being used in commercial transactions, in the payment of wages for building temples, shrines, and the like. The Northern Sung had previously forbidden the export of these coins, when the trade had become so extensive as to present a potential problem; but the prohibition was lifted in 1074, in the reign of Emperor Shen Tsung. Export volume immediately increased. Sporadic attempts to limit the export of coins proved impractical in light of the great demand. In 1171, during Southern Sung emperor Hsiao Tsung's reign, there was a final, unsuccessful attempt at prohibition.

Coins from the mainland were most likely received in trade by

---

84 Yasuda, *Insei to Heishi*, p. 171.

owners of *shōen* in the Kyushu area, who then used the money to pay *shōen* rents and other fees due to capital proprietors, so that the coins ultimately came to be concentrated in Kyoto. Of course, money also moved through the hands of Kyoto merchants to nobles and priests and into the possession of powerful members of rural society. Contemporary documents show that these people had money for the purchase of land. Similarly, coins filtered into the hands of nonagricultural merchants, craftsmen, and the like. From the middle of the twelfth century on, Sung copper coins spread rapidly throughout Japan.[85]

One of the main reasons for the increased demand for Sung coins was Japan's inability to produce enough gold and silver. When coins stopped being minted in Nara and early Heian, gold and silver came to be employed quite widely by Heian nobles. Both were used to purchase goods from Chinese trading vessels at Dazaifu. When gold and silver production dropped, and these metals no longer functioned as substitutes for minted coins, the demand for Sung coins naturally rose, not only among nobles and clerics but also among new local landholders and members of the peasant class involved in crafts production and commerce.[86]

This did not go unnoticed by the ruling noble class. The increasing development of a monetary economy threatened their control of society. A serious attempt was made to curtail the import of Sung coins; there was a sense that people were becoming overly concerned with the acquisition of money. It was said that society was suffering from a "money malady" (*zeni no yamai*).[87] This, of course, simply reflected a considerable degree of societal change, which presaged the rise of lower-stratum members of Japanese society, a development that was to become more obvious in medieval times. The nobility was aware that nonaristocrats were obtaining unprecedented economic power and, further, that nonagricultural groups – merchants, craftsmen, and the like – were expanding. But ultimately the nobility was too greedy for domestic and foreign produce to stop this process.

THE *INSEI* IN RETROSPECT

Since the work of early historians like Jien and Chikafusa, Japanese scholars have focused on the late Heian period as a time when re-

---

85 Miura, "10 seiki–13 seiki no Higashi Ajia to Nihon," pp. 266–67.
86 Miura, "10 seiki–13 seiki," p. 267.
87 Miura, "10 seiki–13 seiki," p. 267; Yasuda, *Insei to Heishi*, p. 174.

tired emperors dominated the political system. They have used the term *insei* to characterize this political form, in which the emperor, after abdication, established an *in-no-chō*, which was the repository of state power.

There has been an attempt to link the *insei* with Fujiwara regency politics (*sekkan seiji*), which reached a high point under the Fujiwara ministers Michinaga and Yorimichi. Not long ago, it was common to claim that under regency politics, national administration was privatized, and the household Administrative Office (*mandokoro*) of the Fujiwara regent's house in effect replaced the constituted offices of the state, with its documents deciding important issues. *Insei* was seen as a form of government in which these functions shifted from the Fujiwara *mandokoro* to the *in-no-chō*, with ex-emperor documents replacing imperial edicts. Though not without some truth, this was a rather mechanistic view of Heian politics according to which consciously instituted changes in the governmental structure compromised imperial authority. Both traditional and modern scholars were consequently critical of *sekkan seiji* and *insei* as aberrations from the political norm.

In the last few decades, however, there has been considerable revision of this viewpoint in Japan and the West. Neither *sekkan seiji* nor *insei* now is believed to have been a cohesive system of political control.[88] Fujiwara documents did not replace imperial edicts, nor were decisions of state the personal prerogative of the Fujiwara regent's house. The *in-no-chō*, especially during the Shirakawa and Toba eras, was not an instrument of national government but, rather, a body for the furtherance of imperial house interests, similar to the *mandokoro* of the *sekkanke* and other noble houses. The late Suzuki Shigeo demonstrated that through 1183, *in-no-chō* documents did not replace imperial edicts but dealt essentially with estate holdings of the members of the imperial kin group and their clients. The private decrees of the ex-emperor (*inzen*), however, were powerful enough to move the Council of State to action.[89]

In short, contemporary scholarship sees both *sekkan seiji* and *insei* in a new light. Neither replaced the old governmental structure but used it to further the political fortunes of the Fujiwara in one case and the imperial house in the other. In particular, the *insei* resulted

---

[88] See, for example, Hashimoto Yoshihiko's articles on *sekkan seiji* and *insei* in his *Heian kizoku shakai no kenkyū* (Tokyo: Yoshikawa kōbunkan, 1976), pp. 85–114.

[89] Suzuki's work is mentioned in the studies by Takeuchi and in Hashimoto (see note 88), but the fullest exposition of his work remains the thesis mentioned in note 55.

in control over the constituted offices of the traditional government by making *in* officials of courtiers holding important posts, or conversely, having *in* officials appointed to posts close to the emperor or to lucrative provincial governorships. The patron–client relationships cultivated between the ex-sovereign and his retainers were crucial in controlling the Heian political system.

Of course, the key was the ability to appoint *in* officials to important posts. What was the nature of the position of ex-emperor in Heian society – and even later – that made such appointments possible? It was not spelled out in the imperial codes, but neither was the role of the emperor set down clearly. At least two points should be raised here, both of which have been touched upon in the earlier discussion.

First, the familial role of the ex-emperor developed over the early Heian period. The ex-emperor, as father or grandfather of the emperor, normally served as paterfamilias of the imperial kin group, and parental authority over family members was quite strong. Some scholars have tried to equate the positions of regent and ex-emperor. The regent, by virtue of his maternal relationship with the emperor – maternal grandfather or uncle – exercised a kind of parental authority over the sovereign. That is why the *sekkanke* favored young emperors. The ex-emperor, working from the paternal side, could enjoy a similar familial control over an emperor, especially with the beginning of a shift from a matrilocal to a patrilocal marriage system in late Heian times. It was difficult for an ex-sovereign to exercise much familial authority over a brother who was emperor, or over an adult sovereign.

The ability to control an emperor through the exercise of natural familial authority is only part of the explanation, however; there was a very real difference between the respective positions of the regent and the ex-emperor. As was pointed out earlier, one cannot easily step down from the highest position in any complex organization, especially a dynasty, and return to a common existence. Authority tends to remain with a person. Thus in Japan, one who had been sovereign, not merely the recognized symbolic head of the state structure but also the religious link in a monarchy considered to be descended from the Sun Goddess, enjoyed an exalted position.

From the beginning, there was considerable confusion as to the respective roles of the sovereign and abdicated sovereign. We have seen that before the late Heian period, ex-emperors were often able to make their will known through edicts and verbal commands and to exercise substantial power and influence. Examination of historical materials allows us to conclude that sovereignty remained largely with the emperor – if for no other reason than that there had to be an emperor, while an abdicated emperor was not a political necessity.

Two well-known examples give evidence of the confusion over authority. In 1163, a dispute broke out between the local officials in the province of Kai and Yashiro-no-shō of the Kumano Shrine.[90] The province tried to abolish the *shōen* on the basis of the regulation ordinance issued a few years before, during Go-Shirakawa's reign. The *shōen* officials claimed exemption on the grounds of a document from ex-emperor Toba's *in-no-chō*. In the capital, Doctor of Law Nakahara no Naritomo was ordered to consider the case. In his opinion, Naritomo wrote that there was no distinction between the emperor and the retired emperor, and therefore retired emperor documents were equivalent to imperial edicts.

In another famous example, Kujō Kanezane records in his diary a conversation with Minamoto no Yoritomo in 1190, when the latter made his first visit to the Heian capital since he had been exiled as a youth.[91] According to Kanezane, Yoritomo recognized that ex-emperor Go-Shirakawa controlled politics and said that Emperor Go-Toba was like a crown prince. This captured the reality of the day perfectly – and Yoritomo noted that since both Go-Toba and Kanezane were young, their best chance for political success would come when Go-Shirakawa died and control passed to Go-Toba. There are other documents indicating that for virtually all of the Heian period imperial edicts were, strictly speaking, more authoritative, more orthodox than ex-sovereign documents. But obviously there was uncertainty in many quarters, and the distinction may be clearer to us today than it was then.

What historians call the *insei* was not a legally based system of political control but a more informal order of organization, which sought to utilize the existing political system. With the development of the *insei* the imperial house acquired the familial resources that other noble houses (*kemmon seika*) enjoyed as private interest groups. To be a *kemmon* it was necessary to have (1) a well-organized house administrative structure; (2) *shōen* holdings as an economic base; (3) private military forces; and (4) the principle of patriarchal control by the house head.[92]

90 Takeuchi, *Bushi no tōjō*, pp. 188–89.   91 *Gyokuyō*, vol. 3, p. 635, Kenkyū 1/11/9.
92 Kuroda Toshio, *Shōensei shakai*, vol. 2 in *Taikei Nihon rekishi*, 6 vols. (Tokyo: Nihon hyōronsha, 1967–68), pp. 114–15.

The *in-no-chō* provided a structure for such a private house organization for the imperial house, but during the heyday of Fujiwara clan power, the imperial house was strongly hampered from expanding this familial organization. From Go-Sanjō's time on, however, Fujiwara control over the royal house was broken, and successive heads of the imperial house, whether emperor or ex-emperor, exerted great efforts to increase family power and wealth. Attracting numerous clients, including warriors, and building up considerable estate holdings and other forms of wealth, the imperial house enjoyed tremendous power and influence in the years before military rule came to Japan. The head of the house could rule with almost equal political influence as emperor (*shinsei*) or through the emperor as ex-emperor (*insei*).[93]

Although the *in-no-chō* never lost its private function, serving primarily as a private organ for the management of royal estate holdings, at some point the abdicated emperor became the acknowledged leader in national affairs; as a result, the *in-no-chō* came to play a more public role. Exactly when this shift took place is extremely hard to discern, since it was an informal rather than a legal development. Most scholars agree that the *in-no-chō* was not a national form of government in the time of either Shirakawa or Toba, although the power and authority of the ex-emperor increased.[94] The shift came during Go-Shirakawa's tenure as ex-sovereign.

Some scholars will point to an 1174 *in-no-chō* order issued to Tōdaiji's Kuroda-no-shō in Iga Province, deciding a dispute between local officials and the estate owner.[95] There is also an 1176 order addressed to the local officials of all the provinces rather than to a specific addressee in one estate or local office. This is an indication that ex-sovereign authority was extending into broader areas of jurisdiction, transcending its earlier, narrower role.

The main national issue in late Heian and early Kamakura was *shōen* and provincial control of productive lands throughout Japan. The *in-no-chō* seems to have exercised great authority in this area – understandably, since it had almost always been connected with *shōen* management. Sometime in Go-Shirakawa's era, its functions expanded to deal more broadly with the regulation and control of

---

93 Kuroda, *Shōensei shakai*, pp. 110.
94 See, for example, Ishimaru Hiroshi, "Inseiki chigyōkokusei ni tsuite no ichikōsatsu," in Kurokawa Takaaki and Kitazume Masao, eds., *Kamakura seiken*, vol. 4 in *Ronshū Nihon rekishi* (Tokyo: Yūseidō, 1976), p. 17.
95 Ishimaru relies on both of these examples to conclude that the *in-no-chō* becomes an instrument of national policy in Go-Shirakawa's era, p. 19.

land. In the opinion of some scholars, the *in-no-chō* may have become a body possessing final authority to decide disputes during Go-Shirakawa's era.[96] Perhaps it happened during the Gempei War, when the Taira fled the capital with the young emperor Antoku, and Go-Shirakawa became the supreme authority and greatest defender of noble interests against the rising eastern warriors. An examination of extant documents shows that from this time *in-no-chō kudashibumi* and *inzen* are addressed to a broader audience and cover a greater range of affairs than before.[97]

National government was not a necessity in the *insei* period. Land and labor had fallen under the control of influential noble houses and local proprietors. Besides defense against foreign attack, what was really necessary at a national level was the ability to mediate disputes among the noble houses and local proprietors, and to suppress rebellions that would upset the balance of power. "Thus national power was a tool to support the private control of the influential noble houses."[98] Given that virtually all once-public functions and offices had been privatized, it is not so strange that the privatized family organization of the ruling house enjoyed the greatest degree of power and authority among the private groups at court in late Heian times.

The *insei* may be a classic case of what Kent Flannery, in his discussion of the evolution of civilizations, has called "promotion."[99] Promotion is an evolutionary mechanism induced by socioenvironmental stresses. "An institution may rise from its place in the control hierarchy to assume a position in a higher level; it may in the process go from 'special purpose' to 'general purpose.'"[100] This is essentially true for the *in-no-chō*, which started as a special purpose institution for the organization of imperial house interests. In the twelfth century, as the crises facing the Japanese state became acute – there was a loss of central power, a rise of provincial warriors, and increasing lawlessness among the unruly monks of the great temples – it was "promoted," or, rather, promoted itself, to a general interest institution. It became less system-serving and more self-serving.

Insei is a term that has a long history. It refers to a series of de-

---

96 Ishimaru, "Inseiki," p. 19.
97 See the appropriate periods in both *Heian ibun* and *Kamakura ibun*.
98 Kuroda, *Shōenshi shakai*, p. 117.
99 Kent Flannery, "The Cultural Evolution of Civilizations," *Annual Review of Ecology and Systemics* 3 (1972): 399–426.
100 Flannery, "Cultural Evolution," p. 413.

velopments in late Heian and Kamakura Japan when aristocratic control of the social and economic resources of the country started seriously to weaken in the face of the rise of a new class with fundamentally different values. Out of this situation rose several ex-emperors whose dominant personalities allowed them to exercise considerable influence over the affairs of the day and create political configurations that distinguish this period of Japanese history from all others.

CHAPTER 10

THE RISE OF THE WARRIORS

ORIGINS OF THE WARRIORS

The term for the Japanese warrior, *bushi* ("martial servitor"), which became common from the late Heian period on, was preceded in earlier centuries by the words *tsuwamono* and *musha*.[1] *Bushi*, like the other two words, specified the professional warrior as distinguished from peasant conscripts, court military officials, and palace guards. *Tsuwamono* is a native Japanese noun of unknown morphology, and *musha* (or *musa*) a Sino-Japanese binom meaning "martial one."

The professional warriors were private fighters who at first fought entirely in their own interests and for their own ends. They later entered the personal retainerships of court nobles or, more commonly, military lords, the greater of whom were called *tōryō*, another Sino-Japanese word, the constituents of which denoted "rooftree and rafters," that is, the chief members of a roof and, by extension, also "chief person." The term was commonly used to mean the chieftain of a major clan or family. As private fighters, the *tsuwamono* were fundamentally different in character from government troops, who were conscripted by authority of the state and fought solely for it.

During the seven hundred years from the twelfth century to the nineteenth, Japanese society was dominated by warriors, who first appeared as a potent independent political force in the country at the time of the revolt of Taira no Masakado in the mid-tenth century. Masakado and many of his supporters and opponents were profes-

---

[1] This chapter was translated by Patricia Sippel and adapted and expanded by Regine Johnson and the editors. It is based on Japanese primary and secondary works cited in the following footnotes. Studies in English on warriors of the Heian period include William Wayne Farris, *Heavenly Warriors: The Evolution of Japan's Military, 500–1300* (Cambridge, Mass.: Harvard East Asian Monographs, 1992); Karl F. Friday, *Hired Swords: The Rise of Private Warrior Power in Early Japan* (Stanford, Calif.: Stanford University Press, 1992); and George B. Sansom, *A History of Japan to 1334* (Stanford, Calif.: Stanford University Press, 1958).

sional fighting men, mounted archers descended in their skills perhaps from the prehistoric hunters found in the archaeological record of the eastern provinces. Mounted warriors are known in Japan from before the seventh century, but they first became professional and a locus of autonomous political power during the tenth century, when their arms were employed not on behalf of the government for its purposes but in pursuit of private interests. As the organizational skills of such warriors grew, they formed retainer-based military bands of increasing size and power, structures that eventually enabled them to contend for control of the country. Their triumph over a weakened imperial court in the twelfth century led to the establishment of a new, warrior-ruled system of government in the Kamakura period (1185–1333).

The popular modern image of the Japanese warrior has been shaped largely by colorful literary and pictorial representations of fifteenth- and sixteenth-century battles in which swordplay figured prominently, and also by the knightly figure of the samurai as found in the status system of the Tokugawa bakufu. The Heian warrior was neither. He was primarily a mounted archer who wielded the dagger and sword when his supply of arrows was gone and fighting had become hand-to-hand. At this time the bow rather than the sword was the weapon of choice. The warrior's status was not, like that of the Edo-period samurai, clearly established near the top of a centralized military society, nor did he see himself, his superiors, or his society in the ideal categories employed by later Confucian pedagogues. Derived from a verb meaning to attend on a superior, *samurai* was used in that sense (in its earlier pronunciation of *saburai*) in an early-eighth-century chronicle to designate civilian attendants assigned to the old or infirm or in the menial service of the sovereign, and it continued to be used in that nonmilitary sense in the Heian period for low-ranking servants of the nobility. As a title within court society, *samurai* was also applied to military attendants.

The main forces of the statutory (*ritsuryō*) imperial court in the eighth century were peasant conscripts, mostly a foot soldiery organized into units of three hundred or fewer to a thousand or more men. Military service was a heavy economic burden for the conscripts, who were required to furnish their own weapons, clothing, and other equipment, specified by law to include a bow, bowstrings, arrows, a quiver, two swords, leggings, boots, a reed hat, a whetstone, and containers for water, food, and salt. Each ten-man unit was also required to supply a tent, tools, cooking equipment, and moxa.² The conscription of a single man, it was said, could bring about the collapse of his entire family.

Modeled on the armies of T'ang China, the statutory conscript system provided the imperial court with a well-articulated military force, lightly armed and trained. But the operation of the system was plagued with trouble from the beginning; individual units sometimes degenerated into little more than work gangs in the employ of officials. In the absence of major internal enemies after the middle of the eighth century and the fading of the perceived threat of Chinese and Korean aggression, the system was generally abandoned in 780 and 792, retained then only in what were considered strategic "frontier" areas, namely, the northeast (the provinces of Dewa and Mutsu) and the Dazaifu provinces of Kyushu. It was partially replaced by small groups of "stalwart youths" (*kondei*), elite mounted fighting men who first appeared in the eighth-century east, where their martial skills were likely learned in some part from their redoubtable Emishi enemies, especially in the matter of fighting from horseback. (For an account of the expeditions against the tribal Emishi in the northeast around 800, see Chapter 1.)

Little is known about *kondei* duties and functions. In 733, three hundred conscripts from Mutsu and Dewa skilled in mounted archery were named *kondei*. It is significant that *kondei* were first appointed in the military districts responsible for the subjugation of the Emishi, and that mounted archers were recognized as being more effective than foot soldiers in combat with those tribal people. The *kondei* of 792 and after were members of powerful local families (*gunji*, "district officials") and cultivators sufficiently prosperous to equip, mount, and support a warrior, recruited from what was likely a substantial pool of hunters in the area.³ Provisions and two grooms (*batei*) aged seventeen to twenty were supplied for each *kondei*, one of the grooms actually functioning perhaps as a batman.⁴

Although the *kondei* were no doubt militarily superior to the peasant conscripts of the old system, their small numbers nationwide indicate that they could not have fully replaced the conscripts. There were fewer than four thousand scattered in units of twenty to two hundred throughout Japan, and they could have functioned, one

---

2 *Ritsu. Ryō no gige, (Shintei zōho) Kokushi taikei*, ed. Kuroita Katsumi, vol. 22 (Tokyo: Yoshikawa kōbunkan, 1939), pp. 183–85.
3 Takeuchi Rizō, "Tōgoku no 'tsuwamono,' " *Miura kobunka*, 25, 5 (1979).
4 *Ruijū sandai kyaku, (Shintei zōho) Kokushi taikei*, vol. 25 (1936), kan 18, p. 548, 22/11/Enryaku 14 (795), and pp. 553–55, 3/11/Tenchō 3 (826).

may assume, only as a constabulary in the protection of government facilities and operations.⁵ The central government had in effect ceded responsibility for the preservation of the public peace outside the vicinity of the capital to the landed class.

The conscript system was not disbanded in Kyushu until 928, replaced there in part by units of "select youths" (*senshi*), who were similar to the *kondei* in origin and presumed functions but were somewhat better attended.⁶ Although there were fewer horses and archers in Kyushu than in the east, the creation of *senshi* units stimulated a similar, if belated, development of a warrior class there, too.

The disestablishment of the conscript armies and their replacement by small units suitable only for the security of government offices and facilities signaled the abandonment of state responsibility for the peace of the country. Reflecting that shrinkage of government intention, the sources for the period record no actions involving either *kondei* or *senshi*. The name *kondei* office (*kondeidokoro*) survived within provincial-government structures until the end of the Heian period, but the offices came to have merely titular existences.

The development of a warrior class in the tenth century and after cannot be directly linked to either the *kondei* or *senshi,* but the men of those units were clearly products of socioeconomic circumstances similar to those that led to the emergence of the private professional warrior. They were mounted fighters and shared common origins with the direct ancestor of the warrior class, the *tsuwamono*. Both the *kondei* and the *tsuwamono* came largely from a prosperous landed class, especially in the east, which was accustomed to hunting from horseback and had a long tradition of bearing arms. Where the *kondei* were insufficient in number to suppress banditry, provincial landlords became more active in military preparedness. They relied increasingly on arms also to settle their disputes and to extend their holdings when they found the opportunity.

Under the statutory laws the provincial governor was conceived of as a civilian authority and his staff was not permitted to bear arms. However, in the ninth century, because of lawlessness in the countryside, governors of certain provinces were granted permission to engage armed men to protect themselves and their headquarter compounds and to enforce their orders. By the beginning of the tenth century and perhaps earlier, when serious disorders occurred

---

5 *Ruijū sandai kyaku*, kan 18, pp. 558–59, 14/6/Enryaku 11 (792).
6 *Ruijū sandai kyaku*, kan 18, pp. 553–54, 3/11/Tenchō 3 (826).

in a province, the court issued additional police or military titles to the governor or his deputies to empower them to raise and lead warriors in order to apprehend miscreants and restore order. These special commissions were intended to be temporary to meet emergencies, but they often became long-term and sometimes hereditary. In the eleventh century, provincial headquarters continued to develop as military centers, regularly garrisoned, and the governor was authorized to engage the services as needed of professional warriors (*tsuwamono*) of the locality.

The word *tsuwamono* in its earliest known uses referred broadly to the means of warfare – weapons, provisions, and skills – and also to the persons who made use of those to wage war – warriors. By the ninth century, the term was restricted to the human element of the definition, the fighter, and in the tenth century *tsuwamono* came to designate more specifically the professional fighter. It was in that sense that Taira no Masakado's "fame as a *tsuwamono*" was recorded in *Shōmonki*.[7] *Tsuwamono* acquired retainers (*rōtō*, "lads" or, more literally, "young companions"), but initially not in the relationship of a lord to his vassals. The term *rōtō* referred rather to the fellow *tsuwamono* whose interests were in common with those of their leader and who fought under him. Since they were not strictly subordinate to their leader, they are perhaps better described in their earliest form as companions. Rudimentary organizations of *tsuwamono* and *rōtō* developed by the middle of the tenth century, thereafter growing in size and strength, but *rōtō* tended to maintain their relationship with their leader only as long as it served their own interests, a tendency that remained to some extent even after the subsequent development of personal bonds of loyalty and subordination had led to the formation of the large-scale warrior retainerships that dominated the political history of the twelfth century.

In acquiring retainers, *tsuwamono* may have been following the example of provincial governors. At any rate, the first occurrence of the word *rōtō* is the case of a former governor of Tosa, Ki no Tsurayuki, who mentions *rōtō* among his retinue as he sets off on his return voyage from Tosa to the capital in 934. *Rōtō* are not found with *tsuwamono* until a few years later, at the time of Masakado's revolt. The practice of acquiring retainers seems to have been widespread among governors. The value of retainers to the governor came to be more than simply personal security; they were employed for admin-

---

7 *Shōmonki*, in *Kodai seiji shakai shisō*, ed. Yamagishi Tokuhei, Takeuchi Rizō, Ienaga Saburō, and Osone Shōsuke, vol. 8 of *Nihon shisō taikei*, 67 vols. (Tokyo: Iwanami shoten, 1979), p. 213.

istrative work and were also available for police or military functions. They appear to have been key instruments in the extraction of wealth from a province. In one case, it is reported, the dispersal of a governor's retainers after his death resulted in the impoverishment of his family. But a governor was a civil official, and when his term of office expired, his retainers might remain to serve the next governor or seek employment with the governor of another province. The *tsuwamono*, on the other hand, was a professional, hereditary warrior vested with interests in land, and his *rōtō* might continue in service with him and his family indefinitely.

The *tsuwamono* warrior was the product of sweeping changes in landholding that in the eighth century and after transformed the public, imperial lands and people of the statutory regime into a stratified society of wealthy, powerful private landholders and a subservient peasantry.[8] The new landholders were in some cases local in genesis, their lands and labor force growing from an original family and its state allotment of land, and in other cases stemming from external authority, descending from officials and military officers appointed in a province by the central government. As the holdings of the new lords expanded and control of an increasingly independent peasant workforce grew more difficult, and as commendation converted land into *shōen* estates with complex and often conflictive external relationships, military might became a useful and necessary adjunct of landholding. The nucleus of the military forces created on the great landholdings was the *tsuwamono*, who enforced the will of the landholder, defended the holding against external threats, official and private, and kept the peace.

The earlier *shōen* were owned by higher nobles and by major temples and shrines that, as absentee landlords, sent a manager to oversee cultivation and remit revenues. However, by the tenth century, most new *shōen* were established by families, local or newly arrived from the capital, who commended land to a high noble or religious institution or member of the imperial family (*ryōke* or *honjo*) with influence enough to protect the *shōen* from interference by provincial authorities and from provincial exactions. In return the owner-manager paid his protector a percentage of the rents collected from farmers. Both the new *shōen* and the older type founded by an owner in the capital required local military force to keep order on the *shōen*, to collect rents and taxes from the cultivators, to stave off the gover-

[8] On statutory landholding institutions, see *Cambridge History of Japan*, vol. 1, chapter 8. On the evolution of these institutions in the early Heian period, see Chapters 3 and 4 of this volume.

nor's men, to resist encroachment by nearby *shōen*, and to expand into *kokugaryō* (lands of the provincial government) or other lands as opportunity arose. *Tsuwamono* were often the owners or managers of *shōen*. In the tenth and eleventh centuries they were also found increasingly among the administrators in the offices of the provincial headquarters and managers of the province's lands.

As military might became a necessary element in successful landholding, two noble warrior clans established themselves as *tsuwamono* both in the vicinity of the capital and in the provinces, especially and most fatefully in the east. Their success was partly attributable to their family lineage, the multiple lines of both clans originating from imperial offspring removed from the imperial family in the cost-cutting of Emperor Saga's time or after and given the noble clan names of Minamoto or Taira. (On that process, see Chapter 1 and Chapter 2.) Many of those demoted princes remained in the capital pursuing conventional court careers, they and their descendants sometimes rising to high office and rank, while others sought their fortunes in the provinces, turning there to the profession of arms. But the most prominent of these warriors maintained their connections at court and, from time to time, held guard or police offices in the capital.

The Minamoto name was granted to one or more princes by eleven emperors from Saga (r. 809–23) to Sanjō (r. 1011–16). The multiple lines created in that manner are distinguished in nomenclature according to the name of the ancestral emperor: Saga Genji, Murakami Genji, and so on, "Genji" being the Sino-Japanese reading of the characters with which "Minamoto clan" is written. The bakufu of the Kamakura period (1185–1333) was founded by the line of the Minamoto usually known as the Seiwa Genji, so called because they were descended from a prince named Tsunemoto (d. 961), who was supposed to be a grandson of Emperor Seiwa. But a document discovered in the nineteenth century indicates that Tsunemoto was actually a grandson of Yōzei (and thus a great-grandson of Seiwa). Not all students of the subject accept the testimony of the document, but if it is correct, we may suspect that the name of the criminally inclined and finally deposed Yōzei was avoided by family historians in favor of a more auspicious genealogical origin for the great line.[9] Tsunemoto's son, Mitsunaka (912–97), served the North-

---

9 "Iwashimizu Tanaka-ke monjo, Kawachi-no-kami Minamoto no Yorinobu kômon," in Takeuchi Rizō, ed., *Heian ibun*, Komonjo-hen, vol. 3 (Tokyo: Tōkyō-dō, 1963), p. 775; and Hoshino Tsune, "Yo no iwayuru Seiwa Genji wa Yōzei Genji naru kangae," in *Shigaku sōsetsu* (Tokyo: Fuzambō, 1909), pp. 108–47.

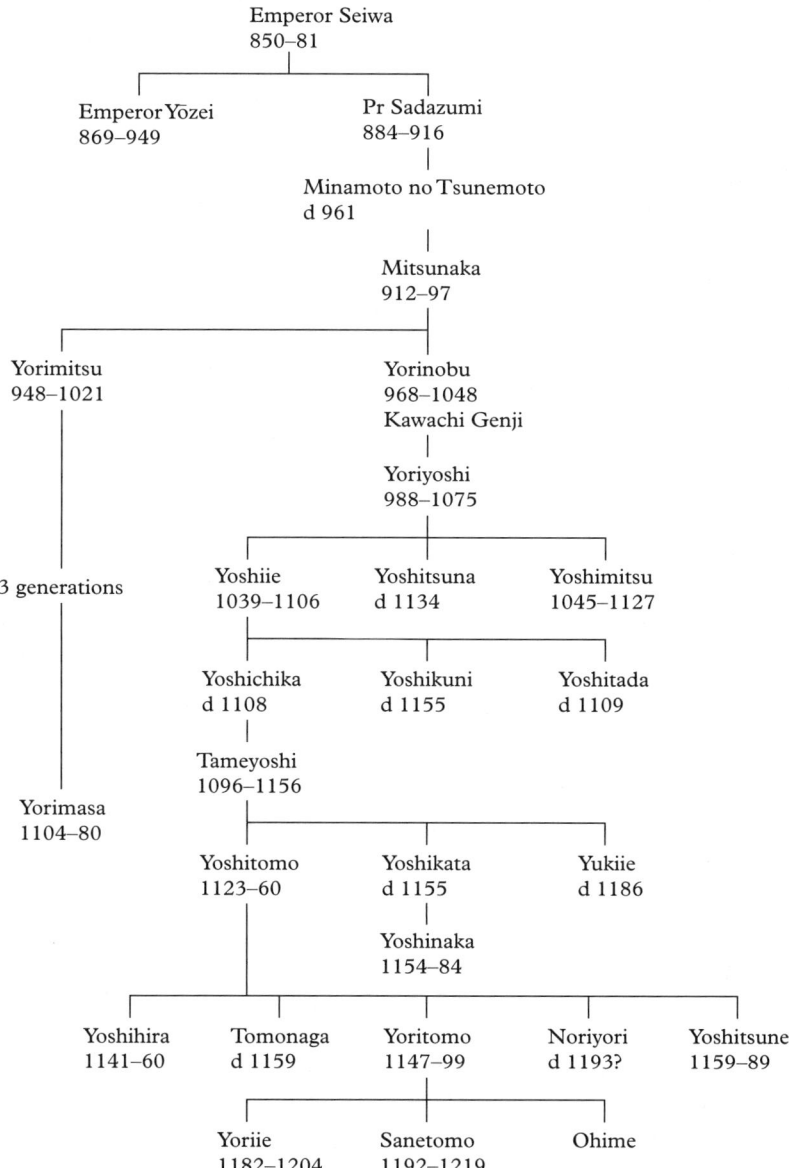

Figure 10.1. Genealogy of the Seiwa Genji (Minamoto). Adapted from *Kodansha Encyclopedia of Japan*.

ern (regental) House of the Fujiwara as its military arm in overawing its rivals. For three more generations until the end of the eleventh century the Seiwa Genji held court positions in the guards, appointments to lead punitive expeditions, and rotations as provincial governors, and gained a reputation as the most formidable warriors in the land.

"Minamoto" was a common noun meaning "source of water, origin." In the clan name, it was used in the sense of "source of court officials." An alternative interpretation assumes that the choice of the name by Saga, its first grantor, was influenced in the court of that sinophile emperor by Chinese precedent, giving it the sense "of the blood." The precedent occurred in China in the reign of an emperor of the Northern Wei (386–534), who, in recognition of the common Hsien-pei origins of a Mongolian prince with himself and the officers of his court, bestowed as a family name on the prince the character with which Minamoto is written – Yüan (in a modern Chinese pronunciation).

The princely recipients of the clan name of Taira were typically of a remoter degree of imperial descent than their Minamoto counterparts: they were never sons of emperors (as Minamoto usually were), but grandsons or genealogically even further removed from the throne. There were several lines of the clan, springing like the Minamoto from the progeny of different emperors (Kammu, Kōkō, Nimmyō, and Montoku), but it was the first created lines, the four Kammu Heishi lines (Heishi is the Sino-Japanese reading of "Taira clan," descending from Emperor Kammu, that produced the Taira who figured most prominently in the history of the period. See Taira genealogy Figure 9.7). First bestowed in the ninth century, the Taira name, in its orthography and Sino-Japanese reading, echoed that of Kammu's new capital at Heian, the characters for which were sometimes also read "Taira no Kyō" or "Taira no Miyako."

Less closely related to emperors than most of the Minamoto and more thoroughly excluded from the higher offices of the court, some Taira early left the capital for the provinces, where their prospects were more encouraging. There were two chief branches of the Kammu Heishi, one a courtier line of mostly minor and middling-level officials; the other, founded by Kammu's great-grandson Takamochi (fl. 889), became a warrior line that included many of the best-known military men of the final century of the Heian period, and it is almost always Takamochi's line that is meant when the term "Kammu Heishi" is used. Takamochi was appointed vice-governor of Kazusa around the end of the ninth century, married locally in the province of his appointment, and expanded his landholdings in Kazusa and Shimōsa. His descendants included in the third generation Masakado, whose campaigns, from 935 to 940, may be said to have marked the emergence of professional-warrior power in Japan.

REVOLTS OF MASAKADO AND SUMITOMO

The revolt in the east began inconspicuously in 935 as an armed squabble among members of a Taira family who had settled in the Kanto area perhaps forty-five years earlier. They had grown into great landowners there, exercising control over a broad area that included the provinces of Kazusa, Hitachi, and Shimōsa (the northern part of Chiba Prefecture and the southern half of Ibaraki). As the conflict evolved in fits and starts, one of the Taira leaders, Masakado, emerged from his Shimōsa base as the chief military power and principal arbiter of disputes throughout the southern Kanto area.[10] The disputes in which he involved himself centered on the resistance of landowners to provincial exactions, Masakado taking the part of the aggrieved landholders. The fighting increasingly assumed the nature of rebellion against provincial authorities, who were mostly Masakado's kinsmen. But perhaps because the eastern provinces had a long history of banditry, unrest, and minor revolts, the central government at first paid scant heed to Masakado and his fighting, intervening only when a suit was brought against him by one of his victims, and then simply to assess a mild punishment that was almost immediately canceled in a general amnesty.

The military forces of Masakado and his opponents comprised the leader's close followers (*jusha*), a permanent bodyguard or army of mounted warriors (400 in the case of Masakado), *banrui* (allies), and provincial troops recruited from among the cultivators. *Banrui* were minor warriors, usually mounted, who were independent collaborators and quick to retire from the battlefield when the fighting went against them. Both Masakado and his enemies used the tactic of burning down the houses of their opponents' *banrui* and peasant foot soldiers and destroying their stored grain to weaken their re-

---

10 The principal source concerning Masakado's uprising is the *Shōmonki* (see note 7), an account in *hentai kambun* ("variant Chinese"), believed by most scholars to have been completed a few months after Masakado's death in 940. See Judith N. Rabinovitch, trans., *Shōmonki: The Story of Masakado's Rebellion*, Monumenta Nipponica Monograph 58 (Tokyo: Sophia University, 1986).

solve, from which we can understand that they were men of meager resources.

Although the organization of the armies of Masakado and his enemies were generally the same, they differed in one decisively important respect: the anti-Masakado forces were an alliance of warrior leaders, at times as many as five or six Taira and also a Minamoto and a Fujiwara, each with his own group of close followers. These alliances were known as *tō* (associations), largely egalitarian leagues of warriors that joined together to further their common interests. (The term *tō* is used in modern times to refer to political parties.) Shortly before Masakado's time, for instance, pack-horse haulers had formed "hire-horse associations" (*shūba no tō*) and were terrorizing and looting agricultural villages along the roads of the Tōkaidō and Tōsandō, their depredations becoming so intolerable that the court established barrier stations (*sekisho*) at key eastern passes to exercise some control over their movements. Nonhierarchical in membership at first, such leagues in the twelfth century developed into small, loosely knit warrior bands like the famous Seven Musashi Associations (*Musashi shichitō*) in the Kanto or the Matsura Association of Kyushu.

Professional warriors of Masakado's time were archers on horseback. They did not by choice engage in hand-to-hand combat with swords. Nor did the mounted men carry lances, as they did in Europe. Masakado's forces also included peasant foot soldiers armed with spears and shields, employed in mass tactics, in the tradition of the earlier imperial conscript armies.

The fighting between Masakado and his opponents, as it evolved through its several stages, was destructive and murderous, but the participants continued throughout the first years to appeal to the court at Kyoto for justice. Imperial authority, although conspicuous by the absence of its physical presence in the east, was still recognized even by Masakado himself. Then, at the end of 939, Masakado became involved in a dispute over taxes between a member of the local gentry in Hitachi and the governor of the province. Before the affair ended, he had burned the provincial headquarters, seized the official signet of the province, and made off with the key to the provincial storehouse. Even the inward-looking court at Heian could scarcely ignore so direct a challenge to its authority or income.

At the urging of a certain Prince Okiyo, a former provincial official in Musashi who had thrown in his lot with Masakado in the course of another dispute with local officials in 939, Masakado set out then to seize control of all the eight Kanto provinces, acting on

Okiyo's famous observation that the punishment for rebellion in many provinces was no worse than for that in one.[11] Claiming that he was obeying an oracle from the Great Bodhisattva Hachiman and justifying his action on the ground that he was a descendant of Emperor Kammu, Masakado proclaimed himself the "New Emperor" (*shinnō*), in contradistinction to the old *tennō* at Heian. Masakado appointed new officials to the provinces and he also began to fashion a rustic version of the central statutory government centered in Shimōsa.

Masakado sent a message to the capital addressed to Fujiwara no Tadahira, under whom in his youth he had enrolled himself as a follower. He sought the regent's understanding of his actions, and also suggested that his ambitions did not extend beyond the Kanto, thus proposing in effect a division of the country between the regental Fujiwara and his own warrior family. By that time, however, the authorities at court were thoroughly alarmed, convinced that Masakado's forces would soon be descending on Kyoto. They adopted a three-pronged policy aimed at ending the rebellion: (1) prayer; (2) the appointment of Pursuit and Apprehension Agents (*tsuibushi*) in the eastern provinces and, in the spring of 940, three or four months after Masakado's attack on the Hitachi provincial headquarters, the dispatch of a court commander, Fujiwara no Tadafumi, to the east; and (3) promises of reward to provincial leaders who succeeded in subduing Masakado. Significantly, it was the third prong of the policy – reliance on provincial warrior leaders – that actually brought Masakado down, although the court subsequently insisted on attributing its success to the divine efficacy of the first. While the specially deputed court commander was still en route to the east at the beginning of 940, Masakado was surprised at his base in Shimōsa with a depleted force and was killed by the joint forces of his cousin, Taira no Sadamori, and the Shimotsuke Suppression and Control Agent (*ōryōshi*) Fujiwara no Hidesato.

The failure of the revolt seems to have been chiefly a result of organizational weakness. Masakado's lack of a retainership system meant that his coalition force of antigovernment landholders tended to fragment after initial successes had achieved the aims of the landholders, and the dispersal of his large force of cultivators to their agricultural pursuits left him exposed at a critical moment to the overwhelming alliance of hostile forces. (The *Shōmonki* says

11 *Shōmonki* (text), p. 208.

that Masakado's force, which had once numbered as many as six thousand, had been reduced to a thousand men.)

The imperial court's military response to the revolt may not have been as ineffective as it seems. The punitive expedition dispatched from the capital against Masakado arrived at the scene after his defeat, but its expected advent in the fighting presumably entered into the calculations of the contending sides. Hidesato participated in the fighting as an imperially appointed officer, holding one of the key titles recently created by the court as it reconstituted its military.

Following the abandonment of the conscript-army system in the late eighth century and afterward, the statutory regime continued as before to rely for military strength on the richer and more powerful elements of rural society, asserting authority and control through a loose, evolving structure of ad hoc and permanent titles that deputized individual warriors to exercise force in defense of the regime or for the maintenance of public order. The social and provincial origins of the regime's military strength remained much the same as earlier. But the nature of the military's relationship to the court shifted from the *employed* service of the Nara period, when men were recruited at the government's pleasure and recompensed for their labor, to *deputized* agency in the ninth and tenth centuries, when the power of private warriors was confirmed and legitimatized by conferral of court titles that may have been useful in the building of retainership systems. Such deputized warriors might fight the battles of the court and enforce its laws, but first and foremost they fought in their own interests and took the offensive when they had most to gain.

The titles awarded to warriors and the functions of the title holders as the functions evolved during the period gave the government's military arm more than simply a paper existence. The resulting military and police system enabled the regime to survive rebellion and rampant banditry for close to four centuries, and the new system was in that sense a successful adaptation of statutory institutions to a changing society. But lacking significant numbers of men and weapons, and having no major military leaders of its own, the court at Heian was able to do little more than survive. It did not have the strength, certainly, to impose its unilateral will on the society.

The dispatch by the court of a force under the command of a senior noble to put down Masaskado's revolt continued the military traditions of the statutory regime, but the ineffectiveness of that effort signaled the approaching end of the traditions. The commander of the army subsequently led a more successful imperial army against the pirate-rebel Sumitomo at the Dazaifu, but after that there were no more such armies.

Instead, there came to be four chief, continuously filled titles given to warriors entrusted with military and police duties outside the capital. One, "General of the Pacification and Defense Headquarters" (*chinjufu shōgun*), was a title of the Nara period that acquired a markedly different meaning as it came to be used during the Heian period. Another, "Offenses Investigation Agent" (*kebiishi*), was originally created for police purposes in the capital city in the ninth century, but in the tenth it expanded nationwide, such agents then being established in each province by the local government. Two new titles formed the backbone of imperial military framework: "Suppression and Control Agent" (*ōryōshi*) and "Pursuit and Apprehension Agent" (*tsuibushi*).

The Pacification and Defense Headquarters had been established in Mutsu Province in the first half of the eighth century to provide security for Japanese colonizers against Emishi in the region. Its large army of conscript soldiers from other provinces played a crucial role in the subjugation of the Emishi, continuing operations against rebellious and bandit elements all through the ninth century. It was staffed by four grades of military officers, headed by a general (*shōgun*). Beginning in the tenth century, the office of General of the Headquarters tended to become hereditary, remaining in a single clan or family line for as many as five successive generations. The title fluctuated between lineages but remained always in three leading warrior families directly descended from high nobility at the capital: sublineages of the Uona line of the Fujiwara, the Kammu Heishi, and the Seiwa Genji.

When the Emishi submitted to the Japanese presence in the northeast during the ninth century, the Pacification and Defense Headquarters (*chinjufu*) lost its military raison d'être, becoming thereafter mainly a civil administrative organ, little or no different perhaps from a normal provincial-government office. The holder of the title of General typically held concurrent appointment to the governorship of Mutsu, which in the eleventh century was associated with great wealth. Despite the loss of the office's primary military function, there was no other military title that brought so much prestige to an eastern warrior, but the title seems to have been primarily a recognition of existing power and a reward for military exploits, not a grant of power or the commission of military duties.

In response to the upsurge of banditry in the countryside, the police and judicial powers of the provincial governments came to be separated and vested in special officers called, like their counterparts in the capital, Offenses Investigation Agents. Such officers existed at latest by the middle of ninth century, and by the tenth they are found in nearly one-third of all provinces, from Musashi in the east to the Dazaifu in Kyushu. Multiple *kebiishi* appointments might be made for a single province, and two, presumably especially lawless provinces, are known to have installed *kebiishi* also at the subprovincial, or district, level. Initially selected from rich and powerful families in a province, by the tenth century rankless peasants were holding the title, and their appointments, which had originally been made by the central government, were in the hands of the provincial headquarters. The appointees then tended to be functionaries of the headquarters.

Fujiwara no Hidesato held the title of Suppression and Control Agent when he and Taira no Sadamori defeated and killed Masakado in 940, and Minamoto no Tsunemoto (d. 961), the ancestor of the Seiwa Genji who was a member of the court's army dispatched against Masakado, held the title of Pursuit and Apprehension Agent. The two titles had emerged in the ninth and tenth centuries as ad hoc court appointments of private warriors to mobilize and lead their own and sometimes other local military forces in the suppression of revolts and banditry. Originally different in function, the two titles came to be substantively the same in the tenth century, when they lost their ad hoc character and were continuously filled, each appointee having jurisdiction in a single province (Hidesato was, for instance, the *ōryōshi* of Shimotsuke) and in principle acting under the direction of the provincial-government headquarters. Appointed by order of the central government, the agents were usually chosen from among powerful local families, frequently from those whose members were already part of the provincial headquarters staff. The posts often became hereditary, and as officials actually resident in a province, appointees were often able in the late Heian period to take over the military and administrative authority of the provincial government.

During the half year before Masakado set the fateful fire at the Hitachi provincial headquarters, the court had been rocked by news of a major revolt by resettled Emishi in Dewa and a renewed outbreak of piracy in the west, in the Inland Sea (Seto Naikai) area, where piracy had been a continuing problem since the last half of the ninth century. The piracy was soon contained, but then just two weeks after word of the burning of the Hitachi headquarters reached Kyoto, the court learned from the vice-governor of Bizen that a powerful pirate leader named Fujiwara no Sumitomo, a great-grandson of Mototsune's biological father, Nagara, and therefore a distant cousin of the current regent, was about to take to the sea again. A few days later came the terrifying news that Sumitomo had caught up with the vice-governor in Settsu as the latter was returning from Bizen to the capital, cut off his ears and slit his nose, killed his son, and taken prisoner his wife. Buffeted by alarming reports from east and west, the court seems to have been on the verge of panic, fearing that Sumitomo and Masakado were acting in concert and that their joint forces would soon be assaulting the virtually defenseless capital itself.

However, Sumitomo was not a *tsuwamono* of the Masakado type. His rebellion followed its own course in its origins and resolution. Sumitomo had formerly held a minor provincial post in Iyo (present Ehime Prefecture) on the island of Shikoku, where he built a large piratical following that was active from as early as 936. Sumitomo organized bands of pirates operating in the area, most of whom were likely poor fishermen and petty seamen, and he began to plunder the sea lanes and ports of the Inland Sea, the transportation routes for the movement of government revenues and products from the western provinces to the capital.

After the renewal of his activities in 939, he attacked governmental headquarters in the provinces of Shikoku and along the Honshu coast, burned ships, and spread havoc throughout the coastal areas. Sumitomo's extensive control of the sea grew into a direct challenge to governmental authority, but it was not until after the defeat of Masakado in early 940 that the central government was able to turn its full attention to the pirate chief. The authorities in Kyoto had earlier attempted to check his depredations by appeasement (he was granted Fifth Rank), but now a government force made up of provincial leaders finally succeeded in attacking and, with the aid of a turncoat, reducing Sumitomo's stronghold in Iyo. The pirate leader fled then to Kyushu, where he occupied and sacked the lightly defended Dazaifu headquarters, continuing his predatory ways until at Hakata he suffered another disastrous defeat in 941 at the hands of court-dispatched land and sea forces supported by deserters from his own ranks and he met his death.[12]

---

12 On Fujiwara no Sumitomo, see John W. Hall, *Government and Local Power in Japan, 500 to 1700* (Princeton, N.J.: Princeton University Press, 1966), pp. 129–31.

The revolt of Masakado and the piracy of Sumitomo proved to be not as serious threats as the court imagined; but some key elements in the origins, prosecution, and suppression of the revolts were emblematic harbingers of the great historical changes that came during the following two and a half centuries. The suppression of Masakado's revolt did not result in an assertion of court authority in the east. Rather, the revolt and its suppression confirmed the private wealth and military strength of the local leaders. Masakado and his principal opponents, Taira no Sadamori, Fujiwara no Hidesato, and Minamoto no Tsunemoto (the vice-governor of Musashi who brought the initial charge of rebellion against Masakado at court), were the ancestors of most of the important warrior leaders in the east during the remainder of the Heian period, and it was from the east that the decisive military power flowed in the fateful twelfth century. All four men were alike in being descendants of the highest strata of the court nobility (the imperial line and the Fujiwara clan). Their ancestors had received appointments in the ninth and tenth centuries to provincial or military posts in the east and had settled and prospered there after the terms of their offices had expired.

In the typical case of the founder of a major warrior family in the east, an ancestor of noble extraction first came to the area with the court-conferred title of General of the *chinjufu* in Mutsu, and his descendants often continued to hold that title after him in a limited hereditary fashion. The powers of the office of the *chinjufu* General in the tenth century probably depended mostly on an appointee's own private military resources, but it was a title of great prestige, conferring on its holder what amounted to the titular leadership of eastern warriors, and its official civil-military functions were still important. Although the Emishi had been decisively defeated by Japanese forces in the ninth century, large numbers in the northern and central parts of Dewa and Mutsu continued to live in a semi-independent tribal society beyond the purview of regular provincial and district officials. It was the responsibility of the *chinjufu* to manage and control them.

Bearing the old and distinguished title of *chinjufu* General, or the somewhat less grand title of governor or vice-governor of a province, and tied to the court not only by blood but also by occasional employment at the capital in court or noble-family military functions, these men and their descendants quickly became major loci of armed power in the eastern provinces, providing military protection for local gentry against their enemies and contending among themselves for domination in an area. Sometimes called "military nobles" (*gunji kizoku*) by historians, they were also, in a sense, trouble waiting to happen, ready to join in any fray that promised to be of advantage to their own interests, as Masakado did in the spring of 939 when he rushed to the relief of a district official in Musashi who had come under attack by a provincial governor bent on the collection of revenues and other wealth. Masakado himself was a professional warrior, a *tsuwamono* in the contemporary lexicon, a predecessor of the late-Heian *bushi*. "He gathered many fierce *tsuwamono* as his companions and engaged in battles as his occupation," in the words of a story about him in the twelfth-century *Konjaku monogatari-shū*.[13] He differed from the earlier warrior of the statutory state who was in fundamental ways an employee of the state who fought for its purposes. The professional warrior of the tenth century and after was a private fighter who did battle as his own interests dictated, legitimizing his actions when he could as government business.

The failure of the two tenth-century revolts is attributable chiefly in both cases to the fragmentation of the rebel forces, alliances chiefly, in Masakado's case, of a warrior leader and rural gentry, and, in Sumitomo's, of a renegade official and local piratical forces. After Masakado's successes against the provincial government forces of Hitachi and other Kanto provinces, the local gentry, their chief purpose achieved, dispersed, leaving Masakado with fewer than a thousand men in his final, losing battle with Sadamori and Hidesato. The pattern was similar in the case of Sumitomo, who lost two of his pirate chieftains and twenty-five hundred men to the bribes of the governor of Iyo in 936 and who was later routed when his subcommander surrendered to government forces and led them to the rebel's base in Iyo Province. There were no adequately cohesive social bonds to hold the rebel forces together once their individual interests were served. Such bonds emerged only with the strong vassalage system that in the late eleventh and twelfth centuries transformed rural society.

Although the government's forces were perhaps inherently no stronger than the rebels', the court was able, nevertheless, to field punitive forces sufficiently powerful to suppress the revolts, thanks to

---

13 Yamada Yoshio, Yamada Tadao, Yamada Hideo, and Yamada Toshio, eds., *Konjaku monogatari-shū*, vols. 22–26 of *Nihon koten bungaku taikei* (Tokyo: Iwanami shoten, 1962), vol. 4, *kan* 25, story 1, p. 362. Fascicle 25, devoted to tales about Heian warriors, has been translated by William Ritchie Wilson, "The Way of the Bow and Arrow: The Japanese Warrior in the *Konjaku Monogatari*," *Monumenta Nipponica* 28 (1973): 190–233, see p. 190.

its own surviving military and financial resources and to its success in allying itself with private warriors very like the rebels themselves – provincial "military nobility" with strong familial and formal ties to the court. For such figures, their services to the government in the suppression of rebels must have seemed simply the continuation in a different framework of the private battles that marked the expansion of warrior strength in the provinces.

The revolts of Masakado and Sumitomo, although not revolutionary in effect, were true watersheds – in the opinion of some, the beginning of the "middle age" (*chūsei*). At least they were the first major efforts by provincial military leaders to assert their autonomous strength. As the old ties of the military nobility with Kyoto weakened and the strength and unity of the provincial military grew, the court's position became ever more isolated and precarious, maintained perhaps as much by ideological, religious, and sentimental values as by any important material strength.

The Masakado rebellion marked the advent of the private professional warrior in Japanese political history, and with his appearance seems also to have emerged the first lineaments of a recognizable warrior ideal. The loose code of conduct that in the Meiji era became generally known as *bushidō* ("way of the warrior") is not directly traceable to the *tsuwamono*, but several prized attributes of the *tsuwamono* may be thought of as having constituted an initial essay at a warrior ethic. Knowledge of the early ideal is slender, since the men left little personal record of themselves, and other sources are problematic, existing as unique, single texts of uncertain authenticity, as in the case of *Shōmonki,* or surviving as tales probably oral in origin and collected over a century after Masakado's time (*Konjaku monogatari-shū*). The picture found in such sources is sketchy, with none of the detail of knightly perfection displayed for our admiration in later sources from the thirteenth century and after, but some important elements are already in place.

Defining characteristics of the *tsuwamono*'s conception of himself are early seen in a letter written at the beginning of 940 by the prototypical *tsuwamono* Taira no Masakado. Written just at the time of his assumption of a royal title at the head of his newly established state in the east, and addressed in explanation of his actions to the imperial regent at Heian, the letter as recorded in *Shōmonki* justifies the new state on three grounds: (1) the precedents of the past, history having recorded earlier instances of usurpation of central authority by arms; (2) Masakado's descent from an emperor, a lineage that could entitle him to exercise sovereignty over the country; and (3) his military power, with which he had been endowed by Heaven, not by any governmental authority.[14] Masakado's argument followed a rationale suited to an age when the government had largely abdicated its defense and peacekeeping responsibilities, and the security of the country was by default mostly in the hands of *tsuwamono*, or so they claimed.

The *bushi* of later ages was depicted as placing supreme value on loyalty to his lord, but the *tsuwamono* as represented in Masakado's letter found his central values in historical practice, familial descent, and military might. Those values underlay, or were expressed in, several characteristics of the ideal *tsuwamono*. Familial descent perhaps more than anything else determined the warrior's status, for the profession of arms, like all other professions at the time, was hereditary and closed at least in its upper reaches to those outside the *tsuwamono* families, the "houses of martial valor" (*buyū no ie*) or "bow-and-arrow houses" (*yumiya no ie*), as they were sometimes called. There was in consequence a strong emphasis on family honor and a tendency to attribute one's accomplishments to the family line. On being praised and rewarded by his master the crown prince for a seemingly impossible arrow shot that killed a fox on the roof of Fujiwara no Kaneie's house one night, Minamoto no Yorimitsu (948–1021), a court warrior and founder of a major sublineage of the Seiwa Genji, is said to have responded, "It was not I alone who shot that arrow. I was aided by my family's guardian deity in order not to bring shame on my ancestors."[15] Prayer to the guardian deity of a family and to the family ancestors was essential. That centrality of the family line led to the warrior's ritual proclamation before battle of the names of his more notable ancestors, a practice that became customary by the twelfth century, at least in literary accounts. That recitation of ancestral names reflected an ancient belief in "word spirit" (*kotodama*), according to which words were thought to be endowed with spirit and the intoning of a name gave the speaker the protection and aid of the spirit of the name's referent.

Although military might may have been in practice the most significant trait of the *tsuwamono*, victory in battle was not necessarily the highest goal. What seems to have been prized most in a warrior

---

14 *Shōmonki* (text), pp. 210–13; Rabinovitch, trans., *Shōmōnki* pp. 113–16.
15 *Konjaku monogatari-shū*, vol. 4, kan 25, story 6, p. 382.

was his readiness to lay down his life in battle, to lead his men himself on the battlefield, and his ferocious tenacity in the face of overwhelming odds. His utter disregard for his own life in pursuit of military honor could require him to be indifferent even to the welfare of his own children. A well-known *Konjaku* tale tells the story of an eleventh-century hero named Fujiwara no Chikataka, who was reprimanded for his weakness when he reported to the renowned warrior and governor of Chikataka's province, Minamoto no Yorinobu, that his son, a child of only five or six, had been taken hostage and was being held under threat of death by a desperate gang of bandits trapped at his house. Yorinobu laughed and said:

> I understand your tears, but they do no good. A warrior must be resolved to grapple with anyone, be he devil or god. Blubbering away like that is stupid. Let them kill him – he's just one child. A *tsuwamono* has to be prepared for that. He's not worth much if he lets concern for wife and children give him pause. Fearlessness depends on thinking neither of oneself nor of one's wife or children.[16]

On the other hand, other *Konjaku* and *Shōmonki* stories exemplify that the true *tsuwamono* spared and protected women.[17]

REVOLT OF TADATSUNE

Following the defeat and death of Masakado in 940, the Taira line descending from Kammu continued to exercise a wide dominion over the eastern provinces. Sadamori, who had overthrown his cousin Masakado, was appointed governor of Mutsu and *chinjufu* General in 974, signifying his leadership of eastern warriors. Four of his sons received appointments as governor or vice-governor of an eastern province. His influence was further expanded by the adoption of numerous grandsons and nephews. He and his clansmen are said to have treated the eastern provinces as their private domain.

The death of Masakado in 940 failed to bring peace in the east. Governmental authorities there came under repeated attack, the sorely tried governor of Shimōsa in 950 complaining, "Lawless bands rage everywhere in the eastern provinces, looting and inflicting injury, so that there is no peace day or night."[18] Accompanied to

---

16 *Konjaku monogatari-shū*, vol. 4, *kan* 25, story 11, p. 391.
17 *Konjaku monogatari-shū*, vol. 4, *kan* 25, story 5, pp. 374–81; *Shōmonki* (text), pp. 216–17; Rabinovitch, trans., *Shōmonki*, pp. 124–26.
18 *Chōya gunsai (Shintei zōho) Kokushi taikei*, vol. 29, 1 (1938), *kan* 22, p. 511, 20/2/Tenryaku 4 (950).

their provinces by large retinues of grasping relatives, friends, and officials, the governors themselves sometimes contributed to the general turmoil of the countryside by their own rapacious behavior. One famous late-tenth-century case was so extreme that the district officials and cultivators of a province were forced to appeal for relief directly to the central government, citing some thirty illegal acts of the governor on which they sought justice. But violence and fighting remained small-scale, and no major armed defiance of governmental authority occurred anywhere in Japan throughout the heyday of the Fujiwara regency. Then in 1028, just months after Michinaga's death, revolt broke out again in the east. This revolt, too, was led by a Taira, a son of a cousin of Masakado and Sadamori named Tadatsune (967–1031).[19] Vice-governor at one time of both Kazusa and Shimōsa, Tadatsune seems to have become involved in the plunder of government tax receipts in those two provinces. The same area had been the scene of another attack on provincial authority a little more than two decades earlier. That attack on the Shimōsa provincial headquarters in 1003 by Taira no Koreyoshi (d. 1022) had ended in Koreyoshi's flight before a court-dispatched Suppression and Control Agent (*ōryōshi*), but Koreyoshi was subsequently granted court rank and given appointment as *chinjufu* General, apparently in response to generous gifts he made to the great Fujiwara leader Michinaga.[20]

Tadatsune's plundering was not so easily managed. He had inherited a vast domain in the east, the official levies on which he had refused to pay to the provincial authorities, and his large force of warriors quickly turned back the meager troops the provincial governor could call upon to demand payment.

In 1028 Tadatsune's rebellion spread rapidly through Shimōsa, Kazusa, and Awa (roughly Chiba Prefecture). Tadatsune occupied the government headquarters in Kazusa, then burned the Awa headquarters and killed the governor there. In 1030 he put such fear in the new governor of Awa that that unfortunate official fled the province, abandoning the provincial seal, enabling Tadatsune to requisition supplies from the peasantry and obtain the tax-storehouse keys. His rebellion became as formidable as that of Masakado.

19 Sources include Minamoto no Tsuneyori's diary, *Sakeiki*; Fujiwara no Sanesuke's diary, *Shōyūki* (*Ouki*); and *Konjaku monogatari-shū*. For further information, see Ōmori Kingorō, *Buke jidai no kenkyū* (Tokyo: Fuzambō, 1923), vol. 1, pp. 196–240; and Ishimoda Shō, *Kodai makki seijishi josetsu* (Tokyo: Miraisha, 1964), vol. 1, pp. 182–96.
20 Takeuchi Rizō, *Bushi no tōjō*, vol. 6 of *Nihon no rekishi*, ed. Inoue Mitsusada, 31 vols. (Tokyo: Chūō kōronsha, 1973), p. 20.

As usual, it was the stoppage of tax payments that moved the court to action. Dependent for military force on *tsuwamono*, the court dispatched against Tadatsune two warriors of the *kebiishi* office, the senior of whom was Taira no Naokata, a great-grandson of Sadamori. (See the Taira genealogy, Figure 9.7.) Naokata had actively sought the commission, as he hoped to eliminate Tadatsune as a rival for power among the Taira in the east, and to gain a conclusive victory in the long-standing feud between their two families. The court, on its part, adopted the same tactic it had used in the Masakado and Koreyoshi uprisings, sending a Taira warrior to suppress an insurgent from a rival Taira family. Notwithstanding the urgency of the situation, it was nearly two months after Naokata was ordered to the attack before he sallied forth from the capital with a core force of some two hundred men under his command. His departure had been delayed by the Fujiwara Minister of the Right Sanesuke, who insisted that in a matter of such importance it was essential that the expedition wait for a calendrically auspicious day on which to set out. The greater part of his force was recruited in eastern provinces. After two years of inconclusive fighting, the government force had still not succeeded in suppressing Tadatsune. The two principal commanders were cashiered and Minamoto no Yorinobu (968–1048), then governor of Kai, was appointed in their place.

Although Minamoto penetration of the east had begun well before Yorinobu's day, it was from his time that the clan began to establish its dominance in the region. Yorinobu was a "warrior of the capital," a son of the Mitsunaka who had earlier served Michinaga.[21] He and his father were ideally situated to initiate the creation of the powerful, enduring retainership system of landholding *tsuwamono* that eventually contributed to the establishment of the Kamakura bakufu in the time of Yorinobu's sixth-generation descendant Yoritomo (see Figure 10.1). A chief goal of the *tsuwamono* was the protection of their land from taxation and governmental interference, protection that Mitsunaka and Yorinobu could help obtain because of their official positions and high connections in the central government. Both held military offices, and both served in the household of the regent. Those positions, their high birth, their appointment to lucrative gubernatorial posts in the provinces with the attendant opportunities that such appointments provided for developing a retinue of followers, and the broad, court-conferred military authority they

---

21 Takeuchi, *Bushi no tōjō*, p. 35.

were given, all encouraged the establishment of a vassalage system under them. The system was the *ikusa*, or, as it is now more frequently called, the *bushidan*, the "warrior band."

Like Naokata before him, Yorinobu delayed his departure for the east several months after his appointment to command the court forces fighting Tadatsune, perhaps in response to messengers Tadatsune sent to the capital to plead the case that he was not in revolt against the government. The court's decision went against him, and his messengers were arrested, putting him on notice that he could soon expect another major assault by court forces. By the late spring of 1031, Yorinobu had arrived in Kai with a son of Tadatsune, a monk, in his train. He was about to launch a campaign against Tadatsune when the rebel suddenly appeared before him. Tadatsune had taken Buddhist vows, changed his name to Jōan, and with two sons and three *rōtō*, surrendered without a fight.

Yorinobu, in his report on the campaign addressed to the guardian deity of his clan, boasted that he had achieved victory "without causing the people to flee or laying waste the land, without beating drums or unfurling banners, without drawing bows or loosing arrows, neither hiding nor attacking." "Just by being there," he crowed, "I captured the enemy."[22]

Although Yoshinobu claimed that his reputation as a warrior was reason enough for Tadatsune to surrender, there seem to have been other considerations as well. In submitting, Tadatsune may have been honoring the obligation of a personal-service bond made with Yoshinobu some two decades earlier (to be discussed later). However, exhaustion may have been a consideration in the surrender: the provinces of Awa, Kazusa, and Shimōsa were by that time devastated from the protracted fighting: in Kazusa, it was reported, there was almost no paddy left in cultivation.[23] This may be why Tadatsune, while holding off the attacks of Naokata, had tried to negotiate with the court and then had taken religious vows as a signal that he did not wish to continue his resistance.

En route to the capital in the custody of Yorinobu, Tadatsune became ill and died. However, his surrender to Yorinobu secured the survival of his family: his sons became retainers of Yorinobu, and in the twelfth century, his descendants, by then known as the Chiba, played a major role in the rise of Yorinobu's descendant Yoritomo.

---

22 "Minamoto no Yorinobu kōmon," *Heian ibun*, vol. 3, p. 777.
23 Takeuchi, *Bushi no tōjō*, pp. 32–33.

The explanation that Tadatsune submitted to Yorinobu in 1031 because he was under a personal obligation to him derives from an incident described in the *Konjaku monogatari-shū*. About twenty years earlier, when Yorinobu was vice-governor of Hitachi and attempting to exercise his influence in the neighboring provinces of Kazusa and Shimōsa, Tadatsune, who held lands in Shimōsa, was flouting his obligation to forward taxes to the provincial headquarters. In the *Konjaku* story, he boasted: "My influence is extremely far-reaching. In Kazusa and Shimōsa, I do as I please. I do not pay public duties, nor do I give heed to the governor of Hitachi." Yorinobu found this behavior intolerable and resolved to chastise Tadatsune. He made common cause with a local strongman, Taira no Koremoto, who had old scores to settle with his rival clansman. Yorinobu with two thousand horsemen and Koremoto with three thousand (certainly inflated numbers) advanced quickly on Tadatsune's base. In the face of this overwhelming force, Tadatsune surrendered without a fight, proffering his name tag (*myōbu*) and a written message of apology for his deeds. Name tags, inscribed with a man's name, official title, and rank, were conventionally presented by a subordinate taking service with a superior, as when someone became a functionary in a noble household, or a disciple pledged himself to a master, or a warrior became a follower of a military lord. Men who presented name tags were known as "house men" (*kenin*) of the recipients of the tags. In the *Konjaku* story, the tag was presumably offered in token of Tadatsune's submission to Yorinobu.[24]

Although the *Konjaku* story may contain fictional elements, the resolution of the conflict by the presentation of a name tag points to a conspicuous feature of the emerging warrior society. In the Heian period, house men were initially of diverse types. They might themselves be nobles or warriors, and they could also include kin of the house. They were like the lads (*rōtō*) in being personal retainers of the lord, but superior in status because of their greater autonomy: they did not usually live in the lord's house or vicinity, but maintained a separate existence. The scope of the term's usage narrowed in the late Heian period, coming then to refer primarily to warrior retainers, a nomenclatural development that was eventually incorporated in the name used of the shogunal retainers of the Kamakura bakufu, the *gokenin*.

Yorinobu may have delayed his departure from the capital in 1031

---

24 *Konjaku monogatari-shū*, vol. 4, kan 25, story 9, p. 387.

because Tadatsune was his *kenin* and he wished to afford him additional time to negotiate with the court. Yorinobu's personal loyalties may have taken precedence over service to the state, an indication of the increasing strength of the *bushidan* relationships, according to some scholars. However, Yorinobu's appointment to replace Naokata as commander of the expedition against Tadatsune probably came after it became known in Kyoto that Tadatsune was seeking a way to surrender, and that this outcome was being resisted by Naokata, who wanted his destruction. As the court hoped, Yorinobu's old relationship with Tadatsune enabled him to bring about Tadatsune's surrender and an end to the destructive struggle that had continued for almost four years.

Tadatsune's submission to Yorinobu was a shock to the Taira, who had long acted as if they owned the Kanto. From this time on they fomented no further rebellions in the east. Instead, many became followers of the Minamoto, with their own groups allying with other military groups under the head of the Minamoto family. The prestige that came to Yorinobu for his "victory" over Tadatsune, together with his noble ancestry, attracted other warrior groups in the east to ally themselves with his *bushidan* organization. The Minamoto became increasingly influential in the remainder of the eleventh century, particularly in the time of Yorinobu's son, Yoriyoshi (988–1075).

Although Yorinobu had effectively carried out his mission, the court, which had little regard for warriors, useful though they were, was slow to reward him. A year later he was appointed governor of Mino, his second-choice position.

In 1046, as governor of Kawachi, the elderly Yorinobu began the worship at Iwashimizu Hachiman Shrine of the martial Hachiman as tutelary god of the Genji. Since 859, when religious practices were imported from the Hachiman Shrine at Usa in Kyushu, there had been some aristocratic support of the shrine. However, Yorinobu was the first to claim the deity as a patron. He explained his decision as an act of reverence toward his ancestors and their marvelous history of defending the country, tracing his lineage back twenty-two generations to the legendary emperor Ōjin, said to have participated in the conquest of Silla while still in the womb of Empress Jingū. Ōjin was considered an avatar of the bodhisattva Hachiman, god of archery. Shrines to Hachiman soon sprang up throughout the country wherever there were Minamoto to invoke his name. Yorinobu's son Yoriyoshi attributed his success in the Earlier Nine Years' War to Hachiman and in 1063 secretly erected a shrine to

Hachiman at Yui-no-gō in Sagami, moved to Kamakura by Yoritomo in 1191.

EARLIER NINE YEARS' WAR

Two lengthy wars followed the Tadatsune revolt at twenty-year intervals, keeping the east – in this case the far northeast end of Honshu beyond the Kanto provinces – in a state of unrest for nearly sixty years. The two later eleventh-century wars are called the "Earlier Nine Years' War" (*zen kunen no eki:* 1051–62, or 1056–62 according to some) and the "Later Three Years' War" (*go sannen no eki:* 1083–87). There is disagreement between these traditional designations and the dates given, even when one allows for reckoning based on a count of calendar years.[25]

Since early times a major concern of the court had been the subjugation of the tribal people who occupied the far northeast. They were called Ezo (or in earlier times usually referred to as Emishi or Ebisu), names indicating that they were "eastern barbarians." (On their names and characteristics, see Chapter 1.) The vast, untamed territory that they inhabited was divided into two very large provinces: Mutsu (present Fukushima, Miyagi, Iwate, and Aomori Prefectures) on the east, and Dewa (present Yamagata and part of Akita Prefectures) on the west. The Ezo continued a dogged resistance for centuries, harassing the encroaching settlers and launching raids by mounted archers on the government's palisades and administrative bases. The innumerable expeditions of conscript troops sent against the Ezo in the eighth century had few successes until the government recruited skilled horsemen from the Kanto area and adopted some of the combat tactics of the enemy. In 801, with the large expeditionary force led by Sakanoue no Tamuramaro (758–811), the Barbarian-subduing Generalissimo (*seii taishōgun*), conquest was almost complete. The Mutsu Ezo, against whom the court had concentrated its efforts, soon ceased resisting.

The way was then open for officials appointed by the court to exploit the territory and its people. The biographer of Fujiwara no Yasunori (825–95), governor of Dewa, writing in 907, said: "The fields (of Dewa) are fertile, and there are many rare products. There is no limit to the land a powerful official can acquire, on which he se-

---

25 On the two wars, see Toyoda Takeshi, ed., *Tōhoku no rekishi*, vol. 1 (Tokyo: Yoshikawa kōbunkan, 1967), pp. 173–84; and Takahashi Tomio, *Kodai Ezo: sono shakai kōzō* (Tokyo: Gakuseisha, 1974).

cretly raises taxes and conscripts as much labor as he desires."[26] The administration of Yoshimine no Chikanari, vice-governor of the Akita Fortress in Dewa was so oppressive that there was a revolt in 878 in a twelve-village area along the Noshiro River. The rebels were unable to coordinate their efforts, however, and the uprising was soon suppressed.

The cost of dispatching expeditionary forces to put down rebellions of this kind and to maintain armies stationed in the area was prohibitive.[27] A different method of maintaining order in the conquered area was essential. To this end Yasunori, the Dewa governor, introduced a compromise policy that proved effective in the long term.[28] He disbanded the army that had been sent to control the area, keeping only a small force of about a thousand *tsuwamono* divided into three units strategically placed. The Ezo chief who had surrendered was charged with the responsibility of administering his people. "Using the barbarian to control barbarians," the land was divided into villages and districts, all with Ezo heads. The resultant landscape of numerous independent units was similar to the depiction of Japan in the first century as described in *Han shu*, the official Chinese history. Thanks to this policy, rebellions in the northeast gradually decreased.

A similar policy was in effect in Mutsu from the time of the Dewa uprising. The chieftain of the local Abe clan was appointed district magistrate in Mutsu in 878, and the Abe held this position for generations. During this time the Abe built at least twelve palisades (*saku*) at strategic points, and the area came to resemble a semi-independent region. Even in 939, when the Dewa Ezo revolted again, peace was maintained in Mutsu.

The Abe lineage is unclear. According to the *Mutsu waki*, a chronicle of the Earlier Nine Years' War compiled shortly after the event, the Abe were Ezo who had submitted to the court.[29] It was a rare exception to the court's policy in Heian times to entrust the administration of a region to a powerful local family. Once it was entrenched in an official position, it was difficult to check the family's appetite to increase its influence and wealth. Before the middle of the eleventh century, the Abe chieftain, who had been entrusted with the admin-

---

26 *Fujiwara no Yasunori den*, in *Kodai seiji shakai shisō*, p. 68.
27 Takeuchi, *Bushi no tōjō*, pp. 47–48.   28 *Fujiwara no Yasunori den*, pp. 64–69.
29 *Mutsu waki*, in *Kodai seiji shakai shisō*, see p. 230. For an annotated translation, see Helen Craig McCullough, "A Tale of Mutsu," *Harvard Journal of Asiatic Studies* 25 (1964–65): 178–211.

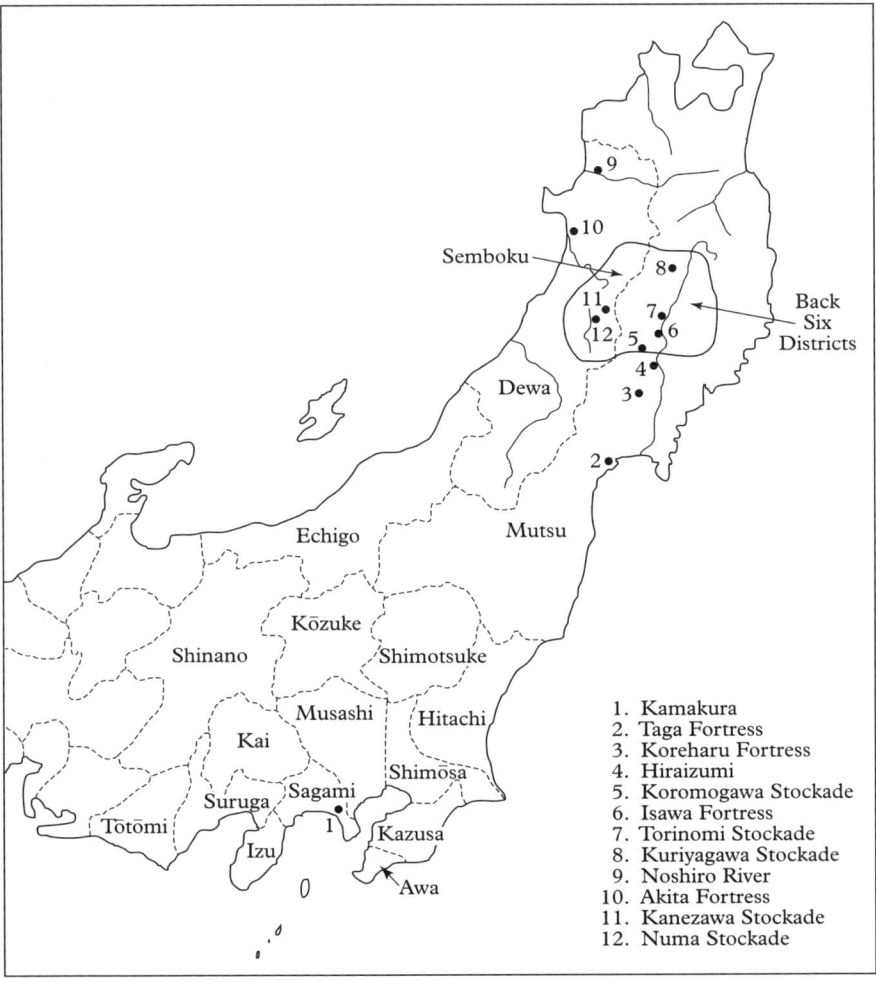

Map 10.1. Battle sites in the northeast.

istration of the "Back Six Districts" (*Okurokugun*) north of Koromo-gawa Fort (near the site of the modern city of Hiraizumi in southern Iwate Prefecture), further extended the area under his control toward the south. Provoked by the chieftain's disobedience and his refusal to pay taxes and corvée dues, the governor of Mutsu and the vice-governor of Akita Fortress attacked him with a force of "several thousand" men, but suffered a crushing defeat. The court then turned to a famed and wealthy warrior, Minamoto no Yorinobu's eldest son, Yoriyoshi, who was dispatched to Mutsu in 1051 as governor of that province and General of the *chinjufu*. He led a force made up of eastern warriors recruited by court order, as well as warriors, also from the eastern provinces, who were his retainers.

Twenty years earlier, Yoriyoshi had aided his father in suppressing the rebellion of Tadatsune. He then served at court, where his exceptional skill in archery made him a favorite hunting companion. His talents apparently caught the eye of Taira no Naokata (leader of the first force sent against Tadatsune), who offered Yoriyoshi his daughter's hand in marriage. It was through Naokata's gift of land around Kamakura in Sagami – land Naokata had acquired while leading the expeditionary force – that the Minamoto first established themselves in Sagami, which was to become their stronghold.

When Yoriyoshi and his force reached Mutsu, the Abe chief, Yoritoki, took advantage of a general amnesty that was proclaimed to submit to the powerful new governor without a fight.[30] Peace continued until the last year of Yoriyoshi's tenure in 1056, when fighting erupted, supposedly initiated by Yoritoki's son Sadatō (1019–62) because of a personal affront, but perhaps actually provoked by Yoriyoshi himself. The court responded by again issuing an imperial order calling for the suppression of the Abe, raising troops for that purpose, and reappointing Yoriyoshi governor of Mutsu.

In the course of Yoriyoshi's offensive, Yoritoki was killed in 1057 at Torinomi Stockade by assimilated Ezo who had been recruited by Yoriyoshi. Sadatō tenaciously continued his resistance and, two months later, defeated Yoriyoshi's undermanned force. It was not until 1062, when Yoriyoshi succeeded in obtaining the help of the Kiyohara, a powerful, partially assimilated Ezo family that controlled Dewa, that he was able at last to prevail against the Abe. In the summer of that year, Kiyohara no Takenori arrived in Mutsu with an army of "more than ten thousand men," divided into seven units, each commanded by a family member. By fall this force and Yoriyoshi's "three thousand"-man army had taken the last Abe stronghold at Kuriyagawa (on the site of the modern city of Morioka in Iwate Prefecture) and killed Sadatō, bringing an end to the Earlier Nine Years' War.

Yoriyoshi's term as governor of Mutsu had expired before the end of the war and, in the view of the court, he fought the final battles as

---

30 An amnesty was declared because of the illness of Michinaga's daughter, Jōtōmon-in – Fujiwara no Shōshi, 988–1074. When he submitted, the Abe chieftain, out of respect, took the name Yoritoki in place of his former name, Yoriyoshi, pronounced the same as the governor's name.

a private warrior. Nonetheless he was promoted to the Fourth Rank and appointed governor of Iyo. His son Yoshiie (1039–1106) became Fifth Rank and governor of Dewa. Even when rank meant little more than title, it served to impress local *tsuwamono*. The Fifth Rank was sought after by warriors; it brought eligibility for appointment as governor or *chinjufu shōgun* and could, on occasion, be purchased.

The real victor in the war was Kiyohara no Takenori, whose large force, and also whose knowledge of conditions in the northeast, were probably crucial to Yoriyoshi's success. The court placed the Back Six Districts of Mutsu under Takenori's control, gave him Fifth Rank, and appointed him to the old and prestige-laden title General of the *chinjufu*, the first man of local extraction to receive this distinction. Together with his original Semboku domain in Dewa (the eastern part of Akita Prefecture) adjoining the west boundary of Mutsu, that expansion of Kiyohara power gave the family control of both Mutsu and Dewa.

It had been policy from Nara times to relocate Ezo who surrendered to Dazaifu. The court followed precedent, deciding not to execute the surviving Abe leaders but to remove them to Iyo on Shikoku and Dazaifu. As a result of this dispersion, Abe descendants proliferated in other parts of the country and became powerholders in the medieval period. Like Taira no Masakado, who came to be worshipped as a deity after his failed insurrection, the Abe also achieved a belated fame. Although disdained by the court, the Abe left a legacy of two centuries of strong leadership and cultural attainment in the remote northeast. Several Abe had been "frontier lecturers" (*sakai no kōshi*), monks with religious duties in Ezo territory. Two fanciful anecdotes are sometimes cited as evidence of the Abe's ability to compose poetry. At the Battle of Koromo River a poetic exchange with Sadatō moved Yoshiie not to release his notched arrow at the fleeing Sadatō, according to the *Kokon chomonjū* (1254). In the *Heike monogatari*, Sadatō's brother, the captive Munetō, composed a poetic response to jeering crowds in the capital.[31] The culture that took root during the long peace before the Earlier Nine Years' War was a forerunner of the twelfth-century efflorescence of Hiraizumi, seat of the so-called Ōshū Fujiwara.

The Kiyohara are thought to have been descendants of Kiyohara no Yoshimochi, who accompanied Fujiwara no Yasunori to Dewa in 879 at the time of the Emishi insurrection. That line of the Kiyohara

---

31 Takeuchi, *Bushi no tōjō*, pp. 62–64.

traced its ancestry to Emperor Temmu's son, Prince Toneri. Although there is no reliable evidence on the point, it is unlikely that the court would have given the title of General of the *chinjufu* to the head of the Dewa Ezo in 1062 if he had not been able to trace his lineage to the Kyoto nobility.[32]

LATER THREE YEARS' WAR

The peace achieved in Mutsu and Dewa in 1062 was upset two decades later in the time of Takenori's grandson Sanehira, when his attempt to strengthen his authority as head of the Kiyohara clan's main line caused dissatisfaction among clan members. A doyen of the clan, Kimiko no Hidetake, refused to accept the arrogant behavior of his junior, Sanehira, and moved into open opposition to him. Hidetake acted not only out of an old man's sense of propriety and amour propre, but also in resistance to a restructuring of clan power that was replacing the more egalitarian practices of the kin alliance or confederation of Takenori's day with a hierarchy culminating in clan lordship by the head of the main line. Sanehira launched a punitive attack in 1083 on his refractory senior relative in Dewa, only to find himself assaulted in Mutsu by his half-brother Iehira and by his stepbrother Kiyohira (1056–1128), to both of whom Hidetake had appealed for support. Kiyohira was a son of Fujiwara no Tsunekiyo, who had fought for Abe no Yoritoki and had been executed at the end of the earlier war. His young son Kiyohira and his widow, a daughter of the Abe chief, Yoritoki, went as spoils of war to Takenori's son, Takesada. He adopted Kiyohira and took the widow as wife; she subsequently bore him Iehira. Hence, Sanehira, Kiyohira, and Iehira were all half- or stepbrothers, but none of them a full brother to either of the others. (See Figure 10.2, the genealogies of the Kiyohara and Ōshū Fujiwara.)

Confronted by hostile forces in Dewa and on his rear in Mutsu, Sanehira remained at his headquarters in the northern Mutsu districts until the new governor of the province, Minamoto no Yoshiie, now head of the Seiwa Genji, arrived at his post in the autumn of 1083. Yoshiie had a towering reputation as a skilled and courageous warrior, earned in the service of his father Yoriyoshi in the earlier war. Yoshiie was quick to intervene in the Kiyohara family feud, ostensibly as a mediator on Sanehira's behalf, but in fact he intended

[32] Takeuchi, *Bushi no tōjō*, pp. 65–66.

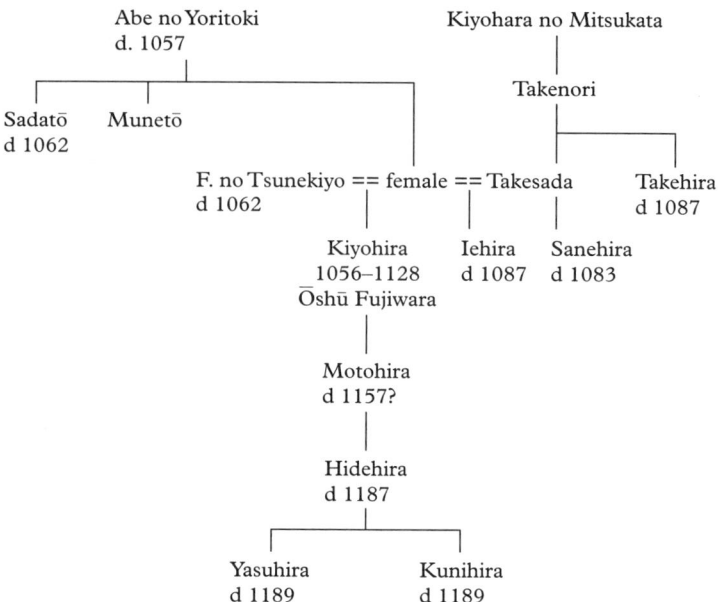

Figure 10.2. The Kiyohara and Ōshū Fujiwara.

to supplant Kiyohara power in Dewa and Mutsu. Yoshiie petitioned the court for a commission to subdue Iehira, which would authorize him to mobilize troops and requisition supplies in neighboring Kanto provinces. The court refused to intervene, declaring the conflict a private Kiyohara affair. Unlike rebels such as Masakado, Tadatsune, and the Abe, the Kiyohara had obeyed the orders of the provincial governors, paid their taxes, and performed their official duties. The court saw no reason for punitive action. Yoshiie was not dissuaded from intervening.

Assured of Yoshiie's backing, Sanehira at last set off to attack Hidetake in Dewa. Taking advantage of Sanehira's absence, Kiyohira and Iehira attacked his headquarters but were in turn assaulted and routed by Yoshiie. Sanehira fell ill and died en route to Dewa, however, obviating further hostilities, and the two half brothers thereupon submitted to the authority of Yoshiie. He mediated the issue of the governance of the Back Six Districts of Mutsu by assigning three districts to each brother. This decision irked Iehira, who now considered himself head of the Kiyohara, while Kiyohira, as the only survivor of the Abe clan remaining in the northeast, may have considered himself heir to the Six Districts. Friction between the brothers mounted, and when Ieharu's forces raided Kiyohira's base and slaughtered his wife and children, Kiyohira appealed to Yoshiie.

In the fall of 1086, Yoshiie besieged Iehira in Numa Stockade with a force of "three thousand mounted warriors." Heavy snow, cold, and hunger forced Yoshiie to lift the siege. His younger brother, Yoshimitsu, left his post at the capital to come to his aid, and after a larger force was collected, they laid siege to Iehira, now in Kanezawa Stockade, a short distance to the north (at what is now the city of Yokote in southeastern Akita Prefecture). After another difficult siege the brothers prevailed at the end of 1087. Iehira was slain, and the main Kiyohara line was at an end[33] (see Map 10.1).

The court again denied Yoshiie's request for rewards for himself and his men and official recognition of their hard-earned victory, maintaining with much justice that the fighting was a private quarrel. Yoshiie had used his considerable resources as governor of Mutsu, which was the principal center of gold mining, to conduct the war and provision his troops. He was now obliged to compensate his retainers and recruits from his own resources. Furthermore, the court disciplined Yoshiie, ending his appointment as governor of Mutsu the next year and requiring him to repay tax revenues from the province that he had diverted to support the war.

Fighting had its own, more important rewards for Yoshiie and his descendants. His victory over Kiyohara no Iehira further enhanced the prestige of his Minamoto line in the eyes of eastern warriors. In the two wars in the northeast, first Yoriyoshi, and then Yoshiie recruited relatives, retainers, and allies in the east to mount campaigns against tribal chieftains. In the first war Yoriyoshi, as recipient of a court commission, had troops requisitioned on court orders, a force he commanded as provincial governor, and garrison guards he led as General of the *chinjufu*. In the second war Yoshiie was able to raise and later compensate an army using mostly his own resources. The wars were long and arduous, at least in part because the Minamoto's forces did not have numerical superiority. In both wars victory came in the end thanks to alliances made with contending local tribal forces. The Minamoto leaders, nonetheless, gained fame as unrivaled warriors.

The combined governorships of Mutsu and Dewa, which may have been one of Yoshiie's goals, went instead to Kiyohira. He profited spectacularly from the war. As the sole survivor of the Abe and

---

[33] For a fuller discussion of the wars, see Toyoda, *Tōhoku no rekishi*, vol. 1, pp. 185–205.

Kiyohara families, he gained the lands once held by both families in Mutsu and Dewa, and was appointed General of the *chinjufu*. He resumed the Fujiwara clan name of his father (who claimed descent from the Hidesato who defeated Masakado). Kiyohira moved his residence to the former base of his erstwhile Abe relatives south of the confluence of the Kitakami and Koromo rivers, a militarily strategic point in the southern part of modern Iwate Prefecture that had figured in the early Heian campaigns against the Emishi and had also more recently been the scene of fighting in which Kiyohira's father, Tsunekiyo, had participated. Known, probably from Kiyohira's time, as Hiraizumi, the site grew into a vigorous urban cultural center distinguished by its prolific, luxurious religious architecture, its Buddhist art, and its landscape gardens, modeled in good part on the style and standards of the imperial capital at Heian. The remarkable flowering of Hiraizumi culture under the lordship of the Ōshū Fujiwara (the "Fujiwara of Mutsu"), as Kiyohira and his three direct lineal descendents are called, depended on the political and military supremacy of those lords in Dewa and Mutsu, and on the great wealth they were able to extract from that large, rich territory, especially gold but also horses and agricultural produce. (The warmer climate prevailing at the time probably made the region better farming land than it was subsequently.)

Kiyohira himself established or, according to temple legend, reestablished, the Chūsonji Temple at Hiraizumi, perhaps for the salvation of the war dead in the recent battles fought in the area. Under the Ōshū Fujiwara, the temple's mountain precincts came eventually to encompass scores of buildings and hundreds of monastic cells, the buildings including most notably the Konjikidō ("Golden Hall"), one of the best-known surviving historical structures in Japan. Constructed in 1124, the chapel-like hall provides beneath the altars of its Amidist statuary a final resting place for the mummified remains of the first three Ōshū Fujiwara lords (Kiyohira, Motohira, and Hidehira) and for a severed head that is tentatively identified as that of the fourth and last lord, Yasuhira (1155–89). The hall and a scripture storehouse were the only Chūsonji structures to survive a wildfire that swept the mountain in 1337, but even by itself, the hall's artistry is more than sufficient to impress upon a modern visitor a keen sense of the puissance, wealth, and cultural ambition of its Fujiwara patrons.

Some understanding of the organization of the private warriors, mounted archers, recruited by the Minamoto leaders during the two wars can be gained from two sources: the *Mutsu waki* on the earlier war and the commentary on the twelfth-century hand-scroll painting concerning the Later Three Years' War.³⁴ These works show that the *rōtō* were organized more systematically than in Masakado's time, and that they formed the core of the *bushidan* (warrior band). Many of the *rōtō* recruited as retainers by Yoriyoshi and his son Yoshiie were from the provinces of Sagami and Mikawa. The *Hōgen monogatari* (ca. 1219–22) quotes the warrior Kamata no Masakiyo as stating that he began his service to the Minamoto when Yoriyoshi was governor of Sagami; at this time he would have been a *kenin*. Thereafter he came to address Yoshiie and then Yoshiie's son and grandson as "master," which indicates that he had placed himself under Yoshiie's protection and was considered a *rōtō*.

The primary change in the *bushidan* involved the strengthening of the lord–vassal relationship. There are numerous tales of vassals who, having accepted service with a lord, willingly sacrificed their lives against hopeless odds defending him.³⁵ Similar tales do not appear in the earlier *Shōmonki* or *Konjaku monogatari-shū*. They are evidence that loyalty to one's lord, the keystone of the later warrior ethic (*bushidō*, was being articulated as a guiding principle, at least in literary accounts. The commitment of vassals grew stronger when they looked to lords to guarantee their rights to land in return for military service. Bonds between lord and retainer were also forged in the hardships and sacrifices they suffered together in the long and arduous campaigns of the two wars. As the lord came to have more control over his vassal's life, he assumed greater responsibilities toward him. In 1091 Yoshiie and his brother Yoshitsuna, who had once been companion in arms in campaigns of the Earlier Nine Years' War, were on the verge of combat over a land dispute between their respective *rōtō*. This incident is often cited as evidence of the strong commitment of mutual support between lord and vassal in the *bushidan* of this time.

CONDITIONS IN THE CAPITAL

Outlawry had been a daily occurrence in the life of Heian-kyō since the ninth century, requiring an extensive system of military guards

---

34 *Go sannen kassen ekotoba*, ed. Komatsu Shigemi and Miya Tsugio, vol. 15 of *Nihon emaki taisei*, 27 vols. (Tokyo: Chūō kōronsha, 1977).
35 See, for example, stories in *Mutsu waki*, pp. 236–37, 250; "A Tale of Mutsu," pp. 192, 203.

and attendants to provide security for the court and its officers.[36] The statutory code provided for several bodies of guards to man the many gates of the imperial palace and to serve as ceremonial escorts for the emperor. Their effectiveness, however, largely evaporated in the Heian period as their manpower dwindled, leaving even the palace itself vulnerable to arson, robbery, and murder. The government had sought since the Nara period to assure the personal safety and dignity of higher officials by assigning attendants (*toneri*) to them for guard and escort duty in numbers varying according to their ranks, ranging from twenty at the lower end of the scale up to four hundred at the highest.[37] Although the *toneri* attendants were merely provincial conscripts and had minimal military skills, their use by nobles for private purposes came to be disruptive of public order,[38] and they were replaced in the case of the highest officials with somewhat better-born guard-officials called *zuijin* ("escorts"), who were organizationally attached to the Imperial Bodyguards. Fewer in number than the *toneri*, the handsomely uniformed *zuijin* escorts were prized more for their appearance than for their military accomplishments, and great nobles were typically forced to augment their security with privately recruited forces of *tsuwamono* warriors.

Police officers known as *kebiishi* (Offenses Investigation Agents) are first mentioned in 816. Their mission was the maintenance of public order in the capital and its environs and the investigation of crimes. By 834 a *kebiishi* office was established within the palace grounds as Imperial Police. The remarkable expansion of the office's functions and its involvement in activities in other provinces is discussed in Chapter 1. And yet it seems to have fallen short of meeting all of the needs for security in Kyoto. Various guard units continued to proliferate within the Great Imperial Palace and elsewhere in the capital. Not even the emperor felt safe. In 890, to protect himself from the deposed and dangerously hostile emperor Yōzei, Emperor Uda found it expedient to establish a special unit of Imperial Bodyguards called the *takiguchi* ("water spout"), supposedly named after the location of the headquarters for the group near the entrance of a stream or irrigation canal into the grounds of the Seiryōden, the chief ceremonial palace of the Emperor's Residential Compound. Numbering only ten men at its founding, the *takiguchi*

---

36 Tanimori Tomoo, *Kebiishi no chūshin to shitaru Heian jidai no keisatsu jōtai* (Tokyo: Kashiwa shobō, 1921), pp. 56–121.
37 *Ritsu. Ryō no gige*, pp. 196–97.
38 *Ruijū sandai kyaku, kan* 20, pp. 636–37, 11/4/Engi 2 (902).

group expanded to thirty in the reign of Go-Shirakawa. Its members were non-nobles of the Sixth Rank attached to the Chamberlains' Office (*kurōdodokoro*), in the late Heian period the appointments becoming hereditary in warrior lines of the Taira and Minamoto clans.

Two similar guard groups were instituted for the palaces of the retired emperors, the first either in the time of Uda (ex. emp. 897–931) or later by En'yū (ex. emp. 984–91), and the second under Shirakawa (ex. emp. 1087–1129). The earlier group, called the *mushadokoro* ("Martialists' Office") was initially composed of ten warriors recruited mainly from the ranks of the *takiguchi*, its complement gradually increasing until by the time of ex-emperor Shirakawa it numbered thirty. The second, later, group was called the *in-no-hokumen*, or simply *hokumen* ("north face"). Organized from low-ranking officers without imperial audience privileges, the *hokumen* became the core of the military strength of the ex-emperors, including in its ranks most notably Taira no Masamori, the grandfather of the first military dictator, Kiyomori. As the Taira moved into high offices at court in the twelfth century, acquiring audience privileges and establishing themselves as the paramount warriors of the capital, the importance of the guards declined, and *hokumen* appointments instead came to be used as a means of bringing otherwise socially debarred favorites and useful supporters into the court of the ex-emperor: artists and performers, *kebiishi*, and provincial officials. The poet Saigyō (1118–90), for instance, was a *hokumen*. After the Taira seized control of the government, the *hokumen* under ex-emperor Go-Shirakawa served as personal attendants of the ex-emperor, becoming an important focus of anti-Taira sentiment; they were involved, for example, in the Shishigatani plot of 1177.

The official *kebiishi* and guard groups were not always able to ensure the safety of even the most exalted court figures, as ex-emperor Kazan discovered in 996 when he is reported to have come under arrow attack at the direction of a disgruntled Fujiwara lover. Lesser leaders of the society were even more vulnerable to the outlawry of the times. Princes, regents, chief ministers, and other prominent nobles often found it necessary to establish private guard units within their own palaces and mansions in quarters called the *saburaidokoro* ("Attendants' Office"). They recruited *tsuwamono* who had proved their prowess in fighting. *Tsuwamono* who attended (*saburau*) court nobles at their beck and call came to be called *saburai*, which later became *samurai*. This name for the hired guards at first lacked the honor associated with the word *tsuwamono*. But warriors who previously may have used and sharpened their military skills in banditry or revolt could thus sometimes find themselves transformed into defenders of their former enemies and victims. Enrollment in the service of a great noble at the capital brought high political connections and prestige that could be used in attracting retainers into a warrior's own service, and the chieftains (*tōryō*) of the warrior clans were thus willing to accept service with regents and ministers. But as the might of the warriors came to be increasingly decisive in the affairs of the capital, and as the warriors themselves rose in government rank and office, they posed an ever growing threat to the political authority of their noble lords.

The court was frequently under threat from the armed monks (*sōhei*) of the great temples near the capital. Although Buddhist teachings forbade monks to carry arms, that proscription had early been ignored in China, and clerical warriors were known also in Japan by the eighth century. But it was not until the tenth century, following a rapid growth in temple populations, that larger, wealthier temples organized armies to protect and assert their own interests and to control and manage a not always peaceable brotherhood. The armies were recruited from the more unruly elements within the temples themselves and also from the temples' *shōen*.

In 1006, Kōfukuji in Nara fielded a fighting force of three thousand men. By 1113, Kōfukuji and Enryakuji were said to have mobilized "tens of thousands" of armed monks in a dispute over the appointment of a priest trained at Enryakuji as chief administrator (*bettō*) of Kiyomizudera, a branch temple of Kōfukuji. Armed monks of the Enryakuji (overlooking the capital on the northeast) and Onjōji (in present Ōtsu), being close to Kyoto, were especially prominent in the history of the eleventh century, when their large bands marched into the capital in order to press petitions and demands (*gōso*), backed by the threat of imminent violence, on the court or on individual courtiers.[39] The belligerent intrusions of the monks were usually supported and protected by displaying symbols of the temples' guardian shrines, the Kōfukuji monks carrying at the head of their procession the "divine tree" (*shimboku*) of the Kasuga Shrine, and the Enryakuji monks descending from Mount Hiei bearing the sacred palanquin (*mikoshi*) of Hie Shrine. Armed monks descended on the capital sixty times during the years of the retired emperors Shirakawa, Toba, and Go-Shirakawa. To counter the threat of these religious institutions,

39 Tsuji Zennosuke, *Nihon bukkyōshi* (Tokyo: Iwanami shoten, 1944), vol. 1, pp. 765–920.

the court relied on the Imperial Police, the *hokumen* warriors, and, increasingly, on the *tōryō* of the Minamoto and Taira clans. *Heike monogatari* quotes Shirakawa as lamenting: "Three things refuse to obey my will: the waters of the Kamo River, the fall of backgammon dice, and the monks of Enryakuji Temple."[40] (For more on the actions of the armed monks, see Chapter 7.)

The heads of the military branches of the Minamoto and Taira were regarded as proper chieftains (*tōryō*) only if they had demonstrated superior martial prowess. Of equal importance were connections with the highest levels at court. Hence they maintained a base in the capital, where they and their kin were appointed to a succession of court titles related to guard offices and they served as private protection for members of the imperial and noble families. The most successful served a succession of province governorships. They built their family's economic strength by acquiring *shōen* in the provinces, some of which they commended to their highest patrons at court. These acts of commendation and gifts of land and horses to their patrons were essential for advancement in court position. The *tōryō* welcomed imperial appointments to lead punitive expeditions to punish enemies of the court, even though they had to recruit most of the military force, because a successful campaign could bring promotion in court rank and position as well as high esteem in the eyes of other *tsuwamono*. Generation after generation, the *tōryō* of the Seiwa Genji were highly successful in this process: Yorinobu settling the Tadatsune uprising, his son Yoriyoshi victorious in the Earlier Nine Years' War, and the latter's son Yoshiie in the Later Three Years' War. Yoshiie was acknowledged as the peerless warrior (*musha*) of the realm. In the words of a popular song, "Of all the Minamoto, Hachiman Tarō [Yoshiie] is the most feared." Yet he remained a *samurai* of the retired emperor.[41]

Shirakawa, who became the first cloistered emperor (*in*) in 1087 (see Chapter 9), was extremely effective both in employing the warrior leaders to his advantage and in balancing rivals against each other to deflect the danger inherent in their increasing strength.

40 Takaki Ichinosuke, Ozawa Masao, Atsumi Kaoru, and Kindaichi Haruhiko, eds., *Heike monogatari*, vols. 32–33 in *Nihon koten bungaku taikei* (1959–60), vol. 1, *kan* 1.4, p. 129. Translation by Helen Craig McCullough, *The Tale of the Heike* (Stanford, Calif.: Stanford University Press, 1988), p. 50.
41 *Chūyūki* (or *Nakauki*), vols. 8–14 in *Shiryō taisei* (Tokyo: Naigai shoseki kabushiki kaisha, 1934), vol. 3, p. 129, 16/7/Kajō 1 (1106); and *Ryōjin hishō*, compiled by Go-Shirakawa, *kan* 2, poem 444, vol. 19 of *Nihon koten zensho* (Tokyo: Asahi shinbunsha, 1953), p. 137. The nickname derives from Yoshiie's coming-of-age ceremony at Iwashimizu Hachiman Shrine.

Yoshiie, after gaining a reputation as a courageous fighter as a young man in the Earlier Nine Years' War, spent many years doing Shirakawa's bidding. However, he was not reappointed to a lucrative position after the Later Three Years' War, from which he emerged as the preeminent warrior. The compensation he gave to his men out of his own resources won the admiration of the warrior class. The court was much concerned to check his power and influence, and the opportunity came when there was the confrontation in 1091 between his powerful *bushidan* and the strong force of his brother Yoshitsuna. The prospect of their forces clashing near the capital alarmed the government, but the regent, Morozane, was able to mediate the dispute. To control Yoshiie he obtained an imperial order forbidding provincial troops from coming up to the capital and also prohibiting landowners from commending additional land to Yoshiie.[42] The prestige of this powerful *tōryō* among provincial landholders posed a threat to the balance of power at court, for the elite had long derived most of its revenue from the possession and commendation of *shōen*.

As commander of the next punitive expedition two years later, Shirakawa turned to Yoshiie's brother and rival and rewarded him with elevation to the Fourth Rank.[43] Five years later Shirakawa mollified Yoshiie by granting him the privilege of entrance to his private quarters. The aristocrats were appalled that a *tsuwamono* was allowed to enter their world on an equal footing.[44]

In 1106, Yoshiie died at the age of sixty-seven, occasioning a struggle to succeed to the position of the Minamoto *tōryō*. By this time the *bushidan* no longer dissolved on the death of the leader, and it became customary for the eldest son to succeed his father. However, Yoshiie's eldest son died young, his second son, the powerful warrior Yoshichika, was exiled for murder while governor of Tsushima, and when another son was killed, Yoshitsuna and his son were rumored to be implicated. Yoshichika's thirteen-year-old son, Tameyoshi (1096–1156), was commissioned to arrest Yoshitsuna, and he was credited with this feat. He succeeded his grandfather as the Minamoto *tōryō*. However, there was little aristocratic support for a young *tōryō*, and the Minamoto *bushidan* weakened significantly. Many of the leaders left the capital for their bases in the provinces. The Minamoto of the

---

42 *Hyakuren shō, (Shintei zōho) Kokushi taikei*, vol. 11 (1929), p. 41; and *Go-Nijō Moromichi ki*, in *Dainihon kokiroku*, series 7, vol. 2 (Tokyo: Iwanami shoten, 1957), p. 132, 12/6/Kanji 5 (1091).
43 Takeuchi, *Bushi no tōjō*, pp. 214–15.
44 *Chūyūki*, vol. 2, pp. 123–24, 23/10/Jōtoku 2 (1098).

generation of Yoshiie and his sons and nephews left a record of violence, lawlessness, and mutually destructive behavior that cost the family its reputation as the leading samurai. Shirakawa, who had fomented Minamoto factionalism as a means of checking their strength, had already chosen the Ise Heishi (Heishi is the Sino-Japanese reading of "Taira clan") as their replacement. Despite a less developed *bushidan*, with Shirakawa's backing the Taira would rise higher and more quickly than the Minamoto.

Although the Taira had originally considered the vast eastern plains their own, they had gradually been absorbed into the Minamoto network after the Tadatsune rebellion. Taira no Korehira was an exception. The ancestor of the Ise Heishi (a branch of the Kammu Heishi) and probably a son or grandson adopted by Sadamori (see Figure 9.7, Genealogy of the Taira), Korehira is believed to have established an estate in Ise when he was appointed governor in 1006. However, his connection with Ise predated this appointment. In 998, Fujiwara no Yukinari's diary *Gonki* records a large-scale dispute over land in Ise between the two renowned warriors, Korehira and Taira no Muneyori (d. 1011), and their many *rōtō*.[45] Both men were summoned to the capital for interrogation by the Imperial Police and detained there. Korehira apologized and, on the recommendation of the Minister of the Right, was appointed governor of Ise. Michinaga, who was allied with the Minamoto, unsuccessfully opposed the appointment.[46] However, he ensured that Korehira's descendants would not be appointed to higher office in the capital than the Imperial Police.

Three generations later, Taira no Masamori was appointed governor of Oki. Unable to derive much revenue from the small island, he developed the family land bequeathed to him by his ancestors in Ise and Iga. In 1098 he commended twenty *chō* (66 acres) of his holdings in Iga to the Rokujō-in, formerly the residence in Kyoto of Shirakawa's favorite daughter, Teishi (Ikuhōmon-in). When she died at the age of twenty, the grieving Shirakawa became a priest and turned the residence into a temple dedicated to her salvation. The act of commendation was probably suggested by Shirakawa's female attendant, the Gion Consort, who was a neighbor of Masamori. This provided Masamori with political backing in his disputes over land with the powerful Tōdaiji and Ise Shrine. It was also the first step by

---

45 *Gonki, Shiryō taisei*, vol. 35 (1939), vol. 1, p. 60, 14/12/Chōtoku 4 (998).
46 Takeuchi, *Bushi no tōjō*, p. 222.

the Ise Heishi toward employment in the capital and political power. After further gifts to Shirakawa, Masamori was employed as a guard in the *hokumen*. This was the first time that a Taira had been employed by a retired emperor.

The fact that the Taira had not been favored by the Fujiwara made them attractive to Shirakawa. Masamori was appointed to lead an attack on Yoshiie's son, the powerful warrior Minamoto no Yoshichika. Yoshichika, who had been accused of murder and plunder while serving as governor of Tsushima and had been exiled to Oki, left his island exile and in 1107 crossed over to Izumo, where he killed a provincial deputy and looted government stores. Masamori, then in the vicinity as governor of Inaba, was commissioned to attack Yoshichika. He distinguished himself by killing Yoshichika and four of his chief retainers, and Shirakawa rewarded him and his sons lavishly. Shirakawa's trusted aide, the Consultant (*sangi*) and literatus Fujiwara no Munetada, complained of the favoritism shown by the retired emperor to such a low-ranking warrior, granting him the governorship of the prized province of Tamba.[47] With Masamori's triumphal return to the capital, the martial reputation of the Taira began to rival the Minamotos'. However, some doubted that a relative unknown could have succeeded so easily against a seasoned warrior. It was suggested that the severed head so prominently displayed had not belonged to Yoshichika.

Masamori received other important commissions. In 1113, he and Minamoto no Tameyoshi fought to defend the capital against armed monks, and Masamori allowed his young son Tadamori (1096–1153) much of the credit. In 1119, while governor of Bizen, Masamori defeated brigands who had threatened the capital, and he also suppressed rebels in Kyushu, for which he was awarded the Fourth Rank.

Tadamori was granted many opportunities to demonstrate his prowess and speed his rise through the ranks. According to *Ima kagami* (1170), Tadamori's wife, the sister of the Gion Consort, spoke to Shirakawa often on his behalf.[48] In 1129, he moved against the pirates of the Inland Sea.[49] These pirates were coordinating raids involving dozens of ships to prey on the shipments by *shōen* of the annual dues to their guarantors and central proprietors in the capi-

---

47 *Chūyūki*, vol. 3, p. 322, 24/1/Tennin 1 (1108).
48 *Ima kagami*, (Shintei zōho) *Kokushi taikei*, vol. 21.2 (1940), kan 4, pp. 100–102. Tadamori's wife, who is referred to in *Chūyūki* as "one who is close to the retired emperor," had been one of Shirakawa's concubines before she was given to Tadamori in marriage.
49 On conditions in the provinces, see Ishimoda, *Kodai makki seijishi josetsu*.

tal.⁵⁰ To judge from tales in *Konjaku monogatari-shū*, however, there does not seem to have been sufficient pirate activity to warrant a court-ordered military campaign against them. It was more likely that Tadamori, as governor of Bizen, had requested permission to confront the pirates.

In 1135, Tadamori led a procession of prisoners through the streets of the capital. According to *Chōshūki*, "Tadamori had taken seventy pirates prisoner. . . . Everyone came to see them. He displayed the head of the pirate Hidaka Zenshi, but most of the captives were not pirates. It is said that Tadamori had taken men and presented them as 'pirate captives'."⁵¹ The forty "pirates" who were not immediately turned over to the Imperial Police were presumably released after the victory procession had served its propagandistic function.

As related in *Heike monogatari*, Tadamori was ridiculed at court for his provincial origins. He realized that military successes were not enough to gain acceptance in elite society, and that he needed also to develop the skills of a courtier. His dancing at the Kamo Festival in 1119 was admired. But in 1130 he was invited to a poetry composition party in the retired emperor's residence, where his poetry was judged "not good."⁵² In 1132, when he built the Sanjūsangendō for Retired Emperor Toba, he was granted the extraordinary privilege of entry into the ex-emperor's private quarters. Tadamori managed to narrow the distance between the worlds of the warrior and the aristocrat. His courtly skills and financial resources compensated in part for the lesser degree of development of the Taira *bushidan*.

In their encounters with the pirates, Masamori and Tadamori had become aware of the profits to be made in foreign trade. Sung and Koryŏ traders negotiated under the jurisdiction of the Dazaifu. By the eleventh century, many of the Dazaifu officials had begun to expand private trade at the expense of official trade. There was a great market for foreign goods. Appointed as an official on Shirakawa's Kanazaki *shōen* in Hizen, Tadamori drew up documents to try to convince the Dazaifu officials that the retired emperor had granted him permission to trade directly with Chinese ships that arrived in 1133.⁵³

---

50 Takeuchi, *Bushi no tōjō*, p. 247.
51 *Chōshūki, Shiryō taisei*, vol. 7 (1934), vol. 2, p. 301, 19/8/Hōen 1 (1135).
52 *Chōshūki*, vol. 2, p. 301, 5/9/Daiji 5 (1130).
53 Mori Katsumi, *Nissō bōeki no kenkyū*, rev. ed., vol. 1 of *Mori Katsumi chosaku senshū* (Tokyo: Kokusho kankōkai, 1975), p. 176.

By the time of his death in 1153, Tadamori had secured a strong economic base for the Ise Heishi in landholding and trade, as well as a leading role among the warrior nobles at court. It was from this privileged position that his son Kiyomori (1118–81) began his spectacular career as warrior and politician, exploiting the factional rivalries among emperors, retired emperors, and Fujiwara families to rise to the highest offices at court.

HŌGEN DISTURBANCE

The military clash that erupted in the capital in the first year of Hōgen (1156) resulted from a quarrel that deeply divided the imperial family and from rivalries within the Fujiwara regental family (sekkanke). The administrative organization of the retired emperor's household, the *insei* or cloister government (see Chapter 9), shaped by Shirakawa, was perpetuated by Toba and Go-Shirakawa, who successively wielded power as senior retired emperor (*hon'in*) until the latter's death in 1192. This unusual system of administration was effective in improving the economic resources of the imperial family and in reducing the influence of the Fujiwara regents, but it led to tensions within the imperial family. The dominant role of the cloistered emperor in governmental matters as well as family affairs was resented by the reigning emperor and his entourage, and by junior retired emperors who were excluded from the powers of the senior position.

Shirakawa controlled the court during the reigns of his son Horikawa, his grandson Toba, and Sutoku, supposedly his great-grandson. (According to the *Kojidan*, a thirteenth-century collection of tales and anecdotes, it was common knowledge that Sutoku, the son of Toba's consort, Shirakawa's "adopted daughter" Taikemmon-in [Fujiwara no Shōshi], was actually fathered by Shirakawa.) Shirakawa required Toba to abdicate in favor of Sutoku.[54] Upon Shirakawa's death in 1129, Toba, succeeding as senior retired emperor, immediately began to undo much of what Shirakawa had accomplished. He replaced Shirakawa's closest retainers, but Taira no Tadamori managed to retain his position as the main military retainer. Toba recalled the former regent, Fujiwara no Tadazane, who had been banished from the court by Shirakawa. Tadazane made plans to reestablish the fortunes of the regental family by reunifying

---

54 Takeuchi, *Bushi no tōjō*, pp. 318–19.

its divided estates, which had diminished under Go-Sanjō and Shirakawa, and by expanding existing *shōen*. In 1150 he also attempted to remove his son Tadamichi from the position of regent in order to entrust leadership of the clan to his favored younger son, Yorinaga. However, Yorinaga was outmaneuvered by his half brother Tadamichi and Toba's consort Bifukumon-in (Fujiwara no Tokushi). Accused of causing the illness of which Emperor Konoe died in 1155 by sticking needles into the eyes of a statue of the emperor, Yorinaga was excluded from the court and a bitter rivalry divided the regental family.

Toba had forced Sutoku to abdicate in 1141 in favor of his younger "brother" Konoe. Sutoku then pinned his hopes on his own son becoming crown prince, but when Konoe died in 1155, Toba selected another of his own sons, Go-Shirakawa, as emperor and the latter's son as crown prince (the future emperor Nijō). Sutoku was still determined that his son should gain the throne, and that, as a consequence, he himself would become the senior retired emperor as father of the reigning emperor. He was supported in this ambition by Yorinaga, who aimed to wrest the leadership of the regental house from Tadamichi. When Toba fell critically ill the next year, Sutoku sought military supporters.

The fraternal quarrels between Go-Shirakawa and Sutoku and between Tadamichi and Yorinaga would likely have been resolved in earlier centuries by maneuver, political manipulation, and a judicious use of exile, but the ready availability now of military forces was a temptation too great for either side to resist.[55] It was rumored that Sutoku and Yorinaga, who were backed militarily by the Minamoto *tōryō* Tameyoshi, and by Taira no Tadamasa (younger brother of Tadamori), were about to "mobilize troops and overthrow the state."[56] Taira no Tadamori's son, Kiyomori, and Tameyoshi's son, Yoshitomo, who was on bad terms with his father, followed by

---

55 On the Hōgen and Heiji disturbances, see Uwayokote Masataka, *Gempei no seisui*, vol. 6 of *Nihon no rekishi bunko* (Tokyo: Kōdansha, 1975), pp. 51–81; and Yasuda Motohisa, *Gempei no sōkoku*, vol. 7 of *Kokumin no rekishi* (Tokyo: Bun'eidō, 1967). The narrative related here generally follows *Hōgen monogatari* and *Heiji monogatari*, semifictional accounts that in their earliest versions seem to date not later than the thirteenth century. The texts used are the Muromachi-period versions printed in vol. 31 of *Nihon koten bungaku taikei*. A partial English translation of another, somewhat different, text of *Heiji* is included in Edwin O. Reischauer and Joseph K. Yamagiwa, *Translations from Early Japanese Literature* (Cambridge, Mass.: Harvard University Press, 1951), pp. 396–446. A complete translation of *Hōgen*, also based on a different, fifteenth-century or later text, is in William R. Wilson, "*Hōgen monogatari*": *Tale of the Disorder in Hōgen* (Tokyo: Sophia University Press, 1971).
56 Takeuchi, *Buke no tōjō*, pp. 344–45, quoting *Heihanki*, the diary of Taira no Nobunori, an important source on the Hōgen clash, in *Shiryō taisei*, vols. 15–18 and 37 (1934–39).

most of the Minamoto *rōtō*, aligned themselves with the imperial faction of Go-Shirakawa. The dying Toba issued orders to his military chiefs, Kiyomori and Yoshitomo, to mobilize their retainers for the defense of his palace near the junction of the Kamo and Katsura rivers south of the city, and also Go-Shirakawa's Takamatsu palace. With the death of Toba on the second day of the seventh month, Sutoku became concerned for his own personal safety and summoned such military support as he could command: Yoshitomo's father, Tameyoshi, and two of Tameyoshi's junior sons; Minamoto warriors from Yamato province; some Taira warriors, most notably Sutoku's favorite Tadamasa; Yorinaga and the armed men he had mustered from his *shōen*; and the armed monks of the Kōfukuji Temple at Nara. The warriors responding to Sutoku's call included formidable fighters, but among them the Yamato Minamoto were taken prisoner by Go-Shirakawa's men before they reached the capital, and the Kōfukuji monks never arrived, so that the total number of fighters defending Sutoku's Shirakawa palace remained small.

The Shirakawa palace was a large establishment east of the Kamo River at the northwest corner of what is now the site of the Heian Shrine. The palace was about a mile and a quarter from Go-Shirakawa's residence and base at the Takamatsu palace north of Sanjō Avenue just southwest of the Greater Imperial Palace. On the night of the eleventh, fighting erupted in a furious attack, launched at nightfall on Shirakawa palace by the forces of Go-Shirakawa. The attacking force included Kiyomori with about three hundred mounted men, Yoshitomo with two hundred, and Yoshiyasu with one hundred. They set fire to the palace, and Sutoku's men fled. Within a few hours both the battle and the war were over.

Sutoku succeeded in escaping to the Ninnaji Temple just beyond the northwest corner of the capital, where he was captured and sent into exile in Sanuki on Shikoku, dying there a bitter man. Hit by a stray arrow during the fighting at Shirakawa, Sutoku's supporter and accomplice Yorinaga died a few days later. Men linked with Yorinaga at court were exiled, and some seventeen of Sutoku's warriors were – against three and a half centuries of bloodless precedent – condemned to execution by imperial order. Despite Yoshitomo's plea for his father Tameyoshi's life, he was ordered to execute him, as was Kiyomori his uncle Tadamasa. This *tsuwamono*-like disposition of prisoners stunned the court, a decision that was urged by Go-Shirakawa's eminence grise, Lesser Counselor Fujiwara no Michinori, known by his Buddhist name Shinzei (1106–

60). Although he was of low rank, he enjoyed the trust of the emperor because his wife had been Go-Shirakawa's wet-nurse, presumably creating the kind of emotional bond that the fiction of the period suggests.

Although the fighting had demonstrated for the first time the effectiveness of the warrior families in determining events in the capital, their rewards were meager. Go-Shirakawa was no more generous in his treatment of Kiyomori and Yoshitomo after the coup than most previous emperors and regents had been in rewarding warriors. From the court's point of view, the warriors who had defended the emperor and stormed the Shirakawa palace were simply useful servants of the throne who could be employed in time of need and otherwise mostly ignored. The rewards publicly granted the two great warriors were insignificant in comparison with their political and economic strength. Kiyomori, the senior warrior representative at court and the heir to a long family tradition of court service, received merely the governorship of Harima; Yoshitomo, the Minamoto chieftain and the architect of the victory at Shirakawa, had to be content with lowly appointment as Provisional Head of the Left Horse Guards, a post of minimal distinction and probably no power or remuneration whatever.

The Hōgen Disturbance resolved sharp conflicts within the imperial and Fujiwara leadership, placing control of the court firmly in the hands of the reigning emperor, but it left unanswered the question of military supremacy as between Go-Shirakawa's two chief warrior leaders, Kiyomori and Yoshitomo, and the further and more fundamental issue of the role of powerful warriors vis-à-vis the imperial court that remained, fatally to the regime, unaddressed.

HEIJI DISTURBANCE

Court politics at Heian in 1159, the first year of the Heiji era, were guided by the complex web of rivalries, ambitions, personal relationships, and alliances that had arisen at court following the Hōgen conflict three years earlier. Go-Shirakawa had come to the throne in 1155 as a stopgap successor transitional to the accession of his son Nijō. When he abdicated in favor of Nijō in the fall of 1158, the relationship between the two was for that reason even more tense than usual in the case of an ex-emperor who would rule as senior retired emperor and a reigning emperor. Bifukumon-in, former mistress of the late ex-emperor Toba and an original supporter of Nijō in the succession struggles, was still alive, exercising a powerful influence at court as a result of her relationship with Nijō and also because of the vast *shōen* wealth that had come to her from Toba.

Emperor Nijō was still young, only fifteen years old, but he had a reputation for quick intelligence, and he was intent on ruling the court in his own right, after the manner of his father, whose wishes he tended to ignore. He was supported in that ambition and advised by two skilled Fujiwara politicians: his maternal uncle, Grand Counselor Tsunemune (1119–89), and his wet-nurse's son, Korekata (fl. 1125–66), the Superintendent of the Imperial Police (*kebiishi no bettō*). Warriors in the emperor's entourage included Minamoto no Yoshitomo's senior kinsmen Mitsuyasu (1095–1160), the father of ex-emperor Toba's last mistress, who had served as a wet-nurse to Nijō, and Minamoto no Yorimasa (1104–80), who had long been in the employ of imperial family members and remained loyal now to his sovereign, even eventually turning his back on his own clan leader to follow Nijō into the embrace of the Taira.

The control of the court that had been exercised by Shinzei since the Hōgen Disturbance was now endangered by the strength of the emperor's party and more particularly by the rapid growth in influence of a new favorite of Go-Shirakawa, Fujiwara no Nobuyori (1133–60), who seemed to be on the verge of usurping Shinzei's formerly dominant role. Shinzei was alive to the danger and endeavored to bring Nobuyori into disrepute with the ex-emperor, denigrating him at every opportunity, but the result was only to incense Nobuyori further against himself. The relations between Nobuyori and Shinzei reached their nadir when Shinzei succeeded in blocking the appointment of Nobuyori to a key office that was usually a stepping-stone to high ministerial rank. Pleading illness, the enraged Nobuyori refused to attend court, staying in seclusion "to practice the military arts."

Toward the end of the first year of the Heiji era, on a day corresponding to a date in January 1160, Taira no Kiyomori, in fulfillment of a vow, left the capital accompanied by his eldest son, Shigemori (1138–79), and a small body of followers on a pilgrimage to Kumano, a well-known and popular sacred site of important shrines, mystics, and mysticism near the west coast of Ise Bay in the southern part of modern Mie Prefecture. The shrines were about 175 miles distant by the circuitous route around the mountains that usually required a minimum five days to traverse.[57]

---

57 Ōmori, *Buke jidai no kenkyū*, vol. 2, p. 188.

Just five days after Kiyomori's departure, his chief rivals at court, Nobuyori and the Minamoto chieftain Yoshitomo, began to move against him and his patron Shinzei. Despite Yoshitomo's critical services at the time of the Hōgen conflict, his fortunes had been checked by Kiyomori acting in league with Shinzei, and he was quick now to join a cause that might offer remedy for that injustice. The Nobuyori–Yoshitomo alliance was joined by other disaffected warriors and by courtiers seeking to strengthen Emperor Nijō's personal control of the court, notably Tsunemune and Korekata. Its military core and most of its strength was Minamoto.

On the ninth of the twelfth month of the Heiji year, a body of mounted men under the command of Yoshitomo and Nobuyori forced ex-emperor Go-Shirakawa to vacate his Sanjō palace and move to the Greater Imperial Palace, where he and Emperor Nijō were held under house arrest. Fire was set to the palace at Sanjō and to Shinzei's residence next door with great loss of life. On the following day, Nobuyori exercised his new power at court to rid the government of Shinzei's sympathizers and to obtain the dismissal of Shinzei and Kiyomori from their official posts. He also obtained for himself a coveted appointment to a high ministerial post and for Yoshitomo the governorship of Harima that had just been snatched from Kiyomori. Shinzei fled to Nara, where a few days later he was caught and executed following a suicide attempt interrupted by his executioners. His severed head was brought back to the capital for public display like that of a common criminal, and the revenge of Nobuyori seemed complete.

Kiyomori, whose absence from the capital had created the opportunity for the conspirators, was at a post station on the Pacific coast toward the tip of the Kii peninsula when a messenger reached him with news of the untoward events at court. After some vacillation, he set out for the capital at the head of his small retinue, now grown with local reinforcement to one hundred mounted men. Picking up the support of three hundred additional men en route, he entered his Rokuhara residence in the city just a few days later, on the seventeenth of the month. He made an initial show of submission to the newly triumphant regime, but when on the twenty-sixth Emperor Nijō, disenchanted with Nobuyori's highhanded ways and advised by Tsunemune and Korekata, managed to slip out of the imperial palace disguised as a woman to join the Taira at Rokuhara, Yoshitomo and Nobuyori were clearly defined as rebels and the Rokuhara Taira acquired the legitimacy of an imperial army. On the same day,

Go-Shirakawa also escaped custody at the imperial palace and fled to the Ninnaji Temple.

The day after the flight of Nijō and Go-Shirakawa, on the twenty-seventh of the month, the Taira force under Shigemori launched an attack on the forces of Yoshitomo and Nobuyori at the Greater Imperial Palace. The attackers withdrew after fierce fighting, luring the Minamoto out of the palace, which the Taira were then able to occupy and secure. The dispossessed Minamoto advanced on Rokuhara, where Kiyomori waited to do battle with them, crushing them and sending them into headlong retreat toward their homelands in the east. After only a few hours of actual fighting between troops of several hundred horsemen, the conflict was over.

The badly frightened Nobuyori, fleeing for his life before the final battle, was caught and executed near Rokuhara on the bed of the Kamo River at Rokujō. His age was just twenty-six. Yoshitomo attempted to flee to the east, but he was betrayed and killed at a refuge in Owari Province. Yoshitomo's two older sons were executed, and the thirteen-year-old Yoritomo would have suffered the same fate but for the plea of Kiyomori's stepmother, Ike no Zenni. He was banished to Izu, placed in the custody of a trusted Taira ally, Hōjō Tokimasa. The infant Yoshitsune was also spared and was assigned to the priesthood. The Taira victory over the Minamoto appeared to be complete and the Minamoto *tōryō* line at an end. But in a remarkable reversal of fate, the brothers Yoritomo and Yoshitsune survived to lead the Minamoto to victory over the Taira twenty-five years later.

The Heiji Disturbance had its beginnings in the rivalries and jealousies among confidants of Retired Emperor Go-Shirakawa and Emperor Nijō, but unlike the Hōgen incident, its action was determined not by commands issued by emperors or court officials, but by warrior chieftains acting on their own personal ambitions. The events revealed to the warriors the powerlessness of the court and the first hints of the political realities of the warriors' military power. Nevertheless, it is probably premature to speak of this time as the beginning of warrior rule, as some historians have. It is at about this time, when the military and political landscape was changing and warriors acted more on their own initiative, that the term *bushi* came into use in referring to warriors. (The term existed in Nara and early Heian times, when it referred neither to warriors or military officials [*bukan*], but rather to literati who were skilled in military arts.)[58]

---

58 *Shoku Nihongi, (Shintei zōho) Kokushi taikei*, vol. 2 (1935), p. 84, 27/1/Yōrō 5 (721).

TAIRA RISE TO POWER

The political history of the two decades following the Heiji Disturbance until the beginning of the war between the Minamoto and Taira (the Gempei War, 1180–85) is discussed more fully in Chapter 9. We are concerned here specifically with the rise to power at court of Taira no Kiyomori and his kinsmen.

In the Hōgen and Heiji conflicts, the Taira mobilized retainers in particular from Bizen and Bitchū provinces (most of what it now Okayama Prefecture) on the Inland Sea and from Iga and Ise (northern Mie Prefecture) southeast of the capital. Those were regions where Taira leaders since the time of Kiyomori's grandfather Masamori had been custodial governors (*zuryō*). Following the decimation of the Minamoto leaders in the Heiji fighting, Kiyomori, as the triumphant hegemon of warriors, had no difficulty in recruiting numbers of the Minamoto's *rōtō* as well as others to his organization. In the following years the Taira developed their network of allies, not only in western Japan and in the capital area, where they had long been prominent, but also in the east. The commission given by Go-Shirakawa to Kiyomori's son, Shigemori, to be prepared to provide military security and police functions wherever needed throughout the country, gave him the opportunity to extend Taira military influence. The economic position of the Taira was also strengthened by their seizing control of some *shōen* of Minamoto and courtier families. The appointment of Taira relatives to more and more provincial governorships also strengthened the financial position of the Taira.

More impressive than Kiyomori's military and economic gains were his rapid promotions in the court hierarchy. In 1160 he received the Third Rank, the first of a warrior family to join the senior nobles (*kugyō*). In 1167 he rose to the post of Chancellor (*daijō daijin*), and the First Rank, the pinnacle of the bureaucratic structure. He arranged the promotion of several Taira kinsmen to the ranks of the senior nobility and membership in the Council of State. He left the chancellorship after a few months, speaking of poor health, and took holy orders; but he had made his point, and continued to assert his influence on court appointments and policy decisions. An adroit politician, Kiyomori took full advantage, after the Heiji affair, of the rivalry for power between the senior retired emperor and his son, Emperor Nijō, both of whom courted him with rewards as they vied for his military support. He also played the game of marriage politics in the Fujiwara style to advance his personal relationships in the highest court circles. His eight-year-old daughter was married to the future regent Motozane in 1164. His connection with Go-Shirakawa became familial when his Taira sister-in-law, Shigeko (Kenshummon-in), bore the retired emperor a son, later enthroned as Emperor Takakura (1161–81, r. 1168–80). Subsequently Kiyomori's daughter Tokushi became Takakura's consort, and their son, the infant Antoku, was placed on the throne by his grandfather, Kiyomori, in 1180, at the height of his control of the court.

Contemporary sources do not, for the most part, comment critically on the rapid advancement of Kiyomori, as a person of warrior lineage, to such high position at court. The explanation of his initial acceptance may lie in prevalence of the rumor, which appears in several sources, that his natural father was actually Emperor Shirakawa. The source considered the most reliable says that the emperor, upon the death of Kiyomori's mother, gave the two-year-old child for adoption to Taira no Tadamori, who thus became his genealogical father.[59]

The *Tale of Heike* (*Heike monogatari*) gives a dramatic account of the "flowering fortunes" of Kiyomori at the height of his success: "Not only did Kiyomori himself attain the pinnacle of worldly success, but his entire family shared his prosperity." The account enumerates the high offices held by three of his sons and the good marriages of seven daughters. "Sixteen Taira ranked as senior nobles, more than thirty were courtiers, and more than sixty held appointments as provincial governors, guards officers, or members of the central bureaucracy. It was as though there were no other people in the world."[60]

Although the key to Kiyomori's ascendancy was ultimately his military strength, he climbed the ranks of court position and advanced his kinsmen by employing the familiar techniques of the civil courtiers rather than by intimidation, at least until 1177. In time, however, Kiyomori's growing power at court caused increasing resentment among courtiers, and Go-Shirakawa in particular sought to check his strength, leading to an organized attempt in 1177 (the so-called Shishigatani plot) by officers of the retired emperor's household, acting in league with some military figures, to move against the Taira

---

59 The statement in the *Heike monogatari* that Kiyomori's mother was Shirakawa's favorite concubine, Gion no Nyōgo, is thought to be incorrect. Rather, it was her younger sister who bore Shirakawa's child, according to documents discovered in modern times. Takeuchi, *Bushi no tōjō*, pp. 388–89.
60 *Heike monogatari*, vol. 1, kan 1.5; in H. McCullough, *The Tale of the Heike*, pp. 28–29.

leader. The plot was discovered and crushed before it could be put into action, however, leaving Kiyomori more powerful than ever but with a heightened enmity toward Go-Shirakawa and his court.

One issue of contention was over control of the landholdings of the regental house. When Regent Motozane, who was married to Kiyomori's daughter, Moriko, died in 1166, Kiyomori arranged for her to inherit most of the estate, passing over Motozane's eldest son, Motomichi, the explanation given being that Motomichi was too young to assume such a responsibility. He was only six years old, it is true, but Moriko herself was just ten. When Moriko died in 1179, the Fujiwara leaders demanded that the holdings revert to Motomichi. At that point Go-Shirakawa intervened in the dispute and confiscated the property. He also confiscated the holdings of Shigemori, Kiyomori's heir, when he died the next month.

Kiyomori countered this threat to his power with a military coup in the eleventh month of 1179. He led several thousand warriors from Fukuhara and paraded them in the capital. He demanded the dismissal of thirty-nine officials, retainers (*kinshin*) of Go-Shirakawa, and replaced them with Taira adherents. The retired emperor was placed under house arrest and moved to the Toba-dono. Kiyomori was declared a traitor by his distraught imperial enemy, but all power was now in his hands. Three months later, Go-Shirakawa's son, Takakura, was forced to abdicate and was replaced as emperor by Kiyomori's infant grandson. Kiyomori's climb to full control of the court had taken two decades, but his victory was short: he died of illness early in 1181.

Takakura, upon his abdication, instead of paying his respects at the nearby shrines of Iwashimizu Hachimangū and Hie (or Hiyoshi), as was the recent custom, went on pilgrimage to a distant shrine under Taira patronage on the small island of Itsukushima off the Inland Sea coast near what is now the city of Hiroshima. The Iwashimizu Hachimangū and Hie shrines were linked by religious and other ties to the powerful Onjōji Temple at Ōtsu, and the temple's angry reaction to the Taira-inspired imperial slight contributed to the formation of a potentially powerful coalition of anti-Taira interests among the armed monks of that temple, their sometime enemies at the Enryakushi on Mount Hiei, and the monks of Kōfukuji, the Fujiwara clan temple at Nara.

Open, military opposition to Taira rule began, however, not in the temples but within the imperial court itself. Among the few Minamoto chieftains to survive the Heiji Disturbance was a remote relative of the clan leader Yoshitomo named Yorimasa (1104–80), an aged warrior-courtier connected also with the Fujiwara through his mother. In the court's neglect of deserving Minamoto warriors following the Heiji fighting, Yorimasa's career had not prospered, but in his old age he had been permitted a considerable degree of court success, rising to the ranks of the senior nobility (the first Minamoto warrior to do so). What Yorimasa's specific motives may have been is not known, but whether they were resentment of past Taira injustice and highhandedness or simply opportunistic personal ambition, in the fourth month of 1180 he persuaded Go-Shirakawa's son Mochihito (1151–80) to issue a call to warriors everywhere for the chastisement of the Taira.

Mochihito's call to arms was a bold and dangerous step, one that soon cost him his life. But in agreeing to take it the prince may have believed he had more than sufficient grievance against the Taira to justify the risk, as well as an adequate prospect for success among the disgruntled, ambitious warriors in the provinces. He may have shared his father Go-Shirakawa's hostility toward Kiyomori, encouraged by his Fujiwara connections, but he also had his own personal complaints against the Taira dispensation. At the time of Kiyomori's coup d'état in 1179, Mochihito suffered the confiscation of a rich landholding. The following year, 1180, his hope of succeeding his cousin Takakura on the imperial throne was dashed when Kiyomori obtained the succession for his grandson. Deprived of his property and disappointed in his fondest hope by the all-powerful Taira leader, Mochihito must have been a willing auditor for any proposal aimed at the destruction of the Taira.

The plot against the Taira became known, however, before the conspirators had their supporters in place, and under threat of arrest and exile, the prince fled the capital to the protection of the Onjōji Temple. The temple responded to his plea for help and attempted to rally also to his cause the armies of the Enryakuji and the Kōfukuji, but when that attempt failed to bring to the prince the hoped-for support, he set out accompanied by Yorimasa and a body of warriors to obtain the backing of the monks at Nara. Overtaken by a large Taira force at Uji, he was slain in the ensuing battle and rout, and his wounded commander Yorimasa was seized and allowed at the age of seventy-six to commit suicide. The first stage of the Taira–Minamoto conflict thus came to an abrupt conclusion the month after the prince's fateful order, but that call to arms had galvanized Minamoto warriors in many regions, preparing the way for the great battles that achieved the prince's aim of removing the Taira from the court.

During the tense and uneasy days just after the deaths of Mochihito and Yorimasa, Kiyomori abrogated the administrative authority of Go-Shirakawa's household office (*in-no-cho*) and announced the transfer of the emperor and two ex-emperors to what he intended to be a new imperial capital at Fukuhara near the Inland Sea coast. Taira men had been the "beneficial holders" (*chigyo*) of the district in which Fukuhara was located since 1162, and after Kiyomori took holy orders in 1168 he had made his residence there, continuing to direct affairs, and receiving visits at his hillside retreat from at least one Chinese trader and also, before their falling-out, from the ex-emperor Go-Shirakawa. It was from Fukuhara that Kiyomori had descended on the capital in 1179 to carry out the palace coup that year. Now, in 1180, after Mochihito's reliance on temple armies in the vicinity of the capital during his attempt to overthrow the Taira, and after a long earlier history of disruption in the city caused by those monks, Kiyomori may have been seeking to escape the threat of the temple forces by the move to Fukuhara some fifty miles distant.[61]

Kiyomori seems to have had a particular interest and involvement in seagoing trade, and in that connection he turned his resources to the improvement and development of an old port near Fukuhara called Ōwada-no-tomari. Little is known about the nature or the volume of the traffic passing through the port, but it lay only about a day's voyage from the entrance to the Yodo River, the shipping route into Heian, and it would have been a convenient port of call for both domestic and foreign bottoms navigating the Inland Sea. Through its waters, one may assume, passed trading ships bearing the Chinese books, the Zen Buddhist texts, and the copper coins that were helping to transform the contemporary intellectual and economic life of Japan.

The emperor and the ex-emperors were temporarily housed in residences of Kiyomori's sons at Fukuhara, and planning for the new capital proceeded apace. After only a few months, however, toward the end of the year of the court's arrival at Fukuhara and at a time when construction of an imperial residential palace had just been completed, the entire project was abandoned, the imperial party and the courtiers and officials all hastening back to Heian. The reasons

---

61 *Heike monogatari*, vol. 1, *kan* 5.11, pp. 379–80; in H. McCullough, *The Tale of the Heike*, p. 193.

for the abandonment of Fukuhara after such a short time remain obscure, but the cramped space of the site, its windswept, dismal location, the ill health of Takakura, and the outbreak at just this time of Minamoto uprisings in the east were possibly key considerations.

The removal of the court and its government to Fukuhara left Heian tattered, dazed, and desperate. The Enryakuji, Heian's guardian temple, was moved to declare itself an enemy of the Taira tyranny, and the many followers of the court, unable to obtain living accommodations at Fukuhara, also had cause to resent the Taira leadership. The city had suffered a devastating fire just three years earlier, and it had become more desolate than ever when people dismantled buildings in order to ship the materials to Fukuhara.[62]

GEMPEI WAR

The several years of warfare following the failed attempt of Mochihito and Yorimasa to overthrow the Taira in 1180, usually known as the Gempei (i.e., Minamoto–Taira) War, has been popularly portrayed as an epic struggle between two great warrior clans for control of the imperial court and its institutions. It is dramatized as a rousing tale of political intrigue and heroic battle, with victory going ultimately to the Minamoto because of the political adroitness and military genius of the Minamoto overlord Yoritomo and the superhuman fighting abilities of the Minamoto generals, aided by the sometimes fumbling cowardice of Taira generals, whose martial valor is supposed to have been corrupted by the genteel life of the court.

That one-dimensional picture of clan rivalry is at once muddied by the presence of Taira and Minamoto warriors on both sides of the conflict and by major intraclan fighting, especially among the Minamoto. Unlike earlier wars in Japan, which were mostly military expeditions sent by the court, the Gempei War was a national civil war, the fighting extending from the Kanto and northeast coast to the western end of Honshu. The war was also part of a broader political, economic, and social upheaval, a revolution that eventually resulted in a changed society, a society that may loosely be called feudal. Dominated by a new class of warriors supported by land

---

62 Kamo no Chōmei, *Hōjōki*, in Nishio Minoru, ed., *Hōjōi. Tsurezure gusa*, vol. 30 of *Nihon koten bugaku taikei* (1957), pp. 26–28; Helen McCullough, trans., "An Account of My Hermitage," in her *Classical Japanese Prose: An Anthology* (Stanford, Calif.: Stanford University Press, 1990), pp. 382–84.

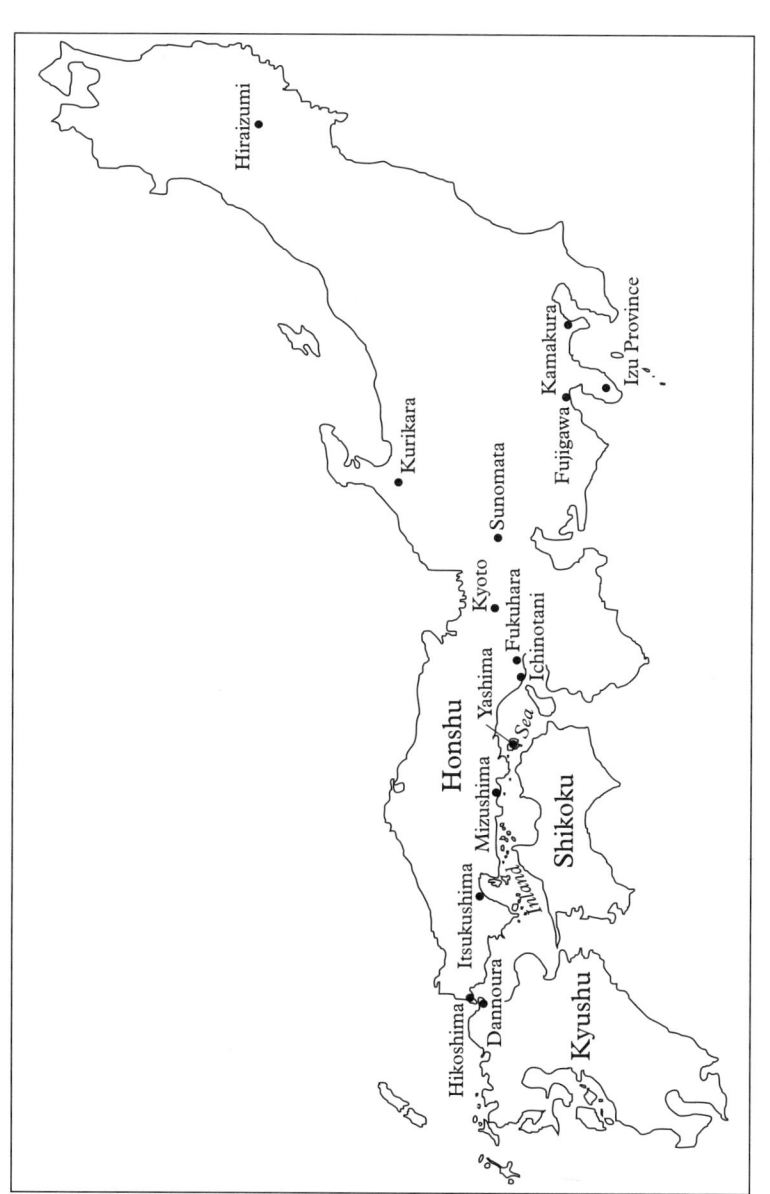

Map 10.2. The Gempei War.

rights conferred or confirmed at least in part by military chiefs, the country under the new regime was governed in large part by a warrior-controlled political structure, at the top of which stood the bakufu shogun in Kamakura.

The first stage of the war followed some months after Mochihito's call to arms in the fourth month of 1180, when warrior uprisings began to challenge and in some instances overthrow Taira authority in many parts of the country. The greatest of the challenges came from two Minamoto cousins, Yoritomo (1147–99) and Yoshinaka (1154–84), grandsons of the Tameyoshi who had been executed after the Hōgen Disturbance. They had escaped the slaughter at the time of the subsequent Heiji Disturbance, and had been living obscurely in the east and north.

Following defeat in the Heiji fighting, Tameyoshi's son Yoshitomo had been killed as he fled eastward; his thirteen-year-old son and heir, Yoritomo, in an act of clemency, was exiled to the distant wilds of Izu Province (the Izu peninsula south of Tokyo). By the time news of Mochihito's call to arms reached Izu in 1180, Yoritomo, now adult and married to Hōjō Masako (1157–1225), a daughter of one of his custodians, Tokimasa (1138–1215), was on such terms with local warriors that, with his father-in-law's backing, he was able in the tenth month to raise a force that attacked and killed the Taira deputy in Izu.

The warriors who rallied to Yoritomo's cause were often not so much partisans of his clan as rebels against the old regime of the imperial court and its control of land rights. The conflict is accordingly best described as a struggle between the military usurpers of that regime, the Taira, and warriors striving to gain secure access to the management of land resources, rallying to the Minamoto. Insofar as the Minamoto fought merely for clan supremacy, or military overlordship, they were fortuitous leaders of a revolution long in the making.

Yoritomo accepted all warriors, whatever their earlier affiliations, if they would pledge allegiance to him. In return he issued, on his own authority, confirmation of their rights to land and office. To usurp the powers of the imperial government in this way was a radical departure. Basing his authority on Mochihito's call and his own ancestral association with the Kanto region, he claimed jurisdiction over all public and private land in the east. He claimed, in essence, to be the ruler of the region. His message to local provincial officials was to oust officials and agents of the central government and seize control of their estates and provinces. In the first two precarious months of Yoritomo's bold program, he was joined by some Taira adherents and opposed by some Minamoto competitors. The promise of secure and permanent confirmation of hitherto uncertain tenures was compelling. Province by province the tide turned in Yoritomo's favor. Some who at first opposed him or would not commit to him now joined his ranks. They were drawn less by the mystique of the Minamoto lineage than by calculations of how their interests could best be served. Yoritomo established a military and administrative headquarters at Kamakura, a site northeast of Izu on Sagami Bay associated with his family for five generations since the time of Yoriyoshi. His offer of confirmations to eastern warriors brought more than troops and the provinces' resources needed for the forthcoming military struggle; it also built a new political organization essential for the long-term goal of ruling the now autonomous eastern region.

In the tenth month the Taira at court dispatched an army under the command of Kiyomori's grandson, Koremori, to subdue the outlaw Yoritomo. Yoritomo advanced to meet the enemy force of 70,000 that waited at the Fuji River, just west of Mount Fuji, with a force of "200,000 horsemen," according to the wildly exaggerated account in the *Tale of Heike*.[63] In any case, Yoritomo may have had a numerical advantage that persuaded the Taira to withdraw without a fight and return to the capital, further encouraging rebellious warriors in the east and in the provinces around the capital to rise against the reeling Taira. Yoritomo decided to consolidate his position in the east rather than to pursue the Taira.

The Taira cause was by no means lost. Shortly after Koremori's retreat, Kiyomori returned the court to Kyoto from Fukuhara, reinstated Go-Shirakawa's administrative authority as senior retired emperor, and moved decisively against the great temples, attacking Onjōji and sending his fifth son, Shigehira, to burn Tōdaiji and Kōfukuji in Nara in retaliation for their armed support of Minamoto forces. That piece of sacrilege, which occurred at the beginning of 1181, deeply offended court society. The Kōfukuji was the clan tem-

---

63 *Heike monogatari*, vol. 1, kan 5.9, pp. 371; in H. McCullough, *The Tale of the Heike*, pp. 187–88. *Azuma kagami (Shintei zōho) Kokushi taikei*, vol. 32 (1932), kan 1, p. 51, also says 200,000. A selected translation of *Azuma kagami* for the years 1180–85 is in Minoru Shinoda, *The Founding of the Kamakura Shogunate 1180–1185* (New York: Columbia University Press, 1960), see p. 187. For a discussion of the size of Heian armies and expeditionary forces, and the tendency of most sources to inflate the numbers, see Farris, *Heavenly Warriors*, pp. 291–93, 300–302, 392–93.

ple of the Fujiwara; the Tōdaiji served a similar role for several other noble families, and it was also revered by the imperial family as the historic Buddhist protector of the state. A month later Kiyomori died.

In the aftermath of the debacle at Fujigawa, the Taira leaders undertook to mobilize military manpower and resources in the nine provinces surrounding and to the east of the capital. Kiyomori's third son, Munemori, was appointed to the new post of commander-in-chief (*sōkan*), and three months later the Taira gained a victory over Yoritomo's uncle, Yukiie, at the Sunomata River (near modern Nagoya). That battle was followed by a two-year lull in the fighting, the effect in part of a famine that hampered the recruiting and provisioning of troops, especially in the west. During this period of preparation for the inevitable confrontation of the military forces, Yoritomo had an advantage in his independence from central authority, being able to seize control of provincial headquarters, lands, and *shōen* in the east to gain the men and supplies he needed. The Taira, as administrators of the central government offices they had usurped, were constrained by the bureaucratic procedures of the court system. They requisitioned troops and supplies from the provincial administrators and *shōen* holders, but the process was slow and cumbersome and they encountered resistance. There was strong resentment of the Taira at court and among the temples, but perhaps more serious was the alienation of many of the provincial warrior class. The new Taira proprietorships in the provinces often reduced land rights and income of the local warriors, the very group that the Taira needed for their armies. The Taira at court did little to champion the interests of the warrior class, while provincial warriors viewed with distrust the rise of the Ise Taira to high court position and intermarriage with court nobility.

The next challenge to the Taira that revealed the weakness of their forces came not from Yoritomo, who continued to consolidate his administration and military strength in the Kanto, but from his cousin Yoshinaka (commonly called Kiso Yoshinaka), who had responded to Prince Mochihito's call a month after Yoritomo. Emerging from his refuge in the Kiso Mountains of Shinano (Nagano Prefecture), he continued to raise troops and won a series of small battles against Taira adherents. The Taira sent a large army led by Koremori against him, but Yoshinaka scored a crushing victory in the fifth month of 1183 at Kurikara in Etchū (near the present boundary of Ishikawa and Toyama prefectures near the Sea of Japan). This victory opened the road to Kyoto. Just three days before Yoshinaka's seizure of the capital at the end of the seventh month, the Taira leader Munemori fled with his nephew, Emperor Antoku, to Kyushu, traditionally a center of Taira strength. Go-Shirakawa, who had evaded the Taira to join Yoshinaka at Mount Hiei the day before Munemori's flight, ordered him and Yukiie to pursue the fleeing Taira, referring now to the Minamoto forces as the "imperial army."[64] Ignoring the absence of the imperial regalia with Antoku in Kyushu, the ex-emperor also installed his three-year-old grandson, Go-Toba (1180–1239, r. 1183–98), on the throne to replace Antoku (although the latter, as the possessor of the regalia, is usually considered to have been the emperor until his death in 1185).

Yoshinaka's occupation of the capital left the country divided into four satrapies, each dominated by a different and hostile military authority: (1) Kyushu, Shikoku, and the Inland Sea provinces ruled mostly by the Taira themselves under Munemori; (2) the capital, nearby provinces, and most of the provinces on the Sea of Japan from Wakasa Bay north of Kyoto northeastward nearly as far as the Mogami River beyond the modern city of Niigata, all held by Yoshinaka; (3) the interior and Pacific seaboard provinces east of the capital to the northern borders of present day Tochigi, Ibaraki, and Gumma prefectures, ruled by the head of the main Minamoto lineage, Yoritomo; and (4) the domain of the Ōshū Fujiwara occupying the upper tip of Honshu north of Yoshinaka's and Yoritomo's spheres.

Yoritomo, at his seat in Kamakura, was the head of the main line of Minamoto warriors, but he was in danger of being relegated to a peripheral status by Yoshinaka's victories. Yoritomo moved to buttress his position, taking several steps to gather the support of principal powers in the capital region. He made friendly gestures toward the great temples whose prayers were accepted as having contributed to the success of Minamoto arms; he returned landed holdings in the east confiscated by the Taira to their rightful temple and noble owners; he followed a policy of leniency in his treatment of captured Taira warriors; and, perhaps most significantly, he established a secret understanding with Go-Shirakawa that led in the tenth month of 1183 to court recognition of both his civil and his military authority in the east. (It is a matter of debate among historians, as to whether the court's recognition of Yoritomo's authority at this point in 1183 was a strengthening or an attempted invasion of his position.)

64 *Gyokuyō, kan* 35, in *Kokusho kankōkai sōsho*, series 1, vols. 53–55 (Tokyo: Kokusho kankōkai, 1906–7), vol. 2, p. 609, 25/7/Juei 2 (1183).

Following his occupation of the capital, Yoshinaka advanced down the Inland Sea coast in pursuit of his Taira foes, but with his army somewhat diminished by the return of warriors to their northern homes and the remainder weakened by months of hard marches and fighting, Yoshinaka was roundly defeated by his enemy midway down the western leg of Honshu at Mizushima Bay (southeast of the modern cities of Okayama and Kurashiki), and he returned to Kyoto.

There, the hostility that his arrogance and his unruly warriors' plundering and looting had provoked throughout Kyoto society coalesced into a rising against him by armed monks from Enryakuji and Onjōji, miscellaneous court warriors, nonwarrior ruffians, and city riffraff, all gathered under the command of a Taira warrior in the service of Go-Shirakawa at the ex-emperor's Hōjūji-dono palace and numbering, it was rumored, twenty thousand men. Yoshinaka's relations with Go-Shirakawa had already been strained by the favoritism the ex-emperor had shown Yoritomo, but his discovery of secret communication between them, the discovery, too, of an assassin dispatched by Yoritomo to the capital to kill Yoshinaka, and the open armed defiance of his rule by the ragtag force at the Hōjūji-dono were no doubt final straws in his burden of resentment. Shortly after the beginning of 1184 he attacked and burned the ex-emperor's palace and easily routed its inexpert defenders. Confining Go-Shirakawa at another palace in the city, he also dismissed from court office the ex-emperor's courtiers and confiscated many of their landholdings. At the same time, he obtained for himself appointment to the long unused court title of "Barbarian-subduing Generalissimo" (*seii taishōgun*), which originally had been conferred directly by the emperor on the leader of an expedition to suppress the Emishi in the northeast. In Yoshinaka's case, it was directed, of course, against Yoritomo as a declaration of war.

Yoshinaka's forceful actions at the beginning of 1184 gave him a nearly complete stranglehold on the Kyoto government, but it also left him isolated and exposed, with only a small army (perhaps as few as six or seven thousand men) to confront enemies on three fronts: the Taira in the west; Yoritomo from the east; and the forces of the Enryakuji nearby.

The unchastened and ever-scheming Go-Shirakawa issued an order to Yoritomo calling on him to punish his wild northern cousin, a task that the Kamakura lord was ready for and probably only too willing to perform. Rather than lead an army against Yoshinaka himself, however, Yoritomo prudently remained as usual ensconced in his eastern stronghold, dispatching to the capital instead a punitive force under the command of his brothers Noriyori and Yoshitsune (1159–89), the latter a general of peerless, if largely legendary, ability and accomplishment. Yoshinaka, his forces outnumbered and still suffering from their recent defeat at Mizushima Bay, went down to defeat in battles at Uji and Seta on the outskirts of Kyoto, and he took his own life. The victory of the Minamoto brothers resulted in the consolidation of anti-Taira forces under the single command of the Kamakura lord. At last Yoritomo turned his attention to fighting the Taira, and the war entered its final stage.

The Taira had regrouped, following their flight from the capital to Kyushu, and had established a base on the small island of Yashima at the northeastern corner of Shikoku (near Takamatsu), from which, with their maritime superiority, they were able to control the Inland Sea. Following their success at Mizushima, they advanced toward the capital and constructed fortifications at Ichinotani near Fukuhara. Less than a month after Yoshinaka's defeat, still in the early part of 1184, Yoshitsune outflanked the Taira at Ichinotani in a daring mounted charge down what had been thought to be an impassable cliff-like route behind the camp, routing the surprised Taira forces with heavy loss of life among the clan's leaders.

In the fall, Yoritomo sent Noriyori's army west from Kyoto down along the Inland Sea coast, and shortly after the beginning of 1185 it reached the province of Bungo in Kyushu behind the Taira island base of Hikoshima in the Shimonoseki Strait. Yoshitsune was ordered to resume his assault on the Taira, which he did in a daring sea attack on their stronghold at Yashima in the second month. Yoshitsune pursued his Taira quarry through the Inland Sea, at the western extremity of which, near the Hikoshima base, the remaining Taira, effectively bottled up by Noriyoshi's army on the Kyushu shore, were finally annihilated in the spring of that year (1185) in a sea battle at Dannoura. Emperor Antoku was drowned at the end of the battle in the arms of his grandmother, it is said, a little more than one month past his sixth birthday.

Yoshitsune's brilliant victories brought the war to a sudden conclusion. But these successes, as well as his fame and popularity at court, fanned Yoritomo's suspicions concerning the loyalty of his half brother. They had been at odds since the previous year when Go-Shirakawa, ever the troublemaker, conferred court title and rank on Yoshitsune in violation of Yoritomo's specific instructions that court offices were not to be granted to his vassals, or accepted by them, without his authorization. The retired emperor had also granted Yoshitsune the rare privilege of entry to his private quarters. Reports continued to reach Yoritomo accusing Yoshitsune of betraying private ambitions. Yoritomo concluded that Yoshitsune and Yukiie, who were reported to be in collusion, should be destroyed. When Yoritomo's attempt to assassinate Yoshitsune in Kyoto failed, Yoshitsune prevailed on Go-Shirakawa to issue an imperial command to attack Yoritomo. The retired emperor appointed Yoshitsune steward (*jitō*) of Kyushu and Yukiie steward of Shikoku to empower them to raise troops. This plan was clearly hopeless. Yoshitsune went into hiding and finally made his way with a few companions to the far northeast, where he found refuge with the Ōshū Fujiwara whose leader, Hidehira, had been his protector during his youth. Unhappily for Yoshitsune, however, his patron died toward the end of the year of his arrival in Hiraizumi (1187). Hidehira's successor, Yasuhira, quailing before Yoritomo's threats, attacked and killed Yoshitsune in the fourth month of 1189 in a desperate attempt to save himself from the wrath of the Kamakura overlord. Yasuhira's treachery failed to secure his own safety, however; he fell before the large conquering army of an outraged and unappeased Yoritomo a few months later. Yoritomo did not rest until he had eliminated the last military power that could challenge his hegemony. The Ōshū Fujiwara's lands in Mutsu and Dewa, which Minamoto no Yoshiie had coveted in vain in the Later Three Years' War more than a century earlier, at last came into the hands of his great-great-grandson.

Yoritomo was the final victor to emerge from the series of military contests that, for the first time since the seventh century, decided political supremacy. Beginning with the Hōgen coup in the capital in 1156, initiatives taken by warriors increasingly overwhelmed civil authority, culminating in the great battles of the Gempei War. Society was fundamentally altered as the warrior gentry of the provinces created a new political structure independent of the imperial court that supported a role for warriors in the administration of land. The court became mostly subservient to the will of Yoritomo, and its economic foundations were much eroded in favor of the warriors. The key relationship in society came to be that between military lord and his kinsmen and retainers.

The Lord of Kamakura (Kamakura-dono) chose to retain his administrative headquarters (the bakufu) in Kamakura, maintaining an identity well separated from the machinations of imperial and noble cliques in Kyoto. Yoritomo seems to have had little need of court honors and titles, often resigning them soon after they were conferred. Following the death in 1192 of Retired Emperor Go-Shirakawa, who opposed the appointment, the emperor gave Yoritomo the title *seii taishōgun*, signifying chief of the warriors, but only two years later Yoritomo expressed his wish to resign the title, a proposal that was not accepted by the court. Yoritomo's bakufu did not replace, for the most part, the ancient civil offices of the court. But he kept under his own control the political and judicial functions he considered essential for his purposes, building until his death in 1199 the institutions and precedents that regulated the military and land-administration functions of the warrior class.[65]

[65] On Yoritomo's governance of the Kamakura regime, see "The Kamakura bakufu" in Kozo Yamamura, ed., *Cambridge History of Japan*, vol. 3 (1990); and Jeffrey P. Mass, *Warrior Government in Early Medieval Japan: A Study of the Kamakura Bakufu, Shugo, and Jitō* (New Haven, Conn.: Yale University Press, 1974).

WORKS CITED

Abe Akio 阿部秋生. *Chūko Nihon bungaku gaisetsu* 中古日本文学概説. Tokyo: Shūei shuppan 集英出版, 1977.
Abe Takeshi 阿部猛. "Heiankyō no keizai kōzō" 平安京の経済構造. In Itō Tasaburō 伊東多三郎, ed. *Seikatsu to shakai keizai* 生活と社会経済. Vol. 2 of *Kokumin seikatsu shi kenkyū* 国民生活史研究. Tokyo: Yoshikawa kōbunkan 吉川弘文館. 1959.
Abe Takeshi 阿部猛. *Heian zenki seijishi* 平安前期政治史. Tokyo: Shinseisha 新生社, 1974.
Abe Takeshi 阿部猛. *Nihon shōen shi* 日本荘園史. Tokyo: Shinseisha 新生社, 1972.
Abe Takeshi 阿部猛. *Owari no kuni gebumi no kenkyū* 尾張国解文の研究. Tokyo: Shinseisha 新生社, 1971.
Abe Takeshi 阿部猛. *Ritsuryō kokka kaitai katei no kenkyū* 律令国家解体過程の研究. Tokyo: Shinseisha 新生社, 1966.
Abe Takeshi 阿部猛. "Sekkanki ni okeru chōzei taikei no kenkyū" 摂関期に於ける徴税体系の研究. In Kodaigaku kyōkai 古代学協会, ed. *Sekkan jidaishi no kenkyū* 摂関時代史の研究. Tokyo: Yoshikawa kōbunkan 吉川弘文館, 1965.
Akimoto Kichirō 秋本吉郎, ed. *Fudoki* 風土記. Vol. 2 of Nihon koten bungaku taikei 日本古典文学大系. Tokyo: Iwanami shoten 岩波書店, 1958.
Akiyama Terukazu 秋山光和. *Emakimono* 絵巻物. Vol. 8 of *Genshoku Nihon no bijutsu* 原色日本の美術. Tokyo: Shōgakukan 小学館, 1968.
Akiyama Terukazu. *Japanese Painting*. New York: Rizzoli International Publications, 1977.
Andrews, Allan A. *The Teachings Essential for Rebirth: A Study of Genshin's Ōjōyōshū*. Tokyo: Sophia University, 1973.
Araki, James T. *The Ballad-Drama of Medieval Japan*. Berkeley and Los Angeles: University of California Press, 1964.
Aston, W. G., trans. *Nihongi: Chronicles of Japan from the Earliest Times to A.D. 697*. 1896. Reprint. London: George Allen and Unwin, 1956.
Azuma kagami 吾妻鏡. Vol. 32 of (*Shintei zōho*) *Kokushi taikei, qv*.
Backus, Robert L. *The Riverside Counselor's Stories: Vernacular Fiction of Late Heian Japan*. Stanford, Calif.: Stanford University Press, 1985.
Besshū fusenshō 別聚符宣抄. Vol 27 of (*Shintei zōho*) *Kokushi taikei, qv*.
Boardman, John, Jasper Griffin, and Oswyn Murray, eds. *Oxford History of the*

Classical World. Oxford and New York: Oxford University Press, 1986.
Bock, Felicia G. *Classical Learning and Taoist Practices in Early Japan: With a Translation of Books XVI and XX of the Engi-shiki.* Tempe: Arizona State University Center for Asian Studies, Occasional Paper No. 17, 1985.
Bock, Felicia, trans. *Engi-shiki: The Procedures of the Engi Era.* 2 vols. Tokyo: Sophia University Press, 1970-72.
Bommōkyō 梵網経 (Ch. *Fan-wang ching*). In *Taishō shinshū daizōkyō* 大正新修大蔵経. Vol. 24. Tokyo: Taishō issaikyō kankōkai 大正一切経刊行会, 1925.
Borgen, Robert. "The Case of the Plagiaristic Journal: A Curious Passage from *Jōjin's Diary*." In Aileen Gatten and Anthony Hood Chambers, eds. *New Leaves: Studies and Translations of Japanese Literature in Honor of Edward G. Seidensticker*, pp. 63-88. Ann Arbor: Center for Japanese Studies, University of Michigan, 1993.
Borgen, Robert. "Ōe no Masafusa and the Spirit of Michizane." *Monumenta Nipponica* 50 (Autumn, 1995): 357-84.
Borgen, Robert. *Sugawara no Michizane and the Early Heian Court.* Harvard East Asian Monographs, 120. Cambridge, Mass.: Council on East Asian Studies, Harvard University, 1986.
Bowring, Richard. *Murasaki Shikibu: Her Diary and Poetic Memoirs.* Princeton, N.J.: Princeton University Press, 1982.
Bowring, Richard. *Murasaki Shikibu: The Tale of Genji.* Cambridge, England: Cambridge University Press, 1988.
Brower, Robert Hopkins. "The *Konzyaku monogatarisyū*: An Historical and Critical Introduction, With Annotated Translations of Seventy-Eight Tales." Ph.D. diss., University of Michigan, Ann Arbor, 1952.
Brower, Robert H., and Earl Miner. *Japanese Court Poetry.* Stanford, Calif.: Stanford University Press, 1961.
Bunka shūrei shū 文華秀麗集. In Kojima Noriyuki 小島憲之, ed. *Kaifūsō. Bunka shūrei shū. Honchō monzui* 懐風藻. 文華秀麗集. 本朝文粋. Vol. 69 of *Nihon koten bungaku taikei* 日本古典文学大系. Tokyo: Iwanami shoten 岩波書店, 1964.
Cambridge History of Japan. Vol. 1. Cambridge, England: Cambridge University Press, 1993.
Cambridge History of Japan. Vol. 3. Cambridge, England: Cambridge University Press, 1990.
Charlier, Michael. *Das Dairi-shiki: Eine Studie zu seiner Entstehung und Wirkung.* Wiesbaden: Otto Harrassowitz, 1975.
Chōshūki 長秋記. Vol. 7 of *Shiryō taisei* 史料大成. Tokyo: Naigai shoseki kabushiki kaisha 内外書籍株式会社, 1934.
Chōshūki 長秋記. 2 vols. In *Zōho shiryō taisei* 増補史料大成. Kyoto: Rinsen shoten 臨川書店, 1965.
Chōya gunsai 朝野群載. Vol. 29.1 of *(Shintei zōho) Kokushi taikei*, qv.
Chūyūki (or *Nakauki*) 中右記. Vols. 8-14 of *Shiryō taisei* 史料大成. Tokyo: Naigai shoseki kabushiki kaisha 内外書籍株式会社, 1934.
Chūyūki 中右記. Vols. 9-15 of *Zōho shiryō taisei* 増補史料大成. Kyoto: Rinsen

shoten 臨川書店, 1965.
Cranston, Edwin A. "*Atemiya*: A Translation from the *Utsubo Monogatari*." *Monumenta Nipponica* 24, 3 (1969): 289-314.
Cranston, Edwin A. *The Izumi Shikibu Diary: A Romance of the Heian Court.* Cambridge, Mass.: Harvard University Press, 1969.
Daianji garan engi narabi ni ruki shizai chō 大安寺伽藍縁起並流記資財帳. In *Dai Nihon Bukkyō zensho* 大日本佛教全書. Vol. 118. Tokyo: Yūseidō shuppambu 有精堂出版部, 1932.
Daibirushanakyō shiki 大毘盧遮那経指帰. In *Taishō shinshū daizōkyō* 大正新修大蔵経, vol. 58. Tokyo: Taishō issaikyō kankōkai 大正一切経刊行会, 1930.
Dai Nihon Bukkyō zensho 大日本佛教全書. 151 vols. Tokyo: Bussho kankōkai 佛書刊行会, 1912-22.
de Bary, Wm. Theodore, ed. *The Buddhist Tradition: in China, India and Japan.* New York: The Modern Library, 1969.
Dengyō Daishi zenshū 伝教大師全集. 5 vols. Sakamoto: Hieizan tosho kankōsho 比叡山図書刊行所. 1926.
Denryaku 殿暦. 5 vols. In Tōkyō daigaku shiryō hensanjo 東京大学史料編纂所, comp. *Dai Nihon kokiroku* 大日本古記録. Tokyo: Iwanami shoten 岩波書店, 1969-70.
Duquenne, Robert. "Daigensui." *Hōbōgirin* 6 (1983): 610-40.
Duquenne, Robert. "Daiitoku myōō." *Hōbōgirin* 6 (1983): 652-70.
Earhart, Byron. *A Religious Study of the Haguro Sect of Shugendō.* Tokyo: Sophia University, 1970.
Eigaku yōki 叡学要記. In *Gunsho ruijū* 群書類従. Vol. 15. Tokyo: Keizai zasshisha 経済雑誌社, 1905.
Eizan Gakuin 叡山学院, ed. *Ganzan Jie Daishi no kenkyū* 元山慈恵大師の研究. Kyoto: Dōbōsha 同朋社, 1984.
Ema Tsutomu 江馬務. *Yūsoku kojitsu* 有職故実. Kyoto: Kawara shoten 河原書店, 1965.
Enchin 円珍. *Yuisei* 遺制, included in *Yohō hennen zasshū* 餘芳編年雑集. In *Dai Nihon Bukkyō zensho* 大日本佛教全集. Vol. 28. Tokyo: Yūseidō shuppambu 有精堂出版部, 1933.
Engi shiki 延喜式. Vol. 26 of (*Shintei zōho*) *Kokushi taikei*, qv.
Ennin 円仁. *Jūsan-jū kanjō hiroku* 十三重潅頂秘録, included in *Tendai kahyō* 天台霞標, *kan* 5, part 1. In *Dai Nihon Bukkyō zensho* 大日本佛教全集. Vol. 126. Tokyo: Bussho kankōkai 佛書刊行会, 1914.
Ennin 円仁. *Nittō guhō junrai kōki* 入唐求法巡礼行記. In *Dai Nihon Bukkyō zensho* 大日本佛教全集. Vol. 113. Tokyo: Yūseidō shuppambu 有精堂出版部, 1932.
Ennin 円仁. *Nittō shingu shōgyō mokuroku* 入唐新求聖教目録. In *Taishō shinshū daizōkyō* 大正新修大蔵経. Vol. 55. Tokyo: Taishō issaikyō kankōkai 大正一切経刊行会, 1928.
Enryaku kōtai shiki 延暦交替式. Vol. 26 of (*Shintei zōho*) *Kokushi taikei*, qv.
Farris, Wayne. *Heavenly Warriors: The Evolution of Japan's Military, 500-1300.*

Cambridge, Mass.: Harvard East Asian Monographs, 1992.
Field, Norma. *The Splendor of Longing in The Tale of Genji*. Princeton, N.J.: Princeton University Press, 1987.
Flannery, Kent. "The Cultural Evolution of Civilizations." *Annual Review of Ecology and Systemics*, 3 (1972), 399-426.
Frank, Bernard. *Histoires qui sont maintenant du passé*. Paris: Gallimard, 1968.
Frank, Bernard. "Kata-imi et kata-tagae: Étude sur les interdits de direction à l'époque Heian." *Bulletin de la Maison Franco-Japonaise*, Nouvelle Série, Tome 5, No. 2-4. Tokyo and Paris: 1958.
Friday, Karl F. *Hired Swords: The Rise of Private Warrior Power in Early Japan*. Stanford, Calif.: Stanford University Press, 1992.
Fujioka Kenjirō 藤岡健次郎. *Kokufu* 国府. Tokyo: Yoshikawa kōbunkan 吉川弘文館, 1974.
Fujiwara no Morosuke 藤原師輔. "*Kujō Ujōshō yuikai*" 九条右丞相遺誡. In Yamagishi Tokuhei 山岸徳平, Takeuchi Rizō 竹内理三, Ienaga Saburō 家永三郎, Ōsone Shōsuke 大曽根章介, eds. *Kodai seiji shakai shisō* 古代政治社会思想. Vol. 8 of *Nihon shisō taikei* 日本思想大系. Tokyo: Iwanami shoten 岩波書店, 1979.
Fujiwara no Nagako. *The Emperor Horikawa Diary*, translated by Jennefer Brewster. Honolulu: University of Hawaii Press, 1977.
Fujiwara no Sukefusa 藤原資房. *Shunki* 春記. In *Tankaku sōsho* 丹鶴叢書. Vol. 1. Tokyo: Kokusho kankōkai 国書刊行会, 1912.
Fujiwara no Yasunori den 藤原保則伝. In *Kodai seiji shakai shisō* 古代政治社会思想. Vol. 8 of *Nihon shisō taikei* 日本思想大系. 67 vols. Tokyo: Iwanami shoten 岩波書店, 1979.
Fujiwara no Yoshifusa 藤原良房 et al. *Daisōzu Kūkai den* 大僧都空海伝. In *Kōbō Daishi zenshū* 弘法大師全集, 3rd ed., rev. and enlarged, *shukan* 首巻. Kōyasan: Mikkyō bunka kenkyūjo 密教文化研究所, 1967.
Fukunaga Mitsuji 福永光司, Ueda Masaaki 上田政昭, and Ueyama Shumpei 上山春平, eds. *Dōkyō to kodai no tennōsei* 道教と古代の天皇制. Tokyo: Tokuma shoten 徳間書店, 1978.
Fukunaga Mitsuji 福永光司, *Dōkyō to Nihon bunka* 道教と日本文化. Kyoto: Jimbun shoin 人文書院, 1982.
Fukuyama Toshio 福山敏男. *Chūsei no jinja kenchiku* 中世の神社建築. Tokyo: Shibundō 至文堂, 1977.
Funao Yoshimasa 舟尾好正. "Suiko no jittai ni kansuru ichikōsatsu: Bitchū no kuni taizei o ōtaru shibōnin chō o chūshin to shite" 出挙の実態に関する一考察：備中国大税を負死亡人帳を中心として. *Shirin* 史林 56.5 (September 1973): 74-102.
Furushima Toshio 古島敏雄. *Nihon nōgyō gijutsu shi* 日本農業技術史. Vol. 1. Tokyo: Jichōsha 時潮社, 1947.
Fusō ryakki 扶桑略記. Vol. 12 of (*Shintei zōho*) *Kokushi taikei*, qv.
Futaba Kenkō 二葉憲香. *Kodai Bukkyō shisō-shi kenkyū* 古代佛教思想史研究. Kyoto: Nagata bunshōdō 永田文昌堂, 1962.

Gempei seisuiki 源平盛衰記. In *Yūhōdō bunko* 有朋堂文庫. Vols. 16-17. Tokyo: Yūhōdō shoten 有朋堂書店, 1911-17.
Genshin 源信. *Ōjō yōshū* 往生要集. In *Taishō shinshū daizōkyō* 大正新修大蔵経. Vol. 84. Tokyo: Taishō issaikyō kankōkai 大正一切経刊行会, 1931.
Gifu ken 岐阜県, ed. *Gifu kenshi* 岐阜県史. *Tsūshihen: kodai* 通史編：古代. Gifu: Taishū shobō 大衆書房, 1971.
Gifu ken 岐阜県, ed. *Gifu kenshi* 岐阜県史. *Tsūshihen: chūsei* 通史編：中世. Gifu: Taishū shobō 大衆書房, 1969.
Go-Nijō Moromichi ki 後二条師通記. In *Dainihon kokiroku* 大日本古記録. Part 7. Tokyo: Iwanami shoten 岩波書店, 1956-58.
Gonki 権記. Vol. 35 of *Shiryō taisei* 史料大成. Tokyo: Naigai shoseki kabushiki kaisha 内外書籍株式会社. 1934.
Go sannen kassen ekotoba 後三年合戦絵詞. Vol. 15 of *Nihon emaki taisei* 日本絵巻大成. 27 vols. Tokyo: Chūō kōron sha 中央公論社, 1977.
Gotō Akio 後藤昭雄, *Heianchō kambungaku ronkō* 平安朝漢文学論考. Tokyo: Ōfūsha 桜楓社, 1981.
Grapard, Allan. "Patriarchs of Heian Buddhism: Kūkai and Saichō." In *Great Historical Figures of Japan*. Tokyo: Japan Culture Institute, 1978.
Grapard, Allan. "Kūkai: Stone Inscription of the śramana Shōdō, who Crossed Mountains and Streams in His Search for Awakening." In *The Mountain Spirit*, edited by Michael Tobias and Harold Drasdo, pp. 50-59. New York: Overlook Press, 1978.
Grapard, Allan. *The Protocol of the Gods*. Berkeley and Los Angeles: University of California Press, 1992.
Grapard, Allan. "Japan's Ignored Cultural Revolution: The Separation of Shinto-Buddhist Divinities and a Case-study: Tōnomine." *History of Religions* 23.3 (1984): 240-65.
Grapard, Allan. "Lotus in the Mountain, Mountain in the Lotus." *Monumenta Nipponica* 14.1 (1986): 21-50.
Grapard, Allan. "Enmountained Text, Textualized Mountain: The Lotus Sutra in the Kunisaki Peninsula." In *The Lotus Sutra in Japanese Culture*, edited by George Tanabe and Willa Tanabe, pp. 159-89. Honolulu: University of Hawaii Press, 1989.
Groner, Paul. *Saichō: The Establishment of the Japanese Tendai School*. Berkeley, Calif.: Asian Humanities Press Buddhist Studies Series, 1985.
Gukanshō 愚管抄. Vol. 86 of *Nihon koten bungaku taikei* 日本古典文学大系. Tokyo: Iwanami shoten 岩波書店, 1967.
Gyokuyō 玉葉. 3 vols. Tokyo: Meicho kankōkai 名著刊行会, 1971.
Gyokuyō 玉葉. Vols. 53-55 of *Kokusho kankōkai sōsho* 国書刊行会叢書. Tokyo: Kokusho kankōkai 国書刊行会, 1906.
Gyōnen 凝然. *Sangoku Buppō denzū engi* 三国佛法伝通縁起. In *Dai Nihon Bukkyō zensho* 大日本佛教全書. Vol. 101. Tokyo: Bussho kankōkai 佛書刊行会, 1913.
Hakeda, Yoshito S. *Kūkai: Major Works*. New York: Columbia University

Press, 1972.

Hall, John W. *Government and Local Power in Japan, 500 to 1700*. Princeton, N.J.: Princeton University Press, 1966.

Hall, John W. *Japan from Prehistory to Modern Times*. New York: Delacorte Press, 1970.

Hamada Takashi 浜田隆. *Zuzō* 図像. Tokyo: Shibundō 至文堂, 1969.

Hanawa Hokinoichi 塙保己一 et al., eds. *Shinkō: Gunsho rujū* 新校群書類従. 24 vols. Tokyo: Naigai shoseki 内外書籍, 1983.

Hanayama Shinshō 花山信勝, trans. *Ōjō yōshū* 往生要集, *Iwanami bunko* 岩波文庫. Vols. 2992-96. Tokyo: Iwanami shoten 岩波書店, 1942.

Harashima Reiji 原島礼次. *Nihon kodai shakai no kiso kōzō* 日本古代社会の基礎構造. Tokyo: Miraisha 未来社, 1966.

Hashimoto Yoshihiko 橋本義彦. *Heian kizoku shakai no kenkyū* 平安貴族社会の研究. Tokyo: Yoshikawa kōbunkan 吉川弘文館, 1976.

Hashimoto Yoshihiko 橋本義彦. "Kizoku seiken no seiji kōzō 貴族政権の政治構造." In *Iwanami kōza Nihon rekishi* 岩波講座日本歴史. *Kodai* 古代 4. Tokyo: Iwanami shoten 岩波書店, 1975.

Hayami Tasuku 速水侑. *Heian jidai kizoku-shakai to bukkyō* 平安時代貴族社会と仏教. Tokyo: Yoshikawa kōbunkan 吉川弘文館, 1975.

Hayashi Rokurō 林陸朗, ed. *Ronshū: Nihon rekishi* 論集日本歴史, 15 vols. Tokyo: Yūseidō 有政堂, 1976.

Hayashi Rokurō 林陸朗. *Jōdai seiji shakai no kenkyū* 上代政治社会の研究. Tokyo: Yoshikawa kōbunkan 吉川弘文館, 1969.

Hayashiya Tatsusaburō 林屋辰三郎. "*Insei*" 院政. *Zusetsu Nihon bunkashi taikei* 図説日本文化史大系. Vol. 5. Tokyo: Shōgakukan 小学館, 1957.

Hazama Jikō 硲慈光. *Tendaishū shi gaisetsu* 天台宗史概説. Rev. by Ōkubo Ryōjun 大久保良順. Tokyo: Daizō shuppan 大蔵出版, 1969.

Heihanki 平範記. 5 vols. In *Zōho shiryō taisei* 増補史料大成. Kyoto: Rinsen shoten 臨川書店, 1965.

Heiji monogatari 平治物語. Vol. 31 of *Nihon koten bungaku taikei* 日本古典文学大系. Tokyo: Iwanami shoten 岩波書店, 1961.

Heike monogatari 平家物語. Vols. 32-33 of *Nihon koten bungaku taikei* 日本古典文学大系. Tokyo: Iwanami shoten 岩波書店, 1959-60.

Hérail, Francine. "Un lettre à la cour de l'empereur Ichijō: Ōe no Masahira (953-1012)," in *Mélanges offerts à M. Charles Haguenauer en l'honneur de son quatre-vingtième anniversaire. Etudes japonaises*. Paris: L'Asiatique, 1980, pp. 369-87.

Hérail, Francine. *Notes journalières de Fujiwara no Michinaga, ministre á la cour de Heian (995-1018): Traduction du Midō kanpakuki*. Hautes études orientales, II, 23. Institut des hautes études japonaises. Geneva: Librairie Droz, 1987.

Hérail, Francine, *Yodo no Tsukai ou le Système de Quatre Envoyés*. Paris: Presses Universitaires de France, 1966.

Hirabayashi Moritoku 平林盛得. *Ryōgen* 良源. *Jimbutsu sōsho* 人物叢書. Vol.

173. Tokyo: Yoshikawa kōbunkan 吉川弘文館, 1976.
Hiraide iseki chōsakai 平出遺跡調査会, ed. *Hiraide* 平出. Tokyo: Asahi shimbunsha 朝日新聞社, 1955.
Hirakawa Minami 平川南. "Zōto to seii" 造都と征夷. In Hashimoto Yoshihiko 橋本義彦, ed. *Komonjo no kataru Nihon shi* 古文書の語る日本史. Vol. 2. *Heian* 平安. Tokyo: Chikuma shobō 筑摩書房, 1991.
Hirano Minoru 平野稔. *Kōshin shinkō* 庚申信仰. Tokyo: Kadokawa shoten 角川書店, 1969.
Hirata Kōji 平田耿二. "Heian jidai no koseki ni tsuite" 平安時代の戸籍について. In Toyoda Takeshi kyōju kanreki kinenkai 豊田武教授還暦記念会, ed. *Nihon kodai chūseishi no chihōteki tenkai* 日本古代中世史の地方的展開. Tokyo: Yoshikawa kōbunkan 吉川弘文館, 1973, pp. 59-96.
Hisaki Yukio 久木幸男. *Nihon kodai gakkō no kenkyū* 日本古代学校の研究. Tokyo: Tamagawa daigaku shuppambu 玉川大学出版部, 1990.
Hochstedler, Carol. *The Tale of Nezame: Part Three of Yowa no Nezame Monogatari*. Ithaca: Cornell University East Asia Papers 22, 1979.
Hōgen monogatari 保元物語. Vol. 31 of *Nihon koten bungaku taikei* 日本古典文学大系. Tokyo: Iwanami shoten 岩波書店, 1961.
Hōgetsu Keigo sensei kanreki kinenkai 宝月圭吾先生還暦記念会, ed. *Nihon shakai keizai shi kenkyū* 日本社会経済史研究. 3 vols. *Kodai chūsei hen* 古代中世編, *Chūsei hen* 中世編, and *Kinsei hen* 近世編. Tokyo: Yoshikawa kōbunkan 吉川弘文館, 1967.
Hōjō Hideki 北条秀樹. "Heian zenki chōzei kikō no ichikōsatsu" 平安前期徴税機構の一考察. In Vol. 3 of Inoue Mitsusada hakushi kanreki kinenkai 井上光貞博士還暦記念会, ed. *Kodaishi ronsō* 古代史論叢. Tokyo: Yoshikawa kōbunkan 吉川弘文館, 1978.
Hōjōki 方丈記. Vol. 30 of *Nihon koten bungaku taikei* 日本古典文学大系. Tokyo: Iwanami shoten 岩波書店, 1957.
Hori Daiji 堀大慈. "Ryōgen no *Nijūrokkajō kishō* seitei no igi" 良源の『二十六箇条起請』制定の意義. *Shisō* 史窓 25 (March 1967): 12-39.
Hori Ichirō 堀一郎. *Kūya* 空也. *Jimbutsu sōsho* 人物叢書. Vol. 106. Tokyo: Yoshikawa kōbunkan 吉川弘文館, 1963.
Hori Ichirō. "On the concept of *Hijiri* (Holy-Man)." *Numen* 5 (1958): 128-232.
Hōryūji garan engi narabi ni ruki shizai chō 法隆寺伽藍縁起並流記資財帳. In *Dai Nihon Bukkyō zensho* 大日本佛教全書. Vol. 117. Tokyo: Yūseidō shuppambu 有精堂出版部, 1932.
Hoshino Tsune 星野恒. "Yo no iwayuru Seiwa Genji wa Yōzei Genji naru kangae" 世の所謂清和源氏は陽成源氏なる考え. In *Shigaku sōsetsu* 史学叢説. Tokyo: Fuzambō 冨山房, 1909, pp. 108-47.
Hurst III, G. Cameron. *Insei: Abdicated Sovereigns in the Politics of Late Heian Japan, 1086-1185*. New York: Columbia University Press, 1976.
Hyakuren shō 百錬抄. Vol. 11 of *(Shintei zōho) Kokushi taikei*, qv.
Ienaga, Saburo. *Painting in the Yamato Style*. New York and Tokyo: John Weatherhill and Heibonsha, 1973.

Iinuma Jirō 飯沼二郎. *Nihon nōgyō gijutsu ron* 日本農業技術論. Tokyo: Miraisha 未来社, 1971.

Iinuma Jirō 飯沼二郎. "Nihonshi ni okeru suki to kuwa" 日本史における犂と鍬. (Kyōto Daigaku jimbun kagaku kenkyūjo) *Jimbun gakuhō* (京都大学人文科学研究所) 人文学報 32 (March 1971).

Ikeda Kikan 池田亀鑑, Kishigami Shinji 岸上慎二, and Akiyama Ken 秋山虔, eds. *Makura no sōshi* 枕草子, *Murasaki Shikibu nikki* 紫式部日記. Vol. 19 of *Nihon koten bungaku taikei* 日本古典文学大系. Tokyo: Iwanami shoten 岩波書店, 1958.

Ima kagami 今鏡. Vol. 21.2 of (*Shintei zōho*) *Kokushi taikei*, qv.

Inagaki Yasuhiko 稲垣泰彦. "Ritsuryōseiteki tochi seido no kaitai" 律令制的土地制度の解体. In Vol. 5 of Takeuchi Rizō 竹内理三 et al., ed. *Taikei Nihonshi sōsho* 体系日本史叢書. Tokyo: Yamakawa shuppansha 山川出版社, 1973.

Inagaki Yasuhiko 稲垣泰彦. "Shoki myōden no kōzō: Yamato no kuni Ōta no Inumaru myō ni tsuite" 初期名田の構造：大和国大田犬丸名について. In Inagaki Yasuhiko 稲垣泰彦 and Nagahara Keiji 永原慶二. *Chūsei no shakai to keizai* 中世の社会と経済. Tokyo: Tōkyō daigaku shuppankai 東京大学出版会, 1962.

Inoue Mitsusada 井上光貞. *Nihon Jōdo-kyō seiritsu-shi no kenkyū* 日本浄土教成立史の研究. Tokyo: Yamakawa shuppansha 山川出版社, 1956.

Inoue Mitsusada 井上光貞. *Nihon kodai kokka no kenkyū* 日本古代国家の研究. Tokyo: Iwanami shoten 岩波書店, 1965.

Inoue Mitsusada 井上光貞. *Nihon kodai no kokka to Bukkyō* 日本古代の国家と佛教. Tokyo: Iwanami shoten 岩波書店, 1971.

Inoue Mitsusada 井上光貞 et al., ed. *Nihon no rekishi* 日本の歴史, 26 vols. Tokyo: Chūō kōron sha 中央公論社, 1973-74.

Inoue Mitsusada 井上光貞, Nagahara Keiji 永原慶二, Kodama Kōta 児玉幸多, and Ōkubo Toshiaki 大久保利謙, eds. *Nihon rekishi taikei* 日本歴史大系. Vol. 1. *Genshi. Kodai*. 原始. 古代. Tokyo: Yamakawa shuppansha 山川出版社, 1984.

Inoue Mitsusada 井上光貞 and Ōsone Shōsuke 大曾根章介, eds. *Ōjō den. Hokke genki*. 往生伝. 法華験記. Vol. 7 of *Nihon shisō taikei* 日本思想大系. Tokyo: Iwanami shoten 岩波書店, 1974.

Inoue Mitsusada hakushi kanreki kinenkai 井上光貞博士還暦記念会, ed. *Kodaishi ronsō* 古代史論叢. 3 vols. Tokyo: Yoshikawa kōbunkan 吉川弘文館, 1978.

Inoue Tatsuo 井上辰雄. *Kodai ōken to shūkyō-teki bemin* 古代王権と宗教的部民. Tokyo: Kashiwa shobō 柏書房, 1980.

Ishida Mizumaro 石田瑞麿. *Jōdo-kyō no tenkai* 浄土教の展開. Tokyo: Shunjūsha 春秋社, 1967.

Ishida Mosaku 石田茂作. *Shakyō yori mitaru Nara-chō Bukkyō no kenkyū* 写経より見たる奈良朝佛教の研究. Tokyo: Tōyō bunko 東洋文庫, 1930.

Ishida Shirō 石田志郎. "Kyōto bonchi hokubu no senjōchi: Heian-kyō sento ji no Kyōto no chisei" 京都盆地北部の扇状地：平安京遷都時の京都の地勢. *Kodai bunka* 古代文化 34.12 (December 1982): 1-14.

Ishii Ryōsuke 石井良助, *Nihon hōseishi gaisetsu* 日本法制史概説. 2nd. ed. Tokyo: Sōbunsha 創文社, 1960.
Ishii Susumu 石井進. "Insei jidai 院政時代." In Rekishigaku kenkyūkai and Nihonshi kenkyūkai 歷史学研究会・日本史研究会, eds. *Kōza Nihonshi* 講座日本史, 10 Vols. 1. Tokyo: Tōkyō daigaku shuppankai 東京大学出版会, 1970.
Ishimaru Hiroshi 石丸熙. "Inseiki chigyōkokusei ni tsuite no ichikōsatsu" 院政期知行国制についての一考察. In Kurokawa Takaaki 黒川高明 and Kitazume Masao 北爪真佐夫, eds. *Kamakura seiken* 鎌倉政権. Vol. 4 of *Ronshū Nihon rekishi* 論集日本歴史. Tokyo: Yūseidō 有精堂, 1976.
Ishimoda Shō 石母田正, "Kodai hō" 古代法. In *Kodai* 古代. Vol. 4 of Ienaga Saburō 家永三郎, Ishimoda Shō 石母田正, Inoue Kiyoshi 井上清, Inoue Mitsusada 井上光貞, et al., eds. *Iwanami kōza: Nihon rekishi* 岩波講座日本歴史. Tokyo: Iwanami shoten 岩波書店, 1962.
Ishimoda Shō 石母田正. *Kodai makki seijishi josetsu* 古代末期政治史序説. Tokyo: Miraisha 未来社, 1964.
Ishimura Teikichi 石村貞吉. *Yūsoku kojitsu kenkyū* 有職故実研究. 3 vols. Tokyo: Yūsoku kojitsu kenkyū kankōkai 有職故実研究刊行会, 1957.
Iyanaga Nobumi. "Daijizaiten." *Hōbōgirin* 6 (1983): 713-65.
Iyanaga Teizō 弥永貞三. "Ritsuryōseiteki tochi shoyū" 律令制的土地所有. In *Kodai* 古代. Vol. 3 of Ienaga Saburō 家永三郎, Ishimoda Shō 石母田正, Inoue Kiyoshi 井上清, Inoue Mitsusada 井上光貞 et al., eds. *Iwanami kōza: Nihon rekishi* 岩波講座日本歴史. Tokyo: Iwanami shoten 岩波書店, 1962.
Izumi Shikibu shū 和泉式部集. In Matsushita Daizaburō 松下大三郎, ed. *Zoku Kokka taikan* 続国歌大観. Tokyo: Kadokawa shoten 角川書店, 1963.
Izumiya Yasuo 泉谷康夫. "Chōyōsei no henshitsu ni tsuite" 調庸制の変質について. In Kodaigaku kyōkai 古代学協会, ed. *Engi Tenryaku jidai no kenkyū* 延喜天暦時代の研究. Tokyo: Yoshikawa kōbunkan 吉川弘文館, 1960.
Izumiya Yasuo 泉谷康夫. "Zuryō kokushi to nin'yō kokushi" 受領国司と任用国司. In Hayashi Rokurō 林陸郎, ed. *Ronshū: Nihon rekishi* 論集：日本歴史. Vol. 3. Tokyo: Yūseidō shuppan 有精堂出版, 1976.
Jinten ainōshō 塵添壒嚢抄. In *Dai Nihon Bukkyō zensho* 大日本佛教全書. Vol. 150. Tokyo: Yūseidō shuppambu 有精堂出版部, 1933.
Johnson, Wallace trans. *The T'ang Code: Volume I. General Principles.* Princeton, N.J.: Princeton University Press, 1979.
Joseishi Sōgō Kenkyūkai 女性史総合研究会, ed. *Nihon josei shi* 日本女性史. Vol. 1. *Genshi. Kodai* 原始. 古代. Tokyo: Tōkyō daigaku shuppankai 東京大学出版会, 1982.
Kagawa Mitsuo 加川光夫 and Fujita Seiichi 藤田晴一, eds. *Usa* 宇佐. Tokyo: Mokujisha 木耳社, 1976.
Kaiei 懐英. *Kōya shunjū hennen shūroku* 高野春秋編年輯録. In *Dai Nihon Bukkyō zensho* 大日本佛教全書. Vol. 131. Tokyo: Bussho kankōkai 佛書刊行会, 1912.
Kakunyo 覚如. *Gaijashō* 改邪鈔. In *Shinshū shōgyō zensho* 真宗聖教全書. Vol. 3. Kyoto: Ōyagi kōbundō 大八木興文堂, 1964.

Kameda Takashi 亀田隆之. *Nihon kodai yōsuishi no kenkyū* 日本古代用水史の研究. Tokyo: Yoshikawa kōbunkan 吉川弘文館, 1973.

Kamens, Edward. *The Three Jewels: A Study and Translation of Minamoto Tamenori's Sanbōe*. Ann Arbor: Center for Japanese Studies, University of Michigan, 1988.

Katsumata Shunkyō 勝又俊教, ed. *Kōbō Daishi zenshū* 弘法大師全集. 3 vols. Tokyo: Sankibō 山喜房, 1968.

Katsumata Shunkyō 勝又俊教. *Mikkyō no Nihon-teki tenkai* 密教の日本的展開. Tokyo: Shunjūsha 春秋社, 1970.

Katsuno Ryūshin 勝野隆信. *Hieizan to Kōyasan* 比叡山と高野山, Tokyo: Shibundō 至文堂, 1959.

Katsuno Ryūshin 勝野隆信. *Sōhei* 僧兵. Tokyo: Shibundō 至文堂, 1955.

Katsuyama Seiji 勝山清次, "Fukosei no saihen to kaitai: jū–jūni seiki no fukosei" 封戸制の再編と解体—十一〜十二世紀の封戸制. *Nihonshi kenkyū* 日本史研究 194 (October 1978): 1-41.

Katsuyama Seiji 勝山清次, "Kōden kammotsu rippō no seiritsu to sono zentei" 公田官物率法の成立とその前提. *Shirin* 史林 70 (February 1987): 1-43.

Kawaguchi Hisao 川口久雄 and Nara Shōichi 奈良正一. *Gōdanshō chū* 江談抄注. Tokyo: Benseisha 勉誠社, 1984.

Kawaguchi Hisao 川口久雄. *Heianchō no kambungaku* 平安朝の漢文学. Tokyo: Yoshikawa kōbunkan 吉川弘文館, 1981.

Kawaguchi Hisao 川口久雄. *Ōe no Masafusa* 大江匡房. Tokyo: Yoshikawa kōbunkan 吉川弘文館, 1968.

Kawasaki Tsuneyuki 川崎庸之. *Jimbutsu Nihon no rekishi* 人物日本の歴史. Vol. 3. *Ōchō no rakujitsu* 王朝の落日. Tokyo: Yomiuri shimbunsha 読売新聞社, 1966.

Kawase Kazuma 川瀬一馬. *Kojisho no kenkyū* 古辞書の研究. Tokyo: Kōdansha 講談社, 1955.

Keene, Donald. *Seeds in the Heart*. New York: Henry Holt, 1993.

Keene, Donald. "*Taketori monogatari*." In J. Thomas Rimer, *Modern Japanese Fiction and Its Tradition*. Princeton, N.J.: Princeton University Press, 1978.

Keirstead, Thomas. *The Geography of Power in Medieval Japan*. Princeton, N.J.: Princeton University Press, 1992.

Ken'i 兼意. *Kōbō Daishi go-den* 弘法大師御伝. In *Zoku gunsho ruijū* 続群書類従. Vol. 8. Tokyo: Keizai zasshisha 経済雑誌社, 1904.

Kikuchi Kyōko 菊池京子. "Tokoro no seiritsu to tenkai" 所の成立と展開. In Vol. 3 of Hayashi Rokurō 林陸郎, ed. *Ronshū: Nihon rekishi* 論集日本歴史. Tokyo: Yūseido. shuppan 有精堂出版, 1976.

Kiley, Cornelius J. "Estate and Property in Late Heian Japan." In John W. Hall and Jeffrey P. Mass, eds. *Medieval Japan: Essays in Institutional History*. New Haven: Yale University Press, 1975.

Kinda Akihiro 金田章裕. "Heian-ki no Yamato bonchi ni okeru jōri jiwari naibu no tochi riyō" 平安期の大和盆地における条里地割内部の土地利用. *Shirin* 史林 61.3 (May 1978): 75-112.

Kinda Akihiro 金田章裕. "Nara Heian-ki no sonraku keitai ni tsuite" 奈良平安期の村落形態について. *Shirin* 史林 54.3 (May 1971): 80-108.

Kinoshita Tadashi 木下忠. "Nōgu" 農具. In Wajima Seiichi 和島誠一, ed. *Nihon no kōkogaku* 日本の考古学. Vol. 3. Tokyo: Kawade shobō 河出書房, 1966.

Kishi Toshio 岸俊男. *Nihon kodai seiji shi kenkyū* 日本古代政治史研究. Tokyo: Hanawa shobō 塙書房, 1966.

Kishi Toshio 岸俊男. *Tojō no seitai* 都城の生態. Vol. 9 of *Nihon no kodai* 日本の古代. Tokyo: Chūō kōronsha 中央公論社, 1987.

Kitanishi Hiromu sensei kanreki kinenkai 北西宏先生還暦記念会, ed. *Chūsei shakai to ikkō ikki* 中世社会と一向一揆. Tokyo: Yoshikawa kōbunkan 吉川弘文館, 1985.

Kiuchi Hiroshi 木内央. *Dengyō Daishi no shōgai to shisō* 伝教大師の生涯と思想. *Regurusu bunko* レグルス文庫. Vol. 56. Tokyo: Daisan bummeisha 第三文明社, 1976.

Kluge, Inge-Lore. *Miyoshi Kiyoyuki: sein Leben und seine Zeit*. Berlin: Institut für Orientforschung, 1958.

Kluge, Inge-Lore. "Fujiwara Morosuke und seine 'Hinterlassene Lehre.'" *Mitteilungen des Instituts für Orientforschung* 1 (1953); 178-87.

Kobayashi, Hiroko. *The Human Comedy of Heian Japan: A Study of the Secular Stories in the Twelfth-Century Collection of Tales, Konjaku Monogatarishū*. Tokyo: The Centre for East Asian Cultural Studies, 1979.

Kōchi Shōsuke 河内祥輔. "Chokushiden ni tsuite" 勅旨田について. In Vol. 2 of Tsuchida Naoshige sensei kanreki kinenkai 土田直鎮先生還暦記念会, ed. *Nara Heian jidaishi ronshū* 奈良平安時代史論集. Tokyo: Yoshikawa kōbunkan 吉川弘文館, 1984.

Kodaigaku kyōkai 古代学協会, ed. *Engi Tenryaku jidai no kenkyū* 延喜天暦時代の研究. Tokyo: Yoshikawa kōbunkan 吉川弘文館, 1960.

Kodaigaku kyōkai 古代学協会, ed. *Sekkan jidaishi no kenkyū* 摂関時代史の研究. Tokyo: Yoshikawa kōbunkan 吉川弘文館, 1965.

Kodansha Encyclopedia of Japan. 9 vols. Tokyo: Kodansha, 1983.

Kōhō 杲宝. *Tōbōki* 東宝記. In *Zokuzoku gunsho ruijū* 続々群書類従. Vol. 12. Tokyo: Kokusho kankōkai 国書刊行会, 1907.

Koizumi Yoshiaki 小泉宣右. "Tōdaijiryō Akanabe no shō" 東大寺領茜部庄. In *Tsūshihen: chūsei* 通史編：中世 of Gifu ken 岐阜県, ed. *Gifu kenshi* 岐阜県史. Gifu: Taishū shobō 大衆書房, 1969.

Kōjō 光定. *Denjutsu isshinkai mon* 伝述一心戒文. In *Dengyō Daishi zenshū* 伝教大師全集. Vol. 1. Shiga-ken, Shiga-gun, Sakamoto: Hieizan tosho kankōsho 比叡山図書刊行所, 1926.

Kokan Shiren 虎関師錬. *Genkō Shakusho* 元亨釈書. In *Dai Nihon Bukkyō zensho* 大日本佛教全書. Vol. 101. Tokyo: Bussho kankōkai 佛書刊行会, 1913.

Kokke no on-tame ni shuhō sen to kou hyō 奉為国家請修法表. Included in *Henjō hakki seirei shū* 遍照発揮性霊集, kan 4. In *Sangō shiiki. Seirei shū* 三教指帰. 性霊集. Vol. 71 of *Nihon koten bungaku taikei* 日本古典文学大系. Tokyo: Iwanami shoten 岩波書店, 1965.

Kokushi daijiten 国史大辞典. 15 vols. Tokyo: Yoshikawa kōbunkan 吉川弘文館, 1979-97.
Kokushi taikei 国史大系. See (*Shintei zōho*) *Kokushi taikei*.
Kon Tōkō 今東光, Kobayashi Takeshi 小林剛, and Gorai Shigeru 五来重, eds. *Rokuharamitsuji* 六波羅蜜寺. Kyoto: Tankōsha 淡交社, 1969.
Kondō Yoshirō 近藤義郎 and Okamoto Akio 岡本明郎. "Nihon no suitō nōkō gijutsu" 日本の水稲農耕技術. In Ishimoda Shō 石母田正, ed. *Kodai no kōza* 古代の講座. Vol. 3. Tokyo: Gakuseisha 学生社, 1962.
Kongōbuji 金剛峯寺 ed. *Kōyasan senhyakunen shi* 高野山千百年史. Kōyasan: Kongōbuji 金剛峯寺, 1942.
Konishi, Jin'ichi, "The Genesis of the *Kokinshū* Style." Trans. Helen C. McCullough. *Harvard Journal of Asiatic Studies* 38, 1 (June 1978): 61-170.
Konishi, Jin'ichi. *A History of Japanese Literature*. 3 vols. to date. Princeton, N.J.: Princeton University Press, 1984-91.
Konjaku monogatari shū 今昔物語集. In Yamada Yoshio 山田孝雄, Yamada Tadao 山田忠雄, Yamada Hideo 山田英雄, and Yamada Toshio 山田俊雄, eds. Vols. 22-25 of *Nihon koten bungaku taikei* 日本古典文学大系. Tokyo: Iwanami shoten 岩波書店, 1959-63.
Kōno Fusao 河野房男. *Heian makki seijishi* 平安末期政治史. Tokyo: Tōkyōdō 東京堂, 1979.
Kubota Osamu 久保田収. *Chūsei Shintō no kenkyū* 中世神道の研究. Kyoto: Shintō-shi gakkai 神道史学会, 1959.
Kudō Yoshiaki 工藤圭章 and Nishikawa Shinji 西川新次. *Amidadō to Fujiwara chōkoku* 阿弥陀堂と藤原彫刻. Vol. 6 of *Genshoku Nihon no bijutsu* 原色日本の美術. Tokyo: Shōgakukan 小学館, 1969.
Kūkai 空海. *Go-shōrai mokuroku* 御将来目録. In *Taishō shinshū daizōkyō* 大正新修大蔵経. Vol. 55. Tokyo: Taishō issaikyō kankōkai 大正一切経刊行会, 1928.
Kūkai 空海. *Go-yuigō* 御遺告. In *Taishō shinshū daizōkyō* 大正新修大蔵経. Vol. 77. Tokyo: Taishō issaikyō kankōkai 大正一切経刊行会, 1931.
Kūkai 空海. *Takao kanjō ki* 高雄潅頂記, included in *Shūi zasshū* 拾遺雑集. In *Kōbō Daishi zenshū* 弘法大師全集. 3rd ed., revised and enlarged. Vol. 3. Kōyasan: Mikkyō bunka kenkyūjo 密教文化研究所, 1965.
Kurata Bunsaku 倉田文作. *Mikkyō jiin to Jōgan chōkoku* 密教寺院と貞観彫刻. Vol. 5 of *Genshoku Nihon no bijutsu* 原色日本の美術. Tokyo: Shōgakukan 小学館, 1967.
Kuroda Toshio 黒田俊雄. "Chinkon no keifu 鎮魂の系譜." In Kuroda Toshio. *Nihon chūsei shakai to shūkyō* 日本中世社会と宗教. Tokyo: Iwanami shoten 岩波書店, 1990.
Kuroda Toshio 黒田俊雄. *Jisha seiryoku* 寺社勢力. Tokyo: Iwanami shoten 岩波書店, 1980.
Kuroda Toshio 黒田俊雄. *Ōbō to buppō* 王法と仏法. Kyoto: Hōzōkan 法蔵館, 1983.
Kuroda Toshio 黒田俊雄. *Shōensei shakai* 荘園制社会. Vol. 2 of *Taikei Nihon rekishi* 体系日本歴史. Tokyo: Nihon hyōronsha 日本評論社, 1967.

Kuroda Toshio 黒田俊雄. "Historical Consciousness and *Hon-jaku* 本迹 Philosophy in the Medieval Period on Mt. Hiei," trans. Allan Grapard. In *The Lotus Sutra in Japanese Culture*. Edited by George Tanabe and Willa Tanabe, pp. 143-58. Honolulu: University of Hawaii Press, 1989.

Kuroda Toshio 黒田俊雄. "Shinto in the History of Japanese Religions." *Journal of Japanese Studies* 7-1 (1981): 1-21.

Kuroita Katsumi 黒板勝美. *Kōtei: kokushi no kenkyū* 更訂：国史の研究. 3 vols. Tokyo: Iwanami shoten 岩波書店, 1931-36.

Kuroita Nobuo 黒板伸夫. "Fujiwara no Tadahira seiken ni taisuru ichikōsatsu" 藤原忠平政権に対する一考察. In Kodaigaku kyōkai 古代学協会, ed. *Engi Tenryaku jidai no kenkyū* 延喜天暦時代の研究. Tokyo: Yoshikawa kōbunkan 吉川弘文館, 1960.

Kushida Ryōkō 櫛田良洪. *Kūkai no kenkyū* 空海の研究. Tokyo: Sankibō Busshorin 山喜房佛書林, 1981.

Kyōhan 経範. *Daishi on-gyōjō shūki* 大師御行状集記. In *Zoku gunsho ruijū* 続群書類従. Vol. 8. Tokyo: Keizai zasshisha 経済雑誌社, 1904.

Kyōkai 景戒, comp. *Nihon ryōiki* 日本霊異記. Edited by Endō Yoshimoto 遠藤嘉基 and Kasuga Kazuo 春日和男. Vol. 70 of *Nihon koten bungaku taikei* 日本古典文学体系. Tokyo: Iwanami shoten 岩波書店, 1967.

Kyoto-shi 京都市, comp. *Kyōto no rekishi* 京都の歴史. Vol. 1. Tokyo: Gakugei shorin 学芸書林, 1971.

Lammers, Wayne P. "The Succession (*Kuniyuzuri*): A Translation from *Utsubo Monogatari*." *Monumenta Nipponica* 37, 2 (1982): 139-78.

Lammers, Wayne P. *The Tale of Matsura: Fujiwara Teika's Experiment in Fiction*. Ann Arbor: Center for Japanese Studies, University of Michigan, 1992.

Lu, David John. *Sources of Japanese History*. New York: McGraw Hill Book Co. 1974.

Manabe Shunshō 真鍋俊照. "Seishuku bijutsu—hoshi mandara 星宿美術—星曼荼羅." *Kobijutsu* 35 (1971): 1-48.

Man'yōshū 万葉集. Vols. 4-7 of *Nihon koten bungaku taikei* 日本古典文学大系. Tokyo: Iwanami shoten 岩波書店, 1957-62.

Marra, Michele. Review of *Il Dio incatenato: Honchō shinsenden di Ōe no Masafusa*, trans. Silvio Calzolari. *Monumenta Nipponica* 41 (Winter 1986): 495-97.

Mass, Jeffrey P. *Warrior Government in Early Medieval Japan: A Study of the Kamakura Bakufu, Shugo, and Jitō*. New Haven, Conn.: Yale University Press, 1974.

Matsumura Hiroji 松村博司, ed. *Ōkagami* 大鏡. Vol. 21 of *Nihon koten bungaku taikei* 日本古典文学大系. Tokyo: Iwanami shoten 岩波書店, 1960.

Matsumura Hiroji 松村博司 and Yamanaka Yutaka 山中裕, eds. *Eiga monogatari* 栄花物語. Vols. 75-76 of *Nihon koten bungaku taikei* 日本古典文学大系. Tokyo: Iwanami shoten 岩波書店, 1964-65.

McCullough, Helen Craig, trans. "An Account of My Hut." In Helen Craig McCullough, comp. and ed. *Classical Japanese Prose: An Anthology*. Stanford,

Calif.: Stanford University Press, 1990.
McCullough, Helen Craig. *Brocade by Night: 'Kokin Wakashū' and the Court Style in Japanese Classical Poetry.* Stanford, Calif.: Stanford University Press, 1985.
McCullough, Helen Craig, trans. *Classical Japanese Prose: An Anthology.* Stanford, Calif.: Stanford University Press, 1990.
McCullough, Helen Craig, trans. *Genji and Heike: Selections from The Tale of Genji and The Tale of the Heike.* Stanford, Calif.: Stanford University Press, 1994.
McCullough, Helen Craig, trans. *Kokin Wakashū: With 'Tosa Nikki' and 'Shinsen Waka.'* Stanford, Calif.: Stanford University Press, 1985.
McCullough, Helen Craig, trans. *Ōkagami, The Great Mirror: Fujiwara Michinaga and His Times.* Princeton, N.J.: Princeton University Press, 1980.
McCullough, Helen Craig, trans. *The Tale of the Heike.* Stanford, Calif.: Stanford University Press, 1988.
McCullough, Helen Craig, trans. "A Tale of Mutsu." *Harvard Journal of Asiatic Studies* 25 (1964–65): 178–211.
McCullough, Helen Craig, trans. *Tales of Ise: Lyrical Episodes from Tenth-Century Japan.* Stanford, Calif.: Stanford University Press, 1968.
McCullough, William H., and Helen Craig McCullough. *A Tale of Flowering Fortunes: Annals of Japanese Aristocratic Life in the Heian Period.* 2 vols. Stanford, Calif.: Stanford University Press, 1980.
McCullough, William. "Japanese Marriage Institutions in the Heian Period." *Harvard Journal of Asiatic Studies*, 27 (1967): 103–67.
Miho Tadao 三保忠夫 and Miho Satoko 三保サト子. *Unshū ōrai Kyōroku bon kenkyū to sōsakuin* 雲州往来享禄本研究と総索引. Osaka: Izumi shoin 泉書院, 1982.
Minamoto, H. *An Illustrated History of Japanese Art.* Kyoto: K. Hoshino, 1935.
Minamoto no Tamenori 源為憲. *Kuchizusami* 口遊. In Vol. 32.1 of *Zoku Gunsho ruijū* 続群書類従. Tokyo: Keizai zasshi sha. 経済雑誌社, 1960.
Minamoto no Tamenori 源為憲. *Sambō ekotoba* 三宝絵詞. In *Dai Nihon Bukkyō zensho* 大日本佛教全書. Vol. 111. Tokyo: Bussho kankōkai 佛書刊行会, 1913.
Misaki Ryōshū 三崎良周. *Taimitsu no kenkyū* 台密の研究. Tokyo: Sōbunsha 創文社, 1988.
Misaki Ryōshū 三崎良周. *Mikkyō to jingi shisō* 密教と神祇思想. Tokyo: Sōbunsha 創文社, 1992.
Misaki Ryōshū 三崎良周. *Nihon・Chūgoku Bukkyō shisō to sono tenkai* 日本・中国仏教思想とその展開. Tokyo: Sankibō 山喜房, 1993.
Misaki Ryōshū 三崎良周. *Taimitsu no riron to jissen* 台密の理論と実践. Tokyo: Sōbunsha 創文社, 1994.
Miura Keiichi 三浦圭一. "10 seiki–13 seiki no Higashi Ajia to Nihon 10世紀–13世紀の東アジアと日本. "*Kōza Nihonshi* 講座日本史. Vol. 2. Tokyo: Tōkyō daigaku shuppankai 東京大学出版会, 1970.
Miyagawa Mitsuru 宮川満. *Ōyama sonshi* 大山村史. 2 vols., *Hommon hen* 本文編

and *Shiryō hen* 史料編. Tokyo: Hanawa shobo 塙書房, 1964.
Miyahara Takeo 宮原武夫. *Nihon kodai no kokka to nōmin* 日本古代の国家と農民. Tokyo: Hōsei daigaku shuppankyoku 法政大学出版局, 1973.
Miyai Yoshio 宮井義雄. *Fujiwara-shi no ujigami-ujidera shinkō to sobyō saishi* 藤原氏の氏神氏寺信仰と祖廟祭祀. Tokyo: Seikō shobō 成甲書房, 1978.
Miyai Yoshio 宮井義雄. *Jōdai no shimbutsu shūgō to Jōdo-kyō* 上代の神仏習合と浄土教. Tokyo: Seikō shobō 成甲書房, 1980.
Miyamoto Tasuku 宮本救. "Ritsuryōsei-teki tochi seido" 律令制的土地制度. In Takeuchi Rizō 竹内理三 et al., eds. *Taikei Nihonshi sōsho* 体系日本史叢書. Vol. 6. Tokyo: Yamakawa shuppansha 山川出版社, 1973.
Miyoshi Tameyasu 三善為康. *Go-shūi ōjō den* 後拾遺往生伝. In Inoue Mitsusada 井上光貞 and Ōsone Shōsuke 大曾根章介, eds. *Ōjō den. Hokke genki* 往生伝. 法華験記. Vol. 7 of *Nihon shisō taikei* 日本思想大系. Tokyo: Iwanami shoten 岩波書店, 1974.
Miyoshi Tameyasu 三善為康. *Shūi ōjō den* 拾遺往生伝. In Inoue Mitsusada 井上光貞 and Ōsone Shōsuke 大曾根章介, eds. *Ōjō den. Hokke genki* 往生伝. 法華験記. Vol. 7 of *Nihon shisō taikei* 日本思想大系. Tokyo: Iwanami shoten 岩波書店, 1974.
Momo Hiroyuki 桃裕行. *Jōdai gakusei no kenkyū* 上代学制の研究. Tokyo: Meguro shoten 目黒書店, 1947.
Montoku jitsuroku 文徳実録. Vol. 3 of *(Shintei zōho) Kokushi taikei*, qv.
Mori Katsumi 森克己. *Nissō bōeki no kenkyū*. 日宋貿易の研究. Rev. ed. Vol. 1 of *Mori Katsumi chosaku senshū* 森克己著作選集. Tokyo: Kokusho kankōkai 国書刊行会, 1975.
Morita Tei 森田悌, "Heian chūki gunji ni tsuite no ichikōsatsu" 平安中期郡司についての一考察. In Vol. 3 of Hayashi Rokurō 林陸郎, ed. *Ronshū: Nihon rekishi* 論集日本歴史. Tokyo: Yūseidō shuppan 有精堂出版, 1976.
Morita Tei 森田悌, *Heian jidai seijishi kenkyū* 平安時代政治史研究. Tokyo: Yoshikawa kōbunkan 吉川弘文館, 1978.
Morita Tei 森田悌, *Nihon kodai ritsuryōhō shi no kenkyū* 日本古代律令法史の研究. Tokyo: Bunken shuppan 文献出版, 1986.
Morris, Dana. "Peasant Economy in Early Japan, 650-950." Ph.D. diss., University of California, Berkeley, 1980.
Morris, Ivan, trans. *As I Crossed a Bridge of Dreams: Recollections of a Woman in Eleventh-Century Japan.* New York: Dial Press, 1971.
Morris, Ivan, trans. *The Pillow Book of Sei Shōnagon.* 2 vols. New York: Columbia University Press, 1967.
Morris, Ivan. *The Tale of Genji Scroll.* Tokyo: Kodansha International, 1971.
Morris, Ivan. *The World of the Shining Prince.* New York: Alfred A. Knopf, 1964.
Murai Yasuhiko 村井康彦. *Heian kizoku no sekai* 平安貴族の世界. Tokyo: Tokuma shoten 徳間書店, 1972.
Murai Yasuhiko 村井康彦. *Kodai kokka kaitai katei no kenkyū* 古代国家解体過程の研究. Tokyo: Iwanami shoten 岩波書店, 1965.

Murai Yasuhiko 村井康彦. "Shōensei no hatten to kōzō" 荘園制の発展と構造. In *Kodai* 古代, Vol. 4 of Ienaga Saburō 家永三郎, Ishimoda Shō 石母田正, Inoue Kiyoshi 井上清, Inoue Mitsusada 井上光貞 et al., eds. *Iwanami kōza: Nihon rekishi* 岩波講座日本歴史. Tokyo: Iwanami shoten 岩波書店, 1962.

Murao Jirō 村尾次郎. *Ritsuryō zaiseishi no kenkyū* 律令財政史の研究. Tokyo: Yoshikawa kōbunkan 吉川弘文館, 1967.

Murayama Shūichi 村山修一. "Heian Bukkyō no tenkai" 平安佛教の展開. In Ienaga Saburō 家永三郎, ed. *Kodai hen* 古代篇. Vol. 1 of *Nihon Bukkyō-shi* 日本佛教史. Kyoto: Hōzōkan 法蔵館, 1967.

Murayama Shūichi 村山修一. *Heian-kyō* 平安京. Tokyo: Shibundō 至文堂, 1957.

Murayama Shūichi 村山修一. *Honji suijaku* 本地垂迹. Tokyo: Yoshikawa kōbunkan 吉川弘文館, 1974.

Murayama Shūichi 村山修一. *Nihon ommyōdō-shi sōsetsu* 日本陰陽道史総説. Tokyo: Hanawa shobō 塙書房, 1981.

Murayama Shūichi 村山修一. *Shimbutsu shūgō shichō* 神仏習合思潮. Kyoto: Heirakuji shoten 平楽寺書店, 1957.

Murayama Shūichi 村山修一. *Yamabushi no rekishi* 山伏の歴史, Tokyo: Hanawa shobō 塙書房, 1970.

Murayama Shūichi 村山修一 and Kageyama Haruki 影山春樹. *Hiei-zan* 比叡山. Tokyo: NHK Bukkusu NHK ブックス, 1970.

Murdoch, James. *A History of Japan*. Vol. 1. 1910. Reprint. London: Routledge and Kegan Paul, 1949.

Mutsu waki 陸奥話記. In *Kodai seiji shakai shisō* 古代政治社会思想. Vol. 8 of *Nihon shisō taikei* 日本思想大系. 67 vols. Tokyo: Iwanami shoten 岩波書店, 1979.

Nachi Taisha 那智大社, ed. *Kumano Sanzan to sono shinkō* 熊野三山とその信仰. 3 vols. Tokyo: Meicho shuppan 名著出版, 1984.

Nagahara Keiji 永原慶二. "Shōensei ni okeru 'shiki' no seikaku" 荘園制における「職」の性格. In *Kodai chūsei hen* 古代中世論. Vol. 2 of Hōgetsu Keigo sensei kanreki kinenkai 宝月圭吾先生還暦記念会, ed. *Nihon shakai keizai shi kenkyū* 日本社会経済史研究. Tokyo: Yoshikawa kōbunkan 吉川弘文館, 1967.

Nagahara Keiji 永原慶二 et al., eds. *Taikei Nihon no rekishi* 体系日本の歴史. 15 vols. Tokyo: Shōgakukan 小学館, 1987-89.

Nagahara Keiji, with Kozo Yamamura. "Village Communities and Daimyo Power." In John Whitney Hall and Toyoda Takeshi, eds. *Japan in the Muromachi Age*. Berkeley and Los Angeles: University of California press, 1977.

Nagayama Yasutaka 長山泰孝. *Ritsuryō futan taikei no kenkyū* 律令負担体系の研究. Tokyo: Hanawa shobō 塙書房, 1976.

Nagazumi Yasuaki 永積安明 and Shimada Isao 島田勇雄, eds. *Kokon chomonjū* 古今著聞集. Vol. 84 of *Nihon koten bungaku taikei* 日本古典文学大系. Tokyo: Iwanami shoten 岩波書店, 1966.

Nakada Kaoru 中田薫. *Shōen no kenkyū* 庄園の研究. Tokyo: Shōkō shoin 彰考書院, 1949.

Nakamura, Kyoko Motomichi. *Miraculous Stories from the Japanese Buddhist*

Tradition: The Nihon Ryōiki of the Monk Kyōkai. Cambridge, Mass.: Harvard University Press, 1972.

Nakano Hatayoshi 中野幡能. *Hachiman shinkō-shi no kenkyū* 八幡信仰史の研究. 2 vols. Tokyo: Yoshikawa kōbunkan 吉川弘文館, 1975.

Nakano Hatayoshi 中野幡能. *Usa-gū* 宇佐宮. Tokyo: Yoshikawa kōbunkan 吉川弘文館, 1985.

Nakano Hideo 中野栄夫. *Ritsuryōsei shakai kaitai katei no kenkyū* 律令制社会解体過程の研究. Tokyo: Hanawa shobō 塙書房, 1979.

Nakao Shumpaku 仲尾俊博. *Dengyō Daishi Saichō no kenkyū* 伝教大師最澄の研究. Kyoto: Nagata bunshōdō 永田文昌堂, 1987.

Needham, Joseph, ed. *Science and Civilization in China.* Vol. 2. *History of Scientific Thought.* Cambridge, England: Cambridge University Press, 1962.

Nihon kiryaku 日本紀略. Vols. 10-11 of *(Shintei zōho) Kokushi taikei), qv.*

Nihon kōki 日本後紀. Vol. 3 of *(Shintei zōho) Kokushi taikei, qv.*

Nihon Montoku Tennō jitsuroku 日本文徳天皇實録. Vol. 3 of *(Shintei zōho) Kokushi taikei, qv.*

Nihon sandai jitsuroku 日本三代実録. Vol. 4 of *(Shintei zōho) Kokushi taikei, qv.*

Nihon shoki 日本書紀. Sakamoto Tarō 坂本太郎, Ienaga Saburō 家永三郎, Inoue Mitsusada 井上光貞, and Ōno Susumu 大野晋, eds. Vol. 67 of *Nihon koten bungaku taikei* 日本古典文学大系. Tokyo: Iwanami shoten 岩波書店, 1967.

Nihonshi kenkyūkai 日本史研究会, ed. *Chūsei no kenryoku to minshū* 中世の権力と民衆. Osaka: Sōgensha 創元社, 1970.

Nihonshi kenkyūkai 日本史研究会, ed. *Chūsei shakai no kihon kōzō* 中世社会の基本構造. Tokyo: Ochanomizu shobō 御茶の水書房, 1958.

Ninchū 仁忠. *Eizan Daishi den* 叡山大師伝. In *Dengyō Daishi zenshū* 伝教大師全集. Vol. 5. Shiga-ken, Shiga-gun, Sakamoto: Hieizan tosho kankōsho 比叡山図書刊行所, 1926.

Nishibeppu Motoka 西別府元日. "Kyū seiki chūyō ni okeru kokusei kichō no tenkan ni tsuite" 九世紀中葉における国政基調の転換について. *Nihonshi kenkyū* 日本史研究 169 (September 1976): 30-54.

Nishimoto Yutaka 西本泰. *Sumiyoshi taisha* 住吉大社. Tokyo: Gakuseisha 学生社, 1977.

Nyūya Tetsuichi 丹生谷哲一. "Zaichi tone no keisei to rekishi-teki ichi" 在地刀禰の形成と歴史的位置. In Ōsaka rekishi gakkai 大阪歴史学会, ed. *Chūsei shakai no seiritsu to tenkai* 中世社会の成立と展開. Tokyo: Yoshikawa kōbunkan 吉川弘文館, 1976.

Ōe no Masafusa 大江匡房. "Bonen no ki" 暮年記. In Yamagishi Tokuhei 山岸徳平, Takeuchi Rizō 竹内理三, Ienaga Saburō 家永三郎, Ōsone Shōsuke 大曽根章介, eds. *Kodai seiji shakai shisō* 古代政治社会思想. Vol. 8 of *Nihon shisō taikei* 日本思想大系. Tokyo: Iwanami shoten 岩波書店, 1979.

Ōe no Masafusa 大江匡房. *Gōdanshō* 江談抄. In *Gunsho ruijū* 群書類従. Vol. 17. Tokyo: Keizai zasshisha 経済雑誌社, 1905.

Ōe no Masafusa 大江匡房. "Zoku honchō ōjōden" 続本朝往生伝. In Inoue Mitsusada 井上光貞 and Ōsone Shōsuke 大曽根章介, eds. *Ōjōden. Hokke genki*

往生伝. 法華験記. Vol. 7 of *Nihon shisō taikei* 日本思想大系. Tokyo: Iwanami shoten 岩波書店, 1974.

Ogi Mitsuo 荻美津夫. *Nihon kodai ongaku shiron* 日本古代音楽史論. Tokyo: Yoshikawa kōbunkan 吉川弘文館, 1977.

Ohase Keikichi 小長谷恵吉. *Nihonkoku genzai shomokuroku kaisetsu kō* 日本国見在書目録解説稿. Tokyo: Komiyama shuppan, 小宮山出版, 1976.

Oka Kazuo 岡一男, ed. *Heianchō bungaku jiten* 平安朝文学事典. Tokyo: Tōkyōdō 東京堂, 1972.

Okada, H. Richard. *Figures of Resistance: Language, Poetry, and Narrating in 'The Tale of Genji' and Other Mid-Heian Texts.* Durham: Duke University Press, 1991.

Okamoto Akio 岡本明郎. "Nōgyō seisan" 農業生産. In Kondō Yoshirō 近藤善郎 and Fujisawa Chōji 藤沢長治, eds. *Nihon no kōkogaku* 日本の考古学. Vol. 5. Tokyo: Kawade shobō 河出書房, 1966.

Okudaira, Hideo. *Narrative Picture Scrolls.* New York and Tokyo: Weatherhill and Shibundō, 1973.

Okuno Nakahiko 奥野中彦. "Hachi kyū seiki ni okeru shiteki tochi shoyūsei no rekishiteki seikaku" 八九世紀における私的土地所有制の歴史的性格. *Nihon rekishi* 日本歴史 279 (August 1971): 53-69.

Okuno Nakahiko 奥野中彦. "Rinji zōyaku no seiritsu to tenkai" 臨時雑役の成立と展開. *Nihon rekishi* 日本歴史 255 (August 1969): 32-49.

Okuno Takahiro 奥野高広. "Go-Sanjō tennō goryō" 後三条天皇御領. In Vol. 4 of *Nihon rekishi daijiten* 日本歴史大辞典. 11 vols. Tokyo: Kawade shobō 河出書房, 1970.

Ōmi no Mifune Genkai 淡海三船元開. *Tō Daiwajō tōsei den* 唐大和上東征伝. In *Dai Nihon Bukkyō zensho* 大日本佛教全書. Vol. 113. Yūseidō shuppambu 有精堂出版部, 1932.

Ōmori Kingorō 大森金五郎. *Buke jidai no kenkyū* 武家時代の研究. Tokyo: Fuzambō 冨山房, 1923

Ōmori Kingorō 大森金五郎. "Ōchō jidai no shigakkō ni tsuite" 王朝時代の私学校に就いて. *Rekishi chiri* 歴史地理 53 (1929): 330-37.

Ono Katsutoshi 小野勝年. *Nittō guhō junrai kōki no kenkyū* 入唐求法巡礼行記の研究. 4 vols. Tokyo: Suzuki gakujutsu zaidan 鈴木学術財団, 1964-69.

Ōno Tatsunosuke 大野達之助. *Jōdai no Jōdo-kyō* 上代の浄土教. Tokyo: Yoshikawa kōbunkan 吉川弘文館, 1972.

Osabe Kazuo 長部和雄. *Ichigyō zenji no kenkyū* 一行禪師の研究. Kobe: Kōbe shōka daigaku 神戸商科大学, 1963.

Ōsaka rekishi gakkai 大阪歴史学会, ed. *Chūsei shakai no seiritsu to tenkai* 中世社会の成立と展開. Tokyo: Yoshikawa kōbunkan 吉川弘文館, 1976.

Ōsaka rekishi gakkai 大阪歴史学会, ed. *Ritsuryō kokka no kiso kōzō* 律令国家の基礎構造. Tokyo: Yoshikawa kōbunkan 吉川弘文館, 1960.

Ōta Seiroku 太田静六. *Shindenzukuri no kenkyū* 寝殿造の研究. Tokyo: Yoshikawa kōbunkan 吉川弘文館, 1987.

Ōyama Kōjun 大山公淳. *Shimbutsu kōshō-shi* 神仏交渉史. Kyoto: Rinsen shoten

臨川書店, 1975.
Ozawa Masao 小沢正夫, ed. *Kokin waka shū* 古今和歌集. Vol. 7 of *Nihon koten bungaku zenshū* 日本古典文学全集. Tokyo: Shōgakukan 小学館, 1971.
Ozawa Masao 小沢正夫, Gotō Shigeo 後藤重郎, Shimazu Tadao 島津忠夫, and Higuchi Yoshimaro 樋口芳麻呂. *Fukuro sōshi chūshaku* 袋草紙注釈. Tokyo: Hanawa shobō, 塙書房, 1974.
Paine, Robert Treat, and Alexander Soper. *The Art and Architecture of Japan.* Pelican History of Art. Baltimore: Penguin Books, 1955.
Pearson, Birger A., ed. *Religious Syncretism in Antiquity.* Missoula: Scholars Press, 1975.
Pekarik, Andrew, ed. *Ukifune: Love in the Tale of Genji.* New York: Columbia University Press, 1982.
Piggott, Joan. "Chieftain Pairs and Co-rulers: Female Sovereignty in Early Japan." In Hitomi Tonomura et al., eds. *Women and Class in Japanese History.* Ann Arbor: Center for Japanese Studies, University of Michigan, 1999.
Pollack, David. *The Fracture of Meaning.* Princeton, N.J.: Princeton University Press, 1986.
Ponsonby-Fane, R. A. B. *Kyoto: The Old Capital of Japan, 794-1869.* Kyoto: The Ponsonby Memorial Society, 1956.
Rabinovitch, Judith N., trans. *Shōmonki: The Story of Masakado's Rebellion.* Monumenta Nipponica Monograph 58. Tokyo: Sophia University, 1986.
Reischauer, A. K. "Genshin's Ojo Yoshu: Collected Essays on Birth into Paradise." *Transactions of the Asiatic Society of Japan.* 2nd series. 7 (1930): 16-97.
Reischauer, Edwin O. *Ennin's Diary: The Record of a Pilgrimage to China in Search of the Law.* New York: Ronald Press, 1955.
Reischauer, Edwin O. *Ennin's Travels in T'ang China.* New York: Ronald Press, 1955.
Reischauer, Edwin O., and Joseph K. Yamagiwa, trans. *Translations from Early Japanese Literature.* Cambridge, Mass.: Harvard University Press, 1951.
Reischauer, Robert Karl. *Early Japanese History (c. 40 B.C.-A.D. 1167).* 2 vols. Princeton, N.J.: Princeton University Press, 1937.
Renondeau, Gaston. *Les Moines Guerriers du Japan.* Paris: Imprimerie Nationale, 1965.
Renondeau, Gaston. *Le Shugendō: Histoire, Doctrines et Rites des Anachorètes Dits Yamabushi.* Paris: Imprimerie Nationale, 1965.
Rheinstein, Max. *Max Weber on Law in Economy and Society.* Cambridge, Mass.: Harvard University Press, 1954.
Ritsu. Ryō no gige 律. 令義解. Vol. 22 of *(Shintei zōho) Kokushi taikei, qv.*
Rohlich, Thomas H. trans. *A Tale of Eleventh-Century Japan: Hamamatsu Chūnagon monogatari.* Princeton, N.J.: Princeton University Press, 1983.
Rotermund, Hartmut O. *Die Yamabushi: Aspekte Ihres Glaubens, Lebens und Ihrer Sozialen Funktion im Japanischen Mittelalter.* Hamburg: Kommissionsverlag Cram, De Gruyter & Co., 1968.
Ruiju kokushi 類聚国史. Vols. 5-6 of *(Shintei zōho) Kokushi taikei, qv.*

Ruiju sandai kyaku. 類聚三代格. Vol. 25 of *(Shintei zōho) Kokushi taikei,* qv.
Ryōgen 良源. *Nijūrokka jō kishō* 二十六箇条起請. In Takeuchi Rizō 竹内理三 ed., *Heian ibun* 平安遺文. Vol. 2. Tokyo: Tōkyō-dō 東京堂, 1964.
Ryōgen 良源. *Tengen sannen Chūdō kuyō gammon* 天元三年中堂供養願文. In *Koji ruien* 古事類苑. Vol. 12. Tokyo: Yoshikawa kōbunkan 吉川弘文館, 1969.
Ryōjin hishō 梁塵秘抄. Go-Shirakawa 後白河, comp. In Vol. 19 of *Nihon koten zensho* 日本古典全書. Tokyo: Asahi shimbunsha 朝日新聞社, 1953.
Ryō no shūge 令集解. Vols. 23-24 of *(Shintei zōho) Kokushi taikei,* qv.
Saeki Arikiyo 佐伯有清. *Dengyō Daishi den no kenkyū* 伝教大師伝の研究. Tokyo: Yoshikawa kōbunkan 吉川弘文館, 1992.
Saeki Umetomo 佐伯梅友, ed. *Kokin waka shū* 古今和歌集. Vol. 8 of *Nihon koten bungaku taikei* 日本古典文学大系. Tokyo: Iwanami shoten 岩波書店, 1959.
Saichō 最澄. *Dengyō Daishi shōrai Esshū roku* 伝教大師将来越州録. In *Taishō shinshū daizōkyō* 大正新修大蔵経. Vol. 55. Tokyo: Taishō issaikyō kankōkai 大正一切経刊行会, 1928.
Saichō 最澄. *Dengyō Daishi shōrai Taishū roku* 伝教大師将来台州録. In *Taishō shinshū daizōkyō* 大正新修大蔵経. Vol. 55. Tokyo: Taishō issaikyō kankōkai 大正一切経刊行会, 1928.
Saichō 最澄. *Kanshō Tendai-shū nembun gakushō shiki* 勧奨天台宗年分学生式, included in *Sange gakushō shiki* 山家学生式. In *Taishō shinshū daizōkyō* 大正新修大蔵経. Vol. 74. Tokyo: Taishō issaikyō kankōkai 大正一切経刊行会, 1931.
Saichō 最澄. *Kenkairon* 顕戒論. In *Dengyō Daishi zenshū* 伝教大師全集. Vol. 1. Shiga-ken, Shiga-gun, Sakamoto: Hieizan tosho kankōsho 比叡山図書刊行所, 1926.
Saichō 最澄. *Kenkairon engi* 顕戒論縁起. In *Dengyō Daishi zenshū* 伝教大師全集. Vol. 1. Shiga-ken, Shiga-gun, Sakamoto: Hieizan tosho kankōsho 比叡山図書刊行所, 1926.
Saichō 最澄. *Naishō Buppō sōjō kechimyaku fu* 内証佛法相承血脈譜. In *Dengyō Daishi zenshū* 伝教大師全集. Vol. 1. Shiga-ken, Shiga-gun, Sakamoto: Hieizan tosho kankōsho 比叡山図書刊行所, 1926.
Saichō 最澄. *Tendai Hokke-shū nembun tokudo gakushō myōchō* 天台法華宗年分得度学生名帳, included in *Jō Kenkairon hyō* 上顕戒論表. In *Dengyō Daishi zenshū* 伝教大師全集. Vol. 1. Shiga-ken, Shiga-gun, Sakamoto: Hieizan tosho kankōsho 比叡山図書刊行所, 1926.
Saitō Tsutomu 斎藤勵. *Ōchō-jidai no ommyōdō* 王朝時代の陰陽道. Tokyo: Sōgensha 創元社, 1947.
Sakamoto Shōzō 坂本賞三. *Nihon ōchō kokka taisei ron* 日本王朝国家体制論. Tokyo: Tōkyō daigaku shuppankai 東京大学出版会, 1972.
Sakamoto Tarō 坂本太郎. *Nihon kodai shi no kisoteki kenkyū* 日本古代史の基礎的研究. 2 vols. Tokyo: Tōkyō daigaku shuppankai 東京大学出版会, 1964.
Sakamoto Tarō 坂本太郎. *Sugawara no Michizane* 菅原道真. Tokyo: Yoshikawa kōbunkan 吉川弘文館, 1962.
Sakamoto Tarō. *The Six National Histories of Japan.* Trans. John S. Brownlee. Vancouver: University of British Columbia Press, 1991.

Sakamoto Tarō hakushi kanreki kinenkai 坂本太郎博士還暦記念会, ed. *Nihon kodaishi ronsū* 日本古代史論集. 3 vols. Tokyo: Yoshikawa kōbunkan 吉川弘文館, 1963.

Sakanoue Akikane 坂上明兼 et al., comps. *Hossō shiyōshō* 法曹至要抄. In Vol. 4 of Hanawa Hokinoichi 塙保己一 et al., eds. *Shinkō: Gunsho ruijū* 新校群書類従. Tokyo: Naigai shoseki 内外書籍, 1983.

Sammon dōsha ki 山門堂舎記. In *Gunsho ruijū* 群書類従. Vol. 15. Tokyo: Keizai zasshisha 経済雑誌社, 1905.

Sandai jitsuroku 三代実録. In Vol. 4 of *(Shintei zōho) Kokushi taikei*, qv.

Sansom, George. *A History of Japan to 1334*. Stanford, Calif.: Stanford University Press, 1958.

Sansom, George. *A Short Cultural History of Japan*. Rev. ed. New York: Appleton-Century, 1943.

Sasaki Keisuke 佐々木恵介. "Dazaifu no kannai shihai henshitsu ni kansuru shiron: omo ni zaisei-teki sokumen kara" 太宰府の管内支配変質に関する試論：主に財政的側面から. In Vol. 2 of Tsuchida Naoshige sensei kanreki kinenkai 土田直鎮先生還暦記念会, ed. *Nara Heian jidaishi ronshū* 奈良平安時代史論集. Tokyo: Yoshikawa kōbunkan 吉川弘文館, 1984.

Sasayama Haruo 笹山晴生. *(Kodai o kangaeru) Heian no miyako* (古代を考える)平安の都. Tokyo: Yoshikawa kōbunkan 吉川弘文館, 1991.

Sato, Elizabeth. "Ōyama Estate and *Insei* Land Policies." *Monumenta Nipponica* 34 (Spring 1979): 73-99.

Satō Shin'ichi 佐藤進一. *Nihon no chūsei kokka* 日本の中世国家. Tokyo: Iwanami shoten 岩波書店, 1983.

Satō Sōjun 佐藤宗諄. *Heian zenki seijishi josetsu* 平安前期政治史序説. Tokyo: Tōkyō daigaku shuppankai 東京大学出版会, 1977.

Schafer, Edward H. *The Golden Peaches of Samarkand: A Study of T'ang Exotics*. Berkeley and Los Angeles: University of California Press, 1963.

Schafer, Edward H. *The Vermilion Bird: T'ang Images of the South*. Berkeley and Los Angeles: University of California Press, 1987.

Scharschmidt, Clemens. "*Unshū shōsoku* oder die Briefsammlung des Unshū." *Ostasiatische Studien* 20 (1917): 20-114.

Schipper, Christofer. "The Taoist Body." *History of Religions* 17 (1978): 355-81.

Seidel, Anna. "La Divinisation de Lao-tseu dans le Taoisme des Han." Publications de l'Ecole Française d'Extrême-Orient. Vol. 71. Paris: Ecole Française d'Extrême-Orient, 1969.

Seidensticker, Edward, trans. *The Gossamer Years: The Diary of a Noblewoman of Heian Japan*. Tokyo and Rutland, Vermont: Charle E. Tuttle Co., 1964.

Seidensticker, Edward. "Murasaki Shikibu and Her Diary and Her Other Writings." *Literature East and West* 18.1 (March 1974): 1-7.

Seidensticker, Edward G. *The Tale of Genji*. 2 vols. New York: Alfred A. Knopf, 1976.

Seiji yōryaku 政事要略. Vol. 28 of *(Shintei zōho) Kokushi taikei*, qv.

Shibata Minoru 柴田実. *Chūsei shomin shinkō no kenkyū* 中世庶民信仰の研究. Tokyo: Kadokawa shoten 角川書店, 1966.
Shibuya Jigai 渋谷慈鎧 ed. *Kōtei zōho Tendai zasu ki* 校訂増補：天台座主記. Tokyo: Daiichi shobō 第一書房, 1973.
Shigematsu Akihisa 重松明久. *Hachiman Usa-gū gotakusen-shū* 八幡宇佐宮御託宣集. Tokyo: Gendai shichōsha 現代思潮社, 1986.
Shikō 志晃. *Jimon denki horoku* 寺門伝記補録. In *Dai Nihon Bukkyō zensho* 大日本佛教全書. Vol. 127. Tokyo: Bussho kankōkai 佛書刊行会, 1915.
Shimada Jirō 島田次郎. "Shōen-teki 'shiki' taisei no kaitai" 荘園的「職」体制の解体. In Takeuchi Rizō 竹内理三 et al., eds. *Taikei Nihonshi sōsho* 体系日本史叢書. Vol. 6. Tokyo: Yamakawa shuppansha 山川出版社, 1973.
Shimaji Daitō 島地大等. *Tendai kyōgaku shi* 天台教学史. Tokyo: Meiji shoin, 1929.
Shimizu, Osamu. "Nihon Montoku Tennō jitsuroku: An Annotated Translation, with a Survey of the Early Ninth Century in Japan," Ph.D. diss., Columbia University, 1951.
Shimode Sekiyo 下出積與. *Dōkyō to Nihonjin* 道教と日本人. Tokyo: Kōdansha 講談社, 1975.
Shimode Sekiyo 下出積与. "Kūkai to Shingon-shū" 空海と真言宗. In *Nihon hen* 日本編. Vol. 2 of Nakamura Hajime 中村元, Kasahara Kazuo 笠原一男, and Kanaoka Shūyū 金岡秀友, eds. *Ajia Bukkyō shi* アジア佛教史. Tokyo: Kōsei shuppansha 佼正出版社, 1974.
Shimode Sekiyo 下出積與. *Nihon kodai no jingi to Dōkyō* 日本古代の神祇と道教. Tokyo: Yoshikawa kōbunkan 吉川弘文館, 1972.
Shimode Sekiyo 下出積与. "Shingon-shū no tenkai" 真言宗の展開. In *Nihon hen* 日本編. Vol. 2 of Nakamura Hajime 中村元, Kasahara Kazuo 笠原一男, and Kanaoka Shūyū 金岡秀友, eds. *Ajia Bukkyō shi* アジア佛教史. Tokyo: Kōsei shuppansha 佼正出版社, 1974.
Shimpen Kokka taikan 新編国歌大観. Shimpen Kokka taikan henshū iinkai 新編国歌大観編集委員会, ed. 10 vols. in 20. Tokyo: Kadokawa shoten 角川書店, 1983-92.
Shinoda, Minoru, trans. *The Founding of the Kamakura Shogunate 1180-1185*. New York: Columbia University Press, 1960.
(*Shintei zōho*) *Kokushi taikei* (新訂増補)国史大系. 60 vols. in 66. Tokyo: Yoshikawa kōbunkan 吉川弘文館, 1929-64.
Shintō taikei hensankai 神道大系編纂会, ed. *Shintō taikei* 神道大系. Vol. 22. Tokyo: Seikōsha 精興社, 1984.
Shioiri Ryōdō 塩入良道 and Kiuchi Gyōō 木内堯央, eds. *Saichō* 最澄. Vol. 2 of *Nihon meisō ronshū* 日本名僧論集. Tokyo: Yoshikawa kōbunkan 吉川弘文館, 1982.
Shirane, Haruo. *The Bridge of Dreams: A Poetics of 'The Tale of Genji.'* Stanford, Calif.: Stanford University Press, 1987.
Shōchūreki 掌中歴. In *Zoku gunsho ruijū* 続群書類従. Vol. 32. Tokyo: Zoku gunsho ruijū kanseikai 続群書類従完成会, 1923-30.

WORKS CITED 733

Shoku Nihongi 続日本紀. Vol. 2 of *(Shintei zōho) Kokushi taikei*, qv.
Shoku Nihon kōki 続日本後紀. In Vol. 3 of *(Shintei zōho) Kokushi taikei*, qv.
Shōmonki 将門記. In *Kodai seiji shakai shisō* 古代政治社会思想. Vol. 8 of *Nihon shisō taikei* 日本思想大系. 67 vols. Tokyo: Iwanami shoten 岩波書店, 1979.
Shōyūki 小右記. Part 10 of *Dai Nihon kokiroku* 大日本古記録. Compiled by Tōkyō daigaku shiryō hensanjo 東京大学史料編纂所. Tokyo: Iwanami shoten 岩波書店, 1959-69.
Sjoberg, Gideon. *The Preindustrial City, Past and Present*. Glencoe, Ill.: Free Press, 1960.
Sockel, Dietrich. *Emakimono: The Art of the Japanese Hand-Painted Scroll*. London: Jonathan Cape, 1959.
Sofū sen'yōkai 祖風宣揚会 ed. *Rankei yuionshū* 蘭契遺音集. In *Kōbō Daishi zenshū* 弘法大師全集, 3rd ed., rev. and enlarged. Vol. 5. Kōyasan: Mikkyō bunka kenkyūjo 密教文化研究所, 1966.
Sonoda Kōyū 薗田香融. "Heian Bukkyō" 平安佛教. In *Kodai* 古代. Vol. 4 of Ienaga Saburō 家永三郎, Ishimoda Shō 石母田正, Inoue Kiyoshi 井上清 et al., eds. *Iwanami kōza: Nihon rekishi* 岩波講座日本歴史. Tokyo: Iwanami shoten 岩波書店, 1962.
Sonoda Kōyū 薗田香融. "Heian Bukkyō no seiritsu" 平安佛教の成立. In Ienaga Saburō 家永三郎, ed. *Kodai hen* 古代篇. Vol. 1 of *Nihon Bukkyō-shi* 日本佛教史. Kyoto: Hōzōkan 法蔵館, 1967.
Sonoda Kōyū 薗田香融. "Saichō to Tendai-shū" 最澄と天台宗. In *Nihon hen* 日本編. Vol. 2 of Nakamura Hajime 中村元, Kasahara Kazuo 笠原一男, and Kanaoka Shūyū 金岡秀友, eds. *Ajia Bukkyō shi* アジア佛教史. Tokyo: Kōsei shuppansha 佼正出版社, 1974.
Sonoda Kōyū 薗田香融. "Suiko: Tempyō kara Engi made" 出挙：天平から延喜まで. In Ōsaka rekishi gakkai 大阪歴史学会, ed. *Ritsuryō kokka no kiso kōzō* 律令国家の基礎構造. Tokyo: Yoshikawa kōbunkan 吉川弘文館, 1960.
Sontsū 尊通. *Chishō Daishi nempu* 智証大師年譜. In *Dai Nihon Bukkyō zensho* 大日本佛教全書. Vol. 28. Tokyo: Yūseidō shuppambu 有精堂出版部, 1933.
Staal, Frits. "Indian Concepts of the Body." *Somatics* (Autumn/Winter 1983-84): 31-41.
Sugawara no Michizane 菅原道真, comp. *Kanke bunsō* 菅家文草. In Vol. 72 of *Nihon koten bungaku taikei* 日本古典文学体系. Tokyo: Iwanami shoten 岩波書店, 1966.
Sumi Tōyō 鷲見等曜. *Zenkindai Nihon kazoku no kōzō* 前近代日本家族の構造. Tokyo: Kōbundō 弘文堂, 1983.
Suzuki Shigeo 鈴木茂男. "Inseiki in-no-chō no kinō ni tsuite: in-no-chō hakkyū monjo o tsūjite mitaru" 院政期院庁の機能について―院庁発給文書を通じて見たる. Unpublished graduation thesis. Tokyo University, 1961.
Suzuki Tomotarō 鈴木知太郎, Kawaguchi Hisao 川口久雄, Endō Yoshimoto 遠藤嘉基, and Nishishita Kyōichi 西下經一, eds. *Tosa nikki* 土佐日記, *Kagerō nikki* かげろふ日記, *Izumi Shikibu nikki* 和泉式部日記, *Sarashina nikki* 更級日記. Vol. 20 of *Nihon koten bungaku taikei* 日本古典文学大系. Tokyo: Iwanami

shoten 岩波書店, 1957.
Taiki 台記. 3 vols. in *Zōho shiryō taisei* 増補史料大成. Kyoto: Rinsen shoten 臨川書店, 1965.
Tajima Isao 田嶋公. "Bokkai to no kōshō" 渤海との交渉. In Hashimoto Yoshihiko 橋本義彦, ed. *Komonjo no kataru Nihon shi* 古文書の語る日本史. Vol. 2. *Heian* 平安. Tokyo: Chikuma shobō 筑摩書房, 1991.
Takada Minoru 高田実. "Chūsei shoki no kokka kenryoku to sonraku" 中世初期の国家権力と村落. *Shichō* 史潮 99 (June 1967): 6-25.
Takada Osamu 高田修 and Yanagisawa Taka 柳沢孝. *Butsuga* 仏画. Vol. 7 of *Genshoku Nihon no bijutsu* 原色日本の美術. Tokyo: Shōgakukan 小学館, 1969.
Takagi Yutaka 高木豊. "Tendai-shū no tenkai." 天台宗の展開. In *Nihon hen* 日本編. Vol. 2 of Nakamura Hajime 中村元, Kasahara Kazuo 笠原一男, and Kanaoka Shūyū 金岡秀友, eds. *Ajia Bukkyō shi* アジア佛教史. Tokyo: Kōsei shuppansha 佼正出版社, 1974.
Takahashi Takashi 高橋崇. *Emishi: kodai tōhokujin no rekishi* 蝦夷：古代東北人の歴史. *Chūkō shinsho* 中公新書 804. Tokyo: Chūō kōronsha 中央公論社, 1986.
Takahashi Tomio 高橋富雄. *Kodai Ezo: sono shakai kōzō* 古代蝦夷：その社会構造. Tokyo: Gakuseisha 学生社, 1974.
Takahashi Toshinori 高橋俊乗. *Nihon kyōiku bunka shi* 日本教育文化史. 1933. Reprint. Tokyo: Kōdansha 講談社, 1978.
Takakusu Junjirō 高楠順次郎, Watanabe Kaigyoku 渡邊海旭, and Ono Gemmyō 小野玄妙, eds. *Taishō shinshū daizōkyō* 大正新修大蔵経. 100 vols. Tokyo: Taishō issaikyō kankōkai 大正一切經刊行会, 1924-34.
Takeuchi Rizō 竹内理三. *Bushi no tōjō* 武士の登場. Vol. 6 of *Nihon no rekishi* 日本の歴史. 31 vols. Tokyo: Chūō kōronsha 中央公論社, 1973.
Takeuchi Rizō 竹内理三, ed. *Heian ibun* 平安遺文. 15 vols. Tokyo: Tōkyōdō 東京堂, 1947-80.
Takeuchi Rizō 竹内理三. "Insei no seiritsu" 院制の成立. In *Kodai* 古代. Vol. 4 of Ienaga Saburō 家永三郎, Ishimoda Shō 石母田正, Inoue Kiyoshi 井上清, Inoue Mitsusada 井上光貞 et al., eds. *Iwanami kōza: Nihon rekishi* 岩波講座日本歴史. Tokyo: Iwanami shoten 岩波書店, 1962.
Takeuchi Rizō 竹内理三, ed. *Kamakura ibun* 鎌倉遺文. 41 vols. Tokyo: Tōkyōdō 東京堂, 1971-90.
Takeuchi Rizō 竹内理三, ed. *Nara ibun* 寧楽遺文. Revised ed. 3 vols. Tokyo: Tōkyōdō 東京堂, 1962.
Takeuchi Rizō 竹内理三. *Nara-chō jidai ni okeru jiin keizai no kenkyū* 奈良朝時代における寺院経済の研究. Tokyo: Ōokayama shoten 大岡山書店, 1932.
Takeuchi Rizō 竹内理三. *Ritsuryōsei to kizoku seiken* 律令制と貴族政権. 2 vols. Tokyo: Ochanomizu shobō 御茶の水書房, 1957, 1958.
Takeuchi Rizō 竹内理三, et al., eds. *Taikei Nihonshi sōsho* 体系日本史叢書. Tokyo: Yamakawa shuppansha 山川出版社, 1973.
Takeuchi Rizō 竹内理三, ed. *Tochi seido shi* 土地制度史. Vol. 6 of *Taikei Nihon shi sōsho* 体系日本史叢書. Tokyo: Yamakawa shuppansha 山川出版社, 1964.

Takeuchi Rizō 竹内理三. "Tōgoku no 'tsuwamono'" 東国の「つわもの」. *Miura kobunka* 三浦古文化 25.5 (1979).
Takikawa Masajirō 滝川政次郎. *Nihon hōseishi* 日本法制史. Tokyo: Yūhikaku 有斐閣, 1960.
Tamura Kōyū 田村晃祐. *Saichō* 最澄. *Jimbutsu sōsho* 人物叢書. Vol. 193. Tokyo: Yoshikawa kōbunkan 吉川弘文館, 1988.
Tamuramaro denki 田邑麻呂傳記. In Hanawa Hokinoichi 塙保己一, comp. *(Shinkō) Gunsho ruijū* (新校) 群書類従. Vol. 3. Tokyo: Meicho fukyūkai 名著普及会, 1977.
Tanabe, George, and Willa Tanabe, eds. *The Lotus Sutra in Japanese Culture.* Honolulu: University of Hawaii Press, 1989.
Tanabe, Willa. "The Lotus Lectures: Hokke hakkō in the Heian Period." *Monumenta Nipponica* 39.4 (1984): 393-407.
Taniguchi Kengo 谷口研吾. "Mino no kuni Ōi no shō ni okeru shōkan ichizoku no ryōshusei: Ōnakatomi no geshishiki sōron o megutte" 美濃国大井庄における庄官一族の領主制：大中臣の下司職争論をめぐって. *Hōsei shigaku* 法政史学 28 1976): 24-37.
Tanimori Tomoo 谷森饒男. *Kebiishi o chūshin to shitaru Heian jidai no keisatsu jōtai* 検非違使を中心としたる平安時代の警察状態. Tokyo: Kashiwa shobō 柏書房, 1921.
Toby, Ronald P. "Why Leave Nara? Kammu and the Transfer of the Capital." *Monumenta Nipponica* 40 (1985): 331-47.
Toda Yoshimi 戸田芳美. *Chūyūki* 中右記. Tokyo: Soshiete そしえて, 1979.
Toda Yoshimi 戸田芳美. "Kokuga gunsei no keisei katei" 国衙軍制の形成過程. In Nihonshi kenkyūkai 日本史研究会, ed. *Chūsei no kenryoku to minshū* 中世の権力と民衆. Osaka: Sōgensha 創元社, 1970.
Toda Yoshimi 戸田芳美. *Nihon ryōshusei seiritsushi no kenkyū* 日本領主制成立史の研究. Tokyo: Iwanami shoten 岩波書店, 1967.
Tōdaiji yōroku 東大寺要録. In *Zokuzoku gunsho ruijū* 続々群書類従. Tokyo: Gunsho ruijū kankōkai 群書類従刊行会, 1909.
Tōji chōja bunin 東寺長者補任. In *Zokuzoku gunsho ruijū* 続々群書類従. Vol. 2. Tokyo: Kokusho kankōkai 国書刊行会, 1907.
Tokoro Isao 所功. *Miyoshi Kiyoyuki* 三善清行. Tokyo: Yoshikawa kōbunkan 吉川弘文館, 1970.
Tokoro Isao 所功. "Ritsuryō jidai ni okeru ikenfūshin seido no jittai" 律令時代における意見封進制度の実態. In Kodaigaku Kyōkai 古代学協会, ed. *Engi Tenryaku jidai no kenkyū* 延喜天暦時代の研究. Tokyo: Yoshikawa kōbunkan 吉川弘文館, 1960.
Tōkyō daigaku shiryō hensanjo 東京大学史料編纂所, comp. *Dai Nihon shiryō* 大日本史料. Series 3, Revised Edition. Tokyo: Tōkyō daigaku shuppankai 東京大学出版会, 1968.
Tokyo National Museum. *Painting 6th-14th Centuries.* Vol. 1 of *Pageant of Japanese Art.* Tokyo: Toto shuppan, 1957.
Torao Toshiya 虎尾俊哉. *Engi shiki* 延喜式. Tokyo: Yoshikawa kōbunkan 吉川弘

文館, 1964.

Torao Toshiya 虎尾俊哉. *Handen shūju hō no kenkyū* 班田収授法の研究. Tokyo: Yoshikawa kōbunkan 吉川弘文館, 1961.

Toyoda Takeshi 豊田武, ed. *Sangyō shi* 産業史. Vol. 10 of *Taikei nihon shi sōsho* 体系日本史叢書. Tokyo: Yamakawa shuppansha 山川出版社, 1964.

Toyoda Takeshi 豊田武. *Tōhoku no rekishi* 東北の歴史. Vol. 1. Tokyo: Yoshikawa kōbunkan 吉川弘文館, 1967.

Toyoda Takeshi kyōju kanreki kinenkai 豊田武教授還暦記念会, ed. *Nihon kodai chūsei no chihōteki tenkai* 日本古代中世の地方的展開. Tokyo: Yoshikawa kōbunkan 吉川弘文館, 1973.

Tsubo Noritada 壷憲惟. *Kōshin shinkō* 庚申信仰. Tokyo: Yamakawa Shuppansha 山川出版社, 1956.

Tsubo Noritada 壷憲惟. *Kōshin shinkō no kenkyū* 庚申信仰の研究. Tokyo: Nihon gakujutsu shinkōkai 日本学術振興会, 1961.

Tsuchida Naoshige 土田直鎮. *Ōchō no kizoku* 王朝の貴族. Vol. 5 of *Nihon no rekishi* 日本の歴史. Tokyo: Chūō kōronsha 中央公論社, 1981.

Tsuchida Naoshige sensei kanreki kinenkai 土田直鎮先生還暦記念会, ed. *Nara Heian jidaishi no kenkyū* 奈良平安時代史の研究. 2 vols. Tokyo: Yoshikawa kōbunkan 吉川弘文館, 1984.

Tsuji Zennosuke 辻善之助. *Nihon Bukkyō-shi: Jōsei hen* 日本佛教史：上世篇. Tokyo: Iwanami shoten 岩波書店, 1944.

Tyler, Royall. *The Miracles of the Kasuga Deity*. Princeton, N.J.: Princeton University Press, 1990.

Uda Tennō 宇多天皇. "*Kampyō goyuikai*" 寛平御遺誡. In Yamagishi Tokuhei 山岸徳平, Takeuchi Rizō 竹内理三, Ienaga Saburō 家永三郎, Ōsone Shōsuke 大曽根章介, eds. *Kodai seiji shakai shisō* 古代政治社会思想. Vol. 8 of *Nihon shisō taikei* 日本思想大系. Tokyo: Iwanami shoten 岩波書店, 1979.

Ueda Masaaki 上田正昭, ed. *Sumiyoshi to Munakata no kami* 住吉と宗像の神. Tokyo: Chikuma shobō 筑摩書房, 1988.

Ueda Takeshi 上田雄. *Bokkaikoku no nazo* 渤海国の謎. Kōdansha gendai shinsho 講談社現代新書, 1104. Tokyo: Kōdansha 講談社, 1992.

Uraki, Ziro. *The Tale of the Cavern*. Tokyo: Shinozaki shorin, 1984.

Ury, Marian, "The Ōe Conversations." *Monumenta Nipponica* 48 (Autumn 1993): 359-80.

Ury, Marian. *Tales of Times Now Past: Sixty-Two Stories from a Medieval Japanese Collection*. Berkeley and Los Angeles: University of California Press, 1979.

Utsuho monogatari 宇津保物語. Vols. 10-12 of *Nihon koten bungaku taikei* 日本古典文学大系. Tokyo: Iwanami shoten 岩波書店, 1959-62.

Uwayokote Masataka 上横手雅敬. *Gempei no seisui* 源平の盛衰. Vol. 6 of *Nihon no rekishi bunko* 日本の歴史文庫. Tokyo: Kōdansha 講談社, 1975.

Verschuer, Charlotte von. *Les Relations Officielles du Japon avec la Chine aux VIIIe et IXe Siécles*. Paris: Librairie Droz, 1985.

Wakamori Tarō 和歌森太郎, Murayama Shūichi 村山修一, Gorai Shigeru 五來重,

Tokawa Yasuakira 戸川安章, and Sakurai Tokutarō 桜井徳太郎, eds. *Sangaku shūkyō-shi kenkyū sōsho* 山岳宗教史研究叢書. 18 vols. Tokyo: Meicho shuppan 名著出版, 1977.
Wakamori Tarō 和歌森太郎. *Shugendō-shi kenkyū* 修験道史研究. Tokyo: Tōyō bunko 東洋文庫, 1972.
Wakita Haruko 脇田晴子. *Nihon chūsei shōgyō hattatsushi no kenkyū* 日本中世商業発達史の研究. Tokyo: Ochanomizu shobō 御茶の水書房, 1969.
Waley, Arthur. *The Tale of Genji: A Novel in Six Parts*. 2 vols. Boston and New York: Houghton Mifflin Co., 1935.
Wamyō ruiju shō 倭名類聚抄. 3 vols. Tokyo: Kazama shobō 風間書房, 1954.
Washio Junkyō 鷲尾順敬. *Kōshitsu to Bukkyō* 皇室と佛教. Tokyo: Daitō shuppansha 大東出版社, 1939.
Watanabe Minoru 渡辺実. *Nihon shokuseikatsu shi* 日本食生活史. Tokyo: Yoshikawa kōbunkan 吉川弘文館, 1964.
Watanabe Shōkō 渡辺照宏 and Miyasaka Yūshō 宮坂有勝, eds. *Sangō-shiiki. Seireishū* 三教指帰. 性霊集. Vol. 71 of Nihon koten bungaku taikei 日本古典文学大系. Tokyo: Iwanami shoten 岩波書店, 1965.
Watanabe Shōkō 渡辺照宏 and Miyasaka Yūshō 宮坂有勝. *Shamon Kūkai* 沙門空海. Chikuma sōsho 筑摩叢書. Vol. 84. Tokyo: Chikuma shobō 筑摩書房, 1967.
Watson, Burton, trans. "Chiteiki" (Record of the Pond Pavilion). In *Japanese Literature in Chinese*. Vol. 1. New York: Columbia University Press, 1975.
Watson, Burton, trans. *Japanese Literature in Chinese: Volume I: Poetry and Prose in Chinese by Japanese Writers of the Early Period*. New York: Columbia University Press, 1975.
Watson, Burton, trans. *Meng ch'iu: Famous Episodes from Chinese History and Legend*. Tokyo: Kodansha International, 1986.
Weinstein, Stanley. "Beginnings of Esoteric Buddhism in Japan: The Neglected Tendai Tradition." *Journal of Asian Studies* 34. 1 (1974): 177-91.
Weinstein, Stanley, "Imperial Patronage in T'ang Buddhism." In Arthur F. Wright and Denis Twitchett., eds. *Perspectives on the T'ang*. New Haven: Yale University Press, 1973.
Wheatley, Paul, and Thomas See. *From Court to Capital: A Tentative Analysis of the Japanese Urban Tradition*. Chicago: University of Chicago Press, 1978.
Whitehouse, Wilfred, and Eizo Yanagisawa. *Ochikubo Monogatari or The Tale of the Lady Ochikubo: A Tenth Century Japanese Novel*. Tokyo: Hokuseido Press. Rev. Ed. 1965.
Willig, Rosette E. *The Changelings: A Classical Japanese Court Tale*. Stanford, Calif.: Stanford University Press, 1983.
Wilson, William Ritchie. *"Hōgen monogatari": Tale of the Disorder in Hōgen*. Tokyo: Sophia University Press, 1971.
Wilson, William Ritchie. "The Way of the Bow and Arrow: The Japanese Warrior in *Konjaku Monogatari*." *Monumenta Nipponica* 28, 2 (Summer 1973): 177-233.
Yabuki Keiki 矢吹慶輝. *Amida Butsu no kenkyū* 阿弥陀佛の研究. Rev. and en-

larged ed. Tokyo: Meiji shoin 明治書院, 1937.
Yamada Hideo 山田英雄. "Sammi no kenkyū" 散位の研究. In Sakamoto Tarō hakushi kanreki kinenkai 坂本太郎博士還暦記念会, ed. *Nihon kodaishi ronshū* 日本古代史論集. Vol. 2. Tokyo: Yoshikawa kōbunkan 吉川弘文館, 1962.
Yamada Yoshio 山田孝雄. *Sambōe ryakuchū* 三宝絵略註. Tokyo: Hōbunkan 宝文館, 1951.
Yamagami Izumo 山上伊豆母. *Nihon geinō no kigen* 日本芸能の起源. Tokyo: Yamato shobō 大和書房, 1977.
Yamagishi Tokuhei 山岸徳平, ed. *Genji monogatari* 源氏物語. Vols. 14-18 of *Nihon koten bungaku taikei* 日本古典文学大系. Tokyo: Iwanami shoten 岩波書店, 1958-63.
Yamanaka Toshiji 山中敏史 and Satō Kōji 佐藤興治. *Kodai no yakusho* 古代の役所. Tokyo: Iwanami shoten 岩波書店, 1984.
Yamanobe Tomoyuki 山辺知行, Okada Jō 岡田譲, and Kurata Osamu 蔵田蔵, eds. *Senshoku, shikkō, kinkō* 染織・漆工・金工. Vol. 20 of *Genshoku Nihon no bijutsu* 原色日本の美術. Tokyo: Shōgakukan 小学館, 1969.
Yasuda Motohisa 安田元久. "Bushidan no keisei" 武士団の形成. In *Kodai* 古代. Vol. 4 of Ienaga Saburō 家永三郎, Ishimoda Shō 石母田正, Inoue Kiyoshi 井上清, Inoue Mitsusada 井上光貞 et al., eds. *Iwanami kōza: Nihon rekishi* 岩波講座日本歴史. Tokyo: Iwanami shoten 岩波書店, 1962.
Yasuda Motohisa 安田元久. *Gempei no sōkoku* 源平の相剋. Vol. 7 of *Kokumin no rekishi* 国民の歴史. Tokyo: Bun'eidō 文英堂, 1968.
Yasuda Motohisa 安田元久. *Insei to Heishi* 院政と平氏. Vol. 7 of *Nihon no rekishi* 日本の歴史. Tokyo: Shōgakukan 小学館, 1974.
Yasuda Motohisa 安田元久. "Kodai makki ni okeru Kantō bushidan" 古代末期に於ける関東武士団. In Yasuda Motohisa 安田元久, ed. *Nihon hōkensei seiritsu no shozentei* 日本封建制成立の諸前提. Tokyo: Yoshikawa kōbunkan 吉川弘文館, 1960, pp. 1-112.
Yasuda Motohisa 安田元久. *Nihon shōen shi gaisetsu* 日本荘園史概説. Tokyo: Yoshikawa kōbunkan 吉川弘文館, 1957.
Yōkan 永観. *Ōjō jūin* 往生十因. In *Jōdo-shū zensho* 浄土宗全書. Vol. 15. Tokyo: Sankibō Busshorin 山喜房佛書林, 1971.
Yoneda Yūsuke 米田雄介, "Gigunji kō" 擬郡司考. In Kodaigaku kyōkai 古代学協会, ed. *Engi Tenryaku jidai no kenkyū* 延喜天暦時代の研究. Tokyo: Yoshikawa kōbunkan 吉川弘文館, 1960.
Yoneyama Toshinao 米山俊直. *Dokyumento Gion matsuri-toshi to matsuri to minshū to* ドキュメント祇園祭-都市と祭と民衆と. Tokyo: NHK bukkusu NHKブックス, 1986.
Yoshida Akira 吉田晶. "Tato no seiritsu ni tsuite" 田堵の成立について. *Historia* ヒストリア 16 (September 1956): 35-46.
Yoshida Mitsukuni 吉田光邦. *Hoshi no shūkyō* 星の宗教. Kyoto: Tankōsha 淡交社, 1970.
Yoshida Sanae 吉田早苗. "Fujiwara no Sanesuke no kazoku" 藤原実資の家族. *Nihon rekishi* 日本歴史 330 (November 1975): 69-85.

Yoshida Sanae 吉田早苗. "Fujiwara no Sanesuke to Ononomiya-tei: shinden-zukuri ni kan-suru ichikōsatsu" 藤原実資と小野宮第：寝殿造に関する一考察. *Nihon rekishi* 日本歴史 350 (July 1977): 50-69.

Yoshida Takashi 吉田孝. "Ritsuryō ni okeru zōyō no kitei to sono kaishaku" 律令における雑徭の規定とその解釈. In Vol. 3 of Sakamoto Tarō hakushi kanreki kinenkai 坂本太郎博士還暦記念会, ed. *Nihon kodaishi ronshū* 日本古代史論集. Tokyo: Yoshikawa kōbunkan 吉川弘文館, 1963.

Yoshida Takashi 吉田孝. "Uji to ie" ウヂとイへ. In Sasaki Junnosuke 佐々木潤之助 and Ishii Susumu 石井進, eds. *Shimpen Nihon shi kenkyū nyūmon* 新編日本史研究入門. Tokyo: Tōkyō daigaku shuppankai 東京大学出版会, 1982. pp. 31-58.

Yoshimura Shigeki 吉村茂樹. *Kokushi seido hōkai ni kansuru kenkyū* 国司制度崩壊に関する研究. Tōkyō daigaku shuppankai 東京大学出版会, 1979.

Yoshioka Saneyuki 吉岡真之. "Kizoku shakai no seijuku" 貴族社会の成熟. In Hashimoto Yoshihiko 橋本義彦, ed. *Komonjo no kataru Nihon shi* 古文書の語る日本史. Vol. 2. *Heian* 平安. Tokyo: Chikuma shobō 筑摩書房, 1991.

Yoshioka Saneyuki 吉岡真之. "Fuyogeyujō to kageyushi ni kansuru shiron" 不与解由状と勘解由使に関する試論. In Vol. 3 of Inoue Mitsusada hakushi kanreki kinenkai 井上光貞博士還暦記念会, ed. *Kodaishi ronsō* 古代史論叢. Tokyo: Yoshikawa kōbunkan 吉岡弘文館, 1978.

Yoshishige no Yasutane 慶滋保胤. *Nihon ōjō gokuraku ki* 日本往生極楽記. In Inoue Mitsusada 井上光貞 and Ōsone Shōsuke 大曾根章介, eds. *Ōjō den. Hokke genki* 往生伝．法華験記. Vol. 7 of *Nihon shisō taikei* 日本思想大系. Tokyo: Iwanami shoten 岩波書店, 1974.

Zō Daisōjō Kūkai Wajō denki 贈大僧正空海和上伝記. In *Kōbō Daishi zenshū* 弘法大師全集. 3rd ed., rev. and enlarged. *Shukan* 首巻. Kōyasan: Mikkyō bunka kenkyūjo 密教文化研究所, 1967.

GLOSSARY-INDEX

abdication, 4, 576-9, 583, 585, 593-5, 600, 621
Abe no Munetō 安倍宗任, warrior, 674
Abe no Sadatō 安倍貞任, warrior, xxi, 673
Abe no Yoritoki 安倍頼時, warrior, xxi, 673
Academy (Daigakuryō 大学寮), 2, 12, 20, 117, 129, 132-3, 159-60, 341, 344, 354, 357, 367-75, 463, 373
Achiki 阿直岐, scholar from Paekche, 343
agricultural communities, 195-9
agriculture: irrigation, 183, 188; diffusion of iron tools, 183-4, 189-90, 192; plows, 183-4, 186-94; fertilizing, 193-4; improved productivity, 184-94; changes in agrarian life, 193-4; *see also* crops; rice
Akō Controversy (阿衡の紛議), xix, 54-6, 76, 379
akusō 悪僧, "rowdy monks," *see sōhei*
allotment fields (*kubunden* 口分田), 57-9, 63-4, 70, 75-6, 78, 91, 98-100, 272, 278-9
Amida 阿弥陀 (Amitābha), 177, 507-8, 572-4
Anna Incident (*Anna no hen* 安和の変), xx, 63-4
Annen 安然, monk, 485, 540-1
Anrakuju-in 安樂寿院, temple, xix, 612-13
anthologies of poetry in Chinese, xix, 357
Antoku 安徳, emperor, xxiii, 629-30, 696-7, 705, 707
archery, 403
architecture: domestic, 391; furnishings, 391-4; *see* Byōdōin, Hōjōji; Ononomiya
armed monks, *see sōhei*
artisans, 166-7
azukaridokoro 預所, custodian of a *shōen*, 249

Banquet Pine Grove (En no matsubara 宴松原), 110, 115
Barbarian-subduing Generalissimo (*seii taishōgun* 征夷大将軍), xviii, 670, 706, 709
Benevolent Longevity Hall, *see* Jijūden
betsumyō 別名, a holding designated for special treatment, 73, 243
bettō 別当, superintendent, 454, 588, 605
Board of Discharge Examiners, *see kageyushi*
Board of Yin and Yang, *see* Ommyōryō
Bommōkyō 梵網経, 465, 470, 473
Buddhism: introduced, 11, 14; used by government, 15-16, 450-1, 454-6; monks and nuns regulated, xviii, 457-61
Buddhist music, 429-31
Buddhist painting, 421-4
Buddhist sculpture, 419-21
Buddhist temples associated with Shinto shrines, 520-3
Bunka shūreishū 文華秀麗集 (imperial anthology of poetry in Chinese), xix, 357
Bunkyō hifu ron 文鏡秘府論 (treatise on the composition of poetry in Chinese), 376
Burakuin 豊楽院 (Court of Abundant Pleasures), 109-11, 174
bushi 武士 warrior, warrior class, 17-19, 644, 663, 694
bushidan 武士団, warrior band, 61, 607, 616, 628, 667, 669, 679, 684-5
buyaku 賦役, corvée (eleventh century), 214
Byōdōin 平等院, temple, xxi, 513

calligraphy, 415-17
cap ranks (*kan'i* 冠位), 3

741

capital transferred to Heian-kyō 平安京, 24, 97-102, 455-6, 459
celestial irregularities, 553-7
Chamberlains' Office, see kurōdodokoro
Chancellor (daijō daijin or dajō daijin 太政大臣), xix, 49, 76-7, 626, 695
chigyōkoku 知行国, possessory provinces, 248, 610-11, 629
childbirth, 150
Chinese calendar, 91
Chinese culture assimilated, 11-14, 17, 82, 343-5
Chinese learning introduced, 343-5
Chinese prosody, 376
chingo kokka 鎮護国家, protection of the state by shrine-temples, 523, 526, 528; Shingon rituals, 533-6; Tendai rituals, 532-3, 538-9
chinjufu shōgun 鎮守府将軍, General of the Pacification and Defense Headquarters, 657, 660, 664, 666
chishiden 地子田, rental fields, 272, 328-9
chō 調, a tax collected as handicraft products, 206, 208, 210, 212, 214, 274
Chōan 長安 (Chinese: Ch'ang-an), a term for the western half of Heian-kyō, 102
Chōdōin 朝堂院 (Court of Government, also known as Hasshō-in), 93, 109-10, 113, 173
Chōkōdōryō 長講堂領, imperial shōen established by Go-Shirakawa, 631-2
chokushiden 勅旨田, imperial grant fields, 284-5, 591
chōshūchō 朝集帳, province's court report, 259
Chōshūki 長秋記, diary of Minamoto no Morotoki, 634, 687
chūgū 中宮, empress, xxi, 69, 70
Chūsonji 中尊寺, temple, xxii, 678
Chūwain 中和院 (Court of Central Harmony), 110, 115
Chūyūki 中右記, diary of Fujiwara no Munetada 藤原宗忠, 596, 602-3, 606, 611
circuit inspector (junsatsushi 巡察使), 292
clans (uji 氏) and the imperial line, 3-4, 7, 14, 16, 18, 24-6, 50-6, 98, 128-31
coins, xxii, 162, 164-5, 636-7
commendation (kishin 寄進), of an interest in a shōen, 10, 133-5, 249-50, 613
conscript system abolished, 42, 645

corvées, see also yō; zōyō; buyaku 208-15, 214, 275-7, 288-9, 322-3
costume, 394-6
Council of State (daijōkan or dajōkan 太政官), 5, 25, 41-2, 70, 75, 77-8, 586-7, 608
court ceremonial and ritual, 180-2
Court of Abundant Pleasures (Buraku-in), 109-11, 174
Court of Central Harmony, see Chūwain
court rank, 3-5, 129-31, 133, 159-61, 255-6, 626
court report of provinces, see chōshūchō
crops: barley, 183, 187; buckwheat, 217; millet, 183, 187; rice, 183, 185-6; soybeans, 187; wheat, 217
custodial governor, see zuryō

daidairi 大内裏 (Greater Imperial Palace), 103, 105, 108-12, 173-5, 179-80
Daigakuryō 大学寮, see Academy
Daigen(sui)hō 大元(帥)法, ritual, 535-6
Daigo 醍醐, emperor, 2, 56, 585
Daigoji 醍醐寺, temple, and the imperial family, 500-2
Daigokuden 大極殿 (Great Hall of State), 110-11, 113, 116, 173-4
daijō daijin or dajō daijin 太政大臣, see Chancellor
daijōkan or dajōkan 太政官, see Council of State
daikeichō 大計帳, province's major accounting report, 259-60
dairi 内裏 (Emperor's Residential Compound), 109, 113-16, 174-5, 621
dairyō 大領, chief magistrate of a district (gun), 257-8, 264
dajō hōō 太上法皇 or hōō, priestly retired emperor, 580
dajō tennō 太上天皇, retired emperor, 580
Dannoura 壇ノ浦, battle, xxiii, 707
Dazaifu 太宰府, Kyushu Government Headquarters, 257, 275-7, 282-3, 659, 674, 687
denso 田租, land tax in rice (seventh-ninth centuries), 201, 205, 210, 212-14, 226-7
Department of Shrines, see Jingikan
Dewa 出羽 Province, 670
diet, 398-9
district (gun or kōri 郡), 2, 9, 208, 239, 243, 326, 333-4
district officials/government (gunji 郡司),

2, 9, 208, 257-8, 261-4, 326, 333-4, 646
Dōkyō 道鏡, Buddhist priest, 26, 49, 453-4, 579
draft animals, 187, 189, 193

Earlier Nine Years' War (zen kunen no eki 前九年の役), xxi, 74, 598, 669-75
Echi-no-shō 愛智荘, 293-6
ecstatic mass movements, 573-4
education of children, 346-54, 385-7
Eiga monogatari 栄花物語 (A Tale of Flowering Fortunes), 14, 393, 395-6, 430-3, 441, 446
eisakushu 永作手, permanent cultivator, 224
emakimono 絵巻物, (horizontal) hand scroll, 413-15
embassies to T'ang, xviii, xix, 84, 344-5, 464, 475, 479
Emishi 蝦夷, ethnic tribes in the northeast, xviii, 646, 657-8, 660, 670; see also Ezo
Emishi campaigns, xviii, 30-2
emperor (tennō 天皇), xvi, 4
Emperor's Residential Compound, see dairi
emperor's role, 3-5, 15, 639
Enchin 円珍, monk, 483-4, 540
Engi shiki 延喜式, xx, 13, 102, 188-9, 193, 203, 207-8, 212, 305-6, 522, 526, 528, 544-6, 550-2, 555
Enkyū 延久 Regulation of shōen, 588, 592
Ennin 円仁, monk, xix, 479-85, 508, 539
En no matsubara 宴松原 (Banquet Pine Grove), 110, 115
Enryakuji 延暦寺, temple, xix, xxi, xxii, 89, 473, 486-7, 522, 528, 682, 706
Enryakuji and Onjōji in conflict, 489-92, 494-7
Enryaku kōtai shiki 延暦交替式 (Enryaku Regulations on the Transfer of Office), 269
En'yū 円融, emperor, 582-3
era name (nengō) changes, 554-5
esoteric Buddhism, 522-3, 532-5
estates, see shōen
examinations of the Academy, 369-73
excursions, 401-2
Ezo 蝦夷, a name for Emishi from mid-Heian, see Emishi

falconry, 401-2

fans, 396-7
fires, 173-5
foreign relations and trade: Sui and T'ang, xviii, xix, 81-4, 87-9; Silla, xviii, xx, 81, 86, 89-90; Po-hai, 81, 90-4; Koryō, xxi, xxii, 95, 633-4; Sung, xxi, xxii, xxiii, 95-6, 632-7, 699; see also embassies to T'ang; trade goods
"former three fusas," 588, 595
fudan nembutsu 不断念佛, uninterrupted contemplation of Amida Buddha, 509
fugō no yakara 富豪の輩, "rich and powerful" (local gentry), 237-9, 280-2, 292, 302-4, 336-7
Fujigawa 富士川, battle, xxviii, 703-4
Fujiwara clan 藤原氏: Ceremonials House (Shikike), 26-7; Capital House (Kyōke), 27; Southern House (Nanke), 26-7; Northern House (Hokke), 25-7, 46, 127-9
Fujiwara Northern House: rise to power, 33, 36-7, 45-8, 59; regency, 49-51, 63, 582-3; dominant, 69-71; administrative office (mandokoro), 638; mansions, 176; temples, 176-9, 534; religious rituals, 520, 526-8, 533, 540
Fujiwara no Akihira 藤原明衡, poet, 385-7
Fujiwara no Fuyutsugu 藤原冬嗣, official, 44, 48
Fujiwara no Hidesato 藤原秀郷, warrior, 61, 655-6, 658, 660
Fujiwara no Kaneie 藤原兼家, regent, xxi, 64-7, 176, 582
Fujiwara no Kanemichi 藤原兼通, regent, 64-5
Fujiwara no Korechika 藤原伊周, official, 67-8
Fujiwara no Kusuko 藤原薬子, 33-5
Fujiwara no Michinaga 藤原道長, regent, xxi, 5, 67-71, 150-1, 176-7, 180, 383, 385, 447, 505, 512-13, 583
Fujiwara no Michinori 藤原通憲 (Shinzei 信西), 619-23, 626, 634, 690, 692-3
Fujiwara no Michitaka 藤原道隆, regent, 67
Fujiwara no Moromichi 藤原師通, regent, 599, 601
Fujiwara no Morosuke 藤原師輔, official, 17, 180, 354, 359, 486, 517-18
Fujiwara no Morozane 藤原師実, regent, 595-6, 598-9, 601
Fujiwara no Motonaga 藤原元命, Gover-

Fujiwara no Motonaga (*cont.*)
  nor of Owari, 211-13, 328-31
Fujiwara no Mototsune 藤原基経, regent, 51-6, 76
Fujiwara no Munetada 藤原宗忠, official, 596
Fujiwara no Nakanari 藤原仲成, official, 33-5
Fujiwara no Norimichi 藤原教通, regent, 585
Fujiwara no Oguromaro 藤原小黒麻呂, official, 97-8, 100
Fujiwara no Sanesuke 藤原実資, official, 144-5, 150-1, 153-8
Fujiwara no Saneyori 藤原実頼, regent, xx, 59, 62-4
Fujiwara no Shōshi 藤原璋子, 609, 611
Fujiwara no Shunzei 藤原俊成 (Toshinari), poet, 439-40
Fujiwara no Sukeyo 藤原佐世, scholar of Chinese, 54, 345
Fujiwara no Sumitomo 藤原純友, pirate, xx, 61, 657, 659, 661-2
Fujiwara no Tadahira 藤原忠平, regent, 59-60, 302, 306-9, 317-18
Fujiwara no Tadamichi 藤原忠通, regent, 611, 619
Fujiwara no Tadazane 藤原忠実, regent, 603-4, 608, 611, 614, 617, 619, 688-9
Fujiwara no Tanetsugu 藤原種継, official, 21, 24, 33, 98, 455
Fujiwara no Tokihira 藤原時平, official, xx, 55-8, 286, 540, 542
Fujiwara no Uchimaro 藤原内麻呂, official, 34, 261
Fujiwara no Yorimichi 藤原頼通, regent, xxi, 70-2, 176-7
Fujiwara no Yorinaga 藤原頼長, official, 619
Fujiwara no Yoritada 藤原頼忠, regent, 65
Fujiwara no Yoshifusa 藤原良房, regent, xix, 36, 45, 48-51
fukandenden 不堪佃田, uncultivatable fields, 325
Fukuhara 福原, 630, 635, 697-9, 700, 703
fumyō 負名, tax manager of a *myō*, 73, 222-3, 233, 337
furnishings, 391-4
furōnin 浮浪人, migrant, 206; *see also* migrants
Futara, Mount 二荒山, 524-5, 566

fuyusoden 不輸租田, fields exempt from land tax, 272

gagaku 雅楽, "elegant music," 425
Gangōji 元興寺, temple, 293, 296
Gembō 玄昉, Buddhist priest, 452-3
Gempei 源平 (Minamoto-Taira) War, 630, 695, 699-708
General of the Pacification and Defense Headquarters, *see chinjufu shōgun*
Genji 源氏, *see* Minamoto
Genji monogatari 源氏物語 (*The Tale of Genji*), xxi, 14, 409, 414, 444-7
Genji monogatari emaki 源氏物語絵巻 (*The Tale of Genji Picture Scrolls*), 413-14, 417
Genshin 源信, monk, 421-2, 510-13, 574
geshi or *gesu* 下司, sub-officer of a *shōen*, 249
Gion festival 祇園祭, 559
Gishin 義真, monk, 463-4, 489, 495
Gōdanshō 江談抄, 389
goe nembutsu 五会念佛, a meditation on Amida, 508
goin 後院, palace of a retired emperor, 591
golden age, 2, 585
goryō 御霊, (cult of) the spirit of a noble who died unjustly, 559; *see also onryō*
Go-Sanjo 後三条, emperor, xxii, 4-5, 71, 339, 576, 583-95
go sannen no eki 後三年の役, *see* Later Three Years' War
Go-Shirakawa 後白河, emperor, senior retired emperor, xxiii, 6, 576, 613-14, 618-32, 681, 689, 690-9, 705-9
Gosho 御所, present Kyoto imperial palace, 175
Go-Toba 後鳥羽, emperor, 630
government buildings, 103-4, 106-19, 173-5
government offices reduced, 38
Greater Imperial Palace, *see daidairi*
Great Hall of State, *see* Daigokuden
Guard-Post Judgments (*jinnosadame* 陣定), 42, 75
gun or *kōri* 郡, district (subdivision of a province), 2, 9, 239
gunji 郡司, *see* district officials/government
guntō 郡稲, *suiko* loan principal controlled by district officials, 208

Hachiman 八幡 cult, xxi, 524, 558-60, 569, 589, 593, 596, 630, 669-70

Haji clan 土師氏, 20, 98
handen shūju 班田収授, rice field allotment system, 215-16; discontinued, 217-21
handicraft produce taxes, *see chō*; *yō*; *kōeki zōmotsu*
Hasshōin 八省院 (Court of the Eight Ministries), 109-10
Hata clan 秦氏, 98
Heian-kyō 平安京, Kyoto: capital, 1, 6, 101; site, 97-101; plan, 102-9; population, 121-3; administration, 170-2; markets, 117-18; residential lots, 119-20, 122
Heiji Disturbance 平治の乱, xxvii, 622-3, 691-5
Heike 平家, *see* Taira
Heike monogatari 平家物語, 602, 628, 698, 703
Heishi 平氏, *see* Taira
Heizei 平城, emperor, xviii, 21, 24, 33-5, 466, 581
Heizei-kyō or Heijō-kyo 平城京, Nara, 21, 102
hereditary offices and professions, 132
Hiei, Mount 比叡山, 169, 462-3, 596, 602; *see also* Enryakuji
Higashi no ichi, Nishi no ichi 東市、西市, East and West Markets of Heian-kyō, 118, 163-4, 167-9
Higashi sanjō dono 東三条殿, a mansion of Fujiwara no Kaneie, 176
hijiri 聖, holy man, 513-14
hiragana 平仮名, syllabary, 13
Hiraizumi 平泉, xxii, 674, 678, 708
historical tales, *rekishi monogatari* 歴史物語, 442, 446
Hizen 肥前 Petition of 881, 281, 283
Hōgen Disturbance 保元の乱, xxiii, 612, 618-19, 688-91
Hōjōji 法成寺, temple founded by Fujiwara no Michinaga, xxi, 71, 79, 177-9, 420-1, 430-1
Hōjō Masako 北条政子, 702
Hōjō Tokimasa 北条時政, 694, 702
Hokekyō 法華経 (*Lotus Sutra*), 461, 469, 484, 488, 512-14, 570
Hōkōin 法興院, a temple founded by Fujiwara no Kaneie, 177
hokumen 北面 (or *in-no-hokumen*), retired emperors's warriors of the northern gate, xxii, 605, 607-8, 614, 646, 681, 683

home provinces, *see* Kinai
Honchō monzui 本朝文粋 (anthology of belles lettres in Chinese), 385
hon'in 本院, senior retired emperor
honjo 本所 or *honke* 本家, highest guarantor of a *shōen*, 250, 649
hōō 法皇, priestly retired emperor, 580
Horikawa 堀河, emperor, 599-600, 604, 608
horsemanship, 402-3
Hossō 法相, school of Buddhism, 463, 469
Hui-kuo 恵果, Chinese master of esoteric Buddhism, 475, 481
Hyōbushō 兵部省, Ministry of War, 110, 112

Ichijō 一条, emperor, xxxi, 69
ichijō 一乗, doctrine of One Vehicle, 468-9, 484
Ichinotani 一谷, battle, xxiii, 707
Iji Fort 伊治城, xviii, 31
iken fuji 意見封事, statement of opinion on successes and failures of government, 380-2
Iki 壱岐 island, xxi
Ikuhōmon-in 郁芳門院, 602, 614
imayō 今様, "modern-style" (songs), 428
imperial anthologies of poetry in Chinese, xix, 357
imperial anthologies of poetry in Japanese (*chokusen waka shū* 勅撰和歌集), 438-41
imperial clan, xviii, 1, 3, 39, 124-5, 129-30
imperial consorts, 69, 126, 128
Imperial Police, *see kebiishi*
imperial rule, 1-3, 580, 585
imperial succession, 123-4, 577-9, 593-5, 597, 618-19
in 院, cloister, retired emperor, 576, 580
in-no-chō 院庁, Retired Emperor's Office, xxii, 6, 17, 572, 588, 604-5, 607, 612, 638, 641-3
in-no-hokumen 院北面, *see hokumen*
insei 院政, cloister government, 6, 576, 632, 638-43, 688
inshi 院司, retired emperor's officials, 581
inzen 院宣, edict of a retired emperor, 604, 614, 638
Isawa Fort 胆沢城, xviii
Ise Heishi 伊勢平氏, a warrior branch of the Taira clan, xxii, 608, 685, 688
Ise monogatari 伊勢物語 (*Tales of Ise*), 441,

Ise monogatari (cont.)
444
Itsukushima Jinja 厳島神社, 619, 635
Iwashimizu Hachiman-gū 石清水八幡宮, xxii, 558, 569, 589, 593, 596, 630
Iyo 伊予, prince, 33-4
Izumi Shikibu 和泉式部, poet, 99
Izumi Shikibu nikki 和泉式部日記 (*Diary of Izumi Shikibu*), 441-2

Jijūden 仁寿殿 (Benevolent Longevity Hall), 114, 116, 174-5
Jimon 寺門, Onjōji branch of the Tendai school, 489
Jingikan 神祇官 (Department of Shrines), 15, 110-12, 518, 520-1, 544, 548
jingūji 神宮寺, shrine-temples, 523-5, 527, 566
jinnosadame 陣定, Guard-Post Judgments, 42, 75
jishiden 地子田, "rental fields," 221
jōden 乗田 "extra fields" (publicly owned but privately operated), 275, 278
jōgō 成功, payment for provincial appointment, 247
jōgyō zammai 常行三昧, a meditation on Amida, 508
Jōhei-Tengyō 承平天慶 Disturbance, xx, 60-1, 653, 663
jōkō 上皇, retired emperor, 580
Jōwa 承和 Incident, xix, 34-7, 550-1
Junna 淳和, emperor, 33, 35, 477
junsatsushi 巡察使, circuit inspector, 265, 292

kabane 姓, hereditary clan title, 3, 130
kachō 加徴, "additional levy" of land tax (tenth century), 41, 211-13
Kagerō nikki 蜻蛉日記 (*Gossamer Journal*), 441
kageyushi 勘解由使 (Board of) Discharge Examiners, 7, 269-71, 300-6
kaidan 戒壇, *see* ordination platform
Kaifūsō 懐風藻 (anthology of poetry in Chinese), 12
kajishi 加地子, "additional rent," 223, 228, 230
kambyakushō 堪百姓, "capable farmers," 304
kammotsu 官物, "official goods," a term for *nengu*, 210, 213, 215, 313-14, 327, 333
kammotsu rippo 官物率法 (or *rippō*), "law of apportionment," set limits on province's taxes, 242
Kammu 桓武, emperor, xviii, 7, 20, 25, 28, 33, 98, 100-1, 103, 169, 228, 455, 457-61, 463-6, 581
Kammu and the Nara temples, 459-60, 463
Kamo Shrine 賀茂神社, xviii, xix, 181-2
kampaku 関白, regent (for adult emperor), xix, xx, 54, 56, 59, 63, 65, 77
kana 仮名, syllabary, 13, 14, 411, 416-17, 432; *see* hiragana
kanden 官田, office fields, 279
Kangakuin 勧学院, Fujiwara clan dormitory and academy, 129, 373-4
kan'i 冠位, cap rank, 3
kannō 勧農, "promotion of agriculture," 236, 239, 261
karae 唐絵, paintings with Chinese subjects, 410
karasuki 唐鋤, animal-drawn, double-stem plow, 186
kata-imi 方忌, directional taboo, 522-3
kata-tagae 方違, directional alternative, 552
Kayanoin 高陽院, a mansion of the Fujiwara regental line, 176
Kazan 花山, emperor, xxi, 66, 984
kebiishi 検非違使, Imperial Police, xix, 7, 17, 43, 170-1, 182, 616-17, 657-8, 666, 680-1
Keikokushū 経国集 (anthology of poetry and prose in Chinese), xix, 357
kemari 蹴鞠, kick ball, 157, 404-5
kemmon seika 権門勢家, powerful noble families, 640
kenin 家人, "house men." 668-9, 679
Kenkairon 顕戒論 (*Treatise on the Precepts*), 473
Kenreimon-in 建礼門院, *see* Taira no Tokushi
Kenrinkaku 乾臨閣 (Celestial Presidence Pavilion), 118
Kinai 畿内, home provinces (Yamato, Yamashiro, Kawachi, Izumi, Settsu), 187
Kinai *shō* 畿内荘, home-provinces type of *shōen*, 228-9
Ki no Kosami 紀古佐美, official, general, 26, 28, 97
Ki no Tsurayuki 紀貫之, official, poet, 13, 931-3, 441
kinshin 近親, retainers of a retired

emperor, 602, 607, 621, 631
Kirokusho 記録所, *see Kiroku shōen kenkeijo*
Kiroku shōen kenkeijo 記録荘園券契所 (Office for the Investigation of Estate Documents), xxii, 589-90, 620
kishin 寄進, *see* commendation
Kiso Yoshinaka 木曾義仲, *see* Minamoto no Yoshinaka
Kitano 北野 cult, 58, 559-64
Kiyohara (Fujiwara) no Kiyohira 清原(藤原)清衡, warrior, xxii, 675-8
Kiyohara no Iehira 清原家衡, warrior, xxii, 675-7
Kiyohara no Sanehira 清原真衡, warrior, 675
Kiyohara no Takenori 清原武則, warrior, xxi, 673-4
kōchōchō 貢調帳, province's tribute-tax report, 260
kōden 公田, public fields, 215, 221, 227, 275, 337
kōeki 交易, "exchange" or barter (of tax-grain for handicraft products), 282
kōeki zōmotsu 交易雑物, "miscellaneous offerings" (tribute paid in products acquired by exchange, tenth century), 208, 210, 262
Kōfukuji 興福寺, temple, xxi, 682, 703, 706
kōgō 皇后, empress, xxi, 69
Kogoshūi 古語拾遺, 520
Kojidan 古事談, 585, 600
Kojiki 古事記, 519, 521, 530, 567, 571
Kokin (waka) shū 古今(和歌)集 (*Collection of Early and Modern Times*), xxii, 13, 417, 433-8, 443
kokubunji 国分寺, provincial branch temple, xviii, 456, 519, 532
kokufu 国府, provincial capital, 236
kokuga 国衙, provincial offices, 236, 243, 298, 337
kokugaryō 国衙領, provincial rice fields, 2, 10, 40, 233, 240, 246
kokutai 国体, "body of the imperial state," 529-30
kokuzu 国図, provincial land register
kōkyū 後宮, "rear palace," women's quarters of palace, 127
kondei 健児, militiamen, provincial guards, 17, 43, 646-7, 262
kondeidokoro 健児所, militia office (of provincial headquarters), 242, 647

konden 墾田, reclaimed rice fields, 215-16, 224, 273, 328
Kongōbuji 金剛峯寺, temple, 409, 477-8, 503-4, 522
Kōnin 光仁, emperor, 20
Konjaku monogatari-shū 今昔物語集 (*A Collection of Tales of Times Now Past*), 184, 238, 446-7, 568, 661-4, 668, 687
Konkōmyōkyō 金光明経 (*Sutra of Golden Light*), 461
Koremune no Kinkata 惟宗公方, doctor of law, 310-11
Kōrokan 鴻臚館, lodgings for foreign emissaries: in Heian-kyō, 93, 107, 117-18; in Dazaifu, 88
koseki 戸籍, population registers, 217-19
Kōya, Mount 高野山, xix, 477-8
kubunden 公分田, allotment household rice fields, 37, 160, 215, 272, 288, 328
Kuchizusami 口遊, textbook, 348-52
kueiden 公営田, publicly operated fields, 275-9, 283
kugetō 公廨稲, stipend *suiko*, 201-2, 260, 265-8, 314-15
kugyō 公卿, senior nobles (Third Rank and above), xxiii, 5, 70, 570, 586-7, 626
kuji 公事, "public duties," a term for *rinji zōyaku* (eleventh century), 210-11, 214-15
Kujō-den no goyuikai 九条殿の御遺誡 (*Testamentary Admonitions of Fujiwara no Morosuke*), 517-18, 542
Kūkai 空海, monk: xviii, xix; early training, 473-4; in China, 475; study of Mikkyō, 467, 475-6; and Saga, 476-7; Shingon chapel at Court, 478; at Tōji and Mount Kōya, 476-7; new rituals, 524-5, 532-8; calligrapher, 416
Kumano 熊野, shrines, 571-2
kuni 国, *see* provinces
Kunisaki 国東 cult, 568-70
kuniyaku 国役, a term for *rinji zōyaku*, 210-12, 230
Kurikara 倶利伽羅, battle, 704
kurōdodokoro 蔵人所, Chamberlains' Office, xviii, 7, 17, 41-2, 45, 313, 588, 681
Kūya (or Kōya) 空也, Buddhist holy man, xx, 514, 574
Kyōshiki 京職, Capital Offices, 170-1
Kyoto 京都, 101

Kyushu Government Headquarters, *see* Dazaifu

land taxes, 201, 205, 210; *see also so; denso; suiko; sozei; nengu; kammotsu*
Later Three Years' War (*go sannen no eki* 後三年の役), xxii, 74, 675-9
law compilations, *see Ryō no gige, Ryō no shūge; Engi shiki*
Limpid Cool Hall, *see* Seiryōden
local administration changes, 236-46
Lotus Sutra, *see Hokekyō*

maguwa 馬鍬, animal-drawn single-stem plow, 186
major accounting report of province, *see daikeichō*
Makura no sōshi 枕草子 (Pillow Book), xxi, 14, 93, 405, 442-3, 445
mandokoro 政所, administrative office of a province or noble family, 242
Man'yōshū 万葉集, 12, 185
mappō 末法, latter days of the Law, 510-11, 572, 603
Markets, East and West, 118, 163-4, 167-9
marriage practices of the nobility, 135-40
masu 升 (*shō*) unit of dry measure (attempt to standardize), 592
measures, 338-40
menden 免田, tax exempt fields, 227
Meng ch'iu (Japanese: *Mōgyū*) 蒙求, a Chinese textbook, 347-8
midō 御堂, Amida Hall, 513
migrants (*rōnin* or *furōnin*), 241, 262-3, 280-3
Mikkyō 密教, esoteric Buddhism, 465
Mimbushō 民部省 (Ministry of Popular Affairs), 112, 317, 319, 324
Minamoto clan 源氏: origins, xix, 7, 39, 129, 650; Murakami Genji (officials), 586-7, 594, 596, 599-601, 650; Seiwa Genji (warriors), 598, 618, 650-1, 683
Minamoto no Mitsunaka 源満仲, warrior, 63-4
Minamoto no Morotoki 源師時, diarist, 634, 687
Minamoto no Motoko 源基子, 597
Minamoto no Shitagō 源順, official and poet, xx, 348
Minamoto no Takaakira 源高明, courtier, xx, 62-4, 601

Minamoto no Tamenori 源為憲, poet in Chinese, 348-54
Minamoto no Tameyoshi 源為義, warrior, xxii, 618-19, 651, 686, 689-90, 702
Minamoto no Toshifusa 源俊房, official, 587, 602
Minamoto no Toshiyori (Shunrai) 源俊頼, poet, 439
Minamoto no Tsunemoto 源経基, warrior, 651, 658, 660
Minamoto no Yorimasa 源頼政, warrior, 630, 651, 692, 698
Minamoto no Yorinobu 源頼信, warrior, 74, 65, 666-9, 672
Minamoto no Yoritomo 源頼朝, warrior, xxiii, 18, 513, 624, 630, 640, 651, 667, 670, 694, 700, 702-9
Minamoto no Yoriyoshi 源頼義, warrior, xxi, 74, 651, 672-4, 677
Minamoto no Yoshiie 源義家, warrior, xxii, 74, 596, 598-9, 607, 651, 663, 674-7, 683-4, 708
Minamoto no Yoshinaka 源義仲 (Kiso Yoshinaka 木曾義仲), warrior, xxiii, 651, 702, 714-17
Minamoto no Yoshitomo 源義朝, warrior, xxiii, 618-19, 622-3, 651, 689-91, 693, 702
Minamoto no Yoshitsuna 源義綱, warrior, xxii, 599, 651, 679, 684
Minamoto no Yoshitsune 源義経, warrior, xxiii, 651, 694, 707-8
Minamoto no Yukiie 源行家, warrior, 651, 704-5, 708
Ministry of Ceremonial, *see* Shikibushō
Ministry of Popular Affairs, *see* Mimbushō
Ministry of War, *see* Hyōbushō
miyako 都 or 京, "the capital," Kyoto, 101
Miyoshi Kiyoyuki 三善清行, scholar, 278, 292, 298-9, 301-4, 309, 335, 365, 379-82
Miyoshi Kiyoyuki's memorial of 914, 80-2, 278, 380
Mochihito 以仁, prince, xxiii, 630, 698, 702
mokudai 目代, deputy supervisor of a province, 242, 253
monoawase 物合, "matching things" (a game), 405-9
mono no aware 物の哀, 414
Montoku 文徳, emperor, xix, 36
Murakami 村上, emperor, 12, 51, 61

Murakami Genji, 586-7, 596, 599-601
Murasaki Shikibu 紫式部, author and poet, xxi, 409, 442, 444-5
musha (or musa) 武者, 644
mushadokoro 武者所, retired emperor's warriors' office, 605
music, 424-8, 430-1
music in shrine rituals, 547
Mutsu 陸奥 Province, 670
Mutsu waki 陸奥話記, 671, 679
myō 名, "a name holding," a unit of tax assessment, 78, 217, 222-3, 229-30, 233, 243, 251-2, 337
myōbō hakase 明法博士, doctor of law, 266
myōshu 名主, tax manager of a myō (eleventh century), 222-3, 229, 233, 251-2

Nagaoka 長岡, 21, 24, 98, 102, 455
nairan 内覧, "private inspection" (regental powers), xxi, 56, 58, 63, 68, 77
Nakatomi uji 中臣氏, Nakatomi clan, 520
Nara 奈良, Heizei-kyō or Heijō-kyō, 21
narrative prose, 441-8
natural occurrences and calamities, 551-2
nembutsu 念仏, 511, 515
nengu 年貢 or kammotsu, combined land tax (tenth century on), 210-11, 213
nenjū gyōji 年中行事, annual ceremonies, 401
Nihonkoku genzai shomokuroku 日本国見在書目録, xix, 345-6
Nihon ryōiki 日本霊異記, 238, 571
Nihon sandai jitsuroku 日本三代実録, xx
Nihon shoki 日本書紀, first of national histories, 29, 343, 354, 359, 519, 521, 530, 567
Nijō 二条, emperor, 622-3
nijūnisha 二十二社, the Twenty-two Shrines, 523-31
Nimmyō 仁明, emperor, 25, 36, 581
Ninkai 仁海, thaumaturgist, 536
Ninnaji 仁和寺 and the imperial family, 500-1
nobility, see court rank
Noto 能登 Province land register (ōtabumi 大田文), 612
nursing practices, 148-55

Ochikubo monogatari 落窪物語 (The Tale of the Sunken Room), 443
ōchō kokka 王朝国家, "Royal Court State," 60

Ōe no Masafusa 大江匡房, scholar, 348, 380, 387-8, 588, 590
Office for the Investigation of Estate Documents, see Kiroku shōen kenkeijo
officials, 159-60, 162, 165-6
Ōjō yōshū 往生要集 (Anthology on Rebirth in Pure Land), xxi, 421-2, 510-13, 574
Ōkagami 大鏡 (The Great Mirror), 14, 397, 446-7
Ōmmyōryō 陰陽寮 (Board of Yin and Yang), 547, 550
Onjōji 園城寺, temple, 483, 596, 682, 697-8, 703
onnae 女絵, feminine paintings, 413-14
Ononomiya 小野宮 Mansion, 144-7, 149, 153, 154-8
onryō 怨霊, "wrathful spirits" cult, 58, 559-64; see also goryō
oracles, 558-9, 561
ordination platform (kaidan), 470, 472-3, 495
ōryōshi 押領使 (Suppression and Control Agent), 655, 657-8, 665
Ōshū 奥州, Mutsu Province
Ōshū Fujiwara 奥州藤原, xxii, xxiii, 674, 478, 705, 708
Ōtemmon 応天門 "Obedience to Heaven Gate" Conspiracy, xviii, 49-50, 109-10
otokoe 男絵, masculine paintings, 413-15
Ōtomo no Otomaro 大伴弟麻呂, official, general, xviii
Ōwada-no-tomari 大輪田泊, 96, 635
Owari 尾張 Province Petition of 988, xxi, 210, 212-13, 221, 321, 326-36
Ōyama-no-shō 大山荘, 111-12, 122, 127, 249, 290, 303-4, 317-20, 323-5

Pacification and Defense Headquarters, see chinjufu shōgun
painting: secular, 409-15; Buddhist, 421-4; Chinese subjects (karae), 410; Japanese subjects (yamatoe), 410-15; feminine subjects (onnae), 413-14; masculine subjects (otokoe), 413-15
palaces of retired emperors, 179-80
paper, 417-18
Park of the Divine Spring, see Shinsen'en
pastimes of court ladies: excursions, 401; monoawase (matching things), 405-8; feminine occupations, 405
pastimes of court nobles: archery, 403;

pastimes of court nobles (*cont.*)
    falconry, 401-2; horsemanship, 402-3; kick ball, 404-5; wrestling, 404
peasant household size, 194-9
pilgrimages to Mount Kōya, 505
Pillow Book, see *Makura no sōshi*
pirates, xx-xxii, 80, 86-7, 89-90, 94-5, 687
plows, 183-94
poetry in Chinese, 12, 351-2, 357-8, 376-8, 383
poetry in Japanese (*waka*), 12-13, 411-12, 431-41
Po-hai 渤海 (Japanese: Bokkai), xix, 81, 88, 90-4, 377, 425, see also foreign relations and trade; trade goods
population, 2, 184, 219, 255
population registers, see *koseki*
position of women in court society, 140-2
possessory provinces, see *chigyōkoku*
priestly retired emperor, see *dajō hōō; hōō; in*
prince-of-the-blood provinces, see *shinnōkoku*
private schools, 374-5
protection of the state, see *chingo kokka*
provinces (*kuni*), 254; administrative officials, 242, 255-7; offices, 263; corvée helpers, 258-9; four provincial reports, 259-60, 264; district (*gun*) administration, 257-8
provincial governor (*kami, kokushi, zuryō*), 238, 316, 599; disciplined, 108, 111-15, 310-11, 496
provincial precedent (*kokurei* 国例), 93, 283, 298
publicly operated fields, see *kueiden*
Pure Land teachings, xxiii, 15-16, 572-4
Pure Land teachings at Hiei, 508
Purple Sanctum Hall, see *Shishinden*

raigō 來迎, "coming to welcome," 16, 422, 423
rain-making rituals, 535-8
rakuchū rakugai zu 洛中洛外図 "pictures of scenes in and around the capital," 102
Rakuyō 洛陽 (Chinese: Lo-yang), a term for eastern Kyoto, Kyoto, or the capital, 101-12
Rampart Gate, see Rashōmon
Rashōmon or Rajōmon 羅城門 (Rampart Gate), 106-7, 175

reallotment of *kubunden*, 278, 283
Records Office, see *Kiroku shōen kenkeijo*, 248-9, 620
regent, 77; see also *sesshō; kampaku; nairan*
regent's income, 78-9
Reizei 冷泉, emperor, 62, 64
rekishi monogatari 歴史物語, historical tales, 442, 446
residential architecture, 142-7; see also Ononomiya
retired (abdicated) emperor, see *dajō tennō; jōkō; dajō hōō; hōō; in; hon'in*
retired emperor's office, see *in-no-chō*
rice: preferred as staple, 183, 186-7; irrigation, 183; seedbed technique and transplanting (*taue*), 184-6; fertilizing, 193-4; harvesting technique, 192-3
"rich and powerful," see *fugō no yakara*
rikiden no yakara 力田之輩 (those who maintain fields), 280, 282
Rikkokushi 六国史, see *Six National Histories*
rinji zōyaku 臨時雑役, "occasional miscellaneous exactions" (tenth century), 210, 213-15, 228, 231, 298, 313-14, 319-22
ritsuryō sei 律令制, statutory system, 3, 7, 24, 37-9, 40-4, 56-7, 59-60, 73, 82, 112, 159-61, 239, 242, 254-65, 286, 338-40, 450, 645, 656
ritsuryō system in decline, 236, 240, 242
rituals privatized, 541-2
rōei 朗詠, recitation of Chinese or Japanese poems, 428
Rokuhara 六波羅, Taira compound in Heian-kyō, 627-8
rōnin 浪人 or *furōnin*, see migrants
rōtō (or *rōdō*) 郎等, follower, companion, 648, 668, 679
Ruijū kokushi 類聚国史, 378
Ryōgen 良源, monk, 486-9
Ryōjin hishō 梁塵秘抄 (*Secret Selection of Songs*), 428
ryōke 領家, high-ranking noble or temple as protector of a *shōen*, 10, 245, 649
Ryō no gige, Ryō no shūge 令義解, 令集解, 364
ryōshu 領主, local lord of a domain, 250
Ryōunshū 凌雲集 (imperial anthology of poems in Chinese), xix, 357

Saga 嵯峨, emperor, xviii, xix, 2, 7, 33-6,

356-7, 466, 476-7, 581-2, 650, 652
sage-kings, 355-9, 366
Saichō 最澄, monk, xviii: early training, 462-4; in China, 464-5; Tendai teachings, 462-4; Mikkyō teachings, 465, 467; relations with Kūkai, 467-9; doctrinal positions, 469; ordination platform at Hiei, 472-3; new rites, 532, 538; and Gishin, 489
Sakanoue no Tamuramaro 坂上田村麻呂, general, xviii, 30, 570
sakushu 作手, cultivator, 223
salons, 443-4
sambumpō 三分法, rule of thirds, 307
Sammon 山門, Hiei (Enryakuji) branch of the Tendai school, 489
samurai 侍, 645, 681
Sangō shiiki 三教指帰, 474
Sanron 三論, school of Buddhism, 463
Sarashina nikki 更級日記 (Sarashina Diary), 442
sato dairi 里内裏, town palace, 175
Sawara 早良, prince, 24, 455
seii taishōgun 征夷大将軍, Barbarian-subduing Generalissimo, xviii, 670, 706, 709
Seiryōden 清涼殿 (Limpid Cool Hall), 174-5, 680
Sei Shōnagon 清少納言, author, xxi, 405, 418, 442-3, 445
Seiwa 清和, emperor, xix, 49-51
Seiwa Genji 清和源氏, see Minamoto
sekkanke 摂関家, Fujiwara regental family, 63, 582, 584, 586, 595, 603, 611, 617, 688
senior noble, see kugyō
senshi 選士, "select youths," militiamen, 647
sesshō 摂政, regent, xix, 49, 54, 59, 63, 77
setsuwa 説話, tales, 446
Sezoku gembun 世俗諺文, textbook, 353-4
shake 社家, shrine family, 520
Shibunritsu 四分律, Buddhist disciplinary code, 469, 472-3
shichibumpō 七分法, rule of sevenths, 298, 307
Shidara 志多羅 cult, 561-2
shiden 私田 "private fields," tax exempt, 221
Shijōkō-hō 熾盛光法, Tendai ritual, 539-41
shiki 職, commission or office, implying proprietary interest, 244-6, 250-1

Shikibushō 式部省 (Ministry of Ceremonial), 110-12
shikisū 式数, suiko quota set by statute, 203
shimbun dosha 神分度者, monks ordained for the worship of kami, 525
shimbutsu shūgō 神仏習合, association of kami with buddhas, 564-75
shindenzukuri 寝殿造, "dwelling house construction," 143, 391, 414, 421
Shingon 真言, school of Buddhism, 473-8; imperial patronage, 500-2
Shingon-in 真言院, Shingon chapel at court, 477-8, 497
Shingon temple rivalries, 499
shinnōkoku 親王国, prince-of-the-blood provinces, 272
Shin sarugakuki 新猿楽記, 385-6
shinsei 親政, direct imperial rule, 580, 585, 641
Shinsen'en 神泉苑 (Park of the Divine Spring), 100, 117-19, 172, 176, 357-8, 376, 538
Shinto shrines associated with Buddhist temples, 520-32
Shinto shrine rituals, 543-4
Shinzei 信西, see Fujiwara no Michinori
Shirakawa 白河, emperor, senior retired emperor, xxii, 6, 247, 576, 593-609, 681, 683-6, 688, 696
Shishigatani 鹿ヶ谷 Plot, xxiii, 628, 696-7
Shishinden 紫宸殿 (Purple Sanctum Hall), 114, 116
shōen 荘園 (or shō), estate, xxii, 5, 10, 18, 37, 43-4, 72-3, 78, 165, 206, 221-35, 245-54, 290-1, 316, 598, 610-13, 620, 629, 631-2, 649, 683-4; early shōen (eighth-ninth centuries) and their decline, 224-7; Kinai shō pattern (tenth century), 227-30; commendation, 249-50, 612; hierarchy of tenures, 249-50; tension between provincial authorities and shōen proprietors, 230-1; regulation, 66, 73, 206, 245-9, 290-2, 588-92, 596, 610-13, 620
Shōmonki 将門記, 648, 655, 662, 664
Shōmu 聖武, emperor, 15
Shōtoku 称徳, empress, 20-1, 579
Shōtoku 聖徳, prince, 11, 14
shōzei 正税, tax grain; suiko rice, 205, 327
shōzeichō 正税帳, tax-grain report of a province, 260, 284
shōzei kōeki 正税交易, tax-grain fund

shōzei kōeki (cont.)
  exchange, 312
Shūi ōjō den 拾遺往生伝, 515
Shukeiryō 主計寮 (Accounting Bureau), 266
Shuzeiryō 主税寮 (Tax Bureau), 266
Sillan refugees, 89-90
Six National Histories (Rikkokushi), xx, 13, 359-64
so 租 (or *denso*), rice land tax, 78, 272-3, 288-9
Sōgō-sho 僧綱所 (Office of the Hierarchs), 470, 477
sōhei 僧兵, armed monks, warrior monks, xx-xxii, 490-4, 596-7, 604, 608, 627, 630, 682, 698-9, 703-4, 706
sokoku 租穀, field-tax grain, 327-8
soku 束, a sheaf (unit of rice measure), 202, 212, 338-40
Sōniryō 僧尼令 (*Administrative Laws Pertaining to Monks and Nuns*), 450-1, 457, 460
sozei 租税, combined land tax in rice (ninth century), 205, 211
sozeiden 租税田, fields subject to land tax (tenth century on), 221, 328-9
stabling draft animals, 193
statutory system, see *ritsuryō sei*
Sugano no Mamichi 菅野真道, official, 269
Sugawara no Michizane 菅原道真, scholar and official, xix, 55-8, 84-5, 272, 297, 344, 353, 358, 370, 372, 376, 559-60; see also Kitano cult
suiko 出挙, rice loans for interest (a tax), 199-205, 208, 210, 212, 214, 227, 266, 273-4, 289
Sukuyōdō 宿曜道 (Way of Lodgings and Planetoids), 553-7
superintendent, see *bettō*
Sutoku 崇徳, emperor, xxiii, 609, 612, 618-19, 688-90
Suzaku 朱雀, emperor, 600
Suzakumon 朱雀門 (Vermillion Sparrow Gate), 106-9
Suzaku ōji 朱雀大路, avenue, 103-7, 173, 175-6

Tachibana no Hiromi 橘広相, scholar of Chinese and official, 54-5
tadokoro 田所, land office of a provincial government, 242
Taga Fort 多賀城, 31-2
Taihō Code 大宝律令, 3, 82, 450

Taikemmon-in 待賢門院 (Fujiwara no Shōshi), 609, 618
Taimitsu 台密 (Tendai Mikkyō), 483, 522, 541
Taira clan 平氏: origins, 7, 39, 615, 650; Kammu Heishi, 652-3; Ise Heishi, xxii, 608, 614-16, 619; and their rise to hegemony, 685-8, 694-7
Taira no Kiyomori 平清盛, warrior, xxiii, 96, 615-16, 619, 622-32, 635, 681, 688-704
Taira no Koremori 平維盛, warrior, 703-4
Taira no Kunika 平国香, xx, 615
Taira no Masakado 平将門, warrior, xx, 18, 61-2, 125, 312, 555, 615, 644, 648, 653-6, 661-2
Taira no Masamori 平正盛, warrior, 607, 614-15, 681, 685-6
Taira no Munemori 平宗盛, warrior, 705
Taira no Naokata 平直方, warrior, xxi, 74, 615, 666, 673
Taira no Sadamori 平貞盛, warrior, xx, 61, 74, 615, 655, 660, 664-5, 685
Taira no Shigemori 平重盛, warrior, 625, 629, 692, 695, 697
Taira no Tadamori 平忠盛, warrior, xxii, 614-17, 686-8, 696
Taira no Tadatsune 平忠常, warrior, 74, 615-16, 664-9
Taira no Tadatsune's Disturbance, 74, 664-9
Taira no Tokushi 平徳子 (Kenreimon-in 建礼門院), 627, 629
Takaosanji 高雄山寺, predecessor to Jingo-ji in Kyoto, 463, 465, 467, 477, 499
Taketori monogatari 竹取物語 (*The Tale of the Bamboo Cutter*), 442
takiguchi 滝口, unit of imperial bodyguards, 680-1
tammai 段米, supplemental land tax (part of *rinji zōyaku*), 214
tan 段, unit of land measure, 203, 212, 338
Taoist influences, 380, 523, 549-50, 554-7
Tao-sui 道邃, patriarch of Chinese Tendai school, 464-5, 495
tato 田堵, land manager, 229, 240-1, 251, 279-80, 323, 337
taue 田植, transplanting rice from seedbeds, 185
taxes: see land taxes; handicraft produce taxes; corvées
tax-grain report of a province, see *shōzeichō*

tax structure: seventh and eighth centuries, 199-202, 210; ninth century, 202-9, 211; tenth century, 210-15
Teishi 禎子, princess (Yōmeimon-in 陽明門院), 583
Temman Daijizai Tenjin 天満大自在天神, 651
Tendai and Fujiwara patronage, 486-7
Tendai Hokke-shū nembun gakushō shiki 天台法華宗年分学生式 (*Bylaws of the Annual Ordinands of the Tendai Hokke School*), 469
Tendai schism, 489-92
Tendai 天台, school of Buddhism, 462, 466
tennō 天皇, "emperor," xvi, 4
Testamentary Admonitions of Fujiwara no Morosuke (*Kujō-den no goyuikai*), 517-18, 542
"three *in*", 609
T'ien-t'ai mountains 天台山, 88, 464
Toba 鳥羽, emperor, senior retired emperor, xxii, xxiii, 576, 600-2, 608-19, 687-9
Tōdaiji 東大寺, temple, xx, 462, 469, 474, 502; Tōdaiji *shōen*, 115, 147, 225-7, 502, 591, 703-4
Toi 刀伊, "Jurchen pirates," xxi, 95, 633
Tōji 東寺, East Temple in Heian-kyō, xix, 107, 117, 477, 499, 501, 522
tokoro 所, offices of a provincial government, 242, 260
Tokuitsu 徳一, Hossō monk, 469, 483
Tōmitsu 東密 (Shingon Mikkyō), 483, 522, 541
tōryō 棟梁, chieftain of a warrior clan, especially the Minamoto and Taira, 616, 644, 682-5
Tosa nikki 土佐日記 (*Tosa Journal*), 13, 441
trade goods: with T'ang, 88, 95-6; Po-hai, 91-2; Koryŏ, 633; Sung, 636-7
tribute-tax report of a province, *see Kōchōchō*
Tsuchimikado 土御門, a mansion of Fujiwara no Michinaga, 70, 79, 176-7
tsuibushi 追捕使, Pursuit and Apprehension Agents, 655, 657
Tsurugaoka Hachiman-gū 鶴岡八幡宮, xxi
tsuwamono, "warrior" (tenth and eleventh centuries, sometimes represented by the graphs 戎, 兵, 武, 勇), 644, 647-50, 661-3, 680
Twenty-two Shrines, 545

Uda 宇多, emperor, xix, 2, 12, 41, 51, 54-5, 59, 582, 585
uji 氏, *see* clans
ujigami 氏神, clan deity, 3
ukimenden 浮免田, "floating exempt fields," 227-8
Unshū shōsoku 雲州消息, textbook, 386-7
Utsuho monogatari うつほ物語 (*The Tale of the Hollow Tree*), 442-3

waka 和歌, *see* poetry in Japanese
Wakan rōei shū 和漢朗詠集 (*Collection of Japanese and Chinese Rōei*), 428
Wake no Hiroyo 和気広世, scholar, 463
Wake no Kiyomaro 和気清麻呂, statesman, 100, 454, 558
wakō 倭寇, "Japanese pirates," 634
Wamyō ruiju shō 和名類聚抄, Japanese dictionary, xx, 188, 348
Wani 王仁, scholar from Paekche, 11, 343
warrior monks, *see sōhei*
wasteland use, 191-2
wrestling, 404
Wu-yüeh 呉越, xx, 88

yamabushi 山伏, mountain ascetics, 541, 549
Yamashiro 山城 Province, 101
yamatoe 大和絵, paintings with Japanese subjects, 410-15
Yashima 屋島, battle, xxiii
yō 庸, tax paid in handicraft products, 206-10, 214, 274
Yōmeimon 陽明門, palace gate, 108-10
Yōmeimon-in 陽明門院, princess, Teishi 禎子, 583, 597
Yōrō Code 養老律令, 3, 80-2, 364, 450
Yoshishige no Yasutane 慶滋保胤, 172
Yōzei 陽成, emperor, 51-3
yui 結 community labor for transplanting rice, 194
yusoden 輸租田, taxable fields, 272

zaichō kanjin 在庁官人, local officials resident at provincial headquarters, 242, 246
zaikeyaku 在家役, resident household levy, 252
zen kunen no eki 前九年の役, *see* Earlier Nine Years' War

zōyaku 雑役, *see rinji zōyaku*
zōyakumen shōen 雑役免荘園, miscellaneous postexemption estate, 614
zōyō 雑徭, corvée (eighth and ninth centuries), 208-10, 213
zuryō 受領, custodial governor, 238, 242, 247-8, 265-71, 590, 605-11